African American National Biography

Editorial Board

Editors in Chief

HENRY LOUIS GATES JR.
Alphonse Fletcher University Professor
Director of the W. E. B. Du Bois Institute for African and African American Research
Harvard University

EVELYN BROOKS HIGGINBOTHAM
Victor S. Thomas Professor of History and of African and African American Studies
Chair of the Department of African and African American Studies
Harvard University

Advisory Board

William L. Andrews
University of North Carolina at Chapel Hill
Vincent Carretta
University of Maryland
Harry J. Elam
Stanford University
Paul Finkelman
Albany Law School
Frances Smith Foster
Emory University
Gerald Gill (deceased)
Tufts University
Farah Jasmine Griffin
Columbia University
Darlene Clark Hine
Northwestern University

Bruce Kellner
Millersville University
David Levering Lewis
Rutgers University
Kenneth Manning
Massachusetts Institute of Technology
Nellie Y. McKay (deceased)
University of Wisconsin
Ingrid Monson
Harvard University
Richard J. Powell
Duke University
Stephanie Shaw
Ohio State University

Subject Editors

Edward E. Baptist
Cornell University
SLAVERY
L. Diane Barnes
Youngstown State University
LABOR HISTORY/LATE ACTIVISM
Elizabeth Beaulieu
Champlain College
LATE WRITING
Edward A. Berlin
Independent Scholar, New York City
EARLY MUSIC
Michael Bertrand
Tennessee State University
LATE MUSIC
Daniel Donaghy
Eastern Connecticut State University
SPORTS
John Ernest
West Virginia University
EARLY JOURNALISM/WRITING
Rayvon Fouché
University of Illinois at Urbana-Champaign
MEDICINE/SCIENCE/INVENTION
Jacqueline Francis
University of Michigan
ART

Tiffany Gill
University of Texas at Austin
BUSINESS
Christina Greene
University of Wisconsin-Madison
CIVIL RIGHTS/LATE ACTIVISM
Valinda Littlefield
University of South Carolina
EDUCATION
Laurie F. Maffly-Kipp
University of North Carolina
RELIGION
Paula Massood
Brooklyn College/CUNY
FILM AND THEATER
Diane E. Pecknold
University of Louisville
LATE MUSIC
Robert A. Pratt
University of Georgia
CIVIL RIGHTS/LATE ACTIVISM
John Saillant
Western Michigan University
EARLY ACTIVISM
David K. Wiggins
George Mason University
SPORTS

African American National Biography

SECOND EDITION

HENRY LOUIS GATES JR.
EVELYN BROOKS HIGGINBOTHAM

Editors in Chief

VOLUME 7: KARENGA, MAULANA – MCCREE, WADE HAMPTON, JR.

OXFORD
UNIVERSITY PRESS

OXFORD
UNIVERSITY PRESS

Oxford University Press is a department of the University of Oxford.
It furthers the University's objective of excellence in research, scholarship,
and education by publishing worldwide.

Oxford   New York
Auckland   Cape Town   Dar es Salaam   Hong Kong   Karachi
Kuala Lumpur   Madrid   Melbourne   Mexico City   Nairobi
New Delhi   Shanghai   Taipei   Toronto

With offices in
Argentina   Austria   Brazil   Chile   Czech Republic   France   Greece
Guatemala   Hungary   Italy   Japan   Poland   Portugal   Singapore
South Korea   Switzerland   Thailand   Turkey   Ukraine   Vietnam

Oxford is a registered trademark of Oxford University Press in the UK and certain other countries.

Published in the United States of America by
Oxford University Press
198 Madison Avenue, New York, NY 10016

© Oxford University Press 2013

Library of Congress Cataloging-in-Publication Data
African American national biography / editors in chief Henry Louis Gates Jr., Evelyn Brooks Higginbotham. – 2nd ed.
p. cm.
Includes bibliographical references and index.
ISBN 978-0-19-999036-8 (volume 1; hdbk.); ISBN 978-0-19-999037-5 (volume 2; hdbk.); ISBN 978-0-19-999038-2 (volume 3; hdbk.);
ISBN 978-0-19-999039-9 (volume 4; hdbk.); ISBN 978-0-19-999040-5 (volume 5; hdbk.); ISBN 978-0-19-999041-2 (volume 6; hdbk.);
ISBN 978-0-19-999042-9 (volume 7; hdbk.); ISBN 978-0-19-999043-6 (volume 8; hdbk.); ISBN 978-0-19-999044-3 (volume 9; hdbk.);
ISBN 978-0-19-999045-0 (volume 10; hdbk.); ISBN 978-0-19-999046-7 (volume 11; hdbk.); ISBN 978-0-19-999047-4 (volume 12;
hdbk.); ISBN 978-0-19-992077-8 (12-volume set; hdbk.)
1. African Americans – Biography – Encyclopedias.   2. African Americans – History – Encyclopedias.
I. Gates, Henry Louis.   II. Higginbotham, Evelyn Brooks, 1945-
E185.96.A4466 2012
920'.009296073 – dc23
[B]
2011043281

1 3 5 7 9 8 6 4 2
Printed in the United States of America
on acid-free paper

African American National Biography

Karenga, Maulana (14 July 1941–), educator, author, social theorist, and activist, was born Ronald McKinley Everett on a farm in Parsonsburg, Maryland, the youngest of fourteen children of Addie and Levi Everett, a Baptist minister. The family's house was supplied by the landowner, who allowed the family half of the produce they harvested. Ronald spent his early years helping on the farm, and he excelled in school, graduating from Salisbury High School in 1958. After moving to Los Angeles, California, in 1959, he attended Los Angeles City College. By 1964 he had earned both a B.A. and an M.A. in Political Science and African Studies from the University of California, Los Angeles (UCLA).

As a student, Everett met MALCOLM X, whose influence on Everett's thinking helped to turn the young man to social activism. Everett began to pursue a doctoral degree, but he stepped away from his studies in 1965, following the Watts riots, to help rebuild the Watts community and to devote himself to the black power struggle. By that time as well he had adopted the names Maulana (meaning "master teacher") and Karenga (meaning "keeper of the tradition"). In 1966 he formed the Organization Us, also known as the US Organization, a black-nationalist group devoted to social change and educational reform.

Organization Us, which still existed in the early twenty-first century, was devoted to, as Karenga stated on the organization's Web site, providing "a philosophy, a set of principles and a program which inspire a personal and social practice that not only satisfies human need but transforms people in the process, making them self-conscious agents of their own life and liberation" (Organization Us). Karenga termed the central philosophy of the organization "Kawaida," a theory he formulated in 1966, which he describes as "an ongoing synthesis of the best of African thought and practice in constant exchange with the world" (Organization Us). Central to this philosophy were the Nguzo Saba, or the Seven Principles: Umoja (unity), Kujichagulia (self-determination), Ujima (collective work and responsibility), Ujamaa (cooperative economics), Nia (purpose), Kuumba (creativity), and Imani (faith). These principles served as the basis for the African American and pan-African holiday known as Kwanzaa that Karenga created in 1966. Kwanzaa is a week-long celebration observed worldwide from December 26 to January 1. But Karenga was influential during the late 1960s in other spheres as well—most notably in the black power conferences he helped organize in Washington, D.C. (1966), Newark, New Jersey (1967), and Philadelphia, Pennsylvania (1968).

But this also proved to be a time of great organizational turmoil and deep personal confusion and error. From its beginnings, Karenga's organization competed for prominence and authority with the Black Panther Party, and the two groups differed greatly on matters of philosophy and methods. In 1969 the two organizations supported different candidates to lead the Afro-American Studies Center at UCLA. A meeting arranged by the Black Student Union to attempt a peaceful negotiation between the two groups ended in tragedy when two members of the US Organization, George P.

and Larry Joseph Stiner, shot and killed two Black Panthers, John Jerome Huggins and Alprentice "Bunchy" Carter. The violence naturally damaged the reputation and undermined the professed philosophies of both Organization Us and the Black Panthers, and commentary on these events was still presented in the early twenty-first century by those critical of Kwanzaa and other black-nationalist initiatives. But this history is rendered more complex by documented evidence that the FBI attempted to encourage violent discord between the two organizations in an effort to disrupt their work and contain their influence.

The events of 1969 might well have contributed to Karenga's own darkest hour, when he and two other men were convicted in 1971 of felony assault and false imprisonment for torturing two women associated with Organization Us. Descriptions of this two-day brutality were both vivid and horrific, and during the trial Karenga's sanity was seriously questioned. The events themselves, including cold cruelty and physical torture, were difficult to associate with the man who had promoted a philosophy of social reform, family, and community. Karenga's mental state at the time was vividly captured in the psychiatrist's report quoted by Judge Arthur L. Alarcon during the sentencing hearing: "This man now represents a picture that can be considered both paranoid and schizophrenic with hallucinations and illusions, inappropriate affect, disorganization, and impaired contact with the environment." Karenga was sentenced to a term of one to ten years, which he began serving in 1971.

By the time he was released from the California State Prison in 1975, Karenga had been heavily influenced by Marxism, and he returned to a revamped Organization Us with a determined socialist focus. He returned as well to his studies and in 1976 earned his first Ph.D. from U.S. International University with a dissertation titled "Afro-American Nationalism: Social Strategy and Struggle for Community."

With a renewed focus on Afrocentric scholarship and a growing international reputation, Karenga in 1982 made one of the most important contributions to African American education, the widely used *Introduction to Black Studies*. Considered by many to be the standard introductory text in the field, *Introduction to Black Studies* provides students with a wide-ranging survey of the scholarship that defined Africana studies as a coherent and comprehensive discipline. The textbook explores the history of student and community activism that led to the creation of black studies programs, presents black history in terms of both its African backgrounds and its American manifestations, and provides an interdisciplinary introduction to the scholarship and debates central to Africana studies, including comprehensive sections on black religion, black sociology, black politics, black economics, black cultural production, and black psychology, and concludes with a section devoted to "reaffirmation and reassessment."

Introduction to Black Studies helped launch a vital new period in Karenga's influence as a scholar. In 1984 he co-hosted with Jacob Carruthers the first Annual Ancient Kemetic Studies Conference in Los Angeles, which led to the development of the Association for the Study of Classical African Civilizations. In 1986 Karenga served as a member of the planning committee for the Pan-African Festival of Arts and Culture, in Dakar, Senegal, and also as the chairman of the delegation of educators and activists of Organization Us to Cuba. In 1987 he served as the co-planner and co-convener of the Annual Ancient Egyptian Studies Conference of the Association for the Study of Classical African Civilizations, Cairo, Egypt, and in that same year he delivered the inaugural lecture in London to establish Black History Month in Britain. By 1989 he had been appointed chairman of the Department of Black Studies at California State University, Long Beach, a position he held until 2002. And his commitment to scholarship was also underscored by his own continuing education, which led to his second Ph.D. in 1994—a doctorate in Social Ethics from the University of Southern California (USC), for which he wrote a dissertation titled "Maat, the Moral Ideal in Ancient Egypt: A Study in Classical African Ethics." In recognition of these various contributions, in 1998 he was awarded an honorary doctorate of philosophy from the University of Durban-Westville, South Africa.

An untiring, committed, and controversial educator and social theorist, Karenga was recognized as one of the most influential scholars and activists of his day. His importance to black communities in the United States was emphasized by his participation in the 1995 Million Man March/Day of Absence, for which he authored the mission statement and sat on the national organizing committee. His importance to the scholarly community was underscored by his numerous publications, his various academic appointments, and his numerous awards for scholarship. His significance worldwide was established by his international lecturing schedule and his participation in various international organizations and events. Determined, insistent, and committed, Karenga rose from a troubled past to a position of international prominence and influence.

FURTHER READING

Alexander, Victor S. "Interview: Dr. Maulana Ron Karenga," *African Commentary* (Oct. 1989).

Brown, Scot. *Fighting for US: Maulana Karenga, the US Organization, and Black Cultural Nationalism* (2003).

Official Kwanzaa Web site, http://www. officialkwanzaawebsite.org/index.shtml (1999–2006).

Organization Us. "The Chair's Message," http://www. us-organization.org/ (1999–2007).

Van Deburg, William L. *New Day in Babylon: The Black Power Movement and American Culture, 1965–1975* (1992).

JOHN ERNEST

Karim, Benjamin Goodman (14 July 1932–2 Aug. 2005), Islamic leader, was born Benjamin Goodman, the only child of Mary Goodman, a hairdresser, and an unknown father in Suffolk, Virginia. Goodman was given his mother's last name because his parents were not married. The family was poor and both he and his mother lived in his grandmother's house. He went to the Easter Graded School in black Saratoga and in 1947 moved to New York for a year. Finding rural Virginia dull, Goodman joined the U.S. Air Force at the age of seventeen and was immediately sent to Flackman Air Force Base in San Antonio, Texas, for training, after which he was transferred to Japan in 1950. He worked as a radar operator in both Japan and Korea, where he experienced discrimination from white American officers. Though acknowledged as the best radar operator for his work in Japan and on the war front in Korea by his fellow airmen, he never received a promotion. He was denied permission to visit his sick mother and later to attend her funeral; that same day, a white airman was allowed to go home to visit his wife who was having a baby. At the end of his tour of duty in 1952 Goodman requested to be discharged in Japan because of the freedom he enjoyed there, but this request was denied and he was released in New Mexico. Through such discriminatory practices, the military failed to comply with President Harry Truman's Executive Order 9981 (1948) that legally eliminated official discrimination and segregation by requiring equal treatment and equal opportunity for blacks in the U.S.

armed forces. Nevertheless the sense of freedom that Goodman had experienced in Japanese society was one he had never felt in his home country.

In November 1952 Goodman moved to Harlem, where he worked various jobs in painting, garment working, gambling, and shipping, occasionally attending church. He was introduced to the Nation of Islam (NOI), but at first rejected it. On 14 April 1957, however, he witnessed MALCOLM X easily quiet an angry black crowd standing in a front of a police station. Founded by W. D. Fard in Detroit in 1930, the NOI was a movement that advocated the creation of a separate black nation in America. It also taught self-esteem, discipline, thrift, and independent economic empowerment to African Americans. NOI adherents were also taught better nutrition, world black history, and public speaking. The organization encouraged the creation of Muslim schools and businesses and rejected white people because they were assumed to be "devils." For many blacks the NOI represented an appealing alternative to Christianity, a religion that was deemed a white man's religion and too close to the racist power structures of America. Malcolm X, who had served as the minister of Temple Number Seven for the NOI since 1954, helped Goodman overcome his stuttering and gambling, a transformation that made him more loyal to his mentor.

Upon his conversion to Islam Goodman was forced to marry his live-in girlfriend, Cora, who also joined the NOI. For a time he continued to visit churches but rejected (black) Christianity because of its emphasis on money, its alleged lack of intellectual sophistication, and its use of white imagery for angels. As an NOI convert Goodman became active in the Fruit of Islam, the NOI auxiliary for men that taught self-discipline and public speaking. Malcolm so appreciated Goodman that he made him assistant minister and later first assistant minister. Goodman became immersed in Islam and he took a job as a building superintendent with less pay in order to find time to read more Islamic literature. He worked hard as an NOI minister, engaging in street preaching and traveling as an itinerant teacher and preacher from Washington to Boston. He found time to serve briefly as assistant minister in Bridgeport, Connecticut, acting minister in Washington, D.C., and temple organizer in Brooklyn and Queens in New York. Soon he became the advance man who opened rallies for Malcolm X and served as a close aide. In 1963 he divorced his first wife and married Linda, with whom he had six children.

In 1963 the NOI had suspended Malcolm X for ninety days because he disobeyed the clear command of ELIJAH MUHAMMAD, NOI national leader, to refrain from making any comments on the death of President Kennedy. After the first suspension Elijah made Malcolm's suspension indefinite. On 12 March 1964 Malcolm left the NOI and his local temple of 3,000 members to found the Muslim Mosque, Incorporated (MMI). Loyal to Malcolm, Goodman and one third of the national memberships of both Temple Number Seven and the NOI throughout the United States joined the MMI. This new Muslim organization left the isolationist stand of the NOI and vowed to work with other civil rights organizations in order to transform American politics. In June 1964 Malcolm founded the Organization of Afro-American Unity (OAAU), a non-Muslim organization whose objective was to fight for human rights for people of color worldwide. Goodman continued to work as a close aide to Malcolm in the MMI. In fact he had introduced Malcolm X at the Audubon Ballroom in New York City on 21 February 1965 moments before NOI members assassinated him.

In 1971 Goodman edited and wrote the introduction to *The End of White World Supremacy*, a collection of Malcolm's speeches. In 1975 he returned to the NOI and was promoted to assistant minister to Wallace D. Muhammad, son and successor of the late Elijah Muhammad, in Chicago. W. D. Muhammad first changed the name of the NOI to the World Community of Al-Islam in the West and later to the American Muslim Mission (AMM). He dropped the nationalist leanings, brought the AMM more in line with traditional Islamic teachings, and welcomed people of all races into the organization. In 1978 W. D. Muhammad gave Goodman the Arabic surname Karim and appointed him minister in charge of the local American Muslim Mission in Richmond, Virginia. He served as adviser to SPIKE LEE for the movie *Malcolm X*. Karim continued to promote Malcolm's teachings and lectured widely until his death.

FURTHER READING

Goodman, Benjamin. *The End of White World Supremacy: Four Speeches* (1971).
Karim, Benjamin. *Remembering Malcolm X* (1992).

DAVID MICHEL

Kaufman, Bob (18 Apr. 1925–12 Jan. 1986), poet, was born Robert Garnell Kaufman in New Orleans, Louisiana, to Joseph Kaufman, a Pullman porter,

and Lillian Vigne, a schoolteacher. Many myths circulate about Kaufman's formative years, perpetuated by word of mouth and scholarly sources alike. The literary scholar Maria Damon debunks many of these in her book *The Dark End of the Street: Margins in American Vanguard Poetry*. The legends, however, bear repeating, as they have become part of Kaufman's biography. The usual story is that Kaufman was born to a German Orthodox Jewish father and Martiniquan Roman Catholic voodoo mother, and that at age thirteen he joined the merchant marine, where he was introduced to literature by a first mate and circled the globe nine times in twenty years.

The truth, according to interviews with Kaufman's brother George, is that their paternal grandfather was part Jewish and that their mother came from an established New Orleans family. The Kaufmans were Catholic, and their thirteen children grew up in a household filled with books. George Kaufman recollects that they had limerick contests and read Proust, Joyce, and Flaubert. Information about Kaufman's early formal education is contradictory; most sources indicate that he achieved an elementary school education or do not mention formal education. However, Kaufman joined the merchant marine at age eighteen, not age thirteen as legend has it. The existent information about his early abandonment of school seems to be a necessary part of this legend.

Kaufman was a merchant marine from 1943 until the mid-1950s. During this time he worked as a labor organizer in the National Maritime Union, primarily in New York City and San Francisco. He also took classes at the New School for Social Research and in 1948 worked in Appalachia as an organizer for Henry Wallace's presidential campaign for the left-leaning Progressive Party. The McCarthy era put an end to Kaufman's union work, and he moved to San Francisco, where he met and married Eileen Singhe in 1958. They had two children, son Parker and daughter Antoinette, and would separate at various times but never divorce.

Settling in North Beach, Kaufman took up poetry in earnest. In a 2000 interview with T. J. Anderson III, Eileen Kaufman said that in 1958 and 1959 Kaufman booked musicians at the Jazz Workshop and began to experiment with bebop rhythms and the spoken word. Performing these works in the streets, Kaufman earned the nickname "The Original Bebop Man" and was arrested repeatedly for disorderly conduct. Kaufman and fellow Beats Jack Kerouac and TED JOANS spontaneously traded poems in North Beach jazz clubs, and Kaufman often recited poems at his hangout, the Co-existence Bagel Shop.

Eileen encouraged Kaufman to write down his oral compositions, and she would continue to play a major role in his literary career, compiling and editing poems and acting as his literary agent. In 1959 Lawrence Ferlinghetti's City Lights Books published three Kaufman broadsides that would become Beat literary classics: *Abomunist Manifesto*, *Second April*, and *Does the Secret Mind Whisper?* a hybrid text composed of legal documents, bebop language, a glossary, an anthem, and a newscast, among other forms, demonstrates Kaufman's commitment to jazz and linguistic experiment as social protest, particularly in the context of the cold war. As Barbara Christian observed in her 1972 article "Whatever Happened to Bob Kaufman?," Abomunism "makes serious fun of *isms* ... [and] is a blueprint for a revolutionary way of life" (27). The other two broadsides employ surrealist image catalogs and Whitman's long line to juxtapose personal, historical, and popular culture events.

In 1959 Kaufman founded *Beatitude* magazine with Allen Ginsberg, John Kelly, and William Margolis. Kaufman did not, however, coin the term "beatnik" as is commonly thought; the *San Francisco Chronicle* columnist Herb Caen coined the term as a pejorative in an article about Kaufman. In 1960 Kaufman's poem "Bagel Shop Jazz" was nominated for the British Guinness Poetry Award, an honor that earned him an invitation to read at Harvard University. T. S. Eliot, however, won the Guinness.

Kaufman moved to New York, where he became part of the Lower East Side avant-garde literary scene. His addiction to drugs and alcohol worsened, as did his relationship with the police. In 1963, having already acquired a substantial record, he was arrested for walking on the grass in Washington Square Park, given numerous shock treatments at Bellevue Hospital, and threatened with a lobotomy. Kaufman moved back to San Francisco, and on 22 November 1963, the day of John F. Kennedy's assassination, he took a vow of silence that would last until the withdrawal of U.S. troops from Vietnam in 1973.

Despite Kaufman's withdrawal from public writing and speaking, his poems continued to be published. In 1965 James Laughlin of New Directions Press published *Solitudes Crowded with Loneliness*, a collection of Kaufman's poetry from 1958 to 1963, and in 1967 *Golden Sardine* was compiled by Mary Beach from Kaufman's manuscripts and published by City Lights Books. T. J. Anderson III characterized *Golden Sardine* as Kaufman's most innovative exploration of a jazz aesthetic, particularly in the use of bebop and scat improvisation and the inclusion of fragmentary work-in-progress. *Solitudes Crowded with Loneliness* would earn Kaufman an international reputation when it was translated into French in 1975, as well as the nickname "the American Rimbaud" or "the Black Rimbaud."

In 1978 Kaufman again withdrew into silence, telling Raymond Foye that "I want to be anonymous ... my ambition is to be completely forgotten" (*The Ancient Rain: Poems, 1956–1978*, 1981, ii). With the help of a grant Kaufman won from the National Endowment for the Arts, Foye edited the collection *The Ancient Rain: Poems, 1956–1978*, in which Kaufman explores themes of death and spirituality through the literary figures Federico García Lorca and Hart Crane.

By now years of substance abuse had damaged Kaufman's body and mind. A. D. Winans remembered that in the 1980s Kaufman was banned from every bar in North Beach except one, and that he "walk[ed] the streets of North Beach twitching, blinking, and mostly unspeaking" (20). Kaufman died of emphysema and cirrhosis. He was honored with a New Orleans–style funeral procession around his North Beach streets, and his ashes were scattered over the San Francisco Bay.

In 1996 Coffee House published *Cranial Guitar: Selected Poems*, a collection of Kaufman's best poems, out-of-print works, and unpublished writing, and his poetry was included in major anthologies of Beat and African American literature. His work influenced innovative African American writers such as ISHMAEL REED, JAYNE CORTEZ, Paul Beatty, HARRYETTE MULLEN, and members of Boston's Darkroom Collective. Arguably one of the best Beat writers, Kaufman's work is notable in that it brought together (and as Damon noted, reworked and defamiliarized) modernist poetry, surrealist poetry, and jazz-inflected writing and performance. His achievement made it impossible to grant him the anonymity he desired.

FURTHER READING

The Howard Gotlieb Archival Research Center at Boston University holds some of Bob Kaufman's papers.

Anderson, T. J., III. *Notes to Make the Sound Come Right: Four Innovators in Jazz Poetry* (2004).

Christian, Barbara. "Whatever Happened to Bob Kaufman?" *Black World* (Sept. 1972).

Clay, Mel. *Jazz—Jail and God: An Impressionistic Biography of Bob Kaufman* (2001).

Damon, Maria. *The Dark End of the Street: Margins in American Vanguard Poetry* (1993).

Damon, Maria. Introduction to "Bob Kaufman: A Special Section," *Callaloo* 25.1 (2002).

Winans, A. D. "Bob Kaufman," *American Poetry Review* 29.3 (May–June 2000).

JENNIFER DRAKE

Kay, Ulysses Simpson (7 Jan. 1917–20 May 1995), composer, was born in Tucson, Arizona, the son of Ulysses Simpson Kay Sr., a barber, and Elizabeth Kay, who was from Louisiana. As a young child he was surrounded with musical sounds—from his parents' singing to his brother and sister practicing music. When it was time for Ulysses Kay to start music instruction, his mother sought advice from Uncle Joe—the legendary cornetist KING OLIVER—concerning trumpet lessons. King Oliver replied, "No, Lizzie. Give that boy piano lessons so's he can learn the rudiments. And then he'll find what *he* wants to do in music" (Slonimsky, 3). Kay began formal piano studies at age six. Besides piano, Kay also played the violin and the saxophone. He was very active in his high school's musical ensembles, playing in the dance orchestra and marching band. Additionally Kay enjoyed listening to the sounds of the contemporary jazz giants Benny Goodman and DUKE ELLINGTON. During the summer he would often attend live concerts of the Tucson Symphony Orchestra and the University of Arizona Concert Band. In 1934 Kay attended the University of Arizona as a liberal arts student. He soon decided to major in music, receiving a bachelor's degree in 1938. Kay continued his graduate education at the Eastman School of Music in Rochester, New York. For two years he studied composition with Bernard Rogers and Howard Hanson. In an interview for *The Black Composer Speaks*, Kay acknowledged three people who had influence on his musical activities: his uncle, King Oliver, WILLIAM GRANT STILL, and Bernard Rogers.

Kay received his master of music degree in Composition from Eastman in 1940. He continued his studies with Paul Hindemith, composing works for orchestra, piano, chorus, brass, and strings. In 1942 Kay enlisted in the U.S. Navy. He was assigned to a band in Rhode Island where he played saxophone, flute, and piano; he also arranged music and composed. After being honorably discharged in 1946 Kay studied with Otto Luening at Columbia University. He received the Prix de Rome in 1949 and 1951, as well as a Fulbright scholarship in 1950. These awards enabled Kay to travel and study in Italy from 1949 to 1952. On 20 August 1949 Kay

Ulysses Simpson Kay, neoclassical composer and professor of music. (University of Massachusetts, Amherst.)

married Barbara Harrison, a fellow musician. Their three daughters were born in 1951, 1957, and 1959.

In 1953 Kay accepted a position as music consultant with Broadcast Music, Inc. He held this position for fifteen years, continuing to compose orchestral works, chamber music, and two operas. In 1968 Kay was appointed distinguished professor of theory and composition at Lehman College of the City University of New York.

Under the auspices of the U.S. State Department, on 17 September 1958 Kay and fellow composers Roy Harris, Peter Mennin, and Roger Sessions traveled to Russia for a monthlong cultural exchange tour with Russian composers and musicologists. During their stay they met with numerous Russian composers, attended live performances, and visited music schools. Their visit culminated with a well-publicized performance of their own compositions.

According to Nicolas Slonimsky, "Ulysses Kay is a composer who refuses to carry a label—technical, racial, stylistic. He writes music that corresponds to his artistic emotions, within a framework of harmony, counterpoint, and orchestration that provides him with the broadest range of expression."

Many Kay scholars have summarized his compositional style. However, in the conclusion to his article "The Choral Works of Ulysses Kay," Robert D. Herrema succinctly analyzed Kay's oeuvre, stating:

A marvelous dichotomy exists in the music of Ulysses Kay: craftsmanship and romanticism, reason and emotion. Occasionally one will give way to the other, but usually both are present in equal amounts. His craft is at once Hindemithian, classical, and Netherlandish; his expressiveness is incredibly romantic and madrigalian. His music can not—and therefore should not—be labeled stylistically, technically or racially. It is modern in the sense that it is contemporary.

Kay described his compositional style "as traditional in terms of materials and attitudes toward them, but personal in expression.... I feel it has evolved to become more chromatic, more free in form and process, and this has happened in order to express newer ideas that have come to me" (Baker et al., 146).

Kay's harmonic language consists of both diatonic and chromatic techniques. Although he did not write atonal music, Kay used dissonance freely and often inventively employed imitative and contrapuntal devices. Kay's melodic writing included the use of diatonic and chromatic lines as well as melodies with irregular interval patterns. He manipulated conventional formal structures for his compositions, giving them a new dimension.

Kay composed more than 130 musical compositions for just about every instrumental and vocal combination. These works include solo instrumental pieces as well as keyboard compositions. His first composition, for solo piano, was entitled *Ten Pieces for Children* (1939). Kay also composed for small instrumental ensembles, string orchestra, chamber orchestra, full orchestra, orchestra with vocalists, concert band, and solo voice. In addition to more than twenty choral works and five operas, Kay wrote several television and film soundtracks.

In the *International Dictionary of Black Composers* (vol. 2, 1999), Lucius Wyatt classified Kay's works into three distinct periods of composition. The early period (1939–1946) includes his ballet *Danse Calinda* (1941), the *Four Pieces for Male Chorus* (1941), his *Suite for Orchestra* (1945), and his first major success, *Of New Horizons: Overture*, which premiered on 29 July 1944 at Lewisohn Stadium in New York with the New York Philharmonic Orchestra and received the American Broadcasting Company prize in 1946. With regard to *Of New Horizons*, Samuel A. Floyd Jr. (*The Power of Black Music*, 163) observes:

As early as 1944, Ulysses Kay's prize-winning orchestral work *Of New Horizons* had begun to move black concert-hall music away from African-American nationalism into a neoclassicism devoid of ring-derived traits. Kay followed this work with *Short Overture* (1946) and *Three Pieces after Blake* (1952), both of which, with their apparent objectivity, restraint, and formal conformity, established Kay as a composer of merit.

According to Wyatt, Kay's middle-period works (1947–1965) "are generally chromatic and adventuresome, melodically and harmonically, as compared to his earlier compositions." This prolific output includes the *Suite for Strings* (1947), *Concerto for Orchestra* (1948), *Sinfonia in E* (1950), *Serenade for Orchestra* (1954) and *Six Dances for String Orchestra* (1954). Kay also composed two operas—*The Boor* (1955) and *The Juggler of Our Lady* (1956)—as well as choral and chamber music.

Kay's late period (1966–1995) includes a work that he considered his most significant composition. *Markings* (1966) premiered on 18 August 1966 with the Detroit Symphony Orchestra, Sixten Ehrling conducting. This work was written in memory of Dag Hammarskjold, the United Nations secretary-general from Sweden. According to Kay, "I feel it is significant because it is big in scope as well as in expression, and I feel it's quite personal in terms of how it's worked out." Other works of the late period include three operas as well as *The Birds* (1966), *Theater Set for Orchestra* (1968), *Scherzi Musicali* (1968), *Facets* (1971), *The Western Paradise* (1976), and *Chariots* (1978).

In addition to his work as a composer, Kay served as a composer-in-residence both in the United States and abroad. Kay was a well-respected conductor, lecturer, adjudicator, consultant, and leader of professional organizations. He received many prestigious awards as well as six honorary doctorates.

After twenty years at Lehman College, Kay retired in 1988. On 14 April 1991 Kay's last opera, *Frederick Douglass* (1979–1985), received its world premiere at Symphony Hall in Newark, New Jersey. Kay lived with his family in Teaneck, New Jersey, until his death in 1995.

FURTHER READING

A number of libraries and resource centers have Kay holdings. One of the largest is the E. Azalia Hackley

Collection, Detroit Public Library, Detroit; there are also holdings at the Music Division, Library of Congress, Washington, D.C. (See *Ulysses Kay: A Bio-Bibliography*, 160–161, for a complete list.)

Baker, David N., Lida M. Bert, and Herman C. Hudson, eds. *The Black Composer Speaks* (1978).

Floyd, Samuel A., Jr. *The Power of Black Music: Interpreting Its History from Africa to the United States* (1995).

Herrema, Robert D. "The Choral Works of Ulysses Kay," *Choral Journal* 11 (Dec. 1970).

Hobson, Constance Tibbs, and Deborra A. Richardson. *Ulysses Kay: A Bio-bibliography* (1994).

Roach, Hildred. *Black American Music: Past and Present* (1992).

Slonimsky, Nicolas. "Ulysses Kay," *American Composers Alliance Bulletin* 7 (1958).

Southern, Eileen. *The Music of Black Americans: A History* (1997).

MARIANNE WILSON

Kearse, Amalya Lyle (11 June 1937–), lawyer, jurist, and champion bridge player, was born in Vauxhall, New Jersey, the daughter of Myra Lyle Smith, a physician and antipoverty director, and Robert Freeman Kearse, a local postmaster. Kearse's parents encouraged her to develop her substantial intellectual skills, and were the catalyst for her dreams of becoming a lawyer and, later, a public servant. Profiled by *Ebony* in 1966, Kearse revealed that her legal aspirations began in childhood. "I became an attorney," she stated, "because I once wanted [as a child] to be an FBI agent." "My father always wanted to be a lawyer," Kearse told the *New York Times* in 1979. "The Depression had a lot to do with why he didn't. I got a lot of encouragement." Kearse's mother hoped her daughter would pursue a career in medicine. "But I couldn't," Kearse explained "I was too squeamish. Besides, I liked going through old law books."

Kearse attended elite Wellesley College, earning her bachelor's degree in Philosophy in 1959. After graduating from Wellesley, and against the advice of college counselors, Kearse enrolled at the University of Michigan Law School. At that time, women and minorities were scarce in law schools across the country. Kearse was the only African American of only eight women in a class of about 350.

While at Michigan, Kearse was elected to the Order of the Coif and was an editor of the law review, where her legal expertise and performance on the Law Review Editorial Board earned her the Jason L. Honigman Prize. During her years as a law student, Kearse became known as a person whose intellect and talents went well beyond the law, and in 1962 she graduated cum laude.

Following her graduation from law school, Kearse moved to New York, choosing to join the esteemed corporate law firm of Hughes, Hubbard, and Reed as an associate trial lawyer specializing in antitrust and business litigation. There, she was one of few African Americans, few women, and even fewer African American women to work on Wall Street. In this competitive atmosphere, Kearse broke down the barrier of white, male privilege.

Seven years later, Kearse became a partner, an unprecedented accomplishment for someone so young, and one that made her the first female African American partner in a major Wall Street law firm. Kearse held the distinction of being both the first African American and the first female in the partnership of Hughes, Hubbard, and Reed. Orville Schell, a senior partner at Hughes Hubbard, offered high praise for his pioneering colleague in 1979: "She became a partner here not because she is a woman, not because she is black, but because she is just so damned good—no question about it."

In June 1979, at the age of 41, Kearse, a Republican at that time, was asked by Democratic president Jimmy Carter to serve on the Second U.S. Circuit Court of Appeals for Manhattan, which serves the states of New York, Connecticut, and Vermont. Even though it meant that she would take a substantial pay cut, Kearse accepted the appointment.

Kearse became the first woman and the second black person to sit on the Second Circuit. She was preceded by THURGOOD MARSHALL, who had been appointed to the Supreme Court in 1967. Judge Kearse soon garnered a reputation as a gifted legal scholar, first-rate legal writer, and a shrewd analyst, and was regarded as a "courtly, low-key, center-left jurist." In 2002 Kearse declared senior status, for which she became eligible at age 65, thus reducing her caseload by half and leaving Kearse more time to spend on nonjudicial activities such as bridge, for which she had developed a great passion.

Kearse impressed liberals and conservatives alike in her role as a federal jurist. This was partly due to her command of the law, and partly because her decisions did not allow her to be predictably categorized. Her votes on social issues often pleased the liberal-leaning groups. Conservatives, on the other hand, were pleased in 1984 when Kearse rendered an opinion that restricted circumstances under which private plaintiffs could seek triple damages in lawsuits brought under the RICO act, and in a decision in 1990, which strengthened the statute of limitations for bringing securities-fraud suits. In Kearse's view, the most significant Second Circuit case of her tenure was *United States v. Yonkers Board of Education*, a decades-long school desegregation case deemed by some to be the most significant case of its kind since *Brown v. Board of Education*.

On several occasions, Judge Kearse was considered for possible appointment to the U.S. Supreme Court. She was one of eight names given to President Reagan by the National Women's Political Caucus for consideration for possible replacement of Justice Potter Stewart. George Herbert Walker Bush considered Kearse, along with CLARENCE THOMAS and others, to fill the vacancy created by the retirement of Marshall. In 1992 her name appeared on a list of persons reviewed by the Clinton administration for the position of U.S. attorney general, a position for which Janet Reno was ultimately nominated. In 1993, when President Clinton was looking for a replacement for Supreme Court Justice Byron White, Kearse was one of the potential appointees. Judge Kearse was considered once again when Justice Harry Blackmun announced his retirement.

In addition to her work as a jurist, Kearse was a gifted athlete and an avid bridge player. In addition to being hoop roller champion at Wellesley, she was a fervent tennis player at the University of Michigan. Kearse was also a world-class bridge player. She took up duplicate bridge while in law school and was later active in the Greater New York Bridge Association in many varied capacities. She won national and world titles and authored books on the subject.

YVONNE L. HUGHES

Keb' Mo'. *See* Moore, Kevin (Keb' Mo').

Kebe, Lamine (1785?–1835?), Muslim teacher who is variously known as Kibbe, Lamen Abd al-Amin, and Paul. Beyond two short notices in the *African [Colonization Society's] Repository* (1835) and a mention in a list of Liberian colonists, all that is known about Kebe was recorded by Theodore Dwight Jr., African colonizationist and a founder and secretary of the American Ethnological Society.

Lamine Kebe was born into a prominent family of the influential Kaba, or Kebe, of the Jakhanke clan of the Soninke or Serahule people. These were the founders of ancient Ghana, according to some accounts, and, more conclusively, twelfth-century converts to Islam from an area near the bend of the Niger River in present-day Mali. A short history of his people by Kebe accurately but sketchily describes the migration of a pragmatic, dedicated Qāadirīya brotherhood of teachers of Islam toward Kebe's Futa Jallon (home of BILALI, another African Muslim enslaved in Georgia, and IBRAHIMA ABD AL-RAHAHMAN, yet another, enslaved in Mississippi). The Jakhanke taught in local languages and without attempting to disrupt native religious practices not in direct conflict with their understanding of Islam. As avid preachers, travelers, and observers, they were necessarily well informed about the lands and peoples they lived among. Kebe, as he reported, trained to be a teacher, taught five years, married, fathered three children, and lost his freedom traveling (probably toward the coast) to buy scarce paper.

Introduced as "Old Paul," Kebe told his first New York City audience in late 1834 that in America he had been sold and moved around many times before a master freed him. It is not known how he got to New York, but it is likely that his stated desire to return to his homeland led to his being sent to this city's branch of the American Colonization Society, dedicated to sending free blacks away from their enslaved relatives. No donations were recorded at this meeting. He did better, however, in May 1835, when he told another audience that his master had freed him because he was literate in Arabic and that he wanted to be a Christian missionary back in Africa. Though a politic lie, Kebe did gain passage to Liberia later that year, after his information about readers of Arabic in the Guinean hinterland created or sparked a thought that became a campaign in 1863—to send Arabic speakers and books with Christian themes into West Africa. An added impetus came from Kebe's correspondence in Arabic with another enslaved African Muslim then in North Carolina, UMAR IBN SAID—instigated, probably, by the secretary of the parent American Colonization Society, Ralph R. Gurley.

Gurley was pleased to report later that the two men had encouraged each other's acceptance of Christianity. In the absence of these letters, it is not possible to know what each actually wrote. But it is doubtful that Kebe would have done more than suggest an apparent conversion. Dwight found him to be an unwavering Muslim. Still, this correspondence was important because Umar sent the unique African-Arabic-American autobiography, labeled by Dwight or another hand "The Life of Omar ben Saeed" (1831), to Kebe. Umar undoubtedly wanted his manuscript in the hands of another Muslim.

Further lines on the soft leather cover, however, declare that Kebe had presented the manuscript to Dwight. When Kebe understood there was an opening for him on a ship to Africa, he must have decided to pass this on to his amanuensis, Dwight, who promised to honestly tell his story. It would be nice to think he also made a copy to take with him to Africa. A "Paul A. Mandingo" from Georgia arrived in Liberia in August 1835. Surely this was Kebe. To the majority of Americans "Mandingo" was synonymous with "Muslim," and Kebe told Dwight that Kebe's mother was a "Manenca." A note added that he soon left the colony for Sierra Leone, closer to his Futa Jallon homeland and fellow *Serahule* Muslims.

In fact, Dwight did respectfully quote from and cite ideas and information gathered from Kebe in two articles. In 1835 Dwight published what may be the only article printed in the antebellum United States on an African's education and pedagogy ("On the Sereculeh Nation, in Nigritia," *American Annals of Education and Instruction*, vol. 5). This introduction to the school system and teachers (male and female) of Futa Jallon and Futa Bundu (Senegal), where Kebe had taught for five years, offered three of Kebe's conclusions from his own experiences teaching multiculturally in Africa, and in response to what he had observed, somehow, in American schools. Students should remain in one school unless a better is needed for their intellectual and moral advancement; teachers should be neither too harsh nor too lenient; and bilingual programs should be adopted for teaching Arabic as well as other languages. He also said—but this was not published until Dwight's second article—that education was universal (for free people, of course), that his aunt was very learned, and that many students taught Arabic and how to write their own languages using Arabic.

In his 1835 pedagogical article, Dwight also declared that much could be learned by Americans about the interesting, almost unknown Africans and their countries by seriously deigning to ask their slaves and servants. An amateur linguist, Dwight appended to these notes, to the limited extent of his ability, a vocabulary and translation of ninety-five words from Kebe's Serahule that may be compared to earlier lists gathered by the Scottish explorer Mungo Park, in his *Travels in the Interior Districts of Africa* (1800), and by Sigismund Koelle in his *Polyglotta Africana: Comparative Vocabulary … in More Than 100 African Languages* (1854). He also included what his ear heard of Kebe's list of twenty-one titles of instructional books (or manuscripts) in Arabic. This list compares favorably with later mid-nineteenth-century lists from West Africa.

Dwight's second article, "Condition and Character of Negroes in Africa" (1864), was more general on African history but made a more pointed argument, that it was reprehensible that Americans had not sought or shared information about Africans and Africa. This undeniably accurate assessment was met, regrettably, with too few details. Kebe would not have been pleased by the fact that for all their conversations, and despite promises to him to do so, Dwight managed to publish very little of what he had gathered—and then only after the Emancipation Proclamation. The only extended quote from Kebe in this article suggests how deeply Kebe would have been disappointed:

> There are good men in America, but all are very ignorant of Africa. Write down what I tell you exactly as I say it, and be careful to distinguish between what I have seen and what I have only heard other people speak of. They may have made some mistakes; but if you put down exactly what I say, by and by, when good men go to Africa, they will say, *Paul* told the truth (78).

The remainder of the article includes references to some European discoveries, lists of names of the best-known African Muslims who had been allowed voices on this side of the Atlantic, and several writings in Arabic and in local languages utilizing Arabic letters written by Africans and emphasizing Umar ibn Said's "Life." It also told of the 1863 campaign raised by the discovery through Kebe that there were many Muslims in and around Liberia who could read Arabic. Dwight and missionary friends, blissfully ignorant of the depth of West African Islam, presumed the latter would surely be converted by shiploads of Bibles in Arabic. Many Bibles, with an improved translation, were sent from Beirut to Liberia around 1864, and in 1866 EDWARD W. BLYDEN, admittedly for broader reasons, began the study of Arabic for instruction in Liberia College. One need not wonder what Kebe would have thought about such a campaign. He knew his people and their religious strengths; no sign of success has been found among followers of the Qāadirīya brotherhood.

When, in 1995, a packet of antebellum papers in Arabic, with translations, were auctioned off in New York, a further Dwight piece on Kebe was found. This was, however, only a corrected galley-sheet preface, unpaginated, from a substantial work Dwight came close to publishing in 1863 or 1864. It states, unequivocally, that Kebe remained sincerely and wholly Muslim. It also includes Dwight's only known description of Kebe: "about six feet high, well formed, of mild and grave countenance, friendly disposition, and dignified but simple demeanor." Daniel Bliss, then president of the young Syria Protestant College (now American University in Beirut), responsible for sending Bibles to Liberia following Dwight's advice while overlooking Kebe's adherence to the religion of his parents, read the proofs and warmly recalled "our old friend" Kebe. Kebe's life and adventures were extraordinary because he was one of a fortunate few enslaved Africans given an opportunity to be heard where it might count in the United States and who managed to gain—though late—an Atlantic Ocean passage back to Africa.

FURTHER READING

Austin, Allan D. *African Muslims in Antebellum America: Transatlantic Stories and Spiritual Struggles* (1997).

Boubakar, Barry. *Senegambia and the Atlantic Slave Trade* (1998).

Diouf, Sylviane A. *Servants of Allah: African Muslims Enslaved in the Americas* (1998).

Dwight, Theodore, Jr., "Condition and Character of Negroes in Africa," *Methodist Quarterly Review* (Jan. 1864).

Sanneh, Lamin O. *The Jakhanke: The History of an Islamic Clerical People of the Senegambia* (1979).

ALLAN AUSTIN

Keckly, Elizabeth Hobbs (Feb. 1818–26 May 1907), slave, dressmaker, abolitionist, and White House memoirist, was born Elizabeth Hobbs in Dinwiddie County, Virginia, the daughter of Armistead Burwell, a white slaveholder, and his slave Agnes Hobbs. Agnes was the family nurse and seamstress. Her husband, George Pleasant Hobbs, the slave of another man, treated "Lizzy" as his own daughter, and it was not until some years later, after George had been forced to move west with his master, that Agnes told Lizzy the identity of her biological father. While her mother taught her sewing, the skill that would make her name and fortune, it was George Hobbs who first instilled in Lizzy a profound respect for learning. Ironically, it was Armistead Burwell who repeatedly told Lizzy she would never be "worth her salt," and thus who probably sparked her ambition to succeed and prove him wrong.

Elizabeth Keckly, slave and dressmaker. She ultimately became a member of the White House staff, where she became a confidante of Mary Todd Lincoln and went on to publish a memoir about her years as a slave and in the White House entitled *Behind the Scenes*. (Courtesy of Documenting the American South, The University of North Carolina at Chapel Hill Libraries.)

As a young girl, Hobbs lived in the master's house, where her earliest tasks were to mind the Burwell's infant daughter, sweep the yard, pull up weeds, and collect eggs. Hobbs benefited from the better diet and clothing and the possibilities for self-improvement that were often afforded to house slaves. Most important, she was taught to read and write. These advantages, added to the relatively stable presence of her extended slave family, contributed to Hobbs's proud bearing and strong sense of self. Nevertheless, living in the master's house was also dangerous. When she was five years old, her mistress, enraged because she had accidentally tilted the baby out of its crib, had her beaten so severely that she never forgot it. At age fourteen, Hobbs was loaned to Burwell's eldest son, Robert, and his new bride, Margaret Anna Robertson. The young Burwells took Hobbs to Hillsborough, North Carolina, where Robert was the minister of the Presbyterian Church and Anna opened a school for girls. Years later Hobbs would speak of her years in Hillsborough as the darkest period of her early life. When she was eighteen, Anna goaded a neighbor and her husband to "break" her with repeated beatings. At twenty she became the sexual prey of Alexander Kirkland, the married son of one of the town's wealthiest slaveholders. For four years she endured a forced sexual relationship, until she gave birth to a son, George, and was sent back to the family in Virginia.

By this time Armistead Burwell had died, and Hobbs and her son rejoined her mother, becoming a slave in the household of Burwell's daughter, Anne, and her husband, Hugh A. Garland. In 1847 Garland moved his household to St. Louis, where he opened a law office. (One of Garland's clients was Irene Emerson, whose slaves, HARRIET and DRED SCOTT, sued her for their freedom.) However, Garland could not make ends meet, and he decided to hire Hobbs out as a seamstress. It was a pivotal moment in Hobbs's life. Being hired out enabled her to hone her skills as a dressmaker, and she soon earned the title of mantua maker for her ability to sew the complicated mantua, whose tight bodice was fitted with a series of tiny, vertical pleats in the back. But above all, sewing for hire gave her opportunities for autonomy that she could not have had working in the master's house. Indeed, during this period Hobbs developed the network of white female clients who, in 1855, lent her money to allow her to pay the twelve-hundred-dollar purchase price for her freedom and that of her son. By this time Hobbs had married James Keckly, whom she had known as a free black Virginian; the marriage quickly soured once she discovered that he was not, in fact, free and that he drank. (Though the conventional spelling of her married name is Keckley, she herself spelled it Keckly.)

Lizzy Keckly remained in St. Louis until 1860, when she moved east alone, leaving James in St. Louis and enrolling her son, George, in Wilberforce University in Ohio. (Her mother had died in 1854.) She arrived in Washington, D.C., in the spring and quickly found work as a seamstress. Within months she had built an impressive list of clients, consisting of the wives of congressmen and army officers. During the secession winter of 1860–1861, Varina Davis, wife of the Mississippi senator Jefferson Davis asked her to move south with her, though Keckly refused.

On the day after President Abraham Lincoln's first inauguration, in 1861, Elizabeth Keckly presented herself at the White House for an interview with Mary Todd Lincoln. One of her clients had recommended her to the new "Mrs. President" in return for a last-minute gown. Over the next few months Keckly made Mary Lincoln fifteen or sixteen new dresses, an enormous task and one that threw the women together for hours at a time for the elaborate fittings that were required. This collaboration was the beginning of a relationship that would deepen over time through the personal and public crises that beset the women. The first crisis they shared occurred in August 1861 when Keckly's son, who had enlisted in the Union army as a white man, was killed in the Battle of Wilson's Creek in Missouri.

A dignified, proud woman, Keckly also established herself as a notable figure in the middle-class black community in Washington. As one of the "colored" White House staff, Keckly was a member of an elite black society, along with the city's leading caterers, barbers, restaurateurs, and government messengers. She boarded with the family of Walker Lewis, a respected messenger and later steward, who had also bought his way out of slavery. She also joined the black Union Bethel Church, second only in stature to the exclusive Fifteenth Street Presbyterian Church (which she joined in 1865). Meanwhile, her dressmaking business grew steadily; at its peak it employed twenty seamstresses.

By 1862 Keckly had become an intimate member of the Lincoln family, looking after the Lincolns' two young sons, combing the president's hair, and advising Mary Lincoln on matters of decorum as well as fashion. After the Lincolns' twelve-year-old son, Willie, died of typhoid fever in February, the grief-stricken Mary Lincoln came to rely more heavily on the steadying presence of Lizzy Keckly.

During this period, Keckly was coming into her own not only as an entrepreneur but also as an activist. In April, after Congress emancipated slaves in the district, she was featured in a syndicated newspaper article about the success stories of recently freed slaves. That summer, she organized church members into the Contraband Relief Association to aid the "contrabands," newly freed slaves who were pouring into Washington by the thousands. In the fall she made her first trip to the North, ostensibly as companion to Mary Lincoln and her youngest son, Tad, traveling to New York and Boston. But she spent much of her time raising funds with black abolitionists, including the Reverend HENRY HIGHLAND GARNET, the Reverend J. SELLA MARTIN, and FREDERICK DOUGLASS, who raised money for her organization in England. She even solicited a donation from the president and Mrs. Lincoln.

Over the course of the four years she was an insider in the White House, Keckly became more comfortable wielding her influence. In 1864 she helped arrange for SOJOURNER TRUTH to meet with Abraham Lincoln in the White House. The Lincolns even visited the contraband camps, where Keckly worked. She was one of the Lincolns' party when they entered Richmond after the Civil War ended.

In 1865, after Lincoln's assassination, Keckly accompanied Mary Lincoln to Chicago and then returned to her business in Washington. In 1867, at Lincoln's request, the two women met in New York City, where Keckly helped Lincoln arrange for a brokerage firm to auction off her old clothes to pay off her debts. Lincoln, who returned to Chicago while Keckly stayed in New York to manage Lincoln's affairs, promised to pay her out of the proceeds of the sale. But the scheme was a disaster; the women lost money on the venture. During this period, with the help of the antislavery journalist James Redpath, Keckly wrote a memoir, devoting the last section to what the newspapers dubbed the "Old Clothes Scandal." The 1868 publication of Keckly's book, *Behind the Scenes; or, Thirty Years a Slave, and Four Years in the White House*, caused Mary Lincoln to break off their friendship.

Behind the Scenes is an invaluable source of information about the Lincolns' private life in the White House. Whatever her motives for writing it, the memoir is unquestionably the expression of Keckly's desire to leave her mark, yet after its publication her business gradually declined, and she turned primarily to teaching sewing. In 1890 she sold her Lincoln mementos to a collector. For several years she headed Wilberforce University's department of sewing and domestic science arts, until she suffered a mild stroke. She died in Washington, D.C., in the National Home for Destitute Colored Women and Children, an institution founded during the war and partly funded by Keckly's contraband association.

FURTHER READING

Keckly, Elizabeth. *Behind the Scenes; or, Thirty Years a Slave, and Four Years in the White House* (1868), ed. Frances Smith Foster (2001).

Fleischner, Jennifer. *Mrs. Lincoln and Mrs. Keckly: The Remarkable Story of the Friendship between a First Lady and a Former Slave* (2003).

JENNIFER FLEISCHNER

Keeble, Marshall (7 Dec. 1878–20 Apr. 1968), preacher, missionary, and educator, was born the son of Robert Keeble, a street cleaner and minister, and Mittie Keeble in Rutherford County, Tennessee. For several generations the black Keeble family had been the slaves of the family of Major Horace Pinkney Keeble, a prominent white lawyer in Murfreesboro, Tennessee. Marshall was named after his grandfather, who served as a personal valet to the Confederate major Keeble during the Civil War. According to some accounts, his grandfather was killed by advancing Union soldiers, but Marshall disputed those accounts, claiming that he knew his grandfather. However, his family must certainly have been favored and personal slaves of the white Keebles because Robert and the elder Marshall were taught to read and write by their masters, which was highly unusual given the widespread prohibition against the education of slaves.

Marshall's grandfather and uncle were both preachers in the interracial—though segregated—Churches of Christ, a religious sect that grew out of the eighteenth-century Restoration movement that rejected all creeds, doctrines, hierarchical structures, or governing regulations that were not, in their view, explicitly found in the New Testament. (The Churches of Christ should not be confused with the more prominent black denomination Church of God in Christ founded by CHARLES HARRISON MASON, a holiness sect, or any of its many offshoots.) In 1882 Robert and Mittie moved their family to Nashville, where for the next thirty years Robert worked as a street cleaner and served as an assistant minister to Preston Taylor at the Gay Street Church. At the age of fourteen Marshall was baptized by Taylor.

When his father purchased a home, Marshall, a bright student, was forced to drop out of school in the seventh grade to help the family meet its new financial obligations. He worked sixteen hours a day in a bucket factory for forty cents an hour. At the age of eighteen he found employment in a soap factory. In 1896 Keeble married Winnie Womack, the daughter of a local minister, S.W. Womack. She was a graduate of Fisk University High School, outspoken in her opinions, and well respected. Keeble and his wife had five children during their thirty-six-year marriage, two of whom died in infancy and three through accidents or disease. Shortly after his wedding in 1896, Keeble assisted the university-trained George Phillip Bowser, Alexander Cleveland Campbell, and his father-in-law S.W. Womack, in founding the Church of

Christ at Jackson Street. These three were among the first black preachers to achieve a modicum of recognition within the Churches of Christ. Elders were the highest officers in the Churches of Christ, and ministers did not use the title "Reverend" but were often called called "Brother," as was Keeble. As Keeble began to gain a reputation as a captivating and persuasive preacher, his wife attempted to refine his speaking style by improving his grammar. He said that she wanted to make a "Fiskite" out of him, but he had discovered a style of communication somewhere between the vernacular argot of the stereotypical black country preacher and the urbane homiletics of a seminarian.

Keeble's thinking and behavior were influenced more by BOOKER T. WASHINGTON than anyone else outside of the church. Keeble had studied *Up from Slavery* closely, and every time Washington spoke in Nashville at the Union Gospel Tabernacle (which later became the Ryman Auditorium, home of the "Grand Ole Opry"), Keeble was in rapt attendance. Washington's political philosophy of gradualism and accommodation meshed neatly in Keeble's mind with the apostle Paul's dicta extolling the patience and sufferance of the righteous.

To support himself and his growing family, Keeble opened a small grocery store. While his wife ran the store, he used their cart and horse to sell coal, produce, and other goods. In 1914 Keeble decided to devote himself entirely to preaching and teaching. David Lipscomb, founder of the Nashville Bible School (which later became Lipscomb University) supported Keeble's efforts by putting him in touch with a white benefactor, A. M. Burton, a founder of the Life and Casualty Insurance Company and a member of the Churches of Christ who was deeply committed to Keeble's evangelical vision. In 1915 they founded a school in Silver Point, Tennessee, but it closed within two years. A second attempt was made in 1920 in Nashville, with the Southern Practical Institute, to provide both religious and vocational training. This endeavor failed within six weeks, in part because the white superintendent of this school for blacks insisted that the students enter through the rear door.

Life on the preaching circuit was fraught with danger and challenges. Since NAT TURNER's failed rebellion in 1831, black preachers had often been suspected of fomenting unrest. In 1926 members of the Ku Klux Klan burst into a prayer meeting that Keeble was leading in Summit, Georgia, to make sure that he was not preaching to an integrated congregation. They then ordered him to read a statement affirming the superiority of the white race. After Keeble read it, he added, "I have always known the white man is superior. They brought us out of Africa, and have lifted us up" (Broking, 23). Similar statements can be found in the poetry of PHILLIS WHEATLEY and other black Christians who expressed gratitude for being taken out of "darkness." But such sentiments were not necessarily a defense of slavery or racism. Keeble certainly believed in the equality of all Christians and their superiority over "heathens," particularly in Africa. In his retelling of this particular incident, four of the Klansmen returned to observe his preaching, and one became saved as a result and submitted to being baptized by Keeble. In another incident, when a white man threatened to strike him, Keeble stood prepared to receive the blow rather than offer resistance or defense. Keeble's noble-minded Christian response shamed his assailant into submission.

In addition to the constant threat of violence, Keeble faced competition from preachers of rival denominations. He never backed down from these confrontations and proved to be a fierce and combative debater. Indeed, his first debate was against his father, Robert, who had joined a group called the Do-Rights, which focused on the efficacy of using water instead of wine or grape juice during communion. On another occasion in Birmingham, Alabama, Keeble held a four-night debate with a holiness preacher on such subjects as proper baptism, the ritual of foot washing, and the nature of the Holy Spirit. He debated a Baptist preacher in Florida, Adventists in Colorado and Oklahoma, and a popular barnstorming preacher in Tennessee. A short, dark man who dressed neatly but simply, Keeble won these debates on the strength of his arguments rather than on eloquence, histrionics, sartorial flare, or humor—although he could always evoke a hearty laugh.

By 1931 Keeble's renowned preaching warranted the publication of *Biography and Sermons of Marshall Keeble, Evangelist*, edited by his colleague B. C. Goodpasture. In 1932 his wife died, and the following year Keeble married Laura Catherine Johnson, a young woman from Corinth, Mississippi. It is said he interrupted his own wedding several times with shouts of "Amen." They lived happily together for the rest of his life, but had no additional children. The Nashville Christian Institute, a school for adult remedial training, was founded in 1939, and in 1942 Keeble became its first president. He served in this position until 1958, and under his leadership the school expanded into a thriving institution serving students from kindergarten through the twelfth grade.

Keeble continued to travel the country during the 1960s, speaking to black and white audiences at churches and colleges. He did not play an active role in the civil rights movement and did not even seem to support the nonviolent tactics used by Dr. MARTIN LUTHER KING JR. Keeble explained: "Anything you have to force a man to do just isn't worth it…. Integration? I would rather we get it slow than get it wrong" (Broking, 75–76).

Yet Keeble never tired of trying to change hearts and save souls by spreading the gospel as he understood it. He made several trips to Africa, where he was made an honorary chief in Nigeria and where a dormitory of the Nigerian Christian Secondary School was named Keeble Hall. In 1962 he published an autobiography with Mary Campbell, *From Mule Back to Super Jet with the Gospel*, a brief testament about his life and his travels in Africa, Europe, the Holy Land, India, Korea, and elsewhere.

In 1965 Keeble received an honorary doctor of law degree from Harding University. When he died at home three years later, he was credited with establishing over two hundred congregations and baptizing over fifteen thousand people, including his own mother. In retrospect, while Keeble seems rather quixotic in regard to integration, he possessed an indomitable spirit in espousing the goals of self-help and the building of black businesses, schools, and churches.

FURTHER READING

A collection of primary documents pertaining to Keeble's life and career, including his correspondence, can be found in the Beaman Library at David Lipscomb University in Nashville.

Keeble, Marshall. *From Mule Back to Super Jet with the Gospel* (1962).

Broking, Darrell. "Marshall Keeble and the Implementation of a Grand Strategy: Erasing the Color Line in the Church of Christ," M.A. thesis, Department of History, East Tennessee State University (2003).

Choate, J. E. *Biography of Marshall Keeble, Roll Jordan Roll* (1974).

Goodpasture, B. C. *Biography and Sermons of Marshall Keeble Evangelist* (1931; rpt.1971).

Phillips, Paul D. "The Interracial Impact of Marshall Keeble Black Evangelist, 1878–1968," *Tennessee Historical Quarterly* 36 (Spring 1977).

Obituary: *Gospel Advocate*, 2 May 1968.

SHOLOMO B. LEVY

Kein, Sybil (29 Sept. 1939–), writer, teacher, musician, and performer, was born Consuela Marie Moore in Luling, Louisiana, to Frank P. Moore, a bricklayer, and Augustine Boudreaux Moore, a homemaker and musician. Kein and her six sisters and seven brothers were raised in New Orleans's Seventh Ward. She, like her family, spoke Creole until she started school. She was then required to speak *bon français*, or good French, which resulted in her losing the ability to speak Creole. Kein's ethnic background was an amalgamation of African American, Spanish, Irish, Native American, French, Jewish, German, and Polish, but Kein identified herself as Creole. She explained, "I like to think of [Creole culture] as epitomizing American culture because we are a mosaic of different cultures" (*Flint* [Michigan] *Journal*, 7 Nov. 1996).

Kein auditioned for the New Orleans Symphony Orchestra in 1958 as a violist, but the orchestra had a whites-only employment policy. She was offered a position in the opera orchestra if she promised not to tell anyone that she was not white. She turned down the position. As she was in this incident, many times in her life Kein was pushed to situate herself based on race (*New Orleans Times-Picayune*, 5 Mar. 1989). But Kein always felt that the Creole identity fit her best. She explained, "Creole by itself stands for it all, I think. The black, white and other color labels simply don't fit us. You're gonna leave somebody out if you put those labels on us" (*Atlanta Journal-Constitution*, 1 Apr. 2001).

Kein decided to study the viola and violin at Xavier University, earning a B.S. in 1964. That same year she studied visual arts at the Aspen School of Arts. Kein married her college sweetheart Felix Provost in 1960; they divorced in 1969 after having three children together, Elizabeth Provost-Small, David Provost, and Susan Provost. While earning an M.A. in Theater Arts and Communications at Louisiana State University at New Orleans, Kein taught classes in public speaking and communication skills. After she received her M.A. in 1972, Kein moved to Michigan to begin a Ph.D. program in American ethnic literature at the University of Michigan, teaching courses in English and theater. She graduated in 1975.

During her time in Michigan, Kein was hit and dragged by a car in a parking lot. The accident resulted in back problems. She was told by a doctor that she would not walk again, a diagnosis that ultimately proved false. During her hospitalization Kein remembered her great-aunt Julia once telling her to curse a childhood illness to speed up recovery. Kein did, cursing her situation in Creole. With help from friends and family and through her own research, she retaught herself the language of her childhood.

Kein continued teaching at the University of Michigan, earning tenure in 1988, but she felt compelled to learn more about her heritage. The Creole language and culture had been written about elsewhere, including in the mystery series by Barbara Hambly featuring the detective Benjamin January and in Anne Rice's *The Feast of All Saints* and *Merrick*, before Kein began writing and joining what she called the "Creole renaissance" (*Atlanta Journal-Constitution*, 1 Apr. 2001). Kein kept an apartment on Magazine Street in New Orleans to allow her to visit, do research, and enjoy events such as Mardi Gras.

Kein became the *chercheur associe* (associate research scholar) at the Centre d'Études Afro-Américaines at the Université de la Sorbonne Nouvelle, Paris, in 1990. She retired from the University of Michigan and moved to New Orleans in January 2000 and then to Natchitoches, Louisiana, to further her research and work on Creole culture. Kein explained, "The Creole people are gorgeous…. That blending of people is so wonderful and the blending of the culture is so wonderful, too" (*New Orleans Times-Picayune*, 26 Aug. 2000).

During her life Kein worked in many service positions. She was the director of the Children's Theater Touring Company in 1972–1974 and was a consultant for the McCree Theater in Flint, Michigan, in 1976–1979. She was a member of the United Teachers of Flint from 1976 to 1979, the Pre-Congress Session on the Arts, Michigan Council for the Arts, in 1978, and the National Council of English from 1978 to 1980. In 1988 she was the producer of *Excerpts from the Jazz Funeral of James Black*. In 1993–1994 she served as a consultant for the documentaries *Storyville* and *Spirit Tides from Congo Square*.

Kein was the recipient of many awards. Her play *Get Together* (1970) won the best playwright award from Louisiana State University in New Orleans in 1970. Her poetry won the Michigan Council for the Arts Creative Artist Award for poetry three different years (1981, 1984, and 1989). She won teaching awards like the Faculty Assembly Award for Excellence in Teaching and Creative/Scholarly Achievement from the University of Michigan (1978), the National AMOCO Outstanding

Teaching Award in Ann Arbor, Michigan (1979), the Michigan Association of Governing Boards Distinguished Faculty Award (1982), and the Loving Award for Professional Development, Teaching, and Service, University of Michigan at Flint (1997–1998).

A prolific writer, her plays include *Saints and Flowers* (1965), *Projection on the Black Box* (1967), *The Christmas Holly* (1967), *Deep River Rises* (1970), *The Reverend* (1970), *When I Grow Up* (1973–1974), and *River Rouges* (1979). She is the author of several books, including *Visions from the Rainbow* (1979), *Gombo People: Poésie Créole de la Nouvelle-Orléans* (1981, 1999), *Delta Dancer* (1984), *An American South* (1997), and *Creole Journal: The Louisiana Poems* (1999). She was the editor of *Creole: The History and Legacy of Louisiana's Free People of Color* (2000). Her work has also been featured in anthologies and literary journals. A recording of her poetry can be found in the National Archives at the Library of Congress. To express her musical talents Kein has recorded several CDs of Creole songs, often with members of her family. Her CDs include *Serenade Creole*, *Creole Ballads & Zydeco*, *Maw-Maw's Creole Lullaby and Other Songs for Children*, *Creole Classique*, *Love Is Forever*, and *Gardenias y Rosas*.

FURTHER READING

Azizian, Carol. "For the Love of Creole Music UM-Flint English Professor Creates Legacy of Sound from Her Past," *Flint* (Michigan) *Journal*, 7 Nov. 1996.

Dawson, Victoria. "Poet's Memories of Creole Childhood Inspire Her Writing," *New Orleans Times-Picayune*, 5 Mar. 1989.

Lane, Cassandra. "Creole Curse Was Blessing for 'Dying' Language—Scholar Helped Revive Tongue after Using It to Ward Off Pain," *Atlanta Journal-Constitution*, 1 Apr. 2001.

Larson, Susan. "Sybil Kein Retired from Her Teaching Job at a Michigan University, Moved Back Home to New Orleans and Committed Her Life to a Cause: Saving Creole Culture," *New Orleans Times-Picayune*, 26 Aug. 2000.

LAURA MADELINE WISEMAN

Keith, Damon Jerome (4 July 1922–), federal judge, was the youngest of six children born to Perry Keith, an automotive worker, and Annie Louise Williams. The family had its roots in Atlanta, Georgia, but Damon was born in Detroit, when his father took a job at the River Rouge Foundry of the Ford Motor Company. Keith has described his father as "the finest man in my life … the epitome of what a human being should be. He was my motivation and my desire to make something of myself."

In 1943 Keith graduated from an historically black college, West Virginia State College. That same year he was drafted into the army and served during World War II in a segregated military, an experience that he later described as "absolutely demeaning." After discharge from the military, Keith attended Howard University Law School, at a time when THURGOOD MARSHALL would practice before his Howard students the arguments he would later make in historic desegregation cases before the U.S. Supreme Court. Keith graduated from Howard Law School in 1949 and worked as a janitor while studying for the bar. Not long after he was admitted to practice in 1950, he married Rachel Boone, a physician from Liberia; they had three daughters, Gilda, Debbie, and Cecile. In 1956 Keith obtained a master of law degree from Wayne State University in Detroit.

During the early part of his career Keith was politically active while he was in practice. Before his appointment to the bench, he was one of the named partners in the firm of Keith, Conyers, Anderson, Brown & Wallis in Detroit. He served on a number of different commissions, including the Detroit Housing Commission, the Civil Rights Commission of the Detroit Bar Association, and the Michigan Civil Rights Commission. Keith was appointed to the federal bench by President Lyndon B. Johnson in 1967 and was elevated to the Sixth Circuit Court of Appeals by President Jimmy Carter in 1977. Although he took senior status, still hearing cases but with a reduced workload, in 1995, Keith has continued to write judicial decisions that record and make history in the United States.

In *United States v. Sinclair* (1971), Keith addressed the abuse of power endemic in the administration of President Richard M. Nixon. Judge Keith's ruling resulted from a criminal trial in which members of the radical leftist White Panther Party were accused of bombing the Ann Arbor, Michigan, offices of the CIA. During the trial it became clear that the federal government had tapped the phone lines of one of the White Panther defendants without obtaining a warrant beforehand. The U.S. attorney general John Mitchell justified the wiretapping on the basis of "national security," but Judge Keith found that Mitchell had exceeded its powers. In particular Keith rejected the Nixon administration's argument that "a dissident domestic organization is akin to an unfriendly foreign power and must be dealt with in the same fashion." Moreover, he added, the "Executive branch … cannot be given the power or the opportunity to investigate and prosecute criminal violations … simply because an accused espouses views which are inconsistent with our present form of Government." Keith concluded that the powers over search and seizure claimed by the Nixon White House were "never contemplated by the framers of our Constitution and cannot be tolerated today." The Supreme Court unanimously upheld Keith's ruling in *United States v. Sinclair*, which came to be known in legal circles as "the Keith decision."

In 2002 Keith returned to the problem of abuses of power in the executive branch, this time by John Ashcroft, President George W. Bush's attorney general. As in *Sinclair*, Keith argued in *Detroit Free Press v. John Ashcroft* that the executive branch had exceeded its powers. In the wake of the 11 September 2001 attacks on the United States, Attorney General Ashcroft had attempted to deport many Muslim non-citizens residing in the United States. The Bush administration also attempted to prevent several Michigan newspapers and Congressman JOHN CONYERS from attending one of those deportation hearings, which was for a Muslim clergyman whose tourist visa had expired. Keith's Sixth Circuit Court of Appeals opinion held that secret deportation hearings that are closed to family, friends, and the press are unconstitutional. Keith concluded by noting that "the Executive Branch seeks to uproot people's lives, outside the public eye, and behind a closed door," and warned that "Democracies die behind closed doors."

Keith is one of a generation of black lawyers who experienced the era of de jure segregation, and used the Constitution to dismantle the systematic oppression of black people. In *Davis v. School District of City of Pontiac* (1970), a school desegregation case, he set for himself the task of deciding "what, if anything, now can be done to halt the furtherance of an abhorrent situation for which no one admits responsibility or wishes to accept the blame." He concluded that the school district of Pontiac, Michigan, "deliberately, in contradiction of their announced policy of achieving a racial mixture in the schools, prevented integration," and recommended busing as a remedy. In *Davis*, Keith then attacked the notion that what had occurred in Pontiac and all over the North was somehow different from legal segregation in the South. "Where a Board of Education has contributed and played a major role in the development and growth of a segregated situation, the Board is guilty of de jure segregation. The fact that it came slowly and surreptitiously rather than by legislative pronouncement makes the situation no less evil."

This sensibility, the awareness of the pernicious effects of discrimination and the importance of giving voice to those who are harmed or injured by discrimination, is also revealed in his dissent in *Rabidue v. Osceola Refining Company* (1986). Keith was credited with introducing the "reasonable woman" standard in sexual discrimination cases. He has, in the words of one of his former law clerks, "reached beyond the subjectivity of his own male experience" and "embraced … the struggle for gender equality."

Keith has received innumerable awards and accolades from his colleagues on the bench and from the major civil rights organizations in the United States. He was given the NAACP Spingarn Medal in 1974, the Thurgood Marshall Award and the Spirit of Excellence Award from the American Bar Association, and the Edward J. Devitt Distinguished Service to Justice Award from the Detroit Urban League, among many others. Keith has been honored not just for the significance of his work as a judge. His dedication to the cause of promoting justice is not restricted to the written page and the decisions he has authored over the years. His appreciation of the importance of history is displayed in the Damon J. Keith Law Collection, an archive established at Wayne State University in 1993. This collection of photographs, documents, personal papers, memorabilia, and interviews documents the contributions of black lawyers and judges to the struggle for racial equality. Part of the collection is a traveling exhibit, Marching toward Justice.

When allegations of discrimination were leveled at a federal judiciary whose clerks were mostly white and predominantly male, Keith provided a model for the proponents of diversity. He employed more women and people of color than any other federal judge, and he chose as his clerks law graduates who practiced different religions and who came from different parts of the world. His former clerks include several law professors and the former attorney general and now governor of the state of Michigan, Jennifer Granholm. In Granholm's words, "All of us are bound by our commitment to issues of justice and civil rights and we all feel a very sincere sense of loyalty to this man who has created a family that is so powerfully driven to change the world."

FURTHER READING

Hale, Jeff A. "Wiretapping and National Security: Nixon, the Mitchell Doctrine, and the White Panthers," Ph.D. diss., Lousiana State University (1995).

Littlejohn, Edward J. "Damon Jerome Keith: Lawyer–Judge–Humanitarian," *Wayne Law Review* 42 (1996): 321–341.

DEBORAH POST

Kelley, Edmond (10 June 1817–?), Baptist minister, was born the slave of Ann White, of Columbia, Maury County, Tennessee. His life narrative gives a detailed account of his struggle to redeem his family from slavery.

Kelley's brief autobiography gives little detail of his early life, experience of slavery, struggle for education and freedom. The majority of his narrative consists of details of his first owner, his marriage to Paralee Walker in 1839, his ordination as a Baptist minister in 1843, the attempt by the Concord Baptist Association to purchase him as a preacher in 1845, and the correspondence associated with his later struggle to purchase his family.

The narrative relates that the Concord Baptist Association first tried to purchase his freedom, but the resolution to raise the money stated that Kelley was "to be held in trust … as the property of this Association." Kelley felt that the resolution was objectionable. The Baptist Association did not purchase him, but he continued to work for them until 1846, himself paying his owner ten dollars a month for his time. In 1846 the estate of Nancy White, daughter of Ann, became insolvent. She urged Kelley to leave Tennessee, to save him being sold. A letter from Hugh Robertson, an attorney of Robertson City, Tennessee, says that White had given him the authority to provide Kelley with a pass to preach anywhere in the United States.

Kelley received the pass on 2 January 1847. It was verified by "Joseph E. Winfield, Clerk of the County Court." Kelley left that district, first for Ohio, then New York, where he received a letter from the Reverend Dr. R. B. C. Howell, the president of the Southern Baptist Convention from 1851 to 1858, instructing him to maintain his humility, modesty, and self-diffidence because these are the greatest attractions he possesses.

Kelley then went to Boston where another letter from Howell urged him to study English and theology under "some of our ministers there,— Stow, or Neale." This second letter also referred to the money the Association had collected for Kelley's purchase, speaking of the need to divert the money to the purchase of his wife and children.

In September 1848 Kelley was invited to New Bedford to preach at Second Baptist Church for a month, after which he became their pastor. A letter from James Avent, chairman of the Concord Baptist Association, reported that the $77.90 collected to purchase Kelley could not be used to purchase his family because it was raised to buy him alone. The letter says that if donors do not request the return of their money by November it would "be appropriated to the beneficiary of this Association at Union University." In a footnote Kelley points out the inconsistency of that argument: if the money cannot be used other than that for which it was given, how can it be used for the "support of a beneficiary at Union University"?

Determined to purchase his family's freedom from James Walker, a wealthy Columbia farmer, Kelley tried to raise the $2,800 purchase price, but Walker refused to sell them as slaves to any but his own family; he would only sell them if they were to be freed. Walker told Kelley that Kelley's family were dear to him and were not treated as ordinary slaves, being more like servants. He insisted that they were happy and comfortable, and stood next in his affections to his own family. He offered to consider selling them if Kelley could provide better conditions for them, but questioned whether Kelley was actually in better circumstances than he was as a slave. He even offered Kelley the opportunity to join his family and live with his wife and children as "nominal slaves." After further correspondence Walker agreed to part with Kelley's wife and her children, except Dolly, whom he gave to his daughter, Annie, to raise as her own. He promised to try to persuade Annie to agree to let Dolly go, but if she refused he would make a deduction on the price. The daughter did consent to let Dolly go and they made the arrangement that, if Kelly could raise the money, he should make payment through Walker's son, J. Knox Walker of Washington City.

In 1850 the Boston Baptist Association appointed Dr. Sharp and Professor Ripley to write to Mr. Walker requesting a lower sale price. He refused and threatened to withdraw his offer unless the money was sent without delay. The Boston Baptist Association appealed to its churches, seeking funds. The appeal letter also contained a list of clergy and eminent friends who supported the appeal, a sentimental hymn written by Kelly, and scriptural passages encouraging compassion. The appeal succeeded and after some complex legal and travel arrangements, Kelley's family arrived in New York on 29 May 1851, coming to New Bedford the next day. Thus after four years he was reunited with his wife and family.

Kelly's life story reflects many of the complex social tensions of the time, providing evidence of the attitudes of a slave, a Baptist association, and slave owners toward manumission. His story reveals some of the practical issues to be faced by individuals who sought to redeem a family from bondage. At a time when the debate over the morality of payment for manumission, compensation to slave owners, the Fugitive Slave Act, and tensions over the policies of the American Colonization Society were dividing opinion, Kelley's narrative illustrates these issues in a specific context. Kelley's narrative reveals that the attitudes of slave owners and Baptist associations toward slavery and slave redemption at the time were based on a complex system of compromises, duplicity, and hypocrisy. Yet through it all Kelley's ability, determination, and love for his family shine through. Whilst Kelley is a minor character on the stage of history his narrative gives profound insights into the social attitudes of the time.

FURTHER READING

Kelley, Edmond. *A Family Redeemed from Bondage; Being Rev. Edmond Kelley, (the Author,) His Wife, and Four Children* (1851). Available at http://docsouth. unc.edu/neh/kelley/menu.html.

Kellow, Margaret M. R. "Conflicting Imperatives: Black and White American Abolitionists Debate the Question of Slave Redemption," in *Buying Freedom: The Ethics and Economics of Slave Redemption*, eds. K. Anthony Appiah and Martin Bunzl (2007).

PAUL WALKER

Kelley, William (1 Nov. 1937–), novelist and educator, was born William Melvin Kelley Jr. in New York City, the son of William Melvin Kelley Sr., a government worker and (in the 1920s and 1930s) an editor for the *Amsterdam (N.Y.) News*, an African American newspaper based in Harlem; and Narcissa (Garcia), who was of Puerto Rican descent. His mother's great-grandfather, Colonel F. S. Bartow, was the first Confederate officer killed at the first battle of Bull Run. Indeed, the Kelleys were the epitome of the melting pot of America. The family lived in a predominantly Italian neighborhood

William Kelley in 1963. (Library of Congress.\ Photographed by Carl Van Vechten.)

in New York. For twelve years William attended the Fieldston School, a mainly white private school in New York, where he excelled academically and athletically, becoming president of the student council and captain of the track team. Although he thrived in this environment, proclaiming himself a "golden boy," and at the time did not think that he had experienced racism, he would later learn that he lived in one of the most racist societies. This realization would guide him to explore issues of race and identity. Kelley's success in high school led him to Harvard University in 1957 to study law. In his sophomore year his desire to enroll in a course of study in which he would not have to complete a final exam decided Kelley on writing. To fit this bill, he enrolled in a prose fiction course taught by writer John Hawkes. Imaginative prose, rhythm, and vivid detail characterized Hawkes's writing. Kelley said of his experience in Hawkes's class, "By the end of that term, I knew I has going to write forever" (Kelley / Wright). Kelley enrolled in several writing classes at Harvard and submitted short stories to various publications. In 1960 he

received the Dana Reed Prize for the best literary work published in an avant-garde publication. In 1961 he started his first novel, *A Different Drummer* (published 1962); however, Kelley was not entirely successful while at Harvard—he passed only his writing classes. After attending Harvard for three and a half years, he was placed on academic probation for a year, and when his probation ended, he decided not to return. Kelley was not fazed by his lack of academic success. He found other ways to hone his craft. In 1962 he received fellowships for the Breadloaf Conference at Middlebury College and for the New York Writers' Conference. In December 1962 he married Karen Isabelle Gibson, a designer. They had two children, Jessica and Ciratikaiji.

In the next eight years Kelley completed five novels. His writing, insofar as it explores how race and identity are constructed, formed, and played out, fits under the classification of postmodernism. His characters exist between two states: the real and the surreal. Kelley incorporated surrealism in his writing when it was a relatively new form, emerging in American literature after World War II. Through surrealism he explores the "what ifs." *A Different Drummer* (1962) is an exploration of the Great Migration and addresses the hypothesis of what might happen if all the black people left, leaving an all-white southern state of the Union. The novel serves as a parable of how even though African Americans are invisible citizens of society, society cannot exist without them. Giving the book mixed reviews, some critics commented on Kelley's distinctive prose and mythic qualities, while traditionalists panned his mixture of reality and fantasy. What most critics agreed on was that his in-depth character development led to the novel's success. In 1963 it earned the Rosenthal Foundation Award of the National Institute of Arts and Letters and the John Hay Whitney Foundation Award. *Dancers on the Shore* (1964) is a collection of short stories chronicling the African American experience. It won the Transatlantic Review Award. *A Drop of Patience* (1965) chronicles the life of a blind jazz saxophone player, Ludlow Washington, who spirals into a destructive life, owing to racism and drugs, but is redeemed through African American culture. In 1965 Kelley was author in residence at the State University of New York at Geneseo.

As the characters in his novels took on political dimensions, Kelley's political position was classified as radical and became more prominent with each book. In an essay entitled "On Racism,

Exploitation, and the White Liberal," Kelley stated his belief that the attempt to assimilate and integrate would lead to color blindness and a loss of what is distinctly black. His novel *dem* (1967) is a satirical account of what might occur if his belief came to fruition. The story follows a well-to-do white couple, Tam and Mitchell. Tam gives birth to twins, one of whom is black. Using revelation, revenge, and white paranoia to create the tale, *dem* is considered the epochal novel produced during the Black Arts Movement. In an interview for *Dissent*, Kelley explained his reason for writing *dem*: "Instead of writing about what American society has done to black people, I've tried to write about American society in terms of what it is doing to itself and what it is" (Kelley / Wright, xxv).

Like so many African American writers and intellectuals before him, Kelley became an expatriate, going to Paris in the mid-1960s to learn French and to complete his "exploration of blackness." In 1968 he was a lecturer in American literature at the University of Nanterre. Moving to Jamaica the following year, from 1969 to 1970 Kelley was a guest instructor at the University of West Indies at Mona.

Dunfords Travels Everywheres (1970) was completed while Kelley was in Europe. The protagonist, Chig Dunford, shares a few similarities with Kelley, a salient one being that the character is a Harvard-educated tourist in Paris. Many readers and critics found the prose difficult to decipher, however, since Kelley wrote it in an African American vernacular and dialect. The book nonetheless was awarded a cash prize for fiction from the Black Academy of Arts and Letters.

Although he did not complete his "exploration of blackness," Kelley returned to the states, in the early 1970s, settling in Harlem. He decided to put writing novels on hold to pursue teaching, becoming a professor of creative writing at Sarah Lawrence College in 1989 and conducting seminars at the Taos Institute of Art in New Mexico.

The resurgence of Kelley and his contemporaries, LeRoi Jones (AMIRI BARAKA), ERNEST GAINES, ISHMAEL REED, Rosa Guy, and CARLENE HATCHER POLITE, in the academy provides readers with a unique way of viewing and interpreting the African American experience. The fact that Kelley wrote all of his novels at the height of the civil rights movement places them in the center of discourse on race, identity, and the stereotypes imposed on African Americans, and his ability to cleverly weave a tale with experimental and rhetorical devices expands the time period, making each novel a timeless piece.

FURTHER READING
Kelley, William. *dem*; foreword by John S. Wright (2000).
Bruck, Peter, ed. *The Black American Short Story in the 20th Century: A Collection of Critical Essays* (1977).
"William Kelley," *Contemporary Authors Online* (2000).
"William Melvin Kelley," *Contemporary Novelists*, 7th ed. (2000).

VALERIE A. GRAY

Kelly, Alexander (7 Apr. 1840–19 June 1907), Civil War soldier and Medal of Honor recipient, was born in Pennsylvania, the son of the Pennsylvania natives David Kelly, a coal miner, and Nancy. The family resided in South Versailles Township, Allegheny County, McKeesport, Pennsylvania, near Pittsburgh, in the heart of coal-mining country. A coal miner like his father, Alexander Kelly, at five feet, three inches, was ideally suited for a profession where working in constricted spaces was the norm. However, he took up another profession, that of soldier, and there too he proved more than able to measure up to the tasks required of him. With the Union army in need of increasingly greater numbers of men, President Abraham Lincoln and the War Department came around to the idea of raising black troops. The idea became policy in May 1863, when General Order Number 143 established the Bureau of Colored Troops, which oversaw activities connected with raising U.S. Colored Troop (USCT) regiments. Indeed recruiters were sent far and wide, including deep into the Confederacy, to recruit black soldiers, and by the time the war was over approximately 178,000 men served in 175 regiments.

In Pennsylvania, which eventually raised ten black regiments, the great impetus to form these regiments came from abolitionist leaders enthusiastic about the idea and willing to raise the money to bring the plan to fruition, perhaps none more so than the citizens, black and white, of Philadelphia. One of these regiments, the Sixth USCT, was organized at Camp William Penn, just outside Philadelphia, from 28 July to 12 September 1863. Two of its first enlistees were Kelly, who enlisted in late July 1863, and the Ohio native THOMAS HAWKINS. What the diminutive Kelly lacked in size he surely made up for with aptitude and toughness, as he was appointed first sergeant in Company F on 3 September 1863, within a week of

Alexander Kelly c. 1900. (Library of Congress.\ Daniel Murray Collection.)

joining the regiment. When the Sixth USCT and Kelly headed for the war zone after completing regimental training in late September 1863, they remained in the Tidewater area of Virginia but saw no combat. This changed when the Sixth was sent to the trenches opposite Confederate fortifications at Richmond in late May 1864 and saw its first real action at Petersburg Heights. However, the true test of courage for Kelly and his men came on 29 September 1864, when they were detailed to take part in a battle to capture several key forts in the Confederate lines around the capital city, including Fort Harrison, located at New Market Heights, and anchor the southern part of the enemy line.

In the dawn hours of 29 September, Kelly's Company F and the rest of the Sixth USCT, in concert with several other USCT regiments, moved out for the assault on Fort Harrison. The battle that developed that day proved to be one of epic proportions; many white company officers were shot down, and the task of leading the men fell on the shoulders of black company sergeants. Many black sergeants, Kelly included, served as standard bearers, carrying the regimental or national colors to help rally their fellow soldiers. Indeed the fighting was so fierce that afterward a swath of dead men no more than six feet wide but several hundred yards long littered the battlefield in front of the Confederate lines. In two days of fighting the Union suffered over five thousand casualties and ended up with a stalemate on its hands, capturing only one of the four forts that were the objectives in what became known as the Battle of New Market Heights (sometimes referred to as the Battle of Chaffin's Farm). However, the capture of Fort Harrison was accomplished by the men of the Fourth, Sixth, Thirty-sixth, and Thirty-eighth USCT Regiments. Fourteen men from these regiments earned the Medal of Honor that day, including Kelly. He was cited for having "gallantly seized the colors, which had fallen near the enemy's line of abatis, raised them and rallied the men at a time of confusion and in a place of the greatest danger" (Civil War Medal of Honor Recipients). His medal was presented on 6 April 1865, six months later. Following this historic action, Kelly and the men of the Sixth USCT were not yet done fighting; they took part in the Battle of Fair Oaks in late October 1864 and later in the assault and capture of Fort Fisher, North Carolina, from December 1864 to January 1865. The regiment took part in further operations in North Carolina and witnessed the surrender of Joseph Johnston's Confederate army on 26 April 1865. Nearly five months later Kelly and the rest of the Sixth USCT were mustered out of the service on 20 September 1865 and returned home to resume their lives as civilians.

Kelly returned to his native Pennsylvania and resumed his occupation as a coal miner in the Pennsylvania hills. The 1870 federal census shows that he was living with his aged parents, his father's occupation still listed as a coal miner even at the age of seventy. Interestingly the entire family was classified as being white. Few other details have been found regarding Kelly's life, though it is known that he continued in the area as a coal miner and was living in Pittsburgh in 1900. After his death in 1907 at the age of sixty-seven, Kelly was buried in Saint Peter's Cemetery in that city. Although he did gain the level of fame achieved by some of the Civil War's other black Medal of Honor winners, his service nonetheless exemplified that of many of the unknown men of the USCT regiments who served capably and honorably in the cause of freedom.

FURTHER READING

U.S. Army Center of Military History. "Civil War Medal of Honor Recipients." Available online at

http://www.army.mil/cmh/html/moh/civwaral.
html.

National Park Service. "Civil War Soldiers and Sailors
System." Available online at http://www.itd.nps.gov/
cwss/.

GLENN ALLEN KNOBLOCK

Kelly, Leontine Turpeau Current (5 Mar. 1920–),
the first black woman ordained a bishop in the
United Methodist Church, was born Leontine
Turpeau in the parsonage of Mount Zion
Methodist Church in Washington, D.C., to David
DeWitt Turpeau Sr., a minister, and Ila Marshall
Turpeau. One of eight children, Leontine Turpeau
was deeply influenced by both of her parents. Her
father, a Catholic turned Methodist, served congregations in Washington, D.C., and Pittsburgh before
moving to Cincinnati's Calvary Methodist Church
in 1928. While there, he was one of the first blacks
in Ohio to serve in the state legislature. During
the segregation era, when all the black Methodist
churches were united into a central jurisdiction,
the Reverend Turpeau never left the denomination
and told his children that they were "staying to try
to just get this church straight because they can't
be the church of Jesus Christ without us." Turpeau's
mother grew up in Louisiana and attended what is
now Dillard University. A gifted speaker, she taught
her children the value of education and community uplift. Life in the large parsonage in Cincinnati
was full, and the family hosted many prominent black leaders, including the college founder
MARY McLEOD BETHUNE and the poet LANGSTON
HUGHES.

In the late 1930s "Teenie," as Turpeau was called,
headed to West Virginia State. She left the college
in 1941, her junior year, to marry Gloster Bryant
Current. The couple moved to Detroit, had three
children, and divorced in 1955. She then returned to
Cincinnati, where she met James Kelly, a Methodist
minister. They married in 1956 and the couple
moved to Richmond, Virginia. There Leontine Kelly
returned to college at Virginia Union University.
She earned her bachelor's degree in 1960 and took
a position as a social studies teacher at Armstrong
High School.

Drawn to preaching and encouraged by her
husband to use her gifts of oratory, Kelly became
a certified lay speaker in the Methodist Church.
When her husband died in 1969 his congregation, Galilee Church in rural Virginia, asked her
to take the helm. She accepted the invitation.
Soon after, she was called to ordained ministry,
earning a master's degree in Divinity from Wesley
Theological Seminary in 1976. She also studied at
Union Theological Seminary in Richmond, living on campus during the week—with her elderly
mother and youngest daughter—and going home
on the weekends to preach.

From 1977 to 1983 she served as pastor of
Asbury-Church Hill United Methodist Church in
Richmond. Kelly's pastorship coincided with wom-
en's growth and visibility in the United Methodist
Church, and she soon became assistant general
secretary of evangelism for the United Methodist
General Board of Discipleship in Nashville.

In 1980 the United Methodist Church elected
its first woman bishop, Marjorie Swank Matthews.
By 1984 women in the church were mobilizing for
further change, and the Women's Clergy Caucus,
Western Jurisdiction, organized a movement to
push for Kelly as bishop. They knew the Southern
Jurisdiction, one of the church's most conservative areas, would very likely never elect a black
American woman as the denomination's second
female bishop, so the female clergy of the West
insisted that Kelly be assigned to the California-
Nevada Conference.

The strategy worked. The Western Jurisdictional
Conference of the United Methodist Church
elected her as the first black woman bishop in her
denomination. She was consecrated in July 1984 at
a ceremony in Boise, Idaho, becoming the church's
second female bishop and the first black woman to
hold such a post in a mainstream religion. The election process was by no means always easy. While
she has said that "there was dancing in the street"
following her ordination, Kelly's election was also
opposed by many who thought she was unfit for the
role because she was a black woman, or because she
was a divorced mother of four. But as she told the
USA Today writer Barbara Reynolds, "Eventually I
felt God called me as I was."

Kelly served as bishop in one of the church's
more liberal regions and as president of the Western
Jurisdiction College of Bishops. In her role she was
the chief administrator and spiritual leader of more
than one hundred thousand United Methodists in
California and Nevada. Since her election Kelly has
been outspoken on issues of social justice and a
role model for men and women all over the world.
She has championed many progressive movements,
including nuclear disarmament, opening up the
church ordination to gays and lesbians, and active
ministry to people living with HIV/AIDS. She was
arrested while rallying against nuclear arms in San

Francisco; in 1995 she protested weapons buildup in Nevada. She was also a vocal opponent of the U.S. invasion and occupation of Iraq.

Another of Kelly's passions was education, and she played a significant role in the development of Africa University, a United Methodist–affiliated college established in Zimbabwe in 1988 to educate young Africans. Kelly is the first black American woman to preside at a General Conference of the United Methodist Church and was officiating in 1988 when the conference passed legislation authorizing the building of Africa University. She was a charter member of the university's development committee and delivered the school's first commencement address in 1994.

Having retired from active ministry in 1988, Kelly continued to serve as a visiting and adjunct professor of religion at Pacific School of Religion in Berkeley, California, and in Hartford Seminary in Hartford, Connecticut. Her spiritual mission has carried her from Japan to Kenya to Italy, where she has preached on civil rights, education, and AIDS compassion. She also served as the first president of the AIDS National Interfaith Network and was president of the Interreligious Health Care ACCESS campaign.

Kelly was named one of the "One Hundred Most Important Women in America" by *Ladies' Home Journal;* was awarded ten honorary doctorates; and won the MARTIN LUTHER KING JR. Drum Major for Justice and Grass Roots Leadership awards from the Southern Christian Leadership Conference. She was inducted into the National Women's Hall of Fame in 2000.

FURTHER READING

Current, Angella P. *Breaking Barriers: An African American Family and the Methodist Story* (2001).

Lanker, Brian. *I Dream a World: Portraits of Black Women Who Changed America*, Tenth Anniversary edition. (1998).

ERVIN DYER

Kelly, Patrick (24 Sept. 1954–1 Jan. 1990), fashion designer, was born in Vicksburg, Mississippi, to Letha Kelly, a home economics teacher, and Danie Kelly, variously a fisherman, cabdriver, and insurance agent, who left the family when his son was a boy. Patrick and his siblings were raised by their mother and grandmother, Ethel Rainey, a maid and cook.

As a young boy Patrick was struck by the absence of black models in the fashion magazines that his grandmother brought home from her work in the homes of local white families. By junior high Patrick was designing and sewing dresses for neighborhood girls, and by high school he was designing display windows and drawing newspaper ads for local stores. Following his 1972 graduation from Vicksburg High School he spent two years at Jackson State University before dropping out and moving to Atlanta, where he volunteered to design the shop windows at the Yves Saint Laurent boutique. He also sorted donations at a used-clothing store, refashioning some of the better pieces and selling them at street fairs and at a local beauty shop. When Kelly met the pioneering black fashion model Pat Cleveland in 1979, she encouraged him to move to New York City. In New York he took a semester of classes at Parson's School of Design but received little encouragement from the design denizens of New York's Seventh Avenue. In 1980 Cleveland intervened for a second time, anonymously giving him a one-way ticket to Paris.

Soon after his arrival in Paris, Kelly found freelance jobs with the designer Paco Rabanne and as a costume designer for Le Palace, the Parisian equivalent of New York's Studio 54. Using a secondhand Singer sewing machine, Kelly began selling his designs to friends and local models and at street fairs. In 1983 he met the Frenchman Bjorn Amelan, a well-connected photographer's agent. The two became lovers and business partners, launching Patrick Kelly Designs. Convinced that he could make chic clothing inexpensively, Kelly invested in a showroom full of jersey material and launched the overriding design principal and tone of his future designs. The appeal of Kelly's simply cut and body-hugging jersey, stretch satin, and Lycra dresses was in their trimmings and decoration. From 1986 until 1990 Kelly adorned his designs with bows, rhinestones, dice, embroidered hearts and lips, gardenias, gummy bears, cue balls, bandanas, plastic fruit, jumbo pearls, miniature Eiffel Towers, and especially buttons, which immediately became his signature. His witty, eccentric, and improvisational clothes were a reflection of his optimistic, effervescent, and unpretentious personality. The bold and extroverted nature of his approach dovetailed nicely with the fashion trends of the mid to late 1980s, which touted conspicuous consumption through color, ornamentation, big hair, and big shoulder pads.

In 1984 the owners of the Parisian boutique Victoire provided the fledgling designer with a showroom and workspace and produced his first collection, which included faux crocodile suits, ribbed black knits with red racing stripes, and "money dresses" covered with gold buttons. A six-page spread in *Elle* magazine in February 1985 brought Kelly to the attention of retailers, including Bergdorf Goodman and I. Magnin, who featured his designs in their store windows. As his career was rapidly gathering speed, Kelly solidified the quirky and friendly image that set him apart from his colleagues. With his down-home charm and unofficial uniform of denim overalls, upturned cap, and colorful high-top sneakers, he was instantly recognizable. Kelly, it was often remarked, made people feel good, lavishing personal attention on friends and clients, who in turn became fiercely loyal supporters.

Dubbed the King of Cling, Kelly showed short tube dresses with stitching in contrasting colors, plunging necklines, and wide, off-the-shoulder collars, stretch animal prints, and bathing suits with big collars and tiaras of feathers. He designed around the pop culture themes of cowboys and Indians, jailhouse rock, and the American tourist in Paris. His offbeat creations included a bustier made of buttons, a mink coat lined in leopard print, an orange-and-black-checked peplum suit with matching orange fur hat, and a bright pink dress with mink bows affixed to the rear and chest. The press lauded his designs as sassy, irreverent, and playful, and awaited his theatrical and enjoyable fashion shows, each of which began with Kelly spray-painting a red heart on a large canvas. His models smiled on the runway and interacted with audiences, and his staff wore his signature button dresses or overalls and baseball caps. A welcome antidote to the often affected world of haute couture, Kelly's informal and inclusive fashion shows broke with convention, culminating in his 1987 Wink-of-the-Eye Haute Couture, a fashion show that parodied fashion shows.

Kelly's personal appeal, wearable fashions, and keen marketing sense made him a good business bet, and in 1987 he signed a $5-million deal with Warnaco, a major United States clothing conglomerate. Benefiting from expanded opportunities to woo media and retailers, Kelly's designs were picked up by 142 distributors and premiere stores, and he signed secondary licensing deals with Vogue Patterns and Streamline Industries for lines of his big buttons. Warnaco's ad campaigns led to further media exposure, including television appearances on NBC's *Today Show*, *Bob Hope's 80th Birthday*, and *Lifestyles of the Rich and Famous*. One of his dresses was worn by a model in a Virginia Slims "You've come a long way, baby" print ad for cigarettes, and his atelier was featured in *Architectural Digest*. Having become a minor celebrity, Kelly was photographed by the premier portraitists Horst P. Horst, William Klein, Annie Leibovitz, Pierre and Gilles, and Oliviero Toscani. Working nonstop Kelly produced three to four annual collections, consisting of up to two hundred pieces each, and made elaborate personal appearances and retail shop visits in Europe and the United States. By 1988 Patrick Kelly Designs employed seventeen people in his workshop on the Rue du Parc Royal and boasted annual revenues of $7 million.

Even with a roster of clients and devotees that included GRACE JONES and IMAN (both of whom regularly modeled in his shows), Bette Davis, JESSYE NORMAN, Isabella Rossellini, Goldie Hawn, Madonna, and Princess Diana, Kelly was an improbable candidate for acceptance by the exclusive European fashion world. But in 1988 he became the first American ever invited to join the Chambre Syndicale de la Haute Couture et du Prêt-à-Porter, the elite governing body of French fashion comprising forty-four design houses, including Dior, Givenchy, and Yves Saint Laurent. Membership in the Chambre Syndicale included an opportunity to show at the Louvre, and Kelly, in a show heavy with crystals, pinwheels, and flower appliqués, used the occasion to spoof the museum's most famous painting, sending Jungle Mona Lisa and Tango Mona Lisa down the runway.

In the world of haute couture, which assiduously ignores issues of race, Kelly put the issue front and center, not only by featuring black popular icons in his designs and black models on his runways, but most particularly in his deliberate crafting of his public persona. He made much of his background in interviews, highlighting and even embellishing his southern black roots and his rags-to-riches story. He attributed his button designs to his grandmother, whom he claimed added extra buttons to divert attention from the mismatched buttons that she used to mend his childhood clothes. He brought fried chicken to Parisian fashion events, and he often spoke in folksy aphorisms, boasting to one journalist, "From one dress in my Baptist church, you could do a whole collection." When the *New York Times* asked about threats he had received from the Ku Klux Klan, Kelly responded, "The Cha Cha Cha ... honey, what do they know about fashion except for a white robe?"

While the French press called him *le mignon petit noir Américain* ("the cute little black American"),

Kelly referred to himself as, among other things, "the black Lucille Ball." After moving to Paris he began collecting black dolls and memorabilia, amassing more than eight thousand items. He was unapologetic about his embrace and employment of stereotypic images of African Americans, offering up images of the pickaninny and golliwog, mammy and Uncle Tom, and watermelons and head scarves. Literally trading in caricatures, he used pickaninny doll pins as his calling card, giving away as many as eight hundred pins a month and festooning dresses with dolls, bandanas, watermelons, and bananas. He selected a cartoonish black face with round white eyes, big red lips, and yellow earrings for his company's logo and in 1989 introduced a line of shopping bags and buttons featuring golliwogs and watermelons. Europeans registered little concern, but in response to objections from some African Americans and other Americans, Kelly told *Essence* magazine in May 1989, "You know why some people are hung up with them? It's because they can't deal with themselves."

Whether Kelly was expanding the reach and legitimacy of racist imagery or whether he was a canny provocateur in the mode of artists like BETYE SAAR and KARA WALKER remains a question of interpretation. Was Kelly a true eccentric, authentic in his joyful and sometimes childlike manner, or was he willfully playing the role of the happy minstrel, entertaining but not threatening his white audiences? What is certain, however, is the deliberateness of his choices with regard to exploiting—or exploding—racial images. For a 1988 *Vanity Fair* portrait taken by the photographer Annie Leibovitz, Kelly appeared as a pickaninny caricature with bows in his hair and two oversize buttons held up as eyes. He was flanked by models in blackface.

Patrick Kelly died in 1990 at the age of thirty-five. At the very height of his career he left unfinished plans for a line of menswear, perfume, and accessories. His death was attributed to bone marrow disease, and in some newspapers to a brain tumor; it is now acknowledged, however, as was rumored at the time, that Kelly died of AIDS. In 2004 the Brooklyn Museum of Art in Brooklyn, New York, mounted a retrospective of his work along with selections from his African American memorabilia collection. The museum included an anecdote that Kelly enjoyed retelling: "One very intelligent woman said she didn't like the Aunt Jemimas because they reminded her of maids. I said, 'My grandmother was a maid, honey.'"

FURTHER READING
Givhan, Robin. "Patrick Kelly's Radical Cheek," *Washington Post*, 31 May 2004.
Silva, Horacio. "Delta Force," *Fashions of the New York Times Magazine*, 22 Feb. 2004.
Obituaries: *Washington Post*, 3 Jan. 1990; *Guardian* (London), 4 Jan. 1990; *International Herald Tribune*, 9 Jan. 1990; *Saint Petersburg (FL) Times*, 9 Jan. 1990; *Independent* (London), 11 Jan. 1990.

LISA E. RIVO

Kelly, Paula (21 Oct. 1942–), dancer, actress, and singer, was the youngest of three girls born to Lehman Clarence Kelly and Ruth Naomi Dempsey in Jacksonville, Florida. When Kelly was six months old, the family, like many other African Americans at this time, migrated from the South to the North seeking a new life. The family settled in the Sugar Hill section of Harlem, where her father became superintendent of the building and famous neighbors included RALPH ELLISON, BILLIE HOLIDAY, BILLY STRAYHORN, and JOHNNY HODGES. The family was close and communicated through a love of music and a joy of life. For Kelly, music was always the thread and remains the catalyst for most of her projects.

Before she was old enough to walk, Kelly would bob her head to the music of COUNT BASIE, DUKE ELLINGTON, and Buddy Johnson. When she was a young child Kelly and her friends would stage talent shows in the alley next to the building in which she lived, imitating the songs and acts they heard on the radio. As a teen she attended Stitt Junior High School and joined the glee club. Her music teacher recognized Kelly's talent and recommended that she audition for the voice program at New York's Music and Art High School.

In 1958, when Kelly was sixteen, she saw her first Broadway show, *West Side Story*. The melding of Leonard Bernstein's musical score and the choreography of Jerome Robbins fueled her determination to be a part of musical theater. During her last year at Music and Art she attended an after-school dance program at the YWHA (Young Women's Hebrew Association), and during the summer before graduation she blossomed under the tutelage of Muriel Manning and Donald McKayle. She was accepted on scholarship to the dance program at the Juilliard School in 1960.

Her teachers, Martha Hill, José Limón, Martha Graham, Pearl Lang, Bertram Ross, Antony Tudor, and Anna Sokolow, were the pioneers of the Juilliard dance program. Mary Hinkson and

Donald McKayle, both soloists in the Martha Graham company and the only African American teachers of the technique at Juilliard, were instrumental in developing and molding Kelly's raw talent. The composer Louis Horst taught dance composition. Even though jazz was not taught at Juilliard, his teachings revealed the relationship between movement and music of all kinds; though particularly jazz for Kelly. While she was in school Kelly's reputation grew to the extent that she was asked to be a soloist on a six-month tour with HARRY BELAFONTE.

Upon graduation in 1964 Kelly was a guest performer with TALLEY BEATTY and ALVIN AILEY and worked with Donald McKayle as soloist and assistant choreographer on numerous television specials. This led to a variety of appearances on *The Carol Burnett Show* and *The Dean Martin Show*. She also danced a duet with Gene Kelly in his CBS television special *New York, New York*. In 1967 she was a featured performer at the grand opening of Caesars Palace in Las Vegas with Jack Benny, Tony Bennett, and Andy Williams. Subsequently she was chosen by the choreographer Bob Fosse for the role of Helene in *Sweet Charity* opposite Juliet Prowse. *Sweet Charity* premiered at Caesars Palace and eventually had a London premiere at the Prince of Wales Theatre, and Kelly won the Variety Award for best supporting actress for her work in the production. In 1968, when Fosse was asked to direct the film version of the musical, he asked Kelly to reprise her role, which she did for the 1969 film. After *Sweet Charity* she was offered a co-starring role in the director Robert Wise's *Andromeda Strain* in 1971. Other film roles during the 1970s included *Soylent Green* (1973), *The Spook Who Sat by the Door* (1973), and *Uptown Saturday Night* (1974).

Kelly alternated her film work with stage roles. She appeared on Broadway in *Metamorphoses* (1973) and was cast as the featured performer in the record-breaking West Coast premiere of Vinnette Carroll's *Don't Bother Me I Can't Cope* at the Mark Taper Forum. For her performance she received the first of three NAACP Image Awards and the Los Angeles Drama Critics' Circle Award for Best Actress. During this time Kelly was cochoreographer with Michael Kidd and danced the role of Tiger Lily in the Hallmark Hall of Fame production of *Peter Pan* starring Danny Kaye.

In the 1980s and 1990s Kelly continued to appear in a variety of roles on television shows and made-for-television movies. During this time she received Emmy nominations for her performances on *Night Court*, *The Women of Brewster Place*, and *The RICHARD PRYOR Special* (1982), and she won a Cable Ace Award for *Uncle Tom's Cabin* (1987). Among her later films, she is best remembered for her role as the octogenarian Ma Pearl, opposite Al Freeman Jr. in Tim Reid's film *Once Upon a Time When We Were Colored* (1995). Kelly also starred opposite GREGORY HINES in the Los Angeles and Las Vegas premiere of *Sophisticated Ladies*. Although she found time to star in film, television, and theater projects throughout the roughly four decades of her professional acting life, *Sophisticated Ladies* reawakened her desire to explore her individual expression through music. This laid the groundwork for her to write and produce her version of a one-woman show, which was acclaimed as unique and beyond category. The California State Assembly cited her for outstanding contributions to the entertainment industry and dedicated community service.

BARON KELLY

Kelly, Sharon Pratt (30 Jan. 1944–), mayor of Washington, D.C., was born Sharon Pratt, the elder child of Carlisle Pratt, a superior court judge, and Mildred Petticord. When Sharon was four years old, her mother died of cancer. With her younger sister, Benaree, and their father, she went to live with her paternal grandmother and aunt. Some years later her father remarried, and Sharon lived with her father and stepmother. She attended Gage and Rudolph elementary schools and McFarland Junior High School and graduated from Roosevelt High School with honors. In 1965 she graduated from Howard University in Washington, D.C., with honors and a B.A. in Political Science; three years later she earned a J.D. from Howard's law school. While in law school, she married her first husband, onetime D.C. council member Arrington Dixon, and they had two daughters, Aimee Arrington Dixon and Drew Arrington Dixon. The couple divorced in 1982. Kelly began her legal career in 1970 as house counsel for the Joint Center for Political Studies in Washington, D.C., before entering private law practice with the legal firm of Pratt and Queen in 1971. From 1972 to 1976 she taught business law at the Antioch School of Law in Washington, D.C., reaching the rank of full professor. After leaving Antioch School of Law, she served as a member of the general counsel's office at Potomac Electric Power Company (PEPCO) from 1976 to 1979, when the company appointed her director of consumer

Sharon Pratt Kelly The Washington mayor flanked by heavyweight champion Riddick Bowe, left, and Jesse Ferguson of Philadelphia, promote the "Heavyweight Debate" on March 24, 1993. (AP Images.)

affairs. In 1986 PEPCO appointed her as its vice president for public policy. In that capacity she worked to develop programs to assist low- and fixed-income residents of the District of Columbia. Her early work in public service also included serving as vice chairman of the District of Columbia's Law Revision Commission.

While representing Washington, D.C., on the Democratic National Committee from 1977 to 1990, Kelly was elected treasurer of the committee, serving from 1985 to 1989. Her close ties to the national Democratic Party furthered her local ambitions, and she launched her mayoral campaign with a lavish, well-attended party during the 1988 Democratic National Convention in Atlanta, Georgia. Defying the odds, on 6 November 1990, Kelly became the first woman elected mayor of Washington, D.C., with a landside 86 percent of the vote. She was also the first African American woman to serve as the chief executive of a major American city.

Commentators credited Kelly's mayoral victory to her demonstrated commitment to the D.C. community over more than twenty years. With her positive campaign slogan of "Yes, We Will," Kelly promised residents an "honest deal" that would restore the city to greatness by improving the quality of life for all of its people. She stunned observers when she promised to fire two thousand midlevel managers immediately, but many citizens were impressed with her eloquence and by the fact that she was an "outsider" with no apparent entanglements in local politics. Most important, she was not an ally of her predecessor as mayor, MARION S. BARRY JR.

In 1978 Barry had inherited a government that was already oversized and undermanaged. After nearly twelve years in office, having failed to tackle those problems and having been convicted of federal charges of cocaine possession, he chose not to run for reelection in 1990. Barry's downfall produced an upsurge of support for reforming the district's government, and Kelly, with her promise to "clean house" and her endorsement by the respected *Washington Post*, rode that political mood to easy victories in both the September Democratic primary and the November general election.

Solving the District of Columbia's myriad problems would not be so easy. The bureaucracy was regarded by many as indifferent to the citizens it was supposed to serve. Like other urban areas, the District of Columbia had a multitude of problems, such as underfinanced, weak public schools; urban economic decay; high unemployment; drug trafficking; and homelessness. Even more disturbing was a financial crisis that had resulted in the city's $300 million deficit at the end of the 1990 fiscal year. The U.S. Congress, as the city's managers, appropriated $100 million in congressional emergency funding for the following fiscal year. Kelly argued that a comprehensive overhaul of city government was also needed.

At first Kelly seemed determined to downsize government and inaugurated programs aimed at restructuring the bureaucracy by automation and retraining. Every category of crime in the District of Columbia declined during her term as mayor. She developed public-private partnerships to facilitate many of her reforms. Area businesses were encouraged to use their ingenuity to help develop programs to serve all of the city's citizens. These partnerships fostered more jobs and encouraged international trade ventures.

By all accounts, however, Kelly's first year was traumatic. Her grandmother died, and a trusted friend and adviser tragically died when a city ambulance went to the wrong address. At the same time, James Kelly, a businessman from New York City whom she had married at the end of her first year, never seemed comfortable in the public spotlight or in playing the supporting role of first spouse. Sharon Kelly was also never able to gain full control of a city still loyal to Barry, and during Kelly's second year in office, Barry backed an initiative to recall her from office. While the recall was unsuccessful, it forced Kelly to retreat from the tough reforms she had promised during her campaign. Kelly blamed Congress for Washington's continuing financial problems and then further alienated Congress by providing it with inaccurate and false information about the city's finances.

Kelly's criticism of Congress for the city's financial woes and her support for D.C. statehood alienated potential Democratic allies who controlled Congress. By 1993 she had also built a palatial office for herself outside the District Building, the usual location of district offices and agencies, and had put a makeup artist on the city payroll. Political observers increasingly saw such extravagance and her lack of political experience as a major problem, prompting some disillusioned voters to encourage Marion Barry's comeback. After Barry had served six months in prison for his cocaine conviction in 1992, he was elected to the city council. In 1994 he defeated Kelly in that year's mayoral election.

Kelly has received an NAACP Presidential Award, the THURGOOD MARSHALL Award of Excellence, and the MARY McLEOD BETHUNE–W. E. B. DuBOIS Award from the Congressional Black Caucus. She has been honored for distinguished leadership by the United Negro College Fund and was the recipient of an award for distinguished service from the Federation of Women's Clubs, whose mission is to improve communities through volunteer service. Although her time in office was not as stellar as she had hoped or predicted it would be, Sharon Kelly will be remembered as the first native of Washington, D.C., and the first African American woman to be elected mayor of a major American city.

FURTHER READING

Borger, Gloria. "People to Watch: Sharon Pratt Dixon," *U.S. News and World Report* (31 Dec. 1990).

French, Mary Ann. "Who Is Sharon Pratt Dixon?," *Essence* (Apr. 1991).

McCraw, Vincent. "Anxious Dixon on Mission to Cure D.C.'s Ills," *Washington Times*, 17 Apr. 1990.

DEBORAH F. ATWATER

Kelly, Wynton (2 Dec. 1931–12 Apr. 1971), jazz pianist, was born in Jamaica. Nothing is known of either his mother or father except that they were both of West Indian heritage. His family moved to Brooklyn, New York, when Kelly was four, and he attended both Music and Art High School and Metropolitan Vocational. In an interview with Gene Lees for *Down Beat*, Kelly said he was unable to study piano at either institution, so he studied string bass and theory instead.

Kelly first worked professionally at age thirteen. By the time he was fifteen, he was touring the Caribbean with the bop tenor saxophonist Ray Abrams. Abrams's combo, which included Kelly, the drummer Lee Abrams (Ray's brother), the baritone saxophonist Cecil Payne, the bassist Ahmad Abdul-Malik, and the alto saxophonist ERNIE HENRY, also worked around Brooklyn. Kelly also played with the tenor saxophonist Hal Singer and the trumpeter HOT LIPS PAGE, Kansas City stylists. Kelly worked for nearly a year with the rhythm and blues tenor saxophonist EDDIE "LOCKJAW" DAVIS. Another experience Kelly himself mentioned was a little-known group called the Three Blazes.

Kelly joined the singer DINAH WASHINGTON as accompanist for three years around the time he first recorded for Blue Note; it is likely that this association is where he formed his penchant for popular song form. His first album as leader was a ten-inch trio recording for Blue Note that was never issued. By 1951 he was leading trio dates for Blue Note with the swing bassists OSCAR PETTIFORD and Franklin Skeete and his former colleague Lee Abrams, a musical collaboration that resulted in the albums *New Faces, New Sounds* and *Piano Interpretations by Wynton Kelly*. Kelly joined DIZZY GILLESPIE in 1952 as pianist for Gillespie's big band, where he played until he was drafted into the army later that year. He also worked with the tenor saxophonist LESTER YOUNG in 1952. Upon his discharge in June 1954, Kelly rejoined Gillespie until late 1957. Kelly was featured on at least four recordings with Gillespie in 1957, most notably *The Big Band Sound of Dizzy Gillespie*.

Kelly recorded and performed with J. J. JOHNSON in 1954 on *The Eminent J. J. Johnson I*, which included the bassist CHARLES MINGUS and the drummer KENNY CLARKE. Kelly was also featured on the tenor saxophonist SONNY ROLLINS's *Sonny Rollins I* (1956) and *Newk's Time* (1958), which is a particularly strong Kelly feature with the bassist Doug Watkins and the drummer PHILLY JOE JONES. Some of Kelly's finest recorded playing is on a 1958 recording by the trumpeter BLUE MITCHELL's sextet, which included Curtis Fuller on trombone, Johnny Griffin on tenor sax, WILBUR WARE on bass, and Philly Joe Jones on drums. Kelly also appeared on the main take of "Naima" on the tenor saxophonist JOHN COLTRANE's milestone album *Giant Steps* (1959).

The trumpeter MILES DAVIS recruited Kelly in 1959 for his rhythm section. He liked Kelly's lyrical simplicity and uncomplicated touch. The transition from Bill Evans to Kelly in the Davis quintet was documented by Kelly's sole performing contribution, the twelve-bar blues "Freddie Freeloader," on *Kind of Blue* (1959), the landmark album that defined the movement known as modal jazz. With the addition of the bassist PAUL CHAMBERS and the drummer Jimmy Cobb, one of jazz's legendary rhythm sections was created. Davis's recording *Someday My Prince Will Come* (1961) showed Kelly's diverse nature as a sideman—a florid, staccato, right-hand melodic style contrasted by a myriad of voicings and a richness of harmonic accompaniment, which remained on top of the beat with a wonderful sense of swing. Another notable recording was a 1960 session in Stockholm, which featured the rhythm section alongside Davis and Coltrane. In 1961 this quintet also performed a concert at Carnegie Hall. Kelly remained with Davis from 1959 until 1963, at which time Davis's entire rhythm section left to further their efforts as a trio.

Kelly had often performed and recorded in a trio setting. A notable recording in 1958, *Wynton Kelly I*, included Chambers, Cobb, and the bass player SAM JONES. The trio recorded several albums together in the early 1960s, including *Kelly at Midnite* (1960), *Autumn Leaves* (1961), and *Wynton Kelly II* (1961). Albums that presented headliners who performed with the trio include *Kelly Blue* (1959), a classic album featuring NAT ADDERLEY on trumpet, Benny Golson on tenor saxophone, and Bobby Jaspar on flute; and *Gettin' Together* (1960), which featured the trio with the saxophonist Art Pepper. *Kelly Great!* (1959) was recorded with a quintet. A favorite addition to the trio was the guitarist WES MONTGOMERY, as shown by the albums *Bags Meets Wes* (1961), with Montgomery and the Modern Jazz Quartet vibraphonist MILT JACKSON; the live album *Full House* (1962), with Montgomery and Johnny Griffin; and two recordings from 1965, *Smokin' at the Half Note* and *Wynton Kelly and Wes Montgomery*.

Throughout the late 1950s and early 1960s Kelly was considered the quintessential sideman, constantly in demand for recording and club dates. He possessed an uncanny ability to comp (accompany

in a jazz setting) with a proper balance of background harmony and melodic material without interfering with the soloist. He recorded as sideman with CANNONBALL ADDERLEY, Coltrane, Art Farmer, Benny Golson, DEXTER GORDON, Johnny Griffin, JIMMY HEATH, Ernie Henry, ILLINOIS JACQUET, Blue Mitchell, Steve Lacy, Art Pepper, WAYNE SHORTER, and CLARK TERRY.

Kelly worked and recorded frequently with several musicians whom he had met through Gillespie's big band. The tenor saxophonist HANK MOBLEY, who had worked with Gillespie initially in 1953, also performed at Davis's 1961 Carnegie Hall concert with Kelly and Chambers. Kelly performed along with the trumpeter LEE MORGAN in Gillespie's big band throughout 1957. The combination of Mobley, Morgan, Kelly, and Chambers was particularly successful, and they recorded together on a number of occasions. Both Kelly and Chambers also served as sidemen with Mobley on four noteworthy recordings for Blue Note during 1960 and 1961, *Soul Station, Roll Call, Workout,* and *Another Workout.*

Kelly remained active as a leader and sideman until his untimely death. He recorded two albums with Claus Ogermann and His Orchestra in 1963 and 1964 as well as the albums *Undiluted* (1965), *Blues on Purpose* (1965), and Kelly's last recording as leader, *Full View* (1967). Kelly's last recorded concert appearance was *Wynton Kelly and George Coleman in Concert* (1968).

Kelly was a heavy drinker throughout his life. In 1971 he experienced an epileptic seizure in Toronto that killed him. He was thirty-nine years old.

Kelly's style was influenced by pianists such as ERROLL GARNER, Bill Evans, PHINEAS NEWBORN, OSCAR PETERSON, Walter Bishop Jr., and McCOY TYNER. He listened to Clyde Hart and BUD POWELL as models for his comping style. Kelly truly loved to comp, which led to his ultimate success as a jazz pianist. Powerfully rhythmic with boundless energy, Kelly propelled the tempo easily with a light sound and a firm, clearly articulated touch that remained underneath the overall texture of the ensemble. Kelly attentively contributed exactly what was needed to enhance a soloist, from simple block harmonies to rhythmic vamps and extended chord clusters. In addition he was one of the few great pianists whose reputation rested on a mastery of the 32-bar popular song form. Complacent yet intelligently calculated, Kelly's style wore the mark of a virtuoso.

A consistent and prudent musician, Kelly was admired by audiences and performers alike. His style influenced countless jazz musicians, such as the entire Marsalis family (Ellis Marsalis, Branford Marsalis, and WYNTON MARSALIS), the bassist and Kelly's cousin Marcus Miller, and several generations of pianists, including the noted contemporaries HERBIE HANCOCK and Tyner.

FURTHER READING

Mathieson, Kenny. *Cookin': Hard Bop and Soul Jazz, 1954–65* (2002).
Piazza, Tom. *The Guide to Classic Recorded Jazz* (1995).
Rosenthal, David. *Hard Bop: Jazz and Black Music 1955–1965* (1992).
Obituary: *Down Beat* 38, no. 11 (1971).

DISCOGRAPHY

Schlouch, Claude. *Wynton Kelly: A Discography* (1993).
This entry is taken from the *American National Biography* and is published here with the permission of the American Council of Learned Societies.

DAVID E. SPIES

Kemp, George (10 July 1832–13 Apr. 1911), musician, was born George Washington Kemp, the son of William and Angerline Moors Kemp, in Sperryville, Virginia. George and his siblings were born into slavery and would become the slaves of Major Armistead Brown and his son, Joseph, of Culpeper, Virginia. George and his family were fortunate to have had a kind master, but he decided to run away after hearing, like many others, of the freedom he could gain by escaping north.

He and seventeen other slaves ran away one night to enlist in the Union Army, under the command of General Oliver Otis Howard. Mr. Kemp soon became an aide to General Howard. After earning the General's trust he was persuaded to come north and work at the Howard farm in Leeds, Maine. This was the beginning of a new life for him. It was now fast approaching the end of the Civil War, and a man born to slavery was finally free.

"Wash," as he was known to his friends, easily fit in with the general's children. They worked to help him learn to read and write and he taught them how to ride and care for their pony. On 22 Jan. 1865 Guy Howard wrote a letter to his father, O. O. Howard:

> I thank the Officers very much indeed for my pony. I could not have received a better or a nicer present. It is just what I have been wanting so long. Wash is a very nice man and takes good care of my pony. I don't know what to name the pony, I have been on him three times, once

I went as far as Capt. Turners. I don't go alone, Wash leads him. The pony likes to play and stand up on her hind feet and put out her fore feet towards Wash. Grace and I are teaching Wash to read. I hope he will stay with us along time.

After working on the farm for one year, George told General Howard that he missed his family and was going to search for them. The general, not wanting to lose his services, said that he would make arrangements to search for Kemp's family. When they reached Virginia, they were told that George's family had been sold and taken deeper into the South. Unfortunately for Maria and her children, their new master was not a kind man and abused them. Maria's son John, even though just a young boy, would carry his wounds with him the rest of his life.

The general commenced to search for Mrs. Kemp and after many months of searching he succeeded in finding her and sent her to Leeds. Christmas afternoon, 1864, while Mr. Kemp was busily engaged doing the farm chores, he looked out of the barn and saw a team approaching with a colored woman in a carriage. He could hardly believe his eyes—his long lost family was finally with him. When he had left the plantation, his daughter Mary was just six weeks old. It was a most joyous time. Wash often remarked that it was the happiest Christmas he ever experienced.

After leaving the Howard farm, Wash and his family bought a farm near Coffin's Mills, in Leeds. They had four more children: Martha, Paul, Charles, and Laura. Only four of their six children would live to adulthood. Although George and Maria could neither read nor write, he insisted that his children get an education. He worked hard at farming, waiting for their children to get an education.

He eventually fulfilled his dream of following his true love, jubilee music. Wash organized the Kemp Family Jubilee Company. This troupe would have a long history of twenty five years on the road. He and his family were well-known as excellent entertainers as they performed throughout Maine, New England, and the Mid-Atlantic States. Wash played the tambourine, and he also danced and patted the juba (slapping of hands, legs, and body to produce a rapid rhythm. Mary played the harp and her sisters, Laura and Martha, played the banjo. They all had wonderful voices. After the concerts a social dance would follow where permitted. The Kemps would provide the music. Martha Kemp loved to tell that they entertained in every town in Vermont and New Hampshire. In Maine, they performed at least two times in almost every town.

The troupe traveled by horse and buggy. Along the way townspeople would invite them to stay for the night, usually at no charge. Most of the trips where uneventful, but one night near the White Mountains in New Hampshire one of their horses fell in the snow. They managed to get the horse back to town, but he died from his injuries. The next day they purchased a new one and continued on. They always had three horses, one for baggage and two for the wagon.

Wash had many ways of advertising his group; the most common was a poster that was put on display announcing his upcoming concert. They also had a picture of Maria, Mary, Martha, and Laura on top of a boxcar (see *Maine's Visible Black History*, p. 218). They continued to entertain until the time of Maria's death in 1901. After the troupe broke up, the girls went back into the labor force as servants and cooks.

Wash married a second time, to Hannah Grice of Lewiston, and they resided in Leeds. He died in Lewiston, Maine at the home of his daughters, Mary and Martha, in 1911, after suffering for nearly a year from Bright's disease. He was well known as a typical Southern gentleman and was sadly missed by all who knew him.

In 1919, the Kemp sisters started "The Bungalow" at Monmouth, Maine. It was a restaurant that offered sit-down meals as well as catering birthday parties, weddings, and other social events. They were well known for their cooking abilities, by the townspeople as well as tourists, and eager to help wherever their services were needed. The Kemps will be forever grateful to General Howard for the act of kindness that he showed their family.

FURTHER READING

Bragdon, Elaine Kemp. "The Kemp Family of Leeds," in Michael C. Lord and W. Dennis Stires, eds. *Androscoggin County, Maine: A Pictorial Sesquicentennial History, 1854–2004*, (2003).

Price, H. H., and Gerald E. Talbot. *Maine's Visible Black History: The First Chronicle of Its People* (2007).

ELAINE KEMP BRAGDON

Kemp-Rotan, Renee (5 January 1953–), trained architect, urban designer, artist, author, musician, and educator, was born Renee Ersell Kemp in Washington, D.C., the only daughter of Reverend Arthur E. Kemp and Ruby E. Dunham. After her parents divorced, she was raised by her mother and her maternal grandparents, who encouraged her early artistic talents through childhood study of piano, violin, and cello. Ruby E. Dunham later married Mohammed Id, a Lebanese neurosurgeon, whose influence provided Renee with a broad international perspective.

Graduating Theodore Roosevelt High School, Washington, D.C., in 1970, Kemp-Rotan studied architecture at Syracuse University in Syracuse, New York. The recipient of an American Institute of Architects (AIA)/Ford Foundation Minority Scholarship, she became the first black female to earn a degree in architecture at Syracuse, graduating *cum laude* in 1975. Syracuse exposed her to European design masters, and immersed her in the German *Bauhaus* aesthetic, a dynamic synthesis of political, social, educational, and artistic development between 1900–1920, that brought together painters, architects, sculptors, writers, dancers and musicians in a creative nexus of cross-pollination.

At the Architectural Association (AA) in London (1972–1974), Kemp-Rotan's studies continued, and were heavily influenced by Paul Oliver, a Fellow of the Royal Anthropological Society, and by Archigram, a British avant-garde design group, which served as her design studio masters. In 1974 she won an AA 3rd Year Travel Research Fellowship to Africa—the first ever awarded to an American. Her solo cultural-geographic field study to Ghana, covering over 1500 miles through many rural villages, followed the anthropological method of ZORA NEALE HURSTON. Photographing and documenting surviving ancient mud architecture building techniques served as grist for her undergraduate design thesis. Years later, at Paul Oliver's request as editor, Renee's work was published as part of the *Encyclopedia of World Vernacular Architecture*, published by Cambridge University Press (1997), which was winner of the prestigious Royal Institute of British Architects' Sir Bannister Fletcher-World History Book Award. Kemp-Rotan gained admittance to the Architectural Association's Diploma School and received the Royal Institute of British Architects (RIBA) Level II Distinction in 1974.

While earning her Masters degree in Planning at Columbia University (1977–1980) Kemp-Rotan worked for the New York City-based Urban Design Group (1975–1979), and ghost wrote *How to Save Your Own Street*, with Raquel Ramati, while working directly with Jacqueline Onassis, who edited the final work. Published in 1981 by Doubleday/Dolphin Books, this book dealt with major urban design projects in New York City, outlining ways to engender community participation in the design process. She was part of the team of advocacy workers in neighborhoods such as the Little Italy Special District, creating zoning for sidewalk cafes, retail use groups, and applying the use of air rights to preserve landmarks and historic districts.

Kemp-Rotan also designed solar houses for Glave, Newman, and Anderson Architects in Richmond, Virginia, while teaching World Art History at Virginia Commonwealth University in that city, under Dr. Murray DePillars—a founder of AfriCobra (an acronym for the Modernist "African Commune of Bad Relevant Artists"), which had emerged in 1970. Kemp-Rotan then left Virginia to teach Urban Design, Tropical Architecture and Architectural History (1981–1985) at Howard University in Washington, D.C., where she produced the American Institute of Architects (AIA) very first conference on "Black Women in Architecture: A Sense of Achievement" in 1983, and directed Design Demonstration and National Design Competition Programs at National Endowment for the Arts/Design Arts (1982–1983). She has also served as a jurist on NEA Panels, and as a constant design consultant for their Design Arts Program.

Kemp-Rotan's article "Being Black and Female in a White Male Dominated Profession" was published in 1984 in the *AIA Journal*, and later her contributions to American architecture were acknowledged in the AIA's archival work *That Exceptional One* (1988). When the *L'Union Internationale des Femmes Architectes* (UIFA) selected her to speak at their 25th Anniversary Conference (in Washington, D.C., 1988) on "Worldwide Contributions of Women in Architecture: Prehistory, Dynasties, Modern Nations," Kemp-Rotan was deemed by the UIFA chair as "the best speaker on the program." Soon afterwards, L. Jane Hastings, FAIA/UIFA Secretary Generale recommended Kemp-Rotan as a member of the "U.S. Women in Environmental Arts Delegation" to visit architecture schools throughout China, but the 1989 Tiananmen Square protests cancelled the excursion.

At Maryland National Capital Park Planning Commission (1985–1991), Kemp-Rotan designed the "pedestrian friendly" Nuclear Regulatory Commission Plaza. She produced a six-week Smithsonian's Distinguished Speaker Series: "The Future of American Suburb Design" in 1988, with icon Robert Stern, FAIA and twenty-one other U.S. designers. Stern (Dean of Architecture, Yale University) later wrote the NEA, urging them "to continue her significant examination of the American Suburb through Kemp-Rotan's Design Advancement Grant." Kemp-Rotan produced her second Smithsonian series "40 Acres and a Mule: The Black American Quest for Land Ownership (1989). In 1992, Tony Wren, the Certified Archivist of the AIA, curator of its Archive of Women in Architecture, and Board Member of the International Archive of Women in Architecture, noted the "dearth of material and scholarship available on women ... in architecture." He further asserted that after being familiar with Renee Kemp-Rotan for more than a decade, she continued to impress him "by her quest for knowledge ... in the Design Arts" and that "her work emanates the seriousness and capability of the ... scholar."

Kemp-Rotan directed Practice Design Education Programs at AIA National Headquarters (1992–1993), overseeing twenty design divisions—Architects in Education, Health, Justice, Urban Design, Historic Preservation, etc.—and turning American design information into cutting-edge programs for national dissemination.

In 1992, Paul Oliver, a lifelong mentor, selected Kemp-Rotan to chair a l'École d'Architecture Paris-Villemin/IASTE panel in Paris, "Segregation or Integration of Gender and Ethnicity in Traditional Environments," as part of the international conference on "Development vs Tradition: The Cultural Ecology of Dwellings and Settlements" co-chaired by Anne Hublin, Dean, l'École d'Architecture, Paris. Soon after, she opened her design firm Urbi et Orbi—*"for the city, for the world"*—in Washington, D.C., and launched several lucrative projects, including the Corcoran School of Art master plan (1989–1990). Her work subsequently convinced Corcoran's president to open her art/jazz salon *Muse de Noire 360* at the Corcoran Museum and to produce painter LOIS MAILOU JONES' first major museum exhibition. By 1992, Kemp-Rotan expanded *Muse de Noire 360*'s productions to include Oscar Brown Jr., Max Beauvoir, and her own docu-drama, "Back of the Big House III" projecting author John Vlach's plantation slides—discovered at the Library of Congress—as backdrop to readings from slave narratives.

In Atlanta, Kemp-Rotan worked as manager of the Corporation for 1996 Olympic Development in Atlanta; as Director, Economic Development (1995); and as Chief, Urban Design/Development (1997–2001), coordinating the Philips Arena, Olympic Park, the Atlanta Aquarium, the Memorial Drive HUD Hope VI, Atlanta's Vending Plan, and her "Civil Rights Street Museum" projects (1995–2001). In 1998, she presented her design casework at Cairo University, Cairo, Egypt (1998) as part of the IASTE's (International Association for the Study of Traditional Environments) conference on

"Manufacturing Heritage, Consuming Tradition: Development, Preservation and Tourism in the Age of Globalization," co-sponsored by the President of Egypt, Department of Architecture, University of Cairo and The Center For Environmental Design Research, University of California, Berkeley.

In 2000, the Smithsonian designated Kemp-Rotan "the Josephine Baker expert" for "Jazz Age in Paris: 1914–1940," following her "Baker: Architecture and Imagination" lectures at the Sorbonne. This was at the behest of Dr. Michel Fabre, Director, Centre d'Études Afro-Américaines et des Nouvelles Litteratures en Anglais (CETANLA; Université Paris III), who praised Kemp-Rotan as "a fine, young scholar and cultural critic in the field of international/interracial/transcontinental interface and influences in the plastic arts ..." in his letter of recommendation to the National Endowment for the Arts.

In 1988, in association with Frank Smith (an AfriCobra painter), Kemp-Rotan won the Stables Building Competition to house the D.C. Arts Commission (1988). In 2002, she led a team including Abdul Halim (Egypt) and Legoretta (Mexico) in the design of the new Grand Egyptian Museum at the base of the pyramids in Giza—intended to be the largest museum complex in the world. Though their design did not win, her team placed twenty-first out of 2227 competitors worldwide, and was published as part of the best entries in the U.N. competition proceedings.

Appointed by the mayor of Birmingham, Alabama, as Director of Capital Projects in 2003, Kemp-Rotan oversees several hundred millions of dollars in public development funds. Her comprehensive plan initiative—the $50 million Railroad Park (2003–2008) and for the New $55 million Fair Park Olympic Village for Children—catalyzed implementation of this public space in once segregated Alabama. Her book *Public Architecture as Artifact: Curation of the New American City* (work in progress) chronicles her interpretive historical/preservation work in public places such as cemeteries, fairgrounds, and viaducts, including her Elegba Project, Atlanta, in 1996.

In 2007, Kemp-Rotan completed her multimedia opera "Will: A Novel Opera Ballet on Self-Determination and the Persecution of Creative Genius"—a twenty-year project based on intellectual challenges faced in her career as design theorist, and her core premise of genius as the most consistently exploited segment of humanity.

Kemp-Rotan's muse also sculpts flesh and human consciousness, via her own creative crucible, as evidenced by her two masterpieces—in collaboration with Eric Rotan (Pharoah Sanders' bassist)—sons Aaron Rotan, U.S. Marine (Digital Designer/Diesel Engineer), and Tai Rotan, Morehouse graduate (Banking and Finance), Digital Musician, IT expert; and derivative works, genius grandsons Jarred, and twins Jacob and Joshua.

FURTHER READING:

Fishkin, Shelley Fisher. "Interrogating "Whiteness," Complicating "Blackness": Remapping American Culture," *American Quarterly*, vol. 47, no. 3 (Sept. 1995), 428–466.

French, Mary Ann. "Josephine, Jazz and Juke Joints," *Washington Post*, 17 November 1994, Home section, p. 14.

Oliver, Paul, ed. *The Encyclopedia of Vernacular Architecture of the World* (1997).

Ostromand, Hans J., and David Macy, eds. (Renee Kemp-Rotan, contributing editor). "Josephine Baker in African American Literature," in *The Greenwood Encyclopedia of African American Literature* (2005).

Y. JAMAL ALI

Kenan, Randall (12 Mar. 1963–), writer, was born Randall Garrett Kenan in Brooklyn, New York, to Clara Lily Dunn Carver and Harry L. Kenan. When he was six weeks old, Kenan was taken to live with his father's parents in the small town of Wallace in eastern North Carolina. As a young boy he came to spend increasingly more time in the nearby farming village of Chinquapin with his great-uncle Redden and his great-aunt Mary, whom Kenan came to know as "Mama." With them he grew up on his family's ancestral land, which the family had owned for five generations. Kenan's large extended family in Duplin County was continuously present during his childhood, and they became a great influence on his writing.

Kenan's family was very much in touch with its ancestral past. Both of his maternal great-grandmothers were alive when he went to high school, and he even knew one great-great-aunt, who was the youngest daughter of Richard Kenan, Randall's great-great-grandfather. Richard Kenan somehow managed to acquire a vast amount of property, scattered across twenty miles throughout Duplin County, and he established in the family the model of the strong black patriarch who created his own economic success. For example, Randall Kenan's grandfather George Washington Kenan was an entrepreneur and jack-of-all-trades who worked as a shipbuilder, renovated and rented old homes, dealt in scrap metal, and built a prosperous dry-cleaning company with business in three counties. Similarly Kenan's "mother" and aunts, several of whom were schoolteachers, provided models of strong black women, who at times contested the concentration of power in the patriarchy (a theme that frequently appears in Kenan's fiction).

Like many other members of his generation in Chinquapin, as a young man Kenan was eager to leave the rural village, a desire made more urgent perhaps by his emerging sexual orientation as a gay man. In 1981 Kenan enrolled in the University of North Carolina at Chapel Hill. His childhood ambition had been to pursue a career in the sciences, botany in particular, and he had also considered the ministry. In his first years at Chapel Hill he was inspired by the early days of the computer revolution. But he eventually chose to pursue a degree in English, and he studied creative writing with Doris Betts and Max Steele. After earning a B.A. in 1985, he moved to New York City, where he worked for Alfred A. Knopf publishers until 1989.

In 1989 Kenan published his own first novel, *A Visitation of Spirits*, in which his great-great grandfather, Richard Kenan, is fictionalized as Ezra Cross. Soon after the publication of his novel, Kenan began teaching creative writing at Sarah Lawrence College and Columbia University. In 1992 he published a collection of stories, *Let the Dead Bury Their Dead*, which was nominated for the Los Angeles Times Book Award, was a finalist for the National Book Critics Circle Award, and was named one of the *New York Times*'s Notable Books of 1992. Like *A Visitation of Spirits*, this work returns to Duplin County and Chinquapin, which he fictionalizes as Tims Creek. The major themes of these books derive from Kenan's childhood in and his continuing attachment to Chinquapin. These themes are the decay of an autonomous black agrarian community, the flight of the "talented tenth," the role of the black Baptist church in the lives of the community, the resistance to white oppression, and the traditional black community's struggles to adjust to change and to accommodate sexual difference.

In 1994 Kenan became the first William Blackburn Visiting Professor at Duke University. This position was followed by a series of distinguished visiting professorships at the University of North Carolina at Chapel Hill, the University of Mississippi in Oxford, and the University of Memphis.

Kenan's concern over what appeared to be the erosion of black communities on a national scale—especially in response to the increased importance of-visual media in the production of images of blackness—led him in 1991 to begin seven years of intermittent travels across the continent, interviewing blacks in a variety of locales both urban and rural, in search of an answer to the question "What does it mean to be black in America today?" His answers to that question were contained in *Walking on Water: Black American Lives at the Turn of the Twenty-First Century* (1999), a book that combines the genres of travelogue, oral history, and spiritual autobiography. *Walking on Water* was nominated for the Southern Book Award.

Kenan's other works include a young adult biography of JAMES BALDWIN (1993); the book-length essay *The Fire This Time* (2007), an homage and update to Baldwin's *The Fire Next Time*; and the text for Norman Mauskoff's book of photographs *A Time Not Here: The Mississippi Delta* (1997).

Kenan's awards included a Guggenheim Fellowship, the Whiting Writers' Award, the Sherwood Anderson Award, the Dos Passos Award, the Mary Francis Hobson Medal for Arts and Letters, and the 1997 American Academy of Arts and Letters' Prix de Rome. In 2003 he returned to his alma mater as an associate professor of English.

FURTHER READING
Kenan, Randall. *Walking on Water: Black American Lives at the Turn of the Twenty-first Century* (1999).
GEORGE HOVIS

Kendricks, Eddie (17 Dec. 1939–5 Oct. 1992), songwriter and falsetto and tenor vocalist, was born Edward James Kendrick to Jonny and Lee Bell Kendrick in Union Springs, Alabama. Aged seven, Kendricks moved to Birmingham, and in 1955, with friends and singing partners Paul Williams (baritone) and Kell Osborne, formed a doo-wop group, the Cavaliers. In 1956, the group moved to Cleveland, Ohio. After moving to Detroit and changing their name to the Primes in 1957 or 1958, they lost Osborne but gained Otis Williams (baritone and tenor), Melvin Franklin (bass), and Elbridge Bryant. Through frequent performances at local dances and singing battles, the Primes soon developed a popular following on the Detroit circuit. A 1960 single, "Oh Mother, Oh Mine," on the Motown affiliate Miracle, sank without a trace. Bryant departed soon after, to be replaced by David Ruffin (tenor), which also precipitated a name

Eddie Kendricks in 1966. Clockwise from bottom left, David Ruffin, Melvin Franklin, Paul Williams, Otis Williams and, in the center, Eddie Kendricks. (AP Images.)

change, with the Primes becoming the Temptations at the behest of BERRY GORDY's secretary, Billie Jean Brown. In 1961 the Temptations signed a contract with Motown. During the early 1960s the Temptations built up a formidable reputation as a live act, owing to their sublime harmonies, tightly choreographed dance moves, and their snappy dress code, which Kendricks oversaw as the group's wardrobe manager. Although early singles failed to transpose this local success to the national charts, in 1964 "The Way You Do the Things You Do," which featured Kendricks on lead vocal, reached number 11 on the *Billboard* Pop Chart and started a long period of chart success for the Temptations.

The Temptations benefited greatly from the competitive atmosphere behind the scenes at Motown, particularly that between SMOKEY ROBINSON and Norman Whitfield, who vied to have their compositions recorded by the band. Robinson's transcendent "My Girl" (1964) was the band's first million-seller, and was followed by a string of Robinson-penned hits. When "Get Ready" (1966) reached only number 29 on the pop chart, Whitfield assumed the writing and producing duties. Ten of the subsequent fifteen Whitfield-produced singles reached the pop top 10 and all

hit the top 5 in the R&B chart. Of these, Kendricks shared lead vocals with David Ruffin on "You're My Everything" (1967) and took lead vocals on "Please Return Your Love to Me" (1968). The departure of Ruffin in 1968, and his replacement by Dennis Edwards, did not affect the group's popularity, nor did Whitfield's decision to adjust the lyrical concerns of its songs. While the Temptations continued to record love songs and ballads, Whitfield and his writing partner Barrett Strong gradually shifted the group's lyrics towards social comment, believing that Motown had a responsibility to address its music to the social concerns of the day. Songs like "Cloud Nine" (1968), "Runaway Child Running Wild" (1969), and "Ball of Confusion (That's What the World Is Today)" (1970), offered pointed commentaries on the social problems of the late 1960s, including drugs, urban disorder, and the collapse of the civil rights movement, all wrapped in a psychedelic update of the Motown sound and topped with Kendricks's immaculate falsetto.

Despite the Temptations' success, Kendricks, like numerous other Motown performers, grew resentful of Berry Gordy's control of Motown finances. Convinced that the Temptations were being underpaid, he began agitating for a greater share of the considerable monies that the group was earning for the label. Tensions between him and the rest of the band—which had rarely been far below the Temptations' smooth veneer—also escalated, precipitating Kendricks's departure for a solo career in 1971, immediately after recording one of the Temptations' finest and most beloved songs, "Just My Imagination (Running Away with Me)," on which he sang lead.

After recording an undistinguished first album, *All By Myself* (1971), Kendricks found solo success with the excellent *People ... Hold On* (1972), and for a brief period became one of Motown's biggest acts. "Keep on Truckin'" (1973) reached number 1 on the pop and R&B charts, selling 3 million copies and receiving a Grammy Award nomination for Best R&B Performance by a Male. "Boogie Down" (1973) and "Shoeshine Boy" (1975) also were big hits, but as with many 1970s soul singers who embraced disco, diminishing commercial and critical returns set in mid-decade. The decline in Kendricks's voice—a consequence of years of heavy smoking—also became audible. Brief associations with Arista and Atlantic Records failed to revive Kendricks's career and in 1982 he rejoined the Temptations for a revival tour, which merely revived the intra-band tensions and perhaps explains why he was not invited to attend the legendary *Motown 25* anniversary show in 1983. After reverting to his family name, Kendricks participated in the 1985 Artists United against Apartheid and Live Aid campaigns and recorded an album with David Ruffin, but none of these projects reignited his fading career. In 1989, Kendricks and his erstwhile colleagues were inducted into the Rock and Roll Hall of Fame but a tour alongside Dennis Edwards and Ruffin failed to build on the momentum. Kendricks's unreliability and increasing drug use did little to help, suggesting that he had succumbed to the very culture that twenty years previously he had critiqued in the Temptations. The revival project was curtailed in 1991 by the death of Ruffin and the news that Kendricks was suffering with lung cancer. After having a lung removed, Kendricks battled the disease for a year, but died in Birmingham, Alabama, aged fifty-two.

Kendricks will best be remembered for his work with the Temptations, arguably the finest vocal group of the 1960s and one of Motown's most successful acts. His soaring falsetto provided the perfect counterpoint to Ruffins's gruff tenor and Franklin's cavernous bass, and was an integral part of the Temptations' most fondly remembered work. Thanks to Norman Whitfield, Kendricks found himself at the forefront of soul music's move towards explicit social comment, a position that he consolidated with *People ... Hold On*. Amongst the most articulate of the early 1970s glut of politicized soul, *People* deserves comparison with MARVIN GAYE's and STEVIE WONDER's contemporaneous work. Unfortunately, owing to a combination of factors, including Motown's decline and his lack of creative input, Kendricks was not able to replicate *People*'s achievement, which perhaps explains why his solo career has been largely forgotten despite its early promise and success.

FURTHER READING
George, Nelson. *Where Did Our Love Go?: The Rise and Fall of the Motown Sound* (1985).
Williams, Otis, with Patricia Romanowski. *Temptations* (1988).
Obituary: *New York Times*, 7 Oct. 1992.
                                    JOE STREET

Kennard, Clyde (20 June 1927–4 July 1963), activist, was born in Forrest County, Mississippi. Kennard's parents, Will Kennard and Leona Smith, worked a small farm, and he had a sister and three brothers. His father died during Kennard's childhood and his mother later married Silas Smith. Kennard

joined the United States Army in 1945 and served for seven years, achieving the rank of sergeant. He studied at Fayetteville Teachers College, a black institution in North Carolina, and later at the University of Chicago, where he enrolled in 1952, at the age of twenty-five. He left the University of Chicago in 1955, the end of his junior year, returning to Mississippi because of his stepfather's illness. From 1957 onward, Kennard was a poultry farmer in Eatonville, Mississippi. He never married.

After he returned to Mississippi, Kennard participated in a National Association for the Advancement of Colored People (NAACP) youth chapter in Hattiesburg, a few miles south of his home. Kennard was then involved with a botched attempt to desegregate Mississippi Southern College (now the University of Southern Mississippi) in Hattiesburg, though without the help of the NAACP. Like many universities in the South, Mississippi Southern College was segregated and did not admit qualified African Americans, though the NAACP was challenging the legal basis of this across the region.

Kennard first applied to Mississippi Southern College in 1956, but his application was deemed incomplete by university officials because it lacked five references from Mississippi Southern alumni, and was therefore rejected. In 1958 Kennard talked about his aim to fill in another application for the university. Rumors about Kennard led the Mississippi State Sovereignty Commission, an agency with extensive investigative powers created in the wake of *Brown v. Board of Education*, to conduct invasive enquiries on Kennard. The commission attempted to find incriminating evidence against Kennard, to pressure local blacks to convince Kennard not to enroll at the university, and to use Mississippi Southern College president, William D. McCain, and even Mississippi Governor J. P. Coleman to coerce Kennard into not applying.

Undaunted by the pressure, Kennard arrived on the campus of Mississippi Southern College on 15 September 1959 with the intent of enrolling in classes as the first African American student at that institution. However, he quickly left campus without enrolling, and was arrested when police found whiskey and wine in his car (probably planted by Southern College constables), and for speeding near campus. For this offense, Kennard was fined $600 and court costs, though he maintained his innocence.

In 1960, when it appeared that he was going to try again to apply to the university, Kennard was arrested for arranging for the theft of, or for arranging with an employee to sell below the actual cost, five bags of chicken feed. The severity of Kennard's punishment was probably connected to his perceived reputation among Mississippi government officials as an agitator. While the only evidence against him was the testimony of a seventeen-year-old employee of the feed store, Kennard was convicted and sentenced to the maximum jail term of seven years. Kennard's alleged feed store accomplice, Johnny Lee Roberts, received a suspended sentence.

On appeal, Kennard's lawyers argued African Americans were excluded from local juries, including the jury that ruled on Kennard's case. The Mississippi Supreme Court declared that an African American on trial was not automatically entitled to have African Americans included on his or her jury. Thurgood Marshall and the NAACP Legal Defense Fund appealed Kennard's case in front of the Supreme Court, which upheld Kennard's original conviction. Life at the notorious Parchman Penitentiary, where Kennard served his sentence, was difficult. Kennard worked all day in the cotton fields, and in his spare time, taught other inmates how to read and write, and also helped them write letters home.

In 1962 Kennard was diagnosed with stomach cancer, with a poor prognosis. He was sent back to jail, with no access to treatment, and continued to work in the Parchman fields. Kennard's friends, including the Mississippi NAACP leader Vernon Dahmer, and the Student Nonviolent Coordinating Committee mobilized on his behalf, and *Jet* magazine published a story describing Kennard's plight. This caught the attention of the activist-comedian Dick Gregory and of Martin Luther King Jr., of the Southern Christian Leadership Conference, who both demanded Kennard's release. In January 1963, Governor Ross Barnett suspended Kennard's sentence indefinitely and Kennard was released from Parchman. Freedom came too late for Kennard, and he died at a University of Chicago hospital on 4 July 1963 at the age of thirty-six.

Activists in Mississippi ensured the memory of Kennard was not forgotten, and he, along with the figures of the lynching victim Emmett Till and assassinated civil rights leaders Dahmer and Medgar Evers, became symbols of the civil rights movement in the state.

FURTHER READING

Extensive records on the investigations by the
Mississippi State Sovereignty Commission on

Kennard are available online at the Mississippi Department of Archives and History: http://mdah. state.ms.us/arrec/digital_archives/

Dittmer, John. *Local People: the Struggle for Civil Rights in Mississippi* (1994).

Eagles, Charles. *The Price of Defiance: James Meredith and the Integration of Ole Miss* (2009).

Obituary: *New York Times,* 5 July 1963.

KRISTAL L. ENTER

Kennedy, Adrienne (1931–), playwright and educator, was born Adrienne Lita Hawkins in Pittsburgh, Pennsylvania, to Cornell Hawkins, an executive secretary for the YMCA, and Etta Hawkins, a teacher. At the age of four Kennedy moved to Ohio, and she spent the rest of her childhood in an integrated neighborhood in Cleveland, Ohio. Kennedy made no note of an unusual childhood. She earned her B.A. at Ohio State University in 1952. As a student at Ohio State, she witnessed the beginning of the civil rights struggles of the postwar era and the growing white backlash against those struggles. The contrast between these tumultuous events and Kennedy's relatively quiet Cleveland childhood shaped her concerns as a playwright.

In 1953 Adrienne married Joseph C. Kennedy. The union produced two sons, Joseph Jr. and Adam. In 1954 Adrienne Kennedy entered Columbia University to study creative writing. She went on to study and write with the American Theatre Wing (1958) and with Edward Albee at the Circle-in-the-Square School (1962). Subsequently Kennedy taught at Princeton, Yale, and the University of California at Berkeley and the University of California at Davis.

Kennedy came of intellectual and creative age during the Black Arts Movement, and her work represents a commitment to issues of race and blackness nationally and globally. From her Obie Award–winning play *Funnyhouse of a Negro* (produced in 1962) to her experimental and fragmented memoir *People Who Led to My Plays* (1987), Kennedy's writing is most often categorized as surrealist. The fragmentary, dreamlike plots of her works are often secondary to the poetic and symbolic imagery they produce. Linear storytelling is not necessarily Kennedy's concern, as is demonstrated by *People Who Led to My Plays*, which is a collection of images woven together by stream-of-consciousness story fragments.

Moreover Kennedy's most famous play, *Funnyhouse of a Negro*, which was written while she was traveling through Europe and Africa during 1960 and 1961, tells the fractured story of a young girl, Negro-Sarah, who is visited by such disparate spirits as Queen Victoria, Jesus, and Patrice Lumumba, the Congolese anticolonial leader. The work explores issues of sexual and physical violence, race, and gender through the character of Sarah during a waking nightmare. The ideas of motherhood, fatherhood, rape, salvation, and power are represented throughout *Funnyhouse*, as in most of Kennedy's work, and point to the complicated nature of an African American identity. For example, Kennedy's work is often transnational and transhistorical, features multiracial characters, and exists in a Freudian dreamscape; these characteristics have also lead to her work being read as postmodern.

Kennedy's plays have been produced in major theaters all over the world, ranging from the Royal Court Theatre and the National Theatre in London to New York's Joseph Papp Public Theater. In short, Kennedy pushed the boundaries of form as well as of black and American identity. Her plays and other writings represent the violence resulting from the clash of race, gender, and culture in the United States.

FURTHER READING

A collection of Kennedy's papers is in the Harry Ransom Center at the University of Texas at Austin.
Kennedy, Adrienne. *People Who Led to My Plays* (1987).
Bryant-Jackson, Paul K., and Lois More Overbeck, eds. *Intersecting Boundaries: The Theatre of Adrienne Kennedy* (1992).

EVE E. DUNBAR

Kennedy, Flo (11 Feb. 1916–21 Dec. 2000), lawyer, feminist, and civil rights activist, was born Florynce Rae Kennedy in Kansas City, Missouri, the second of five daughters of Wiley Kennedy, a Pullman porter, waiter, and taxi-business owner, and Zella (maiden name unknown). The Kennedy family lived in a predominantly white neighborhood in Kansas City that included small enclaves of black families. Although the family owned a modest house in which the three oldest daughters shared not only a room but also a single bed, Kennedy recalled that she and her sisters did not feel poor while they were growing up. In fact their mother made a conscientious effort to maintain an aesthetically pleasing environment in their home. Wiley and Zella Kennedy were not particularly strict with their children and encouraged them to pursue their individual interests, to develop self-confidence, and

to question authority, traits that served Kennedy well in her future career as a "radical loudmouth" and political activist.

Although Kennedy excelled in school and graduated at the top of her class at Lincoln High School, she did not immediately head to college. As she recounted in her autobiography, college was not considered an option for most African Americans in her community then, especially since Kansas University was "almost completely white" at the time. Instead she and her sisters held a variety of jobs, including cleaning homes, hosting a local radio show, and operating a public elevator. Embracing the entrepreneurial spirit of their father, who owned and operated a taxi business, the sisters eventually opened a hat shop called Kay's Hat Shop. Although the shop made money only during the Christmas and Easter holiday seasons, the sisters thoroughly enjoyed the experience, making enough to pay rent and subsist.

In 1938 Zella Kennedy was diagnosed with breast cancer and underwent a mastectomy. Although the cancer was in remission for a while, it recurred and she died in 1940. Two years later Kennedy and her sister Grayce moved to New York City, where they worked at a variety of administrative and clerical jobs.

In 1944 Kennedy began night classes at Columbia University. Disregarding the advice from others to become a teacher or a nurse, she eventually registered full-time as a pre-law student. Regarding her decision, Kennedy said in her autobiography, "I registered immediately as a pre-law student, which I guess was unusual for a Black woman at that time, but I didn't feel particularly Black, and I'd always wanted to be a lawyer—not only to right wrongs, but because most of the people I knew who were lawyers were better off than the others" (38). She received a bachelor's degree in Pre-Law in 1948 from Columbia.

When Kennedy applied to Columbia Law School she was initially rejected despite her excellent academic record. As she recounted in her 1976 autobiography, the school argued that she was denied because she was a woman, not because she was African American. To Kennedy the particulars of the reason did not matter; it still seemed like racial discrimination to her. With a bravado that she eventually became known for, Kennedy met with the dean of the law school and threatened, with the help of the NAACP, to file a racial discrimination lawsuit against the school. When Columbia Law School acquiesced and granted her admission,

Kennedy became one of only eight women in the program and the only African American. In 1951 she became the first African American to graduate from Columbia Law School.

After graduation Kennedy started working for the law firm Hartman, Sheridan and Tekulsky in New York City, where she mainly performed legal clerical work. In 1954, after passing the bar in her second attempt, she opened her own practice, focusing on marital and criminal cases. A few years later she acquired a legal partner, Don Wilkes. During their partnership Kennedy represented the estates of the legendary jazz artists BILLIE HOLLIDAY and CHARLIE PARKER and handled the case of the activist H. RAP BROWN. The partnership with Wilkes was brief, however: he ran away with most of the firm's money, leaving Kennedy mired in debt.

Even though she was never a proponent of the institution of marriage, Kennedy married Charles Dudley Dye, a Welsh science-fiction writer, in 1957. By her account the marriage was a disaster because of Dye's alcoholism and self-loathing. The couple divorced in 1957. Not long afterward Dye died from liver disease.

Representing the Women's Health Collective and 350 female plaintiffs of childbearing age, Kennedy, Nancy Stearns, and Diane Schulder filed a class-action lawsuit (*Abramowicz v. Lefkowitz*) in 1969 challenging New York State's abortion law. They sued the Archdiocese of New York and other related Catholic organizations for violating federal tax law by engaging in active political lobbying against candidates who supported abortion reform. The case became moot when the New York state legislature made abortion legal in 1970. Kennedy and Schulder later documented their experiences with the case in their book *Abortion Rap* (1971).

By the late 1960s Kennedy had become disillusioned with the practice of law. After years of representing working-class underdogs and the Holiday and Parker estates, she concluded that the law was really only about maintaining the status quo. Convinced that the law was not an effective tool for obtaining justice or effecting social change, she changed careers and become a political activist and public speaker.

During the 1960s and 1970s Kennedy was active in the black liberation, women's liberation, gay rights, and prostitute's rights movements and helped establish several organizations. In 1966 she founded the Media Workshop to combat racism in media programming and advertising. She attended all of the Black Power conferences in the late 1960s and attended the first meeting of the National Organization for Women (NOW) in New York City in 1966.

Her involvement with NOW lasted only a few years, as she became increasingly frustrated with the narrow vision of the group. Instead she chose to work with feminist groups that were more radical in their approach and addressed the issues that she deemed important. Believing that feminists needed to be more involved in the electoral process, she founded, with Linda Davall, the Feminist Party in November 1971. The organization's first action was to support SHIRLEY CHISHOLM in her campaign for the U.S. presidency in 1972.

In response to the mainstream media's depiction of the women's movement as exclusively white and middle class, Kennedy and Margaret Sloan formed the National Black Feminist Organization (NBFO) in New York in 1973. The organization articulated a distinct black feminist perspective that simultaneously challenged racism and sexism. The NBFO focused on a variety of issues, including abortion and reproductive rights, child care, employment rights, welfare rights, gay and lesbian rights, and the ratification of the Equal Rights Amendment. Although the national organization lasted for only three years, its chapters in several major U.S. cities, such as Chicago, continued on.

By the 1970s Kennedy was a major draw on the lecture circuit, speaking at rallies, protests, and conferences. She was a much sought-after guest speaker on college campuses across the United States and appeared on numerous national and local television and radio shows. Often outfitted in her trademark garb—Stetson cowboy hat, boots, garish eyeglasses, and T-shirts bearing controversial political slogans—she earned the reputation as the loudest and rudest mouth in America.

Despite her failing health, Kennedy continued to lecture and be involved in political causes during the 1980s and 1990s. In 1981 she and William Pepper published the book *Sex Discrimination in Employment: An Analysis and Guide for Practitioner and Student*. She was a firm supporter of JESSE JACKSON's bid for the U.S. presidency in both 1984 and 1988 and was active in the antiapartheid movement in the 1980s. She produced a cable television political talk show in New York City and was national director of the Voters, Artists, Anti-Nuclear Activists, and Consumers for Political Action and Communication Coalition (VACPAC). In 1985 friends and colleagues paid tribute to her at a roast marking her seventieth birthday.

Kennedy died in New York City at the age of eighty-four. Along with ANGELA DAVIS, Shirley Chisholm, TONI CADE BAMBARA, Frances Beale, and countless others, Kennedy helped build the foundation for black feminist thought and politics in the contemporary United States.

FURTHER READING

Kennedy's papers are housed at the Arthur and Elizabeth Schlesinger Library on the History of Women in America at the Radcliffe Institute for Advanced Study, Harvard University, Cambridge, Massachusetts.

Kennedy, Flo. *Color Me Flo: My Hard Life and Good Times* (1976).

Hanlon, Gail, ed. *Voicing Power: Conversations with Visionary Women* (1997).

Nelson, Jennifer. *Women of Color and the Reproductive Rights Movement* (2003).

Obituary: *New York Times*, 23 Dec. 2000.

KIMALA PRICE

Kennedy, William Jesse, Jr. (15 June 1889–8 July 1985), businessman, civic leader, churchman, and author, was born the eldest son of William Jesse Kennedy, a public school principal, and Katie (Riley) Kennedy, a homemaker, in Andersonville, Georgia. He received his public school training under his father, who was the principal of the local school. Later he was educated at Americus Institute in Americus, Georgia, which was under the auspices of the black Southwestern Georgia Baptist Association, and graduated in 1912. He studied law for a year through textbooks and a correspondence course from LaSalle University, and did special work in business administration through a Columbia University extension course, but did not graduate from either institution. He held a number of jobs ranging from carpenter to meat cutter.

Influenced by an uncle who worked in the insurance industry, he began working at Guaranty Mutual Life Insurance Company of Savannah, Georgia, in 1913, and was employed there for three years. In September 1916, he became associated with North Carolina Mutual Life Insurance Company, which was founded in 1898 by JOHN MERRICK, Dr. Aaron M. Moore, C.C. Spaulding, and five other prominent black leaders in Durham County, and would grow into the largest African American owned insurance company in the nation. Kennedy began his career there as manager of the Savannah, Georgia, district.

On 27 December 1917, he married Margaret L. Spaulding, the sister of CHARLES CLINTON "C.C." SPAULDING, one of the founders of North Carolina Mutual Life. She was a graduate of Barber Scotia Seminary in Concord, North Carolina, and later graduated from Cheyney Normal Teachers College and moved to Durham to teach home economics. She had met Kennedy many times before their marriage when visiting her brother. Three children were born to this union: William J. Kennedy III, Margaret K. Goodwin, and Charlotte K. Sloan.

Kennedy served seven months in a battalion headquarters as Corporal-Clerk at Camp Holabird, located on the Chesapeake Bay, Maryland, during the First World War.

In 1919, the North Carolina Mutual Life Insurance Company transferred him to the home office in Durham, North Carolina, where he served as office manager and assistant secretary. In January 1920 he was elected a director of the company and became involved in all facets of home office operations, and in 1923 he was appointed office manager. From there he quickly passed through the ranks, rising first to vice president-secretary, and then finally, on 2 August 1952, he was elected the company's fourth president upon the death of his brother-in-law "C.C." Spaulding. He served in this position until his retirement on 31 December 1958. In 1959 Kennedy was named chairman of the board and served in that capacity until 1965, remaining as an honorary member until his death. At the time of his transfer to the home office in 1919, the company's assets were $755,000 and its annual income was more than $1.3 million. At the time of his death, North Carolina Mutual's assets had ballooned to more than $200 million, and its insurance in force (that is, policies that are active and represent the total of all insurance carried by the company) was valued at more than $7 billion.

Following his retirement, Kennedy authored the *North Carolina Mutual Story*, which chronicled the history of the company from 1898 to 1970. He was also president of the Bankers Fire Insurance Company and vice president of the Mutual Savings and Loan Association. At various times from the 1930s to the 1960s, he served as a member of the board of directors for the Mechanics and Farmers Bank, Southern Fidelity Mutual Insurance Company, the United Fund, 4-H Foundation of North Carolina Inc., the National Council of the United Negro College Fund, and the board of trustees of Howard University.

In addition to his role in the insurance industry, he was actively involved in the civic affairs of Durham, founding and serving as president of the John Avery Boys' Club, and acting as chairperson of the board of the James E. Shepard Foundation. He also belonged to the Durham Business and Professional Chain, the Algonquin Tennis Club, the Omega Psi Phi Fraternity Inc., the North Carolina Recreation Commission (1945–1956), the North Carolina State Board of Higher Education (1955–1965), and served on the local Selective Service Board (1952–1967).

Active in the civil rights movement, Kennedy helped found the Durham branch of the NAACP in 1919 and the Durham Committee on the Affairs of Black People (1935). Kennedy made the motion to establish this organization and suggested that an executive committee be elected to represent the African American citizenship of Durham in all matters relating to their educational, economic, political, civic, and social welfare.

Kennedy was also involved in the religious affairs of the White Rock Baptist Church, which was famous thanks to its first pastor Dr. MILES MARK FISHER, who had made it one of the best known congregations in the United States because of the church's forceful espousal of a social gospel, and because many of its members were business executives who had national recognition. Kennedy served as a member of the board of trustees of White Rock Baptist Church and as its treasurer from 1925 to 1955. He also served his church as assistant superintendent of the Sunday school and was a teacher of the A.M. Moore Bible Class from 1920 to 1975; on 5 January 1975 the class was renamed the Moore-Kennedy Bible Class and the title of Teacher Emeritus was bestowed upon him by the class. He also received such civil honors as the Boys' Club Silver Keystone Award (1954), the American Recreation and North Carolina Recreation Society citations for meritorious service, and honorary degrees from Shaw University (Doctor of Laws) in 1957, and Virginia State College (Doctor of Laws) in 1958.

Kennedy died on 8 July 1985 at the age of ninety-six and is remembered as a tireless giant in economics, religion, and civic life in Durham.

FURTHER READING

Kennedy's manuscripts are housed in the Southern Historical Collection at the University of North Carolina at Chapel Hill and held jointly with North Carolina Central University.

Kennedy, William Jesse, Jr. *The North Carolina Mutual Story: A Symbol of Progress, 1898–1970* (1970).

North Carolina Mutual Life Insurance. "W. J. Kennedy, Jr., Retires as President," *The Whetstone* (First Quarter 1959).

Troup, Cornelius V. *Distinguished Negro Georgians* (1962).

Vann, Andre D., with Beverly Washington Jones. *Durham's Hayti* (1999).

Weare, Walter B. *Black Business in the New South: A Social History of the North Carolina Mutual Life Insurance Company* (1973).

ANDRE D. VANN

Kennedy, Yvonne (8 Jan. 1945–), educator and politician, as born in Mobile, Alabama. She was the second-youngest of twelve children born to Leroy Kennedy Sr. and Thelma McMillian. Kennedy's paternal grandparents were instrumental in the founding of the Stewart Memorial Christian Methodist Episcopal Church located in Mobile. This church played a large role in Kennedy's life; there she received her early education, was a committed worshipper, and was highly active. Kennedy went on to graduate in the top ten percent of her segregated Central High School class in Mobile in 1962.

That same year, Kennedy enrolled in college at Bishop State Junior College in Mobile, Alabama, where she received an associate's degree in 1964. Soon after, Kennedy transferred to Alabama State University in Montgomery, Alabama. During her second year at Alabama State she received the President's Award for her academic achievements. As a junior, Kennedy joined the Beta Eta chapter of Delta Sigma Theta Sorority. She assumed leadership positions as the president of the Pyramid Club, a group consisting of freshman girls who are interested in the sorority, and then served as the chapter president of Delta Sigma Theta at Alabama State. Kennedy also assumed other positions of college leadership. She was secretary of the Alpha Kappa Mu National Honor Society and editor and chief of the yearbook staff, and was also selected as Miss Alabama State University. Because of her accomplishments, Kennedy was elected to Who's Who among Students in American Colleges and Universities. She graduated in 1966 with a B.A. in English and continued her graduate studies at Morgan State University in Baltimore, Maryland.

While at Morgan State, Kennedy was awarded a two-year graduate assistantship. Still a very active student, she became the advisor to the Alpha Gamma chapter of Delta Sigma Theta Sorority as well as a research assistant in the English department. She graduated in 1968 with a master's degree in English.

Upon completing her master's degree, Kennedy taught English at her alma mater, Bishop State Junior College. Initially serving as an instructor, she rose to the rank of the chair of the department of English, where she was instrumental in helping the college gain accreditation by the Southern Association of Colleges and Schools in 1970. During her tenure at Bishop State, she served as the coordinator of the Higher Education Achievement Program (HEAP). Later she accepted a position as associate director for the Southern Association of Colleges and Schools' cooperative programs and relocated to Atlanta, Georgia. To honor Kennedy for her dedication, the Stewart Memorial CME Church named their largest community outreach project the Yvonne Kennedy Educational Center in 1978, the same year as her father's death.

After two years of working with the Southern Association of Colleges and Schools, Kennedy returned to Bishop State to work as the Title III Coordinator. In 1979 she earned a Ph.D. in Higher Education from the University of Alabama. Within the same year Kennedy ran and was elected as the first African American woman from Mobile County to the Alabama House of Representatives, House District 103 (a position that she continued to hold as of 2011). In 1981 she became the first African American woman to head an Alabama state college, becoming the president of Bishop State Junior College. As president she conducted the college's fist capital campaign and established an endowment for the school. Also, because Kennedy combined the three public two-year colleges in Mobile, Bishop State is now the second-largest institution of higher education in Mobile.

In 1988 Yvonne Kennedy was unanimously elected the national president of Delta Sigma Theta Sorority at the seventy-fifth Diamond Jubilee Convention and was subsequently reelected for a second term served from 1990 to 1992. *Ebony* magazine named Kennedy as one of the "100 Most Influential Black Americans" in 1989 and in 1992.

FURTHER READING

Kimbrough, Walter M. *Black Greek 101: The Culture, Customs, and Challenges of Black Fraternities and Sororities* (2003).

Project Vote Smart. "Project Vote Smart— Representative Yvonne Kennedy." votesmart.org (accessed 14 Nov. 2010).

Smith, Jessie Carney, ed. *Notable Black American Women, Book II* (1996).

AZHIA LONG

Kenney, John Andrew, Sr. (11 June 1874–29 Jan. 1950), physician, surgeon, hospital administrator and founder, author, and medical organizational leader, was born at Redmonds, near Charlottesville, in Albemarle County, Virginia. Kenney was the second of three children born to the ex-slaves John A. and Caroline Howard Kenney. The elder Kenney was a farmer, storekeeper, community leader, and owner of a forty-acre farm. According to unpublished autobiographical sketches in the Kenney Papers, Kenney's parents could not read or write during his youth; however, they were determined that their children would be educated. Kenney's father spearheaded building across the road from his country store a one-room log house, which became the community's first country day school for black children. In addition to school and working in his father's store, Kenney learned all the intricacies of farming, from planting to sales.

The Kenneys experienced a grave loss when John was about fourteen. His father, who according to census records was nearly sixty at John's birth, died, catapulting the family into uncertain financial circumstances. The younger Kenney was thrust into the role of managing the family's farm. He later joined his mother in the household employ of a University of Virginia professor and continued his schooling as time permitted. According to Kenney, he decided to become a physician while observing University of Virginia students as he managed the store of one of his former teachers.

In 1893 Kenney entered Hampton Institute, one of many historically black colleges founded after the Civil War to educate the freedmen. He worked his way through college at on-campus and summer resort jobs in West Virginia. Although practice teaching was a general requirement prior to graduation, he was allowed instead to take college preparatory courses at Shaw University, another historically black college located in Raleigh, North Carolina. Kenney rejoined his Hampton classmates and graduated as valedictorian in 1897.

Shaw University's founder and former president, Reverend Henry Tupper, recognized that physicians of color could contribute greatly to alleviating health care disparities in the black community. As a result, the Leonard Medical School of Shaw University was founded circa 1882, after the Howard University College of Medicine (1868) and Meharry Medical College (1876). The Leonard Medical School became North Carolina's first medical school to accept blacks and one of the country's first to have a graded four-year curriculum. Over four hundred physicians graduated prior to its closure in 1918. Kenney excelled in his studies there, garnering awards in chemistry and physiology prior to graduating in 1901.

Kenney passed Virginia's medical boards in 1901 and began an internship at Freedmen's Hospital, the teaching hospital for Howard University. At the invitation of the noted educator, Tuskegee Institute founder, and principal DR. BOOKER T. WASHINGTON, Kenney accepted the position of resident physician and medical director of the Tuskegee Institute Hospital and Nurse-Training School. The providential partnering of these two Hampton Institute graduates altered the course of health care for thousands of blacks and unveiled extraordinary opportunities for postgraduate education for black physicians and nurses from around the country. Kenney began his tenure at Tuskegee in August 1902. In addition to his school and hospital duties, he became the personal physician of Dr. Booker T. Washington and of the noted scientist and faculty member DR. GEORGE WASHINGTON CARVER. Kenney accompanied Dr. Washington around the country on his goodwill tours and fundraising missions, placing him among some of America's wealthiest and most influential philanthropists and public officials. In December 1902 Kenney married his college sweetheart, Alice Talbot. No children were born to this union.

The professional accomplishments of Dr. Kenney and the history of the National Medical Association (NMA) are inextricably linked. The NMA was founded in 1895 by a group of black health care professionals attending the Cotton States and International Exposition in Atlanta, Georgia. It was at this exposition that Booker T. Washington gave his "Atlanta Compromise" speech. The National Negro Medical Association of Physicians, Surgeons, Dentists, and Pharmacists (which later changed its name to the National Medical Association) was born out of exigency, as its mission statement proclaimed, because of the exclusionary practices of mainstream medical organizations. Although some black physicians were members of the American Medical Association outside of the South, with few exceptions, blacks could not join in the South because they were precluded from membership in its locally affiliated organizations. As a result, black parallel organizations proliferated in medicine,

dentistry, and pharmacy at local and state levels during the period 1890–1930. These parallel organizations provided a much-needed forum for scientific discussions, continuing education, and advocacy.

Kenney joined the NMA at its national meeting in Nashville in 1903 (Kenney, *Journal of the National Medical Association* 38, no. 1 [Jan. 1946]: 29). After his presentation on shock at the meeting, Kenney met Dr. Daniel Hale Williams. Williams had already garnered national recognition as one of the first known surgeons to successfully suture the heart's pericardium (1893). He was also the leading spirit behind founding Provident Hospital in Chicago in 1891. Impressed by Kenney's professionalism and surgical and organizational skills, Williams tapped him to become his preferred anesthetist during his surgical demonstration clinics. Williams also recommended Kenney for NMA secretary; Kenney served in that capacity from 1904 to 1912 (Kenney, *JNMA* Sep. [1941]: 206). Kenney benefited greatly from Williams's sage advice, experience, and professional connections. On visits to Williams in Chicago, Kenney often traveled to the most respected medical centers in the Midwest to observe and participate in postgraduate clinics and surgical demonstrations.

As NMA secretary, Kenney realized that, like the American Medical Association, the NMA needed a journal to serve as a forum for advocacy, scientific research, communication, and medical case studies. In 1908 his proposal to the NMA's executive committee was accepted, and the first issue of the *Journal of the National Medical Association* (JNMA) debuted in early 1909. Kenney tapped Dr. Charles Victor Roman, an eminent and learned black physician and educator, to be the editor-in-chief; Kenney began as managing editor and business manager.

The years 1911–1913 would bring about major changes for Kenney, both professionally and personally. When Tuskegee Institute Hospital outgrew its confines, a gift of $55,000 was procured from Mrs. Elizabeth Mason to erect a new hospital and purchase equipment. Named for Mason's grandfather, the John A. Andrew Memorial Hospital was formally dedicated in 1913. Having keenly observed the demonstration clinics held in conjunction with the annual NMA meetings, Kenney felt that he could enhance the clinical experiences of the members. With the permission of Booker T. Washington, Kenney invited the NMA to hold its 1912 annual session at Tuskegee Institute. He procured eminent physicians—both black and white—to conduct lectures and surgical and clinical demonstrations. Over four hundred patients from several states were treated free of charge during the first John A. Andrew Annual Clinic. In 1912 Kenney authored *The Negro in Medicine*. During the NMA meeting Kenney was elected president for the ensuing year. Tragedy also befell Dr. Kenney in 1912 with the loss of his wife. He married Frieda Armstrong in 1913, and to this union three sons and a daughter were born.

Kenney's editorial responsibilities increased in 1918. When Dr. Roman resigned as *JNMA*'s editor-in-chief, Kenney was elected editor and manager in 1918 (*JNMA* 10(3) [1918], p. 140). Keeping his commitment to enhance educational opportunities for black physicians, Kenney cofounded the John A. Andrew Clinical Society in 1918. Dr. Kenney and the society made history in 1921 by organizing and conducting the first four-week postgraduate course in surgery and medicine for black physicians in the South. As a testament to the high regard in which Kenney was held, eminent physicians from Johns Hopkins, Harvard, Howard, and many leading hospitals from around the country served as lecturers and surgical demonstrators for the John A. Andrew Annual Post-Graduate Course (*The Southern Workman*, July [1923]: 365–366). Kenney's skilled leadership of the John A. Andrew Memorial Hospital also resulted in its designation as a Grade A hospital by the Council on Medical Education of the American Medical Association, making it one of only four black-run hospitals in the country at that time to carry the designation (*New York Age*, 8 Jan. 1921).

The years 1922 and 1923 were tumultuous for both Kenney and Tuskegee Institute. Tuskegee Institute donated three hundred acres to construct a U.S. Veterans Administration (VA) Hospital for wounded black veterans of World War I. Principal Robert R. Moton was led to believe that as soon as possible, the professional staff would be composed of black physicians and nurses. Local white officials opposed this arrangement, and after a rather contentious meeting between both sides, in which Kenney and the administration stood firm in their beliefs, threats of violence escalated. The Ku Klux Klan paraded past the college; Kenney's life was threatened, and a cross was burned on his property. Kenney took his family north for safety reasons, returning several months later. President Harding and the head of the VA reversed their stance on black physicians and nurses for the Tuskegee VA Hospital after several meetings with members of the NMA's executive committee and others (Cobb, p. 176).

Kenney and his family relocated in September 1924 to Newark, New Jersey, where he quickly determined that health care disparities and a lack of hospital privileges for black physicians also plagued this Northern city. Kenney tried to interest several black physicians and a black medical society there in pooling their resources to build a hospital, to no avail. Undeterred, Kenney persevered amid several rejections from financial institutions and was finally granted a personal loan to build a hospital. Named in honor of his parents, the Kenney Memorial Hospital opened in September 1927 on a lot he owned on Kinney Street next to his home. With the addition of its training school for nurses, it grew to provide extraordinary opportunities for black physicians, interns, nurses, and patients. In an effort to truly make it a community hospital, Kenney attempted to sell it to a community hospital association in 1934; however, the group could not reach a consensus on a purchase price. In the true spirit of altruism, Kenney donated the hospital (valued at around $93,000) to the community on Christmas Eve of 1934. Kenney remained as medical director until 1939, at which time he returned to Tuskegee and again headed the John A. Andrew Hospital until 1944.

In 1944 Kenney returned to New Jersey and semi-retired in Montclair. He retired as *JNMA* editor in 1948. In recognition of his outstanding achievements, his portrait was commissioned by the Harmon Foundation for the 1944 Smithsonian exhibit, *Outstanding Americans of Negro Origin*. This exhibit, which traveled around the country, included such notables as CHARLES HAMILTON HOUSTON, RALPH BUNCHE, MARY MCLEOD BETHUNE, and GEORGE WASHINGTON CARVER. Kenney died of bronchial pneumonia and cerebral thrombosis in Glen Ridge, New Jersey. In lamenting his passing, DR. W. MONTAGUE COBB, who succeeded Kenney as *JNMA* editor, stated in part, "Dr. Kenney shiningly exemplified the precepts of Booker T. Washington. He let down his buckets where he was. He lifted himself to noble heights" (Cobb, p. 177).

FURTHER READING

The John A. Kenney Papers are housed at the Tuskegee University Archives in Tuskegee, Alabama.

Cobb, W. Montague. *Journal of the National Medical Association* 42, no. 3 (1950): 175–177.

Richardson, Clement, Ed. *The National Cyclopedia of the Colored Race*, p. 45 (1919).

Obituaries: *The Journal of Negro History* 35, no. 2 (1950): 229–230.

Chicago Tribune, 30 Jan. 1950.

ELVATRICE PARKER BELSCHES

Keppard, Freddie (27 Feb. 1890–15 July 1933), cornetist, was born in New Orleans, Louisiana. His father was a cook; his parents' names are unknown. His older brother, the guitarist and tuba player Louis Keppard, claimed that Freddie was born in 1889 and first played violin, then mandolin and accordion, though he is known to have played guitar. He took up cornet at the age of sixteen. According to Alphonse Picou, he first played cornet in public at a picnic when MANUEL PEREZ became ill. Picking up Perez's cornet, he played blues. It was well received, and thereafter he put aside the guitar. Keppard studied cornet with Adolphe Alexander Sr.

Details of Keppard's activities are confusing. Accounts are casual and conflicting, bands shifted personnel to suit the circumstances of day-to-day life, and musicians and historians have tried to give contributions an enhanced significance by moving the chronology forward. Early on Keppard played with POPS FOSTER and the trombonist Willie Cornish. Substituting for Perez at Leonard Bechet's twenty-first birthday party in April 1907, Keppard played with a young SIDNEY BECHET. Around this time Keppard started and led the Olympia Orchestra with either Picou, GEORGE BAQUET, Bechet, or Jimmie Noone on clarinet. The flexibility of personnel was such that Keppard himself was sometimes replaced by Joe Oliver (not yet KING OLIVER). An engagement at the Tuxedo dance hall happened to anticipate the instrumentation of the Original Dixieland Jazz Band: cornet, clarinet, trombone, piano, and drums. JELLY ROLL MORTON places this event in 1908, but the hall did not open until 1909.

Handing over leadership of the Olympia to the violinist ARMAND JOHN PIRON, Keppard traveled to California to join the bassist BILL JOHNSON in the Original Creole Orchestra (also known as the Creole Band and similar titles) in the spring of 1914. From 1914 to 1918 the band toured on several vaudeville circuits and thereby disseminated an early jazz style nationwide before the first recordings by the Original Dixieland Jazz Band (1917). Initially its instrumentation was violin, cornet, clarinet, trombone, guitar, string bass, and drums. The violinist Jimmy Palao is sometimes called its leader rather than Johnson, who is named as its manager. After a temporary breakup in 1917, the band resumed playing under Keppard's leadership in Chicago and then again on tour. During an engagement in New York (perhaps December 1915, or April 1917,

or later still), Keppard declined an offer to record for the Victor label. Among the reasons given for this seemingly colossal mistake, including a fear that other musicians would copy his style, the most likely was a dispute over money. These may all be excuses to hide a late and for some reason unacceptable effort: "Tack 'em Down," recorded by the unidentified Creole Jazz Band for Victor in New York on 2 December 1918, was never issued.

In 1918 Keppard settled in Chicago, where details of his activities continue to be confusing. The Original Creole Band disbanded in the spring, but Keppard worked briefly at the Royal Gardens with Johnson. He joined the clarinetist Lawrence Duhé's band at the Dreamland Cafe. By the end of 1918 he was the leader at the De Luxe Gardens, billed as King Keppard to rival King Oliver, though on occasion he also played second trumpet in Oliver's own band at the Royal Gardens. At the De Luxe he was joined by Bechet, who temporarily left Duhé's band after an argument over wages. Keppard worked at the Lorraine Club with Noone and concurrently with Mae Brady's band at the Dreamland.

Keppard joined Doc Cook's theater orchestra for two years beginning in the fall of 1922, except for a period with Erskine Tate's Vendome Orchestra, and in June 1923 he recorded two titles with a group drawn from Tate's orchestra. He worked occasionally with the pianist Tony Jackson and was a member of JOHNNY DODDS's group at Burt Kelly's Stable intermittently for six years starting in 1924. He rejoined Cook from late 1925 to early 1926. He recorded four titles, including "Here Comes the Hot Tamale Man," with Noone and JOHNNY ST. CYR in a small group under Cook's name but without Cook in June 1926. Tracks from that same period by the pianist JIMMY BLYTHE, "Messin Around" and "Adams Apple," have been cited as evidence of Keppard's declining abilities, but it is now believed that the unidentified and incompetent cornetist is not Keppard. After leading his own band and making his only recordings as a leader in September 1926, he rejoined Cook from spring 1927 until September of that year. He was again briefly with Tate in early 1928. He led a band in spring 1928, worked with the reed player Jerome Don Pasquall late that year, and toured Illinois and Indiana with his own band. Returning to Chicago, he joined Charlie Elgar at the Savoy Ballroom. Keppard died in Chicago of tuberculosis. He was survived by his wife; details of this marriage are unknown.

According to Morton, Keppard was "about my colour [Morton was light-skinned], Creole accent, a good spender, wore plenty nice clothes, had women hanging around all day long, liked to drink a lot." The singer LIZZIE MILES reported that he was clannish and always spoke to her in patois to prevent others from eavesdropping. The cornetist THOMAS "MUTT" CAREY said Keppard, who was acclaimed for his powerful playing, "could play any kind of song good. Technique, attack, tone, and ideas were all there" (quoted in Shapiro and Hentoff, 45). In addition to improvisatory skills, he had the aural equivalent of a photographic memory, and in an attempt to hide his inability to read music, he would make excuses for not playing a piece well the first time through, only to play it perfectly the next time.

With Keppard having recorded only infrequently and late in his career, there is no surviving aural evidence of his contributions as one of the first "kings" of the jazz cornet. Nevertheless his brief session as a leader in 1926 has sometimes been underappreciated in the literature. For recordings made at a time when the genius of LOUIS ARMSTRONG was already well documented, one cannot get carried away with praise, but certainly Keppard's impressive playing requires no apology. At the opening of "Stockyard Strut" he presents a dignified, polished, relaxed, in-tune, and rhythmically foursquare melody suggesting classic ragtime. Later he loosens the reins to incorporate moments of creative improvisation, sliding "blue notes," and a gentle swing. This contrast is carried further on two versions of "Salty Dog," where Keppard shows himself to be fully in control of the blues idiom and additionally shows sensitivity to instrumental balance by complementing rather than dominating solos by the clarinetist Dodds and the singer Papa Charlie Jackson.

FURTHER READING

Two taped interviews with Louis Keppard are in the archives at Tulane University, New Orleans, Louisiana.

Charters, Samuel B., and Leonard Kunstadt. *Jazz: A History of the New York Scene* (1962).

Chilton, John. *Who's Who of Jazz: Storyville to Swing Street* (1985).

Shapiro, Nat, and Nat Hentoff, eds. *Hear Me Talkin' to Ya: The Story of Jazz as Told by the Men Who Made It* (1955).

This entry is taken from the *American National Biography* and is published here with the permission of the American Council of Learned Societies.

BARRY KERNFELD

Kern Foxworth, Marilyn (18 Feb. 1954–), writer, educator, professional speaker, was born in Toledo, Ohio, but moved to Kosciusko, Mississippi, in 1955 with Jimmie Kern, a housepainter, and Manella Kern, a schoolteacher, who adopted her six years later. The couple had raised ten children of their own (their youngest child was a junior in high school) when they began caring for Marilyn. A very ambitious and high achieving student at Tipton Street High School, Kern hosted a radio program and served as editor-in-chief of the school newspaper, *The Tipton Gazette*. In 1971, Kern and a white student delivered valedictory addresses, after her senior class was forced by a Supreme Court order to integrate the city's white school.

Kern enrolled at Jackson State University (JSU) in August 1971 after receiving a four-year scholarship. Her mother feared for her daughter's safety after the Mississippi State Guard killed two students in May 1971. The bullet holes were still visible in the girls' dorm when Kern moved into the building. Kern majored in Speech Communication at JSU and hosted a radio talk show. She graduated first in her college class.

In 1974, while studying for a master's degree at Florida State University (FSU), Kern read the article "White Backlash to Negro Ads: Fact or Fantasy" by Carl Block, which discussed whether white consumers would refuse to purchase products that used blacks in advertisements. Taking Block's work as her starting point, Kern began writing, researching, and speaking about the portrayals of women, blacks, and other people of color in advertising. While attending FSU her father died suddenly. After a brief tenure as a management trainee for GTE (where she was the first woman to have an office and where she initiated the company's first diversity program), in 1975 Kern began work on her Ph.D. at the University of Wisconsin-Madison. During winter break in 1978, her mother suffered a fatal heart attack. In response to the departure from the university of several African American students (at the time there were 250 African American and 250 African students among the 40,000 attending UW), Kern produced a documentary probing discriminatory and isolating experiences of black students at "Top Ten" universities. The documentary aired on the Wisconsin Public Broadcasting System in January 1980, and again two months later. She met Gregory Lamar Foxworth at UW in February 1980 and married him two years later. (They had one son, Lamar, before divorcing in 1985.) Upon graduation in 1982 Kern Foxworth became the first person of color in the United States to receive a Ph.D. in Advertising and Public Relations.

Kern Foxworth took a job at the University of Tennessee (UT) becoming the first black faculty member in the School of Journalism. In 1983 she became an Amon Carter Evans Scholar, which allowed her to travel to Africa as a participant in the First World Congress on Communication for Africa and the Diaspora. In 1985 she became the first black person to receive the National Faculty Adviser Award from the Public Relations Student Society of America. Kern Foxworth left UT to join the Department of Journalism at Texas A&M University (TAMU) in 1987. By this time she had begun to focus her work on media depictions of women and people of color. In 1988 Kern Foxworth became a Poynter Institute Fellow and an American Press Institute Fellow. Also in 1988, Kern Foxworth was the first woman to receive the prestigious Pathfinder Award from the International Public Relations Institute.

In 1990 Kern Foxworth served as an expert witness for the state in the highly publicized obscenity case *Freeman v. State of Florida*, in which the store owner Charles Freeman was being sued by the state of Florida for selling the album *As Nasty As They Wanna Be* by the rap group 2 Live Crew, which had been deemed lewd and lascivious. In 1991 Kern Foxworth was named an Agnes Harris Postdoctoral Fellow of the American Association of University Women, which allowed her to take a year's leave to finish a book on stereotypical representations of blacks in advertising.

A turning point in Kern Foxworth's career came in 1992 when she was involved with making the acclaimed documentary, *Racism in Advertising: From the Frito Bandito to Power Master*, and wrote the accompanying text, "The Untapped Syndrome: Multi-Ethnic Consumer Markets." In 1993 she became the first minority faculty member to receive the Kreighbaum Under-40 Award for excellence in research, teaching, and public service. Also in 1993, she received the Quill Award for Speech Writing from the International Association of Business Communicators.

Twenty years after the article by Carl Block set the course of her career, Kern Foxworth had become a recognized expert on blacks in advertising and racial relations. She wrote the first book to chronicle the portrayal of blacks in advertising, *Aunt Jemima, Uncle Ben, and Rastus: Blacks in Advertising, Yesterday, Today, and Tomorrow* (1994), with a foreword by ALEX HALEY. This groundbreaking book provided the most in-depth discussion on advertising images and their role in polarizing or bridging race relations. In 1997 Kern Foxworth co-edited *Facing Difference: Race, Gender, and Mass Media*. Also in 1997, she wrote the narrative for the catalog for an exhibition of work by Michael Ray Charles, a noted black artist whose work incorporates black advertising images. The catalog, with a foreword by SPIKE LEE, won several awards, including Best Exhibition Catalog from the American Association of Museums. Throughout these years, Kern Foxworth was affiliated with several women's groups and was a staunch advocate in dispelling misogynistic depictions of women. Such advocacy was a deciding factor in her selection in 1997 as a Leadership Foundation Fellow of the International Women's Forum, an organization comprised of 3,000 of the most influential women in the world.

Kern Foxworth had joined the Association for Education in Journalism and Mass Communication (AEJMC) during the early 1980s; she became active in leading the organization and in 1998 was the first black person elected vice-president of the organization, before being named in 2000 the first black woman president of AEJMC. As president of AEJMC, Kern Foxworth sought to solve the problem of a lack of black women in leadership positions in journalism education by founding the Journalism Leadership Institute in Diversity.

As an expert on black advertising icons, the stereotyping of women and multicultural groups in the mass media, and public relations issues relative to multiracial consumers, Kern Foxworth was frequently featured and her work quoted in local, national, and international media. At the beginning of the twenty-first century, she left the academy and started Kern Foxworth International, a marketing communications firm. Among other major projects, in 2004 the company designed a public relations campaign for the Justice Department and Praxis for the prevention of domestic violence within the African American community, and was hired by the international organization Vital Voices to provide leadership and communications training for Russian and Ukrainian business women. The latter project gave Kern Foxworth an international platform to assist women, which had become her primary passion and mission. In 2007 Kern Foxworth, who had begun writing poetry in the fourth grade, published a book of poems titled

Ebonessence: Dark Daughters of Divine Destiny, that was inspired in part by the firing of Don Imus for making demeaning remarks about the black women college basketball players at Rutgers after their incredible run through the NCAA tournament, and with the general purpose of empowering women worldwide.

FURTHER READING

Barrow, Lionel C. "The Role of Minority Women in the Association for Education in Journalism and Mass Communication from 1968 to 2001" in *Seeking Equity for Women in Journalism and Mass Communication: A 30-Year Update* (2005).

Grunig, Laurissa, Elizabeth Lance Toth, and Linda Childers Hon. "Contributions of Marilyn Kern Foxworth," and "African Americans, Asian Americans, and Hispanic Americans in U. S. Public Relations," in *Women in Public Relations: How Gender Influences Practice* (2001).

Lyons, Michelle. "*Dollars & Sense* Magazine Deems A&M Prof 'Tops:' Dr. Marilyn Kern-Foxworth Was Honored as One of American's Best and Brightest Business Professionals," *The Battalion* (2 Nov. 1995).

LISA K. THOMPSON

Kersands, Billy (1842?–30 June 1915), minstrel entertainer, was born in New Orleans and at an early age moved with his family to New York City. Scant biographical information exists regarding his upbringing before theatrical manager Charles Hicks discovered him in a small Bowery music hall and placed him in his minstrel show, but it has been suggested that he had little formal education and even into his adult life had to be taught the comedic songs and routines for which he became internationally renowned.

Kersands began his career in minstrelsy as a performer in Hicks's Georgia Minstrels in 1870 or 1871. At the time, the popularity of minstrelsy was unrivaled in the United States and Hicks's organization is notable for being one of the first African American minstrel companies to achieve national fame. This troupe adopted the standard tripartite format of the minstrel show as established by white performers in the 1840s: an opening section with the entire company in semicircle on the stage trading jokes, a middle section that highlighted the talents of the individual members of the troupe, and a comedic sketch including all cast members to provide a rousing conclusion. They also kept the content of the show intact, including: rapid-fire punning, the use of tambourines and bones as instruments, and blackface makeup. The benignly racist reception the Georgia Minstrels received, and the kind that dogged Kersands personally for his entire career, is best summed up by a *New York Clipper* review from 1872: "The success of this troupe goes to disprove the saying that the negro can not act the 'nigger.'" Kersands's comedic talents made him a favorite with the crowds and he was quickly elevated to "endman" duties as one of the highlights of the show.

Kersands appropriated and learned many of his signature routines during these early years with the Georgia Minstrels, and he became so famous for them that he was either unable or unwilling ever to drop them from his repertoire. He popularized a "buck-and-wing" dance called "The Essence of Old Virginia," a simple two-step to which he added comic flourishes. The song to which his name was linked for the entirety of his career was James E. Stewart's "Mary's Gone with a Coon," a satirical number in which Kersands played a befuddled man whose daughter has married beneath the family's social standing. In addition to these entertainments Kersands gained notoriety for his enormous mouth. This is no surprise given the antecedents of his style of clowning in minstrelsy, where physical exaggeration was standard practice. He was unique in that he needed neither makeup nor prosthetics for his act. Kersands shocked audiences with the variety of things he could fit in his mouth; newspaper accounts mention everything from billiard balls to an entire cup and saucer. These routines, coupled with his commanding and affable persona, made him one of minstrelsy's top performers for decades.

After permanently leaving the Georgia Minstrels near the end of the 1870s, Kersands hopped between companies on his way to becoming one of the most prominent and well-paid members of the profession. By the mid-1890s Kersands's name was synonymous with minstrelsy. As Tom Fletcher noted in his 1954 memoir *100 Years of the Negro in Show Business*, "In the South, a minstrel show without Billy Kersands was like a circus without elephants" (62). Touring shows that included Kersands were incredibly popular with African American audiences. Black newspapers at the time frequently noted the overwhelming support that Kersands received from African Americans, to the point that some theaters temporarily suspended their segregated seating policies to accommodate the crowds.

In the 1890s Kersands was one of the "Big Four Comedians" with Richard's and Pringles Georgia

Minstrels. The company performed mostly in southern and midwestern cities, though there were several international tours as well. Arguably the most lavish minstrel show of the decade, Richard's and Pringles employed a full band, a contortionist, and an acrobatic team. Even at this middle stage in his career Kersands was known as one of the "old-timers" of minstrelsy. His appeal for audiences continued to be his easygoing charisma, his comic dancing, and his large mouth that featured prominently in both reviews and the company's advertising.

The biggest change in both Kersands's personal and professional life was his marriage in 1896. Little is known about Louise Kersands before she married Billy other than that she hailed from Donaldsville, Louisiana. She traveled with Kersands, performed in the show (including duets with her husband), and, when he later started his own company, became the business manager.

By the turn of the twentieth century Kersands had been treading the minstrel boards for thirty years, mostly by rehashing old material. By the end of the 1902–1903 season he was dropped by Richard's and Pringles due to the stale predictability of his act. Kersands was on the road with his own organization in a matter of months. Reports from members of Kersands's Minstrels claimed that they were having successes, but its route led it into increasingly peripheral regions of the United States, including Texas, Oklahoma, and "Indian Territory." After several full seasons, it disbanded. At the time, the minstrel show had begun losing its audience to vaudeville and motion pictures. Kersands worked infrequently until the end of the decade. By 1910, when another incarnation of the Billy Kersands Minstrels began touring, the marquee star was rightly advertised as "America's Oldest Minstrel." Most of the performers he had originally worked with had either died or retired, but he was still dancing "The Essence of Old Virginia." He traveled with a tent show, played in theaters around Texas for months at a stretch, and departed on an ill-fated trip to Australia in 1912 that was cut short because of low attendance. Despite setbacks, abandonments, and cancellations, Kersands never left minstrelsy. He died in 1915 while on tour, after a performance in Artesia, New Mexico. He had performed in minstrelsy almost constantly for forty-five years.

FURTHER READING
Fletcher, Tom. *100 Years of the Negro in Show Business* (1954).
Sampson, Henry T. *The Ghost Walks: A Chronological History of Blacks in Show Business, 1865–1910* (1988).

Toll, Robert. *Blacking Up: The Minstrel Show in Nineteenth-century America* (1974).

KEVIN BYRNE

Kersee, Jackie Joyner. *See* Joyner-Kersee, Jackie.

Kersey, Kenny (3 Apr. 1916–1 Apr. 1983), jazz pianist, was born Kenneth Lyons Kersey in Harrow, Ontario, Canada. His parents' names are unknown, but Kersey's father was a cellist, and as a child Kersey studied with his mother, who taught piano. During further studies at the Detroit Institute of Musical Art, he took up the trumpet.

Kersey went to New York to work as a trumpeter and pianist in 1936, but physical problems made him give up the brass instrument. He replaced the pianist Billy Kyle in LUCKY MILLINDER's big band in February 1938; later that year he was a member of Billy Hicks and His Sizzling Six. By the year's end he had left Hicks for a brief stay with the singer BILLIE HOLIDAY for the opening of a second Café Society in Greenwich Village. While continuing to work there with the trumpeter FRANKIE NEWTON's band in 1939, he made recordings with Holiday and Newton. Kersey was a member of the trumpeter ROY ELDRIDGE's band at the café in mid-1940 and for recordings from that year. He replaced COUNT BASIE at the clarinetist Benny Goodman's sextet session in December 1940 and had brief solos on "Breakfast Feud" and "I Can't Give You Anything but Love."

Still at Café Society, Kersey joined the trumpeter RED ALLEN in mid-November 1940. A January 1941 review of the band in *Swing* stated:

"Pianist Kersey was fine with Frankie Newton's band when Cafe Society opened, better with Roy Eldridge's great little band of six months ago, and is magnificent with Red Allen. The kid's a virtuoso. He trills and glisses with monumental ease, but never sacrifices good taste to his fluent technique…. Ken's got a wonderful feeling for the rhythm, and really gets the proper percussive flavor out of his instrument." Allen's band broadcast on Henry "Hot Lips" Levine's NBC radio show "The Chamber Society of Lower Basin Street" in February 1941. He recorded "K. K. Boogie" with Allen's band in April, and later that month they gave a concert at Carnegie Hall, "The Art of Boogie Woogie."
While with Allen, Kersey also participated in jam sessions at Minton's Playhouse in Harlem along with swing musicians and practitioners of the incipient bop style. There he recorded "Stardust

II" and "Kerouac" as a member of the trumpeter DIZZY GILLESPIE's quartet, which included the drummer KENNY CLARKE. Kersey left Allen's band in October 1941. He was the pianist in the trumpeter COOTIE WILLIAMS's big band from late 1941 to early 1942, and he recorded a solo on Williams's version of the pianist THELONIOUS MONK's composition "Epistrophy." Kersey's performance was later described by the writer Gunther Schuller as florid in manner and ill suited to Monk's piece.

In May 1942 Kersey replaced MARY LOU WILLIAMS in ANDY KIRK's big band, and he immediately presented Kirk with a big hit in his rendition of his own composition "Boogie Woogie Cocktail." Drafted into the U.S. Army soon thereafter, Kersey was stationed at Camp Kilmer, near New Brunswick, New Jersey, in Special Services, playing in a band that included the trumpeter BUCK CLAYTON. During the mid-1940s he made guest appearances with Kirk, who recalled, "Whenever I'd play the Apollo Theatre he'd come up to New York and I'd bring him on stage in his uniform and the place would go wild." While in the army Kersey also recorded with the alto saxophonist Pete Brown in July 1944 and with the trombonist TRUMMY YOUNG in May 1945.

Discharged in January 1946, Kersey joined the tenor saxophonist Teddy McRae's band, and in February he recorded with the singer Cousin Joe, accompanied by Pete Brown's band. From April 1946 through May 1947 Kersey toured the country with the all-star package show Jazz at the Philharmonic, initially as a member of a rhythm section accompanying Clayton, the tenor saxophonists COLEMAN HAWKINS and LESTER YOUNG, and the singer HELEN HUMES. Among their recorded performances are versions of "JATP Blues" and "I Can't Get Started."

Kersey's association with Jazz at the Philharmonic is said to have extended to early 1949, but during this period he was clearly active elsewhere. He returned to the downtown location of Café Society with Clayton's quintet (soon expanded to a sextet) from May to July 1947. From later that year into 1948 he was again back at the café with the clarinetist EDMOND BLAINEY HALL's band, and he rejoined Eldridge late in 1948.

In April 1949 Hall brought a new band that included Kersey into the Savoy Cafe in Boston. They broadcast from the club, and in December they were recorded there "live," with Kersey's sprightly swing piano melodies and delicate chording featured in solos on "Careless Love" and "Please Don't Talk about Me When I'm Gone." Kersey left Hall early in 1950 and during the spring worked in the reed player SIDNEY BECHET's band in New York City. Kersey rejoined Hall in San Francisco in August; later that month he returned to New York City with Hall to participate in a jam session at the Stuyvesant Casino.

Kersey was with Allen again from 1951 to 1952 and joined the clarinetist Sol Yaged's trio from 1952 to 1954. Around this time he also worked with Clayton, Yaged, and the trombonist Herb Flemming in a band in New York City. He recorded a rhythm and blues session with the trombonist CLYDE BERNHARDT, leading under the pseudonym of Ed Barron in 1953, and he was in jazz sessions with the trumpeter CHARLIE SHAVERS in October 1954, the trombonist Jack Teagarden in November 1954, and the trumpeter Jonah Jones in December 1954. During 1955 Kersey worked with Shavers's band and recorded with the trumpeter Ruby Braff.

In March 1956 Kersey participated in the last of Clayton's acclaimed studio jam sessions for the Columbia label. The relaxed and extended versions of "All the Cats Join In," "After Hours," and "Don't You Miss Your Baby" gave him ample opportunity to perform his swing, blues, and boogie-woogie soloing. He rejoined Yaged's group from 1956 to 1957, and toward the end of the decade he worked at the Metropole with Clayton and at Central Plaza, both in New York City. When a stroke eventually prevented his playing, his daughter took care of him. Details of his marriage or of other children are unknown. He died in New York City.

FURTHER READING
Chilton, John. *Sidney Bechet: The Wizard of Jazz* (1987).
Driggs, Frank. "My Story, by Andy Kirk," in *Jazz Panorama*, ed. Martin Williams (1979).
Schuller, Gunther. *The Swing Era: The Development of Jazz, 1930–1945* (1989).

DISCOGRAPHY
Selchow, Manfred. *Profoundly Blues: A Bio-discographical Scrapbook on Edmond Hall* (1988).
This entry is taken from the *American National Biography* and is published here with the permission of the American Council of Learned Societies.

BARRY KERNFELD

Key, Elizabeth (c. 1630–?), early legal petitioner for freedom, was born near present-day Newport News, Virginia, to an unknown slave woman and Thomas Key, a white Englishman. Key served as a burgess in Virginia's colonial assembly. That Elizabeth's mother is described in colonial records simply as a "slave" is significant for two reasons. First, it means that she was probably not a Christian, since African-born or descended slaves and servants who followed that faith were usually characterized as such in the legal record. Second, it suggests that at least some Africans were being classified as lifetime chattel in Virginia as early as the 1620s, when there were only a few hundred blacks in the colony.

Like that of her mother and of others of African descent in seventeenth-century Virginia, the precise legal status of Elizabeth Key was not clearly defined. Was she free like her father? Or a slave like her mother? Or something in between? A legal document drawn up by Thomas Key in 1636 before he left for England bound his daughter as a servant of Humphrey Higginson, a member of the colonial council of state who was also the child's godfather, for a period of nine years. Sometime before 1655, perhaps because Higginson had died, Elizabeth Key came to be a ward of yet another member of Virginia's colonial political elite, Colonel John Mottram, a justice of the peace in Northumberland County.

When Mottram died in 1655, Key, who was at that time twenty-five years old, sued for her freedom in the Northumberland County Court. Her lawyer, William Grinsted, petitioned the court for her freedom on several grounds. He noted, first, that under English common law children inherited their father's legal condition. Since Thomas Key had been born free, his daughter was also. Second, Grinsted, perhaps drawing on the earlier case involving JOHN GRAWEERE, argued that Elizabeth Key had been baptized as a Christian, preventing her from being enslaved. Finally, under the terms of her father's contract, Key's term of service to Higginson and then Mottram had expired ten years earlier, in 1645. In early 1655 these arguments convinced a jury of twelve colonists, presumably all white, to find in Elizabeth's favor. Her freedom was short-lived, however, following an appeal by the executor of Mottram's estate (another justice of the peace) to the Virginia General Court, which ruled that Elizabeth Key was indeed a slave. Later that year, however, Grinsted sought a hearing for Key's case before the Virginia General Assembly. The assembly then appointed a special committee of burgesses to investigate the matter. The committee agreed with the original decision of the Northumberland County Court, enabling Key to regain her freedom. An appeal by the Mottram estate to the governor of Virginia in 1656 appears to have failed.

It is significant that Key's case divided so many members of Virginia's close-knit colonial political elite. It may be worth noting that Grinsted, her attorney, had also been engaged in an earlier legal dispute with the Mottrams, suggesting that the Key case may have been an extension of that or some other matter. That Key later married Grinsted is also noteworthy. Whether their personal relationship predated their professional one is unknown, but it may have been a factor in Grinsted's determination to pursue the case to the highest level. Yet there is no indication in the legal record that Grinsted—or Key for that matter—viewed their case as a challenge to slavery per se. They argued only that, as in England, the Christian children of freeborn men should also be free. Race or color was irrelevant. For the Mottrams and the members of the general court, however, the Key case represented a direct challenge to the right of white Virginians to enslave all blacks. In the second half of the seventeenth century, the colonists' belief in that right grew directly in proportion to their growing desire for a large, cheap, reliable, and self-reproducing labor force to maximize the profits from cultivating tobacco. Virginia, they argued, was not old England but should instead follow the English colonies in the West Indies, where staple crops like rice and sugar were cultivated by African slaves who were bound for life.

In 1662, only six years after the Key case, it became clear that the Mottrams' view had become the prevailing one in Virginia, with the passage of legislation requiring that the status of a child would be determined by the status of the mother, not the father. Under such a law Key would have been a slave in perpetuity. Further legislation in 1667 assured slaveholders that their slaves would no longer gain their freedom on the grounds of Christian baptism. The Key case thus appears to have prompted Virginia lawmakers to tighten the state's legal codes and prevent future generations of Africans in the colony from achieving even the limited freedoms that she and other early black settlers such as ANTHONY JOHNSON had enjoyed in the early seventeenth century.

FURTHER READING

Billings, Warren M. "The Cases of Fernando and Elizabeth Key: A Note on the Status of Blacks in Seventeenth-century Virginia," *William and Mary Quarterly,* 3rd series, 30 (July 1973): 467–474.

Higginbotham, A. Leon. *In the Matter of Color: Race and the American Legal Process; The Colonial Period* (1978).

Morgan, Edmund S. *American Slavery, American Freedom: The Ordeal of Colonial Virginia* (1975).

STEVEN J. NIVEN

Keyes, Alan (7 Aug. 1950–), conservative activist, diplomat, and radio personality, was born in Long Island, New York, the youngest of the five children of Allison L. Keyes, a U.S. Army sergeant, and Gerthina Quick Keyes, a homemaker. Keyes spent the majority of his childhood on various military bases. He developed a close relationship with his mother, whom he admired greatly for raising a family under difficult circumstances. Both parents instilled in Keyes a strong sense of faith, which would underpin his later political activism.

From an early age Keyes displayed a talent for public speaking, viewing it as an effective means of influencing others, particularly in regards to moral issues. While attending Robert G. Cole High School in San Antonio, Texas, Keyes became active in debating clubs and civic organizations. He competed in numerous speech contests, winning the majority of them. His oratorical skills aided in his elections to student body president and president of Boys Nation, a renowned civics training event for high school students sponsored by the American Legion. After graduating from high school in 1968 Keyes enrolled at Cornell University in a six-year program leading to a Ph.D. in Political Philosophy. After initially intending to speed through higher education, Keyes decided to slow down and take advantage of the stimulating college environment. He participated in glee clubs, debating societies, and student politics.

The late sixties were a time of intense student activism, particularly in opposition to the Vietnam War. During this time Keyes came under the tutelage of Allan Bloom, a conservative scholar, whom he would later credit as the most important teacher in his intellectual formation. Bloom crystallized for Keyes an understanding of the relationship between politics and morality through the exploration of past eras that championed self-reliance.

Politically, Keyes grew up in a Democratic household. Like many in his generation, the civil rights movement of the sixties and the assassinations of John F. Kennedy and MARTIN LUTHER KING JR. shaped his interest in politics. Likes his parents and most African Americans at the time, he identified as a Democrat, but his experiences at Cornell helped make him a conservative Republican. Keyes's close relationship with Bloom, his support of the Vietnam War, and his opposition to the methods of black

Former Republican presidential candidate Alan Keyes addresses opponents of a proposed state amendment which would protect embryonic stem cell research in Jefferson City, Missouri on July 31, 2006. (AP Images.)

nationalist activists on the Cornell campus were not well received. After two years he left the university.

Keyes continued his intellectual development in Paris, where he spent a year working with Bloom, who was on leave from Cornell. Afterwards, Keyes returned to the United States to continue his studies at Harvard University, where in 1972 he completed a B.A. in Government Affairs. He stayed at the university to complete a Ph.D. in Government Affairs in 1979.

After completing his studies Keyes chose to pursue a career in public service. He joined the State Department as a foreign service officer and served as a desk officer to the U.S. consulate in Mumbai, India, in 1979. It was during this time that Keyes met U.N. Ambassador Jeanne Kirkpatrick, a conservative Democrat appointed to the post by the Republican president Ronald Reagan, who served as his mentor. Kirkpatrick, an ardent cold warrior, was integral in promoting

Keyes's rapid ascension through the ranks of the State Department.

In 1981 Keyes married Jocelyn Marcel, whom he had met in India; they would later have three children, Francis, Maya, and Andrew. During this time, Keyes served at the U.S. Embassy in Zimbabwe before returning to the United States as a member of the State Department's Policy and Planning staff. In 1983 he was appointed ambassador to the U.N. Economic and Social Council (UNESCO) and shortly afterward he was appointed assistant secretary of state for international organizational affairs, the youngest person ever appointed to that post.

Keyes was an active supporter of Reagan administration policies. Notably, his political views, particularly on South Africa and apartheid, were at odds with the majority of black Americans. Keyes's willingness to both advocate and articulate positions that were unpopular among most blacks and liberals made him an asset to the conservative Republican administration. By 1987 he had become the highest-ranking African American in the State Department.

In 1988 Keyes left the diplomatic ranks and launched a Senate campaign in Maryland. The odds were heavily against him as a black Republican in a heavily Democratic state going against a popular incumbent, Paul Sarbanes. Although he lost by a landslide, Keyes's ability to invoke biblical rhetoric and articulate the significance of America's founding documents made him a darling of many conservatives, enhancing his national profile. In 1992 Keyes again launched a Senate run against a different Democratic incumbent, Barbara Mikulski, but suffered the same result—a lopsided defeat.

In the wake of his unsuccessful Senate bids, Keyes attempted to continue getting his message out and became the host of the Baltimore-based talk radio show, "America's Wake-Up Call: The Alan Keyes Show." His show was a success among conservatives and he was highly sought after as a public speaker and commentator.

In 1995 Keyes published his first book, *Masters of the Dream: The Strength and Betrayal of Black America*. Riding high on its success, a wave of support generated by his radio show, and a series of speeches circulated throughout conservative outlets, Keyes launched a presidential campaign, becoming the first African American in the twentieth century to seek the presidency as a Republican. His strongest base of supporters was the Christian right, which consisted predominantly of whites. Keyes was defeated in the primaries by Bob Dole. In 1996 he published his second book, *Our Character,*

Our Future. In the late 1990s he turned to the Internet to launch several conservative Web sites.

In 2000 Keyes launched another presidential campaign. Despite showing poorly in the polls, he stayed in the Republican primaries, debating Texas governor George W. Bush and Arizona senator John McCain, and performing surprisingly well. Some commentators even declared him the winner of the debates. Following the election Keyes continued to search for outlets for his conservative message. In 2002 he moved into television as host of the television talk show *Alan Keyes Is Making Sense*, on the cable news channel MSNBC. The show was cancelled in the same year.

In 2004 Keyes pursued another Senate campaign, this time in Illinois against State Senator BARACK OBAMA, who eventually won with more than 75 percent of the vote. Keyes was criticized during the election for negative campaigning and a refusal to congratulate Obama after his victory. Keyes was also criticized for being a last minute Republican candidate who was not an Illinois resident and for negative comments about Vice President Dick Cheney's daughter, who was openly lesbian. The controversy would play a role in the coming out of Keyes's own daughter, Maya. Despite the revelation, Keyes maintained a staunch antigay position.

FURTHER READING

Felder, Raoul and Jackie Mason. "The Key to Alan Keyes." *The American Spectator* 49, February 2000.

MICHAELJULIUS IDANI

Khanga, Yelena (1962–), journalist and broadcaster, was born in Moscow, (then in the Soviet Union), to Abdullah Khanga, a political activist from Zanzibar, and Lily Golden, a former tennis star, historian, and teacher. Khanga's American-born maternal grandparents had joined the Communist Party during the 1920s, when, living in New York City, they faced the prejudice and intolerance often directed at interracial couples. Oliver Golden, a black man with a degree in agronomy from the Tuskegee Institute, was unable to find work in his field and was instead forced to take on the menial tasks available to African Americans at the time, janitorial and domestic work. Bertha Bialek, Khanga's white grandmother, was disowned by her immigrant parents because of her romantic relationship with Oliver. The couple left for the Soviet Union in 1931, convinced that the communist system would free them from the racism that had become endemic in the United States.

Khanga's family eventually made its way from Tashkent in Uzbekistan, near the Afghanistan border—where her grandfather was instrumental in the importation and development of a resilient strain of cotton—to Moscow. When Khanga was two, her father returned on a political mission to Zanzibar and was assassinated. The girl was raised by her grandmother and mother, attending schools in the city. A tennis player like her mother, she was afforded the opportunity to travel throughout the country. She matriculated to Moscow State University and graduated in 1984 with a degree in journalism. Shortly thereafter, she joined the staff of the *Moscow World News*, where she remained until 1987.

In that year, she became the first female reporter to be chosen by the Soviet government to take part in a journalist exchange program with the United States. Khanga was dispatched to Boston, where she joined the staff of the *Christian Science Monitor*. While she was living in the States, news of her unusual story began to attract attention. She was contacted by the *20/20* news magazine program and asked to sit for an interview. A distant relative happened to be watching the program that night and thought she recognized Khanga and her story. The two were soon in contact, and Khanga began to take interest in her American roots. She appealed to the Rockefeller Foundation, which agreed to fund her genealogical research. Soon, she was locating and contacting relatives of the Goldens living across the United States. Her story was picked up by more and more newspapers. She traveled to Yazoo, Mississippi, to visit the farmland once owned by her great-grandfather, who had been born into slavery and managed during the Reconstruction period to become a wealthy landowner. Finally, in 1991 Khanga was the guest of honor at an exuberant (and much-covered) family reunion. Shortly thereafter, she traveled to Tanzania, where she was able to meet some of her father's relatives. In 1992 she turned these experiences into a book, *Soul to Soul: The Story of a Black Russian American Family, 1865–1992*.

Khanga's career since has been a varied one. She splits her time between New York and Moscow. In the 1990s she hosted what is said to be the Soviet Union's first talk show about sex and sex-related topics (among them HIV/AIDS), *About That*, and created something of a public uproar in doing so. In 1992 she became a fellow at the John F. Kennedy Institute of Politics at Harvard and went on to deliver lectures about her own history and the history of black Americans in Russia and the Soviet Union at institutions around the United States. Back in the Soviet Union, she appeared on the program *Shkola zlosloviya* (as herself) in 2005. Details about Khanga's personal life are difficult to come by. The most recent reports suggest that her mother relocated with her to the United States to take on a teaching position at the University of Chicago. Khanga meanwhile continues to exist between two worlds, writing and lecturing and making television appearances.

FURTHER READING

Khanga, Yelena. *Soul to Soul: The Story of a Black Russian American Family, 1865–1992* (1992).

Foner, Eric. "Three Very Rare Generations," *New York Times*, 13 Dec. 1992.

JASON PHILIP MILLER

Khazan, Jibreel (18 Oct. 1941–), civil rights activist, was born Ezell Blair Jr. in Greensboro, North Carolina, the son of Ezell Alexander Blair Sr. and Corene Blair, both teachers. Khazan's father was one of the first members of the local NAACP and made his children familiar with the idea of civil rights activism at an early age. Khazan graduated from Greensboro's Dudley High School, where his father was a teacher, in 1959.

While a student at the all-black North Carolina Agriculture and Technical State University, Khazan was one of four students inciting the famous student sit-ins in a Greensboro Woolworth store. Khazan and his friends DAVID RICHMOND, whom he had known since high school; Joe McNeil; and FRANKLIN McCAIN, all three students at A&T, had been discussing current race relations on a regular basis, their so-called bull sessions, and the idea for action kept recurring during these talks. The doctrine of "separate but equal" was still firmly installed in southern everyday life at that time, despite the *Brown vs. Board of Education* court decision and the Montgomery bus boycott, which had preceded the sit-ins. On the night of 31 January 1960, the four boys spent the evening at the house of Khazan's parents as they often did. Khazan told his mother about their plan and asked how she felt about it. She reports having said, "'I've always said this, that you have a mind of your own. And if you feel that this is the right thing to do, then you should do it. And we are 100% behind you.'" Khazan replied, "'this is all I wanted to know.'"

The next day, the four students headed into the local Woolworth store and after buying a couple of items, sat down at the lunch counter asking to be

Ezell Blair, Jr., center, now known as Jibreel Khazan, discusses legal aspects of the anti-segregation movement with Greensboro dentist and local NAACP leader Dr. George Simkins, right, and fellow North Carolina Agriculture and Technical College student Joseph McNeil, on April 20, 1960, in Greensboro. (AP Images.)

served. At this time, black people could buy food in the store but were not allowed to sit down at the counter. Being denied service they remained in their seats until the store closed, leaving with the promise of coming back the next day. The news about the sit-in spread quickly and by the end of the week the group had grown to about one thousand protesters, with sit-ins extending to other cities across the South. The protesters experienced encouragement as well as verbal and physical abuse from the white community. The protests in Greensboro, after several days reaching beyond the single Woolworth store, brought the city to a virtual standstill, and yet it was five months before the downtown affiliate quietly integrated on 26 July 1960.

The student sit-ins started a mass movement and produced one of the most important civil rights organizations in the 1960s, the Student Nonviolent Coordinating Committee (SNCC). Khazan was

elected to attend the meeting at Shaw University in Raleigh, where the SNCC was formed. Khazan continued to study at A&T, receiving his bachelor's degree in Sociology in 1963. During his time at the university, Khazan served as president of the junior class, the student government association, the campus National Association for the Advancement of Colored People (NAACP), and the Greensboro affiliate of the Congress of Racial Equality (CORE). He attended Howard University's law school for almost one year but was forced to leave the program for health-related reasons.

Afterward, Khazan found it very difficult to find a job in Greensboro because of his reputation as one of the original four of the sit-ins and therefore a troublemaker. He moved to New Bedford, Massachusetts, in 1965. The city was special to him because it was the place where FREDERICK DOUGLASS, a former slave and later leader of the abolitionist movement, had escaped to freedom. He became a member of the New England Islamic Center and took on the name Jibreel Khazan. Over time he worked with the AFL-CIO Trade Council in Boston and the Opportunities Industrialization Center as well as at the Rodman Job Corps Center before ending up at the CETA program in New Bedford, working as a teacher and counselor for developmentally disabled people. In 1994 Khazan received an honorary doctorate from A&T for his involvement in the civil rights movement. The four men reunited for the sit-ins' anniversaries many times. On 2 February 2002 the three remaining men—David Richmond died in 1990—appeared on the A&T campus for the unveiling of a statue honoring them. In 2005 the U.S. House of Representatives paid tribute to the Greensboro Four, as they were known, recognizing their contributions to the civil rights movement.

Khazan had three children with his wife Lorraine France George.

FURTHER READING

Chafe, William H. *Civilities and Civil Rights: Greensboro, North Carolina, and the Black Struggle for Freedom* (1980).

GRETA KÖHLER

Kid Gavilan (6 Jan. 1926–13 Feb. 2003), professional boxer, was born Gerardo Gonzalez in Gamaguey, Cuba. He was known as Kid Gavilan during most of his boxing career. *Gavilan* is the Spanish word for "hawk."

Kid Gavilan started boxing when he was ten years old and had sixty amateur fights before turning pro. He made his professional boxing debut when he was only seventeen years old, defeating Antonio Diaz by a decision after only four rounds. He fought in Cuba until 1946 and also performed in Mexico. His American debut took place in November 1946 and resulted in a victory over Johnny Ryan. By the end of 1947 Kid Gavilan had a record of eleven wins, one defeat, and one draw and was making a name for himself among boxing fans, with *Ring* magazine ranking him as the seventh contender for the world welterweight title. He continued to build up his reputation in a fight with Gene Burton, who had challenged the reigning division champion SUGAR RAY ROBINSON. The ten-round fight ended in a draw, thus showing that Kid Gavilan deserved his ranking. On 30 March 1951 he fought Eugene Hairston in the main event in Madison Square Garden in New York City, which

at the time and in the early twenty-first century was every boxer's dream.

Kid Gavilan's bouts did not always end in victories or draws. He lost back-to-back fights to the lightweight champion at the time, Ike Williams, and to Doug Ratford. However, he was able to defeat Tommy Bell, which secured a fight with one of the best boxers of all time—Sugar Ray Robinson. Gavilan fought Robinson in a nontitle fight in September 1948 and lost by decision. The two fought again the next year, and again Robinson was the winner. Robinson held the welterweight title for two more years before he moved on to the middleweight division. For three years Kid Gavilan was considered the number one contender for the welterweight title.

However, it was not until May 1951 that Kid Gavilan finally got a shot at the title against then champion Johnny Bratton. Gavilan won the fight by a decision and was a dominating champion of the division for four years. He defended his title seven times and defeated such boxing legends as Carmen Basilio and Robinson.

Besides the official defenses of his crown, Kid Gavilan fought twenty times during his title reign, losing only two fights—one to Carl "Bobo" Olson for the world middleweight title on 2 April 1954 in Chicago and the other to Danny Womber on 2 May 1953 in Syracuse, New York. One of his successful defenses was a fight against Bobby Dykes at Miami Stadium in 1952. It was the first fight ever between black and white fighters in then segregated Miami.

Events outside of the ring influenced Kid Gavilan's control of the title. Criminal elements took control of boxing in the 1950s when Frankie Carbo and his assistants took command of the International Boxing Commission (IBC). At the time Johnny Saxton, a rising contender in the welterweight division, was in line for a bout with Kid Gavilan. Saxton's manager was Frankie "Blinky" Palermo, a close friend of Carbo's. Gavilan fought Saxton in a title fight on 20 October 1954 in Philadelphia and lost a controversial decision. Even though the contract called for a rematch, that fight never took place, and Kid Gavilan never got another title shot again. He continued to fight until his retirement in 1958.

Kid Gavilan had a total of 143 professional fights. He won 107, lost 30, and had 6 draws. He knocked out twenty-seven opponents but was never knocked out himself. He was well known for his outstanding stamina, slick defense, timely combinations, and aggression. Boxing fans loved to see him throw his famous right-hand "bolo-punch," which he said he had learned when he was cutting sugarcane as a youngster in Cuba. The bolo was a sweeping punch beginning like a softball pitcher's windup and ending in an uppercut. Kid Gavilan was also a showman in the ring and did a little dance during his fights, which many later compared to the (MUHAMMAD) ALI shuffle.

Kid Gavilan was a popular fighter among boxing fans and once drew a gate of $269,667 for a title defense against Gil Turner, a welterweight record at the time. After his retirement Kid Gavilan returned to Cuba just at the time Fidel Castro was taking power. The Cuban government had confiscated his 39-acre ranch home in Camaguey as well as other real estate and also took his 1949 Lincoln and 1950 Cadillac. He fled Cuba and took up residence in Miami, Florida, in 1968 and worked for Muhammad Ali's camp for a short time. He was one of the first three boxers enshrined into the Boxing Hall of Fame in 1990, along with Sugar Ray Robinson and Jack Dempsey.

From 1999 until his death Kid Gavilan was cared for by the Guardianship Program of Miami-Dade County. Although he had kidney and vision problems, the cause of death was a heart attack. He died penniless and was buried in a pauper's grave in Miami. Later, however, his body was exhumed and buried in a proper grave paid for by funds raised among boxing fans and officials. One contributor was MIKE TYSON. Kid Gavilan was married several times but was estranged from his family.

FURTHER READING

Fitzgerald, Mike, and David Hudson Jr. *Boxing's Most Wanted: The Top 10 Book of Champs, Chumps, and Punch-Drunk Palookas* (2004).

Heller, Peter. *"In This Corner … !": Forty-two World Champions Tell Their Stories* (2004).

Mullan, Harry. *Boxing: The Complete Illustrated Guide* (2003).

Werner, Doug, and Mark Hatmaker. *Boxing Mastery: Advanced Technique, Tactics, and Strategies from the Sweet Science* (2004).

ROBERT JANIS

Kid Norfolk (10 July 1893–1969?), boxer, was born William Ward. His precise date of birth and even the place of his birth are still matters of debate. Some boxing historians claimed that he was born in Norfolk, Virginia (hence his nickname), on 20 September 1895. In 2001, however, a birth certificate was located in Belmont, Trinidad, indicating that William Ward had been born on 10 July 1893 on Norfolk Street in Belmont. The names and occupations of his parents are unknown. As might be imagined from the confusion arising about his birthplace and date of birth, accounts of Kid Norfolk's early life are contradictory. Those who place his birthplace in Virginia tell of early years spent fighting in Battle Royals—a brutal "sport" organized by whites in which several young black boys and men were put in a fighting ring (often blindfolded) and let loose upon one another in a free-for-all in which the last man standing was declared the winner. From there, he supposedly traveled to Baltimore to seek more lucrative fights in the rough-and-tumble shipyards. These bare-knuckle brawls usually matched Kid Norfolk against much older and much bigger men, but his strength and speed usually led to victory. Those who argue for a Trinidad birthplace suggest that he remained there until he was a teenager.

Most sources agree, however, that sometime in 1913 Kid Norfolk was fighting in Panama. A number of good black boxers traveled to the Central American nation for matches. Greater acceptance of black fighters, ongoing construction of the Panama Canal, and a constant flow of international shipping brought in large audiences with money to spend. For nearly four years Kid Norfolk fought exclusively in Panama and most of these fights are now lost to history. However, as he continued to win and his level of competition increased more of his fights were recorded for posterity in local newspapers and sporting magazines. As befit the rather cosmopolitan atmosphere of Panamá, the Kid's opponents ranged from the white, Canadian Arthur Pelkey (whom he knocked out twice), to top African American boxers such as Big Bill Tate (whom he beat by decision), and Sam McVey (who he fought to a no-decision).

Having established his boxing credentials in Panama, in early 1917 Kid Norfolk came to the United States (some would say for the first time) to further his career. It was a calculated gamble. Prizefighting purses could certainly be substantially bigger in America, but for a black fighter the rewards were not always readily attainable. The reign of the first black heavyweight champion, JACK JOHNSON, was fresh in the memories of a white America still seething over the thought of a non-white holding the most important title in all of sports. Kid Norfolk would be allowed to fight at the less prestigious light-heavyweight limit but it was clear that opportunities to fight for the lucrative heavyweight championship were almost nonexistent.

During 1917 Kid Norfolk steadily fought tougher and tougher opposition, including Gunboat Smith twice, Billy Miske once, and in his last fight of the year, the black veteran fighter SAM LANGFORD. Langford took the young boxer to school, knocking him out in the second round. Kid Norfolk regrouped and from 1918 to 1921 he put together a string of impressive victories and called for a fight with the heavyweight champion, Jack Dempsey. Although Dempsey maintained that he would fight any man, white or black, for the title, significantly, he never risked the belt against an African American. Increasingly frustrated, the Kid then laced them up against an unlikely opponent—future middleweight champion Harry Greb, a rugged character nicknamed "the Human Windmill." Although the fight ended in a no-decision, newspaper reports were unanimous in giving the fight to the Kid. He smashed Greb to the canvas in the first round and by the end of the fight was administering a frightful beating. Kid Norfolk's showing against Greb did nothing to convince the Dempsey camp to give him a shot at the title. His desperation increased. Little known outside of his own training camp, the Kid suffered a terrible eye injury when he was thumbed by a fighter in late 1921. He soon completely lost sight in his left eye. In 1922 he threw caution to the wind, agreeing to fight HARRY WILLS, touted by many as the black "uncrowned" heavyweight champion. Like the Kid, Wills had been unable to arrange a fight with Dempsey. The discrepancy in size was immediately and frighteningly apparent—Wills outweighed the Kid by well over fifty pounds. In less than two rounds Wills pounded Kid Norfolk into insensibility.

For all intents and purposes the Wills bout ended Kid Norfolk's dreams of the heavyweight title. He continued to fight competitively, often against good opposition, but in the lighter weight classes. In 1923, for example, he knocked out the future middleweight champion TIGER FLOWERS in one round and then defeated the former light heavyweight king Battling Siki. He also engaged in a wild rematch with Harry Greb in 1924, by which time both men were fighting with just one good eye. Newspaper reports of the fight had the Kid easily winning the first five rounds. At the end of the sixth round, however, Greb committed a flagrant foul by striking Kid Norfolk at least four times after the bell sounded, and was immediately disqualified.

The Greb fight was the Kid's last significant bout. In 1924 he again entered the heavyweight ranks to fight Tommy Gibbons, the man who had gone fifteen rounds with Dempsey just the year before. Gibbons made short work of the aging Kid Norfolk, knocking him out in six rounds. He fought a few more times against undistinguished opposition before retiring in 1926 after a knockout loss. It was reported that he used some of his ring winnings to buy an apartment complex in Harlem and lived off of the income. His death, like his birth, is shrouded in some mystery. One boxing writer claims that Kid Norfolk passed away in 1969, but no official obituary in major newspapers can be located.

FURTHER READING

Ashe, Arthur R. *A Hard Road to Glory: A History of the African American Athlete, 1919–1945* (1988).

Brewer, David. "Willie Ward—Kid Norfolk: Yes, the Great Kid Norfolk Was Born in Belmont," *Trinidad Express*, 19 Dec. 2001.

MICHAEL L. KRENN

Kidd, Mae Taylor Street (8 Feb. 1904–20 Oct. 1999), insurance salesperson, member of the Kentucky legislature, and civil rights activist, was born in Millersburg, Kentucky, to Anna Belle Leer, a domestic, and Charles Robert Jones, a white man and a son of the family for whom Leer worked. Mae was never introduced to her biological father, and he never acknowledged her as his child. Jones eventually married and had his own family, and sometimes they visited Mae and her mother. Mae, however, felt rejected by Jones and wanted nothing to do with him or his family. As the daughter of a white man who denied their relationship, Kidd faced discrimination in both the white and the black communities throughout her life.

When Mae was two years old, her mother married James William Taylor, the man Mae considered to be her father and whose surname name she was given. James Taylor was a tobacco farmer and a chicken breeder, while Kidd's mother had a successful catering business in Millersburg's black community. The family remained in the black community until Mae was in the eighth grade, when her mother was able to secure a house in another part of Millersburg through a white cousin. Being biracial was often difficult for Mae, but sometimes she took advantage of her light complexion and was able to move beyond the restrictions imposed on blacks by Jim Crow laws. As a child she tried on hats in local stores knowing that blacks were not allowed this option when shopping.

As a teenager Mae wanted to help her family financially by seeking employment. Her mother, however, would not allow her to work in white people's homes and insisted that she focus on her education to prepare for better employment options in the future. After Mae completed the eighth grade in 1919, her parents sent her to Simponsville to attend the Lincoln Institute, which provided blacks with the only opportunity for a high school education in Kentucky. After only two years of high school, at age seventeen, she was compelled to return home and help support her family financially.

In 1921 Mae Taylor obtained a job with the Mammoth Life and Accident Insurance Company, a successful black-owned, Kentucky-based company. She walked through black neighborhoods of Millersburg and Carlisle, Kentucky, selling insurance policies and collecting insurance premiums. Because everyone knew her parents in her hometown and older people looked after her in Carlisle, she never had any problems in either community while on duty. Taylor worked as a salesperson for four years before accepting a file clerk position in Louisville at the Mammoth headquarters in 1925. She shared an apartment in the Mammoth building with a friend who had helped her get the clerk position. In Wade Hall's biographical account of Kidd, *Passing for Black*, he reminisced about her pride in being a self-supporting young woman in the city. Yet she remained disheartened by the racial barriers imposed on African Americans, which kept her from using the main public library, for example, and attending movie premieres. "I couldn't use the main public library. I couldn't go to the first-run movie shows on Fourth Street. I had to attend the 'colored' theaters like the Lyric and the Grand" (Hall, 41).

In 1930 she married Horace Leon Street, treasurer for the Mammoth Life Insurance Company. Mae Street was eventually promoted to assistant bookkeeper and then to the policy-issue office, where she supervised the issuance of policies from 1935 to 1943. Shortly after her husband died of heart disease in 1942, she joined the American Red Cross. She was shipped to England, and during World War II she served as assistant director for the black American soldiers' service club, responsible for programming and public relations. In England she met her second husband, the army officer James Meredith Kidd III. They married after the war in 1947 and moved to his hometown of Detroit, Michigan. They had no children.

In Detroit Mae Kidd ran a campaign for a Detroit City Council candidate. This was her first political experience, and her public relations experience

from the Red Cross was crucial to the campaign's success. Kidd served as special representative to the president of Fuller Products, a cosmetics company. She taught Detroit and Chicago sales personnel how to make presentations and promoted the company's products through various marketing venues. She took an eighteen-month course in insurance underwriting that was funded by the Supreme Life Insurance Company in Chicago, which hired her to promote the company and sell insurance. Writing articles and public relations releases, organizing a rail tour to an insurance convention, and organizing the 25-year club, Kidd honed her public relations skills and developed a publicity plan that was recognized by the National Negro Insurance Association (NNIA). As a result the NNIA put her in charge of making public relations plans for all seventy-two member companies, and she was assigned her own office and secretary in 1946. She served in this capacity through 1956.

The Kidds returned to Louisville and the Mammoth Insurance Company in the early 1960s. James Kidd worked first as a teacher in Paris, Kentucky, before accepting a job in Louisville to teach science at the Shawnee Junior High School. Mae Kidd found herself selling insurance again instead of heading public relations. Although she viewed this as a demotion and an insult, her energies and personality resulted in the highest sales in the company's history for three straight years. In 1966 she received national recognition by qualifying for the National Half Million Dollar Round Table, apparently composed of people who sold half a million dollars worth of insurance policies. Now sixty-two, Kidd retired from Mammoth that same year.

Two years after retiring from Mammoth, in 1968, Kidd was elected to the Kentucky House of Representatives. The first bill she sponsored during her first year in the legislature was the open housing bill, one of two bills that bear her name, which made Kentucky the first state in the South to enact open housing laws. Among her other political accomplishments were her low-income housing bill, but she was most proud of her role in getting Kentucky to officially ratify the Thirteenth, Fourteenth, and Fifteenth Amendments to the Constitution, which ended slavery and gave blacks both citizenship and voting rights. She served her Louisville constituents for sixteen years, from 1968 to 1984, sponsoring civil rights legislation and being a voice for those who had often gone unheard. Her many accolades included the National NAACP Women's Conference Unsung Heroine Award, the United Cerebral Palsy Humanitarian Service Award (1974), the Kennedy-King Award (1968), the Top Ten Outstanding Kentuckians Award, and the Louisville Defender Emancipation Exposition Award. She served as president of the Lincoln Foundation and held a lifetime membership in the NAACP. She was also a member of the Louisville Urban League, the Plymouth Congregational Church, and the Iota Phi Lambda sorority, of which she was a charter member. Her second husband died in 1972. She died in 1999 and was buried in the Zachary Taylor National Cemetery.

FURTHER READING

Kidd donated her professional papers and personal memorabilia to Kentucky State University's Paul G. Blazer Library Special Collections.

Hall, Wade. *Passing for Black: The Life and Careers of Mae Street Kidd* (1997).

Henderson, Ashyia N., ed. *Contemporary Black Biography* (2003).

Smith, Jessie Carney, ed. *Notable Black American Women* (1992).

KAREN COTTON MCDANIEL

Kildare, Dan (Nathaniel Augustus) (13 Jan. 1879–21 June 1920), bandleader and pianist active primarily in New York and London in the first two decades of the twentieth century, was one of the first recording artists of African extraction. Little is known of Kildare's early life and education. A Harlem acquaintance, vouching for Kildare's American citizenry on a 1915 passport application, claimed that Kildare was a native of the United States, and Kildare himself claimed that his birth in Kingston, Jamaica, was the result of his parents having been temporary residents there in 1879, but this is apparently untrue. Kildare's brother George was also born in Kingston (5 September 1885) and Dan Kildare claimed while in London that his father had been Paymaster of the Kingston Constabulary. For the last two years of his life he was married to an Englishwoman, and at his death in 1920 the London authorities described him as a British subject.

Dan Kildare appears to have moved to the United States around 1895. According to entertainer Tom Fletcher, in 1901 both were members of J. W. Gorman's "Alabama Troubadours," a traveling show active on the East Coast summer circuit. This troupe also included the dancer BILL "BOJANGLES" ROBINSON and the comedian Sam Lucas at the time, two of the leading performers of the age. In October 1903 Kildare re-entered the United States at Boston on the Admiral Dewey, on a voyage that originated in Port Moresby, New Guinea. This suggests he had been entertaining on the Australia—New Zealand circuit or perhaps in Asia. At that time, he claimed to be a resident of Lowell, Massachusetts. Kildare was described as twenty-four years old and married on the ship's passenger list, but his wife appears not to have been with him. By 1909 Kildare was living in New York; the 1910 U.S. Census listed him with his then wife, a California native who was registered as white, and with his brother, Walter Kildare. Both men were described as "mulattoes" and musicians, Dan working in hotels (presumably ballrooms and cabarets) and his brother in theaters. Dan Kildare would soon become a leader of New York's most important African American musical organization.

In April 1910 under the leadership of conductor and composer JAMES REESE EUROPE, the Clef Club was formed with a mission of musical uplift and the enhancement of the image of African Americans. It soon became one of New York's preeminent musical enterprises, fielding a large, well-drilled orchestra and show band. At the Club's first official meeting, Europe was named president and music director, while Dan Kildare and songwriter Joe Jordan became assistant directors. Kildare's involvement with the Club over the next few years seems to have been casual, yet on 30 December 1913, following Europe's resignation, Kildare assumed the Clef Club's presidency. He retained this position, at least nominally, until leaving for England in March 1915.

Regardless of his Clef Club duties in this period, Kildare was striking out in a more commercial direction. A pervasive dance craze was sweeping the United States and Europe in the years just prior to World War I and accompanying the most celebrated dance stars became the job of choice for the finest African American musicians in New York. They were assumed to be better at playing ragtime for the new American dance steps, and many patrons also preferred them for the tango and the newer fox-trot. James Reese Europe had begun working with the most popular dance team, Vernon and Irene Castle, in the fall of 1913. Kildare himself teamed up with Joan Sawyer, another dance star, at least to the extent of being connected with her for publicity purposes. Victor Records issued the first James Reese Europe recordings in 1914, capitalizing on his connection with the Castles. Columbia Records entered the market by year's end with recordings of "Joan Sawyer's Persian Garden Orchestra," Dan Kildare's band.

The earliest Kildare records, made in May, November, and December 1914, reflect styles that were in vogue in the years shortly before the advent of jazz. Each of the extant sides relates to and names in the title a dance of the day. "Joan Waltz-Hesitation" refers to a modified waltz, as does "Valse Boston." The more ragtime-influenced "When You're a Long Way from Home" is a one-step, a popular dance of the period. Although some of these Kildare recordings are of only historical interest, others, such as "Bregeiro (Rio Brazilian Maxixe)," remain enjoyable many decades after they were recorded. Kildare was soon James Reese Europe's chief rival as a society dance bandleader in New York and was looking beyond New York for a home base. In March 1915 Kildare embarked for England, at the head of a seven-piece band that was booked for a year at London's swank Ciro Club.

Kildare arrived in London at a propitious time, with the dance craze that gripped the United States also an international phenomenon, and his one-year contract led to a residency that lasted two years. He visited New York in April 1916, returning to London with new musicians to replace others who had left his band or died. The tenure of his band at Ciro's was increasingly imperiled, however, as the local press and authorities in London began to take a dim view of the city's rowdier cabarets. In 1917 the club was shut down on the grounds that illegal liquor was being served there. Kildare continued to provide music for London society, but his primary showcase had been shuttered.

Despite less advantageous circumstances, Kildare made additional recordings in London between 1917 and 1919. These reflected an up-to-date repertoire such as songs from recent Broadway shows by current hit-makers such as Jerome Kern. The Kildare group's 1917 recording of W. C. HANDY's "St. Louis Blues" was the first ever made with a vocal, a historic milestone in that three-year-old song's progress toward global popularity. As on the earlier recordings, the sound texture on these records is dominated by the banjo and other plucked-string instruments. This was the same sound palette that James Reese Europe had used in his own small Clef Club and dance units, featuring instruments from such earlier styles as minstrelsy. In the hands of Europe and Kildare's generation of players, these instruments were often turned to the production of ragtime and other more modern dance music.

Kildare's personal life was complicated. His wife Ena and their daughter Francis continued to live in Harlem after Dan moved to London. (It is not known whether Ena was Kildare's first wife.) In 1918, claiming to be a widower although Ena was still living, Kildare married Mary Rose Frances Fink, an English widow with two children. By 1920 relations between the couple were increasingly strained, and Mary sued for divorce in early June. By this time Kildare was drinking heavily and according to some reports was also using drugs. On the evening of 21 June 1920 Kildare entered his wife's pub, the Bell, shot her dead, and then killed her sister and wounded a maid at the bar. Then turning his pistol on a friend of the maid's, he thought better of it and shot himself in the head instead.

The tragedy of Kildare's death should not deflect attention from his accomplishments as a pioneer in the dissemination of post-minstrel African American music beyond the shores of the United States. His legacy is in the recordings he made between 1914 and 1919. Some of the finest of his recordings, such as "Bregeiro," retain their charm, and the first-ever vocal recording of "St. Louis Blues" was a historic milestone. Beyond this, the Kildare recordings open a window on the musical styles of the ragtime era and allow us to hear the music behind the dance craze that characterized the World War I era.

FURTHER READING
Badger, Reid. *A Life in Ragtime: A Biography of James Reese Europe* (1995).
Brooks, Tim. "Dan Kildare" in *Lost Sounds* (2004).
Rye, Howard, and Tim Brooks. "Dan Kildare", in *Storyville* (1996).

ELLIOTT S. HURWITT

Kilgore, Thomas, Jr. (20 Feb. 1913–4 Feb. 1998), church leader and civil rights activist, was born in Woodruff, South Carolina, the sixth of twelve children of Thomas Kilgore Sr. and Eugenia Langston, farmers. He grew up in Woodruff and attended the New Bethel Baptist Church. In 1926 the family moved to Brevard, North Carolina, where Kilgore attended eighth and ninth grades. In 1928 he moved to Asheville, North Carolina, to attend Stephens Lee High School; he graduated in 1930. The same year Brevard's Bethel Baptist Church licensed him to preach. In 1931 Kilgore enrolled at Morehouse College in Atlanta, where he attended Ebenezer Baptist Church, whose pastor was MARTIN LUTHER KING SR. King befriended the young Kilgore, inviting him to his house, where Kilgore met and played with the two-year-old MARTIN LUTHER KING JR. These Atlanta connections served Kilgore well throughout his life.

Morehouse, a black institution, drew a reputation as a progressive school that trained young blacks to be leaders and to defend the interests of the black race. In 1935 Kilgore graduated from Morehouse, was ordained by Bethel Baptist Church, and became the principal of Doggett High School in Rutherford County.

In 1936 Kilgore married Jeanetta Miriam Scott, a public school teacher; they had two daughters, Lynn Elda and Jini Medina. In 1937 Kilgore took his first pastoral charge at New Bethel Baptist Church in Asheville, North Carolina, the first of three pastorates he served in North Carolina. In the summer of 1938 Kilgore resigned from Doggett High to work at a public school in Waynesville, North Carolina, but quickly resigned to take over the pastorate of Friendship Baptist Church in Winston-Salem, where he remained until 1941. There he built new church facilities that were used for a day care center, the first in the town—six other churches used it as a model to create their own programs.

Kilgore also founded a school aimed at increasing adult literacy. He later expanded the school program to include voter registration education—only one hundred out of a black population of about thirty thousand were registered voters. In most southern states a literacy test was required in order to vote, and high levels of illiteracy made it difficult for local African Americans to exercise political rights. In tackling social problems within the black community, Kilgore followed the tradition of postbellum black southern ministers who made it part of their calling to improve the "race." In the fall of 1941 Kilgore took over Walnut Cove's Rising Star Baptist Church. A year later Winston-Salem Teachers College hired him as chaplain. Both positions landed Kilgore opportunities to work with labor unions.

In 1943 Reynolds Tobacco Company workers went on strike, and Jack Atkins, the Teachers College's executive secretary and Reynolds's lawyer, asked Kilgore to use to his ministerial influence to force the workers—mostly female—to return to work. A cautious Kilgore did some fact-finding by contacting a female church member who worked at Reynolds. After being informed of the heavy-duty work of female tobacco workers, he contacted fellow ministers and chose to support the strike. Because black clergy drew their ministerial salaries from people of their own race, they did not fear economic reprisals from white power structures and so could more easily side with black workers on labor issues than could their white counterparts.

Kilgore helped to unionize the workers, which was a first at Reynolds.

During Kilgore's stay at Rising Star he attended Howard University Divinity School for a year (1944–1945) and for two years worked as executive secretary of the General Baptist State Convention of North Carolina. This latter position widened his sphere of influence within black Baptist circles. In the summer of 1947 he was called to Friendship Baptist Church in New York City. While in New York he attended Union Theological Seminary, where he earned the master of divinity degree in 1957. Using Friendship as a base, Kilgore further developed his concerns for the social betterment of African Americans. He raised $6,000 as bail money for Martin Luther King Jr. during the Montgomery bus boycott and journeyed to Montgomery to give his personal support. In March 1957 Kilgore directed the Prayer Pilgrimage for Jobs and Freedom that drew more than fifty thousand people in Washington, D.C. Four years later King set up the New York chapter of the Southern Christian Leadership Conference (SCLC) with Kilgore as founding director (1961–1963). King had founded the SCLC to tackle civil rights issues, such as the employment of blacks in white-owned stores and voter registration. In 1961 both King and Kilgore were instrumental in the founding of the Progressive National Baptist Convention (PNBC), which split from the National Baptist Convention because the latter did not favor limited presidential tenures and protests and marches as a way to gain civil rights. Kilgore further proved himself a devotee of civil rights by being one of the organizers of the 1963 March on Washington.

In 1963 Kilgore ended his New York pastoral tenure and settled in Los Angeles as the new pastor of Second Baptist Church. There he pioneered a child development center, a senior citizens' housing facility, and a nonprofit housing corporation. Upon King's urging, he opened a local SCLC chapter, of which he was the founding director (1964–1969). Four years later he was called to lead prayer at King's funeral in Atlanta. In 1969 Kilgore was elected to a one-year term as the first black president of the American Baptist Convention (ABC), a predominantly white group. The ABC supported the civil rights movement, which led many black ministers to maintain affiliation with both the PNBC and the ABC.

At the ABC's helm Kilgore continued to fight for black improvement. At the 1969 Cincinnati meeting JAMES FORMAN, representative of the National Black Economic Development Conference, asked the ABC for $60 million as reparations for blacks. The request was denied, but the ABC, now under Kilgore's presidency, joined with the PNBC to create the Fund of-Renewal (FOR) to support black colleges and Christian communities in rural and urban areas, and together the denominations raised $9 million for the project. As ABC president Kilgore worked to reduce polarizations between conservatives and liberals within the denomination. In 1973 he served as adviser on community issues to the president of the University of Southern California (USC) and director of special community affairs. Three years later he was elected president of the PNBC.

In 1978 Kilgore developed the Gathering, an interdenominational and interracial group that worked on issues such as affordable housing, affirmative action, voter registration, improved public schools, and improvement of police relations with the community. The following year he created the Black Agenda, a federation of black ministers devoted to working on housing and economic development for black people. Kilgore retired from Second Baptist in 1985 and was made pastor emeritus. He remained active on the boards of various institutions, such as Morehouse, until he died in Los Angeles.

FURTHER READING

Kilgore, Thomas, Jr., and Jini Kilgore Ross. *A Servant's Journey: The Life and Work of Thomas Kilgore* (1998).

Avant, Albert A. *The Social Teachings of the Progressive National Baptist Convention, Inc., since 1961: A Critical Analysis of the Least, the Lost, and the Left-Out* (2004).

Fitts, Leroy. *A History of Black Baptists* (1985).

DAVID MICHEL

Killens, John Oliver (14 Jan. 1916–27 Oct. 1987), writer and activist, was born in Macon, Georgia, the son of Charles Myles Killens Sr., a restaurant manager, and Willie Lee Coleman, an insurance company clerk. Killens attended the local public school for African Americans, Pleasant Hill School, through grade seven, after which he attended Ballard Normal School, a private institution that provided education for African Americans through the twelfth grade, one year longer than the public high schools. Following his graduation in 1933, Killens attended Edward Waters College in Jacksonville, Florida, for one year, after which he transferred to Morris Brown College in Atlanta, Georgia. Killens left Morris Brown during his sophomore year for employment with the National Labor Relations Board (NLRB) in Washington, D.C., where (according to Killens) he was the only black employee at the time. He continued his college education as an evening student at Howard University and Robert H. Terrell Law School.

During World War II, Killens served from 1942 to 1945 in a U.S. Army amphibious unit with duty in the South Pacific for twenty-seven months. He eventually rose to the rank of master sergeant. In 1943 Killens married Grace Ward Jones, with whom he had two children. Following the war Killens, electing to pursue a writing career, abandoned his law studies, even though he was only six months from graduation. To support his family, he returned to the NLRB, where he worked until 1948, when he became a union organizer.

During the summer of 1948 Killens enrolled in Columbia University to study creative writing under Dorothy Brewster. He took up residence in New York City and continued to study at Columbia on the GI Bill. Persisting with creative writing, union organizing, and "soaking up life in Harlem," as he wrote in his autobiography, he was associated with LANGSTON HUGHES, PAUL ROBESON, and W. E. B. DuBois. In the late 1940s or early 1950s Killens joined three of his friends to form the Harlem Writers' Guild. Shortly thereafter he read the first chapter of his first novel, *Youngblood*, to the group; eventually *Youngblood* became the first work of fiction to come from the guild, which nurtured, among others, LOUISE MERIWETHER, Rosa Guy, MAYA ANGELOU, and the playwright-actor OSSIE DAVIS. Meanwhile Killens continued to study writing in seminars taught by Saul Bellow at New York University (NYU), Helen Hull at Columbia, and others. Viola Brother Shore of NYU assisted Killens in contacting editors and publishers.

The publication in 1954 of *Youngblood*, which ranks as Killens's major work, was a success, and he became something of a celebrity. HARRY BELAFONTE bought the screen rights to *Youngblood*, and through book promotion tours, which Hughes helped Killens plan, he met the pianist and singer NAT KING COLE and JOHN JOHNSON, publisher of the *Negro Digest*, *Ebony*, and *Jet* magazines. *Youngblood*, which was reprinted in 1982, is regarded as a classic African American protest novel.

Killens followed this success with *And Then We Heard the Thunder* (1964), based on his World War II experiences as an African American serving in a segregated army. *Thunder* was nominated for a Pulitzer Prize in 1964, but the committee awarded no prize for that year. He suffered the same fate in 1971, the year of the publication of *Cotillion; or, One Good Bull Is Half the Herd*, which was also nominated for a Pulitzer Prize. In all Killens wrote six novels for adults. He also wrote a biography of the poet Alexander Pushkin, titled *Great Black Russian: The Life and Times of Alexander Pushkin* (1988), and two books for children, *Great Gittin' up Morning: A Biography of* DENMARK VESEY (1972) and *A Man Ain't Nothin' but a Man: The Adventures of* JOHN HENRY (1975).

When Killens was not writing, he was fighting injustice and racism. He was active in the Brooklyn NAACP, where he organized a "Night of Stars" as a fund-raiser in 1957. A gentle, soft-spoken man, he was nevertheless unsympathetic with nonviolence and eventually became a follower of MALCOLM X, whom Killens asserted "did not teach nonviolence, but he did advocate self-defense." And while he admired MARTIN LUTHER KING JR., Killens rejected "turning the other cheek" because he was convinced that "people don't respect you unless you fight" (*Macon Courier*, 4 Jan. 1979). Killens also observed that "moral suasion alone has never brought about a revolution."

Killens's writing was an extension of his conviction that he should be of service to his people. As one who used his pen to try to change society, Killens's literary productions, based on the black experience, included the themes of black self-esteem, black manhood, black unity, and even black folklore. To Killens, "All art is social, all art is propaganda, notwithstanding all propaganda is not art." Like RICHARD WRIGHT, whom he greatly admired, he believed that the main goal of art is to attack and thus alter society.

Killens exerted considerable influence on African American writers, whom he always encouraged and assisted. During his service as writer-in-residence at Fisk University (1965–1968), he established one of the first Black Writers' Conferences in the United States. He continued to initiate writers' conferences at Howard University as writer-in-residence from 1971 to 1976 and at Medgar Evers College, where he served as a distinguished professor from 1981 until his death. He also was an adjunct professor at Columbia University from 1970 to 1973. In 1986 he conducted one of his last writing seminars in his hometown of Macon, where his students included Tina Ansa, a best-selling author in the 1990s.

Killens was the recipient of many honors in his lifetime. He served as vice president of the Black Academy of Arts and Letters and as chairman of the Harlem Writers' Guild. Other awards included the Howard University Creative Writers Workshop Award (1974), election to the Black Film Makers Hall of Fame (1976), a National Endowment for the Arts Fellowship (1980), and the Distinguished Writer Award of the Middle Atlantic Writers' Association (1984). Killens died in Brooklyn, New York.

FURTHER READING

Killens, John O. "The Half Ain't Never Been Told," in *Contemporary Authors Autobiography Series*, vol. 2 (1985).
Obituary: *New York Times*, 30 Oct. 1987.
This entry is taken from the *American National Biography* and is published here with the permission of the American Council of Learned Societies.

JOAN B. HUFFMAN

Kilpatrick, Admiral (28 Feb. 1904–20 Feb. 1982), forged a militant commitment to black liberation within a lifelong allegiance to the international socialist movement. In a 1980 interview, the only source of information on his childhood, Kilpatrick said he had been born in Colorado in 1898 to a Native American father (possibly of partly African descent) and a mother who had been enslaved in Kentucky. Information from his Ohio death certificate shows his birth around 1905. Kilpatrick consistently used the birth date of 28 February 1904 for travel by ship to and from Europe in the 1930s. The family moved to Cleveland when he was about six years old, where his father got work for McKerrigan McKinley Steel, which became part of Republic Steel. His father was a socialist and a member of the Industrial Workers of the World (IWW), which young Admiral joined in his teenage years.

He absorbed from his father and other black IWW members that "anyplace you go, where you are working, if anybody is organizing a union, a gutter union or even a dog union, join the union" (Phillips, p. 113). Black coke workers at McKinney steel, affiliated with the IWW, honored the nationwide 1919 steel strike, organized under the American Federation of Labor, by future Communist Party leader William Z. Foster; they later joined the Mine, Mill, and Smelter Workers union. Kilpatrick may have gotten his experience with the steel strike and Attorney General Mitchell

Palmer's generalized raids against unions, socialists, and organizations of foreign-born citizens and residents, among this group of Cleveland metal workers. They were instrumental in preventing violence and turning back the influx of black workers brought from the south by steel companies as strike breakers (Phillips, p. 105).

Kilpatrick remained a member of the IWW, changing jobs often because, as he said, "If I went to a place where there was no union, I would try to organize a union" and "they would kick me the hell out" (Collum, 164). In 1927 he joined the American Communist Party. He was active in the first Unemployed Councils in Cleveland. Both the party and the council challenged racial discrimination: on 5 October 1931 two thousand Unemployment Council members were physically removed from a city council meeting, at the order of the council's president, after marching to City Hall for racial equality and reduced bus fares for children. Kilpatrick was kicked in the back by a patrolman. Neither communist leadership nor black participation interfered with unemployed councils opening in Polish, Czech, and Irish neighborhoods or even in Anglo neighborhoods.

Kilpatrick went to the Soviet Union in 1931 to take courses at the Lenin School (Phillips, p. 203). Returning to the United States on 9 May 1935 aboard the *Paris* from Le Havre, France, he plunged into the work of the Future Outlook League (FOL), organizing African Americans under the slogan "Don't Spend Your Money Where You Can't Work." It was a common theme in northern cities during the 1930s, achieving notable success breaking racial restrictions on hiring. Cleveland FOL organizer John Holly was not a communist, and the party had earlier debated whether this kind of campaign would promote divisions in the working class, but at the time had decided to support it (Phillips, p. 205). FOL relied on Kilpatrick's fellow black communist, Maude White, to teach women members basic methods for picketing and boycotting recalcitrant non-black businesses (Phillips, p. 209).

Less than two years after returning to Cleveland, "the Admiral" left on the *Ile de France* 20 February 1937 on his way to Spain to fight for the Republican government against Franco's fascist armies. He served in a transport unit and then as a front-line ambulance driver. He also served in an intelligence unit, stopping the sabotage of trucks, which involved him in ferreting out not only Franco sympathizers, but also alleged Trotskyites and adherents of the POUM (the Marxist party admired by George Orwell) among the Republican forces. Wounded by shrapnel on a transport assignment at the front lines, he was evacuated from Spain and returned home on the SS *Ausonia* 20 December 1938.

Kilpatrick served during the 1940s as President of Local 735, Mine, Mill, and Smelter Workers Union in Cleveland and then as an international representative. He left the union because he thought his colleagues were backing off from confrontation with the post-war red scare. He went to work at a Westinghouse plant, represented by the United Electrical Radio and Machine Workers, which in 1948 was expelled from the Congress of Industrial Organizations (CIO)—as was Mine, Mill, and Smelter—after refusing to purge its leadership of Communist Party members (Collum, p. 167).

Kilpatrick refused to plead the Fifth Amendment when called to testify before Ohio's own little Un-American Activities Committee, 2–5 December 1953, commenting afterward, "I didn't take no Fifth Amendment. What the hell am I going to take the Fifth? They knew who I was, I didn't give a damn. I had already stated it in open meetings and in delegated bodies to the unions. I've been trying to take the 13th, 14th, and 15th Amendment all my damn life and got nowhere" (Collum, p. 167). This was only one example of Kilpatrick being too militant a communist for the Communist Party; he was expelled in 1960 "because I wasn't going to go along with the fact now all of a sudden you can build a Party with all classes" (Collum, p. 42). Even in the 1930s he considered the line that the Party "was carrying on the traditions of Lincoln, Jefferson, and Douglass" to be "a lot of bull" (Kelley, p. 157).

As a result of his refusal to testify, he was fired from a job at the Wellman Bronze Co. Along with nine other Cleveland residents, he was cited for contempt of the commission but none was tried. His application for unemployment compensation was denied on "grounds related to employment," which he appealed unsuccessfully. Unable to find work—the Federal Bureau of Investigation made a standard practice of visiting the employer of any known communist to strongly suggest that they be fired—Kilpatrick started a small trucking business.

Kilpatrick was a leading organizer of a dissident group within the communist party, Provisional Organizing Committee for a Marxist—Leninist Party in the United States, known for short as POC, both before and after his expulsion from the party, which was the subject of testimony at House Un-American Activities Committee (HUAC) hearings in 1962. In 1972 Kilpatrick was warmly welcomed into the Communist League, which soon after became the Communist Labor Party (CLP). The CLP's Nelson Peery was a generation younger than Kilpatrick, but, like him, a veteran of labor and black liberation struggles and unapologetic socialist internationalism over several decades.

Admiral Kilpatrick died in Cleveland in 1982. Little is known about his family life or whether he ever married, but in 1980 he recounted to an interviewer for the Abraham Lincoln Brigade Archives that he had three daughters and a son, all grown, the youngest twenty-nine years old, so that all would have been born by 1951. An organizer to the very end, he served as chair of the tenant's committee at the senior citizen's housing project, where he spent his last few years.

FURTHER READING

Kelley, Robin D.G. *Race Rebels: Culture, Politics and the Black Working Class* (1996).

Phillips, Kimberley Louise. *Alabama North: African American Migrants, Community, and Working-Class Activism in Cleveland, 1915–1945* (1999).

Collum, Danny Duncan, and Victor A. Berch. *African Americans in the Spanish Civil War: "This Ain't Ethiopia, but It'll Do"* (1992).

CHARLES ROSENBERG

Kilpatrick, Carolyn Cheeks (25 June 1945–), U.S. congresswoman and teacher, was born Carolyn Jean Cheeks in Detroit, Michigan, the third of five children of Marvel Cheeks, a businessman.

When Carolyn was ten years old she decided to become a secretary. In an effort to prepare herself for that occupation, she enrolled in Detroit's High School of Commerce, a nationally acclaimed public high school that prepared students for office-related careers. She was elected president of her graduating class. She married Bernard Kilpatrick. They had two children before the marriage ended in divorce. Hardworking and civic minded, Carolyn Kilpatrick raised her children to have the same values.

After finishing high school in 1963, Kilpatrick worked as a secretary for a short time. She then pursued a teaching certificate. She attended Ferris State College and Western Michigan University, earning a B.S. in Education in in 1972. She earned a master's degree in Education from the University of Michigan in 1977. She taught business education in the Detroit Public Schools until 1978, when she left teaching to pursue a political career.

A protégé of COLEMAN A. YOUNG, the former mayor of Detroit, Kilpatrick began her political career by heading the Political Action Committee at the Shrine of the Black Madonna Church. The church actively worked to further the interests of African Americans. In 1978 she won a seat in the Michigan legislature as a Democrat; she served for eighteen years in the house. During her tenure she broke ground for Detroiters, African Americans, and women. She became the first woman and the first African American appointed to the powerful Michigan House Appropriations Committee. Considered knowledgeable and diplomatic, she gained a reputation among her colleagues for being a hardworking consensus builder.

While serving in the Michigan legislature, Kilpatrick introduced numerous bills and resolutions designed to improve the lives of Michigan citizens, especially Detroiters. One bill called for the formation of empowerment corporations in communities that qualified for a federal empowerment zone designation. Areas with this designation qualified for business and residential grants, low-interest loans, and special tax considerations. Another bill called for improved health coverage and education for citizens living with diabetes. She also introduced a resolution honoring a key organization supporting business education, the National Distributive Clubs of America (DECA).

Kilpatrick was deeply involved in community activities before and during her legislative terms. She served as a member of the board of trustees of Henry Ford Hospital. In 1986 she tried her hand in the business world unsuccessfully. She opened an American Speedy Printer franchise in Lansing, Michigan. Five years later, in 1991, she declared bankruptcy. In 1996 Kilpatrick was elected to the 105th U.S. Congress from Michigan's Fifteenth (now Thirteenth) Congressional District. She was reelected six times. Her son Kwame Kilpatrick was elected to fill her seat in the state legislature, and in 2001 he became the youngest mayor in Detroit's history to date.

Washington quickly took note of the Carolyn Kilpatrick's hard work and political style. She soon became the only Michigan Democrat appointed to the U.S. House Appropriations Committee, which determines the funding for all levels of the federal government. As a member of the Transportation, Treasury, and Independent Agencies Committees, she helped determine the funding for highway projects and transportation programs. Her other memberships included the Foreign Operations Subcommittee, which regulates funding for the

Peace Corps and similar programs. Kilpatrick became the first African American woman to serve on the Air Force Academy board and the first chairwoman of the Congressional Black Caucus. In 2000 an executive order forcing the Department of Defense to open a portion of its $110 million advertising budget to minority contractors was signed by President Bill Clinton thanks in large part to the efforts of Kilpatrick. In 2006 Kilpatrick along with other Democrats, such as Harry Reid, John Kerry, and Robert Menendez, were still trying to get it implemented. Kilpatrick fought to correct the unfair trade policy that China had with the United States. For example, China's laws that govern the automotive industries promoted exports to the United States but required that all parts used in manufacturing vehicles in China be made in China. These policies were directly responsible for the loss of many Michigan jobs. Kilpatrick hosted town meetings and other forums to inform citizens about key issues and to hear citizens' opinions.

As a U.S. congresswoman Kilpatrick was able to do more to serve the interests of her constituents than she could as a state representative, bringing home half a billion dollars to revitalize the Thirteenth District. More programs and funding were available on the federal level. She found funds for her constituents for programs focused on human services, transportation, HIV/AIDS management and research, and mental health. She personally presented the Karmanos Cancer Institute, a part of the Detroit Medical Center, a check for federal funds. Kilpatrick's efforts led to the implementation of a NASA-sponsored engineering and aeronautics program at Wayne State University for Detroit's public school students. She worked with Fannie Mae, a national organization whose mission is to bring affordable housing to low-, moderate-, and middle-income families, to provide millions of dollars for home mortgages to benefit Michigan families. In 2005 Kilpatrick introduced a bill to rename the Thirteenth Congressional District's Federal Homeland Security Office in ROSA PARKS's honor. With much bipartisan support, the bill easily passed.

FURTHER READING
Chapman, Mary M. "Force for Change," *African American Family* (Mar. 2006).

DEBORAH LOIS TAYLOR

Kilson, Martin Luther, Jr. (14 Feb. 1931–), political scientist and public intellectual, was born Martin Luther Kilson Jr. in East Rutherford, New Jersey, the son of Martin Luther Kilson, a Methodist clergyman, and Louisa Laws Kilson. Kilson was raised in Ambler, Pennsylvania, a small factory town outside Philadelphia, where his great-grandfather, a Civil War Colored Infantry Regiment veteran, had settled after the war.

Ambler, a major producer of asbestos textiles, had a small black population and the few black townspeople were generally treated well by the local whites. Kilson experienced little or no overt bigotry during his childhood and adolescence, but he did become aware of structural racism, as his father ministered to Ambler's small black, and mostly poor community. In 1949 Kilson left Ambler for Lincoln University, the nation's oldest historically black university, located in nearby Chester County, Pennsylvania. There he was influenced by the Negritude movement, which had captured the imaginations of many campus intellectuals. In spite of the movement's romanticism, Kilson thought that Negritude had a positive influence on the attitudes of blacks. It forced middle class black students to confront the common historical and cultural bonds that they shared with less fortunate members of their race, and sought to create in them a sense of care and concern. Fraternity life at Lincoln, however, remained untouched by this sense of care and concern; instead it replicated the white America's class and caste distinctions through the enforcement of entry requirements based upon skin complexion. Kilson, a writer for the college newspaper, continually attacked such fraternity elitism.

Graduating magna cum laude and valedictorian in 1953, Kilson entered Harvard University where he earned an M.A. (1958) and a Ph.D. (1959) in Political Science. He married Marion Dusser de Barenne on 8 August 1959. The couple went on to have three children.

During his time as a graduate student, Kilson was a teaching fellow for Harvard's Department of Government from 1957 to 1959. Upon completion of his doctorate, he pursued postdoctoral study at Oxford in 1959. He won a Ford Foundation fellowship for West Africa from 1959 to 1961. He then held a number of appointments—resident fellow at the Harvard Center for International Affairs from 1961 until 1972, tutor of government at Harvard from 1962 until 1967, and visiting professor at the University of Ghana from 1964 to 1965—before he was appointed assistant professor of government at Harvard in 1967. In 1969 he was granted tenure and appointed full professor, achieving historical distinction as the first black tenured faculty member at Harvard.

As a public intellectual, Kilson achieved considerable notoriety. Beginning in 1969 and continuing through the mid-1970s, he engaged in an ongoing and rather vituperative attack on the academic integrity of Harvard's then nascent Afro-American Studies Department. In Kilson's opinion, the Afro-American Studies Department was an ill-conceived product of black student protest demands, which did not measure up to the rigorous standards of Harvard's tradition of academic excellence. Kilson charged that Afro-American studies grades were inflated, that the program lacked academic discipline and was run by a "dictator" and a "cabal" of black militant faculty. The sharp exchanges between Kilson and his main antagonist, Ewart Guinier, the Afro-American Studies Department Chair, were regularly published in the campus newspaper, the *Harvard Crimson*, electrifying and polarizing the Harvard community. Kilson reached a national audience with a feature article in the *New York Times Magazine* (2 Sept. 1973) wherein he took on a new, yet related target: black student life at Harvard and other elite colleges and universities. In "The Black Experience at Harvard," Kilson alleged that black students were in crisis, one engendered by the self-defeating militancy and separatism of ill-prepared students from poor backgrounds and another manifested in exclusive all-black relationships and tense black-white relations. Kilson blamed "politicized" recruitment and admissions policies for the increasing enrollment at Harvard of inner-city blacks who harbored "anti-white feelings" and engaged in "black solidarity behavior" which was "distinctly anti-intellectual and anti-achievement in orientation." In his article, Kilson also continued his trenchant criticism of Harvard's Afro-American Studies Department, declaring that it had become the "main base of operations of black solidarity forces" and "a fervent defender of black separatism." He also alleged that the black solidarity forces exerted "overwhelming" pressure on middle-class students to conform to the symbols and rituals of black solidarity. As a remedy Kilson called for a deemphasis on the recruitment of inner-city African Americans with lower grades to the top American college and the admission of more black students from middle-class backgrounds who, in his view, would be more likely to succeed.

In the late 1960s and early 1970s, Kilson authored *Political Change in a West African State: A Study of the Modernization Process in Sierra Leone* (1966), *Crisis and Change in the Negro Ghetto* (1973), and numerous journal articles. He was an editor or coeditor of the following texts: *The Political Awakening of Africa* (1965); *The Africa Reader*, Volume I: *Colonial Africa*, Volume II: *Independent Africa* (1970); *Apropos of Africa: Afro-American Leaders and the Romance of Africa* (1971); *Key Issues in the Afro-American Experience*, Volumes I and II (1971). Kilson was a consultant to the Fulbright–Hayes International Exchange Program, beginning in 1972 and the Ford Foundation, from 1973 to 1974. He received several honors and awards, including a Phi Betta Kappa scholarship (1974–1975) and a Guggenheim fellowship (1975–76). He was also a fellow of the American Academy of Arts and Sciences, a founding fellow of the Black Academy of Arts and Letters, a member of the American African Studies Association, and a member of the NAACP.

The main foci of Kilson's scholarship were the emergence from colonialism of independent states in Africa and the attendant problems of modernization, development, and democratization; nineteenth-century African American emigrationist thought, specifically attitudes about repatriation or return to Africa; and historical and contemporary African American civic and political issues. Kilson invested twenty-three years of research in his major three-volume work-in-progress, *The Making of Black Intellectuals: Studies on the African American Intelligentsia*.

Exhibiting the acerbic journalism of his Lincoln years, Kilson's opinions touched a raw nerve among many black Ivy League students who, already feeling embattled and besieged by campus elitism and white supremacy, were caught unawares by what they perceived as an unwarranted broadside. Kilson's commentary earned him the enmity of many progressives and the approval of many conservatives, even though Kilson continued to view himself as on the political left and firmly within the civil rights activist tradition. (As a leftist and as a staunch advocate of integration-assimilation Kilson broached no tolerance for nationalism, which he railed against perhaps even more than white racism).

In 1987 Kilson was honored with an endowed chair, the Frank G. Thompson Professorship in Government. Kilson continued to generate controversy, ire, and admiration in the 1990s and the new millennium. The targets of his criticism included several prominent individuals of varying ideological stripes, including the hip-hop intellectuals Michael Eric Dyson and Todd Boyd, the Newark politician Cory Booker, the Princeton philosopher

KWAME ANTHONY APPIAH, the Harvard legal scholar Randall Kennedy, the Harvard literary scholar HENRY LOUIS GATES JR., and the late nationalist intellectual HAROLD CRUSE.

In 1999 Kilson retired from Harvard as Frank G. Thompson Professor Emeritus. During his long career, he mentored several African American leaders, scholars and intellectuals, including most notably JULIAN BOND and his former Harvard student, the philosopher CORNEL WEST.

FURTHER READING

Kitwana, Bakari. "Hip Hop Studies and the New Cultural Wars," *Socialism and Democracy* 36 (July–Dec. 2004).

Winston, Henry. *Marxist-Leninist Critique of Roy Innis on Community Self-Determination and Martin Kilson on Education* (1973).

YUSUF NURUDDIN

Kimbro, Henry Allen (10 Feb. 1912–11 July 1999), baseball player, was born in Davidson County, Tennessee, to Willie Kimbro, a sharecropper and grave keeper, and Sally King, a domestic worker.

Kimbro grew up on the outskirts of Nashville, which made it difficult for him to attend the distantly located all-black high school. Thus his education ended after elementary school.

Often referred to as the "black Ty Cobb," Kimbro, like Cobb, earned a reputation for his explosive and unruly personality. Kimbro insisted that his lack of education made him self-conscious and extremely defensive.

Throughout his youth, Kimbro played the sandlots around Nashville and with a local semi-pro team. In 1935 he married Nellie Bridges. The following year their son Larry was born. For years Kimbro declined offers to leave Nashville to play with other teams. However, in 1936, desperately in need of more income, Kimbro was convinced to leave home for the first time by Jim Taylor, manager of the Chicago American Giants. The following season, the twenty-four-year-old, 5'8", 175-pound outfielder began his professional baseball career and a thirteen-year association with the Elite Giants organization.

Kimbro stayed with the Elites franchise as they moved from Columbus to Washington to Baltimore. In 1937, his first season in the Negro National League, Kimbro hit .276, one of the only times he did not break .300 in his career. Usually the lead-off hitter, his averages of .318 and .310 in 1938 and 1939 were among the league's best. In 1940, his average dipped

to .269. After returning from the Cuban winter league that season, where he hit .294 for the Alamendares team and led the league with eighteen stolen bases, Kimbro was traded to the New York Black Yankees. The following season found him back in an Elites uniform, and his averages rebounded to .288 and .333 for the 1942 and 1943 seasons.

Kimbro's best seasons were 1944–1947. In 1944, he hit .329 and led the league in stolen bases, finishing one run behind league leaders JOSH GIBSON and BUCK LEONARD in runs scored. In 1946, he hit a career best of .371 and led the league in runs scored. The following season he hit .353 and again led in runs scored and tied for most doubles. Back in Havana for winter baseball, he won the Cuban League batting title with an impressive .346 average.

An eight-time All Star, Kimbro averaged .222 in twenty-seven at-bats, with three RBIs and four stolen bases in appearances from 1941 to 1953.

The right-handed throwing, left-handed hitting Kimbro had great upper body strength and consistently hit for power and average. A speedster on the base pads, he ranked high in stolen bases throughout his career. Kimbro was also a force defensively and considered one of the top-rated centerfielders in the league.

In 1950, Kimbro managed the Birmingham Black Barons and then returned to the playing field for seasons 1951–1953.

Kimbro's first marriage ended in divorce in 1948; he married Erbia Mendoza in 1951. Upon his retirement in 1953, the couple had their first of three children.

After his baseball career, Kimbro drove a taxi for Bill's Cab Company in Nashville, a business he later purchased in 1954. Soon after, he purchased a gas station. Kimbro owned the two investment enterprises for twenty-two years, until a series of strokes forced him to sell the companies and retire. He died in Nashville at the age of eighty-seven.

FURTHER READING

Kelly, Brent. *Voices from the Negro Leagues* (1998).

Lester, Larry. *Black Baseball's National Showcase* (2001).

Riley, James A. *The Biographical Encyclopedia of The Negro Baseball Leagues* (1994).

BYRON MOTLEY

Kimbrough, Jack (26 July 1908–13 Apr. 1992), dentist, civil rights activist, and art and book collector, was born Jack Johnson Kimbrough in Lexington, Mississippi, the son of Samuel Gulbridge Kimbrough, a blacksmith, and Mary

Hoover. Jack was named after the famed African American boxer JACK JOHNSON. When he was seven, the Kimbroughs, intimidated by local Ku Klux Klansmen and seeking better economic opportunities, moved from Mississippi to Alameda, California, where relatives resided. After graduating from Alameda High School in 1926 Jack attended Sacramento Junior College. He continued his studies at the University of California at Berkeley, where he studied chemistry while working as a janitor, waiter, cook, and landscaper. His interest in science, as well as the relatively shorter time that it took to earn a dentistry degree than a medical degree, persuaded him to enroll in the University of California Dental School in San Francisco, from which he graduated with a DDS in 1934.

After being told by a prominent black dentist that staking out a practice would be difficult in Los Angeles and that there was no black dentist in San Diego, Kimbrough hitchhiked a ride south in 1935. At the time San Diego was home to 4,400 black inhabitants, and soon after his arrival Kimbrough met the city's only black medical doctor, A. Antonio DaCosta. The two became fast friends, and DaCosta allowed Kimbrough to use a kitchen in one of his rental units as his dental office. Despite the threats of a white resident, Kimbrough and DaCosta later moved their offices to the section of town called Golden Hill, at Twenty-fifth and K streets.

In 1937 Kimbrough married Quincella Nickerson, a schoolteacher; the couple had four children. Though he had built up a thriving practice by the onset of the World War II, Kimbrough nevertheless volunteered for military service. Rather than use his skills, however, the military told him that the greatest need for black medical personnel was on the home front.

Kimbrough's response to a humiliating incident—he was casually refused service at a downtown greasy spoon—led to years of civil rights work. In 1947 he was elected president of the local NAACP. In his first year as NAACP president, Kimbrough recruited black and white students at San Diego State College and, practicing in a restaurant stage set, coached them on how to be legally credible witnesses to acts of racial discrimination. Properly rehearsed, the black students attempted to get served at white-owned restaurants where the white students were already positioned to observe any discriminatory treatment. In this manner thirty-two lawsuits were filed against owners who rejected black customers; Kimbrough and his students prevailed in all but one of these cases. The

judgments for the plaintiffs, usually amounting to three hundred dollars per case, were divided among the students and their attorney. Previously, blacks filing such lawsuits had their claims denied because of lack of evidence.

Kimbrough's most important desegregation triumph began in 1948 when several members of the NAACP met to discuss their recent desegregation victories at the Grant Grill in the U.S. Grant Hotel, then the most prestigious hotel in the city. The restaurant's staff, acting in accordance with management policy, ignored their presence and did not serve them. The following evening the group returned and again were not served. Kimbrough arrived a bit later and sat at the restaurant's counter. After he, too, was ignored, he personally confronted a waitress who, after some discussion with the restaurant's staff, took their orders; Kimbrough and the other blacks were served. In 1953 Kimbrough cofounded the San Diego Urban League and became its first president. He also helped organize the Southeast San Diego YMCA and was on the board of directors of the San Diego Historical Society.

As a dentist his career reached a milestone in 1961 when he became the first African American elected president of the San Diego Dental Society. At the time of his election he was Section Chief of Dental Medicine at San Diego County Hospital, president of the San Diego Society of Clinical Hypnosis, and a member of the executive council of the Southern California State Dental Association. In 1963 Kimbrough was an invited guest of President John F. Kennedy at a White House event celebrating the one-hundredth anniversary of the signing of the Emancipation Proclamation. In 1965 he was appointed to the California State Board of Dental Examiners, and in 1968 he was elected its first black president. In addition to being the first African American to head a major city branch of the American Dental Association, he was one of the earliest African Americans to be named a fellow of the American College of Dentistry.

Kimbrough's home was the scene of numerous cultural events and was a gathering place for the city's black elite. A scholar of African history and culture, Kimbrough amassed one of the largest collections of African art and artifacts on the West Coast. Items from his collection were displayed at the San Diego Museum of Man, the San Diego Museum of Art, San Diego State University, the University of California at San Diego, the Lyceum Theater, and the Heard Museum in Phoenix, Arizona. In 1993 the majority of his African art collection was donated to San Diego Mesa College. Kimbrough also owned an enormous collection of signed first-edition books by black authors, some of whom had visited his home. A captivating speaker with a genial personality, in the early 1980s he was an adjunct professor of Afro-American studies at San Diego State University.

Over the decades Kimbrough served as a mentor to future community leaders, most notably U.S. District Court judge EARL GILLIAM. Kimbrough died of cardiac arrest at Paradise Valley Hospital in National City, California. To preserve his memory the San Diego city school system established the Dr. Jack Kimbrough Pride in Cultural Heritage Award to recognize high-achieving black male students and, in 1997, christened the Dr. Jack J. Kimbrough Elementary School.

FURTHER READING

A transcript of Kimbrough's interview with Robert G. Wright on 11 October 1990 is at the San Diego Historical Society.

"Dental Society Installs Dr. Kimbrough as Pres." *San Diego Union*, 8 Apr. 1961.

"San Diegan Heads Dental Examiners." *San Diego Union-Tribune*, 23 Jan. 1968.

Obituary: *San Diego Union-Tribune*, 15 Apr. 1992.

ROBERT FIKES JR.

Kimmons, Carl Eugene (10 Apr. 1920–), World War II veteran and U.S. naval officer, was born in Hamilton, Ohio, the son of Posey Kimmons and Mary Whitaker. He attended Hamilton High School and graduated in 1939. Afterward Kimmons, like so many other young men at the time, joined the Civilian Conservation Corps and was housed at a local camp, sending home a portion of his earnings on a regular basis. However, he also had another interest sparked by watching the 1937 black and white movie *Submarine D-1* as a teenager. Eager to join the navy, Kimmons's interest was further piqued when another African American from Hamilton, George Morris, came home from the service. A tough-looking submariner dressed in a navy uniform covered with medals and standing over six feet tall, Morris made an indelible impression on Kimmons, who later joked that Morris "didn't tell us how hard it really was" to serve in the navy (Kimmons). Fully hooked, Kimmons enlisted in June 1940 to become an official navy "boot" recruit.

The navy that Kimmons joined in 1940 reflected the racial prejudice rampant throughout American society. Segregation and discrimination were the norm, and black recruits had no choice but to serve in the Steward's Branch of the service. The mess attendant (later steward's mate) and steward ratings were the only available options, whatever a man's skill level, aptitude, or educational level may have been. The job of such men as Kimmons, DORIE MILLER, WILLIAM PINCKNEY, and most black men who joined the navy and saw combat during the war years was to serve the officers' corps. Their job as mess attendants, with promotion available to petty officer status as steward or officer's cook, was to help prepare and serve the officer's meals and clean their quarters. While it is indeed true that the men of the Steward's Branch were fighting men, the navy largely ignored their contributions, and such men were only given a degree of recognition for their service in the late twentieth century. While primarily mess attendants (many of whom were also from the Philippines and the island of Guam), they also served in general quarters (GQ) stations as phone talkers, auxiliary torpedo men, ammunition passers, gunners, and a variety of other posts performing vital military service.

Upon his induction, Kimmons was sent to the boot camp for African American recruits known as Unit B East at Norfolk, Virginia. As the train reached Wheeling, West Virginia, all the black recruits were switched to a segregated rail car. Once his training there ended, Kimmons's stay was extended at Norfolk for duties not as a mess attendant but as a yeoman. In a foreshadowing of his later navy career, Kimmons was employed typing up reports and performing other administrative functions. In September 1940 he was assigned to the destroyer *McFarland*, then being recommissioned at Mare Island, California. While stationed on this ship, Kimmons did unofficial duty as a yeoman in his off-hours, typing reports and handling the ship's log. In fact he "wanted to be a yeoman instead of a mess attendant" and "was eager to do yeoman's work, so I became very good at it" (Knoblock, 309). Because Kimmons had unusual access to a great amount of the ship's paperwork, one day in early 1942 he noticed an unposted memorandum stating that the Submarine Force would now be accepting more blacks. Soon thereafter Kimmons requested submarine duty and was assigned to the USS *Plunger*.

From 1942 to late 1944 Kimmons served on two submarines and made a total of seven war patrols. The first four were conducted on the *Plunger*, where Kimmons's GQ station was in the forward torpedo room on the reload crew (submerged) or as a part of a .50 caliber gun crew (surface). Inexplicably Kimmons was assigned to service on a destroyer after four patrols and served for a short time stateside in Philadelphia. Though deeply disappointed at the change, he did not come away empty-handed during his time back home. In July 1943 he married Thelma Jean Lewis, a high school classmate. The couple had three children, Karen, Larry, and Kimberly. In November 1943 Kimmons was sent back to submarine duty, joining the crew of the new boat *Parche*. He made his final three war patrols on this top-scoring boat, including one in which the skipper, Commander Lawson P. "Red" Ramage, won the Medal of Honor during a furious surface battle while Kimmons and the rest of the crew received the Navy Unit Commendation Award.

The end of the war found Kimmons serving on a new boat, the *Cobbler*, stateside. He stayed aboard until October 1947, when, as a result of President Harry Truman's Executive Order 9981 desegregating the U.S. military issued just months prior, he changed his rate from officer's cook first class to yeoman second class. Even though Kimmons had to accept a reduction in rating, it was the only way he could get the change approved. Although opportunities increased for African Americans in the navy, they were still far from being equal. From this point on Kimmons made history, rising through every enlisted-man rating to become an officer in 1961. He was the only World War II mess attendant to achieve this outstanding feat, retiring as a full lieutenant in 1971 after a thirty-year career.

Upon his retirement, Kimmons and his wife moved to Connecticut, where he earned a master's degree in Education from the University of Connecticut in 1973 and enjoyed a twenty-two-year teaching career that proved just as rewarding as his naval career. Kimmons's eyes lit up when he recalled that great feeling he had every time he was able "to see the light go on in a student's mind," and though qualified as an administrator, he preferred direct contact with his students. Kimmons remained active helping others through his volunteer activities at the local hospital, on the New London submarine base, and as an AARP Drivers Safety classroom instructor.

FURTHER READING

Kimmons, Carl. Interview with author, 2 Mar. 2007.
Knoblock, Glenn A. *Black Submariners in the United States Navy, 1940–1975* (2005).

GLENN ALLEN KNOBLOCK

Kincaid, Jamaica (25 May 1949–), novelist, travel writer, and journalist, was born Elaine Potter Richardson in St. John's, Antigua, daughter of Annie Richardson and Frederick Potter. Annie, who was born in Dominica but moved to Antigua as a young woman, appears in many of Kincaid's fictional and nonfictional writings; she is often referred to in contradictory terms as a loving yet stifling, vituperative, and hostile maternal figure, as well as a dedicated homemaker, gardener, and political activist. Kincaid's biological father was an Antiguan taxi driver who abandoned his family. When Kincaid was a young child, her mother was remarried to a cabinetmaker and carpenter, David Drew, and bore three sons. Kincaid has often referred to Mr. Drew as her father. In 1965, shortly following her sixteenth birthday, Kincaid left Antigua for the United States where she worked as an au pair in Scarsdale, New York. In an article in *Rolling Stone*, "Jamaica Kincaid's New York" (6 Oct. 1977), Kincaid describes her first employers as sympathetic and generous people who, although somewhat patronizing, gave her the freedom to explore New York City. She began to take classes at Westchester Community College in White Plains, New York, and then later at Franconia College in New Hampshire. Her interest in the visual arts prompted her to take photography classes at the New School for Social Research, but ultimately she was drawn into the publishing world when she found a job with *Art Direction* magazine.

Kincaid's first published work of fiction, "Girl," appeared in the *New Yorker* in 1977, thereafter appearing as the lead story in Kincaid's first book, *At the Bottom of the River* (1983). Some critics expressed confusion about the surreal and fragmentary style of this collection, but she was nonetheless heralded as a unique and refreshing voice in American fiction. Kincaid's connection to the *New Yorker* with contributions to the popular weekly Talk of the Town section amplified this positive view. Her reports were energetic and eclectic, as she transported her exciting cultural experiences to the magazine's more traditional pages. A collection of these pieces, *Talk Stories*, was published in 2001.

After the success of this early journalism and fiction, the *New Yorker* published her first novel, *Annie John*, as a series of short stories prior to its publication in 1985. The first-person narrative focuses on the early development of Annie, capturing her adolescent struggles as she confronts predictable mother-daughter and gender roles,

Jamaica Kincaid celebrated with champagne on November 7, 2000, after she won France's Femina Award for a foreign novel for her work "My Brother." (AP Images.)

develops a growing awareness of imperialism, and forms intricate friendships with her peers.

Kincaid's burgeoning literary success in the 1980s paralleled the growth of her family after her marriage in 1979 to the composer Allen Shawn. By the time *Annie John* was published, she had given birth to a daughter, Annie, and in 1988, a son, Harold. That same year she published *A Small Place*, a short, sardonic book that powerfully exposed the Antiguan tourist industry and its historical connection to colonialism, slavery, and globalization so vital to the island's economy. She was informally banned from Antigua following its publication.

Kincaid returned to fiction in 1990 with the publication of *Lucy*. This novel explores similar issues as her previous fiction—exploitation, colonization, and power relations—while picking up where the novel *Annie John* leaves off: a young woman now, Lucy has traded Antigua for a new life in the United States. Shortly thereafter in 1991 Kincaid began a fascinating column in the *New Yorker*, writing about topics such as gardening

and horticulture's link to imperialism, themes that would dominate her writing for decades. The rendition of each flower in its Latin and "street" name underscored her seriousness. Five years later, *My Favorite Plant* highlighted the focus of this column in a collection of articles by various friends of the author and gardeners who described their favorite plant and how it attained that status.

This new path was textually predictable, since Kincaid's fiction had always displayed an intimacy with nature. The very titles in two early texts shout nature's presence—*At the Bottom of the River* followed by *Annie, Gwen, Lilly, Pam and Tulip*. In *Annie John*, a young girl grows up among the sights and smells of luxuriant trees, flowers, herbs, fruits, and vegetables; she wears a turtleberry bandage and a poultice of ground camphor and eucalyptus leaves, rests with her best friend in the shade of a flamboyant tree, and inhales a profusion of aromatic scents. By contrast, Lucy righteously rages at "Daffodils," William Wordsworth's poem that so notoriously symbolizes British imperial education, not only for Kincaid but also for V.S. Naipaul and other contemporary Caribbean authors. Her contempt palpable, Lucy loathes Mariah's insensitive near-worship of the flowers.

In 1996 Kincaid published the novel *The Autobiography of My Mother*. Set in Dominica, it depicts the haunting story of Xuela Claudette Richardson, the daughter of a Carib mother and a half-Scottish, half-African father. Xuela's mother dies giving birth to her, and her father leaves her to be raised by his laundress. Like *Annie John* and *Lucy*, this novel places at center stage a passionate, sad, and frightened woman who survives within a community, historically oppressed by gender hierarchies, class differences, and a painful colonial legacy.

During the mid-1990s Kincaid's brother, Devon Drew, contracted AIDS and died in January of 1996. Kincaid's 1997 memoir, *My Brother*, recounts the story of Devon's life, illness, and death. She describes how she was summoned back to Antigua from Vermont with conflicting emotions: on this visit "home," she wants on one hand to forgive the suffering she attributes to her mother's narcissism and her brother's self-destructiveness, but she feels the need to distance herself from pain and the family's power to consume her life. Furthermore, she poignantly records that another brother, Dalma, lives permanently in the house's back garden because of mother-son tension. Nature and the garden in this case constitute a treasured solitude and solace, with any colonial reference being beside the point.

Kincaid's next novel, *Mr. Potter* (2002), imagines a biological father's life, from the perspective of a daughter. Since the narrator never knew her father, the text reads as a gripping series of speculations and repetitions in Kincaid's inimitable style. Once again she turns to her family tree for inspiration and material: the main character is based on her Antiguan taxi driver father who had left the family when Kincaid was very young.

Kincaid's first full-length text addressing horticulture, *My Garden* (2000), solidified the shift of interest that originated in the *New Yorker* column of 1991. An autobiography of sorts, *My Garden* charmingly documents Kincaid's initial entry into the delights of gardening from her early days in Antigua. Metaphorically she returns home, but this time with a global-based rather than a family-based anger. She's still preoccupied with Annie and Lucy's issues: personal independence, identity, solitude, beauty, and the power of passion. Sharing the soft suspense of her novels, these choric "gardening texts" inquire: how will this new enterprise turn out? In other words, what has critically changed is not the philosophical and political analysis itself but the venue. Kincaid is now able to deliver political critique through discussions of horticulture.

In 2005 two more of Kincaid's publications appeared: she co-edited the essay collection *Best American Travel Writing 2005*, and wrote another stunning "autobiographical handbook" on horticulture called *Among Flowers: A Walk in the Himalay*. The book was quite unlike her other "geographical" text, *A Small Place*. In *Among Flowers*, Kincaid details her adventures with a small group of sturdy seed merchants/gardeners as they navigate the Himalayas at staggeringly high altitudes in search of unusual tropical seeds. A potentially dangerous expedition, it enables us to see Kincaid's psychological and physical courage, a hitherto muted side to the author's character; even a twice-sprained ankle neither fazes nor deters her; numerous porters who trek the group's substantial provisions on their backs or on stretchers receive scant scrutiny. Arguably, *Among Flowers* suggests Kincaid's love of gardening and gardens has shifted into a qualitatively different realm that future writings may illuminate.

In the early twenty-first century, Jamaica Kincaid was a visiting lecturer in African and African American Studies and in English and American Literature at Harvard University.

FURTHER READING
Bloom, Harold, ed. *Jamaica Kincaid* (1998).
Bouson, J. Brooks. *Jamaica Kincaid: Writing Memory, Writing Back to the Mother* (2005).
Covi, Giovanna. *Jamaica Kincaid's Prismatic Subjects: Making Sense of Being in the World* (2004).
Edwards, Justin D. *Understanding Jamaica Kincaid* (2007).
Ferguson, Moira. *Jamaica Kincaid: Where the Land Meets the Body* (1994).
Paravisini-Gebert, Lizabeth. *Jamaica Kincaid: A Critical Companion* (1999).
Simmons, Diane. *Jamaica Kincaid* (1994).
Kincaid, Jamaica. "Jamaica's New York." *Rolling Stone* (6 October 1977).

JUSTIN D. EDWARDS
MOIRA FERGUSON

King, Ada (23 Dec. 1860?–14 Apr. 1964), wife of the eminent geologist, explorer, and writer Clarence King and litigant, was born in or around West Point, Georgia. Though little is known of her early life, she was almost certainly born a slave and as a young girl acquired the name Ada Copeland. In the mid-1880s she migrated to New York City and found work as a nursemaid. In late 1887 or 1888 Copeland met a man who introduced himself as a Pullman porter named James Todd. They were married in September 1888 by the Reverend James H. Cook, a prominent minister with the Union American Methodist Episcopal Church. Although Todd represented himself to Ada as a Marylander of African American descent, this was a false identity. He was in fact Clarence King, a socially and politically prominent white man from Newport, Rhode Island, educated at Yale, who had led the Fortieth Parallel Survey across the western United States, written a popular book called *Mountaineering in the Sierra Nevada* (1872), and served as the first director of the U.S. Geological Survey (1879–1881). His closest friends included the historian Henry Adams and the diplomat John Hay. But neither they nor his white family knew of Ada Copeland's existence until after King's death. And Ada Copeland Todd did not learn her husband's true identity until he confessed it from his deathbed in 1901.

While Clarence King traveled the world as a mining consultant, wrote for scientific and cultural journals, and entertained his friends at New York's Century Club, he lived a double life. His public life transpired in Manhattan, where as a single man he rented rooms in various residential hotels. But as James Todd, the Pullman porter, he lived with his wife in Brooklyn and later in Queens. Between 1889 and 1897 Ada Todd gave birth to five children, the first of whom died as a toddler. By 1900 she and her children were living in a comfortable home in Flushing, with several live-in servants. The following year, believing that his children would face less racial prejudice in Canada, King sent Ada and their four children to Toronto. At about the same time he headed west, hoping to find a cure for his tuberculosis. In the fall, as his death seemed imminent, he wrote to his wife, told her his true name, and suggested she change the children's name to King. He died in Phoenix on 24 December 1901.

Upon her husband's death, Ada Todd returned to New York to gain access to the funds King had promised her and the children. Almost immediately one of King's associates began providing her with a monthly stipend, and in the summer of 1902 he purchased a home in Flushing for her. But Todd sought the trust fund itself, not a small monthly stipend. Beginning in 1902 and continuing for nearly three decades, she pressed her claim to the money she believed her husband had left her. She worked with various Legal Aid Society lawyers, and her quest also brought her into contact with some of the nation's most eminent black attorneys. In 1906–1907 she worked with Everett J. Waring of Philadelphia, the first black man to argue a case before the Supreme Court. From 1909 to 1914 she was represented by J. Douglas Wetmore, an African American attorney in New York who in 1905 had successfully challenged the streetcar segregation laws in Jacksonville, Florida.

Beginning around 1910 Ada King began to use her husband's true surname, and she and her children began to refer to themselves by the family name of King. Issues of racial identity, however, remained central to their family life. While her two sons served in segregated regiments during World War I, King's two daughters sometimes declared themselves white in official records. In 1931 King finally found an attorney to take her case. In November 1933, after a prolonged pretrial discovery phase, she got her day in court. The trial pitted Ada King against the prominent associates of Clarence King's old friend James T. Gardiner, who before his death had served as the conduit for the monthly payments to Ada and her children. To establish her common-law marriage to Clarence King, Ada read his love letters out

loud in the New York courtroom. The public revelation of the marriage triggered a short-lived media frenzy, though nowhere did reporters mention that Clarence King had crafted a false racial identity for himself. In the end the presiding judge ruled that Clarence King had died broke and that the funds Ada King had received every month for thirty years came from King's close friend Hay. Hay had once worked as secretary to President Abraham Lincoln and at the time of King's death served as President Theodore Roosevelt's secretary of state. Following Hay's own death in 1905, his widow and children maintained the secret payments to Ada King to protect Clarence King's public reputation. The trial brought an end to Ada King's monthly stipends, but she received title to the house that Hay had secretly purchased for her in 1902. She continued to live there with two of her children until her death at the age of 103, one of the last living Americans to have been born into slavery.

FURTHER READING

O'Toole, Patricia. *The Five of Hearts: An Intimate Portrait of Henry Adams and His Friends, 1880–1918* (1990).

Sandweiss, Martha A. *Passing Strange: The Secret Life of Clarence King* (2008).

Wilkins, Thurman. *Clarence King: A Biography* (1988).

MARTHA A. SANDWEISS

King, Albert (25 Apr. 1923–21 Dec. 1992), blues singer and guitarist, was born Albert Nelson in Indianola, Mississippi, one of thirteen children of Will Nelson, an itinerant preacher, and Mary (Blevins) Nelson. Why and exactly when he changed his surname to King is not known, but his earliest recordings bear that name. Albert's family worked on plantations in the Delta region and sang in church. In 1931 the family moved to Osceola, Arkansas, where Albert continued to work in agriculture, eventually driving a tractor. He taught himself guitar on homemade instruments. Later with money earned from working, Albert purchased his first electric guitar for $125 from a pawnshop. He began to sing with gospel vocal groups such as the Harmony Kings Quartet. Albert also played roadhouses in the area and was heavily influenced by ROBERT NIGHTHAWK and ELMORE JAMES, both masters of slide guitar. This may account for Albert's later development of a very vocal guitar style, although he himself never used a slide.

Albert moved briefly to St. Louis, Missouri, in the late 1940s but was soon back in Osceola playing nightclubs with the In The Groove Boys. He moved north again in 1952–1953 to Gary, Indiana, where he performed as a drummer for JIMMY REED and John Brim and worked with Homesick James in local clubs. By this time he had adopted the name King and had made his first record for the Parrot label in Chicago. Piano player Johnny Jones from Elmore James's band was present on the session. The single "Bad Luck Blues" was released in 1953 and indicates a style that was somewhat primitive and not fully formed when compared with King's later work. His recordings for Chess Records from this period remained unreleased until long after his subsequent success.

He returned to Osceola in 1954 to drive a bulldozer and play frequent gigs with the In The Groove Boys. He moved back to St. Louis in 1956 and formed his own trio to play local club dates. King recorded for the Bobbin label in St. Louis from 1957 to 1962. He then recorded for the King label and enjoyed his first bona fide hit "Don't Throw Your Love on Me So Strong" in 1962. It reached number 14 on the national rhythm and blues charts. In 1965 he released four singles with the Coun-tree record label to very modest success.

There was a hot blues scene in St. Louis at this time and King competed with strong artists like IKE TURNER and Little Milton Campbell. Around this time King adopted the use of a Gibson Flying V electric guitar that was a futuristic-looking instrument. Its radical design, with a body in the shape of a sideways V, would be associated with Albert King for the rest of his career.

The year 1966 was pivotal for King. He moved to Memphis and signed with Stax Records, which specialized in soul music. OTIS REDDING, Sam and Dave, and RUFUS THOMAS were just a few of the many successful acts on Stax. Backed by Booker T. and the MG's, who had recorded the smash instrumental single "Green Onions" in 1962, and produced by the group's drummer, AL JACKSON, King had contemporary and solid support with funky rhythms. The Memphis Horns, who were the Stax house horn section, embellished and filled out King's new sound. These sessions showcased his smooth, almost crooning vocals and his powerful guitar style. This combined with a strong selection of songs such as "Oh Pretty Woman," "Crosscut Saw," "Personal Manager," and "Born under a Bad Sign"—all blues classics—served to catapult King to national success. He was a late bloomer who finally gained his well-deserved recognition.

Being left-handed, King played a right-handed guitar upside down so that the high strings were on the top. A large man at six-feet four-inches and 260 pounds, King's natural strength and the law of gravity allowed him to pull the high strings down instead of pushing them up as a right-handed player would. This allowed him to achieve almost impossible bends. These unorthodox bends and his vocal-like phrasing created what MUDDY WATERS called "deep blues."

Concert promoter Bill Graham happened to hear Albert King one night and arranged for him to perform at the legendary Fillmore auditorium in San Francisco, California, opening for Janis Joplin and JIMI HENDRIX. Albert had his biggest payday to date then, and really went over well with the mostly white audience. King had spread the rumor that he was B. B. KING's half brother and even went so far as to call his guitar "Lucy" (B. B.'s guitar was famously named "Lucille," and he would always refute Albert's claim of kinship). Whether he really believed it or was just ribbing his main competitor, Albert King made great inroads with white record buyers and blues fans. B. B. King offered an uptown style of the blues that was very polished and contained many elements of jazz. Albert's relatively gutbucket approach seemingly conveyed a more meat-and-potatoes style that rock guitarists tended to emulate.

Jimi Hendrix was already well schooled in Albert's guitar stylings by the time he became popular. In 1967 Eric Clapton mimicked complete phrases of King's in "Strange Brew," a song by the band Cream, on their *Disraeli Gears* album. Other guitarists such as OTIS RUSH and Michael Bloomfield had been quoting Albert King for years. After the song "Blues Power" from the *Live Wire/Blues Power* album was recorded live at one of his shows at the Fillmore in 1968, Albert King became perhaps the most influential electric blues guitarist of all time.

One of a handful of the most innovative and expressive blues guitarists, Albert King harnessed all of his limitations and trebled his strength. Bearing a muscular style that alternately screamed, spoke, and cried, King elicited sounds from his solid-state guitar amplifier that left many a guitarist slack-jawed. That his playing was sparse, simple, and repetitive was easy to understand. He would use under a dozen phrases. It was the way he would drop these phrases in and out of his solos, his mighty thumb wielding tone like Thor's hammer, his subtle variations of pitch, and the squeezing and bending of notes dripping with vibrato that was so difficult for others to duplicate.

King worked tirelessly during the Stax years, appearing on Dick Clark's *American Bandstand* and the *Merv Griffin* television show. He played the best venues across the country including Carnegie Hall and the Newport Jazz Festival. He was featured in a Miller beer commercial and, along with the J. Geils Band and the Allman Brothers Band, was selected to play the final shows at the Fillmore East auditorium in 1971. Two years prior, Albert King was the first blues guitarist to play with a symphony orchestra.

Stax Records went out of business in the 1970s, and King recorded several records for smaller labels like Tomato and Fantasy. Some had disco-style backing and some had more lush arrangements with strings. These records understated his signature guitar tone and were not considered his strongest recordings. His live performances continued to be strong, raw, and satisfying for his adoring fans.

King's career enjoyed a resurgence in the 1980s when he recorded his *I'm in a Phone Booth Baby* album whose title track was cowritten by Robert Cray. Blues rocker Gary Moore covered his classic "Oh Pretty Woman." King's ardent disciple, Stevie Ray Vaughan, who called him "Daddy" and became a rock superstar, probably came closest to imitating Albert's guitar style.

King spoke of being tired and ripped off later in his life and lost interest in recording. He was inducted into the Blues Hall of Fame in 1983. He still played live before enthusiastic audiences and was poised for a European tour with B. B. King and Bobby "Blue" Bland when he died of a heart attack in Memphis. He had performed just two days earlier. Thousands of electric guitarists will forever echo the influence of Albert King but few if any will ever match his simplicity, power, and intensity.

FURTHER READING

Brown, O. "No Kicks Left in Blues for Tired Old Albert," *Courier-Mail* (1990).

Cohn, Lawrence, ed. *Nothing but the Blues* (1993).

Harris, Sheldon. *Blues Who's Who* (1979, 1981).

Palmer, Robert. *Deep Blues* (1981).

Rowe, Mike. *Chicago Blues* (1973, 1984).

Russell, Tony. *The Blues, From Robert Johnson to Robert Cray* (1997).

Sutton, Bob. "Albert King Reshaped Urban Blues," *Toronto Star* (1993).

Obituary: *Blues Notes*, Cascade Blues Association (1992).

DISCOGRAPHY

Blues Records 1943–1970: A Selective Discography (1987).

Born under a Bad Sign (Stax Records 723, 1966).

Live Wire/ Blues Power (Stax Records 2003, 1968).

Years Gone By (Stax Records 2010).

MARK STEVEN MAULUCCI

King, B. B. (16 Sept. 1925–), blues singer and guitarist, was born Riley B. King near Itta Bena, Mississippi, to Albert King and Nora Ella Pully, sharecroppers who worked farms near Indianola. Riley was named after a white planter, O'Reilly, who helped his family when his mother was in labor. The "O" was dropped, his father said, "'cause you don't look Irish" (King, 7). Later, King wanted to be called the Beale Street Blues Boy, but the world came to know him simply as B. B. King.

In 1930 Nora left Albert and the Delta region of Mississippi, taking her five-year-old son to live near Kilmichael in the hill country. There she introduced him to the soulful spirituals of the Elkhorn Baptist Church and the moving testimonials of the Church of God in Christ, a sanctified congregation where his uncle played the guitar as he preached. His uncle Archie Fair taught his nephew to play a few chords, but it was during visits to his aunt Mima that King first heard the sounds of his greatest musical influences, BLIND LEMON JEFFERSON and LONNIE JOHNSON, wailing from a windup Victrola. He was only ten when his mother died, and he lived alone in their cabin until the plantation owner for whom he worked, Mr. Flake Cartledge, lent him fifteen dollars to buy a guitar and instruction manual from the Sears, Roebuck catalog. From then on, King was never really alone again; music became his family and his life. King lived briefly with his father's new family in Lexington, but he soon ran away to Indianola, where he worked in the fields and sang with a group called the Famous St. John Gospel Singers. He was torn between two related musical traditions that had very different career paths. On the one hand, he dreamed his group could emulate the success of the gospel-singing Dixie Hummingbirds, and he thought of becoming a minister, despite the stuttering problem he then had. On the other hand, he found that he could make more money on weekends playing the blues for pedestrians than he made all week driving a tractor. When King heard the electric blues guitar of T-BONE WALKER, his fate was sealed. He dropped out of school in the tenth grade—one of his biggest regrets—and studied the styles of the bluesmen (and blueswomen, such as BESSIE SMITH and MA RAINEY) who performed at local juke joints.

B.B. King in 1970, with his guitar "Lucille." (AP Images.)

In 1944 King married Martha Denton shortly before being drafted into the army during World War II. However, after completing basic training, he was designated as a vital farmworker and released from service. On the train back to the plantation, he and other African Americans were forced to sit behind white German prisoners of war. Of white society at that time he wrote, "You can look at enemy soldiers who were ready to cut your throat, but you can't look at the black American soldiers willing to die for you.... We were seen as beasts of burden, dumb animals, a level below the Germans" (King, 91).

In May 1946 Riley fled to Memphis, Tennessee, after accidentally damaging the tractor he drove. There he found his cousin, the guitarist BUKKA WHITE, who introduced him to the harsh realities of life as a bluesman. After ten months of drudgery, he was dissuaded and went back to his wife and the plantation. Nevertheless, he returned to Memphis in 1948, determined to make it as a bluesman at any cost. His big break came later that year when SONNY BOY WILLIAMSON allowed him to sing on his radio program on KWEM. The enthusiastic response led to offers for local performances, and soon King found himself promoting a tonic called Pepticon; his first jingle was "Pepticon sure is good ... and you can get it anywhere in your neighborhood."

This led to his own radio show on WDIA, called the *Sepia Swing Club*. The name he chose as a disc jockey for this program, B. B. King, stayed with him for the rest of his career.

King recorded his first song, "Take a Swing with Me," at WDIA for Bullet Records in 1949. The company went bankrupt soon after releasing it, and King signed a contract with Modern Records, recording under their Crown and RPM labels for the next decade. He was usually paid about one hundred dollars per song and received no royalties or songwriting credits for these early productions. In 1951 he recorded a version of LOWELL FULSON's "Three O'Clock Blues" that spent three months at the top of *Billboard*'s rhythm and blues chart. With this success, King engaged the promoters Robert Henry and then Maurice Merrit, who arranged bookings on the "chitlin circuit," an informal network of clubs and theaters that hired black performers. By 1952 King was spending so much time on the road that his marriage, which had suffered from distance and infidelity, ended in divorce. In 1958 he married Sue Carol Hall, though in 1966 that marriage also ended in divorce. King acknowledges having fifteen children, none with either of his wives.

King's most enduring and perhaps most passionate relationship was with Lucille, the name he gave to his trademark guitars. He once had to rescue his guitar from a nightclub that had been accidentally set ablaze by two men fighting over a woman named Lucille. King decided that from then on every guitar he owned would be his Lucille. She was personified in song and became the medium through which he could express a range of emotion, from deep pathos to liberating triumph. Drawing on the traditional twelve-bar blues style in which the singer and his guitar converse in a call-and-response counterpoint, King and Lucille became a duet recognized and loved by fans.

King worked throughout his career to overcome the perception of many scholars, critics, and casual listeners that the blues is a simple, unsophisticated art form—one that was even embarrassing to blacks of a certain age and class. He recalled appearing on a bill with some great jazz musicians, and, when his turn to perform came, the announcer told the audience, "Okay, folks, time to pull out your chitlins and collard greens, your pig feet and your watermelons, 'cause here's B. B. King." King's response to this common attitude is characteristically witty: "Being a blues singer is like being black twice" (King, 216–217).

Rock and roll came and went without King, who did not cross over, as did BO DIDDLEY and CHUCK BERRY. Soul music became popular with the Motown sound, but though he often tried new things, King remained a true bluesman. He produced dozens of moderately selling songs like "Sweet Sixteen," and he averaged more than three hundred engagements a year; thus, despite his gambling and problems with the IRS, he was, by the late 1960s, successful. Yet rather than winding down, King's career was about to take off. In 1961 he signed with ABC Paramount. Following his second divorce in 1966, King recorded "Paying the Cost to Be the Boss" and a cathartic rendition of "The Thrill Is Gone" that connected with his widest audience ever. The song reached fifteen on the pop charts and won him the first of thirteen Grammy awards between 1970 and 2002.

His new manager, Sidney Seidenberg, began to book King at what seemed like unlikely venues, but to King's surprise, young white audiences loved him; so did fans in Europe, Asia, and Africa. He welcomed the fame but admitted that he was "disappointed that my people don't appreciate me like the whites" (*Current Biography*, 1970). He became a frequent guest on the *Tonight Show*; had cameos on *Sanford and Son, The Cosby Show, Sesame Street*, and *General Hospital*; and appeared in numerous commercials. He was inducted into the Blues Foundation Hall of Fame in 1984 and into the Rock and Roll Hall of Fame in 1987. King received the Presidential Medal of Freedom in 2006. In April 2005 it was announced that the B. B. King Museum and Delta Interpretive Center would be established in Indianola, Mississippi. Although he was diagnosed with diabetes in 1990, King did not cut back on his full calendar of club dates. When asked at the age of seventy-seven why he continued to work so hard, he said, "If I don't keep doing it, keep going, they'll forget" (Weinraub, 12 Mar.). King exemplifies the best of a long blues tradition that has many admirers but few authentic disciples.

FURTHER READING

King, B. B. *Blues All around Me: The Autobiography of B.-B. King* (1996).

Current Biography Yearbook (1970).

Sawyer, Charles. *The Arrival of B. B. King* (1980).

Weinraub, Bernard. "Spinning Blues into Gold, the Rough Way," *New York Times*, 12 Mar. 2003.

SHOLOMO B. LEVY

King, Ben E. (28 Sept. 1938–), singer, was born Benjamin Earl Nelson in Henderson, North Carolina. Little is known about his early upbringing, including who his parents were. Influenced by gospel and country music, he sang in the church choir, where he first began developing his smooth, gospel-flavored vocal technique. When he was nine years old, in 1947, his family moved to Harlem, where his father opened a restaurant. He pursued his vocal aspirations, singing with a few small gospel groups, and while at James Fenimore Cooper Junior High, he performed with a street-corner doo-wop group called the Four B's. The name stood for the members of the group, Ben Nelson, Billy Davis, Bobby Davis, and Billy Spigner. The Four B's won second place in an Apollo Theater talent contest.

In high school King tried out for the Moonglows, an innovative R&B vocal group, but inexperience doomed his audition. Working at his father's restaurant as a singing waiter led to an invitation in 1955 to sing baritone with the Five Crowns, a regionally popular group formed several years earlier. In 1958 the group performed at the Apollo Theater on the same bill with the Drifters. The Drifters, a nationally acclaimed recording act, had undergone a radical transformation. Particularly devastating was the loss of its lead singer, Clyde McPhatter. Disenchanted with the Drifters in their present state, the band's manager, George Treadwell, fired all of the members. He then transferred the group name, which he owned, to the Five Crowns. The "new" Drifters were born.

Initially, the new group performed before hostile fans who longed for old members. But then the Drifters recorded "There Goes My Baby," written by Nelson, which would become a huge hit on Atlantic Records. By this time Nelson had assumed the pseudonym of Ben E. King (he now shared the surname of his uncle, Jimmy King). "There Goes My Baby" was the first rock 'n' roll song to be fully orchestrated with strings. Brazilian percussive rhythms and vocal passion completed the complex arrangement, creating one of the first true soul records, hitting number two on the pop chart and number one on the R&B chart in 1959, the group's highest-selling record up to that time. Through 1960 King sang lead on the Drifters' classics "Dance With Me," "This Magic Moment," "Save the Last Dance for Me," and "I Count the Tears."

King quit the Drifters in 1961 because of a salary dispute with Treadwell, and started a solo

Ben E. King, American soul singer performs at the Palladium in London, England, on 3 March 1987. (AP Images.)

career, recording with Atlantic's subsidiary label, Atco. He recorded "Spanish Harlem," keeping the Latin percussive facets the Drifters had displayed and reaching the Top Ten. This was followed by "Stand By Me," an even bigger hit, and "Amor" in 1961. Increasingly seeking a larger share of the white record-buying pop market like other African American entertainers crossing over from gospel and R&B, King recorded "Don't Play That Song" in 1962, and "I (Who Have Nothing)" and "I Could Have Danced All Night," both in 1963. He also recorded crossover songs, "Moon River," "What A Difference A Day Made," "Because Of You," and "What Now My Love." Singing his way through the 1960s, this top soul and crossover pop singer released several noteworthy compositions during a decade restless with civil rights changes, the Vietnam War, and the so-called British Invasion. He recorded "It's All Over" in 1964, "Seven Letters" and "The Record (Baby I Love You)," both in 1965, and "What Is Soul" in 1967. In 1969, at age thirty-six, King began to anticipate that the company would drop him because of record-sales trends favoring younger artists; he soon asked to be released from

his Atco contract. Atco granted his wish, and King sought to revive his commercial fortunes.

Early efforts did not materialize. A single and an album on the Maxwell label in 1970, followed by three singles and another album on the Mandala label, did not generate a great deal of attention. Declining interest in his music forced King to join acts on the oldies circuit until Atlantic Records cofounder and president Ahmet Ertegun rescued him from a Miami lounge in 1975. Ertegun asked him to re-sign with Atlantic, which had merged with Warner Brothers and Elektra in 1971. In 1975 King's disco-styled release, "Supernatural Thing, Part I," brought him back from obscurity. The record soared to the top of the R&B charts and reached the pop Top Five, leading to his 1977 collaboration with the Average White Band. The group scored two R&B chart entries. The ensuing albums, *Benny And Us* (1977), *Music Trance* (1980), and *Street Tough* (1981), were less successful. King left Atlantic in 1981 and in 1982 went on tour with a revived version of the Drifters.

At age fifty-five, King's career revived when in 1986 Rob Reiner featured "Stand By Me" in his motion picture of the same title. The song was rereleased as a single and climbed into the Top Ten, going to number one in the United Kingdom. King returned to the recording studio, hoping to exploit the renewed commercial viability of his music. He continued to release new music through the 1990s. In 1991 King emerged in the jazz arena on *Shades of Blue*, performing with a big band featuring Milt Jackson and David "Fathead" Newman as guests. He recorded live at the Blue Note, New York's most prominent jazz club, made a guest appearance on Broadway in *Smokey Joe's Café*, sang at President Bill Clinton's inauguration and performed with the National Symphony's 4 July 1996 PBS Special.

Ben E. King, one of the original inductees of the Rock and Roll Hall of Fame in Cleveland, Ohio, accepted the inductions of his songs "Stand By Me" in 1998 and "Spanish Harlem" in 2002, both on the Atco label. The Hall of Fame cited both songs as two songs that helped shape rock and roll. They also were voted songs of the century by the Recording Industry Association of America. The founder and head of the Ben E. King Stand By Me Foundation, King spent much of his time in the new millennium generating money for musical scholarships, educational programs, and other programs for young people in need.

FURTHER READING

George, Nelson. *The Death of Rhythm & Blues* (1988).
George, Nelson. *Where Did Our Love Go?* (1985).
Guralnick, Peter. *Dream Boogie: Triumph of Sam Cooke* (2005).
Miller, James. *Flowers in the Dust: The Rise of Rock and Roll* (1999).
Otis, Johnny. *Upside Your Head! Rhythm and Blues on Central Avenue* (1993).
Southern, Eileen. *The Music of Black Americans* (1983).

SUNNY NASH

King, Bernice (28 Mar. 1963–), minister and youngest daughter of the slain civil rights leader MARTIN LUTHER KING JR., was born Bernice Albertine King in Atlanta, Georgia. The youngest daughter of Martin Luther King Jr. and CORETTA SCOTT KING, she was named after both her maternal and paternal grandmothers, Alberta Williams King and Bernice McMurray. One of the most memorable images of young King was a Pulitzer Prize-winning photograph of her as a sad girl leaning on her mother during her father's funeral taken by MONETA SLEET JR. and published in *Ebony* magazine. In the shadow of her father's murder, their mother covered King

and her siblings protectively as she promoted her husband's legacy. Every attempt was made to provide a normal upbringing for her and the other three King children. The strength of her family history propelled her desire to chart her professional course in life so that she, in turn, could have an influence on others. In the sixth grade, she decided she wanted to be the first black woman on the U.S. Supreme Court, so King planned to study law.

Having lost her father at such a young age, her memories of him were scant and she didn't feel a strong connection to him. At the age of sixteen, however, she was participating in a youth Bible camp where the 1970 documentary *Montgomery to Memphis*, which detailed the origins of the Civil Rights Movement and Dr. King's role in it, was shown. The brutality and reality of the injustices that African Americans endured to have their voices heard suddenly became real to her and brought her father and his principles closer. The documentary angered King and led her to seek greater understanding of the events that led to her father's death. King had never experienced segregation and violence the way it was depicted on the screen, and it opened up her father's philosophies and the greater struggle for civil and human rights in a new way. When she was introduced to the harsh reality of what life was like for blacks in the South and how violently her father's life was taken from him, she entered a period of deep depression. When she was seventeen, King felt she was called to the ministry but instead entered Spelman College in Atlanta to pursue a degree in psychology. In 1980 she discovered an oratorical gift, not unlike her father's, when she represented her mother at the United Nations in 1980 and spoke out against the system of apartheid that existed in South Africa. She accepted her call to the ministry in 1988 and preached her first sermon at Ebenezer Baptist Church, where her father and grandfather before him were pastors. After receiving her bachelor's degree, King continued her education at Emory University, where she completed her J.D. and MDiv degrees in June 1990, in which year she was ordained into the ministry.

Many of her personal and professional endeavors were influenced by the legacy of her parents and grandparents. Aside from gaining respect and renown as a public speaker, King decided to speak out for important causes without regard for the way she was perceived. Like her father, she placed more emphasis on the goals of fighting injustice than her personal achievement and success. She and her

Bernice King youngest child of Coretta Scott King and the late Dr. Martin Luther King, Jr., joins in singing hymns during her ordination service at Ebenezer Baptist Church in Atlanta, Ga., on May 14, 1990. (AP Images.)

siblings were arrested in 1986 for protesting South African apartheid. She began advocating nonviolent change and world peace and spoke out against the 1991 Persian Gulf War. During that conflict, in January 1992, at the celebration of Martin Luther King Day at the Martin Luther King Jr. Center for Nonviolence and Social Change, she chided President George H.W. Bush and the assembled crowd for celebrating while the ugliness of racism persisted.

In 1994, King joined the ministry at Greater Rising Star Baptist Church in Atlanta, drawn to the congregation by its various outreach programs. She started many programs, including a jail ministry and programs to address teen pregnancy. She maintained her affiliation with her family's church, Ebenezer, while working with Greater Rising Star. She published a book of speeches in 1996, *Hard Questions, Heart Answers: Sermons and Speeches*. In addition to her other degrees, she received an honorary doctor of divinity from Wesley College.

King and her siblings led a campaign to revisit the details of the murder of their father, including supporting a new trial for his convicted killer, James Earl Ray. They felt that the evidence against Ray, which stood for more than thirty years, could have been flawed and that someone in addition to Ray could have been responsible for the civil rights leader's death. Although Ray later succumbed to disease in prison while waiting consideration for their petitions, King and her siblings forgave him for any culpability he may have had in the crime.

When her mother became severely ill, King accompanied her to her cancer and other medical treatments. She and her siblings presided over their mother's nationally televised funeral, and King herself gave the stirring eulogy. She went on to become associate minister at New Birth Missionary Baptist Church under the leadership of Bishop Eddie Long. She continued her outreach ministries to women and prisoners and spoke in both secular and religious circles about family and personal responsibility. She was a member of the board of directors of the Martin Luther King Jr. Center for Nonviolence and Social Change, and was recognized by *Ebony* as one of the fifty leaders of tomorrow.

FURTHER READING

King, Bernice A. *Hard Questions, Heart Answers: Sermons and Speeches* (1996).

Henderson, Ashyia N. "Bernice King," *Contemporary Black Biography*, vol. 4 (1993).

Smith, Jessie Carney. "Bernice A. King," *Notable Black American Women*, book 3 (2002).

SIBYL COLLINS WILSON

King, Boston (1760?–1802), slave, Loyalist during the American Revolution, carpenter, Methodist preacher, and memoirist, was born on a plantation near Charleston, South Carolina, the son of a literate African slave who worked as a driver and a mill cutter and an enslaved mother who made clothes and tended the sick, using herbal knowledge she gained from American Indians. At the age of six Boston King began waiting on his master, Richard Waring, in the plantation house. From age nine to sixteen, he was assigned to tend the cattle and horses, and he traveled with his master's racehorses to many places in America.

At sixteen King was apprenticed to a master carpenter. Two years later he was placed in charge of the master's tools; on two occasions when valuable items were stolen, the master beat and tortured King so severely that he was unable to work for weeks. After the second incident, King's owner threatened to take him away from the carpenter if the abuse was repeated. Over the next two years, King received better treatment and was able to acquire significant knowledge of carpentry. One day during the Revolutionary War, shortly after the British occupied Charleston, King obtained leave to visit his parents, who lived twelve miles away. When a servant absconded with the horse that King had borrowed for the journey, King decided to escape from what would have undoubtedly been cruel punishment by seeking refuge with the British.

Since 1775 the British had promised to free all able-bodied indentured servants and blacks who joined the Loyalist forces. In 1779 Sir Henry Clinton, the British commander in chief, attempted to further deplete the rebel army's resources by issuing the Philipsburg Proclamation, which promised freedom of employment to any slave who deserted from a rebel master and worked within British lines. King felt well received by the British, but after a short taste of freedom he contracted smallpox. Attempting to control the epidemic, the British segregated infected black people from the rest of the camp and left them to languish without food or drink, sometimes for a day at a time. A kindly New York volunteer came to King's rescue and helped nurse him back to health, a favor that King returned a few weeks later when this man was wounded in battle. King nursed him for six weeks until he recovered. King stayed with the British in areas surrounding Charleston for several months, performing a range of personal and military services.

In December 1782 the British left Charleston, taking with them 5,327 African Americans, who relocated to various sites within the British Empire. King sailed to New York, the British military headquarters. He wanted to work as a carpenter, but lack of tools forced him to accept employment in domestic service, where "the wages were so low that I was not able to keep myself in clothes, so that I was under the necessity of leaving my master and going to another. I stayed with him four months, but he never paid me" (King, 355). In these desperate economic straits King met and married a woman named Violet who had been enslaved in Wilmington, North Carolina. A year later he went to work on a pilot boat that was captured by an American whaler; he was transported to New Brunswick, New Jersey, and once again enslaved. Although he was well fed and pleased to find that many local slaves were allowed to go to school at night, he yearned for liberty and grabbed the first chance to escape across the river and find his way back to New York.

Reunited with Violet, King remained in New York until the end of the war. Although he was glad to see the horrors of war come to an end, King and the other former slaves were terrified that they would be sent back to their old masters, as the Americans demanded. However, the British commander in chief, Sir Guy Carleton, insisted that those blacks who had been with the British before the provisional treaty was signed by both sides in Paris on 30 November 1782 would remain free, while those who had sought refuge with the British after that date were to be returned to their American masters. The British compiled a "Book of Negroes," listing the black people whom they were taking with them out of New York. Boston King, a "Stout fellow" aged twenty-three, and Violet King, a "Stout wench" aged thirty-five, "were among the 409 passengers who sailed on 31 July 1783 from New York to Shelburne" in Nova Scotia (King, 367). They settled in a black community called Birchtown, which was built on one side of the Port Roseway Harbour while Shelburne, a white Loyalist town, was built on the opposite side. The British promised land and provisions to the Loyalist settlers, but while "the Whites received farm lands ... averaging 74 acres by November

1786, of the 649 Black men at Birchtown only 184 received farms averaging 34 acres by the year 1788" (Blakeley, 277). Nonetheless, as a skilled carpenter at a time when every family needed to build a house, King appears to have found work plentiful for a time.

During the cold Canadian winter, a religious revival spread throughout Birchtown. Violet King experienced an "awakening" when listening to the preaching of Moses Wilkinson, a blind and lame former slave from Virginia. Boston King soon followed her lead. Taught by Methodist missionaries, such as Freeborn Garretson of Baltimore, "who had manumitted his own slaves immediately upon his conversion in 1775" (Carretta, 368), King in 1785 began to preach to both black and white people. Meanwhile, the black people in Birchtown were in desperate straits. The little land that they were given was so barren that they were forced to work for white farmers, when they could find work at all. A terrible famine set in, and the Kings scrambled to survive. In 1791 King moved to Preston, near Halifax, where he continued preaching and supported himself in domestic service.

Meanwhile, Lieutenant John Clarkson, the brother of the prominent British abolitionist Thomas Clarkson, arrived in Halifax as the agent for the Sierra Leone Company, which intended to resettle former slaves in Africa and to promote trade with Africa. The company promised free passage, thirty acres of land for every married man, and sufficient provisions to sustain the settlers until they were established in Sierra Leone. Although King's preaching in Preston was proceeding to his "great satisfaction, and the Society increased both in number and love" (King, 363), he had long desired to preach to Africans. On 15 January 1792 Boston and Violet King joined 1,188 other blacks who set sail from Halifax in a fleet of fifteen ships. The journey was troubled by terrible storms and disease, and when they arrived in Sierra Leone they found that once again the British had broken their promises. An outbreak of malaria killed people so fast that it was hard to bury them. Violet King died from malaria in April 1792. Boston King grew ill but recovered and found work as a carpenter and preacher.

On 3 August 1793 Governor Richard Dawes appointed King a missionary and schoolteacher at sixty pounds a year and promised to send him to England to obtain the education that he greatly desired (Blakeley, 286). After remarrying, King embarked for England in March 1794 and spent two years at the Kingswood School, a Methodist secondary school near Bristol, where he wrote his memoirs in 1796. A few months later he returned to Sierra Leone, where he worked as a teacher and preacher until his death.

FURTHER READING

King, Boston. "Memoirs of the Life of Boston King, a Black Preacher. Written by Himself, during His Residence at Kingswood School," *Arminian [or Methodist] Magazine* 21 (Mar., Apr., May, and June 1798). Reprinted in *Unchained Voices: An Anthology of Black Authors in the English-speaking World of the Eighteenth Century,* ed. Vincent Carretta (1996).

Blakeley, Phyllis R. "Boston King: A Black Loyalist," in *Eleven Exiles: Accounts of Loyalists of the American Revolution,* eds. Phyllis R. Blakeley and John N. Grant (1982).

KARI J. WINTER

King, Coretta Scott (27 Apr. 1927–30 Jan. 2006), civil rights leader, was born in Heiberger, near Marion, Alabama, the second of three children of Obadiah Scott and Bernice McMurry, who farmed their own land. Although Coretta and her siblings worked in the garden and fields, hoeing and picking cotton, the Scotts were relatively well off. Her father was the first African American in the community to own a truck, which he used to transport pulpwood, and he also purchased his own sawmill, which was mysteriously burned to the ground a few days later. The family blamed the fire on whites jealous of their success.

Wanting a better life for their children, the Scotts sent all three to college. The eldest, Edythe, graduated at the top of her class at Marion's Lincoln High School in 1943 and earned a scholarship to Antioch College in Yellow Springs, Ohio; her brother, Obie, attended Central State University in nearby Wilberforce, Ohio. Coretta, who also graduated at the top of her high school class in 1945, won a scholarship to study elementary education and music at Antioch. She matriculated in 1945 and was one of only three African Americans in her class; the future jurist A. LEON HIGGINBOTHAM was one of the others. Scott was active in extracurricular activities, especially in projects designed to improve race relations. She joined the college chapter of the NAACP and performed onstage at Antioch with PAUL ROBESON, the actor, singer, and activist, who encouraged her to pursue a musical career.

Although Antioch enjoyed a liberal reputation, Scott found that it was not immune to racial discrimination. When she applied to practice as a student teacher, the music department required that she do

Coretta Scott King widow of the Rev. Dr. Martin Luther King Jr., during an interview at the Martin Luther King Jr. Center for Social Change in Atlanta, Ga., in January 1975. (AP Images.)

Moving to Boston changed the course of Coretta Scott's life in more ways than one, for in 1952 a friend there introduced her to MARTIN LUTHER KING JR., an ordained Baptist minister who was attending Boston University's School of Theology. Although she has said that she never wanted to be the wife of a pastor, Scott warmed to the theology student's sincere passion for social justice and also fell for his distinctive line of flattery. She later recalled that King "was a typical man. Smoothness. Jive. Some of it I had never heard of in my life. It was what I call intellectual jive" (Garrow, 45). King, for his part, admired Scott for standing up to his father, who wanted him to marry into one of Atlanta's leading black families. Scott bluntly told the imposing Daddy King that she, too, was from one of the finest families. Soon thereafter MARTIN LUTHER KING SR. accepted his son's choice and performed the couple's wedding ceremony in June 1953. Coretta Scott King asserted her independence, however, by excluding a promise to obey her husband in her wedding vows. In 1954, the year Coretta Scott King graduated from the New England Conservatory of Music, her husband accepted the pastorate of Dexter Avenue Baptist Church in Montgomery, Alabama.

The young couple could not have known that the direction of their lives again would be dramatically altered the following year. On 1 December 1955, ROSA PARKS, a local NAACP official, was arrested for refusing to give up her seat on a city bus in Montgomery. Her arrest changed the course of southern history, for it united and mobilized Montgomery's black community under Martin Luther King's leadership in a mass boycott of the city's segregated bus system. The subsequent national and international press coverage made the young minister and his wife household names, but the limelight brought with it new dangers. During the bus boycott, angry whites made abusive and life-threatening telephone calls at all hours and shot at and bombed the King family home. In 1958 a mentally disturbed black woman attempted to assassinate Martin Luther King by stabbing him in a New York department store.

Like any other couple's, the Kings' married life was not untroubled. Money was a constant source of friction, since Martin paid little heed to financial matters and left his wife to deal with the day-to-day problems of looking after four children. Rumors of her husband's infidelities were also widespread during his lifetime, often encouraged by FBI mischief making. King has always claimed, however,

so at an all-black school system near the campus. The school district in which all other Antioch students did their practice work had no black teachers, and the college administration did not wish to upset the racial status quo in conservative southern Ohio by sending an African American student to teach there. Coretta Scott protested this Jim Crow policy to the office of the college president, but the president refused to support her request. She subsequently agreed to do her internship at the demonstration school on campus.

Scott studied piano and the violin, but focused on singing. She gave her first solo concert in 1948 and graduated with a B.A. from Antioch in Music Education three years later, in 1951. That year she enrolled at the New England Conservatory of Music in Boston, Massachusetts, on a full-tuition fellowship. With assistance from the Urban League, she found part-time work as a clerical assistant and also received out-of-state aid from Alabama, since her home state provided no opportunities for graduate study in music.

that she and Martin "never had one single serious discussion about either of us being involved with another person" (Garrow, 374).

Under such trying circumstances Coretta King developed an iron will and a steely resolve to support her husband's commitment to civil rights. She also supported him by handling mail, telephone calls, and other administrative work, sometimes speaking at engagements that he was unable to attend and participating in musical programs to raise funds for the Southern Christian Leadership Conference (SCLC). King's primary focus in the early years of the civil rights movement, however, was her family. She gave birth to four children: Yolande in 1955, Martin III in 1957, Dexter in 1961, and Bernice in 1963. There were occasions, however, when she resented her husband's full immersion in the civil rights movement. In 1963 she told a reporter that she regretted being absent from many of the era's most important civil rights demonstrations. "I'm usually at home," she remarked, "because my husband says, 'You have to take care of the children'" (Garrow, 308). Other women in the civil rights movement, notably ELLA BAKER, often remarked on the traditionalist—indeed, sexist—view of gender roles held by Martin Luther King and other prominent clergymen. Coretta King was less content to take a back seat when it came to matters of war and peace, as she had been a committed pacifist since her time at Antioch, where visiting speakers like BAYARD RUSTIN had encouraged her nonviolent philosophy. King strongly influenced her husband's evolving opposition to the Vietnam War. In 1961 she attended a disarmament conference in Geneva, Switzerland, as a member of the group Women Strike for Peace. While her husband refrained from publicly challenging the Kennedy and Johnson administrations' foreign policy in the early 1960s, Coretta King attended several peace rallies and picketed the White House in 1965.

Tragically, Coretta Scott King would take center stage in the civil rights movement only after her husband's assassination in Memphis, Tennessee, on 4 April 1968. Four days later she led a memorial march in Memphis, estimated at fifty thousand people. The international media spotlight continued to focus on the slain civil rights leader's family during King's funeral in Atlanta, which was attended by thousands of mourners and watched by millions on television. Coretta Scott King supported several SCLC projects in the wake of her husband's death. In the summer of 1968 she was one of the speakers at the Poor People's Campaign in Washington, D.C., and received national media attention when she, along with others in SCLC, led a protest march by striking hospital workers in Charleston, South Carolina, in 1969.

In the 1970s Coretta King established and chaired the Martin Luther King Jr. Memorial Center for Nonviolent Social Change in Atlanta. This project took her around the world in search of financial support, lecturing to audiences numbering in the hundreds. The King Center, which was dedicated on Auburn Avenue in Atlanta in 1981, contains more than 1 million documents related to the King family's civil rights activities. Several thousand scholars have used its library resources since it was established, but in the 1990s Coretta King and her family came under fire for the way she tightly controlled her husband's legacy, including his image and papers. She was also involved in a feud with the National Park Service over their handling of the King property on Auburn Avenue.

Coretta King's most enduring contribution to American culture has been as chair of the Martin L. King Jr. Federal Holiday Commission. In the late 1970s the King Center collected six million signatures on a petition urging the creation of a Martin Luther King Jr. memorial holiday, and in November 1983 President Ronald Reagan signed the bill designating the national holiday. The center also sponsors an annual celebratory memorial program on his birth date. King's involvement in the civil rights cause continued in the 1980s and 1990s. She was prominent in demonstrations against South Africa's apartheid system and has appeared at anniversary celebrations of her husband's most memorable speech at the 1963 March on Washington. In 1997 she supported a move granting a new trial for her husband's convicted assassin, James Earl Ray, but Ray died before a new trial was scheduled. Her most recent cause was a project to build a memorial for her husband on the National Mall in Washington, D.C. The Alpha Phi Alpha Fraternity, of which he was a member, was also associated with this project.

After suffering a stroke and mild heart attack in August 2005, Coretta Scott King died on 30 January 2006 while being treated at the Hospital Santa Monica in Mexico City. Her funeral service was attended by 115,000 people, including President George W. Bush and the former presidents Bill Clinton and George H. W. Bush. Other attendees included famous civil rights activists and writers, celebrities, and an assortment of politicians. The service took on a political edge (to George Bush and the first lady's obvious discomfort) with pointed reminders of King's advocacy of nonviolence and occasional references to the war in Iraq. The six-hour service was completed with a eulogy delivered by her daughter, Bernice (who was five when Martin Luther King Jr. was assassinated in 1968), who said: "Thank you, mother, for your incredible example of Christ-like love and obedience. We're going to miss you." Throughout her lifetime, Coretta Scott King supported many progressive measures and received many awards and numerous honorary degrees. Perhaps the most prestigious and enduring was not given to her but rather is awarded in her name. The American Library Association's Coretta Scott King Award, established in the early 1970s, is given to highly distinguished African American writers and illustrators of children's literature.

FURTHER READING

King, Coretta Scott. *My Life with Martin Luther King, Jr.* (1969, rev. 1993).

Baldwin, Lewis V. *There Is a Balm in Gilead: The Cultural Roots of Martin Luther King, Jr.* (1991).

Branch, Taylor. *Parting the Waters: America in the King Years, 1954–1963* (1988).

Garrow, David. *Bearing the Cross: Martin Luther King, Jr., and the Southern Christian Leadership Conference* (1988).

Vivian, Octavia. *Coretta: The Story of Mrs. Martin Luther King, Jr.* (1970).

BARBARA WOODS

King, Don (6 Dec. 1932–), boxing promoter, was born Donald King in Cleveland, Ohio, the fifth of seven children of Clarence King, a steelworker, and Hattie King. When Donald was nine years old, his father was killed in an explosion at the steel plant where he worked. His mother baked pies and roasted peanuts to supplement the family's meager income. Donald and his siblings assisted their mother by, among other things, inserting slips of paper with "lucky numbers" into each bag of peanuts like fortune cookies. Thus began his introduction as a minor player in the numbers racket, which operated in many impoverished neighborhoods as a quasi-legitimate part of the underground black economy. After class at Lafayette Elementary School, Donald also delivered live poultry to be slaughtered at Hymie's Chicken Shack. As a student-athlete at John Adams High School, Donald, standing

six-feet-three-inches, had a brief and unimpressive career as an amateur boxer. He had four matches as a flyweight; he won the first two by decision, lost the third by decision, and after being knocked out in his fourth fight decided never to enter the ring as a pugilist again. It is reported that he enjoyed verbal dueling so much that he dreamed of becoming a trial lawyer where he could match wits with opposing counsel in a courtroom instead of a trading blows in a boxing ring. According to some press accounts, he spent a few months at Kent State University and at Case Western Reserve University. In either case, he found the allure of numbers running, with its fast money and flashy lifestyle, too tempting to resist. By the early 1950s he had married Luvenia Mitchell and became known on the streets as "Donald the Kid" because of the amazing speed with which he had risen within the illegal lottery business.

On 2 December 1954 three men tried to rob one of King's gambling establishments. King shot and killed Hillary Brown, one of the stickup men. King argued that he acted in self-defense and the courts ruled that the case was an instance of "justifiable homicide." Over the next decade, his home was bombed, and he suffered a wound from a shotgun blast; but he demonstrated that he could be ruthless as well as generous and that he was as calculating as he was engaging with both his friends and his enemies. On 20 April 1966 King was involved in a street brawl with Sam Garret. When it was over, Garret had been beaten, pistol-whipped, and lay dying on the sidewalk. King claimed that the smaller and unarmed man had attacked him; witnesses—those who did not mysteriously disappear or suddenly lose their memory—testified that King was attempting to collect a gambling debt from the frail Garret. In February 1966 a jury found King guilty of second-degree murder, an offense for which he could have been sentenced to life in prison. Instead, Judge Hugh Corrigan reduced the charge to manslaughter. There were rumors that a secret deal had been made; however, nothing was ever proved and years later, when Judge Corrigan ran for the Court of Appeals, King arranged for MUHAMMAD ALI to make commercials supporting Corrigan's election.

While serving three years and eleven months at Ohio's Marion Correctional Institution, King spent part of his time hauling manure on a work gang, but every spare moment he could find he spent in the prison library reading works by Adam Smith, William Shakespeare, Marcus Aurelius, biographies that raised over $80,000, more than any previous event of its kind. How the money from this benefit was divided remains in dispute; however, it is clear that following this event King and his second wife, Henrietta, were eager to get out of the numbers racket and enter the fight game.

Elbaum was impressed by King's extraordinary business savvy and brought King to the attention of Hank Schwartz, president of Video Techniques, a company that provided closed-circuit broadcasting for lucrative fights. King attended the bout between JOE FRAZIER and GEORGE FOREMAN in January 1973 in Kingston, Jamaica, without any clear mandate. Yet, without title or money he talked his way into both camps; he arrived in the same limousine as the then-reigning champ, Joe Frazier, and left in the limousine of the new champ, George Foreman. King became an important middleman for Schwartz, and soon was hired as a vice president of Video Techniques, largely for his ability to acquire access to the black fighters who had come to dominate the sport. King quickly understood that the fight business, and indeed, much of American capitalism, operated on many of the same principles as the numbers racket that he had mastered years before. Playing by the same rules of his predecessors, King was determined to climb his way to the top of the boxing establishment.

One route to success that King explored was managing and training fighters. He had discovered a rising star in Ernie Shavers, a devastating knockout artist; but when Shavers lost to Jerry Quarry, one of several "Great White Hopes," in the first round, King realized that promoting many fighters was a safer bet than relying on just one. In 1974 he outmaneuvered Bob Arum, a powerful, white Harvard-educated boxing promoter, for the rights to one of the most spectacular moments in boxing history. the showdown between Muhammad Ali and George Foreman. Arum had offered Ali $850,000 to fight Quarry, King offered Ali and Foreman five million dollars each—even though he and Schwartz had no idea how they were going to raise the money. As an incredible testament to King's persuasive ability, he got Foreman to sign seven blank pieces of paper on the promise that King would fill in the details later. After crafting a deal with shady European businessmen and a corrupt African dictator, Mobutu Sese Seko, the fight was held in Zaire, Africa, billed as the "Rumble in the Jungle," and was seen by one billion people worldwide. King's moves outside the ring, including creating his own company, Don King Productions,

Don King in a king costume for a Sportsman's Ball he hosted at Caesar's Palace in Las Vegas, Nev., on June 8, 1978. (AP Images.)

of famous African Americans, and philosophical treatises. As with the sports announcer Howard Cosell, King's penchant for using big words and quoting great authors (sometimes incorrectly) became a hallmark of his persona that was as recognizable as his towering hairdo. King would later say of his prison education, "I didn't serve time. I made time serve me" (Newfield, 22).

After being paroled in September 1971 (he would be given a pardon by Governor James Rhodes in 1983), King renewed his friendship with Lloyd Price, an entertainer who had gained popularity for his songs "Lawdy Miss Clady" and "Stagger Lee." In the spring of 1972 King got the idea of staging a fund-raiser to save Ohio's only black hospital. Lloyd used his influence to get Ali to put on a ten-round exhibition with various opponents. King added a concert that included MARVIN GAYE, WILSON PICKETT, and LOU RAWLS. King had never promoted a boxing event before, but with the help of Don Elbaum—King's early mentor and later rival in the fight business—King hosted an extravaganza were as dazzling as the "rope-a-dope" Ali used in the ring to regain his crown.

Following this achievement, he went on to solidify his three-decade reign as the king of boxing promotion. He produced most of Ali's fights during the remainder of the 1970s, including the final epic battle with Joe Frazier, which he staged in the Philippines and billed as the "Thrilla in Manila" in October 1975. His multimillion-dollar deals with ABC and Caesars Palace casino in Las Vegas broke records. He was the first to bring heavyweight title fights to Home Box Office (HBO). King's ability to deliver title shots with big paydays to hungry fighters allowed him to establish a virtual monopoly on top contenders. His stable of gladiators eventually grew to include Larry Holmes, KEN NORTON, and Mike Weaver in the 1980s, not to mention the infamous but profitable MIKE TYSON in the 1990s. King's dominance as a promoter extended from the heavyweight division to encompass marquee fighters from other divisions such as "SUGAR" RAY LEONARD and Roberto Duran, Julio Cesar Chavez, and Hector "Macho" Camacho. King even briefly branched out into other entertainment venues by promoting concerts of the Jackson Five and representing MICHAEL JACKSON in several major product endorsements.

King's legal battles followed him into boxing. He was the defendant in scores of lawsuits brought by fighters and business associates, most of which he won or privately settled. He was accused of taking kickbacks, manipulating rankings, demanding a large percentage as the promoter, and sometimes pressuring fighters to take his son, Carl, as a manager for an additional share. He also often insisted on cutting in one or more of his subsidiaries, such as King Vision or the Don King Sports and Entertainment Network, for yet more of the profits, and always charging the fighters and others for numerous "expenses." In 1983 the FBI tried to use AL SHARPTON, who worked for King, in an unsuccessful sting against King and the Mafia. The following year, King and his secretary, Constance Harper, were indicted on a variety of tax evasion charges. Harper was convicted, King was acquitted, and he thanked the jury by flying them to London and giving them ringside tickets to one of his fights. In 1994 the FBI tried again to get King, this time on charges stemming from a suspicious insurance claim. The government called eighteen witnesses, the defense only one: King. The case ended in a mistrial but King considered it yet another victory over his persecutors who resented his success as a black boxing mogul.

Having promoted more than five hundred championship fights, King was named "Promoter of the Millennium" by the World Boxing Association in 1999, and he was inducted into both the International Boxing Hall of Fame and World Boxing Hall of Fame. He gave philanthropic support to many civil rights organizations and befriended Democratic and Republican presidents. In 2004 he gave large sums of money to the Republican Party and actively supported the reelection of George W. Bush. Critics charged that he was merely trying to block legislative efforts to bring boxing under greater federal regulations. King, however, retorted that his actions were a patriotic expression of the free enterprise system of this country that allowed him to live the American dream.

FURTHER READING
Lupica, Mike. "Donfire of the Vanities," *Esquire* (Mar. 1991).
Newfield, Jack. *Only in America: The Life and Crimes of Don King* (1995).

SHOLOMO B. LEVY

King, Freddie (3 Sept. 1934–28 Dec. 1976), blues guitarist and singer, was born Freddy Christian, in Gilmer, Texas, the son of J. T. Christian and his first wife, whose name is unknown. The woman he always considered his mother, Ella Mae King, was really his stepmother, having married J. T. Christian when Freddy was five. At six years of age Freddy was introduced to guitar by his uncle, Leon King, and his mother. Growing up in northeast Texas, Freddy performed in school and church and was influenced by the blues records of LIGHTNIN' HOPKINS, MUDDY WATERS, and HOWLIN' WOLF.

In 1950 J. T. Christian moved his family to Chicago. Freddy, a large youngster, was sixteen but looked older. He got a job in a steel mill where he worked for seven years. Chicago was in the midst of a blues explosion, and Freddy frequently went to blues clubs to listen and sit in with the local blues men. He lived behind the Club Zanzibar, where Muddy Waters had a long-term gig. Muddy allowed Freddy to slip in the side door to listen. Freddy sat next to Muddy's guitarist, JIMMY ROGERS, and watched every move he made on the guitar.

Rogers introduced Freddy to the thumb-and-index-finger picking style that he would use his entire career. Freddy would later adopt a plastic thumbpick and metal fingerpick, which gave him his sharp attack. Two other influential Chicago blues guitarists would also help shape Freddy's approach to electric guitar. EDDIE TAYLOR and ROBERT LOCKWOOD JR. were both master accompanists. Taylor made many famous records with JIMMY REED, and Lockwood, then known as Robert Junior Lockwood, was the stepson of ROBERT JOHNSON. Lockwood was a sophisticated player who recorded with many of Chicago's biggest names and imparted some of his jazzy chords and lines to the young Freddy.

Freddy changed his surname to King and began playing as a sideman with many musicians. He recorded with both Little Sonny Cooper and Earl E. Payton's bands for the Parrot label in 1953 and 1954. King began making a name for himself as a forceful singer and guitarist and traded riffs with such peers as OTIS RUSH, BUDDY GUY, and EARL HOOKER while influencing younger up-and-coming guitarists like MAGIC SAM and Luther Allison. Fellow guitarists B. B. KING and ALBERT KING had already mastered single-string soloing and were fronting their own bands, which typically included horn sections. Freddy, though informed by the other two Kings, was ten years younger and was on the cusp of a tougher new generation of more modern, urban blues guitarists. Freddy took his Texas country roots and came of age in the exciting Windy City, which was then the center of the blues universe. Like B. B. King, Freddy was enthralled with the recordings of the singer and sax player LOUIS JORDAN, who fronted a jump jazz-style group. Freddy emulated Jordan's flowing jazz lines and learned to swing in a manner not unlike that of fellow Texas guitarist T-BONE WALKER but with a harder edge. This modern sound was less rhythmic than the electric delta stylings of Muddy Waters and Howlin' Wolf and more citified and cutting.

King recorded his first solo record, "Country Boy," backed with "That's What You Think," for the small El-Bee label in Chicago in 1956. He also recorded for the newly formed Cobra label but nothing was ever issued. In addition, he auditioned for the top blues label, Chess Records, but was turned down because they thought he sounded too much like B. B. King. Then Freddy had the good fortune of being introduced by the guitarist Syl Johnson to Sonny Thompson, A&R (artist and repertoire) man for the King record label. King Records was based in Cincinnati and boasted JAMES BROWN among its successful artists. Freddy was signed to Federal Records, a King subsidiary, in 1960. In August of that year he recorded six of the seventy-seven songs he would record in Cincinnati. The singles were released on Federal and the albums on King. The tunes were produced and arranged by Sonny Thompson, who also played piano on them, backed by the company's studio musicians. King's first and biggest hit was "Hideaway," which reached number 29 on *Billboard*'s Pop charts during a ten-week run. The song had been intended as the B-side to the slow blues vocal "I Love the Woman," but it took off after airplay to become the most famous of King's records. The song's opening melody was based on "Taylor's Boogie" by slide guitarist HOUND DOG TAYLOR and named after Mel's Hideaway Lounge in Chicago. There were several stop verses, in which the band stops and the soloist keeps playing in time, and Freddy quoted the famous "Peter Gunn" theme from the hit television show of the time. He used fancy ninth chords and quick and clever runs that became the blueprint for several dazzling instrumentals to follow, including "San-Ho-Zay," "Sidetracked," "The Stumble," "Just Pickin'," and possibly culminating with "Remington Ride." "Hideaway" remained a staple of blues and rock bands in the early-twenty-first century.

The best-known cover of "Hideaway" was by the British band John Mayall's Bluesbreakers, with Eric Clapton, on their debut album in 1966. Clapton based his tone and his electric guitar style on King's, playing a Gibson Les Paul guitar as did King in his early years, and his tone was the result of pushing the amplifier to distort. Unlike B. B. and Albert King, who played in a sparse and vocal-oriented style, Freddy King's phrases were fast and furious. Fancy and flowing, King's modern sound had a profound influence on the way the electric guitar was played in much popular music. His sound was imitated in teen party music and in the surf music instrumentals of the early 1960s as well as among players like fellow King recording artist Lonnie Mack. Further, King's style became the foundation for British blues guitarists such as Clapton, Peter Green, and Mick Taylor, all Mayall alumni, each of whom covered a King signature instrumental and in turn influenced thousands of aspiring English and American guitarists with their interpretations of King's overdriven tone and phrasing. As if his guitar gifts were not substantial enough, King was blessed with a smooth and smoky singing voice. Songs like "Have You Ever Loved a Woman," "You've Got to Love Her with a Feeling," and "I'm Tore Down" influenced Eric Clapton's singing as much as his guitar playing.

King enjoyed a string of hits through the early 1960s and traveled extensively around the country. He was let go by King Records in 1967; he changed the spelling of his first name to Freddie and signed with Cotillion, an Atlantic Records subsidiary, in 1969. For Cotillion he recorded *Freddie King Is a Blues Master*, produced by the legendary sax player and bandleader KING CURTIS. King was playing a wide circuit of concert halls like the Fillmores, blues festivals, and colleges. In 1972 he was signed to the Shelter label, in which the singer and pianist Leon Russell was a partner. King recorded the powerful song "I'm Going Down," later covered by the Jeff Beck Group. At the peak of his international renown King fittingly signed with RSO Records, which was owned by Eric Clapton's manager, Robert Stigwood.

Though some critics regarded his later work as overproduced, King's live shows never strayed from the intensely driven straight-ahead blues for which he became famous. His ferocious singing and guitar playing were augmented by his impressive showmanship. In contrast to fellow blues master Albert King, who just stood when he played, Freddie felt an obligation to perform as well as play. He put his all into every show and sweated profusely every night. After years of hard touring and living, King succumbed to stomach and liver problems at the age of forty-two. He performed his last show in Texas on Christmas night 1976 and died three days later. Since his death King's wife Jessie, with whom he had seven children, and his daughter Wanda have struggled, both in court and out, to protect the rights to his music from the marketing of bootleg or unauthorized recordings. But his greatest abiding influence, perhaps, can be heard in the playing of tens of thousands of guitarists, many of whom do not even realize it.

FURTHER READING

Fox, Darrin. "Patron Saint, Freddie King," *Guitar Player Magazine* (August 2004).

Gordon, Robert. *Can't Be Satisfied: The Life and Times of Muddy Waters* (2002).

Harris, Sheldon, *Blues Who's Who: A Biographical Dictionary of Blues Singers* (1981).

Jacoubovitch, Daniel. Liner notes to *Just Pickin': Modern Blues Recordings* (1986).

DISCOGRAPHY

Freddie King Is a Blues Master. Cotillion SD 9004 (1969).

Leadbitter, Mike, and Neil Slaven. *Blues Records 1942–1966* (1970).

All His Hits Freddie King. King B0000017B8 (1995).

Just Pickin'. Modern Blues Recordings MB2LP-721 (1986).

MARK STEVEN MAULUCCI

King, Horace (8 Sept. 1807–28 May 1885), bridge designer and builder, was born near Cheraw, South Carolina, the son of Edmund and Susan King, slaves of African, European, and American Indian ancestry. King, his mother, his sister Clarissa (Murray), and his brother Washington were purchased circa 1830 by John Godwin and his wife, Ann Wright Godwin. According to some accounts, King may have been related to Ann's family, the Wrights of Marlboro County, South Carolina. King was already a master carpenter by the time Godwin purchased him, and Godwin expanded King's skills by teaching him how to build bridges. King was literate, although he never attended Oberlin College, as was incorrectly told in family myth.

The Godwins and their slaves moved west in 1832, when Godwin won a contract from Columbus, Georgia, to construct a four-hundred-foot wooden bridge across the Chattahoochee River. They settled in Girard (now Phenix City), at the Alabama end of the bridge. After completing the bridge, Godwin and King constructed much of the infrastructure for west Georgia, east Alabama, and west Florida. By 1840, with Godwin as contractor and King as construction foreman, they had erected cotton warehouses at the port of Apalachicola, Florida; courthouses in Muscogee County, Georgia, and Russell County, Alabama; and three massive covered bridges over the Chattahoochee River at West Point, Georgia; Eufaula, Alabama; and Florence, Georgia. An 1840 advertisement for the new Florence Bridge in Georgia identified its builders as "Honest John Godwin and Horace" (*Columbus (Ga.) Enquirer*, 5 Aug. 1840). Few slave craftsmen in the antebellum South were ever recognized by name (even if just by their first one) in newspapers. King had become a public figure and risen above the anonymity of most slaves.

In March 1837 Godwin transferred the ownership of King and his family to Godwin's wife, Ann, and her uncle and trustee William Carney Wright. He did this perhaps to protect the skilled King from Godwin's creditors, who could have seized King as one of Godwin's assets or because the Wrights had financed the initial purchase of King and his family. Ann and William allowed King to marry a free woman, Frances Gould Thomas, on 28 March 1839. She shared his tri-racial background, and her free status guaranteed freedom for their five children. After 1840, Godwin stayed in Girard, while King, the slave, worked without supervision building bridges hundreds of miles away. King served as the architect and contractor for an $18,000, 420-foot covered bridge across the Tombigee River at Columbus, Mississippi, in 1843, and a $15,000, 600-foot covered bridge across the Coosa River at Wetumpka, Alabama, the following year. The Godwins and King received at least a third of this cost, and the Godwins probably shared this revenue with their skilled slave. Robert Jemison Jr., a Tuscaloosa, Alabama, entrepreneur and legislator, served as a major investor for both of these spans. In early 1845 King, working for one of his owners, William Carney Wright, designed and constructed a covered bridge over the Tallapoosa River at Tallassee, Alabama. These bridges were crucial in expanding the commerce of those three towns. In 1846 King bridged three streams in the vicinity of Steens, Mississippi, for Jemison, who was by then King's close friend. Jemison played a crucial role in freeing King. In general, white southerners feared free blacks, seeing them as potential instigators of slave revolts; thus southern legislatures prohibited owners from freeing their slaves without explicit legislative permission. In February 1846, Jemison pushed King's emancipation bill, in which the Godwins and Wright freed King, through the Alabama legislature. What precisely prompted the Godwins and Wright to free King at this point remains a mystery, but King later testified that he bought his freedom. Freed slaves enjoyed few rights in the antebellum South and were dependent on the kindnesses of their white guardian or neighbors. Because of his reputation as a bridge builder, King faced less hostility and enjoyed more mobility than most free blacks.

As a freedman, King's professional life changed little, although his income increased. In 1851 he was contracted by the state for carpentry work on the Alabama state capitol, and his work included the two graceful circular counter-levered staircases that flank the main entrance. Working for Nelson Tift, an entrepreneur and legislator, King bridged the Flint River at Albany, Georgia, in 1858. In the mid-1850s, he built Moore's Bridge over the Chattahoochee River between Newnan and Carrollton, Georgia, and he retained one-third interest in it. King's wife and the children moved to Moore's Bridge and collected bridge tolls and farmed, while King traveled between Moore's Bridge and Girard and his work sites.

John Godwin died in 1859, and King bought him a grave obelisk. It proclaimed, "This stone was placed here by HORACE KING in lasting remembrance of the love and gratitude he felt for his lost friend and former master" (Godwin's grave, Godwin Cemetery, Phenix City, Alabama). At the time southern newspapers and later secondary accounts interpreted King's gesture as implicit support for slavery. However, King's action might have been motivated by contemporary political events. As the sectional crisis heightened in the late 1850s, white hostility toward freed blacks increased. In 1859, responding to the idea that all African Americans in the South should be under the control of a master, the Alabama and other southern legislatures were debating whether to enslave all free blacks. Perhaps King hoped to prevent his family's enslavement by praising his master, with whom he did enjoy an exceptional relationship. However, nothing about King's unique life can be used to generalize about slavery.

During the Civil War, King wanted to remain a private contractor, but Alabama and Georgia officials forced him under military guard in 1862 to obstruct navigation on the Apalachicola and Alabama rivers. Working for the Confederate Naval Yard and for the Confederate Naval Iron Works in Columbus, Georgia, from 1862–1865, he erected a mill building and supplied large quantities of hewed timbers, sawn lumber, and wooden treenails—the standard building supplies for a bridge builder at that time. His sons avoided impressments into labor gangs as slave-labor by working with their father for the Confederate navy in Columbus after 1864 when Union troops destroyed the town of Moore's Bridge and sacked the King family's outbuildings. Even though King worked for the Confederacy, he remained a Unionist, and in March 1864, he tried in vain to contact Robert Jemison, who was by then a Confederate senator, to ascertain what his fate would be if he stopped working for the Confederacy. In 1878, King unsuccessfully requested federal compensation for property damage done by Union troops at Moore's Bridge (July 1864) and Girard (April 1865). He testified: "I stood on the Union Side and always begged and talked for the Union" (King's Interrogatories).

King's wife died on 21 October 1864, and on 6 June 1865 he married Sarah Jane Jones McManus in Columbus; they had no children. Reconstruction brought change to King, who stepped forward as a natural leader, and the personal friend of several white politicians. King was elected twice, in 1868 and 1870, to the Alabama House of Representatives, but he rarely, if ever, attended the first session, and he played a limited role during subsequent years. He simply undertook too many construction projects that demanded his personal attention. At the same time that he should have been in the legislature he was overextended in rebuilding the Chattahoochee Valley's infrastructure, such as warehouses, wagon and railroad bridges, and mills, which had been torched by Union raiders. These contracts should have brought him wealth, but some corporations and governments paid him in bonds that became worthless, and King, like many southern businessmen during this unstable period, experienced a significant business failure.

In 1872, King's grown sons and daughter moved as a family with him to La Grange, Georgia, where he continued building bridges, stores, houses, and schools until his death in 1885. Obituaries praising his skills and character appeared in the white Columbus, LaGrange, and Atlanta newspapers. King's children continued their father's construction business and became prominent citizens of La Grange. His son John T. King served as a trustee for Clark University from the 1890s to the 1920s and was one of two contractors for the Negro Building at the Atlanta Exposition in 1895.

FURTHER READING

The only extant correspondence of Horace King can be found in the Robert Jemison Jr. Papers, 1797–1898, W.S. Hoole Special Collections Library, University of Alabama, Tuscaloosa, Alabama. Additional King information is located in: Horace King Interrogatories, Near Whitesburg, Carroll County, Georgia, 28 February 1878, Records of the U.S. House of Representatives Case File of the Southern Claims Commission, Commissioners of Claims, no. 19661, National Archives Record Group 233.

Cherry, Francis. "History of Opelika," *Alabama Historical Quarterly*, 15, no. 3 (1953).

Lupold, John S. and Thomas L. French Jr. *Bridging Deep South Rivers: The Life and Legend of Horace King* (2004).

JOHN S. LUPOLD

King, Martin Luther, Jr. (15 Jan. 1929–4 Apr. 1968), Baptist minister and civil rights leader, was born Michael King Jr., in Atlanta, Georgia, the son of the Reverend Michael King (MARTIN LUTHER KING SR.) and Alberta Williams. Born to a family with deep roots in the African American Baptist church and in the Atlanta black community, the younger King spent his first twelve years in the home on Auburn Avenue that his parents shared with his maternal grandparents. A block away, also on Auburn, was Ebenezer Baptist Church, where his grandfather, the Reverend Adam Daniel Williams, had served as pastor since 1894. Under Williams's leadership, Ebenezer had grown from a small congregation without a building to become one of Atlanta's prominent African American churches. After Williams's death in 1931, his son-in-law became Ebenezer's new pastor and gradually established himself as a major figure in state and national Baptist groups. In 1934 the elder King, following the request of his own dying father, changed his name and that of his son to Martin Luther King.

King's formative experiences not only immersed him in the affairs of Ebenezer but also introduced him to the African American social gospel tradition exemplified by his father and grandfather, both of whom were leaders of the Atlanta branch of the National Association for the Advancement of Colored People. Depression-era breadlines heightened his awareness of economic inequities, and his father's leadership of campaigns against racial discrimination in voting and teachers' salaries provided a model for the younger King's own politically engaged ministry. He resisted religious emotionalism and as a teenager questioned some facets of Baptist doctrine, such as the bodily resurrection of Jesus. During his undergraduate years at Atlanta's Morehouse College from 1944 to 1948, King gradually overcame his initial reluctance to accept his inherited calling. Morehouse president BENJAMIN MAYS influenced King's spiritual development, encouraging him to view Christianity as a potential force for progressive social change. The religion professor George Kelsey exposed him to biblical criticism and, according to King's autobiographical sketch, taught him "that behind the legends and myths of the Book were many profound truths which one could not escape." King admired both educators as deeply religious yet also learned men. By the end of his junior year, such academic role models and the example of his father led King to enter the ministry. He described his decision as a response to an "inner urge" calling him to "serve God and humanity." He was ordained during his final semester at Morehouse. By this time King had also taken his first steps toward political activism. He had responded to the postwar wave of antiblack violence by proclaiming in a letter to the editor of the *Atlanta Constitution* that African Americans were "entitled to the basic rights and opportunities

Martin Luther King, Jr. addresses a group of residents in the Watts neighborhood of Los Angeles on August 18, 1965. (Library of Congress.)

of American citizens." During his senior year King joined the Intercollegiate Council, an interracial student discussion group that met monthly at Atlanta's Emory University.

After leaving Morehouse, King increased his understanding of liberal Christian thought while attending Crozer Theological Seminary in Pennsylvania from 1948 to 1951. Initially uncritical of liberal theology, he gradually moved toward Reinhold Niebuhr's neoorthodoxy, which emphasized the intractability of social evil. He reacted skeptically to a presentation on pacifism by the Fellowship of Reconciliation leader A. J. Muste. Moreover, by the end of his seminary studies King had become increasingly dissatisfied with the abstract conceptions of God held by some modern theologians and identified himself instead with

theologians who affirmed the personality of God. Even as he continued to question and modify his own religious beliefs, he compiled an outstanding academic record and graduated at the top of his class.

In 1951 King began doctoral studies in systematic theology at Boston University's School of Theology, which was dominated by personalist theologians. The papers (including his dissertation) that King wrote during his years at Boston displayed little originality, and some contained extensive plagiarism, but his readings enabled him to formulate an eclectic yet coherent theological perspective. By the time he completed his doctoral studies in 1955, King had refined his exceptional ability to draw upon a wide range of theological and philosophical texts to express his views with force and precision. His ability to infuse his oratory with borrowed theological insights became evident in his expanding preaching activities in Boston-area churches and at Ebenezer, where he assisted his father during school vacations.

During his stay at Boston, King also met and courted Coretta Scott (CORETTA SCOTT KING), an Alabama-born Antioch College graduate who was then a student at the New England Conservatory of Music. On 18 June 1953 the two students were married in Marion, Alabama, where Scott's family lived. During the following academic year King began work on his dissertation, which he completed during the spring of 1955.

Although he considered pursuing an academic career, King decided in 1954 to accept an offer to become the pastor of Dexter Avenue Baptist Church in Montgomery, Alabama. In December 1955, when Montgomery black leaders formed the Montgomery Improvement Association to protest the arrest of the NAACP official ROSA PARKS for refusing to give up her bus seat to a white man, they selected King to head the new group. With King as the primary spokesman and with grassroots organizers such as DAISY BATES, the association led a yearlong bus boycott. King utilized the leadership abilities he had gained from his religious background and academic training and gradually forged a distinctive protest strategy that involved the mobilization of black churches and skillful appeals for white support. As King encountered increasingly fierce white opposition, he continued his movement away from theological abstractions toward more reassuring conceptions, rooted in African American religious culture, of God as a constant source of support. He later wrote in his book of sermons, *Strength to Love* (1963), that the travails of movement leadership caused him to abandon the notion of God as a "theological and philosophically satisfying metaphysical category" and to view God as "a living reality that has been validated in the experiences of everyday life." With the encouragement of BAYARD RUSTIN and other veteran pacifists, King also became a firm advocate of Mohandas Gandhi's precepts of nonviolence, which he combined with Christian principles.

After the Supreme Court outlawed Alabama bus segregation laws in late 1956, King sought to expand the nonviolent civil rights movement throughout the South. In 1957 he became the founding president of the Southern Christian Leadership Conference (SCLC), formed to coordinate civil rights activities throughout the region. Publication

of *Stride toward Freedom: The Montgomery Story* (1958) further contributed to King's rapid emergence as a national civil rights leader. Even as he expanded his influence, however, King acted cautiously. Rather than immediately seeking to stimulate mass desegregation protests in the South, King stressed the goal of achieving black voting rights when he addressed an audience at the 1957 Prayer Pilgrimage for Freedom. During 1959 he increased his understanding of Gandhian ideas during a monthlong visit to India as the guest of Prime Minister Jawaharlal Nehru. Early the following year he moved his family, which now included two children, to Atlanta in order to be nearer SCLC headquarters in that city and to become co-pastor, with his father, of Ebenezer Baptist Church. (The Kings' third child was born in 1961; their fourth was born in 1963.)

Soon after King's arrival in Atlanta, the southern civil rights movement gained new impetus from the student-led lunch counter sit-in movement that spread throughout the region during 1960. King dispatched ELLA BAKER to North Carolina to organize students who had staged a protest there. The sit-ins brought into existence a new protest group, the Student Nonviolent Coordinating Committee (SNCC). Its early leaders, such as JOHN LEWIS, worked closely with King, but by the late 1960s STOKELY CARMICHAEL and H. RAP BROWN attempted to push King toward greater militancy. In October 1960 King's arrest during a student-initiated protest in Atlanta became an issue in the national presidential campaign when Democratic candidate John F. Kennedy called Coretta King to express his concern. The successful efforts of Kennedy supporters to secure King's release contributed to the Democratic candidate's narrow victory.

As the southern protest movement expanded during the early 1960s, King was often torn between the increasingly militant student activists and more cautious national civil rights leaders. During 1961 and 1962 his tactical differences with SNCC activists surfaced during a sustained protest movement in Albany, Georgia. King was arrested twice during demonstrations organized by the Albany movement, but when he left jail and ultimately left Albany without achieving a victory, some movement activists began to question his militancy and his dominant role within the southern protest movement.

During 1963, however, King reasserted his preeminence within the African American freedom struggle through his leadership of the Birmingham campaign. Initiated by SCLC in January, the Birmingham demonstrations were the most massive civil rights protest that had yet occurred. With the assistance of FRED SHUTTLESWORTH and other local black leaders and with little competition from SNCC and other civil rights groups, SCLC officials were able to orchestrate the Birmingham protests to achieve maximum national impact. King's decision to intentionally allow himself to be arrested for leading a demonstration on 12 April prodded the Kennedy administration to intervene in the escalating protests. A widely quoted letter that King wrote while jailed displayed his distinctive ability to influence public opinion by appropriating ideas from the Bible, the Constitution, and other canonical texts. During May, televised pictures of police using dogs and fire hoses against demonstrators generated a national outcry against white segregationist officials in Birmingham. The brutality of Birmingham officials and the refusal of Alabama governor George C. Wallace to allow the admission of black students at the University of Alabama prompted President Kennedy to introduce major civil rights legislation.

King's speech at the 28 August 1963 March on Washington, attended by more than two hundred thousand people, was the culmination of a wave of civil rights protest activity that extended even to northern cities. In King's prepared remarks he announced that African Americans wished to cash the "promissory note" signified in the egalitarian rhetoric of the Constitution and the Declaration of Independence. Closing his address with extemporaneous remarks, he insisted that he had not lost hope: "So I say to you, my friends, that even though we must face the difficulties of today and tomorrow, I still have a dream. It is a dream deeply rooted in the American dream that one day this nation will rise up and live out the true meaning of its creed—we hold these truths to be self-evident, that all men are created equal." He appropriated the familiar words of "My Country 'Tis of Thee" before concluding, "And when we allow freedom to ring, when we let it ring from every village and hamlet, from every state and city, we will be able to speed up that day when all of God's children—black men and white men, Jews and Gentiles, Catholics and Protestants—will be able to join hands and to sing in the words of the old Negro spiritual, 'Free at last, free at last, thank God Almighty, we are free at last.'"

King's ability to focus national attention on orchestrated confrontations with racist authorities, combined with his oration at the 1963 March on Washington, made him the most influential African American spokesperson of the first half of the 1960s. Named *Time* magazine's Man of the Year at the end of 1963, he was awarded the Nobel Peace Prize in December 1964. The acclaim King received strengthened his stature among civil rights leaders but also prompted the Federal Bureau of Investigation director J. Edgar Hoover to step up his effort to damage King's reputation. Hoover, with the approval of President Kennedy and Attorney General Robert Kennedy, established phone taps and bugs. Hoover and many other observers of the southern struggle saw King as controlling events, but he was actually a moderating force within an increasingly diverse black militancy of the mid-1960s. As the African American struggle expanded from desegregation protests to mass movements seeking economic and political gains in the North as well as the South, King's active involvement was limited to a few highly publicized civil rights campaigns, particularly the major series of voting rights protests that began in Selma, Alabama, early in 1965, which secured popular support for the passage of national civil rights legislation, particularly the Civil Rights Act of 1964.

The Alabama protests reached a turning point on 7 March when state police attacked a group of SCLC demonstrators led by HOSEA WILLIAMS at the start of a march from Selma to the state capitol in Montgomery. Carrying out Governor Wallace's orders, the police used tear gas and clubs to turn back the marchers soon after they crossed the Edmund Pettus Bridge on the outskirts of Selma. Unprepared for the violent confrontation, King was in Atlanta to deliver a sermon when the incident occurred but returned to Selma to mobilize nationwide support for the voting rights campaign. King alienated some activists when he decided to postpone the continuation of the Selma-to-Montgomery march until he had received court approval, but the march, which finally secured federal court approval, attracted several thousand civil rights sympathizers, black and white, from all regions of the nation. On 25 March, King addressed the arriving marchers from the steps of the capitol in Montgomery. The march and the subsequent killing of a white participant, Viola Liuzzo, dramatized the denial of black voting rights and spurred passage during the following summer of the Voting Rights Act of 1965.

After the successful voting rights march in Alabama, King was unable to garner similar support for his effort to confront the problems of northern urban blacks. Early in 1966 he launched a major campaign against poverty and other urban problems, moving into an apartment in the black ghetto of Chicago. As King shifted the focus of his activities to the North, however, he discovered that the tactics used in the South were not as effective elsewhere. He encountered formidable opposition from Mayor Richard Daley and was unable to mobilize Chicago's economically and ideologically diverse black community. King was stoned by angry whites in the Chicago suburb of Cicero when he led a march against racial discrimination in housing. Despite numerous mass protests, the Chicago campaign resulted in no significant gains and undermined King's reputation as an effective civil rights leader.

King's influence was further undermined by the increasingly caustic tone of black militancy of the period after 1965. Black militants increasingly turned away from the Gandhian precepts of King toward the black nationalism of MALCOLM X, whose posthumously published autobiography and speeches reached large audiences after his assassination in February 1965. Unable to influence the black insurgencies that occurred in many urban areas, King refused to abandon his firmly rooted beliefs about racial integration and nonviolence. He was nevertheless unpersuaded by black nationalist calls for racial uplift and institutional development in black communities. In his last book, *Where Do We Go from Here: Chaos or Community?* (1967), King dismissed the claim of Black Power advocates "to be the most revolutionary wing of the social revolution taking place in the United States," but he acknowledged that they responded to a psychological need among African Americans he had not previously addressed. "Psychological freedom, a firm sense of self-esteem, is the most powerful weapon against the long night of physical slavery," King wrote. "The Negro will only be truly free when he reaches down to the inner depths of his own being and signs with the pen and ink of assertive selfhood his own emancipation proclamation."

Indeed, even as his popularity declined, King spoke out strongly against American involvement in the Vietnam War, making his position public in an address on 4 April 1967 at New York's Riverside Church. King's involvement in the antiwar movement reduced his ability to influence national racial policies and made him a target of further FBI investigations. Nevertheless, he became ever more insistent that his version of Gandhian nonviolence and social gospel Christianity was the most appropriate response to the problems of black Americans.

In November 1967 King announced the formation of the Poor People's Campaign, designed to prod the federal government to strengthen its antipoverty efforts. King, ANDREW YOUNG, JESSE JACKSON, and other SCLC workers began to recruit poor people and antipoverty activists to come to Washington, D.C., to lobby on behalf of improved antipoverty programs. This effort was in its early stages when King became involved in a sanitation workers' strike in Memphis, Tennessee. On 28 March 1968, as King led thousands of sanitation workers and sympathizers on a march through downtown Memphis, black youngsters began throwing rocks and looting stores. This outbreak of violence led to extensive press criticisms of King's entire antipoverty strategy. King returned to Memphis for the last time in early April. Addressing an audience at Bishop Charles J. Mason Temple on 3 April, King affirmed his optimism despite the "difficult days" that lay ahead. "But it doesn't matter with me now," he declared, "because I've been to the mountaintop [and] I've seen the promised land." He continued, "I may not get there with you. But I want you to know tonight, that we, as a people, will get to the promised land." The following evening King was assassinated as he stood on a balcony of the Lorraine Motel in Memphis. A white segregationist, James Earl Ray, was later convicted of the crime. The Poor People's Campaign continued for a few months after his death but did not achieve its objectives.

Until his death King remained steadfast in his commitment to the radical transformation of American society through nonviolent activism. In his posthumously published essay, "A Testament of Hope" (1986), he urged African Americans to refrain from violence but also warned, "White America must recognize that justice for black people cannot be achieved without radical changes in the structure of our society." The "black revolution" was more than a civil rights movement, he insisted. "It is forcing America to face all its interrelated flaws—racism, poverty, militarism and materialism."

After King's death, RALPH ABERNATHY assumed leadership of SCLC, and Coretta Scott King established the Atlanta-based Martin Luther King Jr. Center for Nonviolent Social Change to promote Gandhian-Kingian concepts of nonviolent struggle.

She led the successful effort to honor King with a federal holiday on the anniversary of his birthday, which was first celebrated in 1986.

On 16 October 2011, President BARACK OBAMA officially dedicated the Martin Luther King, Jr. National Memorial in West Potomac Park on the National Mall in Washington, D.C.

FURTHER READING

Collections of King's papers are at the Martin Luther King Jr. Center for Nonviolent Social Change in Atlanta and the Mugar Memorial Library at Boston University.

Branch, Taylor. *Parting the Waters: America in the King Years, 1954–63* (1988).

Branch, Taylor. *Pillar of Fire: America in the King Years, 1963–65* (1998).

Garrow, David J. *Bearing the Cross: Martin Luther King Jr. and the Southern Christian Leadership Conference, 1955–1968* (1986).

Lewis, David Levering. *King: A Biography*, 2d ed. (1978).

Oates, Stephen B. *Let the Trumpet Sound: The Life of Martin Luther King Jr.* (1982).

Washington, James Melvin, ed. *A Testament of Hope: The Essential Writings of Martin Luther King Jr.* (1986).

Obituary: *New York Times*, 5 Apr. 1968.

This entry is taken from the *American National Biography* and is published here with the permission of the American Council of Learned Societies.

CLAYBORNE CARSON

King, Martin Luther, Sr. (19 Dec. 1897–11 Nov. 1984), Baptist pastor and civil rights activist, was born Michael King in Stockbridge, Georgia, the son of James Albert King, an impoverished sharecropper, and Delia Linsey, a cleaning woman and laundress. As a boy King attended school for three to five months a year in an old frame building, where Mrs. Lowe, the wife of the pastor of Floyd's Chapel Baptist Church, taught 234 children in all grades. At Floyd's Chapel, King gained confidence as a singer and began to feel the call to preach. At fifteen, when he delivered a trial sermon at Floyd's Chapel and was licensed to preach, King had learned to read but could not yet write. As a young country preacher he occasionally visited Atlanta. At twenty he left Stockbridge and settled there. He lived in a rooming house and worked at various jobs, including making tires in a rubber plant, loading bales of cotton, and driving a barber-supply truck.

As a young Baptist preacher seeking a start in life, King acquired a Model T Ford to get to small preaching appointments in middle Georgia. In 1919 he met the Reverend Adam Daniel Williams of Atlanta's Ebenezer Baptist Church and began courting his daughter, Alberta Christine Williams. Three years later, at twenty-five, King became the pastor of Travelers Rest Baptist Church in East Point, Georgia; entered Atlanta's Peter James Bryant Preparatory School at the fifth-grade level; and began assisting A. D. Williams at Ebenezer Baptist Church. After graduating from the preparatory school, he entered Morehouse College in 1926. On Thanksgiving Day, King married Alberta Williams and moved into her parents' house on Auburn Avenue. They had three children. In 1930 King received his degree in theology from Morehouse. When his father-in-law died in 1931, King was called to the pulpit of Ebenezer Baptist Church. Steadily, he built it from a congregation of a few hundred people in deep

Martin Luther King, Sr. raises his umbrella as he talks with reporters at the Atlanta University Center on April 17, 1969. (AP Images.)

financial trouble into a prospering congregation of four thousand. In 1934 King attended the World's Baptist Convention in Berlin, Germany, and toured Europe and the Holy Land. After the European trip, King changed his name to Martin Luther King. His ministry occasionally drew criticism, as when he allowed the Ebenezer Church choir, led by his wife, to sing for a gala ball in celebration of the premiere of *Gone with the Wind*. The Baptist choir's appearance was controversial both for its association with social dancing and for its performance in the livery of slaves before an exclusively white audience. As an officer of Atlanta's branch of the NAACP, the Atlanta Civic and Political League, and the Atlanta Baptist Ministers Association between 1935 and 1945, however, King was better known as a leader in the struggle for black voting rights and pay equity for African American public school teachers in the city.

By the late 1940s two of King's children were doing graduate work at northern schools, Willie Christine King at Columbia University and MARTIN LUTHER KING JR. at Crozer Theological Seminary and, later, Boston University. Son Alfred Daniel Williams "A. D." King was working on his degree at Morehouse, where the elder King was on the board of trustees. Young Martin returned to Atlanta each summer to help with the demands at Ebenezer. King would have preferred for his older son to return to Ebenezer full-time, but he accepted his decision to earn a doctorate at Boston and then take another pastorate at Dexter Avenue Baptist Church in Montgomery, Alabama. King's confidence in his older son grew as he led the Montgomery bus boycott and founded the Southern Christian Leadership Conference (SCLC) to spearhead the civil rights movement in the South. The elder King joined the board of directors of the SCLC in 1957 and welcomed his son as co-pastor at Ebenezer Baptist Church in 1960. When Robert F. Kennedy interceded to win the release of Martin Luther King Jr. from the Reidsville, Georgia, state prison later that year, Martin Luther King Sr. endorsed John F. Kennedy in a closely contested presidential race with Richard M. Nixon, which may have influenced the result in several key states. Both supportive of their common cause and concerned for his son's safety, King commonly offered advice on the side of caution, but he respected his son's independent judgment.

King's life was marked by deep tragedy from 1968 to 1976. After his older son was assassinated on 4 April 1968, his younger son, A.D., became his co-pastor at Ebenezer Baptist Church. A. D. King drowned in a swimming accident on 21 July 1969.

A deranged gunman, Marcus Wayne Chenault, shot and killed Alberta Williams King on 30 June 1974 as she played the organ for services at Ebenezer Baptist Church. Two years later a granddaughter, Esther Darlene King, died of a heart attack while she was jogging. King retired from the Ebenezer pulpit in 1975. In retirement he relished his status as an elder statesman of the civil rights movement, playing a significant role in the nomination and election of Jimmy Carter as president in 1976 and supporting the work of his daughter and his daughter-in-law CORETTA SCOTT KING in building Atlanta's Martin Luther King Jr. Center for Nonviolent Social Change. Martin Luther King Sr. died in Atlanta.

FURTHER READING

The papers of Martin Luther King Sr. are in two collections, the Ebenezer Baptist Church Papers and the King Family Papers, both of which are in private hands.

King, Martin Luther, Sr., with Clayton Riley. *Daddy King: An Autobiography* (1980).

Collins, David R. *Not Only Dreamers: The Story of Martin Luther King, Sr., and Martin Luther King, Jr.* (1986).

Obituaries: *Atlanta Constitution* and *Atlanta Journal*, 12 Nov. 1984; *Atlanta Daily World*, 15 Nov. 1984.

This entry is taken from the *American National Biography* and is published here with the permission of the American Council of Learned Societies.

RALPH E. LUKER

King, Preston (3 Mar. 1936–), college professor, political philosopher, and civil rights advocate, was born Preston Theodore King in Albany, Georgia, the youngest of seven sons of Clennon W. King, a civil rights advocate and businessman, and Margaret Slater.

King followed the family view that education was essential and mandatory and proved himself to be a brilliant scholar at an early age. He entered Fisk University in Nashville at age sixteen. He majored in history, languages, and philosophy and graduated magna cum laude with a B.A. He enrolled in graduate school at the London School of Economics & Political Science in England, where he earned an M.Sc. (Econ.), the Leverhulme Award in 1958, and the Mark of Distinction and a Ph.D. in 1966. He also studied during the summers at Atlanta University (1955), Universität Wien in Austria, 1956, 1958 (German language); Université de Strasbourg in France, 1956 (French literature);

and Sorbonne in Paris, 1957 (French literature). He was later awarded an honorary doctorate from Fisk University (1999) and in 2002 was named Honorary Professor of Philosophy at the University of East Anglia in England.

In 1958, Preston King's life changed. He had been a graduate student in London, where he had always mailed in his requests for military deferments, until one vacation. He presented himself before the board, whereupon they demanded that he report immediately for a physical examination for the draft. The board's previous letters had always referred to him as "Sir," but upon seeing that he was a black man, they began to routinely call him by his first name. King has stated that had they called "Mr.," as was common practice, he would have reported for the physical. King wrote them, "Your form of address, 'Dear Preston,' is for intimates. I don't know you; you don't know me; this is official business and I would prefer you to address me in an official way. Change your form of address and I will obey the draft. If you don't change it, I will ignore it." They refused, and so did he. King went back to school in London, where he continued to receive letters from the draft board, which he ignored. When he returned home for another vacation, Preston King was arrested in a predawn raid in December 1960. He was hauled off by two federal marshals, booked, and taken to jail. Because King's brother, C. B. King, was the only black lawyer practicing south of Atlanta, Preston chose him as his attorney. The younger King was tried and convicted of four counts of draft evasion by an all-white jury. Judge William A. Bootle of the U.S. Middle District Court of Georgia sentenced him to eighteen months in prison.

Because of his activities as founder and president of the local chapter of the National Association for the Advancement of Colored People (NAACP) and as a successful businessman, Clennon W. King, after having secured his son's release on bail, advised him that his best move would be to return to London. He felt that Preston would be a target of retaliation if he went to prison.

After fleeing the United States Preston King completed his education at the London School of Economics and Political Science and went on to teach political philosophy at Lancaster University in northern England. He also taught in Australia, Cameroon, Fiji, Ghana, Kenya, Tanzania, Uganda, and New Zealand, but made his home in London, where he continued to evade the draft. He married Murreil Hazel Stern. They had two children, Oona King (born 1967), who was the second black woman elected to the British House of Commons, and Slater King (born 1968), who was named after King's brother, who had died in a tragic car crash. Preston kept in contact with his American family by hosting reunions in Africa and Jamaica and sent his children to stay with his family in Georgia, even though he still could not travel there. After his divorce Preston married Raewyn Stone in 1986. The couple had a son, Akasi Peter.

The Preston King case was given new life when his nephew, Clennon King, a television journalist, began a campaign to get his uncle home. He had been only two when his uncle had fled the country, but had kept in touch by going to the reunions. One day his uncle asked him when he was coming to see him again, and he decided it was time for Preston King to come home. He wrote articles, pitched stories, and put together press conferences. He held a march on Washington for his uncle, which proved dismal in numbers, but had great results. After the Christmas holidays, the media picked up the story and took the cause of Preston King nationwide. With this new push for clemency, Judge Bootle, who had originally sentenced King, proved to be his champion and wrote President Bill Clinton asking him to pardon King. Sadly, it would take another death, King's oldest brother, Clennon, to push the request for clemency to a final conclusion from the White House. On 19 February 2000 President Clinton issued a full pardon and Preston King was allowed to return home for the first time in forty years without the threat of imprisonment.

Within days of returning to the United States, visiting the grave sites of his parents and brothers, and burying his oldest brother, Preston King visited and was greeted warmly by Judge Bootle, who answered his door and said, "Welcome home, Mr. King." On 28 April 2000, at a White House reception, President Clinton welcomed Preston King home, saying, "Professor King, I am so glad that you are back!"

Since receiving his clemency, Preston King has been Scholar-in-Residence at Morehouse University. He also served as distinguished professor at Emory University and served on academic organizations concerned with political thought. He served as editor of *Critical Review of International, Social & Political Philosophy*, authored fourteen books, made documentary films, and wrote extensively for academic journals.

FURTHER READING
John Head, "Patriarch's Legacy of Self-Reliance and Hard Work Leaves an Indelible Mark on Next

Generations: The Kings of Albany," *Atlanta Journal-Constitution*, 26 March 2000.

DELORES WILLIAMS

King, Reatha Clark (11 Apr. 1938–), chemist and corporate leader, was born in Pavo, Georgia, the second of three daughters of Willie Clark and Ola Watts Campbell. Her mother Ola had a third-grade education, and her father Willie was illiterate. Reatha was raised in Moltrie, Georgia, by her mother and aunt after her parents separated when she was young. She had to pick cotton and do the heavy fieldwork that was the typical life in the 1940s for poor sharecroppers' children. African American girls in the rural segregated South had few role models, but she received strong encouragement from her family and community to use her academic ability to overcome social disadvantages.

Clark started school at the age of four in the one-room schoolhouse at Mount Zion Baptist Church. Clark attended the segregated Moultrie High School for Negro Youth. A teacher there encouraged her love of math and science even though the school lacked the lab equipment that the white schools had. She graduated in 1954 as the valedictorian of her class.

Clark received a scholarship to enter Clark College in Atlanta in September 1954, and she went there planning to major in home economics and return to teach in her local high school. These plans changed after her first chemistry course. Her chemistry teacher Alfred Spriggs became her mentor after recognizing her abilities. He encouraged Clark to major in chemistry and to attend graduate school.

During the summer vacations when she was at Clark College, Clark worked as a maid for a woman in upstate New York. This woman became another mentor because she encouraged Clark to visit New York City on weekends. These trips prepared Clark for the transition from a college student in the South to a graduate student in a large city.

In 1958 Clark graduated from Clark College with highest honors. She received a Woodrow Wilson Fellowship for graduate study between 1958 and 1960 and a grant from the state of Georgia to attend graduate school in Chicago (because Jim Crow laws prevented her from attending a public university in Georgia). At the University of Chicago she earned a master's degree in Chemistry in 1960. She then received a National Medical Fellowship to pursue her Ph.D. in Chemistry, which she earned in 1963. Her dissertation was titled "Contributions to the Thermochemistry of the Laves Phases." She also published two articles on thermochemical reactions before completing her Ph.D.

In graduate school Clark met N. Judge King Jr., a native of Birmingham, Alabama, and a graduate of Morehouse College. They married in December 1961 and started a commuter marriage while she was completing her Ph.D. in Chicago and he was going to graduate school at Howard University in Washington, D.C.

After completing her Ph.D., Reatha King moved to Washington, D.C., where she began work at the National Bureau of Standards under George Armstrong, becoming the first African American woman chemist to work for that agency. King remained there for five years and produced many publications of her work before she was thirty-one, which was notable for a young scientist. It was while working at the National Bureau of Standards that she had two sons, juggling work and family life with the help of child care workers.

King moved to New York City when her husband accepted a position as chair of the Department of Chemistry at Nassau Community College in Garden City. She became assistant professor of chemistry at the newly formed York College of the City University of New York and advanced rapidly through the ranks to associate professor of chemistry; in 1970 she was promoted to associate dean for natural science and mathematics. Since the college was only about two years old, there was a lot to do to establish programs of study. She advanced to full professor at York College and managed to conduct research even as she rose to the position of associate dean for academic affairs. It was while working at York College that King went to Columbia University's business school to obtain an MBA.

In 1977 King was nominated for president of Metropolitan State University in Minneapolis, Minnesota. Her husband, who now moved for her career, obtained a position in one of 3M's research divisions in 1978 and became himself a pioneer African American industrial chemist.

In 1988 Reatha King was approached by the CEO of General Mills to become vice president of General Mills and president and executive director of the General Mills Foundation. She accepted this position because she felt that in it she could make a difference in other people's lives. She was responsible for directing the philanthropies of the General Mills Foundation. King retired from General Mills in May 2002 but remained as chair of the board of directors until June 2003. She was one of the few African American women to become a chair of the board of a major corporation. In 2004 she was selected to become a Louis W. Hill Jr. Fellow in Philanthropy at the Hubert H. Humphrey Center of the University of Minnesota.

Through her sixties King continued to serve on numerous corporate and community boards. She served on the boards of Exxon Mobil Corporation and Wells Fargo and Company and on the boards of trustees of Clark Atlanta University, the Congressional Black Caucus Foundation, the International Trachoma Initiative, and the National Association of Corporate Directors (NACD). She became a life trustee of the University of Chicago and a member of the Executive Leadership Council in Washington, D.C.

King received numerous honors and awards, including fourteen honorary doctorate degrees. In 1999 she was named by the *Minneapolis Star Tribune* as one of the one hundred most influential Minnesotans of the twentieth century. In June 2000 the League of Women Voters honored King with the Civic Leader Award for her pioneering efforts to effect social change. In November 2000 she received the Minneapolis 2000 Award for civic leadership. She was chosen by the National Center for Black Philanthropy to be the co-recipient of their 2005 award for Lifetime Achievement in Philanthropy, which was presented on 11 June 2005 at the National Conference on Black Philanthropy.

FURTHER READING

King, Reatha Clark. "Becoming a Scientist: An Important Career Decision," *Sage* 6, no. 2 (Fall 1989): 47–50.

Warren, Wini. *Black Women Scientists in the United States* (1999).

JEANNETTE ELIZABETH BROWN

King, Rodney Glenn (2 Apr. 1965–17 June 2012), taxi driver whose videotaped beating by police officers in March 1991 provoked international outrage, was born in Sacramento, California, to working-class parents. His father was a construction worker and cleaner, and as a child Rodney worked long hours as a cleaner along with his father. His work schedule along with a learning disability contributed to his lack of academic success, and despite considerable athletic ability, he dropped out in 1984 during his senior year of high school. Afterward King found work in construction. During his early adulthood he had two daughters and married Crystal Waters, a woman with two children of her own. Prior to 1991 King was in and out of jail for crimes ranging from robbery to intoxication.

King became an international celebrity and emblem of police abuse in 1991, when a videotape, shot by the amateur cameraman George Holliday, was broadcast by Los Angeles television station KTLA. The video, taped the night of 3 March, showed King being brutally beaten by members of the Los Angeles Police Department (LAPD) after a high-speed police chase, estimated at 110 to 115 miles per hour. During the course of the abuse, fifty-six baton blows and six kicks from four police officers landed on King's body in a two-minute period as seventeen other LAPD and California Highway Patrol (CHP) officers stood by watching. King suffered eleven skull fractures, broken bones, and brain and kidney damage. After the beating he was taken into custody. Four days after the attack King was released, and the charge of felony evading was dropped.

In response to the spectacle of the King case, numerous political figures in the African American community appeared in the media to discuss the events. The former Democratic presidential candidate and Rainbow Coalition founder JESSE JACKSON as well as California's Democratic congresswoman MAXINE WATERS spoke out against the beatings and demanded public accountability.

On 15 March 1991 the four officers involved in the King beating—Sergeant Stacey C. Koon, Officer Laurence M. Powell, Officer Theodore Briseno, and Officer Timothy Wind—were charged with assault with a deadly weapon and excessive use of force. All four officers pleaded not guilty. In the wake of the growing media coverage and the impending trial, Los Angeles police chief Daryl Gates suspended Koon, Powell, and Briseno without pay. Wind was fired. Despite objections from the prosecution, the Superior Court judge Stanley Weisberg ordered the trial of Koon, Powell, Briseno, and Wind moved from Los Angeles to the community of Simi Valley, which included few African Americans and had a disproportionate number of police officers living in the area. One year after the initial beating, the trial for the four police officers began on 5 March 1992. On 29 April a majority white jury found three officers not guilty on all counts; the jury could not agree on a verdict for Powell.

The not guilty verdict sparked the event known as the Los Angeles riots. Looting and violence brewed for six days, overwhelming the city. The riots were one of the greatest civil unrests in California history and the first large-scale, primarily African American rebellion since the Watts riots of 1965. Local and national officials took measures to stem the violence; citywide curfews were instituted by then mayor Tom Bradley.

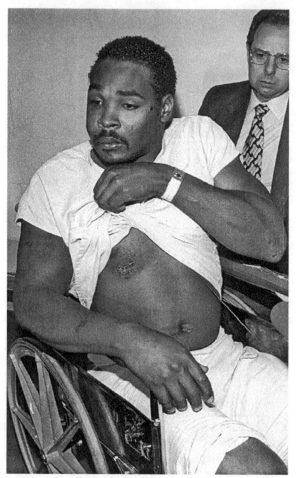

Rodney King shows his bruises in Los Angeles on March 6, 1991. (AP Images.)

Governor Pete Wilson moved four thousand army and marine troops into the city, and President George H. W. Bush federalized the National Guard. Attacks on nonrioting men and women made national headline news. Among the stories was the attack of Reginald Denny, who was pulled from his truck as he stopped to avoid hitting looters and beaten. In total sixty people were killed, and more than two thousand were injured as a result of the rioting. Over eight thousand people were arrested, and there was an estimated $1 billion worth of damage to the city of Los Angeles.

The incident continued to be a matter for the courts. Despite a not guilty verdict in criminal court, federal charges were filed against the officers. In 1993 Koon and Powell were convicted of violating King's civil rights. They both served thirty months in federal prison. King also pursued a civil suit against the city of Los Angeles and in 1994 was awarded $3.8 million in damages. A significant amount of his settlement went to legal fees, but King also used the money to start his own record label, Straight Alta-Pazz Recording Company. The events of 1991 made King a reluctant star. On 1 May 1992, in front of national cameras, he made his famous plea in response to the rioting, "Can we all get along?" a comment often used in black popular culture by comedians and political figures alike. By the end of 1992 his name became a byword for police brutality in the United States. After the trial King joined his daughters outside of Los Angeles. He earned his high school equivalency diploma and went back to a career in construction. He continued to have trouble with the law. In 1991 and 1992 he was arrested for soliciting and domestic abuse, but no charges were filed. Over the next ten years he was arrested for crimes of domestic abuse, vandalism, and driving under the influence.

In April 2012, HarperOne published King's memoir, *The Riot Within: My Journey from Rebellion to Redemption*, in which he claimed that his life was headed in a positive direction with new fiancée Cynthia Kelley, who had been a juror in the civil suit he brought against city of Los Angeles. Two months later, however, Kelley found King lying motionless at the bottom of the swimming pool at the house they shared in Rialto, California. Paramedics rushed him to the hospital, where he was pronounced dead.

FURTHER READING

King, Rodney. *The Riot Within: My Journey from Rebellion to Redemption* (2012).

Owens, Tom. *Lying Eyes: The Truth behind the Corruption and Brutality of the LAPD and the Beating of Rodney King* (1994).

"Rodney King Reluctant Symbol of Police Brutality," CNN.com, http://archives.cnn.com/2001/LAW/03/02/beating.anniversity.king.02/ (3 Mar. 2001).

Tervelon, Jervey, ed. *Geography of Rage: Remembering the Los Angeles Riots of 1992* (2002).

Obituary: *New York Times*, 18 June 2012.

SHANA L. REDMOND

King, Slater (18 July 1927–1969), civil rights activist and real estate entrepreneur, was born in Albany, Georgia, to Clennon King, an entrepreneur, grocer, and activist in local civil rights affairs, and Margaret Allegra Washington. He grew up in a relatively affluent and well-known family, attending local schools. His younger brother PRESTON KING, a political philosopher, refused the draft during the Vietnam War and lived for much of the 1960s and 1970s in England for fear of being arrested. Upon graduation from high school, Slater matriculated at Fisk University in Nashville, Tennessee, from which he graduated in 1946 with a Bachelor of Arts in Economics.

Around that same time King married Valencia Benham and the couple had two sons. King and his family returned to Albany, where King took up the management of his father's store. He also began to build up a real estate brokerage business, slowly at first, eventually securing work through the Aetna Company. His marriage to Valencia dissolved and in 1956 he married Marion Townsend, who worked in his firm and played the role of assistant.

With his business thriving and expanding, King took up his father's cause and became embroiled in local civil rights activities. He joined the Criterion Club, a local community organization and center of growing civil rights activities, and soon found himself at the center of the movement. Meanwhile, 1961 saw the development of one of the most important civil rights movements in the country, the Albany Movement. With roots deep in the history of the state and region, the Albany Movement had its official beginning when members of the Student Nonviolent Coordinating Committee mounted a voter-registration drive that soon blossomed into a far more ambitious effort at citywide desegregation. Soon, the city's civil rights organizations had come together to form what they called the Albany Movement. Protests and other forms of civic action were held. Activists were jailed by the hundreds. In 1961 Slater King was named vice president of the Albany Movement. By the winter of that year, the movement had come to the attention of MARTIN LUTHER KING JR. (no relation), who traveled to Albany and was quickly jailed for taking part in a demonstration. He returned in the summer of the following year and was jailed again. Although ultimately the Albany Movement failed to desegregate the city, the effort provided a model for future movements and groups to emulate, and it was in this environment that Slater King rose to greater prominence as an activist and civil rights leader.

A year later, in 1962, during an errand of mercy for jailed activists held at the Mitchell County prison, Marion King was attacked and beaten by police. She was in the third trimester of a pregnancy at the time, and the assault resulted in a miscarriage. The community was outraged. Martin Luther King Jr. again visited the city and spoke out against the incident.

Thereafter, Slater King's devotion to civil rights causes increased. Alongside his brother, the civil rights lawyer C. B. King, he led protests and coordinated activities for the movement, actions that often led to his arrest and imprisonment. In 1963 he was arrested and tried on charges of conspiracy to obstruct justice, a charge stemming from an organized boycott in reaction to the acquittal of the Baker County sheriff following the shooting of a black man who had already been taken into custody. King's hearing ended in a mistrial, however, and he was ultimately released.

Meanwhile, King used his brokerage firm to redress the problem of housing for African Americans in the Albany area. He worked through the local churches to build houses for the poor and acquired and resold abandoned properties through his own firm. Hoping to further alleviate what appeared to be the intransigent problem of income and skills disparity in the Albany area, he secured funding for and saw to construction of the Dougherty County Resource Center, a job-training and employment assistance center.

King was killed in 1969 in a two-car automobile accident when, on a rainy day, his car skidded out of control and crossed the center line. One of his sons, Alonzo, went on to become a prominent dancer and choreographer. Slater King left behind a legacy of social justice tied to economic and housing reform. His activities brought the Albany Movement to the nation's attention and formed an important piece of the national civil rights picture.

FURTHER READING

Chappell, David L. *Inside Agitators: White Southerners in the Civil Rights Movement* (1996).

McWhorter, Diane. *A Dream of Freedom: The Civil Rights Movement from 1954 to 1968* (2004).

Tuck, Stephen G.N. *Beyond Atlanta: The Struggle for Racial Equality in Georgia, 1940–1980* (2003).

Obituary: *Jet,* 20 Mar. 1969.

JASON PHILIP MILLER

Kirby, John (31 Dec. 1908–14 June 1952), jazz bassist and bandleader, was born in Baltimore, Maryland. Details about his parents are unknown. Abandoned, Kirby had a horrible childhood in an orphanage; it "left him without social graces, and he lacked formal education." He sold newspapers, shined shoes, and groomed horses before securing a job as a Pullman porter on the Pennsylvania Railroad. In 1924 he went to New York with a trombone, which was immediately stolen. He worked in restaurants to buy a tuba and then performed in Harlem, returning to the railroad when opportunities to play were scarce. He was a member of Bill Brown and His Brownies briefly in 1928 and again from 1929 into early 1930. Having begun to play string bass as well as tuba, he switched between both on Brown's recording "What Kind of Rhythm Is This?" (1929).

In April 1930 Kirby joined FLETCHER HENDERSON's big band. "John was a lonely, bewildered kid, who tried hard to be accepted by his peers," the trumpeter REX STEWART wrote. "He finally succeeded because of his hail-fellow-well-met act, but when he was caught off guard, it was plain to see that Kirby really was introspective and a thinker." Having begun to take lessons on string bass from WELLMAN BRAUD, Kirby continued regularly playing both instruments until 1933, when he settled on the string bass and thereafter rarely used the tuba. Not a soloist, he filled the instrument's traditional role of providing a firm rhythmic and harmonic foundation, as on such recordings as "Chinatown, My Chinatown" (1930) and "New King Porter Stomp" (1932), both on string bass, and "I'm Crazy 'bout My Baby" (1931), on tuba. He also recorded late in 1930 with the Chocolate Dandies, a group of Henderson's men under Benny Carter's direction.

After leaving Henderson in March 1934, Kirby joined CHICK WEBB's Orchestra, with which he recorded "Stompin' at the Savoy" and "Don't Be That Way." The following year he briefly led a group before returning to Henderson's orchestra from October 1935 until April 1936. He rejoined Webb in the summer of 1936 and became a member that autumn of the Mills Blue Rhythm Band under LUCKY MILLINDER. From 1935 and extending into 1938 he frequently accompanied BILLIE HOLIDAY on recordings under her name or TEDDY WILSON's.

Kirby's greatest fame came when he began leading a sextet with colleagues from his past big bands. It took shape at the Onyx Club in New York from May to August 1937, during which time its leadership was credited to the trumpeter FRANKIE NEWTON, the singer Leo Watson (who was attempting to play drums), and Kirby. Meanwhile Marietta Williams, singing under the stage name Maxine Williams, had secured a job at the Onyx and a recording date with Claude Thornhill in a septet that included Newton and Kirby but not Watson, who by August had been replaced by O'Neill Spencer. For swing versions of two Scottish tunes the singer was, by a twist of show business logic, given the Irish surname by which she became famous: MAXINE SULLIVAN. "Loch Lomond" was a hit, and by the fall, with Newton having left, Sullivan was starring at the Onyx Club with Kirby's sextet. Comprising the trumpeter CHARLIE SHAVERS, the clarinetist BUSTER BAILEY, the alto saxophonist RUSSELL PROCOPE, the pianist Billy Kyle, Kirby, and Spencer,

the group carved out its own identity, separate from Sullivan's Scotch-Irish jazz but linked to her gentle, subdued swing style.

The sextet memorized (and later wrote out, to accommodate changes in personnel) sprightly arrangements in which coordinated passages for muted trumpet, low- to mid-register clarinet, and sweet-toned alto saxophone alternated with or accompanied brief solos, as on such recordings as "Rehearsin' for a Nervous Breakdown," "Undecided" (both 1938), and "Front and Center" (1939). Its repertoire consisted of popular tunes of the swing era, new themes based on these tunes, and swing-oriented arrangements of classical and light classical material; a piece such as "Beethoven Riffs On" (recorded in 1941), with improvisations and melodic statements based on the slow movement of the Seventh Symphony, was, if less bombastic than many examples of big bands "swingin' the classics," aesthetically equally unsuccessful. Shavers and Kyle were the best soloists; both Bailey and Procope delivered their finest improvisations elsewhere, but given the sextet's orientation toward arrangement, this was not a serious flaw. Kirby as usual concentrated on underpinnings, and Spencer mainly used brushes (rather than sticks) for softness. Exceptions to these stylistic tendencies may be heard on "Royal Garden Blues" (1939), which includes "open" (that is, unmuted) trumpet, a bass solo, and a flamboyant snare drum solo.

By the time of these recordings Sullivan and Kirby were married and had enjoyed a long stand at the Onyx with the privilege of being the first African Americans to secure a sponsored network radio show, *Flow Gently, Sweet Rhythm*. The quiet polish of Kirby's sextet appealed to affluent audiences, and after leaving the Onyx the group was popular at jazz clubs, including the Famous Door in New York, and posh venues, such as the Pump Room of the Hotel Ambassador East in Chicago. The year 1942 marked a turning point in Kirby's life. His marriage ended (they had no children), Sullivan's independent popularity having carried her in another direction, and the sextet was decimated by Spencer's illness (he died in 1944) and the military draft, which took Kyle and, early the next year, Procope. Personnel changed with increasing rapidity, and interest in the sextet's idiosyncratic style declined. By 1947 Kirby was without work, and he had contracted diabetes. He reconstituted the original sextet (with SID CATLETT replacing Spencer on drums) for an unsuccessful concert at Carnegie

Hall in December 1950. After working briefly with HENRY "RED" ALLEN and in the spring of 1951 with BUCK CLAYTON, he moved to the Los Angeles area, where he worked occasionally with Carter. Unhappy and often unemployed, Kirby died in Hollywood from diabetes, its effects compounded by a fondness for alcohol and sweets. He was survived by his second wife, Margaret; her maiden name is unknown.

Having had little impact on the music's history, Kirby's sextet has only a modest stature in jazz. He is remembered mainly as a bassist in the first decade of big band jazz and in ad hoc small groups of the swing era.

FURTHER READING
Garrod, Charles. *John Kirby and His Orchestra; Andy Kirk and His Orchestra* (1991).
Schuller, Gunther. *Early Jazz: Its Roots and Musical Development* (1968).
Schuller, Gunther. *The Swing Era: The Development of Jazz, 1930–1945* (1989).
Shaw, Arnold. *52nd Street: The Street of Jazz* (1977).
Stewart, Rex. *Jazz Masters of the Thirties* (1972).
Obituaries: *Down Beat*, 16 July and 30 July 1952.
This entry is taken from the *American National Biography* and is published here with the permission of the American Council of Learned Societies.

BARRY KERNFELD

Kirk, Andy (28 May 1898–11 Dec. 1992), jazz and popular bandleader and bassist, was born Andrew Dewey Kirk, the son of Charles Kirk and Dellah (maiden name unknown). The family lived in Cincinnati, Ohio, but Kirk may have been born just across the river in Newport, Kentucky; he was unsure. His mother died around 1901, and his father disappeared. Kirk was raised by his mother's half sister, Mary Banion, a domestic who moved her family to Denver in 1904.

In his youth Kirk sang and studied piano but took neither activity seriously. At age sixteen he quit high school. About three years later, while working as a porter and shoe shiner in Sterling, Colorado, he bought a tenor saxophone and taught himself to play. He returned to Denver and, while working as a mailman, became a musician. He acquired other instruments, including a tuba and a string bass, which he played under the bandleader and violinist GEORGE MORRISON. While with Morrison, Kirk performed in New York (1920), worked alongside the visiting pianist JELLY ROLL MORTON (spring 1921), and toured widely (1922 and 1924). On 22 July 1925 Kirk married the pianist Mary Colston, a childhood friend and musical colleague; they had one child.

After less significant affiliations, including an unsuccessful attempt to break into the Chicago jazz scene, Kirk joined the trumpeter Terrence Holder's ten-piece band, the Dark Clouds of Joy, in Dallas around 1927. The band played mainly in Tulsa and Oklahoma City. In January 1929 Holder left the group, and Kirk was elected leader. The saxophonist John Williams, the violinist CLAUDE "FIDDLER" WILLIAMS, and the drummer Edward "Crackshot" McNeil were among the members of Holder's band who stayed with Kirk and the band, renamed the Twelve Clouds of Joy.

The band's first success came at a whites-only venue in Kansas City, Missouri, in June 1929. "Our band didn't stress jazz, though we played it. We emphasized dance music—romantic ballads and pop tunes and waltzes," Kirk explained in his autobiography (Kirk and Lee, 62). After that the Clouds of Joy began touring extensively. At an audition for a record date in Kirk's new home base, Kansas City, the pianist Marion Jackson failed to show up, and Williams's wife, MARY LOU WILLIAMS, sat in with the band. She returned to the studio for the band's first recordings in November 1929, for which she also supplied several pieces, including "Mess-a-Stomp," "Corky Stomp," and "Lotta Sax Appeal." This last title was released under John Williams's name.

In January 1930 the Twelve Clouds of Joy went to New York City to entertain at the Roseland and Savoy ballrooms. In Chicago, at rehearsals for a recording session in April 1930, the producer Jack Kapp noticed Jackson at the piano and insisted on having Mary Lou Williams instead. She thus continued to serve as the band's only pianist on record, including a session in October 1930 that produced "Dallas Blues." The next year, having already participated in some performances, Williams replaced Jackson permanently.

During the early 1930s Kirk's Twelve Clouds of Joy toured the Midwest and the Northeast extensively, returning when convenient to Kansas City, where nightlife flourished under a corrupt administration scarcely touched by the Depression. March 1931 brought recordings for the Victor label that were released under the singer BLANCHE CALLOWAY's name because Kirk was contracted to Brunswick, and the band toured with Calloway in the role of director before Kirk successfully defeated this attempt to wrest the Clouds from his direction.

In these early years Kirk carried the bass line. A photo from 1929 or 1930 shows him holding a conductor's baton and standing near his tuba, tuba mutes, and bass saxophone. By 1934 at the latest, when the tubaist and string bassist Booker Collins joined the band—if not two or three years earlier—Kirk had given up this essential instrumental role and functioned solely as conductor.

Important new sidemen included the trumpeter Irving "Mouse" Randolph (1931 to spring 1934) and a succession of tenor saxophonists: BEN WEBSTER (1933–July 1934), LESTER YOUNG (briefly in summer 1934), and Buddy Tate (late 1934 to summer 1935). Unfortunately the band did not record in this period. Tate's successor, Dick Wilson (1936–1941), who became the Clouds' greatest soloist on record, exhibited a style considerably more original than Kirk's featured soloist and writer Mary Lou Williams. Wilson and Williams figure prominently on such studio recordings as "Walkin' and Swingin'," "Moten Swing," "Bearcat Shuffle," "Christopher Columbus," and "Corky" (all from March 1936); "Wednesday Night Hop" and "In the Groove" (February 1937); and "Ring Dem Bells" (January 1941) and on live recordings from the Trianon Ballroom in Cleveland in 1937.

The other crucial hiring was the singer Pha Terrell, who joined the band in 1933. The version of his romantic ballad, "Until the Real Thing Comes Along," recorded in April 1936, became a huge hit. Further ballads followed, including Terrell's rendition of "Dedicated to You" (December 1936). With the Twelve Clouds now numbering fifteen, including the leader and Terrell, Kirk embarked on his first southern tour in 1937 on the strength of the popularity of "Until the Real Thing Comes Along." From that year through the 1940s the Clouds of Joy toured about fifty thousand miles annually throughout the nation and in Canada while also alternating with the big bands of FLETCHER HENDERSON, LOUIS ARMSTRONG, and EARL HINES for residencies at the Grand Terrace in Chicago from 1936 to 1939. Having earlier expressed disappointment that record companies were not interested in having an African American band record its stylistically white dance repertory (as he described it), Kirk changed his mind after the success of Terrell's vocals and instead expressed regret that there were now fewer opportunities to play jazz.

In 1939 Kirk moved his home to New York City. Important new band members included the tenor saxophonist DON BYAS (1940), the singer June Richmond (1939–1943), and the guitarist Floyd "Wonderful" Smith (1939–1942), whose brilliantly original and eccentric "Floyd's Guitar Blues" featured electric steel guitar playing (March 1939). The tenor saxophonist Al Sears (1941–1942) was replaced by JIMMY FORREST (1942–1948), who at one point played alongside the tenor saxophonist EDDIE "LOCKJAW" DAVIS (1944). Williams and her second husband, the trumpeter Shorty Baker, left Kirk in 1942. The trumpeter HOWARD MCGHEE, featured on "McGhee Special," joined in 1941, and the pianist KENNY KERSEY, featured on "Boogie Woogie Cocktail," was drafted in 1943. Richmond's singing on "Hey Lawdy Mama" was another highlight from this July 1942 recording session.

At some point the saxophonist CHARLIE PARKER joined Kirk briefly. The trumpeter FATS NAVARRO played alongside McGhee in 1944, the pianist Hank Jones joined after Kersey was drafted, and JOE WILLIAMS sang with the band briefly in 1946. Kirk's band had a central role in the movie *Killer Diller* (1948), but his great musicians were gone by this point. The performances are unremarkable, the improvising tenor saxophonists in particular inviting harsh comparisons to soloists who had previously passed through the band. The Clouds of Joy ceased touring in 1949, but Kirk continued to lead bands intermittently into the early 1950s.

In 1952 Kirk went into the real estate business in New York City. The following year he became a Jehovah's Witness, and he subsequently played in Witnesses' orchestras for mass meetings at Yankee Stadium. In the late 1960s he managed the Hotel Theresa in Harlem. During the 1980s he worked for the musicians union in New York City, where he died.

Without leaving a truly remarkable legacy, apart from Wilson's improvisations and Smith's bizarre experiment in amplified sound, Kirk's Clouds of Joy were among the best of the many big bands (whether African American or white) that were comfortable playing in a wide array of jazz and pop styles, from a slow fox-trot to a polka, from the lindy hop to a waltz. During the war years, as the Clouds of Joy diminished in importance, Kirk's band provided a training group for trumpeters and saxophonists who would become prominent in modern jazz.

FURTHER READING

An extensive interview is in the oral history collection of the Institute of Jazz Studies, Newark, New Jersey.

Kirk, Andy, and Amy Lee. *Twenty Years on Wheels* (1989).

Driggs, Frank. "My Story, by Andy Kirk," *Jazz Review* 2 (Feb. 1959): 12–17.

Hester, Mary Lou. *Going to Kansas City* (1980).

McCarthy, Albert. *Big Band Jazz* (1974).

Schuller, Gunther. *The Swing Era: The Development of Jazz, 1930–1945* (1989).

Obituary: *New York Times*, 15 Dec. 1992.

DISCOGRAPHY

Allen, Walter C. *Hendersonia: The Music of Fletcher Henderson and His Musicians: A Bio-discography* (1973).

Garrod, Charles. *John Kirby and His Orchestra; Plus, Andy Kirk and His Orchestra* (1991).

This entry is taken from the *American National Biography* and is published here with the permission of the American Council of Learned Societies.

BARRY KERNFELD

Kirk, Gabrielle. *See* McDonald, Gabrielle Kirk.

Kirk, Rahsaan Roland (7 Aug. 1935–5 Dec. 1977), jazz musician, was born Ronald Theodore Kirk in Columbus, Ohio, the son of Theodore Kirk and Gertrude Broadus. Kirk was blind from infancy. He first demonstrated an interest in music when he was a small boy. Anxious to become the bugler at summer camp, he began blowing the notes of the overtone series on a water hose. Soon his parents gave him a bugle, which he played for a few years before switching to trumpet. He gave up that instrument, however, when his eye doctor decided that the continuous force required to blow the instrument was hard on Kirk's eyes. When Kirk was about twelve, he began playing clarinet in the band at Columbus's Ohio State School for the Blind, learning by listening to the teacher play his parts on the piano. At home he began to practice on the C-melody saxophone; he picked up a few pointers from a friend, but mostly he learned on his own. By age fifteen he was playing tenor saxophone in clubs with a local rhythm and blues band led by Boyd Moore.

At sixteen Kirk had a dream in which he played two instruments at once. In a local music store he found an unusual instrument called the manzello—essentially a soprano saxophone with a slightly curved neck and a forward-facing bell. He bought it and began playing it in simultaneous tandem with his tenor saxophone. A year or two later he acquired a stritch, which is basically a straight alto saxophone. After making a few modifications to his instruments, he was able to play all of them at once, using carefully worked out three-part harmonies. He also used each of them for solo improvisations.

Kirk made his first recording, on the King label, in 1956, but the album was poorly distributed and is little known. He used the name Roland from at least the time of this recording, but why he used it is unknown. He added the honorific Rahsaan, a name that came to him in a dream, in 1970. His second album, *Introducing Roland Kirk* (1960), made after he moved to Chicago, was better distributed and marked his entry onto the national jazz scene. Soon after recording it he played with some world-famous jazz musicians during a short concert tour of Germany. On a subsequent stay in New York City he made another album, *Kirk's Work* (1961), and he worked a three-month engagement with CHARLES MINGUS's group. He also appeared on Mingus's albums *Oh Yeah* and *Tonight at Noon*.

From 1962 until the end of his life Kirk led various jazz combos, often using the title the Vibration Society. He appeared frequently at jazz festivals and in jazz clubs around the world. Along the way he added flute and a variety of unorthodox woodwinds to some forty-five other instruments, many of them homemade. In the fall of 1975 a stroke paralyzed his right side. Despite the disability, he resumed performing within a few months. Although he no longer could play two or three instruments at once, his modifications of his tenor saxophone and the unusual techniques he had developed early in his career enabled him to play one-handed. He also continued playing flute with the aid of a neck-supported holder. He suffered a second stroke in 1976. For a few months in 1977 he and the saxophonist Frank Foster operated the Vibration School of Music in East Orange, New Jersey. Kirk also resumed playing, but with greatly reduced strength and facility. He died in Bloomington, Indiana, shortly after giving two concerts at Indiana University. He was survived by his wife, Dorthann.

Kirk's earliest recording shows that by age twenty-one he had a firm grasp of the bebop musical language, an excellent tone, and a sure command of the supposedly unwieldy manzello and stritch. He also used his two-instrument technique in a thoroughly musical way to state theme choruses and interludes that contrasted effectively with his one-horn improvised solos. Subsequent recordings document an evolving and maturing solo style and the development of his three-horn ensemble technique.

In the years before his stroke Kirk's playing was filled with energy and rhythmic drive. His emotions seemed to burst the bounds of his instruments, as he ended saxophone phrases with audible groans, sang in a frenzied manner while playing flute, and punctuated choruses with blasts on a siren or a whistle (all heard on the album *Three for the Festival* [1968]). Onstage his appearance was unusual, with some instruments hanging from neck straps and others sticking from his pockets or from the bell of his tenor saxophone, all within easy reach. Sometimes he kept his melodic ideas flowing without interruption by means of circular breathing (inflating his cheeks with pockets of air that he used while inhaling through his nostrils). His recording of "Saxophone Concerto" (1972) extends for twenty-one minutes without a break.

Kirk had a passionate interest in all jazz styles, and he paid tribute to SIDNEY BECHET, DUKE ELLINGTON, BILLIE HOLIDAY, LESTER YOUNG, CHARLIE PARKER, Charles Mingus, JOHN COLTRANE, HORACE SILVER, and other jazz greats in his compositions. He also was interested in European classical music of the twentieth century (recording an album titled *Variation on a Theme of Hindemith* in 1963), African music, and music of the Middle East and India. Although his fundamental style was in the bebop idiom, he played New Orleans–style (Dixieland) jazz and free jazz with great facility. A staunch believer in the musical traditions that he represented, he preferred to call his music black classical music rather than jazz.

FURTHER READING

Kruth, John. *Bright Moments: The Life and Legacy of Rahsaan Roland Kirk* (2000).

Obituary:*New York Times*, 6 Dec. 1977.

This entry is taken from the *American National Biography* and is published here with the permission of the American Council of Learned Societies.

THOMAS OWENS

Kirk, Ronald "Ron" (27 June 1954–), U.S. Trade Representative, was born Ronald Kirk in Austin, Texas, the youngest of four children of Lee Kirk, a postal worker, and Willie Mae Kirk, a schoolteacher. Kirk attended public schools in Austin and, like his family, was politically active from a young age. He was elected to serve as president of the student council during his senior year. Following his high school studies, he enrolled at Austin College in Sherman, Texas, where he studied political science and sociology. Kirk received his B.A. in

1976. Afterward, Kirk decided on a career in law and enrolled at the University of Texas Law School. In 1979 Kirk was awarded his law degree and set out to practice in the private sector. He married Matrice Ellis in 1987; the couple had two daughters, Elizabeth and Catherine.

Using his knowledge of the law and his political acumen, Kirk accepted, in 1981, a position on the staff of U.S. Senator Lloyd Bentsen of Texas. This was a tremendous opportunity for Kirk as he learned how to be politically effective and how Washington worked. Taking the knowledge he gained from his service with Senator Bentsen, he left Washington to return to Austin in 1983 to work as a lobbyist. Back in Austin, Kirk employed his ever-growing knowledge of politics and public policy to lobby the state legislature on a variety of legislative matters for both private law firms and the City of Dallas.

By 1994, Kirk was looking for a more active political role. He became the ninety-seventh Texas secretary of state. In this capacity, Kirk worked closely with powerful Democratic governor Ann Richards. When Governor Richards was swept out of office by George W. Bush, Kirk left office and returned to Dallas, where he had considerable political interests and support. Shortly thereafter, he announced his candidacy for mayor of Dallas in the spring of 1995. Ron Kirk became the first African American to be elected mayor of Dallas. He took office in June of 1995 with the support of a broad-based coalition that included minorities, whites, business, and labor. However, being mayor of a large metropolitan city did not come without its difficulties.

As with most cities, Dallas had a strong and very active city council, which the mayor has to contend with in order to accomplish anything. Further, Kirk had to work with the Dallas School Board, which could be equally difficult. Unlike previous Dallas mayor's, Kirk generally was able to keep the peace and transform a city best known as a haven for right-wing extremists and the place where President John F. Kennedy was assassinated, into a thriving metropolis. Kirk ran for reelection in 1999 and was reelected overwhelmingly with 74 percent of the vote. The allure of the being the mayor, however, wore off and Kirk became intrigued with the possibility of replacing Phil Gramm (R-TX) in the U.S. Senate in 2002.

Ron Kirk resigned as mayor in 2001 to run for the Senate. Kirk succeeded in becoming the first African American candidate for the U.S. Senate in Texas when he won the Democratic Party nomination in 2002. His main opponent was Republican John Cornyn, the attorney general of Texas. After a campaign filled with political trench warfare and allegations of race-baiting by supporters of Cornyn, Kirk lost the election, garnering only 43 percent of the vote. Kirk rebounded by returning to private law practice in Dallas. But he remained active in both the Texas and the national Democratic parties.

In 2008 Ron Kirk supported and was heavily involved in the presidential campaign of Senator BARACK OBAMA. In Texas, Kirk worked hard to help Obama defeat U.S. Senator Hillary Rodham Clinton (D-NY). Though Clinton edged Obama in the state's primary, Obama secured more Texas delegates overall as a result of his victory in the caucus part of the election. After President Obama's election in November 2008, Kirk was mentioned by political commentators as a likely candidate for an administration post. On 19 December 2008, at the Drake Hotel in Chicago, President Obama formally nominated Ron Kirk to become the U.S. Trade Representative; the first African American to be so nominated. Along with other Obama nominees, such as Timothy Geithner and Tom Daschle, Kirk ran into political turbulence when political opponents discovered that Kirk had tax problems. The tax issues, however, were cleared up quickly and the U.S. Senate confirmed Kirk 92–5 on 18 March 2009, and he was sworn into office later that day. As trade representative, Kirk served as the primary advisor to the president on all trade-related issues.

FURTHER READING

Boyer Peter J. "The New Texan: Why George Bush Is Scared of Ron Kirk." *New Yorker*, 12 Aug 2002.

Knowlton, Brian. "Trade Diplomat Taps His Deal-Making Past." *New York Times*, 29 May 2009.

Tumulty, Karen. "Can He Rope Texas?," *Time*, 19 Aug 2002.

Biography, U.S. Trade Representative Ron Kirk, http://www.ustr.gov/about-us/biographies-key-officials/united-states-trade-representative-ron-kirk.

DARYL A. CARTER

Kitt, Eartha Mae (17 Jan. 1927–25 Dec. 2008), singer and actor, was born in North, South Carolina. In the late 1990s she learned that she was the illegitimate daughter of Anna Mae Riley, a 14-year-old black Cherokee sharecropper, and a white man. As young children, Eartha and her younger half sister, Anna Pearl, were abandoned by their father and later by their mother. The sisters lived on a farm with a foster family until 1936, when they moved to New York City to live with their aunt, Mamie Lue Riley, a domestic.

As an adolescent, Kitt attended Metropolitan High School (later called the High School of Performing Arts). She relished her unusual voice and facility with language, sang, danced, played baseball, and became a pole-vaulting champion. Eartha left school at age fourteen, and two years later she met KATHERINE DUNHAM, who offered her a dance scholarship and then a spot as a singer and dancer with her troupe. Kitt toured Mexico, South America, and Europe with Dunham and quickly emerged as a soloist. When the tour ended, she remained in Paris, launching a career as a nightclub entertainer. Her provocative and sensual dancing style and her throaty singing voice enthralled audiences from France to Egypt and from Los Angeles to Stockholm.

In 1951 Orson Welles gave Kitt her first role in the legitimate theater when he cast her as Helen of Troy in his stage production *Faust*. Kitt won critical reviews for her performance and toured with the play through Germany and Turkey, after which she returned to New York and audiences at the Village Vanguard and La Vie en Rose. When the producer Leonard Stillman saw her in *Faust*, he was inspired to revive his *New Faces* Broadway revue, and Kitt's debut in *New Faces of 1952* was an instant sensation. Brooks Atkinson of the *New York Times* encapsulated audience reaction to her breakout performance in his stage review: "Eartha Kitt panics the customers with some very combustible singing and performing.... Now we know why the city is so strict about its fire laws in the theater." Stillman's hit show was followed by a 1954 film version, in which Kitt starred, and a best-selling Broadway album featuring Kitt's fiery version of "Monotonous," which began her recording career. Her first solo album, a self-titled record released in 1953, includes a range of songs from "African Lullaby" to "C'est Si Bon" and "I Wanna Be Evil."

Throughout the 1950s and 1960s Kitt flourished in a succession of entertainment media. Smitten by her combination of husky sexiness, talent, and elegant titillation, journalists published a swell of articles and interviews. She performed for sold-out crowds in cabarets and nightclubs throughout the United States and abroad, and she regularly released studio and live albums. Her starring role in the 1955 Broadway play *Mrs. Patterson*, which ran for 101 performances, earned her a Tony nomination. She continued working on Broadway in the musicals *Shinbone Alley* (1957) and *Jolly's Progress* (1959). Hollywood took notice of Kitt's popularity and dynamic presence, casting her in *The Accused* (1957); the W. C. HANDY biographical film *St. Louis*

Eartha Kitt rehearses for a show in Paris, France, Dec. 23, 1950. (AP Images.)

Blues (1958); and the title role, opposite SAMMY DAVIS JR. and NAT KING COLE, in an all-black version of *Anna Lucasta* (1959), for which she earned an Oscar nomination. Kitt's versatility and playful style were perfect for the developing medium of television, and her increasing visibility was due in part to frequent appearances on 1950s variety shows like *The Ed Sullivan Show, Your Show of Shows, Colgate Comedy Hour*, and *Toast of the Town*. A favorite guest of television show hosts, she was equally hospitable to television audiences, even touring her Riverside Drive penthouse for Edward R. Murrow's viewers on *Person to Person*. She made guest appearances on many of the 1960s hit shows, including *I Spy, What's My Line?*, and *Mission Impossible*. During this period, Kitt enjoyed a glamorous and opulent lifestyle. Although she was romantically linked with the Continental playboy Porfirio Rubirosa, the movie theater chain heir Arthur Loew Jr., the cosmetics mogul Charles Revson, and Sammy Davis Jr., Kitt married William McDonald in 1960. The couple had one daughter, Kitt, and divorced in 1965.

In 1968 Kitt was invited to the White House for the "Women Doers' Luncheon," hosted by Lady Bird Johnson and publicized as a discussion on juvenile delinquency. When Kitt's speech linked America's racial and social problems to the war in Vietnam, goodwill toward the star evaporated. Beginning with news reports that claimed her comments had made the first lady cry, Kitt was excoriated in the press. While MARTIN LUTHER KING JR. and other antiwar activists lauded her remarks (some even wore "Eartha Kitt for President" buttons), general attitudes toward the star were critical. Contrary to conventional wisdom, Kitt did continue to work after the incident, primarily overseas, although she was forced to contend with invasive FBI and CIA investigations, press ridicule, loss of popularity, and limited career options. She drew criticism again in 1972, this time from African Americans, when she performed in South Africa after receiving temporary "white status."

In the 1970s and 1980s Kitt worked primarily as a cabaret entertainer and occasionally as an actor. She resumed recording in the 1980s, releasing more than a dozen albums in less than a decade, and returned to Broadway in 1978 in an all-black version of GEOFFREY HOLDER's *Timbuktu*, for which she earned her second Tony nomination. *I Love Men*, Kitt's 1984 album, found an audience with the gay disco crowd and enhanced her reputation as a gay icon. In the 1990s Kitt performed her one-woman show in London and New York, released a five-CD retrospective, *Eartha Quake*, and appeared in cameo roles in several Hollywood films.

Kitt's star rose during a pivotal period for black Americans. That she represented fundamental freedoms—of expression, of movement, of sexuality—at a time when American blacks struggled under legal and de facto segregation, exposes America's complex attitudes toward African Americans in general and African American women in particular. Kitt cultivated a style and persona that simultaneously challenged and tapped into existing stereotypes of black women, specifically historical representations of the "mulatto" and "jezebel" as racially ambiguous, sexual predators, manipulators, and seducers of white men.

Applauded as sophisticated, urbane, and sexually powerful, she was also depicted as a potentially dangerous sex kitten with contempt for her rural and racial past and with a preference for white men. Characterizations of Kitt's "feline" sex appeal began when Kitt played the sexy and independent alley cat Mehitabel in *Shinbone Alley* in 1957. The description stuck, and Kitt's embrace of her sex kitten image can be seen most clearly in her acceptance of the role of Catwoman in the 1960s television show *Batman* and in the naming of her 1991 memoir, *Confessions of a Sex Kitten*, and her 1999 greatest hits album, *Purr-fect*.

Nowhere is Kitt's unique persona more apparent than in her speech. As with many performers, she sought to lose her accent and to perfect standard stage speech. The resulting speech pattern, much like that of SIDNEY POITIER, subverts people's expectations and makes it difficult to locate Kitt's origin. On the subject of her speech, Orson Welles told Kitt: "It's too clear. You don't sound as though you came from anywhere. Everyone sounds as though he's from somewhere, but you—? NO" (Kitt, *Thursday's Child*). Kitt's use of voice control and language—on her first album she sang in English, French, Spanish, Turkish, and Swahili—has allowed her the opportunity, on occasion, to suspend being labeled.

In the late 1990s Kitt charmed New York City taxi riders when she purred seatbelt warnings as one of the original Celebrity Talking Taxi voices. In 2001 Kitt's fairy tale story continued, when she was cast as the Fairy Godmother in the touring production of *Cinderella*. She continued to work in theater, film, and music into her 80s. She died of colon cancer at the age of 81.

FURTHER READING

Kitt, Eartha. *Alone with Me* (1976).
Kitt, Eartha. *Confessions of a Sex Kitten* (1991).
Kitt, Eartha. *I'm Still Here* (1989).
Kitt, Eartha. *Thursday's Child* (1956).
Obituary: *New York Times.* 25 Dec. 2008.

LISA E. RIVO

Kittrell, Flemmie Pansy (25 Dec. 1904–1 Oct. 1980), home economist and university professor, was born in Henderson, North Carolina, to James Lee Kittrell, a farmer, and Alice Mills Kittrell, a homemaker and possibly a farmworker. Both were of Cherokee Indian and African American descent. The seventh of nine siblings and the youngest daughter, Kittrell attended school in Vance County, North Carolina, and received her B.S. degree in 1928 from Hampton Institute (now Hampton University) in Virginia. In 1930 she earned a master's and in 1938 a Ph.D., both from Cornell University. The first African American woman to receive a doctorate in home economics, Kittrell became an influential educator, nutritionist, and philanthropist, a true renaissance woman who epitomized leadership, wisdom, and progressive qualities in her life.

Kittrell was widely published and received many scholarships and awards during her academic career. These included the Rosenwald Scholarship, the General Education Board Scholarship, the Anna Cora Smith Scholarship, and the Price Administration Award for voluntary contribution to President Truman's Price Control Program. Her professional memberships included the Home Economics Advisory Council of Cornell University, the executive committee of the American Association for the United Nations, the American Association of University Women, the American Dietetic Association, the American Association for the Advancement of Science, and the American Home Economics Association. Kittrell was also a member of several honor societies: Omicron Nu, Pi Lambda Theta, Phi Kappa Phi, Sigma Delta Epsilon, and Beta Kappa Chi. For her exemplary achievements and contribution to the field of home economics, in the early 1970s the American Home Economics Association set up the Flemmie P. Kittrell Fellowships.

Kittrell's professional career began as an instructor of home economics in 1928 at Bennett College, Greensboro, North Carolina. She returned to teach at Bennett in 1938, following her graduate studies at Cornell. In 1940 she went back to her alma mater, Hampton Institute, as dean of women and director of the home economics department, where she earned deep admiration from peers and the college's leadership. In 1944 Hampton president Ralph P. Bridgeman praised her contributions: "You have been a pioneer here. Your standards have been the highest and Hampton's personal services to women have been greatly improved under your leadership" (Kittrell Papers, box 104-3, folder 16). For her contribution "to higher education and finer womanhood" (Kittrell Papers, box 104-4, folder 22) Hampton in 1967 instituted the Flemmie P. Kittrell Hall, which later became the School of Pharmacy. Kittrell was also elected to the board of trustees at Hampton in 1955 and received its Alumni Award for outstanding alumna in the same year.

From 1944 to 1971 Kittrell was at Howard University, where she chaired the department of home economics from the year she joined the faculty onward. She gave a solid foundation to home economics by introducing many new courses and developing the department's academic strength. The foundation of Kittrell's home economics philosophy was based on family support and the nurturing of children. She devoted considerable energy at Howard to developing the nursery school, and much of the data gathered from the teaching of children at the school provided a direction for home economics curricula in general. Kittrell also conducted workshops and seminars on child development. Furthermore, she immersed herself in activities on the campus related to community service. Snippets of her success in the academic and curricular arena are gathered from documents of the period, such as letters, that reveal the admiration that her peers and superiors felt for her. The president of Howard University in 1958, MORDECAI JOHNSON, wrote to her "to express deep appreciation for your valuable services" (Kittrell Papers, box 104-6, folder 4). Kittrell served on various committees such as Religious Life and Social Activities. She also contributed to multicultural understanding through her travels abroad and through her interactions with the international community at Howard. For this the university presented her with the International Club Award in 1961. Kittrell spearheaded the effort to construct a new four-story building for the department of home economics (now the School of Human Ecology); the preschool center and the living room were named in her honor. For her vision and dedication in education, community service, and international understanding she was appointed professor emeritus in 1974.

Kittrell taught from 1974 to 1976 at Cornell University, where she was a visiting professor in the College of Human Ecology. Earlier, in 1968 Cornell had awarded her the University Alumni Award for her achievement in the study of human development and quality of environment. And in 1971, prior to beginning her tenure at Cornell, Kittrell was elected to be a member for a three-year term of the Cornell University Council. Cornell honored her service to the university by instituting an annual Flemmie Kittrell Lecture.

Both as an educator and in her private life, Kittrell had a special concern for children's education. She promoted, through her time and her money, the physical and emotional development of African American children. In a 1970 article about children's education she wrote, "Unless we as a society are ready to commit our resources to a long term plan to ensure that every child will have access to the kind of care most appropriate for his needs … we will be a nation drowned in the tears of children" (Kittrell Papers, box 104-12, folder 21). According to available sources she contributed to a milk plan for fifty children during the summer of 1967 (Kittrell Papers, box 104-3, folder 1) and played

a leading role in establishing the nursery school in the department of home economics at Howard University in 1970–1971. Contemporary sources also reveal her commitment to women's issues. She lectured extensively both in the United States and abroad on children's and women's development issues. "What American working mothers do about baby sitters—how frozen foods shorten her working time—and what progress the American Negro is making" (*Washington Post*, 29 July 1958, FPK Vertical File, Clippings), were some of the issues on which Kittrell focused her lectures in Africa.

Some of Kittrell's greatest contributions were on the international scene. In 1947 she was selected by the U.S. Department of State to conduct surveys of the nutrition practices in Nigeria, the Gold Coast, and French West Africa. In 1949 she attended two international conferences: the International Congress in Home Economics in Stockholm, Sweden, and the International League for Peace and Freedom in Copenhagen, Denmark. In 1950 she received a Fulbright Fellowship to spend a year at Baroda University in Madhya Pradesh, India, where she founded the department of home economics and developed its curriculum. "One of Kittrell's contribution [*sic*] was a credit system, for a specific semester's work, so that a young woman, although forced to leave school after a year, or two or three years, would later be able to work toward her degree" (*Washington Afro-American*, 4 Dec. 1954, FPK Vertical File, Clippings). While this system was commonplace in the United States, in India students had to, and still in many institutions must, complete the fours years of undergraduate degree consecutively. Kittrell's greatness lay not just in fulfilling the immediate goals of a project but in looking beyond to establish standards for larger human understanding. As the first black woman to go to India on a Fulbright, according to the dean of the faculty of home science in Baroda, she deserved praise for "trying your best to interpret Indian culture and Indian point of view…. If we can overcome the prejudices towards different nations and races … I am sure we will make progress towards peace" (Kittrell Papers, box 104-4, file 5). For many years after she returned home, Kittrell continued to serve Baroda University's home economics department as an examiner.

In 1957 the Department of State again called upon Kittrell, this time to accompany twenty-two Indian women to Japan and Hawaii to analyze home economics extension techniques. That same year, also for the State Department, she toured West and Central Africa on a cultural tour. In 1960 she conducted a nutrition survey of India and Thailand for the United Nations. In 1961, again at the behest of the Department of State, she went on a cultural tour to Guinea. In the same year she also served as a consultant for the Methodist Church in northern and southern Rhodesia and Mozambique. And between 1961 and 1965 Kittrell served as the home economics consultant to the Congo Polytechnic Institute for the Women's Division of the Methodist Church.

In recognition of her national and international work in the field of home economics Kittrell was listed in the first edition of *Who's Who of American Women* in 1958. In 1961 she received the Scroll of Honor from the National Council of Negro Women. The American Home Economics Association instituted an international scholarship in her name in 1972, and in 1974 the University of North Carolina at Greensboro conferred an honorary doctorate upon her. Kittrell died of a heart attack in Washington, D.C., in 1980 at the Howard University Hospital.

FURTHER READING

The Flemmie P. Kittrell Papers are housed in the Manuscript Division, Moorland-Spingarn Research Center, Howard University, Washington, D.C. Newspaper and journal clippings on Kittrell are also found in the Vertical File (Clippings) of the MSRC's Library Division.

Hine, Darlene Clark, ed. *Black Women in America*, vol. 2, 2d ed. (2000).

Kessler, James, ed., et al. *Distinguished American Scientists of the 20th Century* (1996).

Smith, Jessie Carney, ed. *Notable American Women* (1992).

ANITA NAHAL

Knight, Etheridge (19 Apr. 1931–10 Mar. 1991), poet, was born in Corinth, Mississippi, the son of Etheridge "Bushie" Knight and Belzora Cozart. Knight grew up in Paducah, Kentucky, quit school after the eighth grade, and later ran away from home. During his teenage years he learned various toasts from the older African American men with whom he frequented bars and poolrooms. Toast-telling, or reciting long narrative poems, usually in rhyming couplets, was a social activity Knight enjoyed and later perfected in his prison years.

At age seventeen Knight joined the U.S. Army, serving as a medical technician from 1947 to 1951. He was wounded in Korea and became addicted to morphine, the drug used to treat him. Before his enlistment, however, he had already begun using drugs to escape the pain and disillusionment of growing up in poverty. He continued to abuse narcotics after his discharge and in 1960 was given a ten- to twenty-five-year sentence for armed robbery, committed to support his habit. He served most of his sentence at the Indiana State Prison and was paroled in November 1968. Upon his release from prison, Knight married the poet SONIA SANCHEZ, with whom he had corresponded while incarcerated.

Knight had found among his fellow inmates a receptive audience for the toasts he recited. "The ability to talk is power," he said. "I learned that very young, that the people who could rap and write, you didn't have to fight as much." He soon applied his understanding of the components of a successful toast—interesting subjects, identifiable characters, and specific language—to written poetry. By 1963 he was writing and submitting poetry for publication. He established contacts with black poets, writers, and publishers such as Sanchez, GWENDOLYN BROOKS, and DUDLEY RANDALL. Randall's Detroit-based small press, Broadside, meant as an outlet for black writing, published Knight's first book of poetry, *Poems from Prison*, in 1968.

Knight's emergence as a poet coincided with the rise of the Black Arts Movement, which began in the early 1960s and continued through the mid-1970s. Not since the Harlem Renaissance of the 1920s and early 1930s had such an outpouring of literature and art come from the African American community. Black Aestheticians (as those involved in the movement were called) used their art to encourage racial pride and political involvement, specifically on the part of the working class and the poor. Knight, who certainly wrote on these themes, expressed his reason for writing by saying that he and other poets are naturally meddlers: "The result of a poet's meddling emerges in different ways. Sometimes it's a howl or a scream; sometimes it's a love song or a jubilee; sometimes it's 'arty' intellectual masturbation. But always the main motivation must be loving concern."

Knight's concern for his audience, primarily the African American community, is apparent in poems such as "A Watts Mother Mourns While Boiling Beans" and "For Black Poets Who Think of Suicide" (1973). In the former work, a mother laments the fate of her young son, who has taken to the streets and caused her to endure constant fear for his life. In the latter, Knight urges fellow black poets to "live—not leap from steel bridges (like the white boys do)." Knight said early in his career that the black artist should be accountable only to black people, but he later acknowledged that his poetry evoked feelings of a universal nature and could therefore extend to a wider readership. He was comfortable with the evolution of his work and considered his later poems less narrow instead of less black.

Knight's next book after *Poems from Prison*, *Black Voices from Prison* (1970), contains selections of his poems, letters, and essays as well as work from other prison inmates. In the early 1970s he was writer-in-residence at the University of Pittsburgh, the University of Hartford, and Lincoln University. He received a grant from the National Endowment for the Arts in 1972, and a year later he published *Belly Songs and Other Poems*, which was nominated for both the National Book Award and the Pulitzer Prize. A Guggenheim Fellowship followed in 1974.

Despite his professional success, Knight's personal life continued to be in turmoil. Sanchez divorced him, and his second marriage, to Mary Ellen McAnally in 1973, also ended in divorce after two children were born. He could not shake his drinking and drug problems. In the late 1970s he moved to Memphis, Tennessee, and married Charlene Blackburn, with whom he had a son.

Knight continued to conduct poetry readings and workshops into the 1980s. He received a second grant from the National Endowment for the Arts in 1980, the same year his fourth collection of poetry, *Born of a Woman*, was published. In the preface to this book, Knight admits to making "slight changes in some of the 'older' poems" in order not to offend potential readers. For instance, from the poem "Hard Rock Returns to Prison from the Hospital for the Criminal Insane" (1968), he changed a line containing the phrase "like indians at a corral" to "like a herd of sheep." He did not want to perpetuate racism or sexism in his poems because he felt that to do so was "an evil" that could lead to "artistic and/or actual suicide."

Dorothy Abbott, the editor of *Mississippi Writers: Reflections of Childhood and Youth*, vol. 3, *Poetry* (1988), which includes four of Knight's poems, said of his work that it "reflected the prison, the male experience, and the aesthetic of the 1960s" but with the power of forming "a passionate, loving connection with black and white readers." Knight's most often anthologized poem is "The Idea of Ancestry" (1968), which has been praised as one of the best poems about the African American conception of family history. The poem begins with the narrator describing the pictures of forty-seven family members taped to his cell wall. "I know their dark eyes," Knight comments, "they know mine…. I am all of them, they are all of me"

(Abbott, 165). In this poem as well as many of his others, Knight's use of punctuation and his spacing of words assist the reader in determining how the voice should sound saying the lines. Knight relied strongly on his toast-telling expertise to fill his written poetry with rhythm and a sense of oral speech patterns.

His final collection of poetry, *The Essential Etheridge Knight*, was published in 1986. He died in Indianapolis, Indiana.

FURTHER READING

Abbott, Dorothy, ed. *Mississippi Writers: Reflections of Childhood and Youth*, vol. 3, *Poetry* (1988).

Crowder, Ashby Bland. "Etheridge Knight: Two Fields of Combat," *Concerning Poetry* 16, no. 2 (1983).

Hill, Patricia Liggins. "'Blues for a Mississippi Black Boy': Etheridge Knight's Craft in the Black Oral Tradition," *Mississippi Quarterly* 36, no. 1 (1982–83).

Hurd, Myles Raymond. "The Corinth Connection in Etheridge Knight's 'The Idea of Ancestry,'" *Notes on Mississippi Writers* 25, no. 1 (1993).

Werner, Craig. "The Poet, the Poem, the People: Etheridge Knight's Aesthetic," *Obsidian* 7, nos. 2–3 (1981).

Obituary: *New York Times*, 14 Mar. 1991.

This entry is taken from the *American National Biography* and is published here with the permission of the American Council of Learned Societies.

STACY KLEIN

Knight, Gladys (28 May 1944–), singer and actress, was born Gladys Maria Knight in Atlanta, Georgia, the third of four children of Sarah Elizabeth Woods and Merald Woodrow Knight Sr., who was one of Atlanta's first African American post office workers. The Knights were a musical family; both parents were members of the Wings over Jordan Choir and the Mount Moriah Baptist Church Choir. At four years of age Knight was the youngest member of the Sunbeam Children's Choir, and she performed her first recital in 1948 at Mount Moriah, a benefit concert for the church. At six she toured as a guest soloist with the Mount Moriah Choir and the Morris Brown College Choir. In 1952 eight-year-old Knight attracted national attention when, after winning three consecutive rounds over three weeks, she captured the championship round on the *Ted Mack Original Amateur Hour* television show and received the $2,000 grand prize. Later that year a birthday party led to the creation of a group that ultimately became Gladys Knight and

Gladys Knight with the Pips in 1975. (AP Images.)

the Pips and included Knight's brother Merald ("Bubba") Knight and their cousins Edward Patten and William Guest.

Gladys Knight and the Pips opened for such acts as SAM COOKE and JACKIE WILSON. In 1961, the same year that Knight graduated from Atlanta's Archer High School, where she was a member of the choir, the cheerleading squad, the track team, and the yearbook staff, the group attained its first recording success with "Every Beat of My Heart," a top ten rhythm and blues hit. The next year they enjoyed their second hit, "Letter Full of Tears." The group signed with Motown in 1966 and recorded such classics as "Everybody Needs Love" (1967), "I Heard It through the Grapevine" (1967), "The Nitty Gritty" (1969), "If I Were Your Woman" (1971), "I Don't Want to Do Wrong" (1971), "Make Me the Woman You Go Home To" (1971), "Help Me Make It through the Night" (1972), and "Neither One of Us (Wants to Be the First to Say Goodbye)" (1973). In 1973 Gladys Knight and the Pips left Motown and signed with Buddah Records, where they chalked up hits such as "Midnight Train to Georgia" (1973),

"I've Got to Use My Imagination" (1973), "Best Thing That Ever Happened to Me" (1973), and "On and On" (1974). Beginning in 1980 the group recorded for Columbia/CBS Records and scored several smash singles, such as "Landlord" (1980) and "Save the Overtime" (1983), before moving to MCA Records and recording the hit "Love Overboard" (1987). By the time Gladys Knight and the Pips disbanded in 1989, the phenomenally successful group had starred in a weekly variety show broadcast during the summer of 1975 and earned three Grammy Awards for "Midnight Train to Georgia," "Neither One of Us," and "Love Overboard." The group was inducted into the Georgia Hall of Fame in 1989 and the Rock and Roll Hall of Fame in 1996. The Rhythm and Blues Hall of Fame presented them its Lifetime Achievement Award in 1998. Knight was a versatile entertainer. She made her acting debut in the film *Pipe Dreams* (1976) and later starred with FLIP WILSON in the television sit-com *Charlie and Company* (1985–1986). As an actress Knight also appeared in such television shows as *New York Undercover*, *Living Single*, and *The Jamie Foxx*

Show and starred in *Smokey Joe's Café* on Broadway in 1999 and in various cities in 2000. She produced and starred in the Ace Award–winning *Sisters in the Name of Love* (1986), an HBO special that co-starred PATTI LABELLE and DIONNE WARWICK. Knight collaborated with Warwick, STEVIE WONDER, and Elton John in 1985 on the hit "That's What Friends Are For," which raised money for the American Foundation for Aids Research. It garnered Knight her fourth Grammy Award.

Beginning in 1989 Knight regularly appeared as a solo headliner in Las Vegas. She also continued to tour and record well into the first years of the twenty-first century. Her albums included *Good Woman* (1991), *Just for You* (1994), *Next Time* (1995), *At Last* (2001), which received the Grammy for Best Traditional R&B Vocal Album, and *Before Me* (2006). She received additional Grammy Awards for her collaboration with RAY CHARLES on "Heaven Help Us All," which won Best Gospel Performance in 2004, and for *One Voice*, which won Best Gospel Choir or Choral Album in 2005 and featured Knight as singer and director of the Saints Unified Voices gospel choir. Among Knight's additional accolades were an honorary doctorate of humane letters from Morris Brown College in 1990, a star on the Hollywood Walk of Fame in 2005, and a BET Lifetime Achievement Award in 2005.

Knight, whose marriages to James Newman, Barry Hankerson, and Les Brown ended in divorce, married William McDowell in 2001. Her daughter, Kenya Newman Love, managed her mother's later career, and her son, Shanga Hankerson, administered the Gladys Knight and Ron Winans' Chicken and Waffles restaurants. Knight's first child and former manager, Jimmy Newman, died at the age of thirty-six in 1999. She named her entertainment corporation Shakeji after her three children. Knight established Many Different Roads, a record label that focused on and promoted new talent. In addition Knight remained active in charitable causes. Most notable was her work on behalf of the American Diabetes Association, for which she established the Elizabeth Knight Fund in honor of her late mother. Knight wrote *At Home with Gladys Knight* (2001), which was published by the American Diabetes Association as a cookbook and guide for diabetics.

FURTHER READING

Knight, Gladys. *Between Each Line of Pain and Glory: My Story* (1997).

Dahl, Bill. "Gladys Knight and the Pips," in *Motown: The Golden Years* (2001).

Jackson, Jacquelyn L. "Gladys Knight," in *Notable Black American Women, Book II*, ed. Jessie Carney Smith (1996).

LINDA M. CARTER

Knight, Gwendolyn (20 Apr. 1913–18 Feb. 2005), sculptor, painter, and printmaker, was born in Bridgetown, Barbados, West Indies, the only child of Malcolm, a pharmacist, and Miriam Knight, a homemaker. Knight lost her father when she was two, and her mother suffered a severe leg injury that permanently limited her mobility when a hurricane struck the island while she was still very young. As a result Gwen grew up with foster parents and moved with this family to the United States in 1920, settling in St. Louis, Missouri. Always writing, drawing, and dancing she completed her first paintings between the ages of eight and nine years of age. At thirteen she moved with her family to New York, where she attended Wadleigh Annex and Wadleigh Street School for Girls. She was an avid reader of newspapers and modern literature, especially the work of COUNTÉE CULLEN, Virginia Woolf, and ZORA NEALE HURSTON. She seriously considered becoming a teacher or librarian until she saw an exhibition of paintings by the American portraitist John Singer Sargent and—with the encouragement of a teacher who urged her to follow her dreams—decided instead to become an artist.

Knight enrolled in the art program at Howard University. Living away from home and attending a coed school for the first time she struggled to meet the challenges of study at Howard from 1931–1933, where the painter LOIS MAILOU JONES and the printmaker JAMES LESESNE WELLS were her most supportive teachers. The Great Depression forced Knight to leave Howard in 1933 and return to Harlem. There she worked in the studio-workshop of the sculptor AUGUSTA SAVAGE, working from live models and developing an interest in portraying the human form, animals, and dance. She studied with the painter Angela Straighter and was befriended by the sculptor SELMA BURKE and the painter Georgette Seabrooke. Knight also developed a serious interest in opera, an even deeper affection for dance, and fell in love with the abstract paintings of Arthur Dove that she often viewed during her visits to Alfred Stieglitz's gallery, An American Place, at 509 Madison Avenue in New York.

At the Savage Studio from 1933 until 1937 Knight also worked at the Harlem Art Workshop at 135th Street with the painter CHARLES ALSTON, the first African American supervisor of the federal Works Project Administration (WPA), assisting him on the Harlem Hospital mural project (a children's mural that was never installed). Later, at Alston's WPA studio at 306 West 141st, Knight came into contact with such figures of the Harlem Renaissance as ALAIN L. LOCKE and the artists AARON DOUGLAS, ROMARE BEARDEN, and Jacob Lawrence. Lawrence, who was too young for the WPA projects (he was not yet seventeen), studied under Alston and Bannarn while renting studio space from Alston with funds he received from a Julius Rosenwald Foundation fellowship.

Knight and Jacob Lawrence were married 24 July 1941. Their New Orleans honeymoon was financed by Lawrence's second Rosenwald grant that came immediately after he completed his *Migration of the Negro* series. Gwen had helped gesso the panels. In February 1942 they continued their excursion into the rural South in Lenexa, Virginia, before returning to New York in the summer and settling in Brooklyn. While she did continue to draw and paint Knight posited herself increasingly in a supportive role as her husband's career continued to advance. They were apart for twenty-six months while Lawrence served in the coast guard from 1943 to 1945 as a combat artist. The following summer Knight accompanied him to Black Mountain College, an experimental school near Asheville, North Carolina, where he was invited to teach by the abstract painter Josef Albers. Knight taught dance on an informal basis, instructing students on the basic modern dance techniques she had learned in New York. She and Lawrence rarely left the grounds of the college because of southern prejudice against blacks outside the campus boundaries. In the meantime Knight continued to draw, paint, and dance on her own.

Knight began working at Condé Nast Publications in 1950, initially as an assistant in archives, and later as the assistant to the art director for *Glamour* Magazine. She remained with the company for more than ten years, taking the necessary time off to accompany her husband to teaching appointments at the Skowhegan School of Sculpture and Painting in Maine. Lawrence returned to the New York area to teach at the Five Towns Music and Art Foundation in Cedarhurst, Long Island, and at Pratt Institute in Brooklyn.

Knight began taking classes at the New School of Social Work in 1960, studying off and on under Anthony Toney until 1966. In 1964 she and Lawrence embarked on an eighteen-month African tour, living in Lagos then Ibadaan in Nigeria and traveling to Italy before returning to the United States. Residing in Boston for one year Knight exhibited a selection of her paintings in a show that included work by Lawrence, Savage, and a few additional sculptors. The couple returned to New York in 1966, with Lawrence assuming a teaching position at the New School for Social Research and the next year at the Art Students League, and Knight studying at the Skowhegan School from 1968 until 1970, before relocating permanently in the spring 1971 to Seattle, Washington. With Lawrence taking a professorship at the University of Washington, the couple settled into a home within walking distance of the campus. The move also marked the beginning of a change in the visibility and art career of Gwendolyn Knight.

In 1976 Knight had her first solo exhibition at the Seattle Art Museum, sponsored by the Links, Inc., Greater Seattle Chapter, which financially supported the exhibition. The following year the Francine Seders Gallery organized a show of her work that was presented in Georgia, Oregon, and Washington, D.C. In 1988 she had a solo exhibition at the Lacy Jones Gallery in the Robert W. Woodruff building for the Atlanta University, Inc. The Black Mountain College Museum and Arts Center in Asheville, North Carolina, sponsored an exhibition of her work in May 2001. In 2003 her first retrospective, "Never Late for Heaven: The Art of Gwen Knight," opened at the Tacoma Art Museum in Tacoma, Washington, and traveled to the Museum of Northwest Art in La Conner.

In the early 1990s fellow artist Elizabeth Sandvig encouraged Knight to explore printmaking, a medium to which she would continually return throughout the remainder of her career. One of her best-known images was a lithographed self-portrait completed in 2002. Her prints were included in most of the exhibitions in which she participated after this time, including the Museum of African-American Life and Culture in Dallas, Texas, in 1996; Prints and Monoprints at the Smith Robertson Museum and Cultural Center in Jackson, Mississippi, in 1997; and Gwendolyn Knight, Works from 1941–1999 at Black Mountain Center for the Arts, Black Mountain, North Carolina, in 2001. Other group shows that she participated in include Significant Others: Artist Wives of Artists at the Kraushaar Galleries in New York in 1993, Jacob Lawrence & Gwendolyn Knight: Together in the World at Bumbershoot, Seattle Center in

Seattle, Washington, in 1999, and Lives Connected: Jacob Lawrence and Gwendolyn Knight held at the Minneapolis Institute of Arts in Minnesota.

Knight earned honorary degrees from the University of Minnesota, doctor of humane letters, and Seattle University, doctor of humanities, in 1996. She received the National Honor Award from the Women's Caucus for Art in 1993, Cornish Lifetime Achievement Award (Seattle), Centennial Award of Merit from Arizona State University, and the Pioneer Award from the 12th annual Artist's salute to Black History Month in Los Angeles.

Knight completed roughly 100 works in her lifetime, some of which are held in the permanent collections of the Hampton University Museum in Virginia, Museum of Modern Art in New York, the Phillips Collection in Washington, D.C., Howard University Gallery in Washington D.C., and the St. Louis Museum of Art in Missouri. Gwendolyn Knight Lawrence died at her home in Seattle, Washington.

FURTHER READING

Conkelton, Sheryl, and Barbara Earl Thomas. *Never Late for Heaven: The Art of Gwen Knight* (2003).

AMALIA K. AMAKI

Knox, George Levi (16 Sept. 1841–24 Aug. 1927), slave, barber, politician, newspaper publisher, and writer, was born in Wilson County, Tennessee. His father, Charles Knox, was a slave, and his mother, Nancy (Fisher) Knox, was sold into slavery following her own mother's death. As a young slave, Knox worked on a farm and for short periods of time as a tanner and an apprentice to a shoemaker. In 1861 he worked in a sawmill, and during the Civil War was hired out as a bootmaker. During the war he was also the body servant of a captain in the Tennessee Cavalry. In May 1863, when allowed to visit home, he refused to return to the Confederate army and instead ran away with three other slaves to join the Union army near Murfreesboro, Tennessee. He then served with Union forces in the Indiana Infantry, and in April 1864 while working for a captain on furlough in Indiana, he decided to stay in Indianapolis. In Indianapolis he found work in the Bates House, the city's leading hotel, as a yardman and then as the head porter. In 1864 he began working in the shop of Reuben Gibbs, a well-known black barber, and he saved his earnings to invest in a shop owned by a group of barbers in Kokomo, Indiana. After the end of the Civil War, he opened his own barbershop in Greenfield, Indiana, and on

4 October 1865, he married Aurilla S. Harvey; they had three children.

Knox's business grew, and his Greenfield barbershop became a gathering place for influential white citizens. Among them was the town's first mayor and his son James Whitcomb Riley, later a famous poet, whose poem "Local Politician from Away Back" (1887) contains a reference to Knox's barbershop. Knox became known for his interest in self-improvement and education both for himself and his race. He learned to read with the help of his wife and others. In 1873 he was instrumental in securing the establishment of a Greenfield public school for black children and the next year organized a "colored debating society." Knox promoted the cause of religion among Greenfield's black citizens, helping to organize a Methodist Episcopal Church Sunday school for blacks in 1870 and the Second Methodist Church, which affiliated with the predominantly white Methodist Episcopal Church (Northern Methodist). In the 1880s, he organized interracial camp revival meetings that drew thousands of adherents.

In the 1870s, Knox became active in Greenfield politics. He was one of eleven black men who represented the state of Indiana at a National Conference of Colored Men in May 1879, held in Nashville, Tennessee. The representatives at this meeting hotly debated the exodus of blacks from the South to Kansas, Indiana, and other Western states, a migration of people who became known as "exodusters." Knox defended their right to move to any locality, but opposed any large-scale migration because of practical difficulties certain to result, such as the intensified racial animosity of whites that would worsen the plight of blacks. By 1883 agitation over this exodus had subsided. In 1884, Knox moved to Indianapolis, and with William Bibbs, a well-known black barber, he opened another shop; the shop prospered, and they hired six more barbers. While retaining this establishment, Knox leased the Bates House Barbershop in 1885 and added a ladies annex in 1891. Knox began investing in barbershops in a variety of locations throughout the city. In 1891 he purchased the YMCA Barbershop, and he leased the Grand Hotel Barbershop in 1892. In 1902 he began managing the hotel barbershop in the Denison House, where he continued to work for fifteen years. By the mid-1890s his shops employed more than fifty black men and women. In 1920 Knox sold his last barbershop.

In Indianapolis, around 1885, Knox joined the Simpson Chapel Methodist Episcopal Church. He became active in its Sunday school, was largely responsible for construction of a new church building in the 1890s, and represented the congregation as lay delegate at church conferences convening in Cincinnati and New York City. He remained a prominent figure in the cultural, social, and charitable activities of Indianapolis's black community from the 1880s until his death. He served as president of the Douglass Literary Society for six successive terms, and he was a member of various fraternal orders, was active in the Afro-American League and the Anti-Lynching League, and was a sponsor of the Colored Benevolent Society, which was a subdivision of the Indianapolis Charity Organization. He also helped found the Colored Branch of the Indianapolis YMCA and for a time served as its president.

Knox's political stature grew with his appointment in the early 1890s to the State Republican Central Committee. He was selected as an alternate delegate-at-large to the Republican National Convention in both 1892 and 1896; in 1892 he functioned as a full-fledged delegate when he supported President Benjamin Harrison's bid for renomination. At the convention, Knox influenced southern African American delegates to stay loyal to Harrison, and he minimized the effect of a group of black Indiana Republicans who arrived to support the opponent, James G. Blaine. Knox cited Harrison's support of, and Blaine's opposition to, the Force bill, a proposal to guarantee implementation of the U.S. Constitution's Fifteenth Amendment, which gave men the right to vote regardless of race, color, or previous condition of servitude. In 1904 Knox ran for Congress as an independent candidate. In 1924, after the Ku Klux Klan had become powerful in Indiana's Republican Party, Knox supported the Democratic Party both on the national and local levels.

In 1892 Knox purchased an independent black weekly newspaper, the *Indianapolis Freeman*, and began managing it jointly with his son Elwood in 1893. LILLIAN THOMAS (FOX), a well-known writer and elocutionist, was correspondence editor at the *Freeman*. Proclaiming itself "a national race paper" (Gatewood, 32), the *Freeman* established bureaus in other cities and became an advocate of BOOKER T. WASHINGTON's philosophy of accommodation, which accepted social segregation from whites but favored economic equality with whites. Knox also became active in the Afro-American Press Association. From 1894 through 1895, Knox published his autobiography in serial form in the paper.

In 1913, Knox became director of the newly launched Frederick Douglass Life Insurance Company; he also served as first vice president of the Negro National Business League. During his lifetime as an entrepreneur, Knox acquired substantial wealth and filled speaking engagements around the country, proclaiming his philosophy and formula for success. He preached a Washingtonian philosophy of industriousness, thrift, self-help, personal morality, patience, and persistence, all of which had been the keys to his own success. Knox became a widower in 1910, by which time two of his adult children, William and Nellie, also had died. In 1914 Knox married Mrs. Margaret Nickens, a socially prominent widow in Indianapolis.

In 1927, while visiting a friend in Richmond, Virginia, Knox suffered a paralytic stroke and died the same day; he was buried in Crown Hill Cemetery, Indianapolis. Knox and his family had assumed a place among the black elite of Indianapolis and he became a leader within the black community.

FURTHER READING

Gatewood, Willard B., Jr., ed. *Slave and Freeman, the Autobiography of George L. Knox.* (1979).

Thornbrough, Emma Lou. *The Negro in Indiana before 1900* (1957).

ROSE PELONE SISSON

Knox, William Jacob (5 Jan. 1905–9 July 1995), chemist, was the third of five children born in New Bedford, Massachusetts, to parents whose names are not recorded. The grandson of a former slave, his father worked in the local post office, and his mother was self-educated. His was a close-knit family that embraced education as the main route to economic independence and prosperity. All of the children graduated from high school. Knox's older sister went to normal school, and his brothers earned their doctorates. New Bedford had fewer than one thousand blacks when Knox was a child there, yet it was a prosperous community with black physicians and lawyers and even its own black police force. FREDERICK DOUGLASS had lived there following his escape from slavery, and the town had also been an important stop on the Underground Railroad. Knox's sense of independence and self-reliance was derived from this cultural milieu, and it became the foundation for many of the successes in his future career.

Knox entered Harvard University in 1921. As all freshmen were required to live on campus, he was originally assigned to live in Standis Hall. After returning from a compulsory laboratory exam, he was told there was a mistake in his room assignment and was moved to another location. He found out later that African American freshmen were not permitted to live on campus.

Chemistry was not considered a traditional field of study for blacks in that era. Among the few blacks Knox met at Harvard was PERCY JULIAN, who was studying organic chemistry. Other contemporaries at Harvard included the writer STERLING A. BROWN; ROBERT WEAVER, who became the first black member of a presidential cabinet; A. A. TAYLOR, who was the teacher of the historian JOHN HOPE FRANKLIN; CHARLES HAMILTON HOUSTON, the dean of civil rights attorneys; and WILLIAM LEO HANSBERRY, who taught African cultures and civilizations for many years at Howard University and for whom the Hansberry College of African Studies at the University of Nigeria is named. There were no black women enrolled in science classes during his time there.

Knox enjoyed his classes in economics, literature, and history; he also embraced the intellectual climate, despite the overall racial hostility. George Shannon was his instructor in qualitative analysis, James Bryant Conant taught him organic chemistry, and he also took classes with E. P. Koehler. Knox graduated in 1925 with a baccalaureate degree in Chemistry.

In the 1920s black schools in the South were in great need of teachers in all areas of study, and it was customary for college-educated black men and women to go south to teach as there were few if any openings in the North. In 1925 Knox moved to North Carolina and taught at Johnson C. Smith College in Charlotte. His teaching load included general, analytical, organic, and physical chemistry. His teaching requirements also included teaching Sunday school.

Despite having experienced racial prejudice, Knox was not prepared for the extreme bigotry that permeated life in the South. Nor was he satisfied with the quality of laboratory equipment and teaching resources at his disposal. Socially blacks had to use separate entrances for the movie theaters and had to sit apart from whites in the gallery. Blacks had to ride in the rear of the public buses, and there were even segregated cemeteries for blacks and whites. As a result many students simply stayed on campus; thus the intellectual climate was also stymied. In 1928 Knox enrolled at the Massachusetts Institute of Technology (MIT),

where he earned a master's degree in Chemical Engineering in 1929. Even with this degree he was unable to find professional employment, but with the help of Percy Julian, head of the Chemistry Department at Howard University, he secured a teaching position at Howard. There he met Edna Jordan of Richmond, Virginia, a student in the Art Department, whom he married. After a year at Howard, Knox returned to MIT, where he earned a Ph.D. in 1935. His dissertation, directed by Louis Harris, examined the absorption of light by nitrogen tetraoxide.

Although Knox now had an advanced degree from MIT and applied for several jobs at northern colleges, he continued to be rejected on the basis of his color. He returned to the South to teach at North Carolina Agricultural and Technical College in Greensboro, later moving to Talladega College, which was one of the few liberal arts colleges for African Americans in the United States. On a teacher's salary of $4,000 per year, Knox supported his widowed mother, several of his siblings, and his wife and child.

In 1943 Knox wrote to colleagues at MIT, who then put him in contact with a nuclear research team at Columbia University led by Willard F. Libby. Libby, who later received the Nobel Prize in Chemistry for his radiocarbon dating technique, was leading the Manhattan Project's research into gaseous diffusion techniques for the separation of uranium isotopes, a vital factor in the American effort to build a nuclear weapon. Beginning as a research associate, Knox became interested in trying to find the metals that were the most useful in the development of an atomic bomb. His team helped work out techniques for handling and separating fissionable materials, and he also carried out corrosion and stabilization studies that became his area of expertise. Knox was fascinated with the work and immersed himself in it. When the head of the Corrosion Section moved on, Libby, director of the Manhattan Project, offered the position to Knox.

After World War II ended, Libby recommended Knox for a position working for William Kenyon, head of the Chemistry Department at the Eastman Kodak Company in Rochester, New York. Knox worked on a number of problems involving coating compositions and wetting agents. His solutions helped Kodak keep up with the increasing demand for film and paper stock. Knox amassed nearly two dozen patents in his twenty-five years working at Kodak.

During the postwar years, Knox was also involved in housing and community development issues in the Greater Rochester area, in part because of his own experiences trying to find housing. After moving to Rochester, the only housing he could find was an abandoned former house of prostitution. One of his colleagues took him aside and offered to buy him a home in a nicer neighborhood so Knox could live with his family. This experience spurred Knox's interest in housing and community development. He became active in community relations, writing editorials for the local press, joining and leading the New York Committee against Discrimination, the Housing Advisory Council of Rochester, and both the Urban League and NAACP branches. He also served on the New York advisory council to the federal Civil Rights Commission. His commitment to excellence in education helped spawn a number of scholarships for minority students. In part because of his knowledge of RALPH BUNCHE from his days at Harvard, Knox and another colleague drew up the precepts for the Ralph J. Bunche Scholarship Committee, which still operated in the early twenty-first century.

FURTHER READING

Sammons, Vivian O. *Blacks in Science and Medicine* (1990).

"William Jacob Knox," in *Notable Black American Scientists*, ed. Kristine Krapp (1998).

ROBERT JOHNSON JR.

Knuckles, Frankie (1955–), DJ, producer, and recording and remix artist, was born Frank Warren Knuckles in South Bronx, New York City. Educated at the High School of Art and Design in Manhattan, Knuckles drew tremendous inspiration from the local gay underground music scene. In the early 1970s Knuckles and lifelong friend Larry Levan became regular faces at the Loft, an openly multiracial and bisexual club established by David Mancuso, who played a revelatory mix of soul, rock, African, Latin, and pop music. Mancuso and rival DJ Nicky Siano inspired Knuckles and Levan to start and in 1972 Knuckles took on his first regular gig, at Better Days. Between 1974 and 1976 he played nightly at the Continental Baths, an underground gay club, where he developed his own identity as a DJ, focusing on the slick disco productions of the Philadelphia International label. In March 1977 Knuckles at the opening night of the Warehouse on South Jefferson Street in West Central Chicago, returning as the resident DJ and a partner in the operation in July. Within months, Knuckles had developed a large local following drawn from the gay and black communities and was regularly attracting more than two thousand people on Saturday nights.

By 1979 the *New York Times* and other cultural arbiters had placed disco at the root of the decline of Western civilization. The anti-disco movement peaked in Chicago on 12 July. Local radio DJ Steve Dahl burned a twelve-foot-tall pyre of disco records at Comiskey Park in the middle of a White Sox doubleheader, precipitating a riot and publicly declaring Middle America's hatred for this synthesized, homosexual music. By now though, Knuckles was taking the Warehouse in a different direction, having reassessed how to present the music in a new and dynamic fashion. Noting that crowds reacted best to the instrumental passages of the songs, Knuckles started editing reel-to-reel tapes in order to make these "breaks" last longer. Sometimes Knuckles blended the instrumental section of one record with the a cappella version of another to form a third piece of music. Combining these edits and remixes with robotic European disco and electro, and sometimes using a third turntable to add extra sound effects, Knuckles was defining a new sound. This patchwork became known in Chicago as "house" music in homage to the Warehouse.

In 1982 Knuckles established his own club, the Power Plant, where he started using a drum machine to heighten the rhythmic nature of his mixes to metronomic intensity. Influenced by this sound, some Chicagoans, including Byron Walton (Jamie Principle), Jesse Saunders, and Marshall Jefferson, started producing their own "house" records, which were characterized by unrelenting rhythm— music that was strictly for the Chicago clubs that were following Knuckles's lead. In 1987, anxious to explore new territory, Knuckles returned to New York City. Before leaving Chicago, he had started to experiment with recording his own tracks. Knuckles developed two distinct styles of production. The first featured jacking rhythms and sparse melodies with the occasional spoken vocal. Tracks like "Baby Wants to Ride" (1989) were intensely sexual records that reflected the atmosphere of the clubs in which Knuckles spent his apprenticeship. Knuckles's love of disco and soul—the other important influence on his work—emerged in his other productions, which united house rhythms with a warmer sound and soulful vocals that repeated the lyrical concerns of many disco records: spiritual and physical release, the promise of transcendence through music, and pleas for brotherhood, unity, and understanding. These more commercial tracks won favor with a wider audience, gradually dissolving the erotic, physical tone of early house.

Over the next ten years Knuckles became increasingly popular as a producer and remixer, offering house mixes to numerous pop records; in 1997 he was awarded the inaugural Grammy Award for Remixer of the Year. Between 1991 and 1997 Knuckles was resident DJ at the Sound Factory, New York City, and released two albums of his own material, *Beyond the Mix* (1992) and *Welcome to the Real World* (1995). During the 1990s and 2000s Knuckles released numerous mix albums and served as a governor and trustee of the New York City chapter of the National Academy of Recording Arts and Sciences. A third album of original material, *A New Reality*, appeared in 2004. In August of that year, the city of Chicago honored Knuckles by renaming the street on which the original Warehouse stood as Honorary Frankie Knuckles Way. Widely regarded as one of the leading DJs in the world, Knuckles continued to record and perform into the new millennium, spreading house music to an international audience.

Knuckles's life indicated that house evolved from two forms of exclusion: racial and sexual, that it rejected black nationalism in favor of integration and acceptance, and—contrary to the opinion of many contemporary critics—that it had strong roots in the African American music of the 1970s. While Knuckles frequently emphasized that he did not invent house, his influence on its development was very significant. House was not originally a form of music but was rather an approach *to* music, and Knuckles was one of the pioneers of this approach. In shifting the focus of his sets from melody to rhythm, Knuckles helped to set the artistic template for house music. His Chicagoan audience responded not only by dancing to this music but also by creating their own: house as a style of music emerged at this point of creation, and Knuckles was among the generation of producers who defined the house sound. Attracting a mixed audience to the Warehouse, Knuckles initiated the acceptance of house in the white community, thus fulfilling Mancuso's ambition to deconstruct social barriers through music. Finally, in re-editing and reconstructing the records that he played, Knuckles helped to transform the focus of nightclubs from the music that was played to an emphasis on the DJ's technical skills. In doing so, Knuckles, also known as the "Godfather of House," became a superstar in the process.

FURTHER READING

Garratt, Sheryl. *Adventures in Wonderland: A Decade of Club Culture* (1998).

Lawrence, Tim. *Love Saves the Day: A History of American Dance Music Culture, 1970–1979* (2003).

JOE STREET

Komunyakaa, Yusef (29 Apr. 1947–), poet, was born James Willie Brown Jr. to James Willie Brown, a carpenter, and Mildred Brown in the segregated mill town of Bogalusa, Louisiana, seventy miles northeast of New Orleans, the first of five children. He changed his name for personal reasons (most notably his estrangement from his father, who was abusive and routinely unfaithful to Komunyakaa's mother) as well as for religious ones. His new name, according to family folklore, once belonged to Komunyakaa's grandfather, who came to the United States as a stowaway from the West Indies, most likely Trinidad. After graduating in 1965 from tiny Central High School (then Bogalusa's high school for African American students), Komunyakaa enlisted in the U.S. Army and served a one-year tour of duty in Vietnam as a correspondent and managing editor for *The Southern Cross*, a military newspaper. Honing the sparse, evocative writing style that would later typify his poetry, Komunyakaa reported from the battlefield and wrote feature articles on topics ranging from fellow soldiers to Vietnamese literature and culture. During his tour, Komunyakaa was awarded the Bronze Star. Soon after being discharged from the army, Komunyakaa enrolled at the University of Colorado, where he became seriously interested in poetry writing after signing up for a creative writing workshop with Dr. Alex Blackburn. After earning a bachelor of arts degree from the school in 1975, Komunyakaa went on study at Colorado State University, where he was influenced by the works of poets such as STERLING ALLEN BROWN, COUNTÉE CULLEN, CLAUDE McKAY, and MARGARET WALKER, and where he worked with poet and editor Bill Trembley before earning a master of arts degree in 1978. From there, Komunyakaa went to the University of California-Irvine, where he completed a master of fine arts degree in Creative Writing in 1980. Along the way, Komunyakaa began publishing his poetry, first in literary journals, then in two limited edition collections, *Dedications and Other Darkhorses* (1977) and *Lost in the Bonewheel Factory* (1979). After graduating from UC-Irvine, Komunyakaa joined the staff of the Provincetown Fine Arts Work Center, where he found an atmosphere conducive to developing one's

Yusef Komunyakaa during an interview in Bloomington, Ind., on July 11, 1996. (AP Images.)

own artistic voice. During his time in Provincetown, Komunyakaa rediscovered the influence of southern culture—particularly the racism he experienced and the musical forms of jazz and the blues—on his life. He began to incorporate the cadences of those influences into poems about his years in Louisiana. Later, he would use those same elements when writing about his experiences during the Vietnam War. In 1984, Wesleyan University Press published Komunyakaa's *Copacetic*, which adopts as its title a term coined by African American tap dancer Bill "Bojangles" Robinson to describe the peaceful, self-assured attitude adopted by many jazz and blues musicians of his day. The title is at once an ideal and a challenge; it argues for the place for hope and calmness in a world that is often far from "copacetic," one that is seemingly devoid of any chance for closure. The book's poems are sequenced to provide readers with an arc from suffering to redemption, from the eviscerating effects of racism, bigotry, and betrayal to a resounding hope for and belief in the human spirit's ability to endure and overcome. Ranging

from narratives about family life to lyric meditations on passion and desire, the poems are imbued with the musical forms, phrasings, and structures of jazz and blues. Komunyakaa quickly found critical praise, as he was compared, even in early reviews, to poets ranging from LANGSTON HUGHES and William Carlos Williams to Ezra Pound, T. S. Eliot, and AMIRI BARAKA. Around the time of *Copacetic's* publication, Komunyakaa accepted a position as an English instructor at the University of New Orleans, which afforded him the opportunity to serve as the 1984–1985 Poet-in-the-Schools for the New Orleans Public School system. New Orleans was also where he met the Australian fiction writer Mandy Jane Sayer, with whom he entered into a ten-year marriage in 1985, the same year he left the University of New Orleans and accepted a position as associate professor of English at Indiana University in Bloomington.

The next year, 1986, was the first of four consecutive years in which Yusef Komunyakaa released a new poetry collection. First, Wesleyan University Press published Komunyakaa's fourth volume, *I Apologize for the Eyes in My Head*. Despite the book's title, the collection is anything but an apology. Instead, it is an exploration of common terms and stereotypes that individuals, particularly African Americans, use to define themselves in contemporary society. The book earned the 1986 San Francisco Poetry Center Award and secured Komunyakaa's position as a major contemporary American poet. The following year, Komunyakaa expanded his range of subjects by publishing his first poetry collection about his Vietnam War experiences, *Toys in a Field*, which he followed in 1988 with an expanded collection entitled *Dien Cai Dau* (pronounced "dinkee dow"), which in Vietnamese means "crazy." Along with poets such as Bruce Weigl and W. D. Ehrhart, Komunyakaa emerged in the late 1980s as one of the nation's leading veteran-poets. *Dien Cai Dau* was awarded the Dark Room Poetry Prize and named to the 1988 Young Adults/American Library Association "Best Books for Young Adults" list, and many poems from it—particularly the collection's final poem, "Facing It," which tells the story of an African American's trip to the Vietnam Veterans' Memorial in Washington, D.C.—have been republished in dozens of war literature anthologies. The year 1989 saw another creative departure for Komunyakaa, as his collection *February in Sydney* moved beyond his long past experiences and focused solely on the poet's recent trip to Australia, with special attention given to the influence of American jazz music on Australian culture in general and in particular on remote Aborigine communities. He would return for inspiration to his experiences in Australia for 1998's *Thieves of Paradise*, which was a finalist for the National Book Critics Circle Award.

For his next project, Komunyakaa teamed up with poet and musician Sascha Feinstein to co-edit 1991's *The Jazz Poetry Anthology*. (The two would also co-edit a follow-up volume, *The Second Set: The Jazz Poetry Anthology, Volume 2*, in 1996.) In 1992, Komunyakaa returned to the subjects of Louisiana and Vietnam with a more mature perspective in *Magic City*, which contains two more of his most widely anthologized poems, "Venus's-flytraps," in which Komunyakaa assumes the voice of a five-year-old child, and "My Father's Love Letters," whose speaker is a young boy who composes letters for his illiterate father, who longs for his estranged wife to return. The next year saw the publication of *Neon Vernacular: New and Selected Poems*, which brought Komunyakaa widespread critical acclaim and numerous prestigious awards, including the 1994 Pulitzer Prize for Poetry, the Kingsley Tufts Award, and the William Faulkner Prize from the Université de Rennes.

Komunyakaa remained prolific after releasing *Neon Vernacular*. In addition to three further poetry collections (*Talking Dirty to the Gods* [2000], *Pleasure Dome: New and Collected Poems* [2001], and *Taboo: The Wishbone Trilogy: Part One* [2004]), he co-translated, with Martha Collins, Nguyen Quang Thieu's *The Insomnia of Fire* (1995); released *Blues Notes: Essays, Interviews & Commentaries* (2000); and collaborated with playwright and dramaturge Chad Gracia to create *Gilgamesh: A Verse Play* (2006).

Komunyakaa has emerged as one of the most widely celebrated African American poets since Langston Hughes. In addition to the previously mentioned awards, Komunyakaa has received two Creative Writing Fellowships from the National Endowment for the Arts, fellowships from the Fine Arts Work Center in Provincetown and the Louisiana Arts Council, the Ruth Lilly Poetry Prize, the Thomas Forcade Award, the Hanes Poetry Prize, the Jerome J. Shestack Poetry Prize, and the Robert Creeley Poetry Award. He was elected Chancellor of the Academy of American Poets in 1999 and became a professor in the Council of Humanities and Creative Writing Program at Princeton University.

In 2003, Komunyakaa was faced with a devastating personal tragedy when his fiancée, poet Reetika Vazirani, killed herself and their son.

FURTHER READING

Komunyakaa, Yusef. *Neon Vernacular: New and Selected Poems* (1993).

Komunyakaa, Yusef. *Pleasure Dome: New and Collected Poems* (2001).

Komunyakaa, Yusef. *Talking Dirty to the Gods* (2001).

Koolish, Lynda. *African American Writers: Portraits and Visions* (2001).

Salas, Angela M. *Flashback through the Heart: The Poetry of Yusef Komunyakaa* (2004).

DANIEL DONAGHY

Kornegay, Wade M. (9 Jan. 1934–), physicist, was born in Mount Olive, North Carolina, to Gilbert and Estelle Kornegay, farmers. By the time he reached age six, both of his parents had died and he had gone to live with his maternal grandmother. An excellent student, he was encouraged by his teachers to go to college despite his rather impoverished upbringing, and he managed to obtain a partial scholarship to attend North Carolina Central College (later University), a historically black college in nearby Durham. After receiving a B.S. in Chemistry in 1956, he studied chemistry and physics for a year at the Bonn University in Germany. In 1957 he married Bettie Hunter, with whom he had three children. That same year he entered the graduate program at the University of California at Berkeley. Upon receiving a Ph.D. in Chemical Physics in 1961, he remained at Berkeley for an additional year as a postdoctoral researcher.

In 1962 Kornegay accepted a position with the Massachusetts Institute of Technology's Lincoln Laboratory as a member of its technical staff. At the time, Lincoln was a major consultant to the U.S. Department of Defense, and its research focused on developing methods for protecting the United States from long-range attacks by the Soviet Union. In the early 1960s the greatest threat in this regard was posed by nuclear warheads delivered by intercontinental ballistic missiles (ICBMs) based within the USSR, so Kornegay was assigned to the radar signature studies group. This group was looking for ways to incorporate radar into an early warning system for detecting ICBMs shortly after launch, but there were a number of problems to overcome. One is that the trajectory of an ICBM carries it into outer space, where radar is of extremely limited usefulness. Another problem was the fact that ICBMs, upon reentering Earth's atmosphere, often release chaff (shards of metal foil that resemble large pieces of confetti), thus acting as a "smokescreen" for the warhead itself. A third problem was the use of other evasive tactics such as electronic countermeasures and decoys. Taken as a whole, such problems made it extremely difficult for a radar detection system to identify the precise location of an individual warhead as it hurtled toward its target.

Eventually Kornegay and his colleagues made use of a phenomenon that had been known about for years by atmospheric scientists, the radar signature. When a meteor enters the earth's atmosphere, a radar operator can determine its size and shape from the meteor's bow shock, a radar echo that resembles the wave made in front of a boat as it travels through the water, and the trail of ions it leaves in its wake. Together, these two features give a meteor a specific signature that can be detected by radar. By the late 1960s Kornegay's group had developed methods by which wideband phased-array radars could differentiate between the radar signature of a warhead and the radar signatures of its booster rocket, decoys, and associated debris. Over the next twenty years, Kornegay and his associates developed increasingly sophisticated techniques for detecting radar signatures via wideband radar, thus providing the first line of defense for the United States against an attack by Soviet missiles.

In 1971 Kornegay was named technical group leader of Lincoln's radar signature studies group. In 1990 he won the National Society of Black Engineers' Distinguished Scientist of the Year Award. By 1993 he had become head of the radar measurements division. In 2000 he retired to Burtonsville, Maryland, although he continued to work for the Lincoln Laboratory as a consultant for a number of years thereafter. Most of his research remains classified, so little of it has been published; however, over the years the *Lincoln Laboratory Journal*, which reported on the laboratory's research, published several unclassified versions of his work. In 2003 he was named a Lincoln Laboratory division fellow and a member of the Army Science Board.

FURTHER READING

Kessler, James H., et al. *Distinguished African American Scientists of the 20th Century* (1996).

Krapp, Kristine M., ed. *Notable Black American Scientists* (1999).

Spangenburg, Ray, and Kit Moser. *African Americans in Science, Math, and Invention* (2003).

CHARLES W. CAREY JR.

KRS-One (20 Aug. 1965–), hip-hop artist and social activist, was born Lawrence Kris Parker in Brooklyn, New York's Park Slope neighborhood but was raised largely in the Bronx. At twelve, his mother kicked Kris and his younger brother Kenny out of the house (no further information on his parents is available). Although his brother soon returned to his mother's home, Parker remained on the streets, often seeking shelter in public libraries. The next few years of his life were marked by lawlessness and run-ins with police and other authority figures. Such misadventures came to a head when a routine police stop led to the arrest of Kris and an unidentified partner following an attempt to flee (the pair was hauling drugs for a small-time local dealer). A judge sentenced Parker to a South Bronx juvenile home. There he met Scott Sterling, a social worker and youth counselor who performed hip-hop and rap at local clubs as Scott La Rock. In 1986 Parker, now calling himself KRS-One (a moniker reputedly tied to his background as a graffiti artist), joined forces with La Rock to form the Boogie Down Crew. The two soon altered their name to Boogie Down Productions, or simply BDP, and began to attain a reputation as one of hip-hop's most important foundational groups. In 1987 Boogie Down Productions released its first album, *Criminal Minded*, an early effort in the emergent gangster-rap category. An initial offering from the newly formed B-Boy Records label, *Criminal Minded* offered cuts in the classic hardcore style, such as "9mm Goes Bang" and "South Bronx." Its cover featured KRS-One and La Rock surrounded by firearms. Not surprisingly, the album drew interest and criticism. Sadly, violence of a less-fanciful nature soon intruded on the duo's lives. Not long after the release of *Criminal Minded*, a heated dispute in the Bronx led to the shooting death of La Rock. Instead of ending Boogie Down Productions, however, La Rock's murder had a transformative effect. KRS-One shed much of the first album's violent posturing and pursued a less aggressive vision of rap music that he and La Rock had often discussed but never undertaken. KRS-One abandoned the B-Boy label to join Jive Records, and in 1988 BDP's second album, *By Any Means Necessary*, appeared.

Political to its core, KRS-One's second offering explored themes of the violence endemic in inner-city African American communities and the racism that ran rampant throughout America's public and private institutions. The singles "My Philosophy" and "Stop the Violence" attempted to establish KRS-One as a public philosopher, referenced as "the Teacha." He reconfigured the "KRS-One" moniker to stand for "Knowledge Reigns Supreme Over

KRS-One gives the keynote address to kick-off the Rock and Roll Hall of Fame and Museum's celebration of hip-hop culture on 10 Sept. 1999, at Cleveland State University in Cleveland, Ohio. (AP Images.)

Nearly Everyone." Shortly following the release of *By Any Means Necessary*, KRS-One joined other prominent rap and hip-hop artists to found the Stop the Violence movement to address the problem of violence among young African Americans, a growing social catastrophe that the mainstream press associated with rap and hip-hop.

Two years later, in 1989, KRS-One released *Ghetto Music: The Blueprint of Hip-Hop*, and also began a lecture tour that visited colleges and universities, including Stanford, Yale, and Harvard. KRS-One's status as a leading voice in Afrocentric hip-hop was firmly established, and his high-profile and funky, challenging, and accessible raps helped bring attention to the music's political stance.

Hip-hop of a serious nature, however, generally failed to attract the media attention of gangster rap. In 1990 KRS-One's *Edutainment* made a minimal splash in the market. KRS-One responded by returning to the hard-core rap of *Criminally Minded*, a move that attracted new listeners, yet disappointed a great many of his core fans. *Sex and Violence* appeared in 1992, which would be the last of the BDP records. In its aftermath, KRS-One released a flurry of solo albums, including the highly regarded *Return of the Boom Bap* (1993), *I Got Next* (1997)—with jazzy, driving cuts such as "Over Ya Head," "Can't Stop, Won't Stop," and "A Friend"—and the gospel-inflected *Spiritual Minded* (2002).

The release of his albums also brought controversy. KRS-One relied heavily on shock value in marketing his image. He had earlier, for instance, referred to Christianity as oppressive. Thus his public utterances regarding the terrorist attacks on 11 September 2001 came as little surprise. In October 2004, during a *New Yorker* festival, KRS-One participated in a public discussion about the incident. Asked to reflect on his feelings about the attacks and to address hip-hop's relative silence on the event, KRS-One suggested that New York's smoldering twin towers may have represented a form of poetic justice.

Despite the furor and hyperbole that followed his statement, KRS-One's place among hip-hop's leading lights remained unchallenged. Though they may not have attracted the attention or the sales of the top commercial hip-hop recordings, KRS-One's albums continued to meet with the approval of critics and listeners, and he was considered one of hip-hop's founding fathers and among its most consistent and talented voices.

FURTHER READING

Parmar, Priya. *KRS-One Going Against the Grain: A Critical Study of Rap Music as a Postmodern Text* (2002).

Rose, Tricia. *Black Noise: Rap Music and Black Culture in Contemporary America* (1994).

JASON PHILIP MILLER

LaBelle, Patti (24 May 1944–), singer, actress, and author, was born Patricia Louise Holte in Philadelphia, Pennsylvania, to Henry Holte Jr., a train factory worker, and Bertha Holte, a domestic. Her talent for singing became evident in early childhood and was nurtured in the Beulah Baptist Church choir where she was a regular soloist by the time she was a teenager. She attended John Bartram High School and at age fifteen won a talent contest, which led to her first semiprofessional performance. When she was seventeen years old, an urban renewal project uprooted the residents of the all-black Elmwood neighborhood where she and her family lived. Although forced to relocate to a different part of Philadelphia, her family's move proved advantageous for her musical development.

From the early 1960s until 1976 the direction of her life was closely tied to the singing groups through which she gained her first professional experiences. When she moved with her family from Elmwood to a nearby neighborhood, she met Johnnie Dawson, Yvonne Hogen, and Jean Brown, with whom she formed her first group. Inspired by the Shirelles and other popular girl groups of the day, the four classmates performed at local venues in and around Philadelphia. In 1961 they became known as the Ordettes and signed with manager Bernard Montague.

After Dawson, Hogen, and Brown left the Ordettes, Montague hired Nona Hendryx, Sarah Dash, and Cynthia Birdsong to replace them. Along with Holte, the group formed a new version of the Ordettes, and they toured successfully on the East Coast's so-called chitlin' circuit, which was the limited group of venues open to African American performers in the days before integration. Patricia's performance schedule soon conflicted with her studies, and with her mother's permission, she left high school to pursue her career. In April 1962 the Ordettes signed their first recording contract with the Bluebelle Record Company. Thereafter, Patricia Holte and her group were known as Patti LaBelle and the BlueBelles.

Later that year the group received national exposure on *American Bandstand*, performing "I Sold My Heart to the Junkman." Although legal battles ensued over rightful ownership of the song—the BlueBelles recorded their vocals over the instrumental track from a preexisting version of the song by a different group of the same name—it was considered the group's first hit. Patti LaBelle and the BlueBelles soon followed with other hit records, including "Down the Aisle" (1963) and their arrangement of "You'll Never Walk Alone" (1964).

In 1965 the group toured with the Rolling Stones. Upon returning to Philadelphia, they signed with Atlantic Records, a move which solidified their international status. Atlantic sent the group to perform in London, where LaBelle met Vicki Wickham, producer of England's popular *Ready, Steady, Go* television show. Wickham would later be instrumental in transforming the group's image.

By the late 1960s, the group was undergoing major changes. Birdsong left the BlueBelles to sing with the Supremes in 1967. Both their contract with Atlantic and their management contract with Montague ended in 1969. Also, in July 1969, LaBelle married Armstead Edwards.

Patti LaBelle performs at the Democratic National Convention in Boston, 26 July 2004. (AP Images.)

By the late 1960s, black music had moved away from the innocence and optimism of the doo-wop days. The turbulence of the civil rights struggle shifted the musical tastes of black consumers, who now favored the more revolutionary sounds of the Soul era. By 1969 Patti LaBelle and the BlueBelles were a trio with languishing record sales, considered passé because their name and image were still associated with their girl-group origins. However, their fortunes improved in late 1969 when Wickham, at LaBelle's request, agreed to manage them.

Wickham changed the group's name to LaBelle and completely revamped their image. Once the lead singer of a doo wop–style girl group, Patti LaBelle became the centerpiece of a revolutionary act known for outrageous costumes, political commentary, and edgy rock and gospel stylings. Thus transformed, LaBelle became one of the most edgy groups of the 1970s, along with Earth, Wind & Fire, Parliament-Funkadelic, and Aerosmith. It was during this period of metamorphosis that Patti LaBelle took a brief hiatus from performing to give birth to her son, Zuri Edwards, in July 1973.

During the early 1970s LaBelle was based in New York. The group embarked on successful tours and released its first albums with the Warner Brothers and RCA labels, moving from there to Epic Records. With Epic, LaBelle released her first gold album, *Night Birds* (1974), from which came the international hit single "Lady Marmalade" (1975).

At the height of its success, interpersonal tensions brought the group to an end, so in 1976 Patti LaBelle decided to pursue a solo career. Her early solo releases were lackluster compared to her former success with LaBelle. However, in 1981 a turning point came when she toured with a revival of the stage play *Your Arms Too Short to Box with God*. After nine months on tour, the show made its Broadway debut in 1982, and critics gave Patti LaBelle rave reviews.

Two years after her triumphant performance in *Your Arms Too Short to Box with God*, LaBelle made her film debut in *A Soldier's Story* (1984). During the same year, she had hits with "Stir it Up" and "New Attitude" from the soundtrack of the 1984 film *Beverly Hills Cop*. In 1986 she had a platinum single with Michael McDonald, "On My Own." By 1992 her solo career had come into full bloom with several hit records, five Grammy nominations, and regular appearances on prime-time television shows including NBC's *A Different World* and her own short-lived sitcom, *Out All Night*. However, as she flourished professionally, she endured the loss of three of her siblings and her best friend to cancer. In 1996 she chronicled her triumphs and struggles in her autobiography, *Don't Block the Blessings: Revelations of a Lifetime*. Another book, born of her lifelong interest in cooking, followed in 1999: *LaBelle Cuisine: Recipes to Sing About*. In 2000 she and Armstead Edwards divorced. In 2006 she returned to her church roots with the release of *The Gospel According to Patti LaBelle*, an album featuring the veteran artist along with several younger gospel and secular stars.

FURTHER READING

LaBelle, Patti, with Laura B. Randolph. *Don't Block the Blessings: Revelations of a Lifetime* (1996).
Randolph, Laura B. "Patti LaBelle Gets Down at 50," *Ebony* (Nov. 1994).

TERESA L. REED

Lacy, Rubin (2 Jan. 1901–1972), blues musician and preacher, was born in Pelahatchie, Mississippi. His father, a fireman in Jackson, Mississippi, died in 1911 and Lacy was raised by his grandfather, an African Methodist preacher. He attended school for five years and quickly turned his attention to music. Coming from a musically skilled family, Lacy organized his siblings into gospel quartets while his mother or other siblings played harmonica. He learned to play guitar and mandolin in his early teens from a man named George "Crow Jane" Hendrix, a professional musician. His uncle, Herbert Meiels, a German who was highly educated and spoke five languages, taught Lacy German, history, and politics. At age twenty, Lacy moved to Jackson, Mississippi, to pursue music, but stayed only a short time before he began doing railroad work that took him all over Mississippi and then to Iowa. Lacy moved to Chicago and lived with Meiels for two years as he worked for National Linen Supply. Jobs took Lacy from Kankakee, Illinois, then to Ohio to work on the railroad again. He returned to Jackson shortly thereafter and performed with other blues musicians like Son Spand, Charlie McCoy, Walter Vincent, TOMMY JOHNSON, and Ishmon Bracey. Lacy and his bluesmen became famous locally by playing their music in the streets and on the steps of establishments throughout the towns. Lacy, known as "the Blues King" to some, and his fellow musicians played dances for both blacks and whites during this time. They performed blues, which was predominantly a black style of music, along with waltzes and two-steps, which were predominantly white styles of music.

In 1927 Lacy set out for the Delta to become a successful musician. He became a plantation overseer in Itta Bena, where he met Ralph Lembo, a furniture store owner and music promoter who brought Lacy to Memphis to play for a Columbia recording session. Lacy was not recorded, but Arthur Laibley, who worked for Paramount Records, was also at that session and invited Lacy to come to Chicago to record. Lacy and Lembo went to Chicago in March 1928 and recorded two songs, "Mississippi Jail House Groan" and "Ham Hound Crave"—his only recordings. He continued to work successfully as a musician in the Delta until October 1932, at which time he was severely injured while working at a saw mill. Lacy quit music abruptly and became a preacher, a choice family members felt was a calling ignored by Lacy in his early years. He met his wife in the late 1930s in Tunica, Mississippi, and the two had six children. As a preacher he moved from Mississippi to Arkansas to Missouri. Then in the 1950s he was asked to come to a church in California. He lived his remaining years in the Ridgecrest/Death Valley area preaching and speaking about his life as a blues musician, but never played the guitar again.

FURTHER READING
Evans, David. "Rubin Lacy," *Blues Unlimited* (1967).
The Journal of American Folklore 85.337 (July–Sep. 1972).

KEVIN SLIMAN

Lacy, Sam (23 Oct. 1903?–8 May 2003), sports columnist and editor, was born Samuel Harold Lacy, one of five children of Rose and Samuel Erskine Lacy. Many publications (including his own autobiography) state that Lacy was born in Mystic, Connecticut, but recent research suggests that he may have been born in 1905 in Washington, D.C. His mother, a Shinnecock Indian, was a hairdresser and the family disciplinarian; his father was a notary and legal researcher as well as an avid baseball fan. Lacy was raised in Washington, D.C., moving often within the city during his youth. Although the Lacys were not members of Washington's professionally accomplished African American middle class, they strove to improve their social standing through hard work and education. To that end, Lacy began working when he was about eight years old, shining shoes, selling newspapers, and setting pins at a bowling alley. Later, he shagged fly balls during batting practice for the Washington Nationals (later known as the Senators) baseball team. Popular with many of the ballplayers, Lacy often ran errands for them and eventually worked as a vendor at Griffith Stadium, where he saw major league stars like Ty Cobb and Babe Ruth play, as well as such Negro League stars as OSCAR CHARLESTON and JOHN HENRY LLOYD. Like the rest of America, baseball was rigidly segregated. "I was in a position to make some comparisons," Lacy reminisced in 1990, "and it seemed to me that those black players were good enough to play in the big leagues. There was, of course, no talk then of that ever happening. When I was growing up, there was no real opportunity for blacks in any sport" (Fimrite, 90).

At Armstrong Technical High School, the small, lithe Lacy played baseball, basketball, and football. After graduating in 1924, Lacy played semipro baseball, coached and promoted basketball, briefly attended Howard University, and worked as a part-time journalist and radio announcer. In October 1926 he joined the *Washington Tribune* full-time, soon thereafter becoming its sports editor. In 1927 Lacy married Alberta Robinson; they had one son, Samuel Howe. They were divorced in 1952 and a year later he married Barbara Robinson, a government worker.

During the summer of 1929 Lacy left the *Tribune* to play baseball in Connecticut but returned to the newspaper in 1930, regaining his position as sports editor in July 1933. "By the mid-1930s, married for several years and with the dream of a baseball career no longer a realistic option, I finally was ready to make the move into full-time journalism

Sam Lacy. The sports writer poses in the offices of the *Afro-American* newspaper in Baltimore, Md., on 22 Aug. 1991. (AP Images.)

with the *Washington Tribune*, where I worked from 1934 to 1938" (Lacy, 27).

It was in the mid-1930s that Lacy began agitating for social change, joining contemporaries like the labor leader A. PHILIP RANDOLPH, the law dean CHARLES HAMILTON HOUSTON, and his fellow sportswriter WENDELL SMITH. Indeed, for the rest of his life, having found his voice as a "race man," Lacy criticized a wide variety of racial injustices in the sports world. The list is long, but one of his first big stories came in October 1937, when he reported that Syracuse University's star player, Wilmeth Sidat-Singh, was not in fact a "Hindu," as had been widely reported, but was an American-born black man. Lacy printed the truth, and Syracuse bowed to the University of Maryland's refusal to compete if the player stayed in the lineup. It was a story that elicited criticism, even among African Americans. Lacy stood behind his story, arguing that racial progress demanded honesty. Years later Lacy wrote: "Call 'em as you see 'em and accept the comebacks. Take it in stride, the same as other distractions. That's the way it was. Push forward or get pushed aside" (Lacy, 7).

Baseball, the national pastime and an important cultural institution, was at the forefront of Lacy's agenda. The injustice of the game's racial bigotry and exclusion motivated him. Perhaps encouraged by the response to the Sidat-Singh incident, Lacy met with the Senators' owner, Clark Griffith, in December 1937 to discuss the hiring of black ballplayers. Lacy suggested that Griffith sign the Negro League greats JOSH GIBSON and BUCK LEONARD of the Homestead Grays. Griffith objected, saying that integration would devastate the Negro Leagues "and put about 400 colored guys out of work." Lacy reportedly responded, "When Abraham Lincoln signed the Emancipation Proclamation, he put 400,000 black people out of jobs" (Klingaman, 6A).

A traditionalist, Griffith was not persuaded, partly owing to the profitability of renting his stadium to Negro League teams. Nevertheless, the historian Brad Snyder observes that the meeting with Griffith "marked the beginning of Lacy's campaign to integrate baseball in Washington," and Lacy began to publish a column in the weekly *Washington Tribune* titled "Pro and Con on the Negro in Organized Baseball" (Snyder, 77). Lacy also argued, sometimes didactically, that black ballplayers and those who ran the Negro Leagues needed to be more professional if they were to compete in the major leagues.

In 1940, after a series of disputes with the management of the *Washington Afro-American*, which had bought and absorbed the *Tribune*, Lacy left his wife and young son in Washington and moved to Chicago, where he soon became assistant national editor for the *Chicago Defender*, one of the nation's largest and most influential black papers. While he did not cover sports for the *Defender*, Lacy continued to fight for the integration of professional baseball by intensifying "an already aggressive and voluminous letter campaign directed at major league owners and particularly Commissioner [Kenesaw Mountain] Landis" (*Dictionary of Literary Biography*, vol. 171, 1996, 176). Late in 1943 Landis relented and allowed Lacy to bring a small delegation to speak to the owners at their annual winter meeting. Unfortunately Lacy was upstaged by the publisher of the *Chicago Defender* and by the famous actor-singer PAUL ROBESON and never got to make his case.

Shortly thereafter, a disappointed Lacy became columnist and sports editor for the weekly *Baltimore Afro-American*, a position he held for almost sixty years. Indefatigable, Lacy continued to crusade for the integration of professional baseball in his column and behind the scenes. In March 1945, after Landis died, Lacy wrote to every major league owner suggesting the creation of a committee to reconsider the integration of baseball. Lacy presented his proposal, and the executives agreed to his plan. The Major League Committee on Baseball Integration was established, including Lacy, Branch Rickey of the Brooklyn Dodgers, and Larry MacPhail of the New York Yankees. The committee never met, however, largely because of MacPhail's foot-dragging. Nonetheless, Rickey and JACKIE ROBINSON made history in August 1945, when the latter signed with the Dodgers.

After Robinson made the majors in 1947, Lacy was his close companion for three years. Lacy "chronicled Robinson's first day in the majors, naming those who sat beside him on the Dodgers bench—and how close they sat. He cataloged the insults and debris hurled Robinson's way. He counted brushback pitches. He timed applause. He reported every pulled muscle, broken nail and silver hair on Robinson's prematurely gray head" (Klingaman, 6A). Traveling all over the country with Robinson and other black sportswriters, Lacy suffered numerous racist indignities, yet kept them to himself.

In addition to crusading for the integration of baseball, Lacy wrote about auto and horse racing, boxing, college and professional basketball and football, golf, the Olympics, tennis, and track and field, amounting to roughly three thousand columns in all. A man with an acute sense of fairness, he wrote about racism in accommodations and employment practices, the exploitation of African American student athletes, and numerous other examples of discrimination and injustice.

More than a reporter, Lacy used his sports column to reflect on and to improve the world in which he lived and tried to do something about improving it. He was "a drum major for change—the broad, sweeping sort of social change that helps legitimize this nation's claim to greatness long before the best-recognized civil-rights activists came on the scene. Given baseball's popularity in the '40s, the opening [Lacy helped forge] shattered the myth of white superiority and made it possible for other race-based barriers to crumble" (Wickham, 13A). Lacy won many awards and accolades, including the prestigious 1997 J. G. Taylor Spink Award for meritorious contributions to baseball writing, which earned him a place in the writers' wing of the Baseball Hall of Fame in 1998. Lacy was only the second African American so honored. At a gathering in his honor in 2002, Lacy was lauded by Baltimore's mayor, Martin O'Malley, "for challenging the American conscience and demanding that we live up to our promise as a people" (Kane, 3B).

Though some said he became something of a curmudgeon in his later years, Lacy was a soft-spoken, humble man. "In the case of baseball integration, I just happened to be in the right place at the right time," Lacy observed. "I think that anyone else situated as I was and possessing a bit of curiosity and concern about progress would have done the same thing" (Lacy, 209). Be that as it may, the sports columnist Michael Wilbon convincingly argues, "You can't write the history of sports and race in America without devoting a chapter to Sam Lacy" ("Lacy's Towering Legacy," *Washington Post*, 11 May 2003).

FURTHER READING

Lacy, Sam, with Moses J. Newson. *Fighting for Fairness: The Life Story of Hall of Fame Sportswriter Sam Lacy* (1998).

Fimrite, Ron. "Sam Lacy: Black Crusader," *Sports Illustrated* (29 Oct. 1990).

Kane, Gregory. "A Group of Sports Legends Gathers to Honor the Greatest of Them All," *Baltimore Sun*, 6 Oct. 2002.

Klingaman, Mike. "Hall of Fame Opens Door for Writer," *Baltimore Sun*, 26 July 1998.

Snyder, Brad. *Beyond the Shadows of the Senators: The Untold Story of the Homestead Grays and the Integration of Baseball* (2003)

Wickham, Dewayne. "Journalist's Induction into Hall Long Overdue," *USA Today*, 30 July 1998, 13A.

Obituaries: *Baltimore Sun* and *Washington Post*, 10 May 2003; *New York Times*, 12 May 2003; *Baltimore Afro-American*, 17–23, May 2003; *Sports Illustrated* (19 May 2003).

DANIEL A. NATHAN

Ladd, Florence (16 June 1932–), social psychologist, writer, and administrator, was born Florence Cawthorne in Washington, D.C. to William Cawthorne Jr., a clerk for the board of education, and Eleanor Willis Cawthorne, a special education teacher. Ladd attended the prestigious Dunbar High School in Washington, D.C. While she was a student there, her mother took a course in abnormal psychology. Helping her mother type papers for the class was Ladd's first exposure to the study of psychology and influenced the direction of her later academic work. Ladd went on to study at Howard University, a place well known for its superior psychology program. She spent her junior year abroad in France and Switzerland studying psychological testing and sharing the classroom with white students for the first time. Her experiences abroad began a lifelong fascination with travel and the American expatriate experience. Ladd received a B.S. in Psychology from Howard in 1953.

Ladd moved to New York State to pursue a doctorate in social psychology at the University of Rochester. Upon receiving her Ph.D. in Social Psychology in 1958 (the title of her dissertation was "Activities and Attitudes of Institutionalized Aging Males"), she took a teaching position in psychology at Simmons College in Boston, Massachusetts. In 1959 Ladd married Ulysses Grant Shelton and relocated to Istanbul, Turkey, when her husband was given a Fulbright Scholarship to study there. She taught at the American College for Girls and Robert College in Istanbul until 1964, when she and her husband divorced. Ladd then returned to Boston for a postdoctoral fellowship in community psychiatry at Harvard University. At this time the first critiques of the urban renewal movement were emerging, and Ladd began collaborating with architects and city planners. She became a lecturer at the Harvard Graduate School of Education in 1965 and an associate professor in city planning at the Harvard Graduate School of Design in 1972. From 1970 to 1972 she was also a fellow at the Mary Ingraham Bunting Institute at Radcliffe College, an interdisciplinary center for women scholars. In 1969 she married John Ladd, and in 1970 they welcomed a son, Michael Cawthorne Ladd, who went on to become a respected performance poet and social critic. John Ladd passed away in 1971.

Ladd's association with different academic disciplines allowed her to develop her interest in the intersection of psychology and environmental studies and to contribute to the emerging field of environmental psychology. Developed in part as a response to urban renewal, environmental psychology examined the impact of large-scale renovation of poor urban neighborhoods. The 1960s saw the emergence of strong critiques of urban renewal for its imbedded racism and destruction of inner-city communities. Responses in the field of psychology emphasized the importance of designing for the community, and in 1970 Ladd published the groundbreaking community development study "Black Youths View Their Environments: Neighborhood Maps," in the journal *Environment and Behavior*.

In 1977 Ladd left teaching to become an administrator at the MIT School of Architecture and Planning. By the time she left MIT she had risen to the level of associate dean. She continued her work as an administrator as the dean of students at Wellesley College from 1979 to 1984, encouraging focus on social justice issues and multiculturalism. In 1984 Ladd married William Joseph Harris, an architect and sculptor.

In the mid-1980s Ladd moved away from academics to work for Oxfam America, an international humanitarian aid organization based in Boston. From 1985 to 1987 she served as the educational director and liaison to the United Nations and from 1987 to 1989 as an associate director. Upon leaving Oxfam America, Ladd returned to the Bunting Institute as its director, promoting diversity while fostering a strong sense of community among the fellows. In 1991 Ladd received the Hutchison Medal from the University of Rochester, the highest honor the university bestows upon its alumni.

Although recognized first for her contributions to social psychology, Ladd became known as a writer of fiction and poetry. Her first novel, *Sarah's Psalm*, was published in 1996 and received the Literary Award for Best Fiction from the Black Caucus of the American Library Association. *Sarah's Psalm* follows Sarah Stewart, a young black Harvard graduate who travels to Senegal seeking creative fulfillment and comes to realize that she belongs in Africa. Critics praised the book as a moving first novel that offers an intimate portrait of the journey toward self-realization.

After her retirement as director of the Bunting Institute in 1997, Ladd continued to write and to serve as a member of the board of trustees of Hampshire College, was an overseer of the Boston Museum of Fine Arts, and served as an adviser to a variety of artistic and academic initiatives. Her wide-ranging work in environmental psychology, literature, and as an administrator and mentor distinguishes her as one of the foremost African American champions of the human community.

FURTHER READING

Guthrie, Robert V.. *Even the Rat Was White: A Historical View of Psychology* (1998).

Slaight, Wilma. "Person of the Week: Florence Ladd," *Wellesley College 125th Anniversary Webpage*, 28 Aug. 2000, http://www.wellesley.edu/Anniversary/ladd.html.

Yount, Lisa. *A–Z of Women in Science and Math* (1999).

EMILY A. TEITSWORTH

Ladner, Joyce Ann (12 Oct. 1943–), civil rights activist, sociologist, and university administrator, was born in Battles, Mississippi. She was the youngest of three children born to Annie Ruth Woullard and Eunice Stafford Ladner, a presser for a dry cleaner. After her divorce from Eunice, Annie Ruth married William Coty Perryman, an auto mechanic with whom she had six children. Ladner and her siblings were raised in Palmers Crossing, a segregated rural district outside of Hattiesburg. Ladner grew up in a working-class family surrounded by a tight-knit group of extended relatives and neighbors who provided positive role models. Although separated by distance, she always felt a kinship toward her biological father, whose family came from a long line of Creole farmers, artisans, and craftsmen.

Ladner's childhood experiences with Jim Crow segregation, racial hostility, and economic hardship were mitigated by a supportive black community and a nurturing home environment that bolstered her aspirations and self-esteem. Influenced by her mother and stepfather's optimism and perseverance, she inherited a can-do attitude and defiant spirit at an early age. As a teenager Ladner worked weekends as a domestic in a white household until the day the family's daughter called her a "nigger." Not only did she tell the girl never to speak to her that way again,

she also quit the same day. She credited her parents with preparing her to deal with the challenges of racial discrimination and to succeed in spite of social barriers. Although her mother dropped out of elementary school in order to work on the family farm, she insisted on the importance of education for her children. Seven of Ladner's siblings completed high school and six went on to attend college. An avid student, Ladner would ascend to the highest echelons of academia.

The height of the civil rights movement coincided with Ladner's college years, and her deep involvement in part reflected a reaction to the racism and violent oppression she witnessed growing up in the South. She was eleven years old at the time of the 1954 *Brown v. Board of Education* school desegregation decision and remembered reading headlines in local newspapers proclaiming "Black Monday." Ladner was twelve years old when EMMETT TILL, an African American teenager, was murdered in Mississippi, and the tragedy had an indelible effect upon her worldview. She became engaged in social activism during her teenage years. In 1958 MEDGAR EVERS asked Ladner and her sister Dorie (along with fellow classmate Charles Davis) to organize the Forrest County Youth Chapter of the NAACP while they were students at Rowan High School. After enrolling at Tougaloo, the Ladner sisters also became leading activists involved in the Student Nonviolent Coordinating Committee (SNCC). They and other students helped coordinate efforts to combat racial injustice even as they faced systematic discrimination and opposition. Although legally entitled to vote, blacks in Mississippi were forced to take an extremely rigorous literacy test from which whites were exempt. After failing the examination as a senior in college, Ladner was able to register to vote only after appealing to the federal courts. Despite her frustration and anger, Ladner continued to be heavily involved in the fight for equal rights. For example, she worked behind the scenes in preparation for the historic 1963 March on Washington, raising funds through SNCC offices in New York to provide transportation for as many African Americans as possible. Her early interest in social activism led to a scholarly career in sociology. She majored in sociology at Tougaloo College and joined the Gamma Psi chapter of Delta Sigma Theta Inc. After receiving her bachelor's degree in 1964 she went on to complete her Ph.D. in Sociology at Washington University in St. Louis, Missouri, in 1968.

At Tougaloo, Ladner studied under Dr. Ernst Borinski, an influential figure at the college who played an important role in shaping the sociology department. Ladner benefited from Borinski's social science laboratory and social science forums, which provided graduate students with specialized knowledge and exposure to leading intellectuals in the field (Borinski, 1948). Ladner's scholarly work focused primarily upon the study of race, family structure, value systems, and urban leadership. Her dissertation examined the social adaptations of black female adolescents in a St. Louis housing project. In 1971 she published her first book, *Tomorrow's Tomorrow: Today's Black Woman*, which offered a critical examination of black values and behavior in the ghetto. Breaking sharply with conventional approaches to the study of black communities, Ladner argued for a decolonized perspective that would not compare African American value systems to white middle-class norms. Rejecting the concept of "objective" social science, Ladner was straightforward in her role as a black sociologist: "I decided whose side I was on and resolved within myself that as a black social scientist I must take a stand and that there could be no value-free sanctuary for me" (*Tomorrow's Tomorrow*, xviii). Her study offered a view inside the world of black women that countered many negative stereotypes prevalent in the social science of her day. While earlier research had characterized blacks as suffering from low self-esteem, Ladner empirically demonstrated that many African Americans develop a positive self-image even in the midst of socioeconomic disadvantage and racial discrimination. Moreover, her research presented one of the first substantial challenges to conventional sociological definitions of "deviant" behavior. Ladner argued that black communities affirm the worth of all children, regardless of the marital status of their parents. Further, she reframed African American sexual mores in a positive light and suggested that black women were becoming role models for white women who sought to challenge the traditional institution of marriage.

Ladner began her academic career teaching in Illinois, Connecticut, and Tanzania. She declined job offers from Yale and Berkeley in order to join the faculty at Howard University in 1971. During that time she edited a groundbreaking and controversial volume titled *The Death of White Sociology* (1973), which offered critical perspectives on the intersection of race and social science at the height of the Black Power era. It was also one of the first sociological texts to evaluate the influence of institutional racism and to argue against labeling African Americans as "deviant." In 1973 she married Walter C. Carrington, an ambassador to Senegal and, later, Nigeria. That same year the couple moved to New York where Ladner taught at Hunter College. They adopted their son, Thomas Maigore Ladner Carrington, in 1974, and the family spent a year living in Senegal from 1980 to 1981. Upon returning to the United States, Ladner once again joined the faculty at Howard University, where she would remain professor of sociology at the School of Social Work for seventeen years. A distinguished scholar, Ladner became one of the most influential black sociologists of her time (Conyers, 1996). She also became a single mother after her divorce from Carrington in 1985.

While at Howard, Ladner served as vice president of academic affairs from 1990 to 1994 and was named interim president from 1994 to 1995. Shortly thereafter, President Clinton appointed her to the District of Columbia Financial Control Board, where she worked to coordinate funding for the city's school system and social services. Between 1997 and 2003 Ladner joined the Brookings Institute as a senior research fellow. During her tenure at the institute Ladner completed *The Ties That Bind: Timeless Values for African American Families* (1998), a semiautobiographical book that explores how traditional African American values such as hard work, integrity, self-respect, and perseverance could be passed on to the next generation. In 2001 she wrote *The New Urban Leaders*, which profiles successful leaders of nonprofit organizations in the inner city. And, drawing from her own experiences as a mother, she cowrote *Launching Our Black Children for Success* (2003), a guide to parenting.

Ladner was forced to abandon her scholarly work in 2003 after being diagnosed with fibromyalgia, a condition that causes chronic pain and debilitating fatigue. Although she also suffered from "fibro fog," which severely limited her capacity for analytical thinking, Ladner's right-brain creativity flourished. She moved to Sarasota, Florida, and there she discovered a passion for abstract expressionist painting and jewelry making. Before she became ill, Ladner wrote an unpublished memoir with her sister, Dorie.

Her enduring commitment to improving social conditions for African Americans took root at an early age and has been manifest throughout her life. Ladner's unique sociological perspective emphasizes positive adaptations and successful strategies rather than simply "social problems." As a social activist and distinguished intellectual, she has lectured widely on social issues and has published eight books and more than thirty scholarly articles in addition to contributing regularly to the *Washington Post, Ebony, Essence*, the *New York Times*, and *Black Enterprise* magazine.

FURTHER READING

Additional manuscript materials are held at Washington University in St. Louis, Missouri, and newspaper clippings regarding Ladner and her sister Dorie are stored at the McCain Library and archives of the University of Southern Mississippi. Her complete archives are at the Mississippi State Archives, Jackson, Mississippi.

Roach, Ronald. "Catching up with ... Joyce Ladner," *Black Issues in Higher Education* (May 2005).

Borinski, Ernst. "The Social Science Laboratory at Tougaloo College," *Journal of Educational Sociology* 22 (1948).

Conyers, James E. "Who's Who among Black Doctorates in Sociology," *Sociological Focus* 19.1 (1996).

CRYSTAL MARIE FLEMING

Lafayette, James Armistead (1748?–9 Aug. 1830), slave and Revolutionary War spy, was born James Armistead, a slave belonging to the planter William Armistead of New Kent County, Virginia. Nothing is known of his parents, but it is reasonable to assume that William Armistead also held, at least at some point, James's mother and possibly his father as slaves. James Armistead was a skilled worker whom William Armistead employed in his Richmond offices apparently in a clerical capacity. During the Revolutionary War, William Armistead served as a military supply officer, with James Armistead accompanying him as a body servant. Later William Armistead was a member of the Virginia House of Delegates.

James Armistead accompanied William Armistead to Richmond in the summer of 1781 while William was fulfilling his duties as the commissary of military supplies to the Continental army. American forces, led by the French Marquis de Lafayette, and British troops led by Lord Cornwallis tangled in Virginia through the summer of 1781. In order better to know the movements of the British troops, Lafayette was in search of spies to infiltrate the British command. In Richmond, James Armistead learned that the general was looking for potential secret agents, and he volunteered to become a spy for the American army.

As a slave Armistead was in a unique position to infiltrate the British command. Under General George Washington the American army made limited use of slaves and of African American soldiers generally. By contrast the British encouraged American slaves to run away and join the British army, with the reward of freedom for their service. When Armistead appeared at Cornwallis's camp volunteering to work for the general, he was easily able to gain the trust of the British, who would not have suspected that Armistead was there as an intelligence agent. For a few months Armistead worked as a forager bringing food to British headquarters. By August 1781 Armistead had volunteered to spy on the Americans for the British, thereby improving his access to British military information while allaying any suspicions about his activities.

Several times during the summer and fall of 1781 Armistead relayed important information back to the American camp from Cornwallis's command. General Lafayette learned from Armistead's reports that Cornwallis intended to set up permanently in Yorktown. Additionally, it was partly owing to information gained from Armistead's reports that Lafayette was able to strategize the siege at Yorktown, which resulted in the British surrender on 19 October 1781 that effectively ended the Revolutionary War. In a letter of recommendation dated 21 November 1784, General Lafayette wrote that James Armistead had "done Essential Services to me while I had the Honour to command in this State."

At the end of the war James Armistead returned, still enslaved, to the household of William Armistead. In 1784 and again in 1786 James Armistead submitted petitions to the Virginia General Assembly asking the government to grant him his freedom in return for his service during the war. His petition, he argued, was not only for himself but for others as well—"the just right which all mankind have to Freedom." William Armistead supported both petitions. The second, successful petition was endorsed by the letter of recommendation from the Marquis de Lafayette praising James Armistead's actions during the Revolution. On 9 January 1787 the speaker of the House of Virginia signed a bill making Armistead a free man. In homage to the general whose friendship he valued and whose public statements had helped Armistead secure his freedom, he took the marquis's surname and became James Armistead Lafayette. Later that spring the general assembly agreed to compensate William Armistead for the loss of property in the person of James Armistead Lafayette, granting him 250 pounds sterling. As the historian John Salmon notes, this sum was more than twice the average compensation given to an owner by the state for an executed male slave at this time. As a particularly skilled worker as well as a hero of the Revolution, James Armistead Lafayette was literally and figuratively highly valuable to his owner.

By 1787 Armistead Lafayette had achieved a measure of economic success, owning two horses and three slaves. Slave ownership was not uncommon among free black landowners in Virginia at this time. At some point either before or after his emancipation, Lafayette married and had at least one son. Given laws that defined slavery as a condition inherited from the maternal side and that, legally, enslaved women could not marry, it is entirely possible that Armistead Lafayette was obliged to purchase some of his own family members to secure their freedom. By 1816 Armistead Lafayette owned a parcel of land in New Kent County next to the property of his former owner, William Armistead. As he aged, Lafayette found himself less physically able to work. In 1818 he was back before the General Assembly asking for a veteran's pension. He was awarded a yearly income that he collected twice annually at the office of James E. Heath, the state auditor in Richmond.

After his 1818 petition Lafayette continued to appear in the public eye. Newspapers recounted his nostalgic reunion with the marquis during the marquis's tour of the United States in 1824. As reported in the *Richmond Enquirer*, during General Lafayette's triumphal Jubilee procession through Yorktown, Armistead Lafayette "was recognized by [the Marquis] in the crowd, called to him by name, and taken into his embrace" (Salmon, p. 85). That Armistead Lafayette was even able to remain in the crowd waiting to spot the old general indicates that he held unusual status in Richmond society. A law passed on the occasion of General Lafayette's Richmond visit barred "intoxicated or colored person(s)" from being part of the public display (Gregg Kimball, *Where These Memories Grow: History, Memory, and Southern Identity* [2000], 60).

Also in 1824 the Richmond artist James Blennerhasset Martin painted a portrait of the old Revolutionary War hero. That Martin later made an engraving of the portrait, along with a facsimile of the marquis's 1784 letter of recommendation, indicates that the public was increasingly nostalgic for the passing heroes of the Revolutionary generation.

Martin's oil portrait currently hangs at the Valentine Museum in Richmond. Lafayette College in Easton, Pennsylvania, holds a copy of Martin's engraving, as well as an oil portrait by Jean-Baptiste LePaon depicting the marquis accompanied by a figure thought to be James Armistead Lafayette.

Armistead Lafayette was also memorialized in fiction when in 1828 James Heath, the aforementioned state auditor, published a novel titled *Edge-Hill, or, The Family of the Fitz-royals*. Armistead Lafayette appears as a minor character in the novel in the capacity of a spy for the Marquis de Lafayette. At the end of the novel Heath included a story of the old veteran's reunion with his patron and the general's commendation. Heath and Armistead Lafayette may have met when the latter came to collect his pensions at the auditor's office, but certainly the old patriot was also a well-known public figure in Richmond during Heath's lifetime.

James Armistead Lafayette died at his farm in New Kent County at eighty-two years of age. Although his name faded from public memory for a time, RALPH ELLISON, who wrote a biographical entry on Lafayette for the U.S. Bicentennial Society's Profile of Patriots in 1974, revived his story. Though CRISPUS ATTUCKS may have been the first African American to give his life in the Revolutionary War, James Armistead Lafayette's services to the new nation were more lasting in their effects. Risking life and limb he gathered critical information for the Americans and contributed instrumentally to the American defeat of Cornwallis at Yorktown. His later petitions to the Virginia Assembly stand as eloquent pleas for freedom for all Americans.

FURTHER READING

Ellison, Ralph. "James Armistead Lafayette," in *The Collected Essays of Ralph Ellison* (1995).
Salmon, John. " 'A mission of the most secret and important kind': James Lafayette and American Espionage in 1781," *Virginia Cavalcade* 31. 2 (1981).

ELIZABETH KUEBLER-WOLF

Lafon, Thomy (28 Dec. 1810–22 Dec. 1893), real estate broker and philanthropist, was born free in New Orleans, Louisiana, the son of Modeste Foucher, a woman of Haitian descent. His father may have been Pierre Laralde, who might have been a Caucasian born in France or a free person of color born in Louisiana. Although Lafon was a devout Roman Catholic, no baptismal record has been found, and there is no birth record. He probably took the name Lafon from Barthélémy Lafon, a prominent architect, engineer, and city planner, who was born in Villepinte, France, and took up permanent residence in New Orleans in 1789 or 1790. The connection between Thomy Lafon and Barthélémy Lafon is still unclear; there was a relationship, however, between the elder Lafon and Thomy Lafon's mother.

Most of what has been written about the early life of Thomy Lafon is based on hearsay and conjecture. He was fluent in French, Spanish, and English, but nothing is known of his formal education. Some have said that he was educated in France and was at one time a teacher, but neither of these assertions can be verified. The first published reference to Lafon that has been found is in the New Orleans city directory of 1842; he is listed as a merchant. He is also listed in several later city directories, but it was not until 1868 that he was identified as a broker. The writer of his obituary for the *New Orleans Daily Picayune* said, "He was careful and shrewd in his speculations in real estate, and this is about the only business that he has been ever known to have engaged in" (23 Dec. 1893). At the time of his death he owned vast amounts of property that were located in almost every section of the city.

Lafon never married. The only sibling acknowledged in his obituary and will, the widow Alfee Lafon Baudin, lived with him at the time of his death, and it was said that she had been his "adviser and companion through life." They lived quietly and simply in a modest cottage, even though Lafon was the owner of pretentious dwellings in the city. He dressed well, as befitted a businessman of his stature, but not expensively. He was noted for his courteous and dignified manner. Because of his physical features, he was often taken to be white, but he never encouraged it and chose to be identified as a Creole of color. He avoided social events but was a patron of the arts, especially music, and regularly attended concerts and operas. During the Civil War he favored the Union and later joined Thomas Jefferson Durant's Radical Republican Club. He opposed Andrew Johnson, supported congressional plans for Reconstruction, and favored universal male suffrage and racial integration of the public schools.

Lafon's financial success and philanthropy are well documented. He is remembered for the large bequests to institutions in his will, but he was also generous in life. A contemporary, Rodolphe Lucien Desdunes, the Creole historian, wrote in 1897 that "he gave right and left, for every deserving cause…. There is not a colored charitable institution established in his days that did not receive a donation from him; not a newspaper started in the interest of human rights that did not obtain assistance from his unmeasured liberality." All the institutions that received bequests in his will had previously benefited from his generosity, but it was said that he derived the greatest satisfaction from private donations, being able to assist deserving destitute families and individuals without regard to race or religion. The *Daily Picayune* announced his death under the headline "A Colored Leader in Charity Passes Away" (23 Dec. 1893).

Lafon's bequests included $49,000 in cash and three pieces of property to relatives and friends and $94,000 in cash and twenty-one properties, valued at approximately $400,000, to twelve institutions. Among the institutions were those operated by or for the benefit of both blacks and whites, Protestants and Catholics. The largest gift, however, was to establish a perpetual trust for the benefit of the Sisters of the Holy Family, an order of African American nuns, who operated or would assume operation of several of the Catholic institutions that had received special bequests.

In 1894 the lower house of the Louisiana legislature voted to appropriate funds for a bronze bust of Thomy Lafon to be displayed permanently at Tulane University; the bill died in the senate. However, the Louisiana State Museum possesses a handsome plaster bust of Lafon sculpted by Achille Peretti in 1894 and acquired by the museum in 1909. The name Lafon lives on in a day care center and nursing home operated by the Sisters of the Holy Family, a nursing home of the United Methodist Church, a city street, and a New Orleans public school. Charles Barthelemy Rousséve, the historian, has translated from the French into English prose the last lines of an "Ode to Thomy Lafon," written by Desdunes: "We give thanks, for, because thou didst wed principle and good work, no name, Lafon, shall longer live than thine." Lafon died at his home in New Orleans.

FURTHER READING
Bell, Caryn Cossé. *Revolution, Romanticism, and the Afro-Creole Protest Tradition in Louisiana, 1718–1868* (1997).

Desdunes, Rodolphe Lucien. *Nos hommes et notre histoire* (1911).

Rousséve, Charles Barthelemy. *The Negro in Louisiana: Aspects of His History and His Literature* (1937).

Wynes, Charles E. "Thomy Lafon: Black Philanthropist," *Midwest Quarterly: A Journal of Contemporary Thought* 12 (Winter, 1981).

This entry is taken from the *American National Biography* and is published here with the permission of the American Council of Learned Societies.

CLIFTON H. JOHNSON

LaFontant, Jewel Stradford (28 Apr. 1922–31 May 1997), attorney and civic leader, was born in Chicago into an African American family of successful lawyers. Her father, C. Francis Stradford, was a prominent attorney on Chicago's South Side and the founder of the National Bar Association (NBA), which he established in 1925. In 1940 C. Francis Stradford successfully argued the U.S. Supreme Court's landmark case *Hansberry v. Lee*, which abolished the restrictive covenants that had limited racial integration in Chicago neighborhoods. Her grandfather, J. B. STRADFORD, was a well-known lawyer in the African American community and the owner of the only black hotel in Tulsa, Oklahoma. Her mother, Aida Arrabella Carter Stradford, was an artist and a homemaker. LaFontant's indoctrination to the legal profession occurred early. As a student at Englewood Public High School in Chicago, she spent the summers working in her father's law office. In the autumn of 1939, she followed in the footsteps of her father, grandfather, and grandmother, Bertie Wiley Stradford, and entered Oberlin College. She graduated from Oberlin in 1943, with an AB in Political Science, and entered law school at the University of Chicago in spite of the advice of an admissions counselor, who told her that social work was a more suitable career for a woman. She graduated with a J.D. in 1946.

While attending the University of Chicago Law School, she met fellow student John W. Rogers, and they were married in 1946. A son, John W. Rogers Jr., was born in 1958. LaFontant and Rogers divorced in 1961.

In 1947 LaFontant (then known as Jewel Rogers) and John Rogers went into practice together in the law firm Rogers, Rogers, and Strayhorn (later Rogers, Rogers, Strayhorn, and Harth). Although she was admitted to the Illinois Bar in 1947, she was unable to find employment in any of the major Chicago law firms or to obtain office space in downtown Chicago because of her gender and race. After volunteering at the Social Security Administration for six months in 1947, she went to work as a trial attorney for the Chicago Legal Aid Society, for which she handled landlord-tenant disputes from 1947 to 1953.

After a tenure as the assistant U.S. attorney for the Northern District of Illinois from 1955 to 1958, in 1972 President Richard M. Nixon nominated her to be the United States representative to the United Nations, and from 1973–1975 she was Deputy Solicitor General of the United States. During President George H. W. Bush's administration from 1989–1993, she held the roles of U.S. ambassador-at-large and U.S. coordinator for refugee affairs, and she also served as the vice-chairperson of the U.S. Advisory Commission on International Educational and Cultural Affairs.

LaFontant achieved many firsts as an African American and as an African American female. These were intertwined throughout her forty years of legal experiences. She was the first African American female to attend the University of Chicago Law School, the first African American woman appointed assistant U.S. attorney for the Northern District of Illinois, the first African American and the first woman to be a deputy solicitor general of the United States, one of the first two American women admitted to the International Academy of Trial Lawyers in 1984, and the first African American to address the Republican National Convention in 1988.

Throughout her lifetime, LaFontant was active in a number of legal associations, the foremost of them the NBA; she served as its secretary from 1956 until 1964. She was also active in the Cook County Bar Association, Delta Sigma Theta sorority, the Commercial Club of Chicago, and the Economic Club of Chicago. By 1969 she had sat on the board of fifteen major corporations, including Jewel Foods, Mobil Oil, and Trans World Airlines. She held an office in the National Association for the Advancement of Colored People (NAACP).

In 1961 LaFontant married H. Ernest LaFontant, who died in 1976. In 1989 LaFontant married her third husband, the Egyptian-born Naguib Soby Mankarious. LaFontant died in Chicago of breast cancer. One of her political successors, Senator CAROL MOSELEY BRAUN, said the following words concerning her passing, "We should all be proud of the life that Mrs. Jewel S. LaFontant-Mankarious led. She was a woman of integrity, valor, and achievement, and was a personal heroine and role model to me. She rose above adversity, used her God-given talents to fight for the rights of others, and served as an example for following generations of what a strong heart and mind can achieve" (*Jewel S. Lafontant-Mankarious Daily Digest*, 3 June 1997).

FURTHER READING
The Jewell LaFontant Papers are in the Oberlin College Archives in Oberlin, Ohio.

ELIZABETH K. DAVENPORT

Laine, Henry Allen (10 Jan. 1870–15 Oct. 1955), activist, poet, orator, and teacher, was born in Old Cane Springs, a community in Madison County, Kentucky. He was the son of slave parents. His father was Washington Laine of College Hill, Kentucky, and his mother's maiden name was Amelia Elkins, of Clark County, Kentucky. Commonly addressed as "Mr. Laine," he was always striving to improve the human condition. Although his focus was on improving the plight of blacks in America, his religious upbringing helped to make him a humanitarian for all races and ethnic groups. He was effective in influencing and partnering with white Americans to advance the overall quality of life for people wherever he spoke, visited, or lived.

In his youth he was studious and developed a love of reading and writing at an early age. Even though he had chores to perform and was frequently needed to contribute financially to the success of the family farm, he remained persistent in his quest for literacy. Laine's first official schooling consisted of a two-month subscription school. His primary textbook was the Webster blue-back spelling book. In 1880 he attended a state-supported school held in an old slave cabin. From 1889 to 1897 he attended Berea College. During this time he combined college with extended intervals of work at the Clay City sawmill in order to help his father support the family farm. Laine's work ethic was such that ultimately he was able to help his father pay off the farm. At Berea he worked his way to teaching certificates in 1892 and 1895. He would teach in the Kentucky school system for twenty-one consecutive years. On 22 December 1897 he married Florence Benton; the two would become the parents of eight daughters and one son.

At the turn of the century, when Kentucky's Day Law forced the closure of Berea College to African Americans, Henry Allen Laine lifted his voice in protest to what he decried "as a monument of race hate refuting the glorious doctrine of Christian Brotherhood" advanced by the abolitionist John G. Fee, the founder of Berea. In 1910 Laine was one of the founders of the Madison County Colored Teachers Association. He was the first elected president of this prestigious organization.

In 1915 he organized a farmers club and became largely responsible for forming the County-Institute Chautauqua, which brought to the black community such giants as BOOKER T. WASHINGTON, W. E. B. DuBOIS, and GEORGE WASHINGTON CARVER. These noted speakers drew large crowds, and many were inspired by their presence. Some of the subjects discussed and debated at the meetings were the prevention of soil erosion, the value of fertilizers, winter cover crops, and other subjects that enhanced local farming skills. In 1917 Laine was appointed industrial supervisor of Madison County Colored Schools, a position that subsequently led to his appointment as the first black county agricultural agent in Kentucky.

The most enduring legacy of Henry Allen Laine, however, is that of a writer, poet, and author. His best-known volume of poems, entitled *Foot Prints*, has been so widely read that it has had four printings (1914, 1924, 1947, and 1988). Laine composed his verse in the contemporary style of Negro dialect. He wrote intellectually, but used the slang of the day, to reflect the thoughts and feelings of black people of his era.

Because of his lifetime of service and dedication to his community and the integrity and credibility of his Christian lifestyle, his behavior was emulated by his colleagues and was a model for his students. He was asked to speak on numerous occasions, and he received many awards; in 1947 Laine was proclaimed "Man of the Year" in Richmond, Kentucky. Another significant honor was his nomination and induction, on 29 July 2003, to the Kentucky Civil Rights Hall of Fame, based upon his contributions to black farmers in learning to use farming techniques that would keep fields vital (e.g. rotating crops), being a teacher and speaking to groups about the value of education in advancing the black race, expressing himself in his poetic writings, and giving voice to his religious beliefs that all human beings are God's children.

Laine died after an extended illness. During his lifetime he was invited to countless churches and memorial halls to celebrate and honor many men. Some of these were widely known and others known only to their immediate loved ones and family members, but a line from his own poem "My Kind of Man" is a fitting testimony to the life of Henry Allen Laine: "He looks for the good in men and he / Is the kind of man I delight to see."

FURTHER READING
The Henry Allen Laine Papers are in the Manuscripts Collection of Eastern Kentucky University Library, Richmond, Kentucky. Articles and other materials

are in the archives of Kentucky State University, Frankfort.

Dorris, Jonathan Truman, and Maud Weaver Dorris. *Glimpses of Historic Madison County, Kentucky* (1955). "Kentucky Civil Rights Hall of Fame." Award program, 29 July 2004.

WILLIAM H. HOLLAND
LAWRENCE E. HAMILTON JR.

Lambright, Middleton H. (3 Aug. 1865–21 Mar. 1959), obstetrician and community leader, was born near Moncks Corner, South Carolina, the son of the former slaves John Lambright and Mary Gelzer, farmers. Middleton was one of thirteen children, and although he was born free, more than half his siblings were born into slavery. As a young man he often accompanied his father to Charleston for supplies. Their route took them by the Medical College of South Carolina, and Lambright questioned his father about the young men in white coats walking on the campus. This experience established in him the notion of studying medicine. When a life-threatening accident brought him into personal contact with a physician for a period of several months, he became convinced of his life's ambition. With the support of his family, Lambright eventually graduated from Claflin College in Orangeburg, South Carolina, with an AB degree. In 1898 he received his M.D. from the Meharry Medical Department of Central Tennessee College (now Meharry Medical College). Believing his chances to improve his lot were better outside the South, that fall he migrated to Kansas City, Missouri, where large numbers of blacks and whites were moving to jobs in the shipping and meatpacking industries.

Lambright was joined in Kansas City by James F. Shannon, a friend from his Meharry graduating class, and Thomas Conrad Unthank, another physician who had arrived earlier in the year. They soon encountered some of the same racial divisions that they had hoped to leave behind. Drugstores would not fill prescriptions for black patients, and hospitals would not allow black doctors to practice in them. Finding this situation intolerable, in 1904 the three physicians and one other, John Edward Perry, who had arrived in 1903, opened their own pharmacy and called it the People's Drugstore. The drugstore not only provided medications for black patients but brought together four persons dedicated to helping their community. Perry, in his autobiography *Forty Cords of Wood*, wrote, "It would be difficult to find three men more unselfishly interested in the general welfare of the community as a whole than the late Shannon, Unthank and Lambright." For a number of years Lambright, Shannon, Unthank, and another Meharry graduate, Daniel F. McQueen Carrion, a dentist, shared an office above the pharmacy at Paseo Boulevard and Eighteenth Street. It was the first black-owned business in that part of town, an area that would eventually become the heart of Kansas City's black community.

A second step in unifying the city's black medical profession was the founding of the Kansas City Medical Society in 1909. Lambright, Unthank, Perry, and Shannon were joined by fourteen others "to promote the science and art of medicine, and to bring close together colored physicians of the city … so that they would secure the intelligent unity and harmony in every phase of their labor" (Rodger, 531).

Lambright and his fellow physicians then began to push for access to a public hospital. One particularly persuasive argument for such access was that by neglecting the health of black and Hispanic people, the white citizens were themselves at greater risk for disease. It was a timely request. The city had already decided to build a new public hospital for whites to replace its old Kansas City Municipal Hospital. It was agreed that local black physicians could use the old vacated hospital to serve black and Hispanic patients, although it would remain under the supervision of white doctors. Kansas City General Hospital No. 2 was opened on 1 October 1911.

In 1910 a prominent Kansas City surgeon, Jabez Jackson, brought together a group of specialists who agreed to offer postgraduate training to interested black physicians. Training never before available to them was offered at the hospital in several fields, including surgery, radiology, pediatrics, ophthalmology, and obstetrics. Lambright selected obstetrics and became particularly adept in births that were complicated by malposition of the fetus that required manually turning the fetus to ensure safe delivery. He joined the obstetrical staff and soon became its chief, a position he held until he moved to Cleveland in 1923. In the course of his career at General Hospital No. 2, he trained many nurses and doctors in obstetrics.

In 1908 Lambright had married Bartley Smith Oliver, a native of Paxico, Kansas. They had a daughter, Elizabeth, and a son, Middleton Jr., a surgeon who later became the president of the Academy of Medicine of Cleveland. When his children approached high school age, Lambright decided to move from Kansas City, with its segregated school system, to Cleveland, which at that time was considered one of the least segregated cities in the country. Even so, Lambright arrived in Cleveland in 1923 to find no hospitals available for black physicians to serve their patients. Once again he found himself leading a drive for a racially integrated hospital. It was not until 1939 that Lambright, together with Ulysses Grant Mason and thirty-seven other black physicians, succeeded in organizing the Forest City Hospital Association for the purpose of raising funds for and establishing a hospital. Lambright was treasurer and chairman of the finance committee. Pledges of $500 per trustee, which were paid in installments of $5 and $10, launched the drive.

At Lambright's urging the association solicited successfully from Cleveland's white medical community and industrial leaders. He suggested that a women's auxiliary be formed, a group that became a mainstay of the hospital, and he urged that the physicians and their families take their plight to the churches in an effort to involve the entire black community. In 1957 Cleveland's first racially integrated hospital was opened. To honor his contributions to the founding of the hospital, Lambright was asked to choose its name; it became the Forest City Hospital. Lambright died in Cleveland two years later. In 1960 the Middleton H. Lambright Memorial Lectures were established by the medical staff of the hospital. A total of eighteen annual lectures were delivered at various locations. In 1972 a group of black physicians headed by Doris Evans and Edgar Jackson founded the Middleton H. Lambright Society to honor both Lambright and his son and to promote "the right of quality health care for all."

Lambright was instrumental in establishing interracial hospitals in two separate cities, although neither Forest City Hospital nor General Hospital No. 2 remain. He is representative of the first generation of free black physicians who set about breaking down racial barriers in medicine.

FURTHER READING

Byrd, W. Michael, and Linda A. Clayton. *An American Health Dilemma*, vol. 1, *A Medical History of African Americans and the Problem of Race: Beginnings to 1900* (2000).

Perry, John Edward. *Forty Cords of Wood* (1947).

Rodger, Samuel D. "Kansas City General Hospital No. 2: A Historical Summary," *Journal of the National Medical Association* 54 (Sept. 1962).

Obituary: *Cleveland Press*, 23 Mar. 1959.

This entry is taken from the *American National Biography* and is published here with the permission of the American Council of Learned Societies.

GLEN PIERCE JENKINS

Lampkin, Daisy (1880s–10 Mar. 1965), civil rights and women's suffrage advocate and NAACP leader, was born Daisy Elizabeth Adams, the only child of George S. Adams and Rosa Ann Proctor. Sources differ as to the exact date and place of her birth. Lampkin's obituary in the *New York Times* states that she was 83 years old at the time of her death in 1965, which places her birth in either 1881 or 1882. Other sources claim that she was born on 9 August 1888. It is also uncertain whether she was born in Washington, D.C., or Reading, Pennsylvania, but she completed high school in the latter city before moving to Pittsburgh in 1909. In 1912 she helped organize a gathering for the woman's suffrage movement and joined the Lucy Stone League, an organization connected with the suffrage movement. She became president of the league in 1925 and headed the organization for the next forty years.

In 1912 Daisy Adams married William Lampkin, originally from Rome, Georgia, who ran a restaurant in one of Pittsburgh's wealthy suburbs. During the first years of her marriage, Lampkin worked with her husband in the restaurant business and expanded her activities as a community activist. She made street-corner speeches to mobilize African American women into political clubs, organized black housewives around consumer issues, and was a leading participant in a Liberty Bond drive during World War I, when, as the scholar Edna Chappell McKenzie notes, the black community of Allegheny County, where Pittsburgh is located, raised more than $2 million. She also served on the staff of the Pittsburgh Urban League. Impressed with Lampkin's talents as a fund-raiser, ROBERT L. VANN, editor and publisher of the *Pittsburgh Courier*, solicited Lampkin's help when he was trying to raise money during the early days of the *Courier*. She continued to work for the newspaper in the 1920s and was made vice president in 1929, a position she held for thirty-six years, until her death in 1965.

During and after World War I, Lampkin's activism among black women shaped the black freedom struggle at both local and national levels. She was chair of the Allegheny County Negro Women's Republican League and vice chair of the Negro Voters League. At the national level she was elected president of the Negro Women's Equal Franchise Federation, founded in 1911; she served

Daisy Lampkin was well known as the national field secretary for the NAACP. She also served three decades as the vice president of the Pittsburgh Courier. (Austin/Thompson Collection, by permission of Moorland-Spingarn Research Center.)

as a national organizer and chair of the executive board of the National Association of Colored Women (NACW) and helped organize, with MARY MCLEOD BETHUNE, the National Council of Negro Women.

By the early 1920s Lampkin was a prominent figure in black politics and served as president of the National Colored Republican Conference. In 1924 she was the only woman selected by the NAACP national secretary JAMES WELDON JOHNSON to attend a meeting of black leaders with President Calvin Coolidge at the White House; the meeting was to protest the injustice meted out to African American soldiers allegedly involved in the 1917 Houston riot. She was also elected an alternate delegate at large to the national Republican Party convention in 1926, a remarkable achievement for any black person or any woman at that time, as historian Edna McKenzie notes.

When Lampkin joined the staff of the NAACP in 1927, she linked her championing of black women with that of the NAACP's agenda, focusing on breaking down barriers to full participation in American society. She served as its regional field secretary in the early 1930s; became known as an unflappable, intrepid fund-raiser for the association; and was appointed national field secretary by the NAACP's board of directors in 1935. Using her skills as an organizer and superb speaker, Lampkin worked with black workers during the economic hard times of the 1930s, increasing the NAACP's membership in key cities, such as Chicago and Detroit. She not only revitalized the organization's sagging enrollment but also used her national position and prestige to push the NAACP toward a new approach for attaining civil rights in America.

Lampkin increased NAACP membership at a moment when the association faced perhaps its most severe challenges from both within and without. Within the organization, dissent centered on the fact that the NAACP was not reaching the mass of African Americans. As the Depression deepened in the early 1930s, thousands of African Americans organized themselves through unemployed councils, participated in rent strikes, and joined the CIO's (Congress of Industrial Organizations) rank-and-file industrial unions that were encouraged by President Franklin Roosevelt's New Deal. Some of their actions were encouraged and led by Communist Party organizers, others by groups such as A. PHILIP RANDOLPH's Brotherhood of Sleeping Car Porters. Missing from efforts to mobilize the grassroots was the NAACP, which committed its resources to making appeals in courts on a case-by-case basis and agitated by compiling facts and deluging government officials with information.

Since its founding in 1909, the NAACP had pursued a gradual, legalistic approach to securing African Americans their full citizenship rights. The NAACP's leadership expressed little interest in mass organization of black workers. In 1931 the American Communist Party (CPUSA) challenged the NAACP's narrow agenda by taking on the legal defense of the SCOTTSBORO BOYS, nine working-class African American males who were charged in Scottsboro, Alabama, with the alleged rape of two white women. Because the NAACP had initially refused to take on the Scottsboro Boys case, the Communists convinced at least some African Americans that their party was more in touch with the mood and interests of working-class blacks than the NAACP. Although the CPUSA did not win massive numbers of black converts, their militant approach forced black organizations, and the NAACP in particular to rethink their strategy in challenging racial inequality. The competition between the Communists and the NAACP, historian Mark Naison has argued, was not just for control over the Scottsboro case but also for the "hearts and minds of the black public" (*Communists in Harlem during the Depression* [1985], 62).

As funding from white philanthropists dried up, the NAACP needed to increase its membership within the black community. Daisy Lampkin understood well the threat that Scottsboro posed for the NAACP, and she also had a solution. "The NAACP is being openly criticized by its own members," Lampkin wrote to WALTER WHITE, executive secretary of the NAACP, in 1933. "Some frankly say," she continued, "that the NAACP is less militant" than it used to be. Moreover, Lampkin told White, friends of the NAACP asked her whether she thought the NAACP had outlived its usefulness and whether the time had come for it to give way to another organization with a more "militant program." She advised both Walter White and his assistant, ROY WILKINS, to initiate a more aggressive program in order to meet the "onslaught of the Communists" (letter from Roy Wilkins to Daisy E. Lampkin, 23 Mar. 1935, I-C-80, NAACP Papers, Library of Congress).

Lampkin demonstrated her independence as a leader within the NAACP on another occasion in 1933. A planned boycott of discriminatory practices by the Sears, Roebuck shoe department by "prominent women" in the Chicago branch of the NAACP was aborted by from the national office. Walter White was concerned lest the proposed boycott sully the reputation of the NAACP in the eyes of William Rosenwald, chairman of the board of Sears, whose stock funded the Rosenwald Fund, a major contributor to projects benefiting black Americans. Such concerns did not faze the NACW. When the association met in Chicago in July 1933 for its annual convention, it condemned Sears for its discriminatory policies. Lampkin, running for vice president of the NACW at the time, strongly endorsed the resolution against Sears, which also urged "widespread publicity on the matter" (letter from A. C. MacNeal to Walter White, 29 July 1933, I-G-51, NAACP Papers, Library of Congress).

Perhaps to underscore her concern with the passive approach of the NAACP on this matter, Lampkin, regional field secretary at the time, did not visit the Chicago branch while attending the NACW convention, a slight that led the branch president to complain to White. As Lampkin reminded White in a letter of 22 October 1936, it was because of her influence in the "largest organization of colored women in America" that she was important to the staff of the NAACP. The public was well aware, she said, of her "many other interests," which "account to a very large degree for the success I have in getting people to work with me in campaigns for the NAACP" (NAACP papers, Library of Congress, I-C-68).

By the end of the 1930s, the NAACP had expanded its program to reach a larger number of people, following advice that Lampkin had offered to Walter White and Roy Wilkins in the early 1930s. Lampkin continued to work tirelessly for the NAACP until October 1964, when she collapsed from exhaustion after making yet another strenuous fund-raising appeal for the NAACP. She died a few months later, in March 1965, and was survived by her husband.

The life of Daisy Lampkin exemplifies the important role black women played in twentieth-century campaigns for civil rights. Although Lampkin was best known nationally for her role as a prominent NAACP leader, her contribution to the larger freedom struggles for racial and gender equality extended far beyond that organization. Whatever the venue, the impulse that drove Lampkin's life was to remove barriers that kept African Americans from the full enjoyment of their citizenship rights.

FURTHER READING
Bates, Beth Tompkins. "A New Crowd Challenges the Agenda of the Old Guard in the NAACP, 1933–1941," *American Historical Review* 102.2 (Apr. 1997).
Bates, Beth Tompkins. *Pullman Porters and the Rise of Protest Politics in Black America, 1925–1945* (2001).
McKenzie, Edna B. "Daisy Lampkin: A Life of Love and Service," *Pennsylvania Heritage* (Summer, 1983).
Trotter, Joe William, Jr. *River Jordan: African American Urban Life in the Ohio Valley* (1988).
Obituary: *New York Times*, 12 Mar. 1965.

BETH TOMPKINS BATES

Landry, Pierre Caliste (19 Apr. 1841–22 Dec. 1921), statesman, minister, educator, businessman, and attorney, was born on the plantation of Dr. Francois Marie Prevost near Donaldsonville, Ascension Parish, Louisiana. He is purported to have been born to Rosemond Landry, a white laborer on the Prevost plantation and Marcelite, his slave mistress. He was born with the name Caliste. According to Landry's unpublished autobiography, he resided with a free couple of color and was educated at a school conducted for free children. Despite his owner's wish that he be freed, when Dr. Prevost's estate was settled on 16 May 1854 Caliste was auctioned off to Marius St. Colombe Bringier, a wealthy sugar planter in Ascension Parish. He was sold for $1,665. Landry continued his education on Houmas, the Bringier plantation, and was trusted enough to live in the mansion. He served various roles on Houmas Plantation, eventually earning the position of superintendent of the yard. As a young man, Caliste was taught the trades of confectioner and cook, two trades he employed during his time with the Bringiers. Caliste enjoyed relative freedom at the Bringier plantation, even being given permission to form a business partnership with another slave, the head butler, to run a plantation store. In 1862 Caliste received a release from his yard duties and became an apprentice to both the plantation's head white carpenter and machinist.

In 1866 Caliste changed his name to Pierre for unknown reasons and moved to Donaldsonville. He soon became a prominent member of Donaldsonville's black community. Within his first year there he founded two day schools and a night school for black children. He built the first home owned by a freed slave in Donaldsonville and opened a small but prosperous store. Landry's was one of the first black families in town to own a piano. In 1867 he married Amanda Grigsby. At a 1 January 1867 commemoration of the Emancipation Proclamation a large group of black residents unanimously elected Landry their leader in all matters, social, educational, and political because of his strong leadership and many talents.

In 1868 Landry was elected mayor of Donaldsonville and served for a one-year term, making him the first African American mayor in the United States. He subsequently served as a member of the Ascension Parish School Board, superintendent of schools, and justice of the peace. In 1870 Pierre became president of the Ascension Parish Police Jury and was appointed tax collector for Donaldsonville by Governor Henry C. Warmouth. In 1872 President Ulysses S. Grant appointed Landry as the postmaster of Donaldsonville. That same year he was elected to the State House of Representatives. One of the more notable among his bills to aid black people was the establishment of New Orleans University, the third black private college in Louisiana.

In 1874 he became state senator for the 8th Senatorial District of Louisiana. In his term as a senator he was one of two African American members to dine with President Ulysses S. Grant in 1875. During his tenure in the state senate he also edited a Christian newspaper called the *Monthly Record*. In 1879 he was elected as the delegate from Ascension Parish to the state constitutional convention. He served in the state senate until 1878. Landry had a private law practice for twelve years. He was a founding member of the Board of Trustees for New Orleans University, which later merged with Straight College to form Dillard University.

Landry converted from Catholicism to Methodism through the influence of a local congregation of Methodists. Perhaps this congregation was the Donaldsonville Methodist Episcopal Church, which had been formed in 1844. He was an active member of St. Peter's Methodist Episcopal Church in Donaldsonville. St. Peter's had been founded in 1865 by the Methodist Episcopal Church Society of New York. He was elected a lay delegate from the Louisiana Conference to the General Conference held at Brooklyn, New York, in 1872. He joined the traveling circuit in 1878. He was appointed by Bishop W. L. Harris as pastor of St. Peter's, which he served for three years.

At the Annual Session of the Louisiana Conference at Shreveport in 1881, Bishop C.D. Foss appointed Landry Presiding Elder of the Baton Rouge District, a position he held for four years. In 1885 Bishop W. F. Mallalieu appointed him Presiding Elder of the Shreveport District. After the death of his first wife, Amanda Grigsby, he married Florence Simpkins in 1886. Landry had twelve children with Amanda Grigsby. In 1889 after four years in that position, he was appointed pastor of the St. Paul Church at Shreveport, which he served for three years. After two years he completed the rebuilding of the church after a devastating fire, and rebuilt the parsonage. He supervised the work himself, and at the end of his term he turned over one of the finest pieces of colored church property in the Louisiana Conference. At the Annual Session of the Louisiana Conference of the Methodist Episcopal Church in 1891 he was named Presiding Elder of the south New Orleans District, after which he moved his family to New Orleans.

In 1900 Landry became the dean of Gilbert Academy in Baldwin, Louisiana. Gilbert Academy was a prestigious school begun in 1865 as an agricultural and industrial college for freedmen. The college was under the auspices of the Methodist Episcopal Church. In 1919 Gilbert Academy merged with New Orleans University and was given the name Gilbert Academy High School. The school was located on the campus of New Orleans University on St. Charles Avenue (later the site of De La Salle High). Gilbert Academy eventually acquired the entire campus after New Orleans University merged with Straight College to form Dillard University. Gilbert Academy closed in 1949. Landry served as dean of Gilbert Academy until 1905. That year, his second wife Florence Simpkins died. She and Landry had two children. Landry also served on the board of trustees of Flint Medical College, a Methodist-affiliated institution in New Orleans.

The Reverend Pierre Landry was a minister in the Methodist Episcopal Church for fifty years. The 24 December 1921 issue of the *New Orleans Times Picayune* reported that "He is believed to have preached to more people of his race than any other man." This is not hard to believe as Landry served at St. Peter's Church in Donaldsonville, Bayou Goula, Napoleonville, Woodlawn, Vioron (Belle Rose), Shreveport, New Orleans, and Gonzales. A few years before his death, Landry became a member of the Missionary Baptist Church.

All of his fourteen children went on to receive a higher education. Among them was his son, Lord Beaconsfield Landry, a physician for whom a public school in the Algiers section of New Orleans is named. Several of them became educators.

Pierre Caliste Landry died in the Algiers section of New Orleans, Louisiana. Among the speakers at his funeral was Governor Henry C. Warmouth, and among the pallbearers were Walter L. Cohen and Dr. Charles Vance, two leaders in the New Orleans black community. Landry's place in history became solidified. His life includes time in slavery, emancipation, election to political office, appointment to the pastorate of the Methodist Church, and service as an educator to many.

FURTHER READING

The Dunn-Landry Family Papers (1872–2003) are held at the Amistad Research Center, New Orleans.

Landry, Pierre Caliste. *Always Wanted Cooperation* (Dunn-Landry Family Papers [1873–2003]. Amistad Research Center, New Orleans).

Vincent, Charles. *Black Legislators in Louisiana during Reconstruction* (1976).

Wilson, James David. *Pierre Caliste Landry and African-American Leadership in Louisiana, 1841–1884* (1997).

JARI CHRISTOPHER HONORA

Lane, Dick "Night Train" (16 Apr. 1928–29 Jan. 2002), Hall of Fame football player, was born in Austin, Texas, to Johnnie Mae King, a prostitute, and her pimp, known only as "Texas Slim." King abandoned her baby in a garbage dumpster when he was three months old, and Ella Lane, a widow, discovered and adopted him, naming him Richard. He attended Anderson High School, playing football and basketball and running track. Anderson won the state title in 1944 in the Prairie View Interscholastic League, a league for black high schools in Texas.

After high school, Lane moved to Scottsbluff, Nebraska, to live with his birth mother, who had straightened out her life. Though the town was predominantly white, Lane remembered it as open and friendly to him. In 1947 he signed a professional baseball contract with the Kansas City Monarchs of the Negro Baseball League and was assigned to their farm team, the Omaha Knights. He played only briefly for the Knights before enrolling at Scottsbluff Junior College and joined its football team as offensive and defensive end, earning Junior College All-American honors. He quit after a year to join the army in 1948. After basic training Lane was assigned to the Eighty-fourth Tank Battalion at Fort Ord, California. He played basketball and football for the base team, earning All-Army honors in 1949 and 1950. While in the army Lane married Geraldine Dandridge, a member of the Women's Auxiliary Corps; they divorced in 1959. After his discharge in 1952, Lane remained in California and went to work for North American Aircraft. Lane quickly grew bored with his job at North American and quit. Armed with a scrapbook of his football career in junior college and the army, Lane went to the Los Angeles Rams' front office and asked for a tryout. The Rams had a little foreknowledge of Lane, as a scout had noticed him during an army exhibition game, and they offered him a rookie contract. Unsure of where he best fit, the Rams tried Lane at receiver and cornerback. During his first training camp, Lane had a hard time learning the playbook, so he studied every night with the veteran receiver Tom Fears. Fears and Lane regularly listened to the Buddy Morrow hit "Night Train," so everyone started calling Lane "Night Train." At first, he did not like the nickname, but after a game against the Washington Redskins where he made a devastating tackle on Charlie "Choo Choo" Justice, the newspaper headlines read "Night Train derails Choo Choo." After that, he liked the name. Lane settled

Dick Lane, cornerback for the Chicago Cardinals, catches a football, 1955. (AP Images.)

in at cornerback, becoming a starter his rookie season. His aggressiveness, speed, and gambling style made him the talk of the league, and he set an NFL record with fourteen interceptions.

Lane played one more season in Los Angeles before a trade sent him to the Chicago Cardinals. In 1954, his first season in Chicago, Lane again led the league in interceptions with ten. He played six seasons in Chicago, having only one winning season. He supplemented his football salary by playing poker and opening a series of restaurants in Chicago. After the 1959 season, Lane was traded to the Detroit Lions. He was happy to be back on a winning team and helped the Lions go 7-5 in 1960 and make the inaugural Playoff Bowl, which featured the two divisional second place teams. Detroit beat the Cleveland Browns 17-16, with Lane sealing the victory by blocking a point-after-touchdown kick that would have tied the score. During the 1960 season he married and later divorced Mary Cowser. They had one son.

Though many in the league thought Lane was past his prime, his time in Detroit proved to be his best years in the NFL. The 1960 season was the first of four consecutive All-Pro years for Lane as he was an important part of a dominating Lions defense. He was known and feared around the league for being a vicious tackler, usually delivering hits around the head and face, known as the "Night Train Necktie." After the 1961 season, league officials took notice and banned this practice as well as the grabbing of the facemask, another Lane technique. At the 1962 Pro Bowl, Lane played despite having appendicitis, scoring a touchdown on an interception return. In July 1963 he married jazz singer DINAH WASHINGTON, with the wedding receiving nationwide media coverage. In December, he discovered Dinah in their apartment dead from an apparent drug overdose.

Lane played two more seasons for the Lions before being released during the 1966 training camp. He finished his NFL career with sixty-eight interceptions, ranked third all time. His interception total could have been much higher, but opposing teams regularly avoided his side of the field. Named to six Pro Bowls and the NFL's fiftieth and seventy-fifth anniversary teams, Lane was arguably one of the best cornerbacks to ever play in the NFL. In 1974 he became the second defensive back and seventh African American inducted into the Pro Football Hall of Fame.

After his release, Lions owner William Clay Ford offered Lane a job as special assistant. He worked for Ford until 1972, one of the few black players to move into a front office position after retiring as a player. While Lane was appreciative to Ford for the job, he really wanted to coach and was openly critical of NFL leadership. He believed NFL owners and management were holding back the progress of black players. In 1972 he resigned his position with the Lions and took a coaching job at Southern University in Baton Rouge, Louisiana. He coached for a year at Southern, and then he coached another year at Central State University in Wilberforce, Ohio. In 1974 the comedian REDD FOXX hired Lane as his road manager. Lane moved to Los Angeles and handled Foxx's personal affairs and served as his bodyguard. In 1975 Detroit mayor COLEMAN YOUNG offered Lane a job with the Detroit Police Athletic League (PAL). Lane rose to become executive director of PAL, which offered athletic, tutoring, and mentoring programs to Detroit's inner city youth. In 2000, bothered by chronic knee pain and diabetes, Lane moved into an assisted living facility in Austin. He died of a heart attack shortly before he was to be inducted into the Texas Sports Hall of Fame.

FURTHER READING

Anderson, Dave. *Great Defensive Players of the NFL* (1967).

Burns, Mike. *Night Train Lane: The Life of NFL Hall of Famer Richard "Night Train" Lane* (2000).

Obituaries: *Los Angeles Times* 31 Jan. 2002; *New York Times*, 1 Feb. 2002.

MICHAEL C. MILLER

Lane, Isaac (3 Mar. 1834–5 Dec. 1937), religious leader, college founder, and historian, was born near Jackson, Tennessee, to Cullen Lane, a white slave owner, and Rachel, a slave woman. Although born to a white father, young Isaac, by custom and law, occupied the status of his mother and was thus raised a slave by Rachel and her husband Josh, a slave and field hand. Little is known about young Isaac's parents, and, in fact, his autobiography states that he "was reared almost motherless and fatherless having no parental care and guidance" (Lane, 47). Nevertheless he was a precocious child, eager to learn. At the age of eleven he assumed the surname of his white father.

In his formative years Lane began to educate himself and would eventually learn to read, write, and do math. Denied the advantages of early training, Lane was able to seize a blue-black speller and, through much difficulty, teach himself to read. Although a great risk was involved in Lane's self-education, he was able to conceal the speller and his work from those around him. By writing letters in the sand Lane would eventually learn to write, and soon after he expanded his education by learning to calculate numbers, realizing early on "how much advantage it was to a white person who could read documents and calculate numbers" (Savage, 19).

In his early years Lane also involved himself in what would become a lifelong quest for religious knowledge and spiritual growth. Lane's master and other slave owners attended service at Brown Church each Sunday, leading their slaves to the door of the church to hear the message. Lane's interest in religion deepened as he grew older, and his commitment to Christian service would be realized in his early adulthood. In 1853, at the age of nineteen, Lane met and fell in love with a slave woman from a neighboring plantation, Frances Ann Boyce. Ten months later Lane and Boyce were married.

The union pleased Cullen Lane, whose business affairs with Boyce's owner, Robert Boyce, had much to do with Lane's acquaintance with Frances Boyce. Attracted by her "industry, modesty, neatness of dress, and ladylike bearing," Lane would soon after lead his young bride (and also his mother) into Christian conversion (Lane, 49). For two years of their marriage Lane and his wife were separated as both remained the property of their respective owners; however, Lane eventually convinced Cullen Lane to purchase his family as well as Frances Lane's brother Jupiter for one thousand dollars. Isaac and Frances Lane would eventually become the parents of eleven children who were raised in the Christian faith and would be educated, as Lane made sure, at some of the country's most prestigious institutions of higher education.

During the period of separation from his wife, Lane had, in the mid-morning of 11 September 1854, realized "the presence of the Holy Spirit and the work of the Saving Grace" (Savage, 19). For Lane this moment would not only influence his life and the life of his family but would also encourage his commitment to the ministry. From 1856 to 1861 Lane's reputation as a preacher grew, and the ambitious young man sought to be ordained by the Southern Methodist Conference. Although Southern Methodist authorities initially denied Lane's petition, in 1856, after much deliberation, the conference agreed that, upon passing an examination, Lane would be licensed as an exhorter. In November of that year Lane successfully passed the examination and was licensed as an exhorter by the Southern Methodist Conference. Isaac Lane's professional commitment to the ministry was aided by events during the Civil War that heavily influenced Southern Methodist Church policies. Fearing the loss of their black following, Southern Methodists changed their attitude toward "Negro preaching" and established several slave missions. As a result of these changes within the church and the influence of a postbellum society, Isaac Lane received his license to preach on 25 May 1866. Ministering to diverse congregations would establish Lane as a prominent member of the Methodist Church and celebrated citizen within the state of Tennessee.

In 1866 black members of the Southern Methodist Church split from the organization to form what would become known as the Colored Methodist Episcopal (CME) Church. Establishing a conference known as the Tennessee, North Alabama, and North Mississippi Annual Conference, Lane was an active participant in the forming of the organization, serving as deacon, presiding elder of the Jackson district, and later as leader of the Tennessee delegation. On 19 May 1873 Lane was elected a bishop within the CME Church. Lane continued his ministerial duties while serving as bishop and in 1879 was assigned to the Tennessee Conference. Always concerned with the educational uplift of the black community, Bishop Lane began his quest to aid in the establishment of CME schools. In January of 1880 the Bishop's Council of the CME Church met and agreed, along with Lane, to purchase a four-acre tract of land in north Jackson and open what would be called CME High School. With $1,150 the school was opened and, with the guidance and support of Lane and the CME Church, quickly grew in size and stature. In 1885 the institution's name was changed in honor of its founder and greatest supporter to Lane Institute, and in 1889 would become Lane College. Isaac Lane, a consummate fund-raiser for the college, found time to teach at the college and fulfill his ministerial and administrative duties within the CME Church.

In 1895 Lane's wife of forty-two years died and the following year he married Mary Elizabeth Long Smith of Marshall, Texas. Although the union was met with much contestation from the Lane children, Mary Lane was highly praised for her virtues and dedication to her husband. Tragically, in 1904 and 1915, Lane was preceded in death by two of his children, Dr. William Lane and Mrs. Rebecca Wilson, respectively.

Until his retirement Isaac Lane continued his work for Lane College, where he was instrumental in developing a rigorous curriculum that included a program in theology and a "Farmer's Institute." Within the CME Church, Lane worked diligently and continued to travel the country, ministering even to diverse communities in western parts of the country. In 1914 Lane retired from active service, having ministered to thousands across the country and raised over $100,000 for Lane College. Although retired, Lane continued to actively campaign for Lane College—traveling, lecturing, and fund-raising for the institution. By 1916 Lane had completed and published an autobiography that not only provided information about his life and times but also offered a detailed history of both the CME Church and Lane College.

In 1932 the CME Church instituted the "Lane Centennial Celebration" to celebrate the fifteenth anniversary of Lane College and the accomplishments of the college's founder Bishop Isaac Lane. On 11 November 1932 Isaac Lane was honored for sixty years of dedication to the CME Church, seventy-eight years of Christian service, fifty-nine years of work as bishop, and over ninety years of life. Ever faithful to his church and school, Lane remained committed to the CME Church and Lane College, serving until 1937 as a primary counselor and "ambassador extraordinary of the church" (Savage, 205) until his death at age 103.

FURTHER READING

Lane, Isaac. *Autobiography of Bishop Isaac Lane, L.L.D. with a Short History of the C.M.E. Church in America and of Methodism* (1916).
"Isaac Lane." *Religious Leaders of America*, 2d ed. (1999).
Lakey, Othal Hawthorne. *The History of the Christian Methodist Episcopal Church* (1985).
Savage, Horace C.. *Life and Times of Bishop Isaac Lane* (1958).

DANICA TISDALE

Lane, Lunsford (30 May 1803– ?), entrepreneur, abolitionist lecturer, and autobiographer, was born in Raleigh, North Carolina, the only child of Clarissa Haywood and Edward Lane. Clarissa Haywood was the slave of Sherwood Haywood, an agent for the Bank of Newburn and clerk of the North Carolina State Senate from 1786 to 1798. Edward Lane belonged to John Haywood, the brother of Sherwood Haywood, and though manumitted at the death of John, circa 1830, continued to serve the family as a steward for fourteen years. As a slave, Lunsford Lane was fortunate to be raised by both of his parents who were certainly models for what Lane would later achieve in his life.

About the time that Lane became emotionally aware of his enslaved state, when set to work at the age of ten or eleven, he recalls that his father gave him a basket of peaches which he then sold for thirty cents. This transaction, among others, gave Lane the hope that he could one day buy his freedom, and earning and saving money became the most significant activities of his life. While still enslaved, Lane ran a successful wood-cutting business; taking up a suggestion from his father, he also invented a new mode of preparing tobacco. These products were sold across North Carolina, and Lane became well known as a tobacconist.

In 1828, Lane married Martha Curtis. Within two years, the couple had two of the eventual seven children that would make up the Lane family. At this time, Lane's wife was sold to Raleigh merchant Benjamin Smith. Smith, though benefiting from her labor, refused to provide the basics in food and clothing for Martha and her children. The savings that Lane intended to go toward the purchase of his freedom were thus depleted. However, unexpectedly, Lane's master died. The widow, due to unanticipated financial burdens from her husband's death, allowed Lane to hire out his time. Lane expanded his wood-cutting and tobacco businesses and managed, over the course of time, to save the one thousand dollars needed to buy himself from Mrs. Haywood. Due to the restrictive laws concerning the freeing of slaves in North Carolina, Lane traveled with Mr. Smith to New York where, on September 9, 1835, he became legally free.

Though his freedom permitted him to achieve the economic success required to negotiate the terms of purchase for his wife and children, Lane's trip to New York made him vulnerable to North Carolina laws that forbade free blacks from entering the state. By 1840, Lane, in addition to his own business concerns, worked in the office of the Governor. Though the associations formed through the Governor further confirmed Lane's class allegiance with the elite of Raleigh whom he considered his friends, this level of class and economic success by a black man also drew the attention of less empathetic whites. In 1840, as a free black man, Lane was served with a warrant demanding that he leave the state within twenty days. Because of his work for the Governor, Lane was reprieved until the end of the legislative session. In the meantime, many of the most prominent citizens of North Carolina petitioned the legislature for the passage of a bill allowing Lane to remain in Raleigh. This bill was not passed.

Lane settled in Boston with the one daughter who was permitted to accompany him. Through speaking engagements and donations, he raised the funds to purchase his family and was assured by Benjamin Smith that it was safe to return to Raleigh in order to complete the transaction. However, upon his arrival, Lane was arrested for giving abolitionist lectures. No evidence was found against him, but a mob had formed and Lane was jailed for his own safety. He was released late that night only to be abducted by a group of white men. Though he feared for his life, the men, instead of heading toward the public gallows veered into the woods where they tarred and feathered him. The next morning, Lane and his family, including his mother, boarded a train for Boston.

Paradoxically, Lane's autobiography renders his enslavement as mild and his life as a freeman complex and often violent. The *Narrative* exhibits a commitment to working within the slavocracy by establishing businesses, befriending and working for elite whites, and lawfully purchasing himself and his family. However, the *Narrative* additionally expresses an undertow of bitterness directed at those who forced him to leave Raleigh, along with an antipathy toward whites and their inability to comprehend the feelings of African Americans. Such values set Lane's autobiography apart from other slave narratives of the period—such as the autobiographies of FREDERICK DOUGLASS and WILLIAM WELLS BROWN—which feature slaves as isolated individuals frequently brutalized and repeatedly sold.

Little is known about Lane's life in Massachusetts. A biography written by William G. Hawkins suggests that Lane maintained an interest in entrepreneurial ventures and lectured for the American Anti-Slavery Society. Hawkins's biography, however, is drawn mostly, and often directly, from Lane's autobiography and is centrally concerned with expressing the anti-slavery views of the Reverend Hawkins. John Spencer Bassett's chapter on Lane in *Anti-Slavery Leaders of North Carolina*, though based on the Hawkins' account, is interested in Lane as an economic figure who could have benefited North Carolina during Reconstruction.

FURTHER READING

Many university libraries own one of the original four printings of Lane's autobiography. The autobiography is also available through *Documenting the American South*, an on-line project of the University of North Carolina at Chapel Hill Academic Affairs Library, online at http://docsouth.unc.edu/neh/lanelunsford/menu.html.

Andrews, William L., et al. *North Carolina Slave Narratives: The Lives of Moses Roper, Lunsford Lane, Moses Grandy, and Thomas H. Jones* (2003).

Andrews, William L. *To Tell a Free Story: The First Century of Afro-American Autobiography, 1760–1865* (1988).

Bassett, John Spencer. *Anti-Slavery Leaders of North Carolina* (1898).

Blassingame, John W. *Slave Testimony: Two Centuries of Letters, Speeches, Interviews, and Autobiographies* (2002).

Hawkins, William G. *Lunsford Lane; Or, Another Helper from North Carolina* (1864; reprinted 1969).

Lane, Lunsford. *The Narrative of Lunsford Lane, formerly of Raleigh, N. C. Embracing an account of his early life, the redemption by purchase of himself and family from slavery, and his banishment from the place of his birth for the crime of wearing a colored skin* (1842).

CYNTHIA CURRENT

Lane, Wiley (22 Nov. 1852–16 Feb. 1885), first black Professor of Greek at Howard University, was born in Elizabeth City, North Carolina, the son of Whitmel Lane, a carpenter, and Mary Simonds Lane. Racist legislation initially stalled Wiley Lane's academic career, as blacks in the Antebellum South were denied public schooling. Lane was thus taught at home, where his free parents' religiosity had a profound impact on the values he retained into adulthood. After the Civil War, wider educational opportunities opened up to African Americans, and in 1870 Lane joined the first class of 123 students to enroll in Elizabeth City's new "normal school," which focused on the training of black teachers. The following year, the institution's founding principal, THOMAS W. CARDOZO, singled out three of his graduates and entrusted them to the care of his brother, FRANCIS L. CARDOZO, Professor of Latin at the young Howard University in Washington, D.C. As they matriculated in the black college's Preparatory Department, Cardozo's protégés— Wiley Lane, his brother John, and fellow student Rooks Turner—were introduced to George F. Hoar, later U.S. Senator of Massachusetts, who became one of Wiley Lane's numerous prominent patrons.

An organized and tidy student, Lane demonstrated a remarkable aptitude for ancient Greek and nurtured a lasting fascination with classical cultures. After completing the preparatory program in 1873, he was admitted into Howard's College Department and graduated with his first AB degree in 1877. Lane ranked first in a class of eighteen, and his instructors held him in such high regard that Hoar and Professor Thomas Robinson pushed to have him accepted at prestigious Amherst College. Admitted as a junior, Lane was one of two African Americans in Amherst's student population of four hundred. As at Howard, he applied himself to his books with such zeal that Robinson worried about the student's shaky health. Lane's exertions did not go unrewarded. In 1879 he earned a second bachelor's, finishing his studies in the top third of his class of seventy-six. On the occasion of his graduation, Wiley Lane was invited to the house of Amherst President Julius H. Seelye, and in a further tribute to his scholarship, he became one of five Amherst graduates that year to be elected to Phi Beta Kappa, the nation's oldest Greek-letter honor society. He was the third African American to receive this privilege. Within the next three months, Lane declined an offer to teach at Berea College in Kentucky and instead was hired as a Latin tutor by Howard University, where he simultaneously started working on a master of arts degree.

As Lane moved back to Washington, he continued to excel in the classroom, this time from behind the lectern. Driven by an unwavering sense of duty and delicate consideration of his wards' troubles, he championed their rights and tended to err on the side of leniency. Lane's sensitivity extended also to his friends and family, as he put up two of his sisters and paid for their education. His generosity was grounded in his devotion to the Congregational faith. He participated and later once presided in prayer meetings and would extol the benefits of reading the bible from a young age.

These testimonies to Lane's constancy were, however, contrasted by physical frailty. A massive mustache dominated a smooth face and fragile frame, and the smallness of his hands mirrored his characteristic tenderness. A fashion aficionado, Lane dressed and behaved the perfect gentleman. The bachelor shied away from vulgarity and avoided risqué situations.

Lane's diligence quickly earned him the friendship of former teachers. The youth frequently visited Professor JAMES M. GREGORY's house, and their relationship was close enough for them to be mistaken for family members. Lane also renewed his friendship to Howard classmate GEORGE W. COOK, now a mathematics tutor and influential educator.

In 1881 Lane earned his M.A. He then rose to the position of Principal of the Normal Department, where he taught English. Tentatively, he now ventured into Washington's public arena. Lane's lectures on art impressed civil-rights legend FREDERICK DOUGLASS, and he attracted the attention of other activist giants like FRANCIS JAMES GRIMKÉ. When Lane's first Greek instructor at Howard, Professor Fairfield, retired in 1883, Lane saw an opportunity to turn his passion for classical languages into a means of advancing his race. Many contemporaries considered a grasp of Greek and Latin tantamount to intellectual sophistication and justified racism by pointing to blacks' absence in this field. Lane strove to publicly prove African Americans' equal intellectual facilities by claiming this vacant professorship in the nation's capital. Initially, the trustees opposed his application, but the advocacy of Douglass, Grimké, as well as a former Confederate General, and Lane's many supporters at Amherst and Howard ensured his election. Lane thus became a role model both for racial solidarity and for individual advancement in the face of blatant educational discrimination.

As Professor of Greek Language and Literature—one of only two African American instructors in Howard's College Department—Wiley Lane made up for a scarcity of academic publications through an enthusiastic approach to teaching. He insisted that his students research the full breadth of Greek culture, including archaeology, geography, and mythology in addition to the obligatory grammatical exercises. Personally, he cultivated a curiosity in Greek manners and customs.

In the fall of 1883 Wiley Lane was shocked by the Supreme Court's decision to overturn the 1875 Civil Rights Act. From then on, he would increasingly apply his analytical facilities to political dilemmas, his compassion for the oppressed reaching from India to Ireland and encompassing Native Americans as well as Africans. When Grover Cleveland, the first Democratic president in twenty-three years, took office in 1884, Professors Gregory and Lane jointly addressed the unsettled black public via an interview with the Cleveland Gazette. While they regretted tactical errors committed by the incumbent Republicans and bewailed the return to the presidency of a party traditionally associated with slavery, they did call for optimism in the face of an uncertain future.

When Lane was in his early thirties, Howard University President William W. Patton kindled his curiosity in the American School of Classical Studies at Athens. Fascinated by the prospect of immersing himself in the ruins of a culture he had only cherished from afar, Lane applied his energies toward becoming the first African American to study in this enclave of U.S. classicism in the Greek metropolis. He obtained a twelve-month leave of absence and a *Wanderjahr* seemed within arm's reach. Then, in anticipation of the Mediterranean heat, Lane fell victim to the freezing winter winds of the Middle Atlantic. On the stormy night of Monday, 9 February 1885, he contracted a cold, which the next day worsened into pneumonia. As Patton prayed at Lane's sickbed and Gregory and Cook watched over their ailing friend, severe throat pains kept the dying professor from uttering any last words before he slipped into a coma. He passed away at 1:30 p.m. on Monday, 16 February 1885, only thirty-two years old.

Wiley Lane's death at the peak of his promise confounded Washington's black community. Throngs of students flocked to his funeral on 18 February 1885, and at a memorial meeting on 3 March 1885 a moved Grimké and a tight-lipped Douglass added their eulogies to the mournful speeches of his friends and colleagues. When pioneer black classicist WILLIAM SANDERS SCARBOROUGH applied for Lane's chair, he found passionate support in the black press. Yet Howard's trustees favored well-connected white Oberlin alumnus Carlos A. Kenaston. Lane's remains were returned to North Carolina, where his father outlived him by sixteen years.

FURTHER READING

Wiley Lane's account book is included in the Elisha Overton Papers, University Archives, Elizabeth City State University, Elizabeth City, North Carolina.

Obituary: Addresses on the Occasion of the Funeral of Professor Wiley Lane, Delivered in the University Chapel, Feb'y 18, 1885, by Rev. William W. Patton, D.D., LL.D., President of Howard University, and Hon. George F. Hoar, of Massachusetts, Together with the Addresses of Mr. R. T. Moss, Prof. J. M. Gregory, Prof. F. L. Cardozo, Rev. F. J. Grimké, Hon. Frederick Douglass, Rev. C. H. A. Bulkley, D.D., Mr. G. W. Cook, and Prof. Thomas Robinson, Delivered at the Memorial Meeting Held under the Direction of the Alumni of the College Department in the Fifteenth-St. Presbyterian Church, March 3, 1885. Printed by Order of the College Alumni (1885).

Ronnick, Michele Valerie. "Wiley Lane." *Classical Outlook* 79 pp. 108–109 (2002).

Titcomb, Caldwell. "The Earliest Black Members of Phi Beta Kappa." *The Journal of Blacks in Higher Education* 33 pp. 92–101 (2001).

Obituary: *Cleveland Gazette*, 21 February 1885.

MATHIAS HANSES

Lane, William Henry (1825?–1852), dancer, also known as "Master Juba," is believed to have been born a freeman, although neither his place of birth nor the names of his parents are known. He grew up in lower Manhattan in New York City, where he learned to dance from "Uncle" Jim Lowe, an African American jig-and-reel dancer of exceptional skill.

By the age of fifteen, Lane was performing in notorious "dance houses" and dance establishments in the Five Points district of lower Manhattan. Located at the intersection of Cross, Anthony, Little Water, Orange, and Mulberry streets, its thoroughfare was lined with brothels and saloons occupied largely by free blacks and indigent Irish immigrants. Lane lived and worked in the Five Points district in the early 1840s. In such surroundings, the blending of African American vernacular dance with the Irish jig was inevitable. Marshall Stearns in *Jazz Dance* (1968) confirms that "Lane was a dancer of 'jigs' at a time when the word was adding to its original meaning, an Irish folk dance, and being used to describe the general style of Negro dancing." Charles Dickens, in his *American Notes* (1842), describes a visit to the Five Points district in which he witnessed a performance by a dancer who was probably Lane: "Single shuffle, double shuffle, cut and cross cut; snapping his fingers, rolling his eyes, turning in his knees, presenting the backs of his legs in front, spinning about on his toes and heels like nothing but the man's fingers on the tambourine; dancing with two left legs, two right legs, two wooden legs, two wire legs, two spring legs."

In 1844, after beating the reigning white minstrel dancer, John Diamond, in a series of challenge dances, Lane was hailed as the "King of All Dancers" and named "Master Juba," after the African juba or *gioube*, a step-dance resembling a jig with elaborate variations. The name was often given to slaves who were dancers and musicians. Lane was thereafter adopted by an entire corps of white minstrel players who unreservedly acknowledged his talents. On a tour in New England with the Georgia Champion Minstrels, Lane was billed as "The Wonder of the World Juba, Acknowledged to be the Greatest Dancer in the World!" He was praised for his execution of steps, unsurpassed in grace and endurance, and popular for his skillful imitations of well-known minstrel dancers and their specialty steps. He also performed his own specialty steps, which no one could copy, and he was a first-rate singer and a tambourine virtuoso. In 1845 Lane had the unprecedented distinction of touring with the four-member, all-white Ethiopian Minstrels, with whom he received top billing. At the same time, he prospered as a solo variety performer and from 1846 to 1848 was a regular attraction at White's Melodeon in New York.

Lane traveled to London with Pell's Ethiopian Serenaders in 1848, enthralling the English, who were discerning judges of traditional jigs and clogs, with "the manner in which he beat time with his feet, and the extraordinary command he possessed over them." London's *Theatrical Times* wrote that Master Juba was "far above the common [performers] who give imitations of American and Negro character; there is an *ideality* in what he does that makes his efforts at once *grotesque* and *poetical, without losing sight of the reality of representation.*" Working day and night and living on a poor diet and no rest, Lane died of exhaustion in London.

In England, Lane popularized American minstrel dancing, influencing English clowns who added jumps, splits, and cabrioles to their entrées and began using blackface makeup. Between 1860 and 1865, the Juba character was taken to France by touring British circuses and later became a fixture in French and Belgian *cirques et carrousels*. The image of the blackface clown that persisted in European circuses and fairs continued to be represented in turn-of-the-century popular entertainments as well as on concert stages during the 1920s, in ballets such as Léonide Massine's *Crescendo*, Bronislawa Nijinska's *Jazz*, and George Balanchine's Snowball in *The Triumph of Neptune* (1926).

In the United States, Lane is considered by scholars of dance and historians of the minstrel as the most influential single performer in nineteenth-century American dance. He kept the minstrel show in touch with its African American source material at a time when the stage was dominated by white performers offering theatrical derivatives and grotesque exaggerations of the African American performer. He established a performing style and developed a technique of tap dancing that would be widely imitated. For example, the white dancer Richard M. Carroll was noted for dancing in the style of Lane and earned a reputation for being a great all-around performer; other dancers, like Ralph Keeler, who starred in a riverboat company before the Civil War, learned to dance by practicing the complicated shuffle of Juba. Toward the end of the twentieth century, Lane's legacy continued to be present in elements of the tap dance repertory. Lane's grafting of African rhythms and loose body styling onto the exacting techniques of British jig and clog dancing created a new rhythmic blend of percussive dance that was the earliest form of American tap dance.

FURTHER READING

Stearns, Marshall, and Jean Stearns. *Jazz Dance: The Story of American Vernacular Dance* (1968).

Winter, Marian Hannah. "Juba and American Minstrelsy," in *Chronicles of the American Dance*, ed. Paul Magriel (1948).

This entry is taken from the *American National Biography* and is published here with the permission of the American Council of Learned Societies.

CONSTANCE VALIS HILL

Laney, Lucy Craft (13 Apr. 1854–23 Oct. 1933), educator, was born in Macon, Georgia, the daughter of David Laney and Louisa (maiden name unknown). Both parents were slaves: they belonged to different masters, but following their marriage they were permitted to live together in a home of their own. David Laney was a carpenter and often hired out by his owner, Mr. Cobbs. Louisa, purchased from a group of nomadic Indians while a small child, was a maid in the Campbell household. One of Lucy Laney's most cherished memories was "how her father would, after a week of hard slave work, walk for over twenty miles … to be at home with his wife and children on the Sabbath" (*The Crisis*, June 1934). After the Civil War and emancipation, David Laney, who had served as a slave lay preacher, was ordained as a Presbyterian minister and became pastor of the Washington Avenue Church in Macon, Georgia. Louisa remained in the Campbells' house as a wage earner. The Laneys' newfound income provided the family some comforts that they shared with numerous cousins, orphaned children, and others in need of shelter.

When missionary teachers opened a school in Macon in 1865 Lucy Laney, together with her mother and her siblings, was among the first to enroll. She graduated from the Lewis High School in 1869 and entered Atlanta University, where she received a certificate of graduation from the Higher Normal Department in 1873. In keeping with her strong conviction that "becoming educated [was] a perpetual motion affair" (*Abbott's Monthly*, June 1931), over the course of her career she enrolled in summer programs at the University of Chicago, Hampton Institute, Columbia University, and Tuskegee Institute.

Laney was keenly aware of all the advantages life had afforded her, and she believed that of those to whom much is given much is expected. Emancipation had ushered in new opportunities and responsibilities, and early in life she dedicated herself to her race's advancement. Based on her study of American history, she concluded that the four major components of a realistic program for the "uplift" of blacks were political power, Christian training, "cash," and education. She viewed education as the key to achieving the first three objectives. Her decision to become a teacher was also dictated by the limited employment opportunities available to black women. Following graduation from Atlanta University she accepted a teaching position in Milledgeville, Georgia, and between 1873 and 1883 also taught at schools in Macon, Augusta, and Savannah.

While a student Laney had serious misgivings about the pedagogical practices at the various schools she attended. She had advised her teachers then that "some day I will have a school of my own."

Her experience as a teacher in the public school system intensified her desire to establish a school. She had little patience with "dull teachers … [who] failed to know their pupils—to find out their real needs—and hence had no cause to study methods of better and best development of the boys and girls under their care." She deplored instructors who underestimated "the capabilities and possibilities" of black students and who did not know and/or teach African American history ("The Burden of the Educated Colored Woman," 1899). Moreover, she was convinced that black children needed a thorough Christian education and was disturbed by the public school's failure to address moral and religious concerns.

Laney was one of the first educators to recognize the special and urgent needs of black women in light of their central role in the education of their children. She was convinced that ignorance, immorality, and crime among blacks and perhaps some of the prejudice against them were their "inheritance from slavery." In her opinion, "the basic rock of true culture" was the home, but during slavery "the home was … utterly disregarded … [the] father had neither responsibility, nor authority; mother, neither cares nor duties" ("Educated Colored Woman," 1899). The disregard for home-making and the home environment resulted in untidy and filthy homes that produced children of dubious character. Moreover, the absence of the sanctity of the marriage vow encouraged immorality and disrespect for black women.

While "no person [was] responsible for [her] ancestor's … sins and short-comings," Laney argued that "every woman can see to it that she give to her progeny a good mother and an honorable ancestry." Strengthening the black family and improving its home life was therefore "the place to take the proverbial stitch in time." In addition to their role as wives and mothers, she believed that women were "by nature fitted for teaching the … young" and thus were best suited as teachers in the public school system. She was equally convinced that the teacher "who would mould character must herself possess it" and that those who would be mothers, teachers, and leaders needed to be capable in both "mind and character" ("Address before the Women's Meeting," 1897).

Laney's conviction that educated women were a prerequisite for advancement of her race was the major impetus for the founding of the Haines Normal and Industrial Institute. She began her school with six students in the basement of Christ Presbyterian

Church in Augusta, Georgia, on 6 January 1886. During the following three years the school, as a result of increasing enrollment, was moved to various rented buildings around the city. Haines Institute was chartered by the state of Georgia as a normal and industrial school on 5 May 1888. Although the school was sanctioned by the Presbyterian board, the general assembly provided only moral support, which Laney noted "was not much to go on." In 1889, however, the board purchased a permanent site for the school and erected the institution's first building. Despite numerous problems, by 1887 primary, grammar, and normal divisions had been established, and by 1889 she was able to develop a strong literary department as well as a scientifically based normal program and industrial course. By 1892 Haines Normal and Industrial Institute was recognized as one of the best schools of its type in the nation. John William Gibson and William H. Crogman said of Laney in their classic study, *The Progress of a Race* (1897), "There is probably no one of all the educators of the colored race who stands higher, or who has done more work in pushing forward the education of the Negro woman."

Laney was the foremost female member of the generation born into slavery and educated during Reconstruction who rose to leadership and prominence in the 1880s and 1890s. In addition to being a national race leader, she was a pioneer in the struggles for Prohibition and women's rights as well as in the black women's club movement. She was instrumental in establishing the first public high school for blacks in Georgia, organizing the Augusta Colored Hospital and Nurses Training School, and founding the first kindergarten in the city of Augusta. She was also a leader in the battle to secure improved public schools, sanitation, and other municipal services in Augusta's black community. She was a founding member of the Georgia State Teacher Association and a leader within the regional and national politics of the Young Women's Christian Association. She chaired the Colored Section of the Interracial Commission of Augusta and served on the National Interracial Commission of the Presbyterian Church. An eloquent speaker, she was a distinguished member of the lecture circuit between 1879 and 1930. A number of articles by and about Laney and her school appeared in Presbyterian church publications such as the *Home Mission Monthly*, the *Church Home and Abroad, Women and Mission*, the *Presbyterian Monthly Record*, and the *Presbyterian Magazine* during the years 1886–1933.

Laney, who often stated that she wanted to "wear out, not rust out," died in Augusta, Georgia, and was buried on the campus of the school that she built and to which she had devoted most of her life. The most enduring epithet for Laney, who never married or had children, was "mother of the children of the people," and her most profound contributions were the men and women she educated. Writing in the April 1907 issue of the *Home Mission Monthly* she argued that "the measure of an institution is the men and women it sends into the world. The measure of a man is the service he renders his fellows." Judging by this standard, Lucy Craft Laney and the school she established were eminently successful.

FURTHER READING

Materials regarding Laney are in the Presbyterian Historical Society in Philadelphia and the William E. Harman Collection, Library of Congress.

Brawley, Benjamin. *Negro Builders and Heroes* (1937).

Daniel, Sadie Iola. *Women Builders* (1931).

Griggs, A. C. "Lucy Craft Laney," *Journal of Negro History* (Jan. 1934): 97–102.

Notestein, Lucy Lilian. *Nobody Knows the Trouble I See* (n.d.).

Ovington, Mary White. *Portraits in Color* (1927).

Patton, June O. "Augusta's Black Community and the Struggle for Ware High School," in *New Perspectives on Black Educational History*, eds. Vincent P. Franklin and James D. Anderson (1978).

Obituary: *Augusta* (*Georgia*) *Chronicle*, 23 Oct. 1933.

This entry is taken from the *American National Biography* and is published here with the permission of the American Council of Learned Societies.

JUNE O. PATTON

Langa, Wopashitwe Mondo Eyen we. *See* we Langa, Wopashitwe Mondo Eyen.

Lange, Mary Elizabeth (?–1883), educator and founder of both the oldest Catholic school for African Americans and the first order of African American nuns in the United States, the Oblate Sisters of Providence. The place and date of Lange's birth are unknown. Oral tradition says that she was born on the western part of the island of St. Domingue (now Haiti). Born Elizabeth Lange, she was the offspring of mixed parentage and was a free mulatto. Her mother was Annette Lange; her father's name is unknown. The revolution on the isle of St. Domingue coupled with the Napoleonic revolution forced the emigration of many natives; both black and white refugees fled to other parts of the Western Hemisphere. Lange arrived in the United States educated, refined, and fluent in French. When she arrived on the shores of Maryland, she encountered major problems. She was a free person of color in a slaveholding state, and she spoke French in a country whose native tongue was English. She was a black Catholic and a single woman in a foreign, male-dominated society. In spite of such difficulties, by 1828 Lange had established a school for children of color in Baltimore, St. Frances Academy, still in existence.

The French revolution also caused an influx of European Catholics into the United States. Among the immigrants was a group of priests known as the Sulpician Fathers. In Baltimore the fathers started a seminary for priests, a college for the laity, and a catechism class for black children. The priest in charge, James Marie Hector Nicholas Joubert de La Muraille, himself a refugee from St. Domingue, needed someone to help him with the catechism classes. The problem was not doctrine but reading. In volunteering to teach the children to read, Lange also told Father Joubert of her desire to serve God as a nun. Because no such option was open to black women in 1828, the two decided to start a religious sisterhood for women of African descent. In a rented house at 5 St. Mary's Court, Lange began her new Catholic school. Her pupils consisted of eleven day scholars, nine boarders, and three nonpaying poor students who were called "children of the house." From the outset the curriculum was comparable to ones at private schools for white children. Music and the arts played a major role in the program of studies. Several students who graduated from the school eventually started private schools of their own. These endeavors took place where the average black person was still in slavery. In 1829 Lange and her three companions pronounced vows as Catholic nuns. Lange's name then became Soeur Marie, or Sister Mary. As superior general of the Oblate Sisters of Providence, Lange also became known as Mother Mary Lange.

Soon Lange began taking in homeless children, then widows. Expansion became necessary. Changes in the personnel of the church brought changes into the school and convent of the Oblate Sisters. The reigning archbishop, Samuel Eccleston, suggested that the black women give up the religious life and become good servants in the homes of Baltimore's elite. Lange refused to follow the archbishop's wishes. Poverty and hardship surrounded the infant community. The sisters took in washing, ironing, and sewing to support themselves and their orphans. Then a Bavarian priest, Thaddeus Anwander, asked to help Lange. At first the archbishop asked the priest, "What is the use?" Finally, after much insistence, the bishop gave Father Anwander permission to assist the Oblate Sisters of Providence. Students enrolled at St. Frances, more young black women entered the religious life, and in 1852 a school for African American males was built. News of the sisters' work soon spread to other cities. The Oblate Sisters opened schools in other sections of Baltimore, including Blessed Peter Claver in Fells Point, St. Joseph's in south Baltimore, and St. Michael's on Lombard Street as well as Blessed Peter Claver School in Philadelphia, Pennsylvania, St. Joseph and St. Frances in New Orleans, Guardian Angel in Kansas, St. Elizabeth's in St. Louis, St. Ann's Academy and St. Augustine's in Washington, D.C., and a mission in Cuba, all in the nineteenth century.

Lange died in Baltimore, the city where she had defied the rules, where she succeeded in establishing an educational system for African American youths, and where she brought into existence the first permanent African American Catholic sisterhood. Mother Mary Lange, an immigrant, enriched American culture by enhancing the educational, spiritual, and social structures of nineteenth-century black America.

FURTHER READING

Joubert's original diary, started by the priest and continued by the sisters after his death and covering 1828 to 1874, is in the Oblate Sisters of Providence Archives in Baltimore, Maryland.

Sherwood, Grace. *The Oblates Hundred and One Years* (1931).

This entry is taken from the *American National Biography* and is published here with the permission of the American Council of Learned Societies.

MARY REGINALD GERDES

Langford, George Malcolm (26 Aug. 1944–), cell biologist and professor, was born in Halifax, North Carolina, to Maynard and Lillie Langford, farmers. As a young boy, he exhibited an intense curiosity about the plants and animals on his family's farm, a curiosity that eventually developed into the desire to become a biology teacher. In 1966 he received a B.S. in Biology from Fayetteville State University, a historically black college in North Carolina, and entered the Illinois Institute of Technology, where he received an M.S. in Zoology in 1969 and a Ph.D. in Cell Biology in 1971. After two years of postdoctoral research at the University of Pennsylvania, he accepted a position on the faculty of the University of Massachusetts in Boston. Six years later, he moved to Washington, D.C., to teach biology at Howard University College of Medicine; but he left in 1979 to become a professor of cell physiology at the University of North Carolina School of Medicine. In 1991 he was named the E. E. Just Professor of Natural Sciences at Dartmouth College, a position he held for the rest of his career. In 1968 he married Sylvia Tyler, with whom he had three children.

As a graduate student, Langford conducted research to investigate intermediary metabolism, the enzyme-catalyzed processes within the cells by which energy is extracted from the nutrient molecules and then used to construct cellular components. He was particularly interested in how the intermediary metabolism of *Euglena*, the genus of single-cell green protozoans, breaks down sugar compounds. By the time he had completed his Ph.D., his interests had shifted from intermediary metabolism to intracellular motility, the movement of various biochemical compounds within a single cell. As a postdoctoral researcher, he investigated the movement within cells of organelles, specialized parts of cells that perform specific functions in the cells in much the same way that organs perform specific functions in humans. At the University of Massachusetts, he began studying intracellular motility in nerve cells, and by the time he had moved to Dartmouth he had became a leading expert on neuro-anatomy, the structure of nerve and brain cells.

Like his famous predecessor at Dartmouth, the black biologist ERNEST EVERETT JUST, Langford conducted much of his research during the summer at the Woods Hole Marine Biological Laboratory in Massachusetts. As with most Woods Hole researchers, his research partners changed from one year to the next. In the summer of 1992, for example, he was collaborating with the German cell biologist Dieter Weiss and the Russian cell biologist Sergei Kuznetsov in a study of squid axoplasm, the protoplasm that comprises axons, the appendages of nerve cells that transmit impulses away from the cell. During the course of their research, they discovered the existence of a network for intracellular motility in the endoplasmic reticulum, a major component of the cell membrane. This network consists of filaments composed of actin, a protein that plays an important role in muscle contraction.

Langford and his collaborators also discovered that the biochemical agent responsible for propelling material along the actin network is myosin-V, which is similar to the protein myosin that works in conjunction with actin to govern the motor activities of muscles. What made this discovery remarkable is the fact that, for years, cell biologists were convinced that all intercellular motility took place via a network of structures known as microtubules. To be sure, the majority of intercellular motility in squid axoplasm does indeed take place via microtubules, but the discovery of the actin network demonstrated that much remains to be learned about intercellular motility. Further research by Langford and other researchers suggested that the microtubule network handles the long-range transfer of organelles while the actin network handles short-range movement; however, even these conclusions remain tentative.

Langford served the scientific community in ways other than teacher and researcher. He served as program director for cell biology for the National Science Foundation (1988 to 1989), was chairperson of the Woods Hole science council, and served as secretary of the American Society for Cell Biology (ASCB). He also chaired the ASCB's minorities affairs committee from 1985 to 1990; in this capacity he worked to make it possible for more African Americans and other underserved minorities to pursue careers in science.

FURTHER READING

Kessler, James H., et al. *Distinguished African American Scientists of the 20th Century* (1996).

Krapp, Kristine M., ed. *Notable Black American Scientists* (1999).

Spangenburg, Ray, and Kit Moser. *African Americans in Science, Math, and Invention* (2003).

CHARLES W. CAREY JR.

Langford, Samuel (4 Mar. 1883–12 Jan. 1956), boxer, was born at Weymouth Falls, Nova Scotia, Canada, the son of Robert Langford, a poor black river driver, and Priscilla Robart. He received no formal education, left home at the age of twelve after quarreling with his father, and arrived in the United States on a lumber schooner in 1899. He drifted about New England for several years, working mostly as a stevedore. While panhandling in Boston, he met Joe Woodman, a druggist and small-time boxing promoter. Woodman hired him as a janitor at his gymnasium, and Langford later became a sparring partner and amateur boxer before making his professional debut in April 1902. He was managed by Woodman until 1919.

Weighing only about 140 pounds at the outset of his boxing career, Langford advanced rapidly. By the end of 1903 he had already defeated the lightweight champion JOE GANS and had fought the great Jack Blackburn. In 1904 he twice held Blackburn to draws, defeated Willie Lewis and George McFadden, and fought a draw with the welterweight champion JOE WALCOTT. In 1905 he suffered his first serious defeat at the hands of the heavyweight Joe Jeannette but defeated Blackburn, George Gunther, and Young Peter Jackson. After beating Jeannette in a return bout, Langford engaged the future world heavyweight champion JACK JOHNSON at Chelsea, Massachusetts, on 26 April 1906 in perhaps the most important bout of his career. Johnson, thirty pounds heavier and much taller, won decisively, but after Johnson won the heavyweight title in 1907, Woodman effectively spread the word that Langford had actually had the better of their fight. For years this story was used unsuccessfully to pressure Johnson into defending the heavyweight title against Langford, but it did have the effect of making Langford famous and seemingly too dangerous for Johnson to fight again.

Langford was at the peak of his career from 1907 to 1912. Although weighing only 165 to 170 pounds, he defeated many outstanding heavyweights and traveled throughout the world to find and meet opponents. At this time few white boxers in the United States would fight blacks, and Langford had to meet several tough opponents many times. Langford fought two black rivals, Jeannette and Sam McVea, a dozen or more times each, usually winning. Two white heavyweights who would fight him were Jim Barry and Jim Flynn; he fought Barry twelve times, losing only once, and defeated Flynn twice in their three meetings. In 1911 he knocked out the former light-heavyweight champion Philadelphia Jack O'Brien. Langford traveled to Europe in 1907, 1909, and 1911 and knocked out the British heavyweight champion William "Iron" Hague. He fought in Australia from December 1911 to May 1913 with great success.

Langford, nicknamed the "Boston Tar Baby," was a powerfully built, muscular fighter. His shoulders were extremely broad, and his arms were unusually long. Only five feet eight inches tall, Langford fought aggressively, stalking his foe and throwing short, powerful punches with both hands to head and body. Contemporary descriptions depict him as sleek, pantherlike, and graceful, one of the most impressive fighters in ring history.

Langford is the subject of many legends and stories. He was good-natured and witty. His wit, combined with his awesome reputation, sometimes enabled him to demoralize an opponent with a single remark before the fight even began. It was often said that Langford allowed opponents to stay the distance with him so he could fight them again, but an examination of his record indicates that this could hardly have been true because he won most of his fights by knockout at the peak of his career, and those opponents that he could not knock out were especially formidable.

One of Langford's most interesting fights was a six-rounder in 1910 with the great middleweight champion Stanley Ketchel. This was one of the few times that Langford fought a lighter and faster foe. No official decision was given, but newspaper reporters who witnessed the fight divided about evenly between those who thought Ketchel had won and those who thought it was a draw. Some suggested that Langford held back, but there is no evidence to support this claim.

From 1913 to 1922 Langford, now a heavyweight, declined in his prowess but was still a dangerous opponent. It was in this period that his celebrated series with the much larger Harry Wills took place. They fought sixteen times, including twice in Panama. Their second fight, in Los Angeles in 1914, produced one of Langford's greatest victories, when he came back from eleven knockdowns to knock out Wills in round fourteen. In 1917 he suffered his worst defeat when beaten badly and stopped by Fred Fulton. Langford had impaired vision in his right eye from 1917 onward.

In 1919 Woodman severed his connection with Langford and advised him to retire. But Langford had always quickly spent all the money he had earned, and boxing was his only income. By 1924 he was blind in his right eye and had developed a cataract in his left eye. Although unable to see his opponents clearly, he continued to have a few fights. Langford's last fight was in 1928 at Shawnee, Oklahoma, with Britt Sims, who battered him badly and then knocked him out cold. Langford had almost 300 professional fights over a 26-year period, winning approximately 190 times, with 115 knockout victories and about 50 draws.

The story of Langford's later life is one of poverty and an existence dependent on charity. He had married Martha Burell in 1904 and had one child. After leaving the ring he went back to Boston, where they lived, and opened an athletic gymnasium that soon failed. He then went to New York, where he was injured in an automobile accident in 1935. Soon afterward an operation performed charitably by a surgeon who remembered and admired him improved his vision, but he was soon reduced to living in squalor. In 1942 he became completely blind. Supported by relief, he spent most of his time in his room listening to a radio.

In 1943 an article by a New York sportswriter resulted in the establishment of a fund that provided Langford with a small monthly income for the rest of his life. In 1947 he returned to Boston to live with his daughter, later going into a nursing home in Cambridge, Massachusetts, where he spent all of his time in one room, alternating between a cot and a wheelchair. Despite the privations of his last thirty years, he retained his wit and good humor until he died in Cambridge.

Langford is considered the greatest professional boxer who never held or even fought for a world championship. A combination of factors, including the dominating presence of Jack Johnson during his prime and the limited opportunities available to black boxers of that period, prevented him from winning a title. He was an inaugural inductee into the International Boxing Hall of Fame in 1990.

FURTHER READING
Fleischer, Nat. *Black Dynamite, vol. 4, The Fighting Furies* (1939).
Obituary: *New York Times*, 13 Jan. 1956.
This entry is taken from the *American National Biography* and is published here with the permission of the American Council of Learned Societies.

LUCKETT V. DAVIS

Langhorn, Garfield McConnell (10 Sept. 1948–15 Jan. 1969), Vietnam War soldier and Medal of Honor recipient, was born in Cumberland, Virginia, the son of Garfield and Mary Langhorn. The Langhorn family later moved to Riverhead, New York, where young Garfield grew up and attended school. In high school Langhorn was a track athlete, and his interests as a young man included working on his car and playing the guitar. Garfield Langhorn was also a devout church attendee and was later recalled by many that knew him as "a good Christian who regularly read the Bible and had a heart of gold" (Russell). Langhorn was engaged to be married, but was drafted for military service during the Vietnam War just months after graduating from Riverhead

High School in 1968. Though he was opposed to the war, Langhorn nonetheless went off to war instead of seeking a deferment; his mother Mary later stated that "if he were here, he would say 'I did what I had to do'" (ibid.).

Garfield Langhorn entered the military on 6 May 1968 at Brooklyn, New York, and after completing army boot camp training at Fort Jackson, South Carolina, was assigned to serve in the 17th U.S. Cavalry in Troop C, 7th Squadron (Airmobile), 1st Aviation Brigade. After serving several months stateside, Langhorn was sent to Vietnam by November 1968. Though his service lasted less than a year, Langhorn left the same impression on his fellow soldiers as he did on his friends and family back home. James Napolitano, who was drafted at the same time and served in the same platoon as Langhorn, later commented that he was "a fine young man whom I admired" (Stefans).

On 15 January 1969, Private First Class Garfield Langhorn was serving as a radio operator with his platoon near Plei Djereng, Pleiku Province, in the Republic of Vietnam, where they were dropped into a landing zone to rescue two crewmen of a Cobra helicopter that had been shot down by enemy fire on a heavily wooded hillside. Langhorn and his platoon, making their way through tough terrain, reached the crash-site only to find that the pilots were dead. While transporting the bodies of the servicemen back to the landing zone, the platoon came under heavy enemy fire and was quickly surrounded. Private Langhorn responded by radioing for assistance from nearby helicopter gunships, and subsequently directed the platoon's return rocket fire. He also helped provide cover fire for the wounded while performing his radio duties as night fell on the beleaguered platoon. When an enemy grenade was thrown into their positions, Langhorn protected the nearby wounded by throwing himself on the grenade and absorbing its blast. Though Langhorn died as a result of his quick action, he saved the life of his fellow soldiers.

The service of African American soldiers in Vietnam is significant due to the fact that it was the first war since the Revolutionary War in which African Americans served in fully integrated units from the very beginning and, unlike all previous wars, was one in which their combat performance and leadership skills were rarely in question. The actions of the twenty black soldiers that merited the award of the Medal of Honor, men like Garfield Langhorn, MATTHEW LEONARD, and ROBERT JENKINS JR., are not only important on their own merits, but also exemplify the high level of service performed by African American soldiers in general. This service is even more impressive when the controversies surrounding the Vietnam War's draft and deferment policies are remembered. Not only did blacks serve in disproportionately higher numbers than whites due to draft rates that were nearly double that of eligible white candidates, but they also were granted a disproportionately lower number of educational deferments than those granted to whites.

Private First Class Garfield Langhorn was buried at Riverhead Cemetery in his hometown of Riverhead, New York. Just over a year after his death, he was approved for the Medal of Honor, which was subsequently presented to his family by President Richard Nixon in a White House ceremony on 7 April 1970. In 1993 a bust of Langhorn was erected in front of the Riverhead Town Hall, while in September 2010 the post office in Riverhead was renamed the Private First Class Garfield M. Langhorn Post Office, which building has a portrait of its namesake prominently displayed.

FURTHER READING

Hanna, Charles W. *African American Recipients of the Medal of Honor* (2002).

Russell, Jennett Meriden, "No. 5 Top Story of the Year: Post office renamed for Riverhead hero." *Riverhead News-Review,* 28 Dec. 2010.

Stefans, John. "Post Office Named After Fallen Riverhead Soldier." *Riverhead Patch,* 27 Sept. 2010.

GLENN ALLEN KNOBLOCK

Langston, Charles Henry (1817–21 Nov. 1892), educator, civil rights activist, and politician, was born on a plantation in Louisa County, Virginia, the second son of Captain Ralph Quarles and Lucy Jane Langston. Lucy Langston was Captain Quarles's part-Amerindian and part-black slave, whom he freed with her daughter Mary. Quarles, who died in 1833, left the greater portion of his personal wealth and property to his three sons. Charles Langston's younger brother, JOHN MERCER LANGSTON, wrote that their father gave Charles a start in education that influenced him throughout life. He had a weak body but was compensated with a firm mind and intellectual endowment. Although he had a well-controlled disposition and temper, this did not come to him easily and naturally, and he tended to be impetuous and aggressive. He was restive under discipline and opposition yet resolutely obedient to the training his father gave him because he was interested in his education. Charles was a more accomplished debater and orator than John during his adult years.

Several factors led the three brothers to move from Virginia to Ohio in 1834. First was the increasing restrictions placed on free blacks in Virginia. Second was the opportunity for free blacks to attain higher education, purchase land, and earn wages in Ohio. They settled on a farm bought by their guardian and old family friend, Colonel William Gooch, in Chillicothe, Ohio. Most blacks there worked as farmers, town laborers, domestic servants, or on the Ohio River and canals. In 1842 and 1843 Charles Langston enrolled in the nearby Oberlin Preparatory School, and he later taught black students in Chillicothe, for which he was paid ten dollars per month. Families who patronized the school provided him with room and board. He later lived in both Chillicothe and Columbus, Ohio, where he worked as a teacher and dentist.

Langston was active in several reform-minded and fraternal organizations. As the western representative of the Sons of Temperance in 1848, he promoted education, political rights, and moderate habits. He was also president of a black state convention and served on the "three-man committee of correspondence" that called for a black national convention in Buffalo, New York, in 1852. At that convention he proposed a massive black emigration and colonization from the United States to Central or South America, from where African Americans could pressure the U.S. government to abolish slavery. Charles Langston served as executive secretary of the Ohio State Anti-Slavery Society; his brother John Langston was president.

The Langston brothers came to prominence in the early Ohio Republican Party because they fought for the liberation of John Price during the Oberlin Wellington Rescue. This action reinvigorated the Ohio black movement and critically affected the Ohio Republican Party, with Charles as an antislavery hero and John as the black Republican leader. John Price's rescue brought a grand jury indictment and charges against thirty-seven black and white residents of Oberlin and Wellington accusing them of aiding and abetting in the rescue effort. As one of the party's leaders Langston was tried separately and convicted at the federal courthouse in Cleveland in 1859. During his sentencing the judge asked him to state why the judgment of the law should not be pronounced upon him. His response was a carefully prepared address challenging the racial basis of the American system of justice. John Mercer Langston described his brother's address as powerful, its logic irrefutable. The judge, however, did not agree, and sentenced Charles Langston to twenty days in jail and a fine of one hundred dollars.

Charles Langston wrote to the Cleveland *Plain Dealer* in 1859 to praise the white abolitionist John Brown following his attack on the federal arsenal at Harpers Ferry, Virginia. In Langston's view, Brown's raid was designed to:

> Aid the afflicted and the helpless, to assist the weak and to relieve the poor and needy. To undo the heavy burdens, to let the oppressed go free, to do to others as he would have them do to him. And, above all, to put to death, as the papers tell us, those who steal men and sell them, and in whose hands stolen men are found. His actions then are only the results of his faithfulness to the plain teaching of the word of God (Benjamin Quarles, ed., 12).

At Brown's funeral on 2 December 1859, Langston, a featured speaker, addressed more than two thousand black and white leaders and mourners.

The brief meeting Langston had had with Brown before the Harpers Ferry incident had given him firsthand news about events in Kansas that led him to move to Leavenworth, Kansas, "to work with the contraband" in 1862. An editorial in the *Leavenworth Daily Conservative* on 8 July 1862 claimed that Langston worked with the residents of black and white communities in Leavenworth to organize a day school for the children of the contraband.

During the Civil War in 1862, Langston returned to Ohio to recruit soldiers for the state's first black regiment. He appealed to the loyal people of his district to provide for the necessities of the families of the enlisted black men while they fought for the Union and freedom. Langston was part of a group of black and white abolitionists who fought to ameliorate the condition of the "colored people" of Kansas. He was also active in the Interracial Kansas Emancipation League, which sought to destroy slavery by taking supervision and control of the contraband that were freely coming to Kansas. The group's overall goal was to encourage the growth of industry, education, and moral values among these new black residents and to find them employment.

He campaigned for universal black suffrage for several years until the right of U.S. citizens to vote without restriction on the basis of race, color, or previous conditions of servitude was anchored in the Fifteenth Amendment to the U.S. Constitution. Historians have noted that one of the first attempts to secure voting rights for all came out of a black-sponsored convention in Leavenworth, Kansas, on 1 January 1863, when Langston delivered a major address on the subject. On 8 February 1864 the Kansas House of Representatives asked Langston to speak for forty-five minutes on black suffrage issues. It was followed by a debate with the representative Samuel Newitt Wood of Morris County. Wood argued in favor of women's suffrage but opposed black voting. Addressing the citizens of Kansas, Langston argued that by putting the word "white" in the first section of the fifth article of the Constitution, "colored men" would be denied access to the ballot, thereby losing their personal liberty, civil rights, property, and legal protections. Langston concluded with an eloquent demand for equal rights:

> In the name of that impartial justice which, ignoring all distinctions of race or color, seeks only to establish among men, liberty, equality and fraternity.... We ask at your hands no special privileges. We seek no favor. We do not desire social equality. But we do demand equality before the law. We seek complete emancipation full and perfect enfranchisement absolute legal equality. These are only the natural, inherent, and inalienable rights of man (Sheridan, 1999–2000, 7).

At the end of the war Langston established a store in Leavenworth that stocked fruit, vegetables, fresh butter, and staple and fancy groceries. With commitment and vigor, he continued to make his mark in history fighting for the rights and legal issues of politics, economics, and education that affected the lives of African Americans. He died at age seventy-three in Lawrence, Kansas.

FURTHER READING

Berwanger, Eugene H. "Hardin and Langston: Western Black Spokesmen of the Reconstruction Era," *Journal of Negro History* 64 (Spring, 1979).

Quarles, Benjamin, ed. *Blacks on John Brown* (1972).

Sheridan, Richard B. "From Slavery in Missouri to Freedom in Kansas: The Influx of Black Fugitives and Contrabands into Kansas, 1854–1865," *Kansas History* 12 (Spring, 1989).

Sheridan, Richard B. "Charles Henry Langston and the African American Struggle in Kansas," *Kansas History* 22 (Winter, 1999–2000).

SAM ONYEJINDU OLEKA

Langston, John Mercer (14 Dec. 1829–15 Nov. 1897), political leader and intellectual, was born free in Louisa County, Virginia, the son of Ralph Quarles, a wealthy white slaveholding planter, and Lucy Jane

John Mercer Langston an educator, diplomat, and legislator, between 1860 and 1875. (Library of Congress. Brady-Handy Photograph Collection.)

Langston, a part-Native American, part-black slave emancipated by Quarles in 1806. After the deaths of both of their parents in 1834, Langston and his two brothers, well provided for by Quarles's will but unprotected by Virginia law, moved to Ohio. There Langston lived on a farm near Chillicothe with a cultured white southern family who had been friends of his father and who treated him as a son. He was in effect orphaned again in 1839 when a court hearing, concluding that his guardian's impending move to slave-state Missouri would imperil the boy's freedom and inheritance, forced him to leave the family. Subsequently he boarded in four different homes, white and black, in Chillicothe and Cincinnati, worked as a farmhand and bootblack, intermittently attended privately funded black schools since blacks were barred from public schools for whites, and in August 1841 was caught up in the violent white rioting against blacks and white abolitionists in Cincinnati.

Learning from his brothers and other black community leaders a sense of commitment, Langston also developed a self-confidence that helped him cope with his personal losses and with pervasive, legally sanctioned racism. In 1844 he entered the preparatory department at Oberlin College, where his brothers had been the first black students in 1835. Oberlin's egalitarianism encouraged him, and its rigorous rhetorical training enhanced his speaking skills. As early as 1848 and continuing into the 1860s, Langston joined in the black civil rights movement in Ohio and across the North, working as an orator and organizer to promote black advancement and enfranchisement and to combat slavery. At one Ohio state black convention, the nineteen-year-old Langston, quoting the Roman slave Terence, declared: "'I am a man, and there is nothing of humanity, as I think, estranged to me.' ... The spirit of our people must be aroused. They must feel and act as men." After receiving his B.A. degree in 1849, Langston decided to study law. Discovering that law schools were unwilling to accept a black student, however, he returned to Oberlin and in 1853 became the first black graduate of its prestigious theological program. Despite the evangelist and Oberlin president Charles Grandison Finney's public urging, Langston, skeptical of organized religion, and especially its widespread failure to oppose slavery, refused to enter the ministry. Finding white allies in radical antislavery politics, Langston engaged in local politics beginning in 1852, demonstrating that an articulate black campaigner might effectively counter opposition race-baiting; in mid-decade he helped form the Republican Party on the Western Reserve. Philemon E. Bliss of nearby Elyria, soon to be a Republican congressman, became Langston's mentor for legal study, and in 1854 he was accepted to the Ohio bar, becoming the first black lawyer in the West. That year he married Caroline Matilda Wall, a senior at Oberlin; they had five children. In the spring of 1855 voters in Brownhelm, an otherwise all-white area near Oberlin where Langston had a farm, elected him township clerk on the Free Democratic (Free Soil) ticket, gaining him recognition as the first black elected official in the nation. Langston announced his conviction that political influence was "the bridle by which we can check and guide, to our advantage, the selfishness of American demagogues."

In 1856 the Langstons began a fifteen-year residency in Oberlin. Elected repeatedly to posts on the town council and the board of education, he solidified his reputation as a competent public executive and adroit attorney. In his best-known case, Langston successfully defended EDMONIA LEWIS, a student accused of poisoning two of her white Oberlin classmates (who recovered); Lewis would become the first noted African American sculptor. In promoting militant resistance to slavery, Langston helped stoke outrage over the federal prosecution under the Fugitive Slave Law of thirty-seven of his white and black townsmen and others involved in the 1858 Oberlin-Wellington rescue of the fugitive slave John Price. Immediately, Langston organized the new black Ohio State Anti-Slavery Society, which he headed, to channel black indignation over the case. While his brother CHARLES HENRY LANGSTON, one of the two rescuers convicted, repudiated the law in a notable courtroom plea, Langston urged defiance of it in dozens of speeches throughout the state. Langston supported the plan by John Brown (1800–1859) to foment a slave uprising, although he did not participate in the 1859 raid on Harpers Ferry. Following the outbreak of the Civil War, once recruitment of northern black troops began in early 1863, he raised hundreds of black volunteers for the Massachusetts Fifty-fourth and Fifty-fifth regiments and for Ohio's first black regiment.

After the war, Langston's pursuit of a Reconstruction based on "impartial justice" and a redistribution of political and economic power elevated him to national prominence. In contrast to FREDERICK DOUGLASS, the quintessential self-made man, to whom his leadership was most often compared, Langston represented the importance of education and professionalism, joined to activism, for a people emerging from slavery. In 1864 the black national convention in Syracuse, New York, elected him the first president of the National Equal Rights League, a position he held until 1868. Despite rivalries within the league, Langston shaped it into the first viable national black organization. In 1865 and 1866 he lectured in the upper South, the Midwest, and the Northeast and fought for full enfranchisement not only of the freed people but also of African Americans denied suffrage in the North. In January 1867, on the eve of congressional Reconstruction, he presided over a league-sponsored convention of more than one hundred black delegates from seventeen states to Washington, D.C., to dramatize African American demands for full freedom and citizenship. That spring Langston assumed a signal role in the South as a Republican Party organizer of black voters and the educational inspector-general for the Freedmen's Bureau, traveling from Maryland to Texas. In Virginia, Mississippi, and North Carolina, he helped set up Republican Union Leagues, which instructed freed people on

registration and voting; in Georgia and Louisiana he advised blacks elected to state constitutional conventions on strategy. In almost every southern state, Langston defended Reconstruction policy in addresses before audiences of both races. Insistent on guaranteeing the citizenship and human rights of freed people, he appealed to black self-reliance, self-respect, and self-assertion and to white enlightened self-interest, predicting that interracial cooperation would lead to an "unexampled prosperity and a superior civilization." His charisma, refined rhetorical style, and ability to articulate radical principles in a reasonable tone drew plaudits across ideological and racial lines. Twice, in 1868 and 1872, fellow Republicans, one of whom was white, proposed that Langston run for vice president on the Republican ticket.

In the fall of 1869 Langston founded the law department at Howard University and took up his duties as law professor and first law dean. From December 1873 to July 1875 he was vice president and acting president of the university. He characteristically gained a warm following among students, who were particularly attracted by his manner, which was neither obsequious nor condescending. Despite Langston's accomplishments at Howard, however, the trustees rejected his bid to assume the presidency for reasons that they refused to disclose but that clearly involved his race, his egalitarian and biracial vision, and the fact that he was not a member of an evangelical church. Embittered, he resigned.

Meanwhile Langston continued to function as one of the Republican Party's top black spokesmen. In return, President Ulysses S. Grant appointed him to the Board of Health of the District of Columbia in 1871, and he moved his home from Oberlin to Washington, D.C. He served as the board's legal officer for nearly seven years, during which time he helped devise a model sanitation code for the capital. On another front, at the behest of the Massachusetts senator Charles Sumner, he contributed to the drafting of the Supplementary Civil Rights Act of 1875, which was invalidated by the U.S. Supreme Court in 1883. As radical Reconstruction crumbled, practicality and personal ambition led Langston in 1877 to endorse President Rutherford B. Hayes's conciliatory policy toward the white South. Two years later, however, he condemned the condition of the freed people in the South as "practical enslavement" and called for black migration, the "Exodus" movement, to the North and the West. Langston served with typical efficiency as U.S. minister and consul general to Haiti from 1877 to 1885, winning settlement of claims against the Haitian government, especially by Americans injured during civil unrest, and some improvement in trade relations between the two countries. During his final sixteen months of duty, he was concurrently chargé d'affaires to Santo Domingo.

In 1885 Langston returned to Petersburg, Virginia, to head the state college for African Americans, the Virginia Normal and Collegiate Institute. After his forced resignation less than two years later under heavy pressure from the Democrats who then controlled the state, he announced his intention to run for the U.S. House of Representatives in the mostly black Fourth District, of which Petersburg was the urban center. Running against a white Democrat and a white Republican, Langston waged a ten-month campaign "to establish the manhood, honor, and fidelity of the Negro race." Although the Democratic candidate was initially declared the victor, Langston challenged the election results as fraudulent, and Congress voted in September 1890 to seat him. Within days he was back in Virginia campaigning for reelection to a second term. Again the official count went to the Democrat, a result Langston accepted because he could expect no redress from the new Democratic Congress. The first African American elected to Congress from Virginia, Langston used his three months in the House to put his ideas on education and fair elections into the national record. His most controversial proposal, one intended to head off black disfranchisement, was a constitutional amendment imposing a literacy requirement on all voters in federal elections and a corresponding adjustment in the size of state congressional delegations.

During the remainder of his life, Langston practiced law in the District of Columbia and continued to be active in politics, education, and promoting black rights. He published his autobiography, *From the Virginia Plantation to the National Capitol* (1894), and carried on an active speaking schedule in both the North and the South. He remained hopeful despite legal disfranchisement, segregation, and his own failure to obtain a federal judgeship. In 1896, while raising money to support the filing of civil rights cases, he predicted: "It is in the courts, by the law, that we shall, finally, settle all questions connected with the recognition of the rights, the equality, the full citizenship of colored Americans." He died in Washington, D.C.

FURTHER READING

Langston's papers, together with those of his wife, Caroline W. Langston, and son-in-law James Carroll Napier, are in the Fisk University Library. Valuable scrapbooks of news clippings are in the Moorland-Spingarn Research Center at Howard University.

Langston, John Mercer. *Freedom and Citizenship* (1883, repr. 1969).

Langston, John Mercer. *From the Virginia Plantation to the National Capitol* (1894).

Cheek, William, and Aimee Lee Cheek. *John Mercer Langston and the Fight for Black Freedom, 1829–65* (1989).

Cheek, William, and Aimee Lee Cheek. "John Mercer Langston: Principle and Politics," in *Black Leaders of the Nineteenth Century*, eds. Leon Litwack and August Meier (1988).

This entry is taken from the *American National Biography* and is published here with the permission of the American Council of Learned Societies.

WILLIAM CHEEK AND

AIMEE LEE CHEEK

Lanier, Robert White (c.1908–?), stowaway and thwarted polar explorer, was probably born and raised in Brunswick, Georgia, but had moved to Jersey City, New Jersey, by the mid 1920s. Little is known about his early life. Seeking to become the first African American to reach the South Pole, he hid for three days on the *City of New York*, the flagship of the Byrd Antarctic Expedition. The Byrd Antarctic Expedition was lead by Richard Evelyn Byrd, a native Virginian who was the brother of U.S. Senator Harry Floyd Byrd. The ship left Manhattan on 26 August 1929 with three stowaways, including Lanier. The two other stowaways were found in time to ship them back on a harbor tug. Lanier was discovered three days later in the forecastle head between a crate and a side of the ship. *The New York Times* chronicled his discovery in a series of articles on Boyd's Expeditions between 28 August 1928 and 18 September 1928. A story by W. A. McDonald on 28 August 1928 gave the following account of Mr. Lanier's discovery:

> Shouts from forward reported another stowaway, this one a negro. He lay on the foc'sle head between a spare propeller blade and the side of the ship when the flashlight of Strom, the second officer, showed that he was there. The crew grinned around him. Commander Byrd laughing reached down and shook his hand. The boy's other hand clutched a notebook and half dozen

yellow pencils. "How long have you been there?" someone asked, and he grinned and said "Three days. I wanted to be the first black fellow to get to the South Pole." "When were you coming out?," demanded a man. "When we were so far at sea the captain wouldn't send me back."

Impressed by his tenacity, Commander Byrd let Lanier stay abroad the *City of New York*. A story published in the *New York Times* three weeks later on 17 September 1928 offered a different account of the same events.

Robert White Lanier was the third stowaway to be found on the *City of New York*. In his determination to see the Antarctic continent with Commander Byrd, hid himself for three days in the forecastle head between a crate and the side of the ship. The odor of watermelon, wafted down from the ship's galley, however, proved too much for him on his third day, and he crawled out, went to the captain and begged to be forgiven and taken along.

Only Commander Byrd, Lanier, and the crewmembers know which account is accurate, although the racist implication in the second version that African Americans could not resist watermelon is also clear. Once the decision was made to let Lanier stay on board the *City of New York*, crewmembers and others began investigating his background. When he was discovered, Lanier told Commander Byrd that he was twenty years old and originally from Brunswick, Georgia. On 31 August 1928 an article appeared in the *New York Times* stating that police in Jersey City were uncertain whether Lanier was the same youth found guilty of disorderly conduct in Jersey City in 1926, who received a suspended sentence. Police records showed a Robert Lanier, twenty-one years old, of 29 Orient Avenue, Jersey City, was convicted of using abusive language on 26 November 1926. Lanier later admitted that he currently lived on Orient Avenue in Jersey City, New Jersey.

The Byrd expedition decided that unless Lanier could show a good record he would be removed when the ship reached Panama. He was removed at Panama, with Captain Melville citing a lack of stamina necessary to withstand the rigors of the Antarctic voyage as the main reason. Again the *New York Times* took interest in Lanier and Commander Byrd's expedition. He was quoted—again in the racist style common even in the northern press—as saying "Boy, I sho would like to make de rest of dis trip"

(17 Sept. 1928). Given his quotations in the first *New York Times* article, this quote seems very unlikely.

Not to be deterred on his quest to be the first African American to reach the South Pole, Lanier became a mess boy on the *Golden State*. The ship was headed to Dunedin, New Zealand, to join Commander Byrd's supply ship the *Eleanor Bolling*. While on the *Golden State*, Lanier was charged with stabbing a fellow crewmember in New Zealand and in March 1929 the *New Zealand Truth* wrote an article about Lanier with the headline "Byrd's Mess Boy Charged with Stabbing." During the investigation a diary he kept on the trip from San Francisco was introduced into evidence. The diary provided a glimpse into his life on the *Golden State* and the prejudice he encountered while trying to fulfill his dream and join up with the Byrd Exposition as they headed to the South Pole.

In August 1929 while visiting a friend in Vancouver, British Columbia, Lanier listed his nearest relative as a Ms. Helen Gant (his sister) at 29 Orient Avenue, Jersey City, New Jersey. Unfortunately, Lanier never fulfilled his dream of becoming the first African American to reach the South Pole. George Gibbs, a native of Jacksonville, Florida, joined Byrd in 1937 on this third expedition to Antarctica and fulfilled the dream that Lanier had been chasing for almost a decade.

Lanier continued to his love of adventure and the sea by serving on the *American Scientist* and the *American Jurist* in 1955, traveling to London, Le Havre, France, and Antwerp, Belgium. At that point he disappears from the historical record.

FURTHER READING

"Three Byrd Planes to Be Tested Today." *New York Times*, 31 August 1928.

"Byrd Ship Drops Negro Stowaway." *New York Times*, 17 September 1928.

"Negro's Ambition: First at South Pole, Accepted for Byrd Expedition." *The Argus*, 29 January 1929.

"Legal Barriers on Polar Trip, Byrd's Mess Boy Charged with Stabbing." *NZ Truth*, 21 March 1929.

KENYATTA D. BERRY

Lanier, Willie (21 Aug. 1945–), professional football player, was born in Clover, Virginia. Information about his parents is unknown. He played football at Maggie Walker High School in Richmond, Virginia, becoming a linebacker during his senior season. After graduating in 1963, Lanier originally planned to attend Virginia State University to study business administration. Yet he decided to seek a more racially tolerant environment farther north and enrolled at Morgan State University in Baltimore. He contacted Morgan State football coach Earl "Papa Bear" Banks about the possibility of playing, but Lanier was told there were no scholarships. Scoring in the top 10 percent of his incoming class on his college entrance exam, Lanier had not expected to be a scholarship athlete. Instead, he acquired a student loan and found a work-study job on campus.

Initially making the team as a walk-on, Lanier quickly established himself as an outstanding linebacker and eventually received a scholarship. Already weighing 245 pounds as a freshman, Lanier went on to be named to the Small College All-America team twice. Morgan State won twenty-nine games and lost only three during Lanier's college career, and that season the team began a thirty-three-game winning streak. Morgan State held opponents to only 732 yards in total offense during Lanier's junior year, and he set a school record with twenty-six tackles in one game. When asked if he would have preferred to have attended a major college, Lanier replied that a big school could not have done more for him than Morgan State had. He told the *Houston Chronicle* that he was motivated in college not by athletic glory but by the opportunity to improve his life. Lanier also believed that the Morgan State professors gave him what he needed to be competitive off the playing field.

Following his graduation in 1967, Lanier was selected in the second round of the American Football League (AFL) draft by the Kansas City Chiefs. Because of his intense play as a linebacker, Lanier soon earned the nickname "Contact," given to him by teammate Jerry Mays. Despite playing the most violent position in football, he was durable and missed only one game during his last ten seasons. He missed the final four games of his rookie season after knocking himself out with a head-first tackle, resulting in a week of tests at the Mayo Clinic. Thereafter, Lanier eschewed recklessness in favor of a more cerebral approach to the game, and he also wore extra padding in his helmet.

Lanier was the first African American to play middle linebacker in professional football and the first to become a star while playing that position. Although many linebackers excelled at only one aspect of the game, Lanier was a standout at both stopping runners and defending against the pass. He told the *New York Times* that he was not certain if anyone other than Hank Stram, the Chiefs' coach, would have given him the opportunity to play middle linebacker. His main competition for the position had been another rookie, Jim Lynch. A white player from Notre Dame, Lynch became Lanier's longtime roommate on the road and at training camp. One of the many highlights of Lanier's career occurred during the 1969 American Football League divisional playoff against Joe Namath and the New York Jets, the defending Super Bowl champions. Late in the game Lanier led a goal-line stand that forced the Jets to settle for a field goal, and the Chiefs won 13-6. After beating the Oakland Raiders 17-7 in the league championship game, Kansas City went on to upset the Minnesota Vikings 23-7 in Super Bowl IV behind the brilliant defense led by Lanier (who conceived and administered the defensive alignments), tackle Buck Buchanan, and linebacker Bobby Bell, all three destined for the Pro Football Hall of Fame. A lesser-known aspect of the Chiefs' victory was that 50 percent of the team's players were black, an unusually high number for that era and an indication, according to Lanier, of the organization's commitment to quality regardless of race.

Lanier retired following the 1977 season with twenty-seven career interceptions, including a career high of five in 1975, and fifteen fumble recoveries. He returned two interceptions for touchdowns and also recorded a safety. Lanier was selected to play in the NFL's all-star game, the Pro Bowl, six times and was named the most valuable defensive player in 1971. He also played in two AFL All-Star games before the merger of the two leagues. Lanier was inducted in the Chiefs' Ring of Honor at Arrowhead Stadium in 1984, selected for the Pro Football Hall of Fame in 1988, and named to the NFL's seventy-fifth anniversary team in 1995. In addition to being selected by the *Sporting News* as one of the one-hundred greatest professional football players of the twentieth century, Lanier was also picked by Paul Zimmerman, the professional football expert at *Sports Illustrated*, as one of three linebackers on his all-century team.

Unlike many professional athletes, Lanier saw sports as only one important phase of his life. He told Richmond's *Times-Dispatch* in 1998 that playing in the Super Bowl and being named to the Pro Football Hall of Fame were the highlights of his football career but not his life. He worked in labor relations for Philip Morris in Richmond during the off season, and after leaving football he attended the graduate business school at the University of Missouri-Kansas City but did not receive a degree. Lanier then became an investment banker in Richmond, handling private equity investments across the country. Lanier also served on the board of directors of the Huddle House restaurant chain and Virginia State University's board of visitors. He also supported the United Way of Greater Richmond, the Garfield Child's Fund, the Industrial Development Authority of Chesterfield County, Virginia, and public television station WCVE. Lanier was chosen Virginian of the Year in 1986. The latter honor came nine years after his application to join a Richmond country club was rejected, apparently because of his race. In 2000 Lanier was inducted into the College Football Hall of Fame.

FURTHER READING

Feinstein, John. "Life, Linebacking Still Fun for Lanier," *Washington Post* (Aug. 1977).

Harrington, Denis J.. *The Pro Football Hall of Fame: Players, Coaches, Team Owners and League Officials, 1963–1991* (1991).`

Rhoden, William C. "For Lanier, a Fitting Salute," *New York Times* (Aug. 1986).

MICHAEL ADAMS

Lanusse, Armand (1812–16 Mar. 1868), writer, civil rights activist, and educator, was born in New Orleans, Louisiana. Nothing is known of his personal life except that he married and had five children, four sons and a daughter. A brother, Numa Lanusse, also displayed considerable literary talent until his death at the age of twenty-six in a riding accident.

In New Orleans, the nation's nineteenth-century "Creole capital," Lanusse belonged to a resident coterie of French-speaking Romantic writers whose ranks were reinforced by political refugees of revolutionary upheaval in France and the French Caribbean. Intensely hostile to Louisiana's slave-based racial hierarchy and inspired by the Romantic idealism of the democratic age, Lanusse joined with the native and émigré literati to press for change. In 1843 he played a leading role in the publication of a short-lived, interracial literary journal, *L'album littéraire: Journal des jeunes gens, amateurs de littérature*, which began as a monthly and contained social commentary, poems, and short stories. Lanusse's work and that of other Afro-Creole writers, such as Joanni Questy, CAMILLE THIERRY, Mirtil-Ferdinand Liotau, and Michel Saint-Pierre, dominated the review, while Jean-Louis Marciacq, a white French émigré and director of a school for children of color, appeared as the publisher. In *L'album*, Lanusse and other black Creole contributors, like the Romantic writers in France and the French Caribbean, employed their literary works to attack the evils of contemporary society.

In the short story "*Un mariage de conscience*" Lanusse condemned plaçage (a French-language term referring to a negotiated agreement between a white suitor and a young woman of color that assured the prospective "wife" social and financial security). Though French and Spanish law had prohibited interracial marriage, plaçage had enabled mixed-race couples to enter into stable, quasi-legitimate partnerships. After 1803, however, the decline of Latin European racial attitudes and the mounting conservatism of American Catholicism destroyed plaçage's institutional viability. *L'album's* short stories and poems portrayed plaçage as a form of human bondage that reduced free women of color to the status of prostitutes and threatened the stability of the free black community.

L'album's condemnation of plaçage, its fiery attacks "on the awful condition of Louisiana society," and its aggressive advocacy of the rights of "young Louisianians" prompted one critic to charge the journal with fomenting revolution. An anonymous essayist insisted that *L'album* sought only reform, but the review's content clearly challenged an 1830 state law banning the dissemination of reading materials having a tendency to cause discontent among free blacks and slaves. The periodical apparently ceased publication after only four issues.

With *L'album's* demise, Lanusse conceived of the publication of a collection of poems. Appearing in 1845, *Les cenelles* (the title taking its name from the delectable berries of an indigenous hawthorn bush) contained eighty-five French-language poems by seventeen Afro-Creole authors and conveyed a subdued tone. Lanusse's eighteen contributions, including the dedication and introduction, dominated the book of poetry, and in several of the selections he resumed his attack on the practice of plaçage. He also returned to another issue raised in *L'album*—expanded educational opportunities for the "fine minds" of Louisiana's youth. In *Les cenelles'* introduction, Lanusse pointed to education's value as "a shield against the spiteful and calumnious arrows shot at us."

During the 1840s Lanusse acted upon his advocacy of educational reform when he led a campaign to open a free school for impoverished orphans of color, many of whom were the illegitimate offspring of interracial liaisons. The freewoman of color Justine Firmin Couvent had provided for the establishment of such a school in her 1832 will. Thwarting white opposition to free black education, Lanusse, together with other Afro-Creole leaders, succeeded in executing the terms of Madame Couvent's will. The school, the Sociéte Catholique pour L'Instruction des Orphelins dans L'Indigence, opened in 1848 and became a focal point for some of the city's most radical Afro-Creole activists. In 1852 Lanusse succeeded the freewoman Félicie Callioux as principal of the Couvent School and remained head of the facility until 1866.

Threatened with violence and confiscation of their property in the secession crisis of 1861, Lanusse and other freemen of color joined the Confederate army in a defensive action. When rebel forces withdrew from New Orleans in April 1862, free black soldiers refused to leave and volunteered their services to federal authorities. Against accusations that freemen of color had willingly supported the rebel cause, Lanusse wrote that Afro-Creoles would have been foolish "to offer our cooperation ... to the preservation of a prejudice which, praise be to God, disappears each day from every civilized country of the earth."

Passionately outspoken in defense of his community, Lanusse engaged in bitter disputes with the free black population's detractors in *L'union*, a radical, French-language newspaper founded in 1862 by the Afro-Creole intelligentsia. In retaliation his enemies accused him at one point of desecrating the U.S. flag—a treasonable offense in wartime New Orleans. Cleared of the charge, the irrepressible Louisianian later denounced the U.S. Army after the head of the Department of the Gulf, General Nathaniel P. Banks, forced the resignation of black Union officers in an attempt to appease white conservatives. "Many thought," Lanusse wrote in *L'union*, "that caste prejudice would disappear with the arrival of federal troops in this city." But, he continued, "in every free state of the Union, prejudice is twice as strong as it is here." Lanusse urged people of color to emigrate to Mexico to escape the nation's stifling racial environment.

Lanusse himself remained in the city, and three years before his death there he helped found an interracial political association, the Friends of Universal Suffrage, to press for black voting rights and proportional representation. The organization's advanced positions helped produce one of the Reconstruction South's most radical state constitutions. Despite the strides forward that had been made, Lanusse's wartime admonitions proved prophetic. By 1900 a nightmare of agrarian peonage, legalized segregation, and disfranchisement that endured for more than fifty years had destroyed Reconstruction's promise of equal citizenship.

FURTHER READING

Bell, Caryn Cossé. *Revolution, Romanticism, and the Afro-Creole Protest Tradition in Louisiana, 1718–1868* (1997).

Coleman, Edward Maceo, ed. *Creole Voices: Poems in French by Free Men of Color First Published in 1845* (1945).

Desdunes, Rodolphe Lucien. *Our People and Our History*, trans. and ed. Sister Dorothea Olga McCants (1973).

Roussève, Charles Barthelemy. *The Negro in Louisiana: Aspects of His History and His Literature* (1937).

This entry is taken from the *American National Biography* and is published here with the permission of the American Council of Learned Societies.

CARYN COSSÉ BELL

Larsen, Nella (13 Apr. 1891–30 Mar. 1964), novelist, was born Nellie Walker in Chicago, Illinois, the daughter of Peter Walker, a cook, and Mary Hanson. She was born to a Danish immigrant mother and a "colored" father, according to her birth certificate. On 14 July 1890 Peter Walker and Mary Hanson applied for a marriage license in Chicago, but there is no record that the marriage ever took place. Larsen told her publisher, Alfred A. Knopf, that her father was "a Negro from the Virgin Islands, formerly the Danish West Indies" and that he died when she was two, but none of this has been proven conclusively.

Larsen was prone to invent and embellish her past. Mary Hanson Walker married a Danish man, Peter Larson, on 7 February 1894, after the couple had had a daughter. Peter Larson eventually moved the family from the multiracial world of State Street to a white Chicago suburb, changed the spelling of his name to Larsen, and sent Nellie away to the South. In the 1910 census Mary Larsen denied the existence of Nellie, stating that she had given birth to only one child. The family rejection and the resulting cultural dualism over her racial heritage that Larsen experienced in her youth were to be reflected in her later fiction. Nellie Larson entered the Coleman School in Chicago at age nine, then the Wendell Phillips Junior High School in 1905, where her name was recorded as Nellye Larson. In 1907 she was sent by Peter Larsen to complete high school at the Normal School of Fisk University in Nashville, Tennessee, where she took the spelling "Larsen" and began to use "Nella" as her given name. Larsen claimed to have spent the years 1909 to 1912 in Denmark

Nella Larsen, whose novels explore the complexity of being of mixed race in America. (Library of Congress.)

with her mother's relatives and to have audited courses at the University of Copenhagen, but there is no record of her ever having done so. Her biographer, Thadious M. Davis, says, "The next four years (1908–1912) are a mystery, ... and no conclusive traces of her for these years have surfaced" (67).

In 1912 Larsen enrolled in a three-year nurses' training course at New York City's Lincoln Hospital, one of few nursing programs for African Americans in the country. After graduating in 1915, she worked a year at the John A. Andrew Hospital and Nurse Training School in Tuskegee, Alabama. Unhappy at Tuskegee, Larsen returned to New York and worked briefly as a staff member of the city Department of Health. In May 1919 she married DR. ELMER IMES, a prominent black physicist; the marriage ended in divorce in 1933.

Larsen left nursing in 1921 to become a librarian, beginning work with the New York Public Library in January 1922. Because of her husband's social position, Larsen was able to ascend in the heights of the Harlem social circle, and it is there she met WALTER WHITE, the NAACP leader and novelist, and Carl Van Vechten, the photographer and author of *Nigger Heaven* (1926). White and Van Vechten encouraged her to write, and in January 1926 Larsen quit her job in order to write full-time. She had already begun working on her first novel, *Quicksand*, perhaps during a period of convalescence, and it was published in 1928. Earlier in the 1920s she had published two children's stories in the *Brownies' Book* as Nella Larsen Imes and then two pulp-fiction stories for *Young's Magazine* under the pseudonym Allen Semi. *Quicksand* won the Harmon Foundation's Bronze Medal for literature and established Larsen as one of the prominent writers of the Harlem Renaissance. After her second novel, *Passing*, was published in 1929, she applied for and became the first black woman to receive a Guggenheim Foundation Fellowship. Larsen used the award to travel to Spain in 1930 and to work on her third book, which was never published. After a year and a half in Spain and France, Larsen returned to New York.

Two shocks appear to have ended Larsen's literary career. In 1930 she was accused of plagiarizing her short story "Sanctuary," published that year in *Forum*, when a reader pointed out its likeness to Sheila Kaye-Smith's "Mrs. Adis," a story that had appeared in *Century* magazine in 1922. The editors of *Forum* pursued the charge and exonerated Larsen, but biographers and scholars have concluded that Larsen never recovered from the attack, however unfounded. The second shock was Larsen's discovery of her husband's infidelity early in 1930, although she refrained from seeking a divorce until 1933. Imes supported Larsen with alimony payments until his death in 1941, at which time Larsen returned to her first career, nursing, in New York City. She was a supervisor at Gouverneur Hospital from 1944 to 1961, and then worked at Metropolitan Hospital from 1961 to 1964 to avoid retirement. Since her death in New York City, Larsen's novels, considered "lost" until the 1970s, have been reprinted and reexamined. While she had always been included in the few histories of black American literature, her reputation was eclipsed in the era of naturalism and protest-writing (1930–1970), to be recovered along with the reputations of ZORA NEALE HURSTON and other African American women writers during the rise of the feminist movement in the 1970s.

Larsen's literary reputation rests on the achievement of her two novels of the late 1920s. In *Quicksand* she created an autobiographical protagonist, Helga Crane, the illegitimate daughter of a Danish immigrant mother and a black father who was a gambler and deserted the mother. Crane hates white society, from which she feels excluded by her black skin; she also despises the black bourgeoisie, partly because she is not from one of its families and partly for its racial hypocrisy about the color line and its puritanical moral and aesthetic code. After two years of living in Denmark, Helga returns to America to fall into "quicksand" by marrying an uneducated, animalistic black preacher who takes her to a rural southern town and keeps her pregnant until she is on the edge of death from exhaustion.

In *Passing* Larsen wrote a complicated psychological version of a favorite theme in African American literature. Clare Kendry has hidden her black blood from the white racist she has married. The novel ends with Clare's sudden death as she either plunges or is pushed out of a window by Irene, her best friend, just at the husband's surprise entrance. "What happened next, Irene Redfield never afterwards allowed herself to remember. Never clearly. One moment Clare had been there, a vital glowing thing, like a flame of red and gold. The next she was gone" (271).

Larsen's stature as a novelist continues to grow. She portrays black women convincingly and without the simplification of stereotype. Larsen fully realized the complexity of being of mixed race in America and was able to render her cultural dualism artistically.

FURTHER READING

Larsen's personal papers and books vanished from her apartment at her death, so neither a manuscript archive nor a collection of her private papers exists.

Carby, Hazel. *Reconstructing Womanhood: The Emergence of the Afro-American Woman Novelist* (1987).

Davis, Thadious M.. *Nella Larsen, Novelist of the Harlem Renaissance: A Woman's Life Unveiled* (1994).

Larson, Charles. *Invisible Darkness: Jean Toomer and Nella Larsen* (1993).

Tucker, Adia C.. *Tragic Mulattoes, Tragic Myths* (2001).

This entry is taken from the *American National Biography* and is published here with the permission of the American Council of Learned Societies.

ANN RAYSON

LaSalle, Denise (16 July 1939–), blues and soul singer and performer, was born Denise Craig or Allen in Belzoni, Mississippi, to Nathaniel and Nancy Allen, both farm laborers who made ends meet by picking cotton. She was the youngest of eight. There was a juke joint across the street from the family home, and LaSalle grew up hearing its music pour out onto the street, listening to music programs on the radio (including, she would later note, Nashville's *Grand Ole Opry* program), and singing in her church choir. Her educational record was spotty, and only later did she go on to earn her high school equivalency.

That she did in Chicago, where she moved when she was just thirteen, to live with a cousin. She was determined to make a go in the music business, but the going was rough and she took work serving drinks in a bar to get by. Meantime, she joined a gospel group and sang at churches around the city. She was working at Mixer's Lounge when an executive from the Chess label happened by. LaSalle asked him to listen to one of her songs, he agreed, and before long LaSalle had been offered a recording contract. That, unfortunately, never turned into a recording. For whatever reason, the label never put her voice on tape. Meanwhile, LaSalle's reputation was beginning to grow. She performed in nightclubs around the city and was winning a reputation as a songwriter to reckon with. Billy Emerson, the Chess label executive, encouraged her to enter talent contests around Chicago, which she frequently won. Her exposure grew, and soon she was being offered paying gigs at larger and larger venues. In 1967 she recorded a local hit, "Love's Reputation," for Emerson's small label, but she split with him a year later after he failed to land a spot for her at the Regal. She met and married Bill Jones in 1969. The couple would have no children and divorced in 1974, but in the meantime Jones and LaSalle founded a recording label that frequently showcased LaSalle's songwriting and produced a number of small hits, including Bill Coday's "Get Your Lies Straight." Still, LaSalle was working regular day jobs. When she was signed by the Memphis-based Westbound Records, she was working in a Chicago grocery store. She took vacation time to travel south and recorded what would be her breakout hit, "Trapped By a Thing Called Love." The song hit number one on the R&B chart, landed at number thirteen on the Billboard Hot 100, and eventually went gold. Four years later, 1975, LaSalle was signed to ABC Records. Divorced from Jones, she relocated to Memphis and in 1977 married a popular Jackson, Tennessee, disc jockey named James Wolfe. The couple would have two children.

With ABC, she cut three albums, including 1977's hit *The Bitch Is Bad*, but ABC was soon sold to MCA, and LaSalle's relationship with the label was rocky from the start. She left in 1981 and decided to open a nightclub with Wolfe in Jackson.

Denise LaSalle, a native of Leflore County, Mississippi, speaks with Sen. David Jordan (D-Greenwood), after being honored by the Senate at the Capitol in Jackson, Mississippi, on Feb. 18, 2009. (AP Images.)

Her career, however, was not quite over. In 1980 she'd written a song for Z. Z. Hill and the Malaco label that turned into a modest hit. Malaco wanted more and wanted her to sing again. LaSalle agreed and at last had found a home for her recordings. Indeed, she went on to record a dozen albums with Malaco, including *Rain and Fire* (1986), *Still Trapped* (1990), *Still Bad* (1995), *This Real Woman* (2000), and *Pay before You Pump* (2007), among many others. The 1997 album *Smoking in Bed* was a crossover success and brought LaSalle to the attention of a broader listenership. LaSalle and her husband continue to reside in Jackson, Tennessee, where LaSalle has owned and operated a number of businesses, including a wig shop. She has also sat on the local city council and made herself active in community events and causes, even as she continues to record and play the festival circuit around the United States.

FURTHER READING

Guralnick, Peter. *Sweet Soul Music: Rhythm and Blues and the Southern Dream of Freedom* (1986).

Shaw, Arnold. *Honkers and Shouters: The Golden Years of Rhythm and Blues* (1978).

JASON PHILIP MILLER

Lateef, Yusef (9 Oct. 1920–), saxophonist, oboist, flutist, composer, and educator, was born William Evans in Chattanooga, Tennessee, the son of William Huddleston, a factory worker, and Eva Spicer, a registered nurse; his family moved to Detroit when he was five. He began to play alto saxophone at eighteen; he switched to tenor the following year and studied with Teddy Buckner until 1944. During his years in Detroit he established lifelong friendships with many of the young jazz musicians who lived in the city in those years, notably MILT JACKSON, TOMMY FLANAGAN, BARRY HARRIS, PAUL CHAMBERS, DONALD BYRD, KENNY BURRELL, LUCKY THOMPSON, and THAD JONES and his brothers Elvin and Hank.

In 1946 Lateef played with the LUCKY MILLINDER orchestra, as well as with small groups led by the trumpeters HOT LIPS PAGE and ROY ELDRIDGE; from 1946 until early 1948 he toured with Ernie Fields. Lateef moved to Chicago that year and played in Gene Wright's band; in 1949 he joined DIZZY GILLESPIE's big band in California and stayed with the group for about ten months. He changed his name to Yusef Lateef following his conversion to Islam in the Ahmadiyya movement in 1948. In January 1950 he toured with the Teddy Hill band, returning to Detroit to care for his family during his wife Sadie's illness. Lateef had two children with Sadie, before marrying a woman named Tahira; nothing else is known about these relationships. He studied flute and composition at Wayne State University in the early 1950s.

From 1955 to 1958 Lateef led quintets in Detroit with the trombonist CURTIS FULLER, the bassist Wilbur Harden, the drummer Louis Hayes, the guitarist Kenny Burrell, and others at popular Detroit venues such as Klein's Show Bar. In 1955 Lateef was featured extensively as a recorded soloist for the first time on a Donald Byrd recording. He also continued to expand his musical interests, beginning his study of the oboe in 1958 with Ronald Odemark of the Detroit Symphony Orchestra. By this time Lateef's style and sound were clearly formulated. He possessed a strong, soulful tone and impressive technique, and he was already deeply interested in Middle Eastern music. In 1957 he made his first recording, for Savoy Records, *Prayer to the East*. Tunes such as "Blues in Space," incorporating Arabic inflections, contrasted with others like "Yusef's Mood," a powerful piece rooted in rhythm and blues.

On his next recording, *Jazz and the Sounds of Nature* (1957), Lateef explored Afro-Cuban aspects of jazz, and *Other Sounds*, also from 1957, saw him using Asian scales, microtones, and a variety of African instruments. The Asian influence emerged again that year on *The Sounds of Yusef*, where he used a Chinese gong and made other sound experiments later associated with the avant-garde—the use of 7-Up bottles, for instance, and the squeaky surface of balloons. In Lateef's hands these sounds were accessible and were played within the mainstream jazz tradition.

Lateef's next few albums, all for Riverside Records, clearly affirmed his commitment to tradition, producing both meditative and up-tempo music that was always beautiful and filled with interesting ideas—*Cry! Tender*, *The Three Faces of Yusef Lateef*, and particularly *The Centaur and the Phoenix*. Lateef's interest in Asian music and instrumentation reached fuller expression in 1961's *Eastern Sounds*, an album of Eastern modes

and intervals again situated in a jazz framework; "Blues from the Orient," for instance, is a wonderfully exotic, oboe-driven piece with strong support from his pianist during these years, Barry Harris.

Lateef's personal path had long been as idiosyncratic as his musical one. When he had moved to New York in 1960 he continued his music studies at the Manhattan School of Music. Also in 1960, Lateef played and recorded with CHARLES MINGUS and led his own groups in gigs at Birdland and the Village Gate. From 1962 to 1964 he was a member of CANNONBALL ADDERLEY's group, and also played with the guitarist GRANT GREEN. After he left Adderley he formed a new quintet that included the trumpeter Richard Williams and signed a contract with Impulse! Records, continuing to develop his exploratory style. Even the relatively traditional *Live at Pep's* (2 vols., 1964), an extended set of hard bop originals and jazz classics, mixed sax solos with instruments such as flute, oboe, shenai, and argol. *The Blue Yusef Lateef* (1968) added tamboura and koto to the mix and continued to mine Eastern scale modalities and polyphony. After his return from Africa, Lateef's music took a new turn. He had always been interested in more extended, nonjazz compositions. The Augusta Symphony Orchestra premiered his first orchestral composition, "Blues Suite" (or "Suite 16") in 1969, and the piece was later performed by the Detroit Symphony and recorded by the WDR Orchestra. He earned a B.A. in Music from the Manhattan School of Music in 1969 and an M.A. in Music Education in 1970. He taught in the theory department at Manhattan in 1971 and was an associate professor of music at the Borough of Manhattan Community College from 1972 to 1976. In 1974 the NDR Orchestra commissioned a tone poem, "Lalit," and also premiered and recorded Lateef's Symphony no. 1, *Tahira*. After recording the similar *Ten Years Hence* (1975), a live session from Keystone Korner in San Francisco, Lateef took a long break from performing to live for several years in Africa; his time there was marked by an appointment as a senior researcher at Ahmadubelaa University in Nigeria. Also in 1975 he was awarded a Ph.D. from the University of Massachusetts, Amherst, writing a dissertation titled "An Overview of Western and Islamic Education." After earning his doctorate he became a Five Colleges professor of music in Massachusetts.

Lateef did not abandon jazz performance entirely, but he continued to focus on what he termed "autophysiopsychic" music, or "that which comes from one's spiritual, physical and emotional self." In practice, this style seems to be an extension of his interest in world music, particularly in his collaborations with the composer and percussionist Adam Rudolph from the 1970s and beyond. Lateef founded his own record label, YAL, in the 1980s to give him the freedom to record what he began to refer to as "world" jazz. Many of these efforts also reflected his ongoing fascination with mysticism and were not always well received by jazz audiences, though they always reflected Lateef's own deep-felt musical and philosophical values as well as his undiluted technical skills. Lateef also wrote a concerto for piano and orchestra, and he was awarded a Grammy Award in 1987 for *Yusef Lateef's Little Symphony*, in which he performed all the parts. Lateef also released several more traditional jazz sessions on his label, including recordings with VON FREEMAN (1992), Rene McClean (1993), and Ricky Ford (1994). Some of the best recordings from this period include *The World at Peace* (1995), *Beyond the Sky* (2000), and a session with the group Eternal Wind called *Live at the Luckman Theater* (2001). This last session is a quintet that includes everything from flute and tenor saxophone to table, didjiridoo, gongs, and whistles. On these recordings Lateef's frequently incendiary playing shows his tenor credentials to have been undiminished by time.

Yusef Lateef made more than a hundred recordings in his career, for labels such as Savoy, Prestige, Contemporary, Impulse, Atlantic, and YAL. He performed at colleges and music festivals all over the world and published a novella, two collections of short stories, and several methods books. He was a pioneer in the use of Asian and African instruments and compositional forms in jazz and was a virtuoso performer on tenor saxophone, flute, and oboe and on other instruments that he introduced into jazz ensembles. Lateef's career remains, in the end, unique in jazz history. His playing and composing—from bebop to melodic and mystical world music—have significantly expanded the musical language of jazz. He retired from teaching in 2002 at the age of eighty-one.

FURTHER READING

Lateef, Yusef. *Something Else: Writings of the Yusef Lateef Quartet* (1973).
Feather, Leonard. *The Pleasures of Jazz* (1976).

RONALD P. DUFOUR

Latifah, Queen. *See* Queen Latifah.

Latimer, Lewis Howard (4 Sept. 1848–11 Dec. 1928), engineer and inventor, was born in Chelsea, Massachusetts, the son of George W. Latimer, a barber, and Rebecca Smith, both former slaves who escaped from Norfolk, Virginia, on 4 October 1842. When not attending Phillips Grammar School in Boston, Latimer spent much of his youth working in his father's barbershop, as a paperhanger, and selling the abolitionist newspaper the *Liberator*. Latimer's life changed drastically when his father mysteriously disappeared in 1858. His family, placed in dire financial straits, bound out Latimer and his brothers George and William as apprentices through the Farm School, a state institution in which children worked as unpaid laborers. Upon escaping from the exploitation of the Farm School system, Latimer and his brothers returned to Boston to reunite the family. During the next few years, Latimer was able to help support his family through various odd jobs and by working as an office boy for a Boston attorney, Isaac Wright.

Late in the Civil War, Latimer enlisted in the U.S. Navy. He was assigned to the *Ohio* as a landsman (low-level seaman) on 13 September 1864. He served until 3 July 1865, at which time he was honorably discharged from the *Massasoit*.

After returning from sea, Latimer began his technical career in Boston as an office boy for Crosby and Gould, patent solicitors. Through his assiduous efforts to teach himself the art of drafting, he rose to assistant draftsman and eventually to the position of chief draftsman in the mid-1870s. During this time he met Mary Wilson Lewis, a young woman from Fall River, Massachusetts. They were married in 1873 and had two children.

During his tenure at Crosby and Gould, Latimer began to invent. His first creation, a water closet for railway cars, co-invented with W. C. Brown, was granted Letters Patent No. 147,363 on 10 February 1874. However, drafting remained his primary vocation. One of the most noteworthy projects he undertook was drafting the diagrams for Alexander Graham Bell's telephone patent application, which was approved on 14 February 1876. In 1879 after managerial changes at Crosby and Gould, Latimer left their employment and Boston.

Latimer relocated to Bridgeport, Connecticut, initially working as a paperhanger. He eventually found part-time work making mechanical drawings at the Follandsbee Machine Shop. While drafting at the shop, he met Hiram Stevens Maxim, the chief engineer of the U.S. Electric Lighting Company. In February 1880, shortly after their first meeting, Maxim hired Latimer as his draftsman and private secretary. Latimer quickly moved up within the enterprise, and when the U.S. Electric Lighting Company moved to New York City, it placed him in charge of the production of carbon lamp filaments. Latimer was an integral member of the team that installed the company's first commercial incandescent lighting system, in the Equitable Building in New York City in the fall of 1880. He was on hand at most of the lighting installations that were undertaken by the company, and in 1881 he began to supervise many of their incandescent and arc lighting installations.

Latimer also invented products that were fundamental to the development of the company while directing new installations for the U.S. Electric Lighting Company. In October 1880 Maxim was granted a patent for a filament that was treated with hydrocarbon vapor to equalize and standardize its resistance, a process that allowed it to burn longer than the Edison lamp filament. Latimer began working on a process to manufacture this new carbon filament, and on 17 January 1882 he was granted a patent for a new process of manufacturing carbons. This invention produced a highly resistant filament and diminished the occurrence of broken and distorted filaments that had been commonplace with prior procedures. The filament was shaped into an *M*, which became a noted characteristic of the Maxim lamp. Latimer patented other inventions, including two for an electric lamp and a globe support for electric lamps. These further enhanced the Maxim lamp during 1881 and 1882.

In 1881 Latimer was dispatched to London and successfully established an incandescent lamp factory for the newly founded Maxim-Weston Electric Light Company. In 1882 Latimer left this company and began working for the Olmstead Electric Lighting Company of Brooklyn as superintendent of lamp construction; at this time he created the Latimer Lamp. He later continued his work at the Acme Electric Company of New York.

In 1883 Latimer began working at the Edison Electric Light Company. He became affiliated with the engineering department in 1885, and when the legal department was formed in 1889, Latimer's record of expert legal advice made him a requisite member of the new division. According to Latimer's biographical sketch of himself for the Edison Pioneers, he was transferred to the department "as [a] draughtsman inspector and expert witness as to facts in the early stages of the electric lighting business.... [He] traveled extensively, securing witnesses' affidavits, and early apparatus, and also testifying in a number of the basic patent cases to the advantage of his employers." His complete knowledge of electrical technology was exemplified in his work *Incandescent Electric Lighting, a Practical Description of the Edison System* (1890).

Latimer continued in the legal department when the Edison General Electric Company merged with the Thomson-Houston Company to form General Electric Company in 1892. His knowledge of the electric industry became invaluable when the General Electric Company and the Westinghouse Electric Company formed the Board of Patent Control in 1896. This board was responsible for managing the cross-licensing of patents between the two companies and prosecuting infringers. Latimer was appointed to the position of chief draftsman; however, his duties went far beyond drafting. He assisted inventors and others in developing their ideas. He used the vast body of knowledge he had acquired over the years in their efforts to eliminate outside competition. He remained at this position until the board was dissolved in 1911, after which Latimer put his talents to use for the law firm of Hammer and Schwartz as a patent consultant.

In 1918, when the Edison Pioneers, an organization founded to bring together for social and intellectual interaction men associated with Thomas Edison prior to 1885, was formed, Latimer was one of the twenty-nine original members. A stroke in 1924 forced him to retire from his formal position, and he spent much of his last four years engaged in two other activities that were most important in his life, art and poetry. He died at his home in Flushing, New York, which in 1995 was made a New York City landmark. Latimer was one of very few African Americans who contributed significantly to the development of American electrical technology.

FURTHER READING

Latimer's papers are in the Lewis Howard Latimer Collection at the Queens Borough Public Library in Queens, New York. Copies of many of his papers are located at the Schomburg Center for Research in Black Culture of the New York Public Library.

Norman, Winifred Latimer, and Lily Patterson. *Lewis Latimer: Scientist* (1994).

Schneider, Janet M., and Bayla Singer, eds. *Blueprint for Change: The Life and Times of Lewis H. Latimer* (1995).

Turner, Glennette Tilley. *Lewis Howard Latimer* (1991).

Obituary:*Electrical World* (22 Dec. 1928).

This entry is taken from the *American National Biography* and is published here with the permission of the American Council of Learned Societies.

RAYVON DAVID FOUCHÉ

Latta, Morgan London (1853–1924?), preacher, educator, and activist, was born in Fishdam, North Carolina, one of thirteen children born to slave parents whose names are now unknown but who were owned by the Cameron family. Latta's early years after the Civil War were scarred by the death of his father and oldest brother. By age thirteen he felt the pressure of having to provide food for his entire family and hired himself out as a laborer. Although he worked tirelessly, members of his family often went hungry. He found time to study and occasionally attend school when weather prevented him from working in the fields. As he developed academically, he also began giving speeches from a soapbox in public locations. He continued to take an active interest in politics but refused to run for elected office, believing "that there was nothing in politics for colored people" (Latta, 15).

After deciding against a political career, Latta pursued additional education. Both he and a cousin worked for several years, trying to save enough money to pay for college. They were unsuccessful; however, Latta was determined to attend school and entered Shaw University in Raleigh, North Carolina, which was the oldest historically black college in the South and was affiliated with the Baptist Church. He arrived on campus with one suit, ten cents, and no idea how he was going to pay the matriculation fee that would come due at the end of his first month of school. He approached several of his professors, two of whom offered him work that enabled him to remain in school. Latta felt the sting of poverty when his peers ridiculed him for his poor appearance at Sunday breakfast. This derision led him to perform chores for the cook in return for permission to eat breakfast separately from the other students.

After his first session Latta returned home and opened a summer school, which generated modest income. This income proved so modest that he could only afford to stay in school by opting out of the university meal plan. When intense hunger began to affect his ability to study, he met with the president about his predicament; he allowed Latta to stay on the condition that he teach after completing the session and use the money to repay the university.

Latta took and passed an examination for acquiring a teaching certificate. Better credentialed, he went home and taught at a district school and a night school for three and a half months, then returned to the university with over $100. With academic recognition and enough money to buy respectable clothes, Latta's popularity rose. He was now able to pay for his education. Over the next three years Latta continued at Shaw University as a student and assistant teacher. However, only one term from completing his degree, he became so overtaxed by his workload that his doctor recommended that he not return to school. Latta withdrew and never received his degree. After leaving the university Latta took a variety of posts as a schoolteacher over the next twenty years. He was never without work, having more job offers than time to teach. He worked in district schools, grade schools, and academies.

Undaunted in his passion to educate African Americans, he moved back to Raleigh, where he lived out of a hotel and began raising money for the establishment of Latta University, pursuing both small and large contributions. He insisted that his university would be nondenominational so that it could address the issues of all African Americans. The university's success, he reasoned, could then be credited solely to the achievements of its students and not to any particular religious ideology. Ironically, in the initial stages of his fund-raising for this nonsectarian institution, the local African American population opposed his efforts, but many prominent whites encouraged him. It took two years for the African American community to become convinced of Latta's good intentions and support his undertaking. In 1891 Latta purchased the land that would constitute Latta University. The school was officially founded in 1892 and formally incorporated in 1894. Remembering his early financial troubles, Latta established his university with the aim of admitting all who wanted to pursue an education regardless of their financial status. To facilitate his goal, he set up programs to allow up to one-third of the students to work their way through school without paying tuition. One such program included a marching band for orphan students that would perform in local streets and solicit donations. By 1900 Latta University was able to accommodate 1,400 pupils.

Even though Latta University became one of the largest institutions for African American learning in the South, its long-term viability remained constantly in doubt. Political friction kept it from gaining official accreditation, and the university could not function solely on the fees charged to its students. As a result Latta had to work relentlessly to raise funds to sustain the enterprise. He gave major speeches and raised money for his university in New York City (1892), Detroit (1898), Minnesota (1898), Pawtucket, Rhode Island (1899), Worcester, Massachusetts (1901), Pittsburgh, Pennsylvania (1902), and Danbury, Connecticut (1903). He also visited London, Paris, and several cities in Canada.

In the years that followed the founding of the school, Latta spent much of his time traveling and speaking about what he perceived to be the "Negro problem" (Latta, 37). He emphasized the importance of educating African Americans so that they could be successful and self-sufficient, understanding that the inferior status of his race resulted from the disadvantages imposed upon it. He took the position that there were three things that he endeavored to teach his race: trustworthiness, self-reliance, and punctuality. Latta was always on time and stated that "his heart bled" to know that many African Americans "were wanting in punctuality" (Latta, 79).

As a preacher and educator in the 1890s, Latta had gained both wide-ranging respect and notoriety, especially in his home state of North Carolina. As a result, he was called upon to exercise his influence to help further the political and economic well-being of impoverished African American communities. One notable canvassing campaign was in favor of the Durham and Lynchburg Railroad, which required that two-thirds of registered voters cast ballots before the state could claim the land upon which the railroad was to be built. Initially the African American population of North Carolina opposed the railroad because it was a project favored by white businessmen. However, Latta spearheaded a canvassing campaign that focused on the railroad's economic benefits, with the result that it was approved and built. Latta also became involved in national political issues, such as Prohibition. He canvassed his home state voicing his opposition to Prohibition because of his realistic assessment that abstinence and not legislation was the only way to deal effectively with the nation's alcohol problems.

While the exact year of Latta University's closing and the Reverend Morgan London Latta's death are unknown, it is likely that both these events took place before 1924. In the late twentieth century the importance of Latta and his university was recognized by designating the Latta House—the last remaining building of the university—as a Raleigh Historic Landmark and listing it on the National Register of Historic Places. The house served as a base for community outreach and cultural education until it was destroyed by fire in January 2007.

FURTHER READING

Latta, Morgan London. *The History of My Life and Work* (1903).

JACOB ANDREW FREEDMAN

Lattimore, Benjamin (1761?–28 Apr. 1838), businessman, American Revolutionary War soldier, community leader, property owner, and freedman, was born free in Westersfield, Connecticut, to parents who have not yet been identified. Physical descriptions in early documents suggest that Lattimore (sometimes spelled Latimer) was of mixed racial origin. His family worked on a farm in Lower Ulster County, New York, and ran a ferry service. Benjamin Lattimore was one of only a handful of African American heads of households identified by name as a free person of color during the Colonial era.

The contributions of the black community of early Albany are often forgotten in the context of American history. Many, such as Lattimore, made valuable contributions to the military, to community organizations, and to commerce. In 1776, at the age of fifteen, Benjamin Lattimore joined New York's Third Regiment of the Continental army. The British captured him and forced him into servitude, but he was later recaptured by American troops and released to go home. After the Revolution, he eventually relocated to Albany, New York, where he earned a living as a cart man, cargo handler, and garbage hauler. Lattimore, like other African American heads of households, worked as laborers or in some aspect of the transportation industry. Lattimore held a waggoner's and a cart man's license to transport goods and cargo via wheelbarrow from the docks along the Hudson River to businesses up and down the busy streets of Albany. He provided his clients with this valuable service for the rest of his life.

According to the First U.S. Government Census in 1790, the population of Albany, chartered in 1686, had grown to a population of 3,498. Located along the Hudson River, Albany was a bustling community active in trade and transportation and its population would surge in the next few decades.

The U.S. Census identified 572 of this population as slaves, most of whom were persons of African ancestry; however, among the persons of color were twenty-six free African Americans residing within a total of seven separate Albany households. Evidence in other records—such as civil, business, governmental, church records, and directories—suggests increased numbers of persons of color, especially during the early 1800s. In 1815 Joseph Fry, a New York businessman, compiled a city directory, whose most invaluable feature was the listing of Albany residents that included their first and last names, street addresses, and occupations of some of Albany's African American residents, including Benjamin Lattimore. He became one of those prominent New York middle-class founding fathers who played an integral part in the building of the economy, social structure, and education system of colonial black Albany. Fry's directory reveals that Lattimore, a free black man, owned a home at 9 Plain Street. Lattimore purchased additional parcels of land at Hudson Street and South Pearl Street.

By the early 1800s, Lattimore had become a well-respected member of the local black community. Early documents show that he signed his name with an X, since he never had formal schooling and was not able to read or write. Despite all this, Lattimore saw the value in education and was instrumental in establishing the first Albany school for black children. In 1816 Lattimore successfully petitioned the New York State legislature to establish the Albany School for Educating People of Color. The enrollment reached an impressive number for a community of its size. The school building was built on Lattimore's own property located on South End Street. Unfortunately, owing to the high costs of maintaining the building and the mortgage, the school succumbed to financial difficulties. The Lancaster Society allowed the school to remain open by making provisions for the pupils to meet in the basement of the First African Baptist Church building. The school thrived and offered children of color the opportunity to receive an education formerly reserved for whites.

Benjamin Lattimore and his common law wife, Dina, became members of the Albany First Presbyterian Church, which sanctioned their marriage in 1804. Dina's maiden name and parentage is yet unknown, but she was employed as a maidservant for Dr. Wilhemus Manicus, a distinguished local physician. She and Benjamin had several children, including two sons, Benjamin Jr. and William, and two daughters, Betsy and Mary. Their first son was born eleven years before his parents were married. Benjamin Jr. also made a living as a cart man and continued his father's endeavors in the community and in the church. Benjamin Lattimore eventually changed church memberships to join the Albany African Methodist Episcopal Church. He was also a member of the Albany Temperance Society.

A Revolutionary War veteran, Benjamin Lattimore claimed his pension in 1834 and his will distributed his estate among his three living children. Lattimore died at the age of seventy-eight and was originally buried at the African Methodist Episcopal (AME) Church cemetery, but his remains were later relocated to Albany Rural Cemetery.

FURTHER READING

Bielinski, Stefan. "Benjamin Lattimore," *Colonial Social History Research Project*, New York State Museum, State Education Dept. Available at http://www.nysm.nysed.gov/albany/bios/l/blattimore8200.html.

Bielinski, Stefan. "The Jacksons, Lattimores, and Schuylers: First African American Families of Early Albany," *New York History* (Oct. 1996).

Hughes, Marian I.. *Refusing Ignorance: The Struggle to Educate Black Children in Albany, New York, 1816–1873* (1998).

MELANIE THOMAS

Lattimore, John Aaron Cicero (23 June 1876?–31 Dec. 1959), physician and civil rights activist, was born near Shelby, Cleveland County, North Carolina, the son of John Carpenter Lattimore and Marcella Hambrick, former slaves and farmers. Lattimore graduated from Bennett College in Greensboro, North Carolina, with an AB in 1897. He then attended Meharry Medical College in Nashville, Tennessee, receiving his M.D. in 1901. With a fellow classmate, H. B. Beck, as a partner, he began the general practice of medicine in Louisville, Kentucky. After considerable effort, his practice grew. In 1928 he married Naomi Anthony of Louisville; they had no children.

To provide better care for his patients, Lattimore established the Lattimore Clinic in Louisville. This effort marked the beginning of a professional lifetime devoted to improving medical care for the black community and presaged similar efforts for improving public health measures, hospital care, and educational opportunities for blacks. Lattimore served in the Louisville Health Department from 1928 to 1946. His clinical skills were recognized by his election to the John Andrew Clinical Society of Tuskegee Institute.

During the flood of 1937 Lattimore was appointed to the Mayor's Flood Relief Committee. This experience in administering relief and medical care to large numbers of displaced people led to his appointment in 1937 to the advisory committee of the Central District of the American Red Cross. Lattimore campaigned for the improvement and integration of hospital facilities in the state mental hospitals, resulting in the construction of a new building (begun in 1941) at the Central State Hospital near Louisville. The governor of Kentucky later recognized him for his efforts to obtain the new facilities and to ensure that they were integrated.

By having Kentucky's Day Law amended, Lattimore effected the first step toward obtaining opportunities for professional education for blacks. This law had prohibited blacks and whites from attending school in the same classrooms, but the amendment permitted the integration of professional schools in Kentucky. Lattimore later served on the Governor's Commission on Adult Education.

Through a lifetime of involvement in his profession, the African Methodist Episcopal Church, and several fraternal organizations, Lattimore became identified as a pillar of the black community. He helped organize the Louisville chapter of the NAACP and served on its board until his death. Before 1920 he organized, with others, the Louisville Interracial Group; in 1921 he founded a local Big Brother movement from which arose the local Urban League (1915–1959), a system for furthering race relations in Louisville. He served for the remainder of his life in this interracial group.

Although he never campaigned for or held an elective office, Lattimore did direct a local political maneuver. Initially a Republican, in 1921 he organized a local third party, the Lincoln Party, which assisted black residents in changing their registered political preference to Democrat. It was with some unpleasantness that Lattimore became one of the first black people in Louisville to register as a Democrat.

Lattimore served the black medical profession as an early member, president, and vice president of the Blue Grass Medical Association, which was established in 1899. He helped organize the Falls City Medical Society, serving as its president and vice president. He also became the president, from 1947 to 1948, of the National Medical Association.

Lattimore's many contributions to Louisville and particularly to its black community were recognized over the years. He received the Alpha Phi Alpha Fraternity Award for outstanding leadership (1946 and 1959), he was named Man of the Year by the *Louisville Defender* (1956), the Urban League Guild gave him its Honors Award for initiating health campaigns in Kentucky, and he received an NAACP trophy for outstanding leadership in race relations in Kentucky (1959).

Always modest and unpretentious, Lattimore attributed his numerous contributions to medicine, public health, society, and the civil rights movement to the efforts of others. In an article about him in the *Louisville Courier-Journal* (23 Sept. 1951) in which his accomplishments were summarized, he credited his success to "my confrères, among them the leading white practitioners in the city, without their freely given cooperation in even the tiniest professional matters, I could not have got anywhere." He died in Louisville.

FURTHER READING
Lattimore's papers are at the Ekstrom Library, University of Louisville, Belknap Campus, Louisville, Kentucky.
Obituaries: *Louisville Defender*, 31 Dec. 1959; *Louisville Courier-Journal*, 1 Jan. 1960; *Journal of the National Medical Association* 53 (Sept. 1961).
This entry is taken from the *American National Biography* and is published here with the permission of the American Council of Learned Societies.

EUGENE H. CONNER

Laurie, Eunice Verdell Rivers (12 Nov. 1899–28 Aug. 1986), public health nurse, nursing instructor, and the "scientific assistant" for forty years (1932–1972) for the infamous Tuskegee Syphilis Study, was born in Early County, Georgia, the oldest of three children of Albert Rivers, a sawmill worker and farmer, and Henrietta Rivers. In the small and rural southwest Georgia county where Eunice Rivers was raised, her father did what he could to protect and promote his children's way in the world, especially after the death of his wife when Eunice was fifteen. One night, falsely assuming that Albert Rivers had been involved in aiding another black man's flight from the legal authorities, armed members of the Ku Klux Klan fired upon Rivers's house. Albert Rivers shot back. Less dramatically, though no less importantly, Rivers took his daughter from school to school in various Georgia towns so that the most qualified black teachers he could find could teach her. To reach this goal, one year before her expected graduation from high school he pulled her out of a mission school and sent her across the state border to the Tuskegee Institute in Alabama.

As with many young women who came to Tuskegee, Rivers was at first put into a handicrafts program. Under her father's pressure she switched to nursing, although she claimed later that it was her decision. Public health and work in the community captured her imagination, although jobs for black women in this field were extremely limited. Upon her graduation in 1922 she stayed on in Tuskegee, finding work at first as a private nurse. She then became part of the team on Tuskegee's Moveable School, a truck that took an agricultural agent, a home demonstration agent, and a nurse into the countryside to teach the rural poor new farming techniques and hygiene. Rivers focused on the needs of the women and children, explaining basic health principles for those who had little money and means for sanitation. Her growing knowledge and skill with the rural population brought her to the attention of the state's public health nursing department. Hired as one of only four black public health nurses in Alabama, she worked to upgrade the skills of midwives and began the process of collecting birth records for the state's African American population. These years in the 1920s, spent deep in rural sections of Alabama, taught Rivers to understand and respect the needs of those whose lives kept them uneducated and bound to the land—away from even such centers as Tuskegee.

When the Depression deepened in 1931 the state was unable to keep Rivers in these positions. Returning to Tuskegee Institute, she became a night supervisor at the John A. Andrew Hospital on the Institute's campus. The position never gave her much satisfaction, and she considered leaving the South for another hospital position in New York. But in 1932 DR. EUGENE H. DIBBLE JR., then the medical director of the Tuskegee hospital, who knew of her work on the Moveable School and in the community, had another idea. He asked if she would consider becoming the scientific assistant (as the position was labeled) to the U.S. Public Health Service (PHS) in what would become known as the Tuskegee Study of Untreated Syphilis in the Male Negro.

The study sought to follow 399 black men who were in the late stage of syphilis (and 201 who served as "controls" and did not have the disease) to see how the disease would develop if left untreated. However, the men believed that the aspirins, tonics, and vitamins Rivers was delivering, as well as the spinal taps and exams the doctors provided, were treatments for what was often colloquially referred to as "bad blood."

From 1932 until 1972, when the study was finally closed down in a hail of negative publicity, Rivers was a constant presence in the men's lives. She was responsible for helping to find the subjects, driving them into Tuskegee for the periodic exams, and encouraging them to stay with the study year after year. She sought permission from their families to allow for autopsies by explaining that the PHS was offering burial insurance. She sought to protect the men, whom she saw as her patients, from the arrogance and condescension of the visiting PHS doctors. When there was not enough work on the study to keep her busy, Rivers taught nursing at Tuskegee Institute, worked on a venereal disease control project out of the local health department, and became a stalwart in her local church. In 1952 she married Julius Laurie, a son of one of the participants in the control project at Tuskegee. But for most of her public life she was known as Nurse Rivers.

A monograph published in 1953 entitled "Twenty Years of Follow Up Experience in a Long Range Medical Study" (Rivers et al.), explained what she did to keep the men in the study by her diligent public health work and caring. Although some see her caught up in the logic of the study and as a nurse of her time who was expected just to follow orders, others have argued that her caring gave her a complex way to measure what she could provide against a backdrop of intense poverty and little health care. It is also possible that behind the scenes she was finding ways to get some of the men to treatment, although the evidence for this is still controversial.

In 1958 she was awarded the Oveta Culp Hobby Award from the federal government's then Department of Health, Education, and Welfare for her "notable service" to the project. In the context of the furor that followed the national publicity on the study, Rivers mainly kept her own counsel. Once the story of the study broke in the press and the civil rights attorney FRED D. GRAY sued the federal government and state officials, Rivers retreated into silence. Even when a federal investigation was ordered and Senator Ted Kennedy held hearings that brought Gray and four of the subjects to Washington, Rivers gave no public testimony. Several short oral histories she did with friends in later years merely hint at her motivations and knowledge. Her understanding of what she did was the subject of furious debate in historical monographs, plays, poems, films, historical memory, and classrooms, where the PHS study is used as an example of the worst in American medical research, arrogance, racism, and government deceit. Rivers had little training in venereal disease, but she studied the issues and followed what Dibble and the PHS doctors told her to do.

With little historical record to explain her actions, and because she was the project's only visible woman and African American nurse, commentators have offered many different interpretations of Rivers. Some seek to protect her from responsibility, while others see her as race traitor willing to sell out her own people to keep her job. She was the basis for the main character of David Feldshuh's play and subsequent made-for-television movie *Miss Evers' Boys* (HBO 1997), which suggests that her moral dilemmas deepened over the years of the study. Still others expect her to have stopped the study, even though it took years, national publicity, a federal investigation, and a lawsuit for that to happen. The words of the study survivor Herman Shaw—"she always loved us"—perhaps best sum up the compassion she offered the men. Following her death in August 1986 Eunice Rivers Laurie was buried in Tuskegee, in a graveyard where some of the men she cared for are interred.

FURTHER READING

Gray, Fred D.. *The Tuskegee Syphilis Study: The Real Story and Beyond* (1998).

Jones, James H.. *Bad Blood: The Tuskegee Syphilis Experiment* (1993).

Reverby, Susan, ed. "Rethinking the Role of Nurse Rivers," in *Tuskegee's Truths: Rethinking the Tuskegee Syphilis Study* (2000).

Rivers, Eunice, et al. "Twenty Years of Follow Up Experience in a Long Range Medical Study," *Public Health Reports* 68 (Apr. 1953); reprinted in *Tuskegee's Truths* (2000).

SUSAN M. REVERBY

Lautier, Louis Robert (1897–6 May 1962), journalist, was born in New Iberia, Louisiana, the son of Harry and Ida Lautier (occupations unknown). He grew up Catholic in New Orleans, attended Straight College in New Orleans (which later merged to create Dillard University), and received an AB from Morris Brown College in Atlanta. He later studied law at Howard University. In Washington he married Constance Brawner, a teacher and social worker. They had one daughter, Louise.

As an aide to PERRY W. HOWARD, a politically influential Republican National Committee member from Mississippi and special assistant to the attorney general during the Harding and Coolidge administrations, Lautier became a legal stenographer in the Department of Justice. During World War II he served in the War Department as administrative assistant to WILLIAM H. HASTIE, dealing with matters affecting African American personnel in the army. That position ended with Hastie's resignation in 1943 in protest over biased policies.

During his time as a government employee, Lautier reported on a freelance basis for the black press on a wide variety of subjects, but he focused in particular on the injustices of racial segregation in the capital and the federal government. In 1945 Lautier became head of the Washington bureau of the National Negro Publishers Association (NNPA), holding that post until 1962. Founded by the *Chicago Defender*'s publisher John Sengstacke as a rival news service to the Associated Negro Press, the NNPA had opened a Washington bureau in 1942, and two years later its first Washington correspondent, Harry S. McAlpin, was accredited to attend President Franklin D. Roosevelt's press conferences. The NNPA publishers soon grew dissatisfied with McAlpin's work, however, and hired Lautier to replace him.

Lautier obtained a White House press pass and became the first African American member of the White House Correspondents Association. He also applied to the congressional press galleries, where no African Americans had sat since FREDERICK DOUGLASS and his sons had reported during Reconstruction. In the 1930s the New Deal began generating intense interest in the news from Washington, and black reporters had been applying unsuccessfully for congressional press passes. Press gallery rules required that reporters file stories by telegraph to daily newspapers. So long as the black press consisted entirely of weekly papers, and the general press did not hire African Americans, the rule effectively eliminated all black reporters from the press gallery. Lautier applied in January 1947, when the Senate was debating whether to seat Mississippi senator Theodore Bilbo, a notorious racist. This issue held great interest for his readers, but Lautier had to stand in a long line to get a seat in the crowded public galleries, where he could not take notes. He applied for a press pass, pointing out that the NNPA provided news to the only black daily paper at the time, the *Atlanta Daily World*.

Reporters in the press gallery elected a standing committee of correspondents to judge applicants for admission. The standing committee rejected Lautier on the grounds that the greatest share of his reporting went to weekly papers. He appealed to the Senate Rules and Administration Committee, then chaired by the Illinois Republican senator C. Wayland Brooks—who was seeking the *Chicago Defender*'s endorsement for his race for reelection. After conducting a hearing on the issue, the Rules Committee voted unanimously that Lautier should be accredited to the Senate press gallery. The standing committee complied and also agreed to admit Lautier to the press gallery in the House of Representatives, over which it also had jurisdiction. Since there were at that time no black senators, Lautier chose to make the House press gallery his regular base of operations. From there he covered Congress and the rest of the government. (At the time that Lautier became the first African American member of the newspaper press gallery, the periodical press gallery admitted Percival S. Prattis as Washington correspondent for *Our World*, an African American magazine published in New York.)

Lautier further applied for membership in the all-white National Press Club. "I'm not concerned with carrying on a crusade," he was quoted as saying. "My only reason for asking membership is to have access to the noted speakers at the club" (*Washington Post*, 8 May 1962). The columnists Drew Pearson and Marquis Childs sponsored his application, citing him as a "highly intelligent, respected journalist who will make a good member of the club." In February 1955 the National Press Club held an unprecedented referendum of its entire membership, who voted to admit Lautier by a margin of 377 to 281. A soft-spoken, unassuming man with a wry sense of humor, Lautier was well liked in the Washington press corps. "We looked on Mr. Lautier as an authority on the Negro," commented the *Washington Post* correspondent Edward T. Folliard in an obituary of Lautier, "and we would go to him for help just like you would talk to a science reporter on missiles." Other reporters also appreciated Lautier's stenographic skills, and after press conferences they would often check the accuracy of their notes against his.

The NNPA counted on Lautier's Washington reporting to prove the value of its news service to member papers, but it regretted that his single-handed effort could not generate a greater volume and a variety of copy to out-produce the Associated Negro Press. The ANP's Washington correspondent, ALICE DUNNIGAN, proved a formidable competitor, and she clashed frequently with Lautier. During the Eisenhower administration Lautier, a registered Republican, publicly criticized Dunnigan and ETHEL PAYNE, the two black women members of the White House press corps, for repeatedly pressing President Dwight D. Eisenhower on civil rights. Eisenhower began to ignore both women and call instead on Lautier, who asked less confrontational questions. Ethel Payne scorned the way that Lautier curried favor with the White House, although she credited his more discreet style for having cleared the way for the racial integration of the Washington press corps.

Lautier traveled to Africa in 1957 as part of Vice President Richard Nixon's press contingent. In 1962 he retired from the NNPA and became a special assistant to the chairman of the Republican National Committee. In that post he wrote a column, "Looking at the Record," that the party distributed to the black press. He died in Washington of a heart attack at the age of sixty-five.

FURTHER READING

Ritchie, Donald A.. *Reporting the News from Washington: The History of the Washington Press Corps* (2005).

Washburn, Patrick S. A.. *Question of Sedition: The Federal Government's Investigation of the Black Press during World War II* (1986).

Waters, Enoch P.. *American Diary: A Personal History of the Black Press* (1987).

Obituaries: *Washington Star*, 7 May 1962; *Washington Post*, 8 May 1962; *New York Times*, 9 May 1962.

DONALD A. RITCHIE

Laveaux, Marie (10 Sept. 1801–16 June 1881), voodoo queen, was born in New Orleans, Louisiana, the daughter of Charles Laveaux, a freeman of color who owned a grocery store in that city, and Marguerite D'Arcantel, a freewoman of color about whom very little is known, although it is rumored that she was a spiritualist or root doctor. Certain sources erroneously claim that Charles Laveaux was a prominent white planter and politician. He was not, but he was probably the illegitimate son of Don Carlos (or Charles) Trudeau, a high-ranking official in Spanish-controlled Louisiana and the first president of the New Orleans City Council when the United States purchased Louisiana in 1803. The historical record, which in Marie Laveaux's case is exceptionally imprecise, provides several spellings of her surname, often leaving out the "x," but most archival records suggest that Charles Laveaux used that version of his name and that this spelling was also used in records related to his illiterate daughter.

There is considerable doubt, too, about Laveaux's date of birth. Her 1881 death certificate claims that she died at the age of ninety-eight, suggesting that she was born in 1783, although most accounts give her birth date as 1794. In the late 1990s, however, a researcher found birth and baptismal records of a "mulatto girl child" named Marie Laveaux dated September 1801. This date coincides with information on her marriage certificate, which states that Laveaux was a minor, a month shy of eighteen, when she wed Jacques Paris, a Haitian-born carpenter, in August 1819.

Laveaux's marriage to Paris was short-lived. After her husband's death in the early 1820s, she became known as "the widow Paris" and began a thirty-year relationship with Captain Jean Louis Christophe Duminy de Glapion, a veteran of the War of 1812 usually referred to as a "quadroon" from Santo Domingo. It has often been claimed that the couple had fifteen children, but New Orleans church records suggest that they had only two sons, François and Archange, who died in childhood, and three daughters, Marie Héloïse, Marie Louise, and Marie Phélomise. In addition, Marie Laveaux had a half sister, also named Marie Laveaux, born to Charles Laveaux and his wife, a wealthy member of Louisiana's free colored Creole elite. Many of the legends about the power, wealth, and infamy of Marie Laveaux have arisen because of confusion in oral and literary sources about the women who shared her name, particularly her daughter Marie Héloïse, who was also a voodoo priestess.

In the 1830s Marie Laveaux emerged as a prominent spiritualist and healer at her home; at African American ritual dances on Sundays in New Orleans's Congo Square; and at major religious festivals, such as the midsummer St. John's Eve celebrations on the banks of Lake Pontchartrain, which attracted people of all colors. Laveaux presided over ceremonies that blended elements of Roman Catholicism, such as the invocation of saints and the use of incense and holy water, and traditional African religious dances and rituals involving drumming, chanting, animal sacrifices, and worship of Damballa or Zombi, a snake god. The scanty record of these rituals suggests that Laveaux would blow alcohol on the faces of participants as a blessing and would also wrap a snake around their (usually naked) bodies as a symbol of her control over them. Later accounts of these ceremonies, both in oral tradition and in Robert Tallant's *Voodoo in New Orleans* (1946), highlight the sexual abandon of the participants.

Laveaux's legendary power came less from these infrequent ceremonies, however, than from her skills as an everyday spiritualist who used her charms to bewitch a highly superstitious public. Not unlike J. Edgar Hoover a century later, Laveaux understood that knowledge, particularly knowledge of private indiscretions, equals power. As a hairdresser to prominent women in New Orleans, she had access to gossip about the city's wealthiest and most powerful citizens. She also gained information about the New Orleans elite from African American servants and slaves who, in return for Mamzelle Marie's spiritual protection, brought Laveaux news about their masters' and mistresses' financial, political, and sexual affairs. Laveaux used that intelligence to make herself indispensable to women seeking information on their husbands' philandering, to politicians keen to learn of their opponents' foibles, and to businessmen who relied on her charms and amulets when the hidden hand of the market failed to work its own particular grisgris. Such information—and the spells and potions to rid her clients of what ailed them—provided Laveaux with a steady income, though not the great riches that many of her followers and detractors claimed. It also ensured friends for her in the highest places in Louisiana society, which may explain why, unlike other *voodooiennes*, she was never arrested. Her seeming influence over whites strengthened her influence over black Louisianans and entrenched her position in African American folklore as one of the most powerful women of her time.

Depending on the source, white accounts of Laveaux's mid-nineteenth-century heyday depict her as either saint or whore. After her death in 1881, white Catholics in New Orleans eulogized her saintly role in helping victims of yellow fever and cholera in the 1850s and her tireless work to give comfort to the city's death-row convicts. White Catholics downplayed any African elements in Laveaux's religion and also praised her alleged devotion to the Confederate cause. At the same time, however, an obituary in the white Protestant-controlled *New Orleans Democrat* dismissed these claims for Laveaux's piety, describing her as "the prime mover and soul of the indecent orgies of the ignoble Voudous" (Fandrich, 267). Other newspaper accounts and later folklore suggested that Laveaux had used her Lake Pontchartrain home, the Maison Blanche, as a brothel that served wealthy white men seeking glamorous "high yellow" prostitutes, although it is possible that these accounts confused the elder Marie with her daughter, Marie Héloïse, who reputedly kept a bawdy house.

In death Laveaux remained almost as influential as in life, at least to the thousands who seek out her tomb every year in New Orleans, which, some claim, is the second most visited grave in the United States after Elvis Presley's. Like Presley's followers, Laveaux's pilgrims leave candles, money, and other objects in hope that her spirit will grant their wishes. After the 11 September 2001 terrorist attacks in New York City, Washington, D.C., and Pennsylvania, some disciples even left notes asking that Laveaux administer punishment to the alleged perpetrator, Osama Bin Laden.

FURTHER READING

Fandrich, Ina. "The Mysterious Voodoo Queen Marie Laveaux: A Study of Power and Female Leadership in Nineteenth-Century New Orleans," Ph.D. diss., Temple University (1994).

Raboteau, Albert. *Slave Religion* (1978).

Tallant, Robert. *Voodoo in New Orleans* (1946).

Obituary: *New Orleans Daily Picayune*, 17 June 1881.

STEVEN J. NIVEN

Lawless, Theodore Kenneth (6 Dec. 1892–1 May 1971), medical pioneer and philanthropist who developed groundbreaking treatments for leprosy, syphilis, and cancer, was the eldest son of Dr. Alfred Lawless Jr. and Harriet Dunn. He was born on a farm in Thibodeaux, Louisiana, and with his siblings, Oscar and Helen, grew up in New Orleans.

His interest in medicine began when he was young, working as an assistant to a veterinarian. Lawless's father was a minister and a tireless advocate of civil rights and educational opportunity for African Americans. The Memorial Chapel at Dillard University and Lawless High School in New Orleans were both named in his honor. With such strong influence, it is little wonder that his eldest son, Theodore (known to friends and family as "T.K."), would excel beyond all expectations. He earned a B.A. from Talladega College in 1914 and an M.D. (1919) and M.A. (1920) from Northwestern University, after studying for two years at the University of Kansas. He undertook extensive graduate studies at the Vanderbilt Clinic of Columbia University (1920), Massachusetts General Hospital

and Harvard University Medical School (1921), and worked and studied abroad at hospitals in Paris, France (1921–1922), Frieburg, Germany (1922–1923), and Vienna, Austria (1923–1924).

His medical career revolved around his passion for the study of diseases that affected the skin and had no known cures. After receiving his medical degree in 1919, Lawless joined the Northwestern University medical school staff. From 1919 to 1920 he helped establish their medical laboratories and served as director. From 1928 to 1936 he was an Elizabeth J. Ward Research Fellow. From 1924 to 1941 he was a professor of dermatology and syphilology. In spite of his credentials, international reputation, and acceptance by a multiracial community of patients and peers, the issue of race plagued him throughout his career. He was undoubtedly an exceptional student and physician; however, even his alma mater, Northwestern University, discriminated against him. It denied him students to teach and only allowed him to reach the level of assistant to the chief of dermatology. He left the university in 1941 when the institution failed to award him a promotion.

While working at Northwestern in Evanston, Lawless established residence in nearby Chicago. His private practice, originally established in 1924, moved to the predominantly black Bronzeville community on the Southside in 1937. His choice of a new location came after being repeatedly denied office space downtown and frequently confronted with racial prejudice. The practice continued until 1968 and was one of the largest and most successful in the city. Patients came from all over the United States and represented every social, racial, and economic category. His fees were reasonable for the time, and there was no discrimination against people who could not afford to pay. Lawless often worked day and night and provided services at no charge, particularly to U.S. servicemen. It was not uncommon for his waiting room to be packed and for there to be long lines stretching down the block of people seeking treatment.

In 1936 Lawless devised a treatment known as electropyrexia, an electrically induced fever that was useful for treatment in the early stages of syphilis. He created treatments for people whose skin had been damaged by arsenic-based preparations that were standard treatments for syphilis during the 1920s. He also studied and treated leprosy, sporotrichosis (a fungal infection of the skin that primarily affects people who work with soil, such as farmers and gardeners), tinea sycosis (a parasitic lip infection), and rabbit fever (tularemia), a bacterial infection that thrives in contaminated water and is transmitted by rodents. He also pioneered the use of radium as a treatment for cancer.

Lawless was a senior attending physician at the historic Provident Hospital, which was established in 1891 by the African American physician DANIEL HALE WILLIAMS, the first doctor in the world to successfully undertake open-heart surgery. In 1928 Lawless served as an associate examiner of the National Board of Medical Examiners and on the Chicago Board of Health. Continuing his relationships overseas, he worked abroad as a hospital consultant in Switzerland.

Besides being a brilliant doctor, Lawless was a successful businessman, involving himself in numerous businesses in the banking, insurance, and real estate sectors. He served as director of Marina City Bank and the Supreme Life Insurance Company, an enterprise founded by the publishing magnate John H. Johnson. He was an associate founder, charter member, and president (1951–1953) of Service Federal Savings and Loan Association, which was heavily involved in financing black businesses. He was also president (1945–1953) of the 4213 South Michigan Corporation, a real estate company that promoted low-cost housing on Chicago's South Side.

Lawless was a generous contributor to countless organizations and educational and medical institutions. He sponsored scholarships for African and African American students to study medicine in American schools and served on the trustee boards of Talladega College, Fisk University, Roosevelt College, Dillard University, Huston-Tillotson College, and Rocky Mountain College. He also had a special affinity for Jewish causes because of the support he had received at several stages of his career from Jewish colleagues. He was a board member of B'nai B'rith, donated more than $150,000 to the construction of a dermatology wing at Beilinson Hospital in Tel Aviv, and helped establish a science camp in Rehovoth, Israel.

Lawless's research was routinely featured in professional journals including the *Journal of the American Medical Association*, the *American Journal of Dermatology*, and the *Journal of Laboratory and Clinical Medicine*. Several institutions awarded him honorary degrees, including Talladega College, Howard University, Bethune-Cookman College, Virginia State University, and the University of Illinois. In 1954 he received the NAACP's highest honor—the Spingarn Medal. He died in Chicago after a long illness with no heirs and having never married. His estate, valued in excess of one million dollars, enabled generous gifts to Dillard University in New Orleans and Bielinson Hospital in Israel.

FURTHER READING
Adams, Russell L.. *Great Negroes Past and Present* (1993).
Winslow, Eugene, ed. *Black Americans in Science and Engineering: Contributors of Past and Present* (1992).
                              SHARON LESLIE MORGAN

Lawrence, Jacob Armstead (7 Sept. 1917–9 June 2000), artist and teacher, was born in Atlantic City, New Jersey, to migrant parents. His father, Jacob Lawrence, a railroad cook, was from South Carolina, and his mother, Rose Lee Armstead, hailed from Virginia. In 1919 the family moved to Pennsylvania, where Jacob's sister, Geraldine, was born. Five years later Jacob's brother, William, was born, and his parents separated. Jacob moved with his mother, sister, and brother to a Manhattan apartment on West 143d Street in 1930. Upon his arrival in Harlem, the teenage Lawrence began taking neighborhood art classes. His favorite teacher was the painter CHARLES ALSTON, who taught at the Harlem Art Workshop. This workshop, sponsored by the Works Progress Administration, was first housed in the central Harlem branch of the New York Public Library before relocating to Alston's studio at 306 West 141st Street. Many community cultural workers had studios in this spacious building. Affectionately called "306," Alston's studio in particular was a vital gathering place for creative people. Lawrence met ALAIN LOCKE, AARON DOUGLAS, LANGSTON HUGHES, CLAUDE MCKAY, RICHARD WRIGHT, and RALPH ELLISON at his mentor's lively studio.

In 1935, at age eighteen, Lawrence started painting scenes of Harlem using poster paint and brown paper. Initially chosen for their accessibility and low cost, these humble materials would remain central to the artist's work. The next year Lawrence began what would become his ritual of doing background research for his art projects at the 135th Street branch of the New York Public Library (now the Schomburg Center for Research in Black Culture). Inspired after seeing the play *Haiti* (by the white writer William DuBois) at Harlem's Lafayette Theatre in 1936, he began researching the Haitian Revolution (1791–1804). This eye-opening research culminated in a powerful series of forty-one paintings titled *The Life of Toussaint L'Ouverture*. Completed in 1938, this

Jacob Armstead Lawrence on 31 July 1941. (Library of Congress. Photograph by Carl Van Vechten.)

series dramatically visualized the life of the formerly enslaved man who led the Haitian struggle for independence from France and the creation of the world's first black republic. These paintings also signaled paths the artist would continue to explore in his work, namely, figurative expressionism, history painting, sequential narration, and prose captions. Moreover, the ambitious cycle revealed Lawrence's deep interest in heroism and struggles for freedom.

In September 1938 AUGUSTA SAVAGE, the sculptor and influential director of the Harlem Community Art Center, helped Lawrence gain work as an easel painter on the Works Progress Administration's Federal Art Project. During his eighteen months as a government-employed artist, Lawrence probably produced about thirty-six paintings. In addition, he worked on two more dramatic biographies

of freedom fighters. In 1939 he completed *The Life of* FREDERICK DOUGLASS series. Based on the famous abolitionist's autobiography, the thirty-two painted panels—each accompanied by text—chart the heroic transformation of the escaped slave into a fiery orator and an uncompromising activist. The following year Lawrence completed *The Life of* HARRIET TUBMAN series. Composed of thirty-one panels, this epic visual and textual narrative features the courageous female conductor of the Underground Railroad. Both series were exhibited at the Library of Congress in 1940 in commemoration of the seventy-fifth anniversary of the Thirteenth Amendment to the U.S. Constitution.

In 1941, at age twenty-four, Lawrence completed his signature narrative series, *The Migration of the Negro*, a group of sixty tempera paintings illustrating the mass movement of African Americans from the rural South to the urban North. This historical cycle was done in a modern visual style with its emphasis on strong lines, simplified forms, geometric shapes, flat planes, bold colors, and recurrent motifs. GWENDOLYN KNIGHT, a Barbados-born and Harlem-based artist, helped Lawrence complete the project by assisting with the preparation of the sixty hardboard panels and the accompanying prose captions. The creative couple married in New York on 24 July 1941, shortly after completing this pivotal work. Lawrence's *Migration* series brought him wide public recognition and critical acclaim. Twenty-six of the panels were reproduced in *Fortune* magazine in November 1941. Simultaneously, New York's prestigious Downtown Gallery exhibited the cycle, and, soon after the show opened, Edith Halpert, the gallery's owner, asked Lawrence to join her roster of prominent American artists, which included Ben Shahn, Stuart Davis, and Charles Sheeler. Lawrence accepted Halpert's offer, making him the first artist of African descent to be represented by a downtown gallery. A few months later the Museum of Modern Art (MoMA) purchased half the *Migration* series, and the Phillips Collection in Washington, D.C., bought the other half, marking the first acquisition of works by an African American artist at either institution. In October 1942 MOMA organized a two-year, fifteen-venue national tour of the acclaimed series.

During World War II, Lawrence served in the U.S. Coast Guard, where he continued to paint. In 1944 a group of his paintings based on life at sea was exhibited at MoMA. The following year, while he was still on active duty, Lawrence successfully applied for a Guggenheim Fellowship to begin work on a series devoted to the crisis of war. The fourteen somber panels that make up his *War* series were first shown at the New Jersey State Museum in 1947, and *Time* magazine touted the series as "by far his best work yet" (*Time* 50 [22 Dec. 1947], 61).

Lawrence began his distinguished career as a teacher in 1946 when the former Bauhaus artist Josef Albers invited him to teach the summer session at Black Mountain College in North Carolina. Until his retirement in 1983 Lawrence was a highly sought-after teacher. He taught at numerous schools, including the Skowhegan School of Painting and Sculpture in Maine, Brandeis University in Massachusetts, Pratt Institute, the Art Students League, and the New School for Social Research in New York City. From 1970 to 1983 Lawrence was a full professor of art at the University of Washington in Seattle.

Lawrence's first retrospective began in 1960. Organized by the Brooklyn Museum of Art, the show traveled to sixteen sites across the country. The artist had two other traveling career retrospectives during his lifetime: one organized by the Whitney Museum of American Art in 1974, and another organized by the Seattle Art Museum in 1986.

During the civil rights movement, Lawrence visually captured the challenges of the freedom struggle of blacks in works such as *Two Rebels* (1963). His first venture into limited-edition printmaking, *Two Rebels* dramatized the struggle between black protesters and white policemen through lithography. Over the next three decades the artist would also experiment with other printmaking techniques, such as drypoint, etching, and silkscreen.

In 1962 Lawrence traveled to Nigeria, where he lectured on the influence of traditional West African sculpture on modernist art and exhibited his work in Lagos and Ibadan. Two years later the artist and his wife returned to Nigeria for eight months, to experience life in West Africa and to create work based on their stay.

After working primarily as a painter and a printmaker, Lawrence expanded his range in the late 1970s by also making murals. He received his first mural commission in 1979 when he was hired to create a work for Seattle's Kingdome stadium. He created a ten-panel work titled *Games*. Made of porcelain enamel on steel, the 9½-foot ¥ 7½-foot mural features powerful athletes surrounded by adoring fans. This mural, which was relocated to the Washington State Convention Center in 2000, was followed by others at Howard University (1980, 1984), the University of Washington (1984), the Orlando International Airport (1988), the Joseph Addabbo Federal Building in Queens (1988), and the Harold Washington Library Center in Chicago (1991). The artist's final mural, a 72-foot-long mosaic commissioned by New York City's Metropolitan Transit Authority, was posthumously unveiled in the Times Square subway station in 2001.

When Jacob Lawrence died at home in Seattle at age eighty-two, he was exploring a theme that had captured his imagination at the beginning of his sixty-five-year artistic career. Lawrence was still painting pictures of laborers, their movements and constructions, and their tools. A collection of hand tools—hammers, chisels, planes, rulers, brushes, and a Pullman porter's bed wrench—graced his studio and inspired his work. Concerning his prized collection, the artist explained: "For me, tools became extensions of hands, and movement. Tools are like sculptures. You look at old paintings and you see in them the same tools we use today. Tools are eternal. And I also enjoy the illusion when I paint them: you know, making something that is about making something" (Kimmelman, 210–211).

Jacob Lawrence's lifelong interest in representing work and workers befits a man who left behind a monumental body of work—approximately seven hundred paintings, one hundred prints, eight murals, and hundreds of drawings, studies, and sketches. One of the most widely admired African American artists, he was passionately committed to employing his own expressive tools to creatively visualize historical struggles and modern American life.

FURTHER READING

Jacob Lawrence's papers are housed in the Archives of American Art, Smithsonian Institution, Washington, D.C.

Kimmelman, Michael. *Portraits: Talking with Artists at the Met, the Modern, the Louvre, and Elsewhere* (1998).

Nesbett, Peter T., with an essay by Patricia Hills. *Jacob Lawrence: The Complete Prints (1963–2000): A Catalogue Raisonné* (2001).

Nesbett, Peter T., and Michelle DuBois. *Jacob Lawrence: Paintings, Drawings, and Murals (1935–1999): A Catalogue Raisonné* (2000).

Nesbett, Peter T., and Michelle DuBois, eds. *Over the Line: The Art and Life of Jacob Lawrence* (2001).

Turner, Elizabeth Hutton, ed. *Jacob Lawrence: The Migration Series* (1993).

Wheat, Ellen Harkins. *Jacob Lawrence: American Painter* (1986).

Wheat, Ellen Harkins. *Jacob Lawrence: The Frederick Douglass and Harriet Tubman Series of 1938–40* (1991).

Obituary: *New York Times,* 10 June 2000.

LISA GAIL COLLINS

Lawrence, Margaret Morgan (19 Aug. 1914–), pediatric psychiatrist, was born Margaret Morgan in New York City, the daughter of the Reverend Sandy Alonzo Morgan, an Episcopal priest, and Mary E. Smith, a schoolteacher. Mistrusting segregated southern hospitals, the Morgans temporarily moved from Virginia to Harlem in 1914, living with Morgan's aunt so that their child could be born in New York. Morgan's childhood, however, was spent primarily in Vicksburg, Mississippi, where her father's next congregation was located. She grew up a precocious child, reading at three, and lived in a middle-class black neighborhood with her educated parents.

Every summer Morgan visited her aunts in Harlem, and at the age of fourteen she decided she wanted to live with them so that she could go to a better high school. She had decided to be a doctor, she told people, because her older brother had died in infancy before she was born and she wanted to save babies from dying. With her parents' blessing, she moved to Harlem and attended the Wadleigh School, one of the two classical high schools for girls in New York City that required passing entrance exams. In this predominantly white high school Margaret excelled, and on graduation day the top prize in Greek and Latin was awarded, as the principal put it, to "the Negro girl from Mississippi." She received scholarships from Cornell University, Hunter College, and Smith College and chose Cornell partly because of her state regents scholarship but also for its strong reputation in the biological sciences and, as she told friends, because it had men.

At Cornell in the fall of 1932 Morgan was the only black student in the College of Arts and Sciences. She was not allowed to live in the women's dormitory, but the dean of students found her a room with a business family, where she lived for two years. There, to pay for her room and board, she worked as a servant, wearing a uniform and waiting on the dinner table while she herself ate separately in the kitchen and slept in an uninsulated attic. She was also responsible for the housecleaning, washing, and ironing.

In her junior year Morgan moved in with a faculty family, where she had a large, comfortable room but where, once again, she earned her keep serving as household maid. In her senior year, however, she was taken in by Hattie Jones, a legendary figure in Ithaca's tiny black community. Married to a big-time gambler and driven around town in her flashy car by a good-looking young chauffeur, Jones rented rooms in her big house and cooked huge dinners for students she called "young Negroes coming up" (Lightfoot, 98).

Determined to be a doctor, Morgan preferred courses in organic chemistry and comparative astronomy to ancient history or sociology. In her senior year she worked as a technologist for a researcher in the Agricultural College, which paid the rent and taught her how to prepare tissue specimens for microscopic study. She received excellent grades and was told by the dean of the medical school that she had done "very well" on the medical aptitude test. Medical school seemed certain, and again she chose Cornell.

Cornell Medical School rejected her application. The very same dean stunned her by saying that several meetings of the admissions committee had been devoted to her application, adding that she was a very good student and a promising physician, but still they were turning her down. The dean told her, in words she would always remember, that twenty-five years earlier the medical school had conducted "an experiment," admitting a black student, "and it didn't work out. He got tuberculosis" (Lightfoot, 175).

Morgan was accepted at Columbia, however, and in 1936 she became the third black medical student in that school's history; during her four years there she was the only African American in the school. She did well in her courses and won the respect of her teachers and classmates. Meanwhile, to pay for her meals at the residence hall, she worked in the kitchen drying silverware.

In 1938 Morgan married Charles Lawrence, but her life's goal was still to save babies, so after medical school she sought a residency in pediatrics at New York's Babies Hospital, affiliated with Columbia Medical School. Her application was rejected, because—as she was told and never believed—married interns could not live in the hospital's quarters, even though her husband was then living in Georgia and attending Atlanta University. Instead, she did her pediatric internship at Harlem Hospital and then took a master's degree in Public Health from Columbia in 1943.

In 1944 Lawrence left New York City and returned to the South for four years, teaching pediatrics and public health at Meharry Medical College in Nashville, Tennessee, then the premier medical school for black Americans, while her husband taught sociology at nearby Fisk University. Lawrence and her husband moved back to New York City in 1948. After psychoanalytic training at the Columbia Psychoanalytic Institute, where she was the first black person to go through the institute, she settled into a distinguished career of research, teaching, and clinical work at Harlem Hospital and Columbia Medical School, while her husband became an eminent sociologist at Brooklyn College.

The lucky break that put her on the path to professional distinction was her association at Columbia with a young pediatrician, Dr. Benjamin Spock, during the year she worked for her master's degree in public health. Spock opened Lawrence's eyes to the link between physical health and psychological well-being. From Spock, who was also trained in psychoanalysis, she learned to look at the social and family context of childhood disease. She put these insights to work at Harlem Hospital, where she worked to reconstruct the shattered lives of young black children through treatment and therapy in the Developmental Psychiatry Clinic, which she founded and ran for many years.

Lawrence's most important contribution to child psychiatry was her pioneering advocacy of placing in schools therapeutic teams composed of psychiatrists, neuropsychologists, social workers, and nurses. Her first book, *The Mental Health Team in the School* (1971), describing how visiting teams of mental health specialists could serve children in school, is recognized as a milestone in pediatric psychiatry, as are the programs in child psychiatry she developed in day care centers and hospital clinics.

Throughout her career Lawrence was passionately involved in politics. She was a lifelong activist in the antipoverty and civil rights movements, always seeking to improve, as she never tired of putting it, "the impoverished lives of black babies." She was particularly interested in how poor urban black families coped with adversity and how some black children were able to develop ego strength under stress, themes she explored in her second book *Young Inner City Families* (1975).

Margaret and Charles Lawrence had three children, one of whom, Sara Lawrence Lightfoot, wrote a moving biography of her mother, *Balm in Gilead: Journal of a Healer* (1988). After her retirement at age seventy in 1984 from Harlem Hospital and Columbia University Medical School, Lawrence continued her private child psychiatry practice in Rockland County, New York, while remaining an active crusader to improve mental health for economically disadvantaged children. She has received many honorary degrees, the Joseph Bernstein Mental Health Award (1975), the Outstanding Women Practitioners in Medicine Award (1984), and the Cornell Black Alumni Award (1992).

In the spring of 2002, at the age of eighty-seven, Lawrence returned to Ithaca to give a talk to the Cornell community. She told the rapt audience that she had made it despite her difficulties as a student because "I knew who I was, and I knew my own gifts."

FURTHER READING

Lightfoot, Sara Lawrence. *Balm in Gilead: Journal of a Healer* (1988).

ISAAC KRAMNICK

Lawrence, Robert Henry, Jr. (2 Oct. 1935–8 Dec. 1967), aviator and astronaut, was born in Chicago, the son of Gwendolyn Annette Williams Lawrence, a civil servant, and Robert Henry Lawrence Sr., a disabled veteran. While Lawrence and his sister were quite young, their parents divorced. Their mother married Charles Duncan, who worked as a Veterans Administration underwriter and in periodicals circulation. Robert H. Lawrence Sr. remained a strong influence in his children's lives.

Lawrence, a bright and self-disciplined youngster, attended Haines Elementary School in inner-city Chicago. The family was far from affluent, but the Duncans provided support and intellectual stimulation, nurturing Lawrence's interests in chess, model airplanes, and chemistry. Summers spent at the home of family friends near St. Louis, Missouri, allowed the children to enjoy country surroundings and trips to baseball games and to nearby Lambert Airfield. During the school year in Chicago, visits to museums, concerts, or the zoo were regular weekend events.

At the age of twelve, Lawrence entered Englewood High School. He excelled in chemistry and as a long-distance runner, winning city championships in mile and half-mile races. He graduated in 1952 at the age of sixteen in the top 10 percent of his class. He then enrolled at Bradley University in Peoria, Illinois. There he earned a B.S. in Chemistry and distinguished himself as a cadet lieutenant colonel in the university's Air Force Reserve Officers' Training Corps. Upon graduation in 1956, at the age of twenty, he was commissioned as a second lieutenant in the U.S. Air Force.

Following completion of his flight and flight instructor training, Lawrence was assigned to Fürstenfeldbruck Air Base near Munich, Germany. There he served as a fighter pilot and as a flight instructor for pilots in the German air force. After a fatality occurred during training, Lawrence recommended that the language of instruction be changed from English to German. He reasoned that the pilot trainees could react more rapidly in emergencies if instructed in their native language. The change proved successful, and Lawrence's acumen impressed both the student pilots and the German government.

On 1 July 1958 Lawrence married Barbara Cress, also of Chicago, whom he had first met six years before. They had one son. Lawrence returned to the United States in 1961 and enrolled in a joint program of Ohio State University and the Air Force Institute of Technology at Wright-Patterson Air Force Base. He earned a Ph.D. in Nuclear Chemistry from Ohio State in August 1965. His dissertation explored the conversion of tritium beta rays to methane and ethane gas.

During the 1960s national attention focused on the American space program and on civil rights issues. In 1963 the U.S. Air Force captain Edward J. Dwight Jr., an African American, enrolled in the Aerospace Research Pilot School (ARPS) at Edwards Air Force Base, California, amid much fanfare. Many assumed that Dwight would be selected for astronaut training and eventually be the first African American in space. However, Dwight was not selected for aerospace projects either by NASA or by the air force. Lengthy eligibility disputes and charges of discrimination blighted Dwight's career, and he resigned from the air force in 1966.

After he received his doctorate, Lawrence was assigned to Kirtland Air Force Base, New Mexico, as a research scientist at the Air Force Weapons Laboratory. He accumulated more than 2,500 flight hours, of which two thousand were in jet aircraft. He applied twice to join NASA's astronaut training program, but without success. He then was accepted by the U.S. Air Force Aerospace Research Pilot School at Edwards Air Force Base. In June 1967, upon his successful completion of ARPS training, Lawrence was named to the air force's Manned Orbiting Laboratory (MOL) program.

The air force's space flight program complemented but was not coordinated with NASA's Mercury and Gemini programs. A precursor to the International Space Station program, the MOL program was to equip two astronauts for a thirty-day earth orbit. MOL pilots and NASA astronauts also conducted extensive test flights in various high-performance jet aircraft. Lawrence's research investigated the gliding flight of unpowered aircraft landing from a high orbit. The unpowered steep-descent glide became the landing technique later used by NASA's space shuttle orbiters.

On 8 December 1967, only six months after he joined the MOL program, Lawrence was copilot of a Lockheed F-104 Starfighter during a proficiency flight consisting of a set pattern of steep-descent approaches. The plane crashed on landing. Both officers ejected from the aircraft. The pilot, Major Harvey Royer, sustained serious injuries but survived; Lawrence was killed.

Lawrence was the only MOL pilot killed in the line of duty, but he was the ninth to die in America's combined aerospace programs. Five NASA astronauts were killed in earlier experimental flight tests, and on 27 January 1967 Lieutenant Commander Roger B. Chaffee, Lieutenant Colonel Virgil I. "Gus" Grissom, and Lieutenant Colonel Edward H. White were killed in a flash fire during a test of the *Apollo I* rocket on the launchpad at Cape Kennedy (Cape Canaveral), Florida.

In June 1969 the MOL program merged with NASA's space program, and the seven MOL astronauts who were under thirty-six years of age were transferred to NASA. Had Lawrence lived, he would also have been eligible for transfer to the NASA program.

After Lawrence's death, no minority astronaut candidates were announced until 1978, when an astronaut class of thirty-five included three African Americans, COLONEL GUION S. BLUFORD JR., DR. RONALD E. MCNAIR, and COLONEL FREDERICK D. GREGORY; the first Asian American, Colonel Ellison S. Onizuka; and six women, among them Dr. Shannon W. Lucid, Dr. Judith A. Resnick, and Dr. Sally K. Ride. In 1983 Bluford became the first African American to go into space. Also in 1983 Ride was the first woman in space. Four members of that 1978 group, McNair, Onizuka, Resnick, and Major Francis R. "Dick" Scobee, perished in the *Challenger* shuttle disaster in 1986.

Although informally recognized as the nation's first African American astronaut from the time of his selection for the MOL program, Lawrence was not officially designated an astronaut by the air force until January 1997. On the thirtieth anniversary of his death, in December 1997, Lawrence's name was added to the Astronauts Memorial Foundation Space Mirror at Kennedy Space Center, Cape Canaveral, Florida. Dedicated in 1991, the Space Mirror Memorial honors astronauts who died on American space missions or during mission training.

FURTHER READING

Burns, Khephra, and William Miles. *Black Stars in Orbit* (1995).

Gubert, Betty Kaplan, et al. *Distinguished African Americans in Aviation and Space Science* (2001).

Phelps, J. Alfred. *They Had a Dream: The Story of African-American Astronauts* (1994).

Obituaries: *New York Times, Chicago Tribune*, and *Washington Evening Star*, 9 Dec. 1967.

This entry is taken from the *American National Biography* and is published here with the permission of the American Council of Learned Societies.

CAROLINE M. FANNIN

Lawson, James (22 Sept. 1928–), civil rights activist and minister, was born James Morris Lawson Jr. in Uniontown, Pennsylvania, the oldest boy in a family of nine children. His parents, James Lawson Sr., a minister, and Philane Cover both were immigrants to the United States, Lawson from Canada and Cover from Jamaica. Lawson Jr.'s paternal great grandfather was a runaway slave who settled in Canada and took the last name Lawson to honor the man who helped him escape via the Underground Railroad. Thereafter the family always greatly valued education, and Lawson's father became one of McGill University's first black graduates before he moved to the United States to serve as a minister in the African Methodist Episcopal (AME) Zion Church. Though the Lawsons moved throughout the country, they finally settled in Massillon, Ohio, where young James Lawson grew up.

Raised by a pacifist mother and strict father, Lawson was converted to nonviolence by his mother at the age of ten. After high school Lawson attended an integrated college, Baldwin-Wallace College, located in Berea, Ohio (near Cleveland). During his time at college Lawson honed his commitment to pacifism, joining the Fellowship of Reconciliation (FOR). In 1950, after refusing draft deferments that would have kept him out of jail, Lawson was sentenced to three years in federal prison for violating the military draft laws.

In prison Lawson rediscovered Gandhi and became more committed to his teachings. After his parole Lawson returned to and graduated from college and went to India as a missionary. After serving three years in Nagpur, India, as a campus minister

James Lawson during a labor rally in Oakland Park, Fla., on Feb. 26, 2003. (AP Images.)

and teacher at Hislop College, Lawson remained a Christian and was also a disciple of Gandhi and his nonviolent tactics.

Upon his return to the United States in 1955, Lawson enrolled at Oberlin College's Graduate School of Theology, where he met MARTIN LUTHER KING JR. Upon learning of Lawson's background in nonviolent resistance, King urged him to move to the South and train civil rights activists. Thus in 1957 Lawson opened an FOR office in Nashville, Tennessee, and enrolled in Vanderbilt University's Divinity School. In 1959 Lawson married Dorothy Wood, with whom he integrated a variety of Vanderbilt University's facilities as well as the Nashville Symphony. In addition to pursuing his studies, Lawson ran workshops teaching Gandhian nonviolent tactics of direct action to the city's African American college students. Teaching students not only that nonviolent action worked but also that it was "deeply rooted in the spirituality of Jesus," Lawson helped create the student arm of the civil rights movement. Civil rights movement luminaries such as JOHN LEWIS, MARION BARRY, and DIANE NASH got their start in Lawson's workshops. Using Lawson's principles of nonviolence the student activists staged sit-ins at Nashville's downtown lunch counters. In consultation with Lawson, on 13 February 1960 the student sit-in movement began in earnest.

Not only did the student arm of the civil rights movement desegregate downtown Nashville but it also helped promote an explosion of activism among African American college students. Under Lawson's guidance the student protesters founded the Student Nonviolent Coordinating Committee (SNCC) in October 1960. Indeed, Lawson penned the organization's statement of purpose. Not everyone was pleased with Lawson's activism, and he was expelled from Vanderbilt University; he continued his studies at Boston University and earned a master's degree in Theology.

In 1961, after earning renown for the student activism in Nashville, Lawson became active in the Southern Christian Leadership Conference (SCLC) and the Congress of Racial Equality (CORE). Under the sponsorship of CORE, of which Lawson was the national director, the Nashville Student Group founded the Freedom Rides, which were designed to desegregate interstate transportation. Directly participating in the Freedom Rides, Lawson was jailed in Mississippi, the most dangerous leg of the journey.

During the time of the Freedom Rides, Lawson was pastor to a small Methodist church in Shelbyville, Tennessee, located about fifty miles south of Nashville. In June 1962 Lawson was appointed pastor to Centenary Methodist Church, the largest African American Methodist congregation in the mid-South. During his time in Memphis, Lawson and his toddler son John integrated formerly segregated city parks, and the elder Lawson continued his close association with Martin Luther King Jr. It was Lawson who invited King to Memphis to help dramatize the city's sanitation workers' strike of 1968. In King's final sermon, on the eve of his assassination, he called Lawson "the leading theorist and strategist of nonviolence in the world."

Though Lawson remained in Memphis for more than six years after King's death, in 1974 he became pastor to a large middle-class congregation at Holman Methodist Church in Los Angeles, California, and hosted *Lawson Live*, a weekly radio call-in show. In southern California, Lawson and his wife, Dorothy, raised their three sons. In addition, Lawson visited the man convicted of murdering King, James Earl Ray, and even officiated at Ray's prison wedding. Following his retirement from the ministry Lawson remained actively involved in social justice movements on behalf of labor and minority groups.

FURTHER READING

Halberstam, David. *The Children* (1998).

Norton, Eleanor Holmes. "How the Dream Was Born," *New York Times*, 27 Nov. 1988.

Williams, Juan. *My Soul Looks Back in Wonder: Voices of the Civil Rights Experience* (2004).

JEFF BLOODWORTH

Lawson, James Raymond (15 Jan. 1915–21 Dec. 1996), physicist and university president, was born in Louisville, Kentucky, to Daniel LaMont and Daisy Harris Lawson. Lawson's father, a dean of Louisville's Simmons College, had attended Fisk University where he was a member of the world-renown Fisk Jubilee Singers. Although little is known of his early childhood and education, the younger Lawson followed in his father's footsteps, enrolling at Fisk in 1931. As a mathematics and physics major, Lawson sought the mentorship of Elmer S. Imes. A distinguished physicist, Imes had become the second African American to earn a doctorate in physics when he graduated from the University of Michigan in 1918. Imes had returned to teach at Fisk, his alma mater, in 1930, where he continued to pioneer infrared spectroscopy.

Lawson proved a promising student, graduating Phi Beta Kappa in 1935 with a degree in physics, the first-ever Fisk student to do so.

However, Lawson's successes were not limited to the classroom. An avid sportsman, Lawson held both football and basketball letters. But it was the combination of his leadership experience and intellectual promise that made Lawson an ideal candidate for graduate study. The close ties Imes maintained with the University of Michigan made that school a natural choice for Lawson. As a Julius Rosenwald fellow, Lawson began graduate work at Michigan in 1937, and earned his Ph.D. in Physics in 1939.

Having begun his teaching career at St. Augustine College while he was still a student, Lawson served as an assistant professor at Southern University in Louisiana from 1939 to 1940, then he served as associate professor of physics at Langston University in Oklahoma from 1940 to 1942. Lawson's mentor Imes died unexpectedly that same year, prompting his return to Fisk as associate professor of physics and chair of the department. Continuing the research begun by Imes, Lawson immediately began efforts to establish and develop a research program in infrared spectroscopy. Using his ties with his University of Michigan colleagues, he orchestrated the acquisition of an infrared spectrophotometer for Fisk, similar to a model which was being constructed for University of Michigan departmental research.

By the time the cutting-edge equipment arrived on campus in 1948, Lawson had successfully recruited five Fisk seniors to pursue their masters' of science degrees at the university. As the physics majors conducted their research on the new equipment the infrared laboratory flourished. They were soon presenting their research at major scientific conferences, including the American Physical and American Chemical societies, both of which they effectively integrated. Enabled by grants secured in 1948, 1949, and 1950, both student and faculty research continued to flourish and was formally organized under the codirection of Lawson and Nelson Fuson as the Fisk Infrared Spectroscopy Institute in 1950.

After serving a stint as chair of the department at Tennessee A&I State University (another Nashville historically black institution, later known as Tennessee State University) from 1955 to 1957, Lawson returned to Fisk as a full professor and department chair in 1957. In 1966 he became vice president of the university until 1967, when he was selected as the university's eighth president, following his eighteen-month service as acting-president. As the university's first alumnus president, Lawson assumed the leadership of his historically black alma mater amid the social turmoil of the late 1960s. DR. MARTIN LUTHER KING JR.'s nonviolent ethos was steadily eclipsed by the emergent Black Power movement's popularization of the right to armed self-defense as well as its demands for stronger black cultural identity. Fisk students were no exception to the spirit of the age. Despite leading the institution to secure its largest-ever enrollment of 1,500 students, Lawson continued to face student protests throughout his seven-year presidency. Open student dissent only further served to alienate the university's historical white philanthropist financial base, whose support had continued to wane since the beginning of Fisk's nonviolent student activism of the early 1960s. With a dwindling endowment, Fisk experienced salary cuts of 20 percent and operational budget cuts of 25 percent. Following sharp decreases in student, staff, and faulty enrollment and serious illness, Lawson resigned in 1975.

Over the course of the decade that followed, Lawson resided in Washington, D.C., where he worked for the Energy Research and Development Administration (a forerunner to the Department of Energy) as special assistant to the director of the office of university programs. Later, he served as head of NASA's University Affairs Office and associate director of the Institute for the Study of Educational Study at Howard University before a series of illnesses forced him into full retirement. Soon after, Lawson returned to Nashville where he later died. A member of numerous professional organizations throughout his life, Lawson was a member of the American Physical Society, American Association of Physics Teachers, American Institute of Physics, Sigma Xi, and a board member of the Oak Ridge Associated Universities as well as a member of the Kappa Alpha Psi fraternity, Inc. Married to the former Lillian Arcaeneaux of Opelousas, Louisiana, Lawson had four children: Ronald Raymond and James Edward Lawson, both of whom went to Fisk, as well as daughters Daryl and Elizabeth Lawson.

FURTHER READING

The papers of James R. Lawson are housed in the Special Collections and Archives of the Fisk Franklin Library in Nashville, Tennessee.

Collins, L. M. *One Hundred Years of Fisk University Presidents, 1875–1975* (1989).

"James R. Lawson," *Fisk Herald* (Oct. 1934).

Mickens, Ronald E. "James Raymond Lawson," *Physics Today* (Oct. 1997).

"The Inauguration of James Raymond Lawson as Eighth President of Fisk University," printed program (6 Oct. 1968).

Yates, Jon. "James Lawson, ex-president of Fisk, dies," *Nashville Tennessean*, 23 Dec. 1996.

CRYSTAL A. DEGREGORY

Lawson, John (16 June 1837?–3 May 1919), Civil War sailor and Medal of Honor recipient, was born John Henry Lawson in Pennsylvania to parents from Delaware. Nothing is known about his early life, and even his date of birth is uncertain. Military records indicate that he was born in 1837, while census records state that he was born five years earlier. Census records also reveal that Lawson likely married his wife, Mary (also called Mary Ann), by 1857, the year in which his eldest child, Joseph, was born. John and Mary subsequently had seven other children: Susan, George, Raymond, Mary, Mariah, Gertrude, and Marien.

Like thousands of other black men, both freeborn and freed, Lawson enlisted for Civil War service in the U.S. Navy on 3 December 1863 in New York. Naval records indicate that Lawson was twenty-six years old at the time, a "mulatto" measuring five feet eight inches tall, with his occupation listed as "laborer." His period of enlistment was one year, and he was rated a landsman, the navy's lowest rating for an enlisted man. This designation probably only indicates that Lawson had no experience as a mariner, though it was not uncommon for black enlistees with some maritime experience to be given, because of their race, a rating below that of their actual ability.

Except for one spectacular moment, specifics of Lawson's service in the navy during the war are lacking. Like other men such as AARON ANDERSON and JOACHIM PEASE, he was one of approximately eighteen thousand black men who served in the navy, making up about 20 percent of the navy's manpower during the Civil War. When Lawson joined the navy in late 1863 the number of blacks serving had reached a high-water mark. Early in the war blacks made up only 6 percent of the navy's manpower; from late 1863 to late 1864 the number had risen to 23 percent.

Most black sailors serving in the Union navy—about 75 percent—were born into slavery, though this is not true of Lawson. He was one of approximately twelve hundred blacks from Pennsylvania who served in the navy, and his rating, that of

John Lawson, c. 1900. (Library of Congress.)

landsman, was held by the vast majority of black sailors. Life aboard a Union naval vessel could be difficult for a black man, whether freeborn or freed. Though his duties as a landsman placed him among the lowest level of sailors aboard ship and meant that he was regularly assigned the most menial and backbreaking tasks, Lawson was freeborn and thus may have been treated by his white shipmates with more respect than were his fellow black sailors who had been slaves. Lawson's naval career began when he was assigned to USS *Hartford* on 1 January 1864. This wooden ship was a 2,900-ton sloop of war that served as the flagship of Admiral David Farragut's Western Gulf Squadron. The admiral's job was to shut down blockade runners on the Gulf Coast areas of Mississippi and Alabama that helped keep the Confederacy supplied with materials of war from abroad. Farragut had already accomplished this feat at New Orleans and Vicksburg, and one last port remained to be conquered: Mobile, Alabama.

The *Hartford*, with Admiral Farragut in command and Lawson as one of his sailors, approached Mobile Bay on 5 August 1864 leading a fleet of four monitors and fourteen wooden ships. The entrance to the bay was guarded by two forts and a heavy field of mines (then called torpedoes), and one of the greatest naval contests of the Civil War commenced when Farragut cried, "Damn the torpedoes, full speed ahead," and led his fleet into battle. The action lasted for three hours and was hard-fought. USS *Tecumseh*, going off-course into the minefield, went down with the loss of ninety-four men, while the large Confederate monitor *Tennessee* was sunk by Union forces. Firepower from Fort Gaines and Fort Morgan was heavy, but the Union navy prevailed.

During the course of the action the *Hartford* was hit numerous times. Landsman Lawson took part in the furious battle as a member of his ship's ammunition party, supplying the *Hartford*'s guns with powder and shot, and he was "wounded in the leg and thrown violently against the side of the ship when an enemy shell killed or wounded the six-man crew at the shell whip on the berth deck." In spite of his wounds, "Lawson ... promptly returned to his station and, although urged to go below for treatment, steadfastly continued his duties through the remainder of the action" (United States Bureau of Naval Personnel, 34–35). When the battle was finally over and the smoke had cleared, the Union had won an important victory, and Lawson had earned himself the Medal of Honor—one of eight black sailors in the Civil War to earn the award. By their heroic actions men like Lawson, ROBERT BLAKE, and others dramatically proved the importance of black men in helping to win the Civil War on the high seas.

Several months after the Battle of Mobile Bay, the *Hartford* and Lawson returned to New York. His one-year term of enlistment having expired, Lawson returned home to his wife and family in Philadelphia, Pennsylvania, spending the rest of his life in the area around Philadelphia and Camden, New Jersey. Continuing to work as a laborer wherever he could, Lawson moved frequently about the city and was actually counted twice in the 1870 census.

By 1900, with his wife, Mary, dead and his children all grown, Lawson continued to work as a shop clerk. He died in Philadelphia on 3 May 1919 and was buried in Camden, New Jersey. Despite Lawson's being a Medal of Honor winner, his grave remained unmarked in Mount Peace Cemetery until a local veteran led a successful effort to have a monument erected in 2004.

FURTHER READING

Beyer, Walter F., and Oscar F. Keydel. *Deeds of Valor: How American Heroes Won the Medal of Honor* (1905).

Quarles, Benjamin. *The Negro in the Civil War* (1953)
Reidy, Joseph P. "Black Men in Navy Blue during the Civil War," *Prologue* (Fall, 2001).
United States Bureau of Naval Personnel. *Medal of Honor, 1861–1949, the Navy* (1950).

GLENN ALLEN KNOBLOCK

Layton, John Turner, Sr. (Apr. 1846–16 Feb. 1916), music teacher and conductor, bass singer, Civil War veteran, and active member of the Grand Army of the Republic, author of the first African Methodist Episcopal Church hymnal (working with Bishop James C. Embry), was born in Eulesstown, New Jersey. The 1860 census lists several free families of African descent named Layton, but none have been definitively identified as his. Charles and Harriet Layton, of Warrenville, may have been his parents, but the ages of their children (often the subject of error by census takers) are not a definitive match.

Layton enlisted in the U.S. Navy on 25 August 1864 at Jersey City, giving his occupation as laborer/farmer. Assigned the rating of Landsman, he served on the vessels *Larkspur* and *O.M. Pettit*. Both were tugboats assigned to the South Atlantic Blocking Squadron, towing and repairing ships of the squadron while gathering intelligence on shore, and carrying messages between ships. Most of Turner's military service was off Port Royal, South Carolina.

He pursued musical education after the war, but the exact dates have not been established. Layton attended one or more summer assemblies at Round Lake, New York, organized by the Chautauqua Literary and Scientific Circle, supervised by teachers from the New England Conservatory in Boston. Professor Tinney from the conservatory was among his mentors, and Layton may also have studied in Boston. There are brief contemporary references to musical courses at Northwestern University, which are not confirmed by the incomplete records the university archives retain from the mid-nineteenth century.

Layton settled in Washington, DC, prior to 1870, where he worked for a time as a waiter; an older sister, Mary, boarded at the same address. He worked several more years as a local police officer and in 1880 lived at the boarding house of Esther Bowing, along with an older brother, Alfred. He took special courses in music after moving to the District, under Dr. Kimball and Ernest Kent. He served for many decades as director of the choir of Metropolitan African Methodist Episcopal (AME) church in DC, possibly starting as early as 1873 (according to Metcalf, 1926, Layton held the post for forty-three years).

Layton began teaching music in a primary school in Washington, DC, in 1883, part of the separate school system for students designated as "colored." In 1890 he began teaching music at the high school level. In 1893 Layton married Julia Mason, a primary school teacher and principal in DC public schools, who had also worked for seven years at the Government Printing Office. Mrs. Layton was born in Virginia, with Choctaw, African, and English ancestors. They had two sons, John Turner Layton Jr., born 2 July 1894, and Alfred Mason Layton, born August 1899. Henry and Ann Mason, Julia Layton's parents, lived with their daughter, son-in-law, and grandchildren for the rest of their respective lifetimes.

After several unsuccessful attempts by the bishops of the AME church, starting in 1888, to agree on the compilation and publication of a hymnal, Layton sent a letter to the Bishops' Council in 1895 with a new proposal. A committee was appointed, consisting of Bishop Benjamin Tucker Tanner, Bishop Embry, and Layton. Embry and Layton did the primary work of arranging the hymns and music, with other bishops appointed from time to time to the committee overseeing the project, which was completed and printed in 1897.

Reported as the consummation of a devoutly wished-for "Hymn and Tune Book of our own to be used by our people," it was the first to include full musical arrangement. There were earlier AME hymn books, dating back to one prepared by Richard Allen, Daniel Coker, James Chapman, and Jacob Tapsico in 1818 (*AME Hymn Book*, pp. xi–xv). This book includes a dozen tunes written by Layton, as well as musical pieces for special occasions by Mary E. Church (later Terrell), and Henry F. Gant.

Professor Layton attended the Summer Conservatory of Music at Martha's Vineyard, Massachusetts, in 1896, placing first among forty-seven students, all certified teachers.

In September 1900, Layton was appointed Director of Music for the Colored Schools in Washington, DC, succeeding Mrs. Alice Strange Davis. There was lively debate in the pages of the *The Colored American* over the vacancy created by the death of Mrs. Davis, credited with "the high standard attained in music by the District schools." Layton was described as "The most prominent as well as the most popular candidate for the position" (1 Sept. 1900, p. 12).

Layton was a founder in 1901, and for many years the musical conductor, of Washington's Samuel Coleridge-Taylor Choral Society, intended to "diffuse among the masses a higher musical culture and appreciation of works that tend to refine and elevate" (Mark Tucker, *Ellington: The Early Years*, p. 9). Named for a well known Afro-English composer, the society produced the American premiere of his *Hiawatha* trilogy in 1903, brought the composer himself to conduct concerts of his music in 1904 and 1906, and in 1908 presented Coleridge-Taylor's *The Atonement*, a musical passion play.

Layton was awarded an honorary degree by Wilberforce University in 1906, and was honored by a testimonial dinner in May 1908, in Washington, DC, attended by individuals of many racial designations. He died in Washington eight years later, apparently without having retired from his teaching or choir posts. He was survived by his wife, two sons, and his father-in-law, who was still living in 1920 at age ninety-six. The older son, known professionally as J. Layton Turner, was a successful composer of music and lyrics for vaudeville stars and the Broadway stage, teamed during several years each with Harry Creamer and Clarence Johnstone.

FURTHER READING

The African Methodist Episcopal Hymn and Tune Book (1912).
The Colored American, Washington, DC, 1 Sept. 1900, 12.
Caldwell, A. B. "Julia Mason Layton" In *History of the American Negro*, 233–235 (1921).
Metcalf, Frank J. "History of Sacred Music in the District of Columbia." *Records of the Columbia Historical Society, Washington, D.C.* 28 (1926): 197–198.
Southern, Eileen. *The Music of Black Americans: A History* (1997).

CHARLES ROSENBERG

Lead Belly (15 Jan. 1888–6 Dec. 1949), folk singer and composer, was born Huddie Ledbetter on the Jeter plantation near Caddo Lake, north of Shreveport, Louisiana, the only surviving son of John Wesley Ledbetter and Sally Pugh, farmers who were reasonably well-to-do. Young Huddie (or "Hudy," as the 1910 census records list him) grew up in a large rural black community centered around the Louisiana-Texas-Arkansas junction, and he would later play at rural dances where, in his own words, "there would be no white man around for twenty miles." Though he was exposed to the newer

Lead Belly in 1948. (Library of Congress. Photograph by Austin Wilder.)

African American music forms like the blues, he also absorbed many of the older fiddle tunes, play-party tunes, church songs, field hollers, badman ballads, and even old vaudeville songs of the culture. His uncle taught him a song that later became his signature tune, "Goodnight, Irene." Though Ledbetter's first instrument was a "windjammer" (a small accordion), by 1903 he had acquired a guitar and was plying his trade at local dances. In 1904, when he turned sixteen, Ledbetter made his way to the notorious red-light district of nearby Shreveport; there he was exposed to early jazz and ragtime, as well as blues, and learned how to adapt the left-hand rhythm of the piano players to his own guitar style. He also acquired a venereal disease that eventually drove him back home for treatment. In 1908 he married Aletha Henderson, with whom he had no children, and the pair moved just east of Dallas, where they worked in the fields and prowled the streets of Dallas. Two important things happened to Ledbetter here: he heard and bought his first twelve-string guitar (the instrument that he would make famous), and he met the man who later became one of the best-known exponents of the "country blues," BLIND LEMON JEFFERSON. Though Jefferson was actually Ledbetter's junior by some

five years, he had gained considerable experience as a musician, and he taught Ledbetter much about the blues and about how an itinerant musician in these early days could make a living. The pair were fixtures around Dallas's rough-and-tumble Deep Ellum district until about 1915.

Returning to Harrison County, Texas, Ledbetter then began a series of altercations with the law that would change his life and almost destroy his performing career. It started in 1915, when he was convicted on an assault charge and sent to the local chain gang. He soon escaped, however, and fled to Bowie County under the alias of Walter Boyd. There he lived peacefully until 1917, when he was accused of killing a cousin and wound up at the Sugarland Prison farm in south Texas. There he gained a reputation as a singer and a hard worker, and it was at Sugarland that a prison chaplain gave him the nickname "Lead Belly." (Though subsequent sources have listed the singer's nickname as one word, "Leadbelly," all original documents give "Lead Belly.") At Sugarland he also learned songs like "The Midnight Special" and began to create his own songs about local characters and events. When the Texas governor Pat Neff visited the prison on an inspection tour, Lead Belly composed a song to the governor pleading for his release; impressed by the singer's skill, Neff did indeed give him a pardon, signing the papers on 16 January 1925. For the next five years Lead Belly lived and worked around Shreveport, until 1930, when he was again convicted for assault—this time for knifing a "prominent" white citizen. The result was a six-to-ten-year term in Angola, then arguably the worst prison in America.

In 1933, while in Angola, Lead Belly encountered folk-song collector John Lomax, who had been traveling throughout southern prisons collecting folk songs from inmates for the Library of Congress. Lead Belly sang several of his choice songs for the recording machine, including "The Western Cowboy" and "Goodnight, Irene." Lomax was impressed and a year later returned to gather more songs; this time Lead Belly decided to try his pardon-song technique again and recorded a plea to the Louisiana governor, O. K. Allen. The following year Lead Belly was in fact released, and though he always assumed the song had done the trick, prison records show Lead Belly was scheduled for release anyway because of overcrowding.

Lead Belly immediately sought out Lomax and took a job as his driver and bodyguard. For the last months of 1934, he traveled with Lomax as he made the rounds of southern prisons. During this time he learned a lot about folk music and added dozens of new songs to his own considerable repertoire.

In December 1934 Lomax presented his singer to the national meeting of the Modern Language Association in Philadelphia—Lead Belly's first real public appearance—and then took him to New York City in January 1935. His first appearances there generated a sensational round of stories in the press and on newsreels and set the stage for a series of concerts and interviews. One of these was a well-publicized marriage to a childhood sweetheart, Martha Promise (it is not known how or when his first marriage ended); another was a record contract with the American Record Company. Lomax himself continued to make records at a house in Westport, Connecticut, a series of recordings that was donated to the Library of Congress and that formed the foundation for the book by John Lomax and Alan Lomax, *Negro Folk Songs as Sung by Lead Belly* (1936). For three months money and offers poured in, but complex tensions stemming in part from Lomax's attempts to mold Lead Belly's repertoire in a way that fit the classic folk music image of the day led to an estrangement between Lomax and Lead Belly, and before long the singer returned to Shreveport.

A year later Lead Belly and his wife returned to New York City to try to make it on their own. He found his audience not in the young African American fans of CAB CALLOWAY and DUKE ELLINGTON (who considered his music old-fashioned), but in the young white social activists of various political and labor movements. He felt strongly about issues concerning civil rights and produced songs on a number of topics, the best of which were "The Bourgeois Blues" and "We're in the Same Boat, Brother." Lead Belly soon had his own radio show in New York, which led to an invitation to Hollywood to try his hand at films. He tried out for a role in *Green Pastures* and was considered for a planned film with Bing Crosby about Lomax. The late 1940s saw a series of excellent commercial recordings for Capitol, as well as for the independent Folkways label in New York. His apartment became a headquarters for young aspiring folk singers coming to New York, including a young Woody Guthrie. Martha Promise's niece Tiny began managing Lead Belly's affairs, and his career was on the upswing when, in 1949, he became ill with amyotrophic lateral sclerosis (ALS, or Lou Gehrig's disease). It progressed rapidly, and in December Lead Belly died in Bellevue Hospital in New York City. His body was returned to Mooringsport, Louisiana,

for burial. Ironically, a few months later, his song "Goodnight, Irene" was recorded by the Weavers, a group of his folk-singing friends, and became one of the biggest record hits of the decade.

Lead Belly was one of the first performers to introduce African American traditional music to mainstream American culture in the 1930s and 1940s and was responsible for the popularity and survival of many of the nation's best-loved songs.

FURTHER READING

Lomax, John, and Alan Lomax. *Negro Folk Songs as Sung by Lead Belly* (1936).

Wolfe, Charles K., and Kip Lornell. *The Life and Legend of Leadbelly* (1992).

DISCOGRAPHY

Numerous CDs feature reissues of both the singer's commercial and Library of Congress recordings, notably *Lead Belly: The Library of Congress Recordings* (Rounder 1044–46).

This entry is taken from the *American National Biography* and is published here with the permission of the American Council of Learned Societies.

CHARLES K. WOLFE

Leary, John Sinclair (17 Aug. 1840?–9 Dec. 1904), lawyer, public official, legislator, and law school dean, was the youngest son of five children born in Fayetteville, North Carolina, to Matthew N. Leary, a successful saddler and a staunch abolitionist and philanthropist, and Julia A. Memorell (Menriel). One of Leary's elder brothers was LEWIS SHERIDAN LEARY, a follower of abolitionist John Brown, who was killed in the raid on Harper's Ferry in 1859. Matthew Leary helped local slaves buy their freedom and often educated them, despite legal prohibitions on the practice. According to the 1850 federal census, he personally owned three slaves, though these were held for benevolent reasons.

John Leary's birth year is not certain; the 1850 census records his age as ten, although later reports indicate that he was born as late as 1849. His ethnic heritage was a blend of European, Native American, and African American lineage. His mother, a native of France, migrated as a child to North Carolina from the Bahamas with her French mother. His father, whose family name had been shortened from O'Leary, was reportedly descended from Irish immigrants and Lumbee Indians on one side, and on the other from free African Americans, among them a Revolutionary War soldier, Aaron Revels. John Leary was educated privately for eight years, primarily by white teachers, but he chose at first to enter his father's business, manufacturing horse saddles and harnesses, rather than continue his education.

During the Civil War, John Leary was conscripted by Confederate authorities and forced to helped construct defensive breastworks at Fort Fisher, near the port of Wilmington in North Carolina. After the war ended, he became interested in public affairs and the new Republican Party, and he attended the 1866 statewide convention of African American men. He was selected as a speaker by the national Republican Congressional Committee in 1867. With his father and brother, Leary was among the first African American men allowed to register to vote in Fayetteville in 1867; all went on to hold local office during Reconstruction.

In early 1868 Leary was elected as a Republican to the state house of representatives from Cumberland County. He served in two sessions of the general assembly, 1868–1869 and 1869–1870, and served on the House Committee on Corporations; the Committee on Deaf, Dumb, and Blind Asylum; and the Judiciary Committee. He also served on the Joint Committee on the Public Library. Among a score of African American legislators, Leary was one of a handful who spoke frequently on important issues, offering a unique and innovative perspective. He favored a conciliatory attitude toward former Confederate sympathizers, introducing a resolution instructing North Carolina's newly elected representatives in Congress to restore political rights to the state's penalized citizens during Reconstruction. The resolution, however, did not pass the Republican-controlled House.

Leary's position on issues involving race was moderate. For example he favored a modified voluntary system of racial segregation of the state's public schools, suggesting that children of each race be allowed to choose either segregated or integrated schools, but his amendment to this effect was unsuccessful. Drawing from the extensive legal training he had received from a white Fayetteville lawyer in the late 1860s, he also argued that attempts to codify racial equality in state law were unnecessary and even counterproductive, based on his interpretation of the state's new constitution.

Leary entered the law department of Howard University in Washington, D.C., in 1871. Two years later he received a bachelor's degree in Law. Returning home, he became one of the first African American lawyers to pass the North Carolina bar examination administered by the State Supreme Court. On 9 December 1874 Leary married Alice B. Thomas of Raleigh; the couple had two children, both of whom died in infancy. Following Thomas's death in 1880, Leary married Nannie E. Latham of Charlotte on 14 July 1886. They were the parents of at least five children. While establishing his law practice in Fayetteville, Leary served as a city alderman in 1876–1877 and as a member of the local school committee for both races from 1878 until 1881. Active in the Odd Fellows Order, a British fraternal organization established in the United States in Baltimore in 1819, Leary also participated in Republican affairs, representing Cumberland County as a delegate to state Republican conventions and serving as a district delegate to the Republican national conventions in 1880 and 1884, both held in Chicago.

In the spring of 1881, President James A. Garfield appointed Leary as U.S. deputy collector of revenue for North Carolina's Fourth District, a position he retained until 1885. In that same year Leary was elected president of the North Carolina Industrial Association, the sponsor of an annual statewide fair for African Americans, and he served as the state's honorary commissioner for African Americans to the World's Cotton Exposition, held in New Orleans. In 1888 he was appointed as the first dean of the new law department at Shaw University, a private Baptist institution in Raleigh, North Carolina. He and his family remained in Raleigh until 1892, at which time he moved to Charlotte and established a law practice. Later described as "a ripe scholar and a man of great ability," Leary quickly developed a reputation as one of the state's most effective and accomplished lawyers, respected by members of both races for his "gentle bearing and shrewdness" (*Daily Observer*, 13 Dec. 1904).

Following a brief illness, John Leary died at Charlotte's Good Samaritan Hospital. His funeral was well attended, the immense crowd of mourners of both races spilling out into the streets from the sanctuary of the small Episcopal church he had served as vestryman, lay reader, and Sunday school superintendent. His daughter Rosa recalled in her memoir, *Plum Thickets and Field Daisies* (1996), that every member of the Charlotte bar association attended his funeral, in a rare gesture of respect.

FURTHER READING

Balanoff, Elizabeth. "Negro Legislators in the North Carolina General Assembly, July, 1868–February, 1872" (1972).

Foner, Eric. *Freedom's Lawmakers: A Directory of Black Officeholders During Reconstruction* (1993).

Kenzer, Robert. *Enterprising Southerners: Black Economic Success in North Carolina, 1865–1915* (1997)

Obituary: *Daily Observer*, 13 Dec. 1904.

BENJAMIN R. JUSTESEN

Leary, Lewis Sheridan (17 Mar. 1835–18 Oct. 1859), a free resident of Oberlin, Ohio, was one of the five black men who joined abolitionist John Brown's raid on Harper's Ferry in mid-October 1859. Leary was born in Fayetteville, North Carolina, to free black parents Julie Memriel, the French-born daughter of a Guadeloupian, and Matthew Leary, a harness-maker. On his father's side, Leary's Irish grandfather and free black great-grandfather had fought against the British during the Revolutionary War. Leary attended a school for free blacks in Fayetteville and learned the trade of harness making from his father.

In 1856, at the age of twenty-two, Leary moved to Oberlin, Ohio, where he joined his two sisters, Henrietta and Delilah. Leary worked as a saddler and harness maker and learned to play several musical instruments. In 1858 he met and married Mary Simpson Patterson, an Oberlin College graduate. The couple had a daughter, Lois, in early 1859. Oberlin also was home to several prominent black and white abolitionists, including Wilson Bruce Evans, JOHN MERCER LANGSTON, and James Monroe. Leary joined the abolitionist community and in September 1858 he participated in the Oberlin-Wellington Rescue, when a group of Oberlin and Wellington, Ohio, residents rescued a fugitive slave from a United States marshal who was trying to return him to the South. John Price of Kentucky was seventeen years old and living in Oberlin at the time of his arrest by slave catchers. After seizing Price from the marshal and deputy marshals, the rescuers hid him in an Oberlin home and helped him to reach Canada. Thirty-seven men (including twelve free blacks) were indicted and jailed for their actions in the rescue. Leary was not among them.

A few weeks later, in November 1858, Leary addressed the Oberlin Anti-Slavery Society, telling them, "Men must suffer for a good cause" (Quarles, p. 87). He met John Brown the following spring, in March 1859, when Brown gave a public lecture in nearby Cleveland. In September 1859, Leary recruited fellow Oberlin resident JOHN ANTHONY COPELAND JR., the son of his sister Deliah and her husband, John Copeland Sr., to Brown's cause. Without telling his wife of his plans, Leary left Oberlin with Copeland to join John Brown in Chambersburg, Pennsylvania. Brown was on his way back to his headquarters, the Kennedy Farm near the village of Sharpsburg, Maryland, after visiting Philadelphia for several days. The men met on 12 October 1859 and arrived at the farm early on 15 October.

Late in the evening on Sunday, 16 October, Brown and an interracial band of twenty-two men, including Leary and Copeland, seized the federal arsenal at Harper's Ferry, West Virginia. Brown intended that slaves arm themselves and claim their freedom. He hoped to spark a slave uprising across the South. The band held out against Virginia and Maryland militia for two nights but United States marines stormed the arsenal on the morning of 18 October. Leary was shot during an assault on the rifle factory, which he was holding with Copeland and another raider, John Kagi, a 25-year-old white man from Ohio. Marines then assaulted the engine house, where Brown and most of his men had barricaded themselves. Though mortally wounded, Leary survived for eight hours after marines captured Brown. He was interrogated during those hours. In 1860, OSBORNE PERRY ANDERSON, the only black survivor of Harper's Ferry, remembered that Leary was "generous-hearted and companionable," "brave to desperation" and ready to die for "the most holy principles" (50).

The other black men who joined Brown's band were DANGERFIELD NEWBY and SHIELDS GREEN. Newby was killed at the Ferry and Anderson escaped. Green and Copeland were charged with treason, sentenced to death, and hung on 16 December 1859. The rest of the raiders were white. Of these sixteen men, eight died in the battle, five escaped, and three were executed. Brown was convicted on counts of assault, murder, conspiracy, and treason. He was hung in Charleston on 2 December 1859.

After Leary's death, the abolitionists James Redpath and Wendell Phillips helped raise money for the support and education of his daughter Lois. Leary was buried in a wooden box on the banks of the Shenandoah River opposite the Harper's Ferry arsenal. In 1899 his body was disinterred and reburied at North Elba, New York, near Brown's grave. Oberlin residents held a memorial service for Leary, Copeland, and Green on 25 December 1859 and erected a monument in Westwood Cemetery at Oberlin in 1865. The monument's inscription reads: "These colored citizens of Oberlin, the heroic associates of the immortal John Brown, gave their lives for the slave."

Mary Leary remarried in 1869. Her second husband was the abolitionist CHARLES HENRY LANGSTON. A leader in the rescue of John Price, Langston was tried and convicted for his part in violating the Fugitive Slave Act in 1858. In 1872 the couple had a daughter, Caroline Mercer Langston, who became the mother of poet LANGSTON HUGHES. When Hughes was a child, his grandmother Mary took him to visit the John Brown Memorial Battlefield in Osawatomie, Kansas. In his autobiography, *The Big Sea* (1949), Hughes remembers this trip and explains that Brown's raid was an important part of his family history.

FURTHER READING

Anderson, Osbourne P. *A Voice from Harper's Ferry: A Narrative of Events* (1861).

Hinton, Richard J. *John Brown and His Men* (1968).

Libby, Jean. *Black Voices From Harper's Ferry: Osbourne Anderson and the John Brown Raid* (1979).

Nudelman, Franny. *John Brown's Body: Slavery, Violence, and the Culture of War* (2004).

Quarles, Benjamin. *Allies for Freedom & Blacks on John Brown* (2001).

ZOE TRODD

Ledbetter, Huddie. *See* Lead Belly.

Lee, Andrea (1953–), journalist and fiction writer, was born in Philadelphia, Pennsylvania, to an upper-class family. As a member of the African American elite of the time, she was educated in integrated schools for the privileged classes, undergoing many difficulties to overcome racism and her feeling of being out of place. She then studied at Harvard, where she obtained her bachelor's degree and then her master's degree in English in 1977. While at Harvard she met her future husband, Tom, a specialist in Russian history. Tom was awarded a fellowship to study in Moscow and Leningrad, and they lived there for ten months in 1978–1979. During their stay in the Soviet Union Lee kept a diary whose entries were the core for her first publication, a nonfiction work titled *Russian Journal* (1981).

When they returned to the United States, Lee worked for several years as a staff reporter for the *New Yorker*. She also published short stories and articles in this and other periodicals such as the *New York Times* and *Vogue*. Some of those stories were later collected in her novel *Sarah Phillips* (1984), a semiautobiographical piece of fiction based on her experiences growing up in Philadelphia. By 1984

Lee and her husband had moved to Europe, first living in Rome, then in Paris, and latterly in Turin, Italy, with their two children. In 2002 Lee published *Interesting Women*, a collection of thirteen short stories in which Lee reflected on the everyday realities encountered by well-to-do black women living in Europe. In 2006 she published *Lost Hearts in Italy*, which examined the adulterous relationship between an African American woman and an Italian lover.

As an author Lee was best known for her first two works. *Russian Journal* was awarded the Jean Stein Award from the American Academy and Institute of Arts and Letters in 1984. It describes her sojourn with her husband in the Soviet Union from an unusually fresh viewpoint because, as Lee herself affirmed in the foreword, they "lived on rubles, stood in queues, and rode the metro with ordinary Russians" (vii). However, placing Lee's text within the framework of African American female travel narratives, the book fails to address fundamental issues such as sexism and racism; nor does it offer any serious questioning of the value systems of either the United States or Russia. Although the latter is mainly depicted as the "other," her narration also shows the fascination for American culture on the part of the Russian population.

Lee constantly invoked political neutrality and objectivity in her account, which are easily compromised by the open declaration of her patriotism. Indeed, her version of Russia was greatly influenced by her American beliefs and ideas, to the point that she seemed untouched by her experience there. Another problematic aspect of the text is that she does not acknowledge her racial identity until page 151, in an oblique reference to an African character. This deliberate postponement emphasizes Lee's investment in maintaining a position as a neutral observer, which is nonetheless very unstable. It does, however, inaugurate a new way of relating to personal and communal experience within the contemporary African American literary tradition.

Lee's second book, *Sarah Phillips*, was reissued in 1993 with a prologue by Valerie Smith, the influential African American feminist critic. The novel was a timely and intriguing reflection on the ambiguous legacy of the 1960s. In this bildungsroman the protagonist, Sarah, constantly confronts racial and class differences as she wavers between two worlds, her black neighborhood and her white school. Occupying outsider/insider positions simultaneously, Sarah finds it difficult to make sense of the world surrounding her and to forge an identity of her own. She is confused about her parents' contradictory legacy. On one hand, both of them are active members of the black community: her father is a preacher and a leader in the civil rights movement and her mother a teacher in community service. But on the other, they live in an exclusive neighborhood and do not allow her and her brother to join the historic March on Washington or date interracially, although they are sent to all-white schools. The effects of this privileged status prove devastating to Sarah; she is never able to identify with her father's politics or even with the black cause as a whole. Therefore Sarah's upbringing does not provide her with reliable identity markers that can help her to establish fulfilling racial or class allegiances. For the most part, like the narrator of *Russian Journal*, she seems to be left untouched by her experiences.

Throughout the novel Sarah encounters people from many racial and social backgrounds—from black servants in her exclusive school to Gypsies to the white men she dates while studying at Harvard—who could facilitate a significant step forward in her awareness of herself, but that self-knowledge is continuously deferred. Critics commented in different ways on her inability to react adequately, but what seems to be at stake in the novel is precisely that lack of stability resulting from her refusal to acknowledge her racial and social past. Moreover, Lee also made clear that there cannot be a monolithic identity politics in the black community, underlining the importance of the interconnections between racial and class privilege within it. Coming full circle, the beginning of the novel—each chapter of which deals with a different episode in Sarah's life—testifies to Sarah's uneasiness after she has decided to move to Paris after graduation. Even though she attempts to ignore her "home" and its implications, she ends up falling prey to racist and sexist episodes that lead her back to the United States to continue her quest for wholeness and meaningful selfhood.

Through her writings—and through her explorations of race and class privilege in new locations—Andrea Lee greatly contributed to the African American literary tradition.

FURTHER READING

Enomoto, Don. "Irreconcilable Differences: 'Creative Destruction' and the Fashioning of a Self in *Sarah Phillips*," *Melus* 24.1 (Spring 1999).

King, Nicole. " 'You Think Like You White': Questioning Race and Racial Community through the Lens of Middle-Class Desire(s)," *Novel* 35.2–3 (Spring–Summer 2002).

MAR GALLEGO

Lee, Archy (1840–1873?), fugitive slave, was born in Pike County, Mississippi. His known family—his mother, two brothers, and a sister—were all slaves. There is no evidence that Lee, the slave of the Stovall family of Pike and Carroll counties in Mississippi, ever learned to read or write.

In the summer of 1857 Charles Stovall took Lee to Missouri, where he left him with friends. In the fall he returned to Missouri and traveled with Lee to California. They arrived in Sacramento in October 1857. Before the year's end Stovall advertised in a Sacramento paper for students to enroll in a school he was opening. He also hired out Lee and used part of those wages to support himself. This he did in a city that had an active and stable free black community of workers, ministers, and businesspeople who were in contact with antislavery Sacramento whites.

In January 1858 Stovall decided to return to Mississippi with Lee. At a crucial moment, Lee fled for sanctuary to a hotel run by free blacks. He was arrested there on 6 January 1858.

The laws pertaining to Lee's case were the national Fugitive Slave Law of 1850 and an 1852 California Fugitive Slave Law that stated that a slave owner in California was protected in his ownership of a slave for one year. This law was renewed twice and had expired by April 1855.

The first set of legal moves took place in a county court where the opposing attorneys presented their positions before Judge Robert Robinson. Stovall's attorneys held that Lee was his slave in Mississippi and therefore could be returned there without legal interference. Lee's lawyers countered that because California was a free state Stovall had no legal right to hold Lee and, further, that slavery was only protected for slave owners in transit. Since Stovall had opened a school and also had hired out Lee, he could not be considered in transit. Judge Robinson delayed his decision for fifteen days. Unwilling to wait for the judge's decision, Stovall's lawyers tried to get U.S. commissioner George Penn Johnston, a southerner, to take the case, hoping that his regional sympathies would produce a favorable decision for slavery. But the commissioner concluded that the Fugitive Slave Law of 1850 did not apply to the Lee case because Lee did not cross state boundaries in his strike for freedom.

Judge Robinson's delay and the commissioner's decision propelled the Stovall forces to move in another direction even before the anticipated unfavorable decision was handed down by Robinson. They arranged for the supreme court of the state to take the case, and when Robinson freed Lee, Lee was immediately rearrested, to the surprise of all present. The "Archy case" moved to the highest court in the state. Of the three-member court, two justices were in attendance at the time, both of them southerners with anti–free black and proslavery backgrounds.

Their decision, handed down on 11 February, noted that under existing law Lee was not a fugitive slave, but inasmuch as "this is the first case … we are not disposed to rigidly enforce the rule." Lee was ordered back into slavery, a decision that was received with journalistic derision from coast to coast. The court had completely set aside the fact that Stovall did not qualify as a traveler once he opened a school. The framers of the state's constitution felt that the sojourner requirement was necessary so that slavery could not be introduced surreptitiously into California.

Stovall now had to transport Lee unobserved from Sacramento to San Francisco and conceal him aboard a ship for the return trip to Mississippi. The theatrics that followed became legal history. From 11 February to 5 March the Stovall forces worked covertly to reach San Francisco Bay without detection by either the white antislavery forces or the well-organized, highly alert black community. Black businesspeople and the numerous black maritime workers patrolled the docks night and day during this period. Stovall's forces had every reason to believe that they were not operating in a favorable environment.

When the steamer *Orizaba* left its wharf and moved into San Francisco Bay, a small boat carrying Lee and Stovall moved out from Angel Island to meet it. When the two attempted to board, concealed city police on the ship seized them and brought them to San Francisco, where a new series of court actions began on 8 March. Police officers carried two warrants: one for Archy, to keep him in San Francisco, and the other for Stovall on the charge of kidnapping.

The absurdity of the Archy Lee supreme court decision encouraged the legal and law enforcement community to tolerate the maneuvers that followed Lee's return to San Francisco. The warrants for Lee and Stovall had all the earmarks of ploys to remove Lee from Stovall's control and also to obstruct his efforts to regain control. The pro-Lee forces now had time to position themselves for the next phase of legal struggle.

When the opposing lawyers took their places, representing Lee was one of the most distinguished attorneys in the state, Colonel Edward D. Baker. He was an old friend of Abraham Lincoln and an early member of the new Republican Party and was known as a lawyer who did not fear unpopular causes. Stovall's counsel was James H. Hardy.

After a one-week delay, the case that the press referred to as the "Case of Archy Lee, the Fugitive Slave" resumed on 15 March in a packed courtroom. The lawyers made their opening statements, followed by a variety of arguments by both sides before Judge T. W. Freelon. The fact that Freelon rejected the Hardy request to throw out the entire case suggests that his sympathies were not with the Stovall camp. Baker's strongest statement cast ridicule on the decision of the California Supreme Court to suspend state law because Stovall's obtuseness about the law was a first-time offense.

In this round of exchanges Hardy's main point was that even if the state supreme court's decision was faulty, its decision should be honored. Baker's statement made the legal point that the form in which Stovall's attorneys had presented their case to the supreme court was not in the form of an appeal, and the state supreme court was only an appeals court. He then asked the judge to set Lee free. To everyone's surprise, Hardy did not object, and Freelon declared Lee a free man. Within moments a U.S. marshal rearrested Lee. Stovall's attorney, sensing defeat again, had arranged hours earlier for U.S. commissioner Johnston to once again deal with the case as one coming under the rules of the 1850 Fugitive Slave Law.

Continuances, delays, and adjournments finally concluded on 14 April. By that time Johnston had listened to several Hardy witnesses whose contradictory evidence made it clear that Lee had none of the attributes of a runaway slave from Mississippi. He also heard the Baker ironclad case that Lee was not an interstate runaway and therefore should be freed. Johnston had received by this time the attorney's final briefs and had made his decision. He decreed that the state supreme court had no authority over the Lee case, that Lee's relationship with Stovall en route to California did not support the image of a runaway, and that his strike for freedom was within California state boundaries; therefore, the 1850 National Fugitive Slave Law did not apply. He declared Lee a free man.

Soon on his way to Victoria, British Columbia, Lee joined a large group of California blacks seeking economic opportunity there resulting from the Frazier River gold rush. They also feared impending racist legislation in California. Lee reportedly became a drayman and property owner in Victoria. After the Civil War he returned to California and did not come to public notice again until 1873, when a Sacramento newspaper reported that he had fallen ill. It appears that he died in Sacramento in the winter of that year.

FURTHER READING

Finkelman, Paul. "The Law of Slavery and Freedom in California," *California Western Law Review* 17 (1989): 427–64.

Franklin, William E. "The Archy Case: The California Supreme Court Refuses to Free a Slave," *Pacific Historical Review* 32 (May 1963): 137–54.

Lapp, Rudolph M.. *Archy Lee: A California Fugitive Slave Case* (1969).

This entry is taken from the *American National Biography* and is published here with the permission of the American Council of Learned Societies.

RUDOLPH M. LAPP

Lee, Arthur (7 Mar. 1945–3 Aug. 2006), musician and member of the band Love, was born Arthur Porter Taylor in Memphis, Tennessee, to Agnes Porter, a teacher, and Chester Taylor, a musician. Lee took on the surname of his mother's second husband, Clinton Lee. At the age of five, Lee moved with his parents to Los Angeles. His mother was a schoolteacher, and she taught her child the fundamentals of language. However, Lee found his greatest mode of expression through music.

Lee left school to focus on a musical career. He formed several local outfits, including the LAGs, which then morphed into a group called the American Four, both of which focused mainly on performing R&B cover songs. At the time, Lee also wrote and produced music, including the song "My Diary" for Rosa Lee Brooks, which featured a young JIMI HENDRIX on guitar. In 1965 Lee met another Los Angeles–based artist, Brian Maclean, the road manager for the Byrds. Maclean joined Lee's newest project, the Grass Roots. After a name change, due to another band using the same moniker, the group became a Los Angeles music-scene mainstay, playing clubs on the infamous Sunset Strip as the band Love. The group challenged dominant hierarchies in rock and roll, as Lee and the guitarist Johnny Echols were the sole African Americans in a "white" band. The band's composition was a peculiarity in the Los Angeles and San Francisco rock scenes—scenes that were coming to dominate the sound of the "psychedelic" rock scene of the late 1960s. Before the arrival of Jimi Hendrix, Love was *the* interracial band in a mostly white-dominated musical movement.

The group released four albums on Elektra Records, *Love* (1966), *da capo* (1967), *Forever Changes* (1967), and *Four Sail* (1969). Lee and the band fused psychedelic rock with a folk and garage aesthetic. Raw at times and melodious at others, the music of the band mirrored its complex and esoteric leader. The band experienced numerous personnel changes during the late 1960s, including the departure of Maclean for an ill-fated solo career. Only Lee remained to record under the name Love for two more albums on the Blue Thumb label, *Out Here* (1969) and *False Start* (1970). Lee and the group in its various forms never found widespread commercial success. Just one of their singles, "7 and 7 is," limped into the top-forty singles chart in 1966, and the album critics have labeled their masterwork, *Forever Changes*, peaked at number 152 on the American album charts and number 24 on the British charts.

The lack of initial commercial success, most commonly ascribed to the frequent personnel changes and drug problems that plagued the group, also derived from Lee's reputed reclusive character. The group did not tour extensively outside of California. Yet the legacy of Love still maintained itself. Much of this was due to the continuing musical efforts of Lee. After releasing an unsuccessful solo effort in 1972, *Vindicator*, Lee stepped back from the industry. The band reunited briefly in 1978 and then quickly dissipated once again.

The music of Love influenced numerous bands and artists, such as Television, Lenny Kravitz, the Ramones, Alice Cooper, and Yo La Tengo. In part, Love's influence on such bands and on a variety of musical genres (at various points in its evolution, Love carried the label "grandfathers of punk") was partially responsible for the longevity of its catalog. Lee deserved some of this credit for this as well. The band, through numerous incarnations and periods of long inactivity, survived under the leadership of Lee into the twenty-first century. In the early 1990s Lee, along with a group from Los Angeles called Baby Lemonade, toured as Love. However, continuing legal issues (including assault and drug charges) haunted Lee. The courts sentenced him to eight years in prison after an incident involving the discharge of a firearm during a dispute with a neighbor in 1996. After serving six years, Lee was released in 2001. He rejoined Baby Lemonade and took the Love name out on the road. The group performed the *Forever Changes* album in its entirety on an international tour that included stops in Europe and the United States. Lee continued to tour and record with the group, playing numerous shows and working in the studio until his death in August of 2006 from leukemia. In retrospect, Arthur Lee and Love challenged assumptions of what a rock band should represent regarding issues of race and identity. Along with other acts such as Jimi Hendrix, Love upset notions of the racial line that had formed in popular music, especially after the British Invasion in the early and mid-1960s.

FURTHER READING

Hoskyns, Barney. *Arthur Lee: Alone Again Or* (2003).

Hoskyns, Barney. "Paint Me White: Bad Days, Black Rock, and Arthur Lee's Love Story," in *Rip It Up: The Black Experience in Rock 'N' Roll* (2004).

MATHEW J. BARTKOWIAK

Lee, Barbara (16 July 1946–), politician, was born in El Paso, Texas. Her father was a lieutenant colonel in the U.S. Army. The name of her father and her mother's name and occupation are unknown. As a child in the segregated South she encountered racial discrimination and oppression literally from birth. Her mother was refused admittance to the local hospital when she was in labor with Barbara, almost losing her life as a result. Barbara was prohibited from attending local public schools, attending Catholic school instead. Lee attributes the development of her political consciousness largely to her early encounters with segregation. She moved to California with her family in 1960 and spent her teenage years in San Fernando, California, just outside of Los Angeles, and graduated from San Fernando High School in 1964. The eldest of two girls, she and her sister were raised by both their parents and grandparents.

Despite early challenges in her life that would result in her dependence on public assistance, as a single mother of two sons, Lee continued to work, earning the Bank of America Achievement Award and Rotary Club Music Award, scholarships that supported her as she pursued her educational goals. She graduated from Mills College in Oakland with a bachelor's degree in Psychology in 1973. The previous year she had become excited about the candidacy of SHIRLEY CHISHOLM for president of the United States, and when she learned that Chisholm did not have a campaign office in northern California, Lee started one and became a campaign coordinator. Upon completion of her baccalaureate degree she earned a master's degree in social welfare from the University of California at Berkeley in 1975. Always solution-oriented, while attending graduate school Lee came to recognize the tremendous need for mental health services in traditionally underserved communities and established a community mental health center in Berkeley.

Barbara Lee began her political career as an intern in the office of California Congressman RON DELLUMS in 1975. She later became Dellums's chief-of-staff. In 1990 she was elected to the California State Assembly, and in 1996 she was elected to the California State Senate. When Congressman Dellums retired from Congress in 1998 he urged Lee to run for his seat. She was elected as U.S. Representative to California's Ninth Congressional District, which includes Oakland and Berkeley, with 85 percent of the vote.

As a member of Congress, Representative Lee served as co-chair of the Progressive Caucus, chair of the Congressional Black Caucus Task Force on Global HIV/AIDS, whip of the Congressional Black Caucus, and member of the International Relations Committee and the Financial Services Committee. She authored legislation that provides $15 billion in funding to fight HIV/AIDS, tuberculosis, and malaria around the world. Lee became known in 2001 as the "lone dissenter," the only member of Congress to vote against U.S. House Resolution 64, the legislation that authorized President George W. Bush to use the U.S. armed forces in response to the terrorist attacks of 11 September 2001 in New York and Washington, D.C. The measure passed 98 to 0 in the Senate and 420 to 1 in the House. Although she was sympathetic to the victims of the attack and concerned about threats to international security, Barbara Lee challenged both policymakers and the American public to protect civil liberties and develop alternative strategies to ensure peace, cautioning:

> However difficult this vote may be, some of us must urge the use of restraint…. We are not dealing with a conventional war….
>
> We must not rush to judgment. Far too many innocent people have already died. Our country is in mourning. If we rush to launch a counter-attack, we run too great a risk that women,

children, and other non-combatants will be caught in the crossfire. Nor can we let our justified anger over these outrageous acts by vicious murderers inflame prejudice against all Arab Americans, Muslims, Southeast Asians, or any other people because of their race, religion, or ethnicity.

Finally, we must be careful not to embark on an open-ended war with neither an exit strategy nor a focused target. We cannot repeat past mistakes (U.S. House of Representatives).

Although Lee was attacked by some on the right, including Fox News personalities and radio host Rush Limbaugh, her dissent may have actually increased her popularity in her home district and among political progressives and did not prevent her reelection to Congress in 2002. She also sponsored HR 2929 which passed in July 2007, banning permanent U.S. military bases in Iraq.

Barbara Lee married Reverend Michael Millben. She was the mother of two adult sons, Tony and Craig, and had three grandchildren, Jordan, Joshua, and Jonah.

FURTHER READING

U.S. House of Representatives. "Authorizing Use of United States Armed Forces against Those Responsible for Recent Attacks on the United States," Library of Congress (14 Sept. 2001).

Whitting, Sam. "Facetime: Giving Peace a Chance Local Rep. Barbara Lee on Her National Following," *San Francisco Chronicle* (23 Mar. 2003).

MELINA ABDULLAH

Lee, Canada (3 May 1907–9 May 1952), actor, bandleader, and boxer, was born Leonard Lionel Cornelius Canegata in New York City, the son of James Cornelius Canegata, a clerk, and Lydia Whaley. Lee's father came from a wealthy and politically prominent family in St. Croix, Virgin Islands, whose ancestors had adopted a Danish surname. Lee's grandfather owned a fleet of merchant ships; the family also raced horses. James Canegata shipped out as a cabin boy at eighteen, settled in Manhattan, married, and worked for National Fuel and Gas for thirty-one years. Lee grew up in the San Juan Hill section of Manhattan's West Sixties and attended P.S. 5 in Harlem. An indifferent student, he devoted more energy to fisticuffs than to schoolwork. Lee studied violin from age seven with the composer J. ROSAMOND JOHNSON, and at age eleven he was favorably reviewed at a student concert in Aeolian Hall; his parents hoped he would become a concert violinist.

Lee relished risk and excitement and, like his father, ran away from home, heading for the Saratoga racetracks at fourteen. He worked for two years as a stable hand until a "gyp" (a poor owner who paid his jockeys from winnings only) gave him a chance to race. Lee's unremarkable career as a jockey at the New York tracks (Belmont, Aqueduct, Jamaica) and on a Canadian circuit based in Montreal lasted a further two years, until he grew too tall and too heavy to ride. Returning penniless to New York, Lee encountered a school friend who had become a professional boxer and whom Lee remembered beating regularly in street fights. With his usual decisiveness, Lee turned to boxing. Within two years, under the training of Willie Powell at the Salem Crescent Athletic Club (in the basement of a Methodist church near his parents' house), Lee had won metropolitan, intercity, state, and national lightweight junior championships. In 1925 he turned professional, managed by Jim Buckley. Lee married his first wife, Juanita Waller, in 1926; their son, the actor Carl Vincent (Canegata) Lee, was born in 1928.

When the veteran fight announcer Joe Humphries introduced boxer Lee Canegata as "Canada Lee," Lee acquired the name he would use for the rest of his life. In an eight-year career as a welterweight, Lee fought some two hundred professional bouts, losing only twenty-five. He never won a championship but defeated champions Lou Brouillard, Vince Dundee, and Tommy Freeman in ineligible "over-the-weight" matches shortly before or after they won their crowns. Finally, in a 1931 Madison Square Garden bout intended as a preliminary to a championship bout with Jim McLarnin, Andi Di Vodi landed a blow that left Lee blind in his right eye, which was soon replaced with glass (boxing also left Lee with a broken nose and slightly cauliflowered ears). Always prodigally generous with money, Lee earned more than eighty thousand dollars as a boxer and saved none of it.

Lee returned to music, leading his own big band as violinist and singer (he also played piano). He toured domestically and once filled in for DUKE ELLINGTON at Harlem's famed Cotton Club. In 1933 or 1934 Lee ran a small Harlem nightclub, the Jitterbug, for about six months, at a loss. (Lee later owned the Chicken Coop, a popular Harlem restaurant he ran from 1941 to 1943, where he fed innumerable prizefighters for free.) Broke again in 1934, in the depth of the Great Depression, and too proud to accept Home Relief but reluctant to take an ordinary job, Lee finally went to the Harlem

YMCA employment office. Instead of waiting in line, however, he slipped into the Y's Little Theatre to watch the director FRANK WILSON's auditions for the "Negro unit" of the Public Works of Art Project theater division. Presuming Lee was an actor, Wilson had him audition; Lee found himself with the role of Nathan in Wilson's *Brother Mose* and a new career.

Lee soon succeeded Rex Ingram in the lead role of Blacksnake in a Theater Union revival of Paul Peters's *Stevedore*, which ran for a year at Chicago's Civic Rep. When the Negro unit became part of the Works Progress Administration Federal Theatre Project in 1935, Lee returned to New York as Banquo in Orson Welles's all-black *Macbeth*, a role that won critical notice and confirmed his new vocation. Lee's other Federal Theatre roles included parts in Lewis Stiles Gannett's *Sweet Land* and Kenyon Nicholson's *Sailor, Beware* (1935); Yank in an ill-conceived 1937 revival of Eugene O'Neill's four one-act sea plays; Henri Christophe, Haiti's nineteenth-century liberator and king, in W. E. B. DuBois's 1938 *Haiti*, again following Ingram; an Irish reporter in Ben Hecht and Charles MacArthur's *The Front Page* (1938); and Victor Mason in Theodore Ward's *Big White Fog* (1940). Lee also appeared in *Brown Sugar*, directed by George Abbott in 1937, and bowed on Broadway as Drayton in the 1938 hit by DuBose Heyward, *Mamba's Daughters*, starring the singer ETHEL WATERS. Despite the varying critical success of these largely popular productions, Lee was consistently singled out for notice by reviewers.

Lee also worked extensively in radio in the early 1940s. Harlem's WMCA built a 1944 series, *New World a' Coming* ("vivid programs of Negro life" based on the ROI OTTLEY best-seller), around Lee and made him the voice of the JOHN KIRBY ORCHESTRA. He was featured in WNEW's *The Canada Lee Show*, narrated a series for CBS, and acted in many radio plays for NBC.

The role of Bigger Thomas in the stage adaptation of RICHARD WRIGHT's *Native Son*, directed by Welles in 1941, propelled Lee to stardom; overnight he was acclaimed one of the nation's greatest actors. After a 114-show run and extensive New York–area touring, the play returned to Broadway in 1942–1943 at popular prices. In 1942 Lee also took lead roles in a bill of two mystical Pirandellian one-acts by William Saroyan, *Talking to You* (in which he played a prizefighter) and *Across the Board on Tomorrow Morning*. Lee and his wife were divorced in 1942 after a long separation; Lee continued to raise his son alone.

Lee turned down many stereotypical film parts before accepting the role of Joe, an assistant steward, in Alfred Hitchcock's *Lifeboat* (shot in 1943; released in 1944). Lee insisted on rewriting all his dialogue to eliminate its obsequious Hollywood "Negro dialect." While *Lifeboat* was in postproduction, Lee returned to New York to produce and star in the controversial *South Pacific*, a didactic melodrama directed by Lee Strasberg that allegorized problems of racial integration in the American military (no relation to the famed Rodgers and Hammerstein musical).

As producer and board member of the American Negro Theater, Lee moved Phillip Yordan's *Anna Lucasta* from Harlem to Broadway for 957 performances in 1944 and triumphed in a role far smaller than his star status warranted. Lee won generally good notices also as Caliban, opposite the ballerina Vera Zorina as Ariel, in Margaret Webster's innovative 1944–1945 *The Tempest* and again as the villainous Daniel de Bosola in the director Paul Czinner's 1946 production of John Webster's *The Duchess of Malfi*, said to be the English-speaking world's first "whiteface" role. Lee was also the first African American to produce a straight play on Broadway when he starred in Maxine Wood's 1946 *On Whitman Avenue*, about a black family hounded out of a white neighborhood. The crudely written racial melodrama was a critical flop but a great popular success in New York and on its national tour.

In 1947 Lee costarred opposite John Garfield as the end-of-the-line champ Ben Chaplin in *Body and Soul*, considered the greatest of the classic boxing films (Lee had previously appeared in 1939's *Keep Punching*). To Lee this role represented "the first time the movies have handled an American Negro like any other human being." Lee often said that boxing remained his greatest love. He denied any interest in the sport's brutal aspect and described boxing as an alloy of music, poetry, dance, and psychology, saying he had "approached fighting from an aesthetic angle." Lee believed boxing had taught him balance, fluidity, and rhythm and given him stage presence. He was praised throughout his career for his physical grace and power, command of stage space, imagination, and directness.

Though Lee often told interviewers he had not suffered from discrimination, every aspect of his career was politicized and viewed through the lens of American race relations. He was seen, and saw himself, as a pioneering black actor dedicated to demolishing racial stereotypes. Throughout

Canada Lee performing in a production of *Native Son* on 7 April 1941. (Library of Congress.)

his professional life an outspoken and eloquent defender of social justice, Lee lent his name and his gift for public speaking to such progressive causes as a 1946 American Veterans Committee rally to banish Jim Crow from the theater and numerous campaigns against fascism, racism, and anti-Semitism. As early as 1941 Lee took pains to distance himself publicly from any group with communist affiliations; nonetheless, he was blacklisted, the target of an orchestrated smear campaign in the press, and virtually unable to work in radio, television, or film after 1945. (Stefan Kanfer writes in *A Journal of the Plague Years* [1973] that Lee had been banned from forty radio and television shows by 1952.) The stress Lee endured left him with life-threatening hypertension; he never fully recovered his health.

Lee starred in a production of *Othello* in the summer of 1948 but was unable to secure funding for a Broadway run despite positive notices during the tryout tour, and in 1949 he unsuccessfully attempted to open a school, the Canada Lee Workshop for actors—two of this period's many unfulfilled projects. Lee's last role on Broadway was as George in Dorothy Heyward's 1948 *Set My People Free*. Although Lee was never indicted by the House Un-American Activities Committee (HUAC), an FBI document introduced in evidence at the 1949 trial of Judith Coplon (a government worker indicted for spying) accused him of being a "fellow traveler." Nearly eighteen thousand dollars in debt, Lee appealed to the variety-show host Ed Sullivan in a letter, declaring himself "no more a Communist than an Eskimo." In a press conference called to clear his name, Lee analyzed the racist motive behind HUAC's attack on black leaders, declaring, "Call me Communist and you call all Negroes Communists."

Lee made only two more films, both outside Hollywood. He was powerful in a custom-written role as a Harlem policeman in Louis de Rochemont's controversial *Lost Boundaries* (1949), based on the true story of a light-skinned black doctor and his family who passed for white in a small New Hampshire community. The novelist Alan Paton, impressed with Lee's performance in that film, insisted he be cast as Stephen Kumalo in the film version of Paton's *Cry, the Beloved Country* (1951), the first film ever made about apartheid, shot in Natal, South Africa, in 1950.

Lee married Frances Pollack, his companion of several years, while in London for retakes of *Cry* in 1951. While there, Lee required two operations to reduce his blood pressure. Retakes were further delayed when Lee had to return to New York after his father's death of a heart attack (the same disease that had killed Lee's mother in 1945), though Lee was too ill to attend the funeral. He traveled in Europe briefly to plan several film projects. He was supposed to return to Italy to begin shooting a film of *Othello* in 1951, but he was not permitted to renew his passport. *Cry* was being shown to capacity houses across the United States when Lee died of uremia in his Manhattan home in 1952 at age forty-five. Lee's memorial service at the Henry Street Settlement House was attended by the poet LANGSTON HUGHES, among other black leaders, and included a public denunciation of apartheid.

FURTHER READING

The Manuscripts/Archives and Rare Books Division of the New York Public Library's Schomburg Center for Research in Black Culture possesses collections of production stills from several of Lee's plays and films and all of Lee's personal and professional papers, donated by his widow, including scripts, speeches, correspondence, and photographs.

The Schomburg also holds the complete records

(1952–1954) of the Canada Lee Foundation, set up after his death to aid talented young African Americans in theater.

Smith, Mona Z.. *Becoming Something: The Story of Canada Lee* (2004).

Obituary: *New York Times*, 10 May 1952.

This entry is taken from the *American National Biography* and is published here with the permission of the American Council of Learned Societies.

CHRISTOPHER CAINES

Lee, Everet Astor (31 Aug. 1916–), violinist and conductor, was born in Wheeling, West Virginia, the oldest of two sons of Everett Astor Lee Sr., an accountant, and Mamie Amanda Blue Lee, a homemaker. The children were reared in Cleveland, Ohio.

Lee was the only one in his family to go into the music profession, though his father sang in a college quartet. His career decision was completely supported by his father. Lee graduated in 1941 with a bachelor of music degree from the Cleveland Institute of Music, where he was a violin major and student of Joseph Fuchs. Though one of the school's top violinists, he was unable to get a position with an orchestra. From 1941 to 1948, however, Lee found work as a soloist, chamber musician, and first violinist of the CBS orchestra.

Lee's conducting career began in 1948 when he became leader of the Cosmopolitan Little Symphony, an interracial ensemble that gave concerts for New York's African American community and at such major venues as Town Hall. The Town Hall appearances received considerable praise from the press. An unexpected opportunity arose in 1949 when, as concertmaster in the orchestra for the stage musical *Carmen Jones*, he was asked to substitute as conductor.

Lee served in the military during World War II, and used the GI Bill to study conducting with Max Rudolf. He married Sylvia Olden, a pianist and vocal coach, in 1944, but the couple later divorced. Professionally, his major influence as a conductor was Max Rudolf, but others also mentored him. At Juilliard, after he began his conducting career in 1948, he studied with Fritz Mahler. Through Leonard Bernstein, who had invited Lee to sit in on New York Philharmonic rehearsals, he met Dimitri Mitropoulos, with whom he took private lessons. A German newspaper critic introduced him to Bruno Walter, which led him to sit in on Walter's rehearsals and to get his advice.

In 1952 Lee traveled to Italy on a Fulbright and studied at the Saint Cecilia Academy in Rome. After a brief return to the States he received a German Dank Stipendium in 1956; what was supposed to be a one-year period of study instead lasted for seven years, and included conducting a traveling opera company that performed throughout Germany, France, and South America, as well as conducting orchestras in Brussels and Berlin. He returned to the United States for a few years, but then moved to Sweden in 1963 to accept a ten-year post as chief conductor of the Norrköping Symphony Orchestra.

Lee was asked early on by some Europeans to identify his race. He had features that might not be identified as African American, and his birth certificate identified him as "Mulatto." The Europeans wanted to know how he could call himself a Negro when he had so much European ancestry. Lee responded that in America one was black if one had a single drop of Negro blood.

In the United States, Lee, besides being music director of the Cosmopolitan Symphony, was music director of Symphony of the New World and served as a guest conductor for the Cleveland Orchestra, Dallas Symphony, Atlanta Symphony, Detroit Symphony, St. Louis Symphony, Baltimore Symphony, and the New York Philharmonic. He conducted lyric theater productions for Opera North, Opera Ebony, San Francisco Opera, Cincinnati Opera, and New York City Opera. When, in 1955, Lee conducted Giuseppe Verdi's *La Traviata* at New York City Opera, he became the first African American to conduct a full-scale operatic production at a major American house.

But the bulk of his career, as both orchestra conductor and opera conductor, was carried out in other countries. Along with leading the Norrköping Symphony Orchestra and being guest conductor for orchestras and theaters in Europe and South America, Lee served as music director of the Münchener Opernbühne and conductor of the Nordic Youth Symphony, and held posts at the Royal Swedish Opera and Bogota (Columbia) Philharmonic.

Lee's lyric theater repertoire encompassed sixty scores, mostly from the Italian masters but also including some French and German operas. His concert repertoire was broad, encompassing a wide range of styles, periods, and composers within the symphonic literature. Throughout his career Lee championed the works of African American and American composers.

FURTHER READING

Abdul, Raoul. *Blacks in Classical Music* (1977).

Cheatham, Wallace McClain. *Dialogues on Opera and the African American Experience* (1997).

Gray, John. *Blacks in Classical Music* (1988).

Lee, Sylvia Olden, and Elizabeth Nash. *The Memoirs of Sylvia Olden Lee* (2001).

WALLACE MCCLAIN CHEATHAM

Lee, Fitz (c. June 1866–14 Sept. 1899), U.S. Army soldier and Medal of Honor recipient, was born in Dinwiddie County, Virginia. Though born a free individual in the immediate aftermath of the Civil War, nothing is known of his family background. He is likely the same child that is listed in the 1870 Federal Census for Huntsville, Alabama, born in Virginia and living in the household of Isaac and Agnes Lewis. Interestingly, while Agnes Lewis was born in Virginia like Fitz Lee, her Alabama-born husband, Isaac, worked as a farrier, shoeing horses. Perhaps this would be the impetus for Fitz Lee's later service in the cavalry? In any case, nothing further is known of Lee's early life except that he eventually moved northward as a young man and was working as a laborer in Philadelphia, Pennsylvania, by 1889.

On 26 December 1889 Fitz Lee enlisted in the U.S. Army for a five-year term of service at Philadelphia and was subsequently assigned for duty in Troop M of the 10th Cavalry Regiment. This unit was one of just four regiments in which African Americans could serve at that time, the others being the 9th Cavalry and the 24th and 25th Infantry regiments. These units were segregated, being manned entirely by black enlisted men and noncommissioned officers and were led by white senior officers. Employed almost entirely on the frontier during America's great era of westward expansion, these regiments soon gained the collective nickname "Buffalo Soldiers" as they fought Native American tribes off and on for three decades in a series of conflicts known as the Indian Wars. A newly minted private, Fitz Lee would soon head westward and joined the 10th Cavalry at its headquarters, first in Arizona and later at Fort Leavenworth, Kansas, and Fort Assinniboine in Montana. At the end of his five-year enlistment in 1894, Fitz Lee was rated as a very good soldier, and he immediately reenlisted while stationed in Montana, this time for a three-year term. He would remain a Buffalo Soldier for the rest of his life, enlisting yet again for another three years at Fort Assinniboine on 27 December 1897. Little did Fitz Lee know that just months later, he and his fellow cavalrymen would be assigned new and dangerous duty in wartime conditions.

When the Spanish American War broke out in April 1898, the U.S. Army was in need of experienced troops. Among the veteran units transferred to the Caribbean theater were the Buffalo Soldiers serving out west; it would be hard to find more seasoned and battle-tested regiments in the army than those men that had been employed for years fighting the Indian Wars. As a result, the 10th Cavalry, as well as the three other all-black regiments were sent to Florida in April 1898. On 1 June 1898 Private Fitz Lee was detached from the 10th Cavalry and assigned to the command of Lieutenant Carter Johnson. Chosen to lead a special detachment, Johnson picked fifty men from among the Buffalo Soldier regiments to take part in a mission to provide supplies and reinforcements to Cuban rebels. The American force departed Florida on 25 June and arrived at their chosen landing place near Cienfuegos on 29 June. The first attempt to make a landing was thwarted and a second attempt was made the next day, this time at Tayabacao. Once again, the American landing force faced heavy opposition and had to retreat, this time leaving fourteen men, many wounded, behind and in danger of capture. Several rescue attempts to save these men were subsequently mounted, but each was repulsed, and were it not for the naval bombardment that kept Spanish forces pinned down, the men would surely have been captured. For the fifth rescue attempt Lieutenant Johnson chose four of his best cavalrymen, Fitz Lee, Dennis Bell, WILLIAM THOMPKINS, and George Wanton, to be led by Lieutenant George Ahern, a regular army officer. The mission was a dangerous one, as the Spanish forces were well alert and surely expectant of another rescue attempt. Nevertheless, the small party rowed silently to shore and quickly rescued the men that had been left behind, doing so under heavy gunfire. Lieutenant Johnson would later state that the rescue by the black troopers was "a brave and gallant deed" (Schubert, p. 139), and in Fitz Lee's case perhaps even more so; on the very day of the mission he had begun suffering problems with his vision that would later cripple him. Early the following year, Lieutenant Johnson recommended his men for the Medal of Honor, and by June 1899 the award was approved. Fitz Lee would receive his medal in late June while he was in the hospital at Fort Bliss, Texas.

By the time the Spanish American War had reached its quick end in August 1898 African American troops had proved themselves, as they had during the Civil War and the Indian Wars before, to be every bit the equal of their white counterparts in the army and navy. The highest measure of that service was exemplified in the conduct of such Medal of Honor recipients as Fitz Lee, Edward Baker Jr., and ROBERT PENN. Though largely forgotten figures today, valiant men like this, and many others that served their country honorably without formal recognition, would gradually pave the way for the eventual integration of the U.S. armed forces fifty years later.

Sadly, Fitz Lee did not live long to enjoy his Medal of Honor. Suffering from multiple ailments that seemed to attack him suddenly during his service in Cuba, Lee became nearly blind and crippled. He was subsequently discharged from the army on 5 July 1899 and somehow made his way to Fort Leavenworth, Kansas, where many retired Buffalo Soldiers resided and helped care for their own. Here, Lee was taken in and cared for by fellow soldier CHARLES TAYLOR, a future Negro League baseball manager, and his family. However, Fitz Lee never recovered and died less than three months after his discharge. With the help of his fellow soldiers, both black and white, at Fort Leavenworth, the Medal of Honor recipient was given a proper burial with full military honors at the Leavenworth National Cemetery, where a special headstone and plaque marks his final resting place.

FURTHER READING

Hanna, Charles W. *African American Recipients of the Medal of Honor* (2002).

Schubert, Frank N. *Black Valor: Buffalo Soldiers and the Medal of Honor, 1870–1898* (1997).

GLENN ALLEN KNOBLOCK

Lee, George E. (28 Apr. 1896–2 Oct. 1958), bandleader, singer, and instrumentalist, was born George Ewing Lee Jr. in Boonville, Missouri, the son of George Lee Sr., a violinist who led a string trio, and Katie Redmond. After playing baritone saxophone and piano in an army band in 1917 and working with a vocal quartet, Lee formed a trio that included his sister, the singer and pianist JULIA LEE, who performed with George regularly until 1933. The group played mainly at the Lyric Hall in Kansas City.

The ensemble gradually grew larger, and Lee himself seems to have performed in many guises. Photos and newspapers testify to his playing tuba, guitar, banjo, ukulele, several sizes of saxophone, and clarinet in addition to fulfilling his main roles as

a singer of ballads and novelty songs, an entertaining master of ceremonies, and the band's manager. By 1927, the year of his first obscure recordings, the eight-piece band included the trombonist Thurston "Sox" Maupins, who died in 1928 before documenting the claim of his fellow Kansas City musicians that he was the equal of Jimmy Harrison. When BENNIE MOTEN's band left to tour the East in 1928, Lee found improved opportunities for work. The following year changes in personnel and an expansion to ten pieces involved the hiring of the saxophonist BUDD JOHNSON, who in turn persuaded Lee to ask the temporarily jobless jazz arranger Jesse Stone to update the band's style. Stone became the band's music director, and both he and Johnson contributed substantially to recording sessions made separately under George and Julia's name in November.

The band played for some time at the Reno Club in Kansas City, but it also toured from Texas to the Dakotas. On a visit to Parsons, Kansas, a young BUCK CLAYTON heard Lee: "He sang 'Chloe, If I Could Be with You,' 'Eleven-thirty Saturday Night,' and 'Mississippi Mud.' He looked so sharp in his Oxford-gray coat, pearl-gray vest and gamble stripe pants. When he sang he snapped his fingers. He had a beautiful voice, a strong voice, that could fill up the hall without a microphone. He used a megaphone. He was really sharp" (21). Reports of Lee's personality are contradictory. The clarinetist Herman Walder remembers Lee as overbearing and ungenerous, but Johnson remembers him as a great guy who let the band take off an hour early when FLETCHER HENDERSON's orchestra was playing in town.

During this period Lee regularly traded jobs with Moten, and after sitting in with ANDY KIRK's band in Tulsa at a time when Lee was finishing an engagement at the Pla-Mor Ballroom in Kansas City, he befriended the young Kirk by handing him the job at the Pla-Mor. This sort of arrangement worked to everyone's advantage, because by trading venues a band could find fresh audiences for its musical routines.

Lee's fortunes slowly began to decline in 1931, though his band had a strong soloist in the reed player Tommy Douglas. In 1934 Moten and Lee pooled resources to perform at the new Cherry Blossom nightclub and to produce an elaborate show at the Harlem Club in Kansas City with dancers, comedians, and a chorus line imported from New York. The show failed, and Moten and Lee resumed working separately. Lee toured with a big band into 1935 and then led small groups until the decade's end, when he retired from music and moved first to Detroit and then, after World War II, to San Diego. Before retiring he was in some unknown way the overseer of one of the extraordinary events in the history of jazz. When CHARLIE PARKER left Kansas City in the summer of 1937 to work in Lee's small band at a resort in Eldon, Missouri, he had been laughed at as an incompetent; when Parker returned to the city after his months with Lee, he was hailed as a musical genius. Reportedly Lee was completely paralyzed for the last three years of his life. At his death in Los Angeles, he was survived by his wife Isabelle (maiden name unknown) and a son.

Lee's significance was as a pathbreaker. In the first flowering of jazz and dance music in Kansas City during the Prohibition years, his band was the principal rival of Moten's orchestra. Moten's instrumentalists were superior and his recordings incomparably greater than Lee's, but it was only after hiring JIMMY RUSHING that Moten could compete with George and Julia's singing, which gave Lee's band a great popular appeal in the region.

FURTHER READING

Clayton, Buck. *Buck Clayton's Jazz World* (1986).

Dexter, Dave, Jr. "Moten and Lee Are Patron Saints of Kansas City Jazz," *Down Beat*, 1 Jan. 1941.

Pearson, Nathan W., Jr. *Goin' to Kansas City* (1988).

Russell, Ross. *Jazz Style in Kansas City and the Southwest* (1971).

Obituary: *Kansas City Call*, 7 Nov. 1958.

This entry is taken from the *American National Biography* and is published here with the permission of the American Council of Learned Societies.

BARRY KERNFELD

Lee, Jarena (11 Feb. 1783–?), preacher and evangelist, was born in Cape May, New Jersey. She was not born a slave, but little is known about her family. They were obviously poor enough that at the age of seven Lee was hired out as a live-in maid to a family that lived some sixty miles from her home. She had a religious awakening in 1804, and several years later she recounts achieving rebirth to a life free of sin and focused on spiritual perfection. Each of these spiritual transformations occurred after Lee had experienced physical hardships. Her autobiography describes a long and laborious struggle that led her to the conviction that she should preach. In 1836 she published an autobiographical narrative, *The Life and Religious Experiences of Jarena Lee.*

Jarena Lee, an evangelizing preacher who fought for the ordination of women. (Schomburg Center for Research in Black Culture, New York Public Library.)

The narrative was reprinted in 1839, and in 1849 she produced an expanded version under the title *Religious Experiences and Journal of Mrs. Jarena Lee: Giving an Account of Her Call to Preach the Gospel.*

In the nineteenth century the social order of the United States and Great Britain did not condone women's speaking in public about their spiritual experiences. Few women of any race dreamed or dared to preach publicly. However, Lee felt that she had received from God the command to preach the Christian Gospel, and eventually she began to do so. In search of a community of Christians, Lee had sought to unite with the "English Church," but she felt "there was a wall between me and a communion with that people" (Lee, 4). In 1809, at the age of twenty-six, Lee found in the Bethel African Methodist congregation of Philadelphia, Pennsylvania, a community of people who identified with issues close to her heart. It was in this company of African American Christians that she felt at ease and clear about her mission. She decided that "this is the people to which my heart unites" (5). Lee approached RICHARD ALLEN, the pastor of Bethel, about her desire and call to preach. But he did not grant her a license to preach under the authority of his congregation, because, he said, the congregation still operated under the authority of the white Methodist Episcopal Church, which did not authorize female ministers. But Lee was not deterred and even expressed some defiance at Allen's refusal to recognize her divine charge. She wrote of the incident, "O how careful ought we to be lest through our by-laws of church government and discipline, we bring into disrepute even the work of life. It should be remembered that nothing is impossible with God" (11).

Jarena married the Reverend Joseph Lee in 1811, and they would have two children before Joseph died six years into their marriage. Joseph had not supported his wife's desire to obey her call to preach, and he refused to relocate from the "Coloured Society" in Snow Hill, Pennsylvania, where he had been assigned to serve as pastor. Although she was alone and a single mother after Joseph's death, Jarena Lee was now free to pursue her ministry.

Lee began preaching and met with enough success that in 1817 she renewed her request to Richard Allen for a license to preach under the authority of the newly formed African Methodist Episcopal (AME) Church. There still was no precedent for authorizing women preachers, but by then Allen had seen and heard her preach and was convinced that she was a woman of God. More important, he was now a bishop and was eager to have enthusiastic people who could help the new denomination expand its missionary work. Allen directed Lee to hold prayer meetings and to preach.

Lee undertook her evangelical activity with seriousness and reported that she held many prayer meetings to exhort women and men to Jesus. She felt a bond with the AME Church, even though she never received an official license for her work. However, because Bishop Allen gave her speaking appointments in several Pennsylvania congregations, Lee proceeded with a sense of authority. She traveled with Allen and other AME ministers to denominational meetings in New York and New Jersey. She also traveled alone and with other women to large and small evangelical meetings throughout the Northeast. Lee's steadfast commitment to her divine call, coupled with her preaching success, challenged the male religious hierarchy and set forth new possibilities for the preaching ministry of African American women.

Jarena Lee did not set out to become a revolutionary; she merely wanted to preach the Gospel, but doing that inevitably became a revolutionary act because it challenged the ecclesiastical beliefs and gender roles of her day. Richard Allen was Lee's most powerful friend and ally, even caring for her son for several years while she spread the word. After Allen died in 1831, Lee continued to preach at various Methodist churches and locations, but found herself ostracized from an increasing number of AME churches in Philadelphia. As she wrote, "I seemed much troubled, as being measurably debarred from my own Church as regards this privilege I had been so much used to" (77).

Not much is known of Lee's final years, except that she worked for a time with the New York Anti-Slavery Society. Later in the nineteenth century many African American women within the AME Church and in other denominations followed her lead and realized their call to preach, but it was not until 1948 that Rebecca M. Glover became the first woman ordained by the AME Church. In 2000, with the way paved in part by the consecration in 1989 of BARBARA HARRIS in the Episcopal Church, VASHTI MCKENZIE became the first female AME bishop.

A pathfinder for African American women and a trailblazer among Methodist women, Jarena Lee was the first known black woman to forcefully advocate for the right of women to preach in Methodist denominations. For this feat she must be considered among the vanguard of churchwomen in the United States.

FURTHER READING

Lee, Jarena. *Religious Experiences and Journal of Mrs. Jarena Lee: Giving an Account of Her Call to Preach the Gospel* (1849).

Andrews, William L., ed. *Sisters of the Spirit: Three Black Women's Autobiographies of the Nineteenth Century* (1986).

Peterson, Carla L. "Secular and Sacred Space in the Spiritual Autobiographies of Jarena Lee," in *Reconfigured Spheres: Feminist Explorations of Literary Space*, eds. Margaret R. Higonnet and Joan Templeton (1994).

JUALYNNE E. DODSON

Lee, John Wesley, Jr. (13 Feb. 1924–18 Sept. 2008), pioneer black naval officer, was born in Indianapolis, Indiana, the only child of John

Wesley Sr. and Emma Laverne Scott Lee. His parents also adopted a son, Albert Lee Blount. Lee's parents had a wide disparity of educational attainments. His mother, who had a master's degree, was a schoolteacher. His father, a grocer, had dropped out of elementary school and was barely literate. As a youngster, Lee grew up in Indianapolis and in 1940 graduated from segregated CRISPUS ATTUCKS High School. Lee then attended Indiana University in Bloomington, where he spent three years studying mostly science and mathematics as part of an intended pre-med course. He lived in a rooming house, because the university's dormitories were not open to black students.

In April 1944 Lee enlisted in the navy, influenced to join by his friends and by his brother Albert's experience in that branch of the service. As Lee prepared to leave Indianapolis to begin training, men were selected by lot to go into one of two groups. Half went into general service occupational ratings; Lee was selected to be part of the other group, which would train as cooks and stewards, the traditional roles for African Americans in the navy. He went through recruit training in an all-black section of the naval training station at Bainbridge, Maryland. After brief training as a steward, Lee appealed to a white chief petty officer to let him become a quartermaster or signalman. The chief recommended that he apply instead for the V-12 Naval Reserve officer program that included both college courses and navy training. Lee did and was accepted. He spent some time at DePauw University in Greencastle, Indiana, before attending midshipman schools in New York City and Chicago. Lee was commissioned as a Naval Reserve ensign on 30 July 1945, two weeks before World War II ended in the Pacific.

Lee served brief tours of duty in three Pacific Fleet ships—the oilers USS *Ramapo* and USS *Sepulga* and the attack cargo ship USS *Capricornus*—before being released from active duty in August 1946. He then resumed his education at Butler University in Indianapolis. He left the school to accept the navy's offer of a regular commission. During Lee's time at school the navy informed him that he had been selected for possible commission as an officer in the regular navy, as opposed to the naval reserve. Lee accepted the offer and on 15 March 1947 he was sworn in as the first African American officer in the U.S. Navy, in part because he was in the right age group for his rank as ensign. While the navy had commissioned a few dozen black officers during World War II in response to political pressure,

it now deliberately sought to integrate its officer corps. In July 1947, a few months after he became a regular officer, Lee married Geraldine Virginia Bridgewater. He had met her on a blind date in late 1946 when she and Lee's uncle were working in the same drugstore in Indianapolis. She operated a postal substation in the store, and Lee's uncle was a pharmacist. They subsequently had three children: Deborah Andrea, Cheryl Ann, and John W. Lee III. His wife died in November 2000, and their son died the following month.

Ensign Lee initially attended navy schools for more than a year of additional training. Then the service gave him his choice of duty. He opted for a large warship and was assigned in October 1948 to the aircraft carrier USS *Kearsarge* in the Atlantic Fleet. There he encountered a pattern that was replicated throughout his service career. No one seemed surprised when he showed up at a given ship or shore station. The commanding officers of the units had been queried in advance as to whether they would accept a black officer. This treatment assured that Lee would be welcomed when he reported for duty, but at the same time he disliked it, because it differed from the normal practice for officer assignments. Lee had a cautious approach during his early duty assignments, waiting for other officers to initiate relationships rather than doing so himself. Later in his career he found that behavior no longer necessary.

Lee transferred to the crew of the heavy cruiser USS *Toledo* in June 1950, the month the Korean War broke out. The ship had just returned to California from the Far East but soon returned to the western Pacific. Lee was on board as assistant navigator in September 1950 when the cruiser was flagship for gunfire support operations in connection with the amphibious assault on Inchon, a port on Korea's west coast. In 1952 Lee reported to Washington, D.C., for recruiting duty, specifically to be proactive in publicizing opportunities for minorities in the Naval Reserve Officer Training Corps program. It was a dramatic turnabout from the World War II years in terms of seeking African Americans to become naval officers.

In 1954 Lee earned a bachelor's degree in aerological engineering from the Naval Postgraduate School and became a subspecialist in the area of meteorology. In the same period, through the Scripps Institute, he earned a master's in Oceanography. He served subsequently as aerographer on the aircraft carrier USS *Wright* and as gunnery officer of the destroyer USS *Cotten*. After duty at the Naval

Air Rocket Test Station in Dover, New Jersey, Lee was commanding officer of an oceanographic unit on board the survey ship USNS *Dutton* in 1959–1960. The ship's mission was to do special surveys of the ocean floor to prepare for the advent of the navy's first nuclear-powered submarines armed with Polaris ballistic missiles. In the early 1960s, as a lieutenant commander, Lee served as executive officer (the second in command) and navigator of the cable-laying ship USS *Aeolus*. His final tour of active duty, from 1963 to 1966, was on the staff of the North Atlantic Treaty Organization in Paris.

In 1963 Lee was passed over for promotion to the rank of commander, his greatest professional disappointment. He chose to retire from active duty in June 1966 and seek a second career as a civilian electronics expert. In 1966 and 1967 he worked for the Radio Corporation of America in Indianapolis, and from 1967 to 1989 he was with the Naval Avionics Center, also in his hometown of Indianapolis. With the Avionics Center Lee's work was involved mainly with logistics—supervising the maintenance and repair of ballistic missile guidance systems and airborne communications relay equipment. In that role he made numerous visits to navy ships. During his time in the navy, Lieutenant Commander Lee had a historic role as the service made a dramatic transformation in its attitudes and employment of African American personnel.

FURTHER READING

"Reminiscences of Lieutenant Commander John Wesley Lee Jr., U.S. Navy (Retired)," U.S. Naval Institute oral history (1994). This is a bound volume of the transcripts of oral interviews with Mr. Lee. Copies are on file at the Naval Institute and Naval Academy Library in Annapolis, Maryland, and at the Naval Historical Center in Washington, D.C.

Miller, Dan. "My Letters Ruffled Feathers," *All Hands* (Oct. 1977). [*All Hands* is published by the Bureau of Naval Personnel.]

Nalty, Bernard C. *Long Passage to Korea: Black Sailors and the Integration of the U.S. Navy* (Naval Historical Center, 2003).

PAUL STILLWELL

Lee, Joseph E. (15 Sept. 1849–25 Mar. 1920), Florida Republican political leader, lawyer, and African Methodist Episcopal (ΛME) minister, was born free in Philadelphia, Pennsylvania. Although the names of his parents are unknown, Lee was orphaned while an infant and was raised by Quakers. He attended Cheyney University, then known as the Institute for Colored Youth, the first black high school in the United States. After graduating in 1869, Lee moved to Washington, D.C., to begin a clerkship under the controversial "governor" of the District, Alexander Robey "Boss" Shepherd. Intermittently, Lee attended Howard University Law School in Washington, D.C., a historically black institution established in 1867. Lee attended Howard at a time when African American leaders were clamoring for black lawyers who could help in the struggle to secure the rights of African Americans. He graduated with an LLB degree in 1872.

Lee then relocated to Jacksonville, Florida, and was admitted to the Florida bar in 1873. He quickly became a successful lawyer and an influential Republican Party leader. His political career began after passage of the Civil Rights Act of 1875, which, among other things, granted the right to African Americans to serve on juries and participate in the legal system on an equal footing with whites. The same year he was elected to the state legislature for Duval County. He served in this position until 1876. He then built a lucrative legal practice and returned to the state legislature for six more years, followed by two more years in the state senate. From 1887 to 1889 Lee served as a municipal court judge for Jacksonville. His election proved contentious, and his Democratic opponents fought bitterly to prevent his victory. In an antagonistic move, Democrats discovered that Lee's home in Duval County was just outside the city limits. Since city residency was a requirement for the post, Lee's Democratic enemies asserted that he should be declared ineligible. Catching wind of the new charge, Lee hired a team of carpenters, bricklayers, and other workers to jack his house off its foundation and in the middle of the night move it within the city limits. When city officials surveyed the land, they found—much to their astonishment—that Lee's house was indeed within city limits, and thus Lee retained his judgeship.

Through his expanding political contacts, he was named a collector of customs from 1890 to 1894, and again from 1897 to 1898. He then served as collector of internal revenue from 1898 to 1913, remaining in that office longer than any other African American in a similar position anywhere else in the country. A powerful state Republican leader, Lee served on the state delegation to the Republican National Conventions in 1880, 1884, 1904, 1912, and 1916. With Woodrow Wilson's victory in the 1912 election, however, Lee's political fate was sealed. As soon as President Wilson took office the next year he cleared Republicans from patronage positions, especially African Americans. Men such as Assistant Attorney General of the United States WILLIAM H. LEWIS, Registrar of the Treasury JAMES C. NAPIER, famed Civil War hero ROBERT SMALLS (who was also customs collector in Beaufort, South Carolina), and Lee, collector of internal revenue at Jacksonville, were swept from their offices. Lee then returned to his legal practice in June 1913, and he announced the opening of his office at 32 East Beaver Street in Jacksonville.

Although Lee spent his career helping to lead the Florida Republican Party and served as secretary of the Florida Republican State Central Committee from 1912 until 1920, he served as legal counsel for one side in a disputed seating of a Florida delegation in the Democratic National Convention. He did not appear before the National Democratic Executive Committee, but he did prepare a brief for the side that won its case based on Lee's work. Proud and distinguished in appearance, the bespeckled, dark-skinned Lee was well respected by many in both major political parties and became the most important black Republican of the late nineteenth and early twentieth centuries.

In addition to his career as a lawyer and state political leader, Lee also was a prominent AME clergyman, eventually earning a divinity degree, although no record of the degree-granting institution has been found. He entered the ministry in the fall of 1881 and soon emerged as "one of our leading ministers in the East Florida Conference" (*Christian Recorder*, 28 Aug. 1890). In 1883 Lee worked with other AME church leaders to convince the church to establish a normal school (teacher training) in Florida. He first served at St. Paul's AME Chapel in the Lavilla section of Jacksonville and after 1 July 1892 was the pastor at Jacksonville's Mt. Zion AME Church, which was founded in 1886 on Beaver Street, only a few blocks from where Lee would reestablish his law practice in 1913. In whatever free time remained to him, Lee also was an active PRINCE HALL Freemason and head of the state's Independent Order of Good Templars lodges. Lee did eventually marry; his wife Rose assisted him in church affairs, but nothing else has been uncovered about her. Lee is still honored in his adopted state of Florida. The city of Jacksonville raised a memorial to him, the Joseph E. Lee Child Development Center still serves the city of Jacksonville, and the Joseph E. Lee Republican Club gives out a service award in Lee's name to honor meritorious state political leaders.

FURTHER READING

Akin, Edward N. "When a Minority becomes the Majority: Blacks in Jacksonville, Florida," *Florida Historical Quarterly* (Oct. 1974).

Coppin-Jackson, Fanny. *Reminiscences of School Life and Hints on Teaching* (1913).

Foner, Eric. *Freedom's Lawmaker: A Directory of Black Office Holders During Reconstruction* (1993).

Styles, Fitzhugh Lee. *Negroes and the Law in the Race's Battle for Liberty, Equality and Justice* (1937).

ANTJE DAUB

Lee, Joseph Howard. *See* LoBagola, Bata Kindai Amgoza Ibn.

Lee, Julia (13 Oct. 1903–8 Dec. 1958), blues singer and pianist, was born in Boonville, Missouri, the daughter of George Lee Sr., a violinist, and Katie Redmond. Most published sources cite Julia's birth date as 31 October, but Sheldon Harris cites 13 October as the date on her death certificate. Julia sang with her father's string trio from age four. Around 1913 her parents acquired a piano, and she began studying it with Scrap Harris and Charles Williams. She performed locally from 1916, notably in a group that included the bassist WALTER PAGE. After graduating from Lincoln High School in 1917, she studied piano at Western University beginning around 1918. From 1920 to 1933 her career paralleled that of her brother GEORGE E. LEE, in whose bands she played and sang. With a group drawn from his orchestra, she recorded "Won't You Come Over to My House? (… Nobody Home but Me)" in November 1929. Occasionally during this period she worked on her own, including at an engagement in Chicago in 1923. Sometime during the 1920s Lee married Johnny Thomas; details are unknown. She later married Frank Duncan, a baseball player who played in the Negro Leagues with the Kansas City Monarchs, and with whom she had at least one child, Frank Duncan III.

Julia Lee's career blossomed as her brother's fortunes declined. She held an engagement at Milton's Tap Room in Kansas City from 1933 to 1948, although she left occasionally to perform elsewhere in the Midwest. With JAY MCSHANN playing piano in a session in 1944, she sang a lament, "Trouble in Mind," and a new version of "Come on Over to My House," which included a magnificent alto saxophone solo from Tommy Douglas. In 1945 the record producer and *Down Beat* editor Dave Dexter Jr. included Lee's work in a historical anthology on Capitol Records, and

"Trouble in Mind" was so warmly received that Lee was invited to Los Angeles for further recordings. For the remainder of her career in the studio, Lee herself was the pianist, with occasional featured solos finding her playing variously in blues, boogie-woogie, and swing styles. She sang straightforward popular songs, including a moving version of "When the Real Thing Comes Along" (1947), but most of her hit songs were sexually suggestive, delivered in a restrained manner with biting, crystal-clear enunciation, so that the humorous lyrics could be easily understood. The most clever are her best-selling "King-size Papa," "I Didn't Like It the First Time" (ostensibly about spinach but obviously about sex), and "(Come and See Me Baby, but Please) Don't Come Too Soon" (all from 1947).

While holding engagements in Los Angeles and Denver from mid-1948 through 1950, she continued working and recording in Kansas City. In 1949 she was invited to perform for her admirer and fellow Missourian Harry S. Truman at the White House Press Association dinner in celebration of Truman's election victory. Lee appeared in the film *The Delinquents* in 1957. She died the following year of a heart attack at her home in Kansas City.

Except among devoted fans of rhythm and blues, Lee has been largely forgotten since her death. Carey James Tate described her as "a jolly mother confessor to the depressed spirits of her audiences." Compared to the sexually explicit rap and soul songs of the late twentieth century, Lee's suggestive lyrics seem tame, which makes it difficult to capture the effect they had on audiences of her day. Nonetheless, her renditions offer the additional bonus of fine solos from distinguished jazz and rhythm and blues musicians, including Douglas, Benny Carter, and VIC DICKENSON. When in a serious mood, Lee could convey emotional depth and a plaintive sound.

FURTHER READING

Harris, Sheldon. *Blues Who's Who: A Biographical Dictionary of Blues Singers* (1979).

Pease, Sharon A. "30 Years in KC, Julia Lee Nabs National Fame," *Down Beat*, 15 Jan. 1947.

Tate, Carey James. "Julia Lee: The Last of the Great Blues Singers," *Second Line* 11 (Jan.–Feb. 1960).

This entry is taken from the *American National Biography* and is published here with the permission of the American Council of Learned Societies.

BARRY KERNFELD

Lee, Mollie Huston (18 Jan. 1907–1982), founder, librarian, and civic leader, was the only child born to Corrina Smith Huston and Rolla Soloman Huston, a businessman and politician in Columbus, Ohio. Lee received her early education in Ohio's public school system. Books were plentiful in the Huston's household; as a youth, Lee learned the value of reading books. This belief helped shape her career in which she encouraged African Americans to become more knowledgeable about their heritage through reading, and provided the means for them to do so.

In 1929 Lee earned a B.A. degree from Howard University in Washington, D.C. As a student, she developed a keen interest in Howard's African American collection, serving as a library assistant under EDWARD CHRISTOPHER WILLIAMS. Later, Lee matriculated at Columbia University in pursuit of a library science degree that she received in 1934.

Lee began her career at Shaw University in Raleigh, North Carolina, when she was employed as the university's first African American librarian from 1930 to 1935, an era when public libraries in Raleigh, as in nearly all southern communities, were segregated. She discovered, however, that African Americans were not permitted to use the public Olivia Rainey Library that had been serving whites in Raleigh since 1901. Lee observed that Raleigh consisted of a growing number of African Americans—both non-professionals and professionals—who were avid readers in an environment of two historically black colleges and universities (HBCUs): Saint Augustine's College and Shaw University. Other HBCUs, notably the North Carolina College for Negroes in Durham (changed to North Carolina Central University), were in neighboring cities; therefore, Lee realized that African Americans could gain much knowledge by utilizing a public library. Friends shared Lee's sentiment and rallied around her, meeting in Christ Church to plan for the library.

In 1935, Lee founded the Richard B. Harrison Library, located in Raleigh, North Carolina in Wake County. The library, named in honor of actor Richard Berry Harrison, was opened to serve all ethnic groups. Harrison was an African American who played the role of "De Lawd" in the *Green Pastures*. Richard B. Harrison Library flourished for ten years in downtown Raleigh in the 100 block of East Hargett Street, where several African American businesses were located. Since the library was independently supported, Lee relied on friends to provide funds to purchase equipment, books, and even to rent the building, which was a storefront structure of twenty-five by one hundred feet. With 890 books available to be circulated, Lee devised a plan that she executed when readers were slow in patronizing the library. She often marketed the books, distributing some to businesses and to individuals who were nearby as she hand delivered the books. Lee was determined to have the books read by a vast number of individuals.

Although the city of Raleigh was suffering economically, Lee's leadership and stamina enabled her to succeed in increasing library resources. To meet the growing needs of the community, Lee appealed to the board of directors for another more spacious building, which could accommodate more equipment and collections. Her appeal was granted. In July 1948, this new location for the library was in a framed two-story building on South Blount Street, close to Hargett Street. The library's programs and services enhanced the lives of adults in general, as well as those with special needs. Prominent African American authors frequented the library to lecture and make presentations in their respective fields. Among them were DR. JOHN HOPE FRANKLIN, DR. W. E. B. DuBOIS, LANGSTON HUGHES, ARNA BONTEMPS, ZORA NEAL HURSTON, SAUNDERS REDDING, Jesse Jackson (the author, known for his children's books), and others. Indeed, the Richard B. Harrison Library became recognized throughout the United States with the dedicated efforts of Lee. To serve more African American communities in Wake County, Richard B. Harrison and Olivia Rainey libraries shared a rented bookmobile that traveled to Washington Terrace, Chavis Heights, and Apex to determine if there were enough residents interested in reading and who desired branch libraries in those areas. In 1941, a branch library was established in Apex; it lasted for eight years. Chavis Heights's branch library was opened in 1947, while Washington Terrace's was opened in 1951.

The Richard B. Harrison Library located on South Blount Street for nearly twenty years experienced another transition in 1966. It was no longer operating independently, for, as a consequence of integration, it merged with the Wake County Library System. A new edifice was erected in July 1967, located in the southeast Raleigh neighborhood on New Bern Avenue, where it still exists. Although the Wake County Library System contributed funds to the library annually, the amount was insufficient, so Lee continued to seek financial assistance from other sources. Beatrice Rogers Hamlin, a retired

Raleigh resident and who worked together with Lee approximately twenty years, commented on Lee's dedication. She stated, "When they were trying to build the new library, she (Mrs. Lee) just let her salary go back to help. A lot of people are not that dedicated" (*Carolinian Newspaper*).

All of the support made a positive impact on the growth of the Richard B. Harrison Library. Lecturers of varied ethnic backgrounds participated in programs at the library. More resources, as well as program offerings were accessible to children and adults. The children's story hour improved, and more discussion groups were created for children. Lee was able to extend her adult program to communities in rural Wake County to improve their reading and writing skills and to address current issues that affected their lives in order that their quality of life might be enhanced. Lee's belief that a library should serve its community became more apparent as manifested in her leadership.

The Mollie Huston Lee Collection of Black Literature, containing over 8,000 fiction and nonfiction books about adults and juveniles, was established to enlighten African Americans about their heritage, for the materials are about or written by African Americans. Diverse methods were used in the gradual selection of materials. Several renowned African American authors supported Lee in identifying appropriate materials for the collection, as they corresponded with her regularly. Another method that Lee employed was that she searched for book titles and lists in African American magazines, newspapers, and scholarly journals. Also, she purchased books from a bookshop in New York City and collected personal materials from residents, as well as African American authors. In addition to books, the Lee Collection, which is still in existence, contains newspapers, magazines, brochures, photos and vertical files that capture the local and national culture of African Americans, especially local biographies. The Mollie Huston Lee Collection was officially named in Lee's honor in 1972.

Since more libraries were opening for African American use in the 1940s, there was a need for more librarians. Lee encouraged African American students to become librarians in order that they might be hired in those positions and made provisions for them to receive scholarships. Also, Lee provided students from Atlanta University, North Carolina Central University, and University of North Carolina at Chapel Hill with a rigorous hands-on experience at Richard B. Harrison Library, as she supervised their work in library science.

Mollie Huston Lee, the first black librarian in Wake County, North Carolina, poses in the stacks at the Richard B. Harrison Library. (Richard B. Harrison Library/Mollie Huston Lee Collection.)

Lee founded the North Carolina Library Association in 1934, to improve professional development for African American librarians, and later she became supervisor of local public libraries. She was affiliated with the Democratic Women's Club and the League of Women's Voters; she engaged herself in public service projects through Delta Sigma Theta Sorority and the Links, Inc.

Lee's honors include her listed in *Who's Who in America* and *Who's Who Among American Women*, publications in well-known journals, and numerous honors from organizations. Some of the organizations are the American Library Association, Zeta Phi Beta Sorority, Wake County Library Trustee Board, and the Wake County Commissioners.

In Raleigh, North Carolina on 23 July 1935, Lee married Dr. James Sumner Lee, who was chair of the biology department at North Carolina Central University. The couple had one son, James S. Lee, Jr.

Lee retired from Richard B. Harrison Library after thirty-seven years of service in 1972, but never from public service. Posthumously, Lee received the Road Builders Award in 1989. She died in Durham County Medical Center, Durham, North Carolina.

Lee's work in library science chronicles the services she provided, especially for the African American community. Mollie Huston Lee laid the foundation for numerous African American libraries, most notably the Richard B. Harrison Library in Raleigh, North Carolina; she was its founder and librarian for over thirty-seven years.

FURTHER READING

Some documents such as unpublished dissertations and correspondence are housed in the School of Library and Information Sciences North Carolina Central University, Durham, North Carolina. Web site available at http://web.co.wake.nc.us/lee/

Moore, Ray Nichols. "Mollie Huston Lee: A Profile," *Wilson Library Bulletin* 49 pp. 432–439 (February 1975).

Speller, Benjamin F. Jr. "Mollie Huston Lee (1907–1982): Librarian, Civic Leader, Organizing Leader," In Jessie Carney Smith, ed. *Notable Black American Women, Book II* (1996).

Obituary: *The Carolinian* (Raleigh, North Carolina), 4 Feb. 1982.

PATRICIA WILLIAMSON NWOSU

Lee, Raphael Carl (29 Oct. 1949–), plastic surgeon, biomedical engineer, and educator, was born in Sumter, South Carolina, the son of Leonard Powell Lee, a physician, and Jean Maurice Langston, a visual artist. His father had grown up in rural coastal South Carolina, part of a large family in which he and all his siblings, despite the limited opportunities available, earned higher degrees and went into either teaching or medicine. His mother came from a line of successful entrepreneurs with real estate interests in and near Philadelphia, Pennsylvania, and Washington, D.C.

As South Carolina's public schools remained racially segregated until 1963, Lee's parents enrolled him in a private Roman Catholic "mission" elementary and middle school for blacks. In the fall of 1963 he was among the first group of blacks to enter St. Jude High School in Sumter; he remained there for two years before attending Bishop England High School, also a Catholic institution, in Charleston (1965–1967). The environment at these two schools was hostile at times, he recalls, because of a vocal minority of local whites opposed to racial integration. Undeterred, he went on to earn a bachelor's degree in Electrical Engineering at the University of South Carolina (1971). Lee then moved north to Philadelphia, where he earned a master's degree in Biomedical Engineering at Drexel University (1975) and an M.D. at Temple University (1975); in 1979 he received an ScD in Biomedical Engineering at the Massachusetts Institute of Technology.

Lee's professional interests began to take shape while he was a junior at the University of South Carolina. He took a wide range of courses—biology and other premedical units, in addition to electrical engineering—and discovered the excitement and rewards of interdisciplinary study. The potential medical applications of laser beams, for example, piqued his interest. As a result, Lee entered one of the nation's first combined engineering and medicine programs at Drexel and Temple. This experience motivated him to pursue a career in academic surgery, and he went on to serve as an assistant resident in surgery at the University of Chicago Hospitals between 1975 and 1977. While at Chicago, he developed a special interest in wound healing and plastic surgery—particularly the relationship between electromagnetic fields, fluid mechanics, and human connective tissues—which led him to interrupt his clinical training for a period of research at the Massachusetts Institute of Technology (MIT). He earned his doctorate at MIT in two years with a thesis titled "Cartilage Electromechanics: The Relationship of Physicochemical to Mechanical Properties." He then completed his surgical training at the University of Chicago Hospitals, as resident in surgery (1979–1980) and chief resident in general surgery (1980–1981).

Lee returned to the Boston area in 1981 for further specialized training. He was senior assistant resident in plastic surgery at Massachusetts General Hospital (1981–1982), after which he held three academic appointments simultaneously: assistant professor of electrical engineering and bioengineering at MIT, assistant professor of bioengineering and surgery at Harvard–MIT Division of Health Sciences and Technology, and assistant professor of surgery (plastic) at Harvard Medical School. These multiple appointments reflected the interdisciplinary emphasis of his work but also stretched him thin at times—requiring a determined balancing act that was "barely possible," he felt, in the competitive environments of Harvard and MIT. In 1989 he returned to the University of Chicago as associate professor of surgery, anatomy, and organismal biology (biomechanics). He was promoted to full professor in 1992. Since 1991 he has also served as director of the Electrical Trauma Program and medical director of the Burn Unit at the University of Chicago Hospitals.

Lee's research has resulted in several important developments in the surgical management of severe trauma, particularly electrical shock, thermal burns, and wounds (see Lee et al., *Electrical Trauma: The Pathophysiology, Manifestations, and Clinical Management* [1992]). He also established the usefulness of copolymer surfactants in repairing damaged cells after trauma (see Lee et al., "Surfactant-Induced Sealing of Electropermeabilized Skeletal Muscle Membranes In Vivo," *Proceedings of the National Academy of Sciences* 89 [1992]: 4524–4528). The mechanism involves sealing damaged cell membranes—a powerful illustration of how Lee's engineering and surgical background and interests came together in deeply practical ways in the medical field.

Other important outgrowths of his research include pharmaceutical strategies to reduce scarring, the use of mechanical stress to control engineering of tissues, and surgical procedures for gynecological reconstruction. (On the second of these topics, see, for example, Lee et al., "A Review of the Biophysical Basis for the Clinical Application of Electric Fields in Soft Tissue Repair," *Journal of Burn Care and Rehabilitation* 14 [1993]: 319–335.) Lee has founded two companies—Avocet Polymer Technologies, Inc. (1996), and Maroon Biotech,

Inc. (2000)—to develop and market the scarring and surfactant discoveries, respectively, and he holds about a dozen related patents. Also important is a software package that he and a group of his students created to measure body surface area injury. This was the first technique to use three-dimensional simulation of individual patients to calculate burn involvement, complication, and survival rates in a vastly more accurate way than had been possible with traditional methods of visual estimation or with two-dimensional models.

Lee married Kathleen M. Kelley in 1983. Dr. Kelley holds joint appointments in the departments of psychiatry and pediatrics at the University of Chicago and is an occasional research collaborator with her husband. They have two children—Rachel Kelley Lee and Catherine Marie Lee.

A fellow of the American College of Surgeons and diplomate of the American Board of Surgery and American Board of Plastic Surgery, Lee has held office in a number of professional associations. He was a charter member, membership chairman (1986–1988), and scientific council member (1991–1993) of the Bioelectric Repair and Growth Society; scientific council member (1994) of the Bioelectromagnetics Society; chairman of the plastic surgery section (1989–1991) of the National Medical Association; president (1996) of the Society for Physical Regulation in Biology and Medicine; and member of the research and education committee (1998) of the American Association of Plastic Surgeons. Among his numerous awards, he received a grant from the MacArthur Foundation in 1981, the first year of the prestigious MacArthur Fellows Program. Lee was selected for his original, creative research combining techniques and knowledge in surgery, electrical engineering, biophysics, and electrochemistry. *Science Digest* included him in its 1984 list of America's Top 100 Young Scientists. He was also one of four engineers featured in a 1988 exhibit—Black Achievers in Science—designed by the Museum of Science and Industry in Chicago. In 1991 he received an honorary doctorate from his alma mater, University of South Carolina, in recognition of his distinguished career.

FURTHER READING

The MIT Museum has a small biographical file, mostly clippings, photographs, and news releases, relating to Lee's early career as a faculty member at MIT.

Williams, Clarence G., ed. *Technology and the Dream: Reflections on the Black Experience at MIT, 1941–1999* (2001).

CLARENCE G. WILLIAMS

Lee, Samuel J. (22 Nov. 1844–1 Apr. 1895), politician and lawyer, was born a slave on a plantation in Abbeville District, South Carolina. Of mixed race, he was probably the son of his owner, Samuel McGowan, and a slave woman, whose name is unknown. When McGowan entered Confederate service during the Civil War, Lee attended him in the camps and on the battlefield. Lee was wounded twice, at Second Manassas in 1862 and later near Hanover Junction, Virginia. After emancipation, he farmed in Abbeville District and then in Edgefield County, South Carolina, having settled in Hamburg. By 1870 Lee had accumulated at least $500 in real estate and $400 in personal property. Sometime before February 1872 he married a woman identified in legal documents as R. A. Lee; her maiden name is unknown.

Though not formally educated as a youth, Lee had learned to read and evidently developed talents as a debater and orator fairly early. When the Reconstruction Acts of 1867 allowed freedmen new opportunities for formal political participation, he made the most of his skills. He served as a registrar in 1867 and became an Edgefield County commissioner in 1868. That same year he was elected to represent his black-majority county in the South Carolina house of representatives. A Republican, Lee sat in the legislature for the next six years—after 1871 as the representative of Aiken County, which had been formed from portions of Edgefield and several other counties. In his early years in the legislature, he was a party regular, consistently voting for legislation that strengthened Republican power and black political rights in South Carolina, but he was somewhat less apt than other black Republicans to support measures pressing integration of transportation facilities. Yet as a trustee of the University of South Carolina beginning in 1873, he participated in the opening of that college to African Americans (this experiment in biracial education, which prompted the resignation or dismissal of some white faculty members, was ended by Democrats as soon as Reconstruction collapsed).

As African Americans increasingly demanded and won leadership positions in the South Carolina Republican Party, Lee rose to become speaker of the state house of representatives in 1872. He brought a noted polish to the position, being termed by one Yankee journalist an "elegant and accomplished" officer "who would have creditably presided over any commonwealth's legislative assembly." Lee did not, however, use his authority as speaker to increase the number of black committee chairmen. Regrettably, too, at a time when ethical standards were none too high among American politicians and in a place where opportunities for black Republicans to prosper were few, Lee submitted to abundant temptation. He later admitted to taking money for his vote on a bill and to converting state funds to personal use. Further accusations of corruption were lodged against him, including that he outfitted his home in Aiken with furniture purchased by the state.

Lee resigned the speakership and left the legislature in 1874 to give full time to a second profession, one that would prove less clouded than his political career. He had read law while serving in the General Assembly, had been admitted to the bar by 1872, and had established a practice in Aiken. Initially, though, the baggage he had accumulated as a Reconstruction politician weighed the young attorney down. In 1875 Lee was convicted of fraud in his handling of funds as a county commissioner. Elected solicitor of the Second Circuit in 1876, he had to resign after Democrats made accusations regarding a large bribe he had allegedly taken as a legislator. After an indictment for conspiracy to defraud the state was brought by the newly installed Democratic administration in 1877, Lee left South Carolina and worked in Alabama, investigating land claims for the federal government.

The conspiracy case seems never to have been brought to trial, and by the following year Lee had returned to settle in Charleston. At first he worked for a white attorney there, but within a few years he established his own firm and became the busiest black lawyer in South Carolina. Chiefly practicing criminal law, Lee attracted more clients and did better by them than any other African American attorney in the state (forty-six blacks were admitted to the South Carolina bar between 1868 and 1895, the year of Lee's death). Not confining his work to Charleston, he appeared before the state supreme court in Columbia several dozen times between 1880 and 1894.

Lee did not entirely abjure politics and public life after South Carolina was "redeemed" by white conservatives. He was a member of a delegation of black southerners who conferred with President-elect James Garfield in 1881, and the following year he competed with ROBERT SMALLS for a Republican congressional nomination (both men lost to a third candidate, who was white). Having been active in the Reconstruction-era state militia, he served in the early 1890s as general of a black militia brigade in Charleston.

For all his ability and grace in the courtroom, Lee's black clients could not pay him well, if at all, and he did not prosper financially in his legal practice. At the time of his sudden death from heart failure in Charleston, his estate amounted to some $230 worth of law books and $115 in cash. Though his potential was somewhat dimmed by the temptations of office, the implacability of Democratic opponents, and the poverty of the African American community he served, Lee remains a conspicuous figure in the opening of politics and the professions to African Americans in the post-emancipation South.

FURTHER READING

Bryant, Lawrence C.. *Negro Legislators in South Carolina, 1868–1902* (1967).

Foner, Eric. *Freedom's Lawmakers: A Directory of Black Officeholders during Reconstruction* (1993).

Holt, Thomas. *Black over White: Black Political Leadership in South Carolina during Reconstruction* (1977).

Oldfield, J. R. "A High and Honorable Calling: Black Lawyers in South Carolina, 1868–1915," *Journal of American Studies* 23 (1989).

Underwood, James L., and W. Lewis Burke, eds. *At Freedom's Door: African American Founding Fathers and Lawyers in Reconstruction South Carolina* (2000).

This entry is taken from the *American National Biography* and is published here with the permission of the American Council of Learned Societies.

PATRICK G. WILLIAMS

Lee, Spike (27 Mar. 1957–), filmmaker and screenwriter, was born Shelton Jackson Lee in Atlanta, Georgia, the eldest of four children of Bill Lee, a jazz composer and musician, and Jacquelyn Shelton, a schoolteacher. During Lee's youth, his family moved to Brooklyn, New York, where they lived in the neighborhoods of Crown Heights, Cobble Hill, and Fort Greene. Lee later used his intimate knowledge of these racially integrated Brooklyn neighborhoods to dramatize in his films the relations between African Americans and their non-black neighbors. Movies and television, such as the Anglo-American *The Partridge Family* and the African American *Good Times*, informed Lee's understanding of popular culture. "I-can remember my mother, Jacquelyn, taking me to see James Bond movies," he reminisced. "She liked them. I used to like 007 myself. I remember seeing *Help!* with the Beatles and *A Hard Day's Night*" (*By Any*

Spike Lee poses for photographers in Cannes, France on 15 May 1991. (AP Images.)

Means, 2). Lee's fiction film *Crooklyn*, which he cowrote with his siblings, documents the influence television had on them. In 1975 Lee enrolled at his father's alma mater, Morehouse College in Atlanta, Georgia. He graduated in 1979 with a B.A. in Mass Communications. That summer Lee interned with Columbia Pictures, and the following fall he entered the Tisch School of the Arts at New York University, where he cultivated a working friendship with cinematographer Ernest Dickerson. "We came in together," Lee later recalled. "He was from Howard. I was from Morehouse.... We were the only blacks at NYU" (*Gotta Have It*, 32).

Lee produced his first student film, *The Answer* (1980), in response to D. W. Griffith's 1915 film *The Birth of a Nation*. The following year his MFA thesis project, the forty-five-minute film *Joe's Bed-Stuy Barbershop: We Cut Heads*, which Dickerson shot, won the Academy of Motion Pictures Arts and Sciences' Best Student Film Award and became the first student film ever included in the Lincoln Center New Directors, New Films series.

In 1980 Lee and Monty Ross, a friend from Morehouse, established the production company Forty Acres and a Mule Filmworks. Named after the historically inaccurate, but often cited, "promise" made by the U.S. government to newly emancipated slaves, Lee's company name expresses the consternation of African Americans at America's broken promises and racist policies. The company's first production, Lee's first feature-length film, *She's Gotta Have It* (1986), with its mixture of humor and intensity, its bold exploration of sexuality and race, and its strong visual style, won the Cannes Film Festival's Best New Director Prize. Shot in ten days for $175,000, the film made more than $7 million at the box office. Lee himself played one of the film's key roles, the fast-talking, big glasses–wearing bicycle messenger Mars Blackmon. Blackmon reappeared in a series of Lee-directed Nike commercials aired from 1988 to 1993 and reprised in 2003 upon the retirement of MICHAEL JORDAN.

In 1988 Lee reflected on his Morehouse College experiences with *School Daze*, a musical set in an historically black college. Controversial in its treatment of color and class divisions within the black community, the film pits wealthy, light-skinned "gammas" against working-class, dark-skinned "jigaboos." *School Daze* was Lee's first studio film, and after the production costs reached $4 million, Island Pictures pulled out, but Lee managed to secure additional financing from Columbia Pictures. The film eventually grossed $15 million.

With *Do the Right Thing* (1989), Lee won an Oscar for Best Screenplay and established himself as a filmmaker of unique vision and distinctive voice. The film, which Lee wrote and starred in, explores African American cultural life in the flashy and confident visual style that came to distinguish Lee's work. Featuring OSSIE DAVIS, RUBY DEE, Danny Aiello, and John Turturro, *Do the Right Thing*, like *School Daze*, mines divisions and differences within the African American community and beyond. In the film, a Brooklyn pizza shop becomes the nexus of escalating racial tension between Italian Americans and African Americans. The action takes place on the hottest day of the summer and climaxes with a street riot and the killing of a black youth by white policemen. Unlike most American films, *Do the Right Thing* refuses to resolve its plot or its political conflicts. Instead, it ends with contradictory on-screen quotations from MARTIN LUTHER KING and MALCOLM X.

Lee's next film, *Mo' Better Blues* (1990), about a jazz musician inspired by Lee's father, marked the beginning of his collaboration with leading man DENZEL WASHINGTON, who later starred in *Malcolm X*, *He Got Game*, and *Inside Man*. In *Jungle Fever* (1991), about the romance between a married, black architect and his Italian American secretary, Lee presents another bold treatment of race and class.

Malcolm X (1992), based on ALEX HALEY's biography and a script begun by JAMES BALDWIN, engendered controversy even before production began, most notably through attacks from AMIRI BARAKA. When it went over budget, Lee turned to black celebrities, including OPRAH WINFREY, Michael Jordan, and BILL COSBY, for funds. The film reputedly cost $35 million but it became Lee's highest grossing film, earning $48 million at the box office. The finished film drew praise from critics and audiences, but controversies remained, including concern over Lee's refusal to implicate LOUIS FARRAKHAN and the Nation of Islam explicitly in Malcolm X's death. Although Denzel Washington earned an Oscar nomination for his performance in the title role, the film received no other recognition from the Academy. However, the film's influence on the public's perception of the leader is unequivocal, as was its effect on the marketplace. Promotional merchandise and tie-ins for the film, including clothing, toys, posters, and books, were marketed by Lee himself.

Lee followed *Malcolm X* with the smaller coming-of-age drama, *Crooklyn* (1994), and the darker *Clockers* (1995). In 1996 Lee released both *Girl 6*, written by SUZAN-LORI PARKS, about an unemployed actress who takes a job as a phone sex worker, and *Get on the Bus*, about a busload of black men heading to Washington, D.C., for the 1995 Million Man March. Lee again tapped Denzel Washington for a leading role in his next film, the father-son drama *He Got Game* (1998). *Summer of Sam* (1999), set in the Bronx in the summer of 1977, has a predominantly white cast led by John Leguizamo.

Lee confronts the history of the representation of African Americans head on with the satire *Bamboozled* (2000). The film stars Damon Wayans as an Ivy League–educated black network television writer who unintentionally creates a popular hit with a purposefully offensive modern-day minstrel show featuring black actors wearing blackface. While many viewers and critics complained about the film's descent into melodrama, *Bamboozled* was praised for its fierce exposé of racism in the media. "On a deeper level," wrote Steven Holden in the *New York Times*, "*Bamboozled* addresses the broader issue of minstrelsy and American culture and poses unanswerable questions about black identity, assimilation and the give and take between white and black cultures" (6 Oct. 2000).

In addition to his fiction projects, Lee has directed a number of documentary films. He won an Academy Award for Best Documentary with *4 Little Girls* (1997), about the events surrounding the September 1963 bombing of the Sixteenth Street Church in Birmingham, Alabama, that killed four African American girls. In 2000 Lee captured the stand-up work of comedians Steve Harvey, D.L. Hughley, Cedric the Entertainer, and Bernie Mac in the box-office hit *The Original Kings of Comedy*, and in 2002 he produced and directed JIM BROWN: *All American*. For HBO, Lee directed a television adaptation of John Leguizamo's one-person Broadway show, *Freak*, in 1998. Three years later he directed a television adaptation of Roger Guenveur Smith's Obie Award–winning off-Broadway solo performance in *The* HUEY P. NEWTON *Story*. Lee's other television projects include filming the 1998 and 1999 *Pavarotti & Friends* concerts, organized to raise funds for children in Liberia, Guatemala, and Kosovo. In 2006 HBO aired Lee's documentary depicting the events surrounding Hurricane Katrina, titled *When the Levees Broke: A Requiem in Four Acts*. The documentary chartered the devastation from a multitude of perspectives, and delivered a startling critique of the federal government's response.

Family loyalty helped launch the acting career of Lee's sister, Joie, and the careers in the technical areas of filmmaking of his brothers, Cinqué and David. Lee commissioned his father to write the original scores for many of his films, including *She's Gotta Have It, School Daze, Do the Right Thing, Mo' Better Blues,* and *Jungle Fever.* Most of Lee's films dramatize family and neighborhood issues. One also finds these themes in *25th Hour* (2002), which explores a young Irish American working-class man's ties with his friends, family, and girlfriend on the day before he enters prison for a seven-year term. A critical success marked by a polemical soliloquy from Ed Norton, *25th Hour* was also one of the first full-length films to reference the events of 9/11. Further acclaim came in 2006 with the release of *Inside Man,* Lee's biggest commercial success.

In 1993 Lee married Tanya Lynette Lewis. The couple has two sons, Satchel and Jackson. For more than twenty-five years Spike Lee has maintained his status as one of only a few American filmmakers whose work articulates a personal visual style and moral vision. He is one of a small number of African American filmmakers from the East Coast who received their film-school training in the 1980s and who produce interesting films about ordinary people, showing that those lives are not so banal as many Hollywood films would have audiences believe.

FURTHER READING

Aftab, Kaleem, and Spike Lee. *Spike Lee: That's My Story and I'm Sticking to It* (2004).

Fuchs, Cynthia, ed. *Spike Lee: Interviews* (2002).

Lee, Spike. *By Any Means Necessary: The Trials and Tribulations of the Making of Malcolm X* (1992).

Lee, Spike. *Five for Five: The Films of Spike Lee* (1991).

Lee, Spike, and Lisa Jones. *Spike Lee's Gotta Have It: Inside Guerrilla Filmmaking* (1987).

Levy, Ariel. "The Angriest Auteur," *New York* (21 Aug. 2006).

McGrath, Charles. "He Makes His Own Movies (Just Don't Try to Label Him)," *New York Times* (29 July 2004).

MARK A. REID

Lee, Sylvia Olden (29 June 1917–10 Apr. 2004), pianist and vocal coach for opera, oratorio and concert, was born in Meridian, Mississippi. Sylvia's parents were graduates of Fisk University. Her mother, Sylvia Alice Ward Olden, was a successful concert artist. Her father, James Clarence Olden, was a minister and civil rights activist. In addition to studying theology at Fisk, James Clarence Olden studied classical singing and was a member of the university quartet with Roland Hayes, Charles Wesley, and Lemuel Foster. Lee's mother, who was very light-skinned and could pass for white, was offered an audition with the Metropolitan Opera shortly before her graduation from Fisk. Elizabeth Merry, one of Lee's grandmothers, was a Fisk Jubilee singer and one of the school's first graduates, in 1870.

Lee began piano lessons with her mother at age five and remained under her mother's tutelage for ten years. In 1933, at Howard University, where Lee spent her freshman year, she studied piano and organ with Cecil Cohen and William Duncan Allen. In 1935 she went to Oberlin as a scholarship student, under the guidance of Frank Shaw. At Oberlin, Lee performed in recital on both piano and organ.

Lee's first job, immediately after graduating in 1938, was at Talladega College in Talladega, Alabama, as professor of piano and organ. Established in 1867, Talledega was the oldest historically black college in Alabama. One of Lee's students there was CAROL BRICE, the eminent contralto and the first black musician to win the Naumburg Music Award.

Lee became a professor of piano at Dillard University in 1942. Dillard, also an historically black college, was established in 1930. One of Lee's students at Dillard was Geneva Handy Southall, a distinguished musicologist, pianist, and professor at the University of Minnesota. It was also during this time that Lee toured with PAUL ROBESON and played at the White House for Eleanor Roosevelt.

By 1944 Lee was in New York, studying piano as a scholarship student with Victor Wittgenstein, accompanying in the studios of Elisabeth Schumann, Eva Gautier, Konrad Bos, Rosalie Miller, and Fritz Lehmann; and preparing singers for the New York City Opera and the Metropolitan Opera. It was also in 1944 that she married the violinist and conductor Everett Lee. Sylvia Lee continued her career in the studios and began to assist her husband in preparing opera performances for his Cosmopolitan Little Symphony and the Columbia University Opera Workshop. She also coached at Tanglewood with Boris Goldovsky and served as technical adviser for the world premier of Benjamin Britten's *Peter Grimes.* In 1952 Lee was a Fulbright scholar at the Santa Cecilia Academy in Rome. There she worked with singers and saw many productions at the Rome opera.

In 1954, at the invitation of Max Rudolf, then assistant to Rudolf Bing, Lee became a staff member, remaining there for two seasons, in the Kathryn Turney Long School at the Metropolitan Opera; her selection was a breakthrough for African Americans and women.

Before her appointment to the Metropolitan staff, she confronted Max Rudolf at his home about the chances of a black singer getting on the roster. The confrontation was dropped after Rudolf told her that the time would come, that the first African American must have the greatest of talent with the best of training, the greatest voice in the first place, a good knowledge of all the languages, dramatic ability, and the first appearance must be in a character visually believable.

After Lee was no longer on the Metropolitan staff she continued to work privately with Metropolitan singers, and was, in 1985, invited by James Levine to coach for the Metropolitan's premiere of *Porgy and Bess.*

Along with her husband, in 1956, Lee received a grant from the German government to study at the Munich Conservatory of Music. Sylvia studied lieder (German art songs) and opera with the eminent Gerhard Huesch. What was expected to be one year of involvement became seven years of productivity. She became Huesch's accompanist; prepared a recital of Negro spirituals that toured throughout Germany; served as official accompanist for the annual Munich international vocal competition; became musical producer for a television special in Munich, Stuttgart, and Berlin; and directed an interracial group of singers that performed excerpts from Broadway musicals.

A return to the United States became a brief sojourn. In 1963 Lee moved to Sweden with her husband, who had become conductor of the Norrköping Symphony. She performed as a piano soloist with the maestro throughout Scandinavia and Germany.

In 1967 Sylvia Lee returned to the United States to accept an appointment as voice coach at Cincinnati College-Conservatory of Music. Everett Lee remained in Sweden, and the couple eventually divorced. She remained in this position until 1970, and then at the invitation of Max Rudolf, moved to Curtis Institute, where she remained for twenty-three years. Lee's situation at Curtis permitted her to accompany and coach in other settings. Some of the colleges and universities at which she gave master classes in opera, lieder, and spirituals were the University of Minnesota, University of Michigan, Bethune Cookman College, Lincoln University, and Spelman College. In 1983 Lee was asked by Sarah Caldwell, opera conductor and founder of the Boston Opera Company, to make a trip to Russia and coach, in English, *Porgy and Bess.*

In the early 1980s Lee worked at the Philadelphia College of the Performing Arts as a vocal coach and in the 1990s at Howard University as a teacher of vocal interpretation and style. She remained professionally active until very shortly before her death, working with scholars at Philadelphia's Marian Anderson Historical Society. Her legacy will live through film, writings, arts organizations that bear her name, and several generations of students.

FURTHER READING

Lee, Sylvia Olden, and Elizabeth Nash. *The Memoirs of Sylvia Olden Lee* (2001).

Cheatham, Wallace McClain. *Dialogues on Opera and the African American Experience* (1997).

WALLACE MCCLAIN CHEATHAM

Lee, Ulysses Grant (4 Dec. 1913–7 Jan. 1969), educator, army officer, and author, was born in Washington, D.C., the son of Ulysses Lee, a businessman and grocery store owner, and Mattie Spriggs. He graduated from Dunbar High School in Washington in 1931, attended Howard University in Washington, joined the Reserve Officers' Training Corps, earned his B.A. in 1935, and was also a commissioned graduate and a U.S. Army reservist. Remaining at Howard, Lee taught as a graduate assistant in English in 1935 and 1936 and earned his M.A. in 1936. Lee also studied briefly at the University of Pennsylvania and became a member of the faculty as an instructor and then as an assistant professor of English at Lincoln University in Pennsylvania from 1936 to 1948. During these years he was twice on leave.

From 1936 to 1939 Lee was a research assistant, a consultant, and an editor with the Federal Writers' Project, for which he helped produce a book on Washington, D.C., as a city and as the national capital, and another book on African Americans in Virginia. During part of the time between 1936 and 1942 he was also a Rosenwald fellow and an Alvia Kay Brown fellow at the University of Chicago as a doctoral student in the history of culture. In 1940 he was a visiting professor at Virginia Union University in Richmond. With STERLING A. BROWN and ARTHUR P. DAVIS he coedited *The Negro Caravan: Writings by American Negroes* (1941), an anthology of 1,082 pages containing short stories and selections from novels, poems, folk literature, drama, speeches, pamphlets, letters, autobiographies, biographies, and essays (historical, cultural, and personal), together with informative introductory material. The anthology abundantly achieves its announced purposes of presenting artistically valid writings that depict African American character and experience in America, and of assembling in one volume key literary works that have influenced African American thought—and, to a lesser degree, the thought of Americans as a whole. *The Negro Caravan* was still a widely used textbook at least fifty years after it appeared.

Called to active duty in 1942 as a first lieutenant, Lee began a distinguished military career. That same year he married Vivian Gill. He was one of the first officers assigned to the Information and Education Department of the U.S. Army. During World War II he was an education officer, an editorial analyst in the field, and an Army Service Forces officer. In this last capacity he wrote parts of and edited the manual *Leadership and the Negro Soldier* (1944). Its purpose was to aid in training African American soldiers and to diminish attitude and disciplinary problems, so as to maximize "efficient troop utilization." It was written in a tactful manner, to avoid the real possibility of public controversy. In 1946 Lee was appointed a staff historian in the Office of the Chief of Military History, Department of the Army. While still in the army, Lee found the time and energy to complete his dissertation on the plight and accomplishments of African American soldiers between World War I and World War II. He retired from the army in 1952 with the rank of major. The University of Chicago awarded him a Ph.D. in 1953 in the field of history of culture.

Resuming his academic career, Lee taught at Lincoln University in Jefferson City, Missouri, from 1953 until 1956. He then taught at Morgan State College in Baltimore. While working enthusiastically at Morgan, he used his dissertation as the beginning of the most significant writing of his career, *The Employment of Negro Troops*, which had twenty-two chapters in 738 two-columned pages, along with many illustrations and maps. It was published in 1966 by the Office of the Chief of Military History of the U.S. Army as part of the United States Army in World War II series. In his book, Lee reviews the experiences of African American troops in World War I, problems between the wars with respect to their segregation and duty assignments, and military plans for their phased integration and maximum "utilization" in World War II. He discussed problems connected with the requirement that African American soldiers have separate facilities, difficulties with regard to training and leading them, their physical fitness and morale, disturbing incidents connected with the use of facilities, "camp town" prejudice, and transportation. He discussed African American troops overseas, often in menial service units but also dramatically involved in heroic ground and air combat. To accomplish his research, Lee consulted masses of material, both published and unpublished. The result is a landmark work of enduring historical value; it is scholarly, impressive, and authentic. Without assigning blame, Lee clearly presented evidence of African American soldiers' patience and bravery despite lingering prejudice both inside and outside the army. Reviewers unanimously praised his writing for being dispassionate and judicious.

In 1965 Lee lectured under the auspices of the American Society of African Culture in Nigeria, Sierra Leone, and Cameroon. The most outstanding essay among several he published is "The Draft and the Negro" in *Current History* 55. In it he discussed the African American's historical position with respect to the draft, draft riots and race riots, and African Americans and the draft in World War I, World War II, and later. He concluded that African Americans had been chronically disadvantaged for military service when drafted because of "rankling [social, educational, and vocational] inequities" in the private sector. In 1968–1969 Lee taught concurrently at Morgan State and the University of Pennsylvania. In his limited leisure he studied the art of cooking, classical and jazz music, cocker spaniels, and American railroads. One day as he was leaving the campus at Morgan to return to his home in Washington, he suffered a heart attack and was pronounced dead a few minutes later at a Baltimore hospital.

FURTHER READING
Lee's papers are in the Moorland-Spingarn Research Center at Howard University.
Obituaries: *Washington Post*, 9 Jan. 1969; *New York Times*, 11 Jan. 1969.
This entry is taken from the *American National Biography* and is published here with the permission of the American Council of Learned Societies.

ROBERT L. GALE

Lee, William (c. 1750–c. 1810), slave of George Washington, attending to him throughout the War of Independence, was likely born in Virginia and was initially the slave of Colonel John Lee of Westmoreland County, Virginia. After his owner's death in 1767, William Lee, who would retain his former master's surname for his entire life, was purchased by George Washington at auction in October 1767. The purchase price of William was high for the time, over sixty-one pounds, and was paid by Washington with a bond that came due in April 1769. At this same time, Washington also purchased from the Lee estate William's brother, Frank, described much like William as a "mulatto," and two "negro" boys, Adam and Jack (Wiencek, 131). Subsequently transported to their new home at Washington's Mount Vernon estate, Adam and Jack were likely employed as field hands, while William and Frank Lee were set to work inside the mansion, Frank as a butler and William as Washington's personal valet or manservant. From his obscure beginning and enslaved condition, William Lee would soon be involved in the events of the War of Independence and witnessed first hand the birth of a new nation. William Lee's life provides an interesting window into the mind-set of the United States' most prominent founding father, George Washington, and further demonstrates the vast contradictions engendered by the institution of slavery even at the republic's very inception. Indeed, while Washington struggled to gain America her freedom, his constant attendant was a man bought and paid for who had never known freedom.

As a valet to Washington, William Lee's day began and ended with that of his master; in the morning he likely helped Washington dress and groom himself, as well as attending to his other comforts. He accompanied Washington almost everywhere he went, as was customary for a gentleman's manservant in that era, traveling with his master on business to the House of Burgesses in Williamsburg, Virginia, as well as farther afield on an Ohio surveying expedition in 1770, and to the First Continental Congress in Philadelphia in 1774. George Washington was also an expert horseman and avid foxhunter, and employed William Lee as his hound-keeper (or huntsman). Like Washington, Lee was a skilled, and perhaps reckless, horseman; and Washington's nephew would later recall that "Will … rode a horse called *Chinkling*, a surprising leaper, and made very much like its rider, low but sturdy, and of great bone and muscle … mounted on *Chinkling* … this fearless horseman would rush, at full speed, through broke or tangled wood" (Hirschfeld, 99).

Most interesting is the fact that William Lee accompanied General George Washington in almost all of his travels, expeditions, and battles during the War of Independence; always in the background, and always at the ready, Lee "rode alongside Washington in the thick of battle, ready to hand over to the general a spare horse or his telescope or whatever else might be needed" (Hirschfeld, 111). William Lee bore silent witness to historical events at Valley Forge, Long Island, Trenton, Princeton, Brandywine, Yorktown, Monmouth, and numerous others; he surely gained some insight into the character of Washington's generals and those serving with him in the Continental Congress. Because of this service, William Lee is also depicted in some of the most recognized paintings of the American Revolution. The most notable of these are John Trumbull's 1780 portrait of Washington, with William Lee standing behind him and Thomas Sully's 1813 painting of the crossing of the Delaware River depicting Lee on horseback.

For all his travels, north and south, there is no record that William Lee ever attempted to escape to freedom. Perhaps he was content with his lot in life; though enslaved, he surely knew he was better off than the average field hand. However, maybe he did contemplate gaining his freedom. Like Martha Washington's personal slave, ONA JUDGE STAINES, William Lee surely had sympathetic friends in the black communities of a city such as Philadelphia, and Lee would have been certainly well received if he made a successful dash to the British lines. An examination of the facts, however, reveals just how difficult such an escape may have been psychologically. Although it is undeniable that William Lee was a recognizable figure and such an escape would not have gone long undetected, the historian Henry Wiencek provides an even more plausible theory: fear. William Lee no doubt knew of the dire consequences for those slaves that failed in an escape attempt; when Washington captured a runaway named Tom in 1776, within weeks he sold the man to the West Indies, likely to an early death slaving on one of the sugarcane plantations that were "disease-ridden pestholes" (Wiencek, 132).

By the end of the War of Independence, William Lee was married to a free black from Philadelphia, Margaret Thomas, who had formerly worked as a servant in Washington's headquarters. When Washington and William Lee later returned south, all slaves.... [H]e did not believe that the slaves were inherently inferior people; he believed that the apparent deficiencies in African Americans were the result of their enslavement" (Wiencek, 356). Stoic though he was, surely Washington was motivated to free William Lee for reasons both of logic and of the heart. Either way, Lee was given a thirty-dollar annual pension by Washington for the remainder of his life, and was given the opportunity to stay at Mount Vernon. Aged and infirm, Lee chose to stay on the Washington estate, there living the remainder of his life. William Lee was buried in the slave cemetery at Mount Vernon, likely without military honors and with his valiant and faithful service but a distant memory.

FURTHER READING

Hirschfeld, Fritz. *George Washington and Slavery: A Documentary Portrayal* (1997).

Wiencek, Henry. *An Imperfect God: George Washington, His Slaves, and the Creation of America* (2003).

GLENN ALLEN KNOBLOCK

Lee, William Mack (12 June 1835–?), body servant and minister, was born a slave at Stafford House, on the Potomac River in Westmoreland County, Virginia. The names of Lee's parents are not known, but shortly after the death of his mother he was taken to the Arlington Heights, Virginia, home of Robert E. Lee, later to command the Confederate army of northern Virginia during the Civil War. William Mack Lee married in 1855, but his brief autobiography does not mention the name of his wife, who died in 1910, nor the names of his eight daughters, the youngest of whom was born in 1875. The couple also had twenty-one grandchildren and, as of 1918, eight great-grandchildren.

Lee does not state precisely when he began serving "Marse Robert," whom he describes as "one of the greatest men in the world," but his autobiography notes, erroneously, that Robert E. Lee freed all of his slaves "ten years before the war" (4). In December 1862, just three days before the U.S. president Abraham Lincoln announced the Emancipation Proclamation, General Lee did emancipate around two hundred slaves belonging to his father-in-law, who had died in 1857 and had left instructions in his will for the manumission of all of his slaves within five years. Since none of these slaves bore the surname Lee, however, it is probable that William Mack was not among those emancipated in 1862. William, then, was most likely still

William Lee with George Washington. (Library of Congress.)

the general tried to arrange to have Margaret Lee move to Mount Vernon with her husband, but it is unknown whether or not the move was ever made. The postwar years were not kind to William Lee; he injured one knee on a surveying expedition with Washington and hurt the other several years later after a fall. When Washington was elected to the presidency and traveled to New York for his inauguration, Lee initially stayed behind for medical treatment and would eventually have steel braces for his knees that allowed him some mobility. However, his horseman days were now over and for much of the remainder of his life he would stay at Mount Vernon, working as a cobbler and chatting with the many Revolutionary War veterans that stopped by to visit.

William Lee was given his freedom upon George Washington's death in 1799, the only one of Washington's slaves so manumitted; perhaps Washington granted this freedom out of gratitude for Lee's long and faithful service, perhaps out of a general "sense of justice that extended to a slave at the outbreak of hostilities in 1861 when at age twenty-six he set off for the front as Robert E. Lee's cook and body servant. Lee remained by the general's side throughout the war, including at both battles of Bull Run (Manassas). He was also with General Lee on 9 April 1865 when the general surrendered to the Union forces at Appomattox, Virginia.

William Mack Lee's autobiography, written—or perhaps dictated—in 1918, his eighty-third year, devotes more space to the Confederate generals and politicians whom he served during the war than to his own experience of the conflict. The short pamphlet includes a list of thirty prominent Confederates for whom he cooked and notes that Robert E. Lee cried upon hearing of the loss of General Thomas "Stonewall" Jackson, who had been mistakenly killed by his own troops. William himself received wounds to his head and hip in 1863 when a Union shell exploded near the general's tent just as William was bringing him his horse, Traveler.

A newspaper article appended to William Mack Lee's autobiography also reveals the only time that "Marse Robert ever scolded me" in the four years that William served him (Lee, 8). As William Mack Lee told the story in 1918, the general reprimanded him on 3 July 1863 at Petersburg, Virginia, for catching, killing, and cooking with butter and bread stuffing Little Nellie, a black hen that had reliably produced eggs for more than two years at the front. William had feared that his meager supplies of flannel cakes, tea, and lemonade would be insufficient for gentlemen like generals Lee, Stonewall Jackson, Wade Hampton, and George Pickett. Robert E. Lee, William recalled, told him that he was a "fool to kill de [hen] whut lay de golden egg. Hit made Marse Robert sad ter think of anything bein' killed, whedder 'twas one of his soljers, or his little black hen" (8).

Though this story may have some basis in fact, it is likely that William Mack Lee embellished it. For one thing, the date, 3 July 1863, which William claimed to "remembah ... jes lak it was yestidy" (7), is almost certainly incorrect. Stonewall Jackson had been dead for nearly two months by that date, at which time Lee and Pickett were engaged in the third day of fighting at Gettysburg, Pennsylvania, several hundred miles from Petersburg. Given that William was in his mid-eighties when he told the tale, he may simply have misremembered it. But it may also be more than a simple coincidence that the exact date of his master's greatest military reversal

up to that point remained in William's memory. On that day General Lee accepted full responsibility for his tactical failures at Gettysburg, which historians now view as the decisive turning point in the Civil War. Little Nellie may not have died on that day, but thousands of Lee's troops certainly did, and with them died the hopes of the Confederacy. William Mack Lee was probably far too politic to point that out to southern white reporters, who in 1918 viewed him as "a negro of the old type, distinguished looking [and] polite in manner" (Lee, 4).

Published sources about William Mack Lee's views are limited to his brief autobiography, but it is certainly possible that his expressed love for his master and for the Confederacy was sincere. A minority of African American slaves and free people of color living in the South during the Civil War did, in fact, express loyalty to the Confederacy at the time, though their number is less than that claimed by many modern-day apologists for the cause. William Lee's chief reason for publishing his autobiography in 1918 is, however, instructive. At that time he was attempting to secure funds for the completion of a Baptist church that he established near Norfolk, Virginia. Indeed, he devoted many more decades of service to the black Baptist Church than to General Robert E. Lee. William had begun to preach two years before the war, and he furthered his education by attending one of the many church-funded schools established in Virginia. The funds for his schooling were bequeathed by Robert E. Lee, for whom William continued to work until the general died in 1870.

William Mack Lee "studied hard at the letter" (5), but as a man approaching middle age, he found schooling difficult. He regretted that he did not enjoy the advantages of younger African Americans, who had benefited from the expansion of public education by Reconstruction-era state governments and from the missionary efforts of former abolitionists who established church schools for the southern freedmen. Lee, as ever, did not provoke his intended white southern conservative readership by pointing out these facts. Instead, he preferred to tell them that "obedience to God is service to man" (6).

Ordained as a minister in Washington, D.C., in July 1881, he helped raise the $3,000 needed to establish the Third Baptist Church, Northwest. Over twenty years he increased the size of his pastorate from 20 to 500 members, and he helped found another church in the District of Columbia that boasted an additional two hundred members after only two years. To these he added a church near Baltimore, Maryland, whose congregation rose to more than 350, and in 1912 he began to raise the $5,500 necessary to establish a stone-front church in Churchland, near Norfolk, Virginia. By preaching in eighty-four counties throughout Virginia and the Carolinas, Lee managed to raise $5,000 of the funds needed for his Churchland pastorate between 1912 and 1915.

It was in search of the final $500 for the Churchland building that the Reverend Lee traveled to Bedford, Virginia, where he announced his intention to publish a short memoir of his Civil War experiences with Robert E. Lee and others. It was a skillful business stroke, since southern white—and indeed northern white—interest in the military campaigns of the Civil War had never been greater. Southern whites were often disdainful of the Reverend Lee when he first approached them, limping, his threadbare cap doffed, appealing for funds for his church. Things changed, however, when they heard that the old man's limp was caused by a Yankee bullet and when they learned of his closeness to the most revered Confederate war hero. According to one white newspaper report, Lee would ask them, "Ain't gwine ter turn away Ole Marse Robert's nigger, is yer?" (7). Invariably the former Confederates, or more likely the sons of former Confederates, could not. They listened to his tales; some even made a contribution to his church.

Whether the Reverend Lee was quite as obsequious in his pursuit of funds as this account suggests is unclear. He clearly had other powers of persuasion, given his success in raising, chiefly from African American sources, money for several churches and given his successful organization and leadership of benevolent insurance associations in the District of Columbia, Virginia, West Virginia, and Pennsylvania. He may have genuinely believed, as he states in his memoir, that "if we colored people want to get along well with the white people, we must show our behavior to respect and be obedient to them" (7). Or it could be that William Mack Lee was, like many born into slavery, highly skilled in the arts of "puttin' on ole massa." There is no recorded date of William Mack Lee's death.

FURTHER READING

Lee, William Mack. *History of the Life of Rev. Wm. Mack Lee, Body Servant of General Robert E. Lee through the Civil War, Cook from 1861 to 1865* (1918).

Jordan, Ervin L., Jr. *Black Confederates and Afro-Yankees in Civil War Virginia* (1995).

STEVEN J. NIVEN

Lee-Smith, Hughie (20 Sept. 1915–23 Feb. 1999), painter, printmaker, and educator, was born Hughie Lee Smith in Eustis, Florida, the son of Luther Smith and Alice Williams, a singer. His parents separated soon after his birth, and his mother moved her son to Atlanta, where he was raised by his paternal grandmother, Queenie Victoria Williams, until the age of nine. Hughie's relatives encouraged his early interest in drawing, and when his mother remarried and brought him to Cleveland, Ohio, she enrolled him in a Saturday children's art class at the Cleveland Museum of Art, where he was the only African American student. In junior high and high school he joined art and drama clubs, the debate team, and the track team, a fellow member of which was the future Olympian JESSE OWENS. While at East Technical High School, a classmate suggested that he hyphenate his name to make it seem less common.

Upon winning a one-year National Scholastics Art Competition scholarship during his senior year in high school in 1934, Lee-Smith commenced study at the Detroit Society of Arts and Crafts. Two scholarships from the Gilpin Players allowed him to graduate in 1938 with a certificate from the Cleveland School of Art (later the Cleveland Institute of Art), where he honed his drawing, painting, and portraiture techniques under the instruction of Carl Gaertner, Rolf Stoll, and Henry Keller. Lee-Smith took art courses at night at the John Huntington Polytechnical Institute. He also taught art classes at the Karamu House, a cultural center founded by and for African Americans in Cleveland. He also did some acting with the Karamu Players and some solo dancing.

In the closing years of the Great Depression Lee-Smith found work as a printmaker in a WPA-sponsored art education project. In 1939 he was hired by Claflin College, a small, historically black school in Orangeburg, South Carolina, to develop an art curriculum. The following year he married Mabel Louise Everett, and the couple moved to Detroit, where a daughter, Christina, was born. Lee-Smith spent the first few years of World War II employed by the Ford Motor Company at its River Rouge plant working as a sand molder producing Wright airplane engines in support of the war effort. He spent his evenings and weekends studying and painting. In 1944 he was called to active military service in the U.S. Navy. During his nineteen-month stint in the navy as seaman first class, Lee-Smith, while on duty at the Great Lakes Naval Base near Chicago, painted murals, portraits of the navy's first African American naval officers, including WESLEY A. BROWN and SAMUEL L. GRAVELY JR., and morale-boosting subjects. Lee-Smith eschewed the abstract expressionism that was in vogue in the mid-twentieth century in favor of his idiosyncratic brand of social realism and, later, surrealism. Early in his career his themes addressed the plight of the working class, the dispossessed, and the marginalized. His paintings from the late 1930s and 1940s have been compared to those of the American realist painter Edward Hopper and also show the influence of certain French classicists and Depression-era realists, while his paintings from the 1950s and later are more akin to those of the surrealists, particularly the Italian Giorgio de Chirico and the German Kurt Seligmann.

His often stark, blighted urban landscapes inspired by the poor neighborhoods of Cleveland, Chicago, and Detroit evoke themes of alienation, isolation, and loneliness and present an unrelenting dreamlike world of empty spaces and dreary, desolate environs sparsely populated with emotionless, detached individuals who do not interact. Among his most familiar and acclaimed paintings are *Girl with Balloon* (1949), *Boy with a Tire* (1952), *Man Standing on His Head* (1970), and *The Dreamer* (1999). His commissioned portraits include those of the freedom fighter HARRIET TUBMAN, the U.S. Supreme Court justice THURGOOD MARSHALL, and the New York mayor DAVID DINKINS, whose portrait hangs in New York's city hall. A traveling retrospective exhibit organized by the New Jersey State Museum in 1988 greatly enhanced Lee-Smith's fame.

In the early 1940s Lee-Smith was receiving prizes and favorable critical response to his work. His first one-man show was at the Snowden Gallery in Chicago in 1945. By the early 1950s he had moved from social and romantic realism to surrealism and began to establish himself as one of the nation's leading African American painters, one whose signature style was instantly recognized and had universal appeal. Along with fame came numerous awards and recognitions, including the Founders Prize of the Detroit Institute of Arts (1951), the National Academy of Design Clarke Prize (1959), the Ranger Fund Purchase Prize (1963 and 1977), four awards from Audubon Artists Inc. in the 1980s, and election to the National Academy of Design, thirty years after HENRY OSSAWA TANNER had achieved this honor.

With the aid of the GI Bill, Lee-Smith earned his bachelor's degree in Art Education at Detroit's Wayne State University in 1953. He taught art at several schools in the Midwest and on the East Coast, most notably at the Art Students League in New York City from 1972 to 1987, and he was artist in residence at Howard University from 1969 to 1971. His works are held in several important institutions, including the National Museum of American Art and the Corcoran Museum of Art in Washington, D.C., and the Schomburg Center for Research in Black Culture and the Metropolitan Museum of Art in New York City.

Lee-Smith once reflected, "In my case, aloneness, I think, has stemmed from the fact that I'm black. Unconsciously, it has a lot to do with a sense of alienation" (Bearden and Henderson, 332). This statement notwithstanding, and though it has been observed that with few exceptions the black and white subjects in his painting maintain an anxious distance from one another, he recalled having suffered little personal discrimination because of his race but was keenly aware of those who had. He was known for his donations in support of the civil rights movement of the 1960s. Very much an Anglophile, Lee-Smith frequently visited England and spoke with a decidedly British accent. Divorced from his wife, Mabel, in 1953, his second marriage, in 1965, to Helen Nebraska ended in divorce in 1974. He married a former student, Patricia Ann Thomas-Ferry, in 1978, and by the early 1990s they were living in a retirement community in Cranbury, New Jersey. Lee-Smith died of cancer at a hospice in Albuquerque, New Mexico.

FURTHER READING

Bearden, Romare, and Harry Henderson. *A History of African-American Artists: From 1792 to the Present* (1993).

Brenson, Michael. *Hughie Lee-Smith: An Overview 1949–1995* (1995).

Marion, Sara L.. *Stages of Influence: The Universal Theatre of Hughie Lee-Smith* (2001).

New Jersey State Museum. *Hughie Lee-Smith Retrospective Exhibition* (1988).

Simon, Virginia Spottswood. "Qualities of Loneliness and Light," *International Review of African American Art* (1999).

ROBERT FIKES JR.

LeFlore, John L. (17 May 1903–30 Jan. 1976), civil rights leader and politician, was born John Luzine LeFlore in Mobile, Alabama, the son of Dock LeFlore and Clara Barber. The fifth of five children, John LeFlore was born two years after the ratification of Alabama's Sixth Constitution. Aware of the limited opportunities afforded to blacks, Dock LeFlore taught his family to be proud and hardworking, and he brought them into Mobile's black middle class. Although he died when John LeFlore was only nine months old, his values and work ethic had a lasting influence. John LeFlore sold newspapers at the age of ten and landed a job at the local shipyard at thirteen.

In 1920 LeFlore graduated from Owens Academy in Mobile, one of the few good schools for black students. In 1922 he married Teah Jessie Beck and began work as a postal worker. While riding on the city's railcar in 1925 a white patron demanded that LeFlore vacate his seat. By his own account LeFlore would have given his seat to a woman, but that this was an able-bodied man convinced LeFlore that the demand was based solely on his race. His refusal to yield the seat resulted in a brawl. LeFlore soon began to revive the Mobile NAACP, whose charter had been revoked in 1924. His conviction that Mobile needed an active organization led him to petition the NAACP national office. In August 1926 a new local branch was approved, and a month later the Mobile NAACP was rechartered. This branch became the primary instrument for African American political activism in Mobile.

LeFlore rose through the ranks of the Mobile NAACP, serving as executive secretary for thirty years. He earned a reputation as one of Alabama's most fearless advocates of racial equality. Although his life was repeatedly threatened, LeFlore worked with the national office to increase the number of blacks employed as civil servants in Mobile County, fought for better accommodations for blacks on the Missouri and Southern Pacific Railroads, and investigated lynchings, which occasionally led to arrests. In 1941 LeFlore received an award at the NAACP National Convention in Houston, Texas, for his outstanding work. While serving as the Mobile NAACP executive secretary, LeFlore chaired the Regional Conference of Southern Branches, served as vice president of the Alabama Conference, and worked as a staff correspondent for the *Chicago Defender*.

In 1942 LeFlore led the NAACP in one of the first bus boycotts in the South, following the murder of a black patron by a white driver. The victim, Henry Williams, was a soldier in the U.S. military. Although military and local police officials investigated the killing, their efforts were halfhearted at best. Determined to improve conditions on Mobile's buses, LeFlore demanded that the city bus line accept seven "recommendations." LeFlore informed ROY WILKINS, secretary (director) of the national NAACP, that Mobile's black community was ready to boycott. This Mobile bus boycott, proposed thirteen years prior to the famed Montgomery bus boycott, was canceled when the bus company accepted five of the seven recommendations. LeFlore's efforts also swelled the ranks of the local NAACP. Between late 1942 and spring 1943 Mobile's chapter recruited more than a thousand new members. By 1944 more than fifteen hundred names were on its membership roster.

LeFlore next worked to win voting rights for Alabama's blacks. While protesting the poll tax, he opposed Alabama's Democratic primary, which was based on a tradition of discrimination. The 1870 the Fifteenth Amendment granted voting rights to black men, and with its ratification southern blacks went to the polls. The 1870 Alabama census counted 521,384 whites and 475,510 blacks, but more than twice as many blacks as whites were registered to vote: 114,704 blacks versus 53,409 whites. Conscious of their growing political clout, blacks were the deciding factor in Alabama's constitutional convention held in Montgomery in 1867. As blacks began to vote, white conservatives worked to disenfranchise them. Although by the early 1900s Alabama had more than 120,000 black men who met the legal requirements, the number of registered black voters had dwindled to 3,000. The Sixth Constitution of Alabama, enacted in 1901, gave white Alabamians the exclusive right to vote. With constitutional support, white southerners used the Democratic primary to force blacks out of party politics.

In *Smith v. Allwright* in 1944, the United States Supreme Court abolished the Democratic primary in Texas. The import of the decision was driven home by THURGOOD MARSHALL, special counsel for the NAACP. Convinced that *Allwright* was critical to ending black disenfranchisement, Marshall contacted the Mobile branch about preparing a strategy. LeFlore's work with Marshall led to the abolition of the Democratic primary in 1946 in Alabama and to the largest number of African American voters in half a century.

By the late 1940s LeFlore had turned his attention to equal pay for black teachers. He led a delegation of blacks to discuss with city leaders the disparity in salary between black and white high school and college teachers. In 1947 the Mobile County public school system equalized the salaries of black and white teachers.

During the mid-1950s LeFlore organized Mobile's Committee of One Hundred. He also founded and directed the division of casework for the Non-Partisan Voters League (NPVL), the political arm of Mobile's NAACP. LeFlore used these groups to integrate Mobile's municipal golf course, public library, medical society, Girl Scout council, Young Women's Christian Association, and lunch counters and restaurants.

In 1960 LeFlore headed a group of protesters against segregation at the Montgomery, Alabama, municipal airport, which resulted in fourteen segregation cases. At the same time his suit against the Mobile Trailways Bus Station resulted in landmark changes in public transportation. From 21 February 1961 to 1 October 1961 LeFlore investigated discrimination in local and interstate travel. The results of his investigations led to groundbreaking legislation in statewide and interstate bus and railroad travel.

The process of integration also expanded to the civil service. LeFlore led the call for more black policemen, more firemen, and the first black bus drivers. In 1960 Mobile added ten African American firemen, and by 1963 there were two fire stations staffed by twenty-two blacks. In 1961 three black policewomen and a black county traffic police officer were hired. The city also hired several black census counters.

Although he had worked with other leaders to desegregate the city's public education system, little progress had been made by the early 1960s. In 1960 the NPVL and the Citizens' Committee denounced the Mobile County school board's refusal to ease the overcrowding of one of Mobile's all-black schools. Determined to end segregation in public education, LeFlore recruited young blacks to test desegregation laws. In April 1961 LeFlore informed Marshall that the Mobile NPVL planned to file a lawsuit against the Mobile County school board. The NPVL's efforts culminated in the *Birdie Mae Davis v. Mobile County School Board* case. In April 1963 the case was heard in federal court. Attorneys for the plaintiffs were Jack Greenberg, CONSTANCE BAKER MOTLEY, and DERRICK ALBERT BELL JR. of the NAACP and local attorneys Vernon Crawford and Clarence Moses. In 1963 Mobile's Murphy High School became the first desegregated high school in Alabama.

LeFlore's interest in ending school segregation extended to higher education. In 1952 he wrote Thurgood Marshall and the national branch of the NAACP on behalf of William Powell, who wanted to enter the University of Alabama's law school. By the mid-1950s other civil rights efforts had resulted in the admittance of AUTHERINE LUCY [FOSTER] to the University of Alabama's graduate school. Lucy's offer of admission was rescinded following objections by whites. In 1961 LeFlore encouraged blacks in Mobile to apply to the University of Alabama's undergraduate school. One of his recruits, VIVIAN MALONE, was accepted in the summer of 1963 and matriculated the following fall. In 1965 Malone became the first African American graduate of the University of Alabama.

By the mid-1960s LeFlore's reputation as a civil rights pioneer was established. Still, he went on to serve on the Alabama State Advisory Committee to the U.S. Commission on Civil Rights, the Mobile Housing Board, the Alabama Advisory Council for Comprehensive Health Planning, and the Mobile Committee for the Support of Public Education. In 1975 he became one of only two African Americans to win election to the Alabama House of Representatives from Mobile since Reconstruction. LeFlore died of a heart attack in 1976.

LeFlore's activism spanned half a century. Although he lived in a state notorious for its violence, he used negotiations rather than demonstrations. He believed that success came more from "talking than walking." He understood that without an organization, blacks were in no position to effect change. His vision proved that a vigorous civil rights organization could bring political and economic power.

FURTHER READING

LeFlore's papers are located at the University of South Alabama Archives, Mobile, Alabama.

Autrey, Dorothy. "Can These Bones Live? The National Association for the Advancement of Colored People in Alabama, 1918–1930," *Journal of Negro History* 82.1 (22 Dec. 1997).

Bullock, Henry Allen. *A History of Negro Education in the South: From 1619 to the Present* (1967).

Rogers, William Warren, Robert David Ward, Leah Rawls Atkins, and Wayne Flint. *Alabama: The History of a Deep South State* (1994).

TIMOTHY M. BROUGHTON

Leftwich, John C. (8 June 1867–14 July 1923), educator and newspaper editor, was born John Carter Leftwich in Forkland, Alabama, the eldest of the eight children of Frances Edge and Lloyd Leftwich.

From 1872 to 1876 Lloyd Leftwich served as one of Alabama's last black state senators. John Leftwich and his siblings grew up on the 122-acre farm his parents purchased from Lloyd Leftwich's former owner. The former slaves instilled in their children the importance of religion and education. Not only did the couple learn to read and write after the Civil War but they also donated a portion of their property for the construction of Lloyd Chapel Baptist Church and Lloyd Elementary School. Remarkable for the time period, most of their eight children became college graduates.

In 1886 Leftwich entered Selma University in Selma, Alabama. Unhappy there, he wrote to BOOKER T. WASHINGTON for permission to transfer to Tuskegee Institute, and he offered to perform any kind of work in order to pay for his board. However, Leftwich remained at Selma and earned a bachelor of arts degree in 1890. Upon graduation, he moved to Montgomery, Alabama, and in 1891 he married Annie E. Davis, a widowed seamstress with four children. During his time in Montgomery, Leftwich held several different jobs. Between 1893 and 1895 he edited the *Baptist Leader*, the official newspaper of the Alabama Colored Baptist State Convention. Located on Dexter Avenue in Montgomery, the paper's office was only a few blocks away from the state capitol and the Dexter Avenue Baptist Church, which would later be pastored by DR. MARTIN LUTHER KING JR. Beginning in 1895 Leftwich gave lectures for the National Temperance Society. During this time, he was also active in Republican politics, and in 1896 served on the Republican State Executive Committee. In 1897 the new U.S. president William McKinley appointed him receiver of public monies for the Montgomery office of the Department of the Interior. Leftwich maintained this office for the duration of McKinley's time in office.

In 1899 he organized a conference for African American farmers near Montgomery. Unknown to Leftwich, Booker T. Washington viewed the conference as undesirable competition with his own Tuskegee Negro Conference. Later that year, Leftwich purchased two hundred acres of land outside Montgomery to establish the black town of Klondike. He hoped to receive support from Washington in his endeavor, but received nothing tangible. Washington did mention the town in an article about Negro progress, so Leftwich did receive some publicity, but the town ultimately failed. Finally, in 1902 President Theodore Roosevelt followed Washington's suggestion to remove Leftwich from his post in the Department of the Interior. Jobless, racked with debt, and staring at the impending disfranchisement of blacks in Alabama, Leftwich moved sans his wife to Oklahoma City in the Oklahoma Territory for a fresh start. It is unclear whether they legally divorced, but Annie Leftwich referred to herself as either married or widowed until her death in 1934. Possibly a bigamist, Leftwich married at least once more during his years in Oklahoma and had two children.

Leftwich jumped directly into the political scene by corresponding with the then-territorial governor Thompson B. Ferguson and stumping across Oklahoma and Indian Territories in support of the Republican Party and industrial education for African Americans. He also used his new newspaper, the *Western World*, to broadcast his positions on African American participation in territorial politics and education. Through his efforts, Leftwich hoped to secure himself a bureaucratic position in the Republican-dominated territorial government. He was not successful in getting a political appointment, but in 1904 he was offered the presidency of Sango Baptist College, a small black school in Muskogee, Indian Territory. This appointment commenced Leftwich's almost twenty-year career in education. His first year at the school seemed to end satisfactorily enough, but he overstepped his boundaries by promising that Governor Ferguson would speak at the school's final exercises. This embarrassment may have been a factor in his abrupt exit from the college after only one year.

In the fall of 1905 he moved on to the black town of Boley and secured a donation of five acres of land upon which he founded the Creek Seminole College. Using Booker T. Washington's teaching days at Hampton Institute as a model, Leftwich endeavored to give an industrial and agricultural education to black and Indian children in Oklahoma. In 1907 Oklahoma's new state constitution mandated the segregation of these groups in the public schools. These laws had no effect on Leftwich's vision of his student body, and his school, a private institution, remained interracial. He traveled all over Oklahoma and the Northern states to solicit money for his college. Unfortunately, his inability to manage the money he raised mired him in controversy. In 1910 his political maneuvering increased his notoriety. That year, after the mostly Republican blacks in Oklahoma were disfranchised, Leftwich switched his party loyalties from Republican to Democratic. His new political identity helped him maintain a degree of access to Oklahoma's powerbrokers, but it did not help him achieve his ultimate goal of getting the state to take over the school, a move which would have legitimized his efforts and secured the school's funding. However, with a black college already in Langston, Oklahoma, state legislators had no interest in further investing in black higher education and the school's interracial model did not help his cause either. In 1912, after five students died in a devastating fire, Leftwich rebuilt his college in the black town of Clearview, Oklahoma.

In 1918, while still operating the school in Clearview, Leftwich opened the Bookertee Agricultural and Mechanical College in Bookertee, Oklahoma, a black town named after his deceased mentor. By 1919 he sold the Creek Seminole College and focused his energies on Bookertee. Initially he imagined Bookertee serving black World War I veterans, but it evolved into a manual training school for dependent and neglected children. Among his student body were more than forty children displaced by the 1921 Tulsa Race Riot. Financial difficulties continued to plague Leftwich and eventually led to his violent death. Unable to pay his teachers, Leftwich dismissed the entire faculty during a school assembly. The school's principal, Samuel White, followed Leftwich to his office after the meeting and shot and killed him in front of several students. Leftwich was buried on Bookertee's campus and the school ceased operations a few years later.

FURTHER READING

Brown, Charles A. "Lloyd Leftwich: Alabama State Senator," *Negro History Bulletin* 26.5 (Feb. 1963).

MELISSA NICOLE STUCKEY

Leidesdorff, William Alexander (1810–May 1848),

pioneer, diplomat, and businessman, was born in St. Croix in the Danish Virgin Islands, the son of William Leidesdorff, a Danish planter, and Anna Marie Sparks, an Afro-Caribbean slave. He was educated by his owner, who reportedly treated him more like a son than a slave. As a young man he was sent to New Orleans to work for his uncle's cotton business as a master of ships sailing between New York and New Orleans. Both his father and his uncle died soon after, leaving Leidesdorff a sizable inheritance. His newly acquired wealth allowed him to propose to a white woman he had been courting, Hortense, who accepted. The engagement ended painfully shortly before the wedding date when Leidesdorff told his fiancée of his partial African descent. She called off the wedding, and he left New Orleans.

Arriving in California in 1841 aboard his schooner the *Julia Anna*, Leidesdorff settled in San Francisco, then known as Yerba Buena. In addition to using the *Julia Anna* to make regular visits to the West Indies until 1845, Leidesdorff ran a shipping route between California and Hawaii. In 1843 he obtained two large land grants on the corner of Clay and Kearney streets in San Francisco from the Mexican government, which then controlled California. On this land he constructed an adobe building that served as both his home and a retail store. He became a Mexican citizen in 1844 and with his citizenship acquired a third grant: the Rancho Rio de los Americanos, a 35,500-acre lot on the American River at what is now Folsom. His pro-U.S. sentiments caused his appointment in October 1845 as U.S. vice consul of San Francisco, his Mexican citizenship notwithstanding. American interest in California was growing quickly, and preparations for war with Mexico were beginning. John Frémont, the explorer and surveyor, was sent to the region by the U.S. government ostensibly to survey the Sacramento River valley, but in reality as a political and military leader in the event of a U.S. invasion. Leidesdorff met with and advised Frémont. Leidesdorff obtained a fourth land grant from the Mexican government in 1846—a lot on California Street and the street that would later be named Leidesdorff Street, where he constructed a warehouse.

In July 1846 U.S. marines, led by Captain John Montgomery, landed in California and declared the region the property of the United States. Leidesdorff translated Montgomery's declaration into Spanish. As a prominent Mexican citizen, he was given care of the Mexican flag that had flown over the plaza of the city and of certain official papers. As an American sympathizer and government official, two months after the invasion he hosted a grand ball in honor of the U.S. naval commander Commodore Robert Field Stockton. Leidesdorff continued to develop his land. He constructed a hotel on one lot and bought a house in-which he would live permanently. In 1847 he launched his boat, the *Sitka*, on the San Francisco Bay, the first steamer ever to sail there.

In addition to his business involvements, Leidesdorff was active in city politics. He was elected to the city council in 1847 and served as town treasurer in 1848. He became chair of San

Francisco's school board, presiding over the opening of the first public school in California in April 1848. He died in San Francisco of typhus.

Shortly before Leidesdorff's death, gold was discovered on his land at the Rancho Rio de los Americanos. Captain Joseph Folsom, negotiating to buy the stake, traveled to the West Indies to bargain directly with Leidesdorff's mother. Not until meeting her did Folsom, or anyone in San Francisco, realize that Leidesdorff was of African descent. Having no way of knowing the value of her son's estate, she sold the claim to Folsom for $75,000. When Folsom returned, he registered the property with the deed listing its value as $1.5 million. Leidesdorff is thus sometimes cited as the first African American millionaire; however, although since the wealth did not materialize until after his death, the claim is debatable.

FURTHER READING

"The First Negro Millionaire," *Ebony*, Nov. 1958.

Katz, William Loren. *Black People Who Made the Old West* (1977).

This entry is taken from the *American National Biography* and is published here with the permission of the American Council of Learned Societies.

ELIZABETH ZOE VICARY

Leiper, Fanny (1811–?), free woman of color, property holder, and washerwoman, was born into slavery in Natchez, Mississippi. The exact date of her birth is not now known. She was born to an enslaved woman, Hannah Frey, and to J. S. Miller, a white planter who lived outside of Natchez near the small town of Washington. Mrs. Margaret Overaker, a white woman, and her husband, George, owned Leiper and her mother. While Leiper was still a young girl, her mother was manumitted, but Leiper herself remained enslaved. Sometime around 1831, when Leiper was approximately twenty or twenty-one, she was freed, reportedly at the insistence of her father, who paid her owner $300. In 1834 or thereabouts, following the instructions of her white father, she was taken by boat up the Mississippi River to Cincinnati, Ohio, in the footsteps of her mother.

As was the case with most property-holding free women of color in Natchez, Fanny Leiper was of mixed race. As one Natchez resident put it, "She appears at first to be of pretty near white blood, but when you come to converse with her you discover the contrary" *(Leiper v. Huffman)*. Since Leiper was known in Natchez as a free woman of color, her occupational choices were quite limited. She was employed at one point as a washerwoman. Her white father contributed to her support as well, and it is likely that her father financed her purchase of a house and lot in Natchez.

In 1834 Leiper paid $100 to John R. Wells for a city lot located near the bluff, with the agreement that she would pay an additional installment of $75. She next contracted with the firms of Neibert & Gemmel and then Bryant & Luke to construct a six-room wood-frame house. She hired Daniel Lippencott to build the brick chimney and piers upon which the house was supported. The property additionally consisted of a kitchen, an outhouse, and enclosures that, including the house, cost Leiper $1,562. It appears that she paid at least another $100 for fruit and ornamental trees to adorn the yard. All in all the property that Leiper paid taxes on and occupied from 1834 until 1845 cost her nearly $2,000.

Fanny Leiper's relationships with men had a significant impact on her experience as a free, propertied woman. Apparently in her young adulthood she married a free mixed-race man, who gave his wife her surname of Leiper. It appears that he died shortly thereafter. She then became involved with a man named Gustavas Howard, who may have been white. It is unclear precisely when they began their relationship, but Leiper laundered his clothes and he lived with her periodically. There was a rumor circulating in Natchez that they were married, and it is quite possible that when Leiper moved to Cincinnati in 1845, Gustavas Howard went with her.

One relationship Leiper had with a man proved to cause her considerable grief. Some time in the mid-1830s Leiper began an association with Joseph Winscott, a white engineer on the steamboat *Hail Columbia*. He periodically passed through Natchez for a day or two at a time on his way up the Mississippi River from New Orleans or on the return trip. Some Natchez residents claimed to see him staying at Leiper's home quite comfortably when he was in town and it was understood that she was his mistress. For a number of possible reasons, his name and Leiper's appeared together on the deed of the property, and this issue became a central question concerning the ownership of the lot and the house that sat upon it.

In 1845 Leiper decided to move from Natchez to Cincinnati, Ohio. She hired an agent, Samuel R. Hammet, to manage her property, rent it out, and collect the monthly rent of $8 for her. It was not long after her departure that Malvina Huffman, another free woman of color and Leiper's next-door neighbor, recognized the opportunity to take advantage of Leiper's absence in Natchez. In the latter part of 1846, Malvina Huffman's white lover, Oliver Bemiss, disclosed to Hammet that he had purchased the property for Huffman from Joseph Winscott of New Orleans for $100 or $125. Later Huffman requested Hammet to send her the keys. At that time Hammett, not realizing that the transaction had occurred without Leiper's permission, surrendered the keys to Huffman, who took possession of the house.

In the next year, 1847, Leiper filed a petition against Huffman and her three associates for fraudulently cheating her of her property. Leiper charged that Huffman, with full knowledge of Winscott's name on the deed, falsely informed him that Leiper was in actuality a slave who could not hold property. She then convinced him that Leiper had fled Natchez and that the property was going to ruin. She maintained that since the property fully belonged to him and his name was on the deed, he could sell it to her. He did.

Leiper informed the court that she had paid more than $1,700 for the property and could have sold it for at least $1,000. Huffman refused to remit the house and lot to Leiper, and further, she questioned Leiper's legal freedom. Leiper lost the case she brought before the Southern District Chancery Court in Natchez and was not entitled to any relief. However, she appealed the decision before the Mississippi High Court of Errors and Appeals and eventually won her claim that she had been wrongfully defrauded of her property. After this point, Fanny Leiper is lost in the historical record.

FURTHER READING

Mississippi High Court of Error and Appeals, *Leiper v. Huffman et al.*, case #6185 (1851).

Sydnor, Charles. "The Free Negro in Mississippi before the Civil War," *American Historical Review* 32 (1927).

NICOLE S. RIBIANSZKY

Leland, Frank C. (1860?–1910?), Negro Baseball League officer, was a graduate of Fisk University in Nashville, Tennessee. Virtually nothing is known of his early or personal life—not where he was born,-nor precisely when, nor his parents' names and occupations, nor if he was ever married himself or had children. It is known that Leland played

outfield for three seasons, from 1887 to 1889, with the Chicago Unions. He had actually started his baseball career with the Washington, D.C., Capital Cities in 1887, but when westward expansion of the black teams took place, he moved to Chicago, where he helped to form a total of five teams there.

Information about Negro League teams is in general sketchy, but it is known that from 1887 to 1890, the Chicago Unions operated part-time, as a weekend enterprise, relying on passed-hat contributions from the spectators to meet their expenses. To attract top opponents—including white semi-professional teams—Leyland and the Chicago Unions offered various incentives. Besides dividing gate receipts with the opposing team, the Unions would offer a side bet—ranging from twenty-five to fifty dollars, and sometimes as high as one hundred dollars—to the team that won the game. Another way the team earned money was with side promotions, which added to the day's festivities. For example, in one game between the Brightons and the Unions, the latter promoted a foot race between players from each club. The winner received fifty dollars plus an extra ten dollars from the Chicago Amateur Baseball Association (CABA). In another game between the Unions and the Models, the winning team received a gold ball and a silver-mounted ebony bat.

By 1890 the Unions' season was a nearly fulltime operation, as the team would barnstorm through Midwestern states during the week, returning to Chicago for Sunday games. Leland functioned as the team's traveling manager, while William Peters, the club's general manager from 1890 to 1900, remained in Chicago. Their travels took the club though a wide swath of the Midwest; during one stretch they went on a seven-game winning streak against the best teams in Michigan.

Coming from Nashville, and the South in general, where black baseball clubs already existed, Leland gave many people in the Midwest their first exposure to black baseball. He was instrumental in organizing and developing five successful baseball teams in Chicago: the Union Base Ball Club in 1888, Chicago Unions (1898), Chicago Union Giants (1901), Leland Giants (1905), and the Chicago Giants (1911). His efforts were fueled by his deep-seated belief that black baseball leagues could be a viable business alternative to the white-dominated leagues. Leland pooled his resources with other African American entrepreneurs who believed that their success would depend on economic cooperation, as no help in obtaining capital could be expected from white America. These baseball owners understood that they had to go where the money could be made. At that time, this meant scheduling games with Chicago's white semi-pro clubs, as well as securing leasing agreement with white park managers.

In 1901 Leland combined the Unions with the Columbia Giants to form the team that carried his name, the Leland Giants, a successful team that enjoyed a forty-eight-game winning streak during the 1905 season. In some years Leland both played for the team himself and managed it. In 1907 he lured pitching superstar RUBE FOSTER to Chicago to take the reins of the team as both mound ace and manager. In Foster's first eleven starts he won every game, with four shutouts, even though the Giants had entered the tough integrated city league. Even though in 1909 Foster broke his leg midseason, causing him to miss the playoffs, the Giants went on to win the eastern championship pennant, although the team lost the western championship to the St. Paul Colored Gophers. After his recovery Foster culminated the 1909 season by arranging a postseason series against the Chicago Cubs. Although the Leland Giants lost the three-game series, the games were closely contested, proving that black teams could compete against clubs from organized (white) baseball.

The next season, in 1910, the Leland Giants were the talk of the Midwest, but Foster and Leland separated and formed two distinct teams. Both managers claimed the rights to the pennant won the previous season, as well as to the official name of the club, the Leland Giants. The dispute required legal rulings before accord was reached. Leland's team, because he had a numerical majority of players from the previous season, won the right to fly the pennant. On the other hand, Foster's team won the right to retain and use the name Leland Giants, which caused much confusion, with Foster's team being called the Chicago Leland Giants and Leland's team being referred to as Leland's Chicago Giants. Causing still more confusion, although Foster won the legal right to retain the name of Leland Giants for the 1910 season, he chose to change the club's name to the American Giants during the 1911 season. This move altered the future of the team, and Foster lured five of Leland's players away from Leland's Chicago Giants and developed a new club he could run his own way, with some support from white tavern owner John Schorling. Foster believed the main goal of the Negro Leagues was to prepare for integration; when that day arrived he wanted

African American athletes to be ready to step forward. Leland also renamed his team the Chicago Giants, which became a charter member of the Negro National Leagues formed in 1920.

Leland was one of the earliest pioneers of black baseball and had a career that spanned a quarter century, from 1887 to 1912.

FURTHER READING

Heaphy, Leslie A.. *The Negro Leagues, 1869–1960* (2003).

Hogan, Lawrence D. *Shades of Glory: The Negro Leagues and the Story of African-American Baseball* (2006).

Riley, James A.. *The Biographical Encyclopedia of the Negro Baseball* (1994).

LUKE NICHTER

Leland, Mickey (7 Nov. 1944–7 Aug. 1989), U.S. congressman, was born George Thomas Leland in Lubbock, Texas, to Alice Lewis and George Thomas Leland II. After the separation of his parents Leland, along with his mother and brother, moved to the Fifth Ward of Houston, Texas. His mother worked in a drug store and later became a teacher. A "mousey" lad who was nicknamed Mickey after the world's most famous cartoon mouse, Leland attended the public schools of Houston—Atherton Elementary, Ryan Junior High, and PHILLIS WHEATLEY High School—before entering Texas Southern University in Houston in 1965. During his time there, Leland became a campus activist involved in a number of civil rights, health, and social issues. He led numerous demonstrations on campus and chided his fellow students for their apathy toward social issues and their lack of involvement in civil rights activities. In north Houston he sought to improve the health system for Hispanics and African Americans and helped to initiate a free community health clinic called Jensen Medical Referral Services. There Leland helped to set up a door-to-door outreach campaign to inform people about available medical care and preliminary screenings. Meanwhile he majored in pharmacology and received a bachelor's degree in 1970. Upon graduation Leland served for a year as an instructor of clinical pharmacy at his alma mater.

Driven by his desire to help the poor and downtrodden, Leland became involved in civil rights activities that catapulted him into a political campaign for a seat in the Texas House of Representatives in 1972. Encouraged by friends and supported by the philanthropist John de Menil, Leland won the election for representative from the

Eighty-eighth District in Houston and was twice reelected. As a state representative Leland advocated employment opportunities for minorities and health care for the poor. He helped to author a bill to organize the Health Maintenance Organization of Texas and is especially remembered for promoting legislation that allowed the state health care system to purchase less expensive prescription generic drugs. While serving in the Texas House, Leland was vice chairman of the Joint Committee on Prison Reform and held membership on the Labor, State Affairs, and Human Resources Committees.

When BARBARA JORDAN, Texas's first black U.S. congressperson, decided not to run for reelection in 1978 Mickey Leland, who earlier that same year had organized the National Black-Hispanic Democratic Coalition, became a candidate in the Eighteenth Congressional District. Success in this election afforded Leland the opportunity to represent his native Fifth Ward and also to expand his role in eradicating poverty, hunger, and inequity. Leland, who was known in the Texas legislature for his flamboyant style with his dashiki, Afro haircut, and eccentric hats, abandoned those unconventional characteristics when he got to Congress. But despite Leland's change in style and dress he never wavered in his commitment to the less fortunate. In Congress he would become an advocate for civil rights, health care, children, and the elderly.

Upon his arrival in Congress Leland's leadership abilities were soon recognized, as he was chosen to be freshman Majority Whip in his first term and later served twice as at-large Majority Whip. He also was appointed to the Interstate and Foreign Commerce (later Energy and Commerce) Committee, the Civil Service Committee, and was chairman of the Sub-Committee on Postal Operations and Services. In addition to his regular committee responsibilities, Leland was chairman of the Congressional Black Caucus for the Ninety-ninth Congress. As chairman, on 12 November 1984, he staged a demonstration against apartheid in front of the South African Embassy and successfully urged passage of stronger sanctions against the South African government.

Despite all of these accomplishments, Mickey Leland is best remembered as a spokesperson for the problems of hunger in the United States and throughout the world. He had expressed interest in the issue of hunger since his days at Texas Southern University, but became increasingly concerned as congressman when he visited soup kitchens and a makeshift homeless shelter. The opportunity to do something about this problem presented itself in 1984 when Leland co-authored legislation, with Representative Ben Gilman of New York, to establish the House Select Committee on Hunger. Speaker Thomas P. "Tip" O'Neill named Leland chairman when the bill was enacted to carry out the Committee's mandate: "to conduct a continuing, comprehensive study and review of the problems of hunger and malnutrition." Although it had no legislative jurisdiction, the committee brought attention to the issues of hunger and poverty in the United States. Much of the committee's influence stemmed from Leland's personal ability to generate awareness of complex hunger alleviation issues and to exert moral leadership. Leland's legislative initiative helped to create the National Commission on Infant Mortality, offered better access to free food for at-risk women, children, and infants, and established the first comprehensive services for the homeless.

Leland's sensitivity to the immediate needs of the poor soon made him a spokesman for hungry people on an international scale. Reports of acute famine in Sub-Sahara Africa in 1985 prompted Speaker O'Neill to ask Leland to lead a bipartisan congressional delegation to assess conditions and relief requirements. When Leland returned he brought together entertainment personalities, religious leaders, and private voluntary agencies to generate public support for the Africa Famine Relief and Recovery Act of 1985. This legislation provided $8 million in food and humanitarian relief supplies. Coupled with this effort, in 1987 Leland met with Pope John Paul II to discuss food aid to Africa and to propose a joint United States food initiative to Mozambique. The latter came as a result of the first congressional delegation (of which Leland was a member) to the Soviet Union.

As chairman of the Select Committee on Hunger, Leland organized fund-raising efforts for Africa famine victims and worked to establish health care in third world nations. The fund-raiser for which he was most noted was the 1985 Band Aid Concert in Philadelphia in which he presented the Black Caucus Award to the rock music producer Bob Geldof, who had helped to organize the benefit concert for Ethiopian famine relief. At the same time, Leland strove to keep food aid from being used as a political tool. To this end, he advocated communication between those nations that were friendly toward the United States as well as those who were perceived to be anti-American. His aim was to further humanitarian goals and to support the right of United States citizens to provide humanitarian assistance of food and health care to citizens of any nation. As a result Leland's successful initiative helped to expand the funding for primary health care in developing countries, including UNICEF's child survival activities and Vitamin A programs supported by the U.S. Agency for International Development (USAID). Under Leland's leadership, the Select Committee successfully championed expanding credit to the poorest individuals in third world countries and using the proceeds from the sale of donated U.S. commodities to improve health and education.

Of all Leland's effort to feed the hungry, his trip to the Sudan in the spring of 1984 was perhaps the most memorable and significant. The trip marked the beginning of his tenacious efforts to aid Sudanese refugees in Ethiopia. In the summer of 1989, however, on his sixth visit to Africa Leland, as he had often done before, traveled to Ethiopia to visit a refugee camp which sheltered thousands of children fleeing the civil conflict from neighboring Sudan. On 7 August his plane crashed in a mountainous region in Gambela, Ethiopia, killing Leland and the other eight passengers aboard. He died trying to fulfill the one cause he had championed above all others during his life—providing for the poor and helpless. Leland was buried in Houston's Golden Gate Cemetery.

Mickey Leland received several honors posthumously. His alma mater, Texas Southern University, established the Mickey Leland Center on World Peace and Hunger. On 8 August 2000 Energy Secretary Bill Richardson renamed the Minority Initiative of the Office of Fossil Energy the Mickey Leland Energy Fellowship. This fellowship was dedicated to supporting minority students in academic disciplines related to Fossil Energy. Likewise, in 1992, the Texas Water Commission in partnership with the Texas Water Development Board, the Texas General Fund Office, the Texas Chemical Council, the Council of American Electronic Association, and numerous private corporations established the Mickey Leland Environmental Internship Program. The purpose of this program was to expose minority undergraduate and graduate students to environmental issues and offer them opportunities to gain professional experience. Leland was survived by his wife, Alison Clark Walton, and one son. Twin boys were born after his death.

FURTHER READING

Leland's Papers are located at Texas Southern University, Houston, Texas.

Obituary: Austin (Texas) *American-Statesman*, 12, 15 Aug. 1989.

MERLINE PITRE

Lemon, Meadowlark (25 Apr. 1933–), professional basketball player, member of the Harlem Globetrotters, and minister, was born George Meadow Lemon III in Wilmington, North Carolina. Neither his parents' names nor their occupations are known. When he was eleven years old, Lemon went to the local movie house and saw a short reel about Abe Saperstein's famous Harlem Globetrotters basketball team and decided that one day he would be a member. Lemon attended public school in Wilmington, where he excelled at basketball and football. In 1952, while still a high school student, he wrote the Globetrotters to request a tryout and was given one, but he failed to make the team.

That same year Lemon matriculated at Florida A&M University, but he spent only a few weeks there before he was drafted into the U.S. Army. He spent two years in the service, and as luck would have it, was stationed in Germany when the Globetrotters passed through on an international tour. Lemon again tried out for the team and this time was successful, although he was initially assigned to a Globetrotters developmental team called the Kansas City Stars. Then he was transferred to the less-prestigious East Coast touring team rather than the main Globetrotters unit. Upon his discharge from the army in 1954, and after a single season with the Stars, Lemon joined the main touring team in a backup role and remained there until the resignation of REECE "GOOSE" TATUM, who had been the team's reigning "Clown Prince." As professional basketball's racial barriers had begun to fall with African American CHUCK COOPER being drafted by the NBA in 1950, an ever-increasing number of the Globetrotters' best athletes were drawn away to the professional leagues. Barnstorming teams such as the Globetrotters had begun to resort to on-the-court clowning and other colorful antics to continue to draw audiences and sell tickets. Though all of the Globetrotters were skilled basketball players—their late 1940s victories over the all-white Minneapolis Lakers were the stuff of basketball legend—especially important to the team was its Clown Prince, a kind of hardwood impresario whose trick shots, crowd-pleasing antics, and comedic stunts (usually at the expense of the other team or the officiating crew) formed a kind of ridiculous in-game circus act.

Meadowlark Lemon of the Harlem Globetrotters offers a pretzel to a referee during a game at Madison Square Garden in New York City on 18 February 1978. (AP Images.)

Lemon had long wished for this assignment; and during his years with the touring team he refined not only his basketball skills but also his clowning. In 1957 he finally graduated from Williston High School, and he was brought up to the main Globetrotters squad, and in 1958 he was named Clown Prince—a perfect decision in a pivotal time for the Globetrotters. In the years following the entrance of Chuck Cooper and JOHN HENRY "POP" LLOYD into the NBA, the Globetrotters had been in decline. Competition from the NBA and other professional sports leagues drove away much of the Globetrotters' audience. To maintain its financial viability, the team was forced to tour year-round, averaging more than three hundred games a year. They remained on the road constantly throughout the United States and abroad. Lemon led the team during the difficult civil rights era of the early 1960s but remained notably apolitical. Many black observers accused the team of being Uncle Toms who clowned and goofed for white audiences and for the club's white owner. Still, Lemon's skill and

showmanship helped rebuild the team's reputation as solid entertainment, and by the 1970s the Globetrotters had emerged as national icons and instantly recognizable media figures with their red, white, and blue uniforms and "Sweet Georgia Brown" theme song. The team's games were featured in highly popular installments of ABC's *Wide World of Sports*, and the Hanna-Barbera animation company produced a Harlem Globetrotters cartoon (1970 to 1973), among the first animated Saturday morning television fare to feature black characters. In these cartoons Lemon had a starring role, along with other famous Globetrotters of the era such as Fred "Curly" Neal and Bobby Joe Mason. In the 1970s Lemon also appeared in numerous television programs, talk shows, and motion pictures. He had roles in *The Harlem Globetrotters Popcorn Machine* (1974), *The Fish That Saved Pittsburgh* (1979), and on the TV series *Diff'rent Strokes* (1979), often playing himself. Lemon was named player-coach in 1970, and remained with the team until 1979. In his twenty-four years as a Globetrotter, Lemon had played in more than 9,000 games and had traveled to more than ninety countries around the world. He was married to Dr. Cynthia Lemon, whose maiden name is unknown, and together the couple would have ten children—five boys and five girls.

After his years with the Globetrotters, Lemon would become a founding member of a number of Globetrotter imitators, notably the Bucketeers, the Shooting Stars, and the Harlem All-Stars, which Lemon owned. In 1986, however, he became an ordained minister and went on to earn his doctor of divinity degree from Vision International University, an unaccredited Christian school in Ramona, California, founded in 1974 as a Pentecostal-Charismatic institution. For much of his post-basketball career he was involved in youth ministry for at-risk children. Lemon had his own program on the Trinity Broadcasting Network and opened a mobile youth camp called Camp Meadowlark. In 1994 Lemon returned as a player for a fifty-game season with the Globetrotters. In 2000 he was awarded the Jon Bunn Award given by professional basketball's Naismith Memorial Basketball Hall of Fame, and in 2003 Lemon was officially inducted into the Hall of Fame itself, gaining much-deserved recognition as a legendary contributor to professional basketball.

FURTHER READING

George, Nelson. *Elevating the Game: Black Men and Basketball* (1992).

Green, Ben. *Spinning the Globe: The Rise, Fall, and Return to Greatness of the Harlem Globetrotters* (2005).

JASON PHILIP MILLER

Lenoir, J. B. (5 Mar. 1929–29 Apr. 1967), blues singer and songwriter, was born near Monticello, Lawrence County, Mississippi, the son of Dewitt Lenoir and Roberta Ratliff, farmers. He grew up in a musical family, in which both parents played guitar. He was particularly inspired by his father's blues singing and later claimed that he could play his first song, "Jim Jackson's Kansas City Blues," before he was big enough to sit in a chair and hold the guitar. His father quit playing blues after dreaming that he was chased by the devil, but Lenoir carried on the family musical tradition, sharpening his performance skills at house parties and picnics. Although he recalled few local influences besides his father, he was clearly influenced by the style of Mississippi-born ARTHUR "BIG BOY" CRUDUP, whose records in the late 1940s helped bring the electric guitar to the forefront as a blues instrument.

In his early teens Lenoir left home, ending up in New Orleans, where sometime around 1944 he encountered the guitarist ELMORE JAMES and the harmonica player Aleck Miller, better known as SONNY BOY WILLIAMSON, possibly sitting in with them at the New York Inn. Unhappy with conditions in the South, Lenoir moved from job to job, ranging as far north as New York City and eventually settling in Chicago in the late 1940s. Working as a meatpacker by day, he began to check out the city's music scene by night, thus becoming a younger protégé of the guitarist and fellow Mississippian BIG BILL BROONZY, who allowed Lenoir to sit in with his band and helped him meet other artists, such as MEMPHIS MINNIE and MUDDY WATERS. As he began to gain recognition, Lenoir formed his own band and in 1951 made his first recordings, cutting four sides, including the topical commentaries "Korea Blues" and "Deep in Debt Blues," for the J.O.B. label. Other J.O.B. sessions in fall 1951, late 1952, and early 1953 yielded four more singles, but they did little for him financially. In October 1954 he switched to Parrot, a label owned by the Chicago disc jockey Al Benson. Among the sides cut for Parrot in 1954 and 1955 was another topical single, "Eisenhower Blues," which was summarily pulled off the market—legend has it that "government interference" prompted the action—and recut as "Tax Paying Blues," minus any direct references to

the president. Of greater significance to his career, Lenoir cut "Mama, Talk to Your Daughter" in 1954. It became his signature piece, his only song ever to make the R&B charts, and a continuing classic in the Chicago blues tradition. He reworked variations of the piece throughout his career. At a 1955 recording session, Lenoir brought together the two saxophone players he would work with for the next three years, Alex Atkins and Ernest Cotton. The two-horn, guitar-boogie combination produced a distinctive sound that became Lenoir's musical trademark. In 1955 he began a three-year affiliation with Checker, a subsidiary of Chess Records, where he teamed up with the bassist, songwriter, and producer WILLIE DIXON. However, their material was out of sync with current R&B tastes and did not sell.

Lenoir's stark protest compositions covered hard times, poverty, taxes, war (both Korea and Vietnam), and racial discrimination. Some critics likened him to blues artists who switched from ethnic material to "folk songs" in the 1950s and 1960s, but his songs were more personal than so-called folk material and at times were even surreal. Moreover, Lenoir wrote protest material throughout his career, not as a response to changing public tastes in music.

Lenoir delivered his material in a keen, high-pitched voice that could be as boisterous as the saxophones in his band or as sensitive as the subject matter in his social commentaries. A competent guitarist, he initially used variations of a walking bass boogie figure for his upbeat numbers. Later he developed a style that he referred to as "African hunch," which he often used on acoustic guitar.

In seeming contrast to his talent for sensitive composition, Lenoir had a real flair for showmanship, wearing imitation tiger-skin tails, a matching bow tie, and a gold earring; he often used a harmonica rack to hold his microphone so he could jump off the stage to dance and sing at a club patron's table. Lenoir's longtime friend Dixon, writing in his autobiography, recalled: "He was a helluva showman, because he had this long tiger-striped coat with tails. We used to call it a two-tailed peter."

In the late 1950s Lenoir operated and partially owned a blues club, the Club Lolease, but it went under along with his investment. In the summer of 1958 he recorded a single with the harmonica player JUNIOR WELLS, but the record did not sell, nor did a 1960 Vee-Jay single. In the early 1960s, however, Lenoir recorded for a European label and played acoustic guitar on a documentary album compiled by the British researcher Paul Oliver, foreshadowing a shift into the folk and blues-revival markets. After one final R&B single, a 1963 venture produced by Dixon, Lenoir recorded almost exclusively for European, documentary, and revival-era labels. He began to play white or mixed clubs such as Big John's and the Fickle Pickle on Chicago's north side. He traveled to Europe in 1965 as part of the American Folk Blues Festival and was particularly well received in England, where he inspired the blues rocker John Mayall. A second tour with the American Folk Blues Festival in 1966 reinforced his status in Europe, but back in Chicago he struggled to make a living with music. He moved downstate to take a job as a kitchen worker at the University of Illinois in Urbana. Commuting between the university and Chicago in April 1966, he was involved in an auto accident and apparently sustained injuries that were more serious than first believed. Three weeks after the accident he suffered an apparent heart attack and was pronounced dead at Mercy Hospital in Urbana, Illinois. His wife, Ella Louise and his three children had his body shipped to his birthplace, where he was buried in the Salem Church Cemetery.

FURTHER READING

Broven, John. "J. B. Lenoir," in *Nothing but the Blues*, ed. Mike Leadbitter (1971).

Leadbitter, Mike, Leslie Fancourt, and Paul Pelletier. *Blues Records 1943–1970*, vol. 2, *The Bible of the Blues* (1994).

This entry is taken from the *American National Biography* and is published here with the permission of the American Council of Learned Societies.

BILL MCCULLOCH AND
BARRY LEE PEARSON

Lenoire, Rosetta (8 Aug. 1911–17 Mar. 2002), actress, singer, and producer, was born Rosetta Olive Burton, the daughter of Harold Charles Burton and Marie (Jacques) Burton in New York City's Hell's Kitchen (now Clinton) neighborhood. Her father was a licensed engineer and plumber and was active in the political arena both locally and nationally. When Rosetta was very young, her mother fell desperately ill after giving birth. The nearest hospital refused to admit her because of her race, and she died of pneumonia.

As a youngster, LeNoire suffered from rickets, a weakening of the bones usually caused by inadequate vitamin D and/or calcium in the diet. Doctors reset her legs, but she wore leg braces until 1924 when she was thirteen. At this time she began

to take music lessons from the legendary composer EUBIE BLAKE, who continued to be a mentor and friend until he died in 1983. BILL "BOJANGLES" ROBINSON was her godfather, and she affectionately referred to him as "Uncle Bo." Bojangles suggested that LeNoire begin dancing as a way to strengthen her legs, and by age fifteen she had earned a place in the chorus of Robinson's dance troupe, the Time Steppers.

In 1929, when she was eighteen, she married William LeNoire; the couple would have one son, William. Although the marriage ended in divorce in 1943, LeNoire continued to use the name Rosetta LeNoire professionally throughout her life. LeNoire made her theater debut in 1936 as a witch in Orson Welles's acclaimed all-black version of *Macbeth*, as a part of the Federal Theater, a Works Progress Administration (WPA)-funded project supporting live theater and other artistic performances during the Great Depression. Her Broadway debut came three years later in *The Hot Mikado* in 1939, which featured her godfather, Bojangles Robinson. Few employment opportunities existed for blacks in the theater then, and those that did exist usually entailed roles as servants or slaves. While LeNoire would accept such undesirable roles on Broadway and in film, she became known for bringing a sense of dignity and humanity to her performances.

From 1944 to 1946 she appeared as Stella in *Anna Lucasta* on Broadway, where she choreographed the dance that HILDA SIMMS performed in the title role. She reprised this role in the 1947 revival along with SIDNEY POITIER in the role of Lester, twelve years before his powerful Broadway performance as Walter Lee in LORRAINE HANSBERRY's *A Raisin in the Sun*. In 1948 LeNoire married Egbert Brown, an owner of a fleet of taxicabs. The marriage lasted until Brown's death in 1974.

She continued to work on Broadway into the 1950s, appearing in *Finian's Rainbow* in 1955, and in 1959 LeNoire reprised her role in *Anna Lucasta* in the film production starring EARTHA KITT, SAMMY DAVIS JR., and FREDRICK O'NEAL. Around this time, she was also a pioneer in television, appearing as Noah's wife in the Hallmark Hall of Fame production of *Green Pastures* and in episodes of the television program *Studio One*.

In the 1960s and 1970s her Broadway career continued to flourish. She garnered a role in LANGSTON HUGHES's musical, *Tambourines to Glory* (1963), and in JAMES BALDWIN's play *Blues for Mr. Charlie* (1964). In 1968, using her own savings, she founded the Amas Repertory Theatre (*amas* is Latin for "you love"). According to the theater's Web site, "Amas Musical Theatre is devoted to the creation, development and professional production of new American musicals, the celebration of diversity and minority perspectives, the emergence of new artistic talent, and the training and encouragement of inner-city young people" (www.amasmusical. org). LeNoire's innovative spirit put her in the forefront of producing works utilizing nontraditional casting, which was based on talent without regard to race, ethnicity, or nationality. She served as the founder, producer, and artistic director of Amas.

In 1972 she performed in the Broadway musical *Lost in the Stars* and appeared in other Broadway and Off-Broadway stage productions such as Tennessee Williams's *Streetcar Named Desire* in 1973. LeNoire also found work on TV soap operas in the early 1970s, including *The Guiding Light* (1971 to 1972), *Another World* (1971 to 1973), and *Ryan's Hope* (1975). *Bubbling Brown Sugar*, conceived and produced by LeNoire at Amas, was produced on Broadway in 1976. Around this time LeNoire also made guest television appearances on *Fantasy Island, Benny's Place, The Father Clements Story*, and the television version of *Guess Who's Coming to Dinner* (1975). She appeared in the films *The Sunshine Boys* (1975), *Moscow on the Hudson* (1984), *The Brother from Another Planet* (1984), and *Brewster's Millions* (1985).

In the 1980s LeNoire continued her television career, appearing regularly in *Gimme A Break* (1985 to 1987), on *Amen* (1987 to 1989), and on *Family Matters* (1989 to 1997). During the 1990s she continued to support the award-winning projects of the Amas Repertory, often with her own paychecks. In 1995, in conjunction with Amas, she produced the Broadway musical play *Robeson*, a biographical drama about the life of actor, singer, and political activist PAUL ROBESON.

In 1988, Actors' Equity Association, the union for American professional actors and stage managers, established an award in honor of LeNoire, who also happened to be the award's first recipient. According to Actors' Equity Association Web site (www.actorsequity.org), "The Rosetta LeNoire Award is given in recognition of outstanding artistic contributions, made by either an individual or an institution, to the universality of the human experience in the American Theatre, through either nontraditional casting or affirmative casting of actors of color, females and actors with disabilities." She also received the Theatre World Special Award in 1993, and the National Medal of the Arts, presented to her by President Clinton in 1999. In 2002 she died at the age of ninety in Englewood, New Jersey, from complications associated with diabetes.

FURTHER READING

Norflett, Linda Kerr. "Rosetta LeNoire: The Lady and her Theatre," *Black American Literature Forum* (Summer, 1983).

Norflett, Linda Kerr. "The Theatre Career of Rosetta LeNoire," Ph.D. diss., New York University, 1983.

Schwartz, Bonnie Nelson. *Voices from the Federal Theatre* (2003).

Obituary: *New York Times*, 20 March 2002.

JOAN F. MCCARTY

Leonard, Buck (8 Sept. 1907–27 Nov. 1997), baseball player, was born Walter Fenner Leonard in Rocky Mount, North Carolina, the son of John Leonard, a railroad fireman, and Emma Sesson. Although his parents called him "Buddy," his younger brother mispronounced the name as "Buck," and that became his lifelong nickname. As a young child he learned about baseball while watching white minor league games through the gaps in a stadium fence. When a black ballpark was built in Rocky Mount around 1915, Buck became the batboy for a semi-professional team. Following his father's death during the influenza epidemic in 1919, Leonard quit school to help his family financially. As a teenager he shined shoes, and from 1923 to 1933 he worked for the Atlantic Coastline Railroad shop, installing brake cylinders on boxcars. While working full-time for the railroad, he played semiprofessional baseball in the evenings. Leonard quickly established himself as a hometown star, and at the age of seventeen he was named team manager. He later recalled that he began playing first base in 1931: "One reason why I did that was … I would be close to the umpire for some arguing and I wouldn't have to come all the way in from center field. That's a heck of a reason, but that's how I got started playing first base."

In 1933, with the onset of the Great Depression, Leonard was fired from his job at the railroad shop. There being no other employment available, he decided to go on the road playing semiprofessional baseball. He spent three months with the Portsmouth Firefighters and then jumped to the Baltimore Stars, whose manager promised him a percentage of the gate receipts for every game. But the team experienced serious financial difficulties, and the players often went without food; when the team's two automobiles were impounded and auctioned off in New York City for failure to pay a hotel bill, Leonard and his teammates were left stranded and almost penniless. So Leonard joined the Brooklyn Royal Giants. While in New York, he frequented a Harlem bar where SMOKEY JOE WILLIAMS, a former star pitcher in the Negro leagues, worked as a bartender. Williams saw Leonard play and recommended him to the Homestead Grays in the Negro National League in 1934.

With the Grays, Leonard played a grueling schedule of around 210 games per season, taking the field against both amateur and Negro League teams. He later recalled a typical itinerary:

A lot of times we would play three games in one day, and each one in a different town. We would play a ten-o'clock game in the morning, a three-o'clock game, and a twilight game at six-thirty.… [After a game] we changed sweatshirts and got in the bus, and the business manager would have a sandwich for everybody.… Now, we didn't change clothes, we just changed sweatshirts. We'd keep the uniform on and go out there and start the [next] game. The crowd was already there waiting for us when we got there.

Leonard estimated that in 1941 the Grays logged between thirty thousand and forty thousand miles of road travel. During the winter, he usually played an additional ninety games with barnstorming teams in Cuba or Venezuela. In spite of the wearying effects of a year-round baseball season, Leonard gained a reputation for being one of the hardest-playing and most consistent Negro Leaguers. He was named the Grays' captain during his rookie season, a position that he retained until the team folded in 1950.

A muscular left-hander with an exceptionally quick bat, Leonard often hit third in the lineup, with the slugging catcher JOSH GIBSON hitting fourth; they were known, respectively, as "the black Lou Gehrig" and "the black Babe Ruth." "Sometimes people asked us what the difference was between them and us," he later recalled:

Well, the only thing that we said was, they were white and we were black.… They were white and could play in the major leagues, and we had to play black baseball. That was the only difference.

Leonard and Gibson helped the Grays to become the most dominant club in the Negro National League, winning nine straight championships between 1937 and 1945. Although statistics for the Negro Leagues are notoriously incomplete, newspaper reports suggest that Leonard hit .500 during the first half of the 1937 season and .489 for the first half of 1938. His full-season batting average in 1939 was .363, and in 1940 it was .372. Between 1936 and 1943 he averaged 34 home runs per season. In 1948, when he was 41 years old, Leonard led the Negro Leagues with a .395 batting average. During his career he was selected 11 leagues times to play in the annual East-West All-Star game, a major cultural event for black Americans that often drew 50,000 fans; no other player was chosen as frequently.

Although reporters from the Communist Party–U.S. newspaper *The Daily Worker* urged Leonard to agitate for the integration of Major League Baseball, he refused, arguing that if white owners and white players were forced to accept blacks prematurely, conditions for blacks in the majors would be intolerable. In the handful of exhibition games that he played against major league barnstorming teams, which were led by stars such as Dizzy Dean and Lefty Grove, he batted .382. In 1936 he played on an all-black team in the "Little World Series," a tournament that featured several white players with major league experience; after winning seven straight games and the championship, the Negro Leaguers were barred from future tournament play, and they were never awarded the $5,092 first prize. Around 1938 Leonard and Gibson were called into the office of the Washington Senators owner Clark Griffith, who told them that he was flirting with the idea of signing them to play for his last-place team; although they expressed their interest in the plan, they never heard back from him. In 1952, five years after JACKIE ROBINSON broke the color barrier, St. Louis Browns owner Bill Veeck offered Leonard a major league contract, but he turned it down. "I knew I was over the hill," he later recalled. "I didn't try to fool myself." The following season, at the age of 46, he played a few games of integrated baseball in the Class B minor league Piedmont League and batted .333. Two years later he retired after slugging 13 home runs in 62 games in the Central Mexican League.

Leonard was married twice, to Sarah Wroten, a schoolteacher, from 1937 until her death in 1966, and to Eugenia (maiden name unknown) in 1986. He had no children. After retiring from baseball, Leonard delivered cigars for a tobacco company in Rocky Mount and then worked for twelve years as a truant officer. In 1966 he was licensed to sell real estate, and in 1970 he opened the Buck Leonard Realty Agency. A devout Christian, he was a member of the St. James Baptist Church in Rocky Mount for approximately seventy years. In 1972 he and Josh Gibson were inducted into the National Baseball Hall of Fame; along with SATCHEL PAIGE, they were the first Negro League players so honored. Leonard proudly called his induction the greatest moment in his life. During his later years, he was actively involved in organizing reunions of Negro League players; although he suffered a stroke in 1986, he continued to attend Hall of Fame ceremonies in Cooperstown in his wheelchair. Leonard died in Rocky Mount.

FURTHER READING

Leonard, Buck, as told to James A. Riley. *Buck Leonard: The Black Lou Gehrig* (1995).

Peterson, Robert. *Only the Ball Was White* (1970)

This entry is taken from the *American National Biography* and is published here with the permission of the American Council of Learned Societies.

THOMAS W. COLLINS JR.

Leonard, Harlan "Mike" (2 July 1905–1983), jazz saxophonist and bandleader, was born Harlan Quentin Leonard in Butler, Missouri, not Kansas City, as is commonly given. Nothing is known of his parents. Leonard's nickname was "Mike," for reasons unknown. He attended public schools in Butler and Kansas City, where at age thirteen he enrolled at Lincoln High School, playing clarinet in a school band. Later he studied alto saxophone with George Wilkenson and Eric "Paul" Tremaine. He worked briefly with the bandleader GEORGE E. LEE in 1923, the year he graduated. Leonard married in the mid-1920s. His wife's name is unknown; the couple had two children.

Leonard was the lead alto saxophonist, doubling on clarinet and soprano sax, in BENNIE MOTEN's ensemble from 1923 to late 1931, as it evolved from a small dance band into one of the pioneering jazz big bands. His first recorded solo with Moten was on "She's Sweeter than Sugar," from May 1925. Among numerous subsequent solos, he played jaunty, sweet-toned melodies on "The Jones Law Blues" and "Small Black," both recorded in October 1929, and he led the saxophone section through their featured portions of "Oh! Eddie" and "That Too, Do" in October 1930. After a slow-growing dispute over finances and stylistic direction, Leonard and several other members of Moten's band, including the trombonist Thamon Hayes, became part of a new band, Hayes's Kansas City Sky Rockets. In forming the band, Leonard received financial help from his mother-in-law.

In May 1932 Hayes's group defeated Moten's reorganized ensemble in a battle of the bands at the El Paseo Ballroom. As a consequence of this victory Hayes obtained a booking for the summer at Fairyland Park, on the outskirts of Kansas City. In 1932 and 1933 they worked at the Pla-Mor, a ballroom for whites only, while also performing in many African American social clubs. They left Kansas City for brief tours of the Midwest and the South.

After an abortive job in Chicago, Hayes, disgusted, went home, and Leonard took over leadership of the band. They performed at the Cotton Club in Chicago in 1935 and then in Kansas City until 1937, when Leonard disbanded the group and formed a new ensemble that included sidemen who had previously played with the tenor saxophonist Jimmy Keith and the clarinetist Tommy Douglas.

With Moten dead, Lee's big band having disbanded in 1935, COUNT BASIE's big band having set off for New York in 1936, and ANDY KIRK's band touring nationally from 1937, Leonard's Kansas City Rockets became the leading jazz band in the city. In January 1937 the young alto saxophonist CHARLIE PARKER joined the group, but he was always late to the job, and Leonard, who at this point was serving mainly as conductor, was obliged instead to play the lead alto saxophone part; he soon fired Parker. In September, when the tenor saxophonist Henry Bridges joined, the band signed with the Music Corporation of America (MCA). Their first recordings, made in January 1940, included a version of "My Gal Sal" on which both Bridges and the trombonist Fred Beckett make something special of improvisations on this potentially corny tune. Among four titles recorded on 11 March were "Ride My Blues Away," featuring the blues shouter Ernest Williams and Bridges on tenor saxophone, and "Parade of the Stompers," with Bridges in especially fine form. In this same period the band performed in Chicago and New York.

The arranger TADD DAMERON and the string bassist Billy Hadnott joined that summer; they later had distinguished careers of their own in jazz and in rhythm and blues, respectively. Leonard told the writer Leonard Feather: "One day I ran into Tadd Dameron at the Woodside Hotel [in Harlem]. He was broke, and looking for work. I took him along with me to Kansas City and for a while he played piano in the band as well as writing a lot of our arrangements." Recordings of Dameron's work include "Rock and Ride" and the ballad "A-la-Bridges," both from 15 July 1940. That same year Leonard's band toured the East and the Midwest.

Over the next three years Leonard alternated between engagements at Kansas City venues and regional touring. Moving to the Los Angeles area, he worked at local clubs from May 1943 until early in 1945. He then disbanded, unable to secure enough musical work to support his family. To avoid the temptation to resume playing, he sold his instruments. In January 1949, after working in a defense job for Lockheed and at the post office, he joined the cashier's section at the Los Angeles office of the Department of Internal Revenue. He eventually became chief of the section. He retired around 1970 and did some unspecified interracial work in Los Angeles, where he died. The date of his death is unknown.

As an alto saxophonist, Leonard was admired for his beautiful tone, his feeling for lyrical melodies, his accurate reading skills, and his confident manner of leading ensemble passages. He was not a significant jazz improviser and never claimed to be. Leonard's big band recordings from 1940 are modeled after Basie's, with an emphasis on repeated riffs and improvised solos. But the riffs lack the special creative spark heard in Basie's pieces, and the improvisations are far inferior, with the exception of the consistently excellent tenor saxophonist Bridges, who alone assures Leonard's importance as a bandleader. Many other solos, including those of the perhaps overrated trombonist Fred Beckett, suffer from stiff, sloppy, or awkward moments, including a number of melodic clunkers as an instrumental soloist fails to accord with the accompanying harmony. If anything, a reasonably good band such as Leonard's makes one realize how difficult it actually was for Basie's state-of-the-art ensemble to achieve its seemingly effortless perfection.

FURTHER READING

Driggs, Frank, and Chuck Haddix. *Kansas City Jazz: From Ragtime to Bebop* (2005).

Pearson, Nathan W., Jr. *Goin' to Kansas City* (1994).

Russell, Ross. *Jazz Style in Kansas City and the Southwest* (1997).

Schuller, Gunther. *Early Jazz: Its Roots and Musical Development* (1986).

This entry is taken from the *American National Biography* and is published here with the permission of the American Council of Learned Societies.

BARRY KERNFELD

Leonard, Matthew (26 Nov. 1929–28 Feb. 1967), Korean and Vietnam War soldier and Medal of Honor recipient, was born in Eutaw, Alabama, the son of Lawrence and Matilda Leonard. While he was still a small boy, Matthew Leonard and his family moved ninety miles north to the industrial city of Birmingham, Alabama. Here, Matthew, nicknamed "Bill" by his family, attended local public schools, and it was in the eighth grade that he became sweethearts with Lois Mae Coats, who was two years his junior and would be his future wife. When his father was stricken with cancer, Matthew dropped out of A. H. Parker High School to help support his family. Leonard was working as bicycle deliveryman for a local drugstore when he enlisted in the army on 27 August 1947 in Birmingham.

Soon after completing boot camp training, Matthew Leonard was sent to Japan as part of the U.S. occupation forces of that nation. In November 1950 he was married in Birmingham to Lois Coates while he was home on leave, but soon thereafter was sent overseas to fight in the Korean War. Leonard subsequently served in Korea for about a year, earning four bronze service stars. Following this, Leonard was assigned for duty in Germany, where he served for several years, accompanied by his family. By the mid-1950s, Matthew Leonard was a seasoned army professional who was rising through the ranks of enlisted men. Indeed, his career is indicative of that of many African Americans who enlisted in the immediate post–World War II years, men like CORNELIUS CHARLTON and EUGENE ASHLEY JR., especially after President Truman issued Executive Order 9981 in 1948, which ordered the desegregation of America's armed forces. Now, black soldiers would have equal opportunities to rise to leadership positions in the army based on their skills as a soldier alone. While it is true that remnants of the old army racism surfaced at times, and that full desegregation was not achieved until after the beginning of the Korean War, Matthew Leonard had only positive experiences and, as his wife recalls, "he loved the army."

By the mid-1960s, Sergeant Matthew Leonard, now serving in the army's most celebrated infantry unit, the 1st Infantry Division (nicknamed "The Big Red One"), 1st Battalion, 16th Infantry Regiment, was a veteran platoon leader and devoted family man. The father of five children (Carl, Lavon, Brenda, Wanda, and Paula), Leonard was also a devout church member, but his leadership responsibilities were just as important to him. Like any successful sergeant in the army, Leonard paid attention to all the details, large and small; indeed sergeants like Leonard were (and still are) the backbone of the army hierarchy. Lois Leonard humorously recalls that though she was responsible for most domestic chores, when it came to the washing and care of her husband's uniform that was *his* job, to make sure it was properly cleaned and pressed; after all, her husband said, "How can I expect the best from my men if I don't show it myself?" This was an attitude he would soon demonstrate to his men under the most dire of circumstances. By late 1965 Leonard was stationed with his unit at Fort Leonard Wood in Missouri, during which time he was assisting his wife long-distance in their attempt to purchase a family home in Birmingham. However, before the sale could be finalized, Leonard was assigned for duty in Vietnam, arriving there by early 1966.

On 28 February 1967, Sergeant Matthew Leonard and his platoon were operating near Suoi Da in the Republic of Vietnam when they were attacked by a superior force. Though he was wounded early on in the battle, Leonard rallied his platoon, and they repulsed the initial enemy attack. In the lull that followed, Sergeant Leonard organized the defense and inspired his men with his leadership. When it was discovered that a wounded soldier was outside their defensive perimeter, Leonard dashed out to drag the man to safety, only to have his left hand shattered by a sniper's bullet. Though painfully wounded, Leonard refused medical treatment and led his men in battling yet another enemy assault on their position. Indeed, Leonard seemed to be everywhere, directing fire and encouraging his men. When an enemy machine gun was moved into position to sweep the American perimeter, and the platoon's own machine gun malfunctioned, Leonard made his way to the gun position to try and fix it. While he was doing so, his gunners in the area were wounded by enemy fire, whereby Sergeant Leonard took matters into his own hands and stormed the enemy gun position and, though wounded yet again, succeeded in destroying the emplacement. Now badly wounded, Leonard propped himself up against a nearby tree and continued his fight with the enemy until he expired from his wounds. While Leonard was killed in action, his courageous leadership inspired his men to hold their position until reinforcements arrived.

Matthew Leonard was buried in Shadow Lawn Cemetery in his hometown of Birmingham, and was subsequently awarded the Medal of Honor, which was presented to his family at a Pentagon ceremony on 19 December 1968. Leonard was the fourth African American soldier to earn the Medal of Honor during the Vietnam War, and one of twenty black soldiers overall to be so honored. After his death, his widow, Lois, purchased their dream home in Birmingham, her husband having told her this was what he wanted if he didn't return from Vietnam; on the living room wall to this day may be found hanging Matthew Leonard's Medal of Honor and other mementos highlighting his long army career. Matthew Leonard's heroism, like that of many other Vietnam War veterans, has faded from public memory over the years, but briefly made the news again in 2003, when Lois Leonard was in danger of losing her home due to a looming bank foreclosure. When the plight of Sergeant Leonard's widow came to the notice of local veterans and civic groups, the necessary funds were raised, with the result that Lois Leonard still lives in the house that her husband always wanted her to have.

FURTHER READING

The author gratefully acknowledges the assistance of Lois Leonard during the writing of this article. A telephone interview was conducted on 7 April 2011, with subsequent follow-up correspondence. All quotes herein are from this interview.

Hanna, Charles W. *African American Recipients of the Medal of Honor* (2002).

Lynne, Diana. "War Hero's Widow Gets Reprieve." *World Net Daily,* 18 Feb. 2003. http://www.wnd.com/news/article.asp?ARTICLE_ID=31095.

GLENN ALLEN KNOBLOCK

Leonard, Sugar Ray (17 May 1956–), boxer, was born Ray Charles Leonard in Wilmington, North Carolina, the fifth of the seven children of Cicero and Getha Leonard. His parents were fans of RAY CHARLES, and they named their son after the famous musician. His mother hoped that Ray would grow up and pursue a singing career. When Ray was eleven the family moved to Palmer Park, Maryland, and bought their first house. Ray's three older brothers, Roy, Kenny, and Roger, were active in sports and pressured Ray to accompany them to the local gym. Ray was shy and preferred comic books to physical challenges, and when he initially tried sparring, he found it scary. He did, however, begin to develop his athletic abilities at the school gym. In 1970, to keep kids away from crime and drugs, Palmer Park authorities opened a recreation center with the help of a retired boxer, Dave Jacobs. Leonard's brother Roger frequented the club, which pleased their father, who had been a successful amateur boxer while in the U.S. Navy. Searching for his father's approval, Leonard began

Sugar Ray Leonard, welterweight boxer, tapes his hands before a workout in the boxing ring at the community center in Capitol Heights, Maryland, 8 August 1979. (AP Images.)

taking boxing lessons at the center. To learn the sport quickly, he took on bigger, more experienced opponents and as a consequence developed an outstanding defensive technique that was heavily influenced by MUHAMMAD ALI. Rapidly improving, Leonard began to condition himself physically, and with his increased strength and skill he gained self-confidence as he left his preteen years behind.

When Dave Jacobs began to enter the center's boxers in local contests, Ray Leonard immediately attracted attention. Most gratifying, perhaps, was the approval of his father, who recognized his son's immense talent after seeing him win his first amateur fight. In 1972 Leonard won the local Golden Gloves as a lightweight. He continued to be driven to improve and did so by competing above his age level. As a result, although underage, Leonard was allowed to join a U.S. team that in Las Vegas fought a team from the Soviet Union. Leonard won his match with a knockout. In 1972 he hoped to make the U.S. Olympic team, but he lost a

qualifying match on points in a controversial decision. Despite this loss he acquired the nickname Sugar Ray, after the world boxing champion SUGAR RAY ROBINSON, and returned home determined to become an Olympian in 1976.

The road to the 1976 Olympics was not smooth. Leonard suffered from sore hands that swelled after boxing. He was also offered a contract to become a professional boxer, and he found the lure of money especially hard to turn down when his girlfriend and schoolmate Juanita Wilkinson became pregnant. The families decided that Leonard would be acknowledged as the father, but the two did not marry and continued to live separately. Leonard, affected by the stress of parenthood, lost three straight fights after the birth of his son, Ray Leonard Jr., in 1973.

Following this turbulent period Leonard rebounded to make the 1976 U.S. Olympic team as a light welterweight. With pictures of Ray Jr. and Juanita tucked in his socks, he won the gold medal for his weight class. Although he was a popular medalist, Leonard did not plan to continue his boxing career. Rather, he wanted to attend the University of Maryland. However, when his mother had a heart attack and his father fell ill, Leonard needed money. At twenty years of age he had two families to support.

Because Muhammad Ali advised him not to sign with any single manager, Leonard turned down an offer from DON KING; instead he sought business advice from his friends Charles Brotman, a public relations expert, and Mike Trainer, a lawyer. The three decided that Leonard should incorporate and formed Sugar Ray Leonard Boxing, Inc., for which Leonard acquired an initial loan of $21,000 and drew a weekly salary of $475. In February 1977, working with Ali's former trainer Angelo Dundee, Leonard made his professional debut against Luis Vega at the Baltimore Civic Center and won before a sellout crowd and a television audience of millions. The earnings from this fight made Sugar Ray Leonard Boxing, Inc., financially solvent.

In smaller venues over the next two years Leonard fought frequently, winning twenty-six fights between his debut and his November 1979 World Boxing Council (WBC) championship match against Wilfred Benitez. This was the first welterweight fight to pay each fighter more than a million dollars and was the first of many matches with record-setting purses that would be negotiated by Sugar Ray Leonard Boxing, Inc. With money in the bank and millions more on the horizon, Leonard married Juanita in January 1980. They had two children but divorced in 1990. Leonard was remarried to the model Bernadette Robi in 1993.

Leonard returned to the ring in March 1980 to defend his title, knocking out David Green in the fourth round. That June in a fight promoted by Don King, Leonard was challenged by the Panamanian fighter Roberto Duran, who had a reputation as a dirty fighter with little respect for the rules. Duran reinforced this image by swearing at Leonard in Spanish and making rude gestures at Juanita before the fight. Duran quickly drew Leonard into his street-fighting style and proved too strong, winning a decision on points in fifteen rounds. Although he was badly beaten, Leonard earned approximately nine million dollars for the fight.

A lucrative rematch was fought in November. In this fight, which came to be known as the *no mas* fight, Leonard refused to be drawn in by Duran. Drawing on his effective defensive style, quick footwork, and feinting skill, Leonard outfought Duran, who retired from the fight in the eighth round, gasping, "*No mas, no mas*" ("No more, no more"). Leonard was again WBC welterweight champion. After defending his title against Larry Bonds, Leonard switched weight classes and became the World Boxing Association (WBA) junior middleweight champion after beating Ayube Kalule in nine rounds.

With the WBC welterweight and WBA junior middleweight crowns, Leonard turned his attention to a fight with THOMAS "HIT MAN" HEARNS in September 1981 that would unite the WBC and WBA welterweight titles. The winner would be the undisputed welterweight champion of the world. Hearns jumped out to an early lead, but Leonard came back in the later rounds. The referee stopped the fight in the fourteenth round and declared Leonard the winner. Leonard subsequently defended his title against Bruce Finch but suffered a detached retina while training for a second defense against Roger Stafford. As a result he retired in November 1982.

Retirement was not permanent, and after spending time as a television commentator and boxing manager, Leonard reentered the ring against unranked Kevin Howard. Leonard won, but not easily. During the fourth round he was knocked down for the first time in his professional career. He announced his re-retirement following the fight. Years later, Leonard admitted that drug and alcohol problems had played a part in his poor performance. He continued to battle drugs and alcohol during his intermittent retirements in the 1980s.

Unhappy with the way he had left boxing, Leonard returned to the ring in 1987. His terms were that he would fight Marvelous MARVIN HAGLER, and as a middleweight. Leonard won a split decision after twelve rounds and became the WBC middleweight champion. Both Hagler and Leonard retired after the fight. However, when his rival Hearns won a world title in a fourth weight class, Leonard returned to the ring yet again. Hearns was attempting to become the first fighter to win a world title in five separate weight classes. Leonard, not wanting to be outdone, decided to pursue the same distinction. Fighting against Danny Lalonde in 1988 for the WBC light heavyweight and super middleweight titles, Sugar Ray made his comeback. After trouble in the early rounds, Leonard hit his pace, knocking Lalonde to the mat twice in the ninth round before the referee declared Leonard the winner.

Days before Leonard won his fourth and fifth weight classes against Lalonde, Hearns won his fifth. With public interest piqued by their accomplishments the rivals scheduled a rematch for June 1989. In this bout both boxers hit the mat twice and after twelve rounds the fight ended in a draw. Leonard fought just once more in the super middleweight class, defeating Duran in their third encounter. In 1991 he fought Terry Norris for the WBC junior middleweight crown. The thirty-four-year-old Leonard lost by a wide margin in a twelve-round decision on points and retired after the fight, only to attempt yet one more comeback in March 1997, at the age of forty, against Hector "Macho" Camacho. Leonard lost by a technical knockout in the fifth round and afterward retired permanently, though he remained active in the boxing world as a television commentator and through promotion and managing with his company, Sugar Ray Leonard Boxing, Inc.

Leonard's illustrious career made him the second-highest-earning boxer of all time, behind MIKE TYSON. Handsome and clean-cut, he was the star that rose to replace Muhammad Ali in the 1980s. Leonard was inducted into the International Boxing Hall of Fame in 1997, and he continued to be one of only two fighters to win world titles in five separate weight classes.

FURTHER READING
Bouchard, S. H. *Sports Star, Sugar Ray Leonard* (1983).
Cavendish, Marshall. *Boxing Greats* (1997).
Gloeckner, Carolyn. *Sugar Ray Leonard* (1985).
Haskins, James. *Sugar Ray Leonard* (1982).

Rosenthal, Bert. *Sugar Ray Leonard, the Baby-Faced Boxer* (1982)

JACOB ANDREW FREEDMAN

Leonard, Walter J. (3 Oct. 1929–), educator, was born Walter Jewell Leonard in Alma, Georgia, to Rachel Jewel (Kirkland) Leonard and Francis Albert Leonard. His mother was a practical nurse and his father was a carpenter. He was named for his father's first cousin, WALTER "BUCK" LEONARD, a first baseman with the nine-time Negro League champion Homestead Grays. Like his namesake, Leonard became a champion in his own right, using the college campus as his field of dreams.

Leonard was home-schooled by his grandfather during the early years of the Great Depression and entered the racially segregated public schools of Savannah, Georgia, in the fifth grade. Despite the separate and unequal public school facilities he and his classmates endured, Leonard graduated from Beach-Cyler High School in 1947. He later enrolled in the Georgia State Industrial College for Colored Youth (later Savannah State University), where he met Betty E. Singleton. The two married on 16 June 1951 and eventually had two children.

After completing some coursework at Georgia State Industrial College, Leonard relocated to Atlanta to attend Morehouse College. He later went on to earn a graduate degree in Business Administration from Atlanta University.

Leonard remained in Atlanta to participate in the burgeoning civil rights movement. He was one of sixty people who attended the founding conference for the Southern Christian Leadership Conference (SCLC) held in Atlanta from 10–11 January 1957. Leonard worked as an independent consultant to SCLC and was also an adviser to the NAACP Youth Division of the Southeast Region headquartered in Atlanta. He worked closely with Donald Hollowell, a civil rights lawyer who, along with CONSTANCE BAKER MOTLEY, led the campaign that desegregated the University of Georgia in 1961. Inspired by the legendary CHARLES HAMILTON HOUSTON, Leonard moved his family to Washington, D.C., and enrolled in Howard University School of Law in 1965.

Leonard was a member of the *Howard Law Journal* and a research assistant to CLYDE FERGUSON JR., then law school dean and later U.S. ambassador to Uganda. Leonard also wrote a law

Walter J. Leonard, president of Fisk University, with John Hope Franklin, center, and U.S. Circuit Court Judge Leon Higginbotham, in Chicago on March 9, 1979. (AP Images.)

review note about New York congressman ADAM CLAYTON POWELL JR. that was cited by the U.S. Supreme Court in 1969's *Powell v. McCormick* decision. In 1968 Leonard earned a J.D. and accepted a position as assistant dean at Howard Law School. One year later Leonard relocated his family to Cambridge, Massachusetts, to accept a position as assistant dean at Harvard Law School. This appointment made Leonard the first African American dean in that law school's 152-year history.

Leonard served as assistant dean for two years, during which time he convened the Conference of Black Lawyers in America Today in November 1970. Seven years later Leonard authored *Black Lawyers: Training Results, Then and Now*, one of the first books about African Americans and the legal profession. When Derek Bok, dean of the law school, accepted the position as president of Harvard University in 1971, he hired Leonard as his special assistant, a position he held from 1971 to 1977.

Leonard chaired a Harvard committee in 1973 that wrote a final report to President Bok in support of the establishment of a W. E. B. DuBois Institute for Afro-American Research. He also persuaded Harvard University in 1974 to invest $45 million of its employee life insurance coverage in Atlanta Life and North Carolina Mutual, two African American-owned insurance companies. Leonard chaired the Harvard University Committee on Equal Employment Opportunity for six years and was the principal drafter of the famous Harvard Plan, an affirmative action policy cited favorably by the U.S. Supreme Court in the 1978 *Regents of the University of California v. Bakke* decision. The Harvard Plan was a university policy that allowed race and ethnicity to serve as a factor, although not the main factor, in the admissions decision-making process. It was later adopted by major universities throughout the country. Leonard left Harvard in 1977 to become president of Fisk University, a historically black private university in Nashville, Tennessee, and the alma mater of Harvard's first black Ph.D. recipient, W. E. B. DuBois. When Leonard became president of Fisk University the institution was on the brink of insolvency. Having honed his skills as an administrative maverick at Harvard, Leonard sidestepped the traditional methods for securing funds. Instead, he took out a $1.5 million insurance policy on his life and used the money to keep the university open (a possible first for any president of an American university). During his tenure from 1977 to 1984 Leonard raised $12 million for the school.

In addition to his administrative work Leonard was a visiting lecturer at several law schools, including the University of Virginia and the University of Pennsylvania. He was also a member of or adviser to several boards including the Ford Foundation, the National Urban League, and the U.S. Naval Academy, where he was chairman of the academy's Board of Visitors in 1983. Leonard received over 250 awards and five honorary doctorates. In recognition of his achievements in higher education, the governing body of Wolfson College at Oxford University elected him a visiting scholar and a fellow at the Centre of Socio-Legal Studies in 1997. Oxford University also created the Walter J. Leonard Research Fellowship and the Walter J. Leonard Visiting Fellowship. The Kuumba Singers of Harvard College in 2004 renamed its annual event the Walter J. Leonard Black Arts Festival. All of these honors commemorate Leonard's contributions to the field of American higher education.

GERARD ROBINSON

Lester, Julius (27 Jan. 1939–), writer and activist, was the second of two sons born to Reverend W. D. Lester, a Methodist minister, and Julia (Smith) Lester in St. Louis, Missouri. When he was two years old the family moved to Kansas City, Kansas. His father, seeking dignity, invariably wore a suit and tie, teaching his sons that separate "colored" facilities were demeaning and never to be used. The family spent its summers in the South at the rural home of Lester's maternal grandmother in Pine Bluff, Arkansas.

Lester's early precocity manifested itself in his love for reading and a propensity to challenge teachers. A childhood spent deep within the folds of the black community did not shield him from terror and anger. He later wrote that under segregation, "Hope was the name some dreamer bestowed on a daughter, ... change was what the white man at the store *might* give you when you bought something, and progress was merely another incomprehensible word on a spelling test" (*Lovesong*, 5).

In 1953 Lester's father took a job as director of Negro Affairs for the Board of Evangelism of the Methodist Church, and the family moved to Nashville, Tennessee. Upon entering Fisk University in Nashville in 1956, Lester became persuaded intellectually of atheism but experienced disquietude in the absence of faith. After spending a term as an exchange student at San Diego State College, he immersed himself briefly in the beat poetry scene in San Francisco in 1959. Abstaining from the sit-ins that swept Nashville in 1960, he graduated from Fisk with a degree in English, after which he worked at the Highlander Folk School, a civil rights and folk music center then located in Monteagle, Tennessee.

In 1961 Lester moved to New York City and worked at a bookstore, for the welfare department in Harlem, and at a Catskills summer camp. In 1962 he married Joan Steinau, the future biographer of Congresswoman ELEANOR HOLMES NORTON. They would have two children, Jody and Malcolm. An aspiring musician, Lester was part of the New York folk scene in the mid-1960s, playing with Guy Carawan, Phil Ochs, Judy Collins, Tom Paxton, and Pete Seeger, with whom he wrote an instruction manual, published in 1965, called *The 12-String Guitar as Played by Leadbelly*. He wrote for the folk music magazines *Sing Out!* and *Broadside* and released two blues-folk albums on the Vanguard label.

From 1963 onward Lester devoted himself more intensively to the freedom movement. He led songs at Freedom Schools and mass meetings in Mississippi in 1964, worked at the national office of the Student Nonviolent Coordinating Committee (SNCC) in Atlanta in 1966, and traveled to Vietnam, Cuba, and throughout the South as a movement photographer. From 1967 to 1969 he wrote a weekly column for the *National Guardian*, a radical newspaper.

At the same time Lester was at the forefront of efforts to imagine a new black children's literature. He recast traditional fables and black history in such works as *To Be a Slave* (1968, recipient of the second Newbery Honor Citation ever awarded to a book by a black author), *Black Folktales* (1969), *Long Journey Home: Stories from Black History* (1972, a National Book Award finalist), and *The Knee-high Man and Other Tales* (1972). In *Look Out, Whitey! Black Power's Gon' Get Your Mama!* (1968) and *Revolutionary Notes* (1969) Lester wrote in a vernacular voice fusing black consciousness with new left radicalism. He taught at the New School for Social Research from 1968 to 1970, hosted a weekly radio show from 1968 to 1975 on New York's listener-supported station WBAI, and presided over a live television show on WNET from 1970 to 1972. A firestorm of criticism engulfed Lester in 1968 and 1969 when he declined to denounce anti-Semitic statements made by guests on his radio show during and after the Ocean Hill-Brownsville dispute, which pitted a mostly Jewish teachers' union against black demands for community control of schools.

Beginning in 1969 Lester's prominence as a black radical writer prompted increasing inner turmoil. He began to feel "a prisoner of the black collective" living a life "others needed me to live" (*Lovesong*, 66, 74). He resented it when blacks repeatedly faulted him for marrying a white woman, a subject explored in a thinly disguised self-interview in *Evergreen Review* in 1969. He dissented from what he considered the adventurism of the Black Panther Party. In the end he renounced Black Power itself for making blacks think of themselves as victims, diminishing moral self-examination, and denying whites' humanity.

The declension of Lester's radicalism, combined with the dissolution of his marriage in 1970, led to confusion and soul-searching. For a time he explored Roman Catholic mysticism inspired by the writings of the monk Thomas Merton. In 1971 Lester published a two-volume edition of W.E.B. DuBois's writings and began teaching Afro-American Studies at the University of Massachusetts Amherst. He moved permanently to Massachusetts in 1975. In the 1970s, Lester experienced depression and had difficulty writing, but a turnaround coincided with his 1979 wedding to Alida Carolyn Fechner, a psychotherapist, who brought a daughter, Elena, to the marriage and with whom he had a son, David Julius.

In 1979 a controversial essay by Lester appeared in the *Village Voice* defending Jews and Israel against black criticism in the wake of ANDREW YOUNG's resignation as ambassador to the United Nations. When Lester decided to teach a course on blacks and Jews that year, he realized his growing attraction to Judaism. He studied Jewish texts and history, attended synagogue, and reflected on his genealogy. His maternal grandmother in Arkansas, who to all appearances was white, was one of five children born to Maggie Carson, a "half-black, half-Indian, ex-slave," and Adolph Altschul, a German Jewish immigrant peddler (*All is Well*, 15). Consciousness of this ancestry contributed to Lester's conversion—or homecoming—to Judaism in 1982.

Lester's changed outlook presaged a rupture with his Afro-American Studies colleagues at the University of Massachusetts Amherst. When Lester criticized remarks made by JAMES BALDWIN at the university as anti-Semitic, the department voted unanimously in 1988 to request that he be reassigned. Lester retorted, "I didn't fight against whites trying to limit and define me to turn around and have blacks try to limit and define me" (*New York*

Times, 30 Nov. 1991). Nevertheless, he was transferred to the Judaic Studies program in 1988. He retired from the university as emeritus professor in 2003, having received several prestigious teaching awards.

After his second marriage ended in divorce in 1993, Lester married Milan Sabatini in 1995, becoming stepfather to her daughter, Lián. From 1992 to 2006 Lester led a small synagogue, Congregation Beth El, in St. Johnsbury, Vermont. As an African American and a Jew, Lester participated in several dialogues about why black–Jewish solidarity gave way to discord after the early 1960s.

Although he published adult fiction and poetry, Lester was best known for his children's writings, to which he returned in 1987, when he issued the first in a series of four books reclaiming the Uncle Remus folktales from their racist origins. These works did not escape criticism; JUNE JORDAN criticized the Uncle Remus project as a "misbegotten resurrection" and "terrible waste of very considerable talents" (*New York Times*, 17 May 1987). However Lester's two dozen children's books received many awards and acclaim from most reviewers for their tenderness, whimsy, and wisdom. The author appeared to live by the motto he set down in *John Henry* (1994), a Caldecott Honor Book: "Dying ain't important. Everybody does that. What matters is how well you do your living."

FURTHER READING

Lester, Julius. *All is Well* (1976).

Lester, Julius. *Lovesong: Becoming a Jew* (1988).

Lester, Julius. *On Writing for Children and Other People* (2004).

Lester, Julius. *Search for the New Land: History as Subjective Experience* (1969).

CHRISTOPHER PHELPS

LeTang, Henry (19 June 1916–26 April 2007), tap and theatre dancer, teacher, and choreographer, was born in Harlem, New York, the second son of five children of Clarence and Marie, both of whom were from the Virgin Islands. Clarence and Marie LeTang owned a radio and phonograph repair shop in Harlem, where Clarence built and designed phonographs. Music and dancing were a family pastime, and so the LeTang children were all encouraged to play an instrument. As a young boy LeTang attended a dance recital that began his love of tap. He started dancing when he was seven years old and it became his life. LeTang started touring and at the age of fifteen and danced in the Sophie Tucker stage show.

LeTang went to the Lafayette Theatre almost every weekend to watch the stars of the time, including such great headliners as STEPIN FECHIT, Buck and Bubbles, Earl SNAKE HIPS TUCKER, and Butter Beans and Suzy. LeTang learned too from the pioneers in tap, especially JOHN W. BUBBLES, a tap master. Through observation, imitation, and practice LeTang learned the steps that began his tap dancing career. By the age of seventeen LeTang had developed his own technique, and in 1937 he opened a studio and began teaching tap. His ability to introduce tap style and choreograph made him a popular dance teacher with both professional performers and novices.

Tap performers were legion, but teachers of the craft seemed always to be in short supply. LeTang earned his reputation as master tap teacher and practitioner through his technique of teaching tap. He had a special way of working with novices as well as experienced performers, using their knowledge of tap, however limited, "to give them a nice line" (*New York Guide*, 6 Nov. 1978). LeTang trained and choreographed routines for a roster of performers that included LENA HORNE, Milton Berle, HARRY BELAFONTE, Bette Midler, SUGAR RAY ROBINSON, and LOLA FALANA. Additionally he trained the dancers GREGORY HINES and Maurice Hines, Chita Rivera, Peter Gennaro, Eleanor Powell, and Betty Hutton. He was also credited with choreographing a nightclub revue for the boxer JOE FRAZIER.

Although LeTang was a master dancer and teacher, he was equally well known for his choreographic contributions to several successful Broadway shows. He choreographed eight tap dance routines performed by Gregory and Maurice Hines for the musical *Eubie*. This popular, lucrative production garnered national attention and earned LeTang a Drama Critics Award nomination. LeTang also worked with EUBIE BLAKE on his first musical, *Tan Manhattan*, performed at the Apollo. He created the tap sequences for the Tin Man ("Slide Some Oil to Me") in *The Wiz*, and won an Outer Critics Circle Award for Outstanding Tap Choreography for *Sophisticated Ladies*, featuring JUDITH JAMISON and Gregory Hines. Both *Eubie* and *Sophisticated Ladies* were nominated for Tony Awards, but it wasn't until 1989 that LeTang won a Tony for the best choreographer for *Black and Blue*. During the 1980s LeTang extended his choreography talents to film and is credited with arranging the dancing on three films, *The Cotton Club* (1984), *Tap* (1989), and *Bojangles* (2001), the latter for Showtime television.

LeTang was a recipient of numerous awards to honor his contributions to dance education. In 2003 the Oklahoma City University School of American Dance and Arts Management presented him with an honorary doctorate. In his later years LeTang continued teaching dance, most notably in a workshop series dedicated to his second wife, Ellie, who worked as his choreographic assistant and died in 2003. That same year LeTang won the Educator of the Year Award at the eighth annual American Choreography Awards in Los Angeles. LeTang died in Las Vegas at the age of 91.

FURTHER READING

Hill, Errol, and James Hatch. *A History of African American Theatre* (2005).

Loften, Mitchell. *Black Drama: Story of American Negro in the Theatre* (1967).

Manning, Susan. *Modern Dance, Negro Dance: Race in Motion* (2004).

BARBARA TOOMER DAVIS

Levington, William (1793–23 May 1836), minister, teacher, missionary, and abolitionist, was born free in New York City during the spring of 1793. His parents and the circumstances of his childhood are unknown. Around 1800 Levington relocated to Philadelphia, Pennsylvania, where he spent most of his adolescence and worked in the bookstore of Sheldon Potter. There he became a friend and pro-tégé of Sheldon's brother, Alonzo Potter, who even-tually became the Episcopal bishop of Pennsylvania and who helped secure Levington's entry into the Protestant Episcopal ministry. In 1819 Levington moved to Albany, New York, under Potter's men-torship. Potter became a professor at Union College and he unofficially instructed Levington part-time there until he returned to Philadelphia in 1822. In Albany, Levington was employed as a teacher in a school for African American children and he attended St. Peter's Church. It was likely through his teaching position that Levington was asked to give an abolitionist speech in 1822 to the Female Benezet Philanthropic Society of Albany on the anniversary of the end of the international slave trade, which Britain outlawed in 1807. Levington's speech, later published, was articulate and religiously inspired. He denounced the evil and brutality of slavery, but he also thanked God who, in His providence, used Parliament to outlaw the international slave trade.

The object of Levington's studies, and his ear-nest desire, was to be ordained. Potter sent let-ters on behalf of Levington, inquiring about the possibility of his settlement as minister of the African American Church of St. Thomas in Philadelphia; interest in Levington was expressed by one of that church's vestry members. Levington also wished to return to Philadelphia, perhaps because the New York bishop John Hobart was unwilling to ordain Levington, presumably on account of his race. The people who knew Levington in Albany all wrote of his intelligence, diligence, and piety.

Back in Philadelphia by 1823, Levington continued his education and preparation for ordination under the Reverend Jackson Kemper and on 14 March 1824 was ordained a deacon of the Episcopal Church by Bishop William White. Shortly after his ordination Levington traveled to Baltimore, Maryland, with the intention of forming a black Episcopal church and school. Several factors made Baltimore a likely city for such an undertaking. It was a prosperous port town with many free and enslaved African Americans. A large proportion of enslaved workers were hired out as seasonal workers in both skilled and unskilled jobs. In some cases male slaves were allowed to live on their own, earn wages, and pay set amounts to their master who lived outside the city. When Levington came to Baltimore, there were already two black churches, the Bethel African Methodist Episcopal Church and the Sharp Street Methodist Episcopal Church. The church that Levington founded was the first black Protestant Episcopal Church founded in the southern United States.

His church, however, required his continual labor and was always plagued by a lack of funds. On 23 June 1824 Levington found a location to perform services and hold his school, but in the first nine months after his arrival he was unable to muster the means required for the construction of a church. Even some of his early supporters were pessimistic. Finally, generous support came from members of the white community. James Bosley Esq. donated a piece of land worth $2,000. Others gave monetary donations, and Mr. George Whipple gave five thousand bricks to be used in building the edifice. As with all the money raised for the church, these gifts came as a result of the tireless work of Levington, who raised most of the money needed but who did not receive a salary for his labors. The St. James First African Protestant Episcopal Church was consecrated by Bishop Kemp on 31 March 1827 and the congregation in attendance was substan-tial. On 23 March 1828 Levington was ordained a priest by Bishop White at the Church of St. Thomas. Levington was only the third African American to be ordained to the Episcopal priesthood.

On most weekdays Levington taught eighty black children, of mostly free parents. Every Sunday he also taught two sessions of Sabbath school, which included instruction in reading and writing, and he performed services at eleven and four o'clock. He maintained this rigorous schedule every week, except during those times when he traveled to raise funds to pay off church debt. These trips took him to Philadelphia, Boston, New York, Connecticut, and Rhode Island, but in Providence, Levington experienced northern racism when he was not allowed to preach in its Episcopal Church, as was customary for visiting pastors.

Levington's greatest challenge was facing a congregation divided over its own governance. The church constitution gave both free and slave male church members an equal vote, although only free men could be elected to the vestry. Some free African Americans objected to this arrangement, wanting to make church governance solely the responsibility of free men. Levington and Bishop Kemp would not, however, waver in their convictions to maintain the church's rough impartiality. As a result of this division, a letter was sent to the Standing Committee of the Episcopal Church that alleged some unspecified and unsubstantiated charges against Levington's moral character. An investigation was initiated, but the charges eventually were dropped for lack of evidence.

With peace reestablished and the church running normally, Levington continued in his ministerial and teaching duties. He also gave more attention to abolitionist work, especially in opposing the colonization societies that encouraged free African Americans to migrate to Africa. Sadly, only eight years after his ordination, Levington died at the age of forty-three in Baltimore. Befitting his self-sacrificial character, Levington died without enough money to cover his funeral costs, which were instead met by his friend, the Reverend J.-P.-K.-Henshaw, who much admired Levington for his steadfast character and for his work as a pioneering African American within the Episcopal Church.

FURTHER READING

Bragg, George F. *The First Negro Priest on Southern Soil* (1909).

Bragg, George F. *History of the Afro-American Group of the Episcopal Church* (1968).

Chandler, Phyllis L. *Heritage of Hope and Sacrifice: The Remarkable Journeys of Rev. William Levington* (2002).

Phillips, Christopher. *Freedom's Port: The African American Community of Baltimore, 1790–1860* (1997).

RICHARD J. BOLES

Levy, James Richelieu (28 July 1861–20 Jan. 1936), political activist and doctor, was born in Camden, South Carolina, one of the three sons and six children of James and Susan Levy. Dr. Levy's great-grandmother was a native African. James Levy attended public school in Camden and for a short time the University of South Carolina. When the school closed its doors to black students, he had to find another university. James began his career as a teacher in Mayesville in the early 1880s. During Reconstruction he was a page in the House of Representatives in South Carolina and a student at a preparatory school for boys for entrance to State University. In 1886, he taught school in Arkansas and later entered Fisk University in November 1886. Levy graduated from Fisk University in 1891 and entered the College of Physicians and Surgeons at Chicago (now University of Illinois College of Medicine) that same year. He completed his medical degree in 1894 and relocated to Florence, South Carolina, to practice medicine. There he married Maggie O. Harris, the daughter of Mr. and Mrs. Richard Harris of Nashville, Tennessee, on 12 April 1894. Miss Harris attended Fisk University as well. They were parents of three children, Camille, Myrtle, and Carl. Camille also attended Fisk University. Levy did postgraduate work at Harvard Medical School in 1894 and 1895.

In 1896 Levy was one of the four founders of the Association of Colored Physicians of South Carolina with Dr. Charles Catlett Johnson of Aiken, Dr. Alonzo Clifton McClennan, and Dr. Lawrence A. Earle of Charleston. The organization was founded in response to the exclusion of black medical practitioners from the American Medical Association. In 1946, the organization was renamed the Palmetto Association of Physicians, Pharmacists, and Dentists of South Carolina, and continues to exist. Around 1910, Dr. Levy became Treasurer of the National Medical Association, which was founded in 1895 to advance the art and science of medicine for people of African descent. He held that position until his death

Dr. Levy was active in the politics of Florence, South Carolina. His field of activity covered education, religion, health, politics, and the economic well-being of African Americans in South Carolina. He was the chairman of the Republican

Committee for the Sixth South Carolina district. He was a trustee of Clafin University, a historically black institution founded in 1869 and affiliated with the United Methodist Church, and of another historically black school, the Voorhees Institute in Denmark, South Carolina. He served as a delegate to the Republican convention in Chicago, where he claimed that an estimated 95 percent of the state's black population was for Theodore Roosevelt. In 1916, Dr. Levy was on stage with Charles Evan Hughes, a Republican nominee for President, when he accepted the nomination at Carnegie Hall. In 1920, he was a delegate to the General Conference of the Methodist Episcopal Church. As noted in his obituary, "He was identified with, and a leader of every movement in Florence for the betterment of our group. His field of activity covered education, religion, health, politics and the economic well-being of the group." It also mentioned that "[f]or years he was active in State and National Politics, and was a delegate from South Carolina to five Republican National Conventions." Dr. Levy died on 20 January 1936 in Florence, South Carolina.

FURTHER READING

Caldwell, Arthur Bunyan. *History of the Negro and His Institutions: South Carolina Edition* (1919).

Casdorph, Paul D. *Republicans, Negroes, and Progressives in the South 1912–1916* (1981).

Obituary: "Editorials," *The Journal of the National Medical Association* (1936): 75–76.

KENYATTA D. BERRY

Levy, John (11 Apr. 1912–20 Jan. 2012) bassist, personal manager, record and concert producer, was born in New Orleans, the only child of Laura Hagen, a midwife, and John Levy, a railroad stoker in New Orleans, who later worked as a stockyard laborer in Chicago. Part of the great northern migration during and after World War I, the Levy family moved to Chicago in 1919.

A well-intentioned teacher told Levy to get a job at the post office so that he'd have a secure future, but he had bigger ideas; he imagined himself sitting behind a big desk. He didn't know what he'd be doing at that desk, but he knew that he would be in business. Levy was an entrepreneur before the word became popular. Without completing high school, he did work for brief time at the post office, throwing mail, and as a special delivery messenger, but that was too limiting for a young man with ideas. He bought a bread slicer and made a deal with a bakery to sell sliced bread. He organized dances for social clubs, hiring bands and charging admission. NAT KING COLE's eighteen-piece band was one of the most popular he hired; he paid the band ten dollars. It was while organizing a turkey raffle that he met his first wife, Gladys Gilbert. They married in 1932 and the first of three children was born the following year.

Levy also loved music—particularly jazz—and soon found that he could earn money playing upright bass. Throughout the 1930s he worked in the midwest with a number of artists until the head of the black musician's union recommended him to work with jazz violinist STUFF SMITH. The trio, which included pianist Jimmy Jones, was booked to play at the Onyx Club. Levy never looked back.

He was a good bass player and had the privilege of working with many of the jazz greats, including BEN WEBSTER, ERROLL GARNER, and MILT JACKSON. He also appeared with BILLIE HOLIDAY at her comeback Carnegie Hall concert in 1948. The following year, George Shearing heard him play at the famed Birdland club, and soon after Levy became the bassist in the original George Shearing Quintet. Touring the country with one of the hottest groups of the day, he not only played bass but also acted as Shearing's road manager. His business acumen and promotional astuteness won out; in 1951 he put down his bass to become a full-time personal manager—the first black personal manager in the pop or jazz music field. John Levy Enterprises, Inc. was open for business with John behind his desk.

Despite the obstacles inherent in being a black businessman during that time, his transition from the ranks of jazz instrumentalist to eminence in the personal management field was a smooth one. The rare combination of musical talent and shrewd business savvy made it possible for Levy to discover new talent and develop it to its maximum potential without the usual precarious trial and error struggle experienced by most artists.

By the 1960s, Levy's client roster not only included George Shearing, but also Dakota Staton, Nancy Wilson, CANNONBALL ADDERLEY, WES MONTGOMERY, JOE WILLIAMS, SHIRLEY HORN, Ramsey Lewis, and others. Most weeks, you could find one or more of Levy's clients listed in the top ten of *Billboard* magazine's pop music charts. Back then, jazz was the popular music.

In addition to his varied experiences in personal management, John repeatedly found himself in the roles of concert promoter and record producer, often without credit. He did produce a number of shows under his own banner, however. "Free Sounds of '63" opened for a week at the Apollo Theater, followed by performances at Howard Theater in Washington, D.C., and the Uptown in Philadelphia to capacity crowds. Other shows followed: "Free Sounds of 1970," "Black Music '71," and "Free Sounds of 1971" at the Fisher Theater in Detroit.

Levy was an original member of the National Board of Directors of JESSE JACKSON's PUSH organization (People United to Save Humanity), and in 1972 handled the production of PUSH's Black Expo main entertainment event featuring SAMMY DAVIS JR., the Jackson Five, the Temptations, and ISAAC HAYES.

While his career moved steadily upward, his personal life was somewhat rockier. After his first marriage ended in divorce in 1964, Levy married actress GAIL FISHER in 1965; they raised two daughters and divorced in 1972. He married Cora Utterbach in 1978; they had no children, and separated in 1998. Their divorce was final in 2000 and in 2003 Levy married Devra Hall, who had been working with him for twenty-four years.

Some of the most successful jazz luminaries in the music world testify to the exceptional success of his all-encompassing methods that included public relations and publishing. Levy was among the first managers to encourage musicians to retain the publishing rights to their own compositions and set up individual publishing companies for each of his clients.

Other artists among the more than eighty-five clients on Levy's impressive roster of notables handled over a sixty-year period include Brook Benton, Andy & the Bey Sisters, BETTY CARTER, Randy Crawford, Lou Donaldson, ROBERTA FLACK, ARSENIO HALL, HERBIE HANCOCK, DONNY HATHAWAY, EDDIE HARRIS, JOHNNY HARTMAN, Freddie Hubbard, AHMAD JAMAL, Henry Johnson, ETTA JONES, YUSEF LATEEF, ABBEY LINCOLN, Herbie Mann, Letta Mbulu, Les McCann, Billy Paul, Dianne Reeves, Marlena Shaw, Billy Taylor, STANLEY TURRENTINE, SARAH VAUGHAN, and Maxine Weldon.

In 1980, Levy, along with MUHAMMAD ALI, KAREEM ABDUL-JABBAR, ROY CAMPANELLA, EllaFITZGERALD, and ALEX HALEY, was saluted for projecting "positive images that give black people stability, confidence and hope." Los Angeles Mayor THOMAS BRADLEY made the presentations at the "Testimonial to the Pioneers of Black Positive Images" held at the Century Plaza Hotel.

In the fall of 1997, at the age of 85, Levy's contribution to the world of jazz was formally recognized as he was inducted into the International Jazz Hall of Fame. The National Endowment for the Arts awarded him an NEA Jazz Master Fellowship in 2006. His years of success in all areas has earned him an impeccable reputation in the entertainment industry, respected and admired by other managers, booking agents, concert promoters, entertainment lawyers and accountants, record company executives, and, last but not least, the artists themselves.

FURTHER READING

2006 NEA Jazz Master John Levy, online at http://www.nea.gov/national/jazz/jmCMS/master.php?id=2006_07.

2006 NEA Jazz Master John Levy Video, online at http://snapsizzlebop.com/look-and-listen/nea-jazz-master-videos/.

Fishko, Sara. "John Levy, Jazz Master," *NPR*, 13 January 2006, online at http://www.wnyc.org/shows/fishko/episodes/2006/01/13.

Levy, Devra Hall. *Strollin': A Jazz Life through John Levy's Personal Lens* (2008).

Levy, John, with Devra Hall. *Men, Women, and Girl Singers: My Life as A Musician Turned Talent Manager* (2001).

Mitchell, John. Interview with John Levy, 10–11 December 2006, Jazz Oral History Program Collection, Archives Center, National Museum of American History, Smithsonian Institution, online at http://www.smithsonianjazz.org/oral_histories/pdf/joh_JohnLevy.pdf.

DEVRA HALL LEVY

Levy, Levi Ben (18 Feb. 1935–9 Apr. 1999), rabbi and educator, was born Lawrence Albert McKethan, to West McKethan and Lilly (Blue) McKethan, farmers in Cumberland County, North Carolina. The future rabbi traced his ancestry back to Chattie Blue, a slave who came with the Hodges family from England to North Carolina in the nineteenth century. She obtained her freedom and gave birth to six children, including his fraternal grandmother, Lucy Blue, who was a revered midwife to black and white women in the county. Lucy married a man named Duncan McKethan and gave birth to eight children including one named West. After the death of his first wife, Flora, West married Lilly, a woman of Cherokee ancestry. They had fourteen children, including Levy.

Levy grew up on a small farm with eighteen older siblings and one younger sibling. He was a bright, adventurous child who taught himself to sing and play the piano by ear. His father was one of the pillars of the emerging black community who founded the Antioch Free Will Baptist Church in Cumberland County and, because federal and state support for the education of black children was virtually nonexistent, also helped establish the Antioch Elementary School. The community rebuilt the school three times after it was destroyed (twice by flood and once by fire). Such was the determination of Levy's parents and their neighbors to insure that their children received a basic education.

Religion was as common a feature of Levy's life as the southern pines that surrounded him. His father was a deacon; church attendance was mandatory; and most social functions were sponsored by a church. The churches were as racially segregated as the schools. Since the Civil War, laws requiring black churches in the South to have white overseers had been repealed. This newfound freedom established the black church as the most autonomous institution in the black community. In a cultural sense, black churches often differed from their white counterparts in their modes of religious expression. Reveling in the musical traditions of spirituals and gospel, black churches featured call-and-response singing between the preacher and the congregation. Black preachers, particularly those who were popular during Levy's youth, also placed great emphasis on the Old Testament or Hebrew Bible. Although it is not surprising that American slaves and their descendents would find a strong affinity between themselves and the slaves of the Old Testament, there is no evidence that they imagined the Hebrew slaves to be black people. In fact, Levy was implicitly taught that all the people in the Bible were white because that was how they were depicted in illustrations and portraits.

At the age of fifteen Levy abandoned the family farm to join older siblings in New York City. He found employment with a small restaurant chain called Nedicks and soon became a manager of a local franchise. His heart, however, was still in North Carolina, and it was set on a hometown girl named Roxanna Byrd. With their parents' permission he and Roxanna were married by a justice of the peace on 22 August 1953 and returned to New York shortly thereafter. They would eventually have six children. With his family growing so rapidly, Levy became more anxious about his career. He took evening classes at City College to further his education; he briefly became part owner of a gas station with a brother-in-law; and he even thought of becoming a police officer before joining the track department of the Long Island Rail Road in 1957. It was there that he met a black Jew named Arnold Manot who would change the course of his life.

Manot invited him to attend the Commandment Keepers Congregation in Harlem, New York. It was there that he met the person who would have the most profound effect on his life, Chief Rabbi WENTWORTH MATTHEW. Levy first became a member of the congregation, then he was invited to joins its secret society known as the Royal Order of Ethiopian Hebrews Sons and Daughters of Culture. After completing his Hebrew studies, his teachers and the mothers of the congregation encouraged him to enter the Ethiopian Hebrew Rabbinical College in 1960. Through much hard work and sacrifice, he graduated six years later and was ordained by Chief Rabbi Matthew with great public acclaim in 1967.

Immediately upon graduation and ordination Levy felt he was destined to do great things. He felt that it was his life's mission to awaken the "lost House of Israel." The latter term in his parlance referred to black people who did not yet know that they were Jewish (Papers of Chief Rabbi Levi Ben Levy at the Schomburg Center for Research in Black Culture). With Matthew's blessing, Levy started his first congregation, which he called Beth Shalom, in the living room of his Queens apartment with only eight members. For the first few years, as more people wanted to worship with his new congregation, they rented halls at various locations before acquiring their first building at 609 Marcy Avenue in Brooklyn, New York. In 1968 Levy negotiated an arrangement with the Young Israel of Williamsburg that allowed him to move his congregation into the present home of Beth Shalom E. H. Congregation at 730 Willoughby Avenue. There the congregation flourished to over three hundred members, operated a day care center, drug rehabilitation program, and a Talmud Torah Hebrew School.

In 1971 Levy, along with Rabbi Yisrael, Rabbi Yahonatan, Rabbi Woods, and Rabbi Paris—all students of Chief Rabbi Matthew—set out to revive their alma mater, the Ethiopian Hebrew Rabbinical College that had been established in 1925. They expanded the curriculum and renamed their college the Israelite Rabbinical Academy. By this time the term Ethiopian had been become exclusively associated with the country instead of being used as a synonym for black, as it had been early in the century. As other rabbis joined their ranks, a unified organizational body emerged known as the Israelite Board of Rabbis. Their organization became national when Rabbi Levy established a chapter in Chicago among black Jews led by Rabbi James Hodges, Rabbi Abihu Reuben, and his protégé Rabbi CAPERS FUNNYE. In 1977 the board became international when the Zion House of Israel was established in Barbados and Levy was elected its new Chief Rabbi four years after the death of Chief Rabbi Matthew.

Now at the height of his career, Levy published the *Hakol* newsletter, ran a half-hour radio program on radio station WWRL, appeared on television programs such as *Black Pride* and *Good Morning America*, and often spoke to international audiences—including over one hundred B'nai Brith lodges. Theologically he continued the traditions of Rabbi Matthew, adding new rituals to Jewish practice that made this denomination culturally distinct. He brought the services into closer alignment with Orthodox Jewry by using a standard prayer book while retaining black musical traditions and other customs of spiritual expression such as fiery sermons, anointing, and unscripted supplication. Politically he retained the group's nationalism, which emphasized the historical origins of Judaism with people of color, while vehemently rejecting the rising tide of anti-Semitism and black separatism that were prominent during the period. In addition he elevated women to more prominent positions. His wife, Deborah Levy, became known as a "Rabbinit," a title he invented to describe the leadership role that such women occupied. Although he opposed the ordination of women, he invited esteemed women such as Rabbinit Leana Yahonatan to teach in the Israelite Rabbinical Academy.

In 1983 Levy retired from Beth Shalom because of irreconcilable differences with the congregation's board. Levy was of the belief and tradition that the rabbi is the leader of the congregation, not an employee of it. He subsequently founded his second synagogue, Beth Elohim Hebrew Congregation, in Queens, New York. In 1988 he installed his eldest son, Rabbi Sholomo Levy as the spiritual leader of the congregation. Throughout the 1990s, Levy provided counsel and direction from his retirement home in North Carolina to those who sought his wisdom. In his latter years Levy delved deeply into a branch of Jewish mysticism known as Kabbalah. After being diagnosed with a form of leukemia, Levy returned to New York to seek treatment at Mount Sinai Medical Center. After a few months of unsuccessful therapy he succumbed to his illness and was buried with full Jewish rites at Beth David Cemetery on Long Island. His passing was mourned in both the white and black press.

FURTHER READING

The largest collection of papers and documents belonging to Chief Rabbi Levi Ben Levy and about black Jews is to be found at the Schomburg Center for Research in Black Culture at the New York Public Library. Smaller collections are at the American Jewish Archives in Cincinnati.

Brotz, Howard. *The Black Jews of Harlem: Negro Nationalism and the Dilemmas of Negro Leadership* (1970).

Landing, James E. *Black Judaism: Story of an American Movement* (2002).

Ottley, Roi. *New World A-Coming: Inside Black America* (1943).

Shapiro, Deanne Ruth. "Double Damnation, Double Salvation: The Source and Varieties of Black Judaism in the United States," master's thesis, Columbia University (1970).

Obituary: *New York Times*, 13 April 1999; *The Forward*, 16 April 1999; *New York Amsterdam News*, 16 April 1999.

SHOLOMO B. LEVY

Lew, Barzillai (or Barsillai) (5 Nov. 1743–1822) professional musician and soldier in the French and Indian War and War of Independence, was the freeborn progenitor of a large Groton, Massachusetts, family. The family later spent time in Dracut and Pepperell, where they owned land. His father, Primus Lew, was a skilled artisan (a cooper, or barrel maker) and it is unclear if he was ever a slave and later freed, or was himself freeborn. The historian BENJAMIN QUARLES claimed that Barzillai Lew was also a cooper, and it has been claimed that Primus was also a musician. His mother was named Margret; nothing else about her is known. Father and son both served in the French and Indian War, with Barzillai (also known as "Zeal") serving for thirty-eight weeks in 1760 under the command of Thomas Farrington. In 1768 he married Dinah Bowman, whose freedom he bought for $400. They later had at least thirteen (according to some accounts, sixteen) children and lived in Chelmsford, Massachusetts, early in their marriage. At some point along the way, Lew learned to be an outstanding musician.

In 1775, a few months after the Battle of Lexington and Concord, Lew joined the Twenty-Seventh Massachusetts Regiment, for which he fought and played the fife. Under the command of Captain John Ford, Lew served at the Battle of Bunker Hill. Gary B. Nash, professor emeritus of history at the University of California, Los

Angeles, described Lew as "tall and strong," and claimed that "Barzillai Lew was typical of the free black patriot under arms" in that he enlisted several times (Nash, 7). For a period of time early in the Revolutionary War, George Washington had barred black enlistment for fear of arming slaves, but reversed his stand after Great Britain promised freedom to blacks who agreed to serve the Crown. In Lew's next enlistment, in 1777, he joined Joseph Varnum's militia, which was from Dracut, with which he marched to Fort Ticonderoga in New York where he fought under Benedict Arnold.

After the war the Lew family performed as a traveling band all across northeastern New England. Lew's son Zadock was also known as a particularly talented musician. It is not clear exactly what sort of music this band played. There is a frequently repeated, but apparently apocryphal, story of Lew's band performing at George Washington's inauguration. Lew's half-legendary musicianship may have inspired DUKE ELLINGTON to compose a piece called "Barzillai Lou" in 1943. It is unclear if the piece was ever recorded, but the manuscript of the music is in the Smithsonian. Ellington also mentioned Lew in his autobiography, *Music is My Mistress* (1973).

The Lew family settled in the area that was to become Lowell, Massachusetts. They owned a farm and lived on Totman Road, which then was known as "Old Zeal Road," "Old Zeal" being Lew's nickname later in life. Lew (and his sons) worked on the construction of the (now defunct) Middlesex Canal from 1793 to 1805. He was also a musician with the Pawtucket Society Church, which later became a local center of abolitionism.

When Lew died in 1822, his property was divided between two of his sons, Zimri and Zadock. The Lew family went on to thrive in Massachusetts throughout the nineteenth and twentieth centuries, producing many prominent citizens. There is a portrait in the State Department building in Washington, D.C., titled "The Flutist" that may be a portrait of Barzillai Lew.

FURTHER READING

Nash, Gary B. *The Forgotten Fifth: African Americans in the Age of Revolution* (2006).

Quarles, Benjamin. *The Negro in the American Revolution* (1961).

Robertson, Tatsha. "A Rare Lineage: A Black Family Boasts Early Massachusetts Roots," *Boston Globe*, 21 Feb. 1999.

PAUL DEVLIN

Lewis, Carl (1 July 1961–), track and field athlete, was born Frederick Carlton Lewis in Birmingham, Alabama, the third of four children of William Lewis and Evelyn Lawler, both of them teachers and coaches who had been outstanding athletes themselves at Tuskegee Institute. Lewis's father was an excellent pass receiver in football and sprinter in track and field, while his mother was a nationally ranked hurdler who was expected to compete in the 1952 Olympic Games in Helsinki before an injury cut short her career.

In 1963 Lewis's parents, after brief stints as teachers in Montgomery, Alabama, following their graduation from Tuskegee Institute, moved the family to Willingboro, New Jersey, to further their professional careers and improve their social and economic positions. It was in Willingboro that Lewis honed his enormous physical talents and first garnered national attention for his exploits in track and field. Training alongside his sister Carol, who became a nationally ranked long jumper, and coached by his parents at their Willingboro Track Club, Lewis evolved into the top-ranked long jumper and one of the best interscholastic sprinters in the country. In 1979 he established a national high school record in the long jump with a leap of 26 feet 6 inches and captured a bronze medal in the same event at the Pan American Games.

Carl Lewis in an undated photograph. (AP Images.)

His accomplishments on the track were so extraordinary that Lewis was offered dozens of athletic scholarships by several prestigious colleges and universities. He ultimately decided to attend the University of Houston so that he could train under the highly respected coach Tom Tellez. Lewis blossomed athletically at Houston, capturing many championships and establishing numerous records in the sprints and long jump using the hitch-kick technique introduced to him by Tellez. In 1980 Lewis won the first of two consecutive indoor and outdoor National Collegiate Athletic Association (NCAA) long-jump championships and was chosen to compete on the 4¥100 United States Olympic relay team. Unfortunately, Lewis, along with FLO HYMAN and other American athletes, was denied the opportunity to compete in the Moscow Olympics because of President Jimmy Carter's decision to boycott the games as a result of the Soviet Union's invasion of Afghanistan. The following year Lewis broke the world record in the long jump with a leap of 27 feet 10½ inches at the Southwest Conference championships, captured NCAA titles in the 100 meters and long jump, and garnered the first of many of his titles in the 100 meters and long jump at the Track Athletic Congress (TAC) championships. In 1982 Lewis left the University of Houston and joined the famed Santa Monica Track Club. The change in venue only seemed to fuel Lewis's competitive spirit and enhance his talents on the track. He won titles in the 100 meters, long jump, and 4¥100 meter relay at the 1983 World Championships in Helsinki and in the same year captured the 200 meters in a time of 19¾ seconds and the long jump with a distance of 28 feet 10¼ inches at the TAC championships. In 1984 Lewis realized lasting fame by winning gold medals in the 100 meters, 200 meters, long jump, and 4¥100 meter relay at the Los Angeles Olympic Games. His four-gold-medal–winning performance in Los Angeles was particularly significant since it matched the victories of JESSE OWENS in the 1936 Berlin Games and thus helped revitalize interest in the track legend and the political controversy surrounding Adolf Hitler and the Berlin Olympics. Lewis's triumphs recalled the memory of Owens and the symbolic importance of his victories in a country espousing beliefs in Aryan racial superiority.

Lewis spent some time away from the track honing his artistic talents following his great performance in the Los Angeles Olympic Games. In 1986 he studied voice, dance, and acting at Warren Robertson's Theater Workshop in New York. Always interested in the entertainment business, Lewis formed his own band and produced several records that sold particularly well in Sweden and Japan. In 1988, however, Lewis was once again devoting himself full-time to track and field. At the Seoul Olympics in 1988, he captured a gold medal in the long jump, a silver medal in the 200 meters, and won the gold medal in the 100 meters after Canadian Ben Johnson was disqualified for drug use. In a subpar Olympic performance by his standards, Lewis was denied an opportunity to win another medal at Seoul when the United States 4¥100 meter relay team failed to get to the finals because of a mishandled baton pass in the first qualifying round.

Lewis continued his Olympic success in the 1992 Barcelona Games by winning the gold medal in the long jump with a leap of 28 feet 5½ inches and by anchoring the gold-medal–winning 4¥100 meter relay team. Lewis closed out his Olympic career in grand style at the 1996 Games in Atlanta by winning the gold medal in the long jump. At the athletically old age of thirty-five, he overcame the challenges of archrival MIKE POWELL and a host of much younger jumpers. Lewis thrilled the Atlanta crowd by leaping 27 feet 10¾ inches to become the only track and field performer in Olympic history besides the discus thrower Al Oerter to garner four gold medals in a single event. This victory also made him only the fourth man in history to win nine gold medals in the Summer Games, the others being the Finnish runner Paavo Nurmi, the American swimmer Mark Spitz, and Ray Ewry, an American who competed in the long jump, the high jump, and the triple jump.

Lewis finally ended his competitive track and field career in 1997. He retired with ten Olympic medals (nine gold, one silver), ten world records, and eight titles in major championships. He also retired as the most decorated man in the history of track and field. He was the recipient of the 1981 Sullivan Award, 1982 Jesse Owens Award, 1982 and 1984 Track and Field News World Athlete of the Year Award, 1983 and 1984 Associated Press Male Athlete of the Year awards, and 1999 World Sports Award of the Century for track and field. He was, moreover, a 1985 inductee into the United States Olympic Hall of Fame.

Lewis has enjoyed a busy and largely successful post-athletic career. Although he was arrested for a second time in 2003 for driving drunk and was never able to endear himself to the American public because of his perceived aloofness and arrogance, Lewis has found success in business and has devoted a great deal of time to charitable organizations and causes. He is a National Court Appointed Special Advocate Association spokesperson for abused and neglected children. He founded the Carl Lewis Foundation, which supports a number of charities, including the College Fund (formerly the United Negro College Fund), the Wendy Marx Foundation (organ donor awareness), and the Walkathon in Houston. He is also a board member of the Best Buddies program, which integrates people with special needs into society.

FURTHER READING

Lewis, Carl, with Jeffrey Marx. *Inside Track: My Professional Life in Amateur Track and Field* (1990).
Lewis, Carl, with Jeffrey Marx. *One More Victory Lap* (1996).

DAVID K. WIGGINS

Lewis, Channing (c. 1862–1941), cook and laborer, was born in Lawrenceville, Virginia, probably in 1862 or 1863. The names of his parents have not been recorded, and it is not known whether or not they were enslaved at the time of their son's birth. Indeed, but for the discovery of a package of letters written to Channing Lewis by Alice Hanley, a white Irish American woman, his life would have been largely lost to history. The letters, enclosed in a black lace stocking, fell from the attic of a house undergoing renovation in Northampton, Massachusetts, in spring 1992. When workmen opened up a hole in the ceiling, the stocking fell. Its contents provide a unique perspective on the southern black migrant experience and on the everyday life of black and white working-class people in New England at the turn of the twentieth century.

The letters also reveal a far from everyday love affair between a black man and a white woman at a time when such unions were taboo in New England and were profoundly dangerous in the South. In 1907, the first year of the couple's correspondence, Benjamin Tillman of South Carolina took to the floor of the U.S. Senate to denounce interracial sexual relationships. In a graphic—indeed, pornographic—speech, Tillman denounced "Negro brutes" and "beasts," who, in his view, "roamed" throughout the land in search of white women to rape and ravish. " 'I have three daughters,' Tillman cried, 'but so help me God, I had rather find

either one of them killed by a tiger or a bear … in the purity of her maidenhood, than to have her … tell me the horrid story that she had been robbed of the jewel of her womanhood by a black fiend' " (Williamson, 116–117). In reality, there was no upsurge in nonconsensual or consensual sex between the races, but such pronouncements from national leaders like Tillman fueled many of the more than 2,500 lynchings of African Americans between 1880 and 1920.

Little is known about Lewis's life before 1879 or 1880, when he first appears in the Springfield, Massachusetts, city directory. Since he would have only been in his late teens at that time, it is probable that he had remained in Virginia until then but joined the exodus of thousands of African Americans from the South following the end of Reconstruction in 1877. Lewis was luckier than many southern migrants in that two of his brothers, Edward and George, had been established in Springfield for several years. Edward, who was seventeen years older than Channing, had served in the Ohio Volunteers of the U.S. Colored Infantry during the Civil War and had made a relatively prosperous living for himself in Springfield, first as a peddler and then, by the time Channing arrived, as a button maker. Edward later worked as a coal and wood dealer and eventually became an engineer; he has been credited with inventing the Lewis Smoke Device, a means of regulating the exhaust from steam engines. As a Union army veteran, Edward enjoyed not only an annual pension of $120 but also membership in the E. K. Wilcox Post of the Grand Army, a prestigious veterans organization. He was also a member of the city's leading colored Masonic lodge and of the Third Baptist Church, which was popular among recent southern migrants.

His older brother's connections undoubtedly eased Channing's transition to life in the North. He soon found a job as a laborer in a paper and cloth factory in Springfield, and he lived at first in an apartment rented by Edward, his wife, and their three children. George Lewis, his wife, and their two children lived in an apartment in the same building, an extended family arrangement that enabled the Lewises to pool resources and share responsibility for child care and housework. Perhaps in search of a degree of independence, Channing moved out of his brother's home in 1880 and lived in a number of lodgings over the next two years. He also worked a series of poorly paid laboring jobs during the same period, since African Americans, who made up about 2 percent of Springfield's population, were routinely excluded from better-paying and unionized skilled trades like bricklaying and plumbing, as well as from most white-collar jobs. Unlike his brother Edward, who had arrived in Springfield in the 1860s, Channing Lewis also faced far greater competition for jobs from the hundreds of white European immigrants who had started arriving in the city. The bonds of Protestantism, abolitionism, and support for the Union, which had once united whites and African Americans in Springfield, were weakening. In the 1880s and 1890s in New England, as in the South and West, the common bond of white skin and its privileges had become far more important.

In 1882 Lewis married an African American woman named Amelia Peters, with whom he had daughter, Grace, born in November 1882, and a son, Channing, born in March 1884. Tragically, but not atypically, both children died within four months of each other in the spring and summer of 1884, shortly followed by their mother, who died of tuberculosis in August of that year. By the mid-1880s Lewis had found regular work as a cook, and he probably met his second wife, Josephine Murphy, whom he married in 1890, through his contacts in the restaurant trade. Murphy was white, the daughter of an Irish American cook.

Interracial marriage, which had been legalized in Massachusetts in 1843, was relatively rare but was more common than in other northern states. In Philadelphia and New York City only 1 percent of African Americans had white spouses; the figure in Boston was 10 to 13 percent. Springfield had only a handful of interracial marriages at this time; as in Boston, most of these were between black men and white women. It is unknown how either the Murphy or the Lewis families responded to the marriage, or to the birth of their only child, Josephine, who was born in 1892 and who died in 1909. Lewis continued to find work as a cook, while his wife worked as a laundress. Between 1896 and 1898, however, Lewis also maintained a residence twenty miles away in Northampton, where he was working in a restaurant. He returned to Springfield the following year, but the couple separated in 1903.

By 1907, though perhaps by as early as 1903, Lewis began a love affair with another Irish American woman, Alice Hanley. The letters sent by Hanley to Lewis between 1907 and 1908 reveal a wealth of information about their relationship, though unfortunately no copies of his replies to her have been found. Northampton was smaller than Springfield

and had far fewer African American residents. Openly interracial relationships were also far less common in Northampton, where the couple rarely appeared together in public. Instead, Hanley usually traveled to Lewis's home in Springfield, which was racially mixed. The relationship was a loving one, though the correspondence makes clear that it was not always harmonious. On one occasion Lewis may have beaten Hanley, and there were many disputes about money and about Hanley's request that Lewis buy her clothes. Lewis did what he could to provide for Hanley, but he may also have had to provide for his daughter, Josephine, who lived with her mother, from whom he never divorced. Indeed, divorce may have been an even greater taboo than interracial marriage for Josephine Murphy and her family, who were Roman Catholics.

Although Hanley in her letters twice calls herself Lewis's wife, there is no record that they ever married. In 1913 when Lewis and Hanley were still living together, Massachusetts passed a law prohibiting out-of-state residents from marrying. The new law would not have directly affected the couple, but it had been passed primarily to prevent interracial couples from marrying in Massachusetts. The couple may also have been aware of the fate of the world champion boxer JACK JOHNSON who in 1913 was sentenced to one year in federal prison under the Mann Act for transporting a white woman across state lines for allegedly immoral purposes. Maintaining an interracial relationship was certainly more difficult and more dangerous in 1915 than it had been a quarter of a century earlier when Lewis had married Josephine Murphy.

Lewis and Hanley separated in 1916. Hanley moved to a nearby rooming house, and later that year she married Thomas Brennan, who was eleven years her junior but shared her race, religion, and ethnicity. Lewis remained in Springfield until 1918, but he may have spent some time outside the state between then and 1922, when the city directory lists him as a cook. His whereabouts are unclear for the late 1920s and early 1930s, but by 1934 he had moved to Boston, where he died aged seventy-eight.

FURTHER READING

Horowitz, Helen Lefkowitz, and Kathy Peiss, eds. *Love across the Color Line: The Letters of Alice Hanley to Channing Lewis* (1996).

Williamson, Joel. *The Crucible of Race: Black-White Relations in the American South since Emancipation* (1984).

STEVEN J. NIVEN

Lewis, Cudjo (Kossola) (1841–26 July 1935), slave and freeperson, storyteller, and community organizer, was born in what is now Benin, Africa. He was smuggled into Mobile, Alabama, aboard the schooner *Clotilda* in July 1860, over fifty years after the abolition of the North Atlantic slave trade in the United States. The *Clotilda* was the last known slave ship, and Lewis and the others were the last known Africans brought to America as slaves. Although Lewis's grandfather owned land, livestock, and a few slaves in Africa, his father Oluale and mother Nyfond-lo-loo lived humble lives. Nyfond-lo-loo was Oluale's second wife and Lewis their second child. Nyfond-lo-loo had five other children. Oluale also had nine by his first wife and three by his third wife.

As a young boy, Lewis enjoyed playing with his siblings and playing the drums. At the age of fourteen he began training to become a soldier, learning how to track, hunt, camp, shoot arrows, and throw spears. Lewis claimed that the goal of this training was to protect the community, not to attack others. As an adolescent Lewis was initiated into the *oro*, the secret society for Yoruba men that was in charge of policing the community. His duties included disposing of criminals, which could include selling them into slavery or having them executed, accusing sorcerers and witches, administering justice, and invoking spiritual forces for the protection of the community. By the time he was nineteen, Lewis began showing interest in a young woman, but before he could marry her he was swept up by a Dahomey raid and sold into American slavery.

The raid that captured Lewis and 109 other Africans occurred on or around 16 February 1860. Due to colonial countries declaring the slave trade illegal, the number of slaves transported across the Atlantic from Dahomey declined from 20,000 in the 1600s to around 12,000 in the early 1800s. Instrumental in the trade was King Ghezo, who ruled Dahomey from 1818 to 1856. Although pressure from Great Britain had forced Ghezo to sign a treaty to end his state's foreign slave trade activities in 1852, he nevertheless continued to participate in the trade. Ghezo had threatened to attack Lewis's town because it had refused to pay tribute to the Dahomey king. When Ghezo was killed in 1858 while returning from a military campaign, his son Badohun, who took the name Glele, carried out the attack. Lewis told ZORA NEALE HURSTON, who spent two months interviewing him in Mobile in 1928, that the Africans

were marched to the coast and were forced to look at the decapitated heads of their relatives and friends. Lewis and the others were held in a slave pen, or barracoon, in Ouidah for three weeks and eventually sold for $100 each.

The voyage from West Africa to Mobile lasted around forty-five days. By the time the ship docked, word of the Africans' arrival had spread throughout Mobile. The spark that had launched the *Clotilda*'s journey had been a wager made by Timothy Meaher, a shipbuilder who owned several lumber mills and cotton plantations. In 1859 Meaher bet "a thousand dollars that I myself can bring a ship full of niggers right into Mobile Bay under the Officers' noses" (Pettaway, 27). Meaher used wood processed by his lumber mills to build the ship. Now, to hide the evidence of the schooner, the *Clotilda*'s captain set it on fire in nearby Bayou Canot; Sylviane Diouf noted that the ribs of the Clotilda remained visible at low tide for the next 75 years.

Upon arrival in Mobile, the Africans were scattered. Of the 110 Africans aboard the *Clotilda*, sixteen males and sixteen females became the property of Timothy Meaher. Burns Meaher, Timothy's brother, received ten couples. His other brother, James, received eight slaves, one of whom was Lewis. Eighteen Africans went to live with William Foster, the ship's captain, and Thomas Buford received seven Africans. The others were sold to slave dealers outside the Mobile area. The name "Cudjo Lewis" was a result of the slave owner's inability to pronounce his African name, Kossola Oluale. When James Meaher had a problem calling him Kossola, Lewis asked Meaher to start calling him Cudjo, which means, "born on a Monday." Kodjo was a common boy's name in Benin. Oluale, the name of his father, was the name Cudjo would most likely have inherited had he remained in Africa. Because his name sounded like the English "lu," his last name became "Lewis."

After the Civil War freed all slaves in the United States, many of the *Clotilda* Africans hoped that the Meaher brothers would give them the resources to return to Africa. However, they soon realized that they would have to provide for themselves. Lewis and other former slaves organized a community they called African Town (later Africantown) in 1868. Lewis approached Timothy Meaher about providing them with the land to build their community. The Meahers refused, and Timothy became incensed when

Lewis broached the idea. For several years the Africans rented the land. However, by 1870, they had saved enough money to buy several acres. Lewis purchased almost two acres in 1872 for $100 from Meaher.

Abile, the woman whom Lewis married after slavery had ended, had also been one of the *Clotilda* Africans. Lewis came to know Abile while on Meaher's plantation. When slavery ended, he proposed to her, and she accepted. Together they had six children (Aleck, James, Pollee Dahoo, David, Cudjo, and Celia Es-bew-O-see). The Lewis family endured many tragedies. All of the children died within fifteen years. Three children died within four months of each other. Celia became sick and died in August 1893. Cudjo Jr. was murdered in a melee when two deputies raided a craps (dice) game at the Lewis home in August 1902. In 1905 David was decapitated by a train, Pollee suddenly disappeared a short time after David's death, and James died of paralysis in November. Aleck, the eldest, died in December 1908, shortly after his mother. After over forty years of companionship, Abile died on 14 November 1908. Lewis believed that she had died of a broken heart over the tragic deaths of her children. Lewis never remarried.

After gaining their freedom, Lewis and his shipmates worked in Timothy Meaher's lumberyards. They worked eleven hours a day for one dollar a day. Although Meaher allowed them to work eleven hours a day for wages, he required each laborer to work an additional hour each day without wages. Lewis was a shingle maker, as was his eldest son. Much as they had in Africa, Lewis and the men in Africantown harvested their own corn, beans, yams, English peas, blackberries, figs, scuppernong, grapes, and peaches. They also hunted possum, raccoons, and rabbits, and they raised chickens, cows, and hogs. The women mostly worked as cooks, selling meals to people in surrounding communities.

Lewis and four of his former shipmates became the governors of Africantown. Their rule was based on seniority and respect for the elders. The residents used African terms of respect when speaking to the elders. The people in Africantown called Lewis "Uncle Cudjo." A man with a sense of purpose, Lewis valued hard work, community service, and dedication to family and God. He did not tolerate stealing and dishonesty, and often told folktales, such as the tale of the tortoise—an animal that Lewis saw as wise, disciplined, and frugal—to teach invaluable life lessons. Lewis was revered for his ability to share stories with people of his community. Blacks and whites would come just to hear him speak. Blessed with a remarkable memory, he kept the stories of his native Africa alive through his ability to tell "his story" from Africa to America.

Records show that although Lewis had been exposed to Christianity, he did not lose his respect for his native religious practices. After his arrival in Mobile, Lewis participated in religious ceremonies on the "Praying Grounds," a wooded area used for communicating with the gods. It was not until 1869 that Lewis formally integrated his African religious traditions with Western Christianity when he joined Mobile's Stone Street Baptist Church, a black church that had been established before the Civil War. In 1872 Lewis and others formed the Old Baptist Church, which in 1903 became Union Baptist Church. This church was erected on the site of the "Praying Grounds." After Lewis was injured by a train rail and became unable to work, the congregation of Union Baptist Church made him the church sexton. He faithfully rang the church bell every Sunday morning.

Lewis was one of only a few people to have been born in Africa and to live through slavery, the Civil War, Reconstruction, and Jim Crow. He helped organize the only self-governing African settlement in Alabama. A man of enormous integrity and wit, one who was described as "dignified, lovable, and intelligent," he was always proud of being African (*Mobile Press*, 2 Oct. 1977). His ultimate desire was to return to his native land to see old friends or their children. Perhaps the closest he would come to returning home was talking with Ellen Carter, a white Baptist missionary who spent eighteen months in Nigeria and who often conversed with him in his native language. His dying words were spoken in a whisper, but expressed sentiments that had been shared by millions of Africans who had been torn from their homeland: "Will you see that Cudjo gets back home?" (*Mobile Press*, 2 Oct 1977) In 1959 a bust of Lewis was unveiled in front of Union Baptist Church to commemorate his life and those of the original denizens of Africantown. In 1977 a bronze plaque was placed at Mobile's Bienville Square by the Amoco Foundation and the Association of Afro-American Life and History, Inc., to honor the memory of Lewis and of Africantown. In 1997 the African Town Community Mobilization Project was created to establish an Africantown historic district and to encourage the ongoing development of the site.

FURTHER READING

Mobile Public Library Local History of Genealogy maintains most documents on *Clotilda*, Lewis and his shipmates, including personal interviews (Zora Neale Hurston's among them), ship records, personal notes, and letters of Timothy Meaher and Foster, newspaper articles, periodicals, and photographs.

Diouf, Sylviane. *Dreams of Africa in Alabama: The Slave Ship Clotilda and the Story of the Last Africans Brought to America* (2007).

Glennon, Robert M. *Kudjo: The Last Slave Voyage to America* (1999).

Pettaway, Addie E. *Africantown USA: Some Aspects of Folklore and Material Culture of An Historic Landscape* (1985).

Roche, Emma Langdon. *Historical Sketches of the South* (1914).

TIMOTHY M. BROUGHTON

Lewis, David Levering (25 May 1936–), historian and biographer, was born in Little Rock, Arkansas, to John Henry Lewis and Alice Ernestine Bell, both originally from Atlanta. When John Henry Lewis sacrificed his job as principal of Little Rock's black high school to protest inequities in teachers' salaries based on race, the family moved to Wilberforce, Ohio. Lewis spent ages seven to nine in the community of Wilberforce University, where his father was the dean of theology. Named after the British abolitionist William Wilberforce, the university is the oldest African American institution of higher education. At the age of twelve, Lewis met W. E. B. DuBois, a fraternity brother of his father's and one of his mother's teachers at Atlanta University. The famous scholar and activist asked the young Lewis what he intended to do with his life. In a historical twist, the young boy who was left speechless by the question would go on to dedicate more than fifteen years of his life to writing the biography of the man who asked it. The Lewis family returned to the South in the late 1940s as John Henry Lewis assumed the presidency of Morris Brown College in Atlanta, one of the five schools of Atlanta University. Lewis attended Booker T. Washington High School, following the path set by MARTIN LUTHER KING JR. only a few years before. Also like King, Lewis left the high school early to attend Fisk University's Early Entrants Program. If it seems odd that the biographer of W. E. B. DuBois attended a high school named for the man's great nemesis, BOOKER T. WASHINGTON, it then seems fitting that Lewis went on to DuBois's alma mater

David Levering Lewis on April 16, 2001, after he won the 2001 Pulitzer Prize for biography for the second volume of his biography, *W.E.B. DuBois: The Fight for Equality and The American Century*. (AP Images.)

of Fisk University in Nashville, Tennessee. Named to honor General Clinton B. Fisk of the Tennessee Freedmen's Bureau, Fisk was founded in 1866 with the help of the American Missionary Association to educate newly emancipated African Americans.

After arriving at Fisk in 1952, Lewis quickly became interested in international issues and student leadership. Lewis's time there coincided with that of such prominent faculty members as August Meier and the thriving presidency of CHARLES S. JOHNSON. Lewis graduated Phi Beta Kappa with a bachelor's degree in History and Philosophy in 1956. He briefly attended the University of Michigan Law School but quickly realized that the law was not a good fit for him. He then entered the graduate program in history at Columbia University, where he wrote his master's thesis on John Fiske, the American philosopher and historian, and graduated with a master's degree in History in 1958. He spent the following summer working with Meier researching the history of the African American elite in Atlanta. Their work resulted in an essay that appeared in the *Journal of Negro Education* (Spring,

1959). That fall Lewis entered a doctoral program at the London School of Economics to study European history with a specialization in modern France. He wrote his dissertation on French liberal Roman Catholicism and was awarded the doctorate in 1962. In the fall of that same year Lewis reported to Fort Benning, Georgia, for service in the United States Army. He spent the next year in Germany as a psychiatric technician for the military before returning to a career in academia.

Lewis held positions at the University of Ghana, Howard University, and the University of Notre Dame teaching European history. He then accepted a tenured position at Morgan State University in Baltimore and was asked by an editor at Penguin Books to write a biography of Martin Luther King Jr. Lewis was initially skeptical, given that his area of academic specialty was European history, but he agreed to the project, and *King: A Critical Biography* was published in 1970. In the same year he accepted an associate professorship at the University of the District of Columbia (UDC) and added courses on the civil rights movement to his repertoire. After ten years at UDC, he moved on to the University of California, San Diego (UCSD), and taught there for the next five years. While on the faculty at UCSD, Lewis completed *When Harlem Was in Vogue* (1981), a well-received account of the Harlem Renaissance that traces the explosion of black cultural production during this period. In 1968 Rutgers University had created an endowed professorship in memory of Martin Luther King Jr., and Lewis accepted the chair in 1985. Two years later he published *The Race to Fashoda: European Colonialism and African Resistance in the Scramble for Africa*.

In the late 1980s Lewis continued to work on the biography of DuBois he had begun a decade earlier with the help of Guggenheim and Woodrow Wilson International Center fellowships. In addition to interviewing hundreds of people, Lewis traveled to three continents and more than twenty archives conducting research on DuBois. Lewis also drew on more than 115,000 pieces of correspondence that the University of Massachusetts at Amherst had acquired from SHIRLEY GRAHAM DUBOIS, W. E. B. DuBois's wife, to which previous biographers had not had access. In 1993 Lewis completed the first volume of the biography, titled *W. E. B. DuBois: Biography of a Race, 1868–1919*, which won him the Pulitzer Prize, the Parkman Prize in History, and the Bancroft Prize in American History and Diplomacy. The book traces the life of DuBois from his childhood in Great Barrington, Massachusetts, to his experiences at Fisk and Harvard; his seminal work, *The Souls of Black Folk*; and his leadership of the National Association for the Advancement of Colored People and the organization's publication, the *Crisis*. When the second volume, *W. E. B. DuBois: The Fight for Equality and the American Century, 1919–1963*, was published in 2000, Lewis became the first author to win two Pulitzer prizes in Biography for back-to-back volumes. The second installment of the biography considers DuBois's conflict-laden relationships with other leaders of the time, most notably Booker T. Washington and MARCUS GARVEY, work with the Pan-African movement, DuBois's time in Nazi Germany, and his death in Ghana. As Lewis has noted in interviews, he "didn't want to defend DuBois," but to "present a conflicted figure whose attempt to achieve his ideals caused him to contradict many of them" (*Rutgers Focus*, Feb. 2001). Lewis also edited DuBois's study *Black Reconstruction*, an anthology titled *The W. E. B. DuBois Reader*, and a collection of DuBois's correspondence. He also wrote the introduction to the one hundredth anniversary edition of DuBois's classic, *The Souls of Black Folk*.

A recipient of the coveted MacArthur Fellowship in 1999, Lewis has written on such diverse topics as the history of the District of Columbia (*District of Columbia: A Bicentennial History*, 1976), housing in Great Britain (*New Housing in Great Britain*, 1960, coauthored with Hansmartin Bruckmann), a cache of photographs selected by DuBois at the turn of the twentieth century (*A Small Nation of People: W. E. B. DuBois and African American Portraits of Progress*, 2003, coauthored with DEBORAH WILLIS), and the Dreyfus affair (*Prisoners of Honor: The Dreyfus Affair*, 1994). He has also edited anthologies regarding the civil rights movement (*The Civil Rights Movement in America: Essays*, 1986) and the Harlem Renaissance (*Portable Harlem Renaissance Reader*, 1994, and *Harlem Renaissance: Art of Black America*, 1994, coedited with DAVID DRISKELL). He appears in "America 1900," part of the Public Broadcasting Service's documentary film series *American Experience*, in which he discusses African American life at the turn of the century. He was a scholar in residence at New York University in 2000, and he was a visiting scholar at Harvard University in 2001. In 2003 he joined the faculty at New York University as a university professor and professor of history. He is also a commissioner of the National Portrait Gallery. In 2008 he published *God's Crucible: Islam and the Making of Europe, 570-1215* to critical acclaim. The following year President BARACK OBAMA awarded Lewis the National Humanities Medal.

David Levering Lewis has set the bar for highly readable, accessible, thorough, and layered renderings of periods in American history such as the civil rights movement and the Harlem Renaissance, while his ability to create biographies capturing the complexities of black leaders' lives has earned him deserved acclaim. The recipient of numerous awards and honorary degrees, Lewis has worked for decades to preserve the history of African Americans and their leaders, particularly civil rights icons W. E. B. DuBois and Martin Luther King Jr.

FURTHER READING

Lewis, David Levering. "Ghana, 1963: A Memoir," *The American Scholar* (Winter, 1999).

Lewis, David Levering. "From Eurocentrism to Polycentrism," in *Historians and Race: Autobiography and the Writing of History*, ed. Paul Cimbala and Robert F. Himmelberg (1996).

JENNIFER WOOD

Lewis, Edmonia (c. 1844–after 1909), sculptor, was born to an African American father and a mother of African American and Mississauga descent, whose names are not known. The Mississauga, a Chippewa (Ojibway in Canada) band, lived in southern Ontario. Information about Lewis's early life remains inconsistent and unverified. She was probably born in 1844 or 1845, most likely near Albany, New York. Orphaned by age nine, Lewis and her older brother, Samuel, were taken in by their maternal aunts, Mississaugas living near Niagara Falls. Lewis joined the tribe in hunting and fishing along Lake Ontario and the Niagara River and in making and selling moccasins, baskets, and other souvenirs. Although she later gave her Mississauga name as "Wildfire," Lewis's translation from the Chippewa may have been intended to authenticate her Indian background and appeal to whites. She remained with the Mississauga until age twelve, when Samuel, using earnings amassed during the gold rush in California, arranged for her schooling at New York Central College, an abolitionist school in McGrawville, New York.

In 1859 Lewis entered the ladies' preparatory program at Oberlin College. There she adopted the name Mary Edmonia, using Mary with friends and faculty and Edmonia on her drawings. Lewis proceeded amiably until the winter of 1862, when two of her white housemates accused her of poisoning

Edmonia Lewis's 1867 sculpture *Forever Free*, on display at Harlem's Studio Museum in New York City. (AP Images.)

them with cantharides, or "Spanish fly." Years of antiblack and anti-Oberlin feelings came to a head, and Lewis was badly beaten by a mob and left for dead. JOHN MERCER LANGSTON defended her at a two-day trial, securing a dismissal on the basis of insufficient evidence. The following year, when she was again falsely accused—this time of stealing art supplies—she was unofficially but summarily expelled. Undeterred by her lack of training, Lewis moved to Boston in 1863 with the intention of becoming an artist. Through supporters at Oberlin, she met William Lloyd Garrison and the portrait sculptor Edward Brackett. With the encouragement of Brackett, Lydia Maria Child, and other abolitionists, she learned the basics of clay sculpting. Her first sculptures were clay and plaster portrait medallions and portrait busts of antislavery leaders and Civil War heroes. In 1864 she sold more than one hundred reproductions of her bust of Robert Gould Shaw, the Boston Brahmin who led and died with the black soldiers of the

Fifty-fourth Massachusetts Volunteer Regiment, which included twenty-one men from Oberlin, some of whom Lewis knew. With enough money to travel abroad, in 1865 she sailed for Florence, Italy, where she was assisted by the world-renowned sculptor Hiram Powers. Six months later she settled in Rome, renting a studio once occupied by the neoclassicist Antonio Canova, arguably the greatest sculptor of his time.

Rome in 1866 was home to a vibrant community of American expatriate artists that included Nathaniel Hawthorne, Henry James, and the sculptor William Wetmore Story. Lewis was immediately taken under the wing of the sculptor Harriet Hosmer and her friend the actress Charlotte Cushman, principal members of the social set that Henry James called "that strange sisterhood of American 'lady sculptors'" (James, *William Wetmore Story and His Friends*, 1903, 257). In this group, which included Cushman's companion, Emma Stebbins, Anne Whitney, Louisa Lander, and Margaret Foley, Lewis saw rare examples of financially, sexually, and artistically independent women. Although she caused quite a sensation at Cushman's trendy soirees and benefited from her new friends' generosity, Lewis always remained on the perimeter, considered a bit of a novelty.

Resourceful and fiercely independent, Lewis taught herself to carve marble and established herself as a neoclassical sculptor. She eschewed the custom of employing assistants, fearing that the veracity of her work would be attacked, as had been the case with other black and women artists, including Hosmer and Whitney. Instead, Lewis, who was only four feet tall, undertook by herself what was often very physical work. In the 1860s and 1870s her studio, listed in all the fashionable guidebooks, was a frequent stop for American tourists. She supported herself primarily through commissions for small terra-cotta or marble portrait busts and marble copies of Classical and Renaissance masterworks. Over the years her busts of Abraham Lincoln, Ulysses S. Grant, Henry Wadsworth Longfellow, Senator Charles Sumner, the poet Anna Quincy Waterston, and the abolitionist Maria Weston Chapman were purchased by American collectors. Catering to collectors' tastes, she also produced "conceits" or "fancy pieces" (sculptures using children to convey sentimental themes), of which three survive: *Poor Cupid* (1873, National Museum of American Art [NMAA]), *Asleep* (1871), and *Awake* (1872), both in the San Jose Public Library. After her 1868 conversion to Catholicism,

Lewis received several major commissions for religious works, none of which survive.

Despite her faithfulness to the formal and thematic conventions of neoclassicism, Lewis rendered unique treatments of African American and American Indian themes and figures. Her first large-scale marble sculpture, *The Freed Woman and Her Child* (1866, location unknown), was the first by an African American sculptor to depict this subject. *Forever Free* (1867, Howard University), showing a man and woman casting off the shackles of enslavement, takes its name from a line in the Emancipation Proclamation: "All persons held as slaves shall be then, thenceforward, and forever free." Like *The Freed Woman*, the female figure in *Forever Free* strongly evokes the well-known abolitionist emblem engraved by PATRICK HENRY REASON in 1835, *Am I Not a Woman and a Sister?*, which shows an African American woman on bended knee, stripped to the waist, her head tilted toward the sky, and her clasped hands raised, revealing heavy chains attached at her wrists. While Lewis's figure adopts the pose and gesture of the emblem, her freed slave, unchained and fully clothed, is no longer identifiable as African American by color or physiognomy. Lewis's alterations, made according to the stylistic dictates of the period, simultaneously elide the issue of race and restore the dignity and humanity denied African Americans by slavery.

Lewis made several versions of the biblical figure Hagar, only one of which survives, *Hagar* (1868, NMAA). The Egyptian outcast, though used by other nineteenth-century artists as a symbol of slavery, had particular meaning for Lewis, herself the victim of racial violence and banishment. Reflecting on her sculpture in 1871, she told a journalist, "I have a strong sympathy for all women who have struggled and suffered." Inspired by Longfellow's popular poem "Song of Hiawatha," Lewis produced a number of marble works featuring American Indians. These works include busts of *Minnehaha* and *Hiawatha* (both 1868, Newark Museum), *The Marriage of Hiawatha* (1867, Walter Evans Collection), and *Old Arrow Maker*, also known as *The Wooing of Hiawatha* (three versions survive, made between 1866 and 1872). Lewis broke from strict neoclassical aesthetics by giving the arrow maker idealized but recognizable American Indian features. His daughter, however, appears white, her ethnicity represented only by posture, gesture, and costume. Lewis's depictions of American Indians as proud, dignified, and peaceful countered prevailing images of Indians (and blacks) as half-naked, eroticized savages.

Lewis returned to the United States on several occasions to exhibit and sell her work. Her 1873 cross-country trip terminating in San Francisco, certainly an unusual journey for an unaccompanied black woman, made her one of the first sculptors to exhibit in California. She reached the pinnacle of her career three years later at the 1876 Philadelphia Centennial Exposition with the exhibition of *Death of Cleopatra*, a subject popular with nineteenth-century artists and abolitionists. Lewis's enthroned, lifesize Egyptian queen in the throes of death directly challenged William Wetmore Story's more traditional representation of the same subject also on view at the exposition. *Cleopatra* caused a commotion, provoking strong responses from audiences and critics, including William J. Clark Jr., who wrote in 1878, "The effects of death are represented with such skill as to be absolutely repellant. Apart from all questions of taste, however, the striking qualities of the work are undeniable, and it could only have been produced by a sculptor of genuine endowments" (*Great American Sculptures*). *Death of Cleopatra*, assumed lost until it was rediscovered in 1985, is now on view at the National Museum of American Art.

Ironically, the Centennial Exposition marked the beginning of the end for neoclassical sculpture and, with it, the demand for Lewis's work. By the 1880s romanticism, exemplified by the work of Auguste Rodin, had challenged the stiffness of neoclassical sculpture, bronze had overtaken marble as the fashionable medium, and Paris had become the center of the art world. Lewis, however, remained in Rome, and by 1900 she was all but forgotten. FREDERICK DOUGLASS provided the last substantive account of Lewis's activities, which included, according to his diary, hosting Douglass and his new wife in January 1887. Except for a brief mention in an American Catholic magazine in 1909, no further record of Lewis survives. The date and place of her death remain unknown.

A generation older than the sculptors META WARRICK FULLER and May Howard Jackson and two generations older than ELIZABETH PROPHET, AUGUSTA SAVAGE, and RICHMOND BARTHÉ, Lewis was the first African American sculptor to gain an international reputation. Lewis, who never married, was an independent woman and a skilled survivor, succeeding against unprecedented odds. In all, she created about sixty unique pieces, less than half of which have been located. Remarkably, Lewis succeeded amid a social milieu deeply stratified according to race, gender, and class and within an artistic style exclusively devoted to ideas of Western beauty and history, even while she herself did not conform to any of these standards.

FURTHER READING

Bearden, Romare, and Harry Henderson. *A History of African American Artists: From 1792 to the Present* (1993).

Hartigan, Lynda Roscoe, and the National Museum of American Art. *Sharing Traditions: Five Black Artists in Nineteenth-century America* (1985).

Wolfe, Rinna. *Edmonia Lewis: Wildfire in Marble* (1998).

LISA E. RIVO

Lewis, Edna Regina (13 Apr. 1916–13 Feb. 2006), chef, restaurant owner, author, and teacher, was born in Orange County, Virginia. She was one of eight children, three sons and five daughters, born to Eugene and Daisy Lewis. Her community, called Freetown, was established by her grandfather, Chester Lewis, a farmer, and other freedmen after the Civil War. Her grandfather's home was the site of the community's first school.

Although little is known about Lewis's formal academic education, she learned to cook by observing and assisting her mother and paternal aunt, Jennie. These women cooked in the tradition of their African forebearers: using seasonal ingredients, frying in oil, flavoring vegetables with meat, improvising, and relying on their senses to determine whether food was appropriately seasoned and thoroughly cooked. For example, whether a cake was done could be determined by listening to the sound made by the cake pan. Wonderful dishes were created on a wood stove and without proper measuring implements. Lewis recalled during an interview with *Gourmet Magazine* that she learned to cook using coins as measuring tools.

Following the death of her parents, her father when she was nine and her mother when she was sixteen, Lewis migrated first to Washington, D.C., and then to New York City. Racism restricted her employment opportunities but she did find work in a laundry. One day later, she was terminated for incompetence. Afterward, she was employed by the *Daily Worker*, a communist newspaper. Edna Lewis was married to Steve Kingston, a merchant seaman and a communist who encouraged her to cook for ordinary rather than famous people. He died in the 1970s. Drawing on her skills as a seamstress,

Lewis was able to earn money by copying dresses made by Christian Dior. Among her clients were Marilyn Monroe and the wife of fashion photographer Richard Avedon.

Lewis's entrée into the culinary industry came in 1949 when an acquaintance opened a restaurant. During this period, men dominated the industry and a black, female chef was unheard of. Nevertheless, she was hired as a cook and her simple but delicious food, prepared in the Southern style, was immediately popular among the artists of Manhattan's East Side. As word of her skills spread, celebrities such as authors Tennessee Williams and Truman Capote, actors Marlon Brando and Rita Hayworth, and socialites Diana Vreeland and Gloria Vanderbilt became regular customers. Even the reclusive actress Greta Garbo came to sample Lewis's food after being assured that she would be the only diner present. Lewis remained at Café Nicholson until 1954, when she left to try other business ventures, one of which was a pheasant farm.

While recovering from a broken leg during the 1970s, Lewis began compiling her recipes, a complicated process for someone taught to cook by improvisation. Her first book, *The Edna Lewis Cookbook*, exposed her talents and cooking philosophy to a wider audience and was well received by her colleagues in the industry. Her second publication, *The Taste of Country Cooking*, was as much a history of African American life in Orange County, Virginia, and personal memoir as it was an instructional manual for Southern cooking. Lewis paints a vivid and detailed portrait of farm life, of the creative tactics used by people for survival in harsh economic times, and of the cooperative spirit of the community of Freetown. Particularly informative is her discussion of celebratory times such as Christmas and Emancipation Day, a holiday not widely marked by today's African American community. In 1988 she published *In Pursuit of Flavor*, which included such dishes as lima beans in cream, buttermilk biscuits, and sourdough griddle cakes with warm blueberry sauce and maple syrup.

In 1979 Craig Claiborne, a *New York Times* critic, said her books "revived the nearly forgotten genre of refined Southern cooking" and the resultant popularity served as the impetus for Lewis's return to the restaurant industry. She worked in restaurants in Chapel Hill, North Carolina; Charleston, South Carolina; and Decatur, Georgia. In 1992 she retired after five years as chef at Gage & Tollner in Brooklyn, New York. She continued to be active in the field, however, by providing formal cooking lessons and offering training for individual chefs.

One such chef was a Scott Peacock, a white Southerner, with whom she collaborated on her last book, *The Gift of Southern Cooking*, which was published in 2003. Lewis lived in Decatur, Georgia, with Scott Peacock, who became her caretaker in her declining years.

Peacock and Lewis were instrumental in the organization of the Society for the Revival and Preservation of Southern Food in the mid 1990s. Among the group's goals were encouraging people to use foods in season to obtain maximum taste and devoting the necessary time to cooking to minimize reliance on prepared items from supermarkets and fast food establishments. In addition, Lewis advocated the use of lard for frying, arguing that if done correctly, little fat would be absorbed by the food.

Lewis received numerous awards and recognitions for her culinary talent. In 1986 she was named to Who's Who in American Cooking by *Cook's Magazine* and she received the Lifetime Achievement Award from the International Association of Culinary Professionals. In her field the most prestigious awards came from the James Beard Foundation, which recognized Lewis twice. In 1995 she was the first recipient of the James Beard Living Legend Award and in 2003 she was inducted into the Kitchen Aid Cookbook Hall of Fame. *The Gift of Southern Cooking* was nominated for both the James Beard and the IACP awards.

Perhaps the best description of Lewis's talent came from John Edge, food columnist and contributing editor of *Gourmet Magazine*, who said that her food "pays homage to the frugal South, but it is also worthy of damask dinner cloth."

FURTHER READING

Asimov, Eric, and Kim Severson. "Edna Lewis, 89, Dies; Wrote Cookbooks That Revived Refined Southern Cooking." *The New York Times*, 14 February 2006.

DeMane, Erica. "When Miss Lewis Cooked." *American Legacy Magazine*, Spring 2007.

DONNA TYLER HOLLIE

Lewis, Felix Early (22 Jan. 1892–13 Sept. 1968), preacher, author, publisher, and church administrator, was born in Vanleer, Tennessee. He was the younger of two sons of David and Mary Lena (Street) Lewis, whose parents were born into slavery. Walter Curtis Lewis was Felix's elder brother, only sibling, and early co-worker. The Lewises initially made their home in Vanleer, Dickson County, Tennessee, the Streets' hometown. Vanleer is located about three miles from Cumberland Furnace, and eight miles from the county seat, Charlotte. Dickson County, and especially Cumberland Furnace, Tennessee, is known historically for its production of iron and iron-related products. Dickson County is also known for the mid-1890s relocation of a social-idealist colony known as the "Ruskinites" into Tennessee City near the city of Dickson, the county's largest metropolitan city. In addition to their other agricultural and industrial pursuits, the group, led by John Wayland, operated an extensive printing and publishing business. In all probability, Felix's introduction to and fascination with printing developed from his close proximity to this group when his parents moved to David Lewis's hometown, Dickson, where the two young boys grew up.

Walter and Felix Lewis cofounded with their mother, MARY LENA LEWIS (TATE), the Church of the Living God, the Pillar and Ground of the Truth, Inc. in 1903. In 1908 Mary Lena Lewis called the church's first general assembly at Greenville, Alabama. She was ordained to the bishopric by the elders present and seated as the first Chief Overseer of the organization. This Pentecostal church grew rapidly, primarily in the South (Georgia, Mississippi, Alabama, Florida, Tennessee, Kentucky, and the Carolinas) from 1908 through 1922. During this period of rapid growth and expansion, the church established a sound internal organizational structure and a solid financial base, acquired considerable real estate, and spread into other parts of the eastern United States. Felix and Walter were ordained to the bishopric in 1914 at Quitman, Georgia, and served as two of the first four state bishops of the church. The other two were Bishops J. D. Pagitt and B. J. Scott. Walter Lewis was appointed state bishop of Georgia, where he operated the church's first Saints Home and Rescue Mission. Felix Lewis was appointed state bishop of Florida, which rapidly became the church's most extensive and largest work. The organizational and business acumen of these bishops affected every aspect of the church's growth and development. Walter Lewis died in 1921, a victim of pneumonia contracted while working in the coalmines in Philadelphia, subsequent to his establishment of the church in Pennsylvania.

The church's first publishing effort was the production of a *Revised Decree* book in 1914, which was approved by the Chief Overseer and General Assembly held at Quitman, Georgia, beginning 25 June 1915. This booklet was formally published at Chattanooga, Tennessee, 25 May 1923. In 1923 Bishop Lewis, Bishop Tate, and others located and established the church headquarters in Nashville, Tennessee. Dr. Henry H. Fairfax of Birmingham, Alabama, owned eleven 50-feet-by-140-feet city lots located at 1915 Heiman Street in Nashville. Lewis and a second bishop, B. L. McLeod, negotiated for the purchase of the site, which contained an old brick structure with five large rooms and an old storage barn. In 1923 Lewis established the New and Living Way Publishing Company at this location. The house was renovated and furnished with two large printing presses, paper cutters, print type and type-setting equipment, and considerable other office equipment and furniture. The publishing works engaged the services of a number of apprentices and employed several part-time secretaries and office workers from the African American colleges and universities located nearby in North Nashville. The facility's first major production was the church's *Second and Revised Decree*, published in 1923. During this time, Lewis befriended the publishers at the African Methodist Episcopal (AME) Sunday School Union, touted as the "oldest publishing house of any importance owned by Negroes," (first publication in 1818), which had relocated from Bloomington, Indiana, to Nashville around 1886, and DR. ARTHUR MELVIN TOWNSEND, secretary and publisher at the Baptist Sunday School Publishing Board. Townsend assumed leadership of the board in 1920 and its Nashville edifice was begun in January 1923. Bishop Lewis also became a close friend and ally of DR. HENRY ALLEN BOYD, publisher of the *Nashville Globe* newspaper (1905–1959) and a popular leader in black Nashville. Boyd lived in the same neighborhood as Tate and Lewis on Heiman Street. From 1924 through 1925 the New and Living Way Publishing Company produced the church's doctrinal and organizational treatise, *The Constitution, Government and General Decree Book of the Church of the Living God, the Pillar and Ground of the Truth, Inc.* (1924); at least three periodicals, *The Official Organ, The Present Truth Gospel Preacher*, and the church's Sunday Bible School literature, the *Another Comforter Series*; religious sheet music; and other doctrinal and instructional missives from the Chief Overseer. Thus the publishing house on Heiman Street in Nashville became the first known black-owned publishing facility of a Pentecostal denomination in the United States. Felix Early Lewis was its chief editor.

The New and Living Way Publishing Company was formally chartered in the State of Tennessee in 1943. Because of financial exigencies and property litigation, formal operations were suspended at the Heiman Street location around 1944 to 1950. From 1950 until 1979 the company accomplished publication from the various church branch offices. In 1980 the church acquired a new headquarters site at 4520 Ashland City Highway in Nashville and the New and Living Way Publishing Company resumed its publishing activities from this new location.

After the death of Mary Lena Lewis Tate in December 1930, Felix Early Lewis was selected and seated in May 1931 as one of a triumvirate of overseers ordained by the church's Supreme Executive Council to administer the organization's affairs, a position he held until his death in West Palm Beach, Florida. He is interred in a memorial gravesite in historic Greenwood Cemetery in Nashville.

FURTHER READING

Church of the Living God. *The Constitution, Government, and General Decree Book of the Church of the Living God, the Pillar and Ground of the Truth, Inc.* (1924).

Lewis, Meharry H. *Mary Lena Lewis Tate: VISION! A Biography* (2005).

MEHARRY H. LEWIS

Lewis, Furry (6 Mar. 1893–14 Sept. 1981), blues musician, was born Walter Lewis in Greenwood, Mississippi. His parents' names are unknown. Lewis began his career as a performer in Memphis, Tennessee, the thriving musical center to which he moved at a young age from his family's home in the Mississippi Delta. After teaching himself to play the guitar, by 1910 Lewis was earning a meager living by performing for traveling minstrel and medicine shows that took him around the south and up the Mississippi River. In 1916 he lost a leg in an accident on a train track, and for the rest of his life he wore an artificial limb that undoubtedly added to his allure as a stage performer.

Lewis eventually settled in the Memphis area, scraping out a living from tips from street-corner performances and house parties. He played briefly as a member of the Memphis Jug Band in the late 1920s and accompanied the legendary MEMPHIS MINNIE in the early part of that decade. Lewis allegedly performed alongside W. C. HANDY, the so-called father of the blues; Lewis claimed that Handy gave him his first guitar. In 1922 Lewis took a job as a street cleaner for the Memphis Sanitation Department. He held this job for more than forty years, later boasting facetiously that he had "cleaned up in the music business." During this phase of his career Lewis recorded twenty-three sides for the Victor and Vocalion labels in Chicago, all of which were later rereleased and received warmly by blues critics. Lewis was credited with amalgamating several blues styles distinctive to Memphis on these recordings. Several musicians of the 1960s folk revival, including Joni Mitchell, Don Nix, and Leon Russell, later cited Lewis's recordings as an important influence.

In 1929, after the last of his Chicago recording sessions, Lewis stopped playing professionally, although he continued to practice his craft for the enjoyment of his family and a few select friends. He opened an antique shop and continued to clean the streets of Memphis until he was rediscovered in 1959 by the blues and jazz enthusiast Sam Charters. Lewis then resumed his recording career, becoming a colorful and popular spokesman for the Memphis blues scene almost overnight. Fully appreciating the spotlight that had eluded him for some thirty years, Lewis made up for lost time by joining the touring circuit of coffeehouses and blues festivals spawned by the folk revival of the 1960s. An accomplished storyteller, Lewis delighted audiences—which were composed mainly of white college students—and created a stage persona that gave them exactly what they expected from an old African American bluesman. Lewis appeared in several documentaries in the 1960s and 1970s, and his presence contributed to the popular perception that the only "real" blues musicians were old, grizzled, street-corner veterans who had survived difficult lives and performed their music to express their "blues."

Lewis's success in the folk revival market propelled him to more mainstream popularity. In a sublime example of truth being stranger than fiction, Lewis—only recently an anonymous street-sweeper—appeared several times on *The Tonight Show* with Johnny Carson, became the first African American to be named an honorary Tennessee colonel by the governor of the state, was featured in a 1970 *Playboy* magazine article, and landed a substantial role in the motion picture *W. W. and the Dixie Dance Kings* (1975), starring Burt Reynolds. Lewis deeply enjoyed the attention and took every opportunity to extol the wonders of Memphis blues and blues performers to increasingly wider audiences. He continued to perform in Memphis and advertise the Memphis blues scene elsewhere until he died in his adopted hometown.

Music writers consider Lewis an "accomplished if unconventional guitarist and an intriguing songwriter" (Santelli, 253), particularly adept at challenging slide-guitar riffs and complex finger pickings, and noteworthy for the wit that shone through his songwriting. Critics found in some of Lewis's earliest recorded lyrics the profound sense of rage that characterized much of the recorded blues of the 1920s. But he won enduring fame not for his considerable talents as a musician and songwriter but as an affable showman and raconteur with a wonderful sense of humor—one who helped to introduce a generation of Americans to the rich cultural heritage of Memphis and the Mississippi Delta.

FURTHER READING
Cobb, James C. *The Most Southern Place on Earth: The Mississippi Delta and the Roots of Regional Identity* (1992).
Santelli, Robert. *The Big Book of Blues* (1993).
This entry is taken from the *American National Biography* and is published here with the permission of the American Council of Learned Societies.

TODD MOYE

Lewis, George (14 July 1952–), composer, trombonist, writer, and educator, was born in Chicago, Illinois, the son of George Thomas Lewis, originally from North Carolina, and Cornelia Griffith of Georgia. George attended public elementary school before enrolling at the University of Chicago Laboratory School at age nine, at which time his parents bought him a trombone to assist with what he called "social development." By age twelve George was listening to the music of CHARLIE PARKER, THELONIOUS MONK, and JOHN COLTRANE, learning solos from jazz recordings such as LESTER YOUNG *with the* OSCAR PETERSON *Trio*, and studying improvisation with the trombonist Dean Hey.

At Yale University, from which he earned a B.A. in Philosophy in 1974, Lewis found company in the sextet of the pianist and fellow student ANTHONY DAVIS. After becoming dissatisfied with the artistic boundaries imposed by the music department at Yale, Lewis made a return trip to Chicago in 1971 in search of new creative avenues. It was then that Lewis joined the Association for the Advancement of Creative Musicians (AACM), an internationally known artist cooperative co-founded in 1965 by the pianist and composer MUHAL RICHARD ABRAMS. Lewis studied with Abrams, participated

and collaborated in AACM concerts, and eventually served as chairman of the group in 1975.

The open artistic environment of the AACM aimed, among other things, at removing the limitations of category in music and moving toward what Lewis later described as "the freedom of mobility." Lewis often warned of the "tendentiously posed opposition" that separates "improvised" from "composed" music, preferring a hybrid notion of musical practice: "The very words ['improvised' and 'composed'] have become so charged with meaning, but the people who are really doing creative music aren't paying attention to them" (Rockwell, 29). This legacy of traditional genre classification and hierarchy in arts presentation and funding—issues intrinsically tied to race and class throughout American art history—served as a catalyst for Lewis's approach to his career and music. Recalling his frustrations at Yale and beyond, Lewis stated, "I just want people to take me for what I am. I don't want to be tied to any tradition on the basis of what I look like" (Rockwell, 29).

One of Lewis's fondest experiences during his early career was a typically eclectic gig as a sideman with the COUNT BASIE orchestra in 1976. Lewis recounted the time when, after taking an unusual silent solo during a performance, Basie expressed approval of Lewis's approach, explaining that experimentation had been central to Basie's own experiences of creating music since his days in Kansas City. The theme of art as a product of experimentation has remained central to Lewis's music.

Lewis moved to New York City in 1977 and found voice in the downtown experimental loft scene, exemplified by the Studio Rivbea 1978 recording of a quartet performance of Lewis's interactive acoustic/electronic composition "Chicago Slow Dance," which included longtime AACM collaborator Douglas Ewart. In 1980 Lewis became music director at New York's experimental performance space The Kitchen, remaining at that post until 1982.

Lewis's work often involved interactive and multimedia formats; his interactive computer performance program *Voyager*, which he called "a nonhierarchical, interactive musical environment that privileges improvisation," was featured in performances throughout the world. Yet his musical writing—both improvised and composed—also included works for saxophone quartet ("Ring Shout Ramble," 1998), chamber orchestra ("Collage," 1995), and percussion ensemble ("Virtual Discourse," 1993), as well as collaborative multimedia works involving video, poetry, painting, and landscape architecture ("Information Station no. 1," 2000).

After its inception in 1986 at Amsterdam's Studio voor Elektro-Instrumentale Muziek (STEIM), *Voyager's* performances brought Lewis to the fore of the electronic music field. The composer first became interested in electronic music at the Chicago Laboratory School, listening to Karlheinz Stockhausen's *Gesang Der Jünglinge* and going on to explore the music of Morton Feldman and Milton Babbitt. Lewis's work developed through the decades from multitrack cassette tape collages, homebrew microcomputers, and Micromoog synthesizers to the most advanced available generation of computers. Lewis published some observations on his long-running interaction with *Voyager* in the 2000 article "Too Many Notes: Computers, Complexity, and Culture in *Voyager*" (*Leonardo Music Journal*, vol. 10).

In 1991 Lewis accepted a teaching position in the music department of the University of California, San Diego, where he took a key role in initiating their Critical Studies/Experimental Practices program. Transferring his philosophy of artistic mobility into the institutional environment has been a hallmark of Lewis's academic career. Criticizing past musicological presentations of American experimentalism and attempts to categorize avant-garde music, Lewis observed, "If you read standard histories of music since 1945—by which they mean classical music—you'll find that where African Americans are mentioned, it's usually all on the same page…. That's the kind of thing that, historically, doesn't work anymore" (interview with author, 11 Oct. 2004). In the 1990s Lewis began writing prolifically for academic and art publications. His articles, including "Improvised Music after 1950: Afrological and Eurological Perspectives" and "Teaching Improvised Music: An Ethnographic Memoir," consistently presented an engaging merging of theoretical and cultural analysis with musical practice.

Following awards from the National Endowment for the Arts (1995), the San Diego Arts Commission (1998), the Civitella Ranieri Foundation (1998), and the CalArts/Alpert Foundation (1999), Lewis received a MacArthur Fellowship in 2002. In 2004 Lewis married his artistic collaborator Miya Masaoka; later that year he returned to New York to take an endowed chair in the music department of Columbia University. His first full-length book, *Power Stronger than Itself*, is a history of the AACM.

FURTHER READING
Litweiler, John. "Profile: George Lewis," *Downbeat* (Aug. 1977).
Rockwell, John. "A New Music Director Comes to the Avant-Garde Kitchen," *New York Times*, 14 Sept. 1980.
Shoemaker, Bill. "Mobility Agenda," *Jazz Times* (Oct. 2001).

DISCOGRAPHY
George Lewis: Endless Shout (Tzadik 7054).
This entry is taken from the *American National Biography* and is published here with the permission of the American Council of Learned Societies.

JOHN WRIGGLE

Lewis, George (Joseph François Zeno) (13 July 1900–31 Dec. 1968),

jazz clarinetist, was born Joseph François Zeno in New Orleans, Louisiana, the son of Henry Louis Zeno, a fisherman, and Alice Williams, a domestic servant. He was called George from birth, and the Louis of his father's name became Lewis. He used this name throughout his life. He had a sketchy education. His family home was located behind Hopes Dance Hall, and he grew up hearing the sounds of the bands that played there. At the age of seven he bought his first instrument, a fife; at about age seventeen he bought his first clarinet. Like other New Orleans clarinetists, he played the Albert system clarinet throughout his life because he preferred the larger bore and more flexible tone of these instruments over the Boehm system.

Although he was probably influenced by people like SIDNEY BECHET, a family friend, Lewis taught himself to play clarinet, and in the summer of 1917 he played with his first band, the Black Eagles, in Mandeville, Louisiana. Throughout the 1920s he played with various dance bandleaders, including the trumpeters Buddy Petit and Henry "Kid" Rena and the trombonist KID ORY. He also worked in brass bands like the Eureka, primarily playing the E-flat clarinet. At the time parades, funerals, and festivals provided regular employment for New Orleans musicians. From 1923 Lewis led his own groups, which early on included RED ALLEN on trumpet. From 1929 to 1932 he played with the Olympia Band of the drummer Arnold DuPas. He then went to Crowley, Louisiana, to join the trumpeter Evan Thomas. After Thomas was murdered on the bandstand, Lewis returned to New Orleans. In 1929 Lewis had married Emma (maiden name unknown), with whom he had four children. They separated in 1932, and in about 1934 Lewis married Geneva (Jeannette) Stokes; they had one child.

The 1930s were lean years for playing work. Lewis appeared with Kid Howard's brass band and with BILLIE PIERCE and DE DE PIERCE but worked days loading ships on the river. Musical styles changed as swing gained popularity, but Lewis always held to his personal style, which was rooted in the New Orleans tradition. Although it evolved over time, that tradition stressed direct expression of feeling and close interaction among a group of improvisers. In 1942 William Russell, an important early jazz researcher, came to New Orleans hoping to record that early jazz sound. Although the assembled group centered on the trumpeter BUNK JOHNSON, who had been a member of Thomas's band, Lewis played clarinet on the session. This led to a number of recordings over the next five years, some with Johnson and others and some under Lewis's own name. *Burgundy Street Blues*, recorded in Lewis's home, demonstrates his full tone and lyricism and is considered a classic in the New Orleans jazz style. These sessions for Russell were pivotal for Lewis's career, as they introduced him to listeners outside of New Orleans.

In 1945 a band including Lewis, Johnson, the trombonist JIM ROBINSON, and the drummer BABY DODDS appeared in New York at the Stuyvesant Casino. It was a huge success, owing to a revived interest in New Orleans music. After a year Johnson parted ways with Lewis and the others, who returned to New Orleans and played regularly at Manny's Tavern. The New Orleans revival, sparked by an intellectual interest in the true roots of jazz and the direct, personal style of playing typical of New Orleans musicians, continued into the 1950s, and Lewis was at the center of it. His playing at this time was characterized by much ornamentation as well as his usual sincere expressiveness. He toured with his band around the United States in the 1950s and went to England, Denmark, and Sweden in 1957 and 1959. In the early 1960s he toured Japan. From 1961 on he appeared frequently at Preservation Hall, his last performance being less than three weeks before his death in New Orleans.

Lewis's manner was quiet and polite, but he held strong views about his music. He told his biographer Tom Bethell: "I like my music peppy, and I like four beats to a bar. Something should be going all the time. It's a conversation" (281). Lewis was referring to collective improvisation, which is the hallmark of the New Orleans style. While some listeners may find fault with his technique and his intonation, enthusiasts savor his direct enthusiasm and the unique personality that comes through in a self-taught, natural talent. Regarded as one of the best and most influential clarinetists in the New Orleans tradition, Lewis's name is synonymous with New Orleans–style jazz.

FURTHER READING

Bethell, Tom. *George Lewis: A Jazzman from New Orleans* (1977).

Stuart, Jay Allison. *Call Him George* (1961).

DISCOGRAPHY

Faelt, Lennart, and Häkan B. Haakaansson. *Hymn to George: George Lewis on Record and Tape* (1985).

JAMES KALYN

Lewis, Ida Elizabeth (22 Sept. 1934–), journalist and publisher, was born in Malvern, Pennsylvania, one of six children of Samuel Lewis, a laborer and ship painter, and Grace Walker, a businesswoman who operated an employment agency. Education was of utmost importance to the Lewis family. Ida, who spent summers visiting relatives in Massachusetts, Ohio, and Georgia, would often stay up all night reading when everyone else in her house was asleep. She attended an all-black grammar school, which she credited with giving her a solid grounding in black history.

Upon graduation from Swarthmore High School (which was predominantly white), she decided to pursue her interest in writing and journalism at Boston University's College of Public Relations and Communication, from which she graduated in 1956 with a B.A. in Journalism. "I always wanted to write," she later recalled. "We had a tree in our backyard where I was brought up. I would climb that tree and sit there and dream about all the places that I would visit one day. I used to send little vignettes and short stories to 'The Children's Hour' radio show in the 1940s" (interview with the author, Dec. 2004). In college she considered the idea of writing for the theater, but she realized rather quickly that that was unlikely to happen.

After college Lewis moved to New York City and convinced the *Amsterdam News* editor Jimmy Hicks to hire her as a financial columnist. "I looked at the paper and saw that they did not have any financial news," she recalled; "I thought that perhaps that was a way to get in, because I had minored in economics" (interview with the author, Dec. 2004). Impressed with Lewis but unsure whether the publisher, C. B. Powell, would hire her, Hicks offered to pay her twenty-five dollars per column out of his own pocket for the next several months. When she finally met Powell, and he told her that black people were not interested in finance, she argued that one of the obligations of the black press was to give black people information that they could use in their lives. Powell decided to hire her, at sixty dollars a column. In 1957 Lewis became financial editor of another black newspaper, the *New York Age*. That same year Lewis gave birth to a daughter, Dacia Louise. In 1959 she tried a brief stint as director of research at a Wall Street real estate investment company, after which she decided to focus on freelance writing.

A wealthy entrepreneur seeking business opportunities in West Africa asked Lewis to conduct a feasibility study for him in 1961. Her research took her to Sierra Leone, Liberia, Nigeria, Ghana, and the United Nations at a time when countries all over Africa were gaining their independence. Her observations led to the publication of a book of essays on West Africa, *The Deep Ditch and the Narrow Pit* (1964). Lewis received a major assignment from *Life* magazine to cover the Zanzibar revolution in East Africa in 1964. She was based in the magazine's Paris office during that time. Upon completing her piece back in New York, she returned to Paris in 1965 and lived there for the next five years, writing for French publications, including *L'Express*, *Le Figaro Littéraire*, and *Jeune Afrique*, and interviewing African dignitaries for the BBC African Service. Lewis covered the shifting political and racial landscape in America, as well as African liberation movements. Lewis was still writing for *Jeune Afrique*, a newsmagazine, in New York in 1970 when the founders of *Essence* approached her to be the new magazine's editor in chief. Lewis left the magazine after one year, pushed out by office politics.

In 1972 Lewis realized her dream of establishing her own magazine with the publication of *Encore* (later *Encore American & Worldwide News*), a magazine on domestic and international affairs from a black point of view. Many of Lewis's close friends and colleagues, including the poet Nikki Giovanni, contributed to what was for Lewis "a labor of love" (interview with the author, Dec. 2004). The magazine's name was chosen in homage to John Russwurm, editor of *Freedom's Journal*, the first black newspaper in the United States, who wrote in 1827, "We wish to plead our own cause. Too long have others spoken for us." As Lewis explained, "This is an encore, where we plead our own case."

The first issue's cover story was "America neither Black nor White."

The magazine's format evolved into one similar to that of *Time* and *Newsweek*, with national and international news in the front and arts and entertainment in the back. In 1974 Lewis's role as one of black media's leading figures was recognized when she appeared as a panel member on NBC's *Meet the Press* to interview President Richard Nixon's attorney general, William Saxbe. "I don't think anyone knew what that meant to me," she told a reporter a few months later (Satterwhite, 33). During *Encore's* eleven years of publication, Lewis spun off two other short-lived magazines targeting African Americans: *Good Living*, a health and fitness magazine, and *Eagle & Swan*, about black military life.

After *Encore* ceased publication Lewis took on various consulting jobs. She worked as a press aide for Adam Clayton Powell IV during his campaign for New York State assemblyman in 1986 and for Ross Perot during his presidential bid in 1992. She served as director of communications for Correction Connection, Inc., which distributed DICK GREGORY's Bahamian Diet. In 1998 Lewis became the first female editor in chief of *The Crisis*, the NAACP's journal, founded by W. E. B. DuBois in 1910. Although her tenure there won praise from various quarters, she resigned from the job in 2000. Lewis continued to challenge herself with new projects, teaching at her alma mater, Boston University, and producing a movie about the life of Alexander Pushkin.

FURTHER READING

Satterwhite, Sandra. "The Black Executive: Ida Lewis, Publisher," *New York Post*, 18 Mar. 1975.

PATRICE D. JOHNSON

Lewis, Ira Foster (25 Aug. 1883–4 Sept. 1948), business manager, general manager, and secretary, of the *Pittsburgh Courier* and president of its parent publishing company, the man whose business acumen and salesmanship made the paper solvent and profitable, was born in Lexington, North Carolina, the son of Adelaide Thomas Lewis, who died shortly after he was born. He grew up at the home of his grandparents in Charlotte.

Graduating from high school, he attended Biddle University in Charlotte for a year, then went to Washington, DC, New York, Ohio, and Michigan, where he worked as a hotel waiter. In 1909 he married Michigan native Harriet Eleanor Nicholson, moving to Pittsburgh in 1911. The couple's three children were all born in Pittsburgh, where he found work as a waiter at McCreery's Department Store in the restaurant, while taking secretarial courses.

Lewis first met Robert Lee Vann, the publisher, editor, and eventual majority stockholder of the *Pittsburgh Courier*, in 1912, when Vann hired Lewis as a part-time stenographer for his law practice. In 1914, needing additional income, Lewis applied for a job with the *Courier*. In the first year, he doubled subscriptions and secured substantial new advertising. The board of directors' offer of $3 a month plus a 25 percent commission on advertising was supplemented, after 1917, with a clerkship in the Allegheny County sheriff's office. Vann and Lewis had supported the successful Republican challenger Edward Vose Babcock for mayor of Pittsburgh, over fellow Republican William A. Magee, and a Babcock ally had won the election for sheriff.

As early as 1922, Lewis advised that "the public is really anxious for real live news, with a slight tinge of scandal," a marketing reality in constant tension with Vann's desire for "high standards and ideals" (Buni, p. 132). Although his business, financial, and sales skills were the greatest asset Lewis brought to the *Courier*, during the 1920s and 1930s he wrote "The Passing Review," a column on sports, in which he advocated that Negro Leagues team owners needed to play up the star power of their players to attract fans and revenue—despite fears that star players would go their own way. It was also Lewis's idea to first add photographs in 1928, many of them featuring beautiful young women—it sold papers.

For most of the 1920s and the first half of the 1930s, the *Courier* barely paid its way and was often in debt. Lewis nonetheless advised Vann to spend money that would pay off in the long run—particularly building a printing plant in 1929 so the paper could be printed in-house, and expanding to a twenty-four-page format in 1934. Day-to-day administration of the paper fell in large part to Lewis from 1933 to 1935, while Vann held a position as assistant to the attorney general in Washington.

In 1934 Lewis vigorously advocated that Vann break off the *Courier*'s contract with the William B. Ziff company handling advertising accounts—advice Vann followed in 1935. Ziff, who specialized in securing national advertising for black newspapers, charged commissions of 35 to 50 percent. Lewis found it "almost unbearable to see those birds over there collecting our money and keeping it" (Buni, p. 224). Vann incorporated Interstate United Newspapers to handle national advertising accounts, offering its services to other papers published by and for Americans of African descent. Lewis served for many years as the new agency's president.

When Vann died in October 1940, Lewis took charge of operations, from the positions of general manager, and as the new president of the Pittsburgh Courier Publishing Company. The masthead for years continued to list Robert L. Vann as Editor (Memoria in Aeterna). Vann's interest as majority shareholder was inherited by his widow, Jessie Vann. She took an increasing interest in the paper as her husband's legacy, assuming the positions of publisher and treasurer. Lacking business or editorial experience, she placed confidence in Lewis and in Percival L. Prattis, whom Lewis promoted from managing editor to the new post of executive editor. William G. Nunn succeeded Prattis as managing editor.

In 1944 Lewis represented the *Courier* at a press conference held by President Franklin D. Roosevelt, with publishers of what was then known as "the Negro press." He spoke firmly of "the treatment of our boys in the armed services" who had not "been treated right by civilian police, and by the MP's." A direct statement from the president, Lewis said, "will do more towards strengthening morale and making more for unity and making the Negro citizen believe that he is a part of his great commonweal." Roosevelt acknowledged the problem, but blamed "the attitude of certain white people," which he did not feel he could change (Herbert Shapiro, *White Violence and Black Response: From Reconstruction to Montgomery*, 1988, p. 309).

In 1947 Lewis served as spokesman for a delegation from the National Negro Publishers Association meeting with Secretary of Defense James Forrestal, to press for full integration of the armed forces. The United States, he warned, could not afford another war with one-tenth of its population lacking the spirit to fight.

The historian Rayford W. Logan, who was foreign affairs editor for the *Courier* from 1945 to 1948, and teamed with Prattis to cover the San Francisco Convention of the United Nations in 1945, attributed the financial success of the newspaper to the business management of Ira Lewis, as much as to Robert L. Vann's editorship. Logan pointed out that Vann lost money on other business and publication enterprises, where he did not have Lewis running the business side (Rayford W. Logan, "Robert Lee Vann Family," #486, *The Heritage of Blacks in North Carolina*, pp. 436–437).

The *Courier* did begin to operate at a loss not long after Lewis's death, running out of cash reserves by 1951, three years later. Many factors imposed declining circulation on all weekly papers targeted for African American readers during that period. The *Courier's* largest press run, 357,212 papers, was in May 1947, sixteen months before Lewis died. It remained nearly as high in 1948: 353,913, then falling to 318,208 in 1949, and declining slowly until 1952, when circulation for the first week in May dropped to 237,519, from 309,812 the year before.

Lewis died of a heart attack in New York in 1948. He was survived by his wife; by their children, Adelaide Lewis Scott, Jane Lewis Woodson, and Ira Lewis Jr.; and by his brother, Eugene Lewis.

FURTHER READING

Buni, Andrew. *Robert L. Vann of the Pittsburgh Courier: Politics and Black Journalism* (1974).

Obituary: *Journal of Negro History* 33, no. 4 (Oct. 1948), 503–504.

CHARLES ROSENBERG

Lewis, Joan Tarika (1 Feb. 1950–), visual artist, musician, author, and political activist, was born Joan Angela Lewis in Oakland, California, to JOHN HENRY LEWIS and Florence (Reid) Lewis. She is also known as J. Tarika Lewis, Tarika Lewis, Joan Lewis, and Matilaba. At the time of her birth, her father was a salesman for G&W Refrigeration. He was the first black man to become the light heavyweight champion of the world, a title he held from 1935 to 1939. After retiring as a prize fighter, John Henry Lewis and his father Edward Lewis operated a boxing gym in Oakland.

While attending Oakland Technical High School, Lewis was active in the journalism, music, and athletic programs. She wrote for the school newspaper and played violin in the school orchestra. Lewis was also a member of the swim team and a sprinter on the track team. From the 10th to the 12th grades, she was a concert violinist with the Berkeley-based Young People's Symphony. Lewis was a founding member of the Black Student Union at her high school and, along with her friend Bonnie Pointer, became one of the first students to wear an Afro hairstyle. Pointer later became one of the founders of the Pointer Sisters, a world-renowned singing group.

During the summer of 1967, Lewis became involved with a study group led by David "Mudavanha" Patterson and Fritz Pointer and was active with the Pan African Center, which was located in Oakland at the corner of 42nd Street and Grove Street (later MARTIN LUTHER KING BOULEVARD. At the Pan African Center, Lewis worked as an English and math tutor. In the fall of 1967, at the age of seventeen, Lewis became one of the first females, if not actually the first, to join the Black Panther Party (BPP).

While serving in the organization's Oakland office, she participated in political education classes and received training in weaponry. Within a year of joining the BPP, Lewis was promoted to a section leader position and organized drills for both male and female members. Lewis also became a lieutenant and an assistant to Emory Douglas, an artist, and the organization's minister of culture.

Under the name Matilaba, Lewis published many illustrations in the *Black Panther*, the official newspaper of the organization. Typically, her illustrations in the *Black Panther* featured brave black militants taking action against police officers. One of her first illustrations in the *Black Panther* appeared on 1 January 1968 and one of the last on 25 January 1969. By 8 March 1968, the masthead of the *Black Panther* listed Lewis's non de plume, Matilaba, as the assistant graphic artist. Lewis also published an article titled "To Huey and Our People in the Pig's Pen" and an article titled "From Me to You" in the 2 November 1968 issue of the *Black Panther*. In addition, Lewis published a poem titled "Revolution Bro' n Sis" in the 16 November 1968 issue of the journal. A common theme in her illustrations and writings was the notion that it was imperative for black people to engage in social change and develop an armed resistance movement to police brutality.

During January 1969, the BPP instituted a series of purges with the expressed purpose of enhancing discipline and political education within the organization. Lewis became one of the first victims of this purge program in February of that year. The 9 March 1969 issue of the *Black Panther* reported that Lewis had been removed from the organization along with twenty-nine other people, including such early members as Reggie Forte, Bill Brent, Oleander Harrison, Terry Cotton, and Wendell Wade. Lewis was ousted after complaining that demands and rules applied to the rank and file but not to the interim leadership, especially DAVID HILLIARD. Lewis had also complained about mistreatment of both male and female members of the BPP and how David Hilliard was managing the organization's finances (correspondence with Lewis on 30 April 2007).

After leaving the Black Panther Party, Lewis joined the Nation of Islam in the latter part of 1969 and stayed until the death of Elijah Muhummad in 1975. As did many other members, Lewis maintained involvement with a splinter group of Black Muslims in Oakland after the Nation of Islam split into competing factions following ELIJAH MUHUMMAD's death. That same year, she also got married. Lewis and her husband had a blended family in that both had children from previous relationships. They went on to have one child together (a daughter named Rukiyah), and divorced in 1979. Around 1981, Lewis left the Black Muslim movement because of disillusionment with the local Oakland leadership. She continued her interests in music, art, and education, receiving an A.A. degree in Biology in 1983 from Merritt College in Oakland. In 1988, Lewis received a B.A. degree from California State University, Hayward (later California State University, East Bay) where she majored in fine arts and had two minors in business administration and marketing. That same year, she received a second B.A. in Illustration and Fashion Design from the Academy of Art University in San Francisco.

In 1989, she became an art instructor and counselor for the Healthy Babies Project Inc. in Oakland. Lewis developed a successful art therapy model for women in substance abuse recovery. She created a weekly workshop, which directed her students to visualize on canvas their past, present, and future. Lewis encouraged the women in her workshops to create collages so that they would be involved with the process of transitioning to reveal their problems; the process of transformational thoughts and behavioral changes; and the process of visualizing future plans and long-term goals.

Lewis's artwork and musical skills have been used by a number of sources. Her illustrations have appeared in government sponsored health booklets edited or written by Gene Darling (1994) and Elizabeth Katz (1997). In 1989 Lewis played the violin and sang on the saxophonist John Handy's album titled *Centerpiece*, and played the violin on Paul Tilman Smith's *The Invisible Man* (2004); India. Arie's *Testimony* (2006); Donnie Williams's *Just Like Magic* (2007); and Destiny's *Sacred Bath* (2007).

In 1995 Lewis served as an on-the-set consultant and acted in a small role during the production of Mario Van Peebles's full-length film *Panther*. To help promote the understanding of the film, Lewis also co-authored a book titled *Panther: The Pictorial History of the Black Panther Party* (1995).

From the early 1980s to 2003, Lewis waged a campaign against Yusuf Bey, a prominent Oakland based Black Muslim leader and businessman. Lewis maintained that Bey beat and raped her two step-daughters in the late 1970s and early 1980s. Eventually, Bey was arrested and charged in July 2002 with twenty-seven felony counts of rape and committing lewd acts with four females who were minors at the time. On 26 June 2003, the U. S. Supreme Court, in a five to four decision (*Stogner v. California*) overruled a California law that had suspended the statute of limitations in child molestation cases. Afterwards, all charges against Bey were dropped except those involving one of the four females. Bey pled not guilty to all of the charges, and died in 2003 before the end of the trial involving the remaining charges.

In recognition of her more than thirty years of community service in Oakland and throughout Alameda County, Lewis received several awards. In 2001 Congresswoman Barbara Lee awarded Lewis a Congressional Recognition Award in honor of her activities as a musician and in recognition of community work. Four years later, in 2005, Lewis was selected for the Alameda County Women's Hall of Fame as a result of her work in culture and art. In 2006, Lewis's work in the music business led to her being among the 101 women honored at the eleventh annual African American Excellence in Business Awards.

FURTHER READING

Bailey, Chauncey. "Oakland Muslim Leader Bey Dies," *Oakland Tribune*, 2 Oct. 2003.

Darling, Gene, ed. *Do You Work around Blood or Body Fluids? Cal/OSHA's New Rules* (1994).

Healing through Art. *Crossing the Invisible Line!!: Tellin' It Like It is* (2005).

Katz, Elizabeth. *Using Solvents Safely: A HESIS Booklet* (1997).

Thompson, Chris. "How Oakland Kept the Bey Empire Going," *East Bay Express*, 20 Nov. 2002.

Van Peebles, Mario, Ula Y. Taylor, and Tarika J. Lewis. *Panther: The Pictorial History of the Black Panther Party* (1995).

J. VERN CROMARTIE

Lewis, John (21 Feb. 1940–), civil rights leader and member of Congress, was born John Robert Lewis near Troy, Alabama, the third of seven children. Lewis's father, Eddie, was a sharecropper and small farmer, and his mother, Willie Mae, occasionally did laundry. Both of his parents were deeply

John Lewis, speaking at a meeting of the American Society of Newspaper Editors, 16 April 1964. (Library of Congress.)

religious, which may have helped shape Lewis's life-long commitment to Christianity. As a young man, Lewis recalls, he heard MARTIN LUTHER KING JR. preach on the radio and was inspired to make the ministry his vocation. Starting by preaching in the woods near his home, eventually he was allowed to preach at local churches. In 1957 he became the first of his family to graduate from high school. After graduating, Lewis enrolled in the American Baptist Theological Seminary in Nashville, Tennessee.

In 1958, at the age of eighteen, he met Dr. King, and his life was changed forever: he decided to devote it to the struggle for civil rights. Two months before the famous 1960 sit-ins in Greensboro, North Carolina, Lewis led sit-ins in Nashville. Although he was doused with cleansing powder and abused in other ways, the sit-ins eventually resulted in the desegregation of Nashville lunch counters. After graduating from seminary in 1961, Lewis enrolled at Fisk University, planning to study religion and philosophy. In 1963, however, he dropped out of college to devote his time to work in the civil rights movement. (In 1967 he returned to Fisk to earn

a B.A.) In 1968 Lewis married Lillian Miles; they adopted a son, John Miles.

In the spring of 1960 the Student Nonviolent Coordinating Committee (SNCC) was formed, with several Nashville students in leadership positions, notably MARION BARRY, DIANE NASH, and JAMES LAWSON. By 1961, two northerners, BOB MOSES and JAMES FORMAN, had also emerged as prominent SNCC activists. This interracial organization of black and white college students was created to coordinate student participation in the civil rights movement. Between 1961 and 1965 SNCC played a pivotal role in that movement, working on voter registration campaigns in the most dangerous areas of the rural south. In a sense, SNCC made up the movement's front-line troops, and the young women and men in the organization exhibited extraordinary courage in facing danger and death. But of all the brave people in SNCC, perhaps none exhibited greater courage than Lewis. As Worth Long, a colleague in SNCC, said, "John was the most courageous person that I ever worked with in the movement.... John would not just follow you into the lion's den, he would lead you into it" (Carson, 203). In 1961 Lewis was beaten unconscious in Montgomery, Alabama, in one of the first Freedom Rides to challenge segregated interstate bus travel, and in 1965 he suffered a similar fate as he helped lead a march from Selma to Montgomery in the movement's last great protest. Arrested more than forty times, Lewis invariably responded peacefully and with expressions of Christian faith and love. Many years later, reflecting on Lewis's work in the movement, *Time* referred to him as a "living saint" (Barone, 299). In 1963 Lewis was selected SNCC's second chair, succeeding Marion Barry. (Barry later became mayor of Washington, D.C.) As head of SNCC, Lewis was part of the so-called "Big Six" civil rights leadership group. This informal group attempted to develop and coordinate movement strategy. In addition to Lewis, the group comprised Martin Luther King Jr. of the Southern Christian Leadership Conference, ROY WILKINS of the NAACP, WHITNEY YOUNG of the Urban League, JAMES FARMER of the Congress of Racial Equality, and DOROTHY HEIGHT of the National Council of Negro Women. At the 1963 March on Washington, Lewis, in his capacity as SNCC chair, was among the persons designated to give one of the major speeches. The other leaders thought his prepared text too radical, and he was asked to tone it down. Lewis initially refused, but after much cajoling he agreed to the rewriting of the speech (removing some of the language considered too radical or revolutionary). Nevertheless, the speech as delivered was the most militant of the day, reflecting the fact that SNCC was the most self-consciously radical of the major civil rights organizations.

Ironically, SNCC's evolving militancy and radicalism would lead to Lewis's ouster as SNCC chairman. In 1966 SNCC embraced the philosophy of Black Power. This philosophy, influenced by the ideas of MALCOLM X, called on blacks to form racially separate or independent organizations (which for SNCC meant the ouster of its white members) and to abandon the philosophy of nonviolence. Having embraced this Black Power philosophy, many in SNCC thought that Lewis was unsuited to lead the group in this new direction. In the initial balloting Lewis was easily reelected, but then, in a move that probably violated SNCC rules, the balloting was reopened, and STOKELY CARMICHAEL defeated Lewis. Because of his unwavering commitment to interracialism and nonviolence, Lewis was unsuited to lead SNCC in its new direction, but he was disappointed and angry about the manner in which his colleagues removed him.

After leaving SNCC, Lewis worked with several organizations involved with community organizing and civil rights. From 1970 to 1976 he was executive director of the Atlanta-based Voter Education Project (VEP). The VEP engaged in voter registration and education, a task that represented a blending of Lewis's past civil rights activism with his future political activism. In 1976, when President Jimmy Carter appointed Congressman ANDREW YOUNG of Atlanta as ambassador to the United Nations, Lewis sought to succeed him in the House of Representatives. However, he was defeated rather easily by Wyche Fowler, the white president of Atlanta's city council, although the district had a 65 percent black majority. President Carter then appointed Lewis associate director of ACTION, the umbrella agency with responsibilities for the Peace Corps and domestic volunteer service agencies. When Carter was defeated for reelection, Lewis returned to Atlanta, where in 1981 he was elected to the city council. In 1986 he was elected to the U.S. Congress.

Fowler retired from the House of Representatives in 1986 in order to run, successfully, for the U.S. Senate. Seven candidates sought to succeed him, including Lewis and JULIAN BOND, a state senator, a former SNCC worker, and a historically important figure in the civil rights movement. In the initial primary election Bond led Lewis 47 to 35 percent.

But in the runoff Lewis defeated Bond 52 to 48 percent. Lewis won largely on the basis of the 90 percent support he received from the district's white voters, while Bond carried the black vote 60 to 40 percent. Since his election, Lewis, like most incumbents, has faced little or no opposition and has easily been reelected.

In some ways it was fitting that Lewis won through the support of a multiracial coalition, given his longtime commitment to forming interracial alliances. Because of his status as a genuine American hero, Lewis quickly earned the respect and admiration of his colleagues in the House of Representatives, black and white, liberal and conservative, and Democrats and Republicans. This support facilitated his efforts to build multiracial coalitions.

Lewis was initially assigned to two relatively minor committees, but in 1993 he was appointed to the Committee on Ways and Means, the oldest and most prestigious in the House. Lewis's appointment to this powerful committee (with jurisdiction over taxes, international trade, Social Security, Medicare and Medicaid, and welfare programs) was indicative of the esteem held for him by his Democratic Party colleagues in the House. Further evidence of his stature among his colleagues was his selection as one of four Democratic chief deputy whips. A frequent and passionate participant in House debates on foreign and domestic issues, Lewis has devoted much of his time to persuading Congress to recognize the contributions of African Americans and the civil rights movement to U.S. history. He was active in the establishment of a memorial to Martin Luther King Jr. and has spearheaded plans for the National Museum of African American History and culture, to be part of the Smithsonian Institution. With Lewis's help, the fifty-four-mile Selma-to-Montgomery Voting Rights Trail has been designated a National Historic Trail as well as one of only six "All American" roads. In 1999 he authored, with Michael D'Orso, *Walking with the Wind: A Memoir of the Movement*.

The memoir won the 1999 Robert F. Kennedy Center for Justice and Human Rights Grand Prize Book Award. Throughout the first decade of the 21st century, Lewis was re-elected to the House, usually unopposed by Republicans. While he remained active in Congress, both in the majority and in the minority, and was a passionate liberal voice for social justice and against American unilateralism in foreign affairs, in the 2000s Lewis came to be regarded as one of the last living exemplars of King's "beloved community" of interracial liberalism. His endorsement of a presidential candidate was thus valuable in both the 2004 and 2008 Democratic primaries. In 2004, Lewis backed Massachusetts Senator John Kerry, against the candidacies of Senator John Edwards of North Carolina, and the Reverend AL SHARPTON, the only African American in the field. Edwards defeated Kerry in the first test of southern opinion, South Carolina, with Sharpton receiving around one-quarter of the black vote. Georgia thus became a decisive test of whether Kerry could compete in the South. With Lewis's endorsement and forceful campaigning, Kerry won 62% of the black vote and defeated Edwards, who soon dropped out of the race, leaving Kerry as the presumptive nominee.

In 2007 Lewis initially endorsed Senator Hillary Clinton, the Democratic Senator from New York and former First Lady, in her campaign for the 2008 presidential nomination. After BARACK OBAMA decisively won the Georgia primary in February 2008, with two-thirds of the overall vote and 88 percent of the African American vote, Lewis announced, however, that, as a "Superdelegate" to the Democratic National Convention, he would now vote for Obama, to reflect the views of his constituents. Critics pointed out that Lewis's change of heart was related to his fear of a primary challenge. Lewis's switch to Obama—and Obama's continuing high support among black voters in the primaries that followed—persuaded several of his Congressional colleagues to follow his lead. Reflecting on Obama's victory on the eve of his inauguration and on the day that would have been King's 80th birthday, Lewis connected the historic result with the struggles that had made it possible stating, "Barack Obama is what comes at the end of that bridge in Selma" (Remnick). In 2001 the John F. Kennedy Library honored Lewis with its "Profile in Courage Award for Lifetime Achievement." Ten years later Barack Obama presented Lewis with the nation's highest civilian honor, the Presidential Medal of Freedom.

FURTHER READING

Barone, Michael, and Grant Ujifusa. *The Almanac of American Politics, 1988* (1988).

Carson, Clayborne. *In Struggle: SNCC and the Black Awakening of the 1960s* (1981).

Clay, Bill. *Just Permanent Interests: Black Americans in Congress, 1870–1991* (1992).

Remnick, David. "The President's Hero," *The New Yorker* (2 February 1993) http://www.newyorker.com/talk/comment/2009/02/02/090202taco_talk_remnick#ixzz1clDcT6Si.

Swain, Carol. *Black Faces, Black Interests: The Representation of African Americans in Congress* (1993).

ROBERT C. SMITH

Lewis, John Aaron (3 May 1920–29 Mar. 2001), pianist, composer, and educator, was born in La Grange, Illinois. His parents' names do not appear in readily available sources of information; reportedly, his father was an interior decorator (or, according to some sources, an optometrist), and his mother was a classically trained singer. After the death of his father, Lewis moved with his mother to Albuquerque, New Mexico, as a young child. By the time he was four, his mother had also passed away. Being raised mostly by relatives in a large musical family, Lewis at the age of seven began studying piano with his aunt. As a teenager he performed locally with his cousins and several older musicians. In 1938 he enrolled at the University of New Mexico, where he first majored in anthropology, then switched to music.

After graduating in 1942, Lewis served overseas in the U.S. Army Special Services Musical Branch. While in the army he met the drummer KENNY CLARKE, who had already established himself in New York as a prominent bebop musician. On receiving his discharge in November 1945, Lewis moved to New York and began studying at the Manhattan School of Music. At Clarke's suggestion, he began writing arrangements for the innovative DIZZY GILLESPIE Big Band and in 1946 became the band's pianist, contributing popular arrangements on songs such as "Emanon" and "Two Bass Hits." Two years later he left Gillespie and became a freelance musician. During this period Lewis worked and recorded regularly with the jazz legends CHARLIE PARKER, ILLINOIS JACQUET, LESTER YOUNG, and ELLA FITZGERALD. In 1949 and 1950 Lewis worked as both arranger and pianist on a series of recordings with a nine-piece band headed by the trumpeter MILES DAVIS. The music included on these recordings helped inspire a mid- and late-1950s musical movement known as "cool jazz."

In 1952 Lewis began working with the Modern Jazz Quartet, a group that included members of Dizzy Gillespie's rhythm section and the Milt Jackson Quartet. With Lewis's leadership and the talents of the vibraphonist MILT JACKSON, the bassist Percy Heath, and Clarke, the Modern Jazz

Quartet soon became one of the most successful small groups in jazz history. Lewis believed that by strengthening the music through structure, jazz could reach a wider audience. Heath told the critic Gary Giddins that "John's vision for the group was to change the music from just a jam session, or rhythm section and soloist idea, to something more … to change the whole attitude about the music." In 1955 the percussionist Connie Kay replaced Clarke, and the group's personnel remained unchanged for nearly forty years. The quartet became known for its understated interplay, its sophisticated arrangements, and its ability to present music as serious as Bach or as swinging as DUKE ELLINGTON; at the same time Lewis found a perfect vehicle to showcase his personalized piano style, which favored polyphonic counter lines, subtle embellishments, and a sparseness rare to jazz pianists of the day. In search of a more respectable image, the quartet members performed in tuxedos, and they favored bookings at concert halls and classical music festivals. The group consistently sold albums and filled theaters until their seven-year hiatus that began in 1974 with the departure of Jackson. On Jackson's return in 1981, the quartet reunited and continued to record and perform on a limited level.

Although the Modern Jazz Quartet enjoyed commercial success and longevity, the group had many critics. Some jazz purists and writers found their music pretentious, limited to Jackson's soloing talents, and untrue to the improvisational nature of jazz. In 1963 a concert review in *Time* magazine suggested that Lewis had "gone perilously far in his quest to make jazz more respectable without making it more substantial." Despite their critics, however, the group retained a large loyal fan base, and many of Lewis's compositions with the quartet, such as "Django," "Afternoon in Paris," and "Three Windows," became jazz classics.

Lewis's fame and talents also provided opportunities for him to take on various projects. In the late 1950s he became one of the first modern jazz composers to write for popular films. His 1957 score for the French film *No Sun in Venice* won a Cannes Film Award, and his 1959 score for the film *Odds against Tomorrow* is considered by many to be one of his most successful film efforts. From 1958 to 1983 Lewis was the musical director of the Monterey Jazz Festival. From 1962 to 1965 he was the leader and cofounder of Orchestra U.S.A., which combined a jazz ensemble with strings, and from 1985 to 1992 he held the position of musical director and conductor of the American Jazz Orchestra. Lewis also wrote music for musical theater, ballet, and television. Having obtained a master's degree from the Manhattan School of Music in 1953, he believed strongly in the benefits of music education. From 1957 to 1960 Lewis was head of the faculty for the Lenox School of Jazz in Massachusetts. He also taught improvisation at Harvard University and City College of New York from 1975 to 1982. He received honorary doctorates from the University of New Mexico, Columbia College in Chicago, the New England Conservatory of Music, and Berklee College of Music.

Lewis married a woman named Mirjana, whose maiden name is unknown, in 1962; they had two children and stayed together until his death. Often described as soft-spoken, modest, and sophisticated, Lewis kept his professional life separate from his private life. He was a disciplined and talented man who had a clear understanding of his musical goals despite various criticisms. Despite a long battle with prostate cancer, he continued to pursue his musical activities until the end of his life. He died in New York.

FURTHER READING

Hentoff, Nat. "John Lewis: The Modern Jazz Quartet's Music Director Answers Complaints about the Group and Also Delivers His Music Philosophy," *Down Beat*, Feb. 1957.

Holley, Eugene, Jr.. "Farewell to the Quartet," *Down Beat*, Apr. 2000.

Lyons, Len. *The Great Jazz Pianists Speaking of Their Lives and Music* (1983).

Williams, Martin. *The Jazz Tradition* (1983).

Obituary: *New York Times*, 2 Apr. 2001.

This entry is taken from the *American National Biography* and is published here with the permission of the American Council of Learned Societies.

JAY SWEET

Lewis, John Henry (1 May 1914–14 Apr. 1974), boxer, was born in Los Angeles, California, the son of John E. Lewis and Mattie Drake. His father had been a boxer, runner, and jockey and later operated a gymnasium in Los Angeles and trained the track team of the University of Southern California. In 1918 the family moved to Phoenix, Arizona, where John E. Lewis operated another gymnasium and served as trainer to Arizona university teams. John Henry graduated from Armstrong High School in Phoenix and later attended Arizona State University.

As a child, Lewis often boxed his older brother Christy in public exhibitions. When he was only fourteen years old, he fought professionally for the first time, as a welterweight; by the end of 1931 he had twenty-one fights in Arizona rings, winning twenty and boxing one draw. In 1932 the Lewis family moved to Oakland, California, and John Henry, who had grown into a light heavyweight, immediately began to meet tougher opposition in San Francisco Bay Area rings. Before the year ended, he defeated the light heavyweight contenders Yale Okun, Fred Lenhart, and Lou Scozza and outpointed the future heavyweight champion James Braddock, losing only a nontitle fight to the light heavyweight champion Maxie Rosenbloom.

By this time, although he was only 18 years old, Lewis, at 5 feet 11 inches and 175 pounds, was a highly skilled fighter and had developed the style he would use throughout his career. The boxing journalist Nat Fleischer wrote: "As a defensive boxer, he had few equals. He moved with the speed of a welterweight.... He was versatile in his attack, capable of switching from head to body with no loss of effectiveness, and was a sharp, damaging puncher with either hand, though not a one-punch knockout artist. A boxer, rather than a slugger, he was forever pressing forward with a continuous blinding two-handed attack, and much of his effectiveness was due to the speed and relentlessness of his pace, which gave his ring foes very little rest" (*Black Dynamite*, 206).

In 1933 and 1934 Lewis continued to box in the western states, managed by Frank Schuler, a San Francisco boxing promoter. In return fights he twice outpointed Rosenbloom and defeated many lesser opponents, with only three draws to interrupt his series of successes. In November 1934 he went east under the management of Gus Greenlee of Pittsburgh, owner of a black professional baseball team, and made his debut at Madison Square Garden in New York City on 16 November 1934 against Braddock. The well-trained, greatly improved Braddock gave Lewis his second defeat and became the first opponent to knock him down.

Lewis quickly rebounded from the Braddock defeat and won his next eleven fights, including a decision over Bob Olin, who had succeeded Rosenbloom as light heavyweight champion. In July 1935 Lewis lost decisions to Rosenbloom and Abe Feldman, but he then fought Olin for the world light heavyweight championship in St. Louis on 31 October. Although the fight went the full fifteen rounds, Olin was badly beaten, and Lewis became the champion.

In the years that followed, Lewis fought often and seldom lost, defending his title successfully five times. In 1936 he decisively outboxed the Englishman Jock McAvoy in New York; he then traveled to London and easily beat another Englishman, Len Harvey. In 1937 he knocked out Olin in eight rounds of a title rematch in St. Louis. In 1938 he knocked out Emilio Martinez in four rounds in Minneapolis, Minnesota, and defeated Al Gainer in fifteen rounds in New Haven, Connecticut. He fought and defeated many highly ranked heavyweights, including Johnny Risko, Al Ettore, Patsy Perroni, and Tony Shucco.

Despite his successes, Lewis's ring earnings were comparatively small. The light heavyweight championship was not especially prestigious. In general, attendance at boxing events, and hence ring earnings, were low during the Great Depression. Furthermore, although Lewis was the first African American to win the light heavyweight title, he was greatly overshadowed by JOE LOUIS, whose career began in 1934. While the bigger and much harder-hitting Louis fought important battles in New York and Chicago before enormous crowds, Lewis defended his title and fought nontitle bouts mostly either in smaller cities or in large cities before small crowds.

On 25 January 1939 Lewis and Louis met for the world heavyweight title. Although the two men were said to be friends, the heavyweight champion showed no mercy; he quickly launched a devastating attack that ended the fight in the first round. Landing only two light punches himself, Lewis suffered three knockdowns and a bad beating before the referee stopped the fight. It was the first time he had ever been knocked out, and this proved to be his last fight. In March 1939 he was refused permission to box in Michigan when it was discovered that he was blind in one eye and had poor vision in the other. An attempt to set up a light heavyweight championship rematch with Harvey in England failed when the British Boxing Board of Control banned him from boxing there. Unable to arrange fights, Lewis lost recognition as light heavyweight champion when the New York State Athletic Commission declared the title vacant on 27 July 1939.

Quiet and gentlemanly, Lewis was devoutly religious, abstained from using alcohol and tobacco, and pursued sports and music as hobbies. After his retirement he lived in the Bay Area with his wife,

Florence Anita Reid, with whom he had two children. He died in Berkeley, California.

Lewis fought 117 times, winning 103, 60 by knockout, boxing 6 draws, and losing only 8 times. He was elected to the International Boxing Hall of Fame in 1994.

FURTHER READING

Fleischer, Nat. *Black Dynamite*, vol. 5, *Sockers in Sepia* (1947).

Fleischer, Nat, comp. *The Ring Boxing Encyclopedia and Record Book* (1987).

Obituary: *New York Times*, 19 Apr. 1974.

This entry is taken from the *American National Biography* and is published here with the permission of the American Council of Learned Societies.

LUCKETT V. DAVIS

Lewis, Joseph Vance (25 Dec. 18??–1923), writer, lawyer, and doctor, was born a slave to Doc and Rosa Lewis probably just prior to the Civil War. In his narrative he writes that he was born at a time when "reconciliation was futile and that disruption and secession hung like a cloud over the horizon." The Lewis family was owned by Colonel D. S. Cage Sr., who on the day of Lewis's birth celebrated by recording the event in the family Bible with a short annotation that the birth would increase his wealth by one thousand dollars. For his part Lewis was mostly oblivious to the fact that he was enslaved at all, as he was relatively young when slavery was abolished. The end of slavery was a confusing moment for all the people on Cage's plantation: they were set free but encouraged to remain on the plantation to work for wages. Lewis saw it as a testament to Cage's good temperament and to the loyalty of Lewis's family and friends that most of the former slaves chose to remain on the plantation to work.

Lewis's formal education began when a school was built near his plantation. Spurred on by a competitive and condescending schoolmate, Lewis challenged himself to attend college and finally left Cage's plantation to pursue an undergraduate degree and then a law degree. With his parents deceased, Lewis worked his way through school, successfully graduating from several university programs. He received his first degree from Leland University in New Orleans, where he completed the normal course for teachers, then went to Orange, Texas, where he obtained a teaching certificate. He worked for two years as a teacher in the Cripple Creek School in Angeline County, Texas, and a year as principal of a school in Lufkin, but he was always set on his goal of becoming an attorney. After two terms at Lincoln University in Pennsylvania, he received his law degree from the University of Michigan in Ann Arbor in 1894 and furthered his legal course work at the Chicago College of Law, from which he graduated in 1897.

Lewis began his career doing pro bono work in Chicago so that he could gain some experience and name recognition. His first case was to defend a racist white man against the charge of murder. Lewis won the case, and it gained him national recognition. Soon his career took off, and he was working all across America as a defense attorney in many highly publicized murder trials.

Lewis settled on locating his practice in Houston, Texas, where he thought large-scale growth was imminent. According to Lewis, jealousy was aroused in both the black and white legal communities at the notion of his overwhelming success. Regardless of the motivation of the claimants, Lewis was indicted several times for poor business practices and occasionally was forced to put his criminal practice on hold for short periods. During these times he supported himself by practicing civil law and even once by briefly becoming a physician, which also aroused the anxiety of local professionals.

For six months Lewis was actually prohibited from practicing law, during which time he traveled to Europe, only to be indicted and jailed briefly upon his return to Texas. While in jail, Pauline Gray visited him, and Lewis decided to marry her. Pauline Lewis Lubin, as she would later become known, was herself a significant figure in the Houston African American community. A graduate of Prairie View A&M University and later the librarian at the Carnegie Colored Library, she was a member of the NAACP and an organizer for the Texas Federation of Colored Women's Clubs.

In 1910 Lewis published a memoir, *Out of the Ditch*, the most significant source of information on his life, in which he recounted in great detail and in thoughtful prose the events of his life and the proceedings of many of his court cases. He defended himself against the claims that he had committed fraud in his professional dealings, though it is unclear whether or not the claims brought against him were merely the petty workings of ambitious and jealous competitors. Lewis ended his memoir with a treatise linking religion to the state's responsibility to all its citizens. He moralized as well about the individual's responsibilities within the community and to himself, especially in the black community. His memoir was meant to encourage young men who might have come upon hard times to persevere in their lofty aspirations and to remain on the path of righteousness.

FURTHER READING

Lewis, Joseph Vance. *Out of the Ditch: A True Story of an Ex-Slave* (1910), available online at http://docsouth.unc.edu/neh/lewisj/lewisj.html

Bloomfield, Maxwell. "From Deference to Confrontation: The Early Black Lawyers of Galveston, Texas, 1895–1920," in *The New High Priests: Lawyers in Post–Civil War America*, ed. Gerard W. Gewalt (1984).

LAURA MURPHY

Lewis, Julian Herman (26 May 1891–6 Mar. 1989), physiologist, pathologist, and author, was born in Shawneetown, Illinois, to John and Cordelia Lewis. His father, a former slave, and his mother had both graduated from Berea College in Kentucky, and earned their livelihoods as schoolteachers. Not surprisingly therefore, Lewis was encouraged from a young age to excel in school and to obtain as much education as possible. Instead of attending his parents' alma mater, he entered the University of Illinois, where he studied biology and physiology and received a B.S. degree in 1911 and an M.A. in 1912. Three years later, he completed his doctoral work at the University of Chicago to become the first African American to receive a Ph.D. in Physiology from an American university. In 1917, the same year he received an M.D. from Chicago's Rush Medical College, he was also named a professor of physiology at the University of Chicago, where he remained for twenty-six years.

Lewis's research interests were far-ranging. Most of his research projects were related to pathology, the growth and development of disease, and immunity, the ability of a living organism to resist disease. His most ambitious research in this regard involved anaphylaxis, the tendency of an organism to become increasingly susceptible to the deleterious effects of a foreign protein as its exposure to that protein continues over time, and the ability of lipids, the class of fatty-acid biochemical compounds that includes steroids, to prevent or reduce the effects of anaphylaxis. Other notable research projects of his investigated beef plasma as a safe and suitable substitute for human blood in a transfusion, and studied the effect of epinephrine, a hormone that plays

a role in regulating blood pressure, in the adrenal glands of the human fetus. He was a member of the Society for Experimental Pathology, the American Association of Immunologists, and the American Association of Pathologists and Bacteriologists.

Lewis is best remembered, however, not as a medical researcher but as an author. By the 1930s he had become intensely interested in the degree to which race affects immunology, and in 1942 he published his findings in this regard in *The Biology of the Negro*. It remains unclear to what degree Lewis was responding to the pseudoscience of his day, or to the widespread belief in the white community that people of African descent were biologically inferior to people of European descent. In fact he seems to have been motivated by nothing more than a desire to understand how his own African-ness affected his ability to resist diseases and medical conditions that historically have plagued people outside Africa. Regardless of his motivation, *The Biology of the Negro* was a masterful analysis of the physiological and anatomical differences between African Americans and European Americans. In chapters devoted to anatomy, biochemical and physiological characteristics, medical diseases, surgical diseases, obstetrics and gynecology, diseases of the skin, dental diseases, and diseases of the eye, ears, nose, and throat, Lewis presented in unremarkable prose the findings of other medical researchers concerning blacks and whites and the differences between them. He did not shy away from the fact that, in some cases, blacks do indeed differ physiologically from whites; for example, blacks are much more likely to have Type B blood rather than Type A, which whites are much more likely to possess. Nevertheless, he was clear about the fact that such minor differences in no way suggest that people of African descent are in any way inferior to people of European descent. Although Lewis acknowledged that African Americans suffered more from certain diseases or medical conditions, he also explained that the difference in question often resulted from social or geographical conditions, not physiological ones. *The Biology of the Negro* was almost totally ignored by the white community. The black community, on the other hand, took particular notice of it. The *Journal of the National Medical Association*, the organ of the nation's leading medical association for black physicians, reviewed the book the same year it was published, and applauded its thorough and impartial handling of the subject.

In 1943 Lewis gave up teaching to devote more time to his medical practice. That same year he moved to Dyer, Indiana, where he became the director of the pathology department and the clinical laboratory at Our Lady of Mercy Hospital. He retired from Our Lady of Mercy in the mid-1980s to his home in Dyer, where he died.

FURTHER READING

Salzman, Jack, et al., eds. *Encyclopedia of African-American Culture and History* (1996).

Spangenburg, Ray, and Kit Moser. *African Americans in Science, Math, and Invention* (2003).

CHARLES W. CAREY JR.

Lewis, Kathleen McCree (27 Sept. 1947–16 Oct. 2007), attorney, Detroit area civic leader, and nominee for the sixth circuit federal court of appeals, was born in Boston, Massachusetts, to WADE HAMPTON MCCREE JR. and Dores B. McCrary McCree, and grew up in Detroit, Michigan.

Her father served as a Michigan circuit judge for Wayne County, 1954–1961, and as a federal U.S. district judge 1961–1966, and U.S. sixth circuit court of appeals judge from 1966 to 1977, when he was appointed solicitor general of the United States by President Jimmy Carter. He was the first African American to serve on the sixth circuit court, and the second (after THURGOOD MARSHALL) as solicitor general. Kathleen Lewis attended Detroit public schools, graduating from Cass Technical High School in 1965, then entered Fisk University (*Jet*, 24 Mar. 1966, 39), where Judge McCree was an alumnus, and later a trustee. She transferred to the University of Michigan, where she graduated in 1969 with a bachelor's degree in Political Science, marrying fellow student David Baker Lewis on 17 May 1969. She earned a J.D. at the university's law school in 1973.

She went to work after receiving her law degree for the law firm of Dykema Gosset Spencer Goodnow and Trigg, later known simply as the Dykema Gossett law firm. She remained at the firm for the rest of her life, becoming a full partner, and eventually heading the firm's appellate litigation team. She was admitted to practice in the state and federal courts in Michigan and in the United States courts of appeals for the sixth, seventh, eighth, ninth, tenth, eleventh, and federal circuits, and the United States Supreme Court.

In 1974 she was appointed to the Civil Service Commission of Detroit. The Lewises had two children, Aaron McCree Lewis, born in 1975, and Sarah Susan Lewis, born in 1980. Lewis served on the American Bar Association's Section on Litigation,

editing publications for the section's educational endeavors 1987–1988, and contributing to the Task Force on Children report in 1998 on improving the legal representation of children. She was cochairperson of the section's Litigation Appellate Practice Committee, and a founding member of the State Bar of Michigan Appellate Practice Section. She served two terms, 1986–1992, on the State Bar of Michigan Standing Committee on Appellate Court Administration. In 1992 she received the Wayne County Neighborhood Legal Services Pro Bono Award. A life member of the NAACP, Lewis received, jointly with her husband, the 1995 Learned Hand Award from the Detroit chapter of the American Jewish Committee Institute of Human Rights.

Lewis was nominated on 16 September 1999 by President William J. Clinton to serve on the United States Court of Appeals for the Sixth Circuit. The nomination was never voted on by the senate, in part because Michigan's Republican senator, Spencer Abraham, refused to return the senate's "blue slip" form, indicating approval or disapproval. By the arcane customs of the senate, the Judiciary Committee could not hold a hearing or vote on the nomination until the blue slip was returned. (This custom was abrogated five years later, when Senator Orrin Hatch was chair of the committee, to push through President George W. Bush's nominees.) Abraham preferred a close friend, Judge Gerald E. Rosen, for the vacancy. Abraham also "blue-slipped" the nomination of Helene White to the Sixth Circuit. Clinton resubmitted both nominations in December 2000.

Without mentioning the previous manipulation of senate rules, Republican radio commentator and sometime prosecutor Barbara Olson, in her polemical *The Last Final Days* broadside against the Clinton administration (p. 93), derided the resubmission of Lewis's nomination as fitting "the Clinton pattern of appointing activist judges of liberal persuasion, often with dubious qualifications," and questioned the wisdom of sending this and other nominations to "a United States Senate controlled at that time, although barely, by Republicans." Olson did not offer any empirical background for her characterization of Lewis, but the language exemplifies the political atmosphere that contributed to denying Lewis a hearing, much less a vote to confirm or reject her nomination. Lewis's nomination was formally withdrawn by President George W. Bush, on 19 March 2001.

Continuing to work at the Dykema Gossett firm, Lewis served as president of the American Academy of Appellate Lawyers, 2005–2006, and was named by Michigan Lawyers Weekly in 2006 as one of the state's top ten attorneys.

Lewis died at the age of sixty after a prolonged battle with cancer, survived by her husband and three children. A former coworker at the firm, Jeffrey M. Lipshaw, associate professor of law at Suffolk Law School, and a former attorney at Dykema Gossett, eulogized her as "one of the finest thinkers and writers I ever met," adding that she and her husband David were "truly one of the most elegant couples ever to walk the earth" (http://lawprofessors.typepad.com/legal_profession/2007/10/in-memoriam-kat.html). An award was created to honor her memory by the American Academy of Appellate Lawyers, to "recognize her warmth elegance, and especially her devotion to appellate justice," and to recognize "extraordinary excellence and significant contributions to the appellate process."

FURTHER READING

Congressional Record—Senate, 19 December 2001, 26893; 12 November 2003, 28666, 28715, 28718, 28844, 28865.

Grasso, Kathi L. *A Judge's Guide to Improving the Legal Representation of Children* (1998).

Public Papers of the Presidents of the United States; Administration of William J. Clinton, 2000, April 30, 801.

Scherer, Nancy. *Scoring Points: Politicians, Activists, and the Lower Federal Court Appointment Process* (2005).

Steigerwalt, Amy. *Battle over the Bench: Senators, Interest Groups, and Lower Court Confirmations* (2010).

Obituaries: *Detroit News*, 17 Oct.; 22 Oct. 2007.

CHARLES ROSENBERG

Lewis, Meade Anderson "Lux" (4 Sept. 1905– 7 June 1964), jazz pianist, was born in Chicago, Illinois. His parents' names are unknown. His father, a Pullman porter, played guitar. Lewis spent a part of his childhood in Louisville, Kentucky. In Chicago he studied violin for about six months, but he lacked interest in it. At age sixteen, when his father died, he left school to go to work. He was interested in becoming an automobile mechanic, but he preferred music. Lewis was a teenage friend of the future pianist ALBERT AMMONS. They learned to play piano by listening to such musicians

as Hersal Thomas and Jimmy Yancey and by copying the action of player pianos. Both were strongly attracted to "The Fives," a blues involving strong, repetitive, percussive patterns in the left hand set against equally strong and percussive but less rigorously repetitive counterrhythmic patterns in the right; this piano blues style came to be known as "boogie-woogie." At some point during this period Lewis acquired his nickname. Imitating characters in the comic strip *Alphonse and Gaston*, he would stroke his chin as if he had a goatee and mustache; from this gesture he came to be called "the Duke of Luxembourg," hence "Lux."

Around 1925 Ammons found Lewis a job playing at and supervising the Paradise Inn, a whorehouse in South Bend, Indiana. Lewis regularly returned to Chicago during this time. He played for parties in Detroit for several months in 1927, and he again returned home, where at the end of the year he was given an opportunity to record his greatest boogie-woogie piano piece, "Honky Tonk Train Blues," which features fabulous tensions between oscillating chords in the left hand and counterrhythmic patterns in the right.

Having worked with Ammons at the Silver Taxi Cab company while also playing when opportunities arose, Lewis left Chicago around 1930 or 1931 to entertain in whorehouses in Muskegon Heights, Michigan, and then in Muskegon. Later he had fond memories of the area because he had an opportunity to go fishing every day, and the catch was substantial. He recalled that he was well liked on the job. Although his pianistic skills were limited, he had a good ear and could play any tune from memory if a few bars could be hummed to him.

Lewis stayed in Muskegon until 1932, went back to Chicago, returned to Muskegon, and then returned to Chicago again in 1934. He also worked as a WPA laborer during this period. In Chicago he took a job traveling as a chauffeur for several months. After this job ended, Ammons found him work with a drummer and a trumpeter. This trio was working at Doc Huggins's Club late in 1935 when the record producer John Hammond came looking for Lewis. Ammons directed Hammond to the club (not to a car wash, as is often said; Lewis explained that Hammond made up the story of discovering Lewis at a car wash to make the return from obscurity seem even more colorful). Hammond requested "Honky Tonk Train Blues," and after hearing it, he returned the next night with Benny Goodman and TEDDY WILSON, who played with the trio. Lewis began recording on a regular basis, including the first of several renditions of "Honky Tonk Train Blues." Early in 1936 he recorded "Yancey Special," based on a piece by his forerunner in the boogie-woogie style, Yancey; at this same session he played boogie-woogie on celesta rather than piano. In 1937 Lewis tried a different sort of novelty, "Whistlin' Blues," on which while playing he whistled with the phrasing of a New Orleans jazz cornetist.

With Hammond's support, Lewis made forays to New York to play at the Imperial Theatre in 1936 and at Nick's Club in 1937, but the breakthrough to a general audience came only with the appearance of Lewis, Ammons, and PETE JOHNSON as a boogie-woogie piano trio at the "Spirituals to Swing" concert on 23 December 1938 at Carnegie Hall. With BIG JOE TURNER, the trio worked at Café Society in New York's Greenwich Village and at the Hotel Sherman in Chicago; there also were national radio broadcasts.

In 1940 Lewis recorded his sixth solo piano rendition of "Honky Tonk Train Blues" together with "Bass on Top" and "Six Wheel Chaser." The next year, as a member of the clarinetist EDMOND HALL's quartet with CHARLIE CHRISTIAN on acoustic guitar, he again recorded on celesta, including "Jammin' in Four" and "Profoundly Blue," playing a blues solo on the latter in a delicate, transparent, tuneful manner rather than in his usual two-handed percussive style. From August 1941 he lived in Los Angeles, where he devoted considerable time to fishing and golfing while playing in clubs, for parties, on television, and on soundtracks for movie shorts and cartoons, including the film *New Orleans* (1947). He toured in 1952 with the Piano Parade, which included ERROLL GARNER, ART TATUM, and Pete Johnson. Lewis was killed in an automobile accident in Minneapolis.

Many critics regard Lewis and Ammons, after Yancey, as the best of the boogie-woogie pianists. A technically narrow blues and jazz piano style, their approach was worn out within a few years, but it took on a new vitality as one of the strongest influences on rhythm and blues, urban blues, and rock and roll.

FURTHER READING

Hill, Don. "Meade Lux Lewis," *Cadence*, Oct. 1987.
Ramsey, Frederic, Jr., and Charles Edward Smith, eds. *Jazzmen* (1939).
Obituaries: *New York Times, Down Beat*, 8 June 1964; 16 July 1964.
This entry is taken from the *American National Biography* and is published here with the permission of the American Council of Learned Societies.

BARRY KERNFELD

Lewis, Norman (23 July 1909–27 August 1979), artist, was born Norman Wilfred Lewis in Harlem, New York, the second of three boys born to Wilfred Lewis and Diana Lewis (maiden name unknown). From his earliest school days, Lewis observed how people formed group identities—and noticed the ways he didn't belong. He recalled that Harlem during his boyhood was an Italian and Jewish place where "the only Negroes … were [building] superintendents." Later, as white ethnic residents moved away and more African Americans arrived, he recognized differences within Harlem's "new Negro" community. Lewis was keen to the ways his family's immigrant outlook was distinct from blacks with U.S. roots: his parents came to Harlem from Bermuda, where his father had been a fisherman and his mother ran her own bakery.

At nine years old, Lewis discovered a desire to paint. But his father warned that his racial identity would be an intractable obstacle, and admonished Lewis for dreaming of a "white man's" pursuit. Nevertheless, Lewis continued haltingly towards art. While studying commercial design at the New York Vocational High School, he became discouraged by his inability to emulate popular illustrations. Only later in life would he realize that what he was attempting to render by hand required mechanical equipment (Romare Bearden and Harry Henderson, *A History of African American Artists*, p. 316)

After high school, Lewis surrendered to "drifting." He sought "belonging" in the street culture, masked his "proper" way of speaking with slang, frequented pool halls, and gambled. Lest he be thought "queer," Lewis hid his desire to create and to learn. Around 1929 Lewis found work on a boat and so escaped the street scene. For the first time, he could contemplate the immensity, moods, colors, and textures of natural features like the sea and sky. Sailing to South America, he encountered social class and ethnic relationships he'd never imagined, and began to think differently about his own identity: "I came to realize that it wasn't just black people who were exploited." (Bearden, p. 317)

In the early 1930's, Lewis returned to the U.S., and pursued an artistic path with increasing intensity. While working odd jobs in 1933, Lewis discovered the Uptown Art Laboratory, the storefront art studio and school of AUGUSTA SAVAGE, a black sculptor (and key figure in Harlem's artistic Renaissance). Savage took Lewis on as a pupil. Though he quickly became dissatisfied with her approach, Lewis finally could paint unabashedly. Between 1933 and 1935, he took up and dropped out of formal training programs at Columbia University and the John Reed Art Club. Lewis found he preferred independence, and amassed a collection of art books to guide his studies.

Through involvement in the artistic community, Lewis counterbalanced his solitary bent. In 1933 he was accepted into the Depression-related Work Progress Administration (WPA) arts project. In 1934, he joined the 306 Group, which included notable black artists like ROMARE BEARDEN and RALPH ELLISON. In 1935 he helped found the Harlem Artists Guild. With peers who became lifelong friends, he engaged in a dialogue about "social realist" art. This movement proposed that artistic content should promote change at a time of injustice and economic crisis. So Lewis painted situations that demanded attention, like evictions and soup kitchens, depicting everyday life with recognizable—although simplified and stylized—details.

In 1941, Lewis left New York to serve the World War II effort at a shipyard in the Pacific Northwest. He faced numerous racially motivated incidents, from insubordination to demotion and eventually physical threats—so he quit and returned to New York. Shaken by the experience, Lewis began to doubt whether painting could truly intercede to change real-life conditions. In the aftermath of the war's destruction, many of his artist friends from the WPA came to similar conclusions. They advocated freedom from old expectations. They focused on abstract elements inherent to painting, like color and flat forms. They elevated the individualism and expression of the artist, an approach that promised self-realization to Lewis: "you realize they did just what they wanted to do—so why not me?" (Bearden, p. 321).

Lewis often joined these artists as they gathered downtown to found a new movement called "Abstract Expressionism." Soon, their radical ideas became widely accepted, and Lewis shared some of their early successes. In 1946 he was invited to join Willard, a prestigious Madison Avenue gallery. He exhibited at the Museum of Modern Art (1951) and the Whitney Museum in New York (1958). After he won the popularity prize at a 1955 Carnegie exhibit in Pittsburgh, Lewis imagined much future acclaim.

But his new direction would be resisted by some who believed black artists were obliged to represent racial struggle. While Lewis would defend his freedom to individual expression via abstraction, he addressed social responsibility in other ways. As the sole African American attending "Studio 35," a key gathering of elite art figures in 1950, he felt compelled to ask his peers to consider their relationship to a wider audience. In 1963, he helped found Spiral, a group of black artists addressing race and politics. Above all, he believed his participation in groups like the Student Nonviolent Coordinating Committee (SNCC) and the Congress of Racial Equality (CORE) and in demonstrations achieved more than political paintings.

In 1976, Lewis's first museum retrospective was exhibited at the City University of New York. The show decried Lewis's absence from major collections and his relative anonymity. And although he personally eschewed the socializing that helped propel some fame, Lewis felt racism played a part in his exclusion from circles where connections were cultivated. From 1965 to 1972 Lewis taught art, making a living and remaining involved in the community. Despite his self-professed inclination towards isolation, he would always be highly regarded in the art world. In 1972 he was awarded a grant from the foundation of fellow painter Mark Rothko. He received a National Endowment for the Arts fellowship the same year, and a Guggenheim grant in 1975.

Norman Lewis died in New York in 1979. His abstract paintings are now recognized as essential to modern American art history. Lewis was fascinated with the human urge to follow and belong. So his brushstrokes often evoke figures gathering, with both positive (civil rights marchers) and ominous (the Ku Klux Klan) connotations. Lewis also explored and expressed his individuality by contemplating nature—his tide and seascape paintings suggest he found an inner serenity.

FURTHER READING
Norman Lewis's papers are located in the Smithsonian Archives of American Art in Washington, D.C.
See also, "Oral history interview with Norman Lewis, 14 July 1968." Smithsonian Archives of American Art. [online transcript: http://www.aaa.si.edu/collections/oralhistories/transcripts/lewis68.htm].
Conwill, Kinshasha Holman, David Craven, Ann Eden Gibson, Lowery Stokes Sims, and Jorge Daniel Veneciano. *Norman Lewis: Black Paintings, 1946–1977* (1998).

Gibson, Ann. *Abstract Expressionism Other Politics* (1997).

Euell, Julian, Ann Gibson, and Kellie Jones. *Norman Lewis: From the Harlem Renaissance to Abstraction* (1989).

Obituary: *New York Times*, 29 August, 1979.

TODD PALMER

Lewis, Oliver (c.1863–?), jockey, was born the son of a slave woman sometime during the period shortly before the Emancipation Proclamation. There is little known today about the early years of Lewis, who grew up to become one of the most renowned African American jockeys in horse racing history. Using other accounts and histories from the period, however, speculation about how Lewis came to be such an adept horseman is possible.

After the Civil War, sharecropping replaced slavery as a means for plantation owners to maintain control over their newly liberated charges. Some of these sharecroppers were used as stable hands and exercise boys for the plantation owners' racehorses. The most proficient of these boys (for most of them were barely fourteen or fifteen) were chosen as jockeys, a highly desirable position. Even during slavery times, the title of "jockey" allowed an African American many freedoms that were refused his fellows. African American jockeys both during and after the Civil War were given relative freedom to travel, as well as a sense of dignity and even superiority that was denied most other blacks of the time.

Therefore, it is not difficult to imagine that a mother would hope to provide her son with such advantages by bringing him to the attention of a wealthy racehorse owner. Oftentimes a woman employed by one of these men would bring her son along with her to work. During the course of the mother's workday, the boy would occupy himself, playing in the vicinity of the manor house where his mother performed her duties. The plantation owner might take notice of a particularly agile or strong individual. From there the boy went to live in the owner's stable, sleeping with the horses, caring for them, and developing instincts about the animals that most people today can barely comprehend. By the age of ten or eleven years old, these boys were expert horsemen and spent their days exercising and training the powerful, high-strung racehorses.

Under such circumstances, a few of these young men earned the chance to become jockeys. However, even among these competent horsemen, there were standouts. One such standout was Oliver Lewis. Lewis rode for the McGrathiana stud farm, which was owned by H. Price McGrath. Also employed by McGrath was a trainer named Ansel Williamson. Williamson, born into slavery in Virginia in 1806, was eventually bought and freed by a prominent horse breeder, Robert A. Alexander. Williamson worked for Alexander, buying and training racehorses until Alexander's death in 1867. He then went on to work at McGrathiana, training many famous racehorses as well as developing the young exercise boys into skilled jockeys. Lewis flourished under Williamson's tutelage.

In addition to working for McGrath, Lewis was also employed as a utility rider at inaugural events for the Louisville Jockey Club. On 17 May 1875 Lewis won three races. One of these was the most significant race of his life. Ironically, it was also the race that he was not supposed to win.

H. Price McGrath had two horses entered in the inaugural running of the Kentucky Derby. The horse upon which his optimism rested was a large bay named Chesapeake. His other horse was a smaller chestnut named Aristides. McGrath made the decision that Aristides would be his "rabbit." He would use the speedy horse to tire the others early in the race, leaving room for the late-closing Chesapeake to take the lead near the end. The trainer Ansel Williamson suggested that Lewis should ride Aristides, since he was one of the few jockeys able to hold back the fiery red horse.

The parade to the post, which began the race, found Lewis as one of thirteen African American jockeys in a field of fifteen horses. When the gates opened, beginning the race, McGrath's favorite, Chesapeake, got off to a slow start. As the race progressed, Lewis had all that he could handle trying to hold back the determined Aristides. Meanwhile, Chesapeake never seemed to recover from his poor start. Owner McGrath, seeing the prospect of Chesapeake's victory fading, ordered wildly from the sidelines for Lewis and Aristides to "Go on!" (Saunders and Saunders, 14). This command was all the impetus that horse and rider needed. Lewis gave Aristides free rein, and the pair won the derby, traveling the mile-and-a-half distance in a record time of 2 minutes and 37¾ seconds. McGrath won $2,850 for this race, while Lewis's prize, if any other than the satisfaction of winning, is unknown.

Just a month after his derby win, Lewis was again set up on Aristides as the "rabbit." (It appears that, in most of his races for McGrath, Lewis was used as the "rabbit" rider). This time Lewis and Aristides were to race in the famed Belmont Stakes, one of the jewels in racing's celebrated Triple Crown. As the race commenced, Lewis held his mount back, obeying the explicit orders of the horse's owner. The horse strained to have his head, and the crowd shouted their disapproval, but Lewis kept the horse from taking the lead. Later, when Aristides won the Jerome Stakes and the Withers Stakes in New York, a white jockey, Bobby Swim, not Lewis, rode the tenacious little horse to victory. McGrath, it is reported, favored Swim because of his greater experience.

The remainder of Lewis's career as a jockey is largely unknown. Records indicate, however, that after his racing career, he went on to work as a bookkeeper and later as a racehorse trainer in Lexington, Kentucky. In 1907 a newspaper reporter spotted Lewis at Churchill Downs, the site of the Kentucky Derby. An article in the following day's newspaper related Lewis's appearance as something quite unusual. Interestingly, no one is sure how often Lewis returned to the derby. Perhaps he was a regular attendant, making his visits clandestinely, or maybe he intentionally avoided the site of his most famous race.

After Lewis's derby, fifteen of the twenty-eight following derbies were won by African American jockeys, with some of them, such as JAMES WINKFIELD and ISAAC MURPHY, winning more than once. However, African Americans were slowly being pushed out of the sport. White jockeys, resentful of their success, frequently resorted to dangerous and illegal practices to ensure that black jockeys no longer won races. African American jockeys were cut off, blocked in, jostled, and knocked off their horses to ensure their defeat. Consequently, these actions made horse owners reluctant to hire black jockeys. Eventually, black jockeys all but disappeared from the horseracing world. However, their legacy still remains.

FURTHER READING
Hotaling, Edward. *The Great Black Jockeys: The Lives and Times of the Men Who Dominated America's First National Sport* (1999).
Saunders, James Robert, and Monica Renae Saunders. *Black Winning Jockeys in the Kentucky Derby* (2003).

MONICA R. SAUNDERS

Lewis, Reginald Francis (7 Dec. 1942–18 Jan. 1993), arbitrager and business executive, was born in Baltimore, the son of Clinton Lewis, a skilled worker and small-businessman and Carolyn Cooper. Lewis was strongly influenced by his mother, especially because his parents divorced during his childhood. His mother married Jean S. Fugett Sr. in 1951. An elementary school teacher, Fugett was a graduate of Morgan State College and had five sons and daughters.

Lewis attended a Catholic grade school but was not admitted to a Catholic high school because of low test scores and discrimination against blacks. Instead he attended the black public Paul Laurence Dunbar High School, where he starred in three sports: football, baseball, and basketball. Academically below average because of his weakness in the sciences, Lewis received a football scholarship from Virginia State College in Petersburg, a black public institution. After his freshman year, Lewis withdrew from football because of a shoulder injury; moreover, he had not quite shown star quality in college. His freshman year grades were good but not outstanding. Losing his athletic scholarship, Lewis held a variety of jobs while a student. Rescue from obscurity came in the form of a Harvard Law School summer program for blacks upon his graduation in 1965. Although many of his age cohort entered military service, Lewis was classified 4-F as a diabetic. He maintained a B average at Harvard Law School, graduating in 1968. In 1969 he married Loida Nicolas, a graduate of the University of the Philippines law school whose father was an entrepreneur. The couple had two daughters.

Lewis worked at the well-known liberal New York firm of Paul, Weiss, Rifkind, Wheaton & Garrison from 1968 to 1970. He then became a partner in Wallace, Murphy, Thorpe & Lewis, a black Wall Street law firm. This firm did legal work mostly for the New York Urban Coalition but was gradually adding major corporate clients. As the other partners withdrew, the firm slowly became identified with Lewis. In 1978 the firm became Lewis & Clarkson, but Lewis had recruited Clarkson. Under Lewis's direction, the firm oriented itself more and more toward business, specializing in venture capital work. Lewis adamantly insisted on being paid what his legal services were worth and not less because he was black. Similarly, he did not like receiving legal work specifically because he was black.

Becoming ever more deeply involved in arbitrage, Lewis made the transition from lawyer to financier. In 1975 he tried to buy Parks Sausage, a black-owned publicly traded Baltimore company, but he failed because he lacked a credible financial background and a track record of success, which caused Parks not to take his promises seriously. Typically Lewis sought low-tech, high-cash-flow, well-managed companies for acquisition. He next unsuccessfully tried to buy Almet, a manufacturer of leisure furniture. In 1983 Lewis formed TLC Group, a holding entity, and success came his way soon after. The same year he sought a leveraged buyout of the McCall Pattern Company for $22.5 million. McCall was owned by Esmark, a conglomerate that had purchased McCall Pattern from Norton Simon Industries. Through experience as a corporate lawyer and through preparation, Lewis established his credibility with leading financial intermediaries such as Bear Stearns, who managed the transaction; Drexel Burnham Lambert and others competed for the business, and Bankers Trust lent $19 million. Lewis paid $20 million and a note for $2.5 million in addition to a warrant for 7.5 percent of TLC Pattern Inc. He invested a million in cash, much of it borrowed or obtained from other investors. Lewis netted $50 million for the McCall deal. A highly leveraged acquisition, McCall saw its profits doubled under Lewis's management in 1985 and 1986. McCall did not compete on the basis of price and conceded market share for profit, stressing cash flow to reduce debt. Lewis shared McCall equity with management, but he himself owned more than 80 percent of the equity when McCall went public. Lewis's creative financing and strength as a negotiator obtained him a 90 to 1 gain on equity. A year after Lewis sold McCall for three times his cost, it went bankrupt. Its new owners sued Lewis, alleging fraudulent conveyance, but the suit was dismissed.

Lewis's crowning coup was a leveraged buyout in 1987 of Beatrice International Food Company, a multinational conglomerate holding the international operations of Beatrice Foods. He paid almost $1 billion to the owners, Kohlberg Kravis Roberts, which had pioneered leveraged buyouts in the late 1970s and early 1980s. Michael Milken of Drexel Burnham Lambert acted as the principal financier, and Drexel received 35 percent of the equity for its financial services; Manufacturers Hanover Trust furnished additional credit. Although Lewis did not want to be portrayed as an African American, after the buyout he selected a black-dominated board composed of longtime friends. The closing in December was complicated by the sharp stock market decline the previous October; however, Lewis obtained no price concession. Lewis immediately sold Beatrice assets to finance the buyout and

reduce the Beatrice debt, selling units in Canada, Australia, and Spain for $430 million. By 1989 Lewis had disposed of enough assets to cover 88 percent of the Beatrice buyout. The divestitures left Beatrice with a core food business focused in Western Europe. Having invested $15 million of his own money in the Beatrice buyout, Lewis ended with TLC Beatrice, one of America's largest corporations, in his control.

Living in New York and Paris, Lewis, fluent in French, moved to Paris after acquiring Beatrice. An art collector, he owned paintings by Picasso, Matisse, and others. Lewis became one of the country's wealthiest businessmen, with an estimated net worth of $400 million. He donated $1 million to Howard University, $100,000 to his wife's school, the University of the Philippines, $3 million to the Harvard Law School, and $2 million to the NAACP. Incidentally, he backed various black politicians, including JESSE JACKSON in 1984, and he contributed significantly to Jackson's 1988 presidential campaign.

Doctors diagnosed brain cancer in 1992 but the news was withheld from Beatrice. The public was notified only shortly before Lewis's death in New York a year later. The Lewis family owned 51 percent of Beatrice; his wife, who was chairman and chief executive officer, and his half brother, Jean S. Fugett Jr., assumed the helm of TLC Beatrice.

FURTHER READING

Lewis, Reginald F., and Blair S. Walker. *"Why Should White Guys Have All the Fun?": How Reginald Lewis Created a Billion-Dollar Business Empire* (1995).

Obituary: *New York Times*, 20 Jan. 1993.

This entry is taken from the *American National Biography* and is published here with the permission of the American Council of Learned Societies.

SAUL ENGELBOURG

Lewis, Robert Benjamin (1798–Mar. 1858), inventor, entrepreneur, and historian, was born in what is now Gardiner, Maine, the son of Matthias Lewis, a farm laborer of Mohegan Indian ancestry. Nothing is now known of Lewis's mother. Sometime after 28 July 1800 Lewis's father married Lucy Stockbridge of Pittston, Maine, the daughter of African slaves. It is not known whether this marriage legalized a longstanding relationship or was Matthias's actual second marriage.

Although little is known of Lewis's early life, it appears that he first went to sea in ships that worked the Atlantic rim and the coastal trade down to the Caribbean. It is known that Lewis wanted to become a missionary to Africa; after his death, his neighbors remembered, "it was said … that the Congregational Church in Hallowell [where Lewis moved around 1820] had, in consequence of the intelligence he had manifested in youth, obtained for him an education with a view to his becoming a missionary to Africa" (Pitts, 236). Nothing yet has been unearthed to show that Lewis was ever licensed as a preacher or ordained as a minister; however, he brought away from his studies a thorough knowledge of the Bible as well as classical history.

On 17 March 1835, in the Charles Street Baptist Church in Boston, Lewis married Mary Freeman Heuston of Brunswick, Maine, a month before her eighteenth birthday. She was the fourth of nine children of an escaped Virginia slave who had become a prosperous Maine farmer. The Lewises moved to Old Bath Road in Brunswick; the couple would eventually have three sons and seven daughters. Although he supported his family primarily as a whitewasher, Lewis also exhibited a knack for inventing things. He held three U.S. patents: on 25 April 1836 he patented a "Hair Picker," a machine designed to separate strands of used rope that would be made into the "oakum" used to caulk the seams of the hulls of wooden ships; on 27 June 1840 he patented a "Feather Renovator," described as a "machine for Cleaning and Drying Feathers," that is, decorative feathers—egret, ostrich, peacock, and the like—used to adorn fashionable wardrobes; and on 23 February 1841 he patented a new and improved version of a large brush that could be used in whitewashing. Lewis also invented a number of other things, most notably a product that he would call his "inimitable hair oil"—guaranteed to make hair grow and stay in good condition—sales of which made him a comfortable living. He demonstrated its potency by showing "his long black curls that reached down over his coat collar" that had been "thoroughly greased" with his oil (Pitts, 236).

In 1836 Lewis published a 176-page book entitled *Light and Truth*—the first "history book" about African Americans and Native Americans. *Light and Truth* has been described as "a study in the theological grounds of black nationalism, and an early example of what we would today understand as black liberation theology" (Ernest, 425). Lewis saw it as his mission to search "diligently … in the quest of light, and truth, in ancient, sacred and profane history, translated by English historians …

truths that have long been concealed from the sons of Ethiopia" (Pitts, 238). His book attempted to record "the history of the community defined by white oppression without accepting the defining terms of the white oppressors" (Ernest, 425), which is why he saw African Americans and Native Americans as belonging together. Based on his studies of the Bible and other works, including the *Book of Mormon*, and the Reverend Ethan Smith's *View of the Hebrews* as well as Herodotus, Flavius Josephus, and Thucydides, Lewis asserted that Native Americans were descended from the "Ten Lost Tribes" of Israel—"surely then, the natives of the deserts of America must have been a people who once knew [the] God of Israel!" (Lewis, 267–268). He then took the story of the native African from the Creation to 1840s America and interpreted the Bible (as well as the works of other theologians) to show that Africans had once composed most of the classical world as well as the world of the Bible, further contending that black Africans included such notables as the mathematician Euclid, the philosopher Plato, the general Hannibal, the scientist Boethius, and many more. In November 1843 four African American businessmen of Boston—the clothier Thomas Dalton, the old clothes dealer James Scott, the junk dealer Andress V. Lewis (no relation), and the shoemaker Charles H. Roberts—who called themselves the "Committee of Colored Gentlemen," purchased the copyright for *Light and Truth* and by March of the next year produced it in one volume of four hundred pages. The printer was Charles Roberts's half-brother BENJAMIN F. ROBERTS. Although *Light and Truth* would go through two more printings in 1848 and 1851, the version published by the Committee of Colored Gentlemen is the best known.

In early 1858 Robert Benjamin Lewis sailed for Haiti as ship's cook and steward on the merchantman *Philip Larrabee* of Bath, bound for the capital of Port-au-Prince. Upon the ship's arrival sometime during the month of March, Lewis fell ill, died, and was buried in Haiti.

FURTHER READING

Lewis, Robert Benjamin. *Light and Truth: Collected From the Bible and Ancient and Modern History, Containing the Universal History of the Colored and Indian Race, From the Creation of the World to the Present Time* (1844; repr. 1996).

Ernest, John. *Liberation Historiography: African American Writers and the Challenge of History, 1794–1861* (2004).

Pitts, Reginald H. "Robert Benjamin Lewis," in *Maine's Visible Black History*, eds. H. H. Price and Gerald E. Talbot (2006).

REGINALD H. PITTS

Lewis, Roscoe E. (3 Dec. 1904–1961), chemist, social scientist, and writer, was born in Garfield Heights, Washington, D.C., the son of William Harrison Lewis and Mary (Over) Lewis, of whom little else is known. In 1899 there were only four academic public schools in the segregated Washington, D.C., area, and only one of these was open to African Americans. Lewis attended the noted Dunbar High School, then known as M Street School. Because African Americans with advanced degrees had few other opportunities, during the 1920s three Dunbar teachers held the Ph.D. degree, which was certainly unusual and perhaps unique in American public secondary education.

After attending Dunbar, Lewis graduated from Brown University in Providence, Rhode Island, with a bachelor's degree in Philosophy in 1925. While at Brown, Lewis became the first undergraduate initiate of the Alpha Gamma Chapter of the first African American fraternity, Alpha Phi Alpha. Two years after graduating Lewis received a master of science in Chemistry from Howard University, a historically black university in his hometown of Washington, D.C.

Lewis then began working at the Hampton Institute (later Hampton University) in Hampton, Virginia, as a teacher of sciences in the college's academy in September 1927. During the summers, Lewis continued his graduate work in chemistry at Columbia University in New York City, although it is not known whether he completed his doctoral studies. He was soon promoted to assistant professor in the chemistry department at Hampton, where he taught from 1927 until 1942.

In 1936 Lewis became affiliated with the federal government's Works Progress Administration (WPA) and the Virginia Writers' Project. The WPA was created in May 1935 as a New Deal program to assist in the relief efforts of the Great Depression. The Federal Writers' Project, a WPA program, employed writers and researchers to (among many other things) interview and document the lives of African Americans that experienced slavery. Lewis, already interested in oral histories, was appointed to be the supervisor in charge of recording former slaves' experiences in Virginia. In November 1936 Lewis had gathered together what would become known as the "Virginia Negro Project," a team of sixteen African American workers he assigned to perform interviews throughout the state. Virginia's former slave interviewers proved unique, as in almost every other state the interviewers were white, although ZORA NEALE HURSTON and a few other African Americans did conduct some Florida interviews. From 1936 to 1941, under the direct supervision of Lewis, the Virginia Writers' Project conducted over three hundred interviews of black Virginians, collecting over 1,350 life stories from former slaves. Lewis and members of the writer's project went beyond former slaves' narratives and recorded folklore and musical performances presented by former slave singing groups and individuals. In fact, they collected more than 2,700 songs. Lewis was not only important as the leader of the project but he also set the tone that helped produce some of the most revealing interviews of former slaves collected during the 1930s. He was a personable figure capable of creating a comfortable atmosphere that encouraged the interviewees, many of whom were illiterate and quite poor, to speak freely and without apparent fear of official retaliation—a worry that constrained the responses of many in other states.

The materials collected by the "Virginia Negro Project" formed the basis for the publication of *The Negro in Virginia* in 1940, which described the history and contributions of African Americans in Virginia from the colonial period to the then present day. Lewis wrote the majority of this work and was cited as the editor. His fascination with oral history and with recording the stories of African Americans led him to abandon the field of chemistry in 1941 and to concentrate exclusively in the field of social sciences. To further his understanding of the social sciences, Lewis attended American University from 1941 to 1942 as a Rosenwald Fellow and studied social economy. In 1942 he returned to Hampton Institute as an associate professor of social sciences, then became chairman of the department in 1948.

While performing in his various capacities and continuing his studies in social economy at American University, Lewis remained dedicated to the narratives of former slaves. He continued to conduct interviews with the dwindling number of surviving former slaves in hopes of contributing further publications.

Lewis's extensive contributions to the knowledge of the lives of former slaves in Virginia brought exposure to the words and the experiences of a large segment of the population who had been ignored by scholars. Although never fully recognized for his outstanding contributions, he was able to contribute several professional publications. To extend the public knowledge of the former slaves lives in Virginia, he compiled a catalog of the Virginia Writers' Project at Hampton Institute. Lewis also contributed articles to some of the most prominent African American journals of the time, including *The Crisis, Opportunity, Phylon,* and the *Journal of Negro Education.* He also constructed archival data of interviews with former slaves for publication in several books, including *The Negro Caravan, Lay My Burden Down* and *A Treasury of Southern Folklore.* However, when Lewis died in 1961 at the age of fifty-seven, he still had not fulfilled his goal of publishing the entire collection of interviews. The collected Virginia interviews were finally published in 1976 under the title *Weevils in the Wheat: Interviews With Virginia Ex-Slaves.*

FURTHER READING

Roscoe E. Lewis's papers are housed in the Hampton University Archives, Hampton University, Virginia.

Botkin, B. A., ed. *Lay My Burden Down: A Folk History of Slavery* (1945).

Federal Writers Project of the Works Progress Administration. *Virginia Slave Narratives* (2006).

Virginia Writers' Project, *The Negro in Virginia* (1940; repr. 1994).

KATRINA D. THOMPSON

Lewis, Samella (27 Feb. 1924–), art historian, educator, curator, and artist, was born Samella Sanders in New Orleans, Louisiana, the daughter of Samuel Sanders, a strawberry farm owner and Rachel (Taylor) Sanders, a seamstress. Lewis's childhood in New Orleans exposed her to black history, culture, and art—a background that informed all of her professional activities. Her early experiences with segregation catalyzed the powerful antiracist vision that influenced her entire life. For example, as a young art student, she encountered a major barrier in visiting the Delgado Art Museum, located in a municipal park reserved exclusively for whites. Her teacher, ELIZABETH CATLETT, managed to secure a bus and had everyone in her class move directly from the bus to the museum, technically avoiding the racial restrictions of the park itself. Lewis began her formal art studies at Dillard University, studying with Catlett, who became her lifelong friend and mentor. Transferring to the historically black Hampton Institute (later Hampton University) in Hampton, Virginia, she studied with artist Viktor

Lowenfeld, a refugee from Nazi Germany. In the early 1940s Hampton was an exciting environment for young black artists such as Lewis and JOHN BIGGERS. Lowenfeld encouraged his students to draw from their black heritage and experiences in creating artworks reflecting racial identity and pride.

Following her graduation from Hampton with a B.S. in General Studies, which combined fine arts, art history, and education among other subjects, in 1945, Lewis pursued graduate training at Ohio State University, receiving her M.A. in Fine Arts and Art History in 1948. That same year she married Paul Lewis; the couple later had two sons, Alan and Claude. Switching to art history, she completed her Ph.D. in 1951, with a focus on Asian and African arts and culture. She did postgraduate study in Taiwan in 1962 and then returned to the United States to begin her teaching career in late 1962. She served on the faculty of several colleges and universities, including the historically black institutions Morgan State University in Baltimore, Maryland, and Florida A&M University in Tallahassee, Florida, teaching art history. During her tenure at Florida A&M from 1953 to 1958, she encountered the anticommunist hysteria of the cold war. Like many progressive educators, she declined to sign the required loyalty oath. An early civil rights activist, she had participated in a bus boycott in 1955 in Tallahassee. The result was a pattern of harassment rather than formal blacklisting. For example, she had a Ford Foundation fellowship to Ethiopia withdrawn and was labeled a communist for her outspoken views and activities.

After teaching at the State University of New York at Plattsburgh from 1958 to 1968, Lewis relocated to the Los Angeles area. She served as education coordinator at the Los Angeles County Museum of Art from 1968 to 1969. She taught at various campuses of the California State University system and in 1969 joined the Scripps College faculty in Claremont, California. At Scripps she taught Chinese art history as well as African American art through the Intercollegiate Black Studies Program of the Claremont Colleges.

In California, Lewis produced major books on the history of African American art. Her 1969 two-volume work, *Black Artists on Art,* co-edited with Ruth Waddy, highlighted the efforts of numerous contemporary black artists, including such luminaries as BENNY ANDREWS, Elizabeth Catlett, Alonzo Davis, Dale Davis, DAVID DRISKELL, Eugene Grigsby, David Hammons, William

Pajaud, and BETYE SAAR, among many others who subsequently received national and international acclaim. She complemented her publications with additional efforts to elevate African American art to widespread scholarly and public attention. Beginning in 1976 she served as editor and editor emeritus of the academic journal *The International Review of African American Art* (formerly *Black Art Quarterly*). She also organized several exhibitions throughout the western hemisphere and produced several films about African American art. In 1977 she founded the Museum of African American Art in Los Angeles, an institution dedicated to the exhibition of historical and contemporary black art. Her book *Art: African American*, originally published in 1979 and revised as *African American Art and Artists* in 1990, 1994, and 2003, became a standard text in the field. Her 1984 monograph *The Art of Elizabeth Catlett* was a major work on the artist who had been her teacher, and it placed Catlett among the most distinguished modern American artists. That same year Lewis retired from Scripps College as professor emerita. In 1991 Lewis's *African American Art for Young People* extended her commitment to documenting this tradition for younger audiences. Lewis's numerous books and articles established her as one of the premier African American art historians of the twentieth and twenty-first centuries.

Lewis's creative works added further luster to her iconic status in African American art. The social vision and technical brilliance of Catlett and Mexican muralist Jose Clemente Orozco had a strong influence on Lewis's artistic development. Likewise, her own extensive knowledge of Asian art enabled her to make imaginative formal advances in her paintings and prints. Thematically Lewis's painting focused on several key features of American black life, including workers, religion, women, and family. Above all, her works reflected a powerful commitment to African American dignity, perseverance, and resistance to centuries of racial injustice, oppression, and violence. Her studio efforts augmented her scholarly and community projects in fostering respect for her people and their creative accomplishments. Widely exhibited in both individual and group shows, her paintings and graphic art production were held in many major college, university, and public art museum collections in the United States.

As a pioneering scholar of African American art she fashioned an outstanding and multifaceted career that combined teaching, research, exhibition creation, institution building, and studio art production. Her writing, teaching, and curatorial efforts for well over fifty years reflected her tireless commitment to black artists. Lewis's efforts brought her numerous fellowships, awards, and distinctions, including honorary doctorates from Chapman College (1976), Hampton Institute (1990), the University of Cincinnati (1993), Bennett College (1996), and California College of the Arts (2005).

Her exemplary scholarly and curatorial visibility ironically deflected attention from her reputation as a visual artist. Throughout her career she created a substantial body of paintings, drawings, woodcuts, linocuts, serigraphs, lithographs, sculptures, and mixed-media creations reflecting her commitment to humanity in general and particularly to African American life and culture. Her studio work emerged from the same tradition of African American visual art that she effectively documented and promoted as a scholar and arts administrator. Her artwork typically continued the figurative, narrative, and socially conscious focus of that tradition. Like such distinguished predecessors as JACOB LAWRENCE, ROMARE BEARDEN, CHARLES WHITE, and her teacher Elizabeth Catlett, she combined outstanding artistic training and highly developed techniques with compassionate and socially relevant subject matter. Her art both engaged and educated her viewers, urging them to confront her compelling human and social themes.

FURTHER READING

Bearden, Romare, and Harry Henderson, *A History of African-American Art* (1993).

King-Hammond, Leslie, ed. *Gumbo Ya Ya: Anthology of African-American Women Artists* (1995).

Riggs, Thomas, ed. *St James Guide to Black Artists* (1997).

Von Blum, Paul. *Resistance, Dignity, and Pride: African American Artists in Los Angeles* (2004).

PAUL VON BLUM

Lewis, Shirley A. R. (11 June 1937–), educator and college president, was born Shirley Ann Redd in a coal mining camp in Winding Gulf, West Virginia, and largely reared by her father, Robert F. Redd, a high school teacher at Byrd Prilliman High School in the segregated school system, her grandmother Lottie Bell Redd, her great grandmother Eliza Yates, her paternal uncle "Uncle Bud" and another uncle, "Uncle Bruss." She did not learn that Uncle Bruss was not really related to her by kinship, but instead by friendship and boarding ties, until she was an adult. All of these relatives resided together in Shirley's grandmother's home, a "company house" that she had acquired following the work-related death of her husband. Shirley's mother, Thelma Biggers Redd, was born in Talcott, West Virginia, and worked as a housekeeper in the New York/New Jersey area. Shirley's parents divorced when she was an infant, and she remained primarily in the custody of her father and his family. Despite the physical separation from her mother, Shirley maintained contact through frequent visits, letters, and gifts. Indeed, after her parents divorced, Lewis alternately lived with each parent in various parts of the country, as her mother sought employment and as her father helped augment his teacher's salary through summer work. Lewis consequently lived in Beckley, West Virginia; Harlem, New York; Cambridge, Massachusetts; and other cities in the East, finally settling in Berkeley, California, where her mother acquired a position as a children's nurse.

Shirley's father believed deeply in the power of education, especially for his daughter, whom he was convinced would be successful with the help of a quality education. As such, her father taught Shirley to read one year prior to her entrance into kindergarten. Shirley attended kindergarten in Harlem, New York, at P.S. 186, but when she entered school in Beckley, West Virginia, she was inadvertently "skipped" to the second grade. She attended the second grade through the first half of the fourth grade at the Morton Reeves School. She attended the latter half of her fourth grade year through the seventh grade at the Russell School in Cambridge, Massachusetts, and completed the eighth and ninth grades at Garfield Junior High School in Berkeley, California, where she was the only black student in the school. Shirley attended Berkeley High School in Berkeley, California, and graduated in 1955.

She aspired to become a high school teacher, and entered the University of California at Berkeley in September 1955, majoring in Spanish. She became intimately involved with a program that recruited African American, Hispanic, Native American, and Asian students to the university and worked closely with these students to facilitate their retention at the university. She graduated in 1960 with a bachelor of arts degree.

On 17 August 1963 Redd married Ronald McGhee Lewis, a Ph.D. candidate in Education at Stanford. In 1970 Lewis obtained her master's degree in Social Work from Berkeley, with a focus on community education. She taught at several community colleges in California for a year and in 1971 entered Stanford University's doctoral program in education, specializing in linguistic pluralism. The couple had their only child, Mendi Dessalines Shirley Lewis, in 1973. Both Lewises completed their Ph.D. degrees at Stanford University in 1979. That same year, the family relocated to Nashville, Tennessee, where Lewis's husband had obtained a postdoctoral fellowship at Vanderbilt University. Shirley Lewis taught at Vanderbilt during this time, and in 1984 moved to Meharry Medical College in Nashville, where she became the first associate dean of academic affairs in the School of Medicine and the first woman associate dean at the institution. In 1986 she assumed the position of executive director of the Black College Fund, a program that raised funds on behalf of the nation's Historically Black Colleges and Universities (HBCUs) which was supported by the General Board of Higher Education and Ministry of the United Methodist Church. She was promoted to assistant general secretary in 1991.

Although Lewis initially balked at the notion of becoming a college president, she became the head of Paine College in Augusta, Georgia, in 1994. She went on to distinguish herself as a president who embodied the spirit of the institution's Methodist founders by facilitating access to the college by students from varied academic, economic, and social backgrounds, yet equipped and empowered them to excel both academically and professionally. Not only did Lewis serve as an inspiring leader of her institution but she also served the United Methodist Colleges' Council of Presidents, the United Negro College Fund (UNCF), and other organizations that supported the higher education of African American students. Lewis participated on the planning committee that developed the model for the structure of the education faculty at Africa University in Mutare, Zimbabwe, which opened 24 April 1994. She chaired UNCF's Higher Education Act Reauthorization Committee in 2003 and provided testimony before a number of congressional panels on the continued relevancy and utility of historically black college and university educations. She was also a staunch supporter and proponent of issues related to women in higher education as well as in the professions and was appointed by Secretary of Defense William S. Cohen to the 1998 Defense Advisory Committee on Women in the Services (DACOWITS).

Lewis received the 1994 Outstanding Business and Professional Award from *Dollars and Sense Magazine*, and that same year was awarded the Outstanding Service Award from Rust College. In 1995 she was awarded an honorary doctorate degree from Bethune Cookman College and was the given the Voorhees College Woman of the Year Award. Lewis was a two-time recipient of Dillard University's Distinguished Achievement Award (1989 and 1995), and was the first woman to be named the Thirkield-Jones Lecturer by Gammon Theological Seminary in December of 1998. She was also a lifetime member of Alpha Kappa Alpha sorority, and authored numerous articles and research memoranda on linguistic pluralism and the education of African American students, as was a frequent speaker at commencement exercises and national events.

FURTHER READING

Lewis, Shirley A.R., "A Shared Dream," *The Interpreter* (February-March 1988).

YOLANDA L. WATSON SPIVA

Lewis, W. Arthur (23 Jan. 1915–15 June 1991), economist, development expert, and Nobel Laureate, was born William Arthur Lewis on St. Lucia in the West Indies, the son of George Lewis and Ida Barton, teachers. When Lewis was only seven, his father died, and his mother opened a shop to help support her family of five sons. Financially assisted by the Anglican Church and inspired by his mother's unrelenting determination, the precocious youngster completed the studies required for university admission at fourteen and worked as a government clerk for four years. At eighteen Lewis won the St. Lucia government scholarship for study in Britain and elected to attend the London School of Economics (LSE). Although he had wanted to be an engineer, Lewis knew that neither local industry nor the British government hired blacks in that field. Interested in business and curious about the nature of economics, he chose instead to pursue a bachelor of commerce degree.

In London Lewis discovered his exceptional talent and future career. After receiving his bachelor of commerce degree in 1937, he received an LSE scholarship for a Ph.D. in Economics and rapidly became interested in applying the field's knowledge to practical dilemmas. Especially concerned with the way institutional structures influenced economic problems, he wrote a doctoral thesis on the organization of British industry. The first black at LSE ever appointed as a lecturer, Lewis completed the Ph.D. in 1940, taught at the school (1938–1948), and continued to test economic theory against concrete historical situations.

During the fifteen years following his doctorate, Lewis set in place a basic pattern that would last half a century. Maturing as an intellectual of remarkable range and deep political convictions, he combined his academic endeavors with constant service in government and public administration. Joining the Fabian Society, the intellectual ally of Britain's Labour Party, he wrote pamphlets on the exploitation of indigenous labor in the West Indies and the problems of administering Britain's mixed economy. Working through the United Kingdom's Colonial Office, he argued that Britain should grant political independence and economic assistance to the nations that made up its empire. In 1947 Lewis married Gladys Jacobs, a teacher from Grenada whom he met through the League of Colonial Peoples, an organization much like the American National Association for the Advancement of Colored People (NAACP); they had two daughters.

In 1948 Lewis accepted a position as professor of political economy at the University of Manchester. In addition to publishing his dissertation, he published two more books before the end of the decade, *Economic Survey 1919–1939* and *Principles of Economic Planning* (both 1949). Whereas other scholars described the late 1920s as a period of global prosperity, Lewis's *Survey* noted the weakness of agricultural prices on the world market and provided new answers to questions that historians had typically explored without the benefit of economic analysis. In his treatment of planning, written before cold war tensions made such accounts much more common, Lewis provided a critical argument regarding the problems produced when a central state attempted to control a nation's economy. Noting that centralized planning demanded that a government direct not only the production of a specific good but also all the component parts of its manufacture as well as its substitutes and complements, he argued that coordination would require an army of functionaries and, in the end, result in highly standardized, low-quality goods. A social democrat with an optimistic view of the potential for long-term capitalist growth to improve popular welfare, Lewis rejected both laissez-faire and centralized control in favor of manipulation of the price mechanism and money flows to harness market forces and ensure that the benefits of economic expansion be widely shared.

Lewis's historical analysis and research in problems of political economy won critical acclaim, but his work in development theory made him one of the most influential economists of his generation. In a 1954 article, "Economic Development with Unlimited Supplies of Labour," published in the journal *Manchester School*, he made an intellectual breakthrough that profoundly changed the way both academics and policy makers came to understand the nature of growth in the poorer countries of the world. Where equilibrium models accepted the neoclassical assumption of a limited supply of labor, he argued that many poor nations, unlike the industrialized countries of Western Europe, were characterized by "dual economies." Although the marginal productivity of labor might be high in the small capitalist industrial and commercial sectors of these countries, he claimed that the population engaged in subsistence agriculture, "petty retail trading," domestic service, and informal, sporadic work in urban areas was so large, relative to available resources, that marginal productivity in these areas was negligible. This "disguised unemployment," however, presented a hidden opportunity because workers, including women kept in the home by social mores, could be moved into the commercial and industrial sectors at a wage set by the subsistence level plus an increment just large enough to encourage the transfer. Once this shift started to take place, employment and productivity in the dynamic, capitalist sectors rose, and as long as the labor surplus existed, wages remained constant. As the share of capitalist profits in the nation's income increased, reinvestment and savings promoted rapid economic growth in the poor country until, finally, the labor surplus was exhausted, demand for more workers led to wage increases, and expansion slowed.

Placing that model of development in an open system, Lewis cautioned that attempts to improve productivity in the commercial sector, if directed toward export purposes, could erode the terms of trade. Increasing efficiency in producing crops for foreign markets, he commented, often only lowered prices by raising international supply. Profits and investment, he argued, were the engines of growth; but applying capital to many export industries would only benefit the foreign consumer.

Lewis's dual economy model met with criticism from a range of sources. Many colleagues objected to the idea of a labor surplus so large that a negligible marginal productivity in "subsistence" sectors would allow for labor transfers without output loss. Others claimed that he ignored the fact that the gap between urban and rural wages often grew dramatically and attacked his claim that industrial wages would stay close to rural income. Critics on the left also rejected his assumption that a nascent capitalist class would automatically reinvest profits and lamented the apparent policy implication, later accepted by some African and Asian countries, that import-substituting industrialization could be pursued without attention to problems of rural development.

Lewis did not solve all the problems critics raised. He did argue, however, that he had never meant to endorse an exclusive focus on industrial growth. The path to development, he explained, could be pursued in rural, capitalist agriculture or mining as well as urban industry. His work, moreover, opened up new avenues of inquiry, inspired a massive literature on growth patterns, and was soon applied by economic historians working on India and Japan, for example, and even such problems as illegal immigration in the United States. In elaborating on the problem of foreign capital investment in export sectors, Lewis provided a compelling explanation of the means by which colonialism had helped create a world divided into poorer agricultural nations and wealthy urban industrial ones. In 1955 he expanded on his insights in *The Theory of Economic Growth*, one of the first textbooks in the field of development economics.

Over the next thirty years, Lewis continued to play a major role both in academia and in the formulation of public policy. After leaving Manchester in 1958, he became principal of the University College of the West Indies in 1959 and was appointed vice chancellor of the institution when it was enlarged and made autonomous from the University of London in 1962. In 1963 he moved to the United States to become a professor of economics and international affairs at Princeton University until retiring in 1983. He also continued to dedicate himself to the problems of economic policy making in West Africa and the Caribbean. Between 1957 and 1970 he complemented his academic duties by working as economic adviser to the Ghanaian prime minister Kwame Nkrumah, the deputy managing director of the United Nations Special Fund, and the director of Jamaica's Industrial Development Corporation. Taking a leave from Princeton, he also served as president of the Caribbean Development Bank from 1970 to 1973. Hoping to foster rural development, he argued for democratic institutions over single-party systems.

In later life Lewis continued to publish and from 1978 to 1980 was a member of the Economic Advisory Council of the NAACP. By the time he died, Lewis had become one of the most respected social scientists of his generation. Knighted by Queen Elizabeth II in 1963, he shared the 1979 Nobel Prize in Economics with Theodore Schultz. A thinker and policy maker whose belief that market forces could be harnessed for progressive, reformist goals, Lewis was often at the center of contentious debate. He died in Barbados.

FURTHER READING

Lewis's papers are in Princeton University's Seeley G. Mudd Manuscript Library.

Bhagwati, Jagdish N. "W. Arthur Lewis: An Appreciation," in *The Theory and Experience of Economic Development*, ed. Mark Gersovitz et al. (1982).

Breit, William, and Roger W. Spencer, eds. *Lives of the Laureates: Seven Nobel Economists* (1986).

Leeson, P. F. "The Lewis Model and Development Theory," *Manchester School* 47 (1979): 196–210.

Meier, Gerald M., and Dudley Seers, eds. *Pioneers in Development* (1984).

Obituaries: *Washington Post* and *New York Times*, 17 June 1991.

This entry is taken from the *American National Biography* and is published here with the permission of the American Council of Learned Societies.

MICHAEL E. LATHAM

Lewis, William Charles, II (13 Sept. 1879–5 June 1956), professor, coach, and civic leader, was born in Chester, South Carolina, the eldest of sixteen children of William Charles and Susie (Jackson) Lewis. Only five of the children lived past early childhood. Lewis's father was born on 11 March 1854, the son of an enslaved woman. He was permitted to obtain an education by learning with the white children of the household and, later, by attending public school. He later taught school in Chester County, South Carolina. He and Susie, always a homemaker, raised their surviving children in a two-story house and farm on York Road in Chester.

William Charles Lewis II attended the Brainard Academy in Chester, a private school of the Presbyterian Church. He graduated with a three-year trade certificate in harness making from Virginia's Hampton Normal and Agricultural Institute (later Hampton University) and in 1907 was a football player and coach at South Carolina State College (later South Carolina State University) in Orangeburg. He fulfilled the requirements of the summer school of physical education at the International Young Men's Christian Association College in Springfield, Massachusetts, in 1925.

Lewis married Alethia Minnie Lightner on 9 September 1914 at Mount Carmel Presbyterian Church in Chester. She was the third-youngest of thirteen children and came from a family of well-known builders whose high-quality work can still be seen in houses, churches, and businesses throughout the Carolinas. The Lightner Funeral Home has been a pillar of the Raleigh, North Carolina, community for six generations. She was an inspirational teacher who labored in a one-room schoolhouse in Orangeburg County, South Carolina, for many years, and then as a first-grade teacher in a segregated elementary school in town. She attended the Mather Academy in Camden, South Carolina, graduated from Shaw University in Raleigh with a bachelor's degree, and earned a master's degree from South Carolina State College. Her children's book about the life of GEORGE WASHINGTON CARVER, *A True Fairy Tale* (1952), illuminated the facts and the values that guided this remarkable man's life. W.C. and Alethia Lewis were the parents of two children, ALETHIA ANNETTE LEWIS HOAGE PHINAZEE and William Charles "Pap" Lewis III. "Pap" Lewis, an educator and coach, was the only African American to retain his position as head coach after desegregation in South Carolina. The family also owned and operated a farm in the country, growing and processing virtually all the fruit, vegetables, meat and poultry, milk, cheese, and eggs they consumed until the farm was taken by eminent domain in the early 1950s.

Affectionately known as "Dad," W.C. Lewis was a major contributor to the academic and athletic life of South Carolina State College for forty years, and the engineering building is named for him in recognition of that service. An authoritative and strategic leader, he stressed the mastery of, and taught, the importance of strong fundamentals of football, basketball and tennis. As a football and baseball coach, Lewis, along with Georgia State College President Benjamin J. Hubert and others, saw the need for an organization that would regulate competitions among historically black colleges and universities in the region and founded the Georgia–South Carolina Intercollegiate Athletic Association in 1913. The association later changed its name to the South Atlantic Intercollegiate Athletic Conference, later known as the MEAC–NCAA Division One Mid-Eastern Athletic Conference.

Lewis was also a civic leader and organizer. He was secretary of the Orangeburg Colored County Fair, taking responsibility for organizing the fair, with all of its entertainment and revenues, for many years. The fair was an important source of revenue for local African American businesspeople and entertainers who had few other outlets in the area. In addition to providing leadership to formal organizations, he and a small group of men from the college played croquet every Sunday evening and quietly planned a strategic approach to improving conditions in the segregated life of African American Orangeburg. Picket lines (and later boycotts) were organized at the Sunbeam Bread factory in 1948 to force the issue of hiring black workers. Soon after the *Brown v. Board of Education* Supreme Court decision of 1954, a total boycott of the downtown merchants was implemented. Lewis's role was an important one; on Saturday mornings he would ride out to meet the farmers who were making their weekly shopping trip into town, telling them, "We are not buying even a spool of thread from these folks until they treat us with respect and give us work. If you will give me your shopping lists, I will get what you need from other places. But we will not shop in Orangeburg" (Personal interview with author). The boycott, though protracted and lasting well into the 1960s, was finally successful in changing the power relationships of blacks to whites in Orangeburg.

Deeply spiritual, Lewis taught Sunday school classes at the college for many years. He also was one of the founders of St. Luke Presbyterian Church and served as one of its elders until his death.

RAMONA HOAGE EDELIN

Lewis, William Henry (28 Nov. 1868–1 Jan. 1949), lawyer, government official, and college athlete, was born in Berkley, Virginia, the eldest son of Ashley Henry and Josephine Baker, both former slaves. Not long after William's birth the family moved to Portsmouth, where Ashley Henry became a minister in the Ebenezer Baptist Church. In 1885 William enrolled in the Virginia Normal and Collegiate Institute in Petersburg, a school for the children of Virginia's African American elites established to fulfill a campaign promise made by the Virginia Readjuster Party, which through a coalition of Republican whites and newly freed African Americans had won control of the state government. At Virginia Normal, William found a mentor in the school's president, JOHN MERCER LANGSTON. When Democrats came back into power in Virginia

in 1887, Langston was fired. William Lewis led a delegation of students to Richmond where they received an audience with Governor Fitzhugh Lee. The students won Langston a reprieve, but the victory was short-lived; Langston resigned a few days later.

Lewis left Virginia Normal without graduating and, with Langston's assistance, entered Amherst College in Massachusetts, where he took up football. He became one of the greatest college centers in the game, even though his opponents outweighed him, at times by as much as forty pounds. Popular with his fellow students, he was elected captain twice by his teammates, and he was chosen to give the class speech at his graduation in 1892. Lewis then entered Harvard Law School, where he played football for two years for Harvard. In both years he was named all-American, the first black so honored. For his final game in 1893 his teammates elected him captain, and on Thanksgiving Day, Harvard beat the University of Pennsylvania 26 to 4.

In 1895 Lewis joined Harvard University's coaching staff, becoming the first black coach at a predominantly white college, and possibly even the first black coach ever. He served as defensive and line coach for Harvard through the 1906 season. He wrote one of the first books about the game, *A Primer of College Football* (1896), which was serialized in *Harper's Round Table* magazine in September 1896. When football came under attack by both the media and the public for its violence in 1905–1906, Lewis was one of the principals who proposed changes to the rules to make it safer. His primary contribution was the creation of the "neutral zone" rule, in which before every play the opposing teams were required to keep the length of the ball between them, a rule that remained in force.

After graduating from Harvard Law School in 1895, Lewis married Elizabeth Baker of Cambridge, Massachusetts. The couple had three children, Dorothy, William Jr., and Elizabeth. The family lived in Cambridge, and Lewis practiced law across the Charles River in Boston. Lewis's accomplishments on the gridiron and in the classroom gave him a position of prestige and respect among Boston's African Americans. When Boston's black elites came out in opposition to the programs of BOOKER T. WASHINGTON, Washington came to Boston to meet with them over dinner to discuss their differences. According to T. THOMAS FORTUNE, during "coffee and cigars" Lewis rose and "told Dr. Washington to go back South, and attend to his work of educating the Negro and 'leave to us the matters political affecting the race.' " Three years later, however, Lewis was one of Washington's most prominent supporters, even introducing Washington at a meeting in Boston in July 1903, an event that became known as the Boston Riot. The *Boston Guardian* newspaper publisher WILLIAM MONROE TROTTER and his supporters attempted to denounce Washington, but the confrontation turned into a melee and the publisher was arrested. W. E. B. DuBois later acknowledged the event as the spark that began the Niagara Movement.

DuBois took credit for bringing Lewis and Washington together, but the true force behind their reconciliation had been President Theodore Roosevelt. In 1901 the president wanted to appoint Lewis assistant U.S. attorney for Boston, but he would do so only on the condition that Lewis agree to cooperate with Washington. Lewis told Roosevelt that although he did not support Washington's methods of accommodation, he would agree to work with him "for the benefit of the race." In 1910 President William Howard Taft, fearing that black voters would desert the Republican Party at the midterm elections, named Lewis assistant attorney general of the United States, the highest federal office ever held by an African American. Lewis held the post for more than two years, until the inauguration of the Democratic president Woodrow Wilson, after which the new attorney general, J. C. McReynolds, demanded Lewis's resignation.

Lewis returned to Boston and resumed his law practice. Over the next few years he garnered headlines for his defense of men charged in crimes with racial overtones. In 1916 he defended an African American man in Rhode Island accused of conspiring with two other black men and a white woman to kill her husband, a doctor. The jury acquitted the wife but found the men guilty. In 1921 Lewis defended a Cape Verdean immigrant accused of raping a white woman on Cape Cod and won the first successful motion in Massachusetts history to change venue. Lewis fought side by side with the NAACP to ban the 1915 film *The Birth of a Nation*, unsuccessfully in 1915 and successfully in 1921. He joined the NAACP's legal battles against lynching and race-based property covenants (*Corrigan v. Buckley*). A few weeks before the election of 1924, Lewis, a lifelong Republican, broke from the party, which he believed had fallen under the influence of the Ku Klux Klan. He announced his support of the Democrat John W. Davis for president, even though the Republican candidate, Calvin Coolidge, had been a schoolmate at Amherst.

Lewis by that time had aligned himself with several of Boston's Irish American lawyers, and the association made him quite wealthy. He formed a partnership with Matthew McGrath, a former U.S. marshal, and thanks to their combined connections with the federal courts the firm represented more alleged bootleggers than any other in New England. When one of Boston's leading criminal lawyers, Daniel Coakley, was disbarred in 1922, he began referring many of his high-profile (and high-profit) cases to Lewis, including the defense of the famous swindler Charles Ponzi before the U.S. Supreme Court. In 1930 another Coakley referral gave Lewis his first win before the nation's high court with *U.S. v. Farrar*.

Lewis was able to return the favor to Coakley in 1941 by defending Coakley before the Massachusetts Senate in the commonwealth's first impeachment hearing in more than a century. Lewis continued to practice law until his death. In his final month he appeared on the front page of Boston newspapers conducting a successful defense in what became known as the Revere Bribery Trial; two days before his death the *Berkshire Eagle* wrote of his intention to file an appeal for a client before the U.S. Supreme Court. Lewis died of a heart attack in his Boston apartment. A crowd estimated at more than a thousand, including the governor and governor-elect, attended his high requiem Mass.

FURTHER READING

Fox, Stephen R. *The Guardian of Boston: William Monroe Trotter* (1970).

Langston, John Mercer. *From the Virginia Plantation to the National Capitol, or The First and Only Negro Representative in Congress from the Old Dominion* (1894).

Smith, J. Clay, Jr. *Emancipation: The Making of the Black Lawyer 1844–1944* (1993).

Smith, Ronald A., ed. *Big-Time Football at Harvard 1905: The Diary of Coach Bill Reid* (1994).

EVAN J. ALBRIGHT

Liele, George (c. 1751–1828), pioneering Baptist clergyman and émigré to Jamaica, said of his slave origins, "I was born in Virginia, my father's name was Liele, and my mother's name Nancy; I cannot ascertain much of them, as I went to several parts of America when young, and at length resided in New Georgia" (*Baptist Annual Register*, ed. John Rippon [1793], 332). Liele's master Henry Sharp took him to Burke County, Georgia, as a young man. Liele wrote that he "had a natural fear of God" from his youth. He attended a local Baptist church, was baptized by Matthew Moore, a deacon in the Buckhead Creek Baptist Church about 1772, and was given the opportunity to travel, preaching to both whites and blacks. Liele preached as a probationer for about three years at Bruton Land, Georgia, and at Yamacraw, about a half mile from Savannah. The favorable response to Liele's "ministerial gifts" caused Sharp, who was a Baptist deacon, to free him. Liele remained with Sharp's family until Sharp's death as a Tory officer during the Revolutionary War when the British occupied Savannah.

Upset over his status as a freeman, some of Sharp's heirs had Liele imprisoned. Liele produced his manumission papers and with the aid of a British colonel named Kirkland resumed his public activities. He gathered a small congregation that included African Americans who had come to Savannah on the promise by the British of their freedom. One of Liele's converts was ANDREW BRYAN, who was later responsible for the development of African American Baptist congregations in Savannah. DAVID GEORGE, the pioneering organizer of black Baptist congregations in Nova Scotia and Sierra Leone, also was one of Liele's converts. Despite increasing anxiety over escalating American-British hostilities, Liele continued to hold worship services.

When the British evacuated Savannah in 1782, Liele went as an indentured servant with Kirkland to Kingston, Jamaica. After working two years to satisfy his indebtedness to Kirkland, Liele received a certificate of freedom, and about 1784 he began to preach in a small house in Kingston to what he called a "good smart congregation." It was organized with four other blacks who had come from America. The congregation eventually purchased property in the east end of Kingston and constructed a brick meetinghouse. Liele reported that raising money to pay for the new building was difficult because his congregation was composed mostly of slaves whose masters allowed "but three or four bits per week" out of which to pay for their food. The free people who belonged to Liele's church were generally poor.

Despite initial opposition from some whites, Liele's congregation grew to about 350 members by 1790. It included a few whites. Liele accepted Methodists after they had been baptized by immersion, but in a pragmatic move he did not receive slaves as members without, as he wrote, "a few lines from their owners of their good behavior toward them and religion." Liele assisted in the organization of other congregations on the island and promoted free schools for slaves as well as free black Jamaicans. On his ministerial activities Liele wrote in the early 1790s: "I have deacons and elders, a few; and teachers of small congregations in the town and country, where convenience suits them to come together; and I am pastor. I preach twice on the Lord's Day, in the forenoon and afternoon, and twice in the week, and have not been absent six Sabbath days since I formed the church in this country. I receive nothing for my services; I preach, baptize, administer the Lord's Supper, and travel from one place to another to publish the gospel and settle church affairs, all freely." By 1797 Liele had reason to be more pessimistic. Originally charged with "seditious preaching" because he was the leader of so many slaves, he was thrown into prison where he remained for three years, five months, and ten days. The charge of seditious preaching was dismissed, but his inability to satisfy debts incurred in the building of his church kept him in prison. During Liele's imprisonment his eldest son conducted preaching services.

When Liele was about forty years old he reported that he had three sons and one daughter. His four children ranged in age from nineteen to eleven. His wife, whose name is unknown, had been baptized with him in Savannah. Liele worked as a farmer and teamster besides conducting regular worship services and conducting church business. George Liele has the distinction of being the first regularly ordained African American Baptist minister in America. He is also noteworthy as the founder of the first Baptist church in Jamaica. Liele reported in 1790, "There is no Baptist church in this country but ours." An article sent to British Baptists in 1796 said of Jamaican Baptists whom Liele led: "They preach every Lord's day from 10 to 12 o'clock in the morning, and from 4 to 6 in the evening; and on Tuesday and Thursday evening, from seven to eight. They administer the Lord's supper every month, and baptism once in three months. The members are divided into smaller classes which meet separately every Monday evening, to be examined respecting their daily walk and conversation." Details regarding the last few decades prior to Liele's death in Jamaica are not known.

Liele's pioneering work in establishing the Baptist Church in Jamaica set the foundation for a denominational tradition that continued until the late twentieth century. Apart from being the spiritual father of the Jamaican black Baptist churches, he was the first missionary from any African American church body to the island and may well have been the first African American to be ordained a Baptist preacher. Although nothing is known of his political and social views, he seems to have considered his primary work that of preaching the Christian Gospel and caring for the spiritual welfare of his members.

FURTHER READING

Davis, John W. "George Liele and Andrew Bryan, Pioneer Negro Baptist Preachers," *Journal of Negro History* 3 (Apr. 1918): 119–27.

"Letters Showing the Rise and Progress of the Early Negro Churches of Georgia and the West Indies," *Journal of Negro History* 1 (Jan. 1916): 69–92.

Rusling, G. W. "A Note on Early Negro Baptist History," *Foundations* 11 (Oct.–Dec. 1968): 362–68.

This entry is taken from the *American National Biography* and is published here with the permission of the American Council of Learned Societies.

MILTON C. SERNETT

Lightfoot, George Morton (25 Dec. 1868–24 Dec. 1947), professor of Latin, educator, and editor, was born in the small town of Culpepper in the Blue Ridge Mountains of Virginia. He was the youngest son of James M. and Letetia B. Lightfoot. A teacher in the area, Enoch H. Grastie (also known as Grasty), who had earned a certificate from the Preparatory Department at Howard University in 1872, took an interest in the young Lightfoot and helped him get additional training in Washington, D.C. Lightfoot was able to study at the Howard University Academy from 1884 to 1887. In the fall of 1888 Lightfoot matriculated at Williams College as a sophomore. There he majored in Latin and took German as an elective. Among his professors was Edward Parmalee Morris, who taught Latin from 1885 to 1981 at Williams College. Lightfoot was a member of Williams College's Classical Society and along with fifty-eight other young men was awarded his B.A. degree in June 1891.

With the recommendation of George J. Cummings, principal of the Preparatory Department of Howard University and also professor of Latin and Greek, Lightfoot was appointed to the faculty of the Preparatory Department. This department dated back to 1867, the year Howard University was

founded, and its purpose was the training of students for the Collegiate Department. Lightfoot taught Latin, French and German, history, and mathematics. In 1912 he was appointed as professor of Latin in the college department, where he remained until his retirement in 1939. On 16 July 1916 he married Susie Fry, who hailed from his hometown. They lived in the Vinegar Hill section of Washington, D.C. Both their sons, George M. Lightfoot Jr. and James Cornelius Lightfoot, served in World War II and later pursued professional careers in the civil service and in law.

While teaching at Howard University, Lightfoot attended Catholic University of America as a special student from 1898 to 1900, and in 1901 he enrolled as a regular student in order to pursue his M.A. degree in Latin. His adviser was Professor Roy J. Deferrari, who had earned his Ph.D. at Princeton University in 1915 with a dissertation on the Greek satirist Lucian. Lightfoot wrote his M.A. thesis on Roman satire and, although the original work has disappeared from the archives at Catholic University, a version of his thesis was published in 1923 in the *Howard Review* under the title "The Question of the Roman Satire."

On 9 March 1921 he applied for graduation. A few months later Catholic University of America, which in 1914 began to limit the number of students of African descent on campus, began the process of closing down admission to black students completely. In November of 1921 a sweeping policy of segregation was implemented by executive order and, except for a few nuns who were admitted in 1933, no black students were allowed to attend Catholic University again until 1936. Lightfoot was one of the few students admitted between 1914 and 1921, but the executive order of 1921 ended his hope of earning a Ph.D. in Latin. Lightfoot was permitted to graduate in 1922 with his M.A., but the vice rector instructed Professor Deferrari to mail Lightfoot's diploma to him and to make certain that he was prevented from participating in the official commencement exercises.

During his years at Howard he served his discipline as member of the American Classical League and the Classical Association of the Atlantic States. He also founded the Classical Club at Howard. In 1930 Lightfoot organized a celebration of the 2,000th anniversary of the birth of the Roman poet Virgil and a special program was held on 23 April 1930 in the Andrew Rankin Memorial Chapel, which included a musical accompaniment. He also organized a special exhibit to coincide with the celebration for display in the Carnegie Library on campus. The address he gave for the occasion, *Bimillennium Vergilianum: Vergil through the Ages*, was published by Howard University in 1932 as a twenty-two-page pamphlet.

He was editor-in-chief of the *Howard University Record* from 1919 to 1924, chairman of Howard University's Community Chest, and was appointed by President Theodore Roosevelt to the District of Columbia Board of Charities. Lightfoot was an avid sports fan all of his life and had a particular interest in swimming, baseball, and tennis. In January 1925 he wrote an account of the 1924 Lincoln-Howard football game played in Griffith Stadium that was published in the *Howard University Record*. In the wider community he directed the Howard University Summer School from 1925 to 1932. He was also the faculty sponsor of the Women's Tennis Club.

In January 1938 a number of his friends formed the George M. Lightfoot Portrait Fund Committee. The Committee began to solicit donations toward the goal of six hundred dollars for a portrait to be hung in the Art Gallery or the Founder's Library at Howard University in honor of Lightfoot's forty-seven years of service and his status at that time as the senior member of the faculty. In 1945, with a sum of five thousand dollars, he established the George M. Lightfoot Scholarship Fund in the Department of Classics, which continues today to help an outstanding student of the classics defray college expenses. His name was included among the entries for the *Encyclopedia Africana* planned by CARTER G. WOODSON.

Lightfoot was a member of the Berean Baptist Church for more than twenty-five years and a trustee for at least twelve. He was one of a large group of African Americans from the nineteenth and early twentieth century who trained in classical languages, and then taught them at black colleges and universities across the United States.

FURTHER READING

Nuesse, C. Joseph. "Segregation and Desegregation at the Catholic University of America," *Washington History* (Spring-Summer 1947).

Ronnick, Michele Valerie. "George Morton Lightfoot (1868–1941)," *Classical Outlook* 80 (2002).

Obituary: *Journal of Negro History* 33 (1948); *Pittsburgh Courier*, 3 Jan. 1948.

MICHELE VALERIE RONNICK

Lightner, Gwendolyn (1925–22 Aug. 1999), gospel pianist and arranger, was born Gwendolyn Rosetta Capps in Brookport, Illinois, the daughter of Mase and Florence Capps. Gwendolyn was the fourth of six children. At an early age she manifested some musical disposition by pretending to play piano on her father's razor stand and her mother's sewing machine. Her father died in 1934 and Gwendolyn was raised by her mother. To help the promising Gwendolyn pursue a musical education, a local family donated a piano to her mother. After high school she studied classical music and piano at Southern Illinois University at Carbondale and at the Lyon & Healy Academy of Music in Chicago.

In the early 1940s she settled in Chicago, where she was introduced to gospel music while attending a service at a Shiloh Baptist Church. Chicago was then the emerging national center of black gospel music with a galaxy of stars including THOMAS DORSEY, MAHALIA JACKSON, and Roberta Martin. After hearing gospel music at Shiloh, Gwendolyn went to a music store to buy records. There she met the storeowner, Emma L. Jackson, who hired her as the pianist and arranger for her group, the Emma L. Jackson Singers. At some point in her career the young pianist married Peter Lightner, who might have been her second husband. Some literature assigns her the last name Cooper prior to the latter marriage. She gave birth to seven children.

Lightner toured with SALLIE MARTIN and in 1946 traveled with the Jackson Singers to California. Soon Lightner resettled in Los Angeles, where she founded a music teaching studio, the Los Angeles Gospel Music Mart. By moving to California Lightner served as a channel through which gospel music reached the West Coast. In 1946 the Reverend John L. Branham, pastor of St. Paul Baptist Church, hired her and J. Earle Hines to develop a local church choir, Echoes of Eden. The following year St. Paul Baptist Church began a radio program on KFWB for which Echoes of Eden became the featured choir. In April 1947 Echoes of Eden, with Lightner as pianist, released its first album, *I Am So Glad Jesus Lifted Me*, produced by Capitol Records. Echoes of Eden thus became one of the first gospel choirs to produce a commercial record. Two months later Capitol Records released *What Could I Do If it Wasn't for the Lord*, Echoes's second major album.

Traditionally gospel artists had used blues and jazz, but Lightner blended European music with black singing and developed a unique gospel piano style. Her music sounded different from the Chicago style of gospel by making limited use of rhythm and improvisation. Concurrent with her tenure at St. Paul, Lightner also worked with a female trio, the

Rose of Sharon (1946–1949), and the J. Earle Hines Goodwill Singers (1947–1949). Lightner's musical performances turned her church into the major center of black gospel music on the West Coast. Soon churches from Baptist, Pentecostal, and other denominations developed their own gospel choirs that imitated the Lightner Style, radio programs, and television broadcasts. Lightner's outstanding musical standing won her the title of the "Queen of West Coast gospel piano."

Lightner left St. Paul in 1949 and worked at various times as pianist and choir leader for several churches in the Los Angeles area, including Grace Memorial Church of God in Christ and Mt. Moriah Baptist Church. In 1956 the First Bethany Baptist Church welcomed her as its minister of music. In the 1950s she joined the J. Earle Hines Community Choir and the Sallie Martin Singers. In 1957 she and Thurston G. Frazier organized the Voices of Hope, another community choir that became well known on the West Coast, and with whom she produced two albums on the Capitol label, *We've Come This Far by Faith* and *Walk On by Faith*.

The St. Paul radio broadcast—eventually heard by one million people in seventeen states—and the Echoes albums served as models for numerous church choirs and made Lightner popular within the national gospel music circuit. She performed as guest pianist on Specialty Records albums by the Pilgrim Travelers, the Soul Stirrers, and Brother Joe May. Working with both Baptist and non-Baptist churches and other groups further contributed to the popularization of the Lightner Style, which influenced such great artists as Margaret Pleasant Douroux and Albert A. Goodson.

In the 1960s Lightner provided piano accompaniment for Doris Akers on RCA Records. In 1968 Mahalia Jackson hired her as her pianist, which further increased her fame. Until Jackson's death in 1972 she and Lightner made joint world concert tours and television appearances that publicized the beauty and glamour of black gospel music. In the 1990s Lightner still worked at the First Bethany Baptist Church. She also served as director of music for the Western Baptist State Convention and Congress of Christian Education (CCE) and as pianist for the National Baptist Convention USA and its national CCE. In the late 1990s she became ill with cancer and died in Los Angeles.

FURTHER READING

Dje, Jacqueline Cogdell. "The California Black Gospel Music Tradition: A Confluence of Musical Styles and Cultures," in *California Soul: Music of African Americans in the West*, eds. Jacqueline Cogdell DjeDje and Eddie S. Meadows (1998).

Dje, Jacqueline Cogdell. "Lightner, Gwendolyn," in *Black Women in America: An Historical Encyclopedia*, ed. Darlene Clark Hine (1993).

Goreau, Laurraine. *Just Mahalia, Baby* (1975).

Saffle, Michael, ed. *Perspectives on American Music, 1900–1950* (2000).

Obituary: *Los Angeles Times*, 6 Sept. 1999.

DAVID MICHEL

Lightnin' Hopkins. *See* Hopkins, Lightnin'.

Ligon, Glenn (20 Apr. 1960–), artist, was born in the Bronx, New York, to Clarence Ligon, an auto plant line supervisor, and Andrena Hooks, a nurse's aide. Reared in the South Bronx, Ligon attended Walden School, a progressive private school in Manhattan on scholarship beginning in 1966 and graduating with his high school diploma in 1978. In the fall he enrolled as a studio art major at Wesleyan University in Middletown, Connecticut. Later, in 1981, he also studied briefly at the Rhode Island School of Design in Providence, Rhode Island. It was at Wesleyan that he first exhibited his work—a series of abstract paintings done for his senior thesis—at the school's Davison Art Center in 1982; that same year he earned his bachelor's degree in Studio Art. In the fall of 1984 Ligon studied at the prestigious Whitney Museum Independent Study Program in New York.

Although he began his career as an abstract painter, beginning in the 1990s Ligon's text-based art established his reputation as a conceptual artist. Over the years, Ligon employed a variety of media to explore the representation of race, language, sexuality, and history in his art. In addition to writings by African American authors, Ligon's art borrowed from a wide-ranging historical archive of black cultural sites: runaway slave posters, slave narratives, comedy sketches by RICHARD PRYOR, black-themed coloring books from the 1970s, music, and the Million Man March on Washington, D.C., in 1995. Appropriating and then revising texts representing black experience in the United States, Ligon returned often to the forms, imagery, and words meant to portray and authenticate black life in order to think about how his own black, gay, modern self might correspond with or trouble these artifacts and histories.

In his untitled etchings from the early 1990s, Ligon borrowed sentences or phrases penned by well-known black authors such as ZORA NEALE HURSTON, RALPH WALDO ELLISON, and JAMES BALDWIN. For example, using charcoal dust upon white canvas, Ligon stenciled Hurston's famous words, "I Feel Most Colored When I Am Thrown Against a Sharp White Background," a phrase taken from her essay, "How It Feels to be Colored Me." Reproducing the phrase multiple times and filling the canvas, each descending row of text became less distinct and ultimately, illegible as the stencil picked up and transferred the black medium across the canvas, eventually blurring the distinction between the individual letters and between the black ink medium and the white backdrop. Reproducing a progressively disintegrating and illegible version of the quotation suggested that the representation of blackness always entails a distinct representation of whiteness as well. And the diminishing visibility of the text at the bottom of the canvas suggests that racial blackness has always been a complex interplay between visual spectacle and narrative. In this and in much of Ligon's other work, he confronted the ways that the documenting of black experience has been both delimited and made possible through the way we see as well as how (and what) we read.

Ligon juxtaposed readings of black history and culture with his own autobiography, and Ligon's work both recuperated and reworked earlier narratives and images, for example, his installation, *To Disembark* (1993) referenced the voyage of HENRY BOX BROWN, who mailed himself to freedom in 1849. Various sounds—Ligon reading from Brown's narrative and samples from rap music, spirituals, reggae, African American shout songs, and disco—emanated from a series of boxes marked "Fragile." *Narratives*, a series of lithographs with written descriptions meant to mimic the literary convention and visual form of slave narratives and wanted posters from the 1800s, accompanied this installation. Using nineteenth-century-style illustrations and typefaces, Ligon portrayed the details of his own identity as a modern, black, gay man. Updated with contemporary autobiographical details while retaining the old-fashioned aesthetic of nineteenth-century slave narratives, a mock frontispiece read, "The Narrative of the Life and Uncommon Sufferings of Glenn Ligon, A colored man, who at a tender age discovered his affection for the bodies of other men, and has endured scorn and tribulations ever since. Written By Himself." Evoking the form and titles of early slave narratives like, *The Interesting

Narrative of the Life of Olaudah Equiano, or Gustavus Vassa, the African, Written by Himself*, Ligon cannily revisits elements of the slave narrative genre, providing an autobiographical account of his personal experience as a modern gay black man and at the same time rupturing the formal aspects of those historical and literary documents with his personal history. By reproducing the form and tone of nineteenth-century representations of black subjectivity, Ligon captured the residual effects of racism upon his own experience and suggested other, hidden histories ignored in the formalism and endurance of those early documents of black life.

Taking up a modern depiction of black bodies, originally rendered through the eyes of a white artist, in 1993 Ligon's *Notes on the Margin of the "Black Book"* was exhibited at the Whitney Biennial. This exhibition offered a rereading of photographer Robert Mapplethorpe's *Black Book* by reproducing the erotic images of nude, black men originally captured by Mapplethorpe's camera. In an effort to recontextualize and complicate the representation of sexualized blackness, Ligon displayed Mapplethorpe's work, but with a difference: he added comments, responses, and critiques by notable black intellectuals such as ISAAC JULIEN, BELL HOOKS, and KOBENA MERCER, which were framed and then situated in between two rows of Mapplethorpe's photographs as if to offer a mediating influence and a running critique and conversation along the length of the display.

In 2003 Ligon launched an interactive digital exhibition (www.diacenter.org/ligon), *Annotations*. Much like his earlier work *Feast of Scraps* (1994–1998), Ligon used the personal archive of the family photo album as a way of thinking about the construction of African American identity. *Feast of Scraps* juxtaposed family photos with pornographic images of black men and captions such as "Mother knew," imposing, or perhaps excavating homosexual bodies and desire from the pages of the family photo album, Ligon's assemblage of snapshots recorded what is excluded from the definition of "family" and at the same time documented a wider network of intimate associations outside the boundaries of the family as a vital and neglected part of a gay man's personal history. Similarly, in *Annotations*, clicking on individual photos led the viewer to other "layers" of text, images, and sound that seemingly provided a back story for the initial images and encouraged the reader to reconcile the words and song with varied visual content of the album. The captions neither necessarily identified nor particularized the individuals. Instead, ironic and hopeful phrases such as "Future President of the United States" were written beneath the photo of a young, black unidentified child. What has been preserved in the family archive gives way to other stories, other signatures of memory, and desires that often remain undocumented or unclaimed in the family's need to represent itself.

The year 2006 brought an internationally touring retrospective of Ligon's work titled *Some Changes* organized by Toronto's the Power Plant. The exhibit traveled to the Contemporary Art Museum in Houston, the Andy Warhol Museum in Pittsburgh, the Wexner Center for the Arts in Ohio, and finally to the Musée d'Art Moderne Grand-Duc Jean in Luxembourg.

Ligon won multiple prestigious awards and fellowships, among them the Visual Artists Fellowship from the National Endowment for the Arts (1989 and 1991) and a residency from the Rockefeller Foundation at the Bellagio Study Center in Bellagio, Italy (1994). He has also received a Joan Mitchell Foundation Grant (1997), a John Simon Guggenheim Memorial Foundation Fellowship (2003), the Alphonse Fletcher Sr. Fellowship (2005), awards from the American Academy of Arts and Letters (2006), and the Skowhegan Medal for Painting (2006).

FURTHER READING

Glenn Ligon's art is housed in the permanent collection of the Philadelphia Museum of Modern Art, the Museum of Modern Art, the Whitney Museum of American Art, the San Francisco Museum of Modern Art, and many others.

Ligon, Glenn. *Glenn Ligon—Some Changes* (2005).

Ligon, Glenn. "Narratives," *Yale Journal of Criticism* (1994).

Connor, Kimberly Rae. "'To Disembark': The Slave Narrative Tradition," African American Review (1996).

Firstenberg, Lauri. "Neo-Archival and Textual Modes of Production: An Interview with Glenn Ligon," Art Journal (Spring 2001).

Meyer, Richard. "Borrowed Voices: Glenn Ligon and the Force of Language" (1998). Available at http://www.queerculturalcenter.org/Pages/Ligon/LigonEssay.html.

Middleman, Rachel. "History with a Small 'H': A Conversation with Glenn Ligon," *GLQ: A Journal of Lesbian and Gay Studies* (2006).

JACQUELINE ASHER

Lincoln, Abbey (6 Aug. 1930–14 Aug. 2010), singer, composer, and actress, was born Anna Marie Wooldridge in Chicago, the tenth of the twelve children of Alexander Wooldridge, a home builder, and Evalina (Coffey) Wooldridge, a healer and homemaker. The family lived in rural Calvin Center and then Kalamazoo, Michigan, where the young Anna Marie was drawn to their upright piano and spent hours quietly picking out melodies. A participant in her high school's "Band Follies" and local amateur contests, she eventually graduated to work as a professional supper club singer. After two years in Honolulu, Hawaii, she began to perform at the Moulin Rouge in Los Angeles under the stage name Gaby Lee.

During this time she met the lyricist Bob Russell, who penned such classics as "Crazy He Calls Me" and "Do Nothing Till You Hear From Me." He became her manager, renaming her Abbey Lincoln (Abbey as in London's Westminster Abbey, and Lincoln as in President Abraham Lincoln). Perhaps sensing her literary talents, Russell encouraged Lincoln to read books on semantics and introduced her to the qualities needed for good lyrics: succinctness, coherent storytelling, and originality. His more immediate contributions to her career included securing her first record date and movie appearance. In 1956 she made the album *Affair ... Story of a Girl in Love* under the leadership of the arrangers Marty Paich and Benny Carter, and the film *The Girl Can't Help It*, starring Jayne Mansfield. Her powerful, if mannered, voice was stylistically in keeping with cabaret; however, Lincoln drew as much attention for her appearance as for her musical talent: she posed for the album cover almost upside-down, breasts overflowing from the bodice of her dress. As a result of the movie, she became known as "the black Marilyn Monroe," not only for her great beauty but also because she had worn that starlet's gown from *Gentlemen Prefer Blondes*.

Lincoln's fame had personal consequences as well. She grew uncomfortable with her glamorous yet superficial public image. Moreover, she realized that the standard repertoire offered few alternatives to the usual boy-meets-girl scenarios—many of which seemed to celebrate no-good men—or images of femininity as dictated by white, middle class society. She tossed Monroe's dress into an incinerator, began to wear her hair natural, and reconsidered her choice of material. As an expression of racial pride she started to call herself a jazz singer. In fact, her

Abbey Lincoln performs in New York City during Jazz at Lincoln Center's Higher Ground Hurricane Relief Benefit Concert on 17 September 2005. (AP Images.)

For Nothin' Joe," Brown wrote "Strong Man," which included the verse,

Hair crisp and curly and cropped kind of close
Picture a lover like this.
Lips warm and full that I love the most
Smiling between every kiss.

Lincoln also sang Brown's setting of the PAUL LAURENCE DUNBAR poem "When Malindy Sings" and Weston's setting of the LANGSTON HUGHES poem "African Lady." For some of the instrumental tunes she chose to record, Lincoln ventured to craft her own texts. By the time she recorded *Straight Ahead* for the journalist Nat Hentoff's Candid label (1960), the album included no material from the popular songbook whatsoever.

Top-flight instrumentalists accompanied her on these outings. Roach, in particular, proved highly influential; their tumultuous relationship began around 1957 and the marriage lasted from 1962 to 1970. A bebop pioneer, he introduced her to many of the music's leading artists—Monk, Kenny Dorham, CHARLES MINGUS, and ERIC DOLPHY— and helped her growing technical knowledge of music. Together they also became involved in the civil rights movement. Lincoln was the voice for his historic *We Insist! Max Roach's Freedom Now Suite* (Candid, 1960); she screamed wordlessly on "Protest," a performance renowned for its intensity. Lincoln's involvement in politics included her leadership of the Cultural Association for Women of African Heritage, an organization that sought to address representations of black women and protested the assassination of Patrice Lumumba at the United Nations in 1961.

Lincoln's outspoken views—coupled with the decline in popular interest in, and financial support for, jazz after the British rock invasion—made finding work difficult for her throughout the 1960s. She acted in the films *Nothing But a Man* (1964) and *For Love of Ivy* (1968), in which she starred with SIDNEY POITIER. When her marriage failed, she returned to Los Angeles, began painting, and taught drama at California State University at Northridge.

It was a life-changing trip to Africa in 1972 that renewed the creative spark in Lincoln's musical career. She traveled with the South African singer Miriam Makeba on a two-month tour through Guinea, Ivory Coast, Liberia, and the former Zaire. Guinean president Sekou Tore gave her the name, "Aminata" (the name of the mother of the Christ child), and the Zairean Commissioner of National

change to singing jazz stylistically was a gradual one. It is difficult to discern when her albums became "jazz" as opposed to "pop;" the first was clearly not a jazz effort, but even the second (*That's Him*, 1957) began to show some of the trappings of jazz.

In contrast to the straightforward treatment of songs on *Affair*, Lincoln's Riverside recordings—*That's Him, It's Magic* (1958), and *Abbey is Blue* (1959)—gradually became more conversational and idiosyncratic, and her pitch became flatter, more nasal, more blues-oriented. As vehicles for expression she turned increasingly towards the compositions of her fellow vocalist and playwright OSCAR BROWN JR., the pianists Randy Weston and THELONIOUS MONK, the saxophonist JOHN COLTRANE, and the drummer MAX ROACH, who later became her husband.

In response to Lincoln's request for a song celebrating the kind of men she knew, thus countering the racist descriptions prevalent in lyrics like "Good

Orientation Sacombi Inongo gave her the name, "Moseka" (the god of love in the form of a maiden), which she used in performance in the years thereafter. Lincoln felt as if she had "come home" and credited the trip with freeing her to write her own songs. The first, "People in Me," celebrated her multi-national/ethnic heritage.

Lincoln's climb back within the music industry took more time. She recorded for small independent labels Inner City and Enja. In 1990 Jean-Philippe Allard signed her to Gitanes (the French arm of Universal), resulting in a total of eleven albums to date. Released on Verve in the United States, the albums not only reestablished Lincoln as a major talent but also placed her on a roster of stellar vocal talents critical to the label's revitalization. A number of her projects coupled her with acclaimed guests: the saxophonist Stan Getz (*You Gotta Pay the Band*, 1991), the pianist Hank Jones (*When There is Love*, 1993), and the dancer SAVION GLOVER (*Who Used to Dance*, 1996).

Most of her work after this time was based on her own songs, with lyrics that can be read as social commentary and autobiography. While she did write about romantic love ("Love Has Gone Away" contained some of her most touching lyrics), Lincoln's songs tended to celebrate other subjects: ancestors ("Evalina Coffey," "Song for My Father"), children ("Conversation with a Baby"), and God ("Down Here Below"). Their guiding aesthetics, which shared much with African creative sensibilities, were allegorical and animistic ("Talking to the Sun," "A Turtle's Dream"). Like her own name, they contained rich wordplay ("I Could Sing It For a Song"). From her perspective, women—the ones "who bring the people"—are not objects or victims, but rather the teachers of children, the griots, or storytellers, the "ones who tell us where we came from" (Personal interview with author). Her message of female empowerment simply had no equivalent among the current standards, instead echoing the sentiments of the 1920s blues queens.

Through her refusal to be defined by the words of others, Lincoln developed a powerful alternative to the standard song and used this new approach as the foundation for her own impassioned performances. She received an NEA Jazz Masters Award in 2003 and held honorary doctorates from the University of Rochester and the New School University. In 2001 Columbia University presented a symposium on her life and works titled "For Love of Abbey." Lincoln died in Manhattan in 2010.

FURTHER READING
Lincoln, Abbey, et al. "Racial Prejudice in Jazz," *DownBeat* (1962).
Enstioe, Wayne, and Janis Stockhouse. *Jazzwomen: Conversations with Twenty-One Musicians* (2004).
Griffin, Farah. *If You Can't Be Free, Be a Mystery: In Search of Billie Holiday* (2001).
Monson, Ingrid. *Freedom Sounds: Jazz, Civil Rights, and Africa 1950–1967* (2005).
Porter, Eric. *What is This Thing Called Jazz? African American Musicians as Artists, Critics, and Activists* (2002).
Obituary: *New York Times*, 14 August 2010.

LARA PELLEGRINELLI

Lincoln, C. Eric (23 July 1924–14 May 2000), professor of religion and culture, was born Charles Eric Lincoln in Athens, Alabama. Lincoln never knew his father, and his mother, Bradonia Lincoln, left the family when he was just four years old. Until late in his life Lincoln was removed from his immediate family, which grew to include six half brothers and sisters. Lincoln was reared instead by his maternal grandmother, "Miss Matt," and grandfather, Less Lincoln, on their farm. They were poor, and a nine-year-old C. Eric was forced to take a job, walking nearly three miles every morning as a delivery boy for a dairy farmer for thirty-five cents a week. At a time when most black children in rural Alabama dropped out of school by the sixth grade, Lincoln was able to enroll in Trinity School, a private missionary academy. He was a bright student who finished high school in three years and spent the last in independent study, graduating in 1941.

Lincoln traveled to Chicago, where he earned a living working at odd jobs and freelance writing. Shortly thereafter he enrolled in LeMoyne College, a small Congregational school (later the United Church of Christ) in Tennessee, to study sociology. He received his bachelor's degree in 1947 and then headed off to the University of Chicago to study law, but he struggled financially and never finished. Instead he returned to Tennessee and enrolled at Nashville's Fisk University, earning a master's degree in 1954. While there he pastored the John Calvin Presbyterian Church from 1953 to 1954 and taught at Fisk.

Soon a University of Chicago seminary dean offered him a scholarship to study theology. Lincoln signed up, earning a bachelor's of divinity in 1956. Lincoln's short time in the pulpit taught him that preaching was not his calling. In 1954 he was appointed to teach religion and philosophy at Clark

University in Atlanta. Two years later he headed to Boston University, where by 1960 he had earned a master's in Education and a Ph.D. in Theology. His "gift," he found, was as a teacher and sociologist, studying black life and religion as a way to prepare the black church for the future.

He began his career in 1954 at Clark. He was a dedicated professor, and students flocked to his informal forums on race relations and faith. Two decades later Clark-Atlanta would launch a formal October lecture series devoted to black religion, naming the series for Lincoln. At the time of his death Lincoln's papers and archives were donated to the Atlanta University Center Robert Woodruff Library.

Lincoln, of course, was not the first black scholar to study black religion, but his research, coming amid the fight for social justice and antisegregation, was the first to reach a wide audience. "In the early '60s, no self-respecting theologian could go through school and not read his books," Ronald Peters, director of the Metro-Urban Institute at the Pittsburgh Theological Seminary, told the *Pittsburgh Post-Gazette* before Lincoln came to town to deliver a lecture. Lincoln's forty years of thoughtful, detailed studies also allowed him to form friendships with a number of notable black religious figures, including MARTIN LUTHER KING JR., whom he knew as a young man.

Among Lincoln's most famous texts was his 1961 volume *The Black Muslims in America*, which grew out of his dissertation at Boston University. Lincoln's work is credited with making the study of the black Muslim movement a legitimate field of inquiry for U.S. scholars. It was Lincoln, in 1956, who coined the term "black Muslim" to refer to followers of ELIJAH MUHAMMAD, onetime leader of the Nation of Islam. Before the publication of his book, most Americans saw black Muslims as a devil-worshipping cult or dismissed them as an esoteric black gang with no religious or political significance.

Lincoln's book also helped bring prominence to the Muslim leader MALCOLM X. The two met in Boston before Lincoln's book on Muslims was published and, despite their different faiths, they quickly became confidantes. "We hit it off right away and would visit each other and have conversations all night long," Lincoln told the *Pittsburgh Post-Gazette* in 1998. "We'd solve the problems of the world."

The friendship ended when Malcolm X was gunned down in a Harlem hotel in the winter of 1965. Lincoln, then doing a postdoctoral internship at Brown University, recalled speaking with Malcolm a few days before his assassination to invite him to lecture at Brown. The conversation was an unsettling one. Malcolm was disturbed, Lincoln recalled, and "I had never seen him somber. He told me, 'I'll do anything you ask me to do if I'm alive. [Soon] I may be dead.'" The Sunday following their phone call, during a lecture on racial reconciliation, Malcolm X was shot and killed.

In the decade that followed, Lincoln challenged E. FRANKLIN FRAZIER's prevailing research on the black church, which claimed there were few differences between white and black congregational life. Lincoln had a fuller view. Socially and economically they are worlds apart, he said, documenting the cultural and historical differences in *The Black Church Since Frazier*, which he wrote during a second stay at Fisk from 1973 to 1976.

He continued this debate until the year he left Fisk. While most of the twenty books he published were academic studies of religion, he also published a novel, *The Avenue, Clayton City*, which won the 1988 Lillian Smith Book Award for Best Southern Fiction. Another work, *Race, Religion, and the Continuing American Dilemma*, grew out of a series of lectures he gave after moving to Duke University in 1976.

In 1990 Lincoln released *The Black Church in the African American Experience*, a monumental work co-written with the sociologist Lawrence Mamiya. Basing their work on interviews with more than two thousand ministers from all the major black denominational groups, Lincoln and Mamiya wrote that black churches as a whole were poorly managed, losing male membership, and in need of more theologically trained leaders. Because of the detail and thoughtfulness of the work, Pope John Paul II cited Lincoln in 1990 for his scholarly service to the church.

Lincoln married twice. His first marriage in 1947 to Minnie Coleman ended in divorce. The couple had two children, Joyce Elaine and Cecil Eric. In 1960 he met Lucy Cook, a public school educator in Springfield, Massachusetts. Cook, a graduate of the New England Conservatory of Music, was youth leader for the church in Boston across the street from where Lincoln was writing his dissertation on black Muslims. The couple married in 1961 and had two children, Hilary Ann and Less Charles Lincoln II.

C. Eric Lincoln retired from Duke in 1993 and continued to write, lecture, and serve as a media expert on race relations and religion.

FURTHER READING
Lincoln's papers and archives are housed at the Atlanta University Center Robert Woodruff Library, Atlanta, Georgia.
Obituary: *New York Times*, 17 May 2000.

ERVIN DYER

Lindsay, Inabel Burns (13 Feb. 1900–10 Sept. 1983), social worker and educator, was born in St. Joseph, Missouri, the youngest of six children of Joseph Smith Burns, a farmer, and Margaret (Hartshorn) Burns. Joseph Burns, a native of Kentucky, left the family when Inabel was three years old. His Missouri-born wife had been reared by her formerly enslaved grandparents who migrated from Virginia to Missouri during the Reconstruction era. Possessing only an eighth-grade education, Margaret Burns nevertheless placed top priority on education for her children.

Inabel Burns began to suffer from vision impairment at age three. As a result, she did not attend school. Two older brothers, Weyman and Ocie, were teachers and tutored their sister at home after their workday. Burns's eyesight gradually improved, and at age eight she entered elementary school as a bright but fragile fourth-grader. She was accelerated, graduating from high school at age fifteen. In selecting a college the protective Burns family carefully chose a school at which Inabel would be sheltered and nurtured due to her continuing vision difficulties. They chose Howard University in Washington, D.C., a historically black university with a reputation as a safe, protective, and highly monitored campus environment for collegiate African American women. Burns thrived there both academically and socially, maintaining her academics while engaging in several student strikes. The strikes were the result of increased student activism on black college campuses. During the 1910s and 1920s, Howard students demonstrated their dissatisfaction with various campus rules. Despite her participation in these strikes, she graduated with honors with a B.A. degree in Mathematics in 1920.

Urged by her mother to pursue a career in teaching, Burns instead accepted the advice of a Howard University librarian to pursue social work. Burns was awarded an academic fellowship from the National Urban League, a social advocacy organization founded in 1911, to pursue a two-year certificate at the New York School of Social Work (now Columbia University's School of Social Work). After one year in the program Burns left to fulfill a summer position at the Cleveland Urban League in Ohio. She returned to Missouri in 1921 to be near her ailing mother.

African Americans found that professional opportunities to practice social work were limited, and sometimes nonexistent, in the South. Although still not enthusiastic about teaching, Burns accepted a position at Crispus Attucks Elementary School in Kansas City, Missouri. There she taught fourth- and fifth-grade students with behavioral challenges. The principal of Kansas City's Lincoln High School heard about her effectiveness as a teacher and persuaded her to transfer to the high school in 1923. She taught at Lincoln High School for two years.

During her junior year at Howard University, Burns had met Arnett Grant Lindsay, whom she married in 1925. Arnett, who was Howard University's first graduate to earn a master's degree in Negro history under CARTER G. WOODSON, owned and operated the St. Louis Finance Company. After the wedding she and Arnett relocated to St. Louis, Missouri. But in order to repay the National Urban League for their financial support of her education, she accepted a six-week assignment working on a Springfield, Illinois, racial surveying project with the famed sociologist CHARLES S. JOHNSON, who was the National Urban League's director of research. As his assistant, Lindsay learned a great deal about the need for racial uplift through social work. During her brief position with the Urban League she contributed articles to *Opportunity*, the National Urban League's widely circulated magazine. After completing the National Urban League project Lindsay returned to St. Louis and joined the Provident Association (later the Family and Child Welfare Agency of St. Louis). Provident's caseworkers and caseloads were racially segregated— black caseworkers served black clients and white caseworkers served white clients. Lindsay worked her way up from a position as a caseworker in the all-black district to the rank of district supervisor in the all-white district. Encountering several episodes of racial discrimination, she used her wit and perseverance to overcome them.

Impoverished conditions during the Great Depression created a need for private social welfare associations to enhance their funds using public money. As a result, privately governed associations expanded and became public welfare agencies. Emergency relief agencies formed across the United States. Except for a one-year absence due to ill health, Lindsay remained with Provident

Association until 1936. She then decided to pursue her passion for social work by completing the graduate work she had begun at the New York School of Social Work. Universities in the South did not award graduate degrees in social work to African Americans, so Lindsay headed north to study at the University of Chicago's School of Social Service Administration. During her time in Chicago an academic fellowship paid her tuition while she boarded with her brother Ocie. In 1937 she was awarded a master's degree in Social Work from the University of Chicago.

E. FRANKLIN FRAZIER, an old friend and classmate from the New York School of Social Work—where they had been two of only three black students—invited Lindsay to join the social work staff at Howard University. Frazier, a well-respected sociologist and director of Howard University's sociology program, established the school's social work certificate program in 1935. She accepted his invitation and joined the faculty as program director in social services. During her first years she focused on increasing support for the fieldwork program and strengthening course content. She taught courses on the history of social welfare and awarded students certificates of completion after two years in the program.

Lindsay worked tirelessly to expand Howard University's social work program into a degree-granting program because other graduate social work programs in Washington, D.C., in the 1930s did not accept African Americans. The Howard University Division of Social Work was finally established in 1940 and Lindsay became director. She served one year as acting dean while university administrators sought a male to take on the deanship of the new school. As no qualified male could be found, they appointed Lindsay dean of the School of Social Work in 1945. The program focused on urban social work services—novel for any social work program. She was an advocate for increased faculty, financial, and physical resources and taught courses on racial and cultural factors in social work practice.

Lindsay flourished as a leader in the field of social work. She wrote articles for several scholarly journals. She received a Ph.D. in Social Work from the University of Pittsburgh in 1952 and in 1958 received a Training Specialist grant from the U.S. Department of State to study social work in Norway. She attended the 1966 White House Conference on Civil Rights as a delegate. After more than thirty years at Howard University, she retired in 1967 to become a special consultant to the U.S. Department of Health, Education, and Welfare.

Lindsay served in her Episcopal church and on the social relations board of the diocese of Washington, D.C. She also served in voluntary roles for the American Foundation for the Blind, the Edwin Gould Foundation for Children, the League of Women Voters, the National Urban League, and on the U.S. Senate's Special Commission on Aging and the National Council on Aging. She received alumni awards from her alma maters—Howard University in 1961, and the University of Pittsburgh in 1971. In 1974 she received the Social Worker of the Year award from the Metropolitan Washington chapter of the National Association of Social Workers and in 1982 an honorary doctorate in humane letters from Howard. With tenacity and perseverance, Lindsay paved the way for African American women to serve in leadership roles in the field of social work. Survived by her husband of fifty-eight years, Lindsay passed away of diabetes complications at age eighty-three.

FURTHER READING

Greenlee, Marcia. *Black Women Oral History Project: Transcript of Interview with Inabel Burns Lindsay* (1980).

Shaw, Stephanie J. *What a Woman Ought to Be and Do: Black Professional Women Workers during the Jim Crow Era* (1996).

Smith, Jessie Carney, ed. *Notable Black American Women* (1992).

Obituary: *Washington Post*, 15 Sept. 1983.

LANESHA NEGALE DEBARDELABEN

Lindsay, John (23 Aug. 1894–3 July 1950), jazz string bassist and trombonist, was born in New Orleans, Louisiana. Details of his parents, including their names, are unknown. His nickname was Johnny, and his surname has often (and probably incorrectly) been spelled Lindsey. As a boy he played string bass with his family; his father played guitar and his brother Herb played violin. While John was in his teens, the three men performed with the cornetist FREDDIE KEPPARD at the Hanan Saloon in the Storyville district of New Orleans.

Lindsay was a member of the songwriter and pianist CLARENCE WILLIAMS's group in 1916. From 1917 to 1918 he served in the army. On his return he took up trombone, working for a few months at the Lyric Theatre with John Robichaux around 1920. In the fall of 1920 he joined the violinist ARMAND JOHN PIRON's orchestra, with which he toured to

New York in 1923 and 1924 and recorded "West Indies Blues" (1923). In 1925 he was in trumpeter Dewey Jackson's band on the riverboat *Capitol*, touring between New Orleans and St. Paul, but that same year he settled in Chicago, Illinois. There he recorded "Black Bottom Stomp" and "Grandpa's Spells" as the bassist in JELLY ROLL MORTON's Red Hot Peppers in 1926 and "Boar Hog Blues" as the trombonist in the trumpeter Willie Hightower's band in 1927.

By this time Lindsay was principally a string bassist. From March 1931 to March 1932 he toured nationally with LOUIS ARMSTRONG's big band, with which he recorded "When It's Sleepy Time Down South" and "The Lonesome Road" (1931) and appeared in the film short *Rhapsody in Black and Blue* (1932). He later recorded with the Harlem Hamfats in 1936–1937, the singer VICTORIA SPIVEY in 1936, the reed player SIDNEY BECHET in 1940, the clarinetists JOHNNY DODDS and Jimmie Noone both in 1940, the pianist ALBERT C. AMMONS in 1944, the trumpeter Punch Miller in 1944, and the singer CHIPPIE HILL in 1946. Late in his career Lindsay led his own quartet at the Music Bar and also worked regularly with the reed player Darnell Howard and the guitarist Bob Tinsley. He died in Chicago.

Lindsay would be nothing more than yet another well-accomplished and little-known professional jazz accompanist were it not for the sessions with Morton. The tone of his instrument was tremendously well captured by Victor's studio engineers in an era of low-fidelity recording quality. On these few recordings, Lindsay summarizes the past and future of jazz bass, alternating a ragtime-based two-beat pattern (bass notes sounding on beats one and three of each measure) with an exaggeratedly percussive slapping attack with walking four-beat lines (sounding on each beat of the measure) and a smoothly plucked sound.

FURTHER READING

Charters, Samuel B. *Jazz: New Orleans, 1885–1963: An Index to the Negro Musicians of New Orleans*, rev. ed. (1983).

Schuller, Gunther. *Early Jazz: Its Roots and Musical Development* (1968).

Obituaries: *Down Beat*, 11 Aug. 1950; *Melody Maker*, 23 Sept. 1950.

This entry is taken from the *American National Biography* and is published here with the permission of the American Council of Learned Societies.

BARRY KERNFELD

Lion, Jules (1809?–9 Jan. 1866), artist, was born in France, but the exact place of his birth is unknown. Nothing is known about his parents or his youth, but it seems likely that he received a traditional artistic education in Europe. Lion's lithographs were exhibited at the prestigious Paris Salons of 1831 (four prints, including *L'affût aux canards* [Duck Blind], which won honorable mention), 1834 (four works, including a scene based on Victor Hugo's *Nôtre Dame de Paris*), and 1836 (lithographs after Van Dyck, Jacquand, Waltier, Boulanger, and others). In the mid-1830s Lion immigrated to New Orleans, where the 1837 city directory listed him as a freeman of color and as a painter and lithographer; he worked in a lithography shop opened by the newspaper *L'Abeille* (*The Bee*). Light-skinned, Lion often passed for white and appeared in other records as such. His studio was located at 56 Canal Street, a wide boulevard that divided Creole New Orleans from the flourishing American section of the city.

Lion returned to Paris during the summer of 1839, when Louis Jacques Daguerre distributed a pamphlet detailing his invention of early photographic methods. By 27 September Lion was back in New Orleans producing daguerreotype views of the city. Newspapers praised the clear images that he exhibited at the St. Charles Museum in March 1840; the *Bee* declared that "nothing can be more truly beautiful.... It is a wonderful discovery—one too, that will prove useful, as it is admirable" (14 Mar. 1840). Lion was celebrated for introducing the daguerreotype to New Orleans and for his charming personality: "Mr. Lion is a young French gentleman, after saying which we need not add that he is pleasing, courteous, and polite" (*Daily Picayune*, 20 Mar. 1840). Lion continued to take daguerreotypes of such landmarks as the Levee and the St. Louis Hotel, and in 1842 he advertised his services as a daguerreotypist of sick or deceased persons.

In 1843 Lion opened his own studio at 3 Rue St. Charles, where he made lithographic portraits and miniatures and sold daguerreotypes from Paris. The *Bee* lauded his skill: "Mr. Lion is an artist of superior merit of which anyone can convince himself by an examination of the specimens before the office door" (25 Nov. 1843). Lion also made prints of local scenes, such as *The Cathedral, New Orleans* (1842) and *View of Canal Street* (1846). He exhibited and sold his works at book and frame shops.

Lion's best-known work is a series of more than 150 fine lithographs, executed between 1837 and 1847, of prominent Louisianans and other leaders.

Among Lion's delicate and engaging portraits are those of the most popular Protestant minister in New Orleans, the Reverend Theodore Clapp (1837), of Judge François-Xavier Martin (1837), of the family of the wealthy commission merchant Seaman Field, *Eliza Dubourg Field and Her Daughters Eliza and Odilie* (1838), of William Freret (1839), of Andrew Jackson (1840), and of the legislator James Dunwoody Bronson DeBow (1847). Lion's sitters were Creoles and Americans and included physicians, historians, jurists, mayors, surveyors, and members of the Bringier and Villeré families. Other notable sitters were the artist John James Audubon, the lawyer Charles Conrad, the planter Victor Armand, the poet François Dominique Rouquette, and General Zachary Taylor. One newspaper called the last-named work "remarkable for its likeness and the beauty of the drawing" (*Gazette de Baton Rouge*, 12 Aug. 1837). Lion became the most prolific and admired artist of color in Louisiana in the nineteenth century. He tried to publish many of these portraits in one volume in the 1840s and again in 1860. Although he had numerous patrons, it would appear that he did not have sufficient funds, for the book was never published. However, more than 150 of his portraits exist in a unique leather-bound volume in the Historic New Orleans Collection.

Lion's pastel work, *Asher Moses Nathan and Son* (1845), is a double portrait of a young mulatto man and his white father. The youth may be Achille Lion, the illegitimate son of a woman of color (name unknown), who later became Jules Lion's wife, and Nathan, a Dutch Jewish immigrant and wealthy drygoods merchant. Perhaps to spare his white wife embarrassment and to give his children a European education, Nathan sent Achille and his sister Anna to Paris. After Nathan's wife died, he legally adopted Achille and left his fortune to him and Anna. Jules Lion portrayed his affluent stepson and natural father embracing; they seem to have had a cordial relationship. Thus not only might the composition document the actual paternity of Lion's stepson but it also might allude to the artist's own mixed heritage.

In the mid-1840s Lion was forced to sell property to pay debts. In 1848 he opened an art school with Dominique Canova, a noted muralist and ornamental painter. The *Louisiana Courier* (30 Nov. 1848) commended the undertaking by "two of our most talented artists," but the partnership dissolved after a year.

In 1850 Lion proposed a ceiling painting, altar picture, and pendentive decorations for the new St. Louis Cathedral. He would have liked to paint them for the sake of his art but admitted that he would need payment. Lion assured the construction committee of his ardor: "For Gentlemen, after God, what I love the most is my art" (unpublished letter, trans. Samuel Wilson Jr., Historic New Orleans Collection). It is not known whether Lion did the paintings.

Although Lion continued to work during the 1850s, the press published little about him. In 1852 he taught drawing at Louisiana Academy. The following year he moved from the French Quarter into the Third Municipality, perhaps to save money. It is not known when he married native New Orleanian Maria Ana Muñoz, but the two had a son in 1857.

During the Civil War, Lion lithographed sheet music illustrations of Confederate subjects for several New Orleans music publishers. One work depicts the Free Market, which supplied Confederate New Orleans's indigents. Lion returned to portraiture when the city was occupied by federal forces, then taught drawing at Louisiana Academy to local businessmen in the fall evenings of 1865. He died in New Orleans.

FURTHER READING
Many of Lion's lithographic portraits of prominent Louisianans and some of his sheet music illustrations, as well as his letter to the St. Louis Cathedral committee, are in the Historic New Orleans Collection. His prints and pastels are also in the Louisiana State Museum collection.

Brady, Patricia. "Black Artists in Antebellum New Orleans," *Louisiana History* (Winter, 1991): 5–28.

East, Charles. "Jules Lion's New Orleans," *Georgia Review* (Winter, 1986): 914–916.

Macdonald, Robert R., et al., eds. *Louisiana's Black Heritage* (1979).

Obituary: *L'Abeille*, 10 Jan. 1866.

This entry is taken from the *American National Biography* and is published here with the permission of the American Council of Learned Societies.

THERESA LEININGER-MILLER

Lipman, Wynona M. (17 Nov. 1923?–9 May 1999), politician, was born Evelyn Wynona Moore in LaGrange, Georgia, the second of four children of John Moore Sr., a store owner and bricklayer, and Annabelle Torian. Both John and Annabelle Moore were educated at Clark College in Atlanta, Georgia, at a time when few African Americans had the opportunity to attend college. Evelyn

Wynona Moore's birth certificate was burned in a courthouse fire, and though she never revealed her true year of birth, her family estimates that she was born in 1923.

Wynona Moore grew up in a relatively privileged family where all of the children were expected to go to college. She completed high school at the age of sixteen and attended Talladega College in Alabama. During the late 1930s and early 1940s, when Moore was a student there, Talladega was one of the leading historically black colleges in the nation. She later described Talladega as a place where she was able to compete with other students without the omnipresent specter of race. After graduating from Talladega with a B.A. in French in 1942, Moore pursued an advanced degree at Atlanta University, earning a master's degree in French in 1945. Upon completion of her graduate degree, she became an instructor of French at Morehouse College, an all-male, historically black college in Atlanta. During her tenure at Morehouse she received a prestigious Rockefeller Grant that enabled her to pursue her Ph.D. at Columbia University. While a doctoral student at Columbia, Moore received a Fulbright Fellowship, which allowed her to study at the Sorbonne in Paris from 1950 to 1951.

Moore's time in Paris was filled with excitement, as she shared a house with two women who became legendary in their own right: the singers LEONTYNE PRICE and MATTIWILDA DOBBS. In 1952 her father died, and she married Matthew Lipman, a white doctoral student in philosophy at Columbia who was also in France doing research for his dissertation. The couple married in a small civil service in France, and when her fellowship ended the Lipmans returned to New York. Later that year Wynona Lipman received her Ph.D. in French Literature from Columbia University.

Although both the Lipmans returned to the United States, they lived apart for three years while Wynona returned to her job at Morehouse College and Matthew looked for employment in the New York area. Despite her excellent education Lipman found it all but impossible to secure a professorship at a white northern college. Because interracial marriage continued to be illegal in Georgia during the 1950s, it did not seem feasible for the Lipmans to live together in the South. Once her husband found permanent employment at Columbia University, Lipman left Morehouse and moved to New York City, where she worked at Elizabeth Irwin High School, a private school in Greenwich Village. Eventually the couple settled in Montclair, New Jersey.

After recovering from a brief illness, Lipman resumed her pursuit of a position as a French professor in the New York area. Although prospective employers claimed that they could not hire her because of her lack of an authentic accent, her race was likely the primary reason. In the 1950s African American professors at predominantly white colleges were an anomaly.

In 1959 the Lipmans had their first child, Karyne. A year later a son, William, followed. After the birth of her children Lipman was a homemaker and worked part-time as a French teacher at Montclair High School. It was through her role as a mother and as an actively engaged citizen that she first became involved in New Jersey politics. In Montclair, Lipman was active in both the NAACP and the PTA. She became the first African American PTA president of a school in Montclair. Through her activities as president of the PTA, Lipman came to the attention of the local Democratic Party. Told that she had to "know important people" in order to get anything accomplished, she decided that a better approach was to "become important people" in order to create change.

Lipman's opportunity came when she worked with other mothers in Montclair to prevent the city from dumping dirty snow on a school playground in the town. After organizing the formation of a human chain of mothers around the playground, Lipman was urged by Democratic Party leaders to become active in politics. She began as a Democratic committee member and later served as the chairperson of Montclair's Democratic Party. In 1968 Lipman won office as a freeholder in Essex County. Unique to New Jersey, freeholders govern the counties in the state. Historically New Jersey politics has been dominated by county party politics, and thus her election as a freeholder helped to make her a viable candidate for the state Senate a few years later. Lipman went on to serve as the director of the Essex County Freeholder Board. As one of the few female and African American powerbrokers in New Jersey politics, Lipman took on issues of importance to her diverse constituency in Montclair. She urged other freeholders in Essex County to support prison reform and the reorganization of the very board that she directed. In part because she was unafraid to tackle such issues, local Democrats urged her to run for the state senate.

In 1971 Lipman made history by becoming the first African American woman to become a state senator in New Jersey. She won by just sixty-three votes. Like many other states during the late 1960s and 1970s, New Jersey was undergoing a great deal of turmoil as it struggled to comply with the U.S. Supreme Court rulings that mandated redistricting. Soon after Lipman's election, district lines were drawn that eliminated the district from which she had been elected. Lipman was forced to make a life-altering decision: move from Montclair, where she had made her home for close to twenty years, or face almost certain defeat by trying to run in a different district. Lipman decided to move to Newark in order to be eligible to run for office in the next election. Shortly thereafter she and Matthew Lipman divorced.

In the early 1970s Newark was still reeling from the riots that had crippled it in 1967. Although Newark had been hurt by the riots, it was also at the center of a new political coalition made up of African Americans and Puerto Ricans. In 1970 this coalition helped to elect Kenneth Gibson as Newark's first black mayor. Newark's politicians did not welcome Lipman, however, since they viewed her as a suburbanite moving to the city in order to keep her senate seat. Despite the challenges facing her, Lipman stayed in Newark and won reelection in 1973.

Lipman made her mark on New Jersey politics through her legislation, which centered on the concerns of minorities, women, children, and small-business owners. In the state senate Lipman worked to ensure the passage of a bill creating a commission on sex discrimination after its defeat in the assembly. She then served as the chairperson of the commission, which was charged with modernizing New Jersey's laws and ensuring that they eliminated gender inequities. One of the most important and far-reaching pieces of legislation sponsored by Lipman was the 1981 Domestic Violence Act, which was the first of its kind in New Jersey.

Representing some of the most politically and economically disenfranchised citizens in the state, Lipman also focused on revitalizing the inner city and building an infrastructure that would help Newark's residents address the multifarious issues facing them. Her legislative record included the passage of more than 145 laws, many of which put into place programs for at-risk youth, safer housing standards, and the prevention of domestic violence. Since she viewed money as the biggest problem facing the inner city, she requested and received an appointment to the appropriations committee. Lipman served on the committee for the remainder of her tenure in the state senate and used her position there to press for Newark's economic revitalization.

In 1974 Lipman embarked on a second career in addition to her senate seat. She began teaching business education at Essex County College and working with small-business owners in Newark in an effort to build relationships among minority business owners, government officials, and contractors. Lipman maintained her seat in the New Jersey state senate as well as her teaching position at Essex County College, where she taught many of her constituents, until her death from cancer in 1999.

Lipman entered politics at a crucial juncture in American political history. She took advantage of the growing coalition of white women and of men and women of color to win political office. Once there, she stayed for more than twenty-five years, both shaping the public perception of who could hold office and opening up the political and economic sphere to those with the least access. In 2000 the New Jersey state legislature created the Senator Wynona Lipman Chair in Women's Political Leadership at the Center for American Women and Politics.

FURTHER READING

Lipman's papers are housed at the New Jersey State Senate.

Chason, Alice. "Iron Magnolia," *New Jersey Reporter* (July–Aug 1988).

Cohen, Cathy, Kathleen Jones, and Joan Tronto, eds. *Women Transforming Politics* (1997).

Reuter, Theodore, ed. *The Politics of Race: African Americans and the Political System* (1995).

Springer, Kimberly, ed. *Still Lifting, Still Climbing: Contemporary African American Women's Activism* (1999).

Obituary: New Jersey *Star-Ledger*, 11 May 1999.

STEPHANIE R. WRIGHT

Lipscomb, Eugene Alan "Big Daddy" (9 Nov. 1931–10 May 1963), football player, was born in Detroit, Michigan. The names of his parents are unknown. He never knew his father, who reportedly died in a Civilian Conservation Corps camp when Gene was very young; his mother was stabbed to death by a male acquaintance while she waited for a bus in Detroit in 1942. Raised by his maternal grandfather, Lipscomb recalled that his grandfather "did the best he knew how. But for some reason it was always hard for us to talk together. Instead of telling me what I was doing wrong and how to correct it, my grandfather would holler and whip me." As a youth Gene held a variety of odd jobs to support himself, including a midnight-to-eight shift at a steel mill in Detroit, which he worked before attending classes at Miller High School. He quit school at age sixteen and joined the U.S. Marine Corps.

At Camp Pendleton, California, Lipscomb began to develop his football talents. Having played only one season at Miller High, he learned the fundamentals of the game at a relatively high level of play while in the marines. With 280 pounds filling out his frame of six feet six inches and with unusual speed for a man his size, he soon made a reputation for himself in service football. He got his nickname "Big Daddy" in the marines because he could not remember his teammates' names and called them all "Little Daddy." The Los Angeles Rams of the National Football League (NFL) signed Lipscomb for $4,800 in 1953. He was one of the first extremely large interior linemen with exceptional mobility. But as an unseasoned lineman distracted by personal problems, including marital discord and alcohol abuse, his play was inconsistent, and Los Angeles put him on waivers in 1955.

Sought by several teams, Lipscomb signed with the Baltimore Colts in 1956 as a defensive tackle and came under the tutelage of the head coach Weeb Ewbank, who described him as a "project." Under Ewbank's guidance, Lipscomb learned how to better utilize his size and mobility in interior line play and became one of the outstanding defensive linemen in the NFL. Lipscomb was one of the first black linemen to be widely recognized and acclaimed by fans around the league. While with Baltimore from 1955 to 1960, he was named to the all-NFL team twice and played in two Pro Bowl games. In 1958 and 1959 Lipscomb helped lead the Colts to consecutive NFL championships while anchoring an impressive defensive line that included Art Donovan, Gino Marchetti, and Don Joyce. Baltimore traded Lipscomb to the Pittsburgh Steelers in 1961. He continued to be one of the league's outstanding linemen and played one of his best games in the 1963 Pro Bowl, his third. At the height of his career, Lipscomb earned fifteen thousand dollars per season. During the off-season he earned considerably more money as a professional wrestler, a side job he had begun while in the marines in California.

Although unusually large and aggressive in line play, Lipscomb went out of his way to cultivate an image as a gentle giant. After a tackle, for example, he would help a ball carrier to his feet. "I don't want people or kids to think Big Daddy is a cruel man," he explained. Lipscomb also had the reputation of being something of a homespun philosopher both on and off the field. One of the few NFL players who did not attend college, Lipscomb liked to tell teammates he had played at "Miller Tech," and he once summarized his football technique by saying, "I just grab me an armful of men, pick them over until I find the one with the ball, then I throw them down." On another occasion he remarked: "New York, New York. So big they had to say it twice."

Despite his size, air of confidence, and genial manner, Lipscomb had a difficult personal life. "I've been scared most of my life," he once said. "You wouldn't think so to look at me." In the wake of his dismal childhood, Lipscomb was divorced three times and by the 1950s had a serious drinking problem. He died in Baltimore of an acute reaction to an overdose of heroin. An autopsy showed that a nonintoxicating amount of liquor in his body also contributed to his death. Despite the discovery of a number of recent needle marks on his arms, some of his friends, including the Pittsburgh Steelers owner Art Rooney, suspected foul play. They could not imagine Lipscomb being a drug abuser. Baltimore medical authorities ruled, however, that Lipscomb died of a self-administered overdose of heroin. Lipscomb was one of the first widely known defensive linemen in the NFL. He was also one of the first prominent professional athletes to be linked with drug addiction.

FURTHER READING

Daly, Dan, and Bob O'Donnell. *The Pro Football Chronicle* (1990).

Ewbank, Weeb. *Goal to Go: The Greatest Football Games I Have Coached* (1972).

Schwartz, Daniel. "A Requiem for Big Daddy," *Esquire*, Sept. 1963.

Obituaries: *New York Times*, 11 May 1963; *Time*, 17 May 1963.

This entry is taken from the *American National Biography* and is published here with the permission of the American Council of Learned Societies.

JOHN M. CARROLL

Lipscomb, Mance (9 Apr. 1895–30 Jan. 1976), songster and guitarist, was born on a farm near Navasota, Texas, the son of Charlie Lipscomb, a former slave who became a professional fiddler, and Janie Pratt. Lipscomb learned to play fiddle and guitar at an early age, learning mainly by ear because his musician father was seldom home to teach him. When he was still a preteen Lipscomb supposedly traveled with his father for a time, accompanying him on guitar. However, when Lipscomb was around eleven years old his father stopped coming home altogether, and the youngster went to work on the farm to help his mother.

For the next fifty years Lipscomb worked full-time as a farmer. He took jobs as a farmhand until he was sixteen, then began sharecropping on a twenty-acre tract, raising mainly corn and cotton. Two years later he married Elnora (maiden name unknown); they had one son but raised two sets of grandchildren and several great grandchildren as well. As a sharecropper and later as a rent farmer, Lipscomb worked from before dawn to well past dusk to eke out a slender living for his family. He lived this way until 1956, when he moved to Houston and went to work for a lumber company. Within a year, however, he was injured when a load of lumber fell on him, and he moved back to Navasota, using an insurance settlement to buy a parcel of land and build a small house where he planned to spend his retirement.

As a farmer, Lipscomb was never too far from music. In his early twenties he traveled to the northeastern part of Texas to pick cotton, and on a Saturday night in Dallas he heard the Texas blues virtuoso BLIND LEMON JEFFERSON playing guitar on the street. Lipscomb recalled hearing another Texas native, the slide-guitar evangelist BLIND WILLIE JOHNSON, when Johnson came through Navasota. He also heard obscure local musicians such as Robert Timm, said to be the first Navasota artist to play blues, and Hamp Walker, described by Lipscomb as "about the best guitar man and songster as I ever met," according to the researcher Mack McCormick. At some point Lipscomb began playing guitar and singing at weekend country dances and picnics. Although he became an accomplished musician, his reputation was limited to the Brazos River farming community where he lived.

In the summer of 1960 two researchers, Mack McCormick and Chris Strachwitz, heard about Lipscomb when they traveled out from Houston in search of folk musicians. They went to his house and were waiting for him when he got home after a full day in the fields. "So I came out on the porch with my guitar," Lipscomb later told the author Bruce Cook, "and I played the worst one I could think of just to get rid of them." McCormick and Strachwitz requested more tunes, however, and that night they recorded Lipscomb for almost five hours in his home—recordings that formed the basis for Lipscomb's debut LP on Arhoolie Records.

A farmer all his life, Lipscomb became an overnight celebrity on the folk- and blues-revival circuits at age sixty-five. The year of his first field recordings he played at the Texas Heritage Festival in Houston, initiating a steady schedule of festivals, campus and club bookings, recording sessions, film appearances, and oral history interviews that continued into the early 1970s. His credits included all the major folk and blues festivals—Berkeley in 1961–1963, Monterey in 1963, Newport in 1965, the Festival of American Folklife in Washington, D.C., in 1968, Ann Arbor in 1970, Philadelphia in 1972—and a long list of other events. In addition to further recordings for Strachwitz's Arhoolie label, Lipscomb was featured in the 1971 Les Blank film *A Well Spent Life*. His late-life success as a musician made it possible for Lipscomb to buy a bigger house, where he lived with his wife and one grandchild. As Lipscomb neared eighty, though, failing health curtailed his music career. He died at a hospital near his home and was buried at Rest Haven Cemetery in Navasota.

Discovered well past his prime as a musician, Mance Lipscomb nonetheless possessed both formidable skill as a guitarist and a repertoire of songs that was said to number in the hundreds. As a performer on the folk- and blues-revival circuits during the 1960s, Lipscomb was often regarded as a blues artist—a misnomer that, according to Bruce Cook, caused some young audiences to react with impatience when Lipscomb trotted out such hoary standards as "You Are My Sunshine" and "Shine On, Harvest Moon." In fact, Lipscomb belonged to a Texas songster tradition that drew material from many sources, old and new. Lipscomb sang blues, to be sure; but as Mack McCormick noted, he sang them as part of an unbroken musical stream that included ballads, work songs, breakdowns, and religious songs, in addition to the nineteenth-century standards and dance tunes that he had learned in childhood. Lipscomb, who labeled himself a songster, adorned all of this material with a precise finger-picking style on guitar, and he delivered it with dignified yet intense vocals. He was among the most influential country performers of the revival era.

FURTHER READING

Lipscomb, Mance, with Glen Alyn. *I Say Me for a Parable: The Oral Autobiography of Mance Lipscomb, Texas Bluesman* (1993).

Cook, Bruce. *Listen to the Blues* (1973).

Harris, Sheldon. *Blues Who's Who: A Biographical Dictionary of Blues Singers* (1979).

This entry is taken from the *American National Biography* and is published here with the permission of the American Council of Learned Societies.

BILL MCCULLOCH AND
BARRY LEE PEARSON

Liston, Melba (13 Jan. 1926–23 Apr. 1999), trombonist and arranger, was born in Kansas City, Missouri, the daughter of Lucille Liston, a domestic worker, and Frank Liston, an amateur musician who died when Melba was young. At age six Liston fell in love with a trombone in a pawnshop window. "I picked the trombone visually," she told a reporter forty years later. "I just liked what it looked like in a store window. I became obsessed with the trombone and got one in the school system. I … learned by ear to play 'Deep River,' church, and folk pieces." Melba lived with her grandparents, who also had a young daughter. Liston had approval for her music from her mother, who eventually bought her a trombone. "A child has to have some hobby," Liston said. "My mother worked away … and I had my dear trombone" (interview with the author).

Liston's young aunt liked to listen to blues records, but her grandmother forbade the blues in the house. The girls would listen to them anyway when her grandmother went out. Liston took trombone lessons but did not think her teacher was very good, and she even told her mother not to pay him because he kept giving her misinformation. The family lived in Kansas City at the height of its reputation as a jazz capital, when such greats as the pianist and bandleader COUNT BASIE, the blues shouter BIG JOE TURNER, the pianist and bandleader JAY MCSHANN, and the alto saxophonist CHARLIE "BIRD" PARKER starred there. But Kansas City, a wide-open resort under the rule of the corrupt Boss Pendergast's political machine, attracted gamblers as well as musicians, and Liston was too young to go to the clubs. Her grandmother was so strict that Liston did not even hear jazz until at age ten, in 1937, she moved to Los Angeles with her mother.

At Jefferson High School in Los Angeles, Liston joined the band, which was directed by the teacher Sam Browne and which included a number of talented musicians. Among them was the saxophonist DEXTER GORDON, who befriended her and introduced her to such other musicians as Frank Morgan, Vi Redd, and Ernie Royal. After high school Liston went to Los Angeles City College, which had no pop or jazz classes, so she went back to Sam Browne to study arranging.

When she was sixteen Liston auditioned at the Lincoln Theater in Los Angeles and played there under the direction of Bardu Ali. When the prominent theater closed, the players worked in GERALD WILSON's band in nightclubs. Liston had gained an entrée into the top echelons of jazz, where she met DIZZY GILLESPIE, Count Basie, DUKE ELLINGTON, and Charlie Parker. Liston began recording for Dial records, probably in 1946, on such songs as "Mischievous Lady" and "Lullaby in Rhythm." In 1948 and 1949 she toured with Gillespie's band in the South, but audiences were disappointed that the band played bebop, not blues or dance music. She then toured with BILLIE HOLIDAY and Wilson, again finding a cool reception in the South.

Back in California, Liston got a degree in order to be certified by the board of education. She also married, put down her trombone, and taught school for a while. When her marriage failed, Liston picked up her horn again and returned to the playing scene. Another marriage in the 1950s also failed.

Gillespie took Liston with him on a U.S. State Department tour of the Middle East in 1956 and to South America the following year, because he wanted both a great trombonist and an arranger. Bands loved to take their own arrangers with them because they knew the players' strengths, and nobody had to wait for arrangements to arrive from New York. For Gillespie, Liston arranged "Stella by Starlight," "Annie's Dance," and "My Reverie." She also overcame the antipathy of the band members, who called her a bitch until they heard her arrangements and playing; then they took to calling her "little sister" and "mama," sharing coffee, cigarettes, and drinks with her, and getting her to sew on their buttons and cut their hair.

"Very few women jazz musicians, black or white, survived," she recalled of those months of travel. "It was hard for all. I survived because I was a hardworking, patient, music person…. I learned to build relationships with the men and the jazz world. It's not something you … understand right away." Her memories of spending a month on a bus "sometimes without a hotel, bed or bath," she said, upset her. "And money was short. Or we got stranded when a bus broke down in the snow and cold" (interview with the author).

Gillespie's tours ended in the late 1950s, and Liston married for a third and last time to a junior high school science teacher. "That didn't work either," she later said with a smile. "Nothing works." Analyzing her divorces she mused, "All the guys loved my career," adding, "Men … don't like to be ignored. My last husband was proud if I got a good gig. Then I would ignore him too long, and he would break a dish … and it was time for me to … take care of him" (interview with the author).

She thought that marriage to a musician might have been worse because of competitive feelings. She did fall in love with Gerald Wilson early in her career, but he was a married Catholic, and there may have been other reasons that he would not get a divorce. He and Liston always remained friends.

Between 1959 and 1962 Liston twice toured Europe with QUINCY JONES's band, and she wrote arrangements for Johnny Griffin's album *White Gardenia*, a tribute to Billie Holiday. During this period she also began a long career of writing highly praised arrangements for the pianist Randy Weston. Weston never told her what to do or what size group to write for, and the two worked creatively together for the rest of Liston's life. Liston also worked with, arranged for, and co-led bands with CLARK TERRY, Duke Ellington, Tony Bennett, and Jon Lucien, and she taught at various schools, including the Jamaica School of Music in the West Indies in the 1970s, where many of her students went on to become prominent musicians.

In 1979 Liston played at the Women's Jazz Festival in Kansas City, and then in a women's festival in New York City, as women became more welcome in the jazz world. Tall, strong, and beautiful, dressed in a chic, long, white gown, Liston looked stunning on the bandstand, and her music was as regal as her appearance. By the late 1970s Liston's arrangement of "Soul of Hollywood," done with Weston, had become a collector's item, selling in stores for thirty dollars. Sometimes Liston heard songs on the radio that she knew she had arranged, even though she had just collected her paychecks and left the studios without even remembering the songs' names.

By the early 1980s women were getting slightly more attention and better conditions as jazz players. In 1982 Liston put the finishing touches on her own bands in New York—Melba Liston and Company, and Melba Liston and Friends—with excellent women players. When she suffered a stroke in 1985 she returned to Los Angeles and went back to arranging. At a Carnegie Hall concert honoring Liston, the pianist Junior Mance said of her, "She's not just one of the best women jazz musicians in the world, she's one of the best jazz musicians." "Nice, how nice," said Liston, dipping her head in a characteristically shy bow when she heard the compliment.

FURTHER READING
Gourse, Leslie. *The Golden Age of Jazz in Paris and Other Stories about Jazz* (2000).
Placksin, Sally. *American Women in Jazz* (1982).
Stokes, W. Royal. *The Jazz Scene* (1991).

DISCOGRAPHY
Bogdanov, Vladimir, et al. *The All Music Guide to Jazz: The Experts' Guide to the Best Jazz Recordings*, 4th ed. (2002).
Lord, Thomas. *The Jazz Discography* (1992).
LESLIE GOURSE

Liston, Sonny (8 May 1932–30 Dec. 1970), world champion boxer, was born Charles Liston in rural St. Francis County, Arkansas, to the tenant farmers Helen Baskin and Tobe Liston. Like much in Liston's story, the precise date of his birth and the exact number of his siblings are unknown. He was most likely born between 1927 and 1932, and was probably the tenth of eleven children born to Helen Baskin, and the twenty-fourth of twenty-five children born to Tobe Liston. His nickname, "Sonny," may have been granted in childhood, though most people claimed that it was given to him in prison. Liston received no formal schooling. From an early age, he labored on the tenant farm with his father, who believed that if a child was big enough to sit at the dinner table, he was big enough to chop cotton. Liston rarely spoke of his childhood, except to say, "The only thing my old man ever gave me was a beating" (Tosches, 34). Liston's autopsy would later reveal many whipping welts and the truth of that statement.

In 1946 he moved to St. Louis, Missouri, where his mother had found employment a year earlier. Broad-shouldered, strong, and powerful, Liston occasionally found work as a laborer but more often found himself in trouble for a series of thefts and muggings. In 1950 he was sentenced to five years in the Missouri State Penitentiary on charges of first-degree robbery and larceny. In prison the Catholic chaplain encouraged Liston to box. Liston weighed two hundred pounds, stood six feet one inch tall, and already had a reputation for brawling. Within his first month of training, no other prisoner would step into the ring with him—at least not alone. What Liston lacked in finesse he more than made up for with a powerful left hand; at first he barely used his right, since he did not need it. His only problem was that his fists—fifteen inches in girth—were too large for standard boxing gloves. Most of Liston's contemporaries in prison recalled

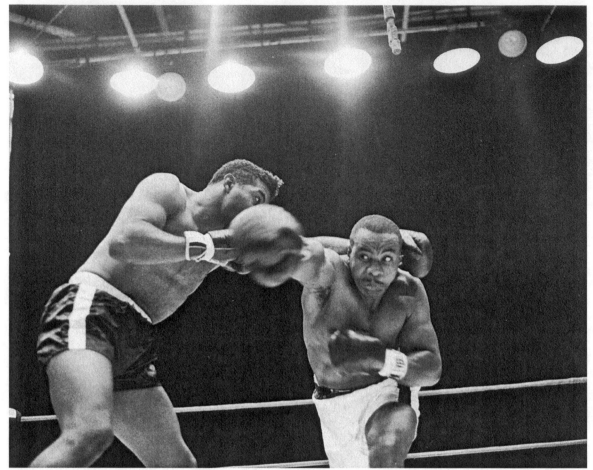

Sonny Liston delivers a left hook to Floyd Patterson in the first round of the World Heavyweight Championship title fight in Chicago, Ill. On 25 September 1962. (AP Images.)

that he was amiable and quiet; Liston, who had experienced far harsher treatment in the Arkansas cotton fields and on the streets of St. Louis, later said that he did not mind his time in jail.

Liston's potential as a heavyweight contender ensured his early release and the keen attention of underworld crime figures. In 1952 he was paroled, thanks to the efforts of a Catholic priest and Frank Mitchell, the publisher of the *St. Louis Argus*, a black newspaper. Mitchell had close ties to John Vitale, the leading mobster in St. Louis, who hired Liston to work at the Union Electric plant as a "head breaker," beating or intimidating workers who, in the view of Vitale and the Teamster leadership, had stepped out of line. Mitchell also hired a former sparring partner of the heavyweight champion JOE LOUIS to work on Liston's technical deficiencies as a boxer. Over the next year Liston defeated a string of amateur opponents, among them Ed Sanders, the

1952 Olympic heavyweight champion. He turned professional in 1953 and won fourteen of his first fifteen fights, seven of them by knockouts. Liston's personal life enjoyed an all too rare period of happiness in 1956, when he met Geraldine Chambers, who had been standing in a downpour waiting for a bus. On seeing her, he immediately reversed his car, jumped out, picked her up, and placed her on the front seat. Chambers did not appear to mind the boxer's presumptuous chivalry, and she married him several months later, shortly before he was sentenced to nine months in the St. Louis workhouse for assaulting a police officer.

In 1958 Liston moved to Philadelphia, Pennsylvania, where he was managed by Frankie Carbo, the most powerful underworld figure in boxing. Four years later, having won twenty consecutive fights, Liston earned the right to challenge the world heavyweight champion FLOYD PATTERSON.

Many in the African American community were wary of Liston replacing Patterson as heavyweight champion. Civil rights leaders viewed the graceful, contemplative Patterson as an ideal spokesman for the race, a man who, like Liston, had grown up in poverty, but one who used his fists only in the ring. Even President John F. Kennedy urged Patterson to fight Liston, telling the champion in the Oval Office, "You've *got* to beat this guy" (Remnick, 14). Yet for all of the media efforts to portray the fight as a battle between good and evil, it was, in fact, a fight between two boxers. Liston was hungrier and knocked Patterson out in the first round with a savage left hook that caught the champion squarely on the jaw. Liston defeated Patterson, again with a first-round knockout, in a July 1963 rematch in Las Vegas.

Although he was the undisputed world champion, Liston did not receive the adulation that other heavyweights had enjoyed. There was no victory parade in Philadelphia, though he did win an audience with Vice President Lyndon Johnson, himself a rough-hewn outsider in Kennedy's Camelot. Foreign boxing fans were more appreciative of Liston and he of them. On a tour of Britain he won standing ovations in several cities and strode through the streets of Glasgow wearing a kilt and playing the bagpipes. Told by Scots reporters that he was a warmer man than they had expected, Liston replied, "I am warm here because I am among warm people.... When I return to the United States, I will be cold again, for the people there ... have treated me badly" (Tosches, 195).

Few expected Liston to lose the heavyweight crown to his young challenger, Cassius Clay, in 1964. Most experts viewed Clay's promise to deliver a "total eclipse of the Sonny" as entertaining bombast at best, but the young fighter proved much fitter and faster than they expected. Clay danced and ducked Liston's lethal jabs, frustrating the champion, cutting his eye, and then landing punch after punch of his own. At the start of the seventh round, Liston refused to leave his stool, claiming that he had an injured left shoulder. Many, including the U.S. Senate, suspected a fix, because victory for Clay would bring a profitable rematch for Liston's underworld backers. The Senate's investigation did not find evidence of collusion, though, and the rematch, in Lewiston, Maine, in May 1965 also resulted in a victory—a first-round knockout—for Clay, who had by then converted to Islam and adopted the name MUHAMMAD ALI. Again, commentators were incredulous that a single blow could knock out Liston. Slow-motion replays revealed, however, that Ali had caught Liston off balance and blindsided, with a corkscrew punch to his left temple.

Liston continued to box after that defeat, and he continued to win, though mainly against second-rate fighters. Rumors circulated about his friendship with gangsters and his involvement in narcotics. On 5 January 1971 his wife returned from a trip to St. Louis to find him dead in their Las Vegas home. He had been dead for a week, and though the coroner's report found evidence of heroin use, medical officials cited heart failure as the cause of death. At his funeral in Las Vegas, the Ink Spots sang "Sunny" in his honor, though Liston would almost certainly have preferred JAMES BROWN's "Night Train," the song that he always listened to while training. Liston's closest friends saw in him a quick, intuitive intelligence and noted his kindness, especially to children. In 1967 the Listons had adopted a three-year-old boy, Daniell. Others saw only Liston's boorishness, his criminal record, and his connection to mobsters. By inducting him into its International Hall of Fame in 1991, the boxing world recognized that Sonny Liston's singular contribution came in the ring, as arguably the hardest-hitting fighter of his generation.

FURTHER READING
Remnick, David. *King of the World: Muhammad Ali and the Rise of an American Hero* (1998).
Tosches, Nick. *The Devil and Sonny Liston* (2000).
Young, A. S. *Sonny Liston: The Champ Nobody Wanted* (1963).
Obituary: *New York Times*, 7 Jan. 1971.

STEVEN J. NIVEN

Little, Booker, Jr. (2 Apr. 1938–5 Oct. 1961), jazz trumpeter and composer, was born in Memphis, Tennessee. Little is known of his parents or his early life. After exchanging clarinet for trumpet at age twelve, the adolescent Little gained experience in his local jazz scene, playing with notable musicians such as PHINEAS NEWBORN and George Coleman. He attended the Chicago Conservatory of Music, graduating with a B.A. in Music in 1958. While in Chicago, Little roomed with the saxophonist SONNY ROLLINS and played in the group MJT+3 with Johnny Griffin.

Rollins had introduced Little to the drummer and bandleader MAX ROACH in 1955, and in June of 1958 Roach invited Little to join his quintet. A central figure in modern jazz, Roach had participated in the full spectrum of its innovations—playing in CHARLIE PARKER's formative bebop groups, MILES DAVIS's *Birth of the Cool* band, and his own hard bop group with the tragically short-lived CLIFFORD BROWN. Indeed it was Brown—a brilliant, brightly toned, and technically gifted trumpeter—whom Little resembled most and to some extent replaced. Little's entrance into Roach's group placed him at the center of the hard bop movement, an East Coast bebop-derivative style that incorporated elements of gospel. Shortly after joining Roach, he made his first recorded appearance on the drummer's EmArcy album, *On the Chicago Scene* (1958). The quintet made three more recordings that year: *Max Roach Plus Four at Newport* for EmArcy, *Award Winning Drummer* for Time, and *Deeds, Not Words* for Riverside. The latter album's title is significant, as among the earliest examples of jazz self-consciously addressing politics. Instrumentally, all three incorporated an unusual ensemble, omitting piano and adding tuba. In October 1958 Little made his first recording as a leader, *The Booker Little 4 and Max Roach*, employing three of his bandmates in addition to the pianist Tommy Flanagan.

After leaving the group in February of the following year, he moved to New York City, where he began freelancing. Throughout the year he worked with the vocalist Bill Henderson, the trombonist SLIDE HAMPTON, and the alto saxophonist Frank Strozier. In April 1960 Little recorded his second album, *Booker Little*, for Time Records. He chose the setting of a quartet, which included the bassist Scott LaFaro. Soon after relocating to Manhattan he met the multi-instrumentalist ERIC DOLPHY. Together they joined Roach on his August 1960 album *We Insist! Max Roach's Freedom Now Suite*, which also included the vocalist ABBEY LINCOLN. The political dimensions implied in the instrumental music of *Deeds, Not Words* were explicitly addressed in the lyrics and screams of "Driva' Man" and "Tryptich: Prayer/Protest/Peace." The group also appeared alongside CHARLES MINGUS at the Jazz Artists Guild concerts, an anti-festival that protested what they saw as the overly commercial hiring practices of the official Newport, Rhode Island, counterpart. The collective was part of a succession of attempts by Mingus and Roach to obtain more control, and thus more monetary reward, for artists over their music.

The collaboration between Little and Dolphy, the most important in the trumpeter's career, came to full fruition in Dolphy's *Far Cry*, recorded in December of 1960. Their partnership evoked a new niche in the evolution of hard bop toward the 1960s avant-garde. While ORNETTE COLEMAN had purged his compositions of prearranged harmony, leaving the soloists the freedom to choose their own tonal region, Little and Dolphy opened up new possibilities within prearranged chord changes. Both would venture into distantly related harmonic areas, utilizing their dissonance for color. At times Little's playing would focus on movement instead of melody, creating spirals from flurries of notes. This type of gestural playing would be expanded further by Little's successor, Freddie Hubbard. He also mastered the use of micro-tones—playing tones in between the standard notes—a device which looked ahead to experiments later in the decade.

The next year Little and Dolphy appeared together on Roach's *Percussion Bitter Sweet* (1961), Little's *Out Front*, and at New York City's Five Spot club. The last engagement, one of the great live recordings, was separated by Prestige into the three albums *At the Five Spot Volume 1*, *Volume 2*, and *The Eric Dolphy Memorial Album*. Little also appeared on JOHN COLTRANE's *Africa/Brass* big band recordings in May and June, the first the saxophonist made for the Impulse label. Little's fourth album as a leader, *Victory and Sorrow*, would be his last. With all but one song written by him, it highlights his talents as a composer. Throughout his themes, he focuses on dissonant, shifting harmonies in the trumpet, trombone, and saxophone against the more consonant, static rhythm section. Suffering from uremia, Little passed away from kidney failure in October at the age of twenty-three. Dolphy would follow him three years later.

Limited as it was, Little's work, especially that with Eric Dolphy, comprised a transition in jazz. His music, incorporating dissonance and non-diatonic gestures, signaled the potential of jazz to develop harmonically and idiomatically while remaining strongly connected to the historic tradition of the rhythm section. Others, such as Miles Davis's second quintet, ANDREW HILL, and much of the avant-garde associated with the Blue Note label in sixties, expanded this idea.

FURTHER READING

Mathieson, Kenny. *Cookin': Hard Bop and Soul Jazz 1954–65* (2002).

DISCOGRAPHY

Saul, Alan. *Booker Little Discography*. Available at http://adale.org/Discographies/Booker.html.

MICHAEL SCHMIDT

Little, Malcolm. *See* Malcolm X.

Little Richard (5 Dec. 1932–), pioneering rock and roll singer, songwriter, and pianist, was born Richard Wayne Penniman in Macon, Georgia, the third of twelve children born to Charles "Bud" Penniman, a brick mason, and Leva Mae (maiden name unknown). His was a family of Seventh-Day Adventist preachers and bootleggers—not the last time that sin and salvation would mix in this performer's life story. As a child, Penniman suffered abuse from his peers because his right leg was shorter than his left. "The kids didn't realize I was crippled," he told his biographer. "They thought I was trying to twist and walk feminine. The kids would call me faggot, sissy, freak" (*Rolling Stone*, 19 July–2 Aug. 1984).

Although he learned to play piano and grew up singing in church with his family (as the Penniman Singers and Tiny Tots Quartet), Penniman was kicked out of the house at age thirteen for homosexual behavior his father thought sinful. Entering the world of carnivals and vaudeville, he was adopted by a white couple, Ann and Johnny Johnson, who ran the Tick Tock Club in Macon, and spent the late 1940s performing in a red evening gown as Princess Lavonne in Sugarfoot Sam's Minstrel Show. Traveling the South, he visited clubs like New Orleans's Dew Drop Inn, where the MC, Patsy Vidalia, was a female impersonator. By the early 1950s rhythm and blues music was spreading across the country. Now known as Little Richard, the performer won an RCA recording contract in 1951 at an audition sponsored by Daddy Zenas Spears of Atlanta's WGST, but these early sessions showed little of the outrageousness to come. Subsequent sessions in 1953 and 1955 with Peacock were equally unsuccessful. Finally, Art Rupe of Specialty Records arranged for Richard to record with a New Orleans band that included such greats as the drummer EARL PALMER and the saxophonist Lee Allen. On 14 September 1955 they recorded "Tutti Frutti" and made history.

The original verses of the song were the kind of material Richard was used to performing in Southern drag queen bars: "Tutti-frutti, good booty / If it don't fit, don't force it / You can grease it, make it easy." Richard was asked to sing it for a white female songwriter, Dorothy LaBostrie, so she could sanitize the lyrics, and the story goes that he was so embarrassed that he sang facing a wall. But the cleaned-up version was a revelation in

Little Richard in 1966. (AP Images.)

itself: over pounding boogie-woogie piano and an ecstatic, gospel-charged, falsetto "whoo," Richard brought matters to a head with the ecstatic yawp "A wop bop a loo bop a lop bam boom!" It might be the quintessential 1950s rock and roll moment.

"Tutti Frutti" sold a half million copies, the bulk of them to white teenagers fascinated by a southern black man wearing mascara and a six-inch pompadour and raving like an out-of-control preacher. There had never been anyone remotely like Little Richard in mainstream pop culture. A bland cover version of "Tutti Frutti" by the white singer Pat Boone went to number twelve on the pop charts, higher than the number seventeen showing of Richard's original. Either way, the result was integrationist: a merger of black and white pop that was felt on radio and in clubs, where kids of all races began partying together.

Others picked up on Richard's barely coded signals. Writing in the 1 April 1997 *Advocate*, Bruce Vilanch argued: "Little Richard was our starter queen, the first flamboyant gay figure of our lives. He may not have been open, but he was open all night. Richard was my hero because he didn't seem to give a damn and I felt he was of my generation." Richard himself has speculated on his explicitly high-camp image: "The people in power maybe felt I wouldn't bother the white girls. Other guys looked more macho, you know, thick and built. JAMES BROWN had a much harder time—by him not having the 'tender look' like me" (*Life*, 1 Dec. 1992).

It is worth remembering Richard's musical innovations as well. Earl Palmer, who drummed on these early sessions, recalled: "I'll tell you, the only reason I started playing what they come to call a rock-and-roll beat came from trying to match Richard's right hand. Ding-ding-ding-ding! ... Little Richard moved from a shuffle to that straight eighth-note feeling ... pounding on the piano with all 10 fingers" (*New York Times*, 25 Apr. 1999). Richard's touring band, the Upsetters, were Macon players with links to James Brown and the subsequent rhythmic upheaval that turned rock and roll into 1960s funk.

Richard had a string of subsequent hits in the late 1950s: "Long Tall Sally," "Slippin' and Slidin'," "Rip It Up," "Reddy Teddy," "She's Got It," "The Girl Can't Help It," "Lucille," "Send Me Some Lovin'," "Jenny, Jenny," "Miss Ann," "Keep a Knockin'," and "Good Golly, Miss Molly" sold an estimated 18 million singles. He was featured in several of the early rock and roll movies, most notably *The Girl Can't Help It* and *Don't Knock the Rock*, both in 1956. Richard has talked about living wildly in this period: for example, being handed ten thousand dollars in hundred-dollar bills by the DJ Alan Freed and putting it all in the trunk of his Cadillac to draw upon as needed; and masturbating while watching his female companion, Angel, have sex with men like the white rock and roller Buddy Holly. Richard's religious beliefs, long buried, started to nag at him, however, and he says that when he saw what turned out to be the *Sputnik* satellite flying across the sky after a show in Australia in 1957, he took it as a sign from God to stop performing rock and roll. He handed his mother the keys to the Cadillac and went back to church.

The rest is anticlimactic. Richard worked in a gospel vein for portions of the 1960s, recording with the great singer SISTER ROSETTA THARPE, the arranger QUINCY JONES, and the Atlantic producer Jerry Wexler. One song from this collaboration, "He Got What He Wanted (But He Lost What He Had)," became something of a trademark for him. He enrolled in Oakwood College, a bible school in Huntsville, Alabama, in 1958.

Yet Richard could never remain out of the spotlight for long, and when the Beatles hit big in 1963, citing him as an influence (now it was Paul McCartney instead of Pat Boone making those "whoos"), he returned to rock and roll. JIMI HENDRIX played in Richard's 1960s touring band for a while, telling him, "I want to make my guitar sound just like your voice" (*Rolling Stone*, 19 July

1984), and perhaps getting a lesson in onstage flamboyance before being fired for upstaging Richard one time too many. Success was more limited for Richard now; his repertoire had barely changed, as he was hauled out to provide nostalgia for the counterculture generation. "I'm the bronze Liberace," he said at a 1970 concert. "Everything we do is '56. We don't do nothing that happened in '66" (Felton, 430).

He had been using drugs since the 1950s, and this began to spiral out of control. Richard continued to put out failed pop material into the 1970s and then returned to Christianity again, after the death of his brother Tony. *People* magazine noted in 1984 that while MICHAEL JACKSON was playing Knoxville, Tennessee, to forty-five thousand people, his musical forefather, Little Richard, was appearing in town on the local *Praise the Lord* TV talk show, telling the host, "I was into homosexuality, and He changed me.... I was into rock 'n' roll, and He changed me."

Richard came back into the limelight once more. In 1986 he was inducted into the inaugural Rock and Roll Hall of Fame and was featured in a cameo performance in the film *Down and Out in Beverly Hills*. Ever since, he has been a kind of rock and roll cartoon, brought in to emote campily in commercials for Revlon, Taco Bell, and Tostitos; playing Giants of Rock package tours; and performing for the first rock president, Bill Clinton, at his inauguration and at a 1994 presidential gala. "I'm the innovator. I'm the emancipator. I'm the originator. I'm the architect of rock 'n' roll," Little Richard likes to say about himself (Dafydd Rees and Luke Crampton, *Q Rock Stars Encyclopedia* [1999], 601). But he never seems to have figured out what his accomplishment meant or reconciled his values, desires, and aspirations.

FURTHER READING

Felton, David. "Little Richard and the Silent Majority," in *The Rolling Stone Rock 'n' Roll Reader*, ed. Ben Fong-Torres (1974).

Lhamon, W. T., Jr. *Deliberate Speed: The Origins of a Cultural Style in the American 1950s* (1990).

Palmer, Robert. *Rock & Roll: An Unruly History* (1995).

White, Charles. *The Life and Times of Little Richard: The Quasar of Rock* (1984).

DISCOGRAPHY

The Georgia Peach (Specialty 7012-2).

Grooviest 17 Original Hits (Specialty 2113).

The Specialty Sessions (Specialty 8508).

ERIC WEISBARD

Little Rock Nine, The, Minnijean Brown-Trickey (11 Sept. 1941–), Elizabeth Eckford (4 Oct. 1941–), Ernest Green (22 Sept. 1941–), MELBA PATILLO-BEALS (7 Dec. 1941–), Thelma Mothershed Wair (29 Nov. 1940–), Gloria Ray Kalmark (26 Sept. 1942–), Dr. Terrence Roberts (3 Dec. 1941–), Jefferson Thomas (1 Sept. 1942–), and Carlotta Walls LaNier (18 Dec. 1942–), were civil rights pioneers, who as teenagers integrated Arkansas's Little Rock (Pulaski County) Central High School on 4 September 1957. They became collectively known as the Little Rock Nine. The students became symbols of the struggle to integrate public education in the U.S. after their enrollment in the previously all-white high school sparked a national controversy, which involved Arkansas governor, Orval Faubus, and President Dwight D. Eisenhower.

After the landmark *Brown v. Board of Education* decision in 1954, in which the Supreme Court ruled that "separate but equal" schools were unconstitutional, school districts throughout the country adopted a slow approach to integration, if they complied with the Court's order at all. In 1955, the Court revisited the issue of desegregation after schools argued that they did not have the resources or infrastructure to facilitate the Court's orders. In 1955, the Court then determined in *Brown v. Board of Education II* (349 U.S. 294), that schools would have to implement desegregation under the auspices of district courts, with "all deliberate speed," a vague expression that did not speak to urgency on the issue; critics said such language held little weight in implementing integration. Prior to *Brown v. Board*, civil rights activists were successful in integration lawsuits in higher and graduate education. In *Sipuel v. Board of Regents of the University of Oklahoma*, the Supreme Court ruled in 1948 the state of Oklahoma had to provide equal education at the state's only public law school, which had previously barred blacks. In the 1950 case *Sweatt v. Painter* the Court ruled that "separate but equal" did not apply in the case of a separate law school for African Americans in the state of Texas, due to a resource disparity between the segregated law schools. NAACP attorney, and later Supreme Court justice, THURGOOD MARSHALL, who was instrumental in *Brown v. Board of Education*, argued both of those law school cases.

In the same year as *Brown II*, the Little Rock School Board decided to integrate Central High School, under a plan proposed by Little Rock School Superintendent Virgil Blossom, beginning with the 1957–1958 school year. Prior to the integration plan, African American children in Little Rock could attend Horace Mann Junior High School and Paul Laurence Dunbar High School. Kalmark, Thomas, and LaNier attended Horace Mann before integrating Central; the other six students attended Dunbar. Central High School, which was the most expensive high school in America when built in 1927 at a cost of $1.5 million to construct, was one of the nation's top secondary schools, with modern science facilities, a gymnasium and nationally renowned publications, when the Little Rock Nine attempted to integrate it. The American Institute of Architects named the school one of the most beautiful high schools in America. In 1929, with funding from the Julius Rosenwald Fund and the Rockefeller General Education Fund, the all-black Dunbar High School opened at a cost of $400,000. The Arkansas state chapter of the NAACP, under the leadership of the state's NAACP president DAISY LEE BATES, organized to file law suits on behalf of black students seeking admission to segregated Little Rock Schools. In 1956, after an attempt to enroll twenty-seven black students in Little Rock public schools, the NAACP filed a lawsuit on behalf of thirty-three children who sought admission to four Little Rock Schools. These attempts were fruitless, after a judge dismissed the cases on the basis that the School Board tried in good faith to fulfill the requests. The organization continued to focus on steps toward integration.

In 1957, Bates and the NAACP began to identify potential students to integrate Central under the Blossom Plan. After interviewing a pool of eligible students, the NAACP selected seventeen students to participate in integration. Eight of the students decided to remain in segregated school. The NAACP proceeded in assisting the Nine with registering at Central; the students were chosen based on their strong academic performance and their individual character. Minnijean Brown-Trickey was born Minnijean Brown to Mr. and Mrs. W. B. Brown in Little Rock. Trickey was 16 years old when she entered Central for her junior year of high school. Elizabeth Ann Eckford was born to Oscar and Birdie Eckford in Little Rock. She was one of six children, and she was fifteen years when she integrated Central. Ernest Gideon Green was born to Ernest G. Green Sr. and Lothaire Green in Little Rock. He was the only student to enter Central as a senior. Thelma Mothershed Wair was born Thelma Jean Mothershed in Bloomberg, Texas, to Arlevis Leander and Hosanna Claire Moore Mothershed. She was fifteen years old when

Nine black students leave Central High School in Little Rock, Arkansas after classes on 25 September 1957. They are being escorted from a side door by troops of the 101st Airborne Division. (AP Images.)

she integrated Central. Melba Joy Pattillo-Beals was born Melba Joy Pattillo in Little Rock to Lois Marie Payton and Howell Patillo. Her mother was one of the first black graduates of the University of Arkansas in Fayetteville. Beals was fifteen years old when she integrated Central. Gloria Ray Kalmark was born Gloria Cecilia Ray in Little Rock. She was fifteen years old when she integrated Central. Terrence James Roberts was born in Little Rock to William and Margaret Roberts. He was 15 when he integrated Central. Carlotta Walls LaNier was born in Little Rock to Juanita and Cartelyou Walls, the oldest of three girls. Her father was a mason and her mother, who had attended the all-black Dunbar High School in Little Rock, worked in the Little Rock office of public housing. The youngest member of the Nine, Carlotta Walls was fourteen when she integrated Central. Jefferson A. Thomas was born in Little Rock to Mr. and Mrs. Ellis Thomas; he was sixteen years old when he integrated Central.

In August 1957, before the commencement of the school year, the all-white Mother's League of Central High School decided to petition GovernorFaubus in opposition to the integration plan. The women opposed the measure based on a fear that integration would lead to interracial sex, particularly between black boys and white girls. Fears of racial mixing played a central role in southern resistance to black social and political equality. The Mother's League filed a motion for a temporary injunction against the plan and a definition on the state's segregation policies. Pulaski County determined that integration was potentially violent and granted the Mother's League request. U.S. District Court Judge Ronald Davies overruled the injunction decision, and he ordered the School Board to continue as planned. On 2 September 1957, two days before the beginning of the school year, Governor Faubus instructed the Arkansas National Guard to bar the students from entering the high school. The School

Board informed the Nine that they could not attend school. Judge Davies ordered desegregation the next day, but Governor Faubus did not relent. The Little Rock standoff became national news as segregationists organized to deliver speeches and demonstrate against the School Board's actions.

On 4 September 1957, the integration issue exploded when the Nine reported for their first day at their new school. Eight of the students arrived together, and Eckford arrived at Central alone. Eckford's family did not have a telephone, and she was not aware of a plan for the children to meet before school and travel to Central in a group. *Arkansas Democrat-Gazette* newspaper photographer Will Counts, who was later nominated for a Pulitzer Prize for his photographs of the crisis, immortalized the resistance to integration in a photograph of Eckford being harassed by an angry mob of anti-integrationists. One of the tormentors was Hazel Bryan Massery, who apologized to Eckford forty years later. Eckford eventually walked to a bus stop with the help of Mrs. Grace Lorch, a white woman. Lorch remained with her until she boarded a bus. Due to the threats and chaos of the previous day, the Nine did not attend school on 5 September 1957. The School Board requested that Judge Davies suspend the order to integrate; two days later Judge Davies denied the request. On 8 September 1957, Governor Faubus declared in an address on national television that integration led to violence and demanded that the federal government no longer intervene on the matter. The next day, Judge Davies filed for an injunction against the Governor and the Arkansas National Guard; he also requested that the United States Justice Department file similar injunctions.

On 14 September 1957, Governor Faubus met with President Eisenhower at the President's vacation home in Newport, Rhode Island, to discuss the integration crisis. On 20 September 1957, the date of Faubus's preliminary junction hearing, Judge Davies ordered Faubus to remove the troops, unless they were going to protect the Nine. The Guardsmen were then replaced by Little Rock police officers. On 23 September 1957, a crowd of more than 1000 protestors swarmed in front of Central to intimidate the Nine and expressed their opposition against integration. The Nine secretly entered the building, but when the crowd heard of their entrance, they were escorted out of the school in police cars. Black reporters covering the story were also targets of the mob. *Tri-State Defender of Memphis* reporter L. Alex Wilson was hit on the head with a brick by

a protestor. Images of the brutal attack on Wilson allegedly roused President Eisenhower to take action against the violence in Little Rock. The next day, on 24 September 1957, President Eisenhower called up the 101st Airborne Division from Fort Campbell, Kentucky ("the Screaming Eagles") to protect the Nine. President Eisenhower also placed the state's National Guard under federal orders to protect the students. On 25 September 1957, U.S. Army General Edwin Walker spoke to the school's white students before the Nine arrived for classes; the Nine were then accompanied into the school by 1200 armed soldiers.

On 1 October 1957, the 101st began to relinquish their duties to the Arkansas National Guard to protect the students. Although the soldiers provided some security, they were not able to protect the students in places such as restrooms, locker rooms and in the school cafeteria. The Nine students endured a challenging school year, marked with intimidation and bullying during the school day, and threats of violence against their families and homes. The Nine faced brutal physical and verbal attacks from students. In December 1957, Trickey was suspended for six days after she poured a bowl of hot chili on a white student who was aggravating her. Trickey was the only student to be expelled from Central. After more confrontations with white students, Trickey was expelled in February 1958. She later transferred to a high school in New York City. The school year continued, and on 27 May 1958, Green became the first black graduate of Central. MARTIN LUTHER KING JR. attended his graduation. Despite fear of violence at the ceremony, Green graduated with no incident. In September 1958, Governor Faubus ordered the closure of the Little Rock Schools for the upcoming school year, as a means of halting further integration. The city of Little Rock voted to support the measure. Other school districts employed this strategy to curb integration; which led to the establishment of private schools in some communities. The schools reopened in August 1959.

After the "lost school year," some members of the Nine returned to Central. Eckford took correspondence courses during the school closure year in St. Louis, Missouri, and earned a bachelor's degree from Knox College in Galesburg, Illinois. She later worked in criminal justice, and served as a probation officer. Green attended Michigan State University, with financial assistance from Michigan State President John A. Hannah, where he became a founding member of the Sigma Chapter of Omega

Psi Phi Fraternity, Inc. He earned a bachelor's of arts in 1962 and a master's degree two years later. He has worked for a building corporation, the Adolph Institute; the A. Phillip Randolph Education Fund; in the office of the Assistant Secretary of Housing and Urban Affairs during President Jimmy Carter's administration; and for the investment services firm, Lehman Brothers. He is both a Boy Scout Eagle Scout and was named a Distinguished Eagle Scout by the Boy Scouts of America. Kalmark earned a bachelor's degree in chemistry and mathematics from the Illinois Institute of Technology. She served as executive director of IBM in the Netherlands, and as a publisher of a European computer journal. She later moved Sweden to work for IBM and founded *Computers in Industry*, a technology journal. After threats of violence and retaliation, Patillo-Beals's mother sent her to live in Santa Rosa, California, with Dr. George and Carol McCabe, Quaker foster parents matched with Patillo-Beals by Bates and the NAACP. Patillo-Beals earned a bachelor's degree from San Francisco State University, and she later earned a master's degree in journalism from Columbia University. She chronicled her experiences in Little Rock in the book *Warriors Don't Cry: A Searing Memoir of the Battle to Integrate Little Rock's Central High School*. She continued to describe her experiences after leaving Little Rock in *White is a State of Mind: A Memoir* (1999). In 2000, she became Program Coordinator for the Communications program at the Dominican University of California in San Rafael. The following year, she was promoted to Assistant Professor and Communications Director of the department. In 2002, Beals was named chair of the newly established Communications Department at Dominican. Roberts did not return to Central; he moved to Los Angeles and attended Los Angeles High School after he left Central. Roberts earned a bachelor's degree in sociology from California State University–Los Angeles in 1967. He earned a master's degree in social welfare from the University of California–Los Angeles in 1967, and a Ph.D. in psychology from Southern Illinois University in 1977. He served as a faculty member and department chair of Antioch University's psychology program in Los Angeles. Thomas returned to Central after it reopened, and he graduated from Central in 1960. He narrated the United States Information Agency's film *Nine From Little Rock* in 1964. This film was among a series of films produced to elevate the profile of the U.S. during the Cold War by highlighting African American progress. After graduating,

Thomas moved to Detroit to attend Wayne State University. He later moved to Los Angeles to attend Los Angeles State College, where he earned a bachelor's degree in business administration. He served in the Vietnam War, and he continued his career with the military as an accountant for the United States Department of Defense. In 2001, he was granted an honorary doctorate from Dominican University.

Trickey earned a bachelor's degree from Southern Illinois University, and after marrying she moved to Ottawa, Ontario, in Canada. She and her husband had six children. In 1999, Trickey returned to the United States and served as a Deputy Assistant Secretary for Workforce Diversity at the United States Department of Interior in President Bill Clinton's administration. She also worked as a diversity consultant and an educator for the Sojourn to the Past Project, which brought students to significant civil rights history sites. Her daughter, Spirit Trickey, served as tour guide for Central, which is on the list of the National Park Service's historic sites. Trickey was the subject of a documentary, *Journey to Little Rock: The Untold Story*, in 2007. Wair earned a bachelor's degree from Southern Illinois University–Carbondale in 1964, and a master's degree in Guidance and Counseling along with an education credential from Southern Illinois University–Edwardsville in 1970. She worked as a home economics teacher for the East St. Louis, Illinois schools and at the Juvenile Detention Center of St. Clair County Jails in Illinois. She retired to Little Rock in 2003. While the Little Rock Schools were closed during 1958–1959, LaNier enrolled in correspondence courses in order to keep up with her schoolwork. She returned to Central the following year and graduated in 1960. LaNier later attended Michigan State University but moved after two years. She completed her bachelor's degree at Colorado State College (now the University of North Colorado) in 1968. She married Ira C. LaNier that year. She worked for the YMCA in administration before establishing a career in real estate. In 1977, she established her own real estate brokerage and served on the Board of Trustees at the University of Northern Colorado.

The Little Rock Nine have been honored in numerous ways for their contributions to Civil Rights and integration. Bates and the Nine were awarded the NAACP Spingarn Medal in 1959, the organization's highest honor for civil rights activities. On 19 August 1977, Little Rock High School was added the National List of Historic Places and on 20

May 1982 it was established as a National Historic Landmark. On 6 November 1998, President Bill Clinton signed a bill to add Central High School to the list of National Historic Sites, citing "the significant role the school played in the desegregation of public schools in the South." One of the school's intersecting streets is named after Bates (Daisy L. Gatson Bates Drive). President Clinton also awarded the Congressional Gold Medal to the Nine on 9 November 1999.

In 2007, HBO Films released a documentary about the school entitled *Little Rock Central: 50 Years Later* in which Central alumni filmmakers, Craig and Brent Renaud, profile the school's contemporary struggle with the school's affluent white student body and poor, African American students and their disparate experiences, as well as the social and economic segregation within Little Rock. The film features Little Rock students, faculty and parents reflecting on the school's successes and failures after integration. Students celebrated the election of African American student Brand Love to the presidency of the student government, yet they highlighted the social segregation among the students. Trickey appears in the film and explains to the students her disappointment upon seeing students self-segregated in a classroom. The population of Little Rock at the time was approximately 55.1 percent white, 40.4 percent black, 2.7 percent Latino or Hispanic. The documentary noted that although the school is among the most racially integrated of all Little Rock public high schools, with a population of 53 percent black students and 42 percent white students, the school's highly rigorous honors and Advanced Placement programs has created two different schools, in which white students participate in the academically advanced courses and African American students struggle to succeed.

On 20 January 2009, seven of the nine activists attended the inauguration of President BARACK OBAMA as honored guests.

FURTHER READING

Bates, Daisy L. *Long Shadow of Little Rock: A Memoir* (1987).

Jacoway, Elizabeth. *Turn Away Thy Son: Little Rock, The Crisis that Shocked the Nation* (2007).

Morrison, Toni. *Remember: The Journey to School Integration* (2004).

Patillo-Beals, Melba. *Warriors Don't Cry: A Searing Memoir of the Battle to Integrate Little Rock's Central High* (1995).

MARCIA CHATELAIN

Livingston, Lemuel Walker (1 May 1861–18 Dec. 1930), physician and diplomat, was born in Monticello, Florida, the son of James and Emily Livingston. After the Civil War, his family moved to Jacksonville, Florida, where Livingston and his older sisters, Julia and Minerva, attended public schools. He became a schoolteacher in Jacksonville while attending that city's Cookman Institute, later merged into Bethune-Cookman University in Orlando. After his graduation from Cookman in 1882, he was recommended by Florida Republican leaders for appointment to the U.S. Military Academy at West Point.

Livingston's quest was detailed by many U.S. newspapers that year, including a memorable sketch in the *New York Sun* (3 Sept. 1882) describing the youth as "conceded to have a bright, intelligent face and a fine physique. If he should prove qualified in his studies, his fellow cadets must not destroy him." Livingston's unexpected nomination surprised the *Sun*, which recalled the recent expulsion of JOHNSON C. WHITTAKER and the courtmartial of HENRY O. FLIPPER, first black graduate of West Point, but the newspaper declared that Livingston "must not be persecuted on account of his race" if he passed the exam.

In early September 1882, Livingston failed the entrance exam at West Point, among fifteen of a group of forty-one applicants rejected that year. But he continued his studies, after being admitted to Howard University's medical department in Washington, DC, later that year. While studying, he was employed as a clerk at the U.S. Treasury Department. He graduated from Howard with an M.D. in 1885. He remained in Washington, continuing his Treasury work while completing studies for a doctorate in pharmacy at Howard, which he received in 1888.

Upon returning to Florida in 1888, he established a medical practice in Key West, and also became principal of the Douglass School, a position that he held for the next seven years. In a letter he wrote that year to the *New York Age* (1 Dec. 1888), after Monroe County had elected a black sheriff and black county judge, Livingston boasted that his new home was "the freest town in the South, and not even Washington excepted," and that the Ku Klux Klan "would be run into the Gulf of Mexico" by local residents. Black Republicans held many local and county offices in the town of Key West and Monroe County, and Livingston himself soon became active in Republican Party politics.

In 1896 Livingston was selected as an at-large state delegate to the Republican national convention in St. Louis, Missouri—one of three blacks in the small Florida delegation—and voted to nominate William McKinley as the party's presidential nominee. Following McKinley's inauguration, Livingston began pressing his bid in the summer of 1897 for appointment as consul to Valparaiso, Chile, with backing from Florida Republican leaders (Washington, DC, *Evening Star*, 7 Jul. 1897). Livingston passed the State Department's consular examination in November 1897, but was nominated instead as U.S. consul to Cape Haitien (Cap-Haitien), Haiti, on 18 December 1897.

Confirmed by the U.S. Senate in January 1898, Livingston assumed his duties in Haiti in February 1898. He held the position for the next two decades, becoming a career employee after the 1906 reorganization of the consular service. In February 1915, he was promoted to Class 9 consul.

Livingston's economic reports from Cape Haitien were widely circulated within the U.S. State Department, and his writing often appeared in the embassy's annual reports from Port-au-Prince. Among Livingston's most memorable accomplishments during his long tenure at Cape Haitien was his role in mediating the cessation of hostilities between rebel forces and the Haitian government in 1915. According to the *New York Times* (3 Oct. 1915), Livingston accompanied the former Haitian interior minister Carlos Zamora and other U.S. officials to a rural area outside the city at Quartier Morin, "and there met the rebel leaders. A formal agreement was drawn and signed" with Livingston's watchful assistance.

Dr. Livingston submitted his resignation as consul in December 1919, but continued to serve until a replacement arrived. He stepped down on 31 March 1920, having served for twenty-two years. He continued to reside in Cape Haitien after his retirement, and died there a decade later.

FURTHER READING

Rivers, Larry E., and Canter Brown Jr. "African-Americans in South Florida: A Home and a Haven for Reconstruction-Era Leaders," *Tequesta: The Journal of the Historical Association of Southern Florida* (1996).

BENJAMIN R. JUSTESEN

Livingston, Myrtle Smith (8 May 1902–15 July 1974), educator and playwright, was born Myrtle Athleen Smith in Holly Grove, Arkansas, to Lula C. (Hall)

and Isaac Samuel Smith. Myrtle attended Manual High School from 1916 to 1920, and studied pharmacy at Howard University in Washington, D.C., from 1920 to 1922. She began attending Colorado Teacher's College in 1923, earning a teaching certificate in 1924 before marrying the physician William McKinley Livingston on 25 June 1925. She left Colorado Teacher's College in 1926 and was hired in 1929 as a physical education instructor by Lincoln University, a historically black college in Jefferson City, Missouri. While at Lincoln, she taught every level of physical education and health and established a formal athletic program for female students, enabling young Lincoln women to participate in organized, competitive sports for the first time. Livingston was a well-respected teacher at Lincoln University for forty-four years, retiring in 1972.

While she spent the majority of her career at Lincoln, Livingston is best known for her play about miscegenation and lynching. Her one-act drama *For Unborn Children* was published in the July 1926 issue of *Crisis* after winning third prize in the magazine's literary competition the year before. Since then, scholars of black drama have recognized the play's value and ensured its continued availability by including it in anthologies. The play centered on LeRoy, a black lawyer who was ready to move north and elope because he and his white fiancée, Selma, could not be together in the South. The action begins with LeRoy's sister and grandmother worrying because he is not home from work and has not telephoned. They believe that his life is always in danger because he is dating a white woman. When LeRoy finally arrives, he says that they will not have to worry much longer because he and Selma have decided to leave town the next night. His sister Marion proclaims, "Well, if you marry her, may God help me never to breathe your name again!" (*The Crisis*, July 1926, 123). Marion runs from the room sobbing, leaving LeRoy with his grandmother, who is equally hurt by his decision but gentler in her response. She tells him that marrying a white woman is a disservice to his unborn children because "a white woman cannot mother a Negro baby!" (*The Crisis*, July 1926, 124). To substantiate her claim, she reveals the family secret he has never known his mother because she was white and chose not to be a part of her "Negro" children's lives. Determined not to risk giving his own offspring such a mother, LeRoy decides not to elope, but the lynch mob is already en route. His fiancée rushes in to warn him, but it is too late. The play ends as the mob yells for LeRoy to step outside, and he exits to meet his death, "victorious and unafraid."

By the time the piece appeared, Livingston was already in Colorado, training to become a teacher. Nevertheless, the play marked her connection to historical movements that helped shape her generation. Coming of age in what came to be known as the New Negro Renaissance, young Myrtle Smith benefited from efforts to develop African American artists. When she attended Howard University, professors ALAIN LOCKE and THOMAS MONTGOMERY GREGORY were working to make the university the nation's training ground for African American theater artists. The university's program encouraged playwriting, and by 1924 interracial political organizations began sponsoring literary contests in their magazines. The Urban League's *Opportunity* magazine announced its competition in August, and *The Crisis*, edited by W. E. B. DuBois, published its call for submissions a month later. In its November 1924 issue, *The Crisis* specifically offered prizes of $75, $40, and $10 for original plays.

Locke, Gregory, and DuBois all were involved with these contests as judges, supporters, and promoters, but they disagreed about what black drama and theater should accomplish. Locke and Gregory promoted "folk" plays that were free of strong political content; they focused on aesthetics because they wanted their students' work to be viewed by the mainstream as truly artistic. DuBois, in contrast, felt that black artists limited themselves by adhering to any aesthetic that ignored art's inherent political power and that denied the importance of directly protesting injustice. Accordingly, he valued so-called race plays, including antilynching plays, because they indicted American racism.

For Unborn Children offered such an indictment and, in doing so, revealed its debt to earlier black women activists and its connection to the Little Negro Theatre movement, which emphasized the need to address black audiences in intimate spaces. *For Unborn Children* never questions the sincerity of LeRoy's and Selma's feelings, but it nevertheless suggests that pursuing interracial love is irresponsible. In recognizing this play with a prize and with publication in *The Crisis*, DuBois clearly saw the value of having his readers debate these issues, just as Livingston's characters do. Livingston clearly believed that black men's vulnerability to white women in the 1920s warranted commentary similar to that offered by black women in the

1890s. Following the example of the antilynching crusader IDA B. WELLS-BARNETT, Livingston set out to show that black men too often willingly destroyed their lives by falling in love with white women. Livingston offers a Wells-inspired critique of LeRoy through his sister's explanation of miscegenation statutes: "Laws would never have been passed against it if states could have believed white women would turn Negro men down, but they knew they wouldn't; they can make fools out of them too easily" (*The Crisis*, July 1926, 123). Wells-Barnett was more diplomatic than Livingston's character, but her investigations revealed that rape was not alleged in most lynch cases. Indeed, Wells-Barnett insisted that when mobs claimed to be motivated by a black man's rape of a white woman, "rape" actually referred to a consensual relationship, often initiated by the woman: "White men lynch the offending Afro-American, not because he is a despoiler of virtue, but because he succumbs to the smiles of white women" (*Southern Horrors*, 54). Livingston and Wells-Barnett both suggested that when white women and black men were intimate, the black man was far from aggressive and violent.

While these arguments saturated Wells-Barnett's protest pamphlets and speeches, Livingston placed them in a play, suggesting that she was not aiming to appeal to integrated audiences of the commercial theater. Indeed, her use of the one-act format indicates that she intended the script to be brought to life in intimate spaces, such as black churches and households—the preferred venues of the Little Black Theatre movement, which was committed to making theater about, by, for, and near African Americans.

Livingston's forty-four years at Lincoln University were similarly marked by her willingness to serve black communities. When she arrived in 1929 as a physical education instructor, she was a "department of one," but by 1936 the program offered girls' baseball, basketball, volleyball, soccer, and tennis as well as archery, golf, track, and hockey. Livingston took particular initiative in offering her students tap dance and interpretive dance, founding a chapter of Orchesis Dance Group in 1936—the first chapter to be formed at a black college. Livingston's troupe offered indoor and outdoor shows in several cities in Kansas and Missouri. In addition to these formal duties, Livingston taught first aid to Jefferson City citizens and wrote several plays and skits that were performed by student groups, including sororities and fraternities; unfortunately, scripts have not been located.

Having always wanted to retire in Hawaii, she moved there with her sister upon leaving Lincoln University, and she died there in 1974 after only a year and a half of retirement. Her ashes were scattered over the Pacific Ocean. Later, Lincoln University trustees named a park in her honor.

FURTHER READING

Correspondence, teaching notes, syllabi, and other manuscript materials as well as articles about Livingston's contributions are preserved in the Lincoln University archives, Jefferson City, Missouri.

Livingston, Myrtle A. Smith. *For Unborn Children: A Play in One Act. (The Crisis,* July 1926).

Burton, Jennifer, ed. *Zora Neale Hurston, Eulalie Spence, Marita Bonner, and Others: The Prize Plays and Other One-Acts Published in Periodicals* (1996).

Hatch, James, ed. *Black Theatre USA: Plays by African Americans,* rev. and exp. ed. (1996).

Wells-Barnett, Ida B. (Jacqueline Jones Royster, ed.) *On Lynchings: Southern Horrors, A Red Record, Mob Rule in New Orleans.* (1997).

KORITHA MITCHELL

LL Cool J (14 Jan. 1968–), hip-hop performer, songwriter, and actor, was born James Todd Smith in New York City. Raised in the St. Albans district of Queens, Smith was the only child of James Smith Jr. and Ondrea Smith, whose turbulent, abusive relationship led to their split when Smith was four years old; the boy and his mother moved in with her parents. Unfortunately, the trouble did not end there: when Smith was four, James Smith Jr. shot his ex-wife in the back and legs as she returned to her parents' house after work, wounding her father in the attack as well. Though both survived, this escalation of violence in his family marked the young James Smith throughout his life, and—according to his 1998 autobiography—he credited this early turmoil (and a later unfortunate reprise, when his mother became the victim of further abuse by a later boyfriend) with helping to shape his persona—and love of musical performance. He sang in his church choir, and, when Smith was eleven, his grandfather bought him a DJ system, offering him the chance to expand upon the rapping ability he had experimented with since age nine. Smith soon crafted his first demo tapes, one of which fell into the hands of fledgling label Def Jam Records.

The energetic sixteen-year-old talent piqued the interest of Def Jam executives, then in the process of building a roster that would quickly make them hip-hop's most powerful record label, and Smith—by then known as LL Cool J, an acronym that stood for "Ladies Love Cool James," or LL for short—released his debut single, the underground smash "I Need A Beat," in 1984. The single sold an astounding 100,000 copies and became Def Jam's first major hit. In 1985, having dropped out of high school to pursue a full-time music career, LL released his debut album *Radio,* an artistic and commercial success that firmly established the young star—and his label—within hip-hop's growing musical and cultural presence. With hit singles "I Can't Live Without My Radio" and "Rock The Bells," *Radio* was an energetic collection of material that immediately set forth LL Cool J's trademark lyrical dexterity and braggadocio, a flirtatious swagger (accompanied by trademark lip-licking, which LL later claimed was a nervous tic) that gained him the reputation as one of hip-hop's most popular artists with female audiences, and also provoked a series of rap-battle conflicts (carried out mostly through the recording of "dis" tracks) that saw LL famously defeat, among others, Kool Moe Dee, whose once-successful career was largely derailed by his unsuccessful attempt to out-rhyme LL Cool J. *Radio* went platinum, and LL earned credit for his ability to match hip-hop's furiously inventive approach with memorable hooks, recognizable song structures, and universal themes.

It also was because of this commercial accessibility that LL became the focus of much unfavorable attention. Critics blamed him, at least in part, for the rise of "pop-rap," a sub-genre he epitomized with the smash single "I Need Love," off his second album *Bigger and Deffer.* The tender love song was one of LL's most lasting singles, and its expressions of devotion and emotional yearning made it exceptional among hip-hop releases. The ongoing ascendance of the subgenre as a successful (and successfully marketed) brand of pop music did not sit well with many of the form's purists. Indeed, his third long-player, 1988's *Walking With A Panther,* was coolly received, particularly in relation to his previous work, though the strutting "I'm The Type Of Guy" reached the top ten. It seemed that, despite a handful of major hits that made LL Cool J a major star, and helped build Def Jam Records in the process, his career had peaked after only three albums.

In 1990, however, LL Cool J rose again. With *Mama Said Knock You Out,* a booming assertion of skill and integrity, and a groundbreaking performance on MTV's *Unplugged* program, LL made the first of his extraordinary returns to the spotlight. The album's ferocious title single (which Bob Dylan later played on the inaugural episode of his radio show) exemplified LL's attempts to engage topics like racial discrimination, police brutality, and the quest for spiritual fulfillment. Despite the album's gravity, the warm, celebratory hit "Around The Way Girl" showed that he still held the title of hip-hop's premiere "loverman." His comeback was sweetened by the arrival of his first two children —Najee (1989) and Italia (1990)—from a relationship with girlfriend Simeone Johnson that ended after Italia's birth. LL later had two more daughters, Samaria (1995) and Nina Simone (2000).

Building on the success of this release, LL Cool J began forays into acting, accepting roles in the films *The Hard Way* (1991) and *Toys* (1992). He continued to act through the latter years of the decade, appearing in Oliver Stone's film *Any Given Sunday* (1999) and the television sitcom *In The House* (1995–1999) Between these acting jobs, he also released hit recordings, including the multiplatinum *Mr. Smith* in 1995; the sultry single "Doin' It" became an award-winning MTV staple. Even as hip-hop underwent significant changes, embracing a variety of styles that, on the surface, had little to do with what made LL Cool J famous, he nonetheless thrived within each context that he chose to release an album, even while most of the genre's biggest and best artists remained in the spotlight for only a short period, burning brightly over the course of a few successful albums. This ability to adapt, the consistent quality of his work, and the continuing appeal of LL's strong-and-sexy persona meant that, even into the twenty-first century, audiences rewarded LL Cool J with warm commercial fortunes and critical appraisal. In 2006 he achieved another level of success by collaborating with Jennifer Lopez on the skittering "Control Myself."

When not making music, LL found time to publish books (including his 1998 autobiography, *I Make My Own Rules*) and start a clothing line, James Todd Smith, which hit clothing stores in 2006. He announced plans to release his final album in 2007. Whether or not it was truly his last, LL Cool J over his long career affirmed his place as one of hip-hop's most important figures, whose artistic achievements and commercial accomplishments helped the genre (and accompanying iconography) reach its dominant position within American cultural life.

FURTHER READING

LL Cool J, with Karen Hunter. *I Make My Own Rules* (1998).

Erlewine, Stephen Thomas. "LL Cool J," in *All Music Guide*, ed. Bogdanov, Vladimir et al (2001).

CHARLES L. HUGHES

Lloyd, Earl Francis (3 Apr. 1928–), basketball player, was born in Alexandria, Virginia, the son of Theodore Lloyd, a laborer, and Daisy (Mitchell) Lloyd, a domestic. The Virginia of Lloyd's youth was deeply segregated. In 1942 he entered Parker-Gray High School in Alexandria, where he played basketball, baseball, and football. At Parker-Gray, Lloyd was profoundly influenced by Lewis Randolph Johnson, who coached all of the school's sports. By 1946, when Lloyd graduated from high school, he had scholarship offers from all of the black colleges and universities along the Atlantic coast. Since Coach Johnson was a graduate of West Virginia State College in Institute just outside Charleston, Lloyd took his mentor's advice and entered the black college in West Virginia. He was the first member of his family to attend college.

At West Virginia State, Lloyd found a caring faculty and another skilled coach, Mark Cardwell. The Yellow Jackets played in the Colored Intercollegiate Athletic conference (CIAA). Because of segregation in the South and racial discrimination in the North, some of the best African American collegiate athletic talent was found in the CIAA. In 1948 and 1949 the Yellow Jackets won consecutive CIAA conference and tournament championships. Lloyd won all-conference honors three times and the *Pittsburgh Courier* placed him on its All-America team in 1949 and 1950. Later he would be honored as the CIAA "Player of the Decade, 1946–1956" and placed on the CIAA Silver Anniversary team. The National Basketball Association (NBA) had just finished its first year of play when Lloyd graduated and it had no African American players. In 1950, however, the New York Knicks purchased the contract of Nat "Sweetwater" Clifton from the Harlem Globetrotters, the Boston Celtics drafted CHUCK COOPER in the second round of the NBA draft, and the Washington Capitols drafted Lloyd in the ninth round. Lloyd had never had a white classmate or a meaningful conversation with a white peer, so his first training camp was also his first significant exposure to white Americans. After surviving training camp, Lloyd, a six-foot six-inch forward, became the first African American to play an NBA game, because Washington was scheduled to play before

Earl Francis Lloyd during a stopover at Chicago's O'Hare Airport on his return to Detroit from Portland, Ore., on Oct. 30, 1972. (AP Images.)

New York or Boston. On 31 October 1950 he scored six points and snared ten rebounds in a 78-70 loss to the Rochester (New York) Royals (the team is now known as the Sacramento Kings). Unlike the attention given to JACKIE ROBINSON when he broke baseball's racial barrier in 1947, Lloyd's presence on Rochester's court generated little response in the media. Most likely this reflected the significant difference in stature of professional baseball and professional basketball, which at the time was still searching for its niche as a spectator sport.

After seven games, Lloyd received his draft notice from the U.S. Army and he would not resume his NBA career until the 1952–1953 season with the Syracuse Nationals (later the Philadelphia 76ers). Lloyd played six seasons with Syracuse where he established himself as a tough rebounded and defender. The Nationals were coached by Al Cervi, a member of the Naismith Hall of Fame, and were led by Dolph Schayes, another Hall of Famer. In 1955 Syracuse won the NBA championship as it squeaked by the Ft. Wayne (later, Detroit) Pistons in a seven-game series. Lloyd and his teammate Jim Tucker were the first African Americans to play on an NBA championship team.

Following the 1957–1958 season, Syracuse traded Lloyd to the Detroit Pistons. In 1960 Dick McGuire, the Pistons' head coach, asked Lloyd to serve as his assistant coach, which made him the first African American to hold this position in the NBA. Lloyd left the Pistons in 1968 to work for the Chrysler Corporation. He returned to the Pistons in the 1971–1972 season as their head coach when Butch Van Breda Kolff left the team after ten games. Up to that time the only other African American to coach an NBA team was BILL RUSSELL, who was named the playing-coach of the Boston Celtics in 1966. Under Lloyd the Pistons won twenty and lost fifty. The following season the Pistons released him after the team lost five of its first seven games.

After his NBA career Lloyd worked for Chrysler, the Detroit Board of Education, and the Bing Group, which was owned by a former star of the Detroit Pistons, Dave Bing. Lloyd was community relations director for the company. On 5 September 2003 Lloyd was inducted into the Naismith Memorial Basketball Hall of Fame as a contributor. He was a basketball pioneer in the truest sense of the word. Lloyd's first contract was for $4,500, which was standard for the early 1950s. Like his white teammates, he endured long train rides and a travel per diem of five dollars. Unlike his white teammates, as an African American he had to endure special burdens. Fans were tough and shouted racial epithets. Hotels refused to let him eat with the team. In an exhibition game played at Wofford College in Spartanburg, South Carolina, Lloyd was not allowed to enter the arena. While Lloyd was the target of racism, he also remembered the kindnesses of white players and coaches. When he was drafted Lloyd did not have a car, but Bill Sharman, later a star with the Boston Celtics (and later still, coach and general manager of the Los Angeles Lakers), picked him up every day so that he did not have to take a bus to training camp. In Fort Wayne the Hotel Ortman had a "whites only" policy in its dining room. Rather than letting him eat alone, Horace "Bones" McKinney joined Lloyd for dinner in the latter's room.

When basketball's Hall of Fame inducted him, it honored him not for his statistics. He averaged 8.4 points over eight years and double figures only once in 1955 (10.2). Lloyd was the consummate team player who understood his role and conducted himself as a professional.

FURTHER READINGS
The Earl Lloyd File is held by the Naismith Memorial Basketball Hall of Fame, Springfield, Massachusetts.
Lloyd, Earl. Oral interview, Naismith Memorial Basketball Hall of Fame in Springfield, Massachusetts (4 Sept. 2003).

Narducci, Mark. "Basketball Honors A Barrier
  Breaker," *Philadelphia Inquirer*, 5 Sept. 2003.
Spears, Mark. "A Footnote in History," the *Denver Post*,
  30 Oct. 2005.
Thomas, Ron. *They Cleared the Lane: The NBA's Black
  Pioneers* (2002).

DOLPH GRUNDMAN

Lloyd, John Henry "Pop" (25 Apr. 1884–19 Mar.
1965), Negro League baseball player and manager,
was born in Palatka, Florida. The names of his parents are not known. His father died when Lloyd
was an infant, and he was raised by his grandmother after his mother remarried. A grade school
dropout, he began his career on the sandlots of
Jacksonville, Florida, at age nineteen.

Mild-mannered, clean-living, and genial, Lloyd
had high cheekbones, a lantern jaw, and piercing
eyes. Similarities in physique, temperament, style,
and talent led to comparisons of Lloyd to white
baseball's preeminent shortstop, and Lloyd was
often called the "black Honus Wagner." Connie
Mack felt that the two were of equal caliber, and
Honus Wagner himself remarked, "After I saw
him, I felt honored that they should name such
a great ballplayer after me." Like Wagner, Lloyd,
at five feet eleven inches and 180 pounds, was a
big man for a shortstop, with long arms and large,
strong hands. Both had wide range in the field
and scooped up unusual amounts of dirt while
fielding groundballs, their strong throws to first
base emerging from clouds of dust. Thus in Cuba
Lloyd earned the nickname "*El Cuchara*" (the
Scoop). He was a devastating left-handed hitter.
Setting himself at the plate with the bat in the
crook of his left elbow, Lloyd unleashed a fluid,
powerful swing, hitting line drives to all fields.
On the bases his loping, awkward gait generated
surprising speed.

Lloyd's hitting prowess gained him great fame
among black fans, both in the United States and in
Cuba, where he played many winters. In November
1910 he matched skills with Ty Cobb, whose Detroit
Tigers played against two Cuban teams that included
several African American players. Not only was
Cobb outhit by Lloyd, .500 to .369, but Cobb was
thrown out three times attempting to steal bases,
prompting him to storm off the field, vowing never
to compete against black players again. Lloyd twice
hit above .400, and as late as 1928, at age forty-four,
he led Negro League hitters with an astonishing
.564 batting average, hitting eleven home runs and
stealing ten bases in only thirty-seven games.

A list of cities in which Lloyd played illustrates
the peripatetic nature of a black ballplayer's career:
Macon, Georgia (Acmes), Philadelphia (Cuban X
Giants, Philadelphia Giants, Hilldales), Chicago
(Leland Giants, Chicago American Giants),
New York (Lincoln Giants, Lincoln Stars, Black
Yankees), Brooklyn (Royal Giants), Atlantic City,
New Jersey (Bacharach Giants), and Columbus,
Ohio (Buckeyes). He rarely stayed with a team so
long as three seasons, and he often left after only
one year. "Where the money was," Lloyd said, "that's
where I was." Lloyd was a key player on some of the
greatest African American teams. The 1910 Leland
Giants compiled a record of 123 wins and 6 losses,
and the following year the Lincoln Giants had 105
wins and 7 losses. Between 1914 and 1919 he played
in three postseason series to determine the unofficial champion of black baseball.

During his early years Lloyd played shortstop,
forming outstanding combinations with second
basemen Grant Johnson and ELWOOD DE MOSS.
In 1924 he shifted to second base, teaming with
shortstop Dick Lundy, and thereafter he played
increasingly at first base. As his career progressed
the African American baseball community affectionately bestowed on him the nickname "Pop." In
1918 he was named player-manager of the Brooklyn
Royal Giants, his first of more than ten years as a
manager. The best team that he managed was the
1923 Hilldales of Philadelphia, champions of the
Eastern Colored League's first season.

After retiring from organized Negro baseball in
1931, Lloyd worked as a janitor in the Atlantic City
post office and public schools, although he continued as a semiprofessional player-manager until
1942. Lloyd and his wife, Nan, had no children,
but Lloyd became active in Little League baseball,
even serving as commissioner in Atlantic City. A
community ballpark built in Atlantic City in 1949
was named after Lloyd in recognition of his contributions to the city's youth. At the dedication
ceremony Lloyd disclaimed any regrets for having
played before JACKIE ROBINSON broke organized
baseball's color line. "I do not consider that I was
born at the wrong time," he said. "I felt it was the
right time, for I had a chance to prove the ability of
our race in this sport, and because many of us did
our very best to uphold the traditions of the game
and of the world of sport, we have given the Negro
a greater opportunity now to be accepted into the
major leagues with other Americans."

Lloyd died in Atlantic City. In 1977 he was
inducted into the National Baseball Hall of Fame

by a committee created to examine the merits of Negro League veterans. Playing at a time when unprecedented black migration to northern cities fostered a vibrant African American baseball community, Lloyd became its first great star. Yet the racism that plagued baseball throughout his brilliant career deprived him of the recognition and acclaim that his uncommon ability would have garnered among organized baseball's white fans. Not only was one of the game's greatest players relegated to the underground of apartheid baseball, but the game itself was diminished.

FURTHER READING
Holway, John. *Voices from the Great Black Baseball Leagues* (1975).
Peterson, Robert W. *Only the Ball Was White* (1970).
Riley, James A. *The All-Time All-Stars of Black Baseball* (1983).
This entry is taken from the *American National Biography* and is published here with the permission of the American Council of Learned Societies.

JERRY MALLOY

LoBagola, Bata Kindai Amgoza Ibn (Bata Kindai Amgoza Joseph Howard Lee Lobagola) (15 Dec. 1887–8 Jan. 1947), entertainer, author, and impostor who posed as an African, was born Joseph Howard Lee in Baltimore, Maryland, the fifth child of Joseph, a cook, and Lucy Cook, a domestic servant. Little is known of Lee's early life other than that he attended the Kasesha Public School for four years and also went to the St. Francis Xavier Roman Catholic church. He went to sea and in 1906 or early 1907 arrived in Liverpool, England, and joined a black touring theatrical company, the Dahomey Warriors, which performed in Scotland and in the English Midlands. After his time with the group he began to re-invent his life as a popular entertainer, describing himself as an African named LoBagola. Twenty-five years later his autobiographical account was published in New York, first in *Scribner's Magazine* (1929), and then as a book entitled *LoBagola. An African Savage's Own Story* (1930).

In his autobiographical account LoBagola mixed truth with much fantasy. He claimed to be a black Jew born in the Sahelian region of West Africa, then a French colony. At the age of six he ran away from home, stowed on board a ship bound for Scotland, where he was adopted and educated by a kindly Glasgow gentleman. Subsequently he fled

his Scottish home, travelled in Europe, returned to Africa, and then earned a living as a vaudeville artiste mainly in the eastern United States. Lee was clearly a clever mimic and persuasive speaker, at one point acting as an informant on West African customs and language to anthropologists at the University of Pennsylvania. In 1918 he secured naturalization papers and briefly joined the U.S. Army, but was discharged for psychiatric reasons. Lee then enlisted in the British Army, serving in a Jewish regiment, and went via Canada and England to Palestine. There he became a Roman Catholic and adopted the name Paul Emanuel LoBagola, which he used for official correspondence in the United States until the early 1930s. He claimed to have been a teacher in both Palestine and Egypt before travelling to West Africa and then in about 1925 returning to the United States. Using his new Roman Catholic identity LoBagola secured a temporary job as a porter and laboratory assistant at Fordham University. By the late 1920s he was earning an uncertain income speaking to high school students about his supposed African adventures, and it was a Brooklyn schoolteacher, Dr. Frederick Houk Law, who helped him write his article for *Scribner's* and then the subsequent autobiography, plus a book of African folk tales—both published by Knopf. The autobiography was dismissed as false in a review by Melville J. Herskovits, but with the help of his New York agent, James B. Pond, who regarded LoBagola as brilliant, his career as a public speaker was successfully promoted among well-heeled clubs and societies in the eastern and midwestern United States and in Canada.

By the mid-1930s, as the Depression began to bite, LoBagola was earning $300 a month with the prospect of higher fees from prestigious institutions, although accumulating debts linked to his gambling and heavy drinking made him an unreliable performer. More damaging to his future career was his pedophilia for which he had been imprisoned a number of times in the United States, the first being a brief sentence in Greenfield, Massachusetts, in 1913. In June 1930 LoBagola pleaded guilty to a charge of sodomy with a New York schoolboy, for which he was sentenced to a term of one-and-a-half to three years imprisonment. Pond, concerned about his bookings and income, and Law both stood by LoBagola and pleaded his case before the state parole board. Emerging from prison in the spring of 1932 LoBagola went to Ohio and tried to resume his speaking career. He only secured small fees and his recent prison record dogged his steps. Moving to Chicago, LoBagola experienced further hard times, reporting to Pond that he was broke. From 1932 to 1934 he had as his agent a young white man. The two men dressed well and stayed in first class hotels, while LoBagola, the poor African American from Baltimore, played the African prince and was thus able to thumb his nose at Jim Crow laws and travel with a white man.

But LoBagola's continued predatory pedophilia resulted in several arrests and his imprisonment in the Wisconsin State Penitentiary at Waupun in September 1934. Since his earlier conviction in 1931 the U.S. Naturalization Service had been checking his identity with a view to his deportation. Interviewed on several occasions in prison LoBagola reluctantly admitted that he had in fact been born in Baltimore. His false persona and his career as a speaker on Africa were in ruins. So was his life. In breach of parole he was subsequently moved to Attica Prison where, convicted of another act of sodomy with a prison inmate, he was sentenced to a further five to ten years. LoBagola's health was poor and perhaps also his mental state, although the prison authorities' low assessment of his intelligence quotient should be treated warily. He died in Attica and was buried in the prison cemetery in plot 29 under his assumed name.

LoBagola was a remarkable man but with a disturbed personality. Born in disadvantaged circumstances and with limited formal education, he escaped into the world of entertainment where his skills as a fantasist and public speaker enabled him to address and charm audiences of well-educated people who generally believed the tales he told. By adopting an African identity LoBagola exploited his blackness and gained access to places and people that would normally have been closed to him. In publicly emphasizing the personal conflict between his supposed savage origins in Africa and his bewilderment with modern civilization he perhaps demonstrated something of the deep racial and sexual tensions within the real life of Joseph Lee.

FURTHER READING

LoBagola, Bata Kindai Amgoza Ibn. "An African Savage's Own Story," *Scribner's Magazine* 85 and 86 (1929).

LoBagola, Bata Kindai Amgoza Ibn. *LoBagola. An African Savage's Own Story* (1930).

LoBagola, Bata Kindai Amgoza Ibn. *Folk Tales of a Savage* (1930).

Killingray, David, and Willie Henderson. "Bata Kindai Amgoza ibn LoBagola and the Making of *An Africans Savage's Own Story*," in *Africans on Stage: Studies in Ethnological Show Business*, ed. Bernth Lindfors (1999).

DAVID KILLINGRAY

Locke, Alain Leroy (13 Sept. 1885–9 June 1954), philosopher and literary critic, was born in Philadelphia, Pennsylvania, the son of Pliny Ishmael Locke, a lawyer, and Mary Hawkins, a teacher and member of the Felix Adler Ethical Society. Locke graduated from Central High School and the Philadelphia School of Pedagogy in Philadelphia in 1904. That same year he published his first editorial, "Moral Training in Elementary Schools," in the *Teacher*, and entered undergraduate school at Harvard University. He studied at Harvard under such scholars as Josiah Royce, George H. Palmer, Ralph B. Perry, and Hugo Münsterberg before graduating in 1907 and becoming the first African American Rhodes scholar, at Hertford College, Oxford. While in Europe, he also attended lectures at the University of Berlin (1910–1911) and studied the works of Franz Brentano, Alexius Meinong, and C. F. von Ehrenfels. Locke associated with other Rhodes scholars, including Horace M. Kallen, author of the concept of cultural pluralism; H. E. Alaily, president of the Egyptian Society of England; Pa Ka Isaka Seme, a black South African law student and eventual founder of the African National Congress of South Africa; and Har Dayal from India—each concerned with national liberation in their respective homelands. The formative years of Locke's education and early career were the years just proceeding and during World War I—years of nationalist uprising and wars between the world's major nation-states. Locke joined the Howard University faculty in 1912, to eventually form the most prestigious department of philosophy at a historically African American university.

In the summer of 1915 Locke began a lecture series sponsored by the Social Science Club of the National Association for the Advancement of Colored People, titled "Race Contacts and Interracial Relations: A Study of the Theory and Practice of Race." Locke argued against social Darwinism, which held that distinct races exist and are biologically determined to express peculiar cultural traits. Locke believed that races were socially constructed and that cultures are the manifestation of stressed values, values always subject to transvaluation and revaluation. Locke introduced a new way of thinking about social entities by conceiving of race as a socially formed category, which, despite its foundation in social history, substantively affected material reality.

Locke received his doctorate in Philosophy from Harvard in 1918 and shortly thereafter wrote "The Role of the Talented Tenth," which supported W. E. B. DuBois's idea that the upward mobility of approximately one-tenth of a population is crucial for the improvement of the whole population. Locke also became interested in the Baha'i faith, finding particularly attractive its emphasis on racial harmony and the interrelatedness of all religious faiths. Locke attended the 1921 Inter-Racial Amity conference on 19–21 May in Washington, D.C., and as late as 1932 published short editorials in the *Baha'i World*. Although he did not formally join the Baha'i faith, he remained respectful of its practices.

Locke went on to help initiate the Harlem Renaissance, a period of significant cultural contributions by African Americans. The years 1924–1925 were a major turning point in Locke's life. He edited a special edition of the magazine *Survey* titled the *Survey Graphic*, on the district of Harlem in New York City. The editor of *Survey* was Paul U. Kellogg, and the associate editor was Jane Addams. That edition became the source for his seminal work reflecting the nature of valuation and the classicism of African American culture, *The New Negro: An Interpretation of Negro Life*, published in 1925. *The New Negro* included a collage of art by Winold Reiss and AARON DOUGLAS and representations of African artifacts, articles by J. A. ROGERS, E. FRANKLIN FRAZIER, CHARLES S. JOHNSON, Melville J. Herskovits, and DuBois, poetry by COUNTÉE CULLEN, LANGSTON HUGHES, ARNA BONTEMPS, and ANGELINA WELD GRIMKÉ, spirituals, and bibliographies. *The New Negro* was intended as a work "by" rather than "about" African Americans, a text exuding pride, historical continuity, and a new spirit of self-respect not because a metamorphosis had occurred in the psychology of African Americans, "but because the Old Negro had long become more of a myth than a man." *The New Negro* embodied Locke's definition of essential features of African American culture, themes such as the importance of self-respect in the face of social denigration; ethnic pride; overcoming racial stereotypes and idioms, such as call-and-response in the spirituals or discord and beats in jazz; and the importance that cultural hybridity, traditions, and revaluations play in shaping cross-cultural relationships. Locke promoted those features of African American folk culture that he believed could be universalized and thus become

classical idioms, functioning, for Locke, as cultural ambassadors encouraging cross-cultural and racial respect. As debates over how to characterize American and African American cultural traits in literature became less a source of intellectual conflict, Locke's interests moved on to issues in education. In 1936 Locke began work on a book series, the Bronze Booklets on the History, Problems, and Cultural Contributions of the Negro, under the auspices of the Associates in Negro Folk Education. Eight booklets were published in the series, which became a standard reference for the teaching of African American history. In one of his frequent book reviews of African American literature for *Opportunity: A Journal of Negro Life*, Locke supported the controversial novel by RICHARD WRIGHT, *Native Son*, in 1941. The novel was controversial because Wright did not portray the lead character, Bigger Thomas, as a peace-loving, passive, and victimized African American, but as a critic of liberals and radicals. Locke's support for Wright's novel represented his belief that race divided America.

Locke published his first extensive article on his philosophy in 1935, "Values and Imperatives," in *American Philosophy: Today and Tomorrow*, edited by Horace M. Kallen and Sidney Hook. Locke argued that values are inherently unstable, always subject to transvaluation and transposition. Locke contended that "All philosophies, it seems to me, are in ultimate derivation philosophies of life and not of abstract, disembodied 'objective' reality; products of time, place, and situation, and thus systems of timed history rather than timeless eternity" (313). Rather than believe that science is an adequate model for reasoning about social reality, Locke presented the view that knowledge is a function of experience and the categories of logic, science, math, and social science are heuristic value fields or distinctions.

Locke published his landmark work on education, "The Need for a New Organon in Education," in *Findings of the First Annual Conference on Adult Education and the Negro* (1938), based on a lecture before the American Association for Adult Education, the Extension Department of Hampton Institute, and the Associates in Negro Folk Education, in Hampton, Virginia, on 20–22 October 1938. Locke proposed the concept of critical relativism (the view that there are no absolutely true propositions, but that we can have standards and criteria for critical evaluations). Locke warned against believing that all relevant knowledge can be acquired through application of formal logic and argued for the need to apply functional methods of reasoning and the importance of value judgments in considering defensible beliefs. Locke actively promoted adult education, working with the American Association of Adult Education in Washington, D.C., from 1948 to 1952.

In 1942 Locke edited, along with Bernard J. Stern, *When Peoples Meet: A Study of Race and Culture*. This anthology used a concept of ethnicity to account for both ethnic and racial contacts. Locke's approach continued his view that racial identities were socially created and were not based on substantive biological categories.

In 1944 Locke became a founding conference member of the Conference on Science, Philosophy and Religion, which published its annual proceedings of debates on the relationship of these areas of thought. He promoted the idea that cultural pluralism was an analogue for why one knowledge field was an insufficient reasoning model for sure knowledge, in other words that different cultures and civilizations supported laudable values just as different disciplines could sustain different spheres of knowledge. For Locke, there was no reason to believe in a unified theory of knowledge—a theory that would tell us about the nature of all forms of knowledge. Rather, a plurality of fields of knowledge and cultural values was a preferable perspective on Locke's account.

Locke was a controversial figure. His aesthetic views contrasted with those of the Black Aesthetic Movement of the 1970s. He was satirized in novels, criticized by ZORA NEALE HURSTON as an elitist interested in controlling the definition of African American culture, reproached for failing to acknowledge the largest Pan-African movement of the 1920s, the MARCUS GARVEY–led Universal Negro Improvement Association, and denounced for placing too great a value on African American literature as a text representing a unique cultural texture.

Locke died in New York City. He lived a controversial life because his ideas of values, race, and culture often challenged popular ideas. His concept of pragmatism was critical of, and different from, the dominant forms represented by William James and John Dewey. Locke's effort to shape the Harlem Renaissance and define the "New Negro" went against those who believed folk culture should not be changed, and his advocacy of value-oriented education within the adult education movement was viewed as a new orientation. Locke's philosophy, promoted by the Alain L. Locke Society, remains a source of controversy and debate.

FURTHER READING
Locke's papers are in the Alain L. Locke Archives, Howard University, Washington, D.C.
Harris, Leonard. *The Philosophy of Alain Locke: Harlem Renaissance and Beyond* (1989).
Harris, Leonard, ed. *The Critical Pragmatism of Alain Locke* (1999).
Holmes, Eugene C. "Alain L. Locke—Philosopher, Critic, Spokesman," *Journal of Philosophy* 54 (Feb. 1957): 113–118.
Linneman, Russell J. *Alain Locke: Reflections on a Modern Renaissance Man* (1982).
Stafford, Douglas K. "Alain Locke: The Child, the Man, and the People," *Journal of Negro Education*, (Winter, 1961): 25–34.
Stewart, Jeffrey C., ed. *The Critical Temper of Alain Locke: A Selection of His Essays on Art and Culture* (1983).
Washington, Johnny. *Alain Locke and His Philosophy: A Quest for Cultural Pluralism* (1986).

LEONARD HARRIS

Locks, John W. (9 Aug. 1818–7 Mar. 1884), entrepreneur, labor leader, and political and social activist, was born free in Baltimore, Maryland, to John and Chaney Locks. It is likely that he attended one of Baltimore's private schools for African Americans, and at the age of eighteen he began a three-year apprenticeship with a carpenter. In 1842 Locks's father died and willed him a house and a $900 account in the Savings Bank of Baltimore. Using his training to obtain employment and his inheritance to finance a variety of business ventures, Locks achieved an unusual degree of economic stability and prosperity for a free black man in a slave society. He worked as a carpenter and a caulker and was promoted to foreman at a white-owned shipyard. With his funds saved in the Freedmen's Bank after the Civil War, Locks began his most profitable enterprise, a livery and hacking business. Shrewdly, he also invested in real estate. By the 1850s he owned five properties; one was his residence and the others housed the stables and equipment for his livery and hack business. So successful was this venture that Locks became treasurer of the predominantly white Hackmen's Association. From his partnership with a free black carpenter and undertaker, the Locks Funeral Home evolved. Still managed by his descendants, it is the oldest African American funeral home in the nation.

Locks lived in Fells Point, near the Baltimore harbor, an international port with a diverse black population—slave and free, native and foreign born. The Oblate Sisters of Providence, the first African American order of nuns, and the African Methodist Episcopal (AME) Bishop Daniel Payne operated schools in the area to educate freedmen openly and slaves surreptitiously. There were numerous benevolent organizations and antislavery societies, many auxiliary to Methodist churches. Baltimore's substantial free black community worked collaboratively to improve the quality of life for the entire black population. Thus Locks was influenced by a community that encouraged and expected him to use his resources and talents for the benefit of others.

Though black men usually dominated the caulking trade, which was considered semi-skilled work, by the 1830s rising European immigration created competition for employment. Since the authorities ignored the physical intimidation of black workers by whites—especially Irish immigrants—bent on eliminating them as job competition, African Americans sought to create an organized form of resistance. In 1838 the Colored Caulkers' Trade Union Society, one of the earliest black labor unions in the United States, was established. The union negotiated a daily wage of $1.75, demanded improved working conditions, and functioned as a social welfare agency and burial society for its members. Locks was an active member and the owner of the Caulkers Union Hall. In 1865 unionized white caulkers, jealous of blacks' economic freedom and control, instigated riots and threatened to strike unless black workers were discharged. Many shipyard owners acceded to their demands. In response to declining employment opportunities John Locks, in concert with other African American caulkers, businessmen, and Methodist and AME activists, founded the Chesapeake Marine Railway and Dry Dock Company in 1866. Money was raised through the sale of stock, with FREDERICK DOUGLASS among the first purchasers. Within six months the company employed three hundred people, black and white, at an average daily wage of three dollars. The company acquired government contracts and discharged its debts by 1871. Locks, the largest stockholder, served as president for twelve years.

Locks also belonged to many fraternal organizations and benevolent societies. Additionally, he was a lay leader and trustee of Bethel AME Church for twenty-five years, and through relationships formed within the Methodist and AME communities worked to ameliorate conditions in his community. A Republican, Locks encouraged black participation in politics and he organized celebrations for

African American Civil War veterans to promote community pride. Locks chaired the delegation to the 1873 National Civil Rights Convention to lobby Republican congressmen in support of a civil rights platform. He also led a delegation to lobby city government leaders for skilled jobs for blacks. Although chosen to represent Baltimore's black Republicans at the 1880 convention, he was excluded by the white delegates. As a result of his political activities, he was the first African American to serve on a federal jury in Baltimore. Locks used his political connections to improve public education for African Americans. Baltimore established public schools for African Americans in 1867, the same years in which Locks was named one of three black trustees of the Howard Normal School. He spearheaded the campaign to hire African American teachers for African American schools and the effort to obtain equal pay for black teachers.

In 1844 Locks married Ann Maria Fernandis, daughter of a Brazilian-born barber. She died in 1856, leaving seven children. In 1858 Locks married Mary Ann Ford, who survived him. At the time of his death the *Cleveland Gazette* called Locks the wealthiest colored citizen of Baltimore and reported that his estate was worth $600,000. In addition to extensive real estate holdings and the hack/livery business, Locks's family inherited stock in the Chesapeake Marine Railway and Dry Dock Company and four other corporations. Eight ministers, including the eulogist, LEVI COPPIN, later an AME bishop, participated in Locks's funeral. Frederick Douglass, befriended by Locks when they worked as caulkers, attended. Political and fraternal leaders of both races were present. The cortege included one hundred fifteen carriages. As a second-generation freedman, John Locks enjoyed a degree of privilege not available to many of his race. As a man of African descent he was still subject to discrimination and oppression. Despite it all, however, he collaborated with blacks of all classes and effectively used positive intra-racial relationships to prosper economically and socially. In so doing he improved the quality of life for African Americans in nineteenth century Baltimore and left a legacy of sharing and service that continued well into the twentieth century.

FURTHER READING

Information related to Locks is held in the Records of the Bethel African Methodist Church and in the Maryland State Archives Special Collections.

Gatewood, Willard B. *Aristocrats of Color: The Black Elite, 1880–1920* (1990).

Graham, Leroy. *Baltimore: The Nineteenth Century Black Capital* (1982).

Phillips, Christopher. *Freedom's Port: The African-American Community of Baltimore, 1790–1860* (1997).

Thomas, Bettye C. "A Nineteenth Century Black Operated Shipyard, 1866–1884: Reflections upon Its Inception And Ownership," *Journal of Negro History* 19.1 (Jan. 1974).

Wayman, Alexander W. *The Cyclopaedia of African Methodism* (1882).

DONNA TYLER HOLLIE

Lockwood, Robert, Jr. (27 Mar. 1915–21 Nov. 2006), guitarist, singer, and songwriter, also known as Junior Lockwood and as Robert Junior, was born in Turkey Scratch, Arkansas, about twenty-five miles from Helena. His parents, Robert Lockwood and Estella Coleman, split up when he was a young boy. He was raised on his grandfather's farm, where he taught himself to play on an old pump organ. Around 1931 his mother began a relationship with the legendary bluesman ROBERT JOHNSON, and it was through Johnson that Lockwood was exposed to the full possibilities of guitar. He had previously regarded the guitar as a limited instrument. Though Johnson was only four or five years older than Lockwood, he became a father figure to the teenage boy. The young Lockwood was impressed with Johnson's ability to make the guitar sound like a full band, playing bass lines, chording, and melodies on the top strings, all the while stomping his foot like a drum. To this Johnson added his voice, eerie, tortured, and high pitched, singing themes about hellhounds on his trail and rambling on his mind; these themes would also become song titles.

Johnson had already synthesized the primitive Delta guitar playing of SON HOUSE and Willie Brown with the more dexterous style of JAMES (KOKOMO) ARNOLD and the haunting sound of SKIP JAMES into a more modern-sounding blues. Johnson's style directly influenced MUDDY WATERS and Elmore James, who essentially electrified Johnson's blues and added rhythm sections for a bigger beat. The rudiments were all there in Johnson's music, and Lockwood was the only person ever to receive personal instruction from Johnson, who jealously guarded his technique. To have a stepfather like Robert Johnson was a life-changing experience for the young Lockwood, who before long could fairly duplicate Johnson's repertoire. This became both a blessing and a curse when Robert Junior, as he was called, later strove to achieve his own identity.

The two Roberts traveled throughout the Delta playing together and separately, working both sides of streets and rivers to make more money. Johnson's records were popular in the region, and he attracted crowds wherever he played. Johnson met an untimely end in 1938 at the age of twenty-seven after being poisoned by a jealous husband. A devastated Lockwood ceased performing in public for a year and a half. The emotional difficulty of playing Johnson's material inspired him to write his own. He began playing again and soon took up with Aleck "Rice" Miller, the brilliant harmonica player and singer later known as SONNY BOY WILLIAMSON. He had been a friend of Johnson's and a frequent visitor to the Lockwood residence. Miller and Lockwood worked the Delta area together, including Helena, Arkansas.

Lockwood also traveled to Memphis and St. Louis and arrived in Chicago for the first time in 1940. There he recorded four of his compositions for the important Bluebird record label. His "Take a Little Walk with Me" and "Little Boy Blue" were modest successes, receiving significant jukebox play in the Delta. His song "Black Spider Blues" was adapted by Muddy Waters as "Mean Red Spider" in 1949, and in 1950 "That's All Right" became a hit for JIMMY ROGERS, who was Waters's guitar accompanist and had been heavily influenced by Lockwood.

Lockwood returned to Helena and with Rice Miller began broadcasting the *King Biscuit Time* show on radio station KFFA. This soon to be legendary program was one of the first African American radio shows in the South. Broadcast daily from noon to twelve-fifteen, the show was widely listened to, and the pair eventually enlisted the aid of the drummer and dance man James "Peck" Curtis and the piano player Dudlow Taylor, with the future Muddy Waters pianist Joe Willie "Pinetop" Perkins sometimes filling in. They would perform their songs and plug their upcoming appearances in the region. This strategy was later used to great advantage by other bluesmen such as HOWLIN' WOLF and B. B. KING.

At this time Miller assumed the "Sonny Boy" moniker, reputedly at the urging of the station manager, to cash in on the success of the Bluebird recording artist John Lee Williamson, a harmonica player and singer based in Chicago who was younger and had a completely different style. To his dying day Miller stubbornly claimed that he was the original and only Sonny Boy Williamson. His likeness adorned the bags of King Biscuit Flour and Sonny Boy Corn Meal, and he became a celebrity throughout the South. Miller's wanderlust led to frequent departures, and an increasingly frustrated Lockwood soon left the show himself to be replaced by his talented guitar disciple JOE WILLIE WILKINS, who stayed with the off-and-on broadcast until the mid-1960s.

In 1948 Lockwood began broadcasting his own show on station KXLR for a competing brand of flour. His increasing fondness for jazz led him to develop a new guitar style, and his single-string approach to playing melody was much like a horn player's. In his quest for his own artistic identity, he transformed himself from a country bluesman into a modern lead guitarist. His electric guitar was the first heard by many throughout the Delta and influenced a young B. B. King, whom Lockwood later instructed. Helena became an important blues center, attracting many blues giants.

After years of crisscrossing the Delta and South and working on the railroad, which brought him to Wyoming, Lockwood moved to Chicago in 1950 and became an important part of the burgeoning blues scene that had its peak during the next ten years. Among his greatest achievements were his contributions as a sideman on landmark recording sessions. Most notable were his Chess Records sessions for LITTLE WALTER and Sonny Boy Williamson (Rice Miller), the two most important and influential blues harmonica players of all time. Lockwood's sympathetic and sophisticated combination of bass lines, chords, and single-string lines helped shape an entire genre of music.

Sonny Boy and Lockwood moved to Cleveland, Ohio, in 1960, but the unpredictable Williamson soon left. Lockwood had moved his wife and children there and worked outside music for much of the 1960s, supporting his family while playing locally. In 1970 he began recording again, amassing a great body of work on several record labels, and continued recording and performing around the world until his death in 2006 at the age of ninety-one. Lockwood received two honorary doctorate degrees, was nominated for a Grammy, received the W. C. HANDY Award, and in 1997 was honored by his adopted city of Cleveland by having a street named after him. "Robert Junior" became Robert Lockwood Jr., a giant in his own right, who was mentored by perhaps the most influential bluesman ever and went on to influence countless others with his modernization of the blues.

FURTHER READING

Harris, Sheldon. *Blues Who's Who* (1981).
Leadbitter, Mike, and Neil Slaven. *Blues Records 1943–1966* (1968).
Palmer, Robert. *Deep Blues* (1981).

DISCOGRAPHY

Complete Trix Recordings (B00000I5F1).
Delta Crossroads (B00004UDEK).
His Best (Little Walter) (B000005KQT).
His Best (Sonny Boy Williamson/Rice Miller) (B000005KQN).

MARK S. MAULUCCI

Lofton, James (5 July 1956–), football player, was born James David Lofton in Fort Ord, California, the son of Michael Lofton and his wife, whose name is unknown. Indeed very little is known about his parents or his early life. James was an all-city quarterback at George Washington High School in Los Angeles before blossoming into an academic All-American at Stanford University, where in 1978 he earned a bachelor's degree in Engineering. Prior to establishing himself as a premier wide receiver under the tutelage of Hall of Fame coach Bill Walsh during his senior year, Lofton was also a top-notch track-and-field athlete. He won the long jump with a record-setting twenty-seven-foot leap as a senior at the 1978 NCAA Track-and-Field Championships. He had previously won the long jump at the 1974 California State Track-and-Field Championships. Although Lofton's outstanding leaping ability helped him become one of the NFL's top wide receivers, it was his speed that truly set him apart. Lofton developed his exceptional speed at Stanford, and in 1976 he sprinted to a fifth-place finish at the U.S. Olympic trials.

Gifted with extraordinary athletic ability, Lofton had a stellar senior year at Stanford. He hauled in twelve touchdown passes while gaining 931 receiving yards on fifty-three catches, and at season's end he was chosen by the Green Bay Packers as the sixth overall pick in the first round of the NFL draft in 1978. He made an immediate impact, becoming the team's primary offensive weapon in his first season. He racked up a team-leading forty-six receptions for 818 yards and six touchdowns en route to a Pro Bowl selection and NFC Offensive Rookie of the Year Award. As his generation's premier deep-threat wide receiver, Lofton was a fixture in Green Bay's lineup and a perennial selection to the Pro Bowl, a postseason honor he received in seven of his nine years as a Packer (1978 to 1986). In 1980 Lofton

James Lofton scores a second quarter touchdown for the Buffalo Bills during the AFC Championship game in Orchard Park, N.Y. on 20 Jan. 1991. He was elected to the Pro Football Hall of Fame on Saturday, 25 Jan. 2003. (AP Images.)

married Beverly Fanning, a former runner-up to Miss Arkansas. Together they raised three children. In his two best seasons with the Packers, 1983 and 1984, Lofton gained 1,300 or more yards each year while leading the league with an average gain of twenty or more yards per reception. Likewise, he caught fifty or more passes in seven of his nine seasons with the Packers, with the only exceptions being his rookie year and the strike-shortened 1982 season. Additionally, he accumulated over 1,000 yards in five of those seasons. Lofton established himself as the most prolific pass catcher in Green Bay Packers' history.

Had it not been for two separate sexual assault scandals in 1984 and 1986, Lofton would have probably spent the remainder of his pro football career with the Packers, a franchise known for its loyalty to players. Although charges in the first case were dropped by the district attorney's office due to a lack of evidence and Lofton was found not guilty in the second incident, his reputation in Green Bay was severely damaged. As a result he was traded to the Los Angeles Raiders where, unfortunately, Lofton failed to perform to his previous high standards. His two seasons for the Raiders (1987 and 1988) were productive, and he managed to hover around the respectable twenty-yard-per-catch average, but he did not top the coveted 1,000-yard mark in either season and was soon released from the team. Although the thirty-two-year-old Lofton was still a speedy and able wide receiver with a keen knowledge of the game, his NFL career appeared to be waning.

In 1989 Lofton was signed by the Buffalo Bills—a team that, like the Packers, reveled in cold weather and was based in a small working-class city. The difference, however, was that Lofton joined Buffalo while the franchise was on a remarkable upsurge. He had played for a Packer team that made the playoffs only once during his nine-year tenure, but he finally got a taste of victory while playing for an explosive Bills team that surrounded him with talented players. He paired with Andre Reed, a superb receiver whose skills nicely complemented Lofton's, and the two formed a fearsome pass-catching duo. The offense was also fueled by two other Hall of Fame-caliber players, quarterback Jim Kelly and running back Thurman Thomas. In 1991, at age thirty-five, Lofton became the oldest wide receiver to gain over 1,000 yards; he had a career-best 220 yards in a single game against the Cincinnati Bengals. Lofton's reputation as a premier wide receiver was reestablished as his career resurrected alongside a Bills franchise that made runs to the Super Bowl during each of the three seasons he played for the team. Lofton would spend one more year in the NFL, splitting 1993 between the Los Angeles Rams and Philadelphia Eagles, both of whom used him sparingly.

Lofton's remarkable sixteen seasons in the NFL saw him bestowed with a number of honors, the greatest of which was his 2003 enshrinement in the Pro Football Hall of Fame. The NFL has also recognized his talents by selecting him, along with JERRY RICE, Steve Largent, and Art Monk, as wide receivers on its 1980s All-Decade Team. Lofton played in eight Pro Bowls, six of which took place during a string of consecutive exceptional seasons in the 1980s. He gained over 1,000 receiving yards six times and caught fifty or more passes in a season nine times. Lofton's cumulative totals as a wide receiver included 233 games played, 764 receptions, and 75 touchdowns. Most impressively, his 14,004 career receiving yards represented an NFL record at the time of his retirement, a record that would later be surpassed by Jerry Rice and Tim Brown.

Upon leaving the gridiron, Lofton spent eight years as a sportscaster and commentator for the CNN, NBC, and FOX television networks. Since 2002 he has worked as an assistant coach specializing in developing wide receivers for the San Diego Chargers. In the early years of the twenty-first century Lofton continued to compete as a runner and long jumper in Masters track and field meets, winning several events.

FURTHER READING

George, Thomas. "Hall Induction of 5 Becomes a Family Affair." *New York Times*, 4 Aug. 2003.

"James Lofton," *Pro Football Hall of Fame*, www. profootballhof.com (7 March 2007).

"James Lofton," *San Diego Chargers*, www.chargers. com/team/coachbio_lofton.cfm (7 March 2007) .

DAVID LUCANDER

Logan, Adella Hunt (Feb. 1863–12 Dec. 1915), educator, suffragist, and clubwoman, was born in Sparta, Georgia, the fourth of eight children of Henry Hunt, a white planter and tanner, and Mariah Hunt, a mixed-race and Cherokee Indian woman of whom little else is known. Logan grew up in a prosperous neighborhood and attended Bass Academy in Sparta. At the age of sixteen, she attended the Upper Normal College (a school for teacher education) at Atlanta University in Atlanta, Georgia. She graduated two years later in 1881, and then taught for two years at an American Missionary School in Albany, Georgia, where she also worked as a city missionary.

Although she was offered a position teaching at Atlanta University in 1883, Logan responded to the call of BOOKER T. WASHINGTON to teach at Tuskegee Institute, Washington's renowned industrial school and college in Tuskegee, Alabama. Although teaching at the well established, urban Atlanta University might have seemed a natural choice for her broad intellectual interests, Logan chose instead to join Washington's mission to educate young African Americans from more impoverished backgrounds for careers in education and the trades.

In 1888 Adella Hunt married Warren Logan, Washington's close friend, who had arrived at Tuskegee a year before her. During Warren Logan's career at Tuskegee, he served as the school's vice president and treasurer. Following her marriage Adella Logan had little time or opportunity to teach. She was occupied attending to the many duties of the wife of a top administrator and to the raising of her family. In 1890 she gave birth to the first of the couple's nine children. Their last child was born in 1909.

Logan soon declared that education was her primary interest. Despite her household duties and frequent pregnancies, she managed to continue leading a number of educational missions at Tuskegee, including the formation of a model school to prepare student teachers for careers in education, and the guidance and administration of Tuskegee's teacher education curriculum and facilities.

In 1895 Logan became a charter member of the Tuskegee Woman's Club. The club, which became an affiliate of the National Association of Colored Women (NACW) in 1896, consisted of educators and staff at Tuskegee Institute. The Tuskegee chapter's mission focused on the social uplift of African Americans in the communities surrounding the school. As a-member, Logan directed and participated in programs to improve the lives and health of African American families, including programs in nutrition, hygiene, civics, and an effort to improve the pre- and post-natal health of mothers and babies. She also advocated prison reform and, always mindful of the need to educate, organized and ran a lending library.

As a Tuskegee educator and as a clubwoman, Logan found ways to integrate civics instruction into everything she taught. Her civics interest led directly to her passion to prepare her students and African Americans in the local community for universal suffrage. Although she was personally discouraged by local and state government attempts to disenfranchise African American men, Logan persisted in educating young men and women for the day when universal suffrage would be achieved.

Logan became captivated by the women's suffrage movement sometime in the early 1890s. In 1895 the National American Woman Suffrage Association (NAWSA) held its annual convention in Atlanta in the hopes of educating white southern men and women about the importance of the ballot for women. At this time, NAWSA was seeking this support because a women's suffrage amendment to the Constitution could not be ratified without the approval of many southern states. NAWSA leaders barred African American women and men from attending all its southern conventions, a move they later claimed was merely in deference to southern whites. African Americans, however, were allowed to hold membership in the organization.

Adella Hunt Logan (third from left) in a family photograph in Tuskegee, Alabama in 1913. (Austin/Thompson Collection and Collection of Adele Logan Alexander.)

Logan traveled to Atlanta during the convention week to hear the NAWSA leader and prominent suffragist Susan B. Anthony lecture at Atlanta University. After hearing Anthony speak, Logan was inspired to dedicate herself further to women's suffrage. Despite NAWSA's explicit racism, Logan revered Anthony throughout the white suffrage leader's life.

While Logan disapproved of NAWSA's accommodation of white southerners' racism, it did not deter her from participating in the organization. Logan became a life member of NAWSA shortly after 1895. By 1897 Logan was using the forum of the Tuskegee Woman's Club to educate and inform her fellow clubwomen about women's suffrage and the activities of the movement. Public support for women's suffrage was nearly nonexistent in Alabama, as would be the case for the next two decades.

She gained knowledge and inspiration from NAWSA conventions, though she commented that African American women's suffrage leaders could have run them better; as she wrote to Emily Howland, a white suffragist who sponsored her membership in NAWSA, "You know a number of colored women would have done it [managed the conventions] more intelligently..." (Alexander, 88). She also contributed financially to NAWSA and wrote articles for *The Woman's Journal*, (NAWSA's primary newspaper), and attended a 1901 NAWSA meeting in Atlanta. Because Logan was light-skinned, as a result of her predominantly white ancestry, her biographer and granddaughter Adele Logan Alexander has suggested that Logan consciously attempted to "pass" for white when she attended NAWSA conventions, which was something she might have justified because of the information she gained to further the cause of African American suffrage. It is not evident from Logan's personal correspondence or letters what her thoughts and feelings were about her attendance at suffrage gatherings. It is evident, however, that her enthusiasm for the ballot for women and the ways in which it could improve the lives of all African Americans was of primary importance to her. Aside from her national suffrage involvement, Logan spoke publicly about women's suffrage to gatherings of African American clubwomen in the South. She lectured at the Alabama Federation of Colored Women's Clubs conventions, the Southern Federation of Colored Women's Clubs, and the National Association of Colored Women (NACW). She was also the leader of the NACW's suffrage section.

In addition to her writings for suffrage journals, she contributed articles about women's suffrage to *The Crisis*, the NAACP's journal edited by W. E. B. DuBois, and the *Colored American* magazine. A major reason for giving African American women the vote, Logan emphasized, was to give them a voice in educational legislation to ensure that African American children would receive their share of public school funds. She argued that black women gaining the right to vote would improve life for all African Americans.

In 1915 Logan experienced a series of misfortunes. She suffered a crippling emotional breakdown, which may have been clinical depression. The death of her good friend and colleague Booker T. Washington in the fall of that year contributed to her despair. On the day of his memorial service, she jumped from the top floor of a Tuskegee Institute building to her death. She died at the age of fifty-two, five years before the Twentieth Amendment became law, thereby guaranteeing women the right to vote.

FURTHER READING

The correspondence of Adella Hunt Logan is housed in the Booker T. Washington Papers, Manuscript Division, Library of Congress, and in the Emily Howland Collection at Cornell University, Ithaca, New York.

Alexander, Adele Logan. "Adella Hunt Logan," in *Notable Black American Women*. Vol. 1 (1992).

Alexander, Adele Logan. "Adella Hunt Logan, the Tuskegee Woman's Club, and African Americans in the Suffrage Movement," in *Votes for Women: The Woman Suffrage Movement in Tennessee, the South, and the Nation* (1995).

JUDITH E. HARPER

Logan, Arthur Courtney (8 Sept. 1909–25 Nov. 1973), physician, surgeon, and civil rights activist, was born on the campus of the Tuskegee Institute in Alabama, one of nine children born to ADELLA HUNT LOGAN. His father, Warren Logan, treasurer of Tuskegee Institute, had begun working as an educator at the Institute when it was established in 1882. Logan remembered an early childhood in bucolic surroundings where he sometimes spent summer days at the side of BOOKER T. WASHINGTON, the founder of Tuskegee Institute.

At the age of ten Logan was sent to New York City to live in Harlem with an older sister and attend the Ethical Culture School on a scholarship. In the 1920s New York City offered blacks a broader spectrum of opportunities than was possible in Alabama. The Ethical Culture School, founded by Felix Adler in 1878, was open to children of all races and religions. Adler was a social activist who promoted the concepts of equality, justice, and intellectual freedom. At Ethical, Logan was exposed to children from many different cultures and socioeconomic backgrounds. Although the school had originally been founded to reach out to the children of the poor, many of New York's wealthiest citizens paid to send their children there as well.

Logan went on to Williams College in Massachusetts, and in 1930 graduated Phi Beta Kappa. He then studied medicine at Columbia University, where Adler held the chair for political and social ethics. When Logan graduated as one of the first black students from Columbia's College of Physicians and Surgeons in 1934, he took with him a commitment to social activism he had learned from years of study in institutions influenced by Adler's progressive ideals. Although he had other opportunities, Logan chose to complete his internship at Harlem Hospital. It was in Harlem that he began his lifelong effort to provide quality medical care for poor and disenfranchised citizens in New York City.

After twelve years in private practice, Logan, along with a small group of other New York physicians, founded the Upper Manhattan Medical Group in Harlem to serve the poorest residents of the city. Founders of one of the nation's first health maintenance organizations, the group served more than thirty thousand subscribers, most of them black. These prepaid subscribers received quality health services that otherwise would have been unavailable to them. Logan remained a partner in the Manhattan Group and served as director of its surgical department until his death.

Although Logan's life was marked by unusual privilege, he was committed to helping those who could not help themselves. The Manhattan Group was just one of many projects Logan took on in order to support the black community. While serving on the surgical staff of several New York hospitals, including Harlem Hospital, Sydenham Hospital, and Knickerbocker Hospital, he dedicated much of his time to organizations like Citizens Organized Against Drug Abuse, which he served as chairman of the board for many years; the New York City Council Against Poverty, in 1965; and United Neighborhood Houses of New York from 1966 until his death. He also worked with the city to develop and implement public projects such as the Manhattanville Health Park, a plan to incorporate health facilities, job training facilities, parks, and low-income housing within civic and commercial areas.

Logan's first marriage to Wenorah Bond ended in divorce in 1947. They had one daughter, Adele. He met his second wife, Marion Taylor of Philadelphia, Pennsylvania, when he was called in to treat her after she became ill at the Apollo Theater where she sang under the name of Marian Bruce. They were married in 1958. Their only child, a son, was named Warren in honor of Logan's father.

In the next decade Logan turned his attention to the civil rights movement. In 1960 he became the director of the Urban League of Greater New York and in 1962 the director of the NAACP Legal Defense and Educational Fund. Logan's membership in New York's progressive elite society allowed him to work behind the scenes along with his wife, who was the only northern-based member on the board of directors of the Southern Christian Leadership Conference (SCLC). Together they opened their fashionable brownstone on West Eighty-eighth Street to raise money to support the movement. Counted among their guests and associates were some of the most important names in civil rights history: MARTIN LUTHER KING JR., ROY WILKINS, the Reverend RALPH ABERNATHY, ELEANOR HOLMES NORTON, VERNON JORDAN, CHARLES RANGEL, and SHIRLEY CHISHOLM. On a single night in April of 1965 the Logans raised eleven thousand dollars at a reception for King.

Five weeks after King's assassination on 4 April 1968 Logan organized and led a team of medical workers to Washington to care for the three thousand demonstrators, mostly blacks, who were camped on the Mall for King's planned Poor People's March on Washington. The tent housing, enmeshed in mud and dubbed "Resurrection City," covered the Mall from 14 May until the federal government razed it on 24 June 1968.

Housing concerns were second only to Logan's dedication to providing adequate quality health care to everyone who needed it. Logan's last undertaking before his death was the Manhattanville project, which called for the expansion of Knickerbocker Hospital along with an array of housing and other civic development. It was at the construction site for this project where Logan's body was found. It is believed that he fell from a viaduct on the Henry Hudson Parkway overlooking the site. Knickerbocker Hospital was renamed the Arthur C. Logan Memorial Hospital after his untimely death at the age of sixty-four.

FURTHER READING

National Cyclopedia of American Biography, vol. 57 (1984).

"Screvane Gets No. 2 Post; Surgeon to Head New Poverty Unit," *New York Times*, 13 May 1965.

Obituaries: *New York Times*, 26 Nov. 1973; *Physicians & Surgeons*, vol. 19 (Summer, 1974).

DONNA M. ABRUZZESE

Logan, Myra Adele (18 Jan. 1908–13 Jan. 1977), physician, surgeon, and medical researcher, was born in Tuskegee, Alabama, the youngest daughter of ADELLA HUNT LOGAN and Warren Logan, well-respected members of black Alabama society and teachers at the Tuskegee Institute. Her father was the first person appointed to the Tuskegee Institute by BOOKER T. WASHINGTON in 1882; Warren Logan was also its treasurer and member of the Board of Trustees. After her retirement from Tuskegee in 1888, her mother, Adella Logan, became an avid suffragist and women's rights activist.

Myra Logan grew up on the Tuskegee campus, attended Tuskegee High School, and graduated with honors in 1923. She was the valedictorian of her class at Atlanta University, where she graduated in 1927. She earned a Master's in Psychology from Columbia University before attending New York Medical College. Encouraged by her brother-in-law, Dr. Eugene Percy Roberts, a well-established physician in Harlem, she applied to medical school. Her medical education was supported by the Walter Gray Crump Scholarship, created in 1928 by a white trustee at the Tuskegee Institute, Dr. Walter Gray Crump, a leading cancer researcher and professor of surgery at New York Medical College. Logan was the first recipient of this scholarship, and the scholarship was the first awarded only for the support of blacks to attend medical school. Logan completed her internship and residency at Harlem Hospital and joined its surgical staff in 1939.

During Logan's internship at Harlem Hospital, a prominent Harlem Renaissance artist, CHARLES ALSTON, was commissioned to paint two murals on the walls of the hospital by the Municipal Art Commission under the New Deal program WPA(Works Progress Administration) Federal Art Project. Logan and Alston met while the artist completed his controversial project, "Magic and Medicine" and "Modern Medicine." Logan and Alston shared a passion for civil rights, he through art and creative expression, she in medicine. They married on 8 April 1943. Logan and Alston were a progressive couple. She did not change her name after they were married and Spinky (Charles's nickname) cooked. They had no children.

Largely because of the actions of her mentor, Harvard Medical School-educated surgeon and civil rights activist Dr. LOUIS TOMPKINS WRIGHT, Logan was appointed to the surgical staff at Harlem Hospital. Dr. Wright, who had been the first black physician hired at Harlem Hospital when he arrived in 1919, was a champion of integration and spent the majority of his medical career building support for black integration into the white medical community. To build his case, he developed a policy of hiring the best and brightest young physicians and believed they would most likely be graduates of already integrated (historically white) medical schools. Wright was in charge of the admissions process at Harlem Hospital at the time Dr. Logan applied for a position. He hired her and thus she became one of the first black women to join the surgical staff at Harlem Hospital. Wright and Logan became close friends as well as colleagues and when Dr. Logan considered resigning from the surgical staff after she experienced gender and racial harassment, Wright gave political guidance and strong support for her intellectual accomplishments. He praised her for her intelligence and her hard work and her promise in surgery. His support gave her the determination not to quit the surgical unit and to fight against transfer to another department in the hospital. In 1943 she was the first woman surgeon to perform open-heart surgery. Dr. Logan was elected a fellow of the American College of Surgeons in 1951.

Mentors were key to the success of the few black women in medicine, providing opportunity where otherwise they were often blocked. Logan's experience of being mentored by Wright in turn influenced her decision to become a mentor for both of Wright's daughters, Jane and Barbara, two younger black women who also became physicians.

In 1948 when a research group at Harlem Hospital led by Dr. Wright conducted a pioneering clinical trial of the antibiotic aureomycin, Dr. Logan was the only woman on the team. Another member of the team studying aureomycin was Dr. Arthur Logan, her younger brother. Her interest in research stayed with her until the 1960s, when she began to focus on breast cancer and to develop a more efficient process of detecting the disease.

She also addressed community issues. Drs. Myra and Arthur Logan were founding partners, along with other physicians in Harlem, of the Upper Manhattan Medical Group of the Health Insurance

Plan of New York, one of the first group medical practices in the United States. For a number of years she served as its treasurer. In 1943 New York Governor Thomas E. Dewey named Dr. Logan to the New York State War Council Committee on Discrimination to study racial discrimination in the workplace during war time. However, in 1944 she resigned along with seven other members after Governor Dewey refused to act on the Committee's findings. Later that same year, she was elected to the Youth Center Administrative Committee, an interfaith organization supervising the care of children whose cases were under review by the New York Children's Court of the Court of Domestic Relations.

Although Logan faced discrimination because of her race and gender, she still was privileged in ways that many other black female physicians at the time were not. In her early life and medical career she benefited from her family's connections in the black community. She came from an influential black family in the South and had support from surgeons Dr. Louis Wright, her brother, Dr. Arthur Logan, and her brother-in-law, Dr. Eugene Percy Roberts in New York City. In addition, her medical education was funded by a scholarship exclusively for blacks. Logan died of lung cancer at Mount Sinai Hospital in New York City.

FURTHER READING

Hayden, Robert C. *Mr. Harlem Hospital* (2003).

Oakes, Elizabeth H. *International Encyclopedia of Women Scientists* (2002).

Obituary: *New York Times*, 15 January 1977.

SUSAN E. BELL AND
MORGAN TAGGART-HAMPTON

Logan, Onnie Lee (c. 1910–10 July 1995), midwife and author, was born Onnie Lee Rodgers near Sweet Water in southwest Alabama to Len Rodgers, a farmer and carpenter, and his wife, Martha (maiden name unknown), a midwife and farmer. Like her fifteen siblings and most rural southerners at the time, Onnie Lee was delivered by an African American midwife, in part because of a lack of practicing physicians outside of the South's major urban centers, and also because black granny midwives had traditionally performed this task since slavery times. In addition to her mother, Logan's maternal and paternal grandmothers, as well as one of her brothers-in-law, were also midwives.

At a time when most of her black neighbors struggled to get by as sharecroppers, Onnie Lee

Logan recalled that her parents owned their own land, a "huge plantation" on which they raised several types of livestock and grew a wide variety of vegetables as well as rice and cotton. Though the family remained cash poor, it also remained self-sufficient and debt free, no mean feat in rural Alabama during the hard times of the 1920s and 1930s. "The Depression depressed us like it did everybody else," Logan recalled in her 1989 memoir, "but we were survivin real good without knowin the sufferin part about it" (17). From an early age the children assisted their parents on the farm, which spared Len Rodgers the cost of hiring additional labor and instilled in the children a powerful work ethic. Logan, who suffered from fainting spells and was excused from laboring in the blistering heat of the cotton fields, spent much of her childhood helping her mother to cook and sew. She also assisted her mother as she traveled throughout Marengo County delivering babies and tending to the sick, often for no financial reward, although some grateful parents paid Martha Rodgers with corn, chicken, or greens. On turning fifteen, Logan began working in Sweet Water as a maid and child nurse for a white couple, and she also looked after several of her nephews and nieces. Determined to become a nurse, she dreamed of finishing high school but was forced to quit after completing the tenth grade in 1928 when her mother died of a stroke.

Depressed by her mother's passing and unable to return to her studies, Onnie Lee remained at home until 1930, when she married her sister's brother-in-law, Elmo Watkins, a railroad worker, and moved to Magnolia, Alabama. She gave birth to her only son, Johnnie, a year later. It was while pregnant and working as a maid in Magnolia that she began to consider a career in midwifery, after helping a white doctor deliver her employer's child. Encouraged by the doctor's praise of her skills, she began assisting several midwives in Magnolia, learning different aspects of the practice from each of them.

Any plans that she may have had to pursue a career in midwifery were briefly stymied in 1934, however, when, shortly after moving to Mobile, Elmo Watkins left her for another woman. She promptly sought a divorce, only to discover that Watkins was still legally married to his first wife. The experience "just killed me as far as men's concerned for a long time," she later recalled, but she was sustained by her Baptist faith and by finding a new job as a maid and nanny for a white Mobile physician, Dr. Mears, his wife, and their three children (Logan, 86). Dr. Mears encouraged her interest in becoming a midwife and allowed her—against his own wife's wishes—to take time off from housework to attend midwifery classes at the Mobile County board of health. Having assisted in several births in Magnolia, she earned her first midwifery license and permit in 1949, and did so quicker than any other midwife in Mobile. Around that time her second husband, Homer George, died. In 1951 she married Roosevelt Logan, with whom she lived until her death.

Though she appreciated that "listenin at the classes … helped a lot," especially about matters of hygiene, nutrition, and prenatal care, Onnie Lee Logan believed that the skills that made her a good midwife came from a "higher power.… God gave me wisdom. Motherwit, commonsense" (Logan, 89). She first experienced that guiding influence a few months before receiving her midwife's license, while assisting a more experienced midwife deliver twins. Unable to get the firstborn child to breathe, Logan's supervisor left him aside, believing that he was dead, to concentrate on the second birth, which was successful. Logan, however, was determined that the first child should live and gave him mouth-to-mouth resuscitation for forty-five minutes until he revived. Not having yet learned mouth-to-mouth resuscitation in class, Logan believed that God had given her the power to save the child.

Logan relied on her faith and her motherwit during the four decades that she worked as a midwife performing home births in Prichard, a predominantly African American suburb of Mobile. Many of her clients lived in desperate poverty and were unable to pay her for her services, which included not only delivering babies but also sanitizing and preparing the mother's birthing room and, as her mother and grandmothers had done before her, cooking meals and cleaning up for the birth family afterward. Although many of the mothers that she attended suffered from poor diets and overwork, Logan lost only four children out of the several hundred babies that she delivered in her career.

Like MARGARET C. SMITH and other African American midwives in the South, Logan's career was profoundly altered by the civil rights movement of the 1960s and the expansion of public health care in the 1970s. After Mobile's main maternity clinic was legally obligated to admit black as well as white mothers, the demand for traditional midwives traveling to home births declined significantly among African Americans. Believing that hospital births were safer than home births, the state of Alabama banned lay midwifery in 1976, but the state allowed some midwives, including Logan, to continue practicing until 1984, when she and all other Alabama midwives were forced to retire.

Though Logan's career as a midwife was remarkable, so too was her determination to tell her life story once the state of Alabama had forced her to retire. In 1989, working with Katherine Clark of the University of Alabama at Tuscaloosa, Logan published a memoir, *Motherwit*, to considerable critical and popular acclaim. Four years later, selections of Logan's memoir appeared, alongside those of Anne Frank, Simone de Beauvoir, and MAYA ANGELOU, in the *Norton Book of Women's Lives* (1993). At the time of Logan's death in Mobile in July 1995, the practice of midwifery had not returned to its former preeminence. But the use of midwives, both at home births and in hospitals, grew considerably during the 1990s, spurred in part by Logan's *Motherwit*, by the historian Laurel Thatcher Ulrich's Pulitzer Prize–winning *A Midwife's Tale* (1990), and by other accounts of the long-neglected history of midwifery in America.

FURTHER READING

Logan, Onnie Lee, as told to Katherine Clark. *Motherwit: An Alabama Midwife's Story* (1989).

Smith, Susan L. *Sick and Tired of Being Sick and Tired: Black Women's Health Activism in America, 1890–1950* (1995).

Obituary: *New York Times*, 13 July 1995.

STEVEN J. NIVEN

Logan, Rayford Whittingham (7 Jan. 1897–4 Nov. 1981), historian of the African diaspora, professor, and civil rights and Pan-Africanist activist, was born in Washington, D.C., the son of Arthur Logan and Martha Whittingham, domestic workers. Two circumstances of Logan's parents are germane to his later life and work. Although he grew up in modest circumstances, his parents enjoyed a measure of status in the Washington black community owing to his father's employment as a butler in the household of Frederic Walcott, the Republican senator from Connecticut. The Walcotts took an interest in the Logan family, providing them with occasional gifts, including money to purchase a house. The Walcotts also took an interest in Rayford Logan's education, presenting him with books and later, in the 1920s and 1930s, introducing him to influential whites in government. Logan grew up on family lore about the antebellum free black heritage of the Whittinghams. It is open to question how much of what he heard was factual; nevertheless, he learned early to make class distinctions among African Americans and to believe that his elite heritage also imposed on him an obligation to help lead his people to freedom and equality.

Both lessons were reinforced by his secondary education at the prestigious M Street (later Dunbar) High School, a public but segregated institution in the District of Columbia. Jim Crow had narrowed the professional options of African American educators, and the faculty included such first-rate intellectuals as CARTER G. WOODSON, JESSIE FAUSET, and ANNA JULIA COOPER; its goal was education for leadership, and among its distinguished alumni were CHARLES HAMILTON HOUSTON, WILLIAM HENRY HASTIE, CHARLES R. DREW, and BENJAMIN O. DAVIS SR. Logan was the valedictorian of the class of 1913. He continued his academic career at Williams College, from which he was graduated Phi Beta Kappa in 1917. After he delivered one of three commencement speeches, he returned to Washington, where he enlisted in the military to fight in World War I.

The First World War was a turning point in Logan's life. Like most African Americans, he followed the lead of W. E. B. DuBois and the NAACP in supporting the war effort with the expectation that blacks' discharging a patriotic duty would bring them full citizenship rights. Logan rose from private to the rank of lieutenant in the segregated 372d Infantry Regiment, one of only four combat units open to black American soldiers; most blacks were restricted to militarized labor units.

Logan saw combat in the Argonne campaign of June 1918 and was wounded; the "war neurosis" that accompanied the injury triggered a series of outbursts by Logan directed at white American officers in retaliation for the accumulated racial humiliation and harassment they visited on him and all black military personnel. He spent the next year fighting the racism of the U.S. military. There were two wars going on—Mr. Wilson [Woodrow Wilson]'s and Mr. Logan's—he asserted in his unpublished autobiography. When he was demobilized in August 1919, Logan chose to remain in France. "My experiences in the army left me so bitter ... that I remained an expatriate in Europe," he later wrote. "I *hated* white Americans."

Between 1919 and 1924 Logan lived in Paris and became a leading member of the Pan-African Congress movement based there. Logan worked closely with W. E. B. DuBois, the movement's principal architect (it was the beginning of a collaboration

that would last into the 1950s), as well as a number of prominent francophone blacks also resident in Paris. The Pan-African Congress, which met four times between 1919 and 1927, espoused the equality of the black race, an end to colonial abuses in Africa, eventual self-government for Europe's African possessions, and full civil rights for African Americans.

In many respects Pan-Africanism between the two world wars was a precursor to America's civil rights movement, as it was supported by the leading black Americans of the day. His five-year European expatriation introduced Logan to the international dimensions of the "race problem," and his interactions with the Haitian diplomat Dantes Bellegarde laid the basis for a lifelong scholarly and political interest in the first independent black republic in the Western Hemisphere.

Having exorcised white Americans from his spirit—largely by avoiding them in Paris—Logan returned to the United States in 1924 determined to pursue the fight for civil rights as both a scholar and an activist. Between 1925 and 1938 he taught at two elite, historically black colleges: Virginia Union University in Richmond (1925–1931) and Atlanta University (1933–1938). In the interim he served for two years as Carter Woodson's assistant at the Association for the Study of Negro Life and History. At Virginia Union, Logan taught French and history and introduced the college's first courses on black history and on imperialism; he earned a reputation as a serious scholar and an engaging teacher.

While on the Union faculty, Logan married Ruth Robinson in 1927; they had no children. He pursued advanced degrees in history, earning his M.A. from Williams College in 1929, and beginning in 1930 the residency and course requirements for his Ph.D. from Harvard University. (He completed them in 1932.) While at Atlanta he researched and wrote his doctoral dissertation, completed in 1936, on the diplomatic relations between the United States and Haiti, a groundbreaking work on race and diplomacy that was published in 1941 as *The Diplomatic Relations of the United States with Haiti, 1776–1891*. He visited Haiti twice and was a firsthand witness to the 1934 end of the American occupation. In the 1920s and 1930s his scholarship on Haiti and colonial Africa earned him national recognition not only in the black diaspora—he was awarded Haiti's Order of Honor and Merit in 1941 for his scholarship and advocacy—but also from influential, predominantly white organizations such as the Foreign Policy Association.

In Richmond and Atlanta—and in Washington, where between 1938 and 1968 he taught at Howard University—Logan engaged in innovative civil rights activity. In the 1920s and 1930s in the first two cities he organized, in conjunction with other outspoken African Americans like LUGENIA HOPE, voter registration drives; the citizenship schools, which taught African Americans how to register to vote and anchored the campaigns, became models for similar activities in the 1960s. On the eve of World War II, he spearheaded a drive of mass rallies and organizing local African American coalitions against the exclusion of African Americans from the U.S. military; the force of the campaign was such that in 1940 he was invited to meet with President Franklin D. Roosevelt on the matter and drafted for the president an order prohibiting the exclusion of blacks from the service.

In 1941 Logan was a leader of A. PHILIP RANDOLPH's March on Washington movement, which pressured Roosevelt into issuing Executive Order 8802 banning racial discrimination in defense industries; Logan participated in the final negotiations over the order. The March on Washington movement declared victory, and the march was canceled. Logan edited *What the Negro Wants* (1944), a collection of essays by fourteen prominent African Americans that helped to bring before the entire American public the demand for a total elimination of segregation. Turning his attention once again to international affairs in the postwar era, Logan, in close alliance with DuBois, fought to orient the United Nations, the United States, and the European powers toward justice and decolonization in Africa. He spent the last decade of his life organizing and editing with Michael R. Winston the *Dictionary of American Negro Biography* (1982).

The central point of Logan's scholarship and activism was the promotion of the dignity and equality of black people throughout the world and the critical examination of American racial hypocrisy. But in an era dominated by the incipient cold war, his scholarship and activism were too strident for the U.S. political establishment, and he often found it difficult to attain a hearing in the white mainstream. *What the Negro Wants* saw life only after he threatened to sue the publisher for breach of contract; two of his other important works, *The Negro and the Post-war World* (1945) and *The African Mandates and World Politics* (1948), were issued privately by Logan because no publisher would bring them out. His best-known work, *The Negro in American Life and Thought: The Nadir, 1877–1901* (1954; revised and republished as *The Betrayal of the Negro* [1965]), which established a useful framework for historians to analyze that period of African American history, was turned down by one publisher, and Macmillan agreed to publish it only after Logan posted a $5,000 subvention.

Rayford Logan was a distinguished and talented intellectual. While he insisted on strict adherence to the historical record and was perhaps conservative in what he considered historical evidence, he knitted his scholarship together with a lifetime of activism. Just as he had hoped that his scholarship would reach a wide audience, he also wanted to be a major civil rights figure. He never reached this position, partly because he was often more strident than the mainstream race advancement organizations of the 1930s, 1940s, and 1950s. He was overlooked by the activists of the 1960s and 1970s in part, he believed, because that generation's impetuousness prevented it from learning from and about the sacrifices and efforts of earlier activists. (In fact, such staples of the 1960s as voter registration drives had been pioneered by Logan three decades earlier.) But there were other reasons, notably his abrasive personality and his chafing at organizational discipline. As a result, he often was on the sidelines, an incisive but little-recognized critic. He perhaps was comfortable in this marginal role because he did not have to implement his visionary, but neglected, plans, but marginality also prevented him from achieving the stature he believed he deserved in both white and black America. He died in Washington, D.C.

FURTHER READING

The major part of Logan's papers are deposited at the Moorland-Spingarn Research Center at Howard University in Washington, D.C. His diaries are deposited in the Manuscript Division of the Library of Congress.

Janken, Kenneth Robert. *Rayford W. Logan and the Dilemma of the African American Intellectual* (1993).

This entry is taken from the *American National Biography* and is published here with the permission of the American Council of Learned Societies.

KENNETH ROBERT JANKEN

Loguen, Jermain Wesley (c. 1813–30 Sept. 1872), bishop of the African Methodist Episcopal Zion (AMEZ) Church and abolitionist, was born Jarm Logue in Davidson County, Tennessee, the son of a slave mother, Cherry, and white slaveholder,

David Logue. After David Logue sold his sister and mother to a brutal master, Jarm escaped through Kentucky and southern Indiana, aided by Quakers, and reached Hamilton, Upper Canada, about 1835. He tried his hand at farming, learned to read at the age of twenty-three, and worked as a hotel porter and lumberjack. It was in Canada that he added an *n* to the spelling of his name to distinguish it from that of his slave master. When creditors seized his farm in 1837, Loguen moved to Rochester, New York, and found employment as a hotel porter.

The black clergyman ELYMAS P. ROGERS urged him to attend Beriah Green's abolitionist school, Oneida Institute, at Whitesboro, New York. Loguen enrolled there in 1839, despite his lack of formal education. He started a school in nearby Utica for African American children and made a public profession of faith. He settled in Syracuse in 1841, opened another school, and married Caroline Storum of Busti, New York. They would have five children. One daughter, Amelia, married Lewis E. Douglass, the son of FREDERICK DOUGLASS; Gerrit Smith Loguen became an accomplished artist; and Sarah Marinda Loguen graduated from the medical school of Syracuse University in 1876.

After being ordained by the AMEZ Church in 1842, Loguen served congregations in Syracuse, Bath, Ithaca, and Troy. He gave his first speech against slavery in Plattsburgh, New York, in 1844 and was enlisted as an itinerant lecturer promoting the Liberty Party. Loguen's sacred vocation now focused on abolitionism, and he devoted less and less time to the local ministry. Working in cooperation with Frederick Douglass of Rochester, the Unitarian minister Samuel May of Syracuse, and the abolitionist and reformer Gerrit Smith of Peterboro in Madison County, Loguen actively aided fugitive slaves passing through upstate New York on their way to Canada. His home became the center of Underground Railroad activity in Syracuse, and in his autobiography, *A Stop on the Underground Railroad* (1859), he claimed to have assisted more than 1,500 runaway slaves.

Loguen was the presiding elder of the AMEZ's Troy district when the Fugitive Slave Law of 1850 was passed. Loguen returned to Syracuse, where he publicly defied the law and vowed resistance. "I don't respect this law," he said. "I don't fear it, I won't obey it! It outlaws me, and I outlaw it, and the men who attempt to enforce it on me. I place the governmental officials on the ground that they place me. I will not live a slave, and if force is employed to re-enslave me, I shall make preparations to meet the crisis as becomes a man." With other members of the Fugitive Aid Society, Loguen participated in the famous rescue of William "Jerry" McHenry in Syracuse in October 1851; fearing arrest for his actions, Lougen fled to St. Catharines, Canada West, where he conducted missionary work and spoke on behalf of the temperance cause among other fugitives. Despite the failure of his appeal of 2 December 1851 for safe passage to Governor Washington Hunt of New York, Loguen returned to Syracuse in late 1852 and renewed his labors on behalf of the Underground Railroad and the local Fugitive Aid Society. Loguen was indicted by a grand jury in Buffalo, New York, but was never tried.

By the 1840s Loguen had moved away from the moral suasion philosophy of William Lloyd Garrison and into the circle of central New York abolitionists who endorsed political means. After the demise of the Liberty Party, Loguen supported a remnant known as the Liberty League. By 1854 Loguen had abandoned the nonviolent philosophy of many of his abolitionist colleagues and joined the Radical Abolition Society. After 1857 he devoted all of his time to the Fugitive Aid Society. He returned to Canada West to attend a convention led by John Brown (1800–1859) prior to the 1859 raid at Harpers Ferry but apparently did not know the details of Brown's plan.

In the early 1860s Loguen served as pastor of Zion Church in Binghamton, New York. He also recruited black troops for the Union army. After the Civil War, Loguen was active in establishing AMEZ congregations among the southern freedmen. He had a special interest in Tennessee, where he believed his mother and sister lived. (Earlier he had refused to purchase the freedom of his mother because her master, Manasseth Logue, his father's brother, demanded that Loguen also purchase his own freedom.) Loguen became bishop of the Fifth District of the AMEZ Church in 1868, with responsibilities for the Allegheny and Kentucky conferences. He supported the work of the Freedmen's Bureau and the American Missionary Association in the South. On the eve of leaving for a new post as organizer of AMEZ missions on the Pacific coast, he died in Saratoga Springs, New York.

FURTHER READING
Loguen's letters are held in the Gerrit Smith Papers, George Arents Research Library, Syracuse University, and are available on microfilm in the *Black Abolitionist Papers*, C. Peter Ripley, ed.

Loguen, J. W. *A Stop on the Underground Railroad: Rev. J. W. Loguen & Syracuse* (1859, 2001).

Hunter, Carol M. *To Set the Captives Free: Reverend Jermain Wesley Loguen and the Struggle for Freedom in Central New York, 1835–1872* (1993)

Sernett, Milton C. "A Citizen of 'No Mean City': Jermain W. Loguen and the Antislavery Reputation of Syracuse," *Syracuse University Library Associates Courier* 22 (Fall, 1987): 33–55.

Obituary: *Syracuse Journal*, 1 Oct. 1872.

This entry is taken from the *American National Biography* and is published here with the permission of the American Council of Learned Societies.

MILTON C. SERNETT

Loguen Fraser, Sarah Marinda (29 Jan. 1850–9 Apr. 1933), physician and pharmacist, was born in Syracuse, New York, the fifth of eight children of Caroline (Storum) and JERMAIN WESLEY LOGUEN, an African Methodist Episcopal Zion (AMEZ) Church bishop. Close friends of FREDERICK DOUGLASS and FRANCES ELLEN WATKINS HARPER, Loguen Fraser's parents were themselves ardent abolitionists and women's rights supporters. Her mother's heritage was free black, Native American, and French Canadian. As her father recounted in his autobiography, *The Reverend J.W. Loguen as a Slave and as a Freeman* (1859), he was conceived after his mother was raped by their white slaveholder in Davidson County, Tennessee. Jermain Loguen escaped North, learned to read, entered the ministry, and vowed to spend his life liberating others from slavery. The Loguens' Syracuse house at East Genesee and Pine Streets was a critical station on the Underground Railroad that sheltered perhaps as many as 1,500 fugitives in all, starting sometime between 1848 and 1851 and possibly continuing into the 1860s.

As a child Loguen Fraser tended the fugitives' illnesses and wounds. At seventeen she nursed her mother through a terminal illness. After graduating from high school, she worked as her father's secretary until his sudden death in 1872. With her two surviving older siblings married and away from home, Loguen Fraser became responsible for providing for her three younger siblings.

Then, in spring 1873, at the Washington, D.C., train station, she witnessed the indifference of the assembled crowd after a wagon struck a child. She called for a doctor until someone finally agreed to treat the boy. As the story goes, on her train ride home to Syracuse, she closed her eyes and vowed aloud to become a doctor so she would never again be helpless to help. As chance would have it, she immediately encountered Michael Benedict, the Loguen family physician and Onondaga County Medical Society president; he had taken the same train. Benedict offered to tutor her so she could apply to Syracuse University School of Medicine (later SUNY Upstate Medical University).

After five months' tutoring, Loguen Fraser was admitted to the School of Medicine; she enrolled in the fall of 1873 and received her medical degree in 1876. She is believed to have been the fourth African American woman to become an M.D., after REBECCA LEE CRUMPLER (1864), Rebecca J. Cole (1867), and SUSAN SMITH MCKINNEY STEWARD (1870). In September 1876 Loguen Fraser started her internship by treating mostly immigrant children and pregnant women at Women's Hospital of Philadelphia, Pennsylvania. Her pediatric patients affectionately nicknamed her "Miss Doc." Apparently a white woman doctor from Nashville, Tennessee, was not so warmly disposed toward Loguen. After the two were told repeatedly that they resembled twin sisters, they discovered they were cousins. The white doctor abruptly resigned from the hospital. In 1876 Frederick Douglass, whose son Lewis had married Loguen Fraser's sister Amelia, introduced her to the pharmacist Charles Alexander Fraser, a Douglass family friend visiting the United States from Puerto Plata, Santo Domingo (later the Dominican Republic). In 1877 the two struck up a correspondence. In fall 1878 Loguen Fraser accepted a six-month appointment at Boston's New England Hospital for Women and Children, where she did work in the dispensary. Shortly thereafter, living in Washington, D.C., with Amelia and Lewis Douglass, she opened her own medical practice on 13th Street, NW.

On 19 September 1882 Charles Fraser and Sarah Loguen were married in Syracuse, then moved to Puerto Plata. As soon as her Spanish was fluent enough, in spring 1883, Loguen Fraser became the first licensed woman physician in Santo Domingo. Her practice and her husband's drugstore prospered. On 23 December 1883 she gave birth to their only child, Gregoria Alejandrina Fraser.

Charles Fraser died in 1894 following a stroke. Loguen Fraser, now the single mother of a ten-year-old girl as well as a widow, closed down her medical practice, took over her husband's pharmacy, and invested the profits. Starting in 1896, Loguen Fraser moved between Washington, D.C., France, and Syracuse to find educational placements for

Sarah Marinda Loguen Fraser with her graduating class at Syracuse Medical College in 1876. (Austin/Thompson Collection.)

her artistically gifted daughter. Loguen Fraser returned to Washington for good in 1907 and reestablished herself in a flourishing private practice. Between 1910 and 1915 she treated patients at the Women's Clinic.

During the 1920s kidney disease and senility increasingly disabled Loguen Fraser, and she died in 1933 at the home she shared with her daughter and son-in-law in Washington. Following her death, the citizens of Puerto Plata lowered their flags to half-mast for more than a week, held a mass in her honor, and placed flowers on her husband's grave. Before her own death in 1963, Loguen Fraser's daughter, the musician Gregoria Fraser Goins, wrote an unpublished biography of her mother, *Miss Doc*.

In 1998 the SUNY Upstate Medical University alumni magazine recounted Loguen Fraser's story. During Black History Month 2000 the campus celebrated her 150th birthday by instituting an annual scholarship award and day in her honor and renaming C-D Street after her. The Syracuse artist Susan Keeter's commissioned oil portrait of Loguen Fraser was unveiled and hung in the library. At the portrait dedication the psychiatrist Sandra Barnett-Reyes read a personal letter to her predecessor, praising Sarah Loguen Fraser as "a 'star' which may have disappeared" but whose "light continues to shine forth and reach us … to create within us concern and passion to serve mankind, a light that helps us to be *better* and *better*, not *bitter*" (Barnett-Reyes, 15).

FURTHER READING

The Gregoria Fraser Goins Papers, Manuscript Division, Moorland-Spingarn Research Center, Howard University contain materials on Sarah Loguen Fraser, including the *Miss Doc* manuscript.

Barnett-Reyes, Saundra. "The Guiding Light of Sarah Loguen Fraser, M.D.," *SUNY Upstate Medical Alumni Journal* (Summer 2000).

Keeter, Susan. "Seeking Dr. Sarah," *SUNY Upstate Medical University Outlook* (Spring 2002).

van der Luft, Eric. "Sarah Loguen Fraser, M.D. (1850–1933): The Fourth African American Woman Physician," *Journal of the National Medical Association* 92.3 (Mar. 2000).

Obituary: *Syracuse Post-Standard*, 14 June 1933.

MARY KRANE DERR

Lomax, Louis Emanuel (16 Aug. 1922–30 July 1970), journalist and social commentator, was born in Valdosta, Georgia, to parents whose names and occupations are now unknown. It is known that Lomax was an only child, and attended local schools. He earned a bachelor's degree in 1942 from Paine College in Augusta, Georgia, an M.A. from American University in Washington, D.C., in 1944, and a Ph.D. in Philosophy from Yale in 1947. After working briefly as an assistant professor of philosophy at Georgia State College, Lomax wrote freelance articles, including several for Chicago's *Daily News*. Although Lomax denied that he had a criminal record, FBI reports showed that he was incarcerated from 1949 to 1954 in Joliet Prison in Illinois for selling a rented car. He was paroled on 28 September 1954 and returned to Chicago to work as a lecturer at writers' workshops, as a reporter for a local nightclub magazine called *Club Chatter*, and as a member of the Associated Writers group. His articles appeared in the *Baltimore American*, the *Chicago American*, and other papers of the Associated Negro Press. Lomax moved to New York City in the late 1950s.

Lomax's journalistic interests focused on black education, culture, and society. He was the first black newscaster hired for WNTA television in New York and he took the lead interviewing role, along with Mike Wallace (later a correspondent for the CBS newsmagazine *60 Minutes*), in the 1959 documentary *The Hate That Hate Produced*, a detailed exploration of the beliefs and personalities of the Nation of Islam. MALCOLM X had initially refused to discuss the issues facing black America with Wallace, a white man (in April 1964 Lomax debated Malcolm X in Cleveland, Ohio, in a forum sponsored by CORE; Malcolm presented the "Ballot or the Bullet" speech at the event). Lomax also narrated a 1961 program for KTVS-TV in Shreveport, Louisiana, titled *Walk in My Shoes*, sponsored by Bell and Howell and produced by ABC News, which featured interviews with African Americans about their lives. Lomax served as executive producer of the show, in addition to conducting all of the interviews. ABC television affiliates in southern states requested a preview of the special and many declined to air it.

Lomax's book *The Reluctant African* (1960) chronicled life in Africa and was awarded the Anisfield-Wolf Award for its frank and realistic coverage. His *The Negro Revolt* (1962) sold well and established Lomax as a major black voice in American society, and was a required text on many college campuses in the 1960s. When race riots broke out in Milwaukee in 1967, one accused rioter claimed that he had been at home reading Lomax's book when the unrest erupted. Lomax wrote about the Black Panthers, the Nation of Islam, civil rights activists, and was an outspoken critic of the war in Vietnam. He took out a full-page newspaper advertisement to announce his refusal to pay income taxes that would fund the war in Vietnam. Lomax was charged with tax evasion by the federal government in 1970, but he would die before the trial could take place.

A third book, *When the Word is Given: A Report on Elijah Muhammad, Malcolm X, and Black Muslim World*, was published in 1963. Lomax spoke at the Conference on Race and Culture in Denmark in 1967 on behalf of the International Association of Authors, Artists and Scientists. His book *Thailand: The War That Is, The War That Will Be* was released in 1967. Lomax entered North Vietnam in 1967 to interview Ho Chi Minh as part of what he termed "a news-gathering mission." Lomax used this phrase in answer to the congressional investigation of his trip. He had been denied a visa for the trip and instead simply entered through another country, denying the U.S. government the right to approve or disapprove his travels. He was one of only two people to be given visas by the Hanoi government (the other was Harrison E. Salisbury of the *New York Times*). Lomax's last book, *To Kill a Black Man: The Shocking Parallel in the Lives of Malcolm X and* MARTIN LUTHER KING, JR., was published in 1968 by Holloway House. Lomax's essays were sometimes featured in the "Speaking Out" column in the *Saturday Evening Post* magazine in the 1960s, and his reviews of black-authored texts appeared in numerous scholarly publications.

The Louis Lomax Show on KTTV-TV Los Angeles, featuring interviews in a talk show format, went on the air in 1959, the first such show to feature an African American newsman. Lomax continued to appear on television in his own biweekly talk show from 1964 until 1968. Subsequently labeled by some media historians as "hate journalism," Lomax's program regularly challenged the actions of the FBI and other law enforcement agencies. He was critical of black colleges for not demanding quality standards for students, and frequently chastised blacks for not achieving in higher education.

After interviewing witnesses for "Mississippi Eyewitness: the Three Civil Rights Workers—How They Were Murdered," an exclusive article published in *Ramparts* magazine in 1964, Lomax joined John Howard Griffin and DICK GREGORY in maintaining that law enforcement could identify the killers of civil rights workers, JAMES CHANEY, Andrew Goodman and Michael Schwerner who had been assigned to work in Meridian, Mississippi, but that no arrests would be made due to pressure from local racists (a charge he would later repeat about the killing of DR. MARTIN LUTHER KING JR.). Lomax spoke and wrote about the U.S. Department of Justice, singling out individuals in the Civil Rights Division for their inability to capture individuals responsible for the bombing of black churches in Southern states. He was critical of Dr. Martin Luther King Jr., charging that King would not be able to keep his supporters united in a movement for non-violence. In stump speeches and debates Lomax predicted that instead, a bloody race revolution would take place in the United States. Lomax, JAMES BALDWIN, and JOHN O. KILLENS represented Artists and Writers for Justice, a group founded by RUBY DEE after the 1963 death of six children in a church bombing in Birmingham, Alabama, that advocated the use of the economic boycott to call attention to racial violence. Lomax's possible links to the Communist Party, beginning in the 1950s, were the topic of lengthy, intensive FBI investigation.

Lomax continued to write articles for a wide variety of magazines and he lectured widely. Hofstra University appointed Lomax writer-in-residence in 1970 after he had taught there for a year as an assistant professor. He was killed in a single-car accident near Santa Rosa, New Mexico, on 30 July 1970, before he could begin the appointment. At the time of his death, he had been working on a three-volume history of blacks in America.

FURTHER READING

The Louis Lomax Papers, 1922–1970, are in the Ethnicity and Race Manuscript collections, at the University of Nevada, Reno.

Carmichael, Stokely (Kwame Ture). *Ready for Revolution* (2003).

Carson, Clayborne. *The Movement: 1964–1970* (1993).

Carson, Clayborne, Bill Kovach, and Carol Polsgrove. *Reporting Civil Rights: American Journalism, 1941–1963*, vol. I, 1963–1973, vol. II (2003).

Jackson, Ronald L., and Elaine B. Richardson. *Understanding African American Rhetoric: Classical Origins to Contemporary Innovations* (2003).

Obituary: *New York Times*, 1 Aug. 1970.

PAMELA LEE GRAY

Long, Donald Russell (27 Aug. 1939–30 June 1966), Vietnam War soldier and Medal of Honor recipient, was born in Blackfork, Ohio, the son of Herman and Mildred (Keels) Long. The Longs had nine children, including Donald; his two brothers, Herman and Billy; and five sisters, Lucy, June, Audrey, Barbara, Marva, and Elsie, and were active in the Union Baptist Church in Blackfork. The congregation of this church, which sits on the former farmland of the Keels family, Donald Long's maternal ancestors, was well known for its activities in support of the Underground Railroad prior to the Civil War. Donald Long would eventually grow up to fight for a different kind of freedom, albeit in a land far from his home.

Donald Long was drafted for service in the Vietnam War on 16 April 1963 and was inducted at Ashland, Kentucky, just across the Ohio River from his hometown. While his early army assignments are unknown, on 19 September 1965 Long was assigned to Troop C, 1st Squadron, 4th Cavalry Regiment at Fort Riley, Kansas, and by 20 October the entire unit was deployed to Vietnam. While there are few details about Donald Long's specific actions prior to 1966, the fact that he had achieved the rank of sergeant in less than three years indicates that he was an accomplished and talented soldier with true leadership skills. Not only is the rank of sergeant the highest position that an enlisted man can achieve, but men in this position serve as the backbone of the army command, training and developing members of their platoon (or troop, as cavalry units are designated) in peacetime, and leading them into battle during time of war. Indeed, of the twenty African American soldiers, men like Donald Long, CLIFFORD SIMS, and MATTHEW LEONARD, to be awarded the Medal of Honor during the Vietnam War, over a third were sergeants. This high level of service is also indicative of how vital African American servicemen were to the modern army overall; no longer encumbered by the racism that was inherent in army life as late as the Korean War, these men developed their skills to the utmost to serve their country to the highest degree possible.

Upon arriving in Vietnam, Donald Long and the 1st Squadron, 4th Cavalry were assigned to the 1st Infantry Division as their reconnaissance squadron and were based at Di An. Not only were they the first elements of the 4th Cavalry to serve in Vietnam, but their deployment was somewhat historic; while many experts thought that Vietnam's terrain was not conducive to the use of armored cavalry units, their early successes proved otherwise, and units of this type were subsequently used on a more widespread basis. The job of the 1st Squadron, 4th Cavalry was primarily to provide security for mission and supply convoys along Vietnam's Route 13, a main route running north from Saigon. On 30 June 1966, Sergeant Donald Long and Troop C were conducting a reconnaissance mission along Route 13 just north of An Lac, near the village of Srok Dong, when forward elements were attacked by the 271st Viet Cong Regiment from concealed positions along the road using mortars and machine guns. The men of Troop C were under heavy fire, but Donald Long leaped from the armored personnel carrier he was riding in to rescue his wounded men and carry them to a waiting helicopter, doing so amid a hail of gunfire. As his platoon and the men of Troop C were subsequently ordered to push northward to relieve the pressure on Troop B, Sergeant Long continuously exposed himself to provide needed supplies and ammunition to the other units, while also using rifle fire and grenades to protect the carrier in which they were riding. When another armored personnel carrier was wrecked by enemy fire, Long again disregarded his own safety and helped bring the wounded crew to safety. As he was reorganizing his men for further attacks, an enemy grenade landed inside their carrier; Sergeant Long quickly shouted a warning, and pushed one man to safety. However, realizing that the men in his platoon were still in danger, Donald Long threw himself on the grenade to absorb the blast. By doing so, he saved the lives of eight of his men, but at the expense of his own.

Sergeant Donald Long was buried at the Union Baptist Church Cemetery in Blackfork, Ohio. He was posthumously awarded the Medal of Honor on 4 April 1968, which was presented to his family at a Pentagon ceremony. He was the third African American soldier to earn the Medal of Honor during the Vietnam War.

FURTHER READING

Baty, Bill. "History of the 4th Cavalry." http://www. quarterhorsecav.org/pg9.htm.

Hanna, Charles W. *African American Recipients of the Medal of Honor* (2002).

GLENN ALLEN KNOBLOCK

Long, Howard Hale (4 Mar. 1888–21 Feb. 1957), educator and psychologist, was born in News Ferry, Virginia, to Annie Vassar and Thomas Long. During his childhood, his family moved to Richmond, where he attended and graduated from Wayland Academy, then part of Virginia Union University. He continued his education at Virginia Union University and transferred to Howard University in Washington, D.C., where he received Bachelor of Science and Bachelor of Education degrees in 1915. He attended Clark University in Worcester, Massachusetts, as a University Fellow, where he received an M.A. in Psychology in 1916 under the direction of G. Stanley Hall, considered one of the founders of American psychology. Long was arguably the first black to receive a postgraduate degree in psychology in the United States.

He was accepted in the doctoral program in psychology at Clark University, which included a scholarship, but did not attend. He taught psychology at Howard University from 1916 to 1917 and married Ollie Mae Guerant in 1917. He served in the U.S. Army from 1917 to 1919 in the 368th Infantry (gas officer and liaison), with the rank of first lieutenant. After his separation from the army he became Dean at Paine College (Augusta, Georgia, 1919–1923) and Professor of Education at Knoxville College (1923–1924). In 1924 he came to Washington, D.C., first as an instructor in Miner Normal School and then as a supervising principal in the Negro schools. In 1925 he became assistant school superintendent for Washington public schools and chief examiner for the divisions 10–13 (i.e., the Negro schools). This position made him responsible for decisions in hiring teachers, clerks, and truant officers.

In the 1920s the results from Army Alpha (intelligence) tests became available. Researchers such as Carl Bingham noted the difference in IQs between northern and southern European immigrants. The same analysis found differences favoring whites over blacks on these tests. Psychologists such as Lewis Terman, who had also studied at Clark University under Hall, assumed these differences were the result of genetic factors that could not be eliminated. Social critics of both races discussed how these analyses ignored the role of environment in these differences. In several articles in *Opportunity* and the *Journal of Negro Education*, Long pointed out statistical and methodological flaws in the analyses of Bingham and Terman.

In 1932 he took a year's leave of absence from the Washington public schools to earn an advanced degree. He received his Doctor of Education degree from Harvard University in 1933, where he was an Austin Scholar and the first black to receive that degree at Harvard. He returned to his position in Washington.

In the 1930s a series of dissertations came out of the University of Cincinnati that demonstrated superior performance of blacks in segregated schools. Although there was disagreement whether these findings applied only to schools that were voluntarily segregated, in an article titled "Some Psychogenic Hazards of Segregated Education of Negroes" in 1935 Hall argued that segregation in any form damaged the psychological development of black children.

During this same period Hall wrote more than twenty articles, primarily in the *Journal of Negro Education*, and he also served on its editorial board. Many of these articles continued to deal with the effects of segregation on Negro children and on the importance of the environment in intelligence. In one study he found that among Negro children in the Washington school system, the longer they had lived in Washington (despite its segregation) the closer their average IQs were to 100 (normal). He concluded from this study, "On any assumption, therefore, the wonder is not that the colored children of Washington fail to equal the whites in I.Q. score, but that their I.Q.'s are as high as they are" (Long, p. 222).

During this time Long also was a member of the Committee on the Participation of Negroes in the National Defense. This group was instrumental in having a clause against racial discrimination written into the Selective Service Act of 1940.

Especially during in his time in Washington, Long was involved in many professional and community organizations. He was a member and Treasurer of the American Teachers Association, an organization concerned with the teaching of black youth. The American Teachers Association worked the National Education Association to gain accreditation for Negro schools and colleges. The American Teachers Association also provided a means for teachers in Negro schools to organize in states where they were forbidden by law from joining white organizations. In 1938 at the organization's convention in Tuskegee, Alabama, Professor Herman Canady proposed a division for Psychology within the American Teachers Association. After unanimous approval, Dr. Long was elected vice chairman.

After his retirement from the Washington, D.C., school system in 1948, Hall became dean of administration at Central State University (Wilberforce, Ohio). He continued his interests in developing equal opportunity in education for all races in the South. During this time he also published articles on various topics in psychology for the *Journal of Human Relations*. He died on 21 February 1957 in Xenia, Ohio, and is buried in Arlington National Cemetery.

FURTHER READING
Guthrie, Robert V. *Even the Rat Was White: A Historical View of Psychology*, 2d ed. (2003).
Long, Howard H. "The Intelligence of Colored Elementary Pupils in Washington, D.C." *Journal of Negro Education*, Vol. 3, 1934, pp. 205–222.
Thomas, William B. "Black Intellectuals' Critique of Early Mental Testing: A Little-Known Saga of the 1920s," *American Journal of Education*, Vol. 90, 1982, pp. 258–292.
Obituaries: *Washington Post*, 24 February 1957; *Washington Star*, 25 February 1957.

STEPHEN A. TRUHON

Long, Jefferson Franklin (3 Mar. 1836–4 Feb. 1901), Reconstruction-era politician, was born a slave of mixed African and Caucasian ancestry in Knoxville, Crawford County, Georgia. The names of his parents and of his owners are unknown. Sometime before the beginning of the Civil War, Long was taken from rural Crawford County to nearby Macon, where he evidently taught himself to read and write and learned a trade. Freed at the end of the war, he opened a tailor shop in Macon, which he and his son operated for a number of years and which provided him a steady income and a position of some eminence in the black community. Long married Lucinda Carhart (marriage date unknown) and had seven children.

Like many who became involved in Republican Party politics in the early years of Reconstruction, Long attended sessions of the Georgia Equal Rights Association, and by the summer of 1867 he was making speeches for that group's successor, the Georgia Equal Rights and Educational Association, urging blacks to register to vote under the terms of the congressional program launched in the spring. In 1868, though not a candidate for any office, Long campaigned diligently for the Ulysses Grant ticket, and though the ticket failed to carry Georgia, Long was rewarded for his efforts with a seat on the Republican state central committee. In 1869 Long and HENRY MCNEAL TURNER, a black minister and politician from Macon, summoned a convention of

Jefferson Franklin Long, U.S. Congressman from Georgia, photographed between 1860 and 1875. (Library of Congress/Brady-Handy Photograph Collection.)

more than two hundred delegates who urged the creation of a public school system and called for higher wages for day laborers and for substantially more favorable terms for tenants in the emerging system of sharecropping.

Before 1870 Long appears to have had only limited roles—organizer, speaker, agitator—in the Reconstruction politics of Georgia. However, just as Republican power was ebbing in the state and at the same time that the Democrats regained control of the legislature, party leaders chose Long as a candidate for Congress from the Fourth District (located in the "Black Belt") in the elections of December 1870. But because Georgia had been denied representation in Congress before 15 July 1870, Long was elected only to the third session of the Forty-first Congress, which met early in 1871; a white Republican was chosen to represent the district for a full term in the Forty-second. It was the Republicans' rather manipulative strategy that year to attract black voters to their ticket by nominating black candidates for the short term and whites for the full one.

Sworn in on 16 January 1871 and serving until the end of the session on 3 March, Long nevertheless was the only black congressman elected from Georgia in the nineteenth century. In his brief tenure, Long also was the first black member to address the House. His short but impassioned speech, widely commented on in the national press, was in opposition to a measure that would relax slightly the restrictions imposed on former Confederates who sought public office. He spoke not to the details of the measure but to the larger question of ongoing racial violence and resistance to Radical Reconstruction in the South. He said:

> Do we, then, really propose here to-day, when the country is not ready for it, where those disloyal people still hate this Government, when loyal men dare not carry the "stars and stripes" through our streets, for if they do they will be turned out of employment, to relieve from political disability the very men who have committed these Kuklux outrages?

Despite Long's speech, the bill passed by a vote of 118 to 90.

Long returned to Macon when Congress adjourned and, though never again seeking or holding a public office, remained active in politics until 1884. He appeared regularly at Republican state and district gatherings and was a delegate to the national conventions in 1872, 1876, and 1880. The remainder of his public career signified his growing dissatisfaction with the white leadership of his party—but he did not advocate black solidarity against all whites in it—and his repeated efforts to transform black voters into a more independent political force. He was particularly critical of the ring control of the state Republican Party and the party's descent into patronage brokering. At the same time, Long realized that black voters would have to reach an accommodation with at least some of the white conservatives who had taken control of Georgia in December 1871.

Soon after Redemption, when the Democratic Party showed signs of splitting between the Regulars and the Independents, who resisted the machinelike control of the party apparatus by powerful bosses, Long supported the Independents and campaigned for William H. Felton, an Independent congressman from a north Georgia district. In 1880, however, when the state Republican Party did not put forth a candidate for governor, Long joined other prominent black Republicans in working vigorously for the incumbent, Alfred Holt Colquitt, a Bourbon Democrat and former Confederate general, instead of for Thomas M. Norwood, an Independent Democrat supported by most white Republicans. Many blacks endorsed Colquitt, who was also a licensed Methodist preacher, partly because of his well-received sermons in black churches and his efforts as governor to protect blacks against white violence, and partly because of their deep hostility to the white manipulation of the Republican Party apparatus. After Colquitt's victory, Long won enthusiastic commendations from the Democratic power brokers.

Within the Republican Party, which was weakened on the one hand by persistent divisions between white officeholders and federal appointees, and on the other by the black rank and file, Long was a steady opponent of what he believed was unprincipled white control. Black dissatisfaction with the party culminated at the state convention in 1880, when the black majority among the delegates—angry because choice nominations and federal appointments usually went to whites, and hostile toward the party leaders' intentions to expand the Republican base by wooing white conservatives—seized control of the central committee, made WILLIAM A. PLEDGER, a young black newspaperman from Athens, the committee chairman, and sent a majority-black delegation to the national convention. Two years later Pledger stepped down as chairman in favor of Alfred E. Buck, a white politician popular with blacks, who held the position until 1898 and adeptly fought off efforts to make the party lilywhite. These convolutions in Republican affairs in Georgia left Long frustrated in his attempts to win meaningful influence for black voters and left him disillusioned with politics itself. In an open letter that he wrote as a parting shot in 1884, he spoke about schoolhouses and churches and about "Christianity, morality, education, and industry" in addressing the unresolved problem of racial advancement in the post-Reconstruction South.

Long lived in Macon the rest of his life, with his-son running his tailor's shop and adding a drycleaning establishment. Long helped organize the Union Brotherhood Lodge, a black mutual-aid society with headquarters in Macon and branches in other towns nearby. Long's daughter Annie Eunice was the wife of Henry Allan Rucker, collector of internal revenue for Georgia from 1897 to 1909. Far more than Long's brief tenure in Congress, his public career in Georgia illuminates the difficulties that confronted black politicians, the weaknesses of Republicanism, and the limitations of the political process in the protection and advancement of black people's interests in the Reconstruction period. Long died in Macon.

FURTHER READING
Drago, Edmund L. *Black Politicians and Reconstruction in Georgia: A Splendid Failure* (1982).
Foner, Eric. *Freedom's Lawmakers* (1993).
Matthews, John M. "Jefferson Franklin Long: The Public Career of Georgia's First Black Congressman," *Phylon* 42 (June 1981):145–156.
Shadgett, Olive Hall. *The Republican Party in Georgia from Reconstruction through 1900* (1964).
Obituaries: *Atlanta Constitution* and *Atlanta Journal*, 5 Feb. 1901.

This entry is taken from the *American National Biography* and is published here with the permission of the American Council of Learned Societies.

JOHN M. MATTHEWS

Long, Sylvester (1 Dec. 1890–19 Mar. 1932), author, actor, and Indian celebrity, was born in Winston, North Carolina, the son of Sallie Long, a nurse and midwife, and Joe Long, a janitor. Sylvester's light-skinned mother was born a slave weeks before the end of the Civil War and was the daughter of a plantation owner and an unknown Lumbee Indian. Long's father, also born into slavery, believed his own mother to be Cherokee and his father white. Their claim to exclusively white and Indian ancestry established the Long family as the social elite of Winston's African American community. After attending elementary school there Sylvester twice joined traveling Wild West circuses, where he passed as an Indian and learned rudimentary Cherokee. After returning to Winston and working as a library janitor Sylvester taught himself to type at night in the white school where his father mopped floors. The principal suggested he apply to the Carlisle Indian School in Pennsylvania, the first and most prestigious off-reservation government boarding school, founded in 1879 to assimilate Native American children into the dominant culture.

After lowering his age by one year and claiming one-half Indian blood in his application, Long entered Carlisle in 1909 and met immediate opposition from the admissions committee who could locate no one in Cherokee County, North Carolina, able to corroborate his ancestry. However, due to the large number of students that the committee needed to investigate and Long's ability to speak some Cherokee when challenged, he was accepted. Students protested and a petition was circulated to expel the "Cherokee nigger" (Smith, 50). Long soon invented new, Indian-sounding names for himself, changing his middle name from Clark to Chahuska and his last name to Long Lance. He graduated as a top student in his class three years later. Now claiming his place of birth as Cherokee County, Long attended the all-white schools of Conway Hall and St. John's Military Academy. He was no longer scrutinized by Indians and his racial identity went unchallenged until he wrote to President Woodrow Wilson, requesting an appointment to the military academy at West Point as a "full-blooded Cherokee." When Wilson accepted him, pending his performance on entrance exams, the news made national headlines. In order to cut off the resulting enquiry into his background, Long may have intentionally failed the exams with scores vastly inferior to his usual academic work. He later claimed that he failed so that he could enlist in the Canadian army and fight in World War I, which the United States had not yet joined.

Long enjoyed respect as an Indian in the Thirty-eighth Battalion and received a quick succession of promotions to acting sergeant, before fighting in the trenches on the Vimy Ridge front, part of the battle of Arras in France. He suffered minor injuries and when released in 1919 chose to live in Calgary, Alberta. He secured a job as a newspaper reporter while further embellishing his personal history. His career as a journalist took him to Indian reservations, where he wrote sympathetic but racially-prejudiced articles, referring, for example, to the Sarcee Indians as "pagans." He was also ceremonially adopted into the Blood tribe and expanded his name to Chief Buffalo Child Long Lance. After moving to Vancouver in 1922 he again claimed full Indian descent, now from the Bloods, and gained entry into reservation communities where white reporters could not. He advocated on behalf of tribes, while presenting himself as a Plains Indian to white audiences, often performing war whoops and dances and parading in city events. Tribal elders regarded him as an outsider. In addition to his writing he toured the lecture circuit and worked as a press representative at an elite Canadian hotel. He made friends with the white clientele, including the editor of Cosmopolitan, who contracted him to write an autobiographical article. After Long's publications expanded to other prestigious magazines, Cosmopolitan invited him to author an adventure novel. Long instead suggested an "autobiography" of his supposed childhood among the last of the traditional Plains Indians. Long Lance was published 1928 to strong sales and stronger reviews, including one from anthropologist Paul Radin. Its first printing sold out and translations appeared in Dutch and German. Long was soon attending Park Avenue parties with New York socialites and dating white actresses and singers, including Elizabeth Clapp, grand-niece of a turn-of-the-century coal baron. The B. F. Goodrich Company contracted him to endorse a new running shoe, the Long Lance Sports Shoe, supposedly modeled on the moccasin. An independent film producer was also struck by Long and hired him to star in The Silent Enemy, designed to reverse Hollywood's stereotypes of Indians as savages.

The fame lead to new scrutiny. When the Commissioner of Indian Affairs was asked by Long's publisher to review the autobiography, he wrote that Long Lance was an interesting and readable work of "fiction." Long also met with challenges during the shooting of The Silent Enemy. His co-star Chauncey Yellow Robe was a nephew of Sitting Bull and suspected him as an imposter, in part because of his boisterousness, punctuality, and easy small talk, as well as errors in his supposedly Plains Indian dancing and sign language. Long altered his history again, explaining that he had been raised by Cherokee adoptive parents in Oklahoma after his Blackfoot clan had broken up. The film was released in 1930 to strong reviews but poor ticket sales. Madison Grant, author of The Passing of the Great Race (1916), which warned against the danger of racial intermarriage and pass-for-white mulattoes, declared The Silent Enemy accurate in every detail. Long toured to promote the film, but the producer's investigation soon revealed his Winston background. Long's party and lecture invitations decreased as rumors of his actual background spread, and his status as the only non-white resident at his elite New York residence was questioned. Though he wished to marry and Elizabeth Clapp encouraged him, he ended their relationship, his most heartfelt, apparently fearing the harm his full exposure would cause her. Long's final performance was played out for California millionaire Anita Baldwin who lived on a sequestered estate near Los Angeles. She employed Long as her personal secretary and bodyguard during a trip to Europe, and although he became repeatedly drunk and violent, she allowed him to stay at her estate and take flying lessons at her expense. In 1932 Long shot himself in the head with a revolver in her private library. He had received a letter from Elizabeth Clapp, announcing her recent wedding, earlier the same day.

Sylvester Long's acts of self-invention enabled him to the escape the enforced limitations of Jim Crow America. By posing as a full-blood member of various Native American tribes, he passed into white society, using the dominant culture's romanticized notions of Indians to his advantage. Though a flamboyant imposter Long could legitimately claim Native American, African American, and European American ancestry, but in the end could not endure the agonies of early twentieth century race construction.

FURTHER READING

Long Lance, Chief Buffalo Child. *Long Lance* (1928).

Smith, Donald B. *Chief Buffalo Child Long Lance: The Glorious Imposter* (1999).

CHRIS GAVALER

Looby, Z. Alexander (8 Apr. 1899–24 Mar. 1972), lawyer, was born Zephaniah Alexander Looby in Antigua, British West Indies, to John Alexander Looby, a fishing boat operator, and Grace Elizabeth Joseph Looby. Looby was among the small number of second-generation black lawyers who began practicing in the southern United States during the 1920s and 1930s. Working individually they provided much of the legal work that led to dismantling systemic local segregation in the late twentieth century.

Looby migrated to the United States in his teens, graduated from Howard University in 1922, and then took a Bachelor of Laws degree (the standard law degree of the day) from Columbia University School of Law in 1925 and a Doctor of Juristic Science from New York University School of Law in 1926. Hired by Fisk University in Nashville, Tennessee, as an assistant professor of economics, he remained on the faculty until 1928 and thereafter taught as an occasional lecturer in jurisprudence at Fisk and at Meharry Medical College in Nashville. In 1929 Looby was admitted to the Tennessee bar and established legal practice in Memphis. Unwilling to work under restrictions imposed by the political machine of Edward H. Crump, he returned to Nashville and taught at Tennessee Agricultural and Industrial State College (now Tennessee State University) from 1932 to 1937, returning periodically to Memphis to court and then marry the schoolteacher Grafta L. Mosby in 1934. He ran unsuccessfully for a Nashville city council seat in 1940, being defeated in a run-off election.

A longstanding member of Omega Psi Phi fraternity, Looby served as the first representative of the fifth district (1938–1941) and as seventeenth Grand Basileus (national president; 1941–1945). With nearly a million young black men serving in uniform, the major challenge of his administration was coping with falling membership due to mobilization. It was not the only challenge posed by the war. After World War II the NAACP, fearing an outbreak of racial conflict similar to what followed World War I, retained him to assist future Supreme Court justice THURGOOD MARSHALL following the first important postwar confrontation involving racial tension, the 26 February 1946 race riot in Columbia, Tennessee. Marshall and Looby led the legal team defending a group of twenty-five black citizens accused of attempted murder following the invasion and destruction of businesses in the "Mink Slide," the city's black commercial district, by Tennessee Highway Patrol officers and "State Guard" members. Twenty-three were acquitted on a lack of evidence and two were granted new trials, making the case among the earliest successful large-scale defenses of black citizens charged with violence across racial lines (no charge was leveled against white participants).

Between 1943 and 1945 Looby chaired Nashville's black bar association, but in 1950 his application to the all-white Nashville Bar Association was rejected. He and Robert E. Lillard were elected to the city council in May 1951, its first black members since 1911. The Columbia case solidified Looby's determination to use the courts to invalidate de facto segregation. He worked steadily to challenge segregation in venue after public venue and built a reputation on successful legal challenges to segregated public amenities like recreation venues and business services. Shortly after the 1954 *Brown v. Board of Education* ruling, he filed an unsuccessful challenge to Nashville's public-school segregation. Five years later a small number of Fisk University students, advised by Rev. JAMES LAWSON, began planning and training for sit-in demonstrations at downtown lunch counters in October 1959. As the sit-in sites multiplied across the city in the spring of 1960, Looby, who was not involved in planning or in protest, nonetheless took a lead providing funds and legal representation to arrested student protestors. Probably because of his support, the Looby home on Meharry Avenue was dynamited on the night of 19 April 1960. Most of the house was destroyed, though miraculously no one was injured. That event became a turning point in Nashville's desegregation effort. A march from Looby's home to city hall protested the city's failure to address equity or halt racial violence. The marchers were met by the politically moderate mayor Ben West, who reluctantly stated publicly that he favored ending segregation at downtown lunch counters. Within days leaders reached an agreement on this first step in civic desegregation, which took effect 10 May 1960. Looby lost a bid to become the first black member of the Tennessee Supreme Court in 1962 but remained on the Nashville City Council and its successor, the Metropolitan Council, for five consecutive terms until declining health prompted his resignation in 1971.

Z. Alexander Looby's contribution to Nashville was commemorated with a branch of the city library named in his honor. The Nashville Bar Association admitted him to membership posthumously in October 1982. A biographical stage drama, *Signs of a New Day*, by playwright Carolyn German premiered in Nashville in January 2010.

FURTHER READING

Lovett, Bobby, and Linda T. Wynn, ed. *Profiles of African Americans in Tennessee* (1996). For the Annual Local Conference on Afro-African Culture and History.

Sarvis, Will. "Leaders in the Court and the Community: Z. Alexander Looby, Avon N. Williams, Jr., and the Legal Fight for Civil Rights in Tennessee, 1940–1970," *Journal of African American History* 88, no. 1 (Winter 2003): 42–58.

Obituary: *Tennessean*, 25 Mar. 1972.

RICHARD SAUNDERS

Lopes, Lisa (Left Eye) (27 May 1971–25 Apr. 2002), rapper, vocalist, dancer, entrepreneur, and founding member of the R&B hip-hop music group TLC, was born in Philadelphia, Pennsylvania, the eldest of three children born to Wanda D. Lopes and Ronald E. Lopes. Her father served in the U.S. military, which resulted in the family's moving frequently during her childhood. She resided in Kansas, Panama, New Jersey, and Florida, before settling in Atlanta, Georgia, in November 1990. There, at the age of nineteen, Lopes responded to an audition ad for the girl band Second Nature, which would morph into TLC.

TLC was an acronym for the phrase "Tender Loving Care" and also the girls' initials: Tionne (T-Boz) Watkins; Lopes; and Rozonda (Chilli) Thomas. The group, which modeled itself after the all-girl trios of the 1960s such as DIANA ROSS and the Supremes, reinvented the girl group for the hip-hop generation, paving the way for later groups such as Destiny's Child, which included Beyoncé Knowles.

The group produced four albums. They released *Ooooooohhh … On the TLC Tip* on 25 February 1992. The album produced three top-ten singles, including "Ain't 2 Proud 2 Beg," "What about Your Friends," and "Baby-Baby-Baby." The trio was also a standard on MTV, creating music videos with vibrant colors and lavish costuming, including multiple outfits in which the girls wore condoms. Lopes also wore a condom over the rim of her left lens in her eyeglasses. The group used their lyrics and the medium of the music video to focus on female empowerment, to educate young women on safe sex, the AIDS epidemic, and about reporting domestic violence. While on tour as the opening act for MC Hammer in 1993, they learned that band member Watkins had sickle-cell disease. Lopes, with the members of TLC, then became an advocate for the Sickle Cell Disease Association of America.

On 2 September 1992, Lopes filed a domestic violence report against her boyfriend Andre Rison, a football player for the Atlanta Falcons, and filed assault charges against him. On 9 June 1994, after a second bout of domestic violence, Lopes doused her boyfriend's sneakers with lighter fluid and ignited them in the bathtub, which rapidly turned into a structure fire of their multimillion dollar home. Lopes was sentenced to five years probation, was ordered to go to rehab for alcoholism, and was charged a fine of $10,000. Out of this experience, Lopes wrote the rap lyrics featured as the bridge to TLC's number one hit song "Waterfalls," which chronicles the story of an urban mother trying to save her son engaged in gang violence, drug dealing (the song discusses crack cocaine addiction) and promiscuous unprotected sex at a young age. The song's protagonist develops HIV and dies in the song's second movement: "One day he goes and takes a glimpse in the mirror/ But he doesn't recognize his own face/ His health is fading and he doesn't know why/ Three letters took him to his final resting place." The third and final movement makes a plea directly to the audience to turn to inner strength and faith (presumably Christianity from the lyrics "And like His promise is true/ Only my faith can undo/ The many chances I blew to bring my life to anew") and reject crime, drugs, and unprotected sexual activity. Three other songs released on the album *CrazySexyCool* also reached the top five spots on the charts in the United States. In

1996 *CrazySexyCool* won a Grammy Award for Best R&B Album and Best R&B Performance by a Duo or Group. The Grammys also nominated the album for Album of the Year.

Lopes actively tried to reinvest money in other African American performance groups and eventually founded Left Eye Productions. She signed the Atlanta group Blaque, which produced hits such as the 1999 song "808" produced by R. Kelly. She also produced songs for mainstream pop groups such as N'Sync.

Between 1999 and 2000, the band completed their third album, *FanMail*, which produced two number one hit singles: "No Scrubs" and "Unpretty." "Unpretty" added a new theme, body image, into the band's focus on female empowerment. The song is an inner monologue sung by a female who is beginning to internalize a negative perception of her body image through a combination of bad relationships and imagery of womanhood in the media. The chorus, which became an anthem for alternative conceptions of feminine beauty at the beginning of the twenty-first century, dealt with issues of consumer products targeted at women to improve their appearance such as hair extensions and plastic surgery. The lyrics spoke to specific attacks on black womanhood and beauty, yet were universally identifiable by women. "You can buy your hair if it won't grow/ You can fix your nose if he says so/ You can buy all the makeup that man can make," yet the final message is that unless "you can look inside you/ Find out who am I too?" that anyone would be able to overpower your self-esteem and "make you feel unpretty too."

Lopes died in an automobile accident on 25 April 2002. She was in the process of shooting a documentary film in Roma, Honduras, that centered on an alternative healing spa, the Usha Nutrition Center, she was attending. By the time of Lopes's death, TLC had sold over 21 million albums and had become the highest grossing girl group of all time in the United States.

FURTHER READING

Pareles, Jon. "Lisa Lopes, Rapper, Dies in Honduras Crash at 30." *New York Times*, 27 Apr. 2002.

"Lisa 'Left Eye' Lopes, Member of Grammy Award–Winning Trio TLC, Dies in Car Crash in Honduras." *Jet*, 13 May 2002, 18, 55.

"Remembering Lisa (Left Eye) Lopes." *Ebony*, August 2002, 136.

RHAE LYNN BARNES

Lorde, Audre (18 Feb. 1934–17 Nov. 1992), poet, writer, and activist, was born Audrey Geraldine Lorde in Harlem, New York City, the youngest of three daughters of Frederic Byron Lorde, a laborer and real estate broker from Barbados, and Linda Bellmar, from Grenada, who sometimes found work as a maid. Lorde's parents came to the United States from the Caribbean with hopes of earning enough money to return to the West Indies and start a small business. During the Depression the realization that the family was going to remain exiled in America slowly set in. Growing up in this atmosphere of disappointment had a profound impact on Lorde's development, as questions of identity, nationality, and community membership occupied her mind.

Ironically, this woman whose living and reputation derived from her skillful use of words had to struggle as a child to acquire speech and literacy. She was so nearsighted that she was considered legally blind. Moreover, her mother feared that she might be retarded, and her first memories of school were of being disparaged for being mentally slow. Either out of fear of her mother, a severe disciplinarian, or because of an undiagnosed speech impediment, Lorde did not begin to talk until she was four years old and was uncommunicative for many years thereafter.

Lorde received her early education at two Catholic institutions in Harlem, St. Mark's and St. Catherine's. In her fictionalized biomythography, *Zami: A New Spelling of My Name* (1982), she recalls the patronizing racism of low expectations, the overt racism of bigotry, and the oppressive learning environment that stifled her creativity. The West Indian dialect and the unusual idioms that she heard at home taught her that words could be used in different and creative ways. Freedom to construct words and sentences as she chose, however, was a right that she would have to fight for. Alternate spellings of her name and the adoption of new names were merely the most visible symbols of her struggle for self-definition. If Lorde was to be a rebel and a contrarian, words would become her weapons of choice.

Lorde began writing poetry in the seventh or eighth grade. At Hunter College High School she met another aspiring poet, Diane de Prima, and they worked together on the school literary journal, *Scribimus*. However, when the school refused to print a love sonnet Lorde had written about her affection for a boy, she sent the poem to *Seventeen* magazine, where it was published. After graduating from high school in 1951, Lorde worked and studied intermittently until 1959, when she received a B.A. degree from Hunter College. During much of the 1950s Lorde supported herself as a factory worker and an X-ray technician and in a number of other unsatisfying positions.

A pivotal experience occurred in 1954, when Lorde spent a year at the National University of Mexico. Although she had had a brief lesbian encounter while working at a factory in Connecticut, it was in Mexico that she began to free herself of the feelings of deviance that had inhibited her sexuality. When she returned to New York the next year, she immersed herself in the "gay girl" culture of Greenwich Village, and she continued to develop her craft as a member of the Harlem Writers Guild, which brought her into contact with such poets as LANGSTON HUGHES. It was also during this period that she became involved with the beat poets Allen Ginsberg, Jack Kerouac, and LeRoi Jones (AMIRI BARAKA).

In 1961 Lorde received an MLS degree from Columbia University's School of Library Service, and in March 1962 she married Edward Ashley Rollins, a white attorney from Brooklyn. They were married for eight years and had two children, Elizabeth and Jonathan, before divorcing in 1970. She held a number of posts at different libraries before becoming the head librarian at Town School Library in New York City, where she served from 1966 to 1968.

Lorde's life took a dramatic turn in 1968 when she received a National Endowment for the Arts grant, resigned her position as a librarian, and accepted a post at Tougaloo College in Mississippi as poet-in-residence. While she was working at this historically black college, Lorde's first book of poetry, *The First Cities* (1968), received critical acclaim for its effective understatement and subtlety. It was at Tougaloo College that Lorde met Frances Clayton, who would become her companion for nineteen years. Lorde's second book, *Cables to Rage* (1970), captures the anger of the emerging Black Power movement and contains the poem "Martha," in which Lorde first confirms her homosexuality in print. From this point on, Lorde observed that different groups (blacks, feminists, lesbians, and others) wanted to claim aspects of her life to aid their cause while rejecting those elements that challenged their prejudices. Of this tendency, Lorde said in an interview: "There's always someone asking you to underline one piece of yourself—whether it's black, woman, mother, dyke, teacher, etc.—because that's the piece that they need to key in to. They want to dismiss everything else. But once you do that, then you've lost" (Carla M. Hammond, *Denver Quarterly* 16, no. 1 [1981], 10–27).

During the 1970s Lorde returned to New York, where she entered a productive period of writing, teaching, and giving readings. Her third book, *From a Land Where Other People Live* (1973), was nominated for the National Book Award for poetry. It was followed in rapid succession by *New York Head Shop and Museum* (1974), *Coal* (1976), *Between Ourselves* (1976), and *The Black Unicorn* (1978). In these works Lorde develops her central themes: bearing witness to the truth, transforming pain into freedom, and seizing the power to define love and beauty for oneself. Never does her work trade in clichés, employ hackneyed metaphors, or evoke saccharine sentiment. Lorde found a new voice in poetry that struck like a hammer but sounded like a bell on issues of race, gender, sexuality, and humanity.

Late in 1978, at the age of forty-four, Lorde was stricken with breast cancer. She had a mastectomy but refused to wear a prosthesis to hide the effects of the surgery. Instead, she chose to face her ordeal openly and honestly by incorporating it into her writing. In many ways *The Cancer Journal* (1980) helped women "come out of the closet" about this disease. Confronted with her own mortality, she published the autobiographical *Zami: A New Spelling of My Name* (1982), which is essentially the story of her early life, and *Sister Outsider* (1984), a collection of speeches and essays. In *Burst of Light* (1988), which won the American Book Award for nonfiction, Lorde explains that "the struggle with cancer now informs all my days, but it is only another face of that continuing battle for self-determination and survival that black women fight daily, often in triumph." Her final book of poems, *The Marvelous Arithmetics of Distance*, was published posthumously in 1993.

In an effort to help other women writers, Lorde cofounded Kitchen Table: Women of Color Press in 1980. She taught courses on race and literature at Lehman College and John Jay College of Criminal Justice, and she was the Thomas Hunter Professor of English at her alma mater, Hunter College, until 1988. Lorde's highest accolade was bestowed in 1991, when she received New York's Walt Whitman Citation of Merit, an award given to the poet laureate of New York State.

Six years after her mastectomy Lorde was diagnosed with liver cancer. She sought treatment in

America, Europe, and Africa before moving to St. Croix in the Virgin Islands with her companion, Gloria I. Joseph. Shortly before her death in November 1992 Lorde underwent an African ritual in which she was renamed Gambda Adisa, which loosely translated means "Warrior: She Who Makes Her Meaning Known."

FURTHER READING

Lorde, Audre. *Zami: A New Spelling of My Name* (1983).

Anderson, Linda R. *Women and Autobiography in the Twentieth Century: Remembered Futures* (1997).

Keating, AnaLouise. *Women Reading Women Writing: Self-Invention in Paula Gunn Allen, Gloria Anzaldúa, and Audre Lorde* (1996).

Steele, Cassie Premo. *We Heal from Memory: Sexton, Lorde, Anzaldúa, and the Poetry of Witness* (2000).

Obituary: *New York Times*, 20 Nov. 1992.

SHOLOMO B. LEVY

Lott, Ronald Mandel "Ronnie" (8 May 1959–), football player, was born in Albuquerque, New Mexico, the oldest of three children born to Roy Lott Sr., an Air Force master sergeant, and Mary Lott. When Lott was five years old, the family moved to Washington, D.C., where his father drove high-ranking Air Force officials to the Pentagon. During his formative childhood years in the inner city of Washington, Lott played baseball in a parking lot and football in the streets, often emulating professional players with his brother, Roy Jr. The family moved to California when Lott was nine, first to San Bernardino, and then settling in Rialto. After playing Pop Warner football, Lott became a standout multisport athlete at Eisenhower High School, garnering honors in football, baseball, and basketball.

The focus of intense recruiting, Lott attended University of Southern California on a football scholarship following his 1977 graduation. At USC, he teamed with the star running back Marcus Allen to lead the USC Trojans to the 1978 national championship and consecutive victories in the 1979 and 1980 Rose Bowls. Lott was a consensus All American his junior and senior years, and as senior team captain, led the Pac-10 with eight interceptions.

The San Francisco 49ers selected Lott as the eighth overall pick in the 1981 draft, citing his speed, strength, and game intelligence as ingredients for a successful player. Lott won the starting left cornerback job out of spring training, and promptly grabbed seven interceptions and three defensive touchdowns over the year, helping the 49ers win their first Super Bowl. Following the season, he was the runner-up in Rookie of the Year voting to the New York Giants linebacker LAWRENCE TAYLOR.

Lott became a defensive mainstay on San Francisco throughout the 1980s, and one of five 49er players, along with his good friend Joe Montana, to be part of the team's four Super Bowl victories during the decade. In 1985 Lott was moved to free safety, a position that more suited his defensive attributes. At the end of the season, he seriously damaged his left pinky in a collision with the Dallas Cowboys running back Tim Newsome. Though he played with his hand heavily bandaged in the wildcard playoff game the following week, Lott faced surgery for 1986. In testimony to his devotion and work ethic, he opted to have part of the finger amputated so he could play a full season. The gamble paid off, and Lott led the league with ten interceptions in 1986 while recording seventy-seven tackles, three forced fumbles, and two sacks. Nodding to Lott's strength on the field, the Hall of Fame wide receiver Art Monk commented, "Most guys would just hit you, but there's something about Ronnie … it's a different feeling" (Falkner).

Along with his tenacity and ferocious hits on the playing field, Lott commanded a role as clubhouse leader with the 49ers, drawing respect from teammates and opponents alike. His off-field charity work with San Francisco–based hospitals and churches also contrasted with his role as a consummate gridiron warrior.

Lott's aggressive style of play came at a cost, however. His various injuries included separated shoulders, pinched nerves, and numerous broken digits, and San Francisco cited the accumulated health risk when not resigning him following the 1990 season. Lott agreed to a free agent deal with the Los Angeles Raiders, where he switched to strong safety. Playing a full season for the first time since 1985, Lott accumulated ninety-three tackles and led the league with eight interceptions, making his tenth and last Pro Bowl team at his third different position. Lott played another season with the Raiders before signing with New York Jets for 1993 and '94. He signed a deal with the Kansas City Chiefs for 1995, but missed the entire season after breaking his leg in an exhibition game and being placed on the injury reserve list. Lott retired in March 1996 with ten Pro Bowl appearances and sixty-three career interceptions.

Lott was voted into the Hall of Fame, appropriately with longtime friend Montana, in 2000, his first year of eligibility. Among other postcareer accolades, Lott was named to the NFL's 75th anniversary team, and had his number retired by the 49ers in 2003.

After serving as a football sportscaster on Fox NFL Sunday, Lott turned his attention to other interests, including starting a private equity firm with former teammates Montana and Harris Barton, helping launch a children's television program, owning car dealerships, and devoting time to various charity organizations.

Lott had two daughters, Hailey and Chloe, and a son, Isaiah, with his wife, Karen Collmer, whom he married in March 1991. He also had a son, Ryan Nece, from a college relationship; though not raised by Lott, Nece became a professional football player as well.

FURTHER READING

Lott, Ronnie with Jill Lieber. *Total Impact* (1991).

Falkner, David. "Passion Play." *The Sporting News*, 24 Oct. 1994.

Lieber, Jill. "Hitter with Heart." *Sports Illustrated*, 23 Jan. 1989.

Silver, Michael. "Together Forever." *Sports Illustrated*, 24 July 2000.

ADAM W. GREEN

Loudin, Frederick Jeremiah (1840–3 Nov. 1904), choir leader, was born in Portage County, Ohio, the son of a farmer whose name is now unknown and whose financial contributions to a nearby college neither overcame the local prejudice nor secured a place for his son among the student body. Educated in Ravenna, Ohio, Loudin went on to train as a printer, only to find his opportunities restricted by white printers who refused to work with him. Even his Methodist church rejected his application to join its choir. For all its positive associations for their kinfolk in the slavery states, mid-nineteenth century Ohio was a hard place for the Loudins, as it had been for FREDERICK DOUGLASS who was mobbed in Columbus, Ohio, when Frederick Loudin was a boy. He was to recall that the "ostracism was even more complete and unchristian in the free than in the slave States" (Marsh, 106).

After the Civil War Loudin lived in Tennessee, and it was there that he learned of the Fisk University choir, which toured in part to gather funds and favorable publicity for the institution. Founded in Nashville in 1866 by General Clinton Fisk, Fisk University housed its ambitious and talented black men and women in barracks once used by the Union army. In 1871 eleven students had

formed a choir that went on to raise $20,000 during a three-month tour. Their next tour took them to Britain, where they spent over three months in London, performing for Queen Victoria, Prime Minister William Gladstone, and numerous members of the aristocracy. Pledges, gifts of books, and thousands of dollars were gathered. The choir, which sang spirituals or jubilee songs, came to be called the Fisk Jubilee Singers.

In 1875 Frederick Loudin became its director. After an unsuccessful tour in the United States, the group again embarked for England, in May 1875, there earning $50,000. Their story was published, with the words and music of 112 songs, and a photograph of Loudin and his nine colleagues. Subsequent books appeared every year, with the bearded Loudin at the center in each year's pose.

Loudin's group started a movement, one through which the outside world gained knowledge of black religious music, and African Americans earned rare respect and recognition for their cultural achievements. Through their successful fundraising, the singers collected more than enough money to rescue Fisk University from financial disaster. So acclaimed were the Jubilee Singers that imposters began to appear and mount tours of their own. Minstrel performers added aspects of spirituals to their routines. Even after the university severed its link with the choir, Loudin's Fisk Jubilee Singers returned to Britain in 1884 for the first part of a six-year world tour that eventually reached Australia.

Loudin's musical direction and daily management were excellent. At recitals he delivered short lectures about the nature of the black experience in the United States, the history of slavery, and the hope and joy that came from hearing and singing spirituals. His demure, neat choir performed with style and inspired generations of listeners. The annual Jubilee Singers books spread the group's genteel gospel music and inspired parlor pianists to play such songs as "Swing Low, Sweet Chariot" and "Oh! Sinner Man." The choir mingled with leading members of high society. On occasions such as their homage at the home of England's anti-slavery campaigner William Wilberforce, in Hull in 1898, they testified brilliantly to the humanity of African people.

Loudin returned to London in the late 1890s. He made contact with the African-British composer Samuel Coleridge-Taylor, an 1897 graduate of the Royal College of Music, who credited Loudin and the Fisk Jubilee Singers with introducing him to spirituals. Coleridge-Taylor brought the music into his symphonic works, arranged some, and published piano versions in Boston, Massachusetts, in 1905. Other people of African descent would also take pride in the strength and wonder of Loudin's choir's songs.

Loudin wrote to the journalist "Bruce Grit" (JOHN EDWARD BRUCE), a former slave, from London, signing himself "Faithfully yours in the great struggle." At that time he and his wife were closely associated with the Pan-African Conference, held in London in July 1900. Also attending from America were W. E. B. DuBois and the African Methodist Episcopal (AME) bishop, ALEXANDER WALTERS. The Loudins served on the committee of the Pan-African Association, with Coleridge-Taylor, John Archer (another British-born black), and the retired U.S. foreign service staffer and writer HENRY DOWNING.

Loudin insisted that his choir members behave as ladies and gentlemen. They distanced themselves from the fun and foolishness of minstrelsy and black-face entertainers. With their polished manners and neat clothing, these refined Christian men and women were welcomed in churches and chapels, palaces and castles, and—with their songs—were hugely influential. The former slave THOMAS LEWIS JOHNSON recalled the choir's visit to the English coastal resort of Bournemouth in October 1900. "Wealthy ladies and gentlemen were making appointments with Mr. Louden [sic] to come and sing before them, for which they [the members of the choir] were remunerated, but it did just seem to me that God sent them to sing" (Johnson, 240–241).

The distinct and developed art form of the spirituals, as sung by Loudin's choir, had many results. As well as enabling Fisk University to overcome what would otherwise have been a terminal financial crisis, it gave African American men and women pride in their people. Their performances took the singers to distant lands and enabled them to see people and places unknown to most Americans. Their audiences heard and saw an artistic creation that, to their ears and eyes, was fresh. To whites, that such music could come from a despised people, served to both reinforce their own shame for their part in slavery and to bolster their respect for the recently freed blacks.

When artistic leaders of the black community in Washington, D.C., managed to satisfy the stringent requirements of Coleridge-Taylor, and welcomed him to the city for concerts there and in Baltimore in mid-November 1904, the concert program included Loudin's name as a member of the committee of patrons. He did not attend, for Frederick Loudin died in Ravenna, Ohio, earlier that month.

Spirituals continued to be performed in the United States and Britain. They became part of the repertory of trained or classical singers. During the 1920s and 1930s they were included in recitals by ROLAND HAYES, PAUL ROBESON, and MARIAN ANDERSON. Fisk University again became formally involved with the Jubilee Singers in the 1950s. Loudin had left a remarkable legacy.

FURTHER READING

Two massive scrapbooks of Loudin's tour to Australia are at the Detroit Public Library. Many of the collected items are press reviews, which repeat the publicity handouts circulated before the concerts.

T. L. Johnson, *Twenty-Eight Years a Slave.* (1909).

J. B. T. Marsh, *The Story of the Jubilee Singers; with their Songs.* (1876).

JEFFREY GREEN

Louis, Joe (13 May 1914–12 Apr. 1981), world champion boxer, was born Joseph Louis Barrow, the seventh of eight children of Munroe Barrow and Lillie Reese, sharecroppers, in a shack in Chambers County, Alabama. In 1916 his father was committed to the Searcy State Hospital for the Colored Insane, where he would live for the next twenty years. Believing that her husband had died, Lillie later married Pat Brooks and moved with their children in 1926 to Detroit, Michigan, where Brooks found a job at the Ford Motor Plant. Like many rural southerners during the Great Migration, Joe Barrow struggled in the new urban environment. Although Alabama had been no racial paradise, Michigan seemed little better. "Nobody ever called me a nigger until I got to Detroit," he later recalled (Ashe, 11). A rural Jim Crow education did not prepare him for the northern public schools, and the decision to place the quickly growing twelve-year-old boy in the fifth grade did not help matters. Shy and with a stutter, he paid little attention to his studies, although one teacher at his vocational school predicted that the boy "some day should be able to do something with his hands" (Ashe, 11). Detroit in the Depression provided few outlets for those hands, but Joe did find work in an automobile factory and as a laborer hauling ice. After a brief flirtation with the violin in his early teens, he took up boxing, and by failing to add his surname to his application to fight as an amateur, he was given a fighting name that stuck, "Joe Louis." Louis lost his first amateur

Joe Louis, nicknamed the Brown Bomber, poses in his boxing apparel in Pompton Lakes, N.J. on 24 Jan. 1937. (AP Images.)

living, nonthreatening image won him a crack at the title. In June 1937 the "Brown Bomber," as the white press had dubbed him, defeated Jim Braddock in an eighth-round knockout to win the world heavyweight championship.

At twenty-three Louis had become a hero to Depression-era blacks. While thousands of northern African Americans took to the streets to celebrate his victory, the southern black response was muted, though no less joyous. President Jimmy Carter recalled that African American neighbors came to his home to listen to the Braddock fight on one of the few radios in Plains, Georgia. Quietly obeying the racial propriety required of them, they showed no emotion at the end of the fight. But on returning to their own homes, as Carter remembers it, "pandemonium broke loose … as our black neighbors shouted and yelled in celebration of the Louis victory" (Sammons, 113).

When Louis defended his title against Max Schmeling in Yankee Stadium in June 1938, the changed international climate encouraged white Americans not only to tolerate Joe Louis but also to embrace him. The 1936 Berlin Olympics had signaled both a resurgent Germany and the willingness of white Americans to appreciate a black athlete, JESSE OWENS. In that light, the media depicted Schmeling against Louis as a battle between fascism and democracy, even though there was precious little democracy for blacks in many American states, including the boxer's native Alabama.

Louis was goaded by racial taunts from the Schmeling camp and was particularly incensed that his only professional loss had been to the German in 1936. Asked if he was scared, he replied: "Yeah, I'm scared. I'm scared I might kill Schmeling" (Ashe, 15). Jack Blackburn often worried that Louis, for all of his finesse and strength, lacked a killer instinct, but when he knocked out Schmeling after only two minutes at Yankee Stadium, it became clear that such fears were unfounded. The Brown Bomber let loose a barrage of quick, savage left jabs and followed up with some stunning right punches to the German's head and body, which, Louis recalled, left Schmeling squealing "like a stuck pig" (Ashe, 16). A left hook backed up by a right to the jaw knocked Schmeling to the canvas.

After that victory Louis defeated fifteen challengers between 1938 and 1941. With the exception of the quick-fisted Irish American Billy Conn, who led on points until Louis knocked him out in the thirteenth round, most of his opponents deserved

fight but won fifty of his next fifty-four bouts, forty-three of them by knockouts. In 1934, on his twentieth birthday, he won the National Amateur Athletic Union light-heavyweight championship and turned professional.

Louis's amateur victories hinted at his promise, but few in the summer of 1934 expected that the gangling, 175-pound boxer would win the world heavyweight championship after only three years as a professional. That he did so was partly because of his trainer, Jack Blackburn, and his managers, Julian Black and John Roxborough, respectable black businessmen by day and numbers kingpins by night. While Blackburn worked on Louis's conditioning and balance, Black, Roxborough, and the white promoter Mike Jacobs crafted a public image for Louis that would enhance his title prospects. Before World War I the heavyweight JACK JOHNSON had so angered whites by gloating over defeated opponents and flaunting white mistresses that no African American since had been allowed to fight for the championship. Black and Roxborough therefore urged Louis never to appear in public with white women and fed the press stories of his deep religiosity and love of family and country. Combined with a remarkable record of thirty victories in thirty-one fights, that clean-the sobriquet "bum of the month," but no heavy-weight champion had ever been so confident in his abilities as to defend his title so often. Because of the huge cut taken by his managers, however, Louis received only a fraction of the more than $2 million that he "won" before 1942. By then he was more than $200,000 in debt to the federal government and to his promoters. The fighter's personal life was also troubled. He had married Marva Trotter in 1935, a few hours before defeating Max Baer, and the couple would have a daughter, Jacqueline, in 1943. Louis's frequent absences and extramarital affairs led to divorce in 1945. Although the couple remarried in 1946 and had a son, Joe Jr., in 1947, they divorced again in 1949.

In the 1940s Louis emerged as the most prominent—and, in the popular consciousness, the most significant—black figure in the American war effort. Within weeks of the Japanese attack on Pearl Harbor, he contributed the entire winnings from his defeat of Buddy Baer to the Navy Relief Fund. In March 1942 he earned nationwide praise for a speech in which he urged all Americans to join the war effort because "we're on God's side." Although he had misspoken—his text had read "God's on our side"—the phrase instantly became one of the most popular slogans of the war effort. In addition to fighting (without payment) in several exhibition bouts, Sergeant Joe Louis appeared in Frank Capra's *The Negro Soldier*, a morale-boosting documentary feature that proved as popular among whites as blacks. Louis was not, however, immune to racism within the American military. At an army camp in Alabama military police ordered Louis and the young boxer SUGAR RAY ROBINSON to sit in the assigned "colored" waiting area for a bus; they refused, were arrested, and were released only when Louis threatened to call contacts in the U.S. War Department. Louis also used his relative influence in Washington, D.C., to highlight the continued discrimination against blacks in the military.

Louis's physical prowess diminished considerably after the war, and in March 1949 he retired after an unprecedented twelve years as heavyweight champion. In the decades that followed, he focused on ways to meet his massive debts, including considerable back taxes. Sadly, but inevitably, this involved a return to the ring in 1950, where he lost to the reigning champion EZZARD CHARLES in 1950. Knocked out by Rocky Marciano in 1951, Louis retired for good. His latter years were spent fighting the IRS, a battle won only after his fourth wife, Martha Malone Jefferson, an attorney, convinced the government that he simply did not have any money. In 1966 Louis moved to Las Vegas, where he worked variously as a greeter in a casino and, ironically, as a debt collector. In his final decade he struggled with cocaine addiction, heart disease, and depression.

On 12 April 1981, one day after attending a world heavyweight championship match, Louis died of a massive heart attack. He was survived by Jacqueline and Joe Jr., children from his first marriage, by his fourth wife, Martha Jefferson, and by four children whom he and Jefferson had adopted. Thousands attended his lying in state at Caesars Palace in Las Vegas, and President Ronald Reagan, who had starred with Louis in the 1943 movie *This Is the Army*, eased military protocol to make possible a burial at Arlington National Cemetery.

In his heyday Joe Louis enjoyed fame and assumed a symbolic significance greater than any other African American. His reign as world champion marked the end of African Americans' exclusion from professional sports and also convinced whites that black achievements need not come at their expense. Most important, his victories in the ring served to inspire even the most powerless Americans, as the Swedish sociologist Gunnar Myrdal discovered when he visited a remote Georgia school in the 1930s. Myrdal interviewed the children and found that none of them had heard of President Franklin Roosevelt, W. E. B. DuBois, or WALTER WHITE. They had all heard of Joe Louis.

FURTHER READING
Louis, Joe, with Edna and Art Rust. *My Life* (1978).
Ashe, Arthur. *A Hard Road to Glory: A History of the African-American Athlete, 1919–1945* (1988).
Mead, Chris. *Champion Joe Louis: Black Hero in White America* (1985).
Sammons, Jeffrey T. *Beyond the Ring: The Role of Boxing in American Society* (1988).
Obituary: *New York Times*, 13 Apr. 1981.
STEVEN J. NIVEN

Loury, Glenn C. (3 Sept. 1948–), author, educator, and economist, was born to Everett Loury and Gloria Cartman (Roosely) Loury and grew up in Park Manor on the South Side of Chicago. Loury attended Northwestern University in Evanston, Illinois, graduating with a B.A. in Mathematics in 1972. He then continued his education as a graduate student in economics at the Massachusetts Institute of Technology (MIT).

Working at MIT under the guidance of the future Nobel laureate Robert M. Solow, Loury began to formulate a theory of "social capital," the idea that family and community characteristics can influence wages regardless of individual ability. This was Loury's explanation for how "equal opportunity" might not guarantee "equal outcome," an important part of the debate surrounding affirmative action. As long as social context was ignored, disparities in incomes between blacks and whites would not be eliminated. In 1976 Loury submitted his dissertation, "Essays in the Theory of the Distribution of Income," and was granted his Ph.D. in Economics.

From 1976 to 1979 Loury served as an assistant professor of economics at Northwestern University, his alma mater. In 1979 he became associate professor of economics at the University of Michigan, earning tenure in 1980. He then moved to Harvard University where he served as professor of economics and Afro-American studies from 1982 to 1984 and as professor of political economy at the John F. Kennedy School of Government from 1984 to 1991. Hired by the department of economics, Loury held the distinction of being the youngest black professor at Harvard to hold tenure. He married Linda Datcher, a fellow labor economist, on 11 June 1983. She later joined the Tufts University Department of Economics in 1984. The couple would have two sons.

A prolific writer, Loury contributed to a variety of academic journals, popular magazines, and newspapers. Besides working in the subfield of microeconomic theory, Loury wrote about political and social issues, at times addressing the normative side of economic issues. Much of his work, critiquing the evils of today's black society, was popular among American conservatives. Loury also provided new insights into the debate over affirmative action policy. For example, he presented racial economic inequality as an example of "market failure," a situation where a "free market" would not produce an efficient outcome, suggesting the need for state intervention.

Loury was arrested for cocaine possession in November 1989, and spent several months in rehabilitation. The public exposure of his addiction contributed to his leaving Harvard in 1991, despite efforts by his colleagues to dissuade him. He moved to Boston University in 1991 as professor of economics and became a University Professor in 1994. Loury's recovery from drug addiction also resulted in-a significant personal transformation; with the help of Pastor Ray Hammond of the Bethel African Methodist Episcopal Church in Boston, he was baptized as a "born-again" Christian. Loury continued his research on race-related issues, writing on subjects such as the "patronization" of blacks, arguing that lowered job standards resulting from affirmative action would serve as a disincentive to invest in skills. In Loury's view, if high-paying jobs were easy for blacks to obtain, then affirmative action would not lead to a change in the relative quality of skills obtained by blacks and whites.

At Boston University, Loury challenged economic theory on moral and ethical grounds. An example is *One by One, From the Inside Out: Essays and Reviews on Race and Responsibility in America* (1995). This work introduced his new view on the Christian religion as the key to solving blacks' economic and political problems. The following year the book won the American Book Award for multicultural diversity from the Before Columbus Foundation and the *Christianity Today* Book Award for outstanding works by Christian authors. Also in 1995 Loury took part in the formation of the Center for New Black Leadership, an organization for black conservatives operating in Washington, D.C. Members included the politician Gerald A. Reynolds and the writer SHELBY STEELE. Loury served as chairman for the center, but he eventually came into conflict with other members when, in 1996, he refused to support California's Proposition 209, the Civil Rights Initiative against Affirmative Action promoted by the University of California's Board of Regents member WARD CONNERLY. In 1997 Loury founded the Institute on Race and Social Division (IRSD) at Boston University, serving as its director until 2002. The IRSD was established as a "multidisciplinary research center" to aid scholarly discussion on "social division" characterized by racial conflict. The IRSD promoted both quantitative study and discussions on morality and ethnic issues.

Loury's career has been distinguished with numerous awards and recognition for his work. In 1994 the members of the Econometric Society elected Loury as a fellow for his contributions to the field of economics. In 1997 the *Journal of Blacks in Higher Education* listed him as the second most frequently cited black economist, after THOMAS SOWELL. He also was elected as a member of the Council on Foreign Relations in 1999 and as a fellow of the American Academy of Arts and Sciences in 2000. In April 2000 he was selected for the W. E. B. DuBois Lecture Series at Harvard

University. His three lectures discussed racial stereotypes, racial stigma, and racial justice, and served as the basis for his 2002 book, *The Anatomy of Racial Inequality*. He spoke on discrimination and redistribution in November 2003 for the James A. Moffett '29 Lectures in Ethics sponsored by the Center for Human Values at Princeton University. In 2005 Loury was honored with the prestigious John von Neumann Award by the Rajk László Szakkollégium (the Rajk László College for Advanced Studies), a student-operated research institution connected with the Budapest University of Economic Sciences and Public Administration in Hungary. That was also the year in which he accepted the position of Merton P. Stoltz Professor of the Social Sciences and professor of economics at Brown University in Providence, Rhode Island. In addition to working in the economics department, Loury also served as an affiliated faculty member for the Africana Studies department and a research associate with the Population Studies and Training Center. He taught courses in labor economics and applied economic theory. Loury continued to publish in prominent magazines, newspapers, and academic journals such as the *American Economic Review, Journal of Economic Perspectives*, and the *Review of Black Political Economy*.

FURTHER READING
Shatz, Adam, "Glenn Loury's About Face," *New York Times Magazine*, 20 Jan. 2002.

JENNIFER VAUGHN

Louveste, Mary (fl. 1840–1865), Civil War Union spy, was born in Virginia and married Michael Louveste around 1840. Nothing is known of her parentage or early life. Both she and her husband were Union sympathizers living in Norfolk at the time of the Civil War. Though some commentaries have described her as a slave during the time of her espionage for the Union, the 1860 U.S. Census lists her and her husband as free inhabitants of the area who could both read and write. The census also records Michael Louveste as a barkeeper possessing a personal estate valued at $1,000.

Mary Louveste's location near the southern coast of Virginia placed her at the heart of Confederate naval operations. She was further well-situated for Union espionage through her employment in Portsmouth, Virginia, at the Gosport Naval Shipyard (renamed the Norfolk Naval Shipyard in 1862). Three days following Virginia's vote to secede from the Union on 17 April 1861, federal

forces abandoned the Gosport Shipyard, burning it and a number of unseaworthy ships docked there. Among the ships burned was a forty-gun steam frigate named the *Merrimack*. While Mary Louveste was employed at the Gosport Naval Shipyard, Confederate naval officials decided to refit the *Merrimack* as an ironclad, rename it the *CSS Virginia*, and use it to attack the Union squadron in Hampton Roads. Literally clad in iron plates, fitted with an iron beak for ramming enemy craft, and armed with seventy guns, it could be a formidable weapon against wooden ships.

It was at this juncture that Mary Louveste's role in U.S. military history became apparent through descriptions provided by a key Union official during the Civil War, the secretary of the U.S. Navy, Gideon Welles. Welles provided two separate accounts of her actions, the first in a letter written by him from his home in Hartford, Connecticut, dated 17 August 1872, to obtain a government pension for her, and the second, in a section of the 1879 publication, *The Annals of the War Written by Leading Participants North and South*. In his accounts, Welles relates that Louveste provided vital information about the *CSS Virginia* that prompted the U.S. Navy to change the plans for its own ironclad, the *USS Monitor*. Though Union officials had required that the *Monitor* be completed and seaworthy within 100 days of its October 1861 contract, that deadline had passed. Meeting the deadline had been considered critical as the Union wanted to capitalize on the element of surprise in its initial plans for the *Monitor*. The initial plan was to have the vessel proceed to Hampton Roads, travel up the Elizabeth River to a position within range of the Gosport Naval Shipyard's drydock, and use its heavy guns to destroy both the drydock and the *CSS Virginia*. With the delay of the *Monitor*'s completion, it was paramount for the Union navy to understand the status of the *Virginia* so it could adjust its strategy accordingly. Consequently, with Mary Louveste's information, not only was the original plan revealed to be futile but the *CSS Virginia* itself also might soon be deployed for attack on nearby Union targets.

Welles reported that Mary Louveste and others at the Gosport Naval Shipyard had carefully observed the development of the Confederate navy's ironclad and that she, in late February of 1862, had shared related information in a private meeting with him after a dangerous journey from Confederate-controlled territory through Union lines. He clearly related how she provided information about the nature of the *CSS Virginia*, that it was near completion and almost out of drydock and poised to be fitted with armament. In addition she presented a document written by a mechanic working on the vessel that not only confirmed the information she had supplied from memory but also provided an estimate of the date of the final completion of the *Virginia*. At the time, the Union navy had only vague information about the *Virginia*, nothing detailed and reliable. Though a few reporters had seen the craft and subsequently published reports, one in a British journal and another in a note in *Scientific American*, the material was too general to guide naval strategy. Dean Burgess, former director of the Portsmouth Public Library and the individual responsible for purchasing the Welles letter for the Portsmouth Library from the Welles estate, has observed that the information in the British journal could never have reached Union officials before the first battle of the ironclads due to the limits of the transportation technology of the time, the steamship. Gideon Welles himself recounted how difficult it had been, prior to Louveste's private meeting, to procure good information. He added that the accompanying uncertainty was a source of anxiety for officials of the Union navy.

Researchers on Mary Louveste may find commentaries listing her surname as Louvestre or Touvestre, but both Gideon Welles and the 1860 Census spelled the name "Louveste." Though historical census records do not always reflect the actual spelling of names, Gideon Welles's contact with Louveste provides additional support on her name being Louveste as opposed to an alternative. As Louveste contacted Welles, not only on the night she shared the information about the *CSS Virginia* but also subsequently through correspondence, one might reasonably assume that the Welles letter reflects the name by which she identified herself.

Mary Louveste's position as a Union spy during the Civil War puts her in the company of other women, some well-known, such as HARRIET TUBMAN and MARY ELIZABETH BOWSER, and others who, by the secretive nature of their work, history may never reveal. Though reliable sources providing background on her early life and the date of her death may not be available, there remains strong evidence of her contribution to key military strategy during the Civil War.

FURTHER READING

Holladay, Mildred, and Dean Burgess. *History of Portsmouth, Virginia* (2007).

McDevitt, Theresa. "African American Women and Espionage in the Civil War," *Social Education* 67.5 (Sept. 2003):254–259.

Tucker, George. "Union Sympathizer's Espionage Saved Nation's Oldest Dry Dock," the *Virginian-Pilot*, 9 Apr. 1995.

Welles, Gideon. Letter with Envelope Missing, 17 Aug. 1872. Historical Collection, Portsmouth Public Library, Portsmouth, Virginia.

Welles, Gideon. "The First Iron-Clad Monitor," in *The Annals of the War Written by Leading Participants North and South* (1879; repr. 1988).

JULIE WALTERS

Love, Edward (21 Sept. 1936–22 Mar. 1999), visual artist and educator, was born in Los Angeles, California, the son of Alyce and Edward Love, about whom little is known. After attending Manual Arts High School, Love, a baseball standout, was slated to be recruited by the San Francisco Giants. The U.S. Air Force proved more attractive to Love than baseball. While serving a five-year stint in the military that ultimately took him to Japan, Love became deeply influenced by Japanese culture. He also developed an affinity for the music of CHARLIE PARKER and MILES DAVIS and the discourse of the Black Arts Movement, as well as a fascination with architectural design.

After an honorable discharge, Love earned a BFA in Sculpture in 1966 and an MFA in Design in 1967 from California State University, Los Angeles. A postgraduate fellowship to study humanities and fine arts at Uppsala University in Sweden soon followed. While there the burgeoning artist explored Europe with his first wife, Winada Chapman Love (whom he married in 1958 and divorced in 1973), and their children, Lori A. Nia and Edward Scott.

Love joined the department of art at Howard University in Washington, D.C., in 1969. By then the primary material he used for his creations were automobile bumpers. The steel of works such as the 1970s sculpture *Monument to* PAUL ROBESON resonated with the struggle and anguish of his people. Love had a distinctive kinship with the "sonic evidence of struggle" found in the works of musicians he admired. He often dedicated his weldings to the likes of the jazz musicians JOHN COLTRANE, ERIC DOLPHY, THELONIOUS MONK, and MAX ROACH and the folk musician Tracy Chapman.

Love challenged his students to cultivate their own perspectives not only to make a good living but also to better themselves and the world around them. A youth advocate, he was integral in the development of the Workshops for Careers in the Arts and the Duke Ellington School for the Arts in Washington, D.C. In addition to teaching at Lorton Prison in Washington, D.C. (also called the Lorton Reformatory), Love produced and hosted a weekly three-hour program on Pacifica Radio—*The Blues, the News, and Other Views!*—for more than ten years.

The Black Arts Movement's commitment to community activism generated a profound sense of justice in Love. Borrowing from the author Neely Fuller Jr., as well as from the visionary and architect R. Buckminster Fuller, Love devised a principal definition of justice: balance between people and environment and balance between people themselves.

By 1987 many believed that Love was a permanent fixture at Howard, for he had founded and guided its undergraduate and graduate sculpture programs. He had also achieved a great deal of professional success, having won a fellowship from the D.C. Commission on the Arts and Humanities, a Guggenheim Foundation fellowship, and the Mayor's Arts Award in Washington, D.C. He surprised many that year when he moved to South Florida to be the dean of the art division of the New World School of the Arts in Miami. He felt called to the riot-torn city and believed that the new school would nurture artists who would flourish in and contribute to multicultural America.

By this time Love's work was more aggressive with its pain and darkness. Pieces like those shown in the exhibition, Signs: The Maximum Security Series, were now making their way around the United States and abroad. Solo exhibitions at the Brickell Square in Miami, the Corcoran Gallery of Art in Washington, D.C., the Forum in Saint Louis, and numerous American and European universities were greeted with acclaim. His significance as an artist was described in Jan Greenberg and Sandra Jordan's *The Sculptor's Eye: Looking at Contemporary American Art* (1993) and in reviews and profiles that appeared in the *New York Times*, *Art in America*, the *International Quarterly*, the *Village Voice*, the *Washington Post*, and the *Los Angeles Times*.

After marrying the author Monifa Atungaye in 1989, Love moved north to Tallahassee, Florida. There he joined the Florida State University faculty and served as professor of art and director of undergraduate studies. These changes also signaled a new approach to his art. The series *The Arkestra* was composed of lightweight steel sculptures resembling the human form in movement. At the height of his career, Love died of a massive heart attack in Tallahassee in 1999.

Love's expansive body of work contained more than four hundred sculptures, a hundred paintings and sketches, scores of theatrical sets, and countless photographs, murals, playgrounds, and costumes. His art and philosophy was the subject of an Emmy-nominated documentary, several CNN programs, *The Best of Black Entertainment Television*, CBS's *Sunday Morning*, and the award-winning video *Kindred Spirits*.

FURTHER READING

Lewis, Samella S., and Ruth G. Waddy. *Black Artists on Art*, vol. 2 (1971).

Love, Monifa, and Jeffrey C. Stewart. *Living Fully, Standing for Justice: Sculptures and Drawings by Ed Love* (2000).

WILLIE HOBBS

Love, Emmanuel King (27 July 1850–24 Apr. 1900), minister, political activist, missionary, writer, and editor, was born a slave near Marion, Alabama. As was the case with many African American men of the post-emancipation era, Love's early schooling was scattershot; still it was substantive enough to prepare him for theological study and a lifelong commitment to service and leadership. Ordained on 12 December 1875, he graduated at the head of his class two years later in 1877 with a B.A. from the Augusta Institute, a forerunner of Atlanta's historic Morehouse College and a training ground for future African American ministers, politicians, and educators.

The highlight of Love's ministry was to pastor the influential First African Baptist Church of Savannah, Georgia, from 1885 to 1900. Tracing its origins to as early as 1773, before the birth of the American nation, First African Baptist was officially instituted in 1788, and it claimed distinction as the oldest continuously running African American congregation in the country, as well as one of the largest. Love's popular sermons attracted as many as one thousand participants to worship services. First African Baptist was a magnet for preachers such as Love who went on to attain state and national prominence as race leaders.

During the 1880s Love served as president of the Baptist Foreign Mission Convention, organized in 1880 by African American Baptist ministers to raise funds, recruit missionaries, and finance scholarships for the establishment of Christian schools and churches in African nations. As an outspoken member of the all-black National Baptist Convention, founded in 1895, Love advocated collaborative linkages with white Baptists. Yet his efforts to initiate a separate publishing house for black Baptists, when white editors of the *Baptist Teacher* refused to accept articles written by him and two other African American ministers, demonstrated his ongoing project of extricating his race from total control by white religious groups and from victimization or neglect as a result of racism. His policies in the Baptist Foreign Mission Convention and National Baptist Convention were imaginative responses to the discrimination, segregation, and civil and political repression that accompanied the end of Reconstruction, and they expressed a sense of obligation to and cultural affiliation with African peoples that black American scholars such as ANNA JULIA COOPER and CARTER G. WOODSON would further articulate at the turn of the twentieth century.

Love backed his nationalist, antiracist religious agenda with similar, sometimes life-threatening, activism in the secular world. For example, on 9 September 1889 he and fellow African American delegates traveling from Georgia to a religious convention in Indiana purchased seats in a segregated, all-white railcar. They barely made it to the meeting with their lives, after a mob stopped the train and beat them. In his adopted home of Savannah, Love stood behind successful efforts to institute a bank patronized by black clients, and to persuade the white state legislature to found the all-black Savannah State College, for which he then nominated his old friend and protégé from the Augusta, Georgia, *Weekly Sentinel*, the Reverend RICHARD R. WRIGHT SR., as its first president.

Finally, Love extended his militancy through the pen. Blurring the distinction between the sacred and secular press, he edited and wrote for a variety of periodical publications including the Albany, Georgia, *National Watchman*, which he founded; the *Weekly Sentinel*, which he cofounded with the Reverends Wright and CHARLES T. WALKER; the *Georgia Baptist*; the *Baptist Truth*; and the *Independent Republican*, another newspaper that he cofounded. Additionally, he published his most provocative sermons as pamphlets for wider dissemination. Topics such as "Emancipation Oration!" (1891) and "A Sermon on Lynch Law and Raping" (1894) epitomized Love's approach of intertwining the religious and political. On the one hand they offer a conciliatory rhetoric and a deference to white southerners reminiscent of BOOKER T. WASHINGTON's public addresses. On the other they propose a practical mandate to both white and black Christian audiences to indict whenever possible the South's increasing racial and sexual violence, and at the same time to insist on extending the full rights and privileges of citizenship to post–Civil War black Americans.

Love's written productions were frequently informed by the ideals of race uplift, the concept that blacks who practiced and upheld such principles as hard work, thrift, home and land ownership, morality, cleanliness, race pride, and education would gradually lift themselves and their fellow African Americans to political and economic parity with whites. This gospel of self-help emerged as the rhetorical centerpiece for national figures such as Booker T. Washington and IDA B. WELLS-BARNETT following the collapse of Reconstruction and the rise of Jim Crow.

Love was still pastor of First African Baptist at the time of his death. He called upon Christian principles to demand religious and secular freedoms and racial self-determinacy, as well as to design a blueprint for future racial advancement and social reform.

FURTHER READING

Love, Emmanuel King. *A History of the First African Baptist Church from Its Organization, January 20, 1788 to July 1, 1888* (1888).

Billingsley, Andrew. *Mighty Like a River: The Black Church and Social Reform* (1999).

Martin, Sandy Dwayne. *Black Baptists and African Missions: The Origins of a Movement, 1880–1915* (1989).

McCaskill, Barbara, and Caroline Gebhard. *Post-Bellum—Pre-Harlem: African American Literature and Culture, 1877–1915* (2006).

Washington, James Melvin. *Frustrated Fellowship: The Black Baptist Quest for Social Power* (2004).

BARBARA MCCASKILL

Love, Josephine Harreld (11 Dec. 1914–12 Sept. 2003), concert pianist, arts administrator, and musicologist, was born in Atlanta, Georgia, into a family of distinguished educators, musicians, and writers. Her maternal grandfather, WILLIAM JEFFERSON WHITE, was the founder of historic Morehouse College. Her poet mother, Claudia Turner (White) Harreld, was one of the first graduates of Spelman College in 1901, where she also taught. Her father, Kemper Harreld, was a renowned violinist. He served for forty-five years as the first director of music of the glee club and of the orchestra at Morehouse College, and for nearly thirty years directed Spelman College's music program. He began teaching his daughter violin when she was three, and he later introduced her to the piano.

Josephine Harreld's concert career as a pianist began when she was twelve and continued intermittently for the next thirty-seven years. She received an impressive education, taking a B.A. in English at Spelman College, while also studying piano with her father and playing the violin and viola in the orchestra; she then completed a BM degree in Piano in 1934 at the Juilliard School of Music; she studied at the Mozarteum Academy in Salzburg, Austria, in 1935; and received an M.A. in 1936 in Musicology from Radcliffe College. She studied composition with Walter Piston at Harvard and piano with Hazel Harrison in Chicago. She taught at Bennett College in Greensboro, North Carolina, from 1936 to 1937; Oakland University in Rochester, Michigan, from 1970 to 1972; the University of Michigan at Ann Arbor from 1987 to 1990. She maintained a private studio in Detroit thereafter.

National audiences were impressed by Harreld's pianistic skills and musical interpretations. Following an after-dinner recital on 13 December 1939 Eleanor Roosevelt wrote, "She has power and a finished technique and plays with real feeling, which made every minute enjoyable to all of us." She presented a varied repertoire featuring Bach, Beethoven, Chopin, Liszt, Debussy, and William Grant Still.

A critic for the *Wichita (Kansas) Beacon* wrote on 4 December 1939: "The artist handled the allegro passages of Bach and Beethoven and the flashing chords of Chopin with verve and dexterity; but it was principally in her interpreting of slow, lyric music that she was outstanding." The music critic Malcolm Miller of the *Knoxville Journal* wrote on 28 January 1940, "Her program was beautifully designed to give full scope to her versatility, imagination and authentic musicianship. The artist's playing was notable for incisive touch, expressive phrasing, elemental power where the music demanded it, delicate tonal effects, and amazing digital dexterity."

From the midpoint to the latter years of Harreld's career, she delivered a lecture-recital enrichment series for the Detroit Public Schools, gave a chamber recital at the University of Michigan, and performed several duo-piano recitals.

In 1940, following a recital at Detroit's Second Baptist Church, she met local physician, William Thomas Love. After a year of correspondence and three social calls they married on 18 June 1941, and eventually had two children.

During the summer of 1969 Love and the textile artist Gwendolyn Harkless Hogue together established an innovative concept for a children's museum—"Your Heritage House"—in the downstairs of Love's home. Though at first financed by its founders, soon grants and contributions were secured from governmental and civic organizations to sustain programs and expand facilities. This laboratory center offered courses in ceramics, fibers, puppetry, soft sculpture, filmmaking, and music; dramatic and musical performances; and a library and exhibitions of "touchable" artifacts. The multidisciplinary environment encouraged children to appreciate the cultural heritages of all ethnic groups, to develop skills, and to experience the joys of self-expression and self-discovery. Its global collection represented the remote and near past as well as the contemporary. Children were able to study African masks and musical sounds; fashion and work Greek, Indonesian, and Javanese puppets; and view dolls of many nationalities and ethnicities in their native costumes.

Throughout her lifetime Josephine Love received numerous awards and honors in acknowledgment of her contributions to the arts, to children, and to the community. She also lectured widely and published several articles, including biographical portraits of AZALIA HACKLEY and Hazel Harrison. The legacy of Josephine Harreld Love is one of artistic sharing through pianistic sounds, educational experiences, and love for children.

FURTHER READING

Smith, Jessie Carney, ed. *Notable Black American Women* (1992).

Southern, Eileen. *Biographical Dictionary of Afro-American and African Musicians* (1982).

Who's Who of American Women, 1st ed. (1964).

MARVA GRIFFIN CARTER

Love, Nat (June 1854–1921), cowboy and author, was born in Davidson County, Tennessee, the son of Sampson Love and a mother whose name is unknown. Both were slaves owned by Robert Love, whom Nat described as a "kind and indulgent Master." Nat Love's father was a foreman over other slaves; his mother, a cook. The family remained with Robert Love after the end of the Civil War.

Nat Love, the cowboy who claimed to be the original "Deadwood Dick" of dime novel fame. (Library of Congress.)

In February 1869 Love struck out on his own. He left because Robert Love's plantation was in desperate economic straits after the war, and he sensed that there were few opportunities other than agricultural work for young former slaves in the defeated South. Although his father had died the year before, leaving him the head of the family, Love nevertheless left because, as he admitted, "I wanted to see more of the world."

After a short stay in Kansas, Love worked for three years on the ranch of Sam Duval in the Texas panhandle. For the next eighteen years (1872–1890) Love was a cowboy on the giant Gallinger Ranch in southern Arizona. He traveled all the western trails between south Texas and Montana herding cattle to market and, as his autobiography reveals, engaged in the drinking, gambling, and violence typical of western cow towns. He became an expert in identifying cattle brands and learned to speak fluent Spanish on trips to Mexico. In 1889 he married a woman named Alice (maiden name unknown), with whom he had one child. The cowboy business was doomed by the westward movement of the railroads. Love recognized this situation and in 1890 secured employment with the Denver and Rio Grande Railroad as a Pullman car porter, one of the few occupations open to black men in the West. For fifteen years Love held this position on various western railroads. His last job, beginning in 1907, was as a bank guard with the General Securities Company in Los Angeles, where he died.

Most of what is known of Love's life is from his 1907 autobiography, *The Life and Adventures of Nat Love, Better Known in the Cattle Country as "Deadwood Dick," by Himself.* The one-hundred-page work seems to have been inspired by the popular and melodramatic dime novels of the day and likely contains more than a bit of fiction itself. Love certainly portrayed himself as a larger-than-life figure. He claimed he could outdrink any man in the West without it affecting him in any way. He depicted himself as one of the most expert cowboys, who could outrope, outshoot, and outride the best of them. He reported that he single-handedly broke up a robbery at an isolated Union Pacific railroad station. "I carry the marks of fourteen bullet wounds on different part [sic] of my body, most any one of which would be sufficient to kill an ordinary man," he boasted," "but I am not even crippled…. I have had five horses shot from under me…. Yet I have always managed to escape with only the mark of a bullet or knife as a reminder." Shot and captured by Indians in 1876, he said he was nursed back to health by them and adopted into the tribe; he was offered the chief's daughter in marriage. But Love had other plans and made his escape one night. He claimed as close acquaintants many western notables such as William F. "Buffalo Bill" Cody, Frank and Jesse James, Kit Carson, and "Billy the Kid" (William H. Bonney). Even as a railroad porter Love made himself out to be one of the best.

The legendary "Deadwood Dick" was created by the western dime novelist Edward L. Wheeler in the 1870s. Several men claimed to be the prototype for the character, including Love, whose autobiography places him in Deadwood in the Dakota Territory on the Fourth of July 1876. In a roping contest, he "roped, threw, tied, bridled, saddled and mounted my mustang in exactly nine minutes," a championship record he said he held until his retirement as a cowboy fourteen years later and a feat, so he claimed, that instantly won him the title of "Deadwood Dick."

The autobiography is consistently upbeat, with the author invariably winning out over those skeptical of his abilities. He mentions no incidents of racial discrimination, although they are known to have occurred in the West. While his accounts of heroic achievements and derring-do are certainly possible, he seems to have stretched the truth, not unlike other western reminiscences. And some of his claims are not verified in other sources. As one student of the West, William Loren Katz, commented, Love's autobiography is "easy to read but hard to believe" (Katz, 323). Yet his life and work do illustrate how a black man of the late nineteenth century could rise from slavery to a satisfying life in the cowboy world, where ability and fortitude did serve to mitigate race prejudice.

FURTHER READING

Love, Nat. *The Life and Adventures of Nat Love, Better Known in the Cattle Country as "Deadwood Dick," by Himself* (1907, repr. 1968).

Durham, Philip, and Everett L. Jones. *The Negro Cowboys* (1965).

Felton, Harold W. *Nat Love: Negro Cowboy* (1969)

Katz, William Loren. *The Black West* (1971).

This entry is taken from the *American National Biography* and is published here with the permission of the American Council of Learned Societies.

WILLIAM F. MUGLESTON

Love, Rose Leary (30 Dec. 1898–2 June 1969), educator and writer, was born in Charlotte, North Carolina, the daughter of JOHN SINCLAIR LEARY and Nannie Latham Leary. The Learys, who were of Irish, French, Scottish, and Native American descent as well as African, were regarded as one of the most prominent African American families in the state, with a collective history of activism stretching back to the American Revolution. LEWIS SHERIDAN LEARY, Love's uncle, a colleague of the abolitionist John Brown, fell mortally wounded in the raid on Harpers Ferry; his cousin JOHN ANTHONY COPELAND JR. was executed for his role in the attack. Love's father was the second African American admitted to the North Carolina bar, dean of the Shaw University Law School in Raleigh, and a Republican state representative; he also handled numerous local responsibilities, including that of school committeeman and Sunday school superintendent. Love's mother raised six children and taught school for more than four decades. Other distinguished relatives included HIRAM RHOADES REVELS, the first African American member of the U.S. Senate, and LANGSTON HUGHES, the renowned poet, who was a cousin.

Love, following her mother's example, attended Scotia Seminary (now Barber-Scotia College), a Presbyterian women's college in Concord, North Carolina. She received her bachelor of arts degree from Johnson C. Smith University in Charlotte and pursued additional coursework in pedagogy at the Hampton Institute in Virginia and at New York's Columbia University. She married George W. Love, a teacher at the Tuskegee Institute and a friend of GEORGE WASHINGTON CARVER. They had one son, the photographer and writer George Leary Love (1937–1995), who later resided in Brazil, where he worked as a magazine editor.

Love taught in the Charlotte-Mecklenburg system from 1925 to 1964, starting at Fairview Elementary School, continuing at Isabella Wyche and Biddleville Schools, and ending at University Park Elementary School, specializing in teaching first-graders. She also taught in Greensboro, where her brother John was a principal; at Livingston College in Salisbury, North Carolina, for its summer school; and in Jakarta, Indonesia, as a second-grade instructor in the International School in 1957 and 1958. Her work in Asia was part of a State Department cooperative exchange program in which her husband participated as a technical adviser.

Before becoming a teacher, Love had dreamed of being a concert pianist. She served as organist and music minister of St. Michael and All Angels Episcopal Church for many years. She was especially fond of Brahms, and her own compositions included "America We Love."

Love published two books: *Nebraska and His Granny* (1936), a children's story published by the Tuskegee Institute Press, and *A Collection of Folklore for Children in Elementary School and at Home* (1964), an eighty-nine-page textbook illustrated with drawings by her students and preserving the stories, rhymes, and games of their ancestors. Both books were praised for Love's noteworthy refusal to resort to dialect or stereotypes in her prose. In *Nebraska*, Love depicts a stable, healthy household headed by Granny, a farmer and quilter, demonstrating the matriarch's skills at raising poultry and vegetables, rearing children, and sewing. Nebraska is an orphan Granny adopted when he was a baby. In establishing Nebraska as a part of Granny's family, Love communicated her belief in a community's obligation to look after all of its children.

However, it was the posthumously published *Plum Thickets and Field Daisies* (1996) that has commanded the interest of scholars since Love's death. Written primarily during the last decade of her life, the manuscript recorded Love's memories of her childhood neighborhood located in Charlotte's Third Ward, called "Brooklyn." (The original title of her memoir was "Brooklyn as I Knew It.") The Brooklyn neighborhood had deteriorated into a slum during Love's lifetime and was demolished during the city's efforts at urban renewal during the 1970s. Love's nostalgic firsthand accounts of everyday life in her once-genteel community have supplied historians and sociologists with vital specifics as they analyze early-twentieth-century southern customs, trends, and practices, such as the mechanics of curing colds and the strategies employed by African American instructors to teach civics. The manuscript was donated to the Public Library of Charlotte and Mecklenburg County by Elizabeth Schmoke Randolph, another prominent African American educator who had worked closely with Love at University Park Elementary School.

Of her earlier writings, Love is perhaps best known for "George Washington Carver: A Boy Who Wished to Know Why," a three-part serial for younger readers featured in the *Negro History Bulletin* from January to March 1967. As with her recollections of her parents and other role models, Love's anecdote-based profile of Carver celebrates his love of education, his determination to succeed, and his commitment to improving life for his brethren. Her other nonfiction credits include an essay about her uncle Sheridan Leary that was also published in the *Bulletin*. Love wrote poetry that appeared in the *North Carolina Teachers Record*, the *Journal of Negro History*, the *South Carolina Journal of Education*, the *Instructor*, and the *Grade Teacher*. The titles of the thirteen poems performed at her retirement tribute give a good sense of the topics dear to her heart: "The Coal Man," "A Joyous Heart," "Dark America Sings," "Flower Seller," "My Old Neighbor," "Our Song to America," "Noises," "The Robin's Song," "Wash Day," "Politeness," "The Circus Is Coming to Town," "Blackberries," and "The Mail Box."

Having moved to the Beatties Ford Road corridor (another historically significant African American neighborhood in Charlotte), Love died at home at age seventy-one. At the time of her death, her unpublished manuscripts included "Little Music Makers" (a collection of songs) and "Under the Mulberry Tree" (a collection of poems).

FURTHER READING

Rose Leary Love's papers are housed in the Carolina Room of the Public Library of Charlotte and Mecklenburg County, North Carolina.

Doar, Harriet. "From Children ... A People's Folklore," *Charlotte Observer*, 28 June 1964.

Smith, Katharine Capshaw. *Children's Literature of the Harlem Renaissance* (2004).

Obituary: *Negro History Bulletin* (Dec. 1969).

PEGGY LIN DUTHIE

Loving, Alvin D., Jr. (19 Sept. 1935–21 June 2005), artist, was born in Detroit, Michigan, to Alvin Loving Sr., a teacher, and Mary Helen Greene, who did quilting work. Alvin Sr. occasionally took work as a sign painter, and he encouraged his son's early artistic bent. Loving attended local schools, including Northern High and Cass Tech High. Alvin Sr., meanwhile, was becoming an important local figure in education. He was already a trailblazer among black educators in Detroit, but when Alvin Jr. was still young he took on a professorship at the University of Michigan that involved overseas trips to India and parts of Africa. He often returned from these with paintings of the local landscapes that he himself had executed, and he sometimes asked his son to paint his own versions.

Loving graduated from Cass Tech in 1954. He took art classes at nearby Wayne State and spent a year in India with his family before returning to the United States intent on pursuing a life in the arts. He matriculated to the University of Illinois, from which in 1963 he took a bachelor's degree in Fine Arts. Two years later, he graduated with his master's in fine arts from the University of Michigan. An early marriage to Eleanor Jean Randles ended in divorce. The couple had two children.

For a short time after graduation, Loving held a lecturer's position at Eastern Michigan State University, but like many young artists, he wished to be at the center of the fine arts world in the United States and so relocated to New York and set about making a name for himself. His style was abstract expressionism—in an era when the movement among African American art was toward more traditionally representational depictions of the black experience—and as such Loving was something of a rarity among its practitioners. His brightly geometric paintings were successful, though, and so he quickly became known around New York as a young talent to watch. He'd only been in the city a year when, in 1969, he was offered a show at the Whitney Museum as part of a larger exhibit of current black art. Loving's work was a sensation, and he soon found his paintings much in demand in galleries in New York and elsewhere. In that same year, 1969, he remarried, this time to Wyn Riser.

The couple would have two children before Riser's death in 1990. It was not the only time that Loving's life would be touched with personal tragedy. A daughter from his first marriage, Lauri, died in 2001. Loving would go on to marry a third time, to Mara Kearney. They had no children, and Kearney survived him.

Loving's career had taken off in a big way. He found himself much in demand as a guest lecturer and resident at universities and art schools across the country. Among these were stints as a guest at the University of California at San Diego, the Maryland Institute, Notre Dame, the University of Kansas, Cornell, and Virginia Commonwealth University, among many others. In 1988 he joined the faculty of the City College of New York, where he remained until 1996. Loving was the recipient of National Endowment for the Arts fellowships in 1970, 1971, 1975, 1976, and 1985. He was awarded a Guggenheim fellowship in 1986. Still, he was beginning to feel the limitations and constraints of his signature style, and he began to experiment and expand. He worked now in what he called "material abstraction," with collage and glass and even cloth. His work also became bigger and more public. His work appeared in Detroit's First National Building, and in 2001 he completed a mosaic for New York's Metropolitan Transportation Authority. The institutions holding his work in their permanent collections included the Whitney, the Metropolitan Museum of Art, and the Detroit Institute of Arts, among too many others to name here. His death was due to complications from lung cancer.

FURTHER READING
Powell, Richard J. *Black Art: A Cultural History* (2003).
Obituaries: *New York Times*, 30 June 2005;
New York Amsterdam News, 7 July 2005.

JASON PHILIP MILLER

Loving, Mildred Delores Jeter (22 July 1939–2 May 2008), a housewife, whose marriage in 1958 to Richard Loving sparked one of the nation's most important civil rights cases, was born Mildred Delores Jeter, of African American and Native American ancestry. Loving was one of five children born to Theoliver Jeter, a sharecropper, and Musiel Byrd, a homemaker. She also had four half brothers. She graduated from Union High School in Bowling Green, Virginia in 1957. In 1958 she married her childhood sweetheart, who was white. Both Jeter and Loving were born in Caroline County, Virginia, an area with a well-known history of black-white

interracial sexual liaisons. As was the local custom, however (and true for most of the South), these unions occurred under cover of darkness and without legal sanction. Many states had laws prohibiting interracial marriages, some with restrictions dating back to the nineteenth century. While enforcement of these laws varied from state to state depending upon the race of the couple involved, the ultimate goal generally was to preserve the sanctity of the white race at all costs. Although both Mildred and Richard Loving were aware of Virginia's legal restrictions on interracial marriage, they apparently were unaware that state statute barred interracial couples from marrying in other states that permitted the practice and returning to Virginia to live as husband and wife. Thus, on 2 June 1958, the happy couple drove across the Virginia state line to be married in Washington, D.C., after which they returned to their home community of Central Point to live.

On the night of 11 July, five weeks after their marriage, their marital bliss was shattered when three law officers acting on an anonymous tip opened the unlocked door of their home, walked into their bedroom, and shined a flashlight in their faces, whereupon Caroline County Sheriff R. Garnett Brooks demanded to know what the two of them were doing in bed together. Pointing to her husband, Mildred Loving answered "I'm his wife," while Richard pointed to the District of Columbia marriage certificate that hung on their bedroom wall. "That's no good here," Sheriff Brooks replied. He charged the couple with unlawful cohabitation and then he and his two deputies hauled the Lovings off to a nearby jail in Bowling Green. The Lovings were formally charged with violating Virginia's 1924 Racial Integrity Act, which stipulated that all marriages between a white person and a colored person shall be absolutely void. The Lovings waived their rights to a trial by jury and pled guilty to the charges. On 6 January 1959, the judge sentenced each of them to one year in jail, but he suspended the sentences on the condition that they leave the state of Virginia and that they not return together or at the same time for a period of twenty-five years. Faced with the difficult decision of having to leave family and friends, the Lovings then moved to Washington, D.C., where they would remain in exile for the next five years raising their three children. The Lovings had not been interested in the civil rights movement up to that point, nor had they ever given much thought to challenging Virginia's law. But with a major civil rights bill being debated in Congress in 1963 (which

Mildred Loving with her husband, Richard P. Loving, 26 January 1965. (AP Images.)

would ultimately become the Civil Rights Act of 1964), Mildred decided to solicit help from Robert F. Kennedy, President John F. Kennedy's younger brother and attorney general of the United States. In her letter she wrote, "5 years ago my husband and I were married here in the District. We then returned to Va. to live. My husband is White, I am part negro, and part indian…. We know we can't live there, but we would like to go back once and awhile to visit our families and friends. We have 3 children and cannot afford an attorney" (Letter from Mildred Loving to Robert F. Kennedy, 20 June 1963 [in author's possession]). The Department of Justice forwarded Mildred's letter to the American Civil Liberties Union. Bernard S. Cohen, a young lawyer doing pro bono work for the ACLU in Alexandria, Virginia, agreed to take the case. He would later be joined by another young attorney, Philip J. Hirschkop.

On 6 November 1963, Bernard Cohen filed a motion asking the trial court judge to set aside the Lovings' conviction and sentence. The motion argued that the Lovings' conviction constituted cruel and unusual punishment and that their banishment from the state violated due process of law. When the trial judge, Leon Bazile, refused to act, Cohen and Hirschkop filed a motion in district court asking for federal intervention. The three-judge panel ruled that the state would have ninety days to render an opinion or the case would be removed to federal court. In January 1965, Judge Bazile finally responded to the motion by upholding his original sentence. He wrote that the Lovings were guilty of "a most serious crime," and that "Almighty God created the races white, black, yellow, malay and red, and he placed them on separate continents. And but for the interference with his arrangement, there would be no cause for such marriages. The fact that he separated the races shows that he did not intend for the races to mix" (Opinion, *Loving v. Commonwealth* [Record No. 6163], 15 [1965]).

On 12 December 1966, the United States Supreme Court agreed to hear the case and oral arguments began on 10 April 1967. The long-awaited decision would not come until 12 June 1967. Writing for a unanimous court, Chief Justice Earl Warren concluded that "The Fourteenth Amendment requires that the freedom of choice to marry not be restricted by invidious racial discriminations. Under our Constitution, the freedom to marry, or not marry, a person of another race resides with the individual and cannot be infringed by the State.... These convictions must be reversed" (*Loving v. Virginia*, 388 U.S. 12 [1967]). The U.S. Supreme Court's ruling in *Loving v. Virginia* also outlawed miscegenation statutes that existed at the time in fifteen other states. Maryland had repealed its ban on interracial marriages only a few months before the decision.

Private and shy people that they were, Richard and Mildred Loving quietly celebrated the court's decision. While they were delighted with the ruling, they seemed oblivious to the broader social implications of the decision and wondered why two people's decision to marry each other had caused such a furor in the first place. The most immediate effect of the decision for the Lovings was that they and their children could return permanently to Caroline County and live together as a family in the new house that Richard had always wanted to build. But on 29 June 1975, the car that Richard Loving was driving was hit broadside by a drunk driver who ran a stop sign; Richard was killed instantly. Also in the car with Richard were Mildred, who lost her right eye in the accident, and her sister Garnet Hill, who suffered minor injuries. The couple had only recently celebrated their seventeenth wedding anniversary and the eighth anniversary of the Supreme Court decision that had validated their marriage.

In the years following the death of her husband, Mildred Loving continued to live in the house that Richard had built for his family. Growing more reclusive over the years, she began granting fewer interviews and relied on her daughter, Peggy, to serve as the family spokesperson. Loving never showed any interest in being a celebrity. She always described herself as an ordinary black woman who fell in love with an ordinary white man, and had the two of them been allowed to be husband and wife, no one would ever have known her name. She will forever be remembered, much in the way that ROSA PARKS has been, as a quiet, shy, but dignified woman who insisted on being treated with a measure of humanity. Loving died at home in Central Point, Virginia, at the age of 68.

FURTHER READING

Newbeck, Phyl, *Virginia Hasn't Always Been for Lovers: Interracial Marriage Bans and the Case of Richard and Mildred Loving* (2004).

Pratt, Robert A. "Crossing the Color Line: A Historical Assessment and Personal Narrative of *Loving v. Virginia*," *Howard Law Journal* 41 (1998).

Wallenstein, Peter. *Tell the Court I Love my Wife: Race, Marriage, and Law: An American History* (2002).

ROBERT A. PRATT

Loving, Neal Vernon (4 Feb. 1916–19 Dec. 1998), aviator and aeronautical engineer, was born in Detroit, Michigan, the third son of Alma (Price) Loving, a homemaker and housekeeper, and Hardin Clay Loving, a railroad conductor and optometrist. Neal Loving had an early love of aviation that remained with him despite family objections. Although he changed elementary schools frequently owing to his family's poverty and related evictions, he read every aviation book and magazine at nearby branches of the Detroit Public Library and raced to watch passing airplanes during school hours. At a schoolteacher's suggestion, he acquired an application for the U.S. Air Corps at the nearest post office, and read it avidly. Deterred by its unequivocal statement that applicants were to be "white, male," he threw away the application and continued to explore. He saved his lunch and movie admission money to buy model airplane materials, and, when the Detroit City Airport opened in 1929, rode the streetcar out to watch the airplane mechanics.

In 1930, at Jefferson Intermediate School, Loving was elected president of the newly formed aeronautics club, despite being the only African American member. That spring, he saved up enough money for his first airplane ride, in an open-cockpit biplane.

In high school he joined the all-black Ace Flying Club; the club's secretary was Earsly Taylor, a woman who would become Loving's longtime business partner. In 1934 Loving graduated from the aeronautics program at Cass Technical High School in Detroit. The same year, inspired by articles in popular mechanics magazines, Loving designed and built a ground trainer (a non-flying aircraft), which received an award from *Mechanix Illustrated* magazine and was exhibited at the annual All-American air show at Detroit City Airport in 1935.

Following this success, he began to design his first full-size glider, but his design work continued slowly, as he was hampered by financial constraints. Job opportunities for African Americans were scarce during the Depression, but in 1936 Loving found a position funded by the Works Progress Administration (WPA) teaching young people at Detroit community centers about the design and construction of model airplanes. By 1938, he had accumulated the funds to begin flight lessons; he was able to solo the following year. In 1939 Loving organized a glider club at the all-black St. Antoine YMCA in downtown Detroit. His next glider, this one airworthy, was designated the Wayne S-1 and was ready to fly in July 1941 That year he also became an aircraft mechanics instructor at the newly founded Aero Mechanics High School, near Detroit City Airport.

As the United States prepared to enter World War II, the Civil Aeronautics Administration, the forerunner of the Federal Aviation Administration, contacted all owners of registered gliders, seeking to purchase aircraft for the military. Although Loving's glider was too small to meet military standards, he offered to build a larger version, designated the S-2, and in 1941 Loving and Earsly Taylor founded the Wayne Aircraft Company in Detroit to manufacture gliders. That same year the United States' Office of Civilian Defense formed the Civil Air Patrol (CAP), a volunteer, civilian branch to provide pre-military training to young people. None of the white CAP squadrons in the Detroit area would accept Loving and Taylor as members; however, in 1942 they were authorized to form an all-black squadron, designated Squadron 639-5 (63rd Wing, Group Nine, Squadron Five). It became known informally as the Parachute Squadron, since it specialized in parachute jump training, in addition to the standard training.

By July 1943 many wartime efforts began to be refocused as it became apparent that the war would eventually be won. Loving's position at Aero Mechanics High School was terminated, so he applied to the Ford Motor Company for an engineering job but was offered only an entry-level engine assembly position. Shortly thereafter he received his draft notice. Loving was certain he would be called to active duty, since he held an active pilot's license and medical certificate, so he increased his efforts to complete the design of the S-2 as quickly as possible. Drafted early in 1944, Loving foresaw no difficulty passing the examinations, but the military physician classified him 4-F,

unfit for military service on the basis of supposed heart problems. Now also realizing that labor union seniority rules would delay his promotion to an engineering position at Ford, Loving appealed to the War Manpower Commission for a statement of availability, so that he might seek a drafting position elsewhere. In the meantime he planned to enroll in Wayne State University in the fall of 1944.

On 30 July 1944, Loving took off for a routine Civil Air Patrol training mission. However, the glider stalled soon after Loving released the towline connecting his glider to the powered plane that had been towing it to the proper cruising altitude of about 175 feet. The resulting crash severely injured his legs, eventually requiring a double amputation. Following a lengthy recovery, Loving acquired two prosthetic limbs and eventually was able once more to fly. During Loving's long recovery the Wayne Aircraft Company closed, but Loving and Taylor soon found another opportunity to use their aviation skills. After World War II, many veterans were learning to fly, using GI Bill benefits for education, but black veterans were routinely rejected by many flight schools. In 1946 Loving and Taylor founded the Wayne School of Aeronautics as an integrated flight school, which continued operation until 1957. By 1947 Loving again began to design aircraft. He focused on midget-class racers, a new category intended to be affordable for those with average incomes. He began to work on his first powered aircraft, the WR-1, later known as *Loving's Love*. The fixed-landing-gear craft with inverted gull wings was completed in 1950, and Loving himself flew the first, nearly flawless, test flight on 7 August 1950.

Loving wanted to enter the WR-1 in the National Air Races on 10 August 1950, but it was not possible for him to complete the ten hours of qualifying flight time required before the start of the races. Nevertheless, he was the first African American to receive a license from the Professional Racing Pilots Association (PRPA). During the racing season of 1951, Loving continued to fly qualifying heats with the WR-1 and he was certified as a racing pilot, receiving a license from the Fédération Aéronautique Internationale (FAI), the oldest international aeronautical licensing organization. Because corporate sponsorship for air racing declined after that year, Loving flew only demonstration flights in 1952. In 1953–1954 Loving flew the WR-1 for the 4,800-mile round-trip from Detroit to Kingston, Jamaica, where Earsly Taylor and her husband, Carl Barnett, had founded a flight school.

In 1954 the Experimental Aircraft Association (EAA) awarded Loving the Most Outstanding Design award for the WR-1.

Loving married Clare Thérèse Barnett in 1955. They later adopted a son and a daughter. He began studying aeronautical engineering at Wayne State University in Detroit in the fall of 1955 and in 1957 closed the Wayne School of Aeronautics in order to study full time. He graduated in 1961 with a bachelor of science degree in Aeronautical Engineering and became an aerospace engineer at the Air Force Flight Dynamics Laboratory, Wright-Patterson Air Force Base, Ohio. While a student, Loving designed the WR-2, a plane that could be folded and towed behind a car; the subsequent WR-3 aircraft was also a "roadable." In 1964, he donated the WR-1 N351C, *Loving's Love*, to the Experimental Aircraft Association Museum in Oshkosh, Wisconsin.

His initial research at Wright-Patterson was primarily in high-altitude clear-air turbulence measurement techniques, for which he became known internationally. He published more than a dozen research papers, most on this subject, and received numerous awards and commendations during his civil service career. Loving retired in 1982, remained active as a public speaker, and continued to fly until 1992. He died in Springfield, Ohio.

FURTHER READING

Neal V. Loving's papers are housed in the Special Collections and Archives, Wright State University, Dayton, Ohio.

Loving, Neal V. *Loving's Love: A Black American's Experience in Aviation.* (1994).

CAROLINE M. BROWN

Lowery, Irving E. (16 Sept. 1850–Dec. 1929), author, Methodist Episcopal Church minister, educator, advocate of black self-help, and champion of Wesleyan perfectionism, was born a slave to Tom and Namie Lowery on the estate of John Frierson in Sumter County, South Carolina. As a young man, Lowery was a house servant for his master and mistress on the Puddin Swamp plantation. He learned to read and write early and developed a deep appreciation for the religious piety of his Methodist owners. He later recalled his close relationship with the Friersons, sleeping in the same room with them on a pallet next to their bed, kindling fires for them, and sounding the plantation's call for work each morning. He also ran errands for the family on a pony bought for his use, and he accompanied his owner on business trips to the county seat. All this,

it appears, gave Lowery certain unique opportunities for a young slave in South Carolina.

Some time before the Civil War, Lowery's father saved enough from the extra wages he earned to purchase his own freedom. Tom Lowery later also bought his own mother out of slavery. At the time Abraham Lincoln issued the Emancipation Proclamation, Lowery's father was working toward the manumission of his wife, Namie. While Irving Lowery was still young, his mother, a devout Christian, had hoped he would become a minister. Although Lowery was occasionally permitted to attend religious services off the plantation, his opportunities for religious fellowship were limited. Years later a close friend of Irving Lowery recalled that the slaves would often gather in Frierson's yard to hear a certified exhorter or religious leader. Those services always took place under the watchful eye of white overseers, who feared that too much religious freedom would lead to insurrection.

Little changed at Puddin Swamp even after the fall of the Confederacy in April 1865. At war's end Lowery was fifteen years old and still living and working on the Frierson plantation. But an incident in fall 1865 altered the young Lowery's life forever. After work one evening, his master's son, Adolphus Frierson, brutally whipped Lowery and threatened to kill him if he ran away. That night Lowery fled, under cover of darkness, with another teenage former slave. The two worked their way through thickets and swampland to the Union garrison at Sumter. Union agents placed Lowery in the custody of his father. In 1866 Tom Lowery enrolled his son in a South Carolina free school, which received support from a New England educational society. Young Irving Lowery came in contact with many Northerners in these years, attending Methodist Episcopal Church (MEC) services as early as 1867 and receiving further education at Baker Theological Institute, operated by the MEC in Charleston. He was also one of the first to register as a student at the newly-founded, MEC-sponsored Claflin University. Like many other Freedman's Aid Society schools, Claflin was staffed, financed, and promoted by Northern philanthropists. For over a hundred years, Claflin was one of the only schools in the South that did not discriminate on the basis of color. For further schooling, Lowery even ventured far north of the Mason-Dixon Line, briefly attending the Wesleyan Academy in Wilbraham, Massachusetts.

Returning to the South, Lowery married a woman, of whom little is known, but whom he described in his diary as light-skinned and from a wealthy family. The couple would have at least five children by the late 1880s. In the 1870s Lowery taught at a Sumter High School, where he later served as principal. Many embittered whites condemned black education and railed against both black and white members of the MEC. Northern Methodists made a concerted effort to draw black members, and African Americans voted with their feet and left southern congregations for the MEC in droves in the postwar years. Detractors considered the MEC little more than a black Republican fellowship. This did not dissuade Lowery, who entered the ministry in 1875 and served MEC churches in Cheraw, Charleston, Aiken, Summerville, and Greenville, South Carolina.

After the war Greenville became a center of holiness activity in the South. Few southerners before the 1870s put much stock in Wesleyan theories of holiness, but in the decades after the war northern-born perfectionism gained headway in the region. True Whittier, a New England Methodist missionary to the South who served as a presiding elder in Charleston, introduced Lowery to Wesleyan sanctification in the 1870s. Lowery soon championed the cause with zeal. He read and wrote for the Boston perfectionist periodical *The Christian Witness*, and he preached holiness to large congregations across South Carolina. The early-twentieth-century black Pentecostal revival owed much to the kind of perfectionism Lowery and others like him preached from pulpits and in newspapers across the region.

Later in life Lowery wrote New South booster articles for newspapers like Columbia, South Carolina's *Daily Record*. He borrowed heavily from BOOKER T. WASHINGTON and other apostles of self-help philosophy and praised white philanthropists and downplayed racism and the crimes against blacks in the South. In 1908 Lowery even lent his support to the United Confederate Veterans and General George W. Gordon, who proposed to erect a monument to the devoted, loyal slave. Lowery's most significant achievement as a writer, his 1911 autobiography, *Life on the Old Plantation in Ante-Bellum Days, or a Story Based on Facts*, painted a rosy picture of the antebellum South, not unlike Joel Chandler Harris's Uncle Remus tales. Nevertheless Lowery's account was a valuable window into plantation life, recalling slave work, celebrations, kinship networks, religious practices, and weddings, among other details. Lowery died in Columbia, South Carolina, in December 1929. It is hard to gauge the full extent of his impact, especially

because historians have paid little attention to his career. Yet he was an influential promoter of Christian holiness among African Americans, and his early efforts laid the groundwork for Southern holiness and Pentecostal growth in the twentieth century.

FURTHER READING

Lowery, Irving E. *Life on the Old Plantation in Ante-Bellum Slavery Days, Or a Story Based on Facts* (1911).

Curry, John W. *Passionate Journey: History of the 1866 South Carolina Annual Conference* (1980).

RANDALL J. STEPHENS

Lowery, Joseph Echols (6 Oct. 1921–), clergyman and civil rights leader, was born in Huntsville, Alabama, to LeRoy Lowery, a store owner, and Dora (Fackler) Lowery, a teacher. Born in the era of Jim Crow, Lowery early had to learn the harsh reality of discrimination against African Americans in Alabama. Lowery grew up with the nurturing influence of the black church, especially Methodism. One of his great grandfathers, Echols Lowery, had founded the local Huntsville Methodist Church and his mother's family included several African Methodist Episcopal Church ministers. In 1928 he began his schooling and in 1936 he enrolled in high school at Alabama Agricultural and Mechanical College's (A&M) laboratory school. After graduating from high school in 1939, Lowery attended Knoxville College and Alabama A&M before transferring to Paine College in Augusta, Georgia, and graduating in 1943 with a B.A. in Sociology. His first job out of college was as a newspaperman on the *Informer* (later the *Mirror*) in Birmingham, Alabama. While working at the newspaper, Lowery attended Paine Theological Seminary part-time. He also met Evelyn Gibson while in Birmingham and they married in 1947, eventually having three children, Cheryl, Karen, and Yvonne. He graduated from seminary in 1950 with a BDiv degree and was ordained a minister in the Central Alabama annual conference of the Methodist Church. In 1952 he became pastor of the Warren Street Methodist Church in Mobile, Alabama, a position he held for a decade.

In 1957 he joined with other Southern African American ministers to form the organization that soon became known as the Southern Christian Leadership Conference (SCLC). It originated out of the success of the Montgomery Bus Boycott and from its inception DR. MARTIN LUTHER KING JR.

Joseph Lowery posed in his office at the Georgia Coalition for the Peoples' Agenda on Mar. 4, 2004. (AP Images.)

was its director. Lowery became a vice president, a post he held until 1967, at which time he became chairman of the board. Lowery was among several SCLC officials sued for libel by local government officials in Montgomery, Alabama, for a fundraising advertisement—a general appeal for financial support and a specific appeal to meet King's legal expenses—that appeared in the *New York Times*. An all-white Alabama jury brought back a collective judgment of $5.6 million against the ministers and the newspaper, of which Lowery—who had not written the ad, nor known that his name was being used—was held responsible for $500,000. The appeal dragged on until 1964, when the U.S. Supreme Court, in its landmark *New York Times v. Sullivan*, overturned the judgment against the ministers and the newspaper. The case was a major victory for freedom of the press, but Lowery suffered financially for several years while the judgment was under appeal. In 1961 Lowery left Mobile for Nashville, Tennessee, where he became administrative assistant for the Methodist bishop CHARLES F. GOLDEN. In Nashville he was involved in the struggle to end the segregated Central Jurisdiction, a racial conference within the Methodist Church, and to desegregate all Methodist annual conferences. In 1964 he became pastor at St. Paul's Methodist Church in Birmingham, Alabama, and he remained there until 1968 when he became the minister of Central United Methodist Church

in southwest Atlanta, the city's oldest and largest predominantly African American UM church. During his eighteen years of service in the church, he worked for economic justice in the local community by overseeing the construction of Central Methodist Gardens, a housing complex for low- and moderate-income families. Although the Central Jurisdiction was phased out as part of the church structure of the new UMC denomination, Lowery continued to work for the elimination of remaining racial annual conferences in the UMC by serving on its Commission on Religion and Race. He was a delegate to the General Conference of the Methodist Church in 1964 and the UMC in 1968.

Lowery remained active in SCLC and the civil rights movement throughout the 1960s. He participated in the 1963 Birmingham campaign, the March on Washington, and the 1965 Selma voting rights campaign. After the assassination of Martin Luther King Jr. in April 1968, the Reverend RALPH D. ABERNATHY became the President of SCLC. However, the subsequent Poor People's Campaign in Washington, D.C., was a dismal failure. By 1977 it had become apparent that Abernathy did not have the leadership skills that SCLC needed in the post-civil rights era and Lowery stepped down as chairman of the board to assume the mantle of president. He was favored over the more militant SCLC staffer HOSEA WILLIAMS who took the newly created position as executive director. When Lowery became president of SCLC, the organization was deeply in debt and its number of affiliated groups had dwindled. The power sharing arrangement between Lowery and Williams lasted only until 1979, when Lowery fired Williams for refusing to resign his seat in the Georgia state legislature while holding a full-time position with SCLC. The board of SCLC upheld Lowery's action and he stayed as the organization president until 1997, when he was succeeded by Martin Luther King III.

In the post-civil rights era, Lowery reversed SCLC's decline through his organizational skills and his gifts as an orator. He was an outspoken defender of affirmative action, opponent of capital punishment, and advocate of public policies to alleviate poverty in America. As such, he connected racial justice with economic justice as King had done at the end of his life. In later years he also sought to fight the spread of AIDS in the African American community and to stop gang violence. In 1979 Lowery became involved in Middle East politics after his former SCLC colleague ANDREW

YOUNG was forced to resign as U.S. ambassador to the United Nations for meeting with a representative of the Palestine Liberation Organization (PLO). Lowery and the Reverend JESSE JACKSON followed with their own meeting with the PLO representative at the U.N. and later met with PLO leader Yasser Arafat in Lebanon. Although Lowery urged the PLO to recognize the state of Israel, his actions and statements angered many American Jews and contributed to a widening gulf between Jewish and African American leaders. Lowery defended his involvement in foreign affairs by pointing to the criticism heaped upon King when he spoke out against the war in Vietnam.

During the 1980s Lowery continued to push against the conservative swing of the national government. However, no cause during this decade was larger than the struggle to end apartheid in South Africa. As he had done many times before in his career as a civil rights leader, Lowery went to jail as a means of building public pressure on the federal government to isolate the South African regime. When apartheid finally ended in the 1990s and Nelson Mandela came to the United States, Lowery served as one of his hosts. Lowery was also a critic of President Ronald Reagan's nomination of Judge Robert Bork to the U.S. Supreme Court.

He retired as pastor of Cascade United Methodist Church in 1992, but remained active in civic and religious affairs. In 1996 he was president of MARTA, the Atlanta Public Transportation System during the Olympics, and in the late 1990s was prominent in the ultimately successful campaign to remove the Confederate Battle Flag (the Stars and Bars) from the Georgia state flag. Lowery received many honors, including the NAACP's Lifetime Achievement Award (1997) and the Walter P. Reuthers Humanitarian Award (2000), of which he was the first recipient. In 2001 Clark Atlanta University established the Joseph E. Lowery Institute for Justice and Human Rights, and the city of Atlanta renamed Ashby Street Joseph E. Lowery Boulevard. Despite his retirement from active ministry and the SCLC, he continued to speak out for civil rights and economic justice. In 2006, at the funeral of CORETTA SCOTT KING, Lowery criticized the economic policies of President George W. Bush, who was in attendance. In January 2009 Lowery delivered the benediction for the inaugural ceremony of U.S. president PRESIDENT BARACK OBAMA; drawing on BIG BILL BROONZY's "Black, Brown and White Blues," Lowery called on God to help Americans "work for that day when black will

not be asked to get in the back, when brown can stick around, when yellow will be mellow, when the red man can get ahead, man; and when white will embrace what is right." In 2009, President Obama presented Lowery with the Presidential Medal of Freedom.

FURTHER READING

Branch, Taylor. *Parting the Waters: America in the King Years, 1954–1963* (1988).

Branch, Taylor. *Pillar of Fire: America in the King Years, 1963–1965* (1998).

Branch, Taylor. *At Cannan's Edge: America in the King Years, 1965–1968* (2006).

Fairclough, Adam., *To Redeem the Soul of America: the Southern Christian Leadership Conference and Martin Luther King, Jr.* (1987).

Garrow, David. *Bearing the Cross: Martin Luther King, Jr., and the Southern Christian Leadership Conference, 1955–1968* (1986).

Lewis, Anthony. *Make No Law: The Sullivan Case and the First Amendment* (1991).

Murray, Peter, *Methodists and the Crucible of Race, 1930–1975* (2004).

PETER C. MURRAY

Lowery, P. G. (11 Oct. 1869–15 Dec. 1942), circus minstrel, vaudeville bandleader, soloist, and entrepreneur, was born Perry George Lowery in Topeka, Kansas, the youngest of eight children of Rachel (Tucker) and Andrew Lowery. "P. G.," as he was known, was so proficient on the cornet that he was called the "World's Greatest Colored Cornet Soloist" by his teacher, Boston Conservatory Professor H. C. Brown (*Indianapolis Freeman*, 22 Feb. 1896).

During Reconstruction, land promoters led wagon trains of newly emancipated black citizens to settle the recently-opened former Indian Territory. The Lowery family was among these, and settled in Reece, near Eureka, Kansas, on a 180-acre plot on Spring Creek in Greenwood County. Soon after their arrival, the Lowery family, who were singers and instrumentalists, organized the Star of the West Brass Band, which became popular in the area. How P. G. learned to play the cornet so well without any formal training is not known, but he once stated that he simply "found a cornet in the attic and began to practice on it" (Kachel, "A Sketch of P. G. Lowery's Life In His Own Words, 1941–1942"). In the mid-1890s, Lowery was hired to play with a show called "Darkest America," thus launching his professional career. He also befriended show owner Ben Wallace of the Cook & Whitby

Circus, laying the groundwork for future appearances. Around 1894 two significant events changed the course of Lowery's musical career. First, he won the prize at the Hutchinson, Kansas, Musical Jubilee for the Finest Rendered Cornet Solo. The coveted prize may have been a scholarship to the Boston Conservatory. Then Lowery was contracted to play a thirty-two-week engagement with the popular Kansas City-based Preston T. Wright's Nashville Students Colored Comedy Company. Two years later, Lowery created a stir and drew attention to himself when he issued "A Challenge to the World." The *New York Clipper* published the following statement, subsequently republished in other newspapers, over his signature: "I claim the honor of being the greatest colored cornet soloist on earth, and will meet any colored cornet soloist in a contest for a purse of from $100 to $600, said challenge expiring Aug. 1." (Eureka, Kansas, *Herald*, 1 May 1896).

Between 1894 and 1897 Lowery studied at Boston Conservatory and worked with the Nashville Students Company. He completed his conservatory studies in 1897. Afterward he played intermittently with the Nashville group for a major portion of his career as soloist and bandmaster (1895 to 1898), briefly as manager (1898), and subsequently (1899 to 1909) as owner of the group.

Lowery left the Nashville Students Company in June 1898 to perform at the Trans-Mississippi and International Exposition in Omaha. His performances were termed "remarkable," and "phenomenal;" the *Indianapolis Freeman* labeled Lowery "The Pride of the Exposition" (*Indianapolis Freeman*, 3 and 17 Sep. 1898). Lowery's reputation got another unexpected boost when he was lured into a "jam" session that turned into a so-called cutting match between himself and cornet player (and "Father of the Blues") WILLIAM CHRISTOPHER (W. C.) HANDY. Handy, bandmaster and virtuoso cornetist of the W.-A. Mahara's Minstrel Band, exclaimed in his subsequent biography, that "from that day his [Handy's] great ambition was to outplay P. G. [Lowery]" (Handy, *Father of The Blues*).

In September 1898 Lowery took a position as "Special Soloist" at the Moorish Café in Omaha and then became band director of the Georgia Up-to-Date Minstrels—a position he held for only about five months—and he opened with the Adam Forepaugh (sometimes spelled as "4-Paw" in advertisements) Circus at Madison Square Garden, New York, in July 1899, which ran until November of that year. Forepaugh, who understood the popular appreciation for black entertainers, was pleased with Lowery's performance and contracted him for the 1900 season. While waiting for the circus season to resume, Lowery set off on another road tour in December with his Nashville Students. On 4 April 1900 Lowery resumed his work with the 4-Paw & Sells Brothers Circus at Madison Square Garden. Responding to public tastes, he began to cast his shows more along the lines of vaudeville. Lowery included such fashionable dances as the One-step, the Slow Drag, and the Cakewalk. He laced his performances with the popular new musical style known as "ragtime." Lowery cultivated a friendship with ragtime composer SCOTT JOPLIN and often featured his music. The sheet music for Joplin's "A Breeze from Alabama, A Ragtime Two Step" (1902) has Lowery's picture on the cover, along with Joplin's statement: "Dedicated to P. G. Lowery, World's Challenging Colored Cornetist and Band Master."

During the 1902 season Lowery became ill and did not tour. He returned to Eureka, and while recovering he organized "P. G. Lowery's Progressive Musical Enterprise," a show development and management company. "The Enterprise," as it was often called, prepared two shows for the 1903 season, and by 1917 it was providing employment for many talented black entertainers in at least three circus sideshows, two minstrel road shows, plus additional smaller projects. Lowery closed with 4-Paw in November 1904, and relocated the Enterprise offices from Eureka to Pittsburgh, Pennsylvania. There, he also conducted W. A. Kelly's thirty-piece band, preparing it for participation in Theodore Roosevelt's 1905 Presidential Inauguration Parade.

The 1905 season opened with Lowery as the attraction in the Great Wallace Circus. Reportedly, his was the best-financed "colored" show on the road (Watkins, 54). The same year, he also composed what was to become his signature piece, the "Prince of Decorah Galop." This composition was one of the most technically challenging examples of music ever written for the circus, and it remained in the standard show repertory. In 1908 the Enterprise hired a female singer named Carrie Gilbert from Columbus, Ohio. She performed several innovative acts, and by 1916 she had become Mrs. Perry George Lowery. Lowery remained in the Wallace show (or the "Carl Hagenbeck-Great Wallace Circus") until 1914 and then returned for the 1916 and 1917 seasons. During the winters, when the circuses were closed, Lowery continued his road show and Enterprise operations. In 1918, because of a railroad restriction caused by World War I, he ended those tours and went to Nitro, West Virginia, where he organized a "colored" concert band to support the war effort.

At the war's end, around 1919, Lowery moved to Cleveland, Ohio, where he joined the Ringling Brothers and Barnum & Bailey Circus and remained there until 1931. Making Cleveland his home, he organized a community music school, coached many of the city's bands and orchestras, and produced a full-blown circus for his fraternal order, the Improved Benevolent and Protective Order of Elks of The World—all while leading what was considered the finest Ringling Brothers side-show band. Lowery closed with Ringling Brothers in September 1931 and then trouped with other shows. He directed a concert band at the 1933 Chicago World's Fair, then played the 1934 season with the Gorman Brothers Circus. In 1935 he joined the Cole Brothers–Clyde Beatty Circus. In 1938 this circus split into two separate shows: the Cole Brothers Circus and the Robbins Brothers Circus. Lowery toured on the Robbins show for only that one single season. When the two shows reunited under the Cole Brothers banner in 1939, Lowery was no longer with either circus.

Lowery's final years proved grueling. He began the 1939 season in August with the Downie Brothers Circus, out of Macon, Georgia. Downie was a hard-luck show that traveled in a convoy of trucks and only made a profit during three days of its entire run. Mercifully, Downie closed in November 1939, and Lowery (who was in declining health) and his troupe were suddenly unemployed. Perhaps out of friendship, the reconnected Cole Brothers Circus rehired the aging Lowery for the 1940 season. The show, including Lowery and his band, made a one-hour radio broadcast from station KLS in Salt Lake City, one of the largest shows of its type ever produced, entertaining ninety thousand war workers. The year 1941 began with promise, but illness struck Lowery and he was, with much difficulty, persuaded by the Cole Brothers management to go home at mid-season to recuperate. A still-ailing Lowery rejoined the Cole show for the 1942 season, struggled through performances and a hospitalization, but completed the tour. He returned to Cleveland mortally ill and then died in December of 1942.

FURTHER READING

Keck, George, and Martin Sherrill, eds. *Feel the Spirit, Studies in Nineteenth-Century Afro-American Music* (1988).

Watkins, Clifford E. *Showman: The Life and Music of Perry George Lowery* (2003).

CLIFFORD EDWARD WATKINS

Lowry, "Tiger" Ted (27 Oct. 1919–14 June 2010), boxer, paratrooper, and prison guard, was born Theodore Adolphus Lowry in New Haven, Connecticut, the fourth and youngest child of James Wesley Lowry and Grace Editha Mathews. His father was born in what is now Beckley, West Virginia, whereas his mother was a native of Brunswick, Maine.

In a sixteen-year boxing career that was interrupted by World War II, Lowry became the only fighter to twice go the ten-round distance with Rocky Marciano, who was known for his knock-out punch and who finished his career as the undefeated world heavyweight champion.

On 1 June 1946 in New Haven, Lowry married Marjorie Frances Parris, whose brother, Fred Parris, was the lead singer of the Five Satins and wrote the hit song "*In The Still of the Night.*" Ted and Marjorie had three sons: Wayne, Kenneth, and Kevin. Ted married Alice Johnson on 11 July 1964 in Norwalk, Connecticut.

When Lowry was ten years old, his father died. His mother took her two youngest children, Ted and his brother, Reynaldo Robert, who was known as Bob, and moved back to Maine where she would have the support of her mother and extended family. Ted's two sisters, Audrey and Editha, had their own families and stayed in Connecticut.

While in Portland, Lowry's athletic ability developed and he became a star running back for Portland High School's football team. He also played other sports, but it was the father of a young woman who caused him to take up boxing.

As Lowry wrote in his autobiography, "*God's In My Corner,*" he was warned by this father to stay away from his daughter, Helen. When Lowry walked Helen home one evening, her father, Mitchell Williams, knocked Lowry down with one punch. Lowry decided to learn how to box so that he could get back at the father. He never did get back at the father and one of Helen's sisters ended up marrying Lowry's brother.

While learning the sport Lowry accepted a dare and entered an amateur boxing tournament. There, he proceeded to knock out three opponents on the same day. He was scheduled to fight a fourth, but that boxer had watched enough of Lowry's prowess and decided withdrawing from the tournament would be a more prudent decision.

Even that success didn't put boxing high on Lowry's agenda. That changed, however, when he was asked to spar with New England middleweight champion Babe Aberilla, who was in Portland preparing for a pending fight. The nineteen-year-old Lowry made such an impression on Aberilla's manager that he signed Ted to a contract and took him to New Bedford, Massachusetts, to train with several other fighters.

His career had begun, and at one point Lowry fought fifteen consecutive weeks, mainly in the Northeast, including ten-rounders. It was while he was in the Army that he really came to believe in himself, when Lowry volunteered to fight then world heavyweight champion JOE LOUIS in an exhibition bout.

In the service Lowry joined the newly created 555th Parachute Infantry Battalion of the 82nd Airborne. As with the Tuskegee Airmen, African Americans were segregated from white paratroop outfits, so the separate battalion was set up, the nation's first all-black parachute infantry test platoon, company, and battalion. The 555th became known as the "Triple Nickels."

Midway through the rigorous combat training in late April 1945, the battalion received new orders, a "permanent change of station" to Pendleton Air Base in Pendleton, Oregon, for duty on a highly classified mission. The Triple Nickels became the world's first smoke jumpers, jumping out of planes to fight forest fires that had been started by Japanese "balloon bombs"—clusters of incendiary bombs and explosives that had traveled across the Pacific Ocean on hydrogen-filled, silk-like bags. The U.S. government kept secret the existence of the "balloon bombs," and, consequently, the existence of the all-black Triple Nickels.

After his discharge from the Army, Lowry resumed his boxing career. Besides Marciano, his opponents included ARCHIE MOORE, Joey Maxim, "Tiger" Jack Fox, Roland LaStarza, and Henry "Kid" Matthews.

Lowry considered Moore his toughest opponent. But it was the Marciano fights that most boxing afficionadois, including Lowry, remember the most.

The two met on 10 October 1949 at the Providence, Rhode Island, Auditorium. The next day the *Providence Journal* reported that Lowry won six of the ten rounds, but Marciano got the victory. "I still think I won the first fight, and so do a lot of people," Lowry said. "But you learn to take the good with the bad. His manager, Al Weill, was very connected. I think that helped him a bit."

Lowry, a defensive specialist, fought wherever there was a fight, in small arenas, small towns, on undercards. Marciano, on the other hand, was the "Great White Hope." The two battled again in November 1950. This time even Lowry admitted Marciano won. But, like their first meeting, Marciano, the great slugger, couldn't stop Lowry.

"I feel as if I was cheated out of my little piece of history," Lowry said of losing the first Marciano fight. "But then I realize I still have a piece of history. Here it is all these years later and reporters still come around and ask about the Marciano fights."

Lowry was far from being just a journeyman boxer. He won both the New England light heavyweight and heavyweight titles. When he retired from the ring in 1955, he said he had won 87 of his 141 fights. Some sources disagree with that record. His last fight, with Johnny Hoye on 18 July 1955, would end in a ten-round loss for Lowry, but as fate would have it, the fight was in Brockton, Massachusetts, one of several cities Lowry fought out of during his career.

Lowry was inducted into the Ring Four's Hall of Fame in 2003. Ring Four is the Boston chapter of the International Veteran Boxers Association.

After he quit the ring, Lowry took a job as a guard at the New Haven County jail. One night an inmate told him about a plot to fly men accused of the Brinks robbery out of the country. When the head jailer ignored his story, Lowry went to the Federal Bureau of Investigation, who acted. Within a month the Brinks robbery was solved.

For years Lowry passed on to children the skills he had learned. He coached at the Greater Norwalk Boxing Association, located at the Norwalk YMCA, before age finally forced him out of that work. During that time he trained two hundred young boxers. Not one to rest on his accomplishments, Lowry and his wife, Alice, both in their eighties, became school bus monitors in Norwalk, Connecticut. In 2008 he was inducted into the Connecticut Boxing Hall of Fame. He died in Norwalk at the age of 90.

FURTHER READING

Biggs, Bradley. *The Triple Nickels: America's First All Black Paratrooper Unit* (1986).
Lowry, Ted. *God's In My Corner: A Portrait of an American Boxer: The Autobiography of "Tiger" Ted Lowry* (2007).

BOB GREENE

Lowry, James H. (28 May 1939–), businessman, was born James Hamilton Lowry in Chicago, Illinois, the younger of two sons of Camille (Caldwell) Lowry, a seamstress and postal worker, and William Abrose Lowry, a postal worker. Jim Lowry's parents had come to Chicago as children from America's rural South during the Great Migration. Grounded by their parents' race-consciousness and southern roots, Lowry and his brother, William Jr., were raised on Chicago's South Side in a comfortable and protected working-class black environment. He thrived in the strange paradox of black ghetto life in the 1940s and 1950s, which was close-knit and economically diverse and where successful black role models were visible and accessible. Lowry went to A.O. Sexton, a neighborhood elementary school, until recruited in 1953 into a high-achieving private school known as the Francis W. Parker School, an overwhelmingly white but relatively egalitarian school on Chicago's affluent North Side. Lowry's classmates included the children of some of Chicago's most illustrious citizens. Campus dating reflected race relations at the time and the fathers of Lowry's girl friends forbade their dating him. His social isolation eroded rapidly, however, when he found that he was an exceptional athlete. Beginning in his sophomore year he was "all city" for three consecutive years and voted among the city's top five players by the *Chicago Sun-Times* and the *Chicago Daily News*.

Lowry attended Grinnell College, a progressive small college situated in the rural and predominantly white community of Grinnell, Iowa, from 1957 to 1961, when he earned a B.A. in Political Science. He roomed with Allison Davis Jr., the son of ALLISON DAVIS, a University of Chicago professor. At Grinnell, as at Parker, the etiquette of race relations isolated Lowry from the majority community until his athletic prowess earned him public esteem as an important campus figure. By senior year, an all-conference in baseball, basketball, and football, he was voted the most outstanding athlete at Grinnell.

Lowry was awarded a scholarship for a fifth year abroad, to travel to Dar es Salaam, where he experienced Tanganyika's (now Tanzania) historic transition from a territory under British control to self-governing independence. Lowry planned to join the Foreign Service after graduating but was recruited by the Peace Corps in 1962 and became an Outward Bound instructor in Arecibo, Puerto Rico. He took a leave and matriculated at the University of Pittsburgh, where he earned an M.A. in Public and International Affairs. Returning to the Peace Corps in 1965, he held the position of associate director for Lima (Peru) Operations until 1967 and learned to speak Spanish. For recreation Lowry played basketball and successfully helped the local Lima basketball club twice win the national championship. During this period he met the then U.S. Attorney General Robert F. Kennedy, who had a profound effect on the next phase of Lowry's life, and with whom he formed a close friendship until Kennedy's assassination in 1968.

In 1967 after returning from Peru Lowry was recruited both by the Ford Foundation and by Robert Kennedy and his aide, *Black Enterprise Magazine* publisher EARL GRAVES, to work on the Bedford-Stuyvesant Restoration Project in Brooklyn, New York. The Bed-Stuy project was the forerunner of the urban development efforts in the 1960s called Community Development Corporations. While working on the Bed-Stuy project Lowry co-hosted a television program, *Inside Bedford-Stuyvesant*, with ROXIE ROKER. In 1968 Lowry took a job with the renowned management consulting firm McKinsey and Company in New York City, becoming the firm's first black consultant. There he worked on projects for inner cities, for the Peace Corps, and eventually, after returning to Tanzania, as a consultant to that country's decentralizing government. In 1969 Lowry married Nettie Anthony, and the newlyweds traveled together to Tanzania, where their daughter Aisha Camille was born. The couple was divorced in 1977.

Lowry returned to the United States in 1972 and attended a professional management development program at Harvard University. The following year he transferred back to his hometown to work in McKinsey's Chicago office and on Richard J. Daley's final mayoral campaign. Daley encouraged Lowry to start his own firm, and in 1975 he established James H. Lowry and Associates (JHLA). During the administration of President Jimmy Carter, the reputation of JHLA flourished when Lowry and his staff wrote the groundbreaking study *A New Strategy for Minority Business Development* (1978) for the U.S. Department of Commerce. The Lowry Report, as it was commonly known, helped increase the department's budget and improve the quality of assistance for minority businesses, and it launched the Minority Business Development Agency (MBDA), formally called the Office of Minority Business Enterprise. JHLA opened offices in Washington, D.C., and Oakland, California, after the impact of his report made Lowry a leading champion of minority business development. With the support of then Congressional Black Caucus President PARREN MITCHELL, Lowry wrote reports for eight federal agencies that built the case for supporting minority business nationwide. Lowry then expanded his vision of minority-majority joint business ventures to the private sector and developed models for minority business development for such companies as PepsiCo, Baxter Travenol Laboratories, Frito-Lay, and Burger King. Lowry was consistently listed among the fifty most powerful people in Chicago business by *Crain's*.

HAROLD WASHINGTON's election in 1985 as Chicago's first black mayor marked the onset of an era of both reform politics and the exercise of political clout by African Americans. Washington appointed Lowry president of the board of the Chicago Public Library, where he oversaw the development of Chicago's central library and the Harold Washington Library and Center. Washington tasked Lowry with designing Chicago's minority business set-aside program, the first of its kind in the nation. This program established benchmark set-aside goals of 25 percent for minorities and 5 percent for women and became the model that cities such as Atlanta, Boston, Oakland, and San Francisco followed.

The political infighting and race-based opposition to Washington's administration, symbolized by Chicago's Council Wars, overflowed into attacks on Lowry. Setting aside 30 percent of municipal contracts for minorities and women was threatening to the white establishment, and Lowry, as the architect of that program, came under fire. His prominence, however, was already established. He hosted and co-produced *MBR: the Minority Business Report*, a television program on Chicago's WGN-TV from 1985 through 1988, and was an adjunct instructor of management at Northwestern University's Kellogg School of Management from 1987 to 1992. He also co-chaired Chicago United, a civic organization of minority and white business leaders that spearheaded major reform of Chicago's public education system.

In 1989 Lowry married Sharon Collins, whose book *Black Corporate Executives* (1997) was inspired in large part by her observations of the evolution of Lowry's career. The couple divorced in 1998. Lowry continued to concentrate his efforts heavily in the private sector, including a project for the Ford Motor Company, which increased Ford's minority procurement from $200 million to over $3 billion. Hoping to end his career by building systems for recruiting and developing large numbers of minorities to work for professional firms, in 2000 Lowry's firm merged with the Boston Consulting Group (BCG). Lowry became president of BCG's Chicago operations and BCG's global diversity director and continued his work on workforce diversity, ethnic marketing, and minority business development and was named a senior vice president of BCG in 2005. In 2000 he married Doris Davenport.

Lowry's civic involvement spanned a wide range of public and private institutions. He served on the boards of Northwestern University Hospital, Northwestern University's Kellogg School of Management, Harvard Business School, and Grinnell College. He was named Chair of the first HBCU's Center for Entrepreneurial Study at Howard University. In 2005 James H. Lowry was inducted into the Inaugural Minority Business Hall of Fame.

SHARON M. COLLINS

Lu Valle, James Ellis (10 Nov. 1912–30 Jan. 1993), chemist, Olympic medalist, and university professor, was born to Isabelle Lu Valle and James Arthur Garfield Lu Valle in San Antonio, Texas. His father was a newspaper editor in Washington, D.C., and an itinerant preacher; his mother was a secretary. Lu Valle's parents separated when he was still young, and James moved with his mother and sister to Los Angeles in 1923. His father traveled worldwide after the separation and was in Europe for a time; Lu Valle remained estranged from him. At a young age he became a voracious reader. A chemistry set given him as a child changed his original interest in the sciences from engineering to chemistry.

James was an excellent student at McKinley Junior High School. His scholastic record there qualified him to attend the competitive Los Angeles Polytechnic High School, where his academic interests in science and math were further cultivated. He distinguished himself academically and athletically, which should have earned him membership into the Ephebian Society, the Los Angeles metropolitan society honoring character, leadership, community service, and scholastic achievement. When James did not become a member of the society for racially restrictive reasons, he was awarded the Willis A. Dunn Gold Medal (because the Ephebian Society barred nonwhites from its membership, the faculty of Polytechnic High had created the Dunn medal for the outstanding all-around student in the senior class). After a serious illness—a ruptured appendix complicated by peritonitis and gangrene—incapacitated him for six months, Lu Valle entered the University of California, Los Angeles (UCLA), in February 1932. Studying chemistry, he maintained a straight 4.0 grade point average and was active in campus life. Lu Valle was President of Blue Key (1936) and elected to Phi Beta Kappa. Captain of the track team in 1935, Lu Valle ran the 100-, 220-, 400-, and 800-meter races. He was the Intercollegiate American Athletic Association quarter-mile champion and National Collegiate Athletic Association 440-meter champion. He established himself as one of the best middle-distance runners in the country and was nicknamed the "Westwood Whirlwind" by the *Los Angeles Herald*. Lu Valle qualified to represent the United States in the 400-meter race on the Olympic Team in 1936. Competing on the same team with JESSE OWENS, he placed third and won the bronze medal.

During this period, Lu Valle wrote an essay entitled "The Lonely Path," dealing with the complex issues faced by light-skinned African Americans or *mulattos*, the term he preferred. It received third prize in the *Atlantic Monthly*'s distinguished essay contest in 1935.

In 1936 Lu Valle entered graduate school at UCLA, where he majored primarily in chemistry but also physics. His thesis focused on the photochemistry of crotonaldehyde, a type of hazardous waste, to prove what photochemical process took place. Lu Valle was instrumental in forming the first graduate student association at that institution. He received his master's degree in Chemistry from UCLA in 1937.

Lu Valle's academic achievements at UCLA prompted professors there to speak with the two-time Nobel laureate Linus Pauling at California Institute of Technology (Caltech), to which Lu Valle was admitted in 1937 and received his doctorate in Chemistry and Mathematics in 1940. His dissertation was entitled *An Electron-Diffraction Investigation Of Several Unsaturated Conjugated Organic Molecules*.

Lu Valle interviewed at several institutions and accepted a position at Fisk University in Nashville, Tennessee, as a chemistry instructor from 1939 until 1941. Backed by Linus Pauling and Professor William Young at UCLA, in 1941 he became the first African American to work at Eastman Kodak as a senior research chemist. He worked in the field of microspectroscopy, which has to do with the size and distribution of photographic grains in a photographic emulsion. Anxious to contribute to the war effort in the days following the attack on Pearl Harbor, Lu Valle accepted an offer to work with the National Defense Research Committee (NDRC) at the University of Chicago. There he tested poisonous gases for use as biological chemical agents. Near the war's end, he married; he and his wife Jean would have three children.

Between the years 1953 and 1975 Lu Valle served as director of the chemistry and photographic departments at Technical Operations, Incorporated, as director of physical and chemical research at Fairchild Camera and Instrumental Corporation, as-well as in several positions at Smith Corona Marchant Corporation, including as director of physical and chemical research and science coordinator, research and development laboratories. From 1975 through 1982 he was the director of undergraduate laboratories in the Department of Chemistry at Stanford University. Lu Valle is the author of thirty-five technical papers and holds several patents in the United States and abroad. Among those are ones for *Photographic Processes* (U.S. Patent 3,219,445), *Photographic Medium and Methods of Preparing Same* (U.S. Patent 3,219,448), and *Sensitizing Photographic Media* (U.S. Patent 3,219,451), all in 1965.

Lu Valle died of a heart attack at the age of eighty.

FURTHER READING

Amateur Athletic Foundation of Los Angeles. *An Olympian's Oral History: Dr. James E. Lu Valle, 1936 Olympic Games, track & field.* (1988).

UCLA Center for Oral History Research. *Founding president of UCLA's graduate student association: James E. Lu Valle.* (1987).

Obituary: *Los Angeles Times*, 12 Feb. 1993.

ALVA MOORE STEVENSON

Luandrew, Albert (Sunnyland Slim) (5 Sep. 1907–17 Mar. 1995), musician, singer, pianist, songwriter, and recording label owner, was born Albert Welton Luandrew in Vance, Mississippi, the son of Thomas Welton Luandrew, a preacher, and Martha Lewis. Best known as Sunnyland Slim, he became one of the creators of and a driving force in post-war Chicago Blues, and towards the end of his life its elder statesman. Albert Luandrew was born into a family of farmers and preachers in the Mississippi Delta. His great-grandfather, a white slave owner, whom Sunnyland would call, "the ol' monster," had a son, Albert Luandrew, with a slave woman in the years before the Civil War. The elder Albert

Luandrew was able to purchase land near Vance, Mississippi, from which he cleared the timber and made crossties he then sold to the up and coming railroads. His father was born in 1887; for his mother precise dates are not known.

Sunnyland spoke fondly of his early childhood, of going to town on the weekends, of his mother and grandfather, his cousins and playmates. The death of his mother of double pneumonia was tragic for the boy of about seven years. His father remarried, and his stepmother Mary, who never liked him, was physically abusive. To escape, Sunnyland took an interest in music. He was intrigued by a small pump-organ in a neighbor's house. To practice, he took an old shoebox onto which he copied the black and white key pattern. On weekends, he heard his father and friends play guitars and sing. Sundays were reserved for going to church. At school, he once played a few songs during a school concert, much to the amazement of his father and stepmother who didn't know he had been secretly practicing the piano.

At ten, Sunnyland ran away from home for the first time. By the time he was thirteen, he lived mostly on his own. He was exposed to several local piano players, such as Jeff Morris, who showed him a Blues in the key of F, and others with colorful names such as Red Eyed Jesse Bell, the Squirrel, and Dough Belly. His first job as a musician was in a movie house in nearby Lambert, Mississippi, at fifteen, where he played the piano while the reels were being changed. In 1923, he met EUREAL "LITTLE BROTHER" MONTGOMERY, a pianist and singer, in a lumber camp in Canton, Mississippi. Sunnyland asked him if he could join him and sing a blues. Little Brother consented and after a few minutes, the room began filling with women asking about the new singer. That night, Luandrew and Montgomery forged a friendship that lasted until Little Brother's death in 1985.

Toward the end of the 1920s, Sunnyland moved to Memphis where Blues was played up and down Beale Street. He heard that GERTRUDE "MA" RAINEY, one of the most successful entertainers of the day, was looking for a piano player. He auditioned with her, got the job, and stayed for about a week. Among the many musicians he met in and around Memphis were such exponents of early Blues as BLIND BLAKE, BLIND BOY FULLER, and Buddy Doyle, as well as musicians he would later encounter again in Chicago, including Rice Miller, Doctor Clayton, and a very young BIG WALTER HORTON. Another memorable encounter was with

ROBERT JOHNSON, the legendary singer and guitarist who was four years his junior.

Around 1929, Luandrew wrote "Lowdown Sunnyland Train." The song talked of the Sunnyland train who "stole away that girl of mine and gone." In real life, the train had run over and killed a white family, and a black family a week later. The image of the little children being killed stayed with Sunnyland for the rest of his life. He would often say "It given me a tender heart." Although he sometimes used other names—Delta Joe, Dudlow (Dudlow Joe was another term for Boogie Woogie), and Doctor Clayton's Buddy—"Sunnyland Slim" became his best-known name. The "Slim" was a natural addition for one who was 6-feet, 5-inches tall.

In the 1930s, he extended his travels farther North, reaching Cairo, Illinois, where he had a gambling joint. Both Little Walter and Honeyboy Edwards profited from his hospitality. He was an expert card, dice, and pool player. When times were lean, he would supplement his income through other sources. For example, he recruited farm-workers in the Deep South and brought them to orchards in the Midwest, and he "ran whiskey" during Prohibition. In 1938, he made his first recording. No trace of it has been found.

By 1942, he had permanently settled in Chicago. He quickly made friends among the established Blues musicians like BIG BILL BROONZY, who gave him work and introduced him to musicians such as TAMPA RED, MEMPHIS MINNIE, and JOHN LEE "SONNY BOY" WILLIAMSON. Sunnyland's band often consisted of a guitarist, upright bassist, drummer, and sometimes horns. Von Freeman (tenor sax) and CLARK TERRY (trumpet) both occasionally played in his band. Sunnyland joined the musicians' union, and in late summer of 1947, recorded for the Hytone label, featuring Lonnie Johnson on guitar. Shortly thereafter, he was asked to record for Aristocrat Records, co-owned by the Chess Brothers. He chose MUDDY WATERS, who was working as a delivery truck driver, to accompany him. According to Luandrew, he got Muddy freed from his job that day by telling the foreman that some close kin of Muddy's had died. In the studio, Sunnyland recorded two songs; when Leonard Chess asked if Muddy could sing, he replied: "He sings like a bird." Muddy cut two sides that day, and went on to establish Chess as the premier Blues label, and himself as the preeminent Chicago Bluesman.

For the rest of the 1940s, the 1950s, and into the early 1960s, Sunnyland recorded for just about every small label in Chicago. He was part owner, along with Joe Brown, of J.O.B. Records, and helped organize many of its sessions. The list of musicians with whom he recorded during those years reads like a Who's Who of post-war Chicago Blues: Floyd and Moody Jones, Little Walter, Big Walter Horton, Jimmy Rogers, Robert Jr. Lockwood, J. B. Lenoir, Snooky Prior, Eddie Taylor, to name a few. Sunnyland became one of the fathers of the emerging Chicago Blues style. His house on South Prairie Avenue was a haven for Blues musicians, a place for gambling, food, socializing and—of course—endless jamming.

In the early 1960s, he began to expand his reputation to a new audience. In November of 1960 he recorded an album for Prestige. It included tenor saxophonist King Curtis and a group of jazz musicians. He also toured with Captain Beefheart, and Canned Heat. In fall of 1964 he traveled to Europe with the American Folk Blues Festival—a tour that included HOWLIN' WOLF, HUBERT SUMLIN, and WILLIE DIXON, and would take them behind the iron curtain. Audiences everywhere greeted him with respect. His overseas travels continued until the mid 1980s, garnering him a dedicated international following. At home, he began playing for a younger and mostly white audience. He traveled the College Circuit with the Chicago Blues All Stars, and in Chicago he played North Side clubs with increasing frequency.

In 1973, he started his own record label, Airway Records. He released four albums and three forty-fives. A fifth album with his Gospel tunes remained unrecorded. By the beginning of the 1980s, Sunnyland had become the elder statesman of the Chicago Blues community. He wrote many songs and recorded well over two hundred sides. His music and his contributions to the Blues began to be recognized. At the 1987 Chicago Blues Festival, he was bestowed the City's Medal of Honor. A year later, he received a National Heritage Fellowship Award from the National Endowment for the Arts. In 1987, on his way to church, he was blown over by a wind gale and broke his hip. Other ailments started but despite more frequent stays at the hospital he continued to perform. His last engagement was at BUDDY GUY's Legends in Chicago in January 1995. Shortly thereafter, he was hospitalized for the last time. He died shortly before midnight on March 17, 1995. He was buried in Mount Vernon Cemetery, Lemont, IL, on March 23, 1995.

Those who knew him speak not only of a great singer and pianist, but of a man who persevered in the face of obstacles, a man who helped countless others, a man of deep faith and conviction.

FURTHER READING
Vaughan, Jack, and Sunnyland Slim. *Sunnyland Blues* (1990).
Whiteis, David. *Chicago Blues, Portraits and Stories* (2006).

SAM BURCKHARDT

Lucas, Bohlen (fl. 1840s–1880s), slave driver, farmer, and Democratic Party activist, was born a slave, probably in Washington County, Mississippi. The names of his parents are not recorded. On the eve of the Civil War, and only sixteen, he was working as a driver of slaves on a Delta plantation, a position generally reserved for experienced laborers in their thirties or forties. That Lucas achieved such a position at such an early age is suggestive of his willingness to work hard and to both obey and command authority. Drivers enjoyed a fair degree of autonomy in their work and occupied a difficult middle position between their fellow slaves and those who owned them, but most understood that the needs and desires of their owners came first. Though some drivers interceded to protect the slaves from harsh treatment by white overseers or masters, a minority abused their position by seeking sexual favors from female slaves or by settling personal grievances. No information is known about Lucas's personal or working relations with his fellow slaves; all that is known is that he worked for a white overseer named James Collier.

After the Civil War, Lucas maintained a close working relationship with his former owners, choosing to remain as Collier's driver on E. A. Fall's plantation in Washington County. Like many former slaves Lucas was ambitious and hoped to own his own land. But unlike many of the freedmen, he placed less faith in the power of the Republican Party or the federal government to help him achieve that goal, preferring instead to cultivate good relations with the native-born whites who continued to hold economic power in the postwar Delta.

He began in 1865 by renting land from his former master's widow, near Deer Creek in neighboring Issaquena County. Unlike Washington County, which large slave-labor gangs had cleared of swamps, dense forests, and canebrakes in the 1840s and 1850s, much of the land on Deer Creek remained uncultivated or had been abandoned during the war. Lucas knew from his employers' experience in Washington County, however, that once cleared, Deer Creek's rich, alluvial, Delta soil would deliver the same high cotton yields that had ensured his employers good profit margins before the war. Although he had to rely primarily on his own labors to clear and cultivate the land, Lucas managed to save one thousand dollars in cash by late 1870, which he paid James Collier as a down payment for a two-hundred-acre farm near Deer Creek. Collier requested only that Lucas pay him the balance of $1,120 by 1 January 1873, and he did not charge his former employee the customary interest.

Lucas might at that point have chosen to make the most of his two hundred acres, for example by diversifying his holdings and becoming self-sufficient like Lewis Spearman, another Delta farmer. He chose instead to expand his acreage of cotton-growing land in the hope of maximizing his investment. By 1872 he had rented more land, cleared it, and purchased plows and other implements, as well as twenty-five mules. As a former slave driver, however, Lucas understood that an adequate labor supply was the key to a successful cotton crop. Unable to pay wages, he entered into sharecropping arrangements with several African American tenants, clearing enough money in cash to pay Collier on time the outstanding balance on his two hundred acres. Now owning forty acres (and several mules) more than the average black landowner in Mississippi, Lucas sought out new lands to cultivate, renting several hundred acres and thirteen horses and oxen from Mrs. E. A. Fall, among others, and leasing and subleasing the land to black tenants. In order to secure cash advances for these ventures he liened his own farm to a local white merchant. Yet as the land under his cultivation increased, so did Lucas's debts. His rental of Mrs. Fall's plantation alone cost him four thousand dollars a year.

Like two-thirds of Mississippi blacks at that time, owners and renters alike, Lucas was illiterate. He thus depended largely on the patronage of white friends and associates to negotiate the many legal contracts and rental agreements he entered into, and at first such assistance was forthcoming. His friends, however, were unable to help him in the mid-1870s when a Mrs. Dingy, claiming to be the widow of a white man he had rented from, sued to repossess the land. Because the courts at first sided with Lucas, believing his claims that Dingy had not married, Lucas continued to cultivate the land, spending money to farm and develop it. When Mrs. Dingy eventually persuaded the Mississippi

Supreme Court that she was the rightful heir to the property, Lucas and his tenants were forced to leave the land and to pay the widow $1,500 plus interest, thus forcing Lucas into greater indebtedness. Unable to repay a loan to his old friend Collier, Lucas was forced to put his two hundred acres up for public auction in 1875; he received only five hundred dollars for it, less than a quarter of what he had paid. Still indebted, and now short of two hundred acres of prime land, Lucas rented more land and earned cash by again working as an overseer on a cotton plantation. Literacy in itself did not ensure success for the Delta's black farmers, but it is perhaps significant that several of the most successful landowners like William Toler learned to read and write, and that WAYNE WELLINGTON COX, one of the wealthiest, attended college before taking up farming.

In 1875 Lucas attempted to help his economic situation by aiding the political ambitions of his white allies, conservative Delta planters who resented Reconstruction and Republican Party rule. Although white Democrats had successfully used intimidation, fraud, and violence in their efforts to weaken Republican rule, the large black voting majorities in Washington and other Delta counties forced the Democrats also to co-opt African American support. To that end the white conservative Taxpayers' League, to whose president Lucas was indebted, appointed him as one of only two black delegates to the 1875 Washington County Democratic Party Convention, where he received the party's nomination for treasurer. This was not Lucas's first foray into politics; four years earlier, when he claimed to be a liberal Republican, he ran unsuccessfully as that party's candidate for sheriff of Washington County. Although the precise methods he employed in the 1875 elections are unclear, Lucas probably used tactics other than moral suasion in marshaling strong black support for Democratic candidates. He personally marched his own tenants to the polls and required that they vote the Democratic ticket. Resenting his actions, and perhaps harboring grudges from Lucas's time as a slave driver, a group of men, probably black Republicans, attacked him as he made his way home on election night, leaving him badly injured.

Once Lucas was in office, his Democratic patrons appointed two white assistants under him, ostensibly because he was illiterate and could not interpret the many legal contracts and deeds that it was his duty to administer. As the Democrats had intended, Lucas enjoyed a political position but no authority.

He at least had a salary, but he lost that on leaving office in 1880, at which time the Democratic Party controlled all but a handful of offices in Mississippi and no longer needed even token black representation. By then Lucas had lost all of the land that he had once owned and now rented only twenty acres, barely enough for him to subsist on. At that point Lucas disappears from the historical record.

Compared to many Mississippi freedmen, Bohlen Lucas enjoyed considerable advantages, not least of which were his close ties to economically powerful whites, which had begun under slavery. Along with his powerful ambition and work ethic, these ties initially enabled him to make good on his goal of owning his own land. Yet after Reconstruction those same qualities—ambition and overdependence on the good graces of whites—ultimately proved to be his undoing.

FURTHER READING

Genovese, Eugene. *Roll Jordan Roll: The World the Slaves Made* (1974).

Van Deburg, William L. *The Slave Drivers: Black Agricultural Labor Supervisors in the Antebellum South* (1979).

Willis, John C. *Forgotten Time: The Yazoo-Mississippi Delta after the Civil War* (2000).

STEVEN J. NIVEN

Lucas, C. Payne (14 Sept. 1933–), activist, writer, and author, was born Cleotha Payne Lucas in Spring Hope, near Rocky Mount in eastern North Carolina. One of fourteen children born to James Russell Lucas and Minnie Hendricks, Lucas worked from an early age shining shoes and picking cotton. Activism came early to Lucas, who became a member of the NAACP during his junior year of high school. Lucas became a youth representative and eventually organized a voter registration campaign in Spring Hope, at a time when few African Americans in eastern North Carolina were able to vote.

Following graduation from C. C. Spaulding High School in 1951, Lucas began classes at Maryland State College, now the University of Maryland Eastern Shore, in Princess Anne, Maryland. In 1953 Lucas left college and joined the U.S. Air Force, serving as a radio technician for four years and achieving the rank of airman. Lucas then returned to Maryland State College, graduating summa cum laude in 1959 with a Bachelor of Art degree in History. In 1961 Lucas earned a Master's degree in Government from the American University in Washington, D.C.

While pursuing his master's degree Lucas worked as an executive trainee for the Office of the United States Secretary of Defense.

Upon completing his master's degree Lucas worked as a research assistant for the Democratic National Committee and joined the Peace Corps at its inception serving under Director Sargent Shriver. Lucas worked for the Peace Corps from 1962 to 1971, working his way up in the organization. Lucas served as assistant country director for the Togolese Republic until 1964. During his tenure in the Togolese Republic, Lucas established a strong relationship with President Hamani Diori. Lucas served as country director for the Republic of Niger from 1964 to 1966. In 1967, based on his work in the Togolese Republic, Lucas was given the President's Award for Distinguished Federal Service by then U.S. President Lyndon Baines Johnson. Lucas served as director of the African Region from 1967 to 1969; as such he was responsible for the operation of Peace Corps offices of over twenty African countries. From 1969 to 1971 Lucas served as director of the office for returned volunteers, coordinating career opportunities and voluntary action programs for former Peace Crops volunteers. Lucas played a key role in the establishment of Peace Corps programs in Uganda and Kenya. Lucas was honored by the Peace Corps as one of the pioneers of the organization. He was awarded the Franklin H. Williams Peace Corps Director Award in 2002.

While working in Niger, Lucas met Dr. William O. Kirker, who founded and established the nonprofit organization Africare, incorporated in Hawaii in 1970. The organization took off when Lucas tried his hand at raising money to aid drought- and famine-stricken Africans. Not only did the wealthy contribute, but some of the poorest people and churches in Washington, D.C., raised money as well. In 1971, Africare was reincorporated in Washington, D.C. Lucas came on board as president and executive director, Dr. Kirker served on Africare's board, and Mr. Diori became Africare's chairman. Since its inception, Africare's focus has shifted from dealing with the realities of drought and offering financial assistance to fight it in Africa to agriculture projects and health care programs; it also assisted in the development of irrigation and water purification systems. In 1978 Africare expanded into South Africa, carefully working around apartheid to help those who too often were overlooked. Africare was able to assist the Ethiopians when they were hit by drought, and in the 1980s was instrumental in bringing the travails of the Somali refugees to worldwide attention. In 1984 President Ronald Reagan awarded Lucas the U.S. Presidential End Hunger Award for Outstanding Individual Achievement.

By the late 1980s Africare shifted its focus to battling the staggering numbers of individuals in Africa who suffered from HIV and AIDS. Efforts were made not only to provide health care, but to educate people as to the causes and ways to combat the spread of HIV and AIDS. In 1989 Africare's Career Development Internship began in South Africa. Under the program, black South Africans were placed in internships in the United States, thus exposing them to opportunities to acquire knowledge and experience they would never have been afforded under the apartheid system of South Africa. Part of the key to the continued success of Africare has been its ability to adapt to the changing needs of the continent of Africa. By the 1990s Africare was teaching poor farmers how to become successful entrepreneurs in Zambia, Zimbabwe, and Mozambique, as well as providing continued literacy programs and HIV/AIDS awareness programs across Africa. Other programs included planting of pest-resistant crops in Uganda and road-building to ensure crops could be sold at local markets. But by far, one of the biggest triumphs occurred in 1997, when Soweto became South Africa's first digital village.

One of Lucas's biggest skills was his ability to get people from all walks of life to contribute funding for programs. Donors include Saudi princes, the Bill and Melinda Gates Foundation, churches, and individuals from across the United States, some of whom could barely afford to give, but who gave because they saw a need greater than their own. Under Lucas's aegis over $710 million dollars was raised and used in support of projects in more than thirty-five African countries. In 2002 Lucas retired as president of Africare turning the reins over to former USAID worker and Africare board member Julies E. Coles. He continued to serve as a board member.

Upon leaving Africare, Lucas formed Lodestar Limited Liability Company (LLC), a consulting company, with his wife Freddie Hill Lucas. Lucas serves as chief executive officer, while Lucas's wife serves as president. Lucas also serves as senior advisor to AllAfrica Global Media, one of the largest providers of African news and information worldwide, and the AllAfrica Foundation, which strives bring to worldwide public attention to issues critical to African development.

While attending Maryland State College, Lucas met Freddie Emily Myra Hill who was working as a physical education teacher at the college. The couple married on 29 August 1964. Lucas has three children Therese, C. Payne Junior, and Hillary (Rouse), and one grandchild Walter Victor Rouse II. Lucas is an avid golfer and an active alumnus of the University of Maryland Eastern Shore not only as a donor but as a member of the University Board of Visitors. Lucas also holds the distinction of being the first African American to receive the Hubert H. Humphrey Public Service Award in 1991. Lucas is the author of *Keeping Kennedy's Promise: The Peace Corps' Moment of Truth* (1978), which discusses fundamental flaws of the Peace Corps.

FURTHER READING

Hamilton, Racine. *The HistoryMakers * Video Oral History Interview with C. Payne Lucas* (2004).

ANNE K. DRISCOLL

Lucas, Sam (7 Aug. 1840–15 Jan. 1916), singer, dancer, comedian, and songwriter, was born Samuel Milady in Washington Court House, Ohio. Nothing is known of his parents except, according to some sources, that they were ex-slaves. Known as the "dean of the Negro stage," Lucas was a multifaceted entertainer who was featured in many of the leading minstrel companies and musical plays of his age including Callender's Original Georgia Minstrels, The Hyers Sisters' *Out of Bondage*, Sam T. Jack's *The Creole Show*, and Cole and Johnson's *A Trip to Coontown*. He also was the first black actor to play the title role in a major stage production of *Uncle Tom's Cabin*, and the first African American to have a leading role in a motion picture.

When he was nineteen Lucas moved to Cincinnati, where he worked as a barber. He sang and played the guitar and soon began performing locally. During the Civil War he served with the Union Army. After the war he briefly attended Wilberforce University and taught school in New Orleans. His first professional show business job was as a guitarist and caller for Hamilton's Celebrated Colored Quadrille Band. Early in his career he also played guitar and sang on riverboats on the Ohio River.

The minstrel show was the most popular form of public entertainment in the mid-nineteenth century. Following the Civil War, a number of all-black minstrel troupes were launched, some of which became enormously popular with both black and white audiences. Capitalizing on his experiences as a riverboat entertainer, Lucas soon became a star of the minstrel circuit, performing with most of the leading black companies of the 1870s. He joined Lew Johnson's Plantation Minstrels in 1871 and two years later he moved to the renowned Callender's Original Georgia Minstrels as a ballad singer. In 1874 he was with Hart's Colored Minstrels. He joined Sprague's Georgia Minstrels in 1878 for a tour that included performances in Havana, Cuba. Lucas then rejoined Callender's company—which had been purchased in 1878 by the flamboyant minstrel entrepreneur J. H. Haverly—for a tour of the western states and, in 1881, a trip to England and Continental Europe.

In 1876 Lucas took a detour from minstrelsy to star in a groundbreaking production by the Hyers Sisters Comic Opera Company, *Out of Bondage*. The singers ANNA MADAH HYERS and EMMA LOUISE HYERS, who had achieved national acclaim for their concert performances, organized one of the first musical theater companies to perform black themed material outside the context of blackface minstrelsy (though never fully escaping minstrelsy's influence). *Out of Bondage* addressed the challenges faced by former slaves on the path to assimilation. Lucas rejoined the Hyers Sisters in 1879 to star in *Peculiar Sam; or, The Underground Railroad*, a musical play about runaway slaves by PAULINE HOPKINS, who later gained acclaim as a novelist and editor. *Peculiar Sam* was the first professional production of a play written by an African American woman. The play reportedly was written specifically to showcase Lucas's talents.

In 1878, Lucas became the first black actor to play Uncle Tom in a major theatrical adaptation of Harriet Beecher Stowe's novel, *Uncle Tom's Cabin*. Stage productions of *Uncle Tom's Cabin* were enormously popular in the later nineteenth century, but the leading black roles were played by white actors in blackface. Producers Charles and Gustave Frohman were searching for a gimmick to rescue a struggling theatrical troupe, and hit upon the idea of staging *Uncle Tom's Cabin* with a black actor in the title role. Apparently anticipating the show might run into trouble, Lucas reportedly was chosen for the role for his personal wealth—some of which he carried with him as a stash of diamonds—as much as for his considerable star appeal and his skills as an actor. Despite Lucas's fame with both black and white audiences, the show did poorly, and Lucas indeed was forced to pawn his diamonds to bail out the stranded troupe. Lucas subsequently played Uncle Tom in

other theatrical productions, including a Hyers Sisters production in which all the black characters were played by African Americans. A bizarre "Double Mammoth" Uncle Tom production starring Lucas in 1882 featured an integrated cast and two performers for some key roles (two Topsys, two Marks, etc.).

Lucas also was renowned as a songwriter, although he did not write all the songs published under his name. Many of the songs attributed to him, such as "Hanna, Boil Dat Cabbage Down" and "Dars a Lock on the Chicken Coop Door," were associated with the minstrel show or were in the "coon song" mold, but some, such as the "Shivering and Shaking out in the Cold," had no specific racial references. One of the most popular and enduring songs attributed to Lucas, "Carve Dat Possum," probably was written by the minstrel performer and songwriter Henry Hart, who sometimes worked with Lucas. Lyrics of songs made popular by Lucas were published in *Sam Lucas' Plantation Songster* (1875) and *Sam Lucas' Careful Man Songster* (1881).

Lucas frequently performed with his second wife, the singer, cornet soloist, and violinist Carrie Melvin Lucas. Between major shows, the coupled toured steadily, performing in venues ranging from lowly dime museums to leading vaudeville theaters. During the rare periods when they were not on the road, the Lucases lived in Boston. Sam formed various short-lived groups, with names such as the Sam Lucas Concert Company, the Sam Lucas Jubilee Concert Company, the Hub Concert Company, and the Colored Ideal Jubilee Concert Company, for performances around the city. The Lucases were on an extended tour of the western states when, in 1880, a daughter was born in Denver. Marie Lucas grew up to become a highly regarded arranger and bandleader.

Lucas pitched the idea of an all-black variety review to the white impresario Sam T. Jack in 1889, and the following year *The Creole Show* had its first performance in Haverhill, Massachusetts. Though it did not stray far from minstrel show conventions, it was noteworthy for replacing men with women in some of the standard minstrel show roles, for its chorus line of sixteen dancers, and for presenting a broader array of African American characters and personalities than was typical of minstrel shows. Performances included sketches, songs, dances, and specialty numbers. Lucas recruited some of the top African American performers of the era, including Carrie Lucas, for the troupe. He appeared in the show as the featured comedian. The successful show ran for seven seasons, though both Sam and Carrie left in 1893.

The 1890s witnessed an explosion of black musical theater, and Lucas had leading roles in many of the major productions. Both Sam and Carrie were featured in *Darkest America*, produced by the white minstrel impresario Al G. Field, in 1896. In 1897–1898 Lucas toured with the Black Patti Troubadours, a variety troupe led by the soprano MADAME SISSIERETTA JOYNER JONES, known as "The Black Patti" in reference to Italian opera singer Adelina Patti. In 1898 he starred in *A Trip to Coontown*, written and produced by Bob Cole and Billy Johnson. Despite a title that is offensive to modern sensibilities, the production was a milestone in African American theater. Featuring some of the leading performers of the time, the show was notable for substantially dispensing with minstrel show conventions. Lucas played Silas Green, the Grand Old Man of Coontown.

Sam and Carrie were divorced by 1899, and she apparently retired from show business. Lucas continued to perform in vaudeville as a solo act and with various female partners. He remained a box office draw, and he was recruited to perform in some of the leading black musical comedies of the first decade of the twentieth century. Lucas toured with Ernest Hogan's *Rastus Rufus* in 1905. In 1906 he was a popular and critical success in his role as Brother Doless in Cole & Johnson's *Shoo Fly Regiment*, which concerned black soldiers in the Spanish-American War. His last major show was Cole & Johnson's *The Red Moon* in 1909.

Lucas retired in 1912, but he returned to show business in 1914 to become the first African American to have a leading role in a motion picture. He agreed to again play Uncle Tom in a full length film directed by William Walter Daly. The script called for his character to jump into a river to save Little Eva. According to Tom Fletcher, a minstrel show and vaudeville performer who worked from time to time with Lucas, while filming the scene he came down with a cold, which he never shook off and which eventually led to his death from pneumonia. "That was the final curtain of a great trouper," wrote Fletcher, "the dean of the colored performers in my book" (p. 76). Others were similarly unstinting in praise for his achievements, "The death of Sam Lucas," James Weldon Johnson wrote, "removes from the theatrical profession the man with the longest and, perhaps, most varied career of all colored performers who have made their reputations in this country" (Johnson and Wilson, p. 126).

FURTHER READING
Johnson, James Weldon, and Wilson, Sondra K. (ed.), *The Selected Writings of James Weldon Johnson, Vol. 1: The New York Age Editorials (1914–1923)* (1995).
Johnson, James Weldon. *Black Manhattan* (1930, reprint 1991).
Fletcher, Tom. *100 Years of the Negro in Show Business* (1954).
Hill, Errol G, and James V. Hatch. A *History of African American Theatre* (2003).
Southern, Eileen. *The Music of Black Americans: A History* (1971).

DAVID K. BRADFORD

Lunceford, Jimmie (6 June 1902–12 July 1947), jazz and popular bandleader, was born James Melvin Lunceford in Fulton, Missouri, the son of a choirmaster. His parents' names are unknown. Before Jimmie enrolled in high school, his family moved to Denver, Colorado, where he studied reed instruments, flute, guitar, and trombone under Wilberforce James Whiteman, the father of Paul Whiteman. Lunceford first worked professionally in the society dance orchestra of the violinist GEORGE MORRISON, with whom he traveled to New York City in 1922 for performances at the Carlton Terrace and for recordings. Soon afterward he entered Fisk University in Nashville, Tennessee, where he excelled at basketball, football, and track while earning a bachelor's degree in Music Education (c. 1926). During summer vacations he worked with Deacon Johnson's band in New York, and early in 1926 he was regularly with the band of the banjoist ELMER SNOWDEN at the Bamville Club in Harlem, playing saxophone and trombone alongside the pianist COUNT BASIE and the trumpeter BUBBER MILEY.

After taking some graduate courses at the City College of New York, Lunceford went to Memphis, Tennessee, in fall 1926 to teach physical education and music at Manassa High School; in Memphis he organized a jazz band that included the bassist Moses Allen and the drummer Jimmy Crawford. During the summers of 1928 and 1929 they played in Lakeside, Ohio, and during the 1929 season the band included the alto saxophonist and singer Willie Smith, the pianist Ed Wilcox, the trombonist and singer Henry Wells (all three having been Fisk students), along with Allen and Crawford. Wilcox also recalled summer engagements at Belmar, New Jersey, and the following year at Asbury Park, New Jersey, the years unspecified. In Memphis the group played professionally at the Hotel Men's

Jimmie Lunceford, jazz and popular music bandleader, New York City, c. August 1946. (© William P. Gottlieb; www. jazzphotos.com.)

Improvement Club Dance Hall and the Silver Slipper nightclub, broadcasting on WREC from the Silver Slipper.

Lunceford finally abandoned education for entertainment. Around 1929 or 1930 the band suffered through an early winter in Cleveland, Ohio, struggling for work. They found a job in Cincinnati, Ohio, and in June 1930 recorded as the Chickasaw Syncopators. After touring in 1931, Lunceford made Buffalo, New York, the group's home base for about three years. In 1932 two additional Fisk alumni joined, the trumpeter Paul Webster and the baritone saxophonist Earl Carruthers. In summer 1933 the band performed at the Caroga Lake resort in upstate New York, and that year Lunceford hired the trumpeter Tommy Stevenson and the man who became his finest soloist, the tenor saxophonist JOE THOMAS.

Up to this point the group had been structured as a cooperative held among Smith, Wilcox, and Lunceford, but when Harold F. Oxley took over management of the band in 1933, questions of business reverted to Lunceford and Oxley alone. By mid-decade the two men had expanded their domain with Lunceford Artists, Inc., managing other orchestras as well as their own.

The arranger, trumpeter, and singer SY OLIVER joined the band in Buffalo, shortly before an engagement at the Lafayette Theatre in Harlem in September 1933. The performance was a disaster, this being the first time that Lunceford's men had played for a choreographed show rather than for dancing, but they survived the experience, toured New England, and returned to New York to record their first well-received recordings, "White Heat" and "Jazznocracy," and more significantly, to follow CAB CALLOWAY's big band as the resident group at the Cotton Club. By January 1934 the trumpeter and singer Eddie Thompkins (often misspelled Tompkins) joined; he was another of Lunceford's men who doubled as a glee club singer in the band.

Lunceford's men broadcast nightly from the Cotton Club for roughly half a year. The band then embarked on years of regular national touring—as well as a Scandinavian tour in February 1937— while recording prolifically. Three titles associated with DUKE ELLINGTON, including Smith's arrangements of "Sophisticated Lady" and "Mood Indigo," show off the virtuosity of the saxophone section and show the band's strong independence from Ellington's conception (other bands of that era having found it quite difficult to perform Ellington's music in an original manner). For this same session of September 1934 Lunceford himself made a rare contribution, his zany and technically demanding composition "Stratosphere." In general his musical involvement was directed toward inspiration and organization rather than the nuts and bolts of playing and writing.

Later sessions exemplify the band's bouncy dance music, including Oliver's arrangements of his own composition "Stomp It Off," Wilcox's arrangement of "Rhythm Is Our Business" (1934), and Oliver's versions of the popular songs "Four or Five Times," "My Blue Heaven" (1935), and "Organ Grinder's Swing" (1936). The band may be seen in action in the film short *Jimmie Lunceford and His Dance Orchestra* (1936).

The arranger, trombonist, and guitarist Eddie Durham had joined in 1935 and contributed scores to the band, but without making the impact that he earlier had with BENNIE MOTEN and later had with Basie. In the fall of 1937 the trombonist TRUMMY YOUNG replaced Durham, and the alto saxophonist Ted Buckner joined; both men are featured on "Margie" (1938). Further hits by Oliver included his compositions and arrangements of "For Dancers Only" (1937) and "Le Jazz Hot" (1939), as well as his arrangement of "'Tain't What You Do (It's the Way That You Do It)" (1939). In 1937 Lunceford married Crystal Tally.

In 1939 Snooky Young replaced Thompkins, and late that year Lunceford was featured with Smith on "Uptown Blues." In mid-1939 the trumpeter GERALD WILSON and the arranger Billy Moore collectively took Oliver's place, and Moore soon gave Lunceford a hit record with his version of "What's Your Story, Morning Glory?" (1940). In its last great moment, Lunceford's orchestra was featured in the movie *Blues in the Night* (1941), the movie's title track providing a hit song for Lunceford and others, including Woody Herman, Jo Stafford with Tommy Dorsey, and HOT LIPS PAGE with Artie Shaw.

By 1940 Lunceford's men were discontented. Crawford claimed that Oxley doled out insufficient salaries. Moore complained that Lunceford routinely appropriated royalty rights for his arrangers' scores, and that Lunceford and Oxley paid the band as little as possible:He was an inspiring leader, from a distance, and he did mould his men into a most effective orchestra; he kept the men on their toes and maintained a fine public image. But he failed to reward the musicians who were mostly responsible for his huge success.... Meanwhile Lunceford bought himself a Lincoln Continental, and then his own plane, which he piloted. (Feather, 170, 172)Considering these and other remembrances, the writer Albert McCarthy speculated that "no musicians of any other major band of the swing era seem to have received such parsimonious salaries as those who worked with Lunceford." Snooky Young, Moses Allen, Smith, and Wilson quit in 1942, and Crawford and Trummy Young quit in 1943. The band continued for several years, but the spark was gone. While signing autographs at a music store in Seaside, Oregon, Lunceford collapsed and soon died of a heart attack. Wilcox and Thomas, and then Wilcox alone, kept the group going for nearly three years before it finally split up permanently.

Lunceford's big band may be rated a notch below the greatest ensembles of the swing era, owing to the absence of highly original improvisers or a consistently original approach to arrangement (Oliver's best scores excepted). The group excelled in its delivery of a relaxed swing beat for dancing, in its presentation of novelty vocal trios (usually sung by Wells, Smith, and Oliver) that became very popular with college students (especially "My Blue Heaven"), and, above all, in its showmanship. The writer George T. Simon reports that among twenty-eight bands playing fifteen-minute sets at the Manhattan Center on 18 November 1940—including the bands of Benny Goodman, Glenn Miller, Count Basie, Les Brown, and Guy Lombardo—Lunceford's band was the only one given such an overwhelming reception that they played beyond their allotted time. They owed this success to their superior antics:

> The trumpets would throw their horns in the air together; the saxes would almost charge off the stage; … the trombones would slip their slides toward the skies; and … the musicians would be kidding and shouting at one another, projecting an aura of irresistible exuberance (Simon, 329).

FURTHER READING

Some Lunceford items are in the Sy Oliver Collection at the New York Public Library for the Performing Arts, Lincoln Center.

Dance, Stanley. *The World of Swing* (1974).

Feather, Leonard. *The Jazz Years: Earwitness to an Era* (1986).

Garrod, Charles. *Jimmie Lunceford and His Orchestra* (1990).

Hoefer, George. "Hot Box: Jimmie Lunceford," *Down Beat* (24 Sept. 1964).

Schuller, Gunther. *The Swing Era: The Development of Jazz, 1930–1945* (1989).

Simon, George T. *The Big Bands* (1974).

Obituary: *New York Times*, 14 July 1947.

This entry is taken from the *American National Biography* and is published here with the permission of the American Council of Learned Societies.

BARRY KERNFELD

Luper, Clara (3 May 1923–8 June 2011), teacher, activist, and writer, was born Clara Sheppard, one of five children born to Ezell and Isabel Sheppard in Okfuskee County, Oklahoma. Violence against blacks and segregation practices were common at that time in rural Oklahoma. Luper's parents were devout Christians who taught their children to love their enemies and anticipate a better America. Ezell Sheppard was a World War I veteran who drove a school bus, picked crops in segregated fields, and worked in a variety of other trades. Isabel Sheppard worked as a maid for white families.

Clara Luper attended Hoffman Elementary, a one-room school where students shared books discarded from white schools. The teacher was also the principal and the janitor. Even as a young child Luper's oratory was impressive. By age eight, she often ended regular church services by reading

Clara Luper on Mar. 1, 2006 in Oklahoma City, Okla.
(AP Images.)

aloud to the congregation. In 1940 she graduated from Grayson High School, then became the first member of her family to attend college. Luper enrolled at Langston University, a black institution in Langston, Oklahoma, in 1940. She joined the NAACP and the Zeta Phi Beta sorority, developing connections that eventually became her financial and intellectual support system during the Oklahoma City sit-ins. At Langston, Luper learned that preparation was necessary before black people could participate fully in American society; she graduated in 1944 with a B.A. degree in Mathematics. She married Bert Luper, an independent electrical contractor, shortly after graduating from Langston. Their first child, Calvin, was born in 1946 and their second, Marilyn, was born in 1947, both would be important figures during the Oklahoma City sit-ins. While married to Bert Luper she balanced the demands of matrimony and motherhood, beginning her career as a classroom teacher, earning her M.A. in Education from the University of Oklahoma, and initiating her role as a civil rights leader. Her marriage ended in divorce during the height of the Oklahoma City sit-in campaign sometime around 1960.

In January 1957 Luper became the Oklahoma City NAACP youth council advisor. She wrote and directed a play about MARTIN LUTHER KING JR. and the philosophy of non-violence. The NAACP youth council performed "Brother President" that May for Negro History Week. A national NAACP representative saw the play and invited the group to come to New York to perform at an upcoming NAACP rally. In St. Louis they experienced their first integrated meal and continued to enjoy integrated services throughout their stay in New York. The trip changed the group forever; returning home

they immediately began negotiations to desegregate public accommodations in Oklahoma City.

Luper had a talent for organizing and inspiring young people. She told them they had a responsibility to become engaged in the struggle for civil rights. After writing letters and asking businesses to integrate for more than a year, the group voted to take action. On 19 August 1958 the NAACP youth, ages six through seventeen, staged a sit-in at Katz Drug Store in Oklahoma City. The police and the press watched as white patrons threatened and insulted the group, but the NAACP youth followed "Martin Luther King's Non-Violent Plans," the foundation of their non-violence training (Luper, 10). Over the next six years Luper led the NAACP youth and hundreds of their supporters through non-violence training workshops, sit-ins, lay-ins, marches, and a boycott. They were spit on, stepped on, slapped, arrested, and once even attacked by a chimpanzee but remained non-violent. The chimpanzee belonged to a "sockless white man" from Stillwater, Oklahoma who warned that the animal had been "trained to bite niggers" (Luper, 139-140). Luper consistently employed creative and dramatic tactics, including staging a funeral procession for Jim Crow; attracting Charlton Heston, the Oscar-winning actor best known for his role as Moses in Cecil B. DeMille's film, *The Ten Commandments* (1956), to lead an Oklahoma City march; and allowing herself to be arrested twenty-six times. One by one, many establishments integrated as a direct result of the pressure from the sit-ins. On 2 June 1964, a month before the U.S. Congress passed the Civil Rights Act of 1964, the city council passed a public accommodations ordinance requiring the holdout restaurants to integrate. On 3 July 1964 the Oklahoma City sit-in campaign declared victory after testing a handful of restaurants and reporting that blacks had been served at each establishment.

Luper became part of the national NAACP network through her Langston University connections. In 1951 she became the first African American to graduate from the social sciences department at the University of Oklahoma. Ada Lois Sipuel had paved the way for blacks to enter the University of Oklahoma when the U.S. Supreme Court ruled in her favor in *Sipuel v. Board of Regents* (1948). THURGOOD MARSHALL and Amos Hall represented Sipuel. Luper befriended Hall and Sipuel at Langston and eventually developed a regular correspondence with Marshall. ROSCOE DUNJEE was an early leader in the Oklahoma NAACP, a Langston graduate, and founder of the *Black Dispatch*, an

Oklahoma City newspaper. Luper considered Dunjee a trusted mentor and the *Black Dispatch* provided crucial support for the NAACP Youth. In 1959 Ezell Blair attended the NAACP national convention, where he heard Luper speak about the Oklahoma City sit-ins. In 1960 Blair participated in a sit-in in Greensboro, North Carolina, often described as the first civil rights sit-in. Luper marched with Martin Luther King Jr. at Selma, Alabama, and the youth council filled two buses for the 1963 March on Washington. She maintained a lifetime friendship with the King family. The Oklahoma City NAACP youth council was voted best in the nation many times under Luper's guidance. Despite her success with the youth, there were occasional tensions between Luper and the state and national NAACP leadership usually over tactics and perceived negative publicity.

Luper's civil rights work continued after the sit-ins ended. On 4 July 1966, she led a 100-mile march from Oklahoma City to Lawton, Oklahoma. The marchers wanted to integrate Lawton's Doe Doe Amusement Park for the soldiers at Fort Sill who were training to fight in Vietnam. In March 1968 Luper founded the Freedom Center, a new home for the NAACP youth. When King was assassinated in April of that year, associates of the Freedom Center patrolled Oklahoma City to prevent rioting. Tensions were high in both black and white communities; Luper received many anonymous threats and the center was bombed in September. Most of the meticulous records kept during the sit-ins were lost, but the center was quickly rebuilt. In 1969 Luper led the Oklahoma City sanitation strike and a citywide Fair Housing Ordinance was passed. In 1971 she began hosting the Miss Black Oklahoma Pageant, and in 1972 she ran unsuccessfully for the U.S. Senate. In 1976 she adopted Chelle Luper, and the following year she married C. P. Wilson, a truck driver from Oklahoma City. *Behold the Walls*, an autobiographical account of her civil rights work, was published in 1979. After a barrier-breaking and distinguished career as a classroom teacher, Luper retired in 1989. She continued working as a public speaker, facilitating the Miss Black Oklahoma pageant, and hosting her Oklahoma City radio show which first aired in the 1950s on the black-owned station KAEZ. Luper's show was later broadcast on KYBE and she hosted "The Clara Luper Radio Show" on KTLV. In 2006 she began raising money to build an African American history plaza at the Oklahoma State Capital, dedicating the effort to the memory of Coretta Scott King, and in 2007 she was inducted into the Oklahoma Hall of Fame. Luper died at her home in Oklahoma City at the age of 88.

FURTHER READING

Luper, Clara. *Behold the Walls* (1979)

Graves, Carl R. "The Right to Be Served: Oklahoma City's Lunch Counter Sit-ins, 1958–1964," *Chronicles of Oklahoma* 59 (1981).

Reese, Linda Williams. "Clara Luper and the Civil Rights Movement in Oklahoma City, 1958–1964," in *African American Women Confront the West, 1600–2000*, ed. Quintard Taylor and Shirley Ann Wilson Moore (2003).

Obituary: *New York Times*. 11 June 2011.

STEFANIE COLE

Lutcher, Nellie (15 Oct. 1915–8 June 2007), singer and pianist, was born Nellie Rose Lutcher in Lake Charles, Louisiana, the third of fifteen children of Isaac Lutcher, a well-known bass player, and Suzie Garrett, a homemaker who briefly studied piano. Through her parents' influence Lutcher started playing the piano at age six and within two years had acquired enough skill to perform for the congregation at her church, New Sunlight Baptist.

To help Lutcher further develop her musical talents her father formed a family band in which Lutcher played piano. She quit school when she was fourteen to play in the family band; in one performance in 1929 she worked with MA RAINEY. A year later she and her father started playing weekend performances with Clarence Hart's Imperial Band. This opportunity led Lutcher to tour with the Southern Rhythm Boys of New Orleans. The group toured throughout Louisiana and Texas before they encountered financial and creative difficulties in Mississippi and disbanded. Following the example of CLEO BROWN, a well-known Los Angeles singer and pianist, Lutcher decided to go to California. Arriving there at the age of twenty, Lutcher quickly found employment as a pianist at the Dunbar Hotel, a popular venue for black performers. She earned two dollars a night, plus tips. Responding to audience requests, she also started to sing while playing and quickly found that listeners enjoyed her distinctive and throaty voice, her jazz scatting, and her rhythm and blues harmonies. In 1936 Lutcher married Leonel Lewis; they later had a son, Talmadge Lewis. After playing at the Dunbar and other local hotels, Lutcher performed with Dootsie Williams and the Chocolate Drops in San Diego. She returned to Los Angeles

Nellie Lutcher performs in New York City, c. 1947. Lutcher gained her greatest recognition playing a jazz-inflected rhythm and blues. (© William P. Gottlieb; www.jazzphotos.com.)

in the 1940s to work at the prestigious Club Bali and later the Club Royale, where she stayed for three years and worked with the notable musicians DEXTER GORDON and Lee Young. Lutcher also gained fame by singing on NAT KING COLE's record *Jazz Encounters* (1945).

Lutcher's big opportunity came in 1947 when she was given a prime spot to sing "The One I Love Belongs to Somebody Else" on a March of Dimes benefit show. The radio broadcast of the show caught the attention of Dave Dexter, a representative of Capitol Records, who had previously heard Lutcher's voice on demo songs with her brother, the saxophonist and singer Joe Woodman Lutcher. Impressed by Lutcher's talent, Dexter signed her to a recording contract with Capitol. On 10 April 1947 Lutcher recorded her first single, "Hurry on Down." The song sold very well and received airplay on jazz, rhythm and blues, and pop radio stations. Fans praised Lutcher's originality of composition and her rhythmic piano arrangements. Later that year Lutcher had another hit song with "Real Gone Guy," a composition of her own that blended blues with witty lyrics.

The accolades continued for Lutcher with her next single "Fine Brown Frame," in 1948. She also recorded a novel version of the pop song "My Mother's Eyes," which utilized blues, jazz, and pop and had widespread appeal. The follow-up singles

"The Song Is Ended (But the Melody Lingers On)," "The One I Love," "The Pig Latin Song," "I Thought about You," and "Imagine You Having Eyes for Me" also received critical acclaim and reached the pop charts. Lutcher's career had reached its zenith. She gave several sold-out performances, including at the Apollo Theater, and formed a trio band to tour the United States and Canada.

As a result of the 1948 Musicians' Union ban on musical recording, Lutcher's singing slowed down. By 1949 she had resumed her musical career and worked at New York's prestigious Café Society. In 1951 her manager Carlos Gastel, who also represented Nat King Cole, arranged for her to tour with Cole in Britain. Meanwhile Lutcher continued recording songs and experimented with the famous Billy May Orchestra on the singles "I Want To Be Near You" and "The Birth of the Blues." Even though Lutcher's songs were popular, her record sales gradually fell and Capitol released her contract in 1952. For the next several years she recorded songs for the Columbia, Liberty, and Imperial labels, but public interest continued to wane. Lutcher retired from performance in 1957 and worked various staff jobs at the Los Angeles Local 47 of the American Federation of Musicians until 1973.

Lutcher returned to performing in 1973 when Barney Josephson, the former owner of the Café Society, offered her a job in his New York restaurant, the Cookery. She accepted, and her appearance there led to performances in numerous clubs throughout the 1970s and 1980s. The 1990s found Lutcher working regularly at California's Vine Street Bar and Grill and the Hollywood Roosevelt Cinegrill. Between performances Lutcher served as a member of the board of directors with the musicians' union of Los Angeles and as manager and owner of an apartment building in California.

To the delight of her fans, *The Best of Nellie Lutcher* CD was released in 1995. Lutcher's timeless talent also led President George H. W. Bush and then-presidental candidate Bill Clinton to extend their congratulations on her eightieth birthday. In that same year her hometown of Lake Charles declared a Nellie Lutcher Day and gave her the key to the city. Lutcher's next significant honor came in 2001 when she received the Jazz Mentorship Award in honor of her lifetime of musical achievement.

Even after her death in Los Angeles, Lutcher's distinctive voice and swing-style rhythms on the piano continued to influence new generations of jazz and blues musicians and listeners.

FURTHER READING

Handy, D. Antoinette. *Black Women in American Bands and Orchestras* (1981).

Kinkle, Roger. *The Complete Encyclopedia of Popular Music and Jazz, 1900–1950* (1974).

DORSÍA SMITH SILVA

Lyle, Ethel Octavia Hedgeman (10 Feb. 1887–28 Nov. 1950), founder of the Alpha Kappa Alpha Sorority, Incorporated, was born in St. Louis, Missouri, one of three daughters of Albert Hedgeman, a community builder who worked for the YMCA, and Maria (Hubbard) Hedgeman, a teacher and homemaker. Her family's ancestry was regarded by longtime Alpha Kappa Alpha Sorority historian Marjorie Parker as "distinguished" (Parker, 21): her paternal grandfather, born in 1824, was an African Methodist Episcopal (AME) minister who helped establish churches from St. Paul, Minnesota, to Denver, Colorado; her maternal grandfather escaped slavery to participate as a Union soldier in the Civil War and became one of the founding members of the historically black Lincoln University in Missouri.

Lyle graduated from St. Louis's Sumner High School in 1904 and received that school's first scholarship to Howard University in Washington, D.C. She attended Howard for a year before withdrawing for one academic year because of an illness. While there, she was active in the university choir, Christian Endeavor, drama productions, and the YWCA.

Lyle was encouraged to develop a sorority by Ethel Robinson, her white counselor at Howard who was a native of Providence, Rhode Island, and had graduated from that city's Brown University where she had participated in sorority activities. Convening eight other Howard women in January 1908, Lyle established the first sorority for African American women. In addition to being the originator, she worked with Margaret Flagg and Lavinia Norman to finalize the organization's constitution, drafted by LUCY DIGGS SLOWE, and designed the ivy leaf, inscribed with AKA as its symbol. After Slowe, the only senior in the new organization, became its first president, Lyle was elected president in fall 1908. After graduating in 1909 with a B.A. in English and Liberal Arts, Lyle moved to Eufaula, Oklahoma, to teach and stayed there until 1910. She was recognized as the first college-trained black woman to teach in a normal school in Oklahoma, and in 1910 the first to receive a Life Teacher's Certificate from the state Department of Education. For the 1910–1911 school year, she taught at a public school in Centralia, Illinois.

On 21 June 1911 she married George Lyle in New York City. They had been students together at Howard, where George Lyle was a member of Alpha Phi Alpha fraternity. Immediately after their marriage they moved to Philadelphia, Pennsylvania, where her husband became a high school principal. They had one son, George Lyle Jr.

In Philadelphia, Lyle founded the Mother's Club of the City, was a charter member of the West Philadelphia League of Women Voters, and was a member of the Republican Women's Committee of Ward 40. In 1937 she was appointed chair of the Mayor's Committee of One Hundred Women and charged with planning the sesquicentennial of the adoption of the Constitution. In addition to her civic and social activities, Lyle also attended graduate school at both the University of Pennsylvania and Temple University.

Lyle resumed her teaching career in Philadelphia, where she taught English in the public schools from 1921 until she retired in 1948. She remained active in her sorority and supported many chapters in addition to growth on a national level. She was a charter member of the Mu Chapter (established in 1922 in Philadelphia) and in 1923 was elected Supreme Tamiouchos, or national treasurer, a position that she held until 1946. She also was a founder and Basileus (president) of the Omega Omega Graduate Chapter (established in 1926) in Philadelphia.

Lyle was named Honorary Supreme Basileus, or national president, by Alpha Kappa Alpha in 1926 and held the honor until her death in Philadelphia in 1950. No other member has been awarded this honor. Lyle was honored many times over the years and was recognized for beginning a sorority that had fifty-eight chapters by 1928, and on the eve of the 100th anniversary had more than 170,000 sorority members. The Ethel Hedgeman Lyle Endowment Fund of the Alpha Kappa Alpha Sorority was named in her honor and at the 1958 Golden Anniversary Boule in Washington, D.C., her two granddaughters were awarded a $1,000 scholarship to attend the college and follow in their grandmother's footsteps. Beginning in January 2008, Alpha Kappa Alpha would hold local, regional, and national celebrations to commemorate 100 years of "service to all mankind" that began with Lyle's vision for virtuous women.

FURTHER READING

Issues of the *Alpha Kappa Alpha Ivy Leaf* are held by at the Moorland-Spingarn Research Center, Howard University, Washington, D.C.

Brown, Tamara L., Gregory S. Parks, and Clarenda M. Phillips, eds. *African American Fraternities and Sororities: The Legacy and the Vision* (2005).

Evans, Stephanie Y. *Black Women in the Ivory Tower, 1850–1954: An Intellectual History* (2007).

McNealy, Ernestine. *Pearls of Service: The Legacy of America's First Black Sorority, Alpha Kappa Alpha.* (2006).

Parker, Marjorie H. *Past is Prologue: The History of Alpha Kappa Alpha, 1908–1999* (1999).

Ross, Lawrence C., Jr. *The Divine Nine: The History of African American Fraternities and Sororities* (2000).

STEPHANIE Y. EVANS

Lymon, Frankie (30 Sept. 1942–27 Feb. 1967), singer, was born Frank Joseph Lymon in Washington Heights, New York City, to Jeannette and Howard Lymon. His father was a truck driver and part-time vocalist with a group called the Harlemaires. At twelve Lymon joined his brothers Lewis and Howie in a group they had formed called the Harlemaires Jr. While working as a grocery clerk in Harlem in 1954 and practicing drums with his brother at Stitt Junior High School, Lymon joined another group that called itself either the Ermines or the Premiers, or sometimes the Coupe de Villes. Lymon sang backup and duets with the group, which included Jimmy Merchant, Sherman Garnes, Herman Santiago, and Joe Negroni.

Exactly how the group was "discovered" is the subject of some conjecture. According to the most romantic version, the Premiers practiced under the apartment window of Richard Barrett, lead singer of a group called the Valentines, leading him to introduce them to the record producer George Goldner so that they could sing in a studio rather than on Barrett's street corner. The group auditioned for Goldner, who especially liked "Why do Birds Sing So Gay," which he renamed "Why Do Fools Fall in Love?" Session saxophone player Jimmy Wright suggested the new group name, the Teenagers, and Lymon moved from harmony to become the lead singer of the group.

The origin of the group's most famous song also has several versions. The original title, "Why Do Birds Sing So Gay," represented the common thread. One story claimed the verse came from a poem written by a girlfriend of a tenant in the apartment building where the group practiced.

Another popular account suggested that Lymon wrote the lyrics after a failed relationship at school, which is the kind of story that music promoters often concocted for use in teen magazines. Lymon also claimed to have written the lyrics as part of a school assignment. According to yet another story, a member of the Premiers singing group found a letter including that phrase and gave it to Lymon. While the song's origins remain murky, a 1992 court decision granted publishing rights to group members Merchant and Santiago, and Lymon's last wife.

In 1955 the single, "Why Do Fools Fall in Love," topped the rhythm and blues chart and entered at number six on the pop chart, eventually selling over two million records. The group released three more singles in 1956: "I Want You to Be My Girl," "I Promise to Remember," and the "ABC's of Love" and all made the top fifty on the charts. The Teenagers suddenly were a hit recording act. Alan Freed invited the group to record songs for his 1956 movie *Rock, Rock, Rock*. The songs recorded for the movie did not sell well in the United States but they were popular in England, so Goldner booked the group on a tour of the United Kingdom in 1957. Their "doo-wop" style of music became an instant hit with fans. The harmonies were tight, and the lyrics often included a series of repeating sounds such as "de (or di) doom wop" or "doe doe." The Teenagers Featuring Frankie Lymon, as the group was now called, was one of the first of its kind and, briefly, the top doo-wop artists in the world.

At the height of their popularity, the Teenagers toured Panama and Europe, made movie and television appearances, and performed for Great Britain's Princess Margaret in a private audience. During his time in London, Lymon made solo recordings that were later released in the United States as group efforts, even though none of the other members had participated.

A new single, "Goody, Goody," was released in 1957 under the name of Frankie Lymon and the Teenagers and reached number twenty on the R&B charts. While the Teenagers were credited, the actual backup personnel for Lymon during the session that produced the song remains a matter of debate. New managers groomed Lymon for adult material, while the Teenagers continued to record adolescent pop without him on the same record label. His popularity as a solo artist lasted nearly two years, but the results, in hindsight, were sporadic. Although he recorded three more albums, his voice began to change in 1958, causing some concern amongst record producers who no longer considered him a marketable commodity. Perhaps unable to handle his sudden rise to fame and its just-as-sudden demise, Lymon increasingly turned to drugs, particularly as his recordings became more infrequent and his performances less in demand. Bob Redcross, his new manager, helped him to enter a drug rehabilitation program for a habit that had begun in 1956 and had expanded to heroin by 1959. Lymon was in the news again in the mid-1960s, after a highly publicized arrest, his second related to drugs. He entered into a brief marriage with Elizabeth Waters in 1964. The following year he married Zola Taylor, lead singer of the popular singing group the Platters (although some accounts claim his marriage to Taylor took place in 1959). Lymon soon left her to enlist in the military, later marrying Emira Eagle in Augusta, Georgia in 1967. He received a dishonorable discharge from the military that same year. In 1968 his new manager Sam Bray appeared to have him poised for a comeback with a recording session scheduled with Roulette Records in New York City, but one day before the session Lymon died from a heroin overdose.

Lymon came back into the popular culture with a 1998 biographical film and hit recordings of "Fools" by James Taylor, Joni Mitchell, and DIANA ROSS. Without doubt, he influenced many who followed in the late 1950s and early 1960s, including such groups as the Jackson 5, with the young MICHAEL JACKSON singing in a Lymon-inspired falsetto lead. Many of the all-male vocal groups of the 1980s and 1990s, such as Boyz II Men, used Teenagers-style arrangements for their harmonies.

Frankie Lymon was the first international black teenage singing star and was inducted into the Rock and Roll Hall of Fame in 1993 and the Vocal Group Hall of Fame in 2000.

FURTHER READING

Warner, Jay. *The De Capo Book of American Singing Groups* (2000).

DISCOGRAPHY

Frankie Lymon and The Teenagers: The Complete Recordings (Bear Family).

PAMELA LEE GRAY

Lynch, Damon, III (18 Mar. 1960–), pastor, community organizer, and activist, was born in Cincinnati, Ohio, the son of Damon Lynch Jr., a pastor and store owner, and Barbara (Davis) Lynch, a former American Airlines reservations supervisor. As a somewhat rebellious and easily bored teen at a boys' parochial school, Lynch ran into opposition when the priests insisted that he shave his facial hair. Lynch bounced from high school to high school before eventually graduating from Woodward High School. Summer jobs in his father's store gave Lynch important entrepreneurial experience that he later drew upon to establish nonprofit organizations in low-income communities. After graduation Lynch held several jobs, including a stint at the United Parcel Service (UPS) where he was taught a serious work ethic. At Burke Marketing and Research, Lynch met his future wife, Johanna Bolden, who also happened to be his on-the-job trainer. The couple married on 3 July 1982, and they later had two sons.

Lynch was also trained as a community organizer through a program called DART (Direct Action and Research Training) in Miami, Florida. At DART his eyes were opened to police misconduct, the need for education reform, and numerous challenges relevant to low-income neighborhoods. Lynch was also the first lead organizer for United Churches Active in Neighborhoods (UCAN).

In 1999 Lynch put his entrepreneurial experience to good use by forming the nonprofit New Prospect Development Corporation (NPDC) in Cincinnati. After years of decline and neglect on Elm Street (located in the Over-the-Rhine neighborhood where Lynch had been pastor of the New Prospect Baptist Church since 1990), NPDC hoped to revitalize the community by developing plans for a health-care facility, a bakery, and low-income housing. The community bakery not only served as a great place to enjoy delicious treats but also provided jobs for local residents. Through the Elm Street Development project an entire inner-city block was acquired, and plans were put in place to renovate this area.

Longtime residents of Cincinnati, particularly African Americans, were aware of racial profiling and police brutality toward blacks. However, the death of Timothy Thomas, a young African American, in April 2001 shone a national spotlight on the problem. Thomas was unarmed and the fifteenth black male killed by Cincinnati police since 1995. In the wake of the Thomas shooting, Cincinnati's inner-city residents began to lose hope in the justice system, and some of them resorted to looting and destruction to express their rage and despair. Cincinnati's mayor Charlie Luken declared a state of emergency and ordered a four-day dusk-to-dawn curfew for all citizens.

In an effort to gain the attention of city officials, the Cincinnati Black United Front (CBUF), led by Lynch, called for a boycott of white-owned Cincinnati businesses on 14 July 2001. The CBUF had formed shortly after fourteen downtown restaurants decided to close during the Ujima Cinci-Bration festival in the summer of 2000. The CBUF was designed to bring economic, social, political, and racial equality to the greater Cincinnati community. By 2004 the economic impact of the boycott was estimated at eighty million dollars in lost revenue for city businesses. This figure included "cancellation of performances by well-known entertainers—the actor-comedian BILL COSBY, the soul singer WILLIAM SMOKEY ROBINSON, the jazz trumpeter WYNTON MARSALIS, and the R&B group the O'Jays" (*Cincinnati Enquirer*, 19 Mar. 2002).

The anger and desolation among black residents following so many police murders of black men sparked Lynch's interest in electoral politics. In 2003 he decided to run for the Cincinnati city council, where he hoped to provide a voice for the voiceless. His campaign got a late start, however, and he finished in ninth place, just shy of winning one of the coveted eight seats. Despite his loss, Lynch's ranking was rather impressive since there were eight incumbents, seven of whom were reelected, out of the twenty-six candidates certified to run. Nor did the defeat dampen Lynch's future plans to seek elected office.

As an adjunct faculty member at Northwestern University's Asset Based Community Development Institute, Lynch traveled the country teaching and training others about community building. He continued to pastor the New Prospect Baptist Church and to address community problems in the city of Cincinnati.

FURTHER READING

Radel, Cliff. "Protester Lynch Becomes Peacemaker Lynch," *Cincinnati Enquirer* (15 Apr. 2001). Accessible at http://www.enquirer.com/editions/2001/04/15/loc_protester_lynch.html

ANGELA M. GOODEN

Lynch, James (8 Jan. 1839–18 Dec. 1872), minister, editor, and politician, was born in Baltimore, Maryland, the son of Benjamin Lynch, a merchant and minister, and Benjamin's wife, a former slave purchased by her husband. Her name is not known. James Lynch attended the elementary school operated by the Reverend DANIEL A. PAYNE of the Bethel African Methodist Episcopal (AME) Church in Baltimore. When Payne left in 1852, Lynch enrolled in the Kimball Union Academy in Meriden, New Hampshire. After about two years, he later testified, his father's business failed, and "we were cut short in our pursuit for knowledge by pecuniary disability" (*Christian Recorder*, 16 Feb. 1867). He taught school on Long Island for a year and then studied for the ministry with a Presbyterian minister in Brooklyn. Struggling with the decision about his future, Lynch moved to Indianapolis to work with Elisha Weaver, an AME minister with whom he later crossed paths—and occasionally swords—at the *Christian Recorder*.

Grateful for his Indiana experience, Lynch committed himself to the ministry, was licensed to preach, and was assigned a small church in Galena, Illinois. In 1860 the now Bishop Payne took him east, where Lynch served a District of Columbia church and completed his studies leading to ordination. Two years later he moved to Baltimore as minister of the Waters Chapel Church, and also that year he married Eugenia Rice.

Lynch's return to the East Coast energized his editorial and speaking talents and brought him denominational attention. Challenging fellow ministers in 1862 to place the care of freedmen above petty theological disputes, he later responded to Bishop Payne's call for southern missionaries, landing in South Carolina in May 1863. Lynch's first opportunity to preach to freedmen came after a mass baptism on Hilton Head Island. He recalled, "My heart was so full I felt like it was overflowing, and there was no trouble for tears and words to run" (*Christian Recorder*, 6 June 1863).

During the next two years Lynch established churches in South Carolina and Georgia, ministered informally and occasionally to several black regiments—including the famous Massachusetts Fifty-fourth—and helped to start schools for freedmen and their children (his sister Jane Margaret Lynch taught in one). Elected secretary of the AME's first southern conference, Lynch traveled incessantly, preached and baptized, chastised and reconciled, introduced parliamentary procedure, and licensed local ministers and exhorters. After the Civil War, Lynch faced threats of violence from defeated rebel forces and grappled with the trauma of hungry, sick, and homeless freedmen. "They need all the help, protection, advice, and prayer, that the Government, philanthropists, and Christians, can grant," he told the *Christian Recorder* (1 July 1865). Lynch had both defamers and defenders; many in the black community believed, as one black minister wrote to the same newspaper, "that Rev. James Lynch has done more for the elevation of the colored people in this department, than any other man" (19 Aug. 1865).

Lynch was appointed editor of the *Christian Recorder* in February 1866 and moved his family to Philadelphia. During his sixteen months with the *Christian Recorder*, it became a lively, issue-oriented paper. Early in 1867, worried by the intransigence of the Methodist Episcopal (ME) Church, South, and fearful of the AME's structural weakness, Lynch tendered his services to the ME Church, North, as a southern missionary.

The AME Church did not give up without a struggle; it offered him the pulpit of the mother church, Bethel Church in Philadelphia, in addition to his editorship—two highly prized and influential positions. He refused both invitations "because I have convictions of duty to my race as deep as my soul" to go south (*Christian Recorder*, 8 June 1867). News of Lynch's denominational switch was slow to reach the faithful, but his appointment as a Republican activist, arranged by party notables, was reported within weeks.

In Mississippi the twin challenge of evangelicalism in religion and politics suited Lynch to perfection. The ME Church provided opportunities, he believed, "where white and black can meet as equals around God's altar," and he asserted that blacks wanted to work with whites but needed the franchise and equality before the law for their own protection (Gravely, *Gilbert Haven*, 183). Elected permanent vice president of the Mississippi Republican Convention in September 1867, Lynch found that his moderate views placed him between the radicals, who wanted to disfranchise former rebels, and the conservatives, who resented blacks as voters and in positions of authority. During 1868, as Republican factions squabbled about proscribing whites and integrating schools, Lynch maintained his stance against proscription and integration. He started the *Colored Citizen Monthly* to appeal to blacks and stayed with the less extreme wing of the party. By mid-1869, as executive council member and vice president of the July convention, Lynch was the foremost African American politician in Mississippi. The convention platform represented his views, endorsing "universal amnesty and universal suffrage," free schools, and free speech.

At the same time, pressured by envious associates, Lynch resigned as the Freedmen's Bureau state assistant superintendent for education before taking up his duties. He refused a nomination as lieutenant governor from the party's splinter wing and accepted the mainstream party's nomination for secretary of state. After a grueling fall campaign, Lynch became the first elected black official in Mississippi. In office he demonstrated his abilities as a responsible and responsive elected official. Besides handling routine duties, Lynch began to unravel the public land confusion, a product of twenty years of neglect, to enable the state to identify taxable lands for schools and for internal improvements. As a member of the Mississippi Board of Education he played a key role in the development of a public school system that rapidly achieved success. Unwilling to depend solely on political solutions to race problems, Lynch denounced the sharecrop system and its credit burden, which, he explained in February 1871, "leaves the laborer at the mercy of the planter, the merchant, and his own ignorance and improvidence" (quoted in Harris, 56). Lynch urged planters to sell surplus lands to blacks, since some planters were already seeking white purchasers for part or all of their holdings.

Lynch did not neglect his denomination. As presiding elder of the Jackson District, he saw a four-year, fourfold increase in membership, even as new districts compressed his own. He was active at the ME's 1872 national conference, opposing a proposal to create a separate conference for Georgia and Alabama blacks and urging that black ministers be considered for the episcopate. "The spirit of the age," Lynch affirmed, demands that we "ignore all questions of color or caste" (*New York Tribune*, 5 June 1872).

Lynch's moderation and his prominence within and without the party exposed him to bitter personal accusations of rape and excessive drinking, the first a specious and the second a probable charge. He consequently failed to win the party's nomination for Congress from the Jackson-Vicksburg district, yet he was reelected secretary of state and remained (with Senator HIRAM REVELS) the state's leading African American. A delegate to the 1872 Republican National Convention, he afterward campaigned for the Ulysses Grant–Henry Wilson ticket in Indiana. Rejecting rumors of political independence, Lynch protested his loyalty, saying that Republicans represent "the only safeguard for the rights of colored people and the only real hope ... for prosperity" (*New York Times*, 14 Sept. 1872).

Lynch's death in Jackson, from both a bronchial infection and Bright's disease, was sudden and unexpected. "He lived exactly at the right time," his eulogist proclaimed, because opportunities to serve his race, his country, and his God could not have been more tailored to his talents. His successor editor at the *Christian Recorder* called him "exceptionally talented—the most far-seeing man of his age we ever knew." Lynch was a builder whose forward-looking posture and performance helped a race and a region and presaged twentieth-century positions that engaged the allies of both BOOKER T. WASHINGTON and W. E. B. DuBois.

FURTHER READING

Gravely, William B. *Gilbert Haven, Methodist Abolitionist* (1973).

Gravely, William B. "James Lynch and the Black Christian Mission during Reconstruction," in *Black Apostles at Home and Abroad*, ed. David W. Wills and Richard Newman (1982).

Harris, William C. "James Lynch: Black Leader in Southern Reconstruction," *Historian* 34 (1971): 40–61.

Payne, Daniel A. *The Semi-Centenary and the Retrospection of the African Methodist Episcopal Church* (1866; repr. 1972).

Walker, Clarence E. *A Rock in a Weary Land: The African Methodist Episcopal Church during the Civil War and Reconstruction* (1981).

Obituary: *Christian Recorder*, 28 Dec. 1872, 16 Jan. 1873. This entry is taken from the *American National Biography* and is published here with the permission of the American Council of Learned Societies.

LESLIE H. FISHEL

Lynch, John Roy (10 Sept. 1847–2 Nov. 1939), U.S. congressman, historian, and attorney, was born on Tacony plantation near Vidalia, Louisiana, the son of Patrick Lynch, the manager of the plantation, and Catherine White, a slave. Patrick Lynch, an Irish immigrant, purchased his wife and two children, but in order to free them, existing state law required they leave Louisiana. Before Patrick Lynch died, he transferred the titles to his wife and children to a friend, William Deal, who promised to treat them as free persons. However, when Patrick Lynch died, Deal sold the family to a planter, Alfred W. Davis, in Natchez, Mississippi. When Davis learned of the conditions of the transfer to Deal, he agreed to allow Catherine Lynch to hire her own time while he honeymooned with his new wife in Europe. Under this arrangement, Catherine Lynch lived in Natchez, worked for various employers, and paid $3.50 a week to an agent of Davis, keeping whatever else she earned.

On Davis's return, he and Catherine Lynch reached an agreement that her elder son would work as a dining room servant and the younger, John Roy, would be Davis's valet. Catherine accepted these conditions, recognizing that she had no alternative. Under this arrangement, John Roy Lynch studied for confirmation and baptism in the Episcopal Church, but the Civil War intervened. Lynch attended black Baptist and Methodist churches during and after the war. Because of a falling-out with Davis's wife, Lynch briefly worked on a plantation until he became ill.

When Union forces reached Natchez in 1863, they freed Lynch, who was sixteen years old. He was visiting relatives at Tacony when Confederate troops overran the plantation and began seizing the former slaves as captives. Lynch convinced the troops that the workers had smallpox, which was a ruse, and the military released them.

Lynch worked at several jobs from 1865 to 1866, including dining room waiter at a boardinghouse, cook with the Forty-ninth Illinois Volunteers Regiment, and pantryman aboard a troop transport ship moored at Natchez. Eventually he became a messenger in a photography shop, where he learned the photographic developing process as a "printer." He continued that line of work with another shop, and in 1866 he took over the full management of a photography shop in Natchez. Briefly attending a grammar school operated by northern teachers, he learned to read by studying newspapers, reading books, and listening to classes given in a white school near his shop. One of the books he studied was on parliamentary law, which fascinated him.

In 1868 Lynch gave a number of speeches in Natchez before the local Republican club in support of the new Mississippi state constitution. The constitution legitimized all slave marriages, including that of his mother and father. In his autobiography Lynch noted that the later constitution, passed by Democrats in 1890, did away with the feature that had legitimized marriages between whites and African Americans but not retroactively.

In 1869 the Natchez Republican club sent Lynch to discuss local political appointments with the state's military governor, Adelbert Ames. Impressed with Lynch's presentation, Ames appointed him justice of the peace, a position Lynch had not sought. Later that year Lynch was elected to the Mississippi house of representatives, where he served through 1873. In his first term he sat on the Judiciary Committee and the Committee on Elections and Education. In his last term he served as Speaker of the house and earned recognition and praise from Republican and Democratic legislators and the local press. During this period he formed an alliance with Governor James L. Alcorn, a white Republican who urged his party to make common cause with black voters. Lynch worked closely with other African Americans in the Mississippi Republican Party, especially BLANCHE K. BRUCE and James Hill. Later he fell into disagreement with Hill, who opposed Lynch's influence in the party.

Lynch was elected to Congress in 1872 and was reelected in 1874. In Congress, he impressed his colleagues with his knowledge of parliamentary procedure, unusual among the small contingent of southern African American Republican members of Congress. Arguing forcefully for the Civil Rights Act of 1875, he called it "an act of simple justice" that "will be instrumental in placing the colored people in a more independent position." He anticipated that, given more civil rights, blacks would vote in both parties and not depend entirely on the Republican Party.

Defeated in the 1876 congressional election, Lynch charged his opponent with fraud. In the election in 1880, through a series of dishonest practices, including lost ballot boxes, miscounts, and stuffed boxes, at least five thousand votes for Lynch were wrongfully thrown out. General James R. Chalmers, a Democrat, claimed victory, but Lynch contested the election. Finally seated late in the term, Lynch served in 1882–1883. Although he was defeated for reelection in 1882 by Henry S. Van Eaton, Lynch was regarded as a political hero by the Republican Party. He was the keynote speaker and temporary chairman of the 1884 national convention. Lynch was the last black keynote speaker at a national political convention until 1968.

In 1884 Lynch married Ella W. Somerville. They had one child before divorcing in 1900. From 1869 through 1905 he was successful in buying and selling real estate, including plantations, in the Natchez region. In 1889 President Benjamin Harrison appointed Lynch fourth auditor of the Treasury for the Navy Department, and he served to 1893.

In 1890 Lynch protested strongly against the "George" scheme, which, under the new Mississippi state constitution, required a literacy test for voting. An "understanding" clause also allowed registrars to pass whites and deny registration to African Americans who could not satisfactorily demonstrate an understanding of the state constitution.

In 1896 Lynch and Hill led competing delegations to the Republican National Convention. Both factions were committed to William McKinley, and through a compromise, delegates from both groups were seated at the convention. One of Hill's delegates bolted the McKinley slate, reducing the influence of the Hill "machine." After the election, McKinley gave Lynch partial control over the distribution of political patronage in the state.

Lynch began to study law in the 1890s and was admitted to the Mississippi bar in 1896. He subsequently obtained a license to practice law in Washington, D.C., where he opened an office with Robert H. Terrell, who had worked with him in the Treasury Department. He continued with this practice into 1898.

With the outbreak of the Spanish-American War, McKinley selected Lynch as an additional paymaster of volunteers with the rank of major in the army. In 1900 Lynch was again a delegate to the Republican National Convention, serving on the Committee on Platform and Resolutions and as chair of the subcommittee that drafted the national platform.

After the war Lynch remained with the army and received a regular commission in 1901. For three years he was assigned to Cuba, where he learned Spanish; then he was stationed for three and a half years in Omaha, Nebraska, and for sixteen months in San Francisco. In 1907 he sailed for Hawaii and the Philippines. In the Philippines a medical examiner claimed that Lynch had a serious heart condition and was therefore unfit for service with only a few months to live. Suspecting racial discrimination, Lynch protested directly to Washington and was reassigned to California.

Lynch retired from the army in 1911 and moved to Chicago. In 1912 he married Cora Williamson, who was twenty-seven years younger than he. They had no children. Admitted to the Chicago bar by reciprocity in 1915, he practiced law for more than twenty-five years. During these years he began writing about the Reconstruction period. An early revisionist, he anticipated the later writings of W. E. B. DuBois and the post–World War II historians, who looked at the achievements of African American politicians in the 1860s and 1870s with more objectivity than prior historians. Lynch published several well-documented works, beginning with *The Facts of Reconstruction* (1914). Initially rejected by several presses, his critique of James Ford Rhodes's history was published in 1917 and 1918 as two articles in the *Journal of Negro History* and was republished in 1922 under the title *Some Historical Errors of James Ford Rhodes*. He also criticized as full of errors Claude G. Bowers's work *The Tragic Era* (1920). He later incorporated a large section of his 1913 history of Reconstruction in his autobiography, *Reminiscences of an Active Life*, completed shortly before his death in Chicago but not published until 1970, edited by JOHN HOPE FRANKLIN.

An accomplished African American author and politician, Lynch was representative of a small group who worked with some success within the existing political and patronage structure to create opportunities for themselves and to fight for civil rights. Considering his childhood as a slave and his lack of formal education, his achievements as a politician, statesman, and historian are notable.

FURTHER READING

Some Lynch correspondence is in the papers of CARTER G. WOODSON in the Manuscripts Division of the Library of Congress.

Bell, Frank C. "The Life and Times of James R. Lynch: A Case Study, 1847–1939," *Journal of Mississippi History* 38 (Feb. 1976): 53–67.

Mann, Kenneth E. "John Roy Lynch, U.S. Congressman from Mississippi," *Negro History Bulletin* 37 (Apr. 1974): 239–241.

Obituary: *New York Times*, 3 Nov. 1939.

This entry is taken from the *American National Biography* and is published here with the permission of the American Council of Learned Societies.

RODNEY P. CARLISLE

Lynk, Miles Vandahurst (3 June 1871–29 Dec. 1956), physician, educator, and advocate for African American physicians, was born near Brownsville, Tennessee, the son of John Henry Lynk, a farmer, and Mary Louise Yancy, both former slaves. Miles's parents, members of the Colored (now Christian) Methodist Episcopal (CME) church, founded in nearby Jackson, Tennessee, named their son after the CME's first two bishops, William Henry Miles and Richard H. Vanderhorst. Miles received basic education from his mother, a country school near Brownsville, a tutor he hired with money he had earned, and a course of self-teaching, which he called attending "Pine Knot College." At age seventeen Miles taught at an African American summer school in a neighboring county and used the money to apprentice himself to Jacob C. Hairston, a local physician and graduate of Meharry Medical College in Nashville. Robert Fulton Boyd, a Meharry professor, was sufficiently impressed with Lynk's entrance examination to admit him to Meharry Medical College in 1889. Lynk finished in two years while the normal course was three years and, by his own account, graduated second in a class of thirteen.

His own man throughout his life, Lynk ignored the advice of friends and opened a practice in Jackson, Tennessee, the site of recent racial unrest. In the racially tense and increasingly segregated late-nineteenth-century South, Lynk personally introduced himself to local white physicians and druggists as a way of defusing their concerns. To forestall adverse reaction to a black physician's presence in Jackson's previously all-white medical profession, Lynk used the tactic other African American physicians of the time employed and, according to his autobiography, "gave each [physician and druggist] my card with the statement that I shall endeavor to practice scientific and ethical medicine" (Lynk, 27–28).

Medicine was becoming a crowded profession, and black physicians were not always given a warm reception by white doctors worried about losing paying patients, black or white. Black physicians often charged lower fees because their predominantly African American clientele usually had low incomes. They thus attracted some white patients more interested in low cost than in their physician's race. In addition to gaining fellow physicians' acceptance, Lynk had to win over the African American population as well. Many African Americans—as a result of biases learned from whites since slavery times, bad experiences with African American healers, or superstitious belief—were reluctant to use black physicians. To overcome such prejudice, Lynk worked diligently in his practice, took the time to educate people about good hygiene and sanitation, gave lectures about health and disease to black teachers and church groups, and generally followed his motto "Do all the good you can to all the people you can in all the ways you can." These approaches seemed to work, and Lynk reported in the Jackson *Daily Sun* that he "soon overcame their [African Americans'] scruples and built up a large and lucrative practice" (12 Dec. 1900). A brief notice in the 26 September 1891 issue of the *Christian Index*, a CME newspaper published in Jackson, attests to his success:

Dr. M. V. Lynk, our Colored physician in this city, has built up such a large practice that it became very necessary that he have a horse and buggy to meet his calls. He now has a splendid outfit and is doing well. Our prediction last winter that a colored doctor would do well here has proven to be true. We are quite glad to see our people giving him their patronage. This is nothing more than right.

From the start of his career Lynk worked not only for his own success but also for the betterment of African Americans, both locally and nationally. At age twenty-one, he established a monthly medical journal for African American physicians, which one black physician from Texas proudly called "a journal of our own" (Lynk, 38). Medical journals of the time ignored the publications and activities of black physicians, medical schools, medical societies, and hospitals. To give African American physicians a voice, Lynk began publishing the *Medical and Surgical Observer (MSO)* in December 1892. In addition to publishing medical articles and reports on black physicians' experiences, it provided Lynk the opportunity to promote his own ideas while bringing a sense of community to often isolated African American physicians around the country. The *MSO* survived for only fourteen issues, until January 1894. Lynk gave no official reason for ceasing publication, though he hinted in editorials at low subscription numbers, lack of article submissions by black physicians, and decreased advertising.

One idea Lynk promoted in the *MSO* that came to fruition was the formation of a national association of black medical professionals. Such an association was needed, Lynk had explained in an editorial in the first issue of the MSO, because black physicians were excluded from the national American Medical Association as well as from southern (and many northern) local and regional medical societies. Black health professionals in Texas and North Carolina, he reported, had established their own societies and were trying to link up with other physicians elsewhere. On 18 November 1895 at the Cotton States and International Exposition in Atlanta, where BOOKER T. WASHINGTON delivered his famous "Atlanta Compromise" speech, Lynk, along with a few other black physicians, and his Meharry professor Robert F. Boyd, held an organizational meeting of what became the National Medical Association.

In 1900, unable to obtain law training in Jackson, Lynk arranged with Lane College, a local CME-sponsored school, for H. R. Sadler, an African American lawyer in Memphis, to offer a law course. Lynk recruited the students, purchased a law library, and allowed his medical office to be used as a classroom. In February 1901, after earning his law degree and passing the Tennessee bar, Lynk founded the University of West Tennessee (UWT), a "college for the professional training of ambitious Negroes." One of the last of fourteen predominantly black medical schools established between Reconstruction and the start of the twentieth century (only Howard and Meharry medical schools survive today), UWT opened in a newly renovated and appropriately equipped house, with newly hired teachers, and offered its African American students medical, dental, pharmaceutical, nursing, and law training. Lynk established his school despite the rising cost of medical education due to the rapid growth of scientific medicine and found UWT's facilities and faculty quickly outdated. The school eventually lost its accreditation—despite a move to Memphis in 1907—and was forced to close in 1923, having graduated 155 physicians and a number of lawyers, nurses, dentists, and pharmacists.

During the 1890s Lynk wrote books and edited a magazine for African Americans. Lynk Publishing House, which he established to print and sell his work, provided employment to about a dozen African American workers. By 1900 he had published *The Afro-American School Speaker and Gems of Literature, for School Commencements, Literary Circles, Debating Clubs, and Rhetoricals Generally* (1896), a collection of black literature, and *The Black Troopers; or, The Daring Heroism of the Negro Soldiers in the Spanish-American War* (1899), which sold more than fifteen thousand copies. He also edited and published several issues of an illustrated monthly literary magazine *Lynk's Magazine* (1898–1899), which was followed some twenty years later by another magazine, *The Negro Outlook* (1919).

Lynk, who was married twice, in 1893 to chemist Beebe Steven, and in 1949 to Ola Herin Moore, remained active in medicine throughout his life. He combated racism and segregation by his own medical, legal, and publishing work and by helping establish black institutions parallel to those in the white medical world—a journal, medical school, and medical society. The National Medical Association, which he helped found in 1895, awarded him its Distinguished Service Medal in 1952. Lynk died in Memphis.

FURTHER READING

Lynk, Miles V. *Sixty Years of Medicine; or, The Life and Times of Dr. Miles V. Lynk: An Autobiography* (1951).

Savitt, Todd L. "'A Journal of Our Own': The *Medical and Surgical Observer* at the Beginnings of an African American Medical Profession in Late Nineteenth-Century America," *Journal of the National Medical Association* 88 (1996).

Savitt, Todd L. "Four African-American Proprietary Medical Colleges: 1888–1923," *Journal of the History of Medicine & Allied Sciences* 55 (2000).

TODD L. SAVITT

Lynn, Conrad J. (4 Nov. 1908–16 Nov. 1995), civil rights lawyer and activist, was born in Newport, Rhode Island. Lynn was one of seven children of Nette (Irving) Lynn, a domestic worker, and Joseph Lynn, a laborer. Lynn's parents were originally from Augusta, Georgia. They had been married in 1904 and migrated north in 1906 when their multimillionaire employer also moved north. Eventually they came to live in Rockville Centre, on New York's Long Island, where they settled in a black ghetto set in a swampy lowland. The mortality rate in Lynn's neighborhood was very high, but even though he was a somewhat sickly young child, he survived.

In 1926 Lynn graduated from Malverne High School as its salutatorian. His academic skills were so exceptional that Syracuse University awarded him a debating scholarship. With funds raised partially from a bake sale, the mothers' club of Lynn's high school presented Lynn's mother with a check for a hundred dollars to cover some of his college expenses.

During the summer of 1926 Lynn worked with his father landscaping and road cutting in order to save money for college. He enrolled in Syracuse University in the fall. Although the school was integrated, racial discrimination prevented him from living on campus, and he rented a room off campus with his remaining funds. Despite the scholarship and support from the mothers' club Lynn struggled financially, and in the early days he was often hungry. Friends and part-time jobs carried him through the most difficult periods, however, and he eventually found his place among the vibrant intellectual atmosphere at Syracuse. Each Sunday the black students at Syracuse met at the Dunbar Community Center on campus and discussed the political, cultural, and historical events of the day. One student was always designated as the "critic" to provide the final word to the discussion. Lynn so impressed his fellow black students that they elected him critic by April of his freshman year, a position he held until graduation.

Lynn's intellectual and political horizons were greatly expanded during his years at Syracuse University. He was increasingly drawn to revolutionary struggles through his debating scholarship. He read Karl Marx's *Communist Manifesto* and by 1928 had become a member of the Young Communist League. Lynn also announced his commitment to militant atheism in the spirit of the radical lawyer Clarence Darrow. After graduation he was accepted into the Syracuse University law school, becoming its first black graduate in

1932. The following year he became a member of the New York bar and immediately began practicing law in New York City. He also supplemented his income by teaching in the Works Progress Administration (WPA), one of the New Deal's most important programs. He remained politically active with Communist organizations during the Depression but was expelled from the Communist Party in 1939 for supporting Trinidadian oil workers in their struggle against Britain.

In 1941 Lynn became heavily involved in the March on Washington movement. A. PHILLIP RANDOLPH, the head of the Brotherhood of Sleeping Car Porters union, had proposed a march to Washington, D.C., to protest racial discrimination and the exclusion of blacks from wartime industries. Lynn was on the executive committee of a young person's group supporting the march. However, upon hearing that Randolph was going to call off the march, Lynn acted quickly to salvage a march for jobs. Despite Lynn's efforts the march was called off even though jobs for blacks in the war industries remained scarce. Lynn later organized a march in 1942 from the Harlem YMCA to Washington, D.C., to protest discrimination.

Lynn's ultimate radicalization as a lawyer occurred when his brother Winfred was drafted into the army during World War II. Winfred refused induction and was arrested. Lynn agreed to become his brother's attorney and tried to recruit the NAACP for help, but the NAACP refused to become involved. The ACLU was more responsive, and Lynn was able to secure the services of the legendary civil liberties attorney Arthur Garfield Hays for his brother's defense.

In 1947 Lynn began participating in freedom rides through the South. Though racial segregation in interstate bus travel had been ruled illegal by the U.S. Supreme Court in 1946, blacks continued to sit in the back of buses when the buses traveled to the South. George Houser of the Congress of Racial Equality (CORE) proposed the so-called "freedom rides" to challenge the tradition and to uphold the new law. Lynn rode a bus from Washington, D.C., that was headed for North Carolina and then for Kentucky. Though Lynn and his contingent made it through Richmond, he was arrested in Petersburg, Virginia, despite the law outlawing segregation. He was victorious at trial, but this did not end segregation on the buses.

In the 1950s and 1960s Lynn continued his political activism, frequently participating in politically controversial legal cases. These included battles against McCarthyism, opposition to the Vietnam War and the draft, and associations with black radicals such as H. RAP BROWN and ROBERT WILLIAMS. Lynn also defended a group of Puerto Rican nationalists in the 1950s who sought independence for the island of Puerto Rico from the United States. They had been charged with shooting at members of Congress while it was in session.

In 1958 Lynn became involved in the so-called "kissing case" in Robert Williams's hometown of Monroe, North Carolina. Lynn represented a ten-year-old young black boy from Monroe who had been charged with rape because he allegedly kissed an eight-year-old white girl during a children's game. In 1964 Lynn became involved in perhaps his most famous case of all, the "Harlem Six." In that case six Harlem youths were put on trial on trumped-up charges involving the murder of a Jewish woman following a neighborhood riot. The case was poisoned with racism that reached all segments of New York and its legal system.

Lynn continued to practice law and demand equal rights for black people until a few months before his death on 16 November 1995. He was survived by his wife Yolanda Moreno Lynn, and their three children.

FURTHER READING

Lynn, Conrad J. *There Is a Fountain: The Autobiography of Conrad Lynn* (1979).
Nelson, Truman. *The Torture of Mothers* (1968).
Tyson, Timothy B. *Radio Free Dixie: Robert F. Williams and the Roots of Black Power* (1999).

BRIAN GILMORE

Lyon, Ernest E. (22 Oct. 1860–17 July 1938), clergyman and diplomat, was born in Belize, British Honduras, a son of Emmanuel and Ann F. (Bending) Lyon, both of Jamaican descent. He moved with his parents in the 1870s to the United States, where he was educated privately in New Orleans, Louisiana, then at the Gilbert Industrial School in La Teche, Louisiana.

Lyon attended Straight University (now Dillard University) and New Orleans University, where he received a bachelor's degree in 1888, and later a master's degree. He later took courses at Union Theological Seminary of New York, and in the 1890s, received a doctorate in Divinity from Wiley University (now Wiley College) in Marshall, Texas. While still an undergraduate, he was ordained as a Methodist Episcopal minister, serving a series of Louisiana pastorates: La Teche in 1883, followed by three New Orleans churches (Mallalieu, Thompson, and Simpson). In 1894 he was appointed conference Sunday School agent, and in 1895, special agent for the Freedmen's Aid and Southern Educational Society.

In 1884 Lyon married Abbie M. Lyon (maiden name unknown) of New York. They had three children—daughters Maude Amelia (Morris) and Annie Belle (Walker) and son Ernest Harrison Lyon, called Harry, all born in Louisiana. The Lyons were divorced shortly after moving to Maryland in 1900. In 1907 his daughter Maude married John Lewis Morris, a Liberian editor and government official, and lived in Liberia until her husband's death in 1935.

In 1896 Lyon was called to serve one of his denomination's most visible black churches, St. Mark's Methodist Episcopal Church, in New York City, assisting senior pastor Dr. William H. Brooks. Lyon soon became politically active as a Republican, appointed in 1896 as an auxiliary member of the Republican National Advisory Committee, advising party leaders on racial matters in the eastern United States. In 1900 he became a full member of the advisory committee.

By mid-1900, Lyon had received an onward assignment to John Wesley Methodist Episcopal Church in Baltimore, Maryland. That same year, he was elected as a vice president of the National Afro-American Council and member of the Council's national executive committee.

Lyon was a close friend and regular correspondent of BOOKER T. WASHINGTON, who recommended him to President Theodore Roosevelt as a replacement for John R. A. Crossland in 1903 as U.S. minister resident and consul general to Liberia. Lyon remained in Monrovia until 1910, becoming dean of Liberia's diplomatic corps, and traveled widely in the country, reporting on both political and economic issues. Minister Lyon also served on the faculty of the College of West Africa, a Methodist seminary in Monrovia. In May 1909, he assisted President William Howard Taft's commission to Liberia, sent to investigate that nation's political crisis.

Lyon's second wife, Clara Florida Bacchus, had once been a boarder in the Lyon home while attending school in Baltimore. They were married in Wilmington, Delaware, on 18 June 1903, shortly before sailing for Liberia. While in Monrovia, Clara Lyon gave birth to a son, Monroe Lyon, in 1905; she died there in 1909.

Lyon returned to the United States in late 1910, resuming his pastorate at John Wesley Church, and remaining in Baltimore until his death. In 1921 he became pastor of Ames Memorial Church, serving there until retirement. A member of the American Academy of Political and Social Science, Lyon lectured on church history and theology at Baltimore's Morgan College, then a private school (now Morgan State University). Beginning in 1914, he edited a weekly religious journal, *Commonwealth*. Lyon wrote numerous short works, including *The Negro's View of Organic Union*, a Methodist pamphlet published in 1915.

In 1902 Lyon also helped found the private Maryland Industrial and Agricultural Institute for Colored Youths on an 87-acre campus near Laurel. During World War I, Lyon was active in the Liberty Bond campaign, raising $200,000 among Maryland's African Americans. He also headed the Afro-American Civic League of Maryland.

From 1911 until his death, Lyon served as Liberian consul general in the United States, a ceremonial role, which Lyon used to testify before Congress in favor of Liberian aid, including loans and economic and educational assistance, sometimes provoking controversy by doing so. He served as an agent for the Board of Education for Liberia.

Reverend Lyon died in Baltimore at age seventy-seven. Months before his death, he was honored with a testimonial dinner featuring congratulatory letters from President Franklin D. Roosevelt and Secretary of State Cordell Hull, among others, for fifty years of public service. Survivors included his third wife, Marie Wright Lyon of Virginia, whom he married in March 1912.

FURTHER READING
Mather, Frank L. *Who's Who of the Colored Race* (1915).
"Ernest Lyon." In *National Cyclopedia of American Biography* (1910).
Obituary: *Baltimore Sun*, 18 July 1938.

BENJAMIN R. JUSTESEN

Lyons, James Leroy (James Jimmy Lyons) (1 Dec. 1931 or 1933–19 May 1986), jazz alto saxophonist, was born in Jersey City, New Jersey, the son of a shipyard worker. Reference works and the usually reliable *Cadence* magazine give his birth year as 1933, but the writer STANLEY CROUCH claims 1931 in his obituary of Lyons in the *Village Voice*. Lyons's parents, whose names are unknown, separated when he was a child, and from around 1941 he was raised by his grandmother, who owned the Chicken Shack restaurant franchise at the Hotel Woodside in Harlem, where COUNT BASIE and many other jazz musicians often stayed.

From around 1945 or 1946 Lyons was once again living with his mother, an amateur pianist, in the Bronx, where he attended parochial school. His uncle, a drummer, showed him some basic percussion techniques that he practiced by playing along with the tenor saxophonist LESTER YOUNG's recordings. He also met the pianists ELMO HOPE and BUD POWELL, who practiced in his neighbor's apartment. The clarinetist BUSTER BAILEY helped Lyons's mother pick out an alto sax for Lyons. Soon he had an opportunity to practice with the pianists Hope and THELONIOUS MONK, who told Lyons that he had a good ear but needed to learn music theory. Both because of and despite these distinguished opportunities for apprenticeship, Lyons's mother dissuaded him from becoming a jazz musician:

> She'd look at a man like Bud Powell, playing the way he was at that time, and the financial situation he was in then—you know, to have nothing. The clothes he had on were raggedy, been slept in for days, and as beautifully as he played, my mother said it would be a crime if I turned out to be a musician.

Lyons finished school, attended college for two years (details are unknown), and also served in the army in Korea for three years; in the course of sixteen months of combat he earned two Bronze Stars. Returning to Harlem, he played professionally on rare occasions but supported himself by working in the post office. Around 1958 or 1959 he studied with the alto saxophonist Rudy Rutherford.

In the summer of 1961 Lyons played five or six nights a week with the bassist Ali Richardson in Greenwich Village at Raphael's, where the free-jazz pianist CECIL TAYLOR was working on weekends with the drummer Dennis Charles and the tenor saxophonist ARCHIE SHEPP. That summer Lyons became a member of Taylor's group, rehearsing and then performing at the Five Spot. At this point many of Lyons's musical friends left him because they were upset that he had turned away from the bop tradition and to Taylor's radical music; in particular Lyons avoided meeting Hope, who was bitter about this stylistic change and whom Lyons did not wish to confront because he honored Hope's former friendship and musical tutoring. That fall Lyons made his first recordings with Taylor, filling one side of the album *Into the Hot*, which was issued under the name of the arranger Gil Evans (although Evans did not participate in the music making) in an unsuccessful effort by Evans to gain greater public acceptance for Taylor's music.

In 1962 Lyons, Taylor, and the drummer Sunny Murray performed in Scandinavia for six months. In Copenhagen the trio recorded *Cecil Taylor Live at the Cafe Montmartre*, and they worked with the tenor saxophonist ALBERT AYLER at the café. They returned to find scarcely any musical work at home. Lyons rehearsed with Taylor twice a week, but he worked perhaps only once every two months over the next decade, including jobs in New York with Ayler, the bassist HENRY GRIMES, and Murray in 1963. In 1966 he recorded Taylor's critically acclaimed free-jazz albums *Unit Structures* and *Conquistador!*

To survive through the 1960s Lyons held jobs outside of music. Taylor brought him out of hard labor at a Chicago copper mill for a few musical jobs, including a residency in 1969 at the Maeght Foundation in Paris, where for the first time Lyons recorded an album of his own, *Other Afternoons*, with the trumpeter LESTER BOWIE, the bassist Alan Silva, and the drummer Andrew Cyrille. While Taylor was on the music faculty at the University of Wisconsin during the academic year 1970 to 1971, Lyons taught music for the Narcotic Addiction Control Commission, a drug treatment center on the Lower East Side in New York. The writer Valerie Wilmer reports that "Lyons found acceptance among street-people who thought he must be an addict and offered him narcotics whenever they saw his horn. He had to fake a habit in order to keep their respect" (135).

Lyons, Taylor, and Cyrille were appointed artists-in-residence at Antioch College in Ohio from 1971 to 1973, and the following year Lyons made tours of Japan, Europe, and America with Taylor. In 1975 he directed the Black Music Ensemble at Bennington College in Vermont and played with Taylor at the Five Spot and at European festivals. Further albums with Taylor included *Dark to Themselves* (1977) and *One Too Many, Salty Swift, and Not Goodbye* (1978).

From 1978 Lyons often performed with his own groups, which recorded the albums *Push Pull* (1978), *Jump Up/What to Do About* (1980), *Wee Sneezawee* (1983), and *Give It Up* (1985). Apart from Lyons's preference for working with the bassoonist Karen Borca, whose instrument gave the ensemble a somewhat distinctive sound, Lyons in his work as a leader continued to pursue the timbres and procedures developed by Taylor. A heavy smoker, Lyons died in New York City of lung cancer.

Taylor told the writer Brian Auerbach that he had often been asked by younger saxophonists if they might join his group, but he always refused, "Because they don't understand the position of Jimmy Lyons within my music. Until that happens, I'm not interested." The writer Gary Giddins offers perhaps the best description of this approach:

> Lyons developed a style that incorporated both the increased fragmentation and permutation of line in the new music with a rhythmic bias derived from Parker, and because he sustained Parker's relative sweetness of tone in the middle register … he brought an unexpected lyricism to Taylor's mercurial writing. His bright, dancing sound provides an unmistakable link with jazz tradition, a link not nearly as accessible in Taylor's piano playing.

FURTHER READING

Jost, Ekkehard. *Free Jazz* (1974; rpt. 1981).

Levin, Robert. "The Third World," *Jazz and Pop* 9 (Aug. 1970): 16–17.

Litweiler, John B. "Profile: Jimmy Lyons," *Down Beat* (16 Jan. 1975): 34.

Wilmer, Valerie. *As Serious as Your Life: The Story of the New Jazz* (1977; rev. ed., 1980).

Obituaries: *Down Beat* 53 (Aug. 1986): 12; *Village Voice*, 19 Aug. 1986.

This entry is taken from the *American National Biography* and is published here with the permission of the American Council of Learned Societies.

BARRY KERNFELD

Lyons, Judson Whitlocke (15 Aug. 1854–22 June 1924), lawyer and public official, was born in Burke County, Georgia, a son of Thomas Lyons and Edy Plummer, who may have been a slave. His birth year, later reported in official biographies as either 1858 or 1860, was most likely several years earlier, in 1854. After the Civil War, he moved to Augusta, where he was educated in the common schools of Richmond County. He graduated from high school at Augusta Institute, which was later moved to Atlanta as Atlanta Baptist Seminary, later becoming Morehouse College.

Lyons began his career as a schoolteacher, working during his student years as a summer teacher in both Georgia and South Carolina and later working full-time in Richmond County, Georgia. His 1874 application for a Freedman's Bank savings account lists his age as twenty; also listed are his parents' names and those of his siblings, including an older sister, Alice Batty, with whom he lived in Augusta.

During the Reconstruction era, Lyons was an early leader in the Georgia Equal Rights Association, and also became active in Republican Party politics.

In 1876 Lyons was chosen as an alternate delegate from Georgia's 8th congressional district to the party's national nominating convention in Cincinnati. Four years later, he became one of the party's youngest voting delegates to the Chicago national convention that nominated James Garfield for president. After Garfield's election, Lyons was appointed as a gauger for the federal Internal Revenue Service in Augusta and Savannah, and later worked on the staff of Georgia's deputy collector of internal revenue.

After his exposure to national politics, Lyons chose to become a lawyer, entering the law department at Howard University in Washington, DC, from which he graduated in 1884 with a bachelor's degree in Law, reportedly with high honors. His classmates at Howard included such rising figures as John C. Asbury of Virginia and Andrew F. Hilyer and Jesse A. Lawson of Washington, DC. After returning to Augusta, Lyons was admitted to the Georgia state bar in November 1884 and established a private practice in Augusta. In 1896 he formed a partnership with Henry Moses Porter, who had attended law school at the University of Michigan.

Lyons married Jane Hope in 1890. They had four children: daughters Hope, Edith, and Alice, born in Augusta between 1893 and 1897, and one son, Judson W. Lyons Jr., born in Washington, DC, in 1906.

Lyons resumed his active participation in Georgia Republican politics, attending every party nominating convention as a district or at-large delegate from 1892 until 1908. In 1896 and 1900, he received the signal honor of being named Georgia's national committee member, the first African American to hold that distinction. As a supporter of William McKinley in 1896, Lyons was among a group of black Republican leaders considered for federal appointments by the new president, and received enthusiastic recommendations from white lawyers and leaders of both parties, at least some of whom expected him to be named as a U.S. consul abroad or in a departmental position in Washington, DC.

In April 1897 President McKinley nominated Lyons as postmaster of Augusta, Georgia, causing an angry reaction among local white leaders. After a lengthy controversy, mediated in part by Postmaster General James A. Gary, Lyons agreed to withdraw his candidacy for the postmastership. In late March 1898, days after the death of U.S. Treasury Register BLANCHE K. BRUCE, President McKinley announced Lyons's nomination to that post, for which he was quickly confirmed by the U.S. Senate. For years he was an active stump speaker in national Republican circles, serving as a fervent advocate among African Americans for President McKinley's reelection in 1900 and publishing a popular booklet titled "Appointments Which Afro-Americans Have Received from President McKinley: An Official Record That Merits a Careful Reading." In 1904 he worked for President Roosevelt's election.

In 1898 Lyons was named to the first subexecutive committee in charge of work by the new National Afro-American Council, a nationwide civil rights organization, and served on the national executive committee until 1901. After retiring from the Treasury register's position in 1906, Lyons briefly practiced law in Washington, before returning to Augusta to become president of the Haines Normal and Industrial Institute, a distinguished high school for African American students. He was an active member of Augusta's Harmony Baptist Church, as well as a thirty-second-degree Mason, and was the first African American elected to the American Academy of Political and Social Science.

Lyons died in Augusta, Georgia, in 1924.

FURTHER READING

Bacote, Clarence A. "Negro Officeholders in Georgia under President McKinley." *Journal of Negro History*, July 1959.

Pipkin, J. J. *The Negro in Revelation, in History, and in Citizenship* (1902).

BENJAMIN R. JUSTESEN

Lyons, Maritcha R. (23 May 1848–28 Jan. 1929), educator, civic leader, feminist, and writer, was born Maritcha Remond Lyons in Manhattan, New York. She was the third of five children (the eldest died before the age of three) born to Albro Lyons Sr., a graduate of the first African Free School in Manhattan and a prosperous businessman, and Mary Joseph Marshall Lyons, a seamstress and hairdresser whose father was from Venezuela and whose mother was a successful businesswoman. The Lyons family lived in a free black community in New York, a community that would become, by the start of the Civil War, economically viable, politically active, socially conscious, and well-educated.

By the time she was eight years old, Lyons's father owned and operated a seaman's home and a seaman's outfitting store that served as a natural cover for her parents' work as conductors on the Underground Railroad. Lyons wrote about her parents' involvement years later in her memoirs, briefly noting that her father had boasted of helping more than one thousand slaves escape to freedom (Bolden, 23). Lyons also wrote about how her godfather, JAMES MCCUNE SMITH, the first university-trained black American doctor, who established an interracial practice and pharmacy in New York and used the back room as a meeting place for antislavery activists, cared for her when she developed a physical disability that kept her out of school until the age of thirteen (Bolden, 20). Growing up among important antislavery leaders shaped Lyons's desire to learn and to resist racism.

Her earliest recorded education began in 1861 at Manhattan's Colored School No. 3 under the direction of CHARLES REASON, one of the first blacks to graduate from college and a former educator at Philadelphia, Pennsylvania's, Institute for Colored Youth. Her family and its business remained largely untouched by the Civil War until the New York Draft Riots of 1863. As the war dragged into a third year, the government made plans to begin drafting able-bodied white men between the ages of twenty and forty-five. In New York City white mobs, angered by exemptions to military service that were available to the well-to-do and by their perception that the war was becoming more about ending slavery than saving the Union, instigated four days of violence and destruction that was centrally located in New York's free black communities. The Lyons home was attacked three times, resulting in such substantial damage that the family was forced to flee to Salem, Massachusetts, where their friends and fellow activists John and Nancy Remond, the parents of well-known antislavery lecturers CHARLES LENOX REMOND and SARAH PARKER REMOND, lived. Lyons was named after the Remonds' daughter Maritcha, one of her mother's bridesmaids and a co-owner of the Salem Ladies Hair Work Salon. Later that fall the family moved back to New York, where Lyons returned to and graduated from Colored School No. 3.

In 1865, when she was ready to enter high school, her family relocated to Providence, Rhode Island. Unfortunately she quickly found that the state did not have a high school for black children. Undaunted, her mother tried to enroll her in the girls' department of Providence High. When she was denied admission her family sued the state, and along with GEORGE DOWNING, a prosperous black businessman from New York and the son of Thomas Downing, a famed New York restaurateur, campaigned for an end to segregated schools. Although they won, Lyons had to formally enter the first grade and pass a written and oral examination before she could officially enter high school. When Lyons graduated in 1869 at age twenty with one of the highest marks in the class, she became the first black person to graduate from Providence High and the first black woman to speak at a high school graduation in the state (Bolden, 39).

Lyons moved back to New York shortly after graduation and accepted a teaching position at Brooklyn's Colored School No. 1, the first African Free School in Brooklyn, under the direction of Charles Dorsey, who later became Brooklyn's school supervisor. This was the beginning of a teaching career that spanned more than fifty years and included a stint as the assistant principal at Brooklyn's Public School No. 83. Lyons also became a prominent women's rights activist who in 1892 cofounded the Women's Loyal Union of New York and Brooklyn, a black women's club that disbursed funds for reform work and acted as an information clearinghouse for the two communities. She also contributed eight biographies to HALLIE QUINN BROWN's *Homespun Heroines and Other Women of Distinction* (1926) and became a well-known writer and public speaker who once won a debate against IDA B. WELLS-BARNETT.

After retiring, Lyons, who never married or had children, moved in with her brother until he passed away in 1906. She them moved in with a nephew. In 1928, a year before she died in Bay Shore, Long Island, Lyons completed the first draft of her memoir. Although it has never been published, it stands as one of the few primary sources that provides details about the lives and times of educated, middle-class, free black women growing up during the nineteenth century.

FURTHER READING

Lyons's memoir, "Memories of Yesterdays: All of Which I Saw and Part of Which I Was" (1928), and photographs of her and her family members (except for her older sister Therese) are included with the Harry A. Williamson Papers at the Schomburg Center for Research in Black Culture, New York Public Library.

Bolden, Tonya. *Maritcha: A Remarkable Nineteenth-Century American Girl* (2005).

Bolden, Tonya. *Tell All the Children Our Story* (2002).

Sterling, Dorothy, ed. *We Are Your Sisters: Black Women in the Nineteenth Century* (1984).

K. WISE WHITEHEAD

Lytle, Lutie A. (1875–1950?), attorney, educator, and activist, was born in Murfreesboro, Tennessee. In 1882 Lytle's parents, John R. and Mary Ann ("Mollie") Lytle, her three siblings, and grandmother moved to Kansas as part of the Exoduster Movement of African Americans to the Midwest and West. While virtually nothing is recorded about Lytle's mother, her father, who owned and operated a barbershop in downtown Topeka, was a highly visible member of the community. The Lytle family settled on Monroe Street in Topeka, where Lytle and her brothers attended the city's high school. Lytle's father was a leader of the anti-Republican progressive Populist Flambeau Club, which he helped to organize in 1893. The club was an arm of the Kansas People's Party, which served as a vehicle for the black and white Populist movements in the mid-1890s, bringing disaffected white Democrats and black Republicans into a shared party. Lytle's father was nominated for register of deeds in Shawnee County by the People's Party as part of a fusion ticket. While he never won public office, the elder Lytle's political activism influenced his daughter. In 1895, at age twenty, Lytle reaped the rewards of patronage through her father's connection with the People's Party and was appointed the party's assistant enrolling clerk in the Kansas state legislature. At the time, she had already been working as a compositor for a local black newspaper in Topeka for several years, which brought her into contact with politicians and other leading members of the community. The following year she decided to move to Chattanooga, Tennessee, where she taught school to pay for her tuition at Central Tennessee College in Nashville. Based on her high school record and teaching experience, she was admitted into the college's Department of Law.

While in Nashville studying law she joined the college glee club and accompanied a number of student musicals on piano. In September 1897, after passing her oral exam, Lytle was admitted to the Criminal Court in Memphis. Newspapers reported that at age twenty-six, Lytle became the first African American woman to be licensed to practice law in Tennessee and only the third in the nation. She returned to Topeka a celebrity, with friends holding receptions about town to honor her educational feat. In Topeka she became the first

Lutie A. Lytle graduated from Central Tennessee Law School in 1897 and was admitted to the Tennessee bar the same year. (Kansas State Historical Society.)

African American woman admitted to the Kansas Bar Association.

Because the Jim Crow South could not sustain more than a few black lawyers, with black clients often preferring white attorneys in discriminatory white-dominated courts, Lytle considered establishing a legal practice in either Chicago, Washington, D.C., or New York City. She longed to use her legal expertise in constitutional law to help African Americans: "The anchor of my race is grounded in the constitution," she noted in an interview. "It is the certificate of our liberty and our equality before the law. Our citizenship is based on it" (*Topeka Daily Capital*, Sept. 1897).

In the fall of 1898, without public explanation, Lytle abandoned her plan to practice law and returned to Nashville to join the faculty at Central Tennessee, becoming the first female professor at a chartered law school in the country. Her decision may have stemmed from her success as a public speaker and the belief that she could make a greater contribution through education than through the legal profession. Lytle's difficulties in finding work as a black female attorney may also have spurred her change in career. While she taught for only one session during the 1898–1899 academic year, she set a precedent for other women to follow, teaching law courses on domestic relations (a specialized field pertaining to marriage, divorce, and custody rights), evidence, real property, and criminal procedure.

Shortly after leaving her teaching post she married Reverend McNeil, a minister in the African Episcopal Church, in 1899. The couple relocated to New Paltz, New York, when Lytle's husband was assigned to a new church. It is not known whether or not Lytle practiced law in New Paltz, but records indicate that she became a member of the Women's Federation in the city, during the heyday of the black women's club movement. Within a few years she remarried, this time to an attorney named Alfred C. Cowan, with whom she moved to Brooklyn, New York. Lytle's father joined the couple in Brooklyn and lived there from 1909 to 1923, running a barbershop and becoming involved in local politics. Lytle's brother Jesse and her sister Corrine soon also moved to Brooklyn to seek better living and working opportunities.

In 1913 Lytle and her husband attended the annual convention of what became the National Negro Bar Association. Newspapers reported that she was the first African American woman to become a member of a national bar organization. In the early 1920s Lytle became a supporter of MARCUS GARVEY, the Jamaican-born leader of the Universal Negro Improvement Association, international advocate for racial equality, and father of contemporary black nationalism. In 1925 Lytle returned to Topeka and addressed a large audience at St. John's AME Church, which she had attended in her youth. Lytle told her audience about the progress of African Americans in New York City, shared examples of integration in the schools and government, and spoke of Garvey's black pride.

Over the next year Lytle lived in Topeka and became involved in the Interstate Literary Association with members from both Kansas and Missouri. She was also invited to give lectures to women's groups and local colleges on issues relating to law and political rights. While she may have returned to New York, it is not known what she did in the final years of her life. She did not have any children and the exact year of her death is unknown.

FURTHER READING

Connolly, Noreen R. "Attorney Lutie A. Lytle: Options and Obstacles of a Legal Pioneer," in *Nebraska Lawyer* (Jan. 1999).

Smith, J. Clay, ed. *Rebel in Law: Voices in History of Black Women Lawyers* (1998).

OMAR H. ALI

Mabley, Moms (19 Mar. 1894?–23 May 1975), comedian, was born Loretta Mary Aiken in Brevard, North Carolina, the daughter of Jim Aiken, a businessman and grocer. Her mother's name is not known. Details of her early life are sketchy at best, but she maintained in interviews she had black, Irish, and Cherokee ancestry. Her birth date is often given as sometime in 1897. Her grandmother, a former slave, advised her at age thirteen "to leave home if I wanted to make something of myself." However, she may have been unhappy over an arranged marriage with an older man. Mabley stated in a 4 October 1974 *Washington Post* interview, "I did get engaged two or three times, but they always wanted a free sample." Her formative years were spent in the Anacostia section of Washington, D.C., and in Cleveland, Ohio, where she later maintained a home. She had a child out of wedlock when she was sixteen. In an interview she explained she came from a religious family and had the baby because "I didn't believe in destroying children." Mabley recalled that the idea to go on the stage came to her when she prayed and had a vision. But in a 1974 interview she said she went into show business "because I was very pretty and didn't want to become a prostitute." Another time she explained, "I didn't know I was a comic till I got on the stage."

In 1908 she joined a Pittsburgh-based minstrel show by claiming to be sixteen; she earned $12.50 a week and sometimes performed in blackface. By 1910 she was working in black theatrical revues, such as *Look Who's Here* (1920), which briefly played on Broadway. She became engaged to a Canadian named Jack Mabley. Though they never married,

she explained she took his name because "he took a lot off me and that was the least I could do."

In 1921 Mabley was working the chitlin circuit, as black entertainers referred to the black-owned and black-managed clubs and theaters in the segregated South. There, she recalled, she introduced a version of the persona that made her famous, the weary older woman on the make for a younger man. The dance duo Butterbeans and Suzie (JODIE EDWARDS and Susan Edwards) caught her act and hired her, polishing her routines and introducing her to the Theater Owners' Booking Association, or TOBA—black artists said the initials stood for "Tough on Black Asses." She shared bills with PIGMEAT MARKHAM, Tim "Kingfish" Moore, and BILL "BOJANGLES" ROBINSON.

In the late 1920s, when Mabley struggled to find work in New York, the black comedian Bonnie Bell Drew (Mabley named her daughter in her honor) became mentor to Mabley, teaching her comedy monologues. Soon Mabley was working Harlem clubs such as the Savoy Ballroom and the Cotton Club and Atlantic City's Club Harlem. She appeared on shows with BESSIE SMITH and CAB CALLOWAY (with whom she had an affair), LOUIS ARMSTRONG, and the COUNT BASIE, DUKE ELLINGTON, and Benny Goodman orchestras. During the Depression, when many clubs closed, she worked church socials and urban movie houses, such as Washington's Howard and Chicago's Monogram and Regal theaters, where she later returned as a headliner.

Mabley had bit parts in early talkies made in the late 1920s in New York. She played a madam in *The Emperor Jones* (1931), based on the Eugene

O'Neill play and starring PAUL ROBESON. In 1931 Mabley collaborated on and appeared in the short-lived Broadway production *Fast and Furious: A Colored Revue in 37 Scenes* with the flamboyant Harlem Renaissance writer ZORA NEALE HURSTON. In the late 1920s she appeared in a featured role on Broadway in *Blackbirds*. She played Quince in *Swinging the Dream* (also featuring BUTTERFLY MCQUEEN) in 1939, a jazz adaptation of *A Midsummer Night's Dream*. Other films include *Killer Diller* (1947), opposite NAT KING COLE and Butterfly McQueen; *Boardinghouse Blues* (1948), in which she played a role much like her stage character; and *Amazing Grace* (1974), in which McQueen and STEPIN FETCHIT had cameos. It was drubbed by critics but did well at the box office.

The most popular Mabley character was the cantankerous but lovable toothless woman with bulging eyes and raspy voice who wore a garish smock or rumpled clothes, argyle socks, and slippers. Though she maintained, "I do the double entendre … and never did anything you haven't heard on the streets," the nature of her material, more often than not off-color, was such that, in spite of the brilliance of her comic timing and gift of ad-libbing, she was denied the route comics such as FLIP WILSON, DICK GREGORY, and BILL COSBY took into fine supper clubs and Las Vegas. A younger brother, Eddie Parton, wrote comedy situations for her, but most of her material was absorbed from listening to her world. Offstage Mabley was an avid reader and an attractive woman who wore furs, chic clothes, and owned a Rolls-Royce, albeit an inveterate smoker, a card shark, and a whiz at checkers.

In 1940 she broke the gender barrier and became the first female comic to appear at Harlem's Apollo Theater, where her act, which included song and dance, played fifteen sold-out weeks. Mabley was mentor to a young PEARL BAILEY and befriended by LANGSTON HUGHES, who wrote a friend that he occasionally helped Mabley financially. Legend has her acquiring the nickname "Moms" because of her mothering instincts toward performers.

Her first album, *Moms Mabley, the Funniest Woman in the World* (1960), sold in excess of a million copies. In 1966 she was signed by Mercury Records. She made more than twenty-five comedy records, many capturing her live performances; others, called "party records," had laugh tracks. She said black and white comics stole her material, then forgot her when they became famous.

Television was late to discover Mabley. Thanks to her fan HARRY BELAFONTE, she made her TV debut in a breakthrough comedy he produced with an integrated cast, *A Time for Laughter* (1967), as the maid to a pretentious black suburban couple. Merv Griffin invited her on his show, and appearances followed with Mike Douglas and variety programs starring Flip Wilson, Bill Cosby, and the Smothers Brothers. Mabley had been known mainly to black audiences. Of this late acceptance, she mused: "It's too bad it took so long. Now that I've got some money, I have to use it all for doctor bills." Mabley was not always career savvy. She passed up an appearance on CBS's top-rated *Ed Sullivan Show*, saying: "Mr. Sullivan didn't want to give me but four minutes. Honey, it takes Moms four minutes just to get on the stage."

Because of her influence with African Americans, Mabley was seriously courted by politicians such as ADAM CLAYTON POWELL JR., whom she called "my minister." She did not aggressively support the 1960s civil rights movement, and she expressed outrage at the riots in Harlem. She was invited to the White House by presidents John F. Kennedy and Lyndon Johnson. Of the latter event, she told a (fictional) joke about admonishing Johnson to "get something colored up in the air quick" (a black astronaut). She said: "I happen to spy him [and] said, 'Hey, Lyndon! Lyndon, son! Lyndon. Come here, boy!'" She brought the house down merely by the gall in her delivery. Mabley maintained she corresponded with and met Eleanor Roosevelt to "talk about young men."

Various articles, which say nothing of a first husband—if there was one—note that Mabley had been separated from her second husband, Ernest Scherer, for twenty years when he died in 1974. The comedian had three daughters and adopted a son, who became a psychiatrist.

Late in her career, Mabley played Carnegie Hall on a bill with the singer Nancy Wilson and the jazz great CANNONBALL ADDERLEY, the famed Copacabana, and even Washington's Kennedy Center (August 1972).

During the filming of her last movie, Mabley suffered a heart attack, and production was delayed for her to undergo surgery for a pacemaker. Her condition weakened on tours to publicize the film, and for six months she was confined to her home in Hartsdale, in New York's Westchester County. She died at White Plains Hospital. Her funeral at Harlem's Abyssinian Baptist Church drew thousands of fans.

FURTHER READING
The Schomburg Center for Research in Black Culture of the New York Public Library and the New York

Public Library for the Performing Arts maintain research files on Mabley.

Bogle, Donald. *Brown Sugar: Eighty Years of America's Black Female Superstars* (1980)

Sochen, June. *Women's Comic Visions* (1991)

Watkins, Mel. *On the Real Side, Laughing, Lying, and Signifying: The Underground Tradition of African American Humor That Transformed American Culture, from Slavery to Richard Pryor* (1994)

Williams, Elsie A. *The Humor of Jackie "Moms" Mabley: An African American Comedic Tradition* (1995)

Obituary: *New York Times*, 25 May 1975.

This entry is taken from the *American National Biography* and is published here with the permission of the American Council of Learned Societies.

ELLIS NASSOUR

Mabson, George Lawrence (Nov. 1845?–4 Oct. 1885), lawyer, federal official, state legislator, and congressional aspirant, was the first of two sons born to a slave mother, Eliza Mabson, and her wealthy white owner, George W. Mabson, in Wilmington, North Carolina. He was educated at an early age in Massachusetts, where he resided until after the end of the Civil War. How George W. Mabson's father arranged to send his oldest son to Massachusetts in the early 1850s is not known, but presumably he either freed the light-skinned youth or smuggled him out of the state. From the age of eight, George reportedly lived with family friends in the Boston area, where he later worked as a waiter after the outbreak of the Civil War. On 15 February 1864, claiming to be eighteen years old, George enlisted in the Union army, joining the Fifth Massachusetts (Colored) Cavalry Regiment's Company G, the state's third African American unit, and mustered in at Camp Meigs in Readville.

Although technically a cavalry unit, the Fifth Massachusetts mostly fought dismounted until the seizure of Richmond, Virginia, and was used essentially as an infantry unit. According to one account, Private Mabson was wounded during the war, probably in 1864 at Petersburg, Virginia, the one major battle in which his regiment participated. Mabson's regiment was then reassigned in June 1864 to guard Confederate prisoners at Point Lookout, Maryland, and was then sent once again to Petersburg in March 1865, and from there to be one of the first regiments to enter Richmond after its evacuation. The regiment's final assignment was to Mexican border duty at Clarksville, Texas. There, on 31 October 1865, Sergeant Mabson and other soldiers were mustered out of the Union army and sent back to Massachusetts for discharge.

Mabson remained in Boston long enough to begin a family with his new wife, Rosa, a Massachusetts native whose maiden name is now unknown. But by 1867, he had moved back to Wilmington, North Carolina, where he immediately became active in Republican politics. Selected as a speaker by the Republican congressional committee in 1867, Mabson was appointed a year later as justice of the peace in New-Hanover County by the Republican governor, William W. Holden.

Mabson now decided to enter the law department of the new Howard University, in Washington, D.C., and for the next two years, juggled legal studies with his public career, both legislative and military. Commissioned in January 1870 by Governor Holden as a lieutenant colonel in the state militia, he commanded African American state guard battalions, under three governors, until his final resignation in 1879.

In the summer of 1870 Mabson also won election as a Republican to the state house of representatives, representing New Hanover County. The General Assembly met for two sessions, from November 1870 to April 1871, and again from November 1871 to February 1872. In between those sessions, Mabson earned his bachelor's degree in Law from Howard in 1871, as one of the school's first ten law graduates. In July 1871 he became the first black attorney admitted to the New Hanover County bar, and one of the state's first licensed black lawyers. He also accepted a federal appointment as U.S. customs inspector for the port of Wilmington, one of six still serving there in 1875, at an annual salary of $1,277.50. In 1874 he assumed additional duties, those of official weigher and gauger, for the customs house.

While in the legislature Mabson had only limited opportunities for service, assigned to just one committee, on penal institutions. But he maintained a high profile, passionately opposing Democratic plans to impeach and remove Governor Holden, an ardent defender of freedmen's rights, from office. "When Gov. Holden is disposed of those whom he protected will be the next victims," Mabson and sixteen colleagues declared in an "Address to the Colored People of North Carolina," in the Raleigh *Sentinel* in December 1870.

Holden was, in fact, removed from office in 1871, but Mabson's fears were not immediately borne out. In 1872, Mabson won election to the state senate, representing the Twelfth District (New Hanover County), and served until that general assembly adjourned its session in February 1874. By coincidence, his younger brother WILLIAM MABSON served in the same legislature, representing his adopted county of Edgecombe in the house of representatives.

George Mabson's final attempt at elective office came in 1874, when the young lawyer sought the Republican nomination for Congress from the state's Third District, seeking to unseat incumbent Democrat Alfred M. Waddell. After losing the nomination to Neil McKay at the district convention, Mabson never sought office again, although he continued to be active in affairs of the race. In 1877 he was elected as vice president of the State Colored Education Convention, a notable gathering of influential statewide leaders in the fields of both politics and teaching.

In April 1881 Mabson was among a group of county and regional leaders calling for a state convention of African Americans in Raleigh to lobby for federal appointments under the new administration of President James A. Garfield. "We have educated young men of our race who are every way qualified to fill positions of profit and trust," read the statewide call signed by Mabson, "yet not a single position of any prominence is accorded them," despite a numerical majority in the state's Republican Party. (*Wilmington Post*, 24 Apr. 1881)

In 1882, Mabson signed a similar statewide call for a convention in Goldsboro, intended to recruit African American candidates for public office in the 1882 state elections, and was one of the primary speakers listed at that convention.

Mabson remained active in local affairs as well. He was an active Freemason, serving as Master of the Giblem Masonic Lodge, Grand Lodge of Colored Masons in North Carolina, in 1879, and a devoted member of St. Stephen's African Methodist Episcopal (AME) Church, on whose building committee he served in 1880. In 1884, he served as local president of the Discharged Union Soldiers Association.

Mabson died of natural causes at his home in 1885, aged forty, and was briefly described by the Wilmington newspaper as a "a colored man of some local prominence as a Republican politician" (Wilmington *Morning Star*, 6 Oct. 1885). In addition to his wife, he was survived by his daughter Robbertta and son George Jr.; his mother, who remained in Wilmington; and several siblings, including William Mabson of Tarboro.

FURTHER READING

Foner, Eric. *Freedom's Lawmakers: A Directory of Black Officeholders during Reconstruction* (1993)

Reaves, William M. *"Strength through Struggle": The Chronological and Historical Record of the African-American Community in Wilmington, North Carolina, 1865–1950* (1998).

Obituary: Wilmington (N.C.) *Morning Star*, 6 Oct. 1885.

BENJAMIN R. JUSTESEN

Mabson, William Patrick (31 Oct. 1846?–20 Dec. 1916), teacher, newspaper editor, labor activist, and state legislator, was one of five children born in Wilmington, North Carolina, to a slave mother, Eliza Mabson, and her wealthy white owner, George W. Mabson. Little is known of his early life or education before the end of the Civil War, only that he left Wilmington in 1865 to enter Lincoln University (formerly Ashmun Institute), in Pennsylvania, where he stayed for three years.

Like his older brother, GEORGE LAWRENCE MABSON, who was educated as a child in Massachusetts, William Mabson returned to North Carolina committed to the advancement of members of his race. There is no official record of his degree from Lincoln University, but he nonetheless became a popular teacher in a number of freedmen's schools across the state, including those in Rockingham, Abbottsburg, Rehoboth, Washington, and Leggetts. In 1870 he settled in Edgecombe County, where he spent the next two decades of his life as an active and often controversial figure in the fields of education, journalism, politics, and labor organizing.

Mabson first taught at the Tarboro Colored Institute, a school constructed by Tarboro's African American community for its children's education. In 1873 he was also named county school examiner for Edgecombe, and during his three-year tenure, issued teaching certificates to 200 new teachers. A strong Methodist, he was active in his local congregation, and some accounts even list him as a minister. He became an active member of the local Republican Party, which selected him in 1872 as its nominee for one of two county seats in the North Carolina House of Representatives.

Mabson won the 1872 election, defeating the Democrat Edward R. Stamps, and served in the 1872–1873 general assembly with his running mate, Willis Bunn of Tarboro, while his brother George served as a member of the state senate representing New Hanover County. State records show that

William Mabson did not complete the term; his seat was declared vacant in January 1874, without explanation, and a new election was ordered, won by Joseph Cobb of Tarboro.

Mabson was married on 15 August 1874 to Louisa Dudley, a native of Greenville, North Carolina. They were the parents of nine children, five of whom lived to adulthood.

By the end of 1874, however, Mabson was back in the general assembly, after chairing the summer's county Republican convention and then winning election as Edgecombe County's first African American state senator, representing the Fifth District, by defeating the Democrat H. C. Brown, with a majority of more than 2,300 votes. One of four African Americans to serve in the 1874–1875 general assembly, Mabson won re-election in 1876, where he was one of five African American senators.

In between his senate terms, Mabson also represented Edgecombe County at the state's 1875 constitutional convention, as one of just six black delegates. In 1876 he served as a delegate from the "Black Second" congressional district to the Republican national convention, held that year in Cincinnati, and at which Ohio governor. Rutherford B. Hayes won the party's nomination for U.S. president.

His political appetite for national office whetted by his convention attendance and by Hayes's narrow victory that fall, Mabson began expressing interest in seeking the Republican nomination for Congress from the "Black Second" district, which had already elected one African American congressman, JOHN ADAMS HYMAN, in 1874. The "Black Second," gerrymandered by the Democratic legislature after the 1870 census in an attempt to contain Republican power as much as possible, stretched unevenly from the Virginia border down to New Bern; all but two of its 10 ten counties had black majorities.

Yet the district's African American voters were not yet completely unified. Hyman had lost his bid for re-election in 1876 to a white Republican. Many black politicians in the district were openly interested, among them eventual nominee JAMES E. O'HARA, who easily turned back Mabson's challenge. O'Hara's controversial record and personal scandals—bigamy and a dubious claim to U.S. citizenship by birth—plus a strong run by the independent black candidate JAMES H. HARRIS, doomed his campaign. Mabson's own personal scandals, tame by comparison, involved his own reckless temper and court fines on two recent occasions for assaulting political rivals. The divided electorate eventually chose a white Democrat, W. H. "Buck" Kitchin.

Following James Garfield's inauguration in 1881, Mabson was named a U.S. gauger, working under the customs collector Elihu A. White. But Mabson did not seek elective office again, confining his relentless energies, for the moment, to education. In January 1882 the Edgecombe County school committee selected Mabson as principal of the new public graded school for African Americans, to be opened in Freedom Hill (later Princeville), just outside Tarboro, despite pleas by a majority of local parents against his appointment for reasons not listed, presumably personal.

Enrollment at the new school reflected that dissatisfaction; by February, Mabson reported just 152 students in class, less than half the total eligible population. During his lengthy career as a teacher, he later estimated, proudly, that he had taught more than 3,000 students.

Mabson took the criticism in stride, and continued teaching. Despite his fiery temper, Mabson had always managed to weather public criticism for his outspoken remarks and occasionally pugnacious behavior. Mabson occasionally embodied conflicting, even contradictory viewpoints at once; in 1879, for example, he enthusiastically encouraged so-called "Exodusters" to leave for better opportunities in the West, but steadfastly refused to leave himself.

Ironically, it was a short-lived strike by local farm workers in September 1889, for higher wages on Edgecombe cotton plantations, which led to Mabson's final departure from North Carolina. The strike collapsed after several weeks, under legal and economic pressure by the planters and county officials, and Mabson, a supporter of the strike, reportedly received at least one death threat for his outspoken actions. In January 1890 he was among 1,600 Edgecombe African Americans who joined the exodus to the West. For the next quarter century, William Mabson worked as a journalist and newspaper editor in Austin, Texas. His death certificate lists his occupation as lawyer, although there is no record of his practice in Texas or elsewhere.

FURTHER READING

Anderson, Eric. *Race and Politics in North Carolina, 1872–1901: The Black Second* (1981)

Foner, Eric. *Freedom's Lawmakers: A Directory of Black Officeholders during Reconstruction* (1993)

Reaves, William M. *"Strength Through Struggle": The Chronological and Historical Record of the*

African-American Community in Wilmington, North Carolina, 1865--1950 (1998).

BENJAMIN R. JUSTESEN

MacAlpine, Arthur (7 Sept. 1914–12 Mar. 1991), poet, boxer, policeman, and journalist, was born Arthur Winslow MacAlpine in Birmingham, Alabama, the third of five children of Francis P. MacAlpine, an Alabamian born in slavery four years before Emancipation, and Mary Winslow, a music teacher from Canada and the first black woman to graduate from the University of New Brunswick. Having met and married in Springfield, Massachusetts, the MacAlpines had moved to Birmingham so that Mary, unable to find employment in the mostly white schools of New England, could teach in a segregated one. In 1919 the promise of a better education for their children persuaded them to return to Springfield, where Francis kept a small convenience store and Mary gave piano and violin lessons.

Poetry and music were paramount in the household. Mary, who knew countless poems by heart, would recite Longfellow, Frost, and the English romantics, sometimes to young Arthur's discomfort. In an interview sixty years later he remarked that some of these poems were "long and important-sounding" and made him feel that he could do better. But it was his mother's piano and violin music that he remembered most clearly, as the musicality of his own poetry bears out. With her encouragement he tried his hand at verse early on, writing what he considered his first complete poem when he was sixteen. His burgeoning gift met with a certain resentment from his teachers and classmates at Classical High, where he and his siblings were among the few black students. Perhaps for this reason he kept his poetry under wraps, preferring to excel, publicly at least, as an athlete. He was an all-city football player and rowed crew into his senior year, but when he was barred from a meet because of his color, he quit the crew team and left school without graduating.

In fall 1931 MacAlpine entered Saint Augustine's College in North Carolina on a football scholarship, but he was obliged to leave the following spring when it was discovered that he lacked a high school diploma. This setback, combined with the hardships of the Depression, prompted him to try earning money in the boxing ring. Working as an amateur at five dollars a fight, and soon as a professional, he boxed from 1933 to 1946, eventually attaining the unofficial title of New England Light Heavyweight Champion and winning ten bouts out of thirteen in the heavyweight division. He fought conservatively, with a deadpan expression, hands held high, and moving in with a minimum of carefully aimed punches—a style that at least one sports writer compared to that of JOE LOUIS (*Springfield Daily News*, 25 July 1935).

Two years into his boxing career he married Victoria Joseph, a childhood neighbor who had studied piano with his mother and with whom he was to have four sons. Between fights he earned thirteen dollars a month with the WPA, played professional footfall, and continued to write poems, occasionally reciting them for friends while Victoria accompanied him on the piano. When World War II took able-bodied white men from the labor force he began a seven-year stint as a machinist at the Chapman Valve Company, where hours of watching a part being honed on a slow cutter gave him time to work on his poetry. It was there that he composed "Man in a Metal Cage," which became the title poem of a book published three decades later. He never mentioned his vocation to his co-workers or fellow boxers. "Nobody ever suspected it," he later said half in jest. "It was one of the deep dark sins that I kept hidden."

By 1946, after defeating Harold Raskin in Madison Square Garden, MacAlpine ranked twelfth as a world heavyweight. He fought his last bout that same year, losing to Elmer "Violent" Ray in a knockout that left him severely injured. After a lengthy recovery he joined the Springfield Police Department, where his boxer's build and skill got him assigned to a tough part of town near the railroad station. His experience patrolling the Gut, as it was called, inspired several poems, among them "Sneaky Pete Alley," in which a splinter of glass from a broken wine bottle commemorates the derelicts who frequented the place:

Remember only that it caught a light,
and briefly matched the brilliance of a star.
And if it's now a fragment of the night,
it is no less than all the dreamers are.

MacAlpine remained on the police force until 1961, when a kneecap shattered in an altercation with a drunk brought him early retirement. His marriage had ended in 1953, and the following year he met and married Madeline Hunter, a nurse with whom he raised three sons and two daughters. During his second marriage he devoted much of his time to journalism, beginning in 1962 as the publisher and editor of a black weekly newspaper, the *New England Sun*, and later writing editorials for the *South Shore Mirror*. In 1968 he moved from journalism to social work, serving with the state rehabilitation commission and tutoring handicapped people at Goodwill Industries. In-spring 1976 his poetry, which until then had remained a mostly private avocation, was heard in a public forum.

This occurred at the county fairgrounds in Northampton, Massachusetts, during a somewhat raucous arts fair in the midst of which a handful of blue-jeaned poets had been trying to read into a portable loudspeaker. At the urging of a friend, the impeccably dressed MacAlpine limped his way forward with his cane, spoke a few poems from memory, and reduced the fairgrounds to near silence. This success brought him invitations to appear on radio and television and at libraries, schools, colleges, a state prison in Connecticut, and Northampton's Broadside Bookstore. There he met the printer and artist Barry Moser, who suggested the possibility of a book. That same evening a friend offered to help finance it, and a limited edition of *Man in a Metal Cage* (1977) was in print within a year.

Illustrated with Moser's wood engravings, the selection included thirty-three of more than two hundred poems that MacAlpine had written and retained, each of them so classically formed as to seem almost anachronistic in an era of free verse and informal diction. Among them were poems of protest, a number of elegies, and several that might be characterized as self-portraits. The protest poems speak out against racism, the threat of nuclear war, and the Holocaust, as in:

> April in Auschwitz–1964
> April slashed the skin of stubborn sod,
> and bled the thick black blood of earth
> a thousand places, broke the pod
> of winter sleep with brutal mirth;
> but turned no blade of grass in odd
> small fields where children wait with just
> their powdered bones to beckon God,
> with silent ash their April's dust.

Possibly because of the loss of his son Mark in 1972, MacAlpine's elegies occasionally address young people missing or deceased. He claimed to have composed one of these beside a cemetery, before he learned that such a person had been buried there that day:

> Requiem for a Young Girl
> Come back from the grape-blued hour
> of dying—walk the dusty grass

> to green, and help me form
> the podded flowers into spring.
> Help me tear the sound of sun
> from these stiff leaves, and tie the silent songs,
> like ribbons, to the April trees,
> where all your dreams were strung.
> Then wait with me on that strident edge
> of birth-green pain, and laugh again at time,
> while all the bright leaves turn to rain.

The poems of self-portraiture depict the poet variously as street singer, rebel, and prisoner. "With importuning hands," the poem "Black Minstrel" begins, "I tugged a sleeve, / and mumbled words against the wind / of history." In "Revolt" MacAlpine calls himself a "fleeing slave" who "threw a stone up at a star" and in so doing "threw away the memory of the lash." Then there is the haunting title poem, "Man in a Metal Cage," the implications of which extend far beyond the machine shop where it was conceived:

> Steel is a spinning, churning mass
> of suns and writhing space between,
> and so is iron, and the shining brass.
> The very walls are merely seen
> as walls, the tiny orbits set
> throughout its width are only lace
> across an empty space—and yet
> my soul cannot escape this place.

The edition of two hundred copies, most of them given away, was quickly consumed, and there were no publications afterward. MacAlpine still gave readings, speaking his poems from memory as always, and continued to write. But the Parkinson's disease that had begun to afflict him some twenty years after his last fight was noticeably worsening. The mid-1980s found him deteriorating rapidly, and at the end of the decade he entered a nursing home. He died there after a year, having achieved a certain renown as a boxer but with his poetry virtually unknown. More ambitious for his poems than for fame, he had made little effort to publish. Even if he had, his formalism might well have kept him from the recognition he deserved. But he was celebrated locally at least, thanks especially to his readings, the final one presented at the nursing home by his wife, Madeline, who recited his poems for the assembled residents as he sat beside her in a wheelchair listening.

FURTHER READING
Chipkin, Robert. "Poetry Is a Way of Taking Life by the Throat," *Springfield Republican*, 20 Jan. 1972.

Faulkner, Frank. "A Boxer Turned Poet," *Springfield Daily News*, 14 Sept. 1976.

HENRY LYMAN

MacDavid, Mary Foster (1895?–6 Jul. 1955), educator and community leader, was born Mary Foster, one of eight children born to Mr. and Mrs. Jiles Foster, a farmer and a housewife in Union County, South Carolina, near Spartanburg. During the 1920s, Mary Foster married Sterling James MacDavid, a teacher and principal in Autauga County, Alabama. They settled in Montgomery, Alabama.

A precocious child, MacDavid entered Tuskegee Institute at an early age and finished high school there in 1907 at the age of twelve under the instruction of Dr. BOOKER T. WASHINGTON. She received her Bachelor's Degree in 1929 during the administration of Dr. ROBERT E. MOTON and her master's degree in 1937 under the tutelage of Dr. FREDERICK D. PATTERSON. MacDavid began her teaching career in the 1910s at the Topeka Educational and Industrial Institute of Topeka, Kansas, and later entered the field of supervision working with the Jeanes Teachers Program in Spartanburg, South Carolina. She served in that capacity for five years before returning to Alabama.

The Jeanes Teachers Program was sponsored by the Jeanes Fund, also known as the Negro Rural School Fund. This was a philanthropic institution established by the Quaker Anna T. Jeanes for the purpose of funding and promoting education for African American children. Jeanes allotted one million dollars for the sponsorship of this program. During the early twentieth century, the Jeanes Fund was one of the most prominent philanthropic organizations in the United States geared toward the education of African American children. The organization employed African American teachers throughout the South, most of them women, whose salaries were augmented by the Jeanes Fund in exchange for their service as community organizers. They also received funding from the General Education Board, a philanthropic institution established by John D. Rockefeller. Financial contributions on the part of individual counties or states varied. The goal of the Jeanes teachers, or Jeanes supervisors as they were sometimes called, was to undertake social projects aimed at the uplift of their respective communities. Among their duties were to teach sanitation, health, and hygiene, as well as industrial and life skills. In 1937 the Jeanes Fund combined with the Virginia Randolph and John F. Slater funds to create the Southern Education Foundation, an entity that still exists today.

After returning to Alabama in the early 1920s, MacDavid took on the role of supervisor of the Jeanes Teachers Program for Macon County. The headquarters for the program under her administration were situated at Tuskegee University. She later became state supervisor of the Jeanes Teachers for the state of Alabama. She served in this capacity for twenty years. During her tenure, the program was based out of Alabama State University in Montgomery, Alabama. As state supervisor, she worked closely in conjunction with the state superintendent of schools to promote and foster quality education for African Americans in the state of Alabama. Among her duties were to establish budgets, consult with local African American communities, fund-raising, and overseeing county training schools. She also supervised the construction of Rosenwald schools. The Rosenwald schools were schools that were built with funds from the Rosenwald School Building Program, a philanthropic entity established in 1912 by Julius Rosenwald, a philanthropist and president of Sears and Roebuck, with the purpose of funding the construction of schools in black communities throughout the South. She also served as a liaison between the black community and white social and political institutions.

In 1939, after serving as state president of the Congress of Colored Parents and Teachers for the state of Alabama, MacDavid was elected president of the National Congress of Colored Parents and Teachers (NCCPT). This organization which was founded by Selena Sloan Butler in 1911 in Atlanta, Georgia, advocated for quality education for African American children and sought to improve standards of living in African American communities. The NCCPT mirrored and worked in close conjunction with the National Association of Parents and Teachers, which was exclusively white. In 1970 the NCCPT merged with the National PTA to form a unified national organization after the end of school segregation.

As president of the NCCPT, MacDavid, along with representatives of the American Federation of Labor, the NAACP, the Congress of Industrial Organizations, the National League of Women Voters, and other organizations, attended the World Congress on Education for Democracy held at Columbia University in New York City in August 1939. During her tenure, the NCCPT was active in the National Anti-Syphilis campaign and assisted in giving TB tests to high school students. Under McDavid's leadership, the NCCPT participated on the National Committee on Education and Defense in which the role of educators in national defense during World War II was discussed. In 1940 MacDavid attended the White House Conference Children in a Democracy. In 1941 a national committee on school lunch programs was launched. Later that year, President Franklin Roosevelt declared October PTA Membership Month. In conjunction with the war effort, the NCCPT national convention theme was "The Place of the PTA in the Total National Defense Program." Training for community leaders was emphasized during the convention.

As a resident of Montgomery, Alabama, since the 1920s, MacDavid made her church home at Saint Paul's African Methodist Episcopal Church, a historical black church in Montgomery, Alabama, and an important center in the civil rights movement. Saint Paul's AME was also the church home of ROSA PARKS, a leader of the civil rights movement and the woman who inspired the 1955 Montgomery bus boycott that led to the historic Supreme Court decision ending segregation of public transportation in the South. MacDavid served as chairman of the official board of Saint Paul's AME Church for four years. She died after a brief illness on 6 July 1955. Her funeral services were held there on 12 July 1955.

Mary Foster MacDavid dedicated her life to the service of African American youth and the African American community. She and other black educators broke down barriers and opened doors of opportunity in the early decades of the twentieth century that fostered the movements for justice and equality that radically restructured American society in the social movements of the 1950s and 1960s.

FURTHER READING
Littlefield, Valinda. *A Quiet Force: Southern African American Women School Teachers and Black Freedom, 1884–1954* (2009).
Woyshner, Christina. *The National PTA, Race, and Civic Engagement, 1897–1970* (2009).
                              BRANDON K. WALLACE

Machito (16 Feb. 1908?–15 Apr. 1984), salsa and jazz bandleader, singer, and percussionist, was born Frank Raúl Grillo in Tampa, Florida, the son of Rogelio Grillo, formerly a cigar maker and then a grocery store owner, and Marta Amparo. In his oral history Machito claimed that 1908 was his year of birth, but in the same interview he claimed to be two years older than Mario Bauzá, which would make 1909 the correct date; 1912, given in some sources, seems less likely (though not impossible), since Machito was already an experienced professional musician in 1928. While he was still an infant, his family moved to Havana, Cuba, where his father ran two restaurants. He was nicknamed Macho because he was the first son after three daughters, one of whom, Graciela, would figure prominently in his career. Immersed in Afro-Cuban music from childhood, he began his career as a singer and maracas player with the group Los Jovenes de Rendición. From 1928 to 1937 he performed in Cuba with María Teresa Vera's El Sexteto Occidente, El Sexteto Agabama, El Sexteto Universo, Ignacio Piñero, and El Sexteto Nacional. During this period he married Luz María Pelgrino. They had one child. In 1937 Grillo came to New York, where he joined Mulato's quartet Las Estrellas Habañeras (Stars of Havana). After holding a residency at the Cadillac Hotel in Detroit, the quartet returned to New York, where Grillo first recorded with the vocalist Alfredito Valdez and Graciela, the latter then in New York as a member of the all-woman group El Septeto Anacaona. Grillo then recorded with El Quarteto Caney, El Conjuncto Moderno, and La Orquesta Hatuey, and he sang with the bands of Noro Morales and Augusto Coen.

Machito, Cuban bandleader, singer, and maracas player, with Graciella Grillo at Glen Island Casino, New York City, c. July 1947. (© William P. Gottlieb; www.jazzphotos.com.)

In 1939 Grillo and Bauzá, his friend from the late 1920s and now a veteran of New York big bands, formed their first Afro-Cuban band to perform at a new nightclub, La Conga. The job fell through for want of a fuse to power the lights. Bauzá joined CAB CALLOWAY, while Grillo sang with Alberto Iznaga and his Orchestra Siboney and also recorded with Xavier Cugat (1939–1940).

Divorced, Grillo married Hilda Esther Porres, from Puerto Rico, in April 1940. They had five children. Grillo modified his nickname from Macho to Machito, and with Bauzá as musical director, he re-formed the Afro-Cubans in July 1940. The ten-man orchestra comprised Machito as singer, two trumpeters, two saxophonists, a pianist, a string bassist, and four percussionists (the leader playing maracas and his sidemen on timbales, bongos, and conga). The Afro-Cubans performed at the Park Palace Ballroom in Spanish Harlem, began an engagement at La Conga on 20 December 1940, and signed a recording contract with Decca. "Sopa de Pichón" (Pigeon soup) and "Tingo Talango," recorded in 1941, became hit songs.

Drafted into the army in 1943, Machito handed the group over to Graciela, who had performed in France, Colombia, and Puerto Rico before returning to Cuba as a member of El Trio García. Now married to Bauzá, she made her debut with the Afro-Cubans during a radio broadcast from La Conga. Machito's position was filled by the singer Polito Galindez, but Machito soon returned, having received an honorable medical discharge after suffering a leg injury. Meanwhile, under Bauzá's influence, the band had begun to blend Afro-Cuban dance rhythms with jazz improvisation and techniques of big band arrangements, notably in its theme song from 1943, "Tanga." The Afro-Cubans recorded regularly from that year onward.

Sharing the stage with Stan Kenton's orchestra, Machito's band was featured at the first Latin jazz concert, given at Town Hall in New York on 24 January 1947. He began recording with guest jazz soloists, including the tenor saxophonist Flip Phillips on "No Noise, Part 1," "Caravan," and "Tanga," the alto saxophonist CHARLIE PARKER on "No Noise, Part 2," "Mango Mangue," and "Okiedoke" (all from December 1948–January 1949), and the trumpeter HOWARD MCGHEE and the tenor saxophonist Brew Moore on "Cubop City" (April 1949). The trumpet and saxophone sections grew in size, each routinely utilizing three or four players, and with jazz musicians incorporated into the band, the Afro-Cubans were billed in alternation with bop groups at Bop City, the Royal Roost, and Birdland in New York and the Harlem Club in Philadelphia. McGhee, Phillips, and the vibraphonist MILT JACKSON were recorded with Machito at the Royal Roost in the spring of 1949. Parker, Phillips, and the drummer Buddy Rich were added for a performance of the composer and arranger Chico O'Farrill's *Afro-Cuban Suite* on 21 December 1950.

Most of the aforementioned Afro-Cuban jazz pieces offer more of a superimposition of genres than a blending, and they are surpassed by recordings of 1948 to 1949 that Machito and his orchestra made on their own. "Vaya Niña," composed by O'Farrill, demonstrates the characteristically repeated and interlocking syncopated instrumental patterns of Latin jazz. Also typical is René Hernandez's piano solo, played in octaves and built in a relaxed but staggered fashion. This track utilizes the mambo dance rhythm, as do several others, including "Tumba el Quinto" and "Llora Timbero," both sung by Machito. O'Farrill's "Gone City," without singing, melds together bop and Cuban styles. The group presents a slower, crisper dance, of the sort that would come to be known as cha-cha, on "Un Poquito de Tu Amor" and "Vive Como Yo," both featuring Graciela, whose voice on these recordings is as bright and cutting as the tone of the Afro-Cuban trumpeters. An outstanding, uncredited arrangement of "The World Is Waiting for the Sunrise" shows how the genre of American popular song might be tastefully Latinized. Here, on these and associated titles, is the Afro-Cuban style that was popularized as salsa in the 1970s, already in full flower roughly a quarter century earlier.

Machito frequently performed at New York's Palladium Ballroom from the late 1940s through the 1950s, and his band made annual tours to Venezuela for fifteen years beginning in 1950. A national craze for mambo also brought steady work in Miami and at resorts in the Catskills as well as a cross-country tour, billed as Mambo U.S.A., together with the band of Joe Loco (1954–1955). From this time onward, if not earlier, Machito was giving considerable time to community work in New York. For the LP *Kenya* (1957; reissued as *Latin Soul Plus Jazz*) he brought in further guest artists, including DOC CHEATHAM, Joe Newman, Johnny Griffin, Herbie Mann, and CANNONBALL ADDERLEY. Griffin, Mann, and the trombonists Curtis Fuller and Sonny Russo contributed to the LP *Afro Jazziac* (1958).

Machito's group toured Japan (1962), Colombia (1965), Panama (1966), Peru (1968), Haiti (1969), and Puerto Rico (1970). In the mid-1970s the popularization of salsa brought him to the attention of a wider and younger audience, for whom he became one of the style's elder statesmen. He performed in New York City's Latin clubs, such as the Cork and Bottle, the Corso, Barney Googles, and El Chico East, and he regularly toured Europe from 1975 onward. In his capacity as a community leader, Machito headed Project Return, which endeavored to rehabilitate drug addicts and juvenile delinquents; he also served as project coordinator for the SCOUT program (Senior Citizens Outreach Unit Team), and he gave concerts for retarded children and adults.

Machito's album *Afro Cuban Jazz Moods*, including O'Farrill's "Oro, Incienso y Mirra," written for DIZZY GILLESPIE with Machito's orchestra, was recorded in June 1975 in a nostalgic and unsuccessful attempt to re-create their early achievements. In December, following a personal disagreement, Bauzá left the band after thirty-five years. He was replaced by Machito's son Mario Grillo. Graciella retired in the late 1970s, and Machito's daughter Paula Grillo took her place. Machito again toured Japan, where in testimony to his international influence the Afro-Cubans appeared with the Tokyo Cuban Boys around 1980. His big band performed at President Ronald Reagan's inaugural ball in January 1981, and that summer he was honored with a concert at City Hall Plaza in New York. The finest album from his last years is *Machito and His Salsa Big Band 1982*, made in the Netherlands during a European tour; it won a Grammy Award. While on yet another European tour, he died in London five days after suffering a stroke. His life was celebrated in the documentary film *Machito: A Latin Jazz Legacy*, completed posthumously and released in 1987.

Machito gave a penetrating description of a difference between Afro-Cuban dance music and jazz: "In Cuban music we never complicate the melody. It is the rhythm that is rich. But in jazz you have all the interest on top of the rhythm." His Afro-Cubans are significant historically as the pioneering ensemble in bringing these two musical streams together. Still more significantly, this was arguably the best Afro-Cuban orchestra, rivaled only briefly by Dizzy Gillespie's big band of the late 1940s.

FURTHER READING

In May 1980 Max Salazar interviewed Machito for the Jazz Oral History Project housed at the Institute of Jazz Studies, Newark, New Jersey

Current Biography (1983).

Roberts, John Storm. *The Latin Tinge: The Impact of Latin American Music on the United States* (1979).

Obituaries: *New York Times*, 17 Apr. 1984; *Jazz Journal International* 37 (June 1984): 7.

This entry is taken from the *American National Biography* and is published here with the permission of the American Council of Learned Societies.

BARRY KERNFELD

Mack, Cecil (6 Nov. 1883–1 Aug. 1944), songwriter, was born Richard C. McPherson in Norfolk, Virginia. Nothing is known of his parents or his early life. He studied at the Norfolk Mission College and at Lincoln University in Pennsylvania and set his sights on the study of medicine at the University of Pennsylvania. At first music was merely an avocation, but he gradually found his musical interests crowding out his medical ones; he began serious music studies in New York with the eminent Melville Charlton, the organist at some of New York's leading churches and synagogues for several decades. His activities during the years around 1900 were manifold, evincing a considerable degree of energy. In addition to his musical activities he was an enthusiastic member of the New York Guard, rising to the rank of lieutenant. He was also later active in the African American entertainment brotherhood known as the Frogs, together with the other leading lights of the theatrical and musical scene in which he traveled.

Beginning his musical career as a songwriter at the age of seventeen, in the years 1901–1906 Mack became a crucial member of a consortium of composers supplying material to the stage acts and recordings of BERT WILLIAMS and GEORGE WALKER, the leading African American stage team of their generation. Among the songs that Mack collaborated on during this period were "Junie," "All In, Down and Out," "Good Morning, Carrie," and "He's a Cousin of Mine." Williams or Walker or both recorded all of them for Victor or Columbia during these years, and the last two were among the biggest hits of the ragtime song genre.

Mack generally wrote only the lyrics for these songs. His collaborators on the music included such leading lights of the African American entertainment scene as CHRIS SMITH and Euday Bowman, as well as the white Tin Pan Alley composer Silvio Hein. Mack also worked with WILL MARION COOK, the eminent classically trained African American musician, during these years. Among their joint efforts were "The Little Gypsy Maid" (1902) and the songs "Brown Skin Baby Mine" and "Molly Green" for the seminal 1903 musical *In Dahomey*. In later years they also combined their energies in a more entrepreneurial direction.

In 1905 Mack founded the Gotham Music Publishing Company. There had been a few other attempts to start such a venture, but none of them had been successful. Gotham merged with a rival firm, Attucks Music, releasing sheet music from the Williams and Walker shows as well as other material by Mack, by Will Marion Cook, and by other major talents of the burgeoning African American music scene. Among the music that Mack composed during these years was "That Minor Strain" in 1910 with FORD DABNEY. His greatest song of this period was "That's Why They Call Me (Shine)," a clever comic song that became a standard and was recorded and performed steadily until at least the 1940s.

A second phase of career success for Mack occurred when the show *Runnin' Wild* took to the stage in 1923, which starred ADELAIDE HALL. Among the songs in this show were "Old Fashioned Love," "Ginger Brown," "Love Bug," "Snow Time," and "Open Your Heart." The music was by the Harlem stride piano giant JAMES P. JOHNSON. The great hit to emerge from this show was "Charleston," which became the ubiquitous dance for flappers and college boys through much of the 1920s. Though the lyrics for this infectious piece were negligible, Mack shared in some of the reflected glory of Johnson's extraordinary inspiration in penning the music.

Mack joined the American Society of Composers, Authors, and Publishers (ASCAP) in 1925, making him one of the first African Americans welcomed into the organization, which monitors performances of music to protect members' copyrights. He founded a vocal organization known as Cecil Mack's Southland Singers, and he later founded the Cecil Mack Choir, which performed in the Lew Leslie production *Rhapsody in Black* (1931). He arranged spirituals for use in this show and also wrote some lyrics for music by others. During the Depression, Mack was less active, although he did contribute the libretto for the Works Progress Administration (WPA)-funded project *Swing It* in 1937. He died in New York. His widow, Gertrude Curtis McPherson, was reputedly the first African American woman dentist licensed to practice in New York City.

FURTHER READING
Jasen, David A., and Gene Jones. *Spreadin' Rhythm Around* (1998).
Morgan, Thomas L., and William Barlow. *From Cakewalks to Concert Halls* (1992).
Obituaries: *New York Times*, 2 Aug. 1944; *Variety*, 9 Aug. 1944.

ELLIOTT S. HURWITT

Mackey, Biz (27 July 1897–22 Sept. 1965), baseball player and manager, was born James Raleigh Mackey in Eagle Pass, Texas, the son of J. Dee Mackey and Beulah Wright. He was raised in Luling, Texas, where he and his brothers Ray and Ernest played for the Luling Oilers in the Prairie League, and where he learned the art of switch-hitting. In 1918 Mackey began his professional baseball career with the San Antonio Black Aces as a catcher. Two years later, when the Negro National League was organized, C. I. TAYLOR, manager of the Indianapolis ABCs, purchased Mackey's contract. In March 1922 Mackey played briefly for the Colored All-Stars against a white major league All-Star team, led by Babe Ruth and Bob Meusel. Mackey batted .333 (11 hits in 33 at bats) with two doubles and a triple. In the 22 games that he played against white major league teams, Mackey hit .326 (27 hits in 82 at bats).

When the Eastern Colored League was formed in 1923, Mackey was traded to Ed Bolden's Philadelphia Hilldale Giants of Darby, Pennsylvania. He led the Hilldale club to three successive league pennants in 1923, 1924, and 1925, hitting .364, .355, and .354, respectively. In 1925, behind Mackey's .375 clutch hitting, the Hilldale club won their first Black World Series title, beating the Kansas City Monarchs in six games.

A master practitioner behind the plate, Mackey was known for his ability to call a game and to frame pitches to influence an umpire's decisions on balls and strikes. He possessed a powerful throwing arm, using a snap-throw release that became popular with catchers in the latter part of the twentieth century. Mackey was strong enough to throw to second base from a sitting position, as he routinely did in pre-inning warm-ups. Although he stood six feet one inch tall and weighed between 220 and 245 pounds, he was surprisingly agile behind the plate, but he lacked speed on the base paths.

In 1927 Mackey made a historic trip to Japan with Lonnie Goodwin's Philadelphia Royal Giants, the first black American team to visit Asia. Mackey became an instant favorite of Japanese fans when he hit the first home run in Tokyo's newly built Meiji Shrine Stadium. Mackey hit three home runs during the Giants' forty-eight-game tour, as they showcased creative gamesmanship to their Japanese counterparts. The diplomatic tour by the black Americans, which took place three years before a similar tour led by Babe Ruth, has been credited by the Japanese baseball historian Kazuo Sayama with inspiring the birth of professional Japanese baseball.

Following the demise of the Hilldale Giants, Mackey began playing for the Baltimore Black Sox in 1929. In 1933 he joined Bolden's new team, the independent Philadelphia Stars. Although the Stars were not a member of the Negro National League, Mackey was voted as a starting catcher, ahead of JOSH GIBSON, to the first East-West All-Star classic in Chicago's Comiskey Park. Mackey played in five more All-Star games, in 1935, 1936, 1938, 1941, and 1947, when he received a ceremonial walk at the age of fifty. In 1934 the Stars joined the Negro National League, and Mackey helped them beat the Chicago American Giants in the playoffs, four games to three, for the league title. Mackey delivered the game-winning hit in the seventh game.

After three seasons with the Stars, Mackey joined the Washington Elite Giants in 1936. When the Elite Giants moved to Baltimore in 1938, he became player-manager and tutor to a promising athlete named ROY CAMPANELLA. "Biz was a great, great catcher in his day," recalled Campanella. "I gathered quite a bit from Mackey, watching how he shifted his feet for an outside pitch, how he threw with a short, quick, accurate throw without drawing back. I didn't think Mickey Cochrane really was the master of defense that Mackey was."

In 1939 Baltimore owner Tom Wilson, satisfied with the progress of the young Campanella, traded the forty-one-year-old Mackey to Effa Manley's Newark Eagles. Although by this time he was past his prime, Mackey was still a bona fide force in the game, hitting over .300 as a part-time catcher from 1940 to 1943. He became the Eagles' manager in 1946. That year the Eagles won both halves of the Negro National League season, earning the right to challenge the Negro American League champs. With clutch hitting from future major leaguers MONTE IRVIN and LARRY DOBY, and superior pitching by LEON DAY and Rufus Lewis, the Eagles defeated the favorite Kansas City Monarchs in a hard-fought seven-game series. Retiring from baseball in 1949, Mackey finished his thirty-one-year playing career with an unofficial .350 average.

In a 1952 poll conducted by the *Pittsburgh Courier*, Mackey was voted the greatest catcher in black baseball by his peers, edging out slugger Josh Gibson as well as LOUIS "BIG BERTHA" SANTOP and Bruce Petway. "For combined hitting, thinking and physical endowment, there has never been another Biz Mackey," recalled CUMBERLAND POSEY, who had managed Gibson yet rated Mackey as the best catcher on his all-time team. Posey added, "He was a tremendous hitter, a fierce competitor; although slow afoot, he is the standout among catchers who have shown their wares in this nation." COOL PAPA BELL, a teammate of Gibson's, once said, "As much as I admired Campanella as a catcher, and Gibson as a hitter, I believe Biz Mackey was the best all-a-round catcher I ever saw."

After retiring from professional baseball, Mackey became a forklift operator for the Stauffers Chemical Company in Los Angeles, California, where he died. In 1959, at a celebration in his honor in Los Angeles, Campanella spoke highly of his mentor, saying, "I couldn't carry his glove or his bat."

FURTHER READING
Barbier, Larry. "Do You Remember Biz Mackey?" *Negro Digest* (Feb. 1951).
Clark, Dick, and Larry Lester, eds. *The Negro Leagues Book* (1994).
Holway, John. *Voices from the Great Black Baseball Leagues* (1975)
Lester, Larry. "Biz Mackey," in Mike Shatzkin, ed. *The Ballplayers* (1990).
This entry is taken from the *American National Biography* and is published here with the permission of the American Council of Learned Societies.

LARRY LESTER

Mackey, John (24 Sept. 1941–6 July 2011), professional football player and union organizer, was born in Roosevelt, on New York's Long Island. He was one of seven children, and his father was a minister. He attended Hempstead High School in New York and played football there. After graduation, he attended Syracuse University and played football with the Orange as a tight end from 1960 to 1962.

Mackey was a standout with quick hands and feet. In just two seasons, he racked up 481 yards and six touchdowns. During his junior year, he recorded 321 yards as a tight end, setting what was then a Syracuse record. Mackey graduated in 1963, and in the same year was taken by the Baltimore Colts in the second round of the National Football

League (NFL) draft. While tight ends function in the modern NFL primarily as short-range receivers, in 1963 NFL teams were just beginning to integrate the passing game into their overall offensive schemes. Up until then, offenses were built largely around running the football. Mackey arrived at just the right moment. He was fast, possessed size, and was an aggressive and effective blocker. He was able to grab both short- and long-range passes. Coaches took note of his success and began to pattern the tight end position after his particular skills. Indeed, to this day NFL tight ends are built around the model he established.

Mackey's ten years with the Colts organization were successful ones. During his rookie year, he caught thirty-five passes, racked up 726 yards, and was named to the Pro Bowl. His quarterback, the legendary John Unitas, began to target Mackey more and more as a long-reception threat. During his stint with the Colts, Mackey enjoyed two seasons with reception averages of twenty yards, a remarkable feat for a tight end (or, indeed, any receiver). In 1971 the Colts squared off against the Dallas Cowboys in Super Bowl V. In that game, Mackey played a key role, catching a tipped (and nearly intercepted) pass from Unitas which he then carried seventy-five yards for a touchdown.

John Mackey, Baltimore Colts Hall of Fame tight end, on the bench in an undated image. (AP Images.)

The Colts went on to win the game. Mackey's catch and scramble set a Super Bowl record and instantly became one of the most legendary plays in NFL history.

Off the field, Mackey's accomplishments were arguably just as valuable as those on the gridiron. A much-liked player, he was in 1970 elected president of the NFL's player union, the National Football League Players Association (NFLPA). He was the first person to hold that position. That same year, a short-lived strike broke out between players and owners. Mackey helped negotiate not only better terms for NFL players but also helped to create the league's first free-agency structure. At the time, the freedom of players to shape their professional destinies was severely limited by League rules. Mackey himself had been on the receiving end of such treatment, once having been ordered to sign a contract. He refused and thereafter remained an advocate of free-agency for NFL players. In the end, the newly established system lasted only a few years—it was abandoned again for a time beginning in 1977—but Mackey's vision helped create the model for what would later become the NFL's free-agency system.

Mackey remained with the Colts until 1972, at which point he was traded to the San Diego Chargers. Over his nine years in Baltimore it appeared that he'd managed to avoid serious injuries, but nagging knee and leg problems led him to retire after only a year in San Diego. For his career, Mackey accumulated 5,236 total yards. He recorded thirty-eight touchdowns, and averaged a remarkable 15.8 yards per reception. He was selected to five Pro Bowls. By the end of his football life Mackey had also become something of a local celebrity on Baltimore television and radio.

Following retirement, Mackey relocated with his wife Sylvia and three children to Los Angeles, where he was successful in a number of business ventures. In 1992 he was selected to the NFL Hall of Fame in his final year of eligibility. He and Mike Ditka were the first tight ends so honored. In the intervening years, however, Mackey's personal behavior was becoming more and more worrying. He was forgetful and languid beyond what could be explained away as the realities of advancing age. He was easily agitated and was banned from several local restaurants for harassing customers. In 2001 Mackey was diagnosed with dementia.

Though no direct link has been established, it was the opinion of Mackey's family and others that his condition was brought on by repeated blows to the head during his time as an NFL player. Over the next few years, Mackey became a leading advocate both for greater safety measures for current players and financial assistance for former players who were suffering the same affliction. In 2006 Sylvia Mackey appealed directly to League commissioner Paul Tagliabue, noting that the increasing cost of John Mackey's healthcare had forced her, at nearly sixty years old, to take on work as a flight attendant. The result of this was the creation of the so-called 88 Plan, a financial entitlement for former NFL players which provides up to $88,000 per year to help offset the costs of their medical care. The plan was named for one of Mackey's jersey numbers. In 2007 the Colts retired that same number, and two years later Mackey was named part of Syracuse's All-Century team.

Mackey's condition eventually became so advanced that his family could no longer care for him on their own, and he was placed in a nursing home. He died in July 2011 due to "frontotemporal dementia." Since the institution of the 88 Plan, the NFL has taken increasingly serious steps to limit the danger of head injuries to its players, including heavy fines levied against players who go helmet-to-helmet against opponents. It is clear that both during his heyday as a player and long after, John Mackey was a pioneer.

FURTHER READING

Neft, David S. *The Football Encyclopedia: The Complete History of Professional NFL Football, from 1892 to the Present* (1991).

Obituaries: *New York Times,* 7 July 2011; *Washington Post,* 7 July 2011.

JASON PHILIP MILLER

Mackey, Nathaniel (25 Oct. 1947–), poet, novelist, and literary critic, was born Nathaniel Ernest Mackey in Miami, Florida, the son of Alexander Obadiah Mackey and Sadie Jane Wilcox. When Mackey was four his parents divorced, and he and his three older siblings moved from Miami to northern California with their mother. In 1958 they relocated to the southern California city of Santa Ana, where Mackey attended high school. Although Mackey neither wrote nor read seriously during these years—in fact, his earliest aspiration was to become a mathematician—weekly trips to his family's Baptist church galvanized in him a deep interest in African American music. His experiences at church, coupled with his discovery of the music of JOHN COLTRANE and ORNETTE COLEMAN during high school, proved formative: black music

would, in all its varying forms, eventually come to represent Mackey's literary bass line. To borrow his own terminology, his "discrepant engagement" with its sounds, its politics, and its connection to traditions of spirituality throughout the African diaspora gives inherence to his wide-reaching and at times challenging body of work.

Mackey enrolled at Princeton University in 1965, and his burgeoning sense of the kinship between music and writing led him to immerse himself in the study of contemporary American literature. Several writers had important influences on his early thinking: the modernist poet William Carlos Williams, whose work he had encountered briefly in high school; the experimental "Projectivist" poets Charles Olson, Robert Duncan, and Robert Creeley; and, most important, the black avant-garde playwright, novelist, and music critic AMIRI BARAKA. While Williams and the Projectivists figured prominently in Mackey's later academic writing, Baraka served as the subject of his undergraduate thesis. As Mackey admitted in an interview in 2000, Baraka's evocations in *The Dead Lecturer* of "an aesthetic analogous to that of [jazz] music—mercurial, oblique, elliptical" inspired him to begin to write and publish in several of Princeton's literary magazines, and Baraka's simultaneous involvement in African American musical, literary, and political cultures led him to examine his potential as a professional writer (Naylor, 659).

Mackey graduated from Princeton in 1969, subsequently returning to California to teach mathematics for a year before entering a doctoral program in English and American literature at Stanford University. In 1974 he began editing a small literary journal called *Hambone*, which published the work of an aggressively cross-cultural mix of poets, fiction writers, and essayists. The venture was discontinued after its first issue, but Mackey successfully resuscitated it in 1982; since then it has both created networks among and gained a wider audience for a diverse range of underexposed writers. After Mackey received his doctorate from Stanford in 1975 he taught briefly at the University of Wisconsin–Madison and at the University of Southern California before settling into a full professorship in literature at the University of California, Santa Cruz. He has taught there since 1979. His academic publications include the anthology *Moment's Notice: Jazz in Poetry and Prose* (1993), which he edited with Art Lange, and *Discrepant Engagement* (1993), a collection of critical essays on writers ranging from Baraka to the Guyanese novelist Wilson Harris to the Barbadian poet Edward Kamau Brathwaite. *Paracritical Hinge*, a collection of essays, talks, and interviews, appeared in 2005.

These works not only are innovative in their ability to create liberating connections among writers, disciplines, and cultures that otherwise remain disparate, even opposed, but also are useful in that they provide a way of understanding the philosophies behind Mackey's better-known poetry and fiction. Indeed, Mackey's literary writings are separable from his academic efforts only in that they are less easy to chronologize in any conventional sense; both share an almost encyclopedic range of intertextual reference (especially to African American music), and both seek to bear witness to his conviction that experimentalism and formal complexity—two fundamental attributes of the traditions of mainstream American literary modernism and postmodernism—are present in the cultural production of socially marginalized groups. Accordingly, Mackey's first two chapbooks of poems, *Four for Trane* (1978) and *Septet for the End of Time* (1983), draw as much on Baraka and the Projectivists as on, for instance, John Coltrane and the tradition of Haitian vodun to create a densely allusive, experimental style of verse that resists categorization. These shorter works—as well Mackey's ongoing serial poems "Mu" and "Song of the Andoumboulou"—were included in his first collection of poetry, *Eroding Witness*, which earned a National Poetry Series selection in 1985. Another book of verse, *School of Udhra*, appeared in 1993, and several other chapbook-length installments of "Mu" and "Song of the Andoumboulou" have since been published. In 1995 Mackey also recorded *Strick: Song of the Andoumboulou: 18–20*, a sequence of poems read to musical accompaniment.

The "Song of the Andoumboulou" series is particularly noteworthy because of its connection to Mackey's fiction. As Mackey has recounted in several interviews, sometime in the late 1970s the phrase "Dear Angel of Dust" came into his head, eventually finding its way into a prose-poem letter—signed by an elusive fictional character named "N."—that eventually became "Song of the Andoumboulou: 6" in *Eroding Witness*. This unconventional narrative form took on a life of its own: Mackey began writing a coherent string of fictional epistolary correspondences from "N." to this mysterious "Angel of Dust" figure in the early 1980s, and the correspondences were collected and published in 1986 as *Bedouin Hornbook*, the first volume of an ongoing series

called *From a Broken Bottle Traces of Perfume Still Emanate*.

Over the next fifteen years Mackey followed up with two more installments: *Djbot Baghostus's Run* (1993) and *Atet A.D.* (2001). Although the letters themselves do not follow a conventional, linear narrative path, their thematic concern always returns to music and its relationship to language, spirituality, and politics—underscoring Mackey's words in a 1995 interview, that "music includes so much: it's social, it's religious, it's metaphysical, it's aesthetic, its expressive, it's creative, it's destructive. It just covers so much" (Funkhouser, 322). Mackey's fiction writing seems to operate with this philosophy in mind.

Mackey married Pascale Gaitet in 1991. He has a stepson named Joe and a younger daughter, Naima—a name perhaps taken from the title of one of John Coltrane's most famous ballad compositions. In 2001 he was elected to the board of chancellors of the Academy of American Poets, and in 2006 his collection *Splay Anthem* was given the National Book Award for poetry, further confirming the significance of his highly experimental, interdisciplinary, and cross-cultural literary endeavors.

FURTHER READING
Funkhouser, Christopher. "An Interview with Nathaniel Mackey," *Callaloo* 18, no. 2 (Spring 1995).
Naylor, Paul, ed. "Nathaniel Mackey: A Special Issue," *Callaloo* 23, no. 2 (Spring 2000).

BRIAN P. HOCHMAN

Madgett, Naomi Long (5 July 1923–), author, poet, and retired professor at Eastern Michigan University was born in Norfolk, Virginia, to Clarence Marcellus, a Baptist minister, and Maude Hilton Long, a former teacher.

Naomi Cornelia Long Madgett was the youngest of three children and her parents' only daughter. Before Madgett turned two years old, her family moved to East Orange, New Jersey, and she graduated from Ashland Grammar School there. Influenced by her parents' love of education and her father's vast library, Madgett discovered her love for poetry as a girl. "I discovered Alfred Lord Tennyson and Langston Hughes at about the same time [while] sitting on the floor of my father's study when I was about seven or eight," Madgett said as quoted in the *Contemporary Authors Autobiography Series*. "I think my early poetry represents something of the variety of interest and style that these two widely divergent poets demonstrate."

Her parents moved to St. Louis, Missouri, in December 1937. At fourteen, Madgett entered the all-black Charles Sumner High School, where she was encouraged to write and authored the poems that appeared in her first volume, *Songs to a Phantom Nightingale*, which was published after she graduated from high school in 1941.

She attended her mother's alma mater, Virginia State University, and pledged the Alpha Kappa Alpha sorority. She graduated with a bachelor's of art and with honors in 1945. She worked as a reporter and copy reader at the *Michigan Chronicle* from 1945 until 1946. Madgett married Julian F. Witherspoon on 31 March 1946. For six years after that, she was a service representative for the Michigan Bell Telephone Company, in Detroit, between 1948 and 1954.

She and Witherspoon divorced 27 April 1949. The couple had one daughter, Jill Witherspoon Boyer, born in 1947. On 19 July 1954, Madgett married William Harold Madgett. A year later, she started teaching at Burroughs Junior High School, then Northern High School. She earned a master's degree in Education from Wayne State University in 1956. She later taught at Northwestern High School for twelve years between 1956 and 1968.

She divorced Madgett on 21 December 1960 but kept his last name.

Madgett introduced the first structured Afro-American literature course in the Detroit Public Schools, according to *Contemporary Authors Online*. She took postgraduate courses at the University of Detroit. In 1961 and 1962 and she was the first recipient of the Mott Fellowship in English, which she used to work as a resource associate at Oakland University in Rochester, Michigan, during the academic year 1965–66. There, she wrote a textbook on African American literature. In 1968 she resigned from the Detroit public schools to take a position as associate professor of English at Eastern Michigan University.

Between 1970 and 1971, Madgett was a visiting lecturer in English at the University of Michigan. She married the elementary school principal Leonard Patton Andrews on 31 March 1972. He died in 1996. She became a full professor of English in 1973.

Madgett wrote nine books of poetry including, *One and the Many* (1956), *Star by Star* (1965), *Octavia and Other Poems* (1988) and *Remembrances of Spring: Collected Early Poems* (1993). Her verses over the years praised the positive aspects of African American communities and were influenced by the civil rights and Black Arts movements as well as the Harlem Renaissance. Her work has been praised for developing what Judi Ketteler referred to in a 2001 review of *Alabama Centennial*, published in Star by Star, as "a political poetics." Ketteler continued in her review for *Poetry for Students*: "Madgett has a deep appreciation for language, whether she is using it to raise her voice in political protest, or to celebrate the beauty of morning dew on a rose." But Pinkie Gordon Lane, writing for the *African American Review* in 1996, said that despite Madgett's lyrical talents and quiet, powerful voice, "it is difficult at times to distinguish between Madgett, the poems' author and Madgett the poems' persona" (Lane, p. 143).

She edited a few other books with Lotus Press, which she founded in 1972. Madgett published authors like Gayl Jones, Haki R. Madhubuti, and E. Ethelbert Miller at Lotus.

According to Kay Vandegrift, who wrote about African American women poets in a 1994 essay published in *Children's Literature Review*, "Madgett made a significant contribution to African-American women's poetry" when, to celebrate the twentieth anniversary of Lotus Press, she collected new poems from fifty-five poets for *Adam of Ifé: Black Women in Praise of Black Men* (1992). "These positive images of strong African-American males, although written by women, are especially important for young African-American men to hear," Vandegrift wrote. Madgett continued to serve as publisher and editor in 2011.

She earned a Ph.D. in 1980 from the International Institute for Advanced Studies (now Greenwich University). She worked as a professor at Eastern Michigan until 1984, when she retired as professor emeritus. According to Madgett's personal biography, Lotus Press's board of directors commissioned Artis Lane to create the life-size bronze sculpture of Madgett that was unveiled in 2005 and now is part of the permanent collection at the Charles H. Wright Museum of African American History.

Madgett has been the recipient of dozens of fellowships and awards for her writing and teaching achievements. Resolutions passed in her honor have been offered twice in both the Michigan State Legislature and the Detroit City Council. She has received citations from the Afro-American Museum of Detroit (1983); the National Coalition of Black Women, and the Black Caucus, National Council of Teachers of English, both 1984; and many more. She won an American Book Award in 1993. She was appointed Detroit's poet laureate on 11 April 2001.

Madgett's poetry has appeared in numerous journals and 185 anthologies in the United States and Europe. She published her autobiography, *Pilgrim Journey*, in 2006.

FURTHER READING

Bell-Russel, Danna C. A Poet's Voice: *Octavia and Other Poems* by Naomi Long Madgett, *Library Journal* (1997).

Ketteler, Judi. Overview of *Alabama Centennial*. In *Poetry for Students*, edited by Michael L. LaBlanc (2001).

Lane, Pinkie Gordon. Reviewed work(s): *Remembrances of Spring: Collected Early Poems* by Naomi Long Madgett, *African American Review* (Spring 1996).

"Naomi Long Madgett." In *Contemporary Authors Autobiography Online* (2002).

"Naomi Long Madgett." In *Notable Black American Women* (1992).

"Naomi Long Madgett." In *Contemporary Authors Autobiography Series* (1996).

Vandergrift, Kay E. "And Bid *Her* Sing: A White Feminist Reads African-American Female Poets." In *African-American Voices in Young Adult Literature: Tradition, Transition, Transformation*, edited by Karen Patricia Smith, pp. 31–77 (1994).

JOSHUNDA SANDERS

Madhubuti, Haki R. (23 Feb. 1942–), author, educator, and poet, was born Don Luther Lee, in Little Rock, Arkansas, to Maxine Lee and an unknown father. In 1943 his family migrated to Detroit, Michigan. Lee's father deserted the family before his baby sister was born. His mother began working as a janitor and barmaid to support her two children. Lee's mother introduced him to the Detroit Public Library, where he spent hours at a time reading. His mother, the person he credits with his interest in black arts, died of a drug overdose when he was sixteen. Upon her death he moved to Chicago, Illinois, and attended Dunbar Vocational High School. His love for reading continued to flourish as he explored works by authors such as CHESTER HIMES, LANGSTON HUGHES, GWENDOLYN BROOKS, and JEAN TOOMER. Lee graduated in 1960 and began selling magazines when he could not find a job. He soon found himself in East St. Louis, Missouri, penniless and in poor health, so he enlisted in the United States Army. During his tenure in the army Lee continued his self-guided literary studies. He was eighteen years old when a white drill sergeant tore the pages of his PAUL ROBESON book *Here I Stand*; this act deepened his commitment to advancing black arts.

In 1963 Lee was discharged from the army and returned to Chicago, where he became an apprentice to MARGARET BURROUGHS, a curator at the DuSable Museum of African History, until 1967. At the same time he enrolled at Wilson Junior College on the South Side of Chicago, now Kennedy-King College. Determined to become a writer, Lee prepared himself by regularly reading a book and writing a book review of two hundred words. He worked retail and held a job at the U.S. Post Office in order to support himself. In 1966 he published his first volume of poetry, *Think Black*. In 1967 Lee, together with poets from the Organization of Black American Culture Writer's Workshop, gathered in Chicago's Woodlawn neighborhood to study with Gwendolyn Brooks. OSCAR BROWN JR., songwriter and producer, had organized the event as part of a weekly poetry workshop he held in collaboration with JEFF FORT and the Black Stone Rangers, a militant organization and gang. Lee had first read Brooks when he was in high school, now age twenty-five, Lee quickly sought and found a mentor in fifty-year-old Brooks.

Lee partnered with the poets Johari Amini and Carolyn Rodgers in 1967 to launch a publishing company, Third World Press, with only $400. Third World Press began in his basement apartment on South Ada Street as an outlet for African American authors and authors of African descent. Lee published two volumes of poetry on his new imprint, *Black Pride* (1968) and *Cry, Scream* in 1969, when he also became a writer-in-residence at Cornell University. During the same year he cofounded the Institute of Positive Education/ New Concept Development Center in Chicago, an Afrocentric school. In 1970 Lee published *We Walk the Way of the New World*, a collection of poems echoing the sentiments of the African American sojourn in America, the ills of self-hatred, and the power of self-love. Lee published three more works in 1971, among them *Dynamite Voices I: Black Poets of the 1960s*, in this collection he defined the role of the black literary critic as essential to the Black Arts Movement. He became poet-in-residence at Howard University in 1973 and published *Book of Life*.

In addition to writing sociopolitical essays and poems, Lee was an active member of several organizations during the Black Arts Movement period such as the Student Non-Violent Coordinating Community (SNCC), the Congress of Racial

Equality (CORE), and the Southern Christian Leadership Conference (SCLC).

In 1974 Lee changed his name to Haki R. Madhubuti. From the KiSwahili language spoken in East African countries Lee chose Haki for his first name, meaning "just" or "justice"; for his last name he chose Madhubuti, which means "precise, accurate, and dependable."

Madhubuti earned an A.A. degree from Chicago City College, attended the University of Illinois and received a master of fine arts in 1984 from the University of Iowa. Upon earning his M.F.A. he became a member of the faculty at Chicago State University. Also in 1984 he published a work about his mentor, *Say That the River Turns: The Impact of Gwendolyn Brooks*, and *Killing Memory, Seeking Ancestors* in 1987.

In 1990 Madhubuti published *Black Men: Obsolete, Single, Dangerous? African American Families in Transition; Essays in Discovery, Solution, and Hope*, which sold over one million copies. With this work he emerged as more of an essayist than a poet. Gwendolyn Brooks was added to Third World's list of major authors in 1991. Pursuant to the controversy caused by the RODNEY KING police brutality case and the ensuing unrest, Madhubuti published *Why L.A. Happened: Implications of the '92 Los Angeles Rebellion* in 1993.

In 2005 Madhubuti published an autobiography, *Yellow Black: The First Twenty-One Year's of a Poet's Life*. An exhaustive list of works by Haki R. Madhubuti is available at Third World Press. He was awarded the Endowment Grant for Poetry (1983), the Distinguished Writer's Award from the Middle Atlantic Association (1984), the American Book Award (1991), and he was the only American chosen to represent the United State in the International Valmiki World Poetry Festival in New Delhi, India (1985). Madhubuti cofounded the Betty Shabazz International Charter School in Chicago (1998) and the National Association of Black Book Publishers. He cofounded and served as chairman of the board of the International Literary Hall of Fame for Writers of African Descent. He is also a founder and director of the National Black Writers Retreat.

In 1990, Madhubuti became the distinguished university professor, founder, and director emeritus of the Gwendolyn Brooks Center for Black Literature and Creative Writing and director of the Master of Fine Arts in Creative Writing Program at Chicago State University.

In 1974 he married Safisha, a professor at Northwestern University, and together they have three children: Lani, Bomani, and Akili. He is also the father of two children from previous unions: Don and Mari.

FURTHER READING
Madhubuti, Haki. *Black Men: Obsolete, Single, Dangerous?* (1990).
Madhubuti, Haki. *Killing Memory, Seeking Ancestors* (1987).
Madhubuti, Haki. *Liberation Narratives: New and Collected Poems* (1966–2009).
McKay, Nellie, and Henry Louis Gates, eds. *The Norton Anthology of African American Literature* (2003).
SAFIYA DALILAH HOSKINS

Magee, James Henry (23 June 1839–29 May 1912), minister, civil rights advocate, and political activist, was born in Madison County, Illinois, to Lazarus, a free black, and Susan, who was a slave until Magee's father earned enough to buy her from her Louisville, Kentucky, owner and move to Illinois, settling in Upper Alton. Like most African Americans James Magee found his opportunities for education limited but managed to acquire more than a rudimentary education. Magee and his siblings attended the local township school with white children until some parents objected and officials forced the withdrawal of the Magee children. They were then provided with an inadequately prepared "colored" teacher. Eventually the Magee children were withdrawn and sent, in the autumn of 1855, to Racine, Wisconsin, where, as the only blacks, they attended for less than a year.

Returning to Shipman in the autumn of 1856 Magee became a teacher in a black Jerseyville school. The following year he moved to Ridge Prairie, where he remained until the fall of 1863. At that time he was ordained a Baptist minister and was called to the Salem Church on Wood River. A year later he moved to the Piasa Church, remaining briefly before being called to the Zion Baptist Church of Springfield. When the senior pastor refused to yield the pulpit to Magee, he resigned and accepted a call to a Baptist church in Atlanta, Canada West, one of the largest black Baptist churches in Canada.

Continuing his own education while teaching Canadian African American children, Magee remained in Canada West throughout the Civil War. At its close, he returned to Illinois. While attending the annual meeting of the Wood River Colored Baptist Association, he participated in one of his earliest important political acts, serving as one of a committee of three assigned to draft a report calling upon the Illinois General Assembly to grant immediate suffrage to its black citizens.

Desiring additional theological education, in 1867 Magee left for England to study at Spurgeon's Pastors College a British Baptist school located in London. Charles Haddon Spurgeon was a noted British Baptist evangelist. Magee returned home after one year and accepted the principalship of the prep school associated with Baptist College in Nashville, Tennessee. While there, he married Mary E. Armsby of St. Louis, Missouri. In 1869 he returned to Alton, Illinois, taught in Alton's colored school, and served as pastor of the Alton Colored Baptist Church. Eighteen months later he became the pastor of the Union Baptist Church in Cincinnati, Ohio, the state's largest black Baptist church. Increasingly strident in his demands for quality education for African American children, Magee urged black participation in mainstream politics. He was particularly concerned with the lack of public funds for the black schools in Cincinnati. He urged all blacks to vote for appropriate school board members and urged them to speak out about the issue of financial support.

Unaccountably, Magee left Cincinnati for Metropolis, Illinois, where he earned $45 a month as the head teacher in the colored school. (White teachers were earning $85 or more per month.) There he became increasingly active in politics, emerging as a leader of black Republicans within the party. In 1878 he was elected to the Massac County Republican Central Committee. In 1882 he became the first African American elected to the Republican State Central Committee. Two years later, in a fierce contest for the Republican gubernatorial nomination, Magee chose to support Richard J. Oglesby, governor and former Civil War general. In February 1884 Magee wrote, "I am a colored man, and a member of the State Central Committee, the first instance of the kind on record in this state. I love the men who went to the front in the hour of our countrie's peril; for such the people delight to honor" (Oglesby Family Papers, Manuscripts Division, Illinois State Historical Library, Box 12). Magee demonstrated his support by issuing a highly partisan broadside urging southern Illinois blacks to vote for Oglesby. Widely in demand as a "race" speaker Magee waived the "bloody shirt" vigorously, reminding African Americans that it was the Republican Party that fought to save the Union and eliminate slavery. During this period he became one of the state's most important black

leaders outside of Chicago. Magee's political activities cost him his position as a teacher in Metropolis. He was rewarded for his work, however, by being offered a clerkship in the Railway and Warehouse Commission offices in Chicago, a position that paid $1,300 a year and gave him ample opportunity to work with the city's black population.

Oglesby and Magee recognized the importance of working with the African American community in order to maintain Republican Party leadership in the state and nation. They became a crucial part of the party's strength, especially after President Rutherford B. Hayes's policy of reconciliation encouraged the Democrats in some areas to appeal for their votes, while withdrawing their right to vote in the former states of the Confederacy through coercion, force, and restrictive legislation. Recognizing the erosion of African American political participation, but at the same time worrying about the Democratic enticements, Magee, at Oglesby's insistence, attended the 1885 Illinois Colored State Convention, despite his own misgivings about encouraging separate institutions. There he made his pitch for loyalty to the party of Lincoln in a powerful speech denouncing those who acted independently of the Republican Party.

During the last thirty years of his life Magee remained highly influential, primarily among the Illinois African American community, and continued as a leader of the AME Church, which he had joined probably sometime in the 1880s. He remained involved in politics, education, and self-help movements. But Magee did not limit his activity on behalf of his fellow blacks to keep them within the party of the "Great Emancipator." In 1890 and 1891 he published Chicago Brotherhood, a weekly periodical devoted to various black fraternal and self-help organizations. In 1898 he became chairman of a Chicago group organized to raise funds for the pursuit of the Alton School desegregation suit, which had begun in 1892 when the city opened an all-black school in Alton. Although the state supreme court ordered the school closed, Alton city fathers defied the court and again opened a segregated school in 1898. In 1899, at the height of the lynching mania gripping the nation, he organized the Black Man's Burden Relief Association to assist in the adoption of stronger anti-lynching legislation. He also lent his support to a movement by Nebraska congressman William J. Connell to provide a federal pension to all aged former slaves, believing them at least as deserving as the Union soldiers who received pensions, and certainly as deserving as ex-Confederate soldiers who were pensioned by many southern states.

By 1901 Magee had moved to Springfield, where he was employed as a printer's expert in the secretary of state's office and organized cultural and self-help movements in the city and lectured on a wide variety of topics. In 1905 he organized and became president of the Illinois Colored Historical Society. It affiliated with the Illinois State Historical Society, headed by Jessie Palmer Weber, the daughter of John M. Palmer, who Magee admired as being only slightly less great than Lincoln and on a par with Oglesby. He actively encouraged black students to attend and to participate in the many activities at the Springfield public high school and issued a pamphlet of outrage when a black girl with the highest marks at graduation was denied the honor of becoming valedictorian. He also helped found and became secretary of the "Stalwart Protective League for the betterment of the race along all lines." For many years he was active in supporting the Ambidexter Institute, which provided vocational educational opportunities for blacks of all ages.

But racism remained so pervasive that Springfield's black population was not even welcome at the massive centennial celebration of the birth of Lincoln, the Great Emancipator, in 1909, nor at the subsequent banquets of the Lincoln Centennial Celebration. Even in 1910, when BOOKER T. WASHINGTON delivered the principle address at the Lincoln Centennial Association's Banquet, African Americans were not welcome, although many did indeed attend. In response Magee organized another massive celebration at the Illinois National Guard Armory, under the auspices of the Colored Historical Society, held on 13 February 1910, at the Union Baptist Church. It was reported that there were more than 5,000 on the floor of the Armory to hear Booker T. Washington address them at the separate celebration. He encouraged his fellow citizens to resist their increased marginalization by encouraging pride through such organizations as the Illinois Colored Historical Society. Magee died of an apparent heart attack. His life and influence were perhaps best summed up by his friend Jessie Palmer Weber, secretary of the Illinois State Historical Society, who wrote, "Dr. Magee believed in the future of his race. He did all in his power to promote its welfare…. He was a good man and an example to the young people and, in fact, to all the race for whose betterment he earnestly labored" ("Death of Dr. J. H. Magee," 317).

FURTHER READING

Magee, James Henry. *High Thoughts and Aims Reach High and Noble Things* (1906?).

Magee, James Henry. *The Night of Affliction and Morning of Recovery. An Autobiography* (1873; repr. 1969).

"Colored Historical Society, Springfield, Ill." *Transactions of the Illinois State Historical Society* 15 (1910).

"Death of Dr. J. H. Magee." *Journal of the Illinois State Historical Society* 5 (July 1912). *Minutes of the … Annual Meeting[s] of the Wood River Colored Baptist Association* (1850–1873).

"Report of Committee from the Illinois Colored Historical Society." *Transactions of the Illinois State Historical Society* 13 (1908).

ROGER D. BRIDGES

Magic Sam (Magic Samuel Gene Maghett) (14 Feb. 1937–1 Dec. 1969), blues singer and guitarist, was born in Grenada, Mississippi, the son of Jessie Maghett and Hetha Anna Henderson, farmers. Sam's mother died when he was still a child. Raised eight miles east of Grenada in a community known as Redgrass, he showed an early aptitude for music, constructing a one-string guitar at age ten. Sam helped his father farm until he was thirteen, at which time he and a brother were sent to Chicago to live with an aunt. In Chicago he became deeply involved with music. A local gambler, James "Shakey Jake" Harris, encouraged Maghett to keep practicing and to work on his singing instead of concentrating solely on guitar.

In his late teens, becoming more confident as a musician, Maghett began singing in a family gospel group in South Side churches while also playing guitar with Harris, by now a blues singer and harmonica player. Harris hired Maghett and Mack Thompson to back him at a club called the Wagon Wheel around 1954. In 1955 Maghett auditioned at the 708 Club, which then featured MUDDY WATERS. The owner promptly booked Maghett to follow Waters, a job that allowed Maghett—or "Good Rocking Sam," as he was billed—to begin expanding his repertoire and develop his own sound.

In 1956 Maghett made his recording studio debut, playing as a sideman on two sides for the short-lived ABCO label, operated by Eli Toscano. Within months he was back in the studio, this time as a featured artist for Toscano's new Cobra label.

Maghett recorded under the new name Magic Sam, and his first single, "All Your Love" backed by "Love Me with a Feeling," was a substantial regional hit. There were three follow-up singles on Cobra, but the records did little to advance Magic Sam's career; he continued to make his main mark in Chicago's blues clubs. Cobra folded in 1959, and that same year Magic Sam was drafted into the army. He deserted and returned to Chicago, but he was captured and imprisoned for six months. Fellow musicians felt that the hiatus hurt his career, affecting both his physical and his mental health. As the guitarist Luther Allison recalled, "The people seemed [like] they had forgotten about him."

Maghett resumed steady work in Chicago's clubs in the early 1960s, sharing billings with Muddy Waters, HOWLIN' WOLF, and OTIS RUSH, among others. He became a regular in the guitar "cutting" contests that were popular in West Side clubs, trying to outplay guitar slingers like Mighty Joe Young, FREDDIE KING, or Allison. Magic Sam resumed recording, too, with several sessions for the German L+R label in 1963 and 1964 and a single for Crash in 1966.

The major event of Magic Sam's career came in 1967 when he recorded an album for the Chicago-based Delmark label, *Magic Sam Blues Band: West Side Soul*. The album, which showcased Maghett's instrumental versatility and his soul vocal stylings, earned a five-star review from *Down Beat* magazine and is considered one of the best urban blues recordings of all time. The album caught the attention of the rock world, leading to bookings far beyond the Chicago club scene. Suddenly Magic Sam was playing at rock palaces on both coasts and touring on the college concert circuit. A follow-up album, *Black Magic*, was recorded for Delmark in the fall of 1968, although it was not released until the next year.

Fueled by the reviews and recognition generated by *West Side Soul*, 1969 began as Magic Sam's most successful year. *Rolling Stone* magazine reviewed his work, and several major labels were said to be eager to sign him. A rigorous schedule, put together by his manager Denny Bruce, kept Maghett on the road, and a European tour with the American Folk Blues Festival was set for later that year. In August he performed at the Ann Arbor Blues Festival, a set so memorable that it elicited comparisons to rock legend JIMI HENDRIX.

With Magic Sam finally nearing stardom, though, his health began to deteriorate under the strain of travel, heavy drinking, and an ongoing heart problem. Collapsing after a concert in Kentucky, he returned to Chicago to recuperate, reportedly spending a week in the hospital and being warned to stop drinking. He went on the European tour, after which he returned to the states and made a trip to California. Back in Chicago in the fall of 1969, he suffered a heart attack in his home and was pronounced dead at St. Anthony Hospital. Sam was buried in Restvale Cemetery in Worth, Illinois. At the time of his death, his finances were in disarray, supposedly because of union problems, and a benefit concert was held on the West Coast to help his common-law wife, Leola, and their four children.

Magic Sam embodied what became known as the "West Side sound," a modern blues style based around three pieces: guitar, bass (or a second guitar), and drums. Simple economics dictated the three-piece format because West Side clubs paid relatively little for live entertainment. The style demanded strong vocals and instrumental virtuosity, and Maghett excelled at both. He possessed an outstanding, soaring blues voice, dramatically effective because of his affinity for minor-chord blues and his soul/gospel vocal inflections. He once told the researcher Jim O'Neal, "I'm a modern type of bluesman, I can play the soul stuff, too"—implying that unlike some older artists he could still appeal to contemporary African American audiences. As a guitarist Magic Sam employed tremolo heavily, played with his fingers instead of with a pick, and displayed a talent for lightning-fast melodic invention within the tight confines of the blues format.

As a writer, Magic Sam was fond of sixteen-bar blues but was equally at home with primitive boogies. He drew material from sources as diverse as LOWELL FULSON, J. B. LENOIR, and LOUIS JORDAN, but he always reshaped the material with his own signature sound. Unlike earlier artists such as Muddy Waters or Howlin' Wolf, who brought fully developed musical traditions from Mississippi to Chicago, Magic Sam developed an urban sound a generation removed from his Mississippi birth.

FURTHER READING

Cappuccio, Robert. "The Magic of Magic Sam," *Living Blues* 13 (Summer 1973): 13.

Franz, Steve. "Magic Rocker: The Life and Music of Magic Sam," *Living Blues* 125 (Jan.–Feb. 1996): 32–44.

Leadbitter, Mike, et al. *Blues Records 1943–1970: "The Bible of the Blues,"* vol. 2, L–Z (1994).

This entry is taken from the *American National Biography* and is published here with the permission of the American Council of Learned Societies.

BILL MCCULLOCH AND
BARRY LEE PEARSON

Mahal, Taj (17 May 1942–) singer, musician, and songwriter, was born Henry St. Clair Fredericks Jr. in New York City, the first of five children born to Henry Fredericks, a jazz musician native to Harlem, and Mildred (Shields) Fredericks, a schoolteacher from South Carolina who spent her life singing in church and in the community. Music permeated the Fredericks's household.

Other family members were influential, including a paternal grandmother from the Caribbean, and a-maternal step-grandmother from the South. At six-months, Fredericks and his family moved to Springfield, Massachusetts, where they bought a house in a mixed race neighborhood. Young Henry experienced relationships with other races at an early age.

Taj Mahal, performing on the Stravinski Stage during the 40th Montreux Jazz Festival in Montreux, Switzerland, 10 July 2006. (AP Images.)

He also experienced loss. When Henry was twelve years old, his father died and his mother and sisters moved back to New York, leaving him and his brothers in a church home. His mother eventually returned to Springfield, and remarried Hughan Williams, a family friend and widower from Jamaica with three sons of his own. Williams and Henry's mother had a son together, and they raised all nine of their children in an upper middle-class environment that appreciated artistic expression. A loner in school, Henry learned guitar privately, quietly strumming it in the attic so as not to awaken others. He eventually met Leonard "Lynwood" Perry, a neighbor who had moved to Springfield from the South, and taught him many blues forms and Southern standards. In high school, he focused on agricultural courses, and on weekends and during summers worked on a dairy farm. In 1961 he entered the University of Massachusetts as an agricultural major.

Shortly after beginning college, following in the tradition of bluesmen like HOWLIN' WOLF and MUDDY WATERS, he adopted a new moniker, Taj Mahal. He wanted a grand name, and so chose to call himself after the famous wonder of the world. The name also served as a means to re-invent himself. At the university, Mahal joined the folklore society as well as a rhythm and blues band made up of students called the Electras, of which he became lead singer. The group performed at fraternity parties throughout the Northeast during Mahal's stint in college. After the band's breakup, Mahal began to follow the burgeoning folk music scene. He listened to fellow University of Massachusetts student Buffy Sainte Marie and popular folksingers like Bob Dylan, Joan Baez, and Bob Gibson.

After graduating in 1963 with a two-year degree in animal husbandry, Mahal moved to the Boston area, where he resumed his musical career. He partnered with the guitarist and singer Jesse Lee Kincaid. As a black and white duo, they drew attention. Yet feeling limited by the folk scene in Cambridge, they relocated to Los Angeles after a brief stay in Detroit. Kincaid was familiar with the area, and introduced Mahal to the guitarist Ry Cooder, who, with the bassist Gary Marker, eventually expanded the duo. The group met success at the Ash Grove, where Mahal met many of the great bluesmen like Reverend GARY DAVIS and LIGHTNIN' HOPKINS. The group now called itself the Rising Sons and was joined briefly by Ed Cassidy—who went on to form the successful rock band, Spirit—on drums. The band played old-time music with a modern sound. In 1967, following

Cassidy's departure, Columbia signed the Rising Sons to a record deal. Unable to develop the group into a mainstream pop act, Columbia dropped it from its roster, leading to the band's dispersal. The company did sign Mahal, who nevertheless maintained a disdain for the commercial aspects of the music business, as a solo artist. He formed his seminal band in the late 1960s and began reaching national and international audiences.

An inveterate jammer, Mahal informally played with many musicians. In Jesse "Ed" Davis, a Native American guitarist, he found a sympathetic foil who contributed immensely to his first three albums. A purveyor of the "less is more" philosophy, Davis, with his deft touch, tasty tone and understanding of space, assisted Mahal in making powerful but easygoing blues. Joined by Gary Gilmore on bass and Chuck Blackwell on drums, this group, fronted by an African American and accompanied by a Native American and two Americans of European descent, truly represented the spiritual foundation of the United States and its music.

Initially, Mahal's arrangements of traditional songs seemed more accessible than his songwriting. Others quickly adapted what he was doing. The Allman Brothers Band, for instance, borrowed his arrangement of BLIND WILLIE McTELL's "Statesboro Blues," which they immortalized on their *Live at the Fillmore East* album in 1971. His versions of "Corrina" and "She Caught the Katy" from his second album, *The Natch'l Blues*, released in 1969, proved difficult to match.

It was a time of great experimentation in rock and jazz that included psychedelia, symphonic, Eastern, and early synthesizer music. Unlike Paul Butterfield who was white and also fronted an influential and integrated blues band, he was the lone young black representative of his generation in the limelight carrying the torch for the blues. In the generation after B. B. KING, artists like OTIS RUSH, MAGIC SAM, and BUDDY GUY, were ten years older than Mahal and had all been reared in the Deep South. In contrast, Mahal was brought up in the Northeast, came at his blues with both the feeling of his forbears and the knowledge of a music historian. Dressed in a denim shirt, bell-bottom blue jeans and a wide-brimmed hat, Mahal maintained a commanding presence that exuded both confidence and an easy, infectious style. Invited in 1968 to perform in England on a BBC special entitled "The Rolling Stones Rock and Roll Circus," Mahal and his band were the only Americans on a bill that included such British artists as John Lennon performing with Eric Clapton,

The Who, Jethro Tull, and of course the hosts, the Rolling Stones. Mahal had attained stardom.

Columbia Records released *Giant Step* in 1969, the year of the first walk on the moon. It was an ambitious, double record set, once again featuring stunning arrangements of other people's songs, including the title song and "Six Days on the Road," a country song by Dave Dudley. Mahal's 1971 record *Happy to Be Just Like I Am*, featured a four-piece tuba section led by Howard Johnson. In 1973 he composed and recorded the soundtrack for the movie *Sounder*. He also had an acting part in the film.

On a tour in Hawaii in 1973, Mahal met Inshirah, born Beverly Geter. They married in 1975 and had seven children together, three of whom died. A previous marriage, to Anna de Leon, had ended in divorce. They lived in Hawaii for many years before separating. Over the years, Mahal fathered fifteen children with seven different women.

Mahal first visited Africa in 1979 and became convinced his ancestors were Kouyates, the main clan of the Mande griots, or storytellers. He studied the music and traditions of these West African caretakers of oral history, and incorporated their style into his own. Having lived in Hawaii for many years, Mahal fused Polynesian influences to his Afro-Caribbean roots. Though the blues remained the thread through his music, Taj Mahal was an international musician who constantly unfolded on his musical journey, seeking to heal himself and others with his music. Nominated for several awards, Mahal won two Grammys for his albums, *Senor Blues* in 1997 and *Shoutin' in Key* in 2000.

An ethnomusicologist and lover of nature, Mahal was a tireless explorer and collaborator, an emissary of world music who left a voluminous body of work. He traveled the world over, playing solo acoustic blues, R&B with the Phantom Blues Band, and his unique blend of island music with the Hula Blues Band, and continually evolving in his artistry. He was one of the first Americans to record reggae music, and was recognized as possibly the first true world musician, exploring his island and African roots and mixing them in his seemingly effortless manner.

FURTHER READING

Mahal, Taj, with Stephen Foehr. *Autobiography of a Bluesman* (2001).

Finigan, Kathleen. "Taj Mahal, Roots and More," *Blues Revue Quarterly*, Issue No. 8 (Spring 1993).

Harris, Sheldon. *Blues Who's Who* (1981)

MARK S. MAULUCCI

Mahoney, Mary (7 May 1845–4 Jan. 1926), nurse, was born Mary Elizabeth Mahoney in the Dorchester neighborhood of Boston, Massachusetts, the eldest of the three children of Charles Mahoney and Mary Jane Steward (or Stewart). Little is known about Mary Mahoney's parents, North Carolina natives and possibly former slaves who migrated to Boston soon after their marriage. In 1855 the Phillips Street School became the first desegregated school in Boston, and the Mahoneys took advantage of this chance to obtain an education for their daughter. At the age of ten Mary Mahoney entered the first grade and apparently continued her education through the eighth grade, at a time when most women, black and white, had less schooling.

Mahoney became an untrained nurse in 1865. A devout Baptist, she may have pursued nursing out of a religious calling, as did many women. Sometime in the 1870s she obtained a job as a cook, washerwoman, and scrubwoman at the New England Hospital for Women and Children (NEHWC). This progressive hospital, founded in 1863 by a group of women physicians led by Dr. Marie Zakrzewska, had a racially mixed patient population and a charter that called for the admission of one African American and one Jew to each nursing class. Although just past the age limit of thirty-one for admittance, Mahoney had the support of a staff physician and enrolled in the hospital school on 23 March 1878. No entrance fee was required.

Students immediately began performing hospital duties for an allowance of one dollar a week for the first six months, which was raised to two dollars for the second six months and three dollars for the final four months. Mahoney learned to take vital signs and apply bandages. She attended a series of lectures on such subjects as manners, food for the sick, disinfectants, obstetrical nursing, and surgical nursing while working a standard 5:30 a.m. to 9 p.m. shift, seven days a week in the medical, surgical, and maternity wards. Each trainee had full responsibility for the care of the six patients in her ward. In the last stage of training, student nurses were sent into the homes of patients for private duty. Mahoney graduated on 1 August 1879, one of only four students in a class of forty-two who completed the sixteen-month training course.

Many Americans saw nursing as a lowly service, only slightly above the level of a servant. Nursing had originated as one of the maternal crafts, a service traditionally performed by women with little or no training who converted their gender-designated roles as nurturers into a livelihood. In the nineteenth and early twentieth century, most nursing took place in homes, with nurses routinely expected to perform such domestic tasks as cooking and cleaning for the elderly and ill.

As one of the earliest women in professional nursing, Mahoney fought against these prevalent notions. As a rare African American woman professional, she had the additional burden of dealing with an attitude among whites that diminished the work of blacks. Never a confrontational person, Mahoney adopted quiet remedies to emphasis her elite status. She did not view nursing as a domestic job and sought to change the perception of the nurse's role in the family of an invalid. Although a notably skilled cook (her favorite dish was plum pudding), she cooked only for her patients and not for their families. Mahoney made it clear to employers that she would not dine at a servants' table with the household help. She answered only "yes," never "yes, sir" or "yes, ma'am." There is no evidence that she ever picked up a dust cloth or a broom in a patient's home.

Although few hospitals would hire black women, the most serious cases of illness in the late nineteenth and early twentieth centuries were still treated at home. Like most nurses, Mahoney depended upon work from a registry of nurses to provide steady income. Her credentials and excellent reputation meant that the wealthiest families in Boston sought her services. Unlike many of her colleagues, she did not charge a higher rate for male patients, and she accepted all cases, including patients with dangerous communicable diseases. A patient's illness would generally last three weeks or more, with a nurse caring for a critically ill patient while often getting only two to six hours of sleep a day. Commended by patients for a calm demeanor, discretion, and loyalty, she was for many years the only black nurse registered in the directory of the Boston Medical Library.

Mahoney, typical of the great majority of professional nurses of her era who regarded nursing as akin to taking religious vows and devoted themselves to their patients, never married. Probably seeking a more reliable source of income and an easier way of making a living in her twilight years, Mahoney briefly left Boston for New York City. She took charge of the historically black Howard Orphan Asylum in King's Park, Long Island, in 1911. She retired in 1912, after a year and a half, and returned to an apartment in the Roxbury neighborhood of Boston.

Infuriated by the continuing low status accorded nursing, Mahoney recognized the need for professional nurses to organize. When the Nurses Associated Alumnae of the United States and Canada formed in 1896 (in 1911 it became the American Nurses' Association), Mahoney became one of its few black members, arriving at the organization through the NEHWC alumnae association. When white nurses would not prioritize the concerns of African American nurses, Mahoney joined black colleagues in recognizing the need for an organization that would serve their needs. Seeking to advance the professional opportunities available to black women, Mahoney helped found the National Association of Colored Graduate Nurses (NACGN) in 1909. She rarely missed a national meeting of nurses or an opportunity to recruit new members. The NACGN established an award in Mahoney's name in 1936, celebrating her efforts to raise the status of black nurses in the nursing profession. The American Nurses' Association, which merged with the NACGN in 1951, now issues the award.

Mahoney's interest in women's equality and women's suffrage may have been sparked by the New England Hospital for Women and Children's philosophy of removing professional barriers based on sex and race. In 1921, at the age of seventy-six, Mahoney was among the first women to register to vote in Boston.

In 1923 Mahoney became ill with metastatic breast cancer. After suffering alone for many months, on 7 December 1925 she entered the New England Hospital for Women and Children and died twenty-five days later. Mahoney's burial place, with a monument later erected to her memory, at Sable Path in the Woodlawn Cemetery in Everett, Massachusetts, is the frequent site of pilgrimages by nursing groups.

FURTHER READING

Carnegie, M. Elizabeth. *The Path We Tread: Blacks in Nursing 1854–1990* (1991).

Chayer, Mary Ella. "Mary Eliza Mahoney, the United States First Professional Negro Nurse," *American Journal of Nursing* (Apr. 1954).

Davis, Althea. *Early Black American Leaders in Nursing: Architects for Integration and Equality* (1999)

Hine, Darlene Clark. *Black Women in White: Racial Conflict and Cooperation in the Nursing Profession 1890–1950* (1989).

Miller, Helen S. *Mary Eliza Mahoney 1845–1926: America's First Black Professional Nurse* (1997)

CARYN E. NEUMANN

Majette, Denise (18 May 1955–), United States congresswoman, lawyer, and judge, was born in Brooklyn, New York, the second of three daughters of Voyd Lee Majette and Olivia Carolyn (Foster) Majette. Her father was a real estate agent and assessor, and her mother was a teacher. Growing up during the civil rights era, Majette was particularly interested in how law was used to effect social change and had early aspirations of becoming a lawyer. She attended Erasmus Hall High School, in Brooklyn, and graduated in the top 10 percent of her class. In 1972 she entered the freshman class at Yale University in New Haven, Connecticut, and despite poor grades during her first semester, she refocused her efforts to perform better. She graduated with a bachelor's degree in History in 1976. Pursuing her childhood dream, Majette enrolled at Duke University Law School in Durham, North Carolina, and graduated with a law degree in 1979. She began her legal career as a staff attorney for the Legal Aid Society in Winston-Salem, North Carolina, and later became a clinical adjunct law professor at Wake Forest University in that city.

In 1983 Majette moved to Stone Mountain, Georgia, and assumed a position as law clerk for Judge R. Keegan Federal at the superior court of DeKalb County, and in 1984 began working for the Georgia Court of Appeals judge Robert Benham. In 1989 she became a partner with the Jenkins, Nelson & Welch law firm and in 1992 worked as an administrative law judge for the Georgia State Board of Worker's Compensation before being appointed by Georgia's governor Zell Miller as a judge on the state court of DeKalb County on 8 June 1993.

On 5 February 2002 Majette resigned from her position as judge and announced her candidacy as a Democrat for a seat in the U.S. Congress against the five-term incumbent Democrat Representative CYNTHIA MCKINNEY. McKinney had garnered negative attention for her statements accusing President George W. Bush of having prior knowledge on the 11 September 2001 terrorist attacks, thereby granting Majette a previously unforeseen advantage. McKinney's supporters criticized Majette as a pawn of conservatives who opposed the liberal and outspoken congresswoman. Majette, however, received a strong endorsement from Georgia's U.S. Senator Zell Miller (a conservative Democrat who supported Bush) and received large financial contributions to her campaign from the Jewish community, which opposed McKinney's support for Palestinian rights and accused her of anti-Semitism. In the 20 August 2002 primary Majette won 58 percent of the vote. McKinney claimed that she was defeated by white Republicans crossing over to vote for Majette in the Democratic primary, but her court challenge to overturn the result was defeated. In the general election Majette gained 77 percent of the vote to defeat her Republican opponent Cynthia Van Auken.

In January 2003, Majette was sworn in to the U.S. House of Representatives. During her tenure she served on the Budget, Education and Workforce, and Small Business committees; she chaired the Task Force on Jobs and the Economy committee. In addition she served as an Assistant Democratic Whip and president of the freshman class of the House Democrats. Majette sponsored legislation for the designation of Arabia Mountain in southeast DeKalb County as a national heritage area. Although McKinney had portrayed Majette as too conservative, Majette opposed President Bush's proposed 2005 fiscal year budget and criticized the administration's education initiatives and record concerning domestic violence against women. As a congresswoman, Majette supported affirmative action, legal status for illegal immigrants working in the United States, and abortion rights; she was opposed to the death penalty and school vouchers. On 29 March 2004 Majette announced her candidacy to occupy the seat being vacated by the retiring senator Zell Miller. She began her campaign at a disadvantage, having a limited statewide fundraising network and being little known outside of the Atlanta area. Majette did not win a majority in the Democratic primary, but she did defeat her millionaire opponent, the businessman Cliff Oxford, in a run-off with a strong grassroots campaign. Ultimately, Majette achieved the distinction of becoming the first African American and the first woman to earn a nomination for the United States Senate from the state of Georgia. But she received only 40 percent of the vote in the general election and lost the vote against the white three-term Republican congressman Johnny Isakson, who was backed by Miller.

In March 2006 Majette reentered the public arena by announcing her candidacy for State School Superintendent of Georgia. In the primary election she defeated Carlotta Harrell, a substitute teacher, by 67 percent of the vote. Majette, however, lost to the Republican incumbent Kathy Cox in the general election. In 2001 Majette was awarded the Judge's Community Recognition Award, and was honored by the Black Law Students' Association and Georgia State University College of Law. In 1998 and 2003 she was honored by the Georgia Association of Black Women Attornies.

In 2000, at the age of forty-five, Majette, an avid runner, completed the New York City Marathon. Majette married Rogers J. Mitchell and they have two sons, Devin and Rogers III, from Mitchell's previous marriage.

FURTHER READING

Eversley, Melanie. "Enormity of Duty Awes Capitol Hill: Georgia's Freshmen Sworn in." *Atlanta Journal-Constitution*, 8 Jan. 2003.

Lewis, Donna Williams. "Majette Makes Appeal for Heritage Area; Designation Would Make as Much as $1 Million per Year Available." *Atlanta Journal-Constitution*, 25 Sept. 2003.

Smith, Ben. "Majette Coming into Her Own in Congress." *Atlanta Journal-Constitution*, 1 May 2003.

SAFIYA DALILAH HOSKINS

Major, Clarence (31 Dec. 1936–), writer and educator, was born in Atlanta, Georgia, the son of Clarence Major, who ran an illicit gambling business, and Inez Huff, an elevator operator. After years of spousal abuse, his mother left the family in 1943 and moved to Chicago, where she passed as white to acquire the best available jobs. Inez Huff divorced her husband and moved Clarence and his sister, Serena, to Chicago in 1946. At age twelve Clarence Major began writing poetry and taking art lessons with the painter Gus Nall.

Major attended the Chicago Institute of Art from 1951 to 1953 on the James Nelson Raymond Fellowship and self-published a collection of poems, *The Fires That Burn in Heaven*, in 1954. After serving in the U.S. Air Force from 1955 to 1957, he founded the literary journal *Coercion Review* in 1958. Editing the journal brought him into contact with authors like William Carlos Williams, Henry Miller, and Allan Ginsberg. Critics subsequently associated Major with these authors, as well as with Ezra Pound, Donald Barthelme, JUNE JORDAN, and ISHMAEL REED, all of whom use imagistic play with language and experiment with form and narrative voice in their work. Major married Joyce Sparrow in 1958; the couple had two sons, Aaron and Darrell, before divorcing in 1964. In the mid-1960s Major taught at several high schools and small colleges in Omaha,

Nebraska, and in New York. During this time he also published anthologies of student writing.

In 1969 Major gained national recognition and became a leader in the Black Arts Movement when he published the novel *All-Night Visitors*, the anthology *The New Black Poetry*, and the television script *Africa Speaks to New York* (1969). The following year he published the *Dictionary of Afro-American Slang* and the poetry collection *Swallow the Lake*, which won the National Council on the Arts Award. In the controversial *All-Night Visitors* Major wrote the first of many surreal and sexually daring explorations into the experiences and consciousness of the contemporary African American male. Major's protagonist is flawed but self-aware, and he refuses to be merely a symbol of racial victimhood or black rage. Instead he engages the nightmarish reality of the novel's world and wrestles with his own humanity—his self-identity, race, sexuality, mortality, morality, and metaphysical loneliness.

Despite pressure to write traditional race novels and obey America's puritanical standards, Major refused to compromise his artistic vision. In his book of essays *The Dark and Feeling* (1974), Major argued that African American authors deserve recognition and respect as individuals, unhampered by racist stereotypes and a fixed black aesthetic. Though Major had been criticized by some African American feminists for his portrayal of women in *All-Night Visitors*, in 1973 he published "On Censorship: An Open Letter to June Jordan," publicly supporting Jordan and her poetry, which also faced criticism and censorship at that time. In the letter, published in the *American Poetry Review*, he defends his poetry against public attacks that had called his work obscene, pornographic, and politically dangerous: "I am against coercion and for freedom of choice…. Believe me, none of the revolutions have been won!" (51). In addition to relating his own experiences, Major challenged mainstream critics and alerted supporters that racism and artistic censorship had not ended and should be vigorously protested.

Major's literary challenges include incorporating slang into his writing, publishing anthologies of unknown African American authors, and mixing genres. During the 1970s his two artistic passions, painting and writing experimental fiction, often influenced each other. Critics have praised his fiction for being expressionistic and collage-like compilations of word-pictures. For example, the dreamlike, nonlinear novel *NO* (1973) merges the world of the imagination with the reality of lived experience to explore human consciousness and African Americans' search for dignity and self-identity. The poems in *The Syncopated Cakewalk* (1974), which includes the Pushcart Prize–winning "Funeral," sketches scenes of social protest and universal humanistic truths. The self-reflexive novel *Reflex and Bone Structure* (1975), a parody of the detective novel genre, throws into sharp relief the subjectivity of reality and the artificiality of fiction. The surrealistic novel *Emergency Exit* (1979), which includes Major's paintings as illustrations, challenges racism, sexism, the myth of the American Dream, and time-honored literary conventions.

Major earned his B.S. at the State University of New York in Albany in 1976 and his Ph.D. in Literature and Art from the Union for Experimenting Colleges and Universities in 1978. He lectured at Queens College, Sarah Lawrence College, Howard University, and the University of Washington before accepting a professorship at the University of Colorado, where he taught from 1977 to 1989. He married Pamela Jane Ritter in 1980, and between 1981 and 1983 he taught at the University of Nice in France on a Fulbright Fellowship. Major continued to push the boundaries of language and form in his fiction, exploring issues of identity in *My Amputations* (1986), which won the Western States Book Award for Fiction. His protagonist, believing that someone has stolen his identity, must struggle to reconstruct his selfhood and his sanity.

Major's subsequent novels examined issues of race, community, and identity from new perspectives. Major chose an African American woman narrator for *Such Was the Season* (1987) and an American Indian narrator for *Painted Turtle: Woman with Guitar* (1988). Major spent several years learning about the Zuni of New Mexico before writing *Painted Turtle* and *Some Observations of a Stranger at Zuni in the Latter Part of the Century* (1989), a poetry collection. In 1989 he won his second Pushcart Prize with the story "My Mother and Mitch."

In 1989 Major began teaching at the University of California, Davis. His published works include the short-story collection *Fun and Games* (1990); *Juba to Jive: A Dictionary of African-American Slang* (1994); a novel, *Dirty Bird Blues* (1996); a poetry collection, *Configurations: New & Selected Poems 1959–1998* (1998); and a creative memoir of his mother's life, *Come by Here* (2002). His later fiction is more straightforward and traditional than his earlier works, but it continues to force readers across social, cultural, linguistic, and stylistic boundaries. Major has succeeded because "he understands well that joy comes from living, always, on a boundary and striving to push beyond it" (Bunge, xviii).

FURTHER READING

Major, Clarence. "On Censorship: An Open Letter to June Jordan," *American Poetry Review*, vol. 2, no. 4 (1973).

Bell, Bernard W., ed. *Clarence Major and His Art: Portraits of an African American Postmodernist* (2001).

Bunge, Nancy, ed. *Conversations with Clarence Major* (2002).

Coleman, James W. *Black Male Fiction and the Legacy of Caliban* (2001)

MATTHEW TEOREY

Majors, Monroe Alpheus (12 Oct. 1864–10 Dec. 1960), physician, civil rights activist, and writer, was born in Waco, Texas, the son of Andrew Jackson Majors and Jane Barringer. In 1869 his family moved to Austin, Texas. After attending public schools in Austin, Majors studied at West Texas College, Tillotson Normal and Collegiate Institute, Central Tennessee College, and finally Meharry Medical College in Nashville, Tennessee, from which he graduated in 1886.

After medical school Majors practiced medicine in Brenham, Dallas, and Calvert, Texas; he was the first African American doctor in Calvert. In 1886 he established the Lone Star State Medical Association for African American physicians in response to the exclusionary policies of the American Medical Association. Because of his prominence as a black doctor and his support of civil rights for African Americans, Majors became a target of racist threats. In 1888 he moved to Los Angeles to escape the rising antiblack violence in Texas and to further his medical career. In Los Angeles Majors participated in various medical societies and was probably the first African American to present lectures at the Los Angeles Medical College. In 1889 he passed the California board medical examination, becoming the first African American to do so. Majors continued his agitation for civil rights while in California. He served as an editor of the *Los Angeles Western News*, through which he successfully encouraged the appointment of African Americans to several civil service positions, including as police officers. In 1889 Majors married Georgia A. Green, a fellow native Texan; they had one daughter.

In 1890 Majors returned to Waco, where he practiced medicine until 1895. He also lectured at Paul Quinn College (1891–1894), edited the *Texas Searchlight* (1893–1895), helped build a hospital, and opened the first black-owned drugstore in the southwestern United States. In 1893 Majors's *Noted Negro Women*, a biographical encyclopedia that was the first of its kind, was published in Chicago. In the mid-1890s Majors wrote several articles for African American newspapers, most notably the *Indianapolis Freeman*, for which he prepared a weekly column. In his journalism he covered numerous topics, including the Ku Klux Klan, black intellectualism, slavery, crime, medicine, and practical advice for African Americans.

In 1898 Majors moved to Decatur, Illinois, where he continued to practice medicine and participate in political reform movements. As a successful black physician, Majors incurred the enmity of the town's white doctors. His life was threatened after he publicly denounced a lynching that had taken place in Decatur shortly before his arrival. Majors then moved to Indianapolis, where he worked as the associate editor of the *Indianapolis Freeman* until 1899.

In 1899 Majors moved back to Texas. For two years he served as superintendent of the Waco hospital that he had helped build. Once again Majors faced racist reactions, including death threats, and in 1901 he moved to Chicago where he lived for thirty-two years. In Chicago, Majors continued to practice medicine and wrote articles and poetry for several African American newspapers, including the *Broad Ax*, the *Chicago Defender*, the *Washington Bee*, the *Peoples Advocate*, and the *Colored American*. From 1908 to 1910 he served as editor of the *Chicago Conservator*. In 1921 Majors's *First Steps to Nursery Rhymes* appeared, a book that is generally considered one of the first publications specifically written for African American children. Having divorced his wife in 1908, Majors married Estelle C. Bond the following year; the couple had one daughter. He later married twice more and had three sons.

In the 1920s failing eyesight curtailed Majors's activities. He discontinued his medical practice in Chicago in 1923 and largely retired from writing. In 1933 he moved back to Los Angeles, where he resumed his medical practice for sporadic periods. Majors died in Los Angeles.

FURTHER READING

Morais, Herbert M. *The History of the Negro in Medicine* (1967).

This entry is taken from the *American National Biography* and is published here with the permission of the American Council of Learned Societies.

THADDEUS RUSSELL

Majozo, Estella Conwill (19 Jan. 1949–), poet, dramatist, and artist, was born Estella Marie Conwill in Louisville, Kentucky, the only daughter of the six children of Mary Luella (Herndon) and Adolph Conwill, of whom little else is known. Growing up during the 1950s civil rights era had a profound impact on the burgeoning writer. Struggling to articulate radical changes in her segregated Louisville community and to explain those changes as one of a handful of blacks in a local Catholic school honed her particular and peculiar voice. Language, ideas, and the spoken word titillated her passion for storytelling. In 1980 that singleness of vision led her to be among the first scholars to earn a doctorate in African American literature from the University of Iowa and to pen several books, including *Come Out the Wilderness: Memoir of a Black Woman Artist* (1999).

An early portion of her memoir related her struggle against becoming a scapegoat because of her nonstandard use of speech, particularly amid the volatile reactions of white teachers and peers during the 1964 march led by MARTIN LUTHER KING JR. and A.D. King for housing equity in Louisville. The strong memory of using her voice, if not her physical self, to support civil rights pressed her to use speech for public advancement. In 1966, when she was graduating from Holy Rosary Academy, Conwill entered a scholarship pageant to win monetary support to attend a historically black college. She wrote and performed a dramatization of the biblical story of Eve and the serpent, titled *Paradise Revisited and Made Real*, and was crowned Miss Black Expo.

When Conwill performed her piece at Holy Rosary, a teacher questioned whether she was indeed the author of her poem and suggested plagiarism. Those kinds of contentions followed her, yet they strengthened her resolve to make her true voice heard and validated. In the following years she left Tennessee State University after a few disappointing weeks, a teaching job at a Catholic elementary school, and a marriage. Yet by 1975 she was pursuing an M.A. in English, raising her young daughter Patrice, and self-publishing *Metamorphosis*, her first collection of poems.

Conwill earned an M.A. from the University of Louisville in 1976 and, encouraged by her mentor, Sister Lucy Friebert, enrolled in a doctoral program in English at the University of Iowa. There she studied under DARWIN TURNER, and her research of black women's autobiographies later inspired her to write her own story.

In 1991 Conwill won a postdoctorate fellowship from the University of Pennsylvania. She subsequently taught literature at Louisville, Iowa, Kentucky State University, and Hunter College in New York City. In addition to mentoring students in creative writing and in women's and African American literature, she developed cultural and literary projects and wrote prolifically. Besides her acclaimed memoir *Come Out the Wilderness*, she authored another book of poetry, *Jiva Telling Rites* (1989); a collection of spiritual testimonies, *Come On Up to Bright Glory* (2001); a text of African American public art and cultural expression, *Libation*; and a drama, *The Middle Passage: 105 Days* (2002).

After the birth of her son Dominic, Conwill began to pen a coming-of-age tale of a black woman and artist. Conwill herself also grappled with issues of domestic violence, single motherhood, and a crisis of faith. She rounded up a community of black artists for both youth instruction and activism, and in the early 1980s she created Blackaleidoscope, a cultural arts center in Louisville. The center was a nucleus that energized a multitude of local artists, musicians, dancers, and writers. A rupture among the artists caused the center to disband, dissolved relationships among friends, and caused her to analyze further ruptures in black artist communities and black political movements. This led in 1988 to the production at the Kentucky Theater of *Purgatory*, a dramatization of such ruptures.

Estella Conwill later added Majozo to her name. It was the combination of the names of three black women she admired: MARY MCLEOD BETHUNE, JOSEPHINE BAKER, and ZORA NEALE HURSTON. Majozo collaborated on public arts projects with her brother, the sculptor Houston Conwill, and with her friend, the architect Joseph De Pace. The three jointly produced cosmograms, consisting of inlaid floor spaces and of inscribed waterfalls, as memorials to the African American and African diaspora experiences. Their productions include *The New Cake Walk* in Atlanta (1989), *Rivers* at the Schomburg Center for Research in Black Culture in New York City (1990), *DuSable's Journey* in Chicago (1991), *The New Charleston* in Charleston, South Carolina (1991), *The New Merengue* at the Brooklyn Museum (1992), *Revelations* in San Francisco (1993), *The Freedom Ring* in Philadelphia

(1994), *The New Ring Shout* at the African Burial Ground in New York (1994), and *The New Calypso* in Miami (1994). For these projects Majozo created poetic histories dedicated to LANGSTON HUGHES, Martin Luther King Jr., the African diaspora community and its languages, and black migrants and immigrants. Much of her work stemmed from ideas and research presented in *Libation*.

FURTHER READING

Majozo, Estella Conwill. *Come Out the Wilderness: Memoir of a Black Woman Artist*, 2d ed. (2000).

SHANNA L. SMITH

Malarcher, David Julius "Gentleman Dave"

(18 Oct. 1894–11 May 1982), Negro League baseball player and manager, was born in Whitehall, Louisiana, the youngest of the eleven children of Martha, a midwife, and Henry Louis Malarcher, a plantation worker. His mother had been a slave in Louisiana prior to the Civil War. Malarcher's family emphasized religious and educational training. His grandparents were founding members of the local black church and his family relocated in order to increase the educational opportunities for their children. As a young boy, Malarcher attended a country school in Union, Louisiana, and played on a local black youth baseball team known as the Baby T's. From 1907 until 1916 Malarcher attended New Orleans University (later Dillard University). There he starred on and served as a coach of the school baseball team, which went undefeated from 1913 until 1916.

Malarcher's stint at New Orleans University was productive both personally and professionally. While there he met his Mabel, whose maiden name is now unknown, a schoolteacher, to whom he was married until her death in 1946. Malarcher also acquired a nickname, "Gentleman Dave," as a result of his commitment to professionalism and his personal distaste for unsavory pursuits such as drinking, gambling, and womanizing. Malarcher's reputation as a true gentleman in what could be a rough-and-tumble game distinguished him among ball players of the era. At New Orleans University, Malarcher also attracted the notice of the Indianapolis ABC manager, CHARLES (C.I.) TAYLOR. Malarcher spent his final years at the University playing for the ABC's in the summer and taking classes in the winter.

In 1918 Malarcher was drafted, along with six of his teammates, and became a soldier in the army's 809th Pioneer Regiment. Malarcher was immediately deployed to France and stayed there until Armistice Day. After World War I ended, he completed his remaining service requirement as a baseball player in the American Expeditionary Force league. After receiving his service discharge in 1919 Malarcher resumed his baseball career with the assistance of RUBE FOSTER, manager of Chicago's American Giants and president of the nascent Negro National League (NNL). From 1920 to 1925 Malarcher played third base for the American Giants and became known as one of the finest third basemen in the league. During those years the Giants dominated the league, often wrapping up the pennant by midseason.

Despite Malarcher's significant accomplishments as a player, he would gain his greatest fame as a Negro League manager. In 1926 Foster became ill and Malarcher succeeded him as the Giants manager, while continuing to play third base. Malarcher proved to be as talented a manager as he was a third-basemen. The Giants won the pennant in Malarcher's first season at the helm. Known as "Cap" to his players, Malarcher gained a reputation as one of the most intelligent and respected men in black baseball. Malarcher compiled an impressive managerial record, leading the American Giants to victories in the 1926 and 1927 Black World Series. After a short two-year retirement, Malarcher returned to helm the Giants in 1931 and subsequently led the team to three successful pennant runs. Unfortunately for Malarcher and the Giants, league president WILLIAM AUGUSTUS GREENLEE overturned their 1933 victory in the Black World Series because the full NNL schedule was not completed. On that basis Greenlee declared the Giants' title illegitimate, and awarded the championship to his own team, the Pittsburgh Crawfords.

Malarcher expected a degree of discipline from his players, requiring them to attend church and to abide by his standards of conduct. Above all he demanded professionalism from the men who played for him and would not tolerate mistakes that reflected a lack of commitment to his baseball strategy. In return, he advocated for his players in order to assist them in garnering raises and shielded them from abusive owners.

An amateur poet after the death of his wife, Malarcher composed numerous works. Among his most notable are a self-published set of poems dedicated to his late wife, an epic poem about World War II, and "Sunset before Dawn," a work that reflects on the promise and obstacles encountered by black baseball players during the segregation of baseball. In "Sunset before Dawn," Malarcher lamented the unfulfilled potential of his fellow Negro Leaguers, men who never had the chance to compete in major league baseball.

Following the conclusion of his athletic career, Malarcher returned to school and became a real estate agent. In order to honor his mother's commitment to education, he established a scholarship fund in her name to benefit further generations of the Malarcher family. Malarcher died at the age of eighty-seven in his adopted hometown of Chicago. As a manager and mentor, he shaped the lives and careers of some of the Negro League's greatest stars, including the Hall of Famers WILLIE WELLS, TURKEY STEARNES, and WILLIAM FOSTER. His commitment to professionalism served as a model for later black ballplayers who would explicitly challenge the segregation policy of major league baseball.

FURTHER READING

The David J. Malarcher Collection of papers, including Malarcher's poetry, correspondence, and photographs, can be found at the Will W. Alexander Library of Dillard University in New Orleans, Louisiana.

Banker, Stephen. *Black Diamonds: An Oral History of Negro Baseball* (1992).

Holway, John. *Voices from the Great Black Baseball Leagues* (1993).

Peterson, Robert. *Only the Ball Was White: A History of Legendary Black Players and All-Black Professional Teams* (1984).

Rogosin, Donn. *Invisible Men: Life in Baseball's Negro Leagues* (1995).

SARAH L. TREMBANIS

Malcolm X (19 May 1925–21 Feb. 1965), Islamic minister and political leader, also known as el-Hajj Malik el-Shabazz, was born Malcolm Little in Omaha, Nebraska, the fourth of five children of Earl Little and Louise (also Louisa) Norton, both activists in the Universal Negro Improvement Association established by MARCUS GARVEY. Earl Little, a Georgia-born itinerant Baptist preacher, encountered considerable racial harassment because of his black nationalist views. He moved his family several times before settling in Michigan, purchasing a home in 1929 on the outskirts of East Lansing, where Malcolm spent his childhood. Their previous home had been destroyed in a mysterious fire. In 1931 Earl Little's body was discovered on a train track. Although police concluded that the death was accidental, the victim's friends and relatives suspected that he had been murdered by a local white-supremacist group. Earl's death left the family in poverty and undoubtedly contributed to Louise Little's mental deterioration. In January 1939 she was declared legally insane and committed to a Michigan mental asylum, where she remained until 1963.

Although Malcolm Little excelled academically in grammar school and was popular among classmates at these predominantly white schools, he also became embittered toward white authority figures. In his autobiography he recalls quitting school in the eighth grade after a teacher warned that his desire to become a lawyer was not a "realistic goal for a nigger." As his mother's mental health deteriorated and he became increasingly incorrigible, welfare officials intervened, placing him in several reform schools and foster homes. In 1941 he left Michigan to live in Boston with his half sister, Ella Collins. In Boston and New York during the early 1940s, Malcolm held a variety of railroad jobs while also becoming increasingly involved in criminal activities, such as peddling illegal drugs and numbers running. At this time he was often

Malcolm X. (Library of Congress.)

called Detroit Red because of his reddish hair. First arrested in 1944 for larceny and given a three-month suspended sentence and a year's probation, Malcolm was arrested again in 1946 for larceny as well as breaking and entering. When the judge learned that Malcolm was involved in a romantic relationship with a white woman, he imposed a particularly severe sentence of from eight to ten years in prison. While in Concord Reformatory in Massachusetts, Malcolm responded to the urgings of his brother Reginald and became a follower of ELIJAH MUHAMMAD (formerly Robert Poole), leader of the Temple of Islam (later Nation of Islam—often called the Black Muslims), a small black nationalist Islamic sect. Attracted to the religious group's racial doctrines, which categorized whites as "devils," he began reading extensively about world history and politics, particularly concerning African slavery and the oppression of black people in America. After he was paroled from prison in August 1952, he became Malcolm X, using the surname assigned to him in place of the African name that had been taken from his slave ancestors.

By 1953 Malcolm X had become Elijah Muhammad's most effective minister, bringing large numbers of new recruits into the group during the 1950s and early 1960s. By 1954 he had become minister of New York Temple No. 7, and he later helped establish Islamic temples in other cities. In 1957 he became the Nation of Islam's national representative, a position of influence second only to that of Elijah Muhammad. In January 1958 he married Betty X (Sanders), who later became known as BETTY SHABAZZ; together they had six daughters.

Malcolm's cogent and electrifying oratory attracted considerable publicity and a large personal following among discontented African Americans. In his speeches he urged black people to separate from whites and win their freedom "by any means necessary." In 1957, after New York police beat and jailed the Nation of Islam member Hinton Johnson, Malcolm X mobilized supporters to confront police officials and secure medical treatment. A 1959 television documentary on the Nation of Islam, called *The Hate That Hate Produced*, further increased Malcolm's notoriety among whites. In 1959 he traveled to Europe and the Middle East on behalf of Elijah Muhammad, and in 1961 he served as Muhammad's emissary at a secret Atlanta meeting seeking an accommodation with the Ku Klux Klan. The following year he participated in protest meetings prompted by the killing of a Black Muslim

during a police raid on a Los Angeles mosque. By 1963 he had become a frequent guest on radio and television programs and was the most well-known figure in the Nation of Islam.

Malcolm X was particularly harsh in his criticisms of the nonviolent strategy to achieve civil rights reforms advocated by MARTIN LUTHER KING JR. His letters seeking King's participation in public forums were generally ignored by King. During a November 1963 address at the Northern Negro Grass Roots Leadership Conference in Detroit, Michigan, Malcolm derided the notion that African Americans could achieve freedom nonviolently. "The only revolution in which the goal is loving your enemy is the Negro revolution," he announced. "Revolution is bloody, revolution is hostile, revolution knows no compromise, revolution overturns and destroys everything that gets in its way." Malcolm also charged that King and other leaders of the recently held March on Washington had taken over the event, with the help of white liberals, in order to subvert its militancy. "And as they took it over, it lost its militancy. It ceased to be angry, it ceased to be hot, it ceased to be uncompromising," he insisted. Despite his caustic criticisms of King, Malcolm nevertheless identified himself with the grassroots leaders of the southern civil rights protest movement. His desire to move from rhetorical to political militancy led him to become increasingly dissatisfied with Elijah Muhammad's apolitical stance. As he later explained in his autobiography, "It could be heard increasingly in the Negro communities: 'Those Muslims *talk* tough, but they never *do* anything, unless somebody bothers Muslims.'"

Malcolm's disillusionment with Elijah Muhammad resulted not only from political differences but also from his personal dismay when he discovered that the religious leader had fathered illegitimate children. Other members of the Nation of Islam began to resent Malcolm's growing prominence and to suspect that he intended to lay claim to leadership of the group. When Malcolm X remarked that President John Kennedy's assassination in November 1963 was a case of the "chickens coming home to roost," Elijah Muhammad used the opportunity to ban his increasingly popular minister from speaking in public.

Despite this effort to silence him, Malcolm X continued to attract public attention during 1964. He counseled the boxer Cassius Clay, who publicly announced, shortly after winning the heavyweight boxing title, that he had become a member of the

Nation of Islam and adopted the name MUHAMMAD ALI. In March 1964 Malcolm announced that he was breaking with the Nation of Islam to form his own group, Muslim Mosque, Inc. The theological and ideological gulf between Malcolm and Elijah Muhammad widened during a monthlong trip to Africa and the Middle East. During a pilgrimage to Mecca on 20 April 1964 Malcolm reported that seeing Muslims of all colors worshiping together caused him to reject the view that all whites were devils. Repudiating the racial theology of the Nation of Islam, he moved toward orthodox Islam as practiced outside the group. He also traveled to Egypt, Lebanon, Nigeria, Ghana, Senegal, and Morocco, meeting with political activists and national leaders, including the Ghanaian president Kwame Nkrumah. After returning to the United States on 21 May, Malcolm announced that he had adopted a Muslim name, el-Hajj Malik el-Shabazz, and that he was forming a new political group, the Organization of Afro-American Unity (OAAU), to bring together all elements of the African American freedom struggle.

Determined to unify African Americans, Malcolm sought to strengthen his ties with the more militant factions of the civil rights movement. Although he continued to reject King's nonviolent, integrationist approach, he had a brief, cordial encounter with King on 26 March 1964 as the latter left a press conference at the U.S. Capitol. The following month, at a symposium in Cleveland, Ohio, sponsored by the Congress of Racial Equality (CORE), Malcolm X delivered one of his most notable speeches, "The Ballot or the Bullet," in which he urged black people to submerge their differences "and realize that it is best for us to first see that we have the same problem, a common problem—a problem that will make you catch hell whether you're a Baptist, or a Methodist, or a Muslim, or a nationalist."

When he traveled again to Africa during the summer of 1964 to attend the Organization of African Unity Summit Conference, he was able to discuss his unity plans at an impromptu meeting in Nairobi with leaders of the Student Nonviolent Coordinating Committee (SNCC). After returning to the United States in November, he invited FANNIE LOU HAMER and other members of the Mississippi Freedom Democratic Party to be guests of honor at an OAAU meeting held the following month in Harlem, New York. Early in February 1965 he traveled to Alabama to address gatherings of young activists involved in a voting rights campaign. He tried to meet with King during this trip, but the civil rights leader was in jail; instead, Malcolm met with CORETTA SCOTT KING, telling her that he did not intend to make life more difficult for her husband. "If white people realize what the alternative is, perhaps they will be more willing to hear Dr. King," he explained.

Malcolm's political enemies multiplied within the U.S. government as he attempted to strengthen his ties with civil rights activists and deepen his relationship with ADAM CLAYTON POWELL JR., JAMES BALDWIN, DICK GREGORY, and black leaders around the world. The Federal Bureau of Investigation saw Malcolm as a subversive and initiated efforts to undermine his influence. In addition, some of his former Nation of Islam colleagues, including Louis X (later LOUIS FARRAKHAN), condemned him as a traitor for publicly criticizing Elijah Muhammad. The Nation of Islam attempted to evict Malcolm from the home he occupied in Queens, New York. On 14 February 1965 Malcolm's home was firebombed; although he and his family escaped unharmed, the perpetrators were never apprehended.

On 21 February 1965 members of the Nation of Islam shot and killed Malcolm as he was beginning a speech at the Audubon Ballroom in New York City. On 27 February more than fifteen hundred people attended his funeral service held in Harlem and OSSIE DAVIS gave a moving eulogy that contrasted the public's perception of an angry Malcolm with the loving and gentle man he knew, a person who gave voice to the pain of his people and gave courage to those who were afraid to speak the truth. Although three men were convicted in 1966 and sentenced to life terms, one of those involved, Thomas Hagan, filed an affidavit in 1977 insisting that his actual accomplices were never apprehended.

After his death, Malcolm's views reached an even larger audience than during his life. *The Autobiography of Malcolm X*, written with the assistance of ALEX HALEY, became a best-selling book following its publication in 1965. During subsequent years other books appeared, containing texts of many of his speeches, including *Malcolm X Speaks* (1965), *The End of White World Supremacy: Four Speeches* (1971), and *February 1965: The Final Speeches* (1992). In 1994 Orlando Bagwell and Judy Richardson produced a major documentary, *Malcolm X: Make It Plain*. His words and image also exerted a lasting influence on African American popular culture, as evidenced in the hip-hop or rap music of the late twentieth century and in the director SPIKE LEE's film biography, *Malcolm X* (1992).

FURTHER READING
Malcolm X and Alex Haley. *The Autobiography of Malcolm X* (1999).
Malcolm X and Alex Haley. *Malcolm Speaks* (1989).
Carson, Clayborne. *Malcolm X: The FBI File* (1991)
Dyson, Michael Eric. *Making Malcolm* (1996).
Myers, Walter Dean. *Malcolm X: By Any Means Necessary* (1994).
Perry, Bruce. *Malcolm: The Life of a Man Who Changed Black America* (1991)
Strickland, William. *Malcolm X: Make It Plain* (1995)
Obituary: *New York Times*, 22 Feb. 1965.

This entry is taken from the *American National Biography* and is published here with the permission of the American Council of Learned Societies.

CLAYBORNE CARSON

Mallory, Arenia Cornelia (28 Dec. 1904–8 May 1977), educator and school administrator, was born in Jacksonville, Illinois, to James Edward and Mazy (Brooks) Mallory. Arenia and her older brother, Edward, were the only two children of this couple, although James Mallory had another daughter from a previous marriage. Mallory was raised in Jacksonville and attended local high school and Newton Baton College. The Mallorys were musical entertainers and their daughter learned how to play the piano and prepared to be a concert pianist at the Whipple Academy of Music (1918–1922) in Jacksonville. Mallory was saved at age sixteen while attending a local revival sponsored by the Church of God in Christ (COGIC), also called the Sanctified Church, in 1920. Her decision to join the Sanctified Church, mostly composed of poor and uneducated people, vexed her mother, who told her to choose between her and the COGIC. Mallory chose to leave home and told her mother that she would use her musical abilities for the Lord. She traveled with COGIC mission workers and soon expressed an interest in going to Africa, then the preferred mission field for African Americans.

In general African Americans felt that because they were black and civilized, they were destined to help fellow Africans. Mallory did not go to Africa as a missionary, however. In 1926 she met Bishop Charles H. Mason, who told her that there was a little Africa in the Mississippi Delta and that his church school needed a piano teacher. Mallory took the position and in October 1926 borrowed money to go to Lexington, Mississippi, where the school was located. The school had been founded around 1914 by Pinkie Duncan, a female COGIC member, who was teaching reading, writing, and arithmetic in a house near Mason's pastorate, St. Paul's COGIC, in Lexington. Mason later invited Duncan to teach in the basement of his church. The school was first named the Holmes County School for Negro Boys and Girls, but in 1917 its name was changed to the Saints Industrial School of Mississippi. Industrial education had been widely promoted in the South, especially by BOOKER T. WASHINGTON. It was believed by many that this was the type of education that could best provide economic freedom to African Americans. James Courts, the school director, died after Mallory's arrival, and she replaced him as school director in 1927. That year she earned a B.S. degree in Education from Simmons College in Louisville, Kentucky. After settling in Lexington, Mallory married J. Pullam, but she was forced by church leaders to divorce him because he was not a COGIC member. On 4 June 1927 she married A. C. Clemmons, a COGIC elder who would divorce her for another woman. Mallory and Clemmons did have one daughter together, Andrea Mazy Clemmons.

When Mallory took over the Saints Industrial School, it was only a simple, one-room school that sat in the middle of a cotton field and had neither indoor plumbing nor electricity. The Saints school building was a structure typical of those that had dotted the South since the end of the Civil War. Many black churches had started such schools to teach freed people and their children how to read. Even laypeople got involved in this type of endeavor. In order to increase enrollment she opened admissions to students outside the COGIC and begged parents to send their children to her school. Many parents in this rural community were farmers and employed their children in the farming industry and so were reluctant to release them. But Mallory won their hearts, and their children enrolled at the Saints. Mallory, as the new director, also faced the sexist attitudes of some within the male-dominated COGIC who felt that another man should have been appointed to head the school. Mallory, a northerner, hired three white teachers for her school, an act that nearly caused her to be lynched because local whites did not believe in racial integration. However, it is possible that Mallory sought only to improve the quality of teaching in her school by employing the services of these white instructors.

Mallory persevered, however, and made raising money for the school a priority. Following in the footsteps of the Fisk Jubilee Singers, she organized a five-member vocal group, the Harmonizers, whose mission was to raise funds through the singing of spirituals. They sang near cotton fields and collected nickels and dimes from farmers. During the Depression, the group went to New York and approached the historic Abyssinian Baptist Church, one of the largest congregations in the country, where Mallory had to wait eight hours before she could talk to the busy pastor, ADAM CLAYTON POWELL SR. Powell was a civil rights leader and a believer in education and invited Mallory to come on Sunday morning and present her vision to the congregation; that Sunday Mallory told the people that she was trying to build the first black high school in Mississippi. The singing group returned Monday night and raised $8,000 from the packed church. After a three-week tour, Mallory returned to Lexington and built Faith Hall, the school's first brick building. The assistance given by Abyssinian to the Saints Industrial School demonstrated that African American Baptists were not as antagonistic to Pentecostals as is often assumed in the literature. In other words, the black self-help philosophy did not know religious boundaries and was instrumental in helping Saints to become the first black high school in Holmes County in 1936. By the mid-1930s Mallory's leadership had so improved Saints Industrial that it owned 350 acres and buildings worth $50,000 and had a reported enrollment of 400 students.

In the educational area Mallory was befriended by MARY MCLEOD BETHUNE, a prominent black educator, who visited Saints many times. As a result, when Bethune founded the National Council of Negro Women (NCNW) in 1935, Mallory joined as a charter member. Through Bethune's connections, Mallory was able to visit President Franklin Delano Roosevelt and his wife, Eleanor Roosevelt, at the White House in 1937 and explain to them the work she was doing in the South. In 1940 and 1945 the NCNW designated Mallory as one of the outstanding women of America. A continuing learner, Mallory earned an M.A. in Business Administration at the University of Illinois in 1950, and four years later this and other efforts allowed Saints to inaugurate a junior college department in 1954. The school endeared itself to the community by offering training for veterans and adults. In the 1960s, Saints won two federal grants of $466,579 and $414,000 to train seasonal farm workers. Those grants allowed

Saints to train men in trades such as carpentry, plumbing, masonry, upholstery, painting, and electricity. Thanks to those grants women were also trained in sewing and basic nursing. Mallory was also appointed to the advisory board of the Child Development Group of Mississippi, a preschool program that supervised day care centers in seventy-five communities. In 1968 Mallory was elected the first black member of the county board of education, clear evidence that many formerly disenfranchised blacks were taking full advantage of the 1965 Voting Rights Act (1965) to elect progressive blacks to positions of power.

Under Mallory's direction, the motto of the Saints Industrial School was "Walk in Dignity, Talk in Dignity, and Live in Dignity." An educated woman, Mallory followed the inspiration of CARTER G. WOODSON, who had created the Association for the Study of Negro Life and History in 1915 and Negro History Week in 1926. Woodson's dream was to educate black people about their own history. Like him, Mallory used history to instill racial pride, leadership skills, and the inspiration to succeed in her students, some of whom later became COGIC officials and leaders in the civil rights movement.

As a woman working in a church that did not ordain women as pastors, Mallory gained much respect as an educator. She not only received an honorary LLD from Bethune-Cookman College in 1951, but also the next year, she asked to be, and was made, a COGIC delegate to the World Pentecostal Conference meeting in London. Mallory's fame went far beyond the COGIC and Mississippi. For three years Mallory served as vice president (1953–1957) for the NCNW. In December 1959 she was appointed representative of the COGIC in Liberia, and she went on to organize Friends of Liberian Youth, whose purpose was to sponsor rural Liberian youths to study in America. While vice president for the NCNW, she was also a member of the National Council of Women. Mallory attended international conferences in Montreal (1954), Austria (1959), Istanbul (1961), and Rome (1962). In 1963 she was appointed manpower specialist by the U.S. Department of Labor and was later invited to White House Conferences on Children and Youth, and another on Aging.

During Mallory's career at the Saints, the school endured at least five fires. Mallory's achievements won her the Governor's Outstanding Mississippian Award in 1974. When she retired in June 1976, the Saints school that she had led for nearly fifty years had educated more than 25,000 students. The college department closed after her retirement and the high school shut down in 1983 after a fire. Ten years later, however, Saints reopened as a Christian academy. A community health center in Lexington was named in her honor.

Upon her retirement, the COGIC made her commissioner of education. She died in Lexington where she spent her life training and giving hope to black children.

FURTHER READING

Bean, Bobby. *This Is the Church of God in Christ* (2001)

Butler, Anthea. "A Peculiar Synergy: Matriarchy and the Church of God in Christ," Ph.D. diss., 2001.

Gist, Sylvia R. "Educating a Southern Rural Community," Ph.D. diss., 1994.

"Mallory, Arenia Cornelia," in *Who's Who in the South and the Southwest* (1973–1974).

Simmons, Dovie Marie, and Olivia L. Martin. *Down behind the Sun: The Story of Arenia Cornelia Mallory* (1983).

DAVID MICHEL

Malone, Annie Turnbo (9 Aug. 1869–10 May 1957), entrepreneur and philanthropist, was born Annie Minerva Turnbo on a farm in Metropolis, Illinois, the tenth of eleven children of Robert Turnbo and Isabella Cook, both farmers. Robert and Isabella owned the land they farmed and were able to provide comfortably for themselves and their children. After her parents died of yellow fever in 1877, Turnbo went to live with an older sister in Peoria, Illinois.

As a young woman, Turnbo grew dissatisfied with the hair-grooming methods then in use by African American women which often involved the use of goose fat, soap, and harsh chemicals for straightening purposes. Stronger products to straighten naturally curly hair generally damaged the hair follicles or scalp. One of the methods recommended by such products advised users to wash their hair and lay it out flat while using a hot flatiron to apply the solutions. Even washed and laid out, the hair of many women was not long enough to iron, and one of the most common beauty complaints among African American women was burned scalps; indeed, many black women suffered from baldness at an early age. In response, by 1900 Turnbo formulated and perfected a product line she named Wonderful Hair Grower which she sold through local stores near her home in Lovejoy, Illinois. Turnbo also invented and patented both a pressing iron and a pressing comb, devices that, when used in conjunction with her products, aided in straightening African American hair. In 1902, in an effort to expand her business opportunities, Turnbo relocated from Lovejoy to St. Louis, Missouri, where she and three assistants began selling her products door-to-door, offering women free, on-the-spot hair treatments. The approach was successful, and Turnbo undertook a highly profitable sales tour of the South in 1903. That same year she married a Mr. Pope but soon divorced him after her new husband attempted to exert control over her thriving door-to-door business. After the divorce, Turnbo opened her own salon, and a year later her products, which she called Poro, were being sold throughout the Midwest.

In 1906 Turnbo copyrighted the name Poro, a West African term that denotes an organization whose aim is to discipline and enhance the body both physically and spiritually. The company name might have another source, however: in advertisements for the company in 1908 and 1909, Annie Turnbo Pope is pictured with a woman named L. L. Roberts. Though there are no records indicating Roberts's relationship to the company, it is possible that "Poro" is a contraction composed of *Pope* and *Roberts*.

The company's sales growth was spurred by Turnbo's understanding and use of modern business practices, including holding press conferences, advertising in African American newspapers, and using female salespeople. By the first decades of the twentieth century, Turnbo's business was thriving, and by 1910 she had opened larger offices in St. Louis. In 1917 she opened Poro College, the first cosmetology school founded to train hairdressers to care for African American hair. The large, lavish facility included well-equipped classrooms, an auditorium, ice cream parlor, bakery, and theater, as well as the manufacturing facilities for Poro products. The college was soon a center of activity and influence in St. Louis's black community, with several prominent local and national African American organizations housed on site. The college offered training courses that included etiquette classes for women interested in joining the Poro System's agent-operator network. By the 1920s the Poro business employed 175 people in St. Louis and boasted of 75,000 agents working throughout the United States and the Caribbean. In 1930 Turnbo opened new headquarters in Chicago that became known as the Poro Block. At the peak of her career, in the 1920s, Turnbo's personal worth reached $14 million.

Turnbo's business success has often been overshadowed by that of her contemporary, MADAME

C. J. WALKER. In fact, Walker's successful use of door-to-door sales agents was a business strategy she learned from Turnbo while employed as a Poro sales agent for several months in 1905. That same year, Walker informed friends that she had learned how to make a hair product that really worked. Perhaps in an effort to avoid direct competition with Turnbo, she moved to Denver early in 1906 to begin her own company.

In 1921 Turnbo married Aaron Malone, a decision that proved disastrous for the company. During much of the 1920s the Malones were engaged in a debilitating, behind-the-scenes power struggle that was kept hidden from all but a few Poro System executives. Before the couple's divorce in 1927 and his subsequent termination from his position as chief manager and president, Aaron Malone sought support in a bid to take over the company. In asking the courts to award him half of the company, Aaron Malone claimed the success of his wife's business was due to connections he had brought to the marriage. While Aaron managed to get support from key members of the black community, Annie Malone, with the help of influential black women leaders, including MARY MCLEOD BETHUNE, succeeded in keeping control of Poro after paying her ex-husband a settlement of around one hundred thousand dollars.

Malone's largesse had certainly helped sway public opinion in her favor. She had become a generous contributor to African American organizations. She supported a pair of black students at every African American land-grant college in the country; orphanages for African American children regularly received donations of five thousand dollars; and during the 1920s alone, she gave sixty thousand dollars each to the St. Louis Colored Young Women's Christian Association, the Tuskegee Institute, and the Howard University Medical School. Within her company Malone was equally magnanimous. Five-year employees received diamond rings, and punctuality and attendance were rewarded as well.

Soon after her divorce, Malone was back in court, when Edgar Brown filed suit against her for one hundred thousand dollars. The case was dismissed for lack of evidence. Ten years later, a former employee successfully brought suit against Malone. These legal and financial troubles exacerbated longstanding management problems at Poro. Poor oversight by Malone, bad hiring choices, rapid expansion, and the prolonged, behind-the-scenes power struggle with Aaron Malone had dire consequences for the company. These battles, both public and private, and her unmatched—and unchecked—generosity spelled the beginning of the end for Malone's Poro empire. Malone was forced to sell her St. Louis property in order to pay for debts incurred in part by her divorce and court settlements. As a result of her failure to pay excise and real estate taxes, the federal government seized control of the company in 1951. Malone died of a stroke in a Chicago hospital six years later, in 1957, at age eighty-seven. Upon her death, her estate was worth only one hundred thousand dollars.

FURTHER READING
Malone's papers are available at the DuSable Museum of African American History in Chicago, Illinois.
Peiss, Kathy. *Hope in a Jar: The Making of America's Beauty Culture* (1998)
Obituary: *Chicago Defender*, 10 May 1957.

NOLIWE ROOKS

Malone, Patti Julia (c.1858–20 Jan. 1897), a renowned vocalist with the Fisk Jubilee Singers, was born near Athens, Alabama, to Mahalia Jackson, a slave. Her father's name is unknown.

"[S]he journeyed around the world, singing in all climes and among all peoples and before all the crowned heads of the land, and wore medals from the most prominent kings and emperors in the world," according to Malone's obituary in the 1897 *Annual Report of the American Missionary Association* (p. 36). During a fifteen-year career, Malone crisscrossed the globe as a member of the Fisk Jubilee Singers and its successor groups, singing in European capitals and remote Asian backwaters. She was one of the most widely traveled and famous African American performers of her age, entertaining audiences in seventeen countries and singing for six European crown heads.

Malone was born a slave around 1858 at Cedars Plantation near Athens, Alabama. Her mother, Mahalia, was a servant in the home of Dr. Thomas Stith Malone, a physician. After emancipation, Patti enrolled in Trinity School, a school for African Americans founded by the American Missionary Association. Her mother continued to work for the Malone family, with the understanding that Patti also would work before and after school. The Malone family, however, attempted to subvert Patti's education by assigning her tasks that kept her from school. The principal of Trinity School, Mary Wells, recognized Patti's deep desire for an education, and offered her a job so she could escape the Malones' influence. Wells, who was later a chaperone for the Fisk Jubilee Singers, subsequently sent Patti as a high school student to Fisk University in Nashville. Fisk was founded in 1866 by the American Missionary Association initially to train African American teachers.

A group of Fisk students, known as the Fisk Jubilee Singers, had toured America and Europe to raise money for the school. In the process they introduced the world to slave era spirituals. The group began as the school's choir, singing conventional choral music arrangements. The choir's director, George White, was deeply moved by the sacred songs he heard students singing among themselves, and encouraged his most promising student, Ella Sheppard, to transcribe them. Although Sheppard and other Fisk students felt that the songs were relics of a past better forgotten, spirituals proved enormously popular with audiences, and the group achieved international acclaim.

The singers conducted two extensive tours beginning in 1871 and 1873. White began recruiting for a third tour in 1875. Malone had a rich mezzo-soprano voice, and White was impressed with her talent, but he left her behind because her health was fragile. In late 1877 he sent for her from Germany to fill the place of a singer who was ill and had to return home. Malone joined the group in Hamburg in January 1878. She got off to a rocky start when, according to Sheppard, she "began in a squeak" on her first solo performance (Ward, p. 360). She recovered, however, and became a valued member of the group for the remainder of the European tour.

Fisk declined to sponsor a fourth tour, so Jubilee member Frederick Loudin and White led a private troupe made up of some of the Jubilees, including Malone, on a "civil rights tour" in support of the Civil Rights Bill of 1875 through the North and parts of the Upper South. The tour ran from September 1879 until May 1882. In 1882 Loudin took full control of the group, and in 1884 Loudin's Fisk Jubilee Singers set out on a six-year world tour.

Malone and the rest of Loudin's troupe began their tour in England. They then spent an extended period in Australia and New Zealand, where Malone reportedly fell in love with a wealthy Australian and considered abandoning the tour to remain with him. Their "homeward bound" tour took them through Ceylon (Sri Lanka); India, where they performed at the Taj Mahal; Burma; Singapore; China; and Japan. The troupe arrived in San Francisco on 20 April 1890, becoming the first African American performance company to complete an around-the-world tour.

Malone died on 20 January 1897 of unspecified causes while on tour with Loudin's group in Omaha, Nebraska. She was eulogized not only in American newspapers, but also in New Zealand, where she and Loudin's troupe were still fondly remembered. According to the *North Otago Times* on 14 April 1897, Patti Malone "was never robust, but always willing to struggle through her work in the path of duty .... She was a true Christian, and the sterling character she bore softened the prejudice of those with whom she came in contact .... No woman of her race ever sang in more countries of the world, and none did her part better."

FURTHER READING
Abbott, Lynn, and Doug Seroff. *Ragged but Right, Black Traveling Shows, "Coon Songs," and the Dark Pathway to Blues and Jazz* (2007).
Ward, Andrew. *Dark Midnight When I Rise: The Story of the Fisk Jubilee Singers* (2001).

DAVID K. BRADFORD

Malone, Vivian Juanita (15 July 1942–13 Oct. 2005), civil rights activist, was born the eldest daughter in a family of eight children and reared in a tight-knit, segregated community near downtown Mobile, Alabama. From early in her childhood, her father, Willie Malone, a carpenter and maintenance man, and her mother, Bertha Malone, a maid at Brookley Air Force Base, impressed upon Malone and her siblings two basic but lasting principles: love God and value education.

As a student at Central High School in Mobile, Malone excelled academically and blossomed socially. As graduation approached Malone turned her attention to the future and began making plans for a college education. Her first choice was the University of Alabama (UA), the state's oldest university, a sprawling, picturesque campus in Tuscaloosa more than 200 miles away from her home. To the frustration of many would-be students and the chagrin of white empathizers, the University of Alabama was also the last institution of higher education in the entire state to shed the confines of segregation. Fueling the effort to keep the university and every other public school separated by race was the recently inaugurated governor, George C. Wallace, a staunch believer in the ways of the old South whose vows against integration had helped him win the election. Malone was more than qualified to meet any academic standards required by UA. Well-rounded and accomplished, boasting a 3.8 grade point average and standardized test scores in the 99th percentile, she would have been an asset to the student body of any college or university. Despite the school's long-standing color barrier and Governor Wallace's outspoken advocacy of race-based separatism, Malone persisted in applying for admission to the University of Alabama. Her determination to be accepted was matched by an equal determination from university administrators to maintain the all-white complexion of the campus. Disappointed but not deterred Malone appealed to THURGOOD MARSHALL, then leader of the NAACP Legal Defense Fund, who responded by naming attorney CONSTANCE BAKER MOTLEY head of Malone's case.

Just four years before Vivian Malone set her sights on admission, the University of Alabama had made an initial (albeit half-hearted) attempt at integration when AUTHERINE LUCY FOSTER became UA's first African American student in 1956, seeking to pursue a graduate degree in library science.

After three days marked by threats and a campus erupting in violence, Lucy was expelled from the university "for her own safety." By the time Malone sought admission, UA had even more students— well over 8,000—most of whom subscribed to the same archaic mind-set and whose passion ran deep enough to jeopardize her well-being, much as it had earlier threatened Autherine Lucy's. Malone's pursuit also came in the wake of the violent unrest in neighboring Mississippi, ignited similarly by the admission of a black student, JAMES MEREDITH, into that state's largest public university. Unmoved by the hostility surrounding her Malone's perseverance never waned and by the time she graduated from high school in 1960, her case was won and the university finally, though no less grudgingly, accepted her as a student.

Although she was technically admitted into the University of Alabama, legal challenges stemming from the state's opposition to federal interference

Vivian Malone, being led into the Foster Auditorium at the University of Alabama in Tuscaloosa, Alabama, in 1963. Malone and classmate James Hood (not pictured) became the first African Americans to enroll at the University, in defiance of over a century of segregation. (AP Images.)

continued to bar Malone from enrolling immediately after graduation. Determined not to let legal red tape stall her pursuit of a degree in business management, she registered at the unaccredited Alabama A&M University, a historically black institution north of Mobile.

Finally, after two long years, a federal court order personally negotiated by President John F. Kennedy and his brother, Attorney General Robert Kennedy, was handed down mandating the long-awaited enrollment of twenty-year-old Vivian Malone and James Hood, another black student. The order barred state governments from impeding the nationwide desegregation of public schools, making the University of Alabama's refusal to admit Malone and Hood an act of illegal defiance. But George Wallace had won the gubernatorial election under the pledge "segregation now, segregation tomorrow, segregation forever," and he intended to honor his word, promising to thwart any attempt to integrate Alabama public schools by physically blocking the doors.

As promised Governor Wallace stationed himself in front of the doors to the Foster Auditorium on 11 June 1963 to prevent Malone and James Hood from becoming the University of Alabama's second and third black students respectively. Media crawled over every inch of the campus as did Wallace supporters, integrationists, and ordinary onlookers. U.S. Deputy Attorney General Nicholas Katzenbach had been assigned to escort Malone and Hood on behalf of the federal government, and 100 soldiers were deployed for their protection, hardly a match for the 600 Alabama police and guardsmen positioned by the state.

Wallace's stance in front of the auditorium doors proved to be much more of a symbolic last stand than a full-fledged confrontation. Brigadier General Henry Graham of the National Guard, by order of the federal government, asked Wallace to step aside from the doors. After reading a final statement proclaiming the state government's right to sovereignty and scolding the powers-that-be for infringing on Alabama's operation as a segregationist state, Wallace moved aside, making way for Malone and Hood to register. Despite the uncertainty and hype surrounding it, the whole incident lasted less than four hours with no instances of violence.

Enrolled in the university as a junior, Malone made the best of what was a tentative situation. She became an object of the media's attention during her first weeks at UA and appeared on the covers of *Time*, *Newsweek*, and *Jet*. A devout Christian, she credited her strength and courage to her faith in and reliance on God. The university gave her a private dormitory room and bathroom, partly for her comfort and partly because other students were opposed to sharing with her. In class, professors excused students offended by her presence; many opted to leave rather than share space with a black student. But Malone readily acknowledged that not everyone at the school treated her negatively, and she was able to make lasting friendships during her time there. She also socialized with students from nearby Stillman College, where she met her future husband, Mack Jones (he had been hired by UA to be her driver). Despite the difficulties and biases enveloping her experience, in 1965 Vivian Malone completed her bachelor of arts degree in Business Administration with honors and became the first African American to graduate from the University of Alabama.

After graduation, Vivian Malone Jones settled into a life that was much quieter but no less important. She took a position in the civil rights division of the Department of Justice in Washington, D.C., but relocated to Atlanta in 1969 when her husband was accepted into the Emory University School of Medicine. Malone raised two children, a daughter, Monica, and a son, Michael, and continued to work for the federal government as the director of civil rights and urban affairs and later as the director of environmental justice for the Environmental Protection Agency. She also acted as executive director of the Voter Education Project. In 1996 Jones retired from a career spanning over thirty years in government work, a fitting profession for a woman who helped to shape and humanize the often-faceless state and federal laws. More ironic was the public apology personally delivered by George Wallace for his open discrimination against Jones thirty-three years earlier. Wallace even selected her as the first recipient of his Lurleen B. Wallace Award of Courage, an honor given to women who had made great contributions to the state of Alabama. Jones accepted both his apology and the award without hesitation. Jones died suddenly from a stroke at the age of sixty-three, a year after her husband's death.

FURTHER READING
Clark, E. Culpepper. *The Schoolhouse Door: Segregation's Last Stand at the University of Alabama* (1995).
Obituaries: *New York Times*, *Washington Post*, and *Mobile Register*, 14 Oct. 2005.

JANELLE HARRIS

Maloney, Arnold Hamilton (4 July 1888–8 Aug. 1955), physician and pharmacologist, was born in Cocoye Village, Trinidad, to Lewis Albert Maloney, a building contractor and grocery chain operator, and Estelle Evetta (Bonas) Maloney, a needlepoint teacher to young women. Maloney has the distinction of being the first African American professor of pharmacology in the nation and the second person of African descent to earn both a medical degree and a doctorate of philosophy in the United States.

Arnold began his career planning to become a druggist in Trinidad. He studied at Naparima College in Trinidad, a school affiliated with Cambridge University in England, where he received the Bachelor of Arts degree in 1909. Maloney had expectations of becoming a druggist in Trinidad; however, after receiving an unexpected letter from his uncle suggesting greater opportunities existed in the United States, he migrated to New York to study medicine. During this same year, while attending Lincoln University in Pennsylvania, Maloney was encouraged to enter the ministry after winning second place in an oratorical contest. In 1910 he enrolled at the General Theological Seminary in New York. Also in 1910 he was afforded the opportunity to earn the Master of Arts degree in philosophy through a reciprocity agreement between Columbia University and the General Theological Seminary.

On his twenty-third birthday, Maloney was ordained at the Cathedral of St. John the Divine with the distinction of being the youngest minister in the Protestant Episcopal Church. His first assignment was serving as minister of St. Anne's Parish Church in Annapolis, Maryland. In 1915 Maloney took charge of St. Phillips Church in Syracuse, New York, where he remained for two years before resigning. Certain aspects of the ministry left Maloney displeased. He thought his congregation consisted of social cliques who too often considered the church a "playhouse." After the Civil War, former field slaves deserted the Black Episcopal Church leaving free blacks and privileged slaves as the two primary groups remaining a part of the congregation. The members of the Black Episcopal Church were viewed as a privileged group and the Church was considered high-status by whites. The ranks of the black Episcopalians included respected old families and people whose education and affluence often set them apart from other blacks. Many of the clergymen were the sons of the most socially prominent families in the church whose influence extended beyond the religious realm. After renouncing the ministry, his view of the clergy was that bigotry, snobbishness, and race prejudice had a firmer hold within the ranks of the clergy than among physicians.

Leaving the ministry in 1922, Maloney turned to teaching and accepted a position as professor of psychology at Wilberforce University in Ohio. He served in this capacity from 1920 to 1925 and decided to continue his education. He enrolled at the Indiana University School of Medicine, graduating with a medical degree (M.D.) in 1929. He then attended the University of Wisconsin as a General Education Board Fellow (1929–1931), attaining a doctorate (Ph.D.) in the field of pharmacology in 1931. He is also the recipient of two honorary degrees, the Doctor of Sacred Theology (S.T.D.) from Morris Brown College (1918) and the Doctor of Law (L.L.D.) from Wilberforce University (1937).

In the same year, Dr. Maloney accepted a position at Howard University, becoming the first African American professor of pharmacology in the United States. He began his tenure as an associate professor of pharmacology, a full professor, and then chair of the Department of Pharmacology. His research involved several areas of pharmacology such as the effects of morphine on the respiratory center; administration of evipal in prolonged surgical anesthesia; contradictory actions of caffeine, coramine, and metrazol; and tissue changes in chronic barbituism, dehydration, and convulsant action. However, his most significant research was the discovery of picrotoxin as an antidote for barbiturate poisoning. His research suggested that the administrating of picrotoxin has the ability to combat the central depression that results from the administration of high doses of barbiturates. The drug is one of the most effective of all the central nervous system stimulants because it reinstates adequate respiration and greatly lessens the degree of anesthesia.

Dr. Maloney authored and co-authored several works in other fields. These include *The Adequate Norm: An Essay on Christian Ethics* (1915), *Some Essentials of Race Relationships* (1924), *Pathways to Democracy* (1945), *Amber Gold: An Adventure in Autobiography* (1946), and *After England–We: Nationhood for the Caribbean* (1949). He also wrote a weekly column for the *Recorder*, "The Indianapolis Negro," and published over fifty articles during his career before retiring in 1953. He was a member of numerous societies and organizations, including the American Negro Academy, American Academy of Political Sciences, National Medical Association,

Medical Reading Club of Washington, Kappa Alpha Psi Fraternity, and Sigma Pi Phi Fraternity.

Maloney retired from Howard University in 1953 and accepted a position as director of the Mental Division of the Knud Hansen Memorial Hospital in St. Thomas, Virgin Islands. He served in this role until his final illness. He died 8 August 1955 in Washington, D.C. He was survived by his wife, Beatrice Johnston Maloney, a son Arnold H. Maloney Jr., and a daughter, Beatrice Louise Maloney.

FURTHER READING

Cobb, W. Montague. *Arnold Hamilton Maloney, M.D., 1888–1955, Journal of the National Medical Association* (1955)

Gatewood, William B. *Aristocrats of Color: The Black Elite 1880–1920* (2000).

Hill, Robert A. *The Marcus Garvey and Universal Improvement Association Papers: Africa for the Africans 1923–1945, Volume X* (2006).

US Department of Health and Human Services, The Office of Minority Health, *Arnold Hamilton Maloney, Physician and Pharmacologist* (2006).

CRYSTAL L. JOSEPH

Malveaux, Julianne Marie (22 Sept. 1953–), writer, journalist, economist, and commentator, was born in San Francisco, California, to Proteone Alexandria Malveaux, a social worker. She received an AB in 1974, an M.A. in 1975 in economics from Boston College, and a Ph.D. in Economics in 1980 from Massachusetts Institute of Technology. Malveaux served as a media intern for WFAA-TV in Dallas, Texas, in the summer of 1975 and as a junior staff economist for the White House Council of Economic Advisers in Washington, D.C., from 1977 to 1978. She was a research fellow for the Rockefeller Foundation in New York City from 1978 to 1980 and an assistant professor of economics at the New School for Social Research in New York from 1980 to 1981. Malveaux's first book, *Black Women in the Labor Force*, appeared in 1980, a collaborative project with Phyllis A. Wallace and Linda Datcher. Malveaux's contributions to the book focus primarily on the history and contemporary material conditions of black female domestic workers, including the casual nature of their employment, their low wages, and what programs exist to help improve their working conditions. This text marked the beginning of Malveaux's lifelong concern with the roles black women play in the workforce.

In 1981 Malveaux returned to San Francisco and began writing a weekly column for the *San Francisco Sun Reporter* while also serving as assistant professor of economics at San Francisco State University from 1981 to 1985. As a columnist Malveaux often concerned herself with both the overt and covert factors that bar women's mobility in the workplace. Malveaux said, "My research has often been infuriating—only by viewing detailed occupational data can the extent of occupational segregation be understood" (*Contemporary Authors Online*). Her columns were syndicated by King Features in the *Philadelphia Inquirer, Denver Post, Los Angeles Times, San Francisco Examiner, Portland Oregonian, Detroit News*, and *Seattle Post-Intelligencer*, and she contributed more than one hundred articles to magazines including *Black Enterprise, Working Woman, Black Scholar, Ms., Black Issues in Higher Education, Progressive*, and *Essence*, for which she was a contributing editor in 1984.

From 1985 to 2001 Malveaux was a visiting professor and research associate for the Department of Afro-American Studies and the Institute for Industrial Relations at the University of California, Berkeley. While at Berkeley, Malveaux published several academic works including *Slipping Through the Cracks: The Status of Black Women* (1986), which she co-edited with Margaret C. Simms; *Sex, Lies, and Stereotypes: Perspectives of a Mad Economist* (1994); *Voices of Vision: African American Women on the Issues* (1996); and *Wall Street, Main Street, and the Side Street: A Mad Economist Takes a Stroll* (1999).

After her tenure at Berkeley, Malveaux moved to Washington, D.C., where she continued to write columns and books. She also maintained a busy schedule of speaking engagements and was a frequent guest on a variety of television and radio programs, including programs on CNN, BET, C-SPAN, MSNBC and CNBC, and Howard University's television show *Evening Exchange*, PBS's *To the Contrary*, ABC's *Politically Incorrect*, and Fox News Channel's *O'Reilly Factor*. She also hosted talk radio programs in Washington, San Francisco, and New York.

In 2002 Malveaux published *The Paradox of Loyalty: An African American Response to the War on Terrorism* with co-editor Reginna A. Green. The book aimed to chronicle not only various responses to the 11 September 2001 attacks on the World Trade Center in New York and the Pentagon but also responses to President George W. Bush's subsequent "war on terrorism" and its relation to historic and contemporary occurrences of racism in the United States. In the book's preface Malveaux and Green poignantly state, "There is no doubt that Americans of color—from those who were enslaved to those who were interned—see the perils of the 'war on terrorism' much more clearly and vividly than those who are members of the privileged class who wage it" (xv). In his foreword to the book CORNEL WEST called Malveaux a "national treasure" who was "the leading multimedia progressive journalist of her generation" (xii, xi). Malveaux's autobiographical essay "Race, Rage, and the Ace of Spades" also appeared in 2002 in Bernestine Singley's *When Race Becomes Real: Black and White Writers Confront Their Personal Histories*. In the essay Malveaux plays with the various connotations of the phrase "playing the race card" and ultimately argues, "If life is a card game, though, we must play the race card. To be sure, we have to be tactical, knowing when to hold 'em and when to fold 'em" (109).

In addition to her prolific writing career Malveaux was a committed activist and civic leader. She served on the boards of the Economic Policy Institute, the National Committee for Responsive Philanthropy, Women Building for the Future—Future PAC, and the Recreation Wish List Committee of Washington, D.C., and held memberships in the American Economic Association, the National Economic Association, the Bay Area Association of Black Journalists, and Delta Sigma Theta.

A self-declared "renaissance person," Malveaux continued to contribute to American society in a variety of ways, and although at times she found it difficult to juggle her many projects, she once said, "I have role models for my efforts though, and when I feel especially overwhelmed I like to think of myself as someone who is following in the footsteps of W. E. B. Du Bois, a scholar/activist and a very lyrical writer" (*Contemporary Authors Online*). Through her role as a writer and commentator, Malveaux continued to be an advocate for racial, gender, and economic equality in America.

FURTHER READING

Malveaux, Julianne. "Race, Rage, and the Ace of Spades," in *When Race Becomes Real*, ed. Bernestine Singley (2002).

Riley, Sam G. "Julianne Marie Malveaux," in *Biographical Dictionary of American Newspaper Columnists* (1995).

West, Cornel. "Foreword," in *The Paradox of Loyalty: An African American Response to the War on Terrorism*, ed. Julianne Malveaux and Reginna A. Green (2002).

MALINDA WILLIAMS

Malvin, John (1795–30 July 1880), abolitionist and political leader, was born in Dumfries, Prince William County, Virginia, the son of a slave father (name unknown) and a free black mother, Dalcus Malvin. By virtue of his mother's status, Malvin was born free. As a boy, he was apprenticed as a servant to a clerk of his father's master; he later learned carpentry from his father. An elderly slave taught John how to read, using the Bible as his primary text. Malvin became a Baptist preacher and later, after moving to Cincinnati, was licensed as a minister, although he never held a permanent position in a church.

Malvin moved to Cincinnati in 1827, and two years later he married Harriet Dorsey. During his four years in Cincinnati, Malvin was active in the antislavery movement and personally helped several escaped slaves find their way north on the Underground Railroad. He agitated against Ohio's Black Laws, which, among other things, restricted black immigration and prohibited black public education and court testimony. Unable to secure the laws' repeal, however, Malvin organized a committee of Cincinnati African Americans to seek permission to resettle in Canada. While he was living in Cincinnati, a vicious race riot took place in which many blacks were attacked and terrorized by whites.

In 1831, during a visit to Louisville, Kentucky, Malvin was arrested as a suspected fugitive slave. Although his "freedom papers" secured his release, this experience and the generally hostile racial climate in Cincinnati led Malvin and his wife to make preparations to move to Canada. Upon learning that conditions for African Americans were much better in northern than in southern Ohio, however, they decided in 1831 to move to Cleveland. Malvin remained in Cleveland for the rest of his life, becoming one of the city's most influential black leaders.

In Cleveland Malvin worked at a variety of occupations, including cook, sawmill operator, carpenter, and captain of barges operating on Lake Erie and the Ohio Canal between Cleveland and Marietta. He also served as an agent for two early black newspapers, the *Colored American* (1837–1842) and the *Palladium of Liberty* (1843). Malvin bought one lake vessel and later sold it at considerable profit. He was successful enough as a businessman to be able to purchase the freedom of his father-in-law, Caleb Dorsey, from a slaveholder in Kentucky.

In 1832, at a time when the state Black Laws did not authorize public funding for educating

African Americans, Malvin helped organize Cleveland's first private school for this purpose. As a result of this success, in 1835 he helped set up the School Fund Society to promote black education throughout Ohio. Under its auspices schools were organized in Columbus, Cincinnati, and Springfield. Malvin continued to assist escaped slaves in securing safe passage to Canada. He was a leading member of the Cleveland Anti-Slavery Society and became well known as a speaker at meetings protesting slavery and the Black Laws; in 1858 he was elected vice president of the Ohio Anti-Slavery Society. Malvin was also active in the Negro Convention movement. In 1843 Malvin and another Clevelander represented the city at the National Convention of Colored Citizens in Buffalo, New York; they were the first black Clevelanders to attend such a convention. The following year Malvin helped organize the Ohio State Convention of Colored Citizens in Columbus, an influential organization whose meetings he regularly attended during the late 1840s and 1850s.

In 1833 Malvin and his wife were among the founding members of Cleveland's First Baptist Church, and two years later Malvin participated in the construction of the church's first permanent home. At that time he was successful in preventing the establishment of a separate "colored gallery" for black members of the church, a practice that was common in the North before the Civil War.

In April 1861, shortly after the Civil War began, Malvin called a meeting of black Clevelanders to organize a black military company. The governor of Ohio refused their offer of enlistment, however, and some of the volunteers from Cleveland went to Massachusetts, where black regiments were being organized. Ohio did not create its own military units for African Americans until 1863. After the war Malvin remained active in the struggle for racial equality, opposing discriminatory state legislation and speaking out in support of the constitutional amendments of the Reconstruction era. After the passage of the Fifteenth Amendment in 1870, he was named chairman of the Cleveland Colored Republican Club, the first political organization of African Americans in the city.

In 1879 Malvin published his *Autobiography*, in which his recounting of stirring events seemed to justify his faith in the triumph of racial justice over oppression during his lifetime. The decline of racism in the North since 1860 had convinced Malvin that racial prejudice in the United States "cannot be lasting, and must sooner or later succumb to the dictates of reason and humanity." At the time of his death in Cleveland he was affectionately known as "Father John" by many Clevelanders, who saw him as a symbol not only of personal achievement but of progress for African Americans as a group.

FURTHER READING

Peskin, Allan, ed. *North into Freedom: The Autobiography of John Malvin, Free Negro, 1795–1880* (1966).

Kusmer, Kenneth L. *A Ghetto Takes Shape: Black Cleveland, 1870–1930* (1976)

This entry is taken from the *American National Biography* and is published here with the permission of the American Council of Learned Societies.

KENNETH L. KUSMER

Mama Dip. *See* Council, Mildred "Mama Dip."

Manley, Audrey Forbes (25 Mar. 1934–), deputy and acting U.S. surgeon general, college president, and advocate for minority, women, and children's health, was born Audrey Elaine Forbes, the eldest of three girls born to Jesse Lee Forbes, a tailor, and Ora Lee Buckhalter, a machine operator and seamstress, in Jackson, Mississippi. As a child Forbes picked cotton in the fields of Tougaloo and watched her mother suffer from mental illness. By the time she was twelve she knew she wanted to become a physician but was told "poor girls, especially poor Black girls from Mississippi, don't become doctors" (Oxygen, 2001).

Undaunted, Forbes held onto her dreams, even after she and her two younger sisters, Yvonne and Barbara, were left with their grandparents as their mother and father searched for work in Chicago. Forbes settled in, taking upper-level math and science classes in junior high school from a teacher named Mr. Caldwell, who taught biology, chemistry, physics, algebra, and geometry. She would later recall, "I was amazed that one man could know all of this" (Scriven interview, 2002). By the time Forbes turned fourteen her ailing grandmother could no longer care for her and her sisters, and the girls moved to Chicago to join their parents, who had by this time divorced. Forbes hated the experience, recounting that she lost at least two years of her education in the process because of inferior instruction (Scriven, 2002).

Whatever education Forbes may or may not have received in Chicago did not deter her from enrolling in college. At age seventeen she graduated as class valedictorian from Wendell Phillips High School and enrolled on a full-tuition scholarship at Spelman College, an all-female, historically black college in Atlanta, Georgia. While at Spelman, Forbes majored in biology with a premed concentration. Concerned that she would not have enough science to get into medical school, she petitioned Spelman's president, Albert Manley, to take advanced chemistry courses at neighboring Morehouse College because Spelman lacked a chemistry curriculum. After graduating from Spelman with honors in 1955, Forbes attended Meharry Medical College in Nashville, Tennessee, on a full-tuition scholarship from the Jesse Smith Noyes Foundation. In 1959, with medical degree in hand, Forbes had fulfilled her childhood dream.

Forbes returned to Chicago in 1963 to complete a pediatric residency at Cook County Children's Hospital. She became the first African American woman and, at twenty-seven, the youngest person to be appointed chief resident. That same year, she traveled with Crossroads Africa as part of a volunteer medical team, operating a thirty-bed children's ward in a government hospital in Nigeria. She delivered similar services to drug-addicted children in San Francisco. After several years of private practice and a brief marriage to a physician that ended in divorce, Forbes returned to the public sector. Less concerned with the financial wealth that being a physician in private practice could provide, Forbes focused on those who had little access to quality health care.

Forbes's sense of community and service also extended back to her undergraduate alma mater, Spelman College. She was often asked to return to the institution to deliver speeches to the students, encouraging them to be socially responsible agents of change. In 1966 Forbes was elected to the Spelman College Board of Trustees, where she would continue to influence the path and direction of the college. However, her influence would extend more personally than her trustee responsibilities. On 3 April 1970, with a twenty-six-year age difference separating them, Forbes married Spelman's president, Albert Manley, the man who had conferred her baccalaureate degree fifteen years earlier. But when she returned to campus and noticed that the number of premed majors had dropped, Audrey Manley turned to her husband and asked, "What can we do?" (Scriven, 2002).

Two black female mathematics faculty, Shirley Mathis McBay and ETTA ZUBER FALCONER, had already asked the same question and were taking action. McBay and Falconer now had an ally in the first lady of the college. By securing support from the American Association of Medical Colleges (AAMC) and the Josiah Macy Foundation, Audrey Manley, McBay, and Falconer established the Health Careers Office. Recalling her own undergraduate experience, Manley reasoned that students needed better counseling on how to navigate the process and understand the system. As she put it, just saying "I think John would make a very good doctor will not get John into medical school" (Scriven, 2002). Spelman began counseling students on course selection and preparation for the medical school entrance exam as well as assisting with their applications and interviewing skills. These efforts paid off. Spelman became one of the top producers of blacks who applied to medical school, second only to Xavier University, a historically black college in New Orleans, Louisiana.

After her husband, Albert, retired from the presidency of Spelman in 1973, the two remained in Atlanta for another three years while Audrey Manley served as chief of medical services for Emory University's family planning unit at Grady Memorial Hospital, the area's largest public health care facility. In 1976, the couple moved to Washington, D.C., where she began a career with the Public Health Service of the U.S. Department of Health and Human Services (HHS). Manley initially directed sickle-cell anemia and other genetic disease programs, and in 1987 became the first woman to direct the National Health Services Corps, a unit within HHS focused on providing underserved communities with health professionals and improved systems of care. That same year, at age fifty-three, Manley earned the master's in Public Health Administration from Johns Hopkins University.

Manley continued to move up the federal government ranks, eventually becoming the first black woman appointed principal deputy assistant secretary for health (1989–1993). In this position Manley was charged with developing public policy, managing a corps of commissioned officers that totaled more than six thousand, and overseeing eight agencies, which included the National Institutes of Health, the Centers for Disease Control and Prevention, and the U.S. Food and Drug Administration, with budgets totaling more than $22 billion. She also used her position to champion the cause of minority health, helping to found the Office of Minority Health as part of the Department of Health and Human Services. In September 1993

Manley was appointed deputy assistant secretary for intergovernmental affairs, and in January 1994, less than six months later, she was promoted to deputy surgeon general and acting deputy assistant secretary for minority health. But even that career milestone would be surpassed within a year. When JOYCELYN ELDERS, the first black female surgeon general, was forced to resign after the furor over her suggestion that teaching masturbation might be a valid part of sex education, President Bill Clinton appointed Manley to acting surgeon general, a position she would hold from January 1995 to July 1997.

It would seem that Manley's rise to the position of the nation's leading health adviser would provide closure to a career that by any standard had been marked by vision and achievement. In addition to her accomplishments with the Public Health Service, she had been elected a fellow with the American Academy of Pediatrics (1967); elected to the National Academy of Sciences (1976); recognized with the MARY MCLEOD BETHUNE Award from the National Council of Negro Women (1979) and the MARTIN LUTHER KING JR. Drum Major for Justice Award from the Southern Christian Leadership Conference (1986); the Distinguished Alumni Award from Meharry Medical College (1989); honorary doctoral degrees from Tougaloo College (1990), Spelman College (1991), and Meharry Medical College (1991); and the Distinguished Service Medal from the United States Public Health Service (1992).

Manley had intentions of retiring from public service at the close of the federal fiscal year on 30 September 1997 and enjoying life with husband, Albert, at their home in Jamaica. But in the spring of 1997 her name surfaced as a candidate in Spelman College's search for a president to replace the magnanimous JOHNNETTA BETSCH COLE, the school's first black female president. Manley had worked in the federal government for most of her professional life and had no experience managing a college or navigating the shared governance structure of academia. Lack of experience notwithstanding, Manley beat out two other contenders, Claudia Mitchell-Kerman, vice chancellor and dean of the University of California, Los Angeles, and HAZEL O'LEARY, former U.S. secretary of energy. It was another pioneering step for Manley: her appointment, scheduled to take effect 1 July 1997, marked the first time an alumna would hold the top post. At age sixty-three Manley knew her time at Spelman would be limited and committed five years to the institution. However, her husband would never see his wife take the helm. Albert Manley died of a heart attack on 28 March 1997 at age eighty-nine at the couple's vacation home in Jamaica.

Alone, Manley returned to lead her alma mater. She used her government networks to secure federal funding to implement a program focused on women's health and wellness and to help complete fund-raising for and construction of the institution's science facility. She also launched a campaign to renovate Sisters Chapel, a historic facility named in honor of the aunt and mother of John D. Rockefeller Jr., a longtime benefactor of the college. Manley would also have her own lasting legacy at Spelman. The science facility, completed in 2002, bears her name. Manley declared that the honor was "the most gratifying thing that will ever happen to me in my life."

As a child Manley was told that black girls didn't become doctors. Her narrative of dreams that would be denied is not unlike many during her generation. However, Manley not only became a physician but rose to become the top health adviser in the country while looking more broadly at mechanisms to help other black women achieve their goals. Reflecting on her career, she noted that,If you're only thinking of yourself, what material and monetary things you can get, if the Mercedes and the fur coat and the big house is what's keeping you going—you're not going to make it. Not too long. You'll have some immediate successes. But for the long term, for life, you really have to have goals that are bigger than you, family, that have to deal with society and making a contribution that's bigger than yourself. (Scriven, 2002)

FURTHER READING

"Doctor Is Successful Despite Age, Sex, Race Background," *Chicago Daily Tribune*, 9 Nov. 1961.

Pure (Oxygen) TV. Oral history interview with Dr. Audrey Forbes Manley in Atlanta, Georgia (Mar. 2001).

"Rear Admiral Audrey F. Manley," *Congressional Record, Proceedings and Debates of the 105th Congress* 143 (12 June 1997).

Scriven, Olivia. Oral history interview conducted with Audrey Forbes Manley in Atlanta, Georgia, 19 Jan. 2002.

OLIVIA A. SCRIVEN

Manly, Alexander (13 May 1866–5 Oct. 1944), editor, alleged provocateur, and Urban League pioneer, was born Alexander Lightfoot Manly near Raleigh, North Carolina, to "Trim" Manly and Corrine

Manly, former slaves of North Carolina Governor Charles Manly, whom Alex claimed as a paternal grandfather. At age 20, having received an elementary education along the way, Alex departed the family farm in Selma Township for Virginia's Hampton Institute, where for a year he worked by day, learned house painting and printing by night, and absorbed the Victorian middle-class values that suffused that institution.

Without graduating from BOOKER T. WASHINGTON's alma mater, Manly left Hampton for Wilmington, North Carolina, the state's largest city and a community where there were more opportunities for black men than in much of the South. There he parlayed his painting proficiency to secure employment with Frederick Sadgwar, who was a house and railroad-trestle builder as well as the pillar of Wilmington's African American community. Working with the well-respected Sadgwar (and courting his daughter, Caroline) guaranteed Manly entry to all social classes within Wilmington's tightly knit community as well as the city's white society. Meanwhile, he took night courses at the Gregory Institute, run by the Congregationalist American Missionary Association.

In August 1895 Manly launched a weekly newspaper, the *Wilmington Record*, perhaps with the financial underwriting of his father-in-law to be, Frederick Sadgwar. It was an auspicious time for a new black-owned newspaper in North Carolina, as the state was then embarking upon the South's boldest post-Reconstruction experiment in interracial political cooperation, as Republicans and Populists fused their electoral tickets to defeat the white supremacist Democratic Party. Since black votes were essential to maintain this so-called Fusion coalition, African American political activity grew dramatically in North Carolina in the 1890s.

The *Record*, whose masthead read "Of the Negro, for the Negro, and by the Negro," devoted much space to announcing the progress of African Americans in North Carolina; there were also advice columns, accounts of recent scientific and engineering achievements, and children's stories. Manly's editorial goal was to preach the middle-class virtues of persistence, prudence, abstinence, frugality, providence, and home ownership. Philosophically, he reflected the egalitarianism of FREDRICK DOUGLASS. The paper diplomatically but effectively campaigned for improvements in the quality of black life at the level of local government. Before long the *Record* was recognized as "a very creditable colored paper" by paternalistic whites

and was patronized by the leading white merchants of Wilmington.

By 1897 the *Record* began to be published statewide as a daily paper, an expansion perhaps assisted by the income Manly received from his appointment as assistant register of deeds in the Populist-Republican administration in Raleigh. By 1898 the *Record* had become not only the voice of African American aspirations within North Carolina's governing Fusion coalition but also one of the nation's leading African American newspapers. Manly's life was transformed, however, on 18 August 1898, following the publication in the Democratic Wilmington *Morning Star* of a quote from Rebecca Felton, the crusading wife of a white Populist leader in Georgia. Speaking of alleged recent "outrages" of white women by black men, Felton stated that "if it needs lynching to protect woman's dearest possession from ravening beasts, then I say lynch, a thousand times a week if necessary." This comment was more than Manly could stand, knowing of his parents' interracial ancestry and awareness from his own experience of consensual sexual relations between white women and black men. For the afternoon edition of his paper he impulsively dashed off what would become known as "The Manly Editorial." In it, he denounced lynching and white hypocrisy concerning miscegenation. He also called upon both races to be judged by the same moral standards and warned: "Don't think ever that your women will remain pure while you are debauching ours. You sow the seed—the harvest will come in due time." Manly's bluntness matched that of the famed antilynching crusader IDA B. WELLS-BARNETT.

Manly's editorial struck a raw nerve. The Democratic press chose to interpret the editorial as a symbolic raping of pure white womanhood. Torrents of abuse and threats rained down upon the outspoken editor. The *Record* was evicted from its white-owned office and white advertising patronage was withdrawn. Although dismayed by the misinterpretation of his message and the virulent reaction to it, Manly resisted pressure from so-called accommodationist black politicians to suspend publication. Instead he sought and secured the support of the black community. The *Record* received asylum in the hall of the fraternal order known as the Grand United Order of Love and Charity, and members of the clergy also offered support. When white threats seemed particularly menacing, black, male supporters turned out en masse to protect their newspaper. Moreover, a group identifying itself as

"An Organization of Colored Ladies" endorsed the paper as "the one medium that has stood up for our rights," according to a Raleigh *News & Observer* report quoting the *Record*.

Even as "The Manly Editorial" became the centerpiece of the Democrats' statewide white-supremacy campaign in 1898, Manly continued to urge black men to perform their duty of registering and voting. Despite an election-day carnival of intimidation and fraud, many black men presented themselves at the polls and cast their ballots, albeit to no avail. The next day an ad hoc committee of white civic leaders carried out a coup d'etat, forcing Wilmington's sitting Fusion officials to resign. Assuming that the danger had passed, the black community was caught by surprise the following day when white vigilantes murdered a number of African Americans—perhaps more than 20—and chased most black leaders out of the community. Only with the aid of a white Episcopal priest was Manly able to escape what became known as the Wilmington Race Riot of 1898.

Manly at first secured refuge with relatives in New Jersey, and then after unsuccessfully seeking sympathy from the McKinley administration in Washington, D.C., Manly considered relocating to New York City with the intent of reestablishing a black daily newspaper in a more hospitable clime. He finally decided to make the nation's capital his new base of operations, since Washington, D.C., had one of the largest black communities in the country and one that still hosted the only post-Reconstruction black congressman, GEORGE H. WHITE. A friend from Manly's Wilmington days, White hired him as his personal secretary. White's support enabled Manly to relaunch the *Record* in Washington in the spring of 1899. Manley's appointment to a patronage position in the Post Office Department helped support the struggling newspaper. Support for the paper also came from members of Manly's family, especially from his brother Frank, who served as the paper's general manager. During the Washington years, Manley also became very active in the local and national Afro-American Council.

Following White's departure from Congress in 1901, Manley married Caroline Sadgwar and moved to Philadelphia, where several family members already resided. Painting jobs came his way, but only when he "passed" for white. The "thing finally became unbearable," Alex told muckraker Ray Stannard Baker, "I preferred to be a Negro and hold up my head." Thus, he dropped his painting

trade and became the janitor of an eight-story apartment building, which paid enough for Manly and his wife to afford a three-room rooftop apartment. Gradually the frugal and industrious Manly created his own painting contracting business and relocated to the Philadelphia suburb of La Mott, which had been a stop on the Underground Railroad and a training ground for black soldiers during the Civil War.

Although he was no longer a newspaper editor, Manly remained active in the civil rights movement. He founded a club of African American voters that allied itself to the city's "good government" movement, and he later organized an association of black tradesmen who came to man most of the electrical generators found in many of Philadelphia's largest buildings. In 1912, with the support of a Quaker meeting, he formed the Armstrong Association (named after the founder of Hampton University) to encourage black youth to enter trades and to aid the assimilation of southern black migrants into Philadelphia's economy and society. When the Armstrong Association became affiliated with the National Urban League, Manly was an active participant, touring the country to create local chapters. Manly died in 1944. His wife later imparted this observation to her sons: "How my poor boy went through all he did and came out cheerful and forgiving is a wonder to me."

FURTHER READING

Alex Manly Papers can be found at East Carolina University in Greenville, North Carolina.

Baker, Ray. *Following the Color Line: An Account of Negro Citizenship in the American Democracy* (1908)

Cecelski, David S., and Tim Tyson, eds. *Democracy Betrayed: The Wilmington Race Riot of 1898 and Its Legacy* (1998)

The Colored American (Aug. 1898).

News & Observer (Oct. 1898).

Prather, H. Leon. *We Have Taken a City: Wilmington Racial Massacre and Coup of 1898* (1984).

Wooley, Robert. "Race and Politics: The Evolution of the White Supremacy Campaign of 1898 in North Carolina," Ph.D. diss., University of North Carolina (1979).

ROBERT H. WOOLEY

Manns Israel, Adrienne (13 Jan. 1947–), student activist, educator, and black studies advocate, was born in Massillon, Ohio, to Mercedes Anna Marie Manns, African American, an office worker for

Illinois Bell Telephone Company. Adrienne grew up with three brothers and a stepfather, Walter Preacely Sr., though she spent most of her youth with her great aunt, Lillian Scott. From an early age Manns valued education, and upon graduation from Washington High School in Massillon, in 1964 she enrolled at Howard University. She expected that this institution would be a place where she could broaden her intellectual horizons while establishing a strong cultural identity. While Manns found Howard's curriculum challenging, she was disappointed that the foundation of her educational experience was immersed in the values of white America. She and other equally disheartened students yearned for an education reflective of the history, culture, and social issues of their communities.

After two years of academic success but increasing frustration with Howard's conservatism, Manns became a founding member of the Black Power Committee, an organization committed to changing the culture and curriculum of the university. Led by professor Nathan Hare, the Black Power Committee focused its energies on overthrowing the old-guard Howard administration and reestablishing the institution as one dedicated to a socially and culturally relevant mission. The administration, hoping to dissolve the organization, acted swiftly and in 1967 dismissed Hare and several other professors and students involved with the group.

In 1968 the Black Power Committee became an even greater force on Howard's campus. Manns used her post as editor of the campus newspaper, the *Hilltop*, to express the group's agenda. That year the Black Power Committee gained strength in numbers when it united with other concerned groups on campus. The newly formed organization, UJAAMA, developed a manifesto expressing its demands on the institution. The group selected Charter Day, the annual observance of the university's founding in 1867, as the deadline for the administration's response to the list of demands, which included the resignation of President JAMES M. NABRIT, the reinstatement of professors fired for their political activism, and the development of a curriculum committed to the study of black people. When the administration failed to respond in the allotted time, UJAAMA disrupted the Charter Day ceremonies and distributed flyers titled "Definition of a Black University." As a result of the counter–Charter Day activities, Manns and other leaders of UJAAMA received judiciary-hearing notices. They in turn planned and executed a takeover of the school Administration building. Manns, a steering committee member and

negotiator for the group of approximately two thousand, helped to orchestrate an impressively organized protest. Following several days of negotiations with the administration, national media coverage of the takeover, and the threat of federal intervention, the negotiation teams for both sides came to an agreement that satisfied many of the student demands. This bold initiative became an important catalyst in the creation of black studies in colleges and universities throughout the country and rooted Manns in a lifelong endeavor to continue the development of black studies curricula.

In 1968, Manns graduated from Howard and started work at the *Washington Post* and *Washington Afro-American* newspapers. One year later, Howard hosted the first "Toward a Black University" conference, which assembled many of the country's key educators and community leaders who developed black studies programs. Manns received an M.A. in African Studies from Howard in 1973 and a Ph.D. in History from Johns Hopkins University in 1984. In the fall of 1982 she accepted a job as a history professor at Guilford College in Greensboro, North Carolina. There she collaborated with students and interested faculty members in developing an African American studies program. In 1984 the college curriculum committee approved African American and African studies as a minor.

On 24 May 1986 Adrienne Manns married Martin L. Israel at the Wells Memorial Church of God in Christ in Greensboro, North Carolina. Manns Israel and her husband remained in Greensboro, where she helped transform Guilford's African American studies minor into a major. In addition to teaching classes such as The Civil Rights Movement, The Underground Railroad, African American History, Africa: Before 1800, and Africa: 1800 to Present, she authored many articles and a book, *Amanda Berry Smith: From Washerwoman to Evangelist* (1998). In 2003 she became vice president and academic dean of Guilford College and remained committed to the black studies movement.

FURTHER READING

Hampton, Henry, and Steve Fayer. "Howard University 1967–1968," in *Voices of Freedom: An Oral History of the Civil Rights Movement from the 1950s through the 1980s* (1990).

Hodge, Natalie Kay. "Fighting for Our Education, Fighting for Our Future: Black Women's Leadership in the Black Studies Movement," master's thesis, Cornell University (2003).

NATALIE HODGE COOK

Manson, Jacob (1851–?), former slave in Warren County, North Carolina, was aged eighty-six years when T. Pat Matthews interviewed him for the federal government's Works Progress Administration Slave Narratives project in 1937. Manson's owner was Colonel Bun Eden. Unlike the majority of his slaveholding brethren in North Carolina, Eden held enough slaves to qualify as a planter. In fact, Manson claimed his master owned more than fifty slaves, which would have placed him in the top 3 percent of North Carolina slaveholders in 1860. Manson paints a very draconian picture of slavery under Colonel Eden, and his discussion of his years in servitude bequeath for posterity a unique first-person look into life on a large Upper South plantation.

Despite living in Warren County, a tobacco-producing region on the border with Virginia, Manson said little about the nature of field work. He did allude to the fact that there existed little gender division of labor on the plantation though. Although older women watched over slave children under Colonel Eden, younger women performed tasks alongside their male counterparts. Slaves worked all day and into the night on a regular basis, though Manson noted that they usually received time off if a storm hit. Manson also recalled that Colonel Eden, a lazy man who lied around in his grand house habitually drunk on whiskey, forced slaves to wash his feet, comb his hair, and in Manson's case, scratch his head while he fell asleep. Manson would sneak away once Eden nodded off so as to avoid waking him and being resummoned, but sometimes the young slave had to fan the flies away from his master so he could slumber.

Manson's account notes that he and his fellow slaves lived in excessive squalor on the Eden plantation. They wore homemade clothing that often failed to include shoes or hats, so when working outside under the hot sun, some slaves resorted to wearing self-spun bonnets or rags tied around their heads. The slave quarters consisted of shoddily constructed cabins, made with stick-and-dirt chimneys, one door, and just one small window in the back. Many had dirt floors. Manson also mentioned the poor quality of the rations fed to slaves and documented how the children were forced to crowd around and eat out of a trough. In keeping with North Carolina law, which prohibited black churches and slave education, Manson recalled books and black religious ceremonies being strictly prohibited. Slaves were allowed to attend white church services. While there, however, they were mainly instructed to be obedient to their masters.

Colonel Eden also took a liking to slave women and girls. He had no white children, and he refused to employ white overseers, as he did not trust them around his slave women. According to Manson, this was not out of the ordinary either—he claimed that one would have been hard-pressed to find a master who did not seek sexual relations with his female slaves. Manson told the story of a slave girl on a nearby plantation who wanted to spurn unwanted sexual advances from her owner, but "her missus told her 'Well, go on, you belong to him'" (Jacob Manson quoted in Hurmence, p. 41). He also recited an anecdote about Jimmie Shaw, a master murdered by his wife because of his affair with a slave girl. These relationships between masters and female slaves gave rise to the "Jezebel myth," which characterized women of African descent as lustful, lewd counterparts to the chaste and virtuous Victorian women. These relationships were widespread and existed with varying degrees of sexual exploitation on behalf of the white master or overseer.

Manson lamented the inhumane treatment that he and his fellow slaves received at the hands of Eden and slave patrollers alike. Manson recalled seeing slaves sold off and many slaves run away, some never to return. Manson recalled being whipped "for any little trifle," including for his sluggish gait, and he recounted the severe thrashing of his uncle by white slave patrols, or "pattyrollers" as many slaves referred to them (Jacob Manson quoted in Hurmence, p. 42). These "pattyrollers" beat Manson's uncle up so badly that they broke his collarbone, an injury from which he never fully recovered. Accordingly, Eden forced the patrols to compensate him for damaging his property.

One morning, the plantation was covered in Union soldiers, who demanded that Manson tell them where his master had hid all of his valuables. When Manson refused, the Yankees "told me I had no Marster, that they had fighted four years to free us and that Marster would not whip me no more" (Manson quoted in Hurmence, p. 42). Following the war, Manson continued to work on plantations, never owning a home of his own. He married Roberta Edwards around January 1886, according to Mrs. Manson. While Jacob remembered having six sons and three daughters, his wife reported that they had five daughters and three sons together. In the early 1930s, he moved to Raleigh to live with his daughter after growing too old to work. Manson summed up his life as follows: "I think slavery wus a mighty bad thing, though it's been no bed of roses

since, but den no one could whip me no more"
(Manson quoted in Rawick, p. 99).

FURTHER READING

Hurmence, Belinda. *My Folks Don't Want Me to Talk about Slavery: Twenty-One Histories of Former North Carolina Slaves* (1984).

Rawick, George P. *The American Slave: A Composite Biography* (1972). See vol. 15, part 2, pp. 95–99.

Taylor, Rosser Howard. *Slaveholding in North Carolina: An Economic View* (1969).

White, Deborah Gray. *Ar'n't I a Woman? Female Slaves in the Plantation South* (1985).

JOHN FRENCH

Manson, Roberta (1863– ?), was seventy-four years old at the time of her Works Progress Administration interview with T. Pat Matthews. Given the unknown status of her exact birth date, the interview could have occurred in either 1937 or 1938. Manson had been a slave, belonging to Weldon Edwards and living on his plantation in Warren County, North Carolina. Born Roberta Edwards in 1863, she was too young to remember her own servitude. Accordingly, everything she knew of slavery had been relayed to her by other former slaves, principally her parents, Lanis and Ellen Edwards. Also owned by Weldon Edwards, Roberta Manson's parents passed down stories that painted the picture of a murderous monster heading up the plantation on which the family lived. Roberta Manson's second-hand narration on American slavery bequeaths to posterity precious insight into the short-term historical memory of someone too young to recall her own servitude.

According to Manson's confidants, her master Weldon Edwards reigned over his plantation with an iron fist and a deadly wrath, and conditions on the plantation worsened when it became readily apparently that emancipation was imminent. Overseers were allowed to flog slaves at their discretion (of which they showed little), and Weldon Edwards himself thrashed Manson's father so severely that the slave had to grease his back in order to remove his shirt. When the slave Harris Edwards had become ill and unable to work for an extended period of time, the overseers Jim Trissel and David Porter forced the issue by dragging him out to be larruped. They beat him to death, leaving his body out for the buzzards to feed on. The plantation mistress, Lucy Edwards, protested, as Harris had worked in her service. She had Trissel relieved of his duties, but not before he left behind a lethal

legacy on the Edwards plantation. During one fit of rage, he knocked Lanis Edwards's hip out of place; and he had once whipped him for crying at the sight of another slave whom Trissel had killed. When the slave Jack Edwards was caught leaving the plantation to tend to his sick wife, he was dragged to the plantation whipping post, where he received a battering so severe that afterward he could only summon the energy to crawl up to the house and die.

To quash any incipient subversion on the plantation, Weldon Edwards imposed strict regulations on the leisure activities of his slaves. Prayer meetings, parties, and literacy were strictly forbidden on the Edwards plantation; no books or papers were allowed in slave possession. The miserly Weldon Edwards shrewdly monitored his expenditures on food, clothing, and shelter for his slaves. The collards and peas served to the slaves had often not even been cleaned prior to cooking. Older slaves often received especially meager rations, and many died as a result of this neglect. Slave cabins had dirt-and-stick chimneys, one small window, and dirt floors, where they were lucky to have a straw bed. Weldon Edwards had no qualms about splitting up slave families. Roberta Manson had four aunts who were sold away from their clan. When her Aunt Millie had cried at the thought of being separated from her baby, she was threatened with brutality. Ultimately, it was decided that she not face corporal punishment in order that she could fetch a better price at auction. After all, it was difficult to sell a slave who had been "skinned up" (Rawick).

These very conditions forced the hands of Roberta Manson's parents after the abolition of slavery; they simply lacked the resources to move elsewhere. Despite all the horror stories her parents had told Manson, they chose to stay on with Weldon Edwards before bouncing around the area sharecropping for several different white families. Since the family had nothing to eat, nothing to wear, and nowhere to go, they had no other options. Her father even had to work alongside his former overseer David Porter. Since the former masters needed labor for their farms and the former slaves had no other options available, postbellum life mirrored antebellum life for the Edwards family.

Roberta married Jacob "Jack" Manson around January 1886. Her husband recalled the couple having nine children, but Roberta stated that she gave birth to eight, only three of whom were alive at the time of her interview. Her opinions and remembrances of slavery were similar to her husband's in that they both testified to draconian treatment, harsh conditions, and limited postwar opportunities for African Americans. Roberta Manson's testimony, however, recalls atrocities normally reserved for history's mass murderers and most nefarious tyrants. While it is clear that callous conditions and ruthless violence existed on Weldon Edwards's plantation, it is nonetheless intriguing and perplexing to note that her parents chose to stay with Weldon Edwards after emancipation. Despite the family's lack of postwar opportunities, they were able to work for several different families in the same time frame. Yet they did choose to stick with Weldon Edwards at least for a while, and this does raise some questions as to the accuracy of Roberta Manson's secondhand account of slavery.

Correct in her belief that masters with large numbers of slaves tended to be crueler, Roberta Manson still lived in a state (North Carolina) that had outlawed the murder of slaves in the eighteenth century. By the mid-nineteenth century, no legal daylight existed between the murder of a slave and the murder of freemen. While overseers generally exhibited malevolent and heartless behavior toward slaves (often sparking conflict with masters concerned about their property values), Roberta Manson's accusations should have raised red flags with local authorities and fellow slave owners, who, in the interest of stability and self-preservation, collectively frowned on such brutal behavior.

As the WPA Slave Narratives contain no death records, there is little or no information on Manson's year of death.

FURTHER READING

Rawick, George P. *The American Slave: A Composite Biography,* vol. 15, part 2, 100–104 (1972).

Stampp, Kenneth R. *The Peculiar Institution: Slavery in the Ante-Bellum South* (1982).

Genovese, Eugene D. *Roll, Jordan, Roll: The World the Slaves Made* (1974).

JOHN FRENCH

Maples, William Lineas (31 Mar. 1869–22 Jan. 1943), physician and musician, was born in Seierville, Tennessee, the son of Edward Maples and Martha Jane Runions. William had one brother, Samuel. Showing a talent for science, oratory, and music, he graduated in the first class of the segregated high school in Knoxville in 1888. He received recognition at graduation for his outstanding oratorical skills and received the Dodson medal for his talent. Upon graduating from high school he taught high school for a year in Austin, Tennessee. He entered medical school at Howard University in Washington, D.C., in 1889 and received his MD in 1893. While he was a medical student he supported himself by a job as a clerk in the federal pension office in Washington, D.C.

In 1893 Maples returned to Knoxville and established a medical practice. During the Spanish-American War, in 1898, he interrupted his practice to serve in the U.S. Army's medical unit of the all-black Third Regiment of the North Carolina Volunteers. He ended his service a year later and returned to Knoxville to resume his practice. In 1896 the Knoxville mayor, S. G. Heiskell, appointed him commissioner of "colored exhibits" at the Tennessee Centennial.

In 1900 agents for the Hawaii Commercial and Sugar Company (HC&S Co.) on Maui traveled through Tennessee and Alabama looking for workers for Hawaii's plantations. They were also seeking a physician to staff the hospital that would be serving the contract workers. Maples was recruited as the anesthetist for the HC&S hospital. Maples's older brother, Samuel, a lawyer, also accepted a position as a leader for the black contract laborers recruited for the HC&S plantations.

Before leaving Knoxville, Maples married Sadie (maiden name unknown), who accompanied him on the voyage to Hawaii. He was assigned to the hospital in Puunene, Hawaii, and for the first few years lived in plantation housing provided to the medical staff. William and Sadie Maples had not planned on staying in Hawaii for more than two contracts, or six years, but William Maples increasingly found the work professionally satisfying. The hospital had installed a new operating room comparable to any found in a small, modern hospital in Tennessee. William and Sadie Maples had two daughters, Gladys and Elizabeth, and the family became active in the community, especially after they purchased a house in the town of Wailuku in 1905. Maples was active as an officer in the Maui chapter, or Valley Isle Court, of the Ancient Order of Foresters, a fraternal and benevolent society founded in England in 1834.

Maples recognized the need for a first-class drugstore in Wailuku and opened Maples Drug Store in April 1905. Advertisements in the *Maui News* boasted that the drugstore carried the finest line of cigars on Maui and had a new soda fountain. The drugstore closed after a few years as Maples's responsibilities at the hospital mounted. Maples was also known locally for his interest in music. In 1911 he became manager of the Navarro orchestra in Wailuku, which provided popular music of the day for the Maui public. He also wrote the Puunene school song in 1931.

Maples was the first African American university-trained physician to practice in Hawaii. He came to Hawaii at a time when, as a new territory of the United States, it offered many opportunities for new immigrants. In Knoxville, legal segregation and racism were rampant. When Maples arrived in Hawaii, there were only a few blacks living in the islands. In Hawaii, professional blacks who sought refuge from segregation and discrimination in America encountered little overt racism. Hawaiian plantation owners were guilty of discrimination against their nonwhite, foreign contract laborers, however, many of whom were Asian. Though most of the black laborers from the South did not renew their initial contracts on the sugar plantations, Maples remained in Hawaii. He worked for the Hawaii Commercial and Sugar Company until his retirement in 1931. William Maples died in Wailuku, Maui, at the age of seventy-three.

FURTHER READING

Jackson, Miles M. *And They Came: A Brief History of Blacks in Hawaii* (2001)

Siddall, John W., ed. *Men of Hawaii* (1917).

Wermager, Paul. "Healing the Sick," in *They Followed the Trade Winds: African Americans in Hawaii*, ed. Miles M. Jackson (2005).

MILES M. JACKSON

Mapps, Grace A. (?–1891), educator and poet, was probably born in Little Egg Harbor, New Jersey, to David Mapps, a wealthy mariner and a respected businessman, and Grace, whose maiden name is unknown. Mapps's parents became Quakers in 1799 and enjoyed great respect within the Society of Friends, welcoming frequent visits from Friends including Charles Osborn, the famous antislavery editor, and Thomas Shillitoe, a British minister. It is said that Isaac Hopper, the abolitionist and participant in the Underground Railroad, once declared at a dinner party that if any of the white guests objected to eating with the Mappses, the offended parties should wait until the end of the event to eat. Everyone dined together that evening. Though the family was embraced by many in the Quaker community, it was highly unusual that they were made members at all. Mrs. Mapps once mourned the difficulties that a black woman encountered in the Society of Friends, wondering how God could have sent her among people who despised her.

Sarah Grimké wrote a similarly scathing article in 1837, criticizing the segregationist practices of the Quaker faith, following her censure by the Friends for sitting next to Grace Mapps's cousin, SARAH MAPPS DOUGLASS, at a meeting.

Grace Mapps enjoyed a relatively privileged childhood, surrounded by people who valued education. After graduating from high school she matriculated at the New York Central College at McGrawville, which was modeled on Oberlin College in Ohio and was founded to serve students regardless of their gender, race, religion, or economic background. When McGrawville opened its doors in 1849, the college faculty included one black male professor and two white female professors. A university building called the farmhouse also served as a station on the Underground Railroad, and McGrawville may have even been chosen as the site of the school because its location was most conducive to that purpose. Mapps graduated in 1852, perhaps making her the first black woman to graduate from a four-year college in America, though MARY JANE PATTERSON, who graduated from Oberlin College in 1862, is often credited with this honor.

After her graduation, Mapps took a job as a teacher at the Institute for Colored Youth in Philadelphia (originally founded by the Quaker philanthropist Richard Humphreys in 1837 as the African Institute); teaching was a popular profession at the time among black educated women despite its low pay. Though the Quakers are known for their abolitionist activities, they were not as committed in the nineteenth century to full equality among the races. Many Quaker schools began to open to students of other denominations, but they were still closed to black students; it was not until the middle of the twentieth century that most Quaker schools admitted black students.

Thus the Institute for Colored Youth served to provide black youth an opportunity to learn the arts, trades, and agriculture and to produce an educated cadre of teachers who could educate future generations of black students. There Grace Mapps was joined by her cousin, Sarah Mapps Douglass, a member of the interracial Philadelphia Female Anti-Slavery Society and an avid proponent of education for African Americans. From 1853 to 1864 Mapps served as the principal of the girls' department of the school. She is said to have studied Greek and taught it at the high school. In 1864 she left the school, which was then suffering from low enrollment caused by the greater job opportunities open to both young men and women during the Civil War. The Institute for Colored Youth became Cheyney University in 1914 and claims to be the nation's oldest historically black institution of higher education.

Grace A. Mapps was also a poet. She was first published in the June 1859 issue of *Anglo-African Magazine*, a race journal founded to provide the black intellectual community a forum for all their academic and political endeavors and to create a link between all people of African descent, whether slave or free. Other authors who contributed to that issue include FRANCES ELLEN WATKINS HARPER, MARTIN DELANY, FREDERICK DOUGLASS, EDWARD BLYDEN, and Sarah Mapps Douglass. The white abolitionists Wendell Phillips and William Lloyd Garrison were said to be admirers of the paper, which also published Martin Delany's *Blake, or The Huts of America* in installments in 1859. Mapps also contributed to several African American periodicals in the years before the Civil War. After a long career as an educator and writer, Grace A. Mapps died in Burlington, New Jersey, not far from her birthplace.

FURTHER READING

Cadbury, Henry J. "Negro Membership in the Society of Friends," *Journal of Negro History* (Apr. 1936).

Grimké, Sarah. *The Subject of Prejudice against Color amongst the Society of Friends in the United States* (1837)

LAURA MURPHY

Marable, Fate (2 Dec. 1890–16 Jan. 1947), musical director, pianist, and riverboat calliope player, was born in Paducah, Kentucky, the son of Elizabeth Lillian, who had taught music as a slave. His mother's maiden name and details about his father are unknown. According to the jazz musician CLARK TERRY, Marable's real name was Marble.

Early on, Marable received strict training in music from his mother. In September 1907, at a time when he was shining shoes in a barber shop, the Streckfus family, owners of the Acme Packet Company, offered Marable a job on the excursion steamer *J.S.*, then in port at Paducah. For dances in the ship's ballroom Marable played piano in a duo with the violinist Emil Flindt. Atop the ship he played the deafening steam calliope. A month later, at a riverboat parade for President Theodore Roosevelt, Marable manned the calliope to play "Turkey in the Straw" while Roosevelt danced a jig on top of the steamer *Mississippi*.

The dance band aboard *J.S.* expanded to four pieces and flourished until the steamship burned to the water in 1910. Marable tried a carnival tour, but he disliked the work and resumed his association with the Streckfus line in 1911. Having replaced an African American pianist, Marable remained a decade later the only African American in the bands of the Streckfus line. Surprisingly—given the separation of riverboat audiences into white and black, the later separation of Streckfus bands into white and black, and wide-ranging racial tensions on the Mississippi—this integrated band seems not to have encountered problems in its reception, perhaps because of Marable's light complexion.

In a move toward the incipient jazz style, Marable in 1917 formed the Kentucky Jazz Band, using players from Paducah on the riverboat *St. Paul*, but he deemed the band musically inadequate. After working on *St. Paul* as its intermission pianist, Marable recruited a new nine-piece band during the steamer's layover in New Orleans in the winter of 1918–1919. His Jazz Syncopators, soon to be called Fate Marable and His Jazz Maniacs, included LOUIS ARMSTRONG, JOHNNY ST. CYR, POPS FOSTER, and BABY DODDS. A photo of the band, taken on the steamer *Sidney*, shows JOHNNY DODDS as well, but he was only a temporary replacement for the clarinetist Sam Dutrey Sr. In May 1919 the band took a train northward to join a black musicians' union and then began touring on *St. Paul*, where Marable, a strict disciplinarian, gave Armstrong, St. Cyr, and Foster ongoing lessons in music-reading skills, general repertory, and professional musicianship. St. Cyr remained in the band until 1920, and Armstrong, Dodds, and Foster remained until 1921. According to St. Cyr, Marable himself grew bored of teaching his musicians and was given a vacation for the winter of 1920–1921.

Marable worked on several boats in the Streckfus line for another two decades. Among his bandsmen were the saxophonist GENE SEDRIC, who later played with FATS WALLER, and the trumpeter Dewey Jackson, who subsequently directed his own groups on the steamers. When in 1927 Jackson received an offer to join CAB CALLOWAY, Jackson's New Orleans Cotton Pickers became Marable's. HENRY "RED" ALLEN was a member of this band in 1928–1929, as was the bassist Al Morgan, who had joined Marable in 1926. By 1930 the band's name had been shortened to Fate Marable's Cotton Pickers. Marable's later bands included the saxophonists Tab Smith (1934) and EARL BOSTIC (1935–1936), with Marable in 1936 codirecting with Charlie Creath.

Marable remained on the boats as a pianist in Creath's band until 1939, when he resumed directing his own band for trips to Pittsburgh. It was at this time that he discovered the pioneering string bassist JIMMY BLANTON. According to his own version, Marable got in touch with DUKE ELLINGTON, who hired Blanton for his band. Marable's health and morale declined when Blanton was fired in 1941; the details of what happened are unknown. Marable played in local clubs and made his home in St. Louis, where he died.

To work with Marable on the riverboats was to attend a floating conservatory of music. He was usually called leader, but since the musically knowledgeable Streckfus family handled financial matters and authorized hiring, as well as supervising the selection of musical repertoire and some aspects of rehearsals, he more accurately should be called musical director. His acclaimed band with Armstrong reportedly played a wide variety of standard dance music scores exactly as written, yet this band was also said to have differed significantly from white bands on the Streckfus steamers and to have been the best on the river. There are no surviving recordings—Marable recorded two insignificant titles in 1924—and it must be inferred from oral testimony how strict reading and varied interpretation might be reconciled. Most probably the band jazzed up standard arrangements by applying a tremendous sense of jazz rhythm to written music and by playing with jazz-oriented instrumental timbres. In doing so, Marable's band had a significant role in disseminating the sound of jazz northward from New Orleans.

FURTHER READING

Dobie, Wilma. "Remembering Fate Marable," *Storyville* 38 (Dec. 1971–Jan. 1972).
Schacht, Beulah. "Story of Fate Marable," *Jazz Record* 42 (Mar. 1946).
Vandervoort, Peter, II. "The King of Riverboat Jazz," *Jazz Journal* 23 (Aug. 1970).
This entry is taken from the *American National Biography* and is published here with the permission of the American Council of Learned Societies.

BARRY KERNFELD

Marcelle, Oliver (21 June 1895–12 June 1949), third baseman in the Negro Leagues, nicknamed "the Ghost," was born Oliver H. Marcelle in Thibodaux, Louisiana. He attended Tomey Lafon Elementary School and New Orleans High School. While in school he played ball on the local sandlots and got his start with the New Orleans Black Eagles. Prior to the start of the Negro National League in 1920

Marcelle handled the hot corner for the Brooklyn Royal Giants and Detroit Stars, becoming one of the league's best defensive third basemen.

Oliver Marcelle played for twelve seasons in the Negro Leagues. During his stint he handled the hot corner for five different teams and hit .293. Marcelle also played in the winter season in Cuba. Marcelle's baseball career in the Negro Leagues began in 1920, the inaugural season of the Negro National League. He played until 1923 with the Bacharach Giants and then played two and a half seasons for the New York Lincoln Giants. He returned to Bacharach mid-season in 1925 and stayed until 1929, when he joined the roster of the Baltimore Black Sox for one season. In 1930 Marcelle played third for the Brooklyn Royal Giants and finished out his final season with the Cuban Stars of the East.

Marcelle hit consistently for every team he played for but he really excelled in the field. Hall of Fame third baseman JUDY JOHNSON felt that Marcelle was a better fielder than he was. His overall strong play caused Hall of Famer JOHN HENRY "POP" LLOYD to name him to his all-time team in 1953. The *Pittsburgh Courier* conducted a poll in 1952 and Marcelle received selection as the best third baseman from the Negro Leagues. Marcelle had great range and a strong arm, to which he added clutch hitting, which made him a valuable man to have on a roster and a dangerous opponent.

Marcelle played in two Negro League World Series for the Bacharach Giants in 1926 and 1927. In the 1926 series Marcelle knocked in six runs in eleven games. The Negro League World Series were generally longer than the Major League series to generate sufficient funds to pay the players and the teams. The games were not just played in the cities of the two teams involved but in other cities to allow more fans to come out and see them compete. In postseason play Marcelle batted .263, with eight runs knocked in and nine walks. He played in twenty games and had only two extra base hits.

During the winter Marcelle either worked or played ball as so many other ball players did. They did not make enough money during the season to survive the winter without a job. He spent seven full seasons in Cuba as well as parts of other years. He hit .307 in his complete seasons and even led the league in hitting in 1923 with a .393 average while playing for the Santa Clara ball club. Santa Clara won the league championship that season with a 36–11 record.

In 1929 Marcelle got the opportunity to play alongside some of the best players in the Negro

Leagues. He became part of what was often referred to as the "million dollar" infield for the Baltimore Black Sox, an infield that helped them earn the American Negro League pennant.

Marcelle loved to play and especially loved to win. He had a legendary temper that sometimes got him in trouble, on and off the field. He had run-ins with umpires and fellow players but still remained popular with the fans and his teammates. One incident involved future Hall of Famer OSCAR CHARLESTON and an argument that resulted in Marcelle hitting Charleston with a bat. In a fight with Frank Wickware during a dice game Wickware supposedly bit off part of Marcelle's nose, leading him to wear a patch to cover up the loss.

After Marcelle retired from baseball he became a house painter in Denver. He also helped get the Kansas City Monarchs invited to play in the *Denver Post* Tournament as the first black team to participate. He died in 1949 without much to show for his career in terms of monetary reward but he had left a record of solid achievement on the baseball diamond.

In 1996 Marcelle received a posthumous honor with his election into the Louisiana Sports Hall of Fame. In 2006 he made the short list for consideration for election into the National Baseball Hall of Fame and although he was not selected the fact that he was considered is testament to his great accomplishments in the Negro Leagues.

FURTHER READING

Patty, Mike. "Riverside Grave Memorial to Honor 'Ghost' Marcelle." *Rocky Mountain News*, 1 June 1991, E3.

Riley, James A. "Marcelle, Oliver H. 'Ghost,'" in *Biographical Dictionary of American Sports, Baseball*, David L. Porter, ed. (2000).

Van De Voorde, Andy. "Ghost Story: A Denver Sports Sleuth Goes Beyond the Grave to Honor a Baseball Legend." *Westword*, 9 July 1991, pp. 4, 6.

LESLIE HEAPHY

Marchbanks, Lucretia (25 Mar. 1832 or 1833–19 Nov. 1911), adventurer, entrepreneur, and cook, was born a slave near Algood, Tennessee, probably the granddaughter of her white master, Martin Marchbanks, and the oldest of eleven children of a slave woman. Trained as a housekeeper and kitchen worker she lived on her white uncle's plantation, until while still quite young she traveled with a Marchbanks daughter to California during the gold rush, gaining first hand impressions of the West and its opportunities. After emancipation she and several siblings sought their fortunes in Colorado. Lured by the discovery of gold in the Black Hills she arrived in Deadwood on 1 June 1876. Unlike most others, however, she never intended to mine gold, having come to believe that there was more profit in offering services to the miners using skills she already possessed. She began her career in the kitchens of the Grand Central Hotel, where she soon became known for her delicious food and her strong, outspoken character. On one famous occasion she reportedly fearlessly confronted a ruffian who had entered the restaurant and was threatening the customers with his gun. Miss Marchbanks's gleaming kitchen knife and the fire in her eye convinced the man he had urgent business elsewhere.

A woman of great character, attractiveness, and stern respectability she was for a time known as "Mahogany," but as she matured she became everyone's "Aunt Lou." At the Golden Gate Hotel, where she held forth in the kitchens, she was known for her excellent cuisine. Later she managed a boarding house owned by the Father DeSmet Mine and cooked for the mine's executive mansion in Central City, earning the excellent salary of $40 a month, and interacting with civic leaders and internationally prominent mining executives.

Lucretia Marchbanks supplemented her income by baking for miners accustomed to paying well for fine food. A mince pie baked for a special customer pleased him so much that he presented her with the stunning black silk dress she wore in a famous photograph from November 1881. An 1879 fund-raising drive to build a Congregational church included the raffle of a diamond ring for the most popular woman in the Hills. Miss Marchbanks won more than half the votes, taking home the jewelry and the title.

In 1883 she opened the Rustic Hotel, a highly successful boardinghouse considered an excellent and respectable address for young men far from home. Her many admirers often compared her to their own mothers. Three years later she purchased a ranch across the Wyoming line between Sundance and Beulah, where she and a younger sister, Martha Ann, raised cattle and horses. There she was reportedly as loved and admired as she had been in Deadwood, and she remained an active member of the community for more than twenty years. Lou Marchbanks never married and her reputation was never touched by scandal. When she died after a brief illness, regional newspapers eulogized her and mourned her passing.

FURTHER READING

Guenther, Todd. "Lucretia Marchbanks: A Black Woman in the Black Hills," *South Dakota History* 31.1 (Spring 2001).

Parker, Watson. *Deadwood: The Golden Years* (1981)

Sundstrom, Jessie. "Black Women in the Black Hills," *Sixth Annual West River History Papers* (1998).

VanEpps-Taylor, Betti C. *Forgotten Americans: African Americans in South Dakota* (forthcoming 2007).

BETTI CAROL VANEPPS-TAYLOR

Marchbanks, Vance Hunter, Jr. (12 Jan. 1905–21 Oct. 1988), aerospace surgeon, was born at Fort Washikie, Wyoming, the son of Vance Hunter Marchbanks Sr., an army cavalry captain, and Mattie (maiden name unknown). Marchbanks Jr. was influenced by the military career of his father, who was a veteran of both the Spanish-American War and World War I. A childhood operation inspired Marchbanks's passion for medicine, after which he operated on cherries in his backyard, opening them up, removing the stones, and sewing shut the incision.

Marchbanks encountered discrimination when he enrolled at the University of Arizona in 1927. Not allowed to live in the dormitories or participate in normal student activities, he lived in an off-campus boardinghouse. He ate at the railroad station restaurant, where he was expected to enter through the back door and was harassed; he often found cockroaches in his soup. Marchbanks graduated in 1931 and was accepted at the Howard University School of Medicine, where he met his future wife, Lois Gilkey, who was an undergraduate at Howard. He received his medical degree in 1937, and then he was an intern and resident in internal medicine at the Freedmen's Hospital in Washington, D.C., for two years.

Still coping with discrimination, Marchbanks "realized that if I stopped looking at the worse side and made an effort, I may be able to see the brighter side of things." His most frustrating experiences with discrimination occurred in the military, where he "experienced it his whole life." He hoped to become a flight surgeon. While serving at the Tuskegee, Alabama, Veterans Administration Hospital, Marchbanks heard that an army air corps flying school would be built at Tuskegee. A field surgeon at Maxwell Air Force Base in nearby Montgomery advised Marchbanks to apply to take an extension course at the School of Aviation Medicine at Randolph Field, Texas.

In 1941 Marchbanks was assigned instead as a first lieutenant in the U.S. Army Medical Corps at Fort Bragg, North Carolina, where he endured "many unpleasant experiences." He later told another generation of black military doctors that "many of you younger physicians have had no such experiences because we paved the way by enduring those hardships and made it possible to abolish many of them."

By December 1942 Marchbanks had completed the army air corps course in aviation medicine and was rated an aviation medical examiner. He was assigned to the station hospital at the Tuskegee Army Air Field, then transferred as a major with the 332nd Fighter Group, known as the Tuskegee Airmen, to Selfridge Field, Michigan. Marchbanks was the group's flight surgeon during campaigns in Italy, becoming one of the first black American flight surgeons and the first in the air force's medical service. He earned a Bronze Star. He also took classes on the medical aspects of atomic explosion and on air base surgery.

Because of his friendship with the Tuskegee Airmen, Marchbanks challenged the military's policy of discharging men who carried the sickle-cell anemia trait. Experts estimate that one of every twelve blacks carries the genetic trait. In a three-year study Marchbanks drew blood from the airmen and analyzed it. He published his results in the article "Sickle Cell Trait and the Black Airman," which helped prove that not everyone who carries the trait has the disease, and he convinced military authorities not to end the careers of black cadets who had the sickle-cell trait.

In 1945 Marchbanks joined the 477th Composite Group of B-52 pilots at Godman Field, Kentucky, as group surgeon. A year later he held the same position at the Lockbourne Army Air Base in Ohio, where he had autonomy at his first station hospital. He applied for a commission in the army and was accepted on his second application, becoming the first black physician commissioned in the army. In 1949 Marchbanks was transferred to the Department of the Air Force when all segregated air force units were disbanded. He became group surgeon of the First Fighter Group at March air force Base in California, then of the Twenty-second Bombardment Group in Okinawa.

Marchbanks accumulated 1,400 hours of flight time during his tour of duty in Okinawa and Korea, where he flew three combat missions. Promoted to the rank of lieutenant colonel, he returned to Lockbourne in January 1951 as hospital commander and wing surgeon for the Ninety-first Strategic Reconnaissance Wing. Three years later he was assigned as deputy commander and chief of professional services at the Air Force Hospital in Nagoya, Japan. This four-hundred-bed facility was the largest air force hospital in Asia.

In 1955 Marchbanks was promoted to the rank of full colonel and was named air force surgeon of Okinawa. He returned to the Strategic Air Command as hospital commander and division surgeon at Loring Air Force Base in Maine. At his various assignments, Marchbanks was a pioneer in aerospace medicine research and received two air force commendation medals for his research projects. He designed an oxygen mask tester, which the air force adopted as a standard piece of equipment on air bases.

During Operation Long Legs in November 1957, Marchbanks accompanied a B-52 jet bomber crew on a 10,600-mile nonstop flight from Florida to Argentina to New York. Spending almost twenty-three hours in the air, he tested the crew for signs of stress and fatigue. He observed that the adrenal hormone content in blood and tissue served as an index to the physical fatigue that often preceded fatal crashes. Marchbanks developed stress tests and a rating system to evaluate air crews in combat—tests and ratings that were later adapted for astronaut training. He told colleagues, "Professionally this was my most rewarding assignment."

Marchbanks also developed a system to identify the remains of numerous casualties from multiple aircraft, as might be found in a war zone. National Aeronautics and Space Administration (NASA) officials cited this achievement as the reason that Marchbanks was selected as an aeromedical monitor and support physician for Project Mercury in 1960. While director of Base Medical Services at the 831 Tactical Hospital at George Air Force Base in California, he was lent to NASA.

As one of eleven specialists assigned to monitor the vital signs of the astronaut John Glenn for his orbital flight, Marchbanks prepared by studying electrocardiography at the School of Aviation Medicine at Brooks Air Force Base in Texas and by familiarizing himself with Glenn's medical history. He also practiced by monitoring the signs of the chimpanzee Enos during his orbit. Marchbanks traveled to the tracking station at Kano, Nigeria, and on 20 February 1962 Glenn, in *Friendship 7*, became the first American to orbit the earth. During the three six-minute periods that Glenn passed over Africa, Marchbanks evaluated his respiration, temperature, and pulse, having the authority to terminate the mission if he detected extreme physical stress. "When he was up there, it was just routine

for us," Marchbanks commented. "We'd been practicing and practicing. I'd studied his EKG for over a year. I hardly realized it was over until it was all over. It was like playing in a game and not realizing you had won until the end." Marchbanks was featured on the cover of *Jet* magazine's 21 December 1961 issue for his aerospace achievements.

While in Nigeria, Marchbanks visited a leper hospital and evaluated medical conditions. Shocked by the lack of books there, he wrote physicians, medical schools, and publishers, asking them to donate medical texts to the country's primary medical training facility, the Hygiene School. Marchbanks collected hundreds of books for Nigeria.

Marchbanks retired from the air force in 1964 and accepted a research position as chief of environmental health services of Hamilton Standard, a division of the United Aircraft Corporation in Windsor Locks, Connecticut. He supervised medical and safety tests of spacesuits and life-support systems for the Apollo moon missions and advised engineers building the equipment about physical and psychological factors crucial for success.

Marchbanks received numerous honors, including the William Alonzo Warfield Award from the Association of Former Interns and Residents of the Freedmen's Hospital. Accruing 1,900 flying hours in propeller and jet aircraft, he collected medical data and published articles for military manuals and research publications. Marchbanks focused on human reactions to speed, noise, and altitude during jet flight. In 1971 Marchbanks addressed the aerospace medicine section at the National Medical Association convention and presented an autobiographical account titled "The Black Physician and the USAF," which was later published in the *Journal of the National Medical Association*.

Marchbanks died in Hartford, Connecticut. He was buried with full military honors at Arlington National Cemetery.

FURTHER READING
"Col. Vance Marchbanks Slated for Medic Award," *Jet* (4 May 1961).
"Space Doctor for the Astronauts," *Ebony* (Apr. 1962).
This entry is taken from the *American National Biography* and is published here with the permission of the American Council of Learned Societies.

ELIZABETH D. SCHAFER

Marichal, Juan (20 Oct. 1937–), baseball player, was born Juan Antonio Marichal Sánchez in

Laguna Verde, Dominican Republic, to Natividad (Sánchez) and Francisco Marichal. His father was a farmer who died when Juan Marichal was three. Marichal was raised by his mother on their large farm, and began playing baseball at six. Dropping out of high school after the eleventh grade, Marichal nominally drove a tractor for the United Fruit Company while pitching for its baseball team. After he dominated the Dominican Air Force team in a 2-1 game, the seventeen-year-old Marichal received a telegram the following day from the son of the dictator Rafael Trujillo, requesting his enlistment in the nation's air force. Much like his job in the fruit industry, Marichal was with the organization for one reason: to pitch. In fourteen months Marichal never flew a plane, but he did develop his pitching skills and attracted the attention of major league scouts. In 1955 he signed with the Escogido Leones, the Dominican affiliate of the San Francisco Giants.

Marichal signed his first big-league contract with the Giants in 1957, and following spring training in 1958 he was assigned to the Giants' Single-A club in Michigan City, Indiana. With his unique high leg-kick delivery already confounding

batters, Marichal quickly acclimated to baseball in America, leading the Midwest League with twenty-one wins and a 1.58 ERA. However, it took him longer to adapt to a still-segregated society and to a language in which he was not yet fluent. Marichal led the Double-A Eastern League the following season in wins, strikeouts, and ERA, and was 11-5 in Triple-A Tacoma in 1960 when he got his call to the big league club. Becoming just the second Dominican native to pitch in the majors, trailing the Washington Senators' Rudy Hernandez by sixteen days, Marichal made his stellar debut on 19 July 1960. Facing the Phillies, Marichal carried a no-hitter into the eighth inning, and finished with a complete-game, one-hit shutout. In his third career start, he beat future Hall-of-Fame southpaw Warren Spahn in a 3-2 ten-inning match. Marichal was a regular starter by 1961, helped the team to the World Series in 1962, and became the staff ace in 1963, when he won twenty-five games, posted a 2.41 ERA, and exceeded 200 strikeouts for the first of six times. With Puerto Rican teammate ORLANDO CEPEDA and superstar WILLIE MAYS, Marichal became one of the cornerstones of a Giants club that would post at least eighty-five

Juan Marichal, on the field with his teammates from the San Francisco Giants, March 1968. (AP Images.)

victories per season throughout the decade. Off the field, Marichal set down roots as well, marrying Alma Rosa Carrajal in 1962, with whom he would later have six children.

Known as "The Dominican Dandy" and "Manito," Marichal combined a stylish delivery and vast repertoire of pitches to make him one of the dominant hurlers of his day. To his misfortune, his best years came at the same time as BOB GIBSON's and Sandy Koufax's; Marichal never won a Cy Young Award, despite posting some of the best seasons of the era. He won at least twenty games in six of the seven years from 1963 through 1969; in 1963 he became the first Latin pitcher to throw a no-hitter, and two weeks later tossed a sixteen-inning shutout against the Milwaukee Braves. He was elected to the All-Star team each year from 1962 through 1969. Back pain hampered his play in 1970, but he bounced back to win eighteen games and an All-Star spot for the last time in 1971.

Marichal's moment of infamy, and one that shadowed his career, was a gruesome brawl with the Los Angeles Dodgers catcher John Roseboro. On 22 August 1965, the rival teams were in the middle of a tight game in which Marichal had repeatedly brushed back Dodgers hitters. When Marichal came to bat in the third inning, Roseboro threw a ball back to pitcher Sandy Koufax, narrowly missing Marichal's ear. As the Dominican ace yelled in protest, Roseboro charged him, and Marichal responded by hitting him on the head with the bat, causing a melee and Roseboro to require medical attention. Marichal expressed deep regret about the incident, and in the 1980s, with the former enemies turned friends, Roseboro became a big petitioner for Marichal's entry into the Hall of Fame.

Following his decline with the Giants, Marichal was sold to the Boston Red Sox before the 1974 season, and caught on with the Dodgers in 1975, where he pitched in just two games before retiring.

Marichal went on to work for the Oakland Athletics' scouting department, and by the early 1980s was operating a camp in the Dominican Republic to train young standout ballplayers. After two years of failing to gain entry to the Hall of Fame, Marichal was elected in 1983. The first Dominican to be received at Cooperstown, he was also the first Latin player to be chosen in a regular election (ROBERTO CLEMENTE and MARTIN DIHIGO were selected under special circumstances). His bilingual inauguration speech was relayed by satellite to the Caribbean.

Marichal's relationship with baseball continued; one of his daughters was briefly married to Cincinnati Reds pitcher Jose Rijo. Leonel Fernandez, the president of the Dominican Republic and longtime fan of Marichal, named the Latin star to be the country's sports minister in 1996. Marichal served until 2000, promoting youth programs, holding relief events for the country after it was devastated by hurricanes, and securing the 2003 Pan-American Games.

In 2005 the Giants unveiled a nine-foot statue of Marichal outside their stadium; with stars of the past in attendance and salsa music broadcast over the speakers, the Giants took the field with "Gigantes" on their uniforms in tribute both to Marichal and the Latin influence in baseball.

At a time when Latin players were beginning to make a name for themselves in the major leagues, Marichal's stardom helped pave the way. With the color line broken, many star players from the Caribbean's fruit and sugar company leagues began to be scouted. Though others had come before him, Marichal established many milestones for Latin pitchers. As a dark-skinned Latino playing in America, he endured hardships he had not grown up with, including segregation, racial epithets hurled at him from opposing fans, and even a manager (Alvin Dark) who banned Spanish from the Giants' clubhouse. His legacy with Latin players remained strong years after he retired: the Dominican ace PEDRO MARTINEZ, when presented by Marichal with his first Cy Young Award on 22 January 1998 at the Boston Baseball Writers' Dinner, turned and gave it back to Marichal out of gratitude, saying "I always thought he should be the first (Dominican) to get it before anybody" (*Patriot Ledger*, 23 Jan. 1998).

FURTHER READING
Marichal, Juan, and Charles Einstein. *A Pitcher's Story* (1967).
Barra, Allen. "With Politics at the Plate, Baseball Went Ballistic," *New York Times*, 20 Aug. 2000.
"The Dandy Dominican." *Time* (10 June 1966).
Livingstone, Seth. "Pedro, Marichal Giving Away the Cy Young," *Patriot Ledger*, 23 Jan. 1998.
                                                    ADAM W. GREEN

Marino, Eugene Antonio (29 May 1934–12 Nov. 2000), clergyman, and the first African American Roman Catholic archbishop in the United States, was born in Biloxi, Mississippi, the sixth of eight children of Jesus Maria Marino, a baker, and Lottie Irene Bradford, a maid. After an elementary and high school education in parish schools, the future prelate studied for the priesthood as a member of a religious community established to minister to blacks and Native Americans. He graduated from St. Joseph's Seminary College in Washington, D.C., and later earned a master's degree at Fordham University. Marino grew up as a religious minority within a racial minority oppressed by segregation in the Deep South. The family was devoutly Catholic in a region of the country that was overwhelmingly Protestant and historically as hostile toward the Church of Rome as it was toward people of African descent. Biloxi's Catholic parish for blacks, Our Mother of Sorrow, constituted the family social life. Parents and children went to 6:30 a.m. daily mass. Mother, father, and eight children would all kneel around their beds at night to pray the rosary.

Family members said that even in grade school Marino wanted to be a priest. Specifically, he wanted to join St. Joseph's Society of the Sacred Heart, a community of religious men established in the United States in 1898 to minister among African Americans. The Josephites, as the organization became widely known, was a spin-off of the St. Joseph's Foreign Mission Society founded in 1868 in England to evangelize in Africa. Marino's seminary education began in 1952 at Epiphany Apostolic College in Newburgh, New York. He completed his theological studies at St. Joseph Seminary in Washington, D.C., and was ordained on 9 June 1962 by Auxiliary Bishop Phillip M. Hannan, who in 1965 became archbishop of New Orleans.

Marino's first assignment was to teach science and religion at his alma mater in Newburgh. The intellectual life continued to be a large part of his ministry. While at Newburgh he furthered his studies in religion. He earned a master of arts degree in Religious Education in 1967 from Fordham University and the next year was appointed spiritual director at the St. Joseph Seminary in Washington, D.C.

In addition to his work as a spiritual guide to Josephite priesthood candidates, Marino used his knowledge and experience with the development of the inner self to aid the archdiocese and the National Conference of Catholic Bishops. He was spiritual director from 1969 to 1971 for the married men who entered the archdiocese's Permanent Diaconate Program. During that same period he helped the U.S. Catholic bishops to develop national guidelines for the training and spiritual development of Catholic laymen, who would then minister as permanent deacons.

In 1971 the Josephites recognized Marino's leadership and elected him vicar general or head of the order. On 16 July 1974 Archbishop William W. Baum of Washington, D.C., announced that Pope Paul VI would appoint the Reverend Eugene A. Marino as one of two new bishops to assist him in the then-thirty-five-year-old archdiocese, whose territory included the District of Columbia and St. Mary's, Calvert, Charles, Prince George's, and Montgomery counties in Maryland. The third African American to join the U.S. Roman Catholic bishops' ranks in a decade, Marino was consecrated on 12 September in a ceremony at the National Shrine of the Immaculate Conception. The onetime Josephite priest at age forty was a bishop at the political center of the U.S. Catholic Church. He served as pastor of St. Gabriel's, a predominantly black parish on Grant Circle in northwest Washington. Along with those duties and the responsibility to preside at church sacramental rites as a bishop, he maintained an administrative involvement in archdiocesan affairs and those of the national church. Marino chaired the National Conference of Catholic Bishops Committee on the Permanent Diaconate. He also served on the Committee for Priestly Formation and as a liaison to committees for the National Office for Black Catholics; the Priest, Religious and Laity; and the Council of Major Superiors of Men.

Since 1964, when New Orleans Auxiliary Bishop Harold Perry was consecrated as the first black U.S. Catholic bishop appointed in the twentieth century, some newspapers speculated about the possibility of a black U.S. cardinal, an elector of the pope. Hopes grew again in 1988 when Pope John Paul II elevated Marino to archbishop of Atlanta. The fifty-four-year-old Marino's appointment to a major southern capital showed the willingness of the Church to offer great challenges and responsibilities to its clergy, regardless of race. The motto beneath his episcopal coat of arms was "Feed My Lambs." A 21,445-square-mile jurisdiction, the archdiocese of Atlanta had been established on 10 February 1962, nearly five months to the day before Marino became a priest. The new archbishop's first great challenge was to deal with a scandal over the sexual abuse of children by clergy. His background as a spiritual director came in handy. The new archbishop began to do what he could to heal those most hurt by the crisis. Within months Marino's administration issued guidelines for the report of clergy abuse allegations and outreach to abuse victims. His administration also provided a long-sought outreach to the Latino population. The media hailed him as a force for spiritual renewal and healing in the city of more than 3 million people. Despite the region's relatively small Catholic population of 99,000, the archbishop worked to bring closer ties with people of other faiths. He accomplished that with high visibility. The Roman Catholic archbishop participated in everything from raising money for causes to interreligious gatherings. The media praised him as a breath of fresh air until he, too, emerged at the center of a scandal.

Marino was installed as the third archbishop of Atlanta on 5 May 1988. Twenty-six months later, on 10 July 1990, he resigned. The initial reported cause was that he suffered from stress and exhaustion. As archbishop emeritus of Atlanta, Marino withdrew to a Midwest treatment center for priests. Less than a month later the Atlanta media reported that the real cause of his resignation was an affair with Vicki Long, a twenty-seven-year-old single mother. Reports surfaced that the couple were married in 1988, and that Long received payments from archdiocesan funds. Later, newspapers reported that she divorced the archbishop. A financial audit led by Marino successor, James P. Lyke, OFM, a Franciscan priest and the nation's second African American archbishop, determined that Long received a little more than $20,000. Ultimately, Marino acknowledged his involvement in an "inappropriate sexual relationship" and dropped out of sight. Despite his episcopal rank he returned to the work he did at the beginning of his career, spiritual direction.

During the first five years after his resignation Marino was a chaplain for the Sisters of Mercy in Alma, Michigan. In 1995 the archbishop became spiritual director of a clergy outpatient program at St. Vincent's Hospital in Harrison, New York, where he conducted retreats and counseled with priests, nuns, and monks who had personal problems. On 11 November 2000 Archbishop Marino conducted a session at St. Ignatius Retreat House in Manhasset, New York. The day ended with a mass in which the prelate anointed the sick. One of the priests that presided at the celebration anointed Marino. Afterward, Marino went to bed. A housekeeper found him dead the next morning.

In 1999 Marino received more than 2,500 letters of tribute and commendation as he was honored for his work with troubled priests, nuns, and brothers at a celebration of his twenty-five-year anniversary as a prelate. The accomplishments of his thirty-eight years in the priesthood eclipsed discussion of the Atlanta scandal. He was hailed as a spiritual man who climbed to the highest ranks of the Roman Catholic Church. He sinned and sought forgiveness by helping others sort out their emotional and spiritual pain. In that life he found peace.

FURTHER READING

Harris, Michael. "A First for Black Catholics," *Time* (28 March 1988; 5 June 2007).

Wood, Elaine. "The Rev. Eugene Marino, First Black Archbishop," *Chicago Sun-Times*, 19 Nov. 2000.

"Obituary for America's First Black Catholic Archbishop." *Independent Catholic News*, 20 Nov. 2000; 5 June 2007.

VINCENT F. A. GOLPHIN

Marion, John C. (9 May 1923–9 Sept. 2010), decorated World War II veteran, born in Chicago, Illinois, was the son of William Marion, a World War I veteran, and Ola Mae Bostick Marion, a homemaker and entrepreneur. Shortly after his birth, his family returned back to Atlanta, Georgia, where he became a lifetime resident. Johnny, as he

Sergeant John C. Marion, World War II veteran and Purple Heart recipient (c.1942). Courtesy of Tina C. Jones.

was fondly called by his family, was an extraordinary young man. He was educated in the Atlanta Public School system and graduated from Booker T. Washington High School. Having a strong aptitude and interest in math and science, Johnny had dreams of becoming a medical doctor. However, after the death of both parents by the time he was eighteen, his responsibilities to his family caused him to amend his plans.

A few years later, he was drafted in the U.S. Army and became a decorated, World War II veteran. Marion served in combat in both the European and Pacific theaters at the rank of sergeant, following the traditions of his military family—both his father and Uncle Rias Bostic, a Purple Heart recipient, served in World War I, and he had ancestors who served during the Civil War and the American Revolutionary War. When Marion returned home from combat in World War II, it was with a bullet-dinged helmet, a chest full of medals, and the promise of a job from the family of a man he saved in battle.

He married Barbara Marion and they had a daughter, Armelia Doris Marion. He cared for his family by working at the H. J. Russell Plastering Co. (now Russell Construction Company) for over thirty-four years. He was a lifetime member of the United Brotherhood of Carpenters and Joiners of America local union for over sixty-two years and held office as past president.

Marion was recognized during a special ceremony held on 10 October 2009 at Arlington National Cemetery (ANC) in the Washington, DC, area, along with his American Revolutionary War patriot ancestor, OSCAR MARION, the first African American patriot to be honored at the ANC, who served alongside the infamous "swamp fox" Brigadier General Francis Marion. Information about his dedicated service to our country has been published in *The Washington Post* newspaper, the *Patriots of the American Revolution* magazine, and the *American Legion* magazine. For his service to the United States, he received the following decorations: (1) European-African-Middle Eastern Service Medal, (2) Asiatic-Pacific Service Medal, (3) Philippines Liberation Ribbon, (4) Good Conduct Medal, and (5) World War II Victory Medal. In 2004, for his eightieth birthday, he received a birthday card from then President George W. Bush and First Lady Laura Bush, and letters of congratulations from Georgia's governor Sonny Perdue and the former Atlanta mayor SHIRLEY FRANKLIN. During this birthday dinner celebration he was

praised for taking on the awesome task of raising his six siblings after the death of both parents. At the young age of seventeen, he volunteered to take the responsibility to keep the family together by officially becoming the legal guardian of his younger brothers and sisters, and cared for each one until they all reached adulthood.

Also in 2004, the American Battle Monuments Commission entered Sergeant Marion into the World War II Registry of Remembrances for participating and helping our nation win the greatest military victory in history. His name has been added to the World War II memorial in Washington, DC.

John C. Marion died on Thursday, 9 September 2010 at Veterans Administration Hospital in Decatur, Georgia, at age eighty-seven. A memorial service was held at the Bethlehem Church of God, Holiness in Atlanta, Georgia, with Bishop James C. Taylor Sr., as the officiant. The internment was at the Georgia National Cemetery (Veterans), Canton, Georgia. Ceremonial documents were received from Governor Sonny Perdue of Georgia, U.S. Senator Johnny Isakson (Georgia), and the Honorable Kasim Reed, mayor of Atlanta, Georgia.

Marion was honored again at a special memorial ceremony held on Tuesday, 12 October 2010 at the Veterans Administration Building in Decatur, Georgi, with full military honors.

FURTHER READING

Jones, Tina C. "Patriot Slave," *American Legion Magazine*, May/June 2010.

TINA C. JONES

Marion, Oscar (c.1742–c.1815), was a Patriot of the American Revolutionary War. Legend has it that Oscar grew up on the same plantation as his famed master and war hero, Brigadier General Francis Marion, in Berkeley County, South Carolina, and that they played together as childhood friends in the 1730s. Francis Marion's family owned the plantation. Francis fondly referred to Oscar by his nickname, "Buddy." In time, these childhood playmates would mature and, as adults, find fame as patriotic heroes and fierce guerrilla fighters in the Revolutionary War. Francis Marion grew up to become the wily general known to his enemies as the "Swamp Fox." Oscar Marion's place fighting alongside Francis has only recently come into full focus, although his role in the war has often been portrayed in art and literature over the past two centuries.

Oscar Marion served in the 2nd Continental Army Regiment of South Carolina. His volunteer service of seven years far exceeded the average enlisted soldier's time on duty, and his combat experience was intense; he was described at the time as a "loyal (and) faithful servant" to General Francis Marion. Oscar served as the General's personal assistant, bodyguard, sous-chef, bugler, courier, confidant, oarsman, and, of course, fighter. Unlike other slaves owned by Francis Marion's family, who left and served with the loyalists, Oscar deliberately chose the path of patriotism.

Oscar Marion was captured on canvas by several of the most famous American artists of the time. John Blake White, William Ranney, and Alonzo Chapel all painted various images of Revolutionary War events that included Oscar somewhere near his master, General Francis Marion.

A soldier by day and sous-chef by night, Oscar is shown roasting sweet potatoes for a British officer in a famous oil painting by John Blake White that later was engraved and printed on South Carolina's $10 Confederate notes and $5 postwar notes.

Oscar can be found rowing as they travel up and down the Pee Dee River. He is seen as a soldier in full uniform, mounted on a horse and armed with a rifle. There is also a provocative painting by William Rainey showing both Marion men sharing a white horse. It appears that Oscar has been wounded and is being assisted by the General; they are crossing shallow water along the Pee Dee River as their horses stop for a drink, and Oscar is carrying a brass bugle around his right shoulder, demonstrating another of his many duties as one of Marion's Men.

It appears that Oscar may have been literate. In their youth, Oscar accompanied Francis Marion to a school run by the Winyah Society in Georgetown, South Carolina. A black slave called "Willibee" is referred to as Francis Marion's wet nurse in several sources, including an early will that has been

Swamp Encampment. General Marion shares a meal of sweet potatoes prepared by his slave, Oscar Marion, with a British officer. Painting by John Blake White, Lithograph by Currier & Ives, 1876. (Library of Congress.)

published by both Broddie and Yeadon. Broddie says Marion was wet nursed by Chloe, who was Buddy's mother. He also identifies June as being Buddy's father. Chloe and Willibee may be the same person or Willibee may be Chloe's mother, because Chloe was alive after 1815. Willibee is listed in the estate of Benjamin Marion (the General's grandfather) as a "girl." Benjamin Marion died in 1735.

Yeadon speaks of talking with "Phoebe," the sister of General Marion's body servant Buddy. Phoebe was over 100 years old at the time and was living with four generations of descendants on the plantation of the widow of the late Francis (Dwight) Marion in St. John's Berkeley (Phoebe died 3 June 1845). Francis Marion had left all his property to Francis Marion Dwight if the boy would drop his last name and take the General's. The will was defective with regard to real estate, but all of the General's personal property, which included Buddy and his family, passed to Francis (Dwight) Marion upon the death of the General's widow. Phoebe was probably the younger sister of Buddy, who was at least as old as the General and probably a year or so older, because he was given the lifelong task of looking after Francis Marion. Phoebe had at least one daughter, Peggy, who was 73 years old in 1845. Peggy (Buddy's niece) had been the personal maid of Mrs. General Marion. The General told Phoebe that his mother had died at his brother's plantation when they were living at a home near Frierson's Lock on the Santee Canal and that she had been buried at Biggin Church.

Buddy, Phoebe, and Chloe all passed to Francis (Dwight) Marion after the death of Mary Esther in 1815, meaning Buddy was over the age of 73 when he died. Buddy's mother, Chloe, died at about 100 years old.

Oscar may have been married, but no references to his immediate family—his wife and children—exist. Oscar may be buried on the plantation of Francis (Dwight) Marion or there may have been a family slave cemetery at Pond Bluff or Bell Isle. Because Yeadon was writing in 1846–1858 and the fifth generation of Phoebe (Buddy's sister) had just been born at the Marion Plantation, those slaves would have been the ones freed at the time of the Civil War. If children of that generation lived to 90 years old, they died in the 1930s or 1940s.

Oscar Marion fought and engaged in several battles and skirmishes throughout the seven-years of the Revolutionary War. More than 225 years later, Oscar's exploits were dramatized in the portrayal of a character named Occam in the 2000 movie *The Patriot*, starring Mel Gibson.

Research efforts by Tina C. Jones (the current author) resulted in the identification of Marion in a famous oil painting that has been on exhibit at the U.S. Capitol building for more than a century; his identity had been previously unknown. Jones presented evidence regarding her collateral ancestor to the U.S. Senate Curator's Office and, after verification, the U.S. Senate curator agreed to update their official records to reflect Marion's identification. After pressing government officials, Jones also received permission to organize a special ceremony to honor her relative's unique contribution to America's military history.

On 15 December 2006, at the U.S. Capitol in Washington, Oscar Marion was finally given post Revolutionary War recognition for service to his country. His family received a special proclamation and certificate from President George W. Bush and U.S. Representative Albert Wynn (D-MD), on behalf of a grateful nation. The program included a musical prelude by the 257th Army Band and remarks from Senate Curator Diane K. Skvarla, NBC News correspondent Tracie Potts, and Smithsonian Institute historian Margaret S. Vining, a consultant for *The Patriot*. Debra Newman Ham, historian and professor at Morgan State University, was the main speaker.

In addition, the program included excerpts from *The Patriot* featuring the character Occam, played by actor Jay Arlen Jones. The ceremony received extensive media coverage, including a front-page story in *The Washington Post*.

An additional honor was bestowed on 10 October 2009 when Marion became the first African American patriot of the American Revolutionary War to be given military honors at Arlington National Cemetery in Arlington, Virginia. The Governor and Lt. Governors of South Carolina issued letters and a declaration that 10 October 2009 is Oscar Marion Day in South Carolina.

FURTHER READING
Jones, Tina C. "Slave Patriot," *American Legion Magazine*, July 2008, http://www.legion.org/national/divisions/magazine.

Moss, Bobby G., and Michael C. Scoggins. *African American Patriots in the Southern Campaign of the American Revolutionary War* (2004).

TINA C. JONES

Markham, Dewey "Pigmeat" (18 Apr. 1904–13 Dec. 1981), comedian and actor, was born in Durham, North Carolina, to unknown parents. As a comedian, his career spanned the eras of minstrel shows, vaudeville, radio, motion pictures, and television.

As a young man Markham began performing in tent shows and minstrel shows. By 1917 he was gaining attention as a comedian on the Chitlin' Circuit, the nickname for the network of theaters and nightclubs in African American neighborhoods, with such performers as BESSIE SMITH and Gertrude "MA" RAINEY.

The origin of his famous nickname is uncertain, although the phrase "Pigmeat" was commonly used as a sexual metaphor in blues songs of the early 1900s. It is known that he was performing under the name Pigmeat by the 1920s.

According to the music historian Bill Dahl, Markham originated his most famous character, Judge Pigmeat, during the late 1920s while performing at the Alhambra Theater in Harlem. This

Motion picture poster for *House-Rent Party*, featuring head-and-shoulders portraits of Pigmeat "Alamo" Markham (right) and John "Rastus" Murray, with stills from the film and a half-length portrait of Alberta Pryne, 1946. (Library of Congress.)

judge was known for entering his courtroom shouting "Here Come de Judge," mangling the English language, and giving ridiculously unfair sentences to people who appeared in his court. While some may have felt this routine was a stereotype of the supposed incompetence of African Americans, most black audiences enjoyed Markham's antics for decades before he became known to white Americans. In the liner notes to Markham's *The Crap Shootin' Rev*, Dahl suggests that Markham based this character on the outlandish racism African Americans often faced in court, particularly from judges in the southern United States at that time. This routine may also have its origins in an earlier routine by the pioneering black comedian BERT WILLIAMS. In his 1919 recording "Twenty Years," which appears on the 2001 Archeophone Records CD *Bert Williams, The Middle Years 1910–1919*, Williams's character Judge Grimes sentences a man who slipped on a banana peel to "twenty years for unlawful speeding" among other outrageous punishments. A casual comparison of this recording to one of Markham's Judge Pigmeat routines indicates that Williams's Judge Grimes was a likely precursor to Judge Pigmeat. Another aspect of Williams's comedy used by Markham was the practice of performing in blackface minstrel makeup. This was a standard practice among black comedians in the late 1800s and early 1900s as a result of the influence of the white minstrel tradition. Although this trend appeared to be on the wane among African American comics by the time of Williams's death in 1922, many black comedians continued to perform in this fashion onstage well into the 1940s. On the 1993 Home Box Office documentary *Mo' Funny: Black Comedy in America*, Markham's contemporary Timmie Rogers recalled that he convinced Markham to discontinue wearing blackface makeup onstage when he asked Markham if he would wear such a costume on the radio.

In the 1940s Markham also became a pioneer in another fashion. He was among the first black comedians to have a major supporting role in a regular mainstream radio program, playing Alamo the Cook on the Andrews Sisters' radio show. The success of this role led to Markham being billed with the double moniker Pigmeat "Alamo" Markham for his appearances in all-black comedies produced for segregated theaters such as *House-Rent Party* (1946), where he teamed with fellow comic John "Rastus" Murray, and *Junction 88* (1947). By 1955 he had made occasional appearances on the popular *Ed Sullivan Show* on television.

Despite this modest success, Markham was not a household name in black or white America and was overshadowed by other African American comics such as DICK GREGORY and REDD FOXX who had more success in mainstream media. This started to change in 1961 when Chess Records began producing albums of his comedy routines given at inner-city theaters and nightclubs such as the Regal in Chicago and the Apollo in Harlem. Some of these albums included *The Trial* (1961), *Anything Goes with Pigmeat Markham* (1962), *Pigmeat at the Party* (1961), and *The World's Greatest Clown* (1965). Portions of the latter were recorded at the Apollo on 21 February 1965 while at the same time human rights activist MALCOLM X was assassinated only a few miles away.

These albums are among the best examples of Markham's legacy as a comedian. They consist largely of ensemble routines typically featuring Markham with Chuck Thompson, who portrayed an intellectual character who recoiled at Markham's onstage antics, fellow comedian "Baby" Seals, and actress Edna Mae Harris, who usually appeared as a femme fatale. The routines were laced with sexual innuendo and double entendre that was considered risqué at the time, but avoided the explicit references and profanity of later comedians. One such routine from *The Trial* featured Markham as Judge Pigmeat hearing the case of a man arrested for indecent exposure. Upon learning that the defendant is the father of nine children, Judge Pigmeat dismisses the case because "This man hasn't had time to put his pants on!"

These recordings made Markham a popular figure in black households, and many African American children of that era would recite his comedy routines in schools and playgrounds in the same manner that a later generation would with rap music. Some of Markham's skits were done in rhyme, and routines such as "I Got the Number" from *Anything Goes with Pigmeat* (where Markham and Thompson rhymed about playing the "numbers game") and "Here Come de Judge" were precursors to rap music, as the first generation of rappers were among those who enjoyed Markham's records in the 1960s and 1970s. The popular rap group Arrested Development sampled "I Got the Number" for their song "Ease My Mind" in the 1990s.

Markham's televised performances as Judge Pigmeat on the 1967 television special *A Time for Laughter: Negro Humor in America*, and a year later on *Rowan and Martin's Laugh-In* finally brought him mainstream celebrity status. In 1969 this success led to a book, *Here Come the Judge!*, co-written with Bill Levinson, filled with Markham's amusing commentary on the political situations of that era. Unfortunately, this success came late in Markham's life when health problems curtailed his career through the 1970s. Younger comedians such as RICHARD PRYOR in the 1990 television special *A Party for Pryor* would cite him as an influence. Markham's death from a stroke on 13 December 1981 showed that he was not forgotten as tributes aired in sources as diverse as *Jet* magazine and the popular syndicated television program *Entertainment Tonight*. He left behind a wife, Bernice, a daughter, Cathy, and a son, Dewey Markham Jr.

FURTHER READING

Markham, Pigmeat, and Levinson, Bill. *Here Comes the Judge!* (1969).

Dahl, Bill. Liner notes to *Pigmeat Markham, The Crap Shootin' Rev* (1970).

Obituary: *Jet* (17 Jan. 1982).

DAMON L. FORDHAM

Marrant, John (15 June 1755–Apr. 1791), minister and author, was born in the New York Colony to a family of free blacks. The names and occupations of his parents are not known. When he was four years old his father died. Marrant and his mother moved to Florida and Georgia; subsequently Marrant moved to Charleston, South Carolina, to live with his sister and brother-in-law. He stayed in school until he was eleven years old, becoming an apprentice to a music master for two additional years. During this time he also learned carpentry. His careers in music and carpentry ended in late 1769 or early 1770, when he was converted to Christianity by the famous evangelical minister George Whitefield.

Over the next few years Marrant converted many Native Americans, including members of the Cherokee, Creek, Choctaw, and Chickasaw nations. In 1772 he returned to his family for a short time. For the next three years Marrant worked as a minister in the Charleston area. There he saw a plantation owner and other white males whip thirty slaves for attending his church school.

With the onslaught of the Revolutionary War, Marrant was impressed as a musician into the British navy in October or November of 1776. Not much is known of his exploits during this period besides the fact that he fought in the Dutch-Anglo War (1780–1784). As a result of his injuries, he was discharged in 1782.

Marrant eventually married. A listing in the New York City Inspection Roll of Negroes in 1783 cited a Mellia Marrant as "formerly the property of John Marrant near Santee Carolina"; this document also states that she "left him at the Siege of Georgetown." Apparently, his wife had been a slave; he bought and freed her in order to marry her. The same listing claimed that Mellia was aboard the *William and Mary* with her children Amelia and Ben, heading for Annapolis Royal, Nova Scotia. There is no evidence to support or deny that they were Marrant's children. The information in this record is all that is known of his marriage and offspring.

To further his opportunities, Marrant moved to London, England, living there between 1782 and 1785. In Bath on 15 May 1785, he was ordained a minister in the chapel of Selina Hastings, countess of Huntingdon and a supporter of the African American poet PHILLIS WHEATLEY. During this time, despite being literate, Marrant told his story to the Methodist minister William Aldridge, who later published it as *A Narrative of the Lord's Wonderful Dealings with John Marrant, a Black (Now Going to Preach the Gospel in Nova-Scotia) Born in New-York, in North-America* (1785). The narrative, in which Marrant describes his conversion and his life as a traveling minister, was so popular that it went through twenty editions by 1835. In 1785 S. Whitchurch and S. Hazard both published *The Negro Convert: A Poem; Being the Substance of the Experience of Mr. John Marrant, a Negro.*

In November 1785 Marrant moved to Birchtown, Nova Scotia, to minister to the black Loyalists who had immigrated there after the American Revolution. For the next two years he was persecuted and harassed by fellow ministers because he preached Calvinistic Methodism to whites, blacks, and Native Americans in Nova Scotia. Despite his persecution, he built a chapel in Birchtown, taught at the Birchtown school, preached to the congregation, and ministered in other towns. In late November 1786 Marrant gave up control of his school because of his exhaustion and decided to concentrate on being a traveling minister. He contracted smallpox in an epidemic in February 1787 and was ill for six months.

In Nova Scotia, Marrant lived a life of poverty and illness. In late January 1788 he moved to Boston, where he preached and apparently taught school. However, Marrant could not escape persecution. On 27 February 1789 he eluded a mob of forty armed men who were attempting to kill him because their girlfriends went to his Friday sermon. In March of that year he became a Freemason in the African Lodge. As a Freemason, Marrant gave a sermon at the Festival of John the Baptist; the sermon was published in 1789. On his way back to England, Marrant wrote his last journal entry on 7 March 1790. The journal was later published as *A Journal of the Rev. John Marrant* (1790), along with Marrant's sermon of a funeral service in Nova Scotia. The preface of the journal gave the publication date of 29 June 1790. Marrant died somewhere in England and is buried at Islington.

In his sermons, Marrant tried to teach people to love God through a comparison of biblical allegories and everyday life. For example, in his *Narrative*, Marrant's travels after his conversion are reminiscent of John the Baptist's sojourn in the wilderness. His theme is clear: let Jesus and God be your guides. This message is stressed when faith saves him from being executed by a Native American nation: "I fell down upon my knees, and mentioned to the Lord his delivering of the three children in the fiery furnace, and of Daniel in the Lion's den, and had close communion with God.... And about the middle of my prayer, the Lord impressed a strong desire upon my mind to turn into their language, and pray in their tongue ... which wonderfully affected the people" (Porter, 437).

In his short life, Marrant dedicated himself to helping others reach their religious potential. Through his published sermons and conversions, Marrant wanted to help humankind the best way he knew how: by giving them God's lessons. Even though he never reaped an earthly reward in his lifetime, his works stand as a model for religious colonial life.

FURTHER READING

Andrews, William L. *To Tell a Free Story: The First Century of Afro-American Autobiography, 1760–1865* (1988)

Gates, Henry Louis, Jr. *The Signifying Monkey: A Theory of Afro-American Literary Criticism* (1988).

Porter, Dorothy. *Early Negro Writing, 1760–1837* (1971)

Potkay, Adam, and Sandra Burr, eds. *Black Atlantic Writers of the Eighteenth Century: Living the New Exodus in England and the Americas* (1995).

This entry is taken from the *American National Biography* and is published here with the permission of the American Council of Learned Societies.

DEVONA A. MALLORY

Marrett, Cora Bagley (15 June 1942–), educator, public intellectual, and advocate, was born Cora Elmira Bagley to Horace Bagley and Clorann

(Boswell) Bagley in Richmond, Virginia, about seventy miles from the family's home in Kenbridge, Virginia. At that time, the small town of Kenbridge lacked decent medical facilities for the 46 percent of its population who were African American, and traveling to Richmond was one of the only options for those needing medical care. Elmira, as her family called her, was the youngest of twelve children, with a multitude of nieces and nephews. Her father, a carpenter and contractor for small building projects, and her mother, who spent most of her years as a housewife but worked from time to time as a maid, recognized in the precocious Elmira a proclivity for learning and an insatiable thirst for knowledge. Her mother especially stressed the importance of reading and constantly provided her with opportunities to hone the skills that would help her excel in school.

After high school Bagley entered the historically black Virginia Union University in Richmond, from which she received her bachelor's degree in 1963. An early interest in science turned to inquiry in the "social laboratory"—that is, in society itself—and she decided to earn a degree in sociology. With characteristic enthusiasm and keen intellect, Bagley proved an exemplary student. As a sophomore she participated in an upper-division course offered by the historian Pearl Oxendine. Despite being surrounded by more advanced students, Bagley distinguished herself in the class and Professor Oxendine soon became her mentor. Bagley had assumed that she would become a schoolteacher—one of the few career paths open at that time to young African American women with academic ambitions. However, while at Virginia Union and under Oxendine's tutelage, Bagley began to see graduate school and higher education as a real possibility for developing her talent and making a positive difference in the world.

On Oxendine's advice and encouragement, she applied and was admitted to the doctoral program in sociology at the University of Wisconsin–Madison. However, the cost was well beyond the means of Bagley and her family—even with a residency waiver and partial assistance offered by the university. Ironically, it was racism that ultimately helped Cora to attend graduate school. Like many southern states at the time, Virginia was willing to provide financial aid to African American students with graduate-school ambitions if they would attend school elsewhere and not challenge the discriminatory in-state admission policies. Taking advantage of this program, Bagley left Virginia and headed to Wisconsin and one of the nation's top universities,

where she earned an M.A. in 1965 and a Ph.D. in 1968. That same year, Bagley married the Jamaican-born agricultural scientist Louis E. Marrett, whom she met while both were attending the university.

Ambitious, dedicated, and talented, Cora Bagley Marrett's story is a litany of accomplishments and service. This eclectic scholar's research, as reflected in her numerous publications and presentations, included studies of complex organizations, social policy, education, institutional relations, and race, ethnicity, and gender dynamics. She began her academic career as assistant professor of sociology at the University of North Carolina at Chapel Hill (1968–1969) and at Western Michigan University (1969–1974), where she was promoted to associate professor. Her zeal and commitment garnered her professional recognition almost from the outset. Indeed, while still only an assistant professor, Marrett was nominated for the presidency of Barnard College. Although she declined the nomination, it was a precursor of this rising star's future.

Acting on a suggestion from her husband, Marrett applied for and was awarded a senior policy fellowship at the National Academy of Sciences (1973–1974). In 1974 she returned to the University of Wisconsin–Madison as a faculty member in sociology and in Afro-American studies and was later promoted to full professor. In 1976–1977 she was a fellow at the Center for Advanced Study in the Behavioral Sciences in Stanford, California. She also served as associate chair of the sociology department (1988–1991) at the University of Wisconsin and was an affiliate of the Energy Analysis and Policy Program and of the Wisconsin Center for Education Research. From 1990 to 1992 Marrett was director of the Andrew Mellon Foundation programs for the United Negro College Fund. From 1992 to 1996 Marrett led the newly created Directorate for the Social, Behavioral, and Economic Sciences at the United States National Science Foundation, which also led to her involvement in the international arena, taking her to France, Japan, Belgium, China, and South Africa.

In 1997 Marrett took up the mantle of senior vice chancellor for academic affairs and provost at the University of Massachusetts–Amherst, as well as professor of sociology and of Afro-American studies. Her stewardship of the university was marked by excellence and acclaim. Another of her accomplishments while in Amherst concerned her role in the establishment of the Berkshire Hills Music Academy, a postsecondary school of musical arts for young adults with Williams syndrome and other cognitive disabilities. Marrett's efforts resulted in the involvement of faculties and students from the area's "Five Colleges" (Amherst, Hampshire, Mount Holyoke, and Smith Colleges, and the University of Massachusetts) and in securing the facility for the academy. In 2001 Marrett returned to the University of Wisconsin as senior vice president for academic affairs, the university system's chief academic officer, and also resumed her title there as professor of sociology. In 2007, while retaining her University of Wisconsin professorship, Marrett returned to the National Science Foundation to lead the Directorate of Education and Human Resources, making her the first person to have headed two of the Foundation's research directorates.

Marrett served on the board of governors of the Argonne National Laboratory; the board of trustees for the Social Science Research Council; the Commission on the Social and Behavioral Sciences and Education of the National Research Council; the Peer Review Oversight Group for the National Institutes of Health (NIH); and the Advisory Council of the Fogarty International Center, NIH's international component. Other public service included, among other things, membership on various committees for the National Academies and the President's Commission on the Accident at Three Mile Island. She also received numerous honors and awards. She was elected fellow of the American Association for the Advancement of Science in 1996 and was inducted into the American Academy of Arts and Sciences in 1998. In 2001 the Quality Education for Minorities (QEM)/Mathematics, Science, and Engineering Network conferred upon Marrett the Giant in Science Award, citing her distinguished research, teaching, and service, and her significant impact on students. In 2005 QEM also bestowed upon her the Erich Bloch Distinguished Service Award for her "singular contributions to the advancement of science and to the participation of groups underrepresented in science through policies, programs, and public service."

Throughout her career, the goal of developing talent remained foremost on her agenda. Viewing higher education as "a place of dreams, action, and leadership" (personal interview with the author), Marrett was a "practical visionary" with concrete plans and goals for encouraging academic excellence and access, developing an educated citizenry, and fostering an environment that engages students and facilitates learning, diversity, and social responsibility.

FURTHER READING
Much of the information for this essay was drawn from personal interviews conducted by the author (25 Feb. 2005, 22 Apr. 2005).
Mervis, Jeffrey. "NSF Fills Education Post," *ScienceNOW* (26 Sept. 2006).
Schalmo, Tom. "Marrett Ready to Join NSF Ranks," *The Badger Herald*, 27 Sept. 2006.
Wright, Patricia. "Clearing the Channels," *UMASS Magazine* (Fall 1999).

CONNIE L. MCNEELY

Marrow, Tracy. *See* Ice-T.

Marrs, Elijah Preston (Jan. 1840–30 Aug. 1910), soldier, preacher, educator, delegate to political and religious conventions, and writer, was born to Andrew Marrs, a free man, and Frances Marrs, at the time considered by law to be the property of one Jesse Robinson, in Shelby County, Kentucky. By law, Elijah Marrs inherited the slave status of his mother.

At the age of seven or eight, Marrs was sent to work serving food in the Robinsons' dining room. Within a few years he was plowing corn fields and taking care of the cows. "Our master was not hard on us," he later wrote, "and allowed us generally to do as we pleased after his own work was done." Mothers, he added, including his own, "were necessarily compelled to be severe on their children to keep them from talking too much. Many a poor mother has been whipped nearly to death on account of their children telling the white children things, who would then go and tell their mothers or fathers" (Marrs, p. 11).

Marrs enlisted the help of white playmates in teaching him the alphabet, learning additional reading and writing at a night school run by "an old colored man on the place by the name of Ham Graves" (Marrs, p. 12). All of his efforts to become literate were illegal at the time. Marrs made a profession of Christian faith around 1851, at a protracted revival meeting conducted by Reverend Charles Wells, pastor of the Colored Baptist Church in Simpsonville.

Marrs had previously attended a Methodist class meeting, overheard his father talking to a pastor about salvation, and heard about sin and salvation from one of Robinson's sons when they were cutting corn stalks in the field together. Still, even after being saved he had to request permission from Mr. and Mrs. Robinson to join the church and to be baptized. At his baptism, Marrs was immersed in a cold stream with ice an inch thick. Robinson, a one-time Baptist deacon, eventually decided he wanted all "the boys" on his farm to learn to read the Bible, the skill of writing being prohibited more severely.

By the outbreak of the Civil War in 1861, Marrs's literacy was widely known. When the federal government began enlisting for the United States Colored Troops, nearly all the soldiers from the local area addressed letters home to family in the care of Marrs, since he would be able to read the letters to them. Marrs became known as "the Shelby County negro clerk" by Confederate rebel sympathizers in the area. Robinson, who opposed secession, warned Marrs he was in danger.

An older brother, Henry Marrs, enlisted in the United States Army. In September 1864, Elijah Marrs decided to do the same, and walked to Simpsonville, along the way enlisting old comrades he met on the Shelbyville Pike. By the time they arrived the party had gained twenty-seven men, and Marrs was elected captain. After arriving at the recruiting office in Louisville 26 September 1864, Marrs recalled "the owner of every man of us was in the city hunting his slaves, but we had all enlisted" (Marrs, p. 20). As newly enlisted men, all became privates. Marrs was assigned to Company L, 12th U.S. Colored Artillery, and was quickly promoted to duty sergeant, because he could read and write. The unit was marched around various parts of Kentucky that continued to be contested by small rebel forces, including Bowling Green, Glasgow, Munfordville, and Elizabethtown. They were apparently never issued any artillery, but fought mainly as infantry. He was discharged 24 April 1866.

Marrs taught school in Shelby County, and served as a delegate to the first State Educational Convention in Louisville in 1867. He was also a delegate to the 1869 Frankfort convention that ratified the Fifteenth Amendment. He married Julia Gray of Shelbyville, 3 August 1871, and was licensed to preach by the New Castle Baptist Church on 16 June 1873. In 1874 Marrs attended the Baptist College (also known as Roger Williams University) at Nashville, Tennessee, returning home after one term. He was ordained a minister on 22 August 1875, and was elected that year to serve as messenger to the General Association of Colored Baptists of Kentucky convention in Paris. The following April, 1876, Julia Marrs died.

With his brother Henry, Marrs opened the Baptist Normal and Theological Institute in Louisville, on 25 November 1879. The school later changed its name to State University, then Simmons University, and finally Simmons Bible College.

A year later he was called to be the first pastor of Beargrass Baptist Church, in Crescent Hill, but disputes within the church led him to accept a call from St. John Baptist Church in Louisville, where he became pastor in April 1881. However, the members of Beargrass reconsidered and asked him to return. "I prayed night and day for the guidance of God in the matter, and the Lord taught me that this was the field for me." He returned to Beargrass on 9 June 1881 with an indefinite call. He also served as a delegate to the state convention of colored men in Lexington in 1882, and to the national convention of colored men in Louisville in 1883.

In 1883, Marrs was invited by the trustees of a school district in Jefferson County, Kentucky, to teach in the district school. He first had to take a state examination, which he passed First Class, First Grade, with an 85 percent average. The *American Baptist*, published by the college he had attended in Nashville, proudly wrote "He has no equals. He had a most difficult examination to pass through, and on that day was the only one who passed. White ladies with tears in their eyes, because of failure, could not see how he could succeed, while they could not.... All over the State white teachers are failing and the colored one passing."

The *Louisville Commercial*, covering the same examination, reported that new commissioner Abner J. Smith, "has determined, in his work of reform, that none shall occupy positions as teachers unless thoroughly qualified," whereas previously almost anyone who applied for a teaching certificate was granted one. The majority of established teachers failed; of "several colored applicants" taking the exam "only one, Rev. E. P. Marrs, passed." He taught for two terms in Jefferson County, then devoted his time primarily to his ministry, though he still found the time to serve as delegate to an educational convention in Frankfort in 1884.

Between 1873 and 1884, Marrs was a delegate to numerous Baptist General Association meetings in Kentucky. He served as a member of the Executive Board of the General Association of Colored Baptists for six years, a member of the Executive Board of the Central District Association, and for twelve years as secretary of the Central District Association. In 1887 he was treasurer of the General Association. He was also president of the Athenaeum Society at State University for one term.

He remarried around 1888, three years after publishing his autobiography. Bettie (or Betty) Marrs's maiden name is undiscovered. She was born in 1864. The couple had six children: James, Elijah Jr.,

Charles, Nellie, Alice, and Andrew. Though unclear, Marrs may have retired from active ministry after receiving a Civil War invalid pension in 1891. He died of chronic bronchitis in 1910. References to him in the same year's census as a "laborer" doing "odd jobs" who was "not employed" can reasonably be attributed to the increasingly strong racism of the early twentieth century; Kentucky mortuary records, which were more heavily scrutinized by state record-keepers, noted his profession as "pastor." Betty Marrs subsequently moved to Detroit, then to Chicago.

FURTHER READING

Marrs, Elijah P. *Life and History of Elijah P. Marrs* (1969). (Reprinted from the original published in 1885).

Lucas, Marion Brunson. *A History of Blacks in Kentucky: From Slavery to Segregation, 1760–1891* (2003).

Simmons, William J., and Henry McNeal Turner. *Men of Mark: Eminent, Progressive, and Rising* (1887).

Wheeler, Edward L. *Uplifting the Race: The Black Minister in the New South, 1865–1902* (1986).

CHARLES ROSENBERG

Mars, James (3 Mar. 1790–?), slave narrative author, was born in Canaan, Connecticut, the child of slaves. James's father, Jupiter Mars, was born in New York State. He had a succession of owners, including General Henry Kiliaen Van Rensselaer, with whom Jupiter served in the Revolutionary War. He was subsequently owned in Salisbury, Connecticut, and later by the Reverend Mr. Thompson, a minister in North Canaan, Connecticut. Mars's mother, whose name remains unknown, was born in Virginia and was owned there by the woman who became Thompson's wife. His mother, who had one child while living in Virginia, was relocated to Connecticut when Mrs. Thompson moved to Canaan to join her husband. The Reverend Thompson married Mars's parents, and they had James and four other children, three of whom died in infancy.

Of Mrs. Thompson, James Mars told his father that "if she only had him South, where she could have at her call a half dozen men, she would have him stripped and flogged until he was cut in strings" (Mars, 5). The Thompsons eventually did move south, leaving the farm to be tended by Mars's parents. In 1798, when James was eight years old, Thompson, who had always preached that slavery was divinely sanctioned, returned to Connecticut, intending to sell the farm and bring his slaves to the South for sale on the southern slave market. The Mars family—James's mother, father, fourteen-year-old older brother Joseph, and younger sister—resisted by escaping to Norfolk, Connecticut. They went deeper into hiding when news arrived that Thompson had hired slave catchers to locate them and transport them to Virginia. After several days, during which the family successfully evaded recapture, Thompson decided to focus his attentions on Joseph and James, since they would bring the highest prices on the slave market.

Thompson, who originally refused to go to Virginia without the boys, eventually proposed a compromise by which Mars's father would agree to sell his sons to owners in Connecticut in exchange for his freedom and that of his wife and daughter. Jupiter Mars was permitted to approve the men to whom his sons would be sold. On 12 September 1798, Joseph was sold to a farmer named Bingham (who had once owned Jupiter), and James was sold to a man named Munger from Norfolk. Thompson received one hundred dollars for each. Under the terms of the sale, the boys would be slaves until the age of twenty-five, the limit to which Connecticut law allowed slaves to be held. James's parents and sister remained in Norfolk, and he was permitted to see them once every two weeks.

By the age of thirteen or fourteen, Mars had grown dissatisfied with his lack of education, his owner's cruelty, and the terms of his servitude in comparison with the terms of indentured white boys, who were bound in service until they were twenty-one and who received one hundred dollars at the conclusion of their terms. On one occasion, when Mars was sixteen, Munger threatened to whip him, and Mars responded saying, "You had better not." Munger backed down, and as Mars tells it, "From that time until I was twenty one, I do not remember that he ever gave me an unpleasant word or look" (Mars, 25). Mars was generally able to live as freely as any of the other boys who lived in the neighborhood.

For the next few years, Mars worked in relative contentment. "I was willing to work, and thought much of the family, and they thought something of me," he later wrote (26). Munger seems not to have been aware that under Connecticut law he could hold Mars in his service after he turned twenty-one, and he made an offer to Mars on the condition that he would stay longer. Mars thought "the offer was tolerably fair. I had now become attached to the family" (27), but Munger withdrew the verbal offer after learning that he had the legal right to keep Mars as a slave until his twenty-fifth birthday, especially since no written agreement could be produced proving otherwise.

Mars was further disappointed when Munger reneged on an agreement to give him some livestock, and he threatened to leave unless Munger would put the agreement in writing. When Munger declined, Mars left the farm for his parents' home. Munger asked Mars to return voluntarily. Instead, Mars and Munger agreed to abide by the decision of three mutually acceptable arbiters. The arbiters ruled that Mars should pay Munger ninety dollars for his freedom. After paying Munger, Mars hired himself out to another family, but after a four-year break he returned to work for the Munger family. After a trip west, he returned to find that Munger had suffered a decline in his fortunes and that his daughter was in poor health. Mars, "accustomed to take care of the sick" (31), remained with Munger's daughter until she died peacefully soon after. "That was a scene that I love to think of. It makes me almost forget that I ever was a slave to her father; but so it was" (32). Although Mars worked where he chose for the next several years, he was frequently at the Munger home and remained in close contact with his former owner until he, like his daughter, died with Mars at his side.

Mars married after Munger's death and fathered eight children. He lived in Norfolk and Hartford, Connecticut, and Pittsfield, Massachusetts. In the appendix to his narrative, Mars notes that his children followed a variety of vocations: one son enlisted in the U.S. Navy; another went to sea and fell out of touch with the family; a third enlisted in the navy at the beginning of the Civil War; and a fourth son enlisted as an artillery man and was most likely killed in the Civil War. One of Mars's daughters went to Africa and became a teacher, and another moved to Massachusetts with her family.

What we know about James Mars comes entirely from his narrative *Life of James Mars, a Slave Born and Sold in Connecticut. Written by Himself*, published in 1864. Mars indicates in his introduction that publication was not his intention when he began writing at his sister's request during the Civil War. His sister, who had lived in Africa for more than thirty years, had been born in freedom and knew little of her parents' and siblings' experiences under slavery. Unlike the narratives published by escaped slaves who wrote, often with abolitionist sponsorship, with the intention of educating readers about the atrocities of the slave system and in the hopes of bringing about its end, Mars's original intentions were entirely personal: "When I had got it written, as it made more writing than I was willing to undertake to give each of them [the members of his family] one, I thought I would have it printed, and perhaps I might sell enough to pay the expenses, as many of the people now on the stage of life do not know that slavery ever existed in Connecticut" (3). In addition to revealing the facts of his own life, Mars's narrative contributes to our understanding of the lives of slaves in the North as well as the peculiarities of slavery in the North. It provides a rare illustration of the economic and social disparities and the grave distinction between the freedom promised by the North and the actual social and economic limitations imposed upon blacks in northern states.

Mars reports that at the age of seventy-nine, he was living on meager savings and unable to work because of a fall he experienced in 1866. He intended his narrative as a testament to the experiences of other slaves who labored in Connecticut, a place that many readers were unaware ever countenanced slavery. Despite the restrictions imposed by the state of Connecticut, Mars tells his readers, he had voted in five presidential elections and twice voted for Abraham Lincoln. Mars concludes his narrative with a condemnation of his home state: "If my life is spared I intend to be where I can show that I have the principles of a man, and act like a man, and vote like a man, but not in my native State; I cannot do it there, I must remove to the old Bay State for the right to be a man. Connecticut, I love thy name, but not thy restrictions" (38). How long Mars lived after his memoir was reprinted in 1868 and the circumstances of his death remain unknown.

FURTHER READING
Mars, James. *Life of James Mars, a Slave Born and Sold in Connecticut. Written by Himself* (1864, repr. 1868); also published in *African American Slave Narratives: An Anthology*, ed. Sterling Lecater Bland Jr., vol. 3 (2001).

STERLING LECATER BLAND JR.

Mars, John N. (22 June 1804–17 Sept. 1884), Methodist minister, antislavery activist, and chaplain in the Civil War, was born in Norfolk, Connecticut, the son of former slaves, Jupiter and Fannie Mars.

Since his parents had escaped from their master, a Presbyterian minister, prior to his birth, John N. Mars grew up as a free man and was able to obtain six months of formal schooling. His brother James, however, born before their parents escape, remained a slave until his twenty-first birthday.

At age nineteen Mars left Connecticut and traveled to Spencertown and Ghent, New York, where he lived and worked for a number of years. Around 1824 he married Silvia Gordon and they had two sons, John S. (born c. 1832) and George (born c. 1835).

While living in the area Mars was converted in the Methodist Episcopal Church (MEC) and soon began to experience a call to preach. He subsequently united with the African Methodist Episcopal Zion (AMEZ) Church and was eventually ordained as an elder. From the late 1830s through 1841 Mars served churches in Newark, New Jersey, and Fishkill and Poughkeepsie, New York. His wife, Silvia, died on 28 December 1838, at age twenty-nine in Athol, Massachusetts, where Mars seems to have established his home.

In 1841 Mars was sent to Salem, Massachusetts, to work with the Reverend Newell S. Spaulding, a white Methodist Episcopal minister, who was organizing a new church in that city. He was apparently successful in ministering to the black population there, as the minutes of the 1843 annual meeting of the AMEZ Church include a resolution to receive the Society of Salem (with 103 members), and Mars was officially assigned to the society for the coming year.

After serving in Salem for two years Mars officially withdrew from the AMEZ Church and went to Upper Canada under the auspices of the Wesleyan Methodist Church as a missionary to the slaves who had escaped to that area. By the end of the first year he had established five large circuits with eight churches, four schools, and temperance societies and Sabbath Day Schools.

Records are sketchy as to just how long he actually stayed in Canada; however, on 14 April 1846, John N. Mars was married in Athol, Massachusetts, to Elizabeth J. Holt, a white woman from Salem, Massachusetts. Following his time in Canada he returned to New England and joined once again with the AMEZ Church and served churches in Springfield and Worcester, Massachusetts, and Hartford, Connecticut.

Throughout all of these years Mars was heavily involved in efforts to improve the quality of life for African Americans in the United States. He supported the development of temperance societies for African Americans and equal educational opportunities for black children. He was active in the Massachusetts and American Anti-Slavery Societies and was an outspoken opponent of the Fugitive Slave Law passed in 1850. He preached across the area at camp meetings and advocated his beliefs whenever the opportunity presented itself.

In 1861, as the Civil War commenced, Mars spoke out strongly about people of color being unable to fight in the war. As soon as President Abraham Lincoln signed the Emancipation Proclamation not only granting freedom to all slaves but also giving all American men regardless of color the right to enlist in the armed services, Mars himself enlisted, even though he was by then nearly fifty-nine years old. He was assigned to the First North Carolina Colored Volunteers as their chaplain. Along with JOHN VAN SURLY DEGRASSE, a black physician from Boston, he became one of the first two African Americans to receive a commission in the Civil War.

During the Civil War, Mars was located in New Bern, North Carolina, where he had the opportunity to participate in a service in which he and the Reverend W. C. Whitcomb, the hospital chaplain, christened and baptized 105 children. According to the 17 August 1863 *Daily Evening Bulletin* (San Francisco), this was the first time a black pastor had been allowed to participate in a service of baptism in the state.

Unfortunately at his age Mars's health was not strong, and he was unable to endure harsh army life. He was assigned to the Army stores at New Bern for a number of months before being transferred to Norfolk and Portsmouth, Virginia, where his chronic rheumatism finally forced him to resign his commission. Mars' son George also enlisted in the Army on 26 December 1863 and was given a disability discharge on 21 October 1865. He died of dysentery ten days later.

In April 1864 Mars realized another "first" in his life when he was received as a probationary member of the New England Conference of the MEC. Before this, African Americans had been allowed to be ordained as deacons and occasionally as elders but were not allowed to become full members of the conference and receive the same rights as their white brothers.

Having seen the work that needed to be done in the South, however, Mars requested that he be allowed to return to Virginia to work under the auspices of the American Missionary Society. He served there until October when he transferred from the New England Conference to the Washington Conference (a newly formed all black conference) to serve the Sharp Street MEC in Baltimore. In 1865 he was received as a full member and appointed Presiding Elder of the Chesapeake District.

Mars served in that position until 1869 and then transferred back into the white New England

Conference where he served a number of appointments before retiring in 1873 to his home in Athol. When he died, he left his wife, Elizabeth, and his oldest son, John, and his family.

Mars's theology of life may be summed up in the verse from a hymn which he once wrote:

All men are equal in God's sight,
The bond, the free, the black, the white;
He made them all, then freedom gave;
He made the *man*—*man* made the *slave*.

FURTHER READING

Brown-Kubisch, Linda. *The Queen's Bush Settlement: Black Pioneers, 1839–1865* (2004).

Eldridge, Joseph, and Theron Wilmot Crissey, comp. *History of Norfolk, Litchfield County, Connecticut 1744–1900* (1900).

Hood, Bishop J. W. *One Hundred Years of the African Methodist Episcopal Zion Church; or The Centennial of African Methodism* (1895).

Norton, John Foote. *The Record of Athol, Massachusetts, in Suppressing the Great Rebellion* (1866).

Ripley, Peter C. *The Black Abolitionist Papers,* vol. 3: *The United States, 1830–1846* (1991).

PATRICIA J. THOMPSON

Marsalis, Wynton (18 Oct. 1961–), trumpeter, was born in Kenner, Louisiana, the second of six sons of Ellis Marsalis, a jazz pianist and teacher, and Dolores Ferdinand. He was named after the jazz pianist WYNTON KELLY. Wynton Marsalis was raised in a musical family with his brothers, Branford (tenor and soprano saxophones), Delfeayo (trombone), and Jason (drums).

Marsalis began playing the trumpet at the age of six, starting on an instrument given to him by the bandleader and trumpeter Al Hirt, with whom his father was then playing. At age eight he was playing in a children's marching band and performing at the New Orleans Jazz and Heritage Festival. A prodigiously talented instrumentalist, Marsalis studied both jazz and classical music from an early age and at age twelve began classical training on the trumpet. His early musical experience was diverse and included playing in local marching bands, jazz groups, and classical youth orchestras. At high school he played first trumpet with the New Orleans Civic Orchestra. He made his professional debut at age fourteen in a performance of Haydn's Trumpet Concerto with the New Orleans Philharmonic Orchestra.

In 1977 Marsalis's performance at the Eastern Music Festival in North Carolina led to his being awarded the festival's Most Outstanding Musician Award. In 1978, at age seventeen, he performed Bach's Brandenburg Concerto no. 2 (on piccolo trumpet) with the New Orleans Symphony Orchestra. In the same year, Gunther Schuller admitted him to the summer-school program at the Berkshire Music Center at Tanglewood, in Lenox, Massachusetts, after he had auditioned with the same Bach concerto. Schuller recounted how Marsalis "soared right through it and didn't miss a note" (Giddins, 158), afterward receiving the school's Harry Shapiro Award for Outstanding Brass Player. In 1979 Marsalis was awarded a scholarship to the Juilliard School of Music in New York City. At that time he also performed with the Brooklyn Philharmonic and the Mexico City Symphony orchestras as well as playing in the pit band for Stephen Sondheim's Broadway musical *Sweeney Todd*.

In 1980, with a leave of absence from Juilliard, Marsalis joined ART BLAKEY's Jazz Messengers. He then toured in a quartet led by HERBIE HANCOCK, performing at the Newport Jazz Festival and on the album *Herbie Hancock Quartet* (1981). In 1983 Marsalis appeared again with Hancock in a quintet that included his brother Branford. By 1982 Marsalis was touring extensively with his own quintet and appearing at such venues as the Kool Jazz Festival at Newport and with the Young Lions of Jazz in New York. In London at the end of the year he appeared at Ronnie Scott's club and made his first classical recordings: trumpet concertos by Haydn, Hummel, and Leopold Mozart, with Raymond Leppard and the National Philharmonic Orchestra. Also in 1982 he recorded his debut album as leader, *Wynton Marsalis*. In the same year, he won the Jazz Musician of the Year Award in *Down Beat*'s readers' poll. In 1984 Marsalis undertook a classical tour, playing with orchestras across the United States and Canada. Also in 1984 he became the first (and only) musician to win Grammy awards in both jazz and classical categories, taking Best Soloist for his jazz album *Think of One*, and Best Soloist with Orchestra for the concerto set with Leppard. He won both awards again the following year.

By the middle of the decade Marsalis was recording prolifically and accumulating significant awards and prizes. This period saw the release of *Hot House Flowers* (1984), *Black Codes (from the Underground)* (1985), and *J Mood* (1986). Subsequent recordings included the first volume of the Standard Time series (1987), *Live at Blue Alley* (1988), *The Majesty of the Blues* (1989), the three-volume *Soul Gestures in Southern Blue* (1991), and *Blue Interlude* (1992). In 1992 Marsalis became artistic director of jazz at New York's Lincoln Center and leader of its Jazz Orchestra (LCJO). In 1997 he was awarded the Pulitzer Prize for Music for his "oratorio," *Blood on the Fields*, which was commissioned by Lincoln Center and premiered there with the LCJO in 1994. Jazz musicians had hitherto been ineligible for the award—it was denied to DUKE ELLINGTON in 1965—and it was a measure of Marsalis's distinction, and the enhanced prestige of jazz, that he should be the first to receive the award. The oratorio, about American slavery, was self-consciously Ellingtonian in style, theme, and scope, recalling Ellington's 1943 suite, *Black, Brown and Beige*.

In addition to his jazz albums, Marsalis has made several classical recordings: *Baroque Music for Trumpets* (1988), a collection of orchestral works by Vivaldi, Telemann, and Biber, with Raymond Leppard and the English Chamber Orchestra

(ECO); *On the Twentieth Century …* (1993), with Judith Lynn Stillman (piano), including works by Ravel, Honegger, Bernstein, and Hindemith; and *In Gabriel's Garden* (1996), with Anthony Newman and the ECO, featuring orchestral works by Mouret, Torelli, Charpentier, and Jeremiah Clarke. Marsalis also composed for dance: in collaboration with Garth Fagan for *Citi Movement* (1993); with Peter Martins and Twyla Tharp for the ballet works on *Jump, Start and Jazz* (1997); and with JUDITH JAMISON of the ALVIN AILEY American Dance Theater (*Sweet Release*), and the Zhong Mei Dance Company (*Ghost Story*), issued together as *Sweet Release & Ghost Story* (1999). His first composition for string quartet, *At the Octoroon Balls* (1999), was performed by the Orion String Quartet conducted by Marsalis.

Although Marsalis has enjoyed phenomenal success as a practicing musician, it is his concomitant "ambassadorial" role that has made him such a crucially significant figure in jazz. An indefatigable

Wynton Marsalis, the first jazz composer to win a Pulitzer Prize for music, playing his trumpet on 17 January, 1997. (AP Images.)

writer, broadcaster, educator, and administrator, he has assumed a position of unprecedented authority in shaping the meaning and value of jazz, particularly through his influential position at Lincoln Center. No one has done more than Marsalis to validate the artistic status of jazz and popularize its cultural standing. An unstinting proselytizer for jazz, he has embraced a pedagogical role through school programs, lectures, workshops, and master classes in addition to the Lincoln Center's education and performance programs and through his involvement with television and radio series, such as PBS's *Marsalis on Music* (1995), NPR's *Making the Music* (1995), and Ken Burns's PBS series *Jazz* (2001). In these endeavors, he found a firm ally and mentor in Albert Murray, the critic and author, who is also on the board of Jazz at Lincoln Center.

In the aftermath of Hurricane Katrina in 2005, Marsalis organized the Higher Ground Hurricane Relief Concert, which raised over $3 million for musicians and cultural organizations affected by the hurricane. Marsalis also played a central role in the Bring Back New Orleans Cultural Commission. In 2009 the French government awarded Marsalis that nation's highest civilian honor, making him a Chevalier of the Legion of Honor. That same year he received an honorary doctorate from Harvard University.

Marsalis's ascendancy as jazz's quasi-official spokesperson occurred during a period in which the condition of jazz appeared in disarray; his star was rising when jazz criticism was increasingly concerned with the compromised integrity of contemporary jazz. Critics complained that jazz had fragmented into hybridized, bastardized subcategories (like fusion), forms corrupted by ersatz electronic instrumentation and produced by MILES DAVIS and other musicians, who were seen to have "sold out" their jazz credentials. Marsalis sought to "reclaim" jazz from what he saw as the depredations of a commercialized popular culture (pop, rap, hiphop) that had led to its marginalization. Hence, he has advocated a traditionalist "neoclassical" agenda and has been both praised and criticized for playing the predominant role in what was often described as a "jazz renaissance" (Sancton, 66). Impeccably attired in retro-tailoring, he is, in himself, reminiscent of swing-era iconography.

Drawing on critical perspectives from his mentor and champion, STANLEY CROUCH, Marsalis's polemical writing has insistently repudiated the white romantic conception of jazz's "*down*" status as the imputed cultural expression of black lowlife.

Marsalis also rejects the spurious stereotype of black musicians' intuitive primitivism, which he calls "the noble savage cliché" (Marsalis, 21, 24). For Marsalis, jazz is—*was*—a cultural form of the highest order, and he has worked assiduously to safeguard its "purism" through his emphasis on the centrality of a highly selective canonical jazz tradition. With an emphasis on jazz purism rather than its pluralism, Wynton Marsalis has marked out the parameters of "what jazz is—and isn't."

FURTHER READING

Marsalis, Wynton. "What Jazz Is—and Isn't," *New York Times*, 31 July 1988.

Marsalis, Wynton, and Carl Vigeland. *Jazz in the Bittersweet Blues of Life* (2000).

Marsalis, Wynton, and Frank Stewart. *Sweet Swing Blues on the Road* (1994).

Marsalis, Wynton, and Selwyn Seyfu Hinds. *To a Young Jazz Musician: Letters from the Road* (2005).

Giddins, Gary. "Wynton Marsalis and Other Neoclassical Lions," in *Rhythm-a-ning: Jazz Tradition and Innovation* (2000): 156–161.

Gourse, Leslie. *Wynton Marsalis: Skain's Domain: A Biography* (1999)

Ratliff, Ben. "The Making of a Jazz Statesman," *New York Times*, 18 Oct. 2004.

Sancton, Thomas. "Horns of Plenty," *Time* (22 Oct. 1990): 64–71.

Seidel, Mitchell. "Profile: Wynton Marsalis," *Down Beat* 49, no. 1 (Jan. 1982): 52–53.

DISCOGRAPHY

Black Codes (From the Underground) (Columbia 40009).

Blood on the Fields (Columbia 57694).

Wynton Marsalis (Columbia 37574).

IAN BROOKES

Marsh, Vivian Osborne (5 Sept. 1897–8 Mar. 1986), civil rights activist, organizer, political activist, and philanthropist, was born Vivian Osborne in Houston, Texas, the youngest of four children of Benjamin J. Osborne and Alice (Estes) Osborne. Marsh attended Houston public schools until the age of sixteen. In 1913, three years after her father's death, the family moved to Berkeley, California, where Marsh enrolled at Berkeley High School and excelled in her studies. In Berkeley, Marsh's mother was an active member of the St. Augustine Church and West Indian Association, which organized community social functions. Marsh would follow her mother's example and become an activist in her own right.

After her graduation from high school in 1914, Marsh enrolled at the University of California, Berkeley, where she was the first black woman to major in anthropology. She entered the university in 1916, the same year that she had a son, Roy Curtis Osborne. There is no official record of his father. Also in 1916 Marsh joined the PHILLIS WHEATLEY Club, the youth branch of the California State Association of Colored Women. Much later, in 1941, she would be chosen as the organization's state president. She earned her B.A. in Anthropology in 1920 from the University of California, Berkeley, and her master's from the same university in 1922.

In 1920, the same year Marsh earned her BA, Lucy Stebbins, the university's dean of women, approached her to determine whether the school's black women had any interest in participating in sororities on campus. Since there was no black sorority on campus, Marsh took the initiative to recruit other women to help her with the 1921 formation of the first black sorority on a western United States campus. They formed the Kappa Chapter of Delta Sigma Theta Sorority.

In 1921 she married military veteran Leon Frederick Marsh. It was Leon's second marriage, and Marsh became stepmother to his son, Gerald. The couple made their home in the Berkeley, California, residence that Leon Marsh had purchased at 2838 Grant Street, where they would live their entire lives. Together, the couple had a son, Leon Frederick Marsh Jr.

In 1929 Marsh organized the Omega Sigma Alumna Chapter to serve members once they left college. She was also instrumental in initiating the formation of black sorority chapters at other universities in the western part of the country. Marsh was an active member and held sorority offices as first president of Kappa Chapter and as first president of Omega Sigma Chapter. She served the parent organization, Delta Sigma Theta Sorority, Inc., as its seventh national president from 1935 until 1939. Marsh maintained her activities in the organization throughout her lifetime.

Marsh was an officer of the National Council of Negro Women, an organization that represented other organizations of black women. She was active in the Young Women's Christian Association, the Young Men's Christian Association, and the Taylor Memorial Methodist Church. Some of Marsh's most important work was with the National Youth Administration, an organization concerned with unemployment among youth. Through her direct efforts, hundreds of African American undergraduate and graduate students received help to complete their educations. The vocational training programs she implemented helped train more than 1,000 young people in useful trades. She also served as a supervisor in the organization and used her access to the California Federation of Colored Women's Clubs as a means to recruit youth into the programs. Her personal relationship with MARY McLEOD BETHUNE proved valuable in those efforts. Marsh made serious gains toward the success of the National Youth Administration during the years 1935 and 1941.

Vivian and Leon Marsh were united in their community work. Respected philanthropists in their Berkeley community, they donated freely to social groups. Among them was a major California Masonic lodge, the Adonis Lodge No. 25, Free and Accepted Masons of PRINCE HALL, which Leon Marsh had organized in 1916. He served as the organization's first master. The couple worked with numerous lodges including the Order of the Eastern Star of the Golden State Grand Chapter Masonic lodge. From 1941 through 1946 Vivian Marsh served that organization as Royal Grand Matron, responsible for conducting its charitable work. Well informed about the inner workings of lodges, Marsh wrote a book called *History of the Order of Eastern Star and the Golden State Grand Chapter, Prince Hall Adoptive Rite*, which was published in 1956. Marsh held positions of honor in several lodges which she and her husband belonged to, in which she organized food drives, student scholarships, and clothing drives and executed fund-raisers to benefit the needy. In the tradition of her mother, Marsh maintained a commitment to community and the betterment of society.

Marsh received many tributes for her work. She was honored with Zeta Phi Beta Sorority's 1947 Woman of the Year award. As a respected professional and well-educated mentor in her community, Marsh was a public speaker in high demand. She often spoke on behalf of organizations to which she belonged. On 14 January 1951 Marsh was invited to speak at the first public appearance of another sorority chapter that she helped to form: the Delta Theta chapter of Delta Sigma Theta Sorority, Inc., Sacramento, California.

A politically active Republican in the 1950s, Marsh held seats on the California State Republican Legislative Council, the County Central Republican Committee, and the Berkeley City Council Planning Commission.

In recognition of her many years of dedication to community service as well as her work on city boards and commissions, Berkeley, California's mayor, Eugene Newport, proclaimed 21 February 1981 Vivian Osborne Marsh Day. Marsh was honored by the military with the distinction of being the only African American person in the United States invited to christen SS *Ocean Telegraph*, a U.S. Navy cargo ship.

While attending a conference of masons in El Centro, California, she suffered a stroke. Marsh received medical treatment at Herrick Hospital in Berkeley where she was flown by helicopter, but she never regained consciousness. She was later transferred to El Cerrito's Shields Convalescent Home, where she died.

FURTHER READING

Broussard, Albert S. *Black San Francisco: The Struggle for Racial Equality in the West, 1900–1954* (1994)

Giddings, Paula J. *In Search of Sisterhood: Delta Sigma Theta and the Challenge of the Black Sorority Movement* (1994)

Smith, Jessie Carney. *Notable Black American Women, Book II* (1995).

Taylor, Quintard. *In Search of the Racial Frontier: African-Americans in the American West, 1528–1990* (1998)

NANCY T. ROBINSON

Marshall, Albert P. (5 Sept. 1914–9 Mar. 2001), educator, university librarian, and historian, was born in Texarkana, Texas, to Early Marshall, a carpenter and railroad worker, and Muskogee, Oklahoma, native Mary (Bland) Marshall. Little is known about Marshall's early life, but his father died when "A.P." was still a boy, and the family moved to Kansas City, Missouri. There Marshall began his library work experience at one of the public library branches while he attended high school. Marshall prepared himself for a professional career by attending Lincoln University at Jefferson City, Missouri (1934–1938), earning a B.A. in English and History. He continued his studies at the University of Illinois at Champaign-Urbana, receiving a B.S. degree in Library Science in 1939.

His foremost contribution to the field of library services was *A Guide to Negro Periodical Literature* (vols. 1–4, Nov. 1941–Dec. 1946), which he began while working as a library assistant in 1939 at Lincoln University and published himself. He used three-by-five cards to create an index to the content of such well-known African American publications as *Crisis, Journal of Negro History, Phylon,* and *Ebony.* Scholarly and popular publications, along with those of fraternal organizations, professional societies, and colleges and universities, are included in the *Guide,* capturing a period for which no other indexing of its kind had been recorded. Included as well are smaller, short-lived, and long-forgotten popular publications that give a unique snapshot of African American culture and politics before World War II. Marshall's *Guide* is patterned after the subject-author arrangement of the *Readers' Guide to Periodical Literature.* Marshall himself worked on the index until 1943, when he entered the U.S. Coast Guard during the war. Others sustained the effort while he was away, and eventually his work was absorbed into conventional indexing services. Nevertheless, this unrivaled reference resource offers a unique glimpse into the past and provides a key to the literature for academic research in African American studies during that era. The original revised and updated is now known as *The Marshall Index: A Guide to Negro Periodical Literature, 1940–1946.*

While still in Jefferson City he married Ruthe Langley, on 12 June 1941, and one daughter was born to the couple.

Marshall went on from Lincoln University to Winston-Salem Teacher's College (now Winston-Salem State University) in North Carolina, where he was the director of libraries from 1941 to 1948. There he was instrumental in the establishment of the North Carolina Negro Library Association and was elected vice president. He earned an M.A. degree in Intellectual History in 1950 with a master's thesis titled "An International Police Force: Development of the Idea from the Paris Peace Conference to the San Francisco Conference."

Marshall returned to Lincoln University in 1950 and served as director of libraries until 1969. He remained an engaged scholar who championed equal access to information in support of the library and information needs of students and faculty. He also continued his own studies, earning a master's degree in History in 1953 from the University of Illinois, Champaign-Urbana.

Marshall moved to Eastern Michigan University at Ypsilanti in 1969 and remained the director of its library until 1972. He served as dean of academic services from 1972 to 1978, and as professor in 1978 until his retirement in 1980. He was successful in strengthening supportive relationships with the faculty and the student body and served as a mentor to many. He had been an active member of the Missouri Library Association, and as a leader of the American Library Association (ALA) in the 1960s, he worked toward gaining full equality of access to information for all, fostering academic professionalism, and fighting discrimination and segregation within the organization. He was nominated president of the American Library Association in 1970, but lost by a very narrow margin, and served as ALA Councilor from 1963 to 1976. He was the first African American to serve as chair of an ALA's Nominating Committee in 1965. Later, the Association of College and Research Libraries would recognize him for his leadership within the ALA. Marshall was also affiliated with many social, professional, church, and civic organizations, including the Ypsilanti Rotary Club, Alpha Phi Alpha fraternal organization, and the Ypsilanti Historical Preservation Commission.

He published many articles and books, including "New Demands on Negro College Librarians" in *Quarterly Review of Higher Education among Negroes* (Oct. 1940), and served as editor of the *Missouri Library Quarterly*. He also wrote a history of Lincoln University, *Soldiers' Dream: A Centennial History of Lincoln University in Missouri* (1966). Even after retirement, the professor emeritus continued to do research and publish books, chronicling the black experience in *The Real McCoy of Ypsilanti* (1989), *Unconquered Souls: The History of the African American in Ypsilanti* (1993), *Helen Walker McAndrew, Ypsilanti's Lady Frontier Doctor* (1996), *and The Legendary 4 Horsemen of the African Methodist Episcopal Church* (1996).

A. P. Marshall sought to bring public attention to the rich body of primary literature on the black experience during the 1940s through his periodical guide. In his local histories and biographies, the events and lives of African Americans who might otherwise have been unknown to researchers and scholars are recorded for posterity. Marshall died at his home at Ypsilanti, Michigan, at age eighty-six.

FURTHER READING

The Albert Prince Marshall Papers, 1943–1951, are housed in the archives of the University of Illinois at Champaign-Urbana.

Newman, Richard. "The First Black Index: Albert P. Marshall and *A Guide to Negro Periodical Literature*," *Harvard Library Bulletin* 11, no. 2, 2000.

Obituary: *Library Juice*, 21 March 2001. Available online at http://www.libr.org/Juice/issues/vol4/LJ_4.10.html#10

MELANIE THOMAS

Marshall, Andrew Cox (c. 1756–11 Dec. 1856), pastor and businessman, was probably born in Goose Creek, South Carolina. His mother was a slave, and his father was the English overseer on the plantation where the family lived; their names are unknown. Shortly after Marshall's birth, his father died while on a trip to England, thus ending abruptly the Englishman's plans to free his family. Marshall, his mother, and an older sibling (whose sex is not revealed in extant records) were subsequently sold to John Houstoun of Savannah, a prominent public official.

Houstoun was the second of five masters that Marshall had during his half century of servitude. Marshall became devoted to Houstoun, whose life he once saved, and Houstoun apparently grew fond of Marshall, for whose manumission Houstoun provided in his will. Nevertheless, when Houstoun, who had twice served as governor of Georgia and later as mayor of Savannah, died in 1796, the executors of his estate refused to honor the manumission provision. When the executors separated Marshall from his wife of nearly twenty-five years (name unknown), selling them to different masters, Marshall rebelled by running away. This led his new master to cancel the purchase, but another purchaser, Judge Joseph Clay (1741–1804), was found. Judge Clay subsequently apprehended the runaway slave, who had sought refuge nearby, but Marshall was never reunited with his wife. He was sold twice more, the last time to Richard Richardson, a Savannah merchant, who facilitated Marshall's manumission by lending him the two hundred dollars needed to purchase his freedom (c. 1806).

After gaining his freedom Marshall operated a very successful dray business that was patronized by Savannah's leading merchants. From this operation he earned income sufficient to repay Richardson, to purchase the freedom of Rachel (his second wife), their four sons, a stepson, and his father-in-law, and to build a home and rental property.

The person who influenced Marshall most was his maternal uncle, ANDREW BRYAN, a slave preacher on Brampton Plantation, who founded the First African Baptist Church there in 1788. In 1825 Marshall was called to the ministry of that church; he was installed the following year. In the ensuing thirty years Marshall operated his dray business and also shepherded his flock with distinction. The same year that Marshall was installed, the Sunbury Baptist Association, a biracial association to which First African Baptist belonged, invited him to preach to its annual convention. This marked the only time that an African American ever received such an invitation. In 1829, less than five years after

Marshall assumed the pulpit of that historic church, his wife, Rachel, died.

By 1830 the membership of First African Baptist Church had reached 2,417, nearly double the size that it was at the time of Bryan's death in 1812. A few years later, however, the church experienced a nasty schism when the Sunbury Baptist Association alleged that Marshall, in allowing Alexander Campbell to preach at his church, had embraced the antislavery and theological views of the Disciples of Christ Church (Campbellites). Marshall was expelled from the association in 1833 and was not allowed to return until he apologized in 1837. As a result of his expulsion, a majority of the deacons in the First African Baptist Church, along with about two hundred members (less than 10 percent of the total membership), left the church and founded the Third African Baptist Church, which was renamed First Bryan Baptist Church after the Civil War.

Marshall's ministry achieved widespread recognition and attracted white visitors from throughout the nation and from Europe. Several such visitors published favorable comments about Marshall's sermons. Sir Charles Lyell, commenting on a sermon that he heard in 1846, said that Marshall compared the probationary state of the pious to that of "an eagle teaching her newly fledged offspring to fly." Marshall assured the congregation that just as a mother eagle, when teaching her young eagle to fly, darts beneath it to keep it from hitting the ground, so does God rescue the pious person whenever he or she is in danger. This is the first recorded instance of a black pastor preaching "An Eagle Feathereth Its Nest," a favorite sermon in black evangelical churches.

In a sermon that Fredrika Bremer heard, Marshall asked his congregation, "Did He [Jesus Christ] come only to the rich?" He then answered his own question: "No! Blessed be the Lord! He came to the poor! He came to us, and for our sakes, my brothers and sisters." In his powerful expository style Marshall preached about sin, salvation, and punishment of the wicked—regardless of color (black or white) and legal status (slave or free). In the fiery style of the Great Awakening ministers, which black evangelical ministers retained long after that movement had died, Marshall preached to the hearts of his congregation, not to their heads. Hence his sermons were therapeutic to the black occupants of both the pulpit and the pews, because everyone was in the same boat and had the same spiritual needs. As

his fame spread, Marshall was invited to preach in other cities, including New Orleans, and to give an address to the state legislature of Georgia (c. 1850). Marshall was the first African American to address that body.

Although Marshall never attended school, he did not allow this deprivation to hinder him. He never learned to write, but he taught himself to read and eventually assembled the largest black-owned library in antebellum Georgia. Under his leadership, the First African Baptist Church, the oldest and largest Baptist church—black or white—in Savannah, remained the leading black church in the lower South. It is said that over the span of his ministry Marshall baptized about 3,800 people, averaging nearly 127 a year, that he converted more than 4,000, and that he married 2,000. In addition to these achievements, Marshall was proud of having served as the coachman and manservant to George Washington during Washington's visit to Savannah in the 1790s. In short, Marshall was the most outstanding African American in antebellum Georgia.

It is small wonder that whites respected Marshall and blacks revered him, which was apparent in the eulogy in the local newspaper following his death in Richmond, Virginia. He was survived by Sarah, his third wife, whom he had married in the early 1830s, a son, and an adopted daughter. Marshall is buried in an impressive red brick vault in Savannah's Laurel Grove Cemetery South. Racially segregated, it was one of few black cemeteries in existence at that time.

FURTHER READING

Daniel, W. Harrison. "Andrew Marshall," in *Dictionary of Afro-American Slavery*, ed. Randall M. Miller and John David Smith (1988).

Johnson, Whittington B. "Andrew C. Marshall: A Black Religious Leader of Antebellum Savannah," *Georgia Historical Quarterly* 69, no. 2 (1985): 173–192.

Thomas, Edgar G. *The First African Baptist Church of North America* (1925)

This entry is taken from the *American National Biography* and is published here with the permission of the American Council of Learned Societies.

WHITTINGTON B. JOHNSON

Marshall, Arthur (20 Nov. 1881–18 Aug. 1968), ragtime composer and pianist, was born in Saline County, Missouri; information about his parents is unknown. The Marshall family had relocated to Sedalia, Missouri, by the time that Arthur was in grade school, and there he befriended another budding musician, SCOTT HAYDEN. Noted ragtime pianist SCOTT JOPLIN lived with the Marshall family for a while, influencing the youngster's interest in ragtime; Arthur also took private lessons in classical piano. Joplin is said to have introduced Arthur to the Maple Leaf Club (the inspiration for Joplin's own "Maple Leaf Rag") while Arthur was still in high school, and Arthur is said to have performed there.

Marshall attended George R. Smith College in Sedalia, where he studied music and then obtained a teaching license. He worked at various parties and gatherings in St. Louis, as well as in the city's red-light district, where ragtime music was much in demand. In about 1901 he is said to have worked with a local minstrel troupe, McCabe's Minstrels, playing piano during their show's intermission. Marshall probably married his first wife, Maude McAdams, around this time; details of their marriage are unknown. Hayden, Joplin, and Marshall spent much time together during this period, collaborating on a projected opera, called *A Guest of Honor*, that was never produced, as well as critiquing each other's works and composing together.

Marshall and Joplin's collaboration, "Swipsey Cakewalk," was published by John Stark in 1900 and shows Marshall's predilection for folk melodies. As in his collaborations with Hayden, Joplin supplied the trio and probably helped give the entire work its formal structure.

In about 1906 Marshall left St. Louis and moved to Chicago because there were more performing opportunities there. Apparently either widowed or divorced, he married Julia Jackson in about 1907, and they had two daughters and a son. Most of Marshall's solo compositions were published while he was living in Chicago, although none was as successful as "Swipsey Cakewalk." "Lily Queen" (1907) was also credited to Joplin, who had arranged to have it published in New York but seems to have had no hand in its creation. Through 1908 Marshall published four other pieces with John Stark, who also published Joplin's works.

In about 1910 Marshall returned to St. Louis, taking the prize for the best ragtime pianist at the contest sponsored by the Turpin family at the Booker T. Washington Theater. Marshall worked for TOM TURPIN at one of his bars for a while and continued to work St. Louis's bars and brothels through 1916. His second wife died at that time, and Marshall relocated to Kansas City, abandoning his musical career. Sometime after 1917 he married for a third and final time; the name of his third wife is unknown.

Marshall's music was much in the style of his mentor Joplin, with perhaps a little more folk flavoring than the elder composer used. Marshall and Joplin's "Swipsey Cakewalk" contains folk-style melodies reminiscent of the earlier cakewalk style popularized in minstrel shows, although it is written in the four-part, formal, classical ragtime style that Joplin pioneered. The final part has the feeling of a barrelhouse ragtime stomp, the kind of music played in the bawdy houses throughout the South and West. Marshall published only five other rags during the heyday of the musical style from 1906 to 1908; unlike Joplin, Marshall actively performed his works and often incorporated crowd-pleasing devices into them, such as bluesy chords, slurred notes, and energetic endings (like the one heard in "Swipsey Cakewalk") that would bring a crowd to its feet.

Ragtime historians Rudi Blesh and Harriet Janis interviewed Marshall in the late 1940s for their landmark work *They All Played Ragtime* (1971); they also recorded him performing some rags for their small Circle label. Blesh and Janis printed in their book three previously unpublished works by Marshall—"Century Prize," "Missouri Romp," and "Silver Rocket"; a fourth work, "Little Jack's Rag," discovered after Marshall's death, was published in 1976.

FURTHER READING

Berlin, Edward A. *King of Ragtime: Scott Joplin and His Era* (1994)

Jasen, David A., and Trebor Jay Tichenor. *Rags and Ragtime: A Musical History* (1978).

This entry is taken from the *American National Biography* and is published here with the permission of the American Council of Learned Societies.

RICHARD CARLIN

Marshall, Bobby (12 Mar. 1880–27 Aug. 1958), athlete and civil servant, was born Robert Wells Marshall in Milwaukee, Wisconsin, the son of Richard Marshall, a railroad porter and laborer, and Symanthia Gillepsie Marshall. The family soon moved to Minneapolis, Minnesota, and Marshall first rose to prominence as an athlete at Minneapolis Central High School (MCHS), where he participated in football, baseball, ice hockey, and track. In 1900 Marshall led the Central High football team to a 0–0 tie against the University of Minnesota varsity, which would go on to capture the Western Conference (later the Big Ten) championship. MCHS completed its 1900 schedule undefeated, and claimed the mythic title of "High School Champions of the West."

Marshall graduated from Central in 1901, and, after working for a year to help support his family, he enrolled at the University of Minnesota. Although most professional sports had been effectively segregated by the twentieth century, Minnesota, like many colleges outside of the South, remained committed to a degree of equal opportunity and continued to field integrated teams. Consequently, Marshall immediately joined the Gopher football squad when he arrived on campus in 1903. Marshall cracked the starting lineup midway through his freshman year, and he remained a mainstay at end for the rest of his collegiate career, quickly gaining a reputation as a formidable presence on the field. Minnesota won a share of the Western Conference championship in 1903, 1904, and 1906 and compiled a four-year record of 41-2-1 during Marshall's tenure. He was one of the team's best defenders and most skilled runners, and, as importantly in an era when field-goals were worth four points and touchdowns were sometimes hard to come by, he was also one of the best kickers in the country. Marshall cemented his place in college football lore in the last game of his senior year during a grudge match against Amos Alonzo Stagg's powerhouse University of Chicago team. In a match that decided the Western Conference championship, which Chicago had taken from Minnesota in 1905, Marshall repeatedly frustrated Chicago's running attack, and, battling muddy and rainy conditions, he booted a forty-eight-yard field goal to account for all of Minnesota's points. The hometown *Chicago Tribune* said simply in a front-page headline: "Gophers Earn Victory by Magnificent Playing of Marshall, Colored End" (11 Nov. 1906).

His gridiron feats did not go unnoticed. Sportswriters routinely placed him on their "All Western" teams, and Walter Camp, the dean of college football scribes, honored Marshall as a second-team "All American" end in both 1905 and 1906. Marshall was the first African American to be named since first-teamer William Henry Lewis of Harvard in 1892 and 1893. Marshall also won varsity letters in baseball and track, and he helped lead the Gopher baseball team to a conference title his senior season. Active in intramural contests, he participated in ice hockey and tennis competitions. Despite his busy schedule, Marshall graduated in 1907 with a law degree.

In a testament to the university's acceptance of equal opportunity, Minnesota hired the knowledgeable Marshall as an assistant football coach after he finished school. He worked the Gopher sidelines

for one season and the following year became head coach at his alma mater, Minneapolis Central High School. In 1909 nearby Parker College (now defunct) engaged him to take charge of its football team, making Marshall one of the few African Americans to coach at an integrated college in the early twentieth century.

Marshall also continued his athletic career after graduation, playing on some of the best semi-professional football and ice hockey teams in the state. Usually the only black athlete on his team, he played quarterback and end in football and cover point in hockey, winning acclaim for his prowess in both sports. An ankle injury led him to give up hockey in 1909, but he was undoubtedly among the first blacks in the country to play the sport competitively. Although he continued to find success in integrated sporting events, such contests were the exception. As the color line hardened, most African American athletes of the era played for all-black teams in segregated competitions. Despite his connections to the white community, Marshall, too, could not escape all such racial limitations, and during his summers after college, he played for many of the region's leading African American baseball squads, including the St. Paul Colored Gophers, the Minneapolis Keystones, the Chicago Leland Giants, and the Chicago Giants.

In between his many sporting commitments Marshall attempted a legal career. For five years after graduating, he struggled—by himself and with various partners—to develop a legal practice, but prospects were not good for a black attorney. In 1911 he abandoned the law and accepted a job as a grain inspector for the state of Minnesota. Seven years later, he married Irene Knott, a recent migrant from the South, who was twenty years his junior. The couple had four children.

Marshall's civil service job kept him busy and limited his athletic commitments. For the next decade, he competed at the highest levels only in football, playing for the strong Minneapolis Marines semi-pro team on weekends. He soon got another opportunity to test his mettle against the best in the country. In the rough and tumble early days of professional football, several teams fielded African American ex-collegians like PAUL ROBESON and FRITZ POLLARD. In 1919 the Rock Island (Illinois) Independents continued this trend and signed the thirty-nine-year-old Marshall, who stayed on the team for three seasons. In 1925 he finished his pro career with the Duluth Kelleys, retiring as one of the dozen black men to play in the early NFL before that league drew the color line in 1933.

Over the next twenty years Marshall occasionally resurfaced in local and semipro games, but he focused on raising his children and coaching at Minneapolis's PHILLIS WHEATLEY House. When he retired from state employment in 1950, six hundred people, including the governor, attended his testimonial dinner. Marshall died eight years later with little fanfare as few remembered his pioneering exploits. Since his death, Marshall's career has been rediscovered. The College Football Hall of Fame inducted the Gopher star in 1971, and twenty years later he was a charter member of the University of Minnesota Athletic Hall of Fame.

FURTHER READING

Bernstein, Ross. *Pigskin Pride: Celebrating a Century of Minnesota Football* (2000)

Hoffbeck, Steven R. "Bobby Marshall," *Minnesota History* (Winter 2004–2005).

Hoffbeck, Steven R., ed. "Opposing the Color Line" in *Swinging for the Fences: Black Baseball in Minnesota* (2005).

Waters, Phil. "Football: Its Defenders and Champions," *The Colored American Magazine* (Apr. 1906).

GREGORY BOND

Marshall, Harriet Gibbs (18 Feb. 1865–25 Feb. 1941), musician, music educator, and author, was born Harriet Gibbs in Victoria, British Columbia, to MIFFLIN WISTAR GIBBS, an abolitionist politician and businessman, and Maria Ann Alexander, a graduate of Oberlin College. Mifflin Gibbs had moved to Canada in 1858; there he was successful in business and politics and was elected to the Victoria City Council for two terms. In 1869 the family moved to Oberlin, Ohio, seeking to take advantage of the educational opportunities available there. Mifflin Gibbs continued his dedication to politics and followed an impressive career that included serving as a municipal judge, as the register of the U.S. Land Office in Little Rock, Arkansas, and as the United States consul to Madagascar. Mifflin and Anna Maria Gibbs set high standards for the family in terms of ambition, diligence, and interest in education and public service. Like their mother, three of the Gibbs's four children attended Oberlin College.

Piano lessons at the age of nine from her older sister Ida prepared Harriet Gibbs for music study at the Oberlin College Conservatory, which she began at the age of eleven. She graduated from the conservatory with a major in piano in 1899, the first African American to achieve this distinction. She received a bachelor of music degree in 1906 when the college began to grant the degree.

In the following years Harriet Gibbs performed as a solo pianist, as an accompanist, and in chamber ensembles, at the same time continuing her piano study in Boston and Paris. In the 1890s she joined the faculty of the Eckstein-Norton University, an industrial school in Cane Spring, Kentucky. At Eckstein-Norton she taught theory, harmony, and piano and was the first director of the school's music conservatory. She was also a participant in fundraising tours to finance the construction of a new building. Living in the South influenced Gibbs significantly, because, as she stated in the Washington Conservatory bulletin of 1931, she listened to Negro melodies and became aware of the abundant untutored talent among local African Americans.

In 1900 she moved to Washington, D.C., where she was appointed assistant director of music in charge of special work for the Washington, D.C., public schools, a system that had separate divisions for white and black students. Gibbs, although she was later promoted to director of music and supervised a staff of seven, took her orders from a white supervisor and found that she had no actual voice in the operation of music in the schools.

In 1903 Gibbs, still in the employ of the Washington, D.C., public schools, founded the Washington Conservatory of Music, which offered music instruction to children and college-level students. The school opened with a staff of seven teachers in True Reformers Hall, a new building in the U Street neighborhood designed by John A. Lankford. The building's prestige, its location, and the fact that the conservatory was the only such school in the city for black students caused the new school to be highly welcomed by Washington's African American community. Within a year of the school's founding, however, the conservatory moved to its permanent home at 902 T Street after Mifflin Gibbs gifted his daughter with the more spacious building. It became the longest-lasting black-owned school offering a comprehensive music program on the college level. Financially this represented quite a struggle, for Gibbs received relatively little financial assistance from philanthropists. After more than one attempt to preserve it, the building was sold to a developer in 2004, forty-three years after the closing of the conservatory in 1961.

The conservatory hired CORALIE COOK to teach elocution and dramatic presentation, skills considered highly necessary for a struggling race. The school became the Washington Conservatory of

Music and School of Expression. The conservatory records reveal that by 1906 about three hundred students, most of them from farther south, studied a wide range of subjects: piano, voice, vocal expression, chorus training, pipe organ, organ building, piano tuning, stringed and wind instruments, ear training, theory, general history of music, Negro music, and public school music. The school's instructors were drawn from the ranks of well-known African American musicians and educators. BOOKER T. WASHINGTON and W. E. B. DU BOIS both endorsed the curriculum, suggesting that it satisfied both sides of the debate over the issue of education for the elite versus more practical education. Graduates became performers and teachers in the public and private schools and colleges.

In 1906 Gibbs married Napoleon B. Marshall, who supported his wife's vision of developing a school and preserving African American music. It also was during this period that Harriet Gibbs Marshall met and began a friendship with the renowned African English composer Samuel Coleridge-Taylor. She regularly included his works on conservatory programs. In fact, from 1903 to 1910 he was the only black composer represented. Her own work *The Last Concerto* (1941) was based on the story of his life. She was also a charter member of the S. Coleridge-Taylor Choral Society of Washington, D.C.

Marshall was one of the first educators to include the study of African American music in the curriculum, thus moving toward the establishment of African American music history as a discipline. The conservatory began a concert series that promoted black composers and performers as early as 1910, thereby introducing the best-known black musicians and classical music written by black musicians to the predominantly African American community. As Marshall developed her interest in African American culture, she took the first step toward the establishment of a national organization for black musicians by inviting recognized musicians to meet for this purpose. After she had written letters of invitation for several years with minimal response, Henry Grant, her protégé and colleague, took over this project and eventually chaired the meeting that led to the National Association of Negro Musicians in 1919.

By 1921 Marshall spoke of plans to expand the building at 902 T Street into the National Negro Music Research Center. She requested and received from publishers numerous copies of works by black composers. But from 1922 to roughly 1928 Marshall remained in charge of the conservatory in name only. During this time she was living in Haiti with her husband, who was a member of the American legation. Her interest in the cultural life of the Haitian people led her to conduct research, to cofound the industrial school L'Oeuvre des Femmes Haitienne pour l'Organization de Labour, and to write a book entitled *A Story of Haiti*, published in 1930.

Upon her return to Washington, Marshall again turned her attention to her vision of a research center. Despite a series of fund-raising campaigns begun in 1921 to benefit the conservatory and the research center, Marshall had collected only $1,100 by 1937, when she nonetheless announced the opening of the National Negro Music Center for the purpose of collecting and providing opportunities for research and study of African American music. Upon Marshall's death in Washington, D.C., in 1941, her cousin, Victoria Muse, became director of the conservatory.

FURTHER READING

Marshall's paper are part of the Washington Conservatory of Music Records located in the Moorland-Spingarn Research Center, Howard University, Washington, D.C.
Jackson, Irene V., ed. *More than Dancing: Essays on Afro-American Music and Musicians* (1985).
McGinty, Doris. "Black Women in the Music of Washington, D.C., 1900–1920," in *New Perspectives on Women in Music: Essays in Honor of Eileen Southern*, eds. Josephine Wright and Samuel Floyd (1992).
McGinty, Doris. "The Washington Conservatory of Music and School of Expression," *Black Perspective in Music* 7, no. 1 (1979).
Richings, G. F. *Evidence of Progress among Colored People*, 8th ed. (1902).
Obituary: *Washington Tribune*, 1 Mar. 1941.

DORIS EVANS MCGINTY

Marshall, Kerry James (17 Oct. 1955–), painter, photographer, printmaker, and installation artist, was born in Birmingham, Alabama, the second son of James Marshall, a postal service worker, and Ora Dee Prentice Marshall, a songwriter and entrepreneur, both of Birmingham. Marshall's family moved to Los Angeles in 1963, living in the Nickerson Gardens public housing project in Watts before settling in South Central Los Angeles.

Marshall's artistic inclinations were kindled by a kindergarten teacher at Birmingham's Holy Family Catholic School, who kept a picture-filled scrapbook for her young charges. This image compendium fed Marshall's obsession with making art. Impressed by his creativity and drive, his elementary, junior high, and high school teachers encouraged him with special opportunities. Marshall learned his first painting techniques from his third grade teacher. Later, an art instructor at George Washington Carver Junior High introduced Marshall to the Los Angeles County Museum of Art and a special summer drawing class taught by George De Groat at Otis Art Institute. There Marshall saw the book *Images of Dignity: The Drawings of* CHARLES WHITE. White's drawings depicting realistic African American subjects with aesthetic richness and highly charged emotion inspired Marshall to reflect his own experiences in art. De Groat took his class to visit White's studio, where Marshall had his first encounter with a living artist. After meeting White, who was on the faculty at Otis, Marshall became determined to attend college there.

Marshall embarked on a self-tutorial to develop his figure-drawing skills. Drawings made when he was about fifteen years old show his emerging technical proficiency. He created his own workspace in the family garage, complete with easel and still-life set-ups. In this "studio" he experimented with egg tempera and made his own charcoal and ink. In the summer of 1972, just before his final year of high school, Marshall enrolled in a Saturday adult painting class at Otis. His instructor, the painter and animator Sam Clayberger, showed Marshall how to analyze pictorial structure. During his final year in high school, Marshall also attended Charles White's life-drawing class at Otis. These artists remained a significant mentoring influence on Marshall, who spent two years after high school graduation in 1973 working as a dishwasher and then for a flooring company. In his spare time he painted in his garage studio and audited White's and Clayberger's classes. College was not a foregone conclusion in Marshall's family; on reaching majority children were expected to earn a living. In fact, with the exception of his Otis experiences, Marshall was not immediately aware of higher-education opportunities. Laid off from the flooring company in 1975, he approached Otis about enrollment and discovered that he needed two years of liberal arts education to enroll. He registered at Los Angeles City College, planning to transfer to Otis as a third-year student, which he did in 1977. Clayberger had given Marshall a glimpse of the kind of education he dreamed of—one based on inquiry, skills, knowledge, and standards. While attending Otis, though, Marshall began to realize that traditional practices and techniques had been subsumed by conceptual and theoretical approaches—notions that were in conflict with Marshall's ideals about formal art education. His discontent with Otis was instrumental in his subsequent formulation of a pedagogical approach emphasizing definition and clarification of skills through the acquisition of knowledge, standards, judgments, and values.

The painter and draftsman Arnold Mesches was Marshall's most challenging influence at Otis, urging Marshall to expand his artistic horizons. His entire senior year was occupied with creating a collage series loosely based on the work of ROMARE BEARDEN. The first, titled *Thirty Pieces of Silver*, symbolically portrayed the artist as Judas with a wide grin. This grin quickly became a signature element in his paintings. After graduation in 1978, Marshall applied to the government-sponsored Comprehensive Employment Training Act program for cultural employment and training opportunities through Brockman Art Gallery and was assigned to Mesches as a paid studio assistant.

In 1980 Marshall created *Portrait of the Artist as a Shadow of His Former Self*, a painting he feels was his first to unify completely process and meaning. *Portrait* signals the beginning of his signature style of the highly stylized, streamlined iconic black persona, rendered in pure black paint, with barely discernible features, except for gleaming white eyes and teeth. A series of paintings featuring stylized black figures followed. These works were exhibited at the art gallery at Los Angeles Southwest College, and on the strength of this show Marshall secured a part-time teaching job there. Additional works from this series were featured in his first commercial gallery exhibition, at James Turcotte Gallery in Los Angeles; the show was reviewed positively by the *L.A. Times* critic William Wilson. Marshall's professional career developed quickly: in 1985 he had his first solo exhibition, at Koplin Gallery in Los Angeles; that same year he was awarded a resident fellowship at the Studio Museum in Harlem. Packing his possessions in a Volkswagen van, he set off with the intention of moving to New York permanently. However, in New York he met his future wife, the Chicago native and actress Cheryl Lynn Bruce. After completing the residency and working for a few months at the print publishers Chalk & Vermilion, he followed Bruce to Chicago in 1987. They married in April 1989.

Also in 1987 Marshall began working with the cinematographer ARTHUR JAFA and his wife, the director JULIE DASH, as production designer for Dash's film *Daughters in the Dust* (1989). Marshall collaborated with Dash and Jaffa on several additional film projects (*Hendrix Project* and *Praise House*, both from 1991); he also worked with Haile Gerima on *Sankofa* (1990). Meanwhile, his work as a visual artist progressed. From his first Chicago residence, a six-by-nine foot room at the Chicago YMCA, he moved with Bruce into an apartment in Hyde Park. Marshall's larger space allowed him to increase the scale of his work dramatically. Large-scale narrative paintings were the focus of a second show at Koplin (1991) and the basis for his successful National Endowment for the Arts (NEA) Visual Art Fellowship grant application. Receiving NEA support was a major career milestone, allowing him to establish his first professional studio outside his home.

The painting *The Lost Boys* (1993) epitomized his next period of artistic growth. Marshall believes that it was in this artwork that he achieved the surface beauty and compositional sophistication he had been striving for. With this work, he began to think in terms of larger narrative series, or installations, rather than individual pictures. The year 1993 marked his first participation in museum exhibitions (Corcoran Gallery of Art in Washington, D.C., and the Museum of Modern Art in New York). He also had his first New York gallery show, at the Jack Shainman Gallery, and received the prestigious Louis Comfort Tiffany Foundation Award in painting. He began teaching at the School of Art and Design at the University of Illinois at Chicago, gaining full professorship and tenure in 1998. His first solo museum show, organized by the Cleveland Center for Contemporary Art in 1994, included a catalog and a four-city tour.

For Marshall, 1997 was a banner year. He received the Alpert Award in the Arts and was given the prestigious MacArthur Foundation's Fellows Program grant. He also was included in Documenta 10, that year's edition of the important international art exhibition held every five years in Kassel, Germany. Marshall's idea for a multifaceted project came to fruition in 1998 with Mementos, organized by the Renaissance Society, University of Chicago. His subject was broad: the tumultuous 1960s, loss, remembrance, and commemoration. Four mural-sized paintings titled *Souvenir* formed the installation's core. Additional components, including paintings portraying MARTIN LUTHER KING JR., John F. Kennedy, and Robert F. Kennedy; a video installation; freestanding sculptures in the shape of giant rubber stamps; and relief prints of popular slogans from the 1960s, such as "Black Is Beautiful" and "We Shall Overcome," conveyed an overall sense of gravity and reverence.

Marshall explored social and political issues further in the show Carnegie International 1999/2000, at the Carnegie Museum of Art in Pittsburgh. His work *Rythm Mastr* consisted of hand-drawn and commercially printed comic book–style narratives that were displayed in a site-specific installation incorporating exhibition cases normally used to show fragile artifacts. These cartoons were later published as a supplement to the Sunday Pittsburgh *Post-Gazette*. As a professional artist, Marshall has always sought to create works that commingle the aesthetics and sociology of African American popular culture. With *Rythm Mastr* he deftly conjoined the worlds of popular culture and fine art. In 1999, twenty-one years after he entered the program, Otis conferred an honorary doctorate on Marshall in recognition of his creativity, dedication, and career achievements.

Marshall's work is indicative of a significant development in twenty-first-century artistic discourse being practiced by a new generation of art makers: a concern with modern and postmodern art idioms combined with social and political content and a profound dedication to classical art traditions. His work is deeply rooted in the great tradition of representation and historical narrative painting, yet is imbued with personal expression and social awareness. Like other artists of his generation, such as LORNA SIMPSON, GLENN LIGON, and CARRIE MAE WEEMS, he has charted a new course based on the solid foundations of the past.

FURTHER READING

Marshall, Kerry James, Terrie Sultan, and Arthur Jafa. *Kerry James Marshall* (2000).
Holg, Garrett. "Stuff Your Eyes with Wonder," *ARTnews* (Mar. 1998).
Reid, Calvin. "Kerry James Marshall," *Bomb* (Winter 1998).
Sultan, Terrie. *Kerry James Marshall: Telling Stories* (1994)
                                                    TERRIE SULTAN

Marshall, Napoleon Bonaparte (1873–5 June 1933), athlete, lawyer, soldier, and civil servant, was born in Washington, D.C., to Alexander Marshall, an employee of the Treasury Department, and Leatha Marshall, a homemaker. He attended the M Street High School, then prepped for a year at New Hampshire's Phillips Exeter Academy, where he was editor-in-chief of the *Phillips Exeter Literary Monthly* and a member of the track team. In 1893 he entered Harvard and immediately joined the Crimson track squad, on which he represented the college for four consecutive seasons, specializing in the 440-meter and quarter-mile runs. In 1894 he finished third in the quarter-mile at the Inter-Collegiate Amateur Athletic Association of America national championships. He competed for three more seasons and became the school's second black varsity athlete behind the football player WILLIAM HENRY LEWIS. Marshall was also an active member of the Harvard Union debating club and was well known on campus for his forensics skill. He helped found and was elected president of Serapion, a literary society devoted to modern English literature, and he studied foreign languages, becoming fluent in French. He graduated in 1897 and subsequently took one year of classes at Harvard Law School.

In 1898 Marshall became the chair of mathematics at the State Normal and Industrial College for Colored Students (later Florida A&M University) in Tallahassee, Florida, but returned to Boston after one year. Though lacking a formal law degree, Marshall passed the Massachusetts bar exam in March 1900. In addition to his legal work Marshall became active in politics. A member of the so-called Boston Radicals, a group of mostly college-educated northern blacks who opposed BOOKER T. WASHINGTON's accommodationist philosophy, Marshall and his allies advocated integration and fought against Washington's policies. He was at the "Boston Riot" in 1903, during which a group of "Radicals" heckled and interrupted a speech by the "Wizard of Tuskegee." In explaining the action of his compatriots Marshall told the *Boston Globe*:

> The movement against Mr. Washington was started by the colored people in Boston, who have been much displeased of late at the method that he has taken of trying to uplift the race. He has advocated the jim-crow car, and shown up unnecessarily the failings of the people. Thus the people took this opportunity of showing to the country their disapproval of Mr. Washington and his methods (*Boston Globe*, 31 July 1903).

Marshall did not limit his activism to the black community. He was one the few contemporary African Americans loyal to the Democratic Party. Black Democrats hoped to split the vote of African Americans to make both major parties pay more attention to their interests. He organized and promoted for the local Democratic Party, and in 1902 he was rewarded with the patronage position of deputy tax collector. He kept this position until 1906, when he moved to Washington, D.C., to marry HARRIET GIBBS MARSHALL, the first black graduate of the Oberlin Conservatory of Music and the founder of the Washington Conservatory of Music, the only such African American school in the country. The couple had no children. While in Washington he remained involved with politics. After the Brownsville Affair, in which interracial violence in Brownsville, Texas, caused 167 black infantrymen from nearby Ft. Brown to be unjustly dishonorably discharged, Marshall raised money for the soldiers' defense and conducted an independent investigation with fellow lawyer Gilchrist Stewart. Around 1910 Marshall began splitting his time between Washington, where he helped his wife manage the Conservatory, and New York City, where he resumed his legal career. He teamed with the attorneys J. Frank Wheaton and Oscar Garrett to form the firm of Marshall, Wheaton, and Garrett, reportedly one of the most influential and successful African American law firms in the country.

During the run-up to the United States' entry into World War I, Marshall decided that military service provided an avenue for African Americans to improve their condition and to demonstrate their patriotism. In 1916, at the age of forty-three, Marshall enlisted in the Fifteenth New York Infantry Regiment, a segregated unit of the national guard. He passed the officer's exam and earned a captain's commission. When the United States entered the war in 1917, the Fifteenth traveled to Spartanburg, South Carolina, for training. Local residents constantly harassed the black soldiers, and a mob once forcibly removed Captain Marshall from a streetcar. In November 1917 the Fifteenth Infantry deployed to France, where it was initially relegated to construction work and menial labor, until the War Department redesignated it as the federal 369th United States Infantry Regiment, and eventually sent it to the front lines where it earned the nickname "Harlem's Hell Fighters." At the front Marshall experienced a poison gas attack and, after recuperating, was reassigned to the 365th Infantry, another segregated unit. On 21 October 1918 he was severely wounded during a nighttime raid on a German machine-gun position. Marshall suffered a serious injury to his spinal cord from which he never fully recovered. In recognition of his heroism he received the prestigious Croix de Guerre from the French government.

After the war Marshall, who apparently had switched political allegiances, served for six years during the Coolidge and Harding presidential administrations as the military attaché to the United States' legation in Port au Prince, Haiti. While overseas his wife gathered material for her well-regarded book, *A Story of Haiti*, published in 1930. Owing to his war injuries, Marshall walked with a cane and wore a steel brace, but his health deteriorated further during the 1920s, forcing him to return to the United States. Although never healthy enough to resume his legal career, he remained active. He served as president of the "Save Haiti League," and he publicly opposed the continuing American occupation of that country. Marshall died in New York City and was buried in Arlington National Cemetery.

FURTHER READING

A small collection of correspondence, chiefly between Napoleon Marshall and Harriet Gibbs Marshall, is held in the Washington Conservatory of Music papers in the Moorland-Spingarn Collection at Howard University.

Marshall, Napoleon B. *The Providential Armistice, A Volunteer's Story: Military Sketch of Captain Napoleon B. Marshall* (1930).

"Athlete and Lawyer," *Boston Globe*, 4 May 1902.

Chalk, Ocania. *Black College Sport* (1976)

Harris, Stephen L. *Harlem's Hell Fighters* (2003)

Scott, Emmett J. *The American Negro in the World War* (1919)

Obituary: *Amsterdam (N.Y.) News*, 7 June 1933.

GREGORY BOND

Marshall, Paule (9 Apr. 1929–), writer, was born Valenza Pauline Burke in Brooklyn, New York, the second of three children of the Barbadian immigrants Samuel Burke, a factory worker, and Ada (maiden name unknown), a domestic. As a child Marshall read the great British novelists Charles Dickens, William Makepeace Thackeray, and Henry Fielding. Their influence is especially apparent in her sense of setting and characterization.

Later, she discovered African American writers such as RICHARD WRIGHT and PAUL LAURENCE DUNBAR. The latter's use of dialect helped to legitimate her use of the cadences and grammatical structures of the vernacular used by the Bajan women of her community. Marshall writes beautifully about these women and their language in her *New York Times Book Review* essay "The Making of a Writer: From the Poets in the Kitchen" (1983).

As a young adult Marshall was greatly influenced by RALPH ELLISON's *Shadow and Act*, which she has called her "literary bible," and by GWENDOLYN BROOKS's lone novel, *Maud Martha*. In addition, she claims JAMES BALDWIN as crucial to her formation as a writer and thinker. These three writers emerged as significant literary figures who received mainstream acclaim in the early 1950s. By the end of that decade, Marshall joined them as the newest and one of the most original voices of the time.

In 1948 Marshall entered Hunter College in New York City, but illness forced her to take time off from her studies. During her recuperation she began writing short stories. Marshall married her first husband, Kenneth Marshall, in 1950; nine years later she gave birth to her only child, a son, Evan Keith. Before long her artistic aspirations began to challenge her domestic life. In 1953 she graduated cum laude with a degree in English from Brooklyn College and was inducted into Phi Beta Kappa. Following graduation Marshall worked as a librarian at the New York Public Library while seeking work in journalism. As is the case with her fictional character Reena, in the novella of the same name, Marshall found that the sophisticated world of Manhattan magazine publishing was still closed to black writers unless they were already well known. Eventually she joined the staff of *Our World* magazine, a black publication, as its only female correspondent. At *Our World* she encountered sexism in both her superiors and her colleagues, who voiced expectations that she would fail. Nonetheless, while at *Our World*, Marshall traveled extensively throughout the Caribbean and South America.

In 1954 Marshall published her first short story, "The Valley Between," the story of a young white wife and mother who, in defiance of her husband, wants to continue her education and eventually pursue a career. The story chronicles the character's ambition as well as her guilt. Marshall later said that she might have made her characters white in order to avoid having to confront the similarities between herself and her protagonist. Against her own husband's wishes, Marshall enlisted the services of a baby-sitter so that she would have time to work on her writing. In 1959 she published her first and best-known novel, *Brown Girl, Brownstones*. In 1963 her marriage ended in divorce.

In *Brown Girl, Brownstones* Marshall renders the speech of a Brooklyn community of Bajan immigrants, as well as African American migrants from the South, with extraordinary beauty and poetry. Along with Gwendolyn Brooks's *Annie Allen* and *Maud Martha*, *Brown Girl, Brownstones*—a portrait of Selina Boyce, a young, strong-willed girl—is one of the first books in American literature to concern itself with the interior life of a young black girl. In addition, *Brown Girl, Brownstones* is also the earliest novel to explore the intricacy of black mother-daughter relationships and one of the first to give such a complex portrait of a community of Caribbean immigrants.

In 1960 Marshall received a Guggenheim Fellowship, which she used to write a collection of four novellas titled *Soul Clap Hands and Sing* (1961). Each novella—"Barbados," "Brooklyn," "British Guiana," and "Brazil"—presents an elderly man who has to come to terms with his meaningless life. The settings range from sites in the United States to Central America, the Caribbean, and South America. Marshall received an American Academy Arts and Letters Award for *Soul Clap Hands and Sing*.

Her next work, the exquisite, complex novel *The Chosen Place, the Timeless People*, is one of Marshall's greatest accomplishments. Set in a fictional Caribbean nation, the novel explores a number of characters, black and white, male and female, North American, West Indian, and European. Through them, Marshall explores larger issues of power and dominance, colonialism, slavery, and neocolonialism. Perhaps most importantly, the novel introduces Merle Kinbona, an eccentric, educated, middle-aged, sensual, radical, intellectual black woman, and one of the most original and complex characters in contemporary fiction.

Fourteen years passed before the publication of Marshall's next novel, *Praisesong for the Widow* (1983). During this creative hiatus she married Nourry Menard, a Haitian businessman. *Praisesong* continues Marshall's portrayal of older women, her concern for characters who have lost their spiritual centers, and her exploration of the relationship between African American and Afro-Caribbean history. If her earlier work focused on specific locations, in *Praisesong for the Widow* she begins to include the Caribbean and Central and South America in her conception of the black South.

Marshall's next novels turn to the children of diaspora. *Daughters* (1991), which received the Columbus Foundation American Book Award, is the story of Ursa MacKenzie, the buppie daughter of a West Indian politician father and a middle-class black woman from the United States. While these are her biological parents, her father's mistress, a childless businesswoman, and his own nursemaid also mother her. But most significantly she is the daughter of Afro-diasporic history; in documenting that history, she gives birth to herself.

Marshall's most recent novel, *The Fisher King* (2000), centers on a little boy, Sonny, who is a true child of the African diaspora. His mother was raised in Paris, and his father is a Senegalese street vendor in Paris. His maternal grandparents are two American expatriates, Sonny Rhett-Payne and a character modeled after LENA HORNE. One of his great grandmothers is an aristocratic African American woman with roots in the Deep South, and another is a stern West Indian woman; both of them live in brownstones on the same Brooklyn block. Thus, Sonny has roots throughout the African diaspora, and as he is brought to live with his great grandmothers in Brooklyn it is tempting to see that Marshall's work has come full circle.

Since 1995 Marshall has divided her time between Richmond, Virginia, and New York City. In addition to teaching creative writing at New York University, she also introduced the School's Paule Marshall and the New Generation Reading Series. The series has featured a number of young writers before they achieved public acclaim. Among these are EDWIDGE DANTICAT, COLSON WHITEHEAD, DANZY SENNA, and A. J. Verdelle. In 1993 she was awarded a MacArthur Foundation Fellowship.

Marshall is a cosmopolitan intellectual whose work traces the complex connections and conflicts among black people throughout the Americas. Long before academics turned their attention to the African diaspora or the "Black Atlantic," Marshall mapped this terrain in novels, novellas, and short stories. Her experience as the child of immigrants, her childhood in a Brooklyn populated by blacks from the Caribbean and the American South, and her travels as an adult throughout the Americas all inform her artistic vision. Her literature underscores the relationship among slavery, colonialism, racism, and neocolonialism and the formation of the modern black subject.

FURTHER READING

Marshall, Paule. "From the Poets of the Kitchen," *New York Times Book Review* (9 Jan. 1983), 3, 34–35.

DeLamotte, Eugenia C. *Places of Silence, Journeys of Freedom* (1998).

Denniston, Dorothy Hamer. *The Fiction of Paule Marshall: Reconstructions of History, Culture, and Gender* (1995).

Hathaway, Heather. *Caribbean Waves: Relocating Claude McKay and Paule Marshall* (1999).

Pettis, Joyce. *Toward Wholeness in Paule Marshall's Fiction* (1995).

FARAH JASMINE GRIFFIN

Marshall, Thurgood (2 July 1908–24 Jan. 1993), civil rights lawyer and U.S. Supreme Court justice, was born Thoroughgood Marshall in Baltimore, Maryland, the son of William Canfield Marshall, a dining-car waiter and club steward, and Norma Arica Williams, an elementary school teacher. Growing up in a solid middle-class environment, Marshall was an outgoing and sometimes rebellious student who first encountered the Constitution when he was required to read it as punishment for classroom misbehavior. Marshall's parents wanted him to become a dentist, as his brother did, but Marshall was not interested in the science courses he took at Lincoln University in Pennsylvania, from which he was graduated with honors in 1930. He married Vivian "Buster" Burey in 1929; they had no children.

Unable to attend the segregated University of Maryland School of Law, Marshall enrolled in and commuted to Howard University School of Law, where he became a protégé of the dean, CHARLES HAMILTON HOUSTON, who inspired a cadre of law students to see the law as a form of social engineering to be used to advance the interests of African Americans. After graduating first in his class from Howard in 1933, Marshall remained in Baltimore, where he opened a private law practice and struggled to make a living during the Depression. Marshall was active in the Baltimore branch of the National Association for the Advancement of Colored People (NAACP), and in 1936 Houston persuaded both the NAACP board and Marshall that Marshall ought to join him in New York as a staff lawyer for the NAACP. After Houston returned to Washington in 1938, Marshall remained and became the chief staff lawyer, a position he held until 1961. Early in his Baltimore practice Marshall had decided to attack the policies that had barred him from attending the state-supported law school. Acting under Houston's direction, Marshall sued the University of Maryland on behalf of Donald Murray. The Maryland state court's 1936 decision ordering the school to admit Murray because the state did not maintain a "separate but equal" law school for African Americans was the first step in a two-decade effort to undermine the constitutional basis of racial segregation. Over the next fourteen years, Marshall pursued his challenge to segregated higher education through two main areas. In *Missouri ex rel Gaines v. Canada* (1938), a case Houston developed and argued, the U.S. Supreme Court directed the University of Missouri to either admit Lloyd Gaines to its law school or open one for African Americans. The

attack culminated in Marshall's case of *Sweatt v. Painter* (1950), in which the Supreme Court held that the law school Texas had opened for African Americans was not "equal" to the well-established law school for whites.

The cases that the Supreme Court decided under the name *Brown v. Board of Education* constituted Marshall's main efforts from 1950 to 1955. Assembling a team of lawyers to develop legal and historical theories against segregation, Marshall had his greatest triumph as a lawyer in *Brown* (1954), in which the Supreme Court held that segregation of public schools by race was unconstitutional. In the 1896 case of *Plessy v. Ferguson*, the Supreme Court had upheld segregation, saying that segregation was a reasonable way for states to regulate race relations and that it did not "stamp the colored race with a badge of inferiority." Examining the background of the Fourteenth Amendment, Marshall's team concluded that the amendment's framers did not intend either to authorize or to outlaw segregation. From this research Marshall came to the conclusion that under modern conditions, given the place of education in twentieth-century life, segregated public education was no longer reasonable. Marshall also relied, though less heavily, on arguments based on the psychological research of KENNETH B. CLARK showing that, *Plessy* notwithstanding, segregation did in fact damage the self-images of African American schoolchildren. During oral arguments Marshall occasionally stumbled over technical and historical details, but his straightforward appeal to common sense captured the essence of the constitutional challenge: "In the South where I spend most of my time," he said, "you will see white and colored kids going down the road together to school. They separate and go to different schools, and they come out and they play together. I do not see why there would necessarily be any trouble if they went to school together."

There was trouble, however, as officials in the Deep South engaged in massive resistance to desegregation. Marshall argued the case of *Cooper v. Aaron* (1958), which arose after the Arkansas governor Orval Faubus sought to circumvent desegregation by closing four Little Rock schools on the first day of class. Marshall pointed out that Faubus's attempts to thwart the Supreme Court directive in *Brown* threatened fundamental American ideas about the rule of law, and he asked the Court to assert its constitutional authority by directing Little Rock officials to reopen and racially integrate the schools. Marshall told the justices that a ruling in favor of Faubus would be tantamount to telling the nine black boys and girls who had endured harassment and intimidation at Little Rock's Central High School throughout the 1957–1958 school year, "You fought for what you considered democracy and you lost…. go back to the segregated school from which you came." Again the Supreme Court agreed with Marshall, and in August 1959 the schools reopened in line with federal desegregation orders.

A gregarious person who was always ready to use an apt, humorous story to make a point, Marshall traveled throughout the segregated South to speak to teachers and NAACP members, and in the 1940s and 1950s he became a major civil rights leader. By the mid-1950s his role as a civil rights leader had superseded his work as an attorney, and he had become a widely sought-after speaker and fund-raiser. He also was active in the Episcopal Church and the PRINCE HALL Masons. His wife died of lung cancer in February 1955, and the following December he married Cecilia Suyatt, a secretary in the NAACP's national office; they would have two children, both boys.

Fending off attacks on the NAACP, its lawyers, and its members as well as attempting to push desegregation forward took a toll on Marshall. His travels kept him away from his family, and his NAACP salary, even when supplemented by gifts from wealthy white members, was inadequate to provide a college education for his sons. Moreover, the emergence of MARTIN LUTHER KING JR., the Southern Christian Leadership Conference (SCLC), and the Student Nonviolent Coordinating Committee (SNCC) shifted the civil rights movement away from the legal strategies Marshall favored toward more direct-action tactics. Because of this, and to ease his financial burden and make more time for his family, in 1961 Marshall accepted an appointment to the U.S. Court of Appeals for the Second Circuit (in New York). Political maneuvering delayed his confirmation for nearly a year, after which he served on the Second Circuit for five years. His opinions were solid but hardly pathbreaking. Aware of his lack of experience in business and tax law, which constituted an important portion of the Second Circuit's business, Marshall took guidance from Judge Henry Friendly in those areas.

In 1965 President Lyndon Johnson named Marshall U.S. solicitor general, the government's chief lawyer before the Supreme Court. Although neither said so explicitly, both Johnson and Marshall expected that Johnson would name Marshall to the U.S. Supreme Court as soon as possible. In 1967

Johnson manipulated Justice Tom Clark into resigning from the Court by naming his son Ramsey Clark attorney general, and that same year, saying it was "the right thing to do, the right time to do it, the right man and the right place," Johnson named Marshall to be the first African American Supreme Court justice.

Marshall joined a Court that was dominated by liberals, but within five years the Court's composition had changed dramatically following the retirement of Chief Justice Earl Warren and the deaths of Justice Hugo Black and Justice John Marshall Harlan. Instead of being active in the coalition that determined the Court's positions, Marshall found himself in a beleaguered minority that opposed the more conservative justices appointed by Richard Nixon and Ronald Reagan. Marshall rarely got the opportunity to write important majority opinions, even when his liberal colleagues led by William J. Brennan were able to cobble together a majority, because such opinions had to appeal to one or two of the justices who were significantly more

Thurgood Marshall, visiting the White House's Oval Office, Washington D.C, 13 June 1967. (Lyndon Baines Johnson Presidential Library.)

conservative than Marshall, and Marshall was relatively uncompromising on matters he cared about.

Marshall's repertoire of stories endeared him to nearly every one of his colleagues, although initially some conservatives, including Lewis F. Powell, were put off by what they saw as Marshall's failure to approach the job with appropriate seriousness. Marshall did delight in puncturing what he took to be Chief Justice Warren Burger's pomposity, occasionally greeting Burger with, "What's shakin', Chiefy baby?" Yet most of Marshall's colleagues came to understand that he used his stories, often about the experiences of black Americans in the nation's court system, to make points about the cases the justices were considering. At the time of his retirement in 1991, Marshall brought more experience as a practicing lawyer to the Court than did any of his colleagues, and he often urged them to take more account of courtroom realities than of abstract deliberations about the Constitution.

Court watchers, particularly those who were unsympathetic to Marshall's positions on constitutional issues, criticized him for delegating too much of his work to his law clerks. Familiar with numerous aspects of the law from his experiences on the court of appeals and as solicitor general, Marshall had a facility for quickly determining the main thrust of each party's contentions and for deciding what result to reach. He would provide a sketchy outline of what an opinion should say; after that, the law clerks did substantially all of the opinion drafting in his chambers, as was the case in other chambers as well. Marshall did not edit his clerks' drafts as closely as other justices did, but he rejected drafts that did not capture the substance or the intensity of his views, and thus the guidance he gave made the opinions his own.

Marshall's most important contribution to constitutional doctrine was his "sliding-scale" theory of the Fourteenth Amendment's guarantee of equal protection of the laws, which he stated in most detail in dissenting opinions in *Dandridge v. Williams* (1970) and *San Antonio Independent School District v. Rodriguez* (1973). The Court's stated doctrine distinguished between two "tiers" of judicial scrutiny. One tier involved "suspect" classifications, such as race or "fundamental" interests; statutes using those classifications received strict scrutiny and rarely were upheld. The other tier contained all other statutes; statutes in this category simply had to have a "rational basis" and rarely were struck down. As the Court grappled with more and more cases involving discrimination against women,

aliens, and nonmarital children, and cases dealing with the provision of public assistance, Marshall pointed out that the rigid two-tiered approach was inadequate, because for one thing, it failed to take account of variations in the importance of different interests; perhaps even more important, it failed to describe the outcomes of the Court's cases. Marshall proposed that the Court adopt an approach that openly balanced the importance of the goals the government was trying to achieve, the nature of the interest(s) affected, and the character of the group adversely affected by the classifications of a given statute. Although the Court did not expressly adopt Marshall's suggestion, some of its decisions seemed implicitly to do so, and many scholars believe that his analysis was more representative of the Court's decision making than was the doctrine that the Court claimed to be applying.

Beyond his specific doctrinal contributions, Marshall provided a voice on the Court, and in the Court's internal deliberations, for black Americans and others with few champions. After he retired, several of his colleagues said that Marshall's opinions had brought the real world into the Court's deliberations. When the Court, in upholding a federal filing fee for bankruptcy (*United States v. Kras* [1973]), suggested that it should not be difficult for a poor person to set aside about two dollars a week to pay the fee, Marshall became indignant, writing in his published opinion, "No one who has had close contact with poor people can fail to understand how close to the margin of survival many of them are."

Marshall drew on his experience as a criminal defense lawyer when he argued that in all cases capital punishment is a form of cruel and unusual punishment barred by the Constitution. After the Court rejected that proposition in *Gregg v. Georgia* (1976), Marshall continued to express his disagreement; his dissents often asserted that the fair administration of justice was compromised in death penalty cases, particularly when defendants facing death sentences had received inadequate legal assistance.

Marshall's overall approach to constitutional law combined Charles Hamilton Houston's view that it is a form of social engineering with a pragmatic grasp of courtroom and practical realities. For example, he refused to deem that the police practice of arresting drunks was unconstitutional, in part because he believed that society had not instituted a better method of dealing with the problem than to lock up drunks until they were sober. He was willing to endorse large-scale reforms through constitutional law, as in attempts to effect desegregation and to rid the law of the death penalty, because *Brown* had taught him that a bold Supreme Court pronouncement often had an indirect but lasting impact on social practices.

Feeling the effects of age, and having lost his closest ally on the Court when Brennan retired in 1990, Marshall announced his retirement on 27 June 1991. The Court was substantially more conservative when Marshall left than when he arrived. During his tenure the nation's political system had drifted to the right; so had the Court, a trend that would continue with the appointment of his successor, CLARENCE THOMAS. Marshall never was able to act as a social engineer on behalf of African Americans and others who had made up the New Deal and Great Society political coalition; instead, he came to occupy a different role on the Court, that of the great dissenter.

Earlier on the day of his retirement Marshall filed his final dissent. In *Payne v. Tennessee* a majority of the Court overruled the controversial decision in *Booth v. Maryland* (1987) and allowed prosecutors to introduce statements about the personal impact that a murder had had on the victim's family and friends. Beginning with the statement "Power, not reason, is the new currency of this Court's decision making," Marshall's dissent bitterly criticized the majority opinion. Although the Warren Court, whose work Marshall had endorsed and contributed to during the 1960s, was not averse to overruling precedents, Marshall believed that those cases were different: old rules that either did not work or were inconsistent with later developments had been displaced. In *Payne*, by contrast, Marshall believed that the only change that had taken place between 1987 and 1991 was the makeup of the Court. To have constitutional law turn on the personalities of the judges was, in Marshall's view, inconsistent with the ideal of the rule of law.

Marshall died at Bethesda Naval Hospital in Maryland. Many tributes noted that he would have deserved a major place in histories of constitutional law even had he not served on the Supreme Court, because his efforts as chief lawyer for the NAACP in leading the Court to restructure constitutional law with regard to race was as important a contribution as any in modern history. Marshall made fewer contributions to constitutional law as a justice, largely because he was not part of the Court's more conservative majority, but his passionate voice for the poor and for African Americans resonated in his dissenting opinions, and he remained an inspiration to those who believed in the possibility of achieving justice through the Constitution.

FURTHER READING
Marshall's professional papers, along with a small number of personal papers, are collected in the NAACP Papers and the Thurgood Marshall Papers, both in the Manuscript Division of the Library of Congress.

Davis, Michael, and Hunter Clark. *Thurgood Marshall: Warrior at the Bar, Rebel on the Bench*, rev. ed. (1994).

Kluger, Richard. *Simple Justice* (1975)

Rowan, Carl. *Dream Makers, Dream Breakers: The World of Justice Thurgood Marshall* (1993)

Thurgood Marshall Commemorative Issue. *Howard Law Journal* vol. 35 (1991): 1–114.

"A Tribute to Justice Thurgood Marshall," *Harvard Law Review* 105 (Nov. 1991): 23–76.

"Tribute to Justice Thurgood Marshall," *Stanford Law Review* 44 (Summer 1992): 1213–1299.

Tushnet, Mark. *Making Civil Rights Law: Thurgood Marshall and the Supreme Court, 1936–1961* (1994)

Tushnet, Mark. *Making Constitutional Law: Thurgood Marshall and the Supreme Court, 1961–1991* (1997)

Obituaries: *New York Times* and *Washington Post*, 25 Jan. 1993.

This entry is taken from the *American National Biography* and is published here with the permission of the American Council of Learned Societies.

MARK TUSHNET

Marshall-Linnemeier, Lynn (1954–), photographer, painter, and writer, was born in Southern Pines, North Carolina, to a domestic worker and a musician. Marshall-Linnemeier began painting as a child; though her father was an amateur photographer, she did not pick up the camera until she was in her early thirties. After attending Spelman College, Marshall-Linnemeier transferred to the Atlanta College of Art, the Southeast's oldest private college of art. The year before she graduated Marshall-Linnemeier worked with Jackson State University, the Center for the Study of Southern Culture at the University of Mississippi, and the Center for Documentary Studies at Duke University on a collaborative project titled Mississippi Self-Portrait. For this, she traveled throughout Mississippi to gather photographs and narratives from local families in order to create a visual archive of southern, black histories. In 1990 Marshall-Linnemeier graduated with honors, a BFA in Photography and a personally invented medium she called "illuminated photography." This mixed-media form integrates traditional photography, painting, and text as a contemporary method of storytelling.

Two years after graduating Marshall-Linnemeier continued her anthropological art with a project about Reynoldstown, an historic Atlanta neighborhood that was settled by freed slaves who came to the city to work on the railroads. She photographed Reynoldstown residents and painted futurist environments over the original backgrounds. Based on this work she was awarded the 1994 Lila Wallace-Reader's Digest Arts International Travel grant for a three-month project in Adelaide, Australia. Like the Mississippi Self-Portrait project, the work in Australia involved photographing local people; here it was southern Australia's aborigines, whose mythology Marshall-Linnemeier studied. Upon returning from Australia, Marshall-Linnemeier joined the Arts in the Atlanta Project as an arts educator. She taught children illuminated photography to help them improve communication skills and develop self-esteem and pride in their communities.

The 1996 Centennial Olympic Games generated Marshall-Linnemeier's second commissioned work. Hartsfield Jackson International Airport in Atlanta commissioned her to create a permanent installation, which she titled *A Guide to Juke in Honor of the Olympics.*

In 1999 Marshall-Linnemeier became one of two artists to participate in Georgia's Fulton County Arts Council's and Artists in Residence International's pilot project in South Africa. She and MILDRED THOMPSON, an abstract expressionist painter who graduated from Howard University and worked as an associate editor of the acclaimed, Atlanta-based visual arts journal *Arts Papers,* traveled to the Caversham Centre for Artists and Writers in Balgowan, South Africa. The fellowship with Caversham, South Africa's first independent fine arts press, provided Marshall-Linnemeier with a printmaking residency as part of the Hourglass Project. She, along with fourteen other artists from around the world, mounted an exhibit of the work made during the residency period. The culminating exhibit, titled The Hourglass Project: A Women's Vision, was first displayed in Atlanta in January 2000. Two years later Marshall-Linnemeier became the only Atlanta artist to be included in

the international exhibit Testimony Through Art, curated by the photographer Roland Freeman, organized by the Group for Cultural Documentation, and displayed at the APEX Museum. The exhibit included work that sought to testify to the women's fight for peace and justice in their war-torn, patriarchal societies. She was also part of a group exhibition with Sistagraphy, an Atlanta-based collective of African American women. The show, A Slave Speaks of Silence/Silence Speaks, was originally mounted as a solo exhibition at Clark Atlanta University in 2001.

In addition to making and teaching art Marshall-Linnemeier lectured on various sociological topics related to race, class, and gender in America. One noteworthy and highly influential research area for Marshall-Linnemeier was the life of ANNA MURRAY DOUGLASS, a free African American woman and FREDERICK DOUGLASS's first wife. Like Marshall-Linnemeier's earlier areas of scholarly and artistic interest, the Anna Murray Douglass story represented the historical and sociological misrepresentation of and the absence of African American women from America's cultural canon. From this research was born a "biographical installation" about the "secret" life of Anna Murray Douglass. Influenced by her visit to Haiti just before the 2004 coup, Marshall-Linnemeier references Haitian Vodoun practices in the installation, titled *The Secret Journals of Anna Murray Douglass.* The piece is composed of several small, colorfully painted wooden box altars that include various ephemera; each altar depicts what Marshall-Linnemeier imagined Anna Murray Douglass's personal journals would reveal.

For her art and community work, Marshall-Linnemeier won numerous awards. Most notable were a Southern Arts Foundation/National Endowment for the Arts Regional Fellowship in Photography and a National Endowment for the Arts Entrepreneurial Program Fellowship, a Georgia Council for the Arts Individual Artist Grant, and numerous residencies in America and abroad. Even as she traveled extensively to mount exhibitions and lecture on key social issues, Marshall-Linnemeier remained close to the local communities of Metro Atlanta.

FURTHER READING

Janich, Kathy. "Faces to Watch: For Versatile Visual Artist, Creativity Is 'What We Are.'" *Atlanta Journal-Constitution,* 26 May 2002.

CRYSTAL AM NELSON

Martin, Archie Alexander "A. A." and Nancy Candler Martin (15 Sept. 1857–29 Feb. 1960) and (22 May 1855?–17 May 1947), were former slaves, housing rights advocates, humanitarians, and leaders of a pioneering family of black Iowans. Nancy was born in Newman, Georgia, to Jake and Angeline Candler, later spelled Chandler. According to family lore passed on from Angeline Candler to her daughter, the family had been slaves of the family of Asa Candler, the Coca-Cola magnate. Nancy passed this and other stories on to her children. One of five siblings, Archie was born in Wilmington, North Carolina, to George Martin, a minister, and Julia Martin. Little is known about the Martins' lives in the period immediately following emancipation. Both embraced Christianity, but neither was afforded the opportunity to attend school. Nancy taught herself to count and to read and write. Archie, however, was only able to write his name, and he apprenticed in plastering as a young man in North Carolina.

By 1887 Archie was established as a plasterer in Austell, Georgia, where he married Nancy, widow of Richard Simmons, already the mother of four, and a restaurateur. By 1900 Archie and Nancy had eight more children. They stressed the importance of education and hard work to their children.

Nancy's small corner restaurant, limited to stand-up window service only, was a landmark, serving both black and white customers. It attracted white Methodist worshippers attending church camps in nearby Lithia Springs, and ill people seeking cures in the medicinal waters at resorts in Austell. White physicians David and Jennie Ghrists, vacationing from Ames, Iowa, dined there, and, impressed by the entrepreneur, promised her higher wages to work for them. Nancy accepted the Ghristses' offer, moving to Ames in 1913. Archie and the children followed her in 1915. In Ames the Chicago and Northwestern (CNW) Railway Company hired him as assistant yardmaster. In 1910, according to the U.S. Decennial Census of Story County, only five of Ames's 4,223 residents were black. The town's principal institution, Iowa State College (now Iowa State University), enrolled 1,723 students (Ross, 422). Between 1894 and 1906, the college graduated two blacks, and in 1914, it graduated one other African American. Black churches, service organizations, and businesses in Ames were nonexistent, and blacks and whites were not socially integrated. Despite being admitted to attend the college, blacks were treated differently—subtly and overtly—but they considered life in Ames more comfortable and opportunities greater than in the South. By 1920 when, according to the census, fifty-one blacks lived in Story County, the Martins formed the core of the black community. Their house, built by sons Archie Jr., Robert, and Paul, stood on Lincoln Way, Ames's major thoroughfare. Black students, among them the future educator and scientist SAMUEL MASSIE, came to them for advice and housing. In notes for his autobiography co-written with ROBERT HAYDEN, Massie said that the Martins owned the only place in Ames where blacks could find housing. Blacks could enroll and attend the college, but could live on campus only with other blacks.

For decades, particularly during the 1930s to the 1950s, the Martins would have been considered deans, residence directors, and counselors, opening their home to male students while their daughter Nellie Martin Shipp and her husband, John Shipp Sr., opened their home to female students. The precise number of students they housed is unknown, but, between 1920 and 1960, Story County's black population leapt from 51 to 127 (Silag, 41)—possibly indicating a rise in the college's black enrollment, especially after World War II.

Although the Martins strived to help all the black students, they could not house them all in their two-story clapboard home. Archie thus made an appointment with R. A. Pearson, the college's president from 1912 to 1926 and convinced him to house blacks in the dormitories. Pearson agreed to house blacks on an equal basis with other students, but Archie learned later that blacks still suffered from housing discrimination at the college. Following further meetings between Martin and Pearson, black students began to have an easier time finding housing on campus. Exactly when the college officially integrated its housing is unknown, perhaps by the late 1940s or early 1950s, but the Martins' housing arrangements are cited as factors in black students coming to Ames to attend school. Ames Mayor Ted Tedesco has noted that "if the Martin family had not been willing to house black students, they probably would not have come to Ames" (Sullivan). Former students housed by the Martins, including the contractor Herbert DeCosta Jr., owner of a *Black Enterprise* magazine "Top 100 Businesses in the Nation," and Dr. James Bowman, former Greater Des Moines Public Schools assistant superintendent, also remarked on the value of the mentoring received in the Martin home. Martin descendants became scientists, inventors, entrepreneurs, engineers, Ph.D. educators, lawyers, doctors/health care professionals, and a high-ranking military officer.

Potentially eligible for inclusion on the National Register of Historic Places, the Martin home has been a haven and cultural touchstone for Caribbean, African, and African Americans matriculating at Iowa State College. The home also served as the unofficial chapter house for black fraternity Kappa Alpha Psi. Many distinguished African American guests or boarders included GEORGE WASHINGTON CARVER; the scientist Dr. Samuel Massie; Dr. FREDERICK PATTERSON, the founder of the United Negro College Fund; Dr. HUBERT B. CROUCH, co-founder of the National Institute of Science and grandson-in-law of Nancy and Archie Martin; Dr. HaroldReasby, the superintendent of Edmonds and Monroe Washington School Districts; Dr. Walter H. Pattillo Jr., Biology Professor, North Carolina Central University, Durham, and great-grandson of WALTER A. PATTILLO, the principal leader of the black Populists of nineteenth-century North Carolina; and Don Smith, a former *Seattle Times* reporter.

In 2002, decades after the Martins died (Nancy in 1947 at age ninety-two, Archie in 1960 at age 102), the city of Ames erected the Nancy and Archie Martin Pier in their honor. In 2004 the State of Iowa Board of Regents named a new $23 million dormitory Martin Hall, honoring the couple's contributions to black students and the university.

FURTHER READING

Information about the Martins is housed in the Iowa State University Library/University Archives, Ames, Iowa, and in the Farwell T. Brown Photographic Archive, in the Ames (Iowa) Public Library.

Brown, Farwell T. *Ames, The Early Years in Word and Picture, From Marsh to Modern City* (1993).

Massie, Dr. Samuel P., with Dr. Robert C. Hayden. *CATALYST: The Autobiography of an American Chemist, Dr. Samuel P. Massie* (2000).

Hill, Thomas, Iowa State University, Vice President, Student Affairs. *Memo to Gregory Geoffroy, President, Iowa State University, 7 July 2004.* Iowa State University Library/University Archives.

Ross, Earle D. *A History of Iowa State College of Agriculture and the Mechanical Arts* (1942).

Silag, Bill, Susan Koch-Bridgford, and Hal Chase, eds. *Outside In: African American History in Iowa, 1838–2000* (2001).

Sullivan, Elizabeth. "Martins Honored for Housing Black Students." *Iowa State Daily*, 8 Feb. 2002.

Sullivan, Elizabeth. "Pier Honoring Martins Revealed." *Iowa State Daily*, 11 Feb. 2002.

Obituary: Martin, Archie Alexander. *Ames Daily Tribune*, 29 Feb. 1960. *Ames Daily Tribune*, 17 May 1947.

DEBRA A. VARNADO

Martin, Graham Edward (18 Jan. 1917–9 May 2006), naval officer, was born in Tobacco Port, Tennessee, the son of Charles, a tobacco farmer, and Carrie Martin; he had two sisters and one brother. For the first few years of his life, Martin lived on a farm in Tennessee, near the Cumberland River. When Martin was about five or six years old, his father died. Because she was unable to keep up the farm, his mother moved to Indianapolis, Indiana, where she became a seamstress. Graham Martin, by then seven or eight, went with his mother, while his siblings remained in Tennessee. He attended segregated public schools and had to deal with the Jim Crow practices of his new home city. For instance, blacks had to sit in the balconies of movie theaters, and the sports teams on which Martin played were not allowed to compete against teams from local all-white schools.

As he recalled in an oral history many years later, he was initially a poor student and was involved in juvenile delinquency. Because Martin's mother's work prevented her from exercising adequate supervision over her son, a judge directed that Martin be placed in an orphans' home. He spent nearly eight years in the orphanage. As he later observed, "That turned out to be my salvation" (Stillwell, 6). His fourth-grade teacher took an interest in him, encouraging him to behave and apply himself to his studies. The discipline he received in the orphans' home and the positive reinforcement in school made all the difference, and from then on he did well in his studies and began reading voraciously. He took his improved study habits with him to Indianapolis's all-black Crispus Attucks High School. In high school Martin was selected as president of several student organizations, among them the student council, French club, and his graduating class.

In 1937 he graduated from high school after being an all-state player in football, and earned an academic scholarship to Indiana University. At Indiana, as a 193-pound tackle, Martin made the varsity team, coached by Alvin "Bo" McMillin. Most of his playing time was in road games rather than those at home in front of the university's faculty, students, and alumni. Martin earned his bachelor's degree in History in 1941 and that same year married Alma Patterson, a graduate of Kentucky State

College. They would have one daughter, Elayne G. Lewis. Alma Martin died in December 1998.

Martin went on to Howard University, where he earned a master's degree in History by writing a thesis on the Underground Railroad for fugitive slaves who used Indiana as a pathway to freedom in the nineteenth century. He subsequently received a second master's degree, in Education, from Indiana University in 1954.

In 1942 Martin enlisted in the navy, which that same year opened its general service ratings to black sailors; previously they had been almost completely confined to being cooks and servants for officers. Martin went through recruit training at the segregated Camp Robert Smalls at Great Lakes, Illinois, and was himself subsequently made part of the training staff. In 1943, as a tackle, he was the lone black player on the Great Lakes Naval Training Station team, a squad that was considered the equal of the best college teams in the country. In January 1944, at Camp Robert Smalls, Martin was one of sixteen black sailors chosen from a pool of approximately 100,000 to take part in the navy's first-ever training course for black officers. He was among the few in the group with a postgraduate degree. In two and a half months, the sixteen men went through a cram course that included training in such areas as navigation, communications, gunnery, propulsion machinery, seamanship, naval history, and the navy disciplinary system. At the conclusion in March 1944 Martin was among twelve men commissioned as Naval Reserve ensigns; one other man became a warrant officer. Years later these pioneers were retroactively titled the "Golden Thirteen." The other three men also passed the course but were not commissioned.

Even with their new commissions, the men faced discrimination both within the navy and in the civilian world. In June 1944, in Chicago, Martin and his wife, Alma, sought to eat in a restaurant. The proprietor served them but put laxative in their food.

Martin was initially stationed at Great Lakes to aid in training black sailors. Subsequently he served in a yard patrol craft and yard oiler in San Francisco. Even though he had received training to qualify him as a seagoing officer, Martin was assigned to craft small enough to be run by all-black crews rather than to a fleet ship. Martin later served in Hawaii and Eniwetok Atoll in the Marshall Islands as an athletic training officer. On Eniwetok he was also in charge of all-black stevedore gangs and served as division officer for his men. His final navy jobs, prior to leaving active service in 1946, were as a public information officer at Great Lakes and in Washington, D.C. While he was in the navy, he spent some of his off-duty time as a semi-professional football player.

Martin's goal in seeking higher education had been to serve as professor and later president of a traditionally black college. Upon leaving the service in 1946, he joined the faculty of Bluefield State College in West Virginia. He was an assistant professor of history and also coached the football and basketball teams. In 1947 he moved back to his hometown and began work at his alma mater, Crispus Attucks High School, as a history teacher, and remained there until his retirement in 1982. For the majority of those years he was also coach of both the football and baseball teams. Recalling how his education had been given a boost by the attention and encouragement he had received in school, Martin passed that gift on to his students during the many years he taught. He took as his guide a motto he had seen on a building at Indiana University—that it is the obligation of a teacher both to instruct and inspire. In his later years, as the Golden Thirteen held reunions and met with later generations of black naval officers, he continued to serve as an inspiring role model. He died in Indianapolis.

FURTHER READING

"Reminiscences of Graham E. Martin, Member of the Golden Thirteen." Transcript of U.S. Naval Institute oral history (1989).

Stillwell, Paul, ed. *The Golden Thirteen: Recollections of the First Black Naval Officers* (1993).

Obituary: *Indianapolis Star*, 12 May 2006.

PAUL STILLWELL

Martin, John B. (c.1890?–1973?), dentist, politician, and Negro Baseball League officer, was born in Memphis, Tennessee. A member of a prominent Memphis family with four brothers who all played roles in baseball in that city and beyond, John B. Martin, a dentist, was a co-owner and a club officer of the Memphis Red Sox and the Chicago American Giants. He also served as the president of three different leagues: the Negro Southern League (NSL), the Negro American League (NAL), and the Negro Dixie League.

Together with his brother, B. B. Martin, also a dentist, John B. Martin took over the Memphis Red Sox in the late 1920s from funeral director Robert S. Lewis and built a ballpark they called Martin Stadium. Martin also owned a hotel next to the park and operated the concession stand.

Beyond baseball, Martin also served the community as a pharmacist, dentist, real estate agent, Republican political leader, and funeral parlor operator. Meanwhile, brother A. T. Martin worked as a general practitioner for more than a half century and was affiliated with the Red Sox organization for more than twenty-five years, while brother William S. Martin was also an officer for the Red Sox and served as president of the NSL and an officer in the NAL.

A personal crisis in 1940 abruptly interrupted John B. Martin's rising fortunes. After spearheading local backing of Republican presidential candidate Wendell Willkie, Martin was ordered to terminate all political activities or face retribution. His light-skinned wife had also offended Memphis commissioner of public safety Joseph Boyle by breaking racial etiquette and sitting in the white section at a local circus. Consequently, the Memphis police department initiated an ongoing campaign of intimidation, searching all customers of Martin's drugstore while claiming that the establishment was a center for illegal narcotics and stolen goods. Despite support from the Memphis daily press, Martin left the city to relocate in Chicago.

Upon his arrival in Chicago he became involved with the Chicago American Giants baseball club, and he soon matched and even surpassed his earlier achievements in Memphis. Earning a substantial income from investments in a life insurance company, real estate, and an undertaking establishment, Martin became one of the richest blacks in the country, reportedly worth more than $250,000 by 1949. Meanwhile, with the Chicago American Giants in increasing disarray following the loss of their park in December 1940, Martin became part of a core of investors who assumed control of the franchise during 1941 and eventually obtained controlling interest from owner Horace Hall.

Martin resumed political activity in Chicago as well. He advanced within the Republican Party in Chicago, receiving nominations for local offices in 1942 and 1944 despite eventual defeats. In 1946 he finally succeeded, becoming the first black to be elected to the nine-member Sanitary District Trustee Board of Chicago, a lucrative position reportedly paying $10,000 annually for a six-year term. Martin was a dedicated figure whose involvement in black baseball seemingly complemented his political aspirations. Yet Martin often appeared unwilling to confront the difficulties in black baseball and was content to keep the leagues running in their imperfect state. Notably, Martin made no attempt to divest himself of his holdings in his league teams while serving as president.

Martin's legacy in baseball was an attempt to bring discipline to the sometimes unruly teams of the Negro Leagues. He cracked down on teams such as Cincinnati's Ethiopian Clowns. He wanted them to play under their real names instead of the burlesque names adopted by the players and to stop painting their faces and play straight baseball. Unfortunately, despite employing several capable ballplayers, the Clowns continued to emphasize comedy during their appearances, featuring performers including Richard King ("King Tut") and later a juggler and a midget. Ironically, as black baseball reached its financial peak, it remained firmly bound to the whims of whites. Most league officials recognized this fact, including Martin, who acknowledged that it was impossible for the clubs to operate unless they played in the big league parks.

During World War II, some observers questioned whether professional baseball could survive the loss of more players to the military or defense work, but Martin remained confident, noting that most of the players either worked day shifts in the defense plants or had medical discharges. In addition, Martin openly expressed support of integration, noting that he could not see where it would injure black baseball.

However, black professional baseball clearly faced a hopeless future by 1951, after four consecutive years of steady deterioration. Most of the country's best black players, including future major leaguers John Roseburo, Maury Wills, and Frank Robinson, proceeded directly from high school or college into organized baseball during the early 1950s, rather than to the Negro Leagues. Although Martin continued to insist that the NAL offered superior pay and a better chance for advancement than lower-level minor leagues, black franchises began to struggle to find capable players, and the inferior caliber of play was soon evident to most observers. By 1959 even the eternally optimistic Martin admitted that attendance had become horrible. In 1963 the NAL finally collapsed, a development that concerned few African American fans, many of whom were unaware of the league's continued existence.

FURTHER READING
Heaphy, Leslie A. *The Negro Leagues, 1869–1960* (2003).
Hogan, Lawrence D. *Shades of Glory: The Negro Leagues and the Story of African-American Baseball* (2006).

Lanctot, Neil. *Negro League Baseball: The Rise and Ruin of a Black Institution* (2004).

LUKE NICHTER

Martin, John Sella (Sept. 1832–Aug. 1876), minister and abolitionist, was born into slavery in Charlotte, North Carolina, the son of Winnifred, a biracial slave, and the nephew of his mother's owner. He had one sister. In an eighteen-year period he was sold eight times. Martin taught himself to read and write. In 1856 he used those skills and his employment as a boatman on the Mississippi River to escape to Cairo, Illinois.

Martin settled in Chicago, where in 1856 he met Mary Ann Shadd (MARY ANN CAMBERTON SHADD CARY) and began his career as an abolitionist. That same year Shadd appointed him as an agent for the *Provincial Freeman*. He eventually moved to Detroit, where he spent nine months studying for the ministry. Martin worked diligently toward perfecting his speaking ability. He quickly earned a reputation for being a natural orator.

Martin served briefly in 1858 as minister of the Michigan Street Baptist Church in Buffalo, New York, before moving on to Boston. Boston was a major center of black activism, with a number of individuals participating visibly in antislavery work. Martin was one of the few ministers who did so.

The pastor of Boston's Tremont Temple, the Reverend Isaac Smith Kalloch, invited Martin to temporarily fill his pulpit in 1859. Kalloch's church was one of the few integrated churches in Boston. That same year Martin became pastor of the First Independent Baptist Church, also known as the Joy Street Baptist Church. The church was also called "abolition church" because it was the site of local antislavery gatherings and black community organizations.

While serving at this church, Martin developed his reputation as a powerful orator and militant antislavery speaker. He endorsed slave insurrections, noting that the only difference between the American Revolution and John Brown's act was that for once someone had used his resources for black men instead of white men. Martin once stated that it was providential that he was born on the same day that NAT TURNER was hanged. He envisioned himself as a replacement for Turner and often made him the subject of his speeches.

Martin took issue with FREDERICK DOUGLASS's assertion that slaves were apathetic and cowardly and would not fight for their freedom. Martin argued in public addresses and in articles in the *Liberator* that blacks had not fully participated in Brown's raid because they had learned hard lessons about the treachery of white men. Blacks felt that they could not trust whites, even when a white person came as a deliverer. Martin also supported the African Civilization Society's emigration program as a legitimate response to America's racist obstinacy, although he would abandon his emigrationist stance just prior to the Civil War.

Martin was an ardent defender of black people, particularly when accusations were made regarding laziness and the inability to learn. He believed that there was no such thing as natural inferiority. The allegation of black inferiority was a red herring concocted to confuse the issue of equality.

In 1861 Martin traveled to Britain to help build support for the Union. In 1862 he returned to Boston with $2,500 to purchase his sister and her two children from a Georgia plantation. After some time he was able to buy their freedom. He eventually resigned as pastor of Joy Street Baptist and took a position with a congregation near London. He used the opportunity to continue his travels and garner support for the Union cause.

Martin returned for a brief time to the United States in 1864, becoming pastor of Shiloh Presbyterian Church in New York City. His transition from Baptist to Presbyterian was facilitated by his association with the Congregationalist chapel in London.

While Martin was living in New York, Abraham Lincoln was assassinated. Martin was appalled at the treatment given to blacks who wanted to participate in the funeral procession march. Many blacks gathered at his church to protest the actions of the city's governing board that had barred blacks from participating. Although the War Department insisted that blacks be allowed to participate, they were placed so far back in the line that Lincoln's coffin had left the city by the time they joined the procession. Martin wrote a letter to the editor of the *New York Evening Post* denouncing the racist actions of the council, but the paper refused to print it.

Martin began work with the American Missionary Association (AMA) in 1864. He traveled to Britain on a fund-raising mission on its behalf. Between 1864 and 1868 he was able to raise thousands of dollars to aid freedmen in the South. As a result of his success, he was put in charge of the AMA's solicitation efforts for all of Europe.

Returning to the United States in 1868, Martin became pastor of the Fifteenth Street Presbyterian Church in Washington, D.C. He became actively involved in the black labor movement, serving as editor of the *New Era*, the official journal of the Colored National Labor Union. He was also elected to the Executive Board of the National Colored Convention.

Between 1870 and 1876 Martin had difficulty finding stable employment. Consequently, he found himself struggling financially. He was appointed as a special agent with the post office in Mobile, a position he held for only a few months. In 1870 he moved to New Orleans, where he worked with the black Republicans in Louisiana. He was named coeditor of the Republican paper the *New National Era*. After the paper merged with another in 1873, Martin was unemployed.

Martin eventually found a position in 1874 as a Treasury Department special agent in Shieldsboro, Mississippi. He held the position for a short time, then moved back to New Orleans. He went to Massachusetts briefly to live with his wife, Sarah, whom he had married in 1858, and their daughter, but he returned to New Orleans in 1876. His family had not lived with him on a permanent basis since they had resided in Washington from 1868 to 1870.

Martin was frequently beset with painful urinary infections. He also had attacks of pleurisy, neuralgia, ague, liver disorder, and catarrhal fever. These ailments often immobilized him and interrupted his work and travel schedule. To relieve his pain and symptoms, he was given prescriptions for opium and laudanum, drugs to which he became addicted. He was found by a servant in his bedroom in New Orleans suffering from irregular breathing. Next to his bed was a half-empty vial of laudanum. Efforts to revive him failed, and he died soon afterward. Autopsy reports revealed little as to the actual cause of death. The evidence suggests that, because of his financial problems, inability to find work, and estrangement from his family, Martin became despondent and committed suicide.

FURTHER READING

Pease, Jane H., and William H. Pease. *They Who Would Be Free* (1974).

Quarles, Benjamin. *Black Abolitionists* (1969)

Ripley, C. Peter, ed. *Black Abolitionists Papers*, vol. 5 (1985–92).

This entry is taken from the *American National Biography* and is published here with the permission of the American Council of Learned Societies.

MAMIE E. LOCKE

Martin, Lazarus "Lesra" (1963–), lawyer, author, and motivational speaker, was born in Queens, New York, to Earl Martin (onetime singer with the doo wop group, the Del Vikings), and his wife Alma Martin. Lesra Martin had seven younger brothers and sisters. The family eventually moved to the Brooklyn neighborhoods of Beauford-Stuyvesant and Bushwick. The Martin family lived in poverty with seven other families in a four-storey house that had long been condemned, and Lesra Martin was illiterate until he was sixteen because he began working at the age of ten to help support his family. One of his brothers died of AIDS in prison after being convicted of manslaughter, while another brother was murdered after intervening in a fight.

Martin's life, however, changed radically at the age of sixteen. A group of Canadian business owners, living in a commune, visited New York City to test a gas-saving device. There, the group, including Sam Chaiton and Terry Swinton, met Martin—who was working in a summer job program—and recognized his potential. The Canadians held antiwar and anticapitalism beliefs, and also identified with the struggles of racism and discrimination against African Americans in America. They convinced Martin's parents to allow the commune to bring him to Toronto, Canada, in September 1979 to fund his education and provide him with better health care. While still able to keep in touch and visit his family, Martin was cared for by the commune, and he graduated from high school in Canada in 1983. He was educated at home by members of the commune for two years, with an additional year at a public school. Martin received his B.A. in Anthropology from the University of Toronto in 1988. He then began studying for a master's degree in Sociology from Dalhousie University in Halifax. Martin next campaigned for admittance to law schools, and was eventually admitted to Dalhousie University, earning his law degree in 1997. He married Cheryl Tynes in 1998.

Martin is most often associated with the release of middleweight boxer Rubin "Hurricane" Carter from prison. Carter, himself from a troubled background, stood wrongfully accused of the murder of a white bar owner and two white patrons at the Lafayette Bar and Grill in Paterson, New Jersey. Carter, sentenced to three consecutive life terms, was imprisoned mostly at Trenton State Prison. Martin first became interested in Carter's case after reading Carter's autobiography, *The Sixteenth Round,* believing that Carter's fate could have easily been his own. Martin wrote a letter to the imprisoned Carter in September 1980. Carter replied, and the pair exchanged several letters. Martin first visited Carter around Christmas 1980, the first visit Carter had received (other than from attorneys) in over five years. A group from the commune, including Martin, again visited Carter in prison in February 1981. The group also sent gifts to Carter, such as food and a robe, to help ease his time in prison. While Martin mainly stayed in Canada to focus on his education, he maintained contact with Carter, and a few of the Canadians moved to New Jersey to provide emotional support to Carter, and financial and legal aid to Carter's lawyers. The commune members examined court documents related to Carter's case and performed paralegal tasks in an effort to exonerate him. With this help, a proceeding commenced in February 1983 that ultimately resulted in Carter's release in 1985 after nineteen years total in prison. Federal District Judge H. Lee Sarokin ruled that the case had been tainted by racial prejudice and corrupted evidence. Upon his release, Carter spent his first Thanksgiving dinner with the Martin family in Brooklyn.

In 1985 Martin began dating women outside of the commune, which was against the rules, and he was forced to leave the commune for a brief period. However, he returned to live in the commune's house in 1993, when he left the University of Dalhousie before studying for his law degree. Carter and Martin would reunite, with Martin acting as Carter's companion when Carter began a tour to help others who had been wrongfully imprisoned. The pair again parted ways when Martin decided to return to Dalhousie University and focus on his law education. After graduating in 1997, Martin established himself as a crown prosecutor in Kamloops, British Columbia. Carter's plight (and Martin's assistance) was dramatized in the 1999 film *The Hurricane,* starring Denzel Washington, though the film took liberties with the legal proceedings involved in Carter's case. Martin then embarked on a career in motivational speaking, and also served as an advocate for literacy, appearing on the *Oprah Winfrey Show* and in front of the General Assembly of the United Nations.

FURTHER READING

Hirsch, James. *The Miraculous Journey of Rubin Carter* (2000).

Chaiton, Sam, and Terry Swinton. *Lazarus and the Hurricane: The Freeing of Rubin "Hurricane" Carter* (1999).

Wice, Paul. *Rubin "Hurricane" Carter and the American Justice System* (2000).

KRISTAL L. ENTER

Martin, Louis E. (18 Nov. 1912–27 Jan. 1997), journalist and Democratic Party activist, was born Louis Emanuel Martin Jr. in Shelbyville, Tennessee, the only son of Louis E. Martin, a physician, and Willa (Hill) Martin. When Louis Jr. was four the Martins moved from his mother's hometown in Tennessee to Savannah, Georgia, whose climate reminded the boy's father of his hometown of Santiago, Cuba. Martin later recalled that he became a civil rights advocate at the age of seven when he witnessed an incident in his father's medical office. Informed that a white man wanted to see him, Dr. Martin, who had been napping, immediately rushed to meet the white man. "I always regretted that my old man got up," Louis told an interviewer decades later. But in showing that "just being a white man made a hell of a lot of difference," the episode also taught young Louis about the centrality of race in American life. From that point on he "kept looking for [racial] signs and studying people closely" in an effort to "understand how crazy this society is" (Poinsett, 1). Although he was initially a mediocre student, one of the nuns at Saint Benedict's Roman Catholic grade school in Savannah encouraged Louis to work harder at his schoolwork after she read one of his essays on Saint Francis of Assisi. With strong encouragement and discipline at school and fear of even stronger discipline by his father, Louis studied hard and was valedictorian of his ninth-grade class. Since there was no accredited high school for blacks in Savannah, Martin's parents sent him back to Tennessee to study at Nashville's Fisk Academy, which was associated with Fisk University. There, unlike in Savannah, he learned about African American history and was also exposed to the writings of Harlem Renaissance authors like CLAUDE MCKAY. The most important intellectual influence during Martin's high school years, however, was Malcolm Nurse, a Jamaican-born Fisk University undergraduate who later adopted the pseudonym GEORGE PADMORE and became a leading Pan-Africanist intellectual. When Fisk Academy was forced to close in 1929, Martin's senior year, he transferred to Pearl High School in Nashville, where he helped launch a student newspaper, the *Pearl High Voice,* before graduating in 1930.

Martin remained in Nashville, taking college classes at Fisk University, but he transferred to the University of Michigan in 1931, having saved enough money to pay his tuition of $127. One of only five black undergraduates on the Ann Arbor campus, Martin majored in English composition and got on well with white students, some of whom shared his increasingly cynical view of American democracy. Upon graduating in 1934 he traveled to Cuba, having informed his father that he would study medicine there, though in truth he planned to write a novel. Both plans were thwarted, however, when Cuba's military leader, Fulgencio Batista, closed the University of Havana following a student and faculty strike. Martin spent the rest of his time on the island playing table tennis and discussing politics and social inequality with young Cubans.

Martin returned to Ann Arbor to pursue graduate study in English in fall 1935, but after one year he left to work for the *Chicago Defender*, the Midwest's leading black newspaper. By June 1936, still only twenty-three, Martin was dispatched to Detroit to serve as editor and publisher of a new black newspaper in that city, the *Michigan Chronicle*, which was printed on the *Defender's* presses in Chicago. During the hectic first months of production—in which Martin was solely responsible for writing copy, building circulation, and securing advertising—he somehow found time to get married. In January 1937 he eloped with Gertrude Scott, a fellow Savannah native who was at that time teaching at Wilberforce University in Ohio. The couple would have five daughters, Trudy, Linda, Anita, Lisa, and Toni.

By 1940 Martin had established the *Chronicle* as Detroit's premier black newspaper, with a circulation of more than 15,000. The paper's editorials, penned by Martin, were strongly pro-organized labor, pro-Democrat, and pro-New Deal. That stance was initially opposed by the conservative and Republican black ministers who had long regarded themselves as the leaders of Detroit's black community and who had cultivated close ties with the anti-union Ford Motor Company. Martin also used the *Chronicle* to promote a biracial, liberal-labor political coalition in Detroit. In 1936 the paper helped elect Michigan's first black state legislator, Charles C. Diggs Jr., and endorsed the efforts of the integrated, pro-civil rights United Auto Workers (UAW) in unionizing both the Chrysler and the Ford automobile plants.

Martin, Diggs, the NAACP, and the UAW also worked together successfully in 1942 to integrate a Detroit federal housing project, thereby alleviating a housing crisis caused by the migration of thousands of whites and African Americans into the city in search of war-related work. Despite these successes Martin was also aware of the city's deep-rooted racial tensions and warned of the potential for violence in an article, "Detroit Is Dynamite," published in *Life* magazine in August 1942. Ten months later

his warning was vindicated by the bloody Detroit riot that left thirty-four people dead, half of them African Americans killed by white policemen. Several of the victims had been shot in the back. The official state investigation of the riot absolved the police of any responsibility, however, and instead blamed Louis Martin's *Chronicle* editorials and the Detroit NAACP for instigating the riots.

Martin's prominent role in Detroit affairs did not go unnoticed. In 1944 WILLIAM L. DAWSON, the nation's only black congressman, invited him to direct the Democrats' national election campaign among black voters. The position provided Martin with an entrée into Washington politics. In addition to meeting President Franklin D. Roosevelt and members of his black cabinet, notably ROBERT WEAVER and WILLIAM HASTIE, Martin also befriended fellow journalists like TED POSTON. These connections proved useful in 1945 when Martin moved to New York City to start a newsmagazine, *Headlines and Pictures*, which focused on the happenings of noteworthy African Americans in politics, business, the entertainment industry, and sports. Although circulation reached 20,000, *Headlines and Pictures* was forced to close in 1947 because of the prohibitive cost of newsprint. Martin then began working as New York bureau chief of the *Chicago Defender* and then served as the *Defender's* editor in chief from 1950 until 1959.

In 1959 Martin took a sabbatical to work as an adviser to the Amalgamated Press, a newspaper company in Lagos, Nigeria, and he attended the official opening of the newly independent country's parliament in 1960. On returning to the United States in summer 1960 Martin accompanied Chief Ayo Rosiji, a high-ranking Nigerian official, on a tour of the United States.

While on that tour Martin was recruited by Pierre Salinger, Senator John F. Kennedy's press secretary, to join the Kennedy presidential campaign. Martin's job was to win over the black press to the Kennedy cause, a difficult task given Kennedy's lukewarm support of civil rights and his close ties to prominent segregationists, including the Alabama governor John Patterson. There was evidence, too, of growing black support for the Republican Party. Republican president Dwight D. Eisenhower had secured less than a quarter of the black vote in 1952 but won nearly 40 percent in 1956. Eisenhower's running mate, Richard Nixon, Kennedy's opponent in 1960, was thus well positioned to increase the GOP's share of the black vote. Nixon, however, ignored the entreaties of his main black adviser, E. FREDERIC MORROW, preferring instead to seek the Southern white vote. Though the Kennedys also feared losing Southern white votes, they agreed with Martin that a strong turnout by blacks in Northern cities like Chicago, Detroit, and Philadelphia could deliver several major states to the Democratic column.

Martin secured from his candidate a series of more positive statements on civil rights matters, which resulted in endorsements for Kennedy from most black newspapers. Martin also played a central role in persuading Kennedy to make a phone call to CORETTA SCOTT KING after her husband, MARTIN LUTHER KING JR., was arrested and imprisoned in a Georgia jail on trumped-up charges. Louis Martin launched a massive press campaign to publicize the phone call, which resulted in King's release, contrasting Kennedy's action with Nixon's failure to intervene. Anecdotal evidence suggests that Kennedy's concern for the civil rights leader persuaded many black Republicans, including King's own father, to abandon Nixon. Equally important was Martin's role in persuading to Kennedy to endorse the moral, as well as the economic and political, case for integration. As Martin had predicted and labored to achieve, a huge turnout by black voters in Illinois, New York, and other industrial states provided Kennedy with a slim margin of victory.

Following Kennedy's inauguration in January 1961, Martin was appointed as the first black deputy chairman of the Democratic National Committee. He held that position for the next eight years, serving as one of the leading civil rights advisers to both President Kennedy and his successor, Lyndon B. Johnson. Martin's key achievement was to stiffen the resolve of Kennedy administration officials who often wavered in their support of the civil rights movement. In 1963, for example, he persuaded Kennedy to support the March on Washington over the opposition of several aides. He also ensured that Kennedy's civil rights bill that year included a section prohibiting racial discrimination in all public accommodations.

Johnson's open support of civil rights and of antipoverty efforts made Martin's job as his election adviser in 1964 easier than it had been four years earlier. Martin nonetheless conducted the campaign as though it would be a close one and helped to secure for Johnson a remarkable 96 percent of the black vote. Working behind the scenes Martin helped engineer a series of high-level presidential appointments of African Americans, including ANDREW BRIMMER, the first black

member of the board of the Federal Reserve; A. LEON HIGGINBOTHAM, the first black member of the Federal Trade Commission; Weaver, the first black cabinet secretary; and, in 1967, THURGOOD MARSHALL, the first African American Supreme Court justice. Martin also brokered a meeting between Johnson and Martin Luther King Jr. to help repair relations between the two men, which had been harmed by the president's increasingly aggressive Vietnam policy and King's increasingly vocal opposition to that policy.

After Richard Nixon was inaugurated president in 1969, Martin returned to Chicago to edit the *Defender*. He maintained close ties with the Washington political establishment through the Joint Center for Political and Economic Studies, a black political think tank founded in 1970, and served as chairman of its board until 1978. That year he returned to the White House as a special assistant to President Jimmy Carter on minority hiring issues. He again played a pivotal role in securing a breakthrough African American appointment when Carter appointed CLIFFORD ALEXANDER as secretary of the U.S. Army. Carter's defeat by the conservative Republican Ronald Reagan in 1980, however, signaled an end to the liberal policies that Martin had championed for nearly five decades. Remaining in Washington he served on the board of the Joint Center and of Riggs Bank, and also as assistant vice president for communications at Howard University. Martin retired from active public life following a stroke in 1988, and he moved with his wife to Diamond Bar, California, where he died, at the age of eighty-four, in January 1997.

Five years before his death, Louis E. Martin's pioneering role in black politics was recognized by the Democratic National Committee, which honored him with the inaugural Lawrence F. O'Brien Award for services to the party. That the award was presented by the DNC's first African American chair, RON BROWN, was a fitting tribute to a man widely known as the godfather of black politics.

FURTHER READING

Information on Louis Martin's political career over several decades can be found in the presidential libraries of John F. Kennedy in Boston, Massachusetts, of Lyndon B. Johnson in Austin, Texas, and of Jimmy Carter in Atlanta, Georgia. There are also tapes and transcripts of ten oral history interviews conducted with Louis Martin between 1981 and 1987 in the Columbia University Oral History Collection in New York City.

Poinsett, Alex. *Walking with Presidents: Louis Martin and the Rise of Black Political Power* (1997)

STEVEN J. NIVEN

Martin, Roberta (12 Feb. 1907–18 Jan. 1969), gospel pianist, composer-arranger, and singer, was born Roberta Evelyn Winston in Helena, Arkansas, the daughter of William Winston and Anna (maiden name unknown). One of six children in the Winston household, Roberta showed an early proclivity for music. When only a toddler, she climbed onto the piano bench and picked out melodies that she had heard. This interest and talent was nurtured by the wife of her oldest brother, who became her first piano teacher.

When Martin was ten years old, her family moved from Arkansas to Chicago. She continued her piano studies with Mildred Bryant Jones in standard keyboard literature and pointed her career toward that of concert pianist or professional accompanist. She graduated from Wendell Phillips High School and was encouraged by Jones to pursue a career in music. Why Roberta chose "Martin" as her surname is not known.

Martin began playing for churches at an early age. Her first experience was at Pilgrim Baptist Church, where she served as pianist for the Sunday school. In 1932 she was invited by THOMAS A. DORSEY—the father of gospel music—and Theodore R. Frye to accept the position of pianist for Chicago's Ebenezer Baptist Church junior choir. Dorsey and Frye, longtime friends, worked together as pianist and director, respectively, for the Ebenezer adult choir. They had heard of Martin's talent and wanted her to play for the younger choir. She was apprehensive because this choir of young people sang only gospel songs. She auditioned with the one gospel song that she knew and was immediately hired.

Dorsey and Frye encouraged and guided Martin in her development of a gospel style of piano playing. In 1933 they assisted her in organizing her first gospel group, the Martin-Frye Quartet, which included the singers Robert Anderson, James Lawrence, Norsalus McKissick, Eugene Smith, and Willie Webb. The group was renamed the Roberta Martin Singers in 1936. By this time Martin had worked with choirs enough to know what type of sound she wanted. In the 1940s she made the quantum leap of combining male and female voices, and was a pioneer in the formulation of a mixed-voice choir. According to Pearl Williams-Jones, "The unique harmonic sound created by this particular voicing was mellow and smooth, with dynamic nuances that ebbed and flowed and a timing that was almost imperceptibly 'behind' the beat" (Reagon, 258). Martin's first female singers were Bessie Folk and DELOIS BARRETT CAMPBELL. Other talented singers were added later. Martin chose outstanding singers who could perform as soloists as well as blend in. This was the beginning of the Roberta Martin "sound," which in the mid-1940s was called "classic gospel." Martin's group established the sound benchmark against which future gospel choirs were measured.

Another of Thomas Dorsey's protégés, SALLIE MARTIN (no relation to Roberta Martin), helped to popularize gospel music through her singing, composing, arranging, and development of choruses. The two Martins operated as a team very briefly and called their chorus the Martin and Martin Gospel Singers. This merger did not last long because neither woman wanted to risk being overshadowed by the other. Dorsey, however, recognizing the talent of both Martins, promoted a gospel-singing contest between the two groups. The contest was held at DuSable High School in Chicago and played to a full house. The fifteen-cent admission charge did not dissuade hundreds from attending and set a precedent of paid admission for gospel concerts that continues today.

In 1939 Roberta Martin expanded her career to include music publishing. She had learned the business from Dorsey, who was one of the first publishers of gospel sheet music. Martin's publishing company thrived because those who heard her group wanted to purchase the arrangements so that they could sing them in their church choirs. Songwriters took their songs to Martin for arranging and publishing because they knew that the music would sell. The oral tradition of gospel music, with its florid piano ornamentation and vocal improvisation, is not easily committed to notation. This fact generated a need for recordings to supplement live performances. The Roberta Martin Singers recorded on the Apollo label and then the Savoy label, winning several gold records for extraordinary sales. People attended the concerts and purchased the sheet music and recordings so that they could imitate the Roberta Martin sound in their singing.

Because Martin was a trained musician who could read, write, and arrange music, she began to compose gospel songs, as well as arrange songs written by others. She arranged songs for other gospel greats, including JAMES CLEVELAND, Lucy Smith Collier, Willie Webb, and Robert Anderson. Martin's first composition, written in 1943, was the familiar "Try Jesus He Satisfies." During the 1940s the Roberta Martin Singers traveled widely and established a reputation as one of the most outstanding gospel choirs in the nation.

In 1947 Martin married James Austin and started a family. She decided to leave the travel circuit so that she could raise their son properly. She turned over the management of the group to Eugene Smith, who was best known for his narrative song introductions during concerts. Lucy Smith Collier, Martin's stepdaughter and protégé, having sung with the group and closely observed Martin's playing style, replaced her as the group's pianist. Austin focused his energies on the financial management of their publishing business so that Martin could spend time with their son and continue her gospel songwriting and arranging. Her compositions include "God Is Still on the Throne," "Have You Found a Friend," "He's Always Right There," "I Don't Mind," "Is There Anybody Here," "I'm Just Waiting on the Lord," "Let It Be," "No Other Help I Know," and "Teach Me Lord."

The Roberta Martin Singers continued to draw huge audiences on their tours. They headlined at the Los Angeles World's Greatest Gospel Caravan in 1959, received the annual Thomas A. Dorsey Award in New York in 1962, served as featured group at the New York Coliseum in 1963, and sang at Italy's Spoleto Festival of Two Worlds in 1963.

After thirty years of singing together, the group retired in 1966. During the Martin era the Singers performed on radio and television and in major concert halls, stadiums, and churches at home and abroad. Individuals who had sung with Martin's groups went on to forge for themselves prominent positions in the musical world. Chief among these were Archie Davis, who traveled widely as guest soloist with the Billy Graham Crusades; DINAH WASHINGTON, who was called the "Queen of Rhythm and Blues"; James Cleveland, a prolific gospel singer and composer who was called the "Crown Prince of Gospel"; and Della Reese, who was nominated for a Grammy Award in gospel music in 1987 and who enjoyed success in the popular music field.

When Martin died in Chicago, more than fifty thousand mourners attended her memorial service. During her lifetime she composed approximately seventy songs and arranged and published approximately 280. After Martin's death Austin continued the still-thriving Roberta Martin Publishing Company to ensure that Martin's songs remained accessible. In 1981 a Black History Month tribute was paid to Roberta Martin for her contributions to gospel music. This tribute was held at the Smithsonian Institution and included a concert series of Martin's songs sung by nine former Martin Singers and a colloquium featuring gospel scholars and colleagues of Martin's. This tribute to Roberta Martin served to highlight the legacy that as performer, composer-arranger, and pianist she left to the gospel community and to the world.

FURTHER READING

Heilbut, Anthony. *The Gospel Sound: Good News and Bad Times* (1971).

Reagon, Bernice Johnson, ed. *We'll Understand It Better By and By: Pioneering African American Gospel Composers* (1992).

Reagon, Bernice Johnson, and Linn Shapiro, eds. *Roberta Martin and the Roberta Martin Singers: The Legacy and the Music* (1981).

This entry is taken from the *American National Biography* and is published here with the permission of the American Council of Learned Societies.

MARY FRANCES EARLY

Martin, Sallie (20 Nov. 1895–18 June 1988), gospel singer, music publisher, and philanthropist, was born in the rural black hamlet of Pittfield, Georgia, to a farming family. Very little is known of her parents or her early life. As a young child she lost her father. She was raised by her grandparents and her mother, a gospel singer who toured small Southern churches. Sallie enjoyed singing at Pittfield's combination schoolhouse-Baptist church, although her formal education ended with eighth grade. When Sallie was sixteen, her mother also died. Sallie then moved to Atlanta in search of work and found jobs in childcare, housework, and laundry. After hearing the expressive, high-energy, frequently spontaneous singing style beloved in Pentecostal congregations since the 1890s, Martin joined the Fire Baptized Holiness Church. Her contralto voice's dramatic power soon made her a popular song leader.

In Atlanta she met and married Wallace Martin, also a Georgia native with Georgia-born parents, when he was seventeen years old and she was twenty. According to his World War I draft registration card, by September 1918, the couple had moved to Cleveland, Ohio, joining in the Great Migration of southern blacks who sought better jobs and living conditions in northern cities. He found work as a laborer. Records from the 1920 census indicate that the Martins were still in Cleveland. He was employed in a nuts-and-bolts factory and she was a homemaker. At some point during the 1920s, the Martins had their only child, a son. They also moved to Chicago in search of better work prospects. There Sallie Martin distinguished herself as a church soloist. In 1929, the year of her first recording, she left her husband, taking custody of their son. She later explained that she disapproved when he added gambling and liquor to the boarding and barbeque enterprises they operated together. Because of the Depression, Martin could not find any work except at a "contagious" hospital (a hospital for patients with tuberculosis).

During the 1930s the gospel songs of THOMAS A. DORSEY, the former pianist for GERTRUDE "MA" RAINEY and music director at Pilgrim Baptist Church, became popular among Chicago's black Protestant congregations. Sallie Martin decided to become a featured soloist with Dorsey. Initially he was put off by her bluntness, her untrained voice, her lack of interest in learning to read music, and her emotive Pentecostal style, which many Baptists considered undignified. Her charisma as a performer and zeal for ministry, however, finally persuaded him. In 1932 he invited her to join and eventually solo with a demonstration trio for his own compositions, which he self-published through the Dorsey House of Music.

Martin showed considerable flair for business as well as performance. She and Dorsey co-founded the National Convention of Gospel Choirs and Choruses (NCGCC) in 1932. From its founding until her death Martin remained vice president. She organized new member groups nationally and marketed Dorsey's sheet music to them; devised careful bookkeeping and inventory methods for his publishing firm; and organized an income-generating company music store and voice lesson program. Under her tutelage the Dorsey House of Music won both profits and national influence. Starting in 1937 Chicago radio station WLFL regularly broadcast Dorsey's University Gospel Singers. Martin and MAHALIA JACKSON were both soloists with this group. During the late 1930s Sallie Martin also performed with the ROBERTA MARTIN (no relation) Singers.

In 1940 Martin broke with Dorsey and moved from Pilgrim Baptist to the First Church of Deliverance. Though eager to run her own music-publishing firm, she lacked start-up funds and still could not notate music. Clarence Cobb, her new pastor, offered her the money on the condition that she partner with Kenneth Morris, his music director and a highly gifted gospel performer, composer, and arranger with formal music training. The two launched the Martin and Morris Music Company.

It published works by such leading gospel composers as JAMES CLEVELAND, SAM COOKE, and LUCIE CAMPBELL along with Morris's own songs, including his well-known "Does Jesus Care," "Just A Closer Walk With Thee," and "Power of the Holy Ghost." He arranged and notated all the company's sheet music, then played and sold it in the Chicago demonstration studio. The chronically-ill Morris left demonstration group tours and audience marketing throughout North America and Europe to the ever-energetic Martin.

Founded in 1940, the Sallie Martin Singers, also called the Sallie Martin Colored Ladies Quartet, was the first all-woman gospel group. Ruth Jones, its first pianist, later achieved fame under the professional name of DINAH WASHINGTON. In 1942 Sallie Martin's son, an Army solider, was killed, and a talented fifteen-year-old named Cora Brewer joined the Singers. With the blessing of Cora's parents, Sallie Martin adopted her. During 1944 the Los Angeles evangelist Aimee Semple McPherson featured the Singers in her mass crusades.

By the late 1950s and early 1960s Sallie Martin had established herself as a generous philanthropist and perhaps the wealthiest woman in gospel. She donated scholarships to struggling young musicians, backed a Baptist-run school in Nigeria as well as the emerging nation's government health program, and contributed large funds to Dr. MARTIN LUTHER KING JR. and the civil rights struggle. King chose her to represent him at Nigeria's independence celebration (1960). Accounts vary, but a Nigerian government ministry or mission school building was reportedly named after her in honor of her generosity.

Sallie Martin received a multitude of honors during her lifetime. The NCGCC dubbed her "Mother of Gospel." In 1969 Chicago's New Covenant Baptist Church presented its musical "This Is Your Life—Sallie Martin" before the woman herself, Dorsey, Morris, Cobb, and other admirers. After selling Morris her share of their company and disbanding the Singers in the early 1970s, Martin still enjoyed performing. At age eighty-three she starred with MARION WILLIAMS in "Gospel Caravan," a nightly show in Paris. Because of popular demand it extended its run seven weeks beyond schedule. With Dorsey, WILLIE MAE FORD SMITH, and other pioneering gospel personalities, Martin appeared in George T. Nierenberg's joyous documentary *Say Amen Somebody* (United Artists Classics, 1982). The Los Angeles County Public Library named Martin an African American Living Legend (1985). Over

1,300 people crowded Chicago's Fellowship Baptist Church to celebrate her ninetieth birthday and sing gospel for five hours.

At age ninety-two Sallie Martin died in Chicago. During the 1990s some of her old recordings were reissued on CD. In 1991 she was inducted posthumously into the Gospel Music Association Hall of Fame. *Ebony* (June 2000) recognized her early popularization of gospel among its "25 Most Important Events in Black Music History." Long before, Sallie Martin had asserted her own intended legacy to numerous Chicago congregations. "If Mahalia Jackson is a Cadillac, then I'm a Model T Ford. I makes it over the hill without shifting gears, and that's what counts, church, I makes it over the hill" (*Chicago Tribune*, 29 Apr. 1979).

FURTHER READING

The Chicago Public Library houses the Martin and Morris Gospel Sheet Music Collection, an almost complete catalog of 1,500-plus songs. The National Museum of American History, Smithsonian Institution, holds the Martin and Morris Music Company Records.

Boyer, Horace Clarence. *How Sweet the Sound: The Golden Age of Gospel* (1995).

Heilbut, Anthony. *The Gospel Sound: Good News and Bad Times* (1997, repr. 2002).

Price, Emmett G., III. "Sallie Martin," in *Encyclopedia of American Gospel Music*, ed. W. K. McNeil (2005).

Reagon, Bernice Johnson. *We'll Understand It Better By and By: Pioneering African-American Gospel Composers* (1992).

Obituary: *New York Times*, 22 June 1988.

DISCOGRAPHY

Eyes Hath Not Seen (Specialty Records 808).

Precious Lord / God Is Here (Vee-Jay Records NVG2-606).

Throw Out the Lifeline (Specialty Records SPCD 7043-2).

MARY KRANE DERR

Martinet, Louis Andre (28 Dec. 1849–7 June 1917), physician, newspaper founder, and attorney, initiated the challenge to Louisiana's "Separate Car Law," which led to the U.S. Supreme Court decision to uphold "separate but equal" public accommodations in *Plessy v. Ferguson* (1896). Martinet was born free, the second of eight children born to Pierre Hyppolite Martinet, a carpenter who arrived sometime before 1850 in St. Martinsville, Louisiana, from Belgium, and his wife, the former Marie-Louise Benoît, a native of Louisiana. Benoît

is generally referred to as a free woman of color, but there is a record in St. Martin Parish Courthouse that Pierre Martinet purchased her freedom on 10 January 1848 from Dr. Pierre Louis Nee, along with her mother and their infant son Pierre. They were married on 7 December 1869 in St. Martin de Tours Catholic Church, St. Martinsville, Louisiana— before the Civil War, Louisiana law did not permit them to marry.

At age twenty-three, Martinet was elected a state representative from St. Martin Parish, serving in that capacity from 1872 to 1875. He lost his seat in April 1875, as part of the compromise engineered by U.S. Representative William A. Wheeler, a New York Republican, seating eleven conservative Democrats and removing the same number of Republicans, most of them colored. In 1876 Martinet graduated from Strait Law School, which claimed him as its "first Negro graduate." He had already passed the Louisiana bar exam in 1875, at the time permitted after one year of law school. He supported himself and paid his tuition by teaching French and Latin courses at Straight. He was one of four people of African descent appointed to the Orleans Parish school board in 1877.

Allied for a time with the former senator and lieutenant governor P. B. S. PINCHBACK, Martinet joined him in supporting the "Redeemer" state constitution of 1879, which replaced Louisiana's 1867 constitution drafted during Reconstruction, laying the groundwork for a new postslavery version of white supremacy. Pinchback, not native to Louisiana, was the son of a free woman of color and an Alabama planter, who at times represented the English-speaking colored population of the state, but made political enemies simply by advancing his own career and patronage network. He offered his support in exchange for the establishment of an all-black Southern University. Martinet was rooted in the free colored population, who drew much of their culture and politics from the legacy of the French revolution. He firmly opposed any acknowledgment of race in the law or public institutions, while some of the darker-skinned English-speaking colored population wanted their own schools.

His father died 1875; in 1880 Louis Martinet remained in his mother's home, with his younger brother Jules, a carpenter like their father, and their brother-in-law Auguste Mora (a constable), married to their sister Mathilde, twenty-three, with a daughter of the same name. His grandmother, Hortense Armand Benoît, and aunt Elmira Lemella also lived with the family. Martinet married Leonora

Jeanne Miller, a New Orleans native teaching at Southern University, on 27 September 1882. The couple had two children, Marie Divonne, who died in infancy, and Leslie Louise. They divorced around 1900. Martinet's mother died in 1886. On 2 June 1885 Martinet was admitted to practice in the U.S. District Court for the Eastern District of Louisiana.

In 1889 Martinet began publishing the *Crusader* in English and French, a weekly newspaper covering civil rights struggles in Louisiana and nationally, which expanded to daily publication. In 1894 it was the only black paper in the United States and the only Republican paper in the southern states, described by Martinet and other editors as "the enemy of wrong and injustice, the friend and defender of right and justice." The editorial style of the *Crusader* is represented by the following report: "Last week in Fayette County, Ga., eight Negroes were killed and six were wounded. Eight whites were shot, but only one fatally. However deplorable these affrays, it is refreshing to see the Negro defending himself, but he must learn to shoot straight." Martinet closed the paper in 1896, shortly after the Supreme Court's ruling in *Plessy v. Ferguson*.

In September 1891, Martinet called for a *Comitée de Citoyens* or Citizens Committee for the Annulment of Act No. 111—the "Separate Car Act" adopted by the Louisiana legislature 10 July 1890. This committee, which continued to have an active role in litigation to turn back racially motivated legislation, gave rise to the American Citizens' Equal Rights Association (ACERA). In ACERA's official protest to the Louisiana legislature, responding to the "Separate Car Act," Martinet openly questioned racial distinction and identity as arbitrary and without scientific basis (Elliott, p. 250). Martinet successfully represented Daniel Desdunes, son of the activist Rodolfe Lucien Dedunes, who openly boarded a "white only" car on a train bound for Mobile, Alabama. Desdunes was acquitted because the Louisiana law was in conflict with federal laws governing interstate commerce. However, when the legal team tested the law on an intrastate train, boarded by HOMER ADOLPH PLESSY, the U.S. Supreme Court ruled 18 May 1896 that the statute did not violate the Thirteenth or Fourteenth Amendments to the federal constitution.

Martinet held an appointment as clerk in the Collector of Customs Office in 1882, as deputy surveyor for the Port of New Orleans in 1883, and as a carrier in the U.S. Post Office in 1885. It was common in post-Reconstruction southern states that Republicans who could no longer win state offices received appointments to federal jobs, and in New Orleans free men of color were among them. Martinet completed a medical degree from Flint Medical College in New Orleans in about 1894. He was able to obtain some appointed state positions, including an appointment by Governor Samuel Douglas McEnery to the Board of Trustees of Southern University, 1889–1897, and served as a Notary Public from 1888 to 1917. In New Orleans, notary was a municipal office, responsible for maintaining records now entrusted to parish clerks of court. His notarial acts are part of the official records of the parish, in eight chronological bound volumes.

FURTHER READING

Binder, Wolfgang. *Creoles and Cajuns: French Louisiana* (1998).

DeVore, Donald E., and Joseph Logsdon. *Crescent City Schools: Public Education in New Orleans, 1841–1991* (1991).

Elliott, Mark Emory. *Color-Blind Justice: Albion Tourgée and the Quest for Racial Equality from the Civil War to Plessy v. Ferguson* (2006).

Fireside, Harvey. *Separate and Unequal: Homer Plessy and the Supreme Court Decision That Legalized Racism* (2004).

Scott, Rebecca J. *Degrees of Freedom: Louisiana and Cuba after Slavery* (2005).

Smith, J. Clay, Jr. *Emancipation: The Making of the Black Lawyer, 1944–1944* (1993).

CHARLES ROSENBERG

Martinez, Pedro (25 Oct. 1971–), Major League Baseball pitcher, was born in Manoguayabo, Dominican Republic, the son of Paolino, a baseball player and janitor, and Leopoldina Martinez, a laundress. One of four brothers and two sisters, Martinez grew up in a three-room house. His father was a former top pitcher on the island and instilled in his sons a great passion for the game. At the age of fifteen, Martinez's older brother, Ramon, pitched for the Dominican Republic Olympic team in Los Angeles. Soon after, he was signed by the Los Angeles Dodgers and sent to their academy in the Dominican Republic.

Martinez, thirteen at the time, attended one of his brother's workouts. The Dodgers recognized his talent, with his fastball topping out at eighty miles per hour, and signed him when he turned sixteen. Physically, however, Martinez did not compare to his brother Ramon. Over the course of his career, Martinez would surprise critics who did not believe that his diminutive body could withstand full major league seasons. In 1990, when Martinez made his minor league debut in Great Falls, Montana, he was five-feet eleven-inches tall, but weighed only 135 pounds.

Martinez played for the Dodgers for two years, pitching almost exclusively from the bullpen; he started only three of the sixty-seven games in which he appeared. The Dodgers saw Martinez's small frame as a liability, and so traded him after the 1993 season to the Montreal Expos.

In Montreal, Martinez became one of the game's greatest pitchers and moved from the bullpen to the starting rotation. As a starter, Martinez excelled with an overpowering fastball with outstanding movement due to his extraordinarily long fingers. It was with the Expos that Martinez began to emerge as perhaps the most dominating pitcher of his size in baseball history. He was carrying thirty-five more pounds on his frame than he had as a minor leaguer, and used that extra weight for both more power and better control. In addition to a fastball that topped out consistently around ninety-five miles per hour, Martinez also had outstanding control of his pitches (which included a devastating circle change-up and a good curveball) and a deceptive delivery that hid the ball from hitters until Martinez was just about to deliver the ball. In 1997 he won the Cy Young Award, given to the best pitcher in each league. He won seventeen games, striking out 305 batters, with a league-leading 1.90 earned run average. The Expos, however, were financially unstable and did not expect to sign Martinez when his contract ran out at the end of the next season. That winter the small-market Expos traded him to the Boston Red Sox, where he signed a seven-year, $82.5 million contract.

In Boston, Martinez continued his domination. In his extraordinary 1999 season, pitching in a hitter's era, Martinez had one of the best records in major league history, finishing the year with a 23-4 record, a 2.07 ERA, and 313 strikeouts. It was the first season in the twentieth century where a pitcher under six feet tall tallied 300 strikeouts in a season (and only the eighth pitcher in modern baseball history to reach the 300 strikeouts mark). In his eight years with the Red Sox, Martinez won the Cy Young award twice and finished in the top five in voting every year but one. Martinez will always be remembered for leading the Red Sox to their first World Series Championship since 1918.

Martinez may best be remembered in Boston for three specific games. He started the 1999 Major League Baseball All-Star Game in Boston. In front of his hometown fans, Martinez struck out the side in the first, fanning Barry Larkin, Larry Walker, and Sammy Sosa. In the second inning, Martinez continued to dominate, striking out Mark McGwire. He left the game after the second, having fanned five in two innings, including the two most prolific homerun hitters of the era, Sosa and McGwire. Martinez was named MVP following the game. He would dominate hitters that whole season and into the play-offs.

In game one of the American League Division Series in 1999, Martinez left in the first inning because of back pain. He was in such pain that he was unable to make his next scheduled start in game five of the series. However, with Red Sox pitchers struggling, and the score tied 8-8 in the fourth inning, Martinez entered the game from the bullpen. Because of the pain, Martinez pitched at a much lower arm angle than typical, throwing almost sidearm at times. Indians hitters, though, were helpless. Martinez threw six innings of no-hit ball and the Red Sox won the game and the series. Red Sox starting pitcher Bret Saberhagen, said after the game, "He couldn't even pick up a ball two days ago, and was almost in tears. He's just the most unbelievable pitcher I've ever seen."

Martinez had a number of memorable games against the New York Yankees, the bitter rival of the Red Sox. His most unforgettable performance had little to do with his pitching. In game three of the 2003 American League Championship Series he squared off against former Red Sox great Roger Clemens. After Martinez hit Yankee outfielder Karim Garcia in the head, Clemens threw a high fastball to Red Sox cleanup hitter Manny Ramirez in the next inning. Both benches cleared and the seventy-two-year-old Yankee bench coach Don Zimmer charged across the field at Martinez. Martinez eluded Zimmer and pushed him to the ground. Uninjured, Zimmer later expressed regret about the incident. The Yankees won the game and would later eliminate the Red Sox from the play-offs.

Martinez, throughout his career, had a number of quirks and a habit of speaking off the cuff. In May of 2003 Martinez, after a shut out of the Yankees, told reporters "Wake up the Bambino [that is, Yankee great Babe Ruth]. Maybe I'll drill him in the ass." In 2004, after a loss to the Yankees, Martinez said, "I just tip my hat and call the Yankees my daddy."

In 2004, he teamed up with newly acquired All-Star pitcher Curt Schilling to form the best one-two combination of pitchers in the game as they ended the team's eighty-six year World Series drought. In 2005 Martinez left the Red Sox and signed as a free agent with the New York Mets. Even as he aged, Martinez continued to dominate hitters. As his fastball gradually lost velocity, from its peak of ninety-seven miles-per-hour, he moved from a power pitcher to more of a finesse pitcher, dazzling hitters with curveballs and changeups.

Martinez never forgot the roots of his baseball career. He donated money for the construction of a church and school in his hometown of Manoguayabo. He married the former Christina Cruz, a sports reporter, in 2005 and in the off-season lived in a compound he built for his extended family in Manoguayabo.

One of the best pitchers in Major League Baseball history, in an era of offense, Pedro Martinez dominated hitters like few in the game.

FURTHER READING

Callahan, Gerry. "Rocket Redux," *Sports Illustrated* (20 Apr. 1998).

Crothers, Tim, and Kevin Cook and Mark Mravic. "The Ballot of Pedro & Pudge," *Sports Illustrated* (29 Nov. 1999).

Doyle, Paul. "King of the Hill Aims Higher," *Sporting News* (11 Oct. 1999).

Elkin, Jack. "Pedro Martinez: A Little Guy Makes It Big Time," *Baseball Digest* (Nov. 1997).

Myles, Stephanie. "Heating Up," *Baseball Digest* (Sept. 1999).

Thorn, John, Phil Birnbaum, Bill Deane, and Rob Neyer. *Total Baseball, Completely Revised and Updated: The Ultimate Baseball Encyclopedia* (2004).

Verducci, Tom. "The Power of Pedro," *Sports Illustrated* (27 Mar. 2000).

LOU MANZO

Marvin X (29 May 1944–), poet, playwright, essayist, and activist, was born Marvin Ellis Jackmon in Fowler, California, near the city of Fresno. He has also used such Arabic names as El Muhajir, Nazzam al Fitnah, Nazzam al Sudan, and Imam Maalik El Muhajir. He was born to Marian Murrill Jackmon, a real estate broker, and Owendell Jackmon, a real estate agent turned florist and also publisher of the *Fresno Voice*, the first black newspaper of California's Central Valley. Marvin Jackmon attended a series of elementary schools in West Fresno and Oakland. After graduating from Edison High School he enrolled at Oakland City College (now Merritt College), where he met HUEY P. NEWTON and BOBBY SEALE, founders of the revolutionary Black Panther Party. Having earned an associate's degree, he then attended San Francisco State College (now San Francisco State University), where he received both a B.A. and an M.A. degree in English. Here he met ED BULLINS, the playwright, producer, and essayist with whom he founded the Black House and the Black Arts/West Theater in San Francisco's Fillmore district (1967). The Black House served as the Panthers' Bay Area headquarters during the 1960s. Both writers, along with figures like Newton, Seale, and ELDRIDGE CLEAVER, are inextricable from the politically charged matrix of Black Power and its artistic wing, the Black Arts Movement.

It was after Jackmon joined ELIJAH MUHAMMAD's Nation of Islam that he changed his name to Marvin X to signal his disdain for a history of white supremacist oppression. An outspoken and controversial figure, he has been an extremely prolific writer, especially during the last three decades of the twentieth century. Among his published works are *Sudan Rajula Samia* (1967), *Black Dialectics* (1967), *Fly to Allah* (his first poetry collection, 1969), *The Son of Man* (proverbs, 1969), *Black Man Listen!* (poems, 1969), *Selected Poems* (1979), *Confessions of a Wife Beater and Other Poems* (1981), *Liberation Poems for North American Africans* (1982), *Love and War* (poems, 1995), and *Land of My Daughters* (poems, 2002). Essay collections include *In the Crazy House Called America* (2002) and *Wish I Could Tell You the Truth* (2005). Marvin X's most noted dramatic works are *Flowers for the Trashman* (or *Take Care of Business*, 1965), *The Black Bird* (*Al Tai Aswad*, 1969), *Resurrection of the Dead* (1969), *The Trial* (1970), *Woman—Man's Best Friend* (musical drama, 1973), and *In the Name of Love* (1981). Other dramatic works include *Come Next Summer* (1969), *How I Met Isa* (1975), and *Sergeant Santa* (2002). Essays, short stories, commentaries, and poetry have appeared in a number of diverse periodicals. These include *Muhammad Speaks*, *Soulbook*, *Black Dialogue*, *Negro Digest/Black World*, *Journal of Black Poetry*, and *Black Theater*. He has received writing fellowships from Columbia University and the National Endowment for the Humanities.

Marvin X's autobiography, *Somethin' Proper: The Life and Times of a North American African Poet* (1998), presents its subject as a witness and survivor of an extremely intense period in American history. With stark honesty and detailed reminiscences of the rise of Black Power, he traces the vicissitudes of his family life and the challenges of growing up as a black revolutionary during the era of civil rights, decolonization and recolonization movements, and the Vietnam War, as well as his own evolution of self-consciousness as a Black Muslim. He begins the work on the occasion of his eldest daughter's wedding. He fathered two sons (Marvin and Darrel, also known as Abdul) and three daughters (Nefertiti, Muhammida, and Amira). Among his wives, partners, and companions are Patricia Smith (now divorced; the mother of Marvin X's sons), Hasani (now divorced; renamed by Marvin X, as he relates in *Somethin' Proper*), and Nisa (briefly mentioned in the acknowledgments of *Somethin' Proper* but not in the text). Marvin X also fondly recalls a former addict named Marsha as his "main woman" (263); she died in 1994 while he was addicted to crack cocaine. His parents also passed away during this period. *Somethin' Proper* lingers upon Marvin X's "revolutionary lover," Ethna Wyatt (Hurriyah Asar), and his flirtations with polygamous marriage, spiritual crises, personal rivalries, and political disillusionment.

In order to avoid the Vietnam War draft, Marvin X took refuge in Canada and Central America prior to being arrested and repatriated to America to serve time. He has often pinpointed his identity as a Muslim as the root of his political persecution. Interwoven into his autobiography are numerous encounters with and references to Black Arts luminaries and related political icons. These are people primarily associated with the period 1960–1970: AMIRI BARAKA, SONIA SANCHEZ, Ben Caldwell, Askia Muhammad Toure, ANGELA DAVIS, NIKKI GIOVANNI, and JAMES BALDWIN, among others. The close ties and occasional frictions among Marvin X, Eldridge Cleaver, and lifelong friend Huey P. Newton also figure in the narrative.

Marvin X's story is one of radical politics and their expression through art and personal commitment. Though the majority of his life work has been based on the West Coast, he has also participated in the East Coast (that is, Harlem's) artistic and social scene. From 1969 to 1972 he served as associate editor of *Black Theater* magazine. He was also contributing editor of the *Journal of Black Poetry* and was founder of Al Kitab Sudan Publishing Company (1967). His career has included work as an instructor of English, African American studies, and theater at such postsecondary institutions as Fresno State University, the University of California (Berkeley and San Diego), the University of Nevada (Reno), San Francisco State University, Merritt College, Laney College, and Mills College. In 1980

he organized the first National Conference of Black Men at Oakland Auditorium, a precursor of LOUIS FARRAKHAN's Million Man March (1995).

After a serious bout with crack cocaine addiction, Marvin X cofounded Recovery Theater with Geoffrey Grier, a postrehabilitation project based in San Francisco. The group focuses on the struggle of recovering addicts. The docudrama *One Day in the Life* (1999) details the path to recovery using a transparently autobiographical premise. As a public presence Marvin X remains an extremely vocal critic of the effect that drugs, violence, racism, apathy, poverty, ignorance, and preemptive despair have had on the psyches of African Americans, especially the younger generations.

FURTHER READING

Marvin X (Marvin E. Jackmon). *Somethin' Proper: The Life and Times of a North American African Poet* (1998).

Idland, Michael E. "Marvin X," in *African American Dramatists: An A-to-Z Guide*, ed. Emmanuel S. Nelson (2004).

Peterson, Bernard L., Jr. *Contemporary Black American Playwrights and Their Plays: A Biographical Directory and Dramatic Index* (1988).

NANCY KANG

Mason, Biddy Bridget (15 Aug.? 1818–15 Jan. 1891), slave, nurse, landowner, and philanthropist, was born a slave in Hancock County, Georgia, of unknown parents. Though her slave name was Bridget, she was almost always called Biddy, and not until she achieved her freedom in Los Angeles, California, in 1865 did she take the surname Mason. It is not definitively known why she chose "Mason," although Amasa Mason Lyman was the company captain on Biddy Mason's journey from Mississippi to Salt Lake City, and later to San Bernardino. Biddy was an infant when she was given or sold to the John Smithson family of Mississippi, to whom she belonged until she was eighteen. Smithson then gave her, along with two other slaves, as a wedding present to his cousin Rebecca when she married Robert M. Smith. Biddy Mason's new duties included nursing care of the frail Rebecca Smith and the making and use of herbal medicines. Although no records exist, Mason family legend says that while in the marshy woodlands collecting herbs, Mason met a Native American man who was the chief, or son of the chief, of a local tribe, perhaps Choctaw, Cherokee, Chickasaw, or Creek. According to the legend, Mason and the Indian man married and her first daughter Ellen, born in 1838, was his child. By 1848, Mason had three daughters: Ellen, age ten; Ann, age four; and baby Harriet. Robert Smith may have been the father of all three.

In the 1840s, Mormon missionaries came to Mississippi. The Smith family converted to the faith (officially named The Church of Jesus Christ of Latter-day Saints), and in 1848 Mr. Smith decided to move two thousand miles to what would soon be the new Utah Territory. He gave his adult slaves the choice of being sold to other masters in Mississippi or going with him to Utah. Mr. Smith could, of course, take the slaves' children, as they were his property. Mason chose to go with the Smiths. They met John Brown, a Mormon who was to be their guide on the journey West, and five other families in Fulton, Mississippi, on 9 March 1848. Mr. Brown recorded who was included in the Smith family group in his daily journal: nine white people, ten black slaves, two yoke oxen, one horse, eight mules, seven milk cows, three wagons. The next morning they set off for Utah with Mason walking behind the wagons to herd the family's animals. For three months, in the rain, wind, mud, dust, and dirt, with her baby on her back or at her breast, Mason walked, cared for the Smith family's needs, and kept the Smith family's animals in line. At the end of May 1848, having traveled 917 miles, the Smith family and all their possessions arrived at the Mormon Winter Quarters, west of the Missouri River, in what would become Nebraska Territory. Then on 1 July 1848 they joined a group of several hundred other people setting out on the Mormon Trail. As before, Mason walked behind her master's wagons, performed her usual duties, and provided nursing care to the group as needed. In October they all arrived at the Great Salt Lake.

The Mormon leadership now found itself facing an unexpected dilemma. There was no law for or against slavery in the Mormon Church, so the church leaders determined that if a slave wished to leave his or her master, the master must allow the slave to go. The leaders noted, however, on 15 February 1851, "all the slaves that are there appear to be perfectly contented and satisfied" (*Our Pioneer Heritage*, vol. 8). It is not known whether Mr. Smith informed his slaves of this opportunity to be free. In any case, Mason and her daughters remained his slaves.

Three years later, in March 1851, Mr. Smith decided to move almost eight hundred miles to Southern California where a new Mormon settlement was "to farm and to plant moral values"

(Minutes, San Bernardino, 6 April 1852). Once again Mason walked behind her master's wagons, arriving in San Bernardino, California, in June. Mason and her daughters (and all Smith's fourteen slaves) were now in the free state of California. Over the next few years Mason met several black people who were not slaves, and she must have given considerable thought to her situation. She was well treated by her own account, but she and her daughters were still, in practice, slaves.

In actuality, as she would learn in 1856, the moment she had entered California she was "at once emancipated" (This and all following quotes are from "Suit for Freedom," *Los Angeles Star*, 2 Feb. 1856). In December 1855 Smith began preparing for a move from California to Texas. At that point Mason, with the help of her friends in the tiny (fewer than fifty people) Los Angeles black community and the Los Angeles County sheriff, ended up in the courtroom of Los Angeles judge Benjamin Hayes. The sheriff, having been told of Smith's plan to "remove to the State of Texas, carrying [Mason et al.] with him into slavery," took all fourteen slaves to the county jail "for their protection" until Judge Hayes could hear the case. In January 1856 Judge Hayes ruled that Mason and all Smith's slaves "are entitled to their freedom and are free forever." Explaining his decision, Judge Hayes wrote a lengthy article in the *Los Angeles Star* in which he said Mason and the others were "ignorant of our laws." He quoted Mason as telling him she was a "pampered house slave," that Mr. Smith had said she "would be just as free in Texas as here," and, she said, "I always feared this trip to Texas since I first heard of it." Judge Hayes concluded that Mr. Smith's claims that his "slaves" had the "pleasant prospect of freedom in Texas" were false and that it was the moral responsibility of the court to ensure "the lawful liberty of the humblest dweller on our soil."

This was a timely decision indeed. The next year the U.S. Supreme Court ruled, in the infamous 1857 DRED SCOTT decision, that a slave was not a person, but property, and that a slave's residence in a free state or territory did not make that slave free. Biddy Mason and her daughters were now free, on their own, and penniless in the rough little cattle town of Los Angeles, but through contacts in the black community and especially through Robert Owens, a wealthy black businessman, Mason immediately found work as a nurse and midwife for Dr. John S. Griffin of Los Angeles. Her skills were obviously highly valued, for she was paid the good salary of $2.50 a day. Mason and her daughters had a place to live (rented from the Owenses), she had a fine job, and she had a dream—to own her own land. In 1866 after ten years of work, Mason bought her first piece of property in Los Angeles for $250. Her purchase was not in the settled and expensive Olvera Street area but farther south, out of town, on Third and Spring streets. She had two rental houses built on her new property, and before long she bought more land even farther south, near Sixth and Olive streets, where she put up additional rental buildings.

In the ensuing years Los Angeles expanded rapidly, with newcomers arriving by wagon train, mule train, stagecoach, foot, and in the 1880s, by railroad. The central business district spread south; Mason's property, now at the center of downtown Los Angeles, was worth a fortune. Biddy Mason became a wealthy woman by selling her property bit by bit (though never her original homestead on Third and Spring, to which she moved in 1884). She continued to work as a nurse and midwife, but now she did it free of charge. She regularly visited the small Los Angeles jail, taking food to the inmates and counseling them to do better. She had already helped found the Los Angeles branch of the First African Methodist Episcopal Church (FAME) in 1872, and in the following years she started a school and day-care center for children, and took into her own home the poor who had nowhere else to go. She bought food and clothes for those who needed them, and she paid taxes for those who could not pay. Her open-hearted generosity was so well known that needy folk of all races formed daily lines outside her door, waiting for her sure assistance. When Mason died in Los Angeles in 1891, the *Los Angeles Times* noted her many charitable accomplishments and her astonishing net worth of $300,000. Her property remained in the family until it was lost in the Depression. Mason is memorialized at the site of her original homestead with both a unique urban park and a dramatic, freestanding wall embedded with artifacts portraying her remarkable life.

FURTHER READING

Biddy Mason's legal documents and photographs are in the University of California Los Angeles (UCLA) Research Library, Special Collections Division.

Black Angelenos: The Afro-American in Los Angeles, 1850–1950 (resource catalog from 1988 exhibit at the California Afro-American Museum, Los Angeles, 1988).

Hayden, Dolores. "Biddy Mason's Los Angeles 1856–1891," *California History* (Fall 1989).

Hayes, Benjamin I. "Suit for Freedom," *Los Angeles Star*, 2 Feb. 1856.

"The Negro Woman in Los Angeles and Vicinity: Some Notable Characters," *Los Angeles Times*, 12 Feb. 1909.

JERI CHASE FERRIS

Mason, Charles Harrison (8 Sept. 1866–17 Nov. 1961), church founder and religious leader, was born in Bartlett, Tennessee, to the former slaves Jerry and Eliza Mason. His parents worked for a plantation owner named Prior Lee, a well-connected planter whose spiritual foundation was in the Baptist Church. After the Civil War the Masons worked as tenant farmers and remained committed Baptists. Throughout Mason's childhood his mother encouraged him to join her in prayer, an experience that left a lasting mark on his understanding of Christian expression. In 1878 a yellow fever epidemic forced the Mason family to leave Tennessee for Plumersville, Arkansas, and the plantation farm of John Watson, where they continued to work as tenant farmers. Unfortunately, in 1879 young Charles's father succumbed to yellow fever, leaving the family to struggle financially. In the early summer of 1880 Charles also fell ill. Fearing for his life his mother prayed that he would be healed, and by late September Mason's health had improved. That near-death experience formally propelled Mason to the altar of Mount Olive Baptist Church, where the Reverend I. S. Nelson baptized him.

The apparently miraculous healing, his baptism, and earnest Baptist faith led him to begin adult life as a lay preacher. In 1891 Mason was licensed and ordained to preach by the Baptist denomination in Preston, Arkansas. Although he believed the ministry was important Mason deferred a full-time ministry to marry Alice Saxton, daughter of his mother's best friend, sometime around 1891. The happiness of this moment was short-lived. She did not embrace the life of a minister's wife and divorced him within two years. He refused to marry again while she was alive, his Holiness-Pentecostal tradition not allowing divorce except in cases of infidelity, but after her death he married Lelia Washington in 1903. This union produced eight children. In 1936 Lelia Mason died, and in 1943 Mason married Elise Washington, who would be his first biographer.

The failure of Mason's first marriage left him devastated. His sense of self-worth plunged and his faith became stagnant; the grief consumed him to the point of considering suicide. It was during that low ebb that Mason turned his focus to education.

He became an avid reader, wishing to expand his mind. One title proved pivotal, the 1893 *An Autobiography: The Story of the Lord's Dealing with Mrs. Amanda Smith ...*, a work that recounted the life and ministry of the former slave and Holiness preacher. Smith's record of ministerial success, which she attributed to the Lord's grace and mercy, as well as her description of the experience of sanctification, by which she was spiritually set apart for the Lord's use, proved transformative for Mason. He believed that the Lord was dealing with him and his faith through that text. He saw in Smith's experiences a closeness to God through sanctification that was lacking in his own faith. During the 1890s the Holiness movement was growing in popularity. Initially an outgrowth of the calls for revival by several Methodist ministers in New Jersey in 1867, the movement evolved into an independent Christian denomination that preached and taught a new Christian way of life and a revival to Christian churches.

Mason enrolled in the Arkansas Baptist Institute on 1 November 1893 but left within one semester for several reasons. His fundamentalist beliefs conflicted with the institute's more liberal biblical foundation. And his steady embrace of the Holiness doctrine increased his suspicions about the growing materialism within Christendom in general and the black church in particular. Over the course of the next few years Mason's hunger for the holy things of God led him to seek out Charles Price Jones, his friend and fellow Baptist minister. Mason and Jones realized that their Christian migrations were similar. They were contemporaries, raised in humble circumstances, and were both devout Baptists. Both, however, had become utterly enthralled with the rising Holiness faith by the early 1890s. Jones had completed training at the Arkansas Baptist Institute in 1891 and was known as a powerful preacher. The two men immediately became friends. In 1895 Jones and Mason started holding revivals at the Mount Helms Baptist Church. Between 1897 and 1899 tensions between Baptist and Holiness advocates rose to a fever pitch, ultimately leading to a permanent split. Jones attempted to maintain control of the Mount Helm Baptist congregation that he had nurtured. He attempted to change the name of the congregation to Church of Christ Holiness, signifying a break with the Baptist Church. Issues of property ownership and legal rights came in to play and Jones and Mason opted to leave Mount Helm and cultivate another fellowship of believers. In March 1897, after a series of revival meetings,

Mason claimed that the Lord had revealed to him the name of their new congregation, the Church of God. Later that year Mason and Jones moved to Memphis, Tennessee, to charter and incorporate their church under that name.

Although both embraced the Holiness doctrine of sanctification as a work of grace, Mason remained unsure about the completeness of the work in himself. News of the Azusa Street revival in Los Angeles, California, operated by WILLIAM SEYMOUR, founder of the Apostolic Faith Mission, offered him the opportunity to test his faith. In April 1907 Mason, along with others, traveled to Los Angeles to experience the revival. He spent over a month at Azusa Street learning about the Pentecostal element of sanctification, and the gift of speaking in tongues (glossolalia), which Pentecostals held was the promised gift of Jesus to the Apostles that empowered them to preach salvation. Upon meeting with William Seymour, Mason realized that this gift was the answer to his question. Unfortunately, Mason's belief in the primacy of glossolalia in the Christian life led to a final division with Jones and a split in the church in August 1907.

By 1909 Jones had formed the Church of Christ Holiness, USA, and Mason formed the Pentecostal Assembly of the Church of God in Christ (COGIC). Mason's COGIC church was an interracial congregation with members in Mississippi, Arkansas, and Tennessee. Mason was elected general overseer and chief apostle, positions he held for more than fifty years. Unfortunately, in 1914 racism split the church, and its white members left to start the Assemblies of God. Nevertheless, the birth of COGIC culminated in the largest, oldest, and most visible African American Holiness-Pentecostal church in the world. Mason's vision embraced egalitarianism with the formation of a Women's Department in 1911, and it cultivated youth and rising ministers.

Over subsequent decades Mason, as the leader of COGIC, built the denomination into one of the largest Pentecostal bodies in the world. When African Americans migrated from the South to northern cities in the early decades of the twentieth century, and later to the West Coast, COGIC established churches in new population centers such as Detroit, Chicago, and Cleveland. By the time of Mason's death in Detroit, Michigan, the church he founded claimed nearly half a million members and had spurred the establishment of at least ten other Pentecostal denominations.

FURTHER READING

Clemmons, Ithiel C. *Bishop C. H. Mason and the Roots of the Church of Christ* (1996).

DuPree, Sherry Sherrod, ed. *Biographical Dictionary of African American Holiness Pentecostals, 1880–1990* (1989).

Mason, Elise Washington. *The Man, Charles Harrison Mason* (1979).

Maxwell, Joe. "Building the Church (of God in Christ)," *Christianity Today* 40 (8 Apr. 1996).

Sanders, Cheryl J. *Saints in Exile: The Holiness-Pentecostal Experience in African American Religion and Culture* (1996).

IDA E. JONES

Mason, E. Harold (5 Dec. 1901–10 Feb. 1994), educator, social worker, and interfaith and interracial relations specialist, was born Eugene Harold Mason in Cythiana, Kentucky, the second son of Thomas Jefferson Mason, an 1894 graduate of the (Kentucky) State Normal School for Colored Persons, and Mary Mahalia Mason. Harold Mason attended secondary school in Kentucky and Ohio. Though he became a familiar figure in several communities, much of what is known about Mason must be drawn from newspaper accounts and his own extensive correspondence. As a result, the dates of some of his achievements can only be approximated. After graduating from high school in 1921 he attended Case Western Reserve University, where he began a long-standing relationship with the Young Men's Christian Association (YMCA), serving as the assistant secretary of the African American branch in Cleveland.

Mason proved early on to be highly committed to civil rights and the religious community. After graduating from Case Western he worked for the YMCA in Buffalo, New York, and became a member of CARTER G. WOODSON's Association for the Study of Negro Life and History (ASNLH), which proved an important influence on his thinking. In 1930, as a member of the ASNLH, he wrote a letter to the editor and publisher of the *Buffalo Evening News*, urging him to capitalize "Negro" each time it appeared in print. A month later the paper's policy was changed.

While working at the YMCA in Buffalo, Mason met Alvin Lucas of San Mateo, California, who convinced Mason to travel to the West Coast and visit the nondenominational churches there. Mason was interested in the idea of community-based fellowship groups as an alternative to small, independent religious sects. Mason arrived in California in January 1932 and remained there for the next decade. From 1932 to 1935 he attended the Berkeley Baptist Divinity School, where he was the first African American man to graduate. While attending divinity school Mason continued his work as a community activist. He taught African American history classes at the historic Beth Eden Baptist Church and at the YMCA in the Berkeley area. He also toured the South, speaking to African American communities there. After receiving his degree he studied in the department of social institutions (later the department of sociology) at the University of California, Berkeley. For seven years he served as a non-salaried visiting chaplain at San Quentin prison, where he counseled prisoners, conducted lectures on a variety of topics, and addressed the needs of black prisoners. When Mason found that the black church groups in the prison were denied resources available to white Christian and Jewish organizations, he campaigned to have stationery, books, and a typewriter donated to them. This achievement, one in which Mason brought together his interests in race and religion, was something that he referenced throughout the rest of his life.

Throughout the 1930s Mason wrote about his accomplishments at the prison and on the lecture circuit for the African American newspaper the *San Francisco Spokesman*. In his *Spokesman* articles he echoed many of the themes of his teaching and lecturing, including economic and political analyses of the African American community, important events in black history, and the need for what he called "practical Christianity" in daily life. In his written work and speeches Mason always balanced his concerns about racial discrimination with attention to historic achievements by African Americans. Likewise, he balanced his interest in popularizing black studies with a call for African Americans to work for the welfare and betterment of all members of society.

In 1943 Mason moved to New York City and became the assistant director of the Intercultural Education Workshop, a race relations group founded in 1941 by Rachel Davis DuBois and run primarily by white educators. Though he served in this position for only four years, it is in his work with interculturalism—a predecessor to multiculturalism—that his efforts are best recorded and his legacy most measurable. Intercultural education stressed interracial tolerance and focused its efforts on transforming race relations in the public schools. Intercultural leaders worked to diversify the curriculum to include the artistic, scientific, and historical achievements of African Americans, as well as to train public school teachers in planning classroom activities that would promote tolerance. In addition, leaders encouraged teachers and students to participate in school assemblies, class visits between different schools, and extracurricular groups in an effort to create stronger, more informed relations between white and African American students. Mason argued that this development in education was not a temporary experiment, but the future standard for education in America. For the first time, Mason contended, the philosophy of education and democratic politics were working in tandem.

In addition to his work in schools, Mason served as a consultant to the Citywide Commission on Harlem, headed by ADAM CLAYTON POWELL JR. and A. PHILIP RANDOLPH, and to the human relations committee for the New York City schools. Through DuBois, a committed Quaker, Mason also came to serve on the race relations committee of the American Friends Society. During the four years in which he served as assistant director of the Intercultural Education Workshop, Mason lectured extensively in New York, Connecticut, New Jersey, and Pennsylvania, speaking to schools, churches, camps, and interracial and interfaith organizations. During this time he published in prestigious education journals, including his article "What Is Intercultural Education?," which was published in *School and Society* (v. 62 [1945]: 241–244). Interestingly, DuBois does not mention Mason in her autobiography, which might suggest that relations between the two leaders were strained.

At some point after 1947 Mason returned to Oakland, California. Though it had inspired the development of multiculturalism in the 1960s, a movement with different politics and greater participation by African Americans at the leadership level, interculturalism began to lose focus and influence in the late 1940s.

In 1956 Mason became the first president of the Carter G. Woodson Society, an Oakland-based group committed to preserving black folklore, history, poetry, and music. The society also strove to establish a black history museum, and Mason was a founding member of the African American Museum and Library established in Oakland in 1965. In July of the same year, Mason helped to found the East Bay branch of the ASNLH. During this time Mason maintained an extensive lecture schedule and often was away for long enough periods of time that he slowed the progress of some of the Carter G. Woodson Society's projects. When he moved to Los Angeles in the late 1960s the group became largely inactive. The deleterious effects of Mason's absence speak to his dynamism and charisma as a leader. Mason continued to serve as a lecturer throughout the 1970s, speaking on topics such as school integration and the growth of urban ghettos. He remained in Los Angeles until his death at the age of ninety-two.

FURTHER READING

E. Harold Mason's papers are housed at the archives at the Schomburg Center for Research in Black Culture, New York Public Library in New York, New York; the African American Museum and Library in Oakland, California; and the William Grant Still Community Arts Center in Los Angeles, California.

JONNA PERRILLO

Mason, Isaac (14 May 1822–28 Aug. 1898), escaped slave, abolitionist, community leader, and autobiographer, was born in the town of George Town Cross Oats in Kent County, Maryland. He was the first of five children born to Zekiel Thompson, a free man and farm hand and Sophia Thompson, a slave. The death of Mason's first owner when Mason was approximately fifteen years old marked the onset of his worst years in slavery. Although Zekiel Thompson was able to secure freedom for his wife and infant daughter, Mason was originally hired out to repay a small portion of his relatives' purchase price and subsequently sold to a new owner. In late December 1846, Mason fled his master's farm. Mason and two other male slaves, with assistance from agents of the Underground Railroad, walked from Kent County to Delaware and Pennsylvania.

Mason worked in Chester County, Pennsylvania, until he found employment in Philadelphia. In 1849 he married Annie (maiden name unknown), and the newlyweds remained in Philadelphia until Mason, while working as a construction worker, saw his master's son in the city. Mason's fear of returning to Maryland and bondage caused him to relocate further north in 1850. Mason and his wife journeyed to Boston, where they stayed with the abolitionist Lewis Hayden and his family until WILLIAM C. NELL, a fellow abolitionist, encouraged the couple to move to Worcester, Massachusetts, where their first child, Eliza Jane, was born in 1851 and where Mason worked on a farm until 15 April of that same year. Renewed fears of being captured led Mason to live in Canada until his wife's illness caused him to return to Worcester. While traveling home, he encountered his former master, yet to Mason's immense relief, the man did not recognize him. Mason returned to Worcester on 2 July 1851. Three years later, Samuel Mason was born. Over the years, Mason worked as a janitor at various municipal buildings. For nearly five decades, Mason was one of Worcester's most prominent African American citizens. He was active in the Anti-Slavery Movement, Republican Party, and A.M.E. Zion Church, as well as two fraternal organizations: the Masons, where he was a member of King David Lodge No. 16 in Worcester; and the Odd Fellows.

In May 1860 Mason, heeding the Scottish-American abolitionist James Redpath's plea for African Americans to emigrate to Haiti, traveled there in search of better economic opportunities. However Mason soon became disillusioned with Redpath's colonization efforts, returned to Worcester, and publically voiced his opposition to the project. After the Civil War, Mason, no longer a fugitive slave, returned to Kent County, Maryland, in 1866 as a member of his church's delegation. The group, led by Reverend G. W. Offley, assisted former slaves. Mason published his narrative, *Life of Isaac Mason as a Slave* in 1893. Five years later, he died on 28 August.

FURTHER READING

Mason, Isaac. *Life of Isaac Mason as a Slave*. 1893. (2009).

McCarthy, B. Eugene, and Thomas L. Doughton, eds. *From Bondage to Belonging: The Worcester Slave Narratives* (2007).

Salvatore, Nick. *We All Got History: The Memory Books of Amos Weber* (1996).

LINDA M. CARTER

Mason, Lena Doolin (8 May 1864–4 Sep. 1924), evangelist and poet, was born Lena Doolin in Quincy, Illinois, to Vaughn Poole Doolin, a black Civil War soldier, and Reida (or Reba) Doolin, a former slave. After the war the Doolin family moved to Hannibal, Missouri. Lena Doolin was the fifth of ten children and grew up with her seven sisters and two brothers in a loving family. Doolin's parents affirmed her as a person and nurtured her in the Christian faith. In January 1872, at the age of seven, she joined the African Methodist Episcopal (AME) Church of Hannibal under the Reverend John Turner. Church leaders and family sensed that Lena had a special God-ordained purpose for her life at an early age,

and by age twelve she was able to interpret scripture as effectively as an adult. Twice during her youth she felt a nudging from God to preach the Christian gospel. Doolin postponed responding to the call while she attended Douglass High School in Hannibal and Knott's School in Chicago. She married George Mason on 9 March 1883, when she was nineteen years old. Four boys and two girls were born to them, but only one child, Bertha, born in 1887, survived to adulthood.

In 1887, at age twenty-three, Lena Mason accepted the call and began her ministry as a preacher and evangelist. Rev. Dr. Cornelius Thaddeus Schaffer, a medical doctor who was also pastor of an African Methodist Episcopal Church, licensed Mason to preach. While the AME Church would not ordain female clergy, several AME pastors had no qualms about giving licenses to women, since they had proven themselves to be effective evangelists. Between 1868 and 1884 local licenses were under the control of the denomination, thus permitting some flexibility on the role of women in the church, and in 1884 the General Conference officially approved the position of female evangelists within the church organization. Mason preached to white congregations during the first three years of her ministry. As her reputation grew, she also preached in interracial settings, as well as in black churches, such as the Wayman Chapel in Chicago (1911), Ebenezer AME in Evanston, Illinois (1911 and 1917), and the Quinn Chapel AME Church in Louisville, Kentucky (1918).

Mason touched many lives as she spread the Gospel during her travels through the West. On the evening of 10 May 1896, she launched a revival in Denver that, according to the *Colorado Statesman*, drew nearly one thousand people who came from all denominations to hear her sermon "The Rejected Stone Made the Head of the Corner." At one service she gave in May 1896 at Denver's Shorter Chapel, she converted William Paul Quinn Byrd, who later went on to become an AME minister. Although she was short in stature, Mason had a powerfully resonant voice and an energetic, eloquent delivery. Her biblical interpretation was solid and sound, and her illustrations and life applications were delightfully refreshing. Mason's Wesleyan orientation was manifested in the manner in which she coupled personal piety with social holiness, and her sermons (and her poetry) spoke of racial equality, political freedom, civil liberties, and spiritual redemption.

Around 1900 Mason conducted a tent camp meeting in St. Paul, Minnesota, and spent five months in-Minneapolis, Minnesota. In August 1908 she preached during the Great Central Chautauqua Meeting in Philadelphia, Pennsylvania, and eventually preached in nearly every state in the Union. More than sixteen hundred persons were converted to Christianity as a result of her ministry, including men and women, white and black, rich and poor, the educated and the uneducated, and her converts came from a variety of denominations. Although some accounts suggest that Mason was affiliated with the Colored Conference of the Methodist Church, her name appears as an original member of the Colorado Branch in the fifth district of the AME Missionary Society, organized by Bishop BENJAMIN T. TANNER.

Mason was widely acclaimed as an orator, songwriter, and poet. In one of her best-known poems, "A Negro in It," she provides history about the role and contributions of African Americans in United States history, including their gallantry in the Civil War and in the battle of San Juan Hill during the Spanish-American War, as well as J. B. Parker's role in the capture of President William McKinley's assassin in 1901. "The Negro in Education" emphasizes the liberating effects of educating the mind, and another poem provides a religious rationale for the futility of lynching.

No conclusive information has been discovered about Mason's last years and the events surrounding her death. The 1920 Federal census showed her living in Philadelphia's Ward 26, and the *Chicago Defender* of 6 September 1924 reported that Mrs. Lena Mason was found dead in her home by the police and services were held at Bethel AME Church on 5 September. That same report indicates that she was survived by her husband and a daughter and son.

FURTHER READING

Dodson, Jualynne E. "African Methodist Episcopal Preaching Women," in *Black Women in America*, ed. Darlene Clark Hine (1993).

"Lena Mason: Methodist Evangelist Credited with Numerous Conversions," in *Profiles of Negro Womanhood*, ed. Sylvia G. L. Dannett, vol. 1 (1964–1966).

"Mason, Lena Doolin," in *Facts on File Encyclopedia of Black Women in America: The Early Years, 1617–1899*, ed. Darlene Clark Hine (1997).

Tait, Jennifer Woodruff. "I Received My Commission from Him, Brother," *Christian History and Bibliography* 82 (Spring 2004).

ARTHUREE MCLAUGHLIN WRIGHT

Mason, Vivian Carter (10 Feb. 1900–10 May 1982), feminist, club woman, social worker, and civil rights activist, was born Vivian Carter in Wilkes-Barre, Pennsylvania, the sixth of eight children and daughter of George Cook Carter, a Methodist minister, and Florence (Williams) Carter, a music teacher. The Carters instilled in their children strong Christian ideals and high moral standards. She was raised in Auburn, New York, the very place HARRIET TUBMAN settled in the last years of her life, and Carter's mother often entertained the famous activist. "As a child I could not realize what a wonderful privilege it was to have known the famed freedom fighter Harriet Tubman. 'Aunt Harriet,' as we called her, would tramp through the ice, snow, and bitter cold of the northern winters from her home on the outskirts to our snug house" (Thurman, 28).

Vivian Carter was educated in Auburn, New York's integrated public schools. While a college student at the University of Chicago, Carter honed her skills as an activist by joining and actively participating in the National Association of Colored Women's Clubs (NACWC), the NAACP, and Alpha Kappa Alpha Sorority. These organizations were prominent opponents of segregation.

While attending the University of Chicago, Carter met her future husband, fellow student William T. Mason, a native of Trinidad, West Indies. After graduating from the University of Chicago in 1924 with a bachelor's degree in both Political Science and Social Work, she pursued graduate work at Fordham University and New York University. In 1925 she and Mason married and later moved to Norfolk, Virginia. In 1926 she gave birth to their only child, William T. Mason Jr., who would later graduate from Howard University Law School and became the first African American U.S. attorney since Reconstruction to represent Virginia's eastern region. William T. Mason Sr. became a resourceful businessman, establishing a lucrative real estate and insurance business that survived the Great Depression. He cofounded Norfolk Community Hospital, and managed to amass a considerable fortune before his death in 1976.

Because of their economic stability, and the ill-equipped condition of schools for African Americans in Norfolk, Virginia, the Masons decided to educate their only child in integrated schools in the North. In 1931 Mason traveled to New York City to secure suitable schooling for her son and a job as a social worker. Mason embarked on a career as a social worker directing welfare programs at the

Young Women's Christian Association (YWCA) in New York City. Through her position at the YWCA, she met many African American leaders of the time including MARY MCLEOD BETHUNE, ADAM CLAYTON POWELL, and A. PHILIP RANDOLPH. Inspired by the contributions of these leaders and many others, Mason worked her way up the ranks to become the first African American woman to direct the administrative division of the New York Department of Welfare. While in the city, Mason organized a committee of women to raise funds to send poor children to summer camp to avoid idleness and influences that might lead them into trouble. This achievement in Mason's career was no easy feat. She counted on the support of like-minded people in other local and national organizations, including the NAACP, the YWCA, and the National Council of Negro Women (NCNW).

In order to devote more time to being a wife and mother, Mason returned to Norfolk, Virginia, in the 1940s. While World War II raged in Europe, African Americans were fighting to reform segregated America, demanding full integration and civil rights. Mason, a trained political scientist, became one of the leading social and political reform activists in Norfolk. At the time Norfolk had no integrated political or social groups, inferior educational facilities for black children, and no African American public officials. Within six months of her arrival, Mason had formed the Women's Interracial Council, an integrated group that advocated for changes in employment, housing, education, and recreation. From 1949 to 1953 Mason served as president of the Norfolk chapter of the NCNW and as national vice president and adviser to the NCNW president DOROTHY B. FEREBEE. One of the most powerful social activists of the twentieth century, Mary McLeod Bethune met and worked closely with Mason and observed her efficiency as an invaluable member of the NCNW. In 1945, during Bethune's tenure as NCNW president, Bethune designated Mason to represent the NCNW at the Council on the International Women's Democratic Federation (IWDF) in Paris, France. Mason continued to serve on the executive board of IWDF becoming vice president of its American affiliate, the Congress of American Women. In 1953 Mason was elected national president of the NCNW. This non-paid position gave Mason an opportunity to make a large impact nationally and internationally. During her tenure as president from 1953 until 1957 the organization grew in membership, stature, and influence. The NCNW's structure incorporated a rather comprehensive program. Its internal composition included local councils and national affiliates, and its cooperative endeavors extended to every major program affecting minorities in America. Mason introduced more efficient and sophisticated order in the headquarters' administrative offices and further developed the organization's programs. She also placed special emphasis on interracial cooperation.

In 1955 the Montgomery, Alabama, bus boycott was the largest successful protest led by African Americans. The National Council of Negro Women led by Mason during this era aided in the success of its efforts by supplying the support needed through NCNW affiliate organizations to the Montgomery Improvement Association led by the Reverend MARTIN LUTHER KING JR. Mason visited Alabama to acquire firsthand information on the boycott and its progress.

In 1971 Mason became the first African American woman appointed to the Norfolk city school board, was awarded the Virginia Press's Women "Newsmaker of 1971 Award," and established the Norfolk Branch of the National Urban League in 1978. Among her numerous local involvements were the Daughters of the Elks, the National Women's Political Caucus Council, Links Inc., the Norfolk Chamber of Commerce, the Norfolk Democratic Committee, the Status of Women Commission, the Tidewater Assembly on Family Life, and many other grassroots organizations. She was honored throughout her life with many awards and is respected today as a renowned advocate for the poor, national and international civil rights leader, crusader, and trailblazer. At the age of eighty-two, Vivian Carter Mason died of a chronic heart condition at the Norfolk Community Hospital.

FURTHER READINGS

A significant amount of information on Vivian Carter Mason can be found at the Mary McLeod Bethune Council House National Historic Site's Archives of Black Women's History, Norfolk State University Archives, and Old Dominion University Libraries Special Collections.

Mason, Vivian Carter. "The Essence and Emphasis of NCNW," National Council of Negro Women Inc., *Women United Souvenir Year Book Sixteenth Anniversary* (1951).

Giddings, Paula. *When and Where I Enter: The Impact of Black Women on Race and Sex in America* (1984)

Thomas, Bettye C. *National Council of Negro Women 1935–1980* (1981).

Thurman, Sue B., ed., National Council of Negro Women Inc., *The Historical Cookbook of the American Negro* (1958).

Obituary: *Virginia Pilot*, 12 May 1982.

JOY G. KINARD

Massaquoi, Hans J. (19 Jan. 1926–), journalist, editor, and writer, was born Hans-Jürgen Massaquoi in Hamburg, Germany, the son of Al-Haj Massaquoi, a businessman from Liberia, and Bertha Baetz, a domestic worker and nurse from Germany. Massaquoi descended from a family with strong political ties and power in the West African capital city of Monrovia. His grandfather Momolu Massaquoi inherited the crown of his parents, King Lahai and Queen Sandimanni.

During the course of his life Massaquoi lived on three continents, but it was his experience of growing up black in Germany, a child of Liberian and German parents, that set the course of much of his life. Massaquoi's father, the consul general to Germany since 1922, had to return to Liberia in 1929, leaving his wife and son behind. Massaquoi was a child during a period when African American culture, and particularly music, had become a source of renewal for the moribund Weimar Republic. Soon, however, the sociopolitical environment would turn increasingly hostile toward people of non-Aryan descent. After Hitler's rise to power as chancellor in 1933, Massaquoi lived in constant fear of Nazi cleansing policies that meant deportation to a concentration camp. Under the care of his loving mother he spent his first twenty-two years in Hamburg. During the 1930s and 1940s he came to idolize African American sports figures such as the boxer JOE LOUIS and the track-and-field star JESSE OWENS. With the 1936 Olympic Games in Berlin and Max Schmeling's series of fights against Louis, the "Brown Bomber," from 1936 to 1938, Massaquoi found some prominent black icons he could proudly identify with.

Miraculously, Massaquoi slipped through the deadly net of the Nazis' persecution of non-Aryans. He survived World War II and the devastating British bomber attacks on Hamburg called Operation Gomorrah physically unscathed. After the surrender of Germany in 1945 Massaquoi and his mother faced starvation and homelessness. In order to survive dire postwar struggles Massaquoi played saxophone in various German jazz bands. In some ways, through his adoption of American styles and attitudes, he fashioned himself into an African American long before he actually became a naturalized citizen.

In 1948 Massaquoi left Germany to reconnect with his African roots in Liberia. Living there for many years, he found his appreciation of African culture to be growing, even if a reunion with his father's side of the family eighteen years after his departure from Germany remained an ambivalent experience. It was not until his arrival in Monrovia that Massaquoi learned of the existence of his brother Morris, whom his father had discredited and abandoned. Disenchanted by these Liberian encounters he embarked with a one-year student visa to the United States. Nine months later Massaquoi joined the U.S. Army as a paratrooper in the Eighty-Second Airborne Division. After two years in the service, a decorated Massaquoi enrolled at the community college in Elgin and later at the University of Illinois in Urbana-Champaign. Having earned a bachelor's degree in journalism and communication sciences, he held some minor editorial jobs before he landed a position with JOHN H. JOHNSON's publication company. Starting as a writer for the weekly magazine *Jet*, he soon worked his way up to the more esteemed, influential monthly *Ebony*, the leading African American magazine and the flagship of the Johnson publishing empire. From his vantage as a managing editor and member of the publication's editorial board, Massaquoi wielded considerable media power. Among his concerns were exploitation, racism, and sociopolitical inequality. He interviewed leading politicians around the world and inveighed against racial stereotypes in the United States, Africa, Europe, Asia, and the Caribbean. His diverse assignments included interviews with the presidents of Nigeria, Botswana, Liberia, and Namibia, civil rights activists like Dr. MARTIN LUTHER KING JR., the Reverend JESSE JACKSON, and MALCOLM X, as well as icons of American culture such as the singer DIANA ROSS, the actor RICHARD ROUNDTREE, the writer ALEX HALEY, and the boxer MUHAMMAD ALI.

Massaquoi developed a keen insight into the latent patterns of racist behavior. His childhood experience as a black child within a basically all-white environment and the open racism of the Nazis fostered in him a lifelong concern for ethnic minorities all over the world. In the United States Massaquoi offered prominent voices from the civil rights movement a popular platform by writing about their visions of social reform in *Ebony*. When Massaquoi saw what he labeled "the ugly side of America," he became active in the civil rights movement, joining, for example, Dr. Martin

Luther King Jr. in his "march for open housing" in Chicago's all-white Gage Park neighborhood.

In 1966 Massaquoi revisited Hamburg for the first time in almost two decades. There he published a two-part article entitled "A Journey into the Past," which touched on aspects of racial equality in democratic West Germany, the native population's ambivalent responses toward Americanization, the German jazz craze from the Weimar Republic to the postwar years, and the so-called "brown babies," the mostly illegitimate offspring of black GIs and German women. During his many returns to Germany he continued to report on the representation of African Americans and ongoing racism on American military bases abroad. In the 1960s and 1970s he served as an important cultural mediator for German radio, TV, and print journalists covering the progress of the civil rights movement in the United States. Massaquoi's transcultural perspective on issues regarding human rights became an important source of inspiration for his colleagues on both sides of the Atlantic.

Massaquoi had two sons with his first wife, Joan De Berry, Steve and Hans Jr. In 1999 he published the first part of his autobiography, *Destined to Witness: Growing Up Black in Nazi Germany*, which became a huge success in Germany under the title *Neger, Neger, Schornsteinfeger*, a reference to a mocking children's song about black kids. The book attracted film directors and spawned a sequel covering Massaquoi's career in the United States, which as of June 2005 had only appeared in a German translation called *Hänschen klein, ging allein … Mein Weg in die Neue Welt* ("Little Hans Left All by Himself … My Way to the New World"). After his first marriage ended, Massaquoi and his second wife, Katharine, relocated to Florida.

FURTHER READING

Massaquoi, Hans. *Destined to Witness: Growing Up Black in Nazi Germany* (1999).

Massaquoi, Hans. *Hänschen klein, ging allein … Mein Weg in die Neue Welt* (2004).

Hopkins, Leroy. "Writing Diasporic Identity: Afro-German Literature since 1985," in *Not So Plain as Black and White: Afro-German Culture and History, 1890–2000*, eds. Patricia Mazón and Reinhild Steingröver (2005).

FRANK MEHRING

Massey, Walter Eugene (Apr. 1938–), physicist, science and engineering administrator, and college president, was born in Hattiesburg, Mississippi, the first of two sons born to Almar C. Massey, a manual laborer for the Hercules Chemical Company, and Essie Nelson, an elementary school teacher and principal. Massey received support and encouragement not only from his parents but also from a cadre of excellent African American teachers, who, as a resolt of restricted employment opportunities in rigidly segregated Mississippi, pursued teaching with passion and dedication. Massey attended the Sixteenth Section Elementary School in Hattiesburg, where his mother taught, and the Royal Street High School in the same city. He excelled in school and entered Atlanta's Morehouse College on a Ford Foundation scholarship after completing the tenth grade. As a student at Morehouse, Massey, like MARTIN LUTHER KING JR. and other African American men who attended the college between 1940 and 1967, came under the influence of the president, the renowned Dr. BENJAMIN MAYS.

Buttressed by the high standards of excellence advocated by Mays and by the mentoring he had received from a cast of outstanding teachers from the Sixteenth Section to Morehouse College, Massey embarked on a journey that led him to an international reputation as an educator and science and engineering administrator. After spending one year in graduate school at Howard University, Massey entered Washington University in St. Louis, Missouri. At Washington University he began work on understanding the behavior of liquid helium with Dr. Eugene Feenberg as his adviser. Massey's interest in liquid helium led later in his career to work for which he is best known as a physicist. This work, in which he collaborated with Humphrey Maris, provided a theoretical explanation for the anomalous dispersion of sound in superfluid helium. He received both a master's degree and a doctorate from Washington University in 1966.

Subsequently he became a staff physicist at the Argonne National Laboratory in Chicago, an institution to which he returned in 1979 as director. Massey joined the faculty at the University of Illinois as an assistant professor of physics in 1968. In 1969 he married Shirley A. Streeter of Chicago, Illinois. The couple had two sons, Keith and Eric. After two years at Illinois, Massey became associate professor of physics at Brown University in Providence, Rhode Island, where he remained for nine years. While at Brown, Massey became professor of physics and served as dean of the college from 1975 until 1979. After leaving Brown he served for five years as director of the Argonne National Laboratory; he also accepted the position of vice president for research at the University of Chicago, where he remained for seven years. In 1991 he became the director of the foremost federal agency for the support of basic research in the physical sciences, mathematics, and engineering, the National Science Foundation (NSF). At the NSF he advocated a stronger coupling between academe and industry in the pursuit of research in science and engineering. In 1993 he joined the University of California system as provost and senior vice president for academic affairs. In 1995 he returned to Morehouse as its ninth president. In this leadership position he has advocated the development of leaders and high academic standards; he has also sought to enhance the stature of the college both nationally and internationally.

Massey's career has been characterized by a number of firsts. He was the first African American to receive a doctorate in physics at Washington University, the first African American dean at Brown University, the first African American director at the Argonne National Laboratory and at the National Science Foundation, the first African American vice president at the University of Chicago, and the first African American provost of the University of California system. As an educator, Massey has taught physics at several universities; however, the leadership he has provided in the development of policy and direction in educational organizations has been more significant. In 1971 and 1972 he served on the executive committee on Physics in the Predominantly Black Colleges for the American Institute of Physics. During the same period he implemented a program at Brown University to prepare teachers to teach science and mathematics in urban school systems. Later in the same decade he served on the board of advisers for the Fund for the Improvement of Post-Secondary Education, the Energy Advisory Committee of the Association of American Universities, and the Commission on Institutional Development and National Affairs of the American Association of Colleges. He has served on the boards of trustees of Washington University, Brown University, and Rockefeller University. In 1996 he became a member of the Annenberg Institute of School Reform and the advisory board of the Georgia Institute of Technology. He joined the board of directors of the Morehouse School of Medicine in 1997. In 1999 he became a member of the National Commission on Mathematics and Science Teaching for the 21st Century and the Gates Millennium Scholars Advisory Council.

Walter Massey's career has been characterized by his willingness to serve in leadership roles in varied organizations. He has not just remained active in professional and civic organizations but has often assumed the mantle of leadership. Notably, he served as president (1988–1989) and chairman (1989–1990) of the American Association for the Advancement of Science and as vice president (1990) of the American Physical Society. He served on the National Science Board from 1978 through 1984 and the President's Council of Advisers on Science and Technology from 1990 until 1992. He rejoined the president's council in 2001. Also in 2001 he became a member of the board of directors of the Rotary Club of Atlanta. Since 1998 he has served as chairman of the Atlanta Committee for Public Education.

At Morehouse, Massey has been actively involved in the college's Minority Research Institute, which has focused on research to strengthen and improve prospects for African American male youth, who at the end of the twentieth century were disproportionately affected by numerous American societal maladies and pathologies. At Morehouse he fostered the development of a formal leadership program and established the goal of being the best liberal arts college as an aim commensurate with the Morehouse legacy. As president of Morehouse, Massey found the ideal arena in which to meet the challenges of Benjamin Mays and that cast of outstanding African American educators who mentored and nurtured him. In 2006 Massey announced that after a decade at the helm, he would retire as president at the end of the 2006–2007 academic year.

FURTHER READING

"Former NSF Director Massey Returns to Alma Mater, Morehouse College, as Institution's New President," *The Scientist* 9 (21 Aug. 1995), 15.

Manning, Kenneth. "Race, Gender and Science," *History of Science Society Online Newsletter*, http://www.hssonline.org/society/about/newsletter/ (1995).

Sammons, Vivian O. *Blacks in Science and Education* (1989).

ROBERT M. DIXON

Massiah, Louis Joseph (10 June 1954–), documentary filmmaker, was born in Philadelphia, Pennsylvania, the youngest of three sons of the engineer and contractor Frederick McDonald Massiah, a native of Barbados, and Edith Lamarre-Massiah from Haiti, who taught French at North Carolina Central College and the Baldwin School in Bryn Mawr, Pennsylvania. Massiah grew up in North Philadelphia near Temple University. He attended Friends Select School, an independent Quaker institution in Philadelphia, from kindergarten through grade 12, and received an undergraduate degree from Cornell University in 1977.

At Cornell, Massiah studied physics and astronomy, but also became interested in media arts. While residing at the University's Risley College for the Creative and Performing Arts, Massiah made the experimental film *Exercise: Swim, Pebble, Martyr, Remember* (1975). During this time, he also started to work at WNET, the public television station in New York City. He later pursued a graduate degree in Documentary Filmmaking at Massachusetts Institute for Technology in Cambridge, where he graduated in 1982 with a thesis entitled "Event and Idea: A Writer's Approach to the Videotape Documentary."

After his graduate studies, Massiah returned to his native Philadelphia and in 1982 founded the Scribe Video Center, a grassroots nonprofit media arts organization that offered low-cost workshops and equipment access to emerging video/filmmakers. The center's mission was to reach communities that traditionally had not had access to video training and production facilities including people of color, women, young people, senior citizens, and those with limited economic resources. Massiah served as executive director of Scribe from its inception. He also devised the Precious Places Community History Project, a citywide oral history project produced collaboratively with 42 neighborhood organizations in and around Philadelphia.

Massiah's first film after graduate school was *Miami Journal: The Haitian Refugees* (1982), a film about the U.S. government's unequal policies toward Haitians and Cubans, with the latter receiving preferential treatment. As a producer and director at WHYY, the public television station in Philadelphia, Massiah produced a variety of documentaries including the acclaimed *The Bombing of Osage Avenue*, about the 1985 Philadelphia police bombing of the MOVE organization headquarters. In the following years, Massiah became a nationally recognized community historian by producing and directing two episodes of the award-winning *Eyes on the Prize II* series (*Power! 1967–1968* and *A Nation of Law? 1968–1971*) produced for HENRY HAMPTON's *Blackside, Inc.* Massiah is perhaps best known for his innovative documentary *W. E. B. Du Bois: A Biography in Four Voices*, completed in 1996. A collaboration with the writers TONI CADE BAMBARA, AMIRI BARAKA, Wesley Brown, and THULANI DAVIS, the documentary captures the complex life and politics of one of the nation's seminal intellectuals, Pan-Africanists, activists, writers, and organizers. Besides internationally renowned individuals such as Du Bois, Massiah also profiled less-known personalities like the African American labor activist and Communist leader LOUISE THOMPSON PATTERSON. Over the course of his career, Massiah made more than 20 historical documentaries. *Haytian Stories* focuses on two centuries of intense and often tragic relations between the United States and the Republic of Haiti.

Over the course of his career Massiah received numerous awards for his work in documentary film and television. He was awarded fellowships from the Pew Trust (1994), the Rockefeller Foundation (1990, 1996), and the John D. and Catherine T. MacArthur Foundation (1996). He also received the PAUL ROBESON Award for Social Justice from Philadelphia's Bread and Roses Community Foundation, as well as awards from Columbia-DuPont, the Corporation for Public Broadcasting, the Global Village Documentary Festival, and the Black Filmmakers Hall of Fame, and several nominations for Emmy Awards. Additionally, Massiah was a lecturer and resident artist at the Princeton University Atelier, Haverford College, and the University of Pennsylvania. In 2006 he joined the faculty of the School of Communication at American University in Washington, D.C., as senior professor of film and media arts.

Massiah emerged as one of the most important African American documentary filmmakers in the United States. A highly gifted storyteller, he was also a brilliant historian with a keen eye for detail as well as a profound sense for setting events into perspective and connecting them to the larger national and global context. In his films, Massiah reported courageously about politically controversial topics and brought us closer to the lives of daring social activists who often paid dearly for their struggle against discrimination, oppression, and injustice.

FURTHER READING

Klotman, Phyllis R., and Janet K. Cutler, eds. *Struggles for Representation: African American Documentary* (1999).

INA J. FANDRICH

Massie, Samuel Proctor, Jr. (3 July 1919–10 Apr. 2005), scientist and first black professor and chemistry department head at the U.S. Naval Academy, was one of three sons born in North Little Rock, Arkansas, to Samuel Proctor Massie and Earlee Jacko Massie. His twin brother died soon after birth. Massie was nurtured in an extended family of educators, devout churchgoers, and community and civic leaders. He learned from his father, an African Methodist Episcopal (AME) preacher and biology teacher, to stand up for himself and to minister to others' needs. His maternal grandmother, Josephine Jacko, a full-blooded Choctaw Indian, was born a slave. She instilled in him a sense of right and wrong and during long conversations helped him to recognize his gift for motivating and guiding others. His maternal grandfather, William B. Jacko, also a schoolteacher and former superintendent of schools in Jefferson Steps, Jefferson County, served in the Arkansas State House of Representatives from 1885 to 1889.

Massie's mother was the impetus behind his early intellectual development and achievements. At four he accompanied her to her job in Keo, Arkansas, where she taught in a one-room schoolhouse. In the classroom, he followed her habitually as she taught, soon beginning to learn to read, spell, write, and do arithmetic. During the week Grandma Josephine took care of his father and the home in North Little Rock while Samuel Massie Sr. taught at the high school for blacks. On weekends the family reunited. Signaling future scholarship and many pioneering firsts, the scientist-to-be entered first grade working at a third-grade level and completed seventh grade when he was nine. Although a precocious youth whose time was spent mostly on academic pursuits, he still enjoyed childhood pleasures. From an early age he always worked to be prepared and qualified for any situation he entered. Keeping this promise and finding a cure for his father's asthma were central goals in his life.

Massie spent his high school years at Paul Laurence Dunbar High School in Little Rock, where his father had begun to teach and to chair the science department. In his father's biology classes, Massie's passion for science skyrocketed. He graduated from high school at thirteen, and at eighteen he graduated summa cum laude and as valedictorian with a bachelor's degree in chemistry, with a minor in mathematics, from the Agricultural, Mechanical, and Normal (AM&N) College, a teaching-oriented, predominantly black school that is now the University of Arkansas, Pine Bluff.

During his last year at AM&N, Massie introduced himself to the Reverend WILLIAM J. FAULKNER, a minister and the dean of religion at Fisk University in Nashville, Tennessee. Faulkner was participating in a conference held at AM&N. In response to Faulkner's questions about his plans after graduation, Massie said that he did not know what he would do and did not have any money. Upon hearing this, Faulkner asked him to come to Fisk and he facilitated his studies by helping him to obtain a federal National Youth Administration Scholarship. Arriving at Fisk in 1939, he found the world of laboratory research opened to him. St. Elmo Brady headed the chemistry department, and under his leadership Massie's scientific talents began to emerge. At twenty-one Massie received an M.A. in Chemistry from Fisk and returned to AM&N for a brief stint as teacher and acting head of the mathematics and physics departments.

In 1941 he decided to enter a doctoral program at Iowa State University (ISU) in Ames. Dr. NATHANIEL O. CALLOWAY, an organic chemist who had graduated from ISU and had been a research fellow there in the 1930s, and Dr. Henry Gilman, a nationally renowned chemist and ISU professor, were responsible for his going to Iowa State. Dr. Calloway had recommended him to the doctoral program and Dr. Gilman had accepted him. Massie's studies at Fisk exposed him not only to the brilliant scholarship and scientific techniques of Calloway and Gilman but also to Dr. Roger Adams and Dr. Louis Fieser, both highly esteemed chemists from Harvard University. These eminent scientists, especially Calloway and Gilman, sharpened his skills and development as a chemist. A lifelong friend, Gilman mentored Massie and introduced him to phenothiazine, the focus of Massie's groundbreaking research and the classic 1954 article "The Chemistry of Phenothiazine" published in *Chemical Reviews*. As the chief source of information on phenothiazine, Massie received more than five hundred requests for reprints of his article from more than fifty countries. He presented professional papers on phenothiazine at conferences held in Brazil, Japan, Mexico, and Switzerland. After two years at ISU, Massie withdrew to serve the war effort as a member of Gilman's team working on the Manhattan Project, developing the atomic bomb. Massie then resumed his studies, graduating in 1946 with a Ph.D. in Organic Chemistry and co-authoring with Gilman six papers published by the American Chemical Society (ACS).

Poverty-stricken and nearly losing his draft deferment, at Ames he withstood separation from his family, social isolation, the death of his father from asthma, and racial discrimination and prejudice. Eventually ISU allowed Massie to conduct experiments in its regular chemistry lab instead of in the dilapidated and vacant biochemistry lab in the building's basement. He was never permitted to live on campus. Archie and Nancy Martin, former slaves and housing rights advocates, aided his adjustment to Ames's racial isolation. For a time he lived in their home, where they looked after him and scores of other black male ISU students between 1920 and 1960.

After completing his PhD, Massie was unable to find work in private industry because no one would hire blacks so he returned to Fisk to teach. His friend, former colleague, and mentor, Dr. Brady had invited him back with high hopes that he would assume the leadership of the chemistry department after Brady's planned retirement in 1947. At Fisk Massie met Gloria Belle Thompkins, president of her senior class of 1947, and his first serious romance. She was to become his wife. Thompkins had asked him to serve as a chaperone at a school function. They began dating and were married in August 1947, a few months after she graduated. Instead of assuming the department's chairmanship, Massie soon left for Langston, Oklahoma, to direct Langston University's chemistry department and to research antimalarial and cancer-fighting drugs. At Langston he was the inspiration behind the 1950 statewide interracial chemistry education conference, and in 1953 he was the first black to be elected president of the Oklahoma Academy of Sciences. Not long after the election, Fisk's president Charles S. Johnson learned of his achievement and invited him to chair the department of chemistry at Fisk. At the end of 1953 Massie and his wife left Langston to return to Fisk. At the helm of the department, Massie lived up to the high standards set by Brady, his predecessor and mentor, and the ambitious goals embraced by President Johnson. He continued to provide high quality education to Fisk students and was innovative, courageous, and forward-looking in achieving Fisk's mission. In 1955 he convened the ASC's sixth chemistry conference, the first time a major scientific gathering was held at a historically black university. In attendance were many distinguished scientists, including a Nobel Laureate.

In 1960 Massie became the first black to hold a prominent position at the National Science Foundation in Washington, D.C. As associate director of advanced science programs he administered the nation's science education and research agenda and oversaw grants to university scientists. Concurrently he served part-time at Howard University as professor and chair of the pharmaceutical chemistry department.

In 1963, with his wife and three sons, including twins, he moved to Durham to become the third president of North Carolina College (now North Carolina Central University), a black liberal arts school. Combining his talents as a science scholar, administrator, and master teacher, he continued the school's tradition of excellence, brought in grants and gifts, increased enrollment to its highest level ever, expanded the faculty, especially with professors holding PhDs, and advocated equal funding for all of North Carolina's schools. In 1966 during the civil rights movement Massie again made history as the U.S. Naval Academy's first black professor, and in 1977 he became head of its chemistry department. Expressing "gratitude to ISU and Dr. Gilman for the chance to show what he could do," Massie said that his experiences in Ames helped him to adjust to the Naval Academy. "Being at Iowa State was my first time living outside a segregated Black community" (Massie and Hayden, 9).

At the Naval Academy, Massie's influence was pervasive. He volunteered to prepare local Annapolis youth to pursue academy training, chaired the academy's first Equal Economic Opportunity Committee, and helped develop the black studies program. As a gubernatorial charter appointee to Maryland's board of community colleges and its president from 1979 to 1989, he helped formulate policies for state schools. He decried the housing discrimination blacks faced, leading officials to establish a human relations commission to investigate discrimination claims.

Massie received numerous honors, among them the Manufacturing Chemists Award as one of the top six U.S. university chemistry teachers (1960), the ISU Alumni Merit (1964) and Distinguished Achievement (1981) citations, and an honorary doctor of laws (1970) from the University of Arkansas—which ironically had rejected his application in 1934 because he was black. He was named Outstanding Professor by the National Organization of Black Professional Chemists and Chemical Engineers (1980), and for his work with the United Negro College Fund and Maryland's Board of Community Colleges, he received a White House Lifetime Achievement Award for Contributions to Science, Technology, and Community Service (1988).

Inducted into the National Black College Hall of Fame (1989), he received the Naval Academy's award for faculty achievement (1990) and the ACS's James Flack Norris Teaching Award (1994).

In 1992 the Annapolis chapter of the National Naval Officers Association designated its scholarship as the Samuel P. Massie Educational Endowment Fund. In 1994 his portrait was hung in the National Academy of Sciences Gallery, and the U.S. Department of Energy endowed the $14.7 million Dr. Samuel P. Massie Chairs of Excellence at ten universities. Soon after his retirement in 1994, the U.S. Congress paid tribute to him in the Congressional Record.

As a scholar and scientist *Chemical and Engineering News* ranked Massie among the top seventy-five chemists of the twentieth century (1998); he received acclaim for research in combating malaria and meningitis, for drugs to fight herpes and cancer, and for foams to protect against nerve gases. He shared a patent for chemical agents effective in treating gonorrhea. From 1990 to 1991 he served as Grand Sire Archon of Sigma Pi Phi Fraternity (the Boule), and in 1996 he received the ACS Award for Encouraging Disadvantaged Students into Careers in the Chemical Sciences. Of his many awards and citations, he ranked at the top the Laurel Wreath (1976) given by Kappa Alpha Psi fraternity to only fifty-one of nearly 110,000 members since 1911. Massie was promoted to professor emeritus in 1994 with his retirement from the Naval Academy. He died eleven years later at age eighty-five in Laurel, Maryland.

FURTHER READING

Materials about Massie are in the Iowa State University archives.

Massie, Samuel P., with Robert C. Hayden. *Catalyst: The Autobiography of an American Chemist, Dr. Samuel P. Massie* (2000).

Obituary: *Washington Post*, 15 Apr. 2005.

DEBRA A. VARNADO

Matheus, John Frederick (10 Sept. 1887–21 Feb. 1983), writer, educator, and scholar, was born in Keyser, West Virginia, the eldest son of John William Matheus, a bank messenger and part-time tannery worker, and Mary Susan Brown Matheus. As a young boy he moved with his family to Steubenville, Ohio, where he developed a great love for literature and reading. As a teenager he read the poets Edgar Allan Poe, Henry Wadsworth Longfellow, and Heinrich Heine and was inspired to write his own verse, some of which was published in two local newspapers. At the age of fifteen he also demonstrated his talent for writing prose by winning a prize for the best history of Ohio in a contest offered by the Woman's Club of Steubenville. He crowned these early achievements by graduating with honors from Steubenville High School in 1905. The following year he began studying at Western Reserve University and in 1910 earned an AB (cum laude), with a concentration in Latin, Greek, German, and Romance Languages.

That same year Matheus and his wife, Maude Roberts, whom he married in 1909 (they never had children), moved to Tallahassee, Florida, where he was professor of Latin and modern foreign languages at Florida Agricultural and Mechanical College. The South offered Matheus new opportunities and experiences, but not all were positive: "I had heard about prejudice but I didn't get my first taste of it until I visited Tallahassee in 1911" (Morris, 6). Undeterred, Matheus stayed there until 1920, but then left to attend Columbia University, where in 1921 he received a master's degree in romance languages and a diploma as a teacher of French. He furthered his education by attending classes at the Sorbonne in Paris in 1925 and doing a summer term at the University of Chicago in 1927.

Matheus was hired to head the Department of Romance Language and Literature at West Virginia Colored Institute (later West Virginia State College) in 1922, a position he occupied until 1953. Early in his stint there he resumed his creative writing in earnest and began submitting short stories, poems, plays, and essays to black literary periodicals. One of his short stories, "Fog," garnered national attention when it won first place in 1925 in a contest conducted by the magazine *Opportunity*. This story, arguably his best-known work, is about a racially diverse group of passengers aboard a trolley car that is involved in an accident on a fog-covered bridge. The passengers' near-death experience unites them and enables them, if only momentarily, to put aside their differences and see one another in a clearer light.

Although Matheus continued to produce a significant number of literary works between 1925 and 1935, his banner year was 1926, during which he won six awards in contests sponsored by *Opportunity*: a first place for his personal experience essay "Sand," a second place for his play '*Cruiter*, and two honorable mentions for his poetry and two for his short stories. In a *Crisis* magazine contest that same year, he won first prize for his short story "Swamp

Moccasin." By then Matheus was acquiring a reputation abroad, and his work reached more international readers when "Swamp Moccasin" and "Fog" were translated into German and French, respectively.

In 1928 Matheus accompanied Clarence Cameron White, a respected composer and music director at West Virginia State College, to Haiti to collect material on native music, folklore, and literature. The result was Matheus's play *Tambour* (1929), for which White supplied incidental music. Matheus also penned the libretto for White's opera, *Ouanga* (1931), which would have its premiere performance in South Bend, Indiana, in 1949.

In 1930 Matheus was traveling again, this time to Africa to investigate charges of forced labor in Liberia. He served as secretary to Dr. CHARLES S. JOHNSON, American member of the International Commission of Inquiry to Liberia, which was sponsored by President Hoover, the U.S. Department of State, and the League of Nations.

After 1935 Matheus occasionally published a poem or short story, but increasingly he turned his attention to scholarly writing and service in academic associations. Among the latter, he served as treasurer of the College Language Association (1943–1975); as president of the West Virginia Chapter of the American Association of Teachers of French (1949–1950); and as president of the West Virginia Chapter of the Modern Language Teachers' Association (1952–1953). The Tau Chapter of Kappa Alpha Psi Fraternity recognized his service by awarding him its 1951 Annual Achievement Award.

Teaching also remained important to Matheus, so when offered the opportunity to use his pedagogical skills in Haiti, he seized it. From 1945 to 1946 was director of the teaching of English in the national schools of Haiti, under the Inter-American Education Foundation. While there he broadcast weekly English lessons and prepared a broadcast on American music. To reward his efforts, the Haitian government decorated him an Officier de l'Ordre Nationale ("Officer of the National Order").

Even after retiring from West Virginia State College in 1953, Matheus still wanted to teach. He came out of retirement to teach at six institutions: Maryland State College, 1953–1954; Dillard University, 1954–1957; Atlanta University System, 1957–1959; Texas Southern University, 1959–1961; Hampton Institute, 1961–1962; and Kentucky State College, 1962.

In 1965 his beloved wife, Maude Roberts, died. He married Ellen Turner Gordon in 1973 (the couple had no children.) That same year he acted as a consultant for Caribbean literature of French expression for a pre-conference workshop offered by the American Council of the Teaching of Foreign Languages. One year later he privately published a collection of his short stories.

In 1980, at the age of ninety-three, Matheus still had not slowed. He was assiduously working on his autobiography (which remains unpublished). Commenting to an interviewer at the time, he said, "I don't know how much longer I have, but as long as I have a life, I want to be working" (Morris, 6).

Matheus died a few years later in Tallahassee, Florida. With his death, the world lost not only a gifted writer but also a respected scholar, teacher, and a man who worked tirelessly for the betterment of himself and others.

FURTHER READING

Some of John Frederick Matheus's papers are housed in the Archives of Drain-Jordan Library, West Virginia State University, Institute, West Virginia; and in Special Collections at Florida A&M University, Tallahassee, Florida.

Morris, Gene. "John F. Matheus—A Man for Many Seasons," *Famuan* (29 Oct. 1980).

Obituary: *Charleston (West Virginia) Daily Mail,* 22 Feb. 1983.

LARRY SEAN KINDER

Mathis, Johnny (30 Sept. 1935–), singer and musician, was born in Gilmer, Texas, to Clem Mathis, a former musician and vaudeville performer, and Mildred Mathis. He was the fourth of seven children. When Mathis was still a young boy, the family relocated to San Francisco, California. Soon thereafter, his father, noticing his son's emerging musical interests and talent, bought a $25 piano. The piano had to be completely dismantled before it would fit through the doorway of the family's basement apartment. The elder Mathis began to teach his eager son the numbers that he had performed in vaudeville and in Texas. Young Mathis sharpened his routines by performing for guests and later found a spot on the church choir. He also sang at school events and at amateur exhibitions and contests around the city.

At thirteen, Mathis began receiving formal voice training from Connie Cox, a classically trained coach. With Cox, he studied not only popular tunes but also opera, lessons that carried over into his later recording and performing career. Several years later, while attending San Francisco State

University to study English and physical education, a fellow student brought Mathis to the Black Hawk nightclub. It was a Sunday, a day when bands were allowed to jam on stage. Mathis's unplanned performance brought him to the attention of the club's owner, Helen Noga, who became the nineteen-year old singer's manager. On several occasions, she approached George Avakian, head of Columbia's jazz division, about her new client. In the fall of 1955 he at last conceded to Noga's insistence and came to see Mathis perform at Ann Dee's 440 Club. Avakian was very impressed and immediately implored Columbia to sign the young singer.

A talented and accomplished athlete who played basketball and excelled in track-and-field events (he bested a high jump record set by BILL RUSSELL), Mathis anticipated a career in organized sports. Officials had invited him to participate in the 1956 Olympic time trials, with a chance to compete in Melbourne, Australia, later that year. When Avakian summoned him to New York for a recording session, Mathis put aside his Olympic ambitions and cast his lot with the record business. His first album, *Johnny Mathis: A New Sound in Popular Music*, appeared later in 1956. A collection of popular standards, the record did not receive rave reviews and sold poorly. Mathis continued to

Johnny Mathis, photographed in March 1958. (AP Images.)

play the New York club circuit, however, and his reputation began to grow. Renowned producer Mitch Miller was one of the people who began to notice the singer's rising status. He thought Mathis's smooth, warm delivery was best suited for romantic tunes. He pushed the singer to go with his strength, and Mathis's next two singles, "It's Not for Me to Say," and "Wonderful, Wonderful," made him a star. The ballad remained among his biggest hits and most requested songs. Soon Mathis signed on to appear and sing in two motion pictures produced by MGM and Twentieth Century–Fox. He then recorded the song that became his signature hit, "Chances Are." The song soared to number one on the *Billboard* charts and brought Mathis to the attention of an even larger audience. Expanding his audience even further, Mathis appeared on Ed Sullivan's televised variety program. Mathis's rise to stardom was quick. He became the youngest African American entertainer to become a millionaire.

In 1958 Mathis moved to Beverly Hills, where he continued to perform and record. By that year he had accumulated enough hit songs to release a greatest hits album (one of the first of its kind in the recording industry), and observers recognized him as one of the top male vocalists in the country, second only perhaps to Frank Sinatra. In 1959 he recorded ERROLL GARNER's "Misty," another tune for which his was to become the standard version. Younger styles, however, predominated on the radio and on the charts, pushing jazz and adult contemporary sounds to the margins of the pop market. In this environment, Mathis's days as an automatic number one hit-maker were largely over. He continued to record with amazing energy, cutting more than 130 albums in styles ranging from jazz to R&B, and from country to several much-cherished and perennially popular Christmas albums. In 1964 Mathis hired Ray Haughn as his new agent (he and Noga had parted ways) and founded Jon Mat Records and Ronjon Productions. His association with Haughn lasted until Haughn's death in 1984. While owning his own record company gave him an entrepreneurial stake in the music business, he continued to record with Columbia during the course of his long career and remained the label's longest-running star.

Among Mathis's many accomplishments were three Grammy Awards (and six nominations), an Oscar nomination for best song (1978's *Same Time, Next Year*), and a star on Hollywood's Walk of Fame. His greatest hits album remained on the

Billboard chart for nearly ten years, an unprecedented feat. His television appearances—both his own specials as well as guest spots on programs like the *Tonight Show*—were too numerous to calculate. Never far from his roots as an athlete, Mathis hosted the Johnny Mathis Track and Field Meet at San Francisco State College, an event held annually beginning in 1982.

In 2010 Mathis's, *Let It Be Me: Mathis in Nashville*, was nominated for a Grammy in the Best Traditional Pop Vocal category. Though his style leaned heavily toward light jazz and romantic standards, Mathis was for many the preferred voice of the American musical era of classic standards. His warmly ingratiating delivery and highly distinctive vocal style put him in the top flight of love song balladeers, along with Frank Sinatra and NAT KING COLE.

FURTHER READING

Jasper, Tony. *Johnny: The Authorized Biography of Johnny Mathis* (1983).

JASON PHILIP MILLER

Matthew, Wentworth Arthur (23 June 1892–3 Dec. 1973), rabbi and educator, is believed to have been born in St. Mary's, St. Kitts, in the British West Indies, the son of Joseph Matthew and Frances M. Cornelius. Matthew gave seemingly contradictory accounts of his ancestry that put his place of birth in such places as Ethiopia, Ghana, and Lagos, Nigeria. Some of those lingering discrepancies were partially clarified when Matthew explained that his father, a cobbler from Lagos, was the son of an Ethiopian Jew, a cantor who sang traditional Jewish liturgies near the ancient Ethiopian capital of Gondar. Matthew's father then married a Christian woman in Lagos, and they gave their son, Wentworth, the Hebrew name Yoseh ben Moshe ben Yehuda, also given as Moshe Ben David. His father died when he was a small boy, and his mother took him to live in St. Kitts, where she had relatives.

In 1913 Matthew immigrated to New York City, where he worked as a carpenter and engaged in prizefighting, though he was just a scrappy five feet four inches tall. He reportedly studied at Christian and Jewish schools, including the Hayden Theological Seminary and the Rose of Sharon Theological Seminary (both now defunct), Hebrew Union College in Cincinnati, and even the University of Berlin, but there is no independent evidence to corroborate his attendance at these institutions. In 1916 Matthew married Florence Docher Liburd, a native of Fountaine, Nevis, with whom he had four children. During World War I Matthew was one of many street exhorters who used a ladder for a pulpit and Harlem's bustling sidewalks as temporary pews for interested pedestrians. By 1919 enough people were drawn to his evolving theology of Judaism and black nationalism that he was able to found "The Commandments Keepers Church of the living God, The pillar and ground of the truth And the faith of Jesus Christ." He attempted to appeal to a largely Christian audience by pointing out that observance of the Old Testament commandments was the faith of Jesus; however, it became apparent that visitors often missed this point and assumed that any reference to Jesus implied a belief in Jesus. To avoid this confusion with Christianity, Matthew ceased to use the title "Bishop" and removed all references to Jesus from the organization's literature and papers of incorporation.

The transition from a church-based organization holding Jewish beliefs to a functioning synagogue that embraced most of the tenets of mainstream Orthodox Judaism was accomplished by Matthew's association with Rabbi ARNOLD FORD. Ford was a luminary in the Universal Negro Improvement Association, the black nationalist organization led by MARCUS GARVEY. Ford offered Hebrew lessons and religious instruction to a number of laypeople and clergy in the Harlem area. He worked with both Matthew's Commandments Keepers Congregation and the Moorish Zionist Congregation led by Mordecai Herman in the 1920s before starting his own congregation, Beth B'nai Abraham. In 1931, after Ford immigrated to Ethiopia, he sent a letter to Matthew granting him "full authority to represent Us in America" and furnishing him with a *Shmecah*, a certificate of rabbinic ordination (Ford to Matthew, 5 June 1931). Throughout the rest of his career, Matthew would claim that he and his followers were Ethiopian Hebrews, because in their lexicon "Ethiopian" was preferred over the term "Negro," which they abhorred, and because his authority derived from their chief rabbi in Ethiopia.

As an adjunct to his congregation, Matthew created a Masonic lodge called the Royal Order of Aethiopian Hebrews the Sons and Daughters of Culture. He became a U.S. citizen in 1924 and the following year created the Ethiopian Hebrew Rabbinical College for the training of other black rabbis. Women often served as officers and board members of the congregation, though they could not become rabbis. In the lodge there were no gender restrictions, and women took courses and even taught in the school. Religion, history, and cultural anthropology, presented from an Afrocentric perspective, were of immense interest to Matthew's followers and pervaded all of his teaching. The lodge functioned as a secret society where the initiated explored a branch of Jewish mysticism called kabbalah, and the school sought to present a systematic understanding of the practice of Judaism to those who initially adopted the religion solely as an ethnic identity. While the black press accepted the validity of the black Jews, the white Jewish press was divided; some reporters accepted them as odd and considered their soulful expressions exotic, most challenged Matthew's identification with Judaism, and a few ridiculed "King Solomon's black children" and mocked Matthew's efforts to "teach young pickaninnies Hebrew" (*Newsweek*, 13 Sept. 1934).

Matthew traveled frequently around the country, establishing tenuous ties with black congregations interested in his doctrine. He insisted that the original Jews were black and that white Jews were either the product of centuries of intermarriage with Europeans or the descendents of Jacob's brother Esau, whom the Bible describes as having a "red" countenance. Matthew argued that the suffering of black people was in large measure God's punishment for having violated the commandments. When black people "returned" to Judaism, he believed, their curse would be lifted and the biblical prophecies of redemption would be fulfilled. Most of the black Jewish congregations that sprung up in the post-Depression era trace their origin to Matthew or to WILLIAM CROWDY, a nineteenth-century minister whose followers also embraced some aspects of Judaism but who, unlike Matthew's followers, never abandoned New Testament theology. Matthew often inflated the size of his community by counting those with only a loose affiliation and who exhibited any affinity to Judaism along with the members who adhered more strictly to his doctrine of Sabbath worship, kosher food, bar mitzvahs, circumcision, and observance of all Jewish holidays. His core supporters probably never exceeded ten thousand followers from a few small congregations in New York, Chicago, Ohio, and Philadelphia, Pennysylvania. Many of his students established synagogues in other parts of New York City; often these were short-lived, and those that thrived tended to become rivals rather than true extensions of Matthew's organization.

Two of Matthew's sons served in the military during World War II, and the congregation watched with horror as atrocities against Jews were reported.

In 1942 Matthew published the *Minute Book*, a short history of his life's work, which he described as the "most gigantic struggle of any people for a place under the sun." Matthew would later create *Malach* (Messenger), a sporadically published newsletter. Having supported the Zionist cause, the congregation celebrated the creation of the state of Israel in 1948, but by the 1950s their dreams of settling in Africa or Israel had been replaced by a more modest vision of establishing a farming collective on Long Island. The congregation purchased a few parcels of land in North Babylon in Suffolk County, New York, and began building a community that was to consist of a retirement home for the aged, residential dwellings, and small commercial and agricultural industry. Opposition from local residents and insufficient funding prevented the property from being developed into anything more than a summer camp and weekend retreat for members, and the land was lost in the 1960s.

When a new wave of black nationalism swept the country during the civil rights movement, there were periods of solidarity between blacks and Jews, but also painful moments of tension in major cities. Matthew maintained a supportive relationship with ADAM CLAYTON POWELL JR. in Harlem, with PERCY SUTTON, who as borough president of Manhattan proclaimed a day in Matthew's honor, and with Congressman CHARLES RANGEL, who was a frequent guest at Commandments Keepers. Matthew also became affiliated with Rabbi Irving Block, a young white idealist who had recently graduated from Jewish Theological Seminary and started the Brotherhood Synagogue. Block encouraged Matthew to seek closer ties with the white Jewish community, and he urged white Jewish institutions to accept black Jews. Matthew applied for membership in the New York Board of Rabbis and in B'nai B'rith but was rejected. Publicly, leaders of the two organizations said that Matthew was turned down because he was not ordained by one of their seminaries; privately, they questioned whether Matthew and his community were Jewish at all. After reflecting on this incident and its aftermath, Matthew said, "The sad thing about this whole matter is, that after forty or fifty years … they are planning ways of discrediting all that it took us almost two generations to accomplish" (Howard Waitzkin, "Black Judaism in New York," *Harvard Journal of Negro Affairs* 1, no. 3 [1967]: 31).

In an effort to circumvent Matthew's leadership of the black Jewish community, the Committee on Black Jews was created by the Commission on

Synagogue Relations. The committee in turn sponsored an organization called Hatza'ad Harishon (the First Step), which attempted to bring black people into the Jewish mainstream. Despite the organizers' liberal intentions, the project failed because it was unable to navigate the same racial and ritual land mines that Matthew had encountered. Matthew had written that "a majority of the [white] Jews have always been in brotherly sympathy with us and without reservation" (*New York Age*, 31 May 1958), but because he refused to assimilate completely he met fierce resistance from white Jewish leadership. As he explained:

> We're not trying to lose our identity among the white Jews. When the white Jew comes among us, he's really at home, we have no prejudice. But when we're among them they'll say you're a good man, you have a white heart. Or they'll be overly nice. Deep down that sense of superiority-inferiority is still there and no black man can avoid it (Shapiro, 183).

Before Matthew's death at the age of eighty-one, he turned the reins of leadership over to a younger generation of his students. Rabbi LEVI BEN LEVY, who founded Beth Shalom E.H. Congregation and Beth Elohim Hebrew Congregation, engineered the formation of the Israelite Board of Rabbis in 1970 as a representative body for black rabbis, and he transformed Matthew's Ethiopian Rabbinical College into the Israelite Rabbinical Academy. Rabbi Yehoshua Yahonatan and his wife, Leah, formed the Israelite Counsel, a civic organization for black Jews. Matthew expected that his grandson, Rabbi David Dore, a graduate of Yeshiva University, would assume leadership of Commandments Keepers Congregation, but as a result of internecine conflict and a painful legal battle, Rabbi Chaim White emerged as the leader of the congregation and continued Matthew's legacy.

Matthew and his cohorts were autodidacts and organic intellectuals who believed that history and theology held the answers to their racial predicament. In their Darwinian view of politics, people who do not know their cultural heritage are inevitably exploited by those who do. Hence, discovery of their true identities was essential to achieving self-respect and political freedom. In this regard, Matthew, NOBLE DREW ALI, and ELIJAH MUHAMMAD agreed in their cultural assessment of the overriding problem facing black people, though they chose different religious paths.

FURTHER READING
The largest collection of papers and documents from Matthew and about black Jews is to be found at the Schomburg Center for Research in Black Culture of the New York Public Library. Smaller collections are at the American Jewish Archives in Cincinnati.

Brotz, Howard. *The Black Jews of Harlem: Negro Nationalism and the Dilemmas of Negro Leadership* (1970).

Landing, James E. *Black Judaism: Story of an American Movement* (2002).

Ottley, Roi. *New World A-Coming: Inside Black America* (1943).

Shapiro, Deanne Ruth. "Double Damnation, Double Salvation: The Source and Varieties of Black Judaism in the United States," M.A. thesis, Columbia University (1970).

SHOLOMO B. LEVY

Matthews, Artie (15 Nov. 1888–25 Oct. 1958), musician and school founder, was born in Braidwood, Illinois. His parents' names are unknown. He spent his childhood in Springfield, Illinois, where his family moved when he was a young child. Matthews early expressed an interest in music, and historical accounts credit his mother as his first piano teacher, although he later took lessons from local teachers. A trip to St. Louis, Missouri, in 1904 exposed Matthews to the major African American performers of ragtime, the dominant popular music then. Upon returning to Springfield, Matthews learned ragtime from local performers.

Sometime in 1907 or 1908 Matthews settled in St. Louis, where he remained for the next seven or eight years, with some excursions to Chicago. While in St. Louis he studied theory, arranging, composition, and organ at the Keeton School of Music. He developed into an excellent pianist, composer, and arranger, and his reputation led to his being sought by a variety of writers and publishers of music, including Barrett's Theatorium and the publisher John Stark. He functioned as arranger for the first published song with "blues" in the title, the singer Baby Seals's "The Baby Seals Blues" (1912). Matthews also served as musical director for TOM TURPIN's Booker T. Washington Theater, where he was responsible for composing and arranging the music for the many variety and vaudeville shows appearing weekly.

During his time in St. Louis, Matthews made outstanding contributions with his own compositions in the genres of blues and ragtime. His blues composition "The Weary Blues" (1915) was very popular and has become an American standard.

Matthews also composed a series of five ragtime compositions known as *The Pastime Rags*. They are recognized as classics in the tradition of ragtime composition and feature innovative and advanced approaches. For instance, "Pastime Rag #4" features dissonant clusters and atonal segments, while "Pastime Rag #1" introduces a walking-bass line in strain C. Matthews made significant contributions to refining and extending the melodic, harmonic, and rhythmic approaches to ragtime composition and performance. In their book *The Art of Ragtime*, William J. Schafer and Johannes Riedel speak of *The Pastime Rags* as "a compendium of ragtime techniques."

In 1915 Matthews moved to Chicago, where he was active as a church organist and studio teacher. In 1916 he settled permanently in Cincinnati, Ohio, accepting a position as organist and choir director for St. Andrew's Episcopal Church. While serving in these capacities Matthews continued to expand his musical skills and knowledge. He studied organ and theory with Professor W. S. Sterling of the Metropolitan College of Music and Dramatic Arts, receiving a diploma in 1918. In 1920 he married Anna Howard; they had no children.

Though Matthews was able to pursue his musical education, he recognized that racism and segregation denied such opportunities to many other African Americans in Cincinnati. In order to provide music education for African Americans that would develop talent and open up new career opportunities, Matthews and his wife—also an accomplished musician and educator—established the Cosmopolitan School of Music in Cincinnati in 1921. The school was divided into four departments of instruction: applied music (performance), theoretical music, music education (public school music), and speech and dramatic art. The school also offered a course in the history of Negro music. The Cosmopolitan School of Music became one of the best-equipped and best-staffed private music schools in the area. Its highest enrollment was more than 150 students, including many who were working toward a college degree.

Along with operating the Cosmopolitan School of Music, Matthews was a leader and activist in the Cincinnati community. He likewise continued to work as a composer and arranger. In 1922 he established the Cosmopolitan School of Music Press and published *Ethiopia*, a religious anthem for voices and organ (piano) or orchestra with a nationalistic theme similar to those expressed by other African American artists of the Harlem Renaissance era. In 1924 he served as musical director for MARIAN ANDERSON'S

first Cincinnati recital. In 1928 he pursued advanced studies in music at New York University, and in 1929 he became choral director for the Cincinnati Public Recreation Commission, a position that he held for seventeen years. The decade of the 1920s also saw Matthews begin thirty years of service as secretary-treasurer for the African American Musicians' Union, Local 814. He continued his involvement with African American sacred music by serving as choir director and organist for various black church congregations.

Despite the death of Anna Howard Matthews in July 1930, the Cosmopolitan School of Music became a major music education institution, establishing cooperative links with Wilberforce University and Knoxville College, both historically black. Matthews's efforts included gaining the support of sensitive whites in the Cincinnati community. In a series of meetings in 1934, Matthews, the Race Relations Committee of the Cincinnati Women's City Club, and administrators at the University of Cincinnati came up with an agreement that placed the Cosmopolitan School of Music on the university's accredited list of affiliated music schools. This agreement afforded African Americans attending the Cosmopolitan School of Music the opportunity to earn a bachelor of music education degree, thus enabling them to pursue careers in music education.

In September 1935 Matthews experienced a personal tragedy when his second wife, Beryl Winston, and their unborn child died during childbirth, just fifteen months after their marriage.

In 1938 Matthews's contributions were recognized when Wilberforce University conferred an honorary doctor of music degree on him. That same year Matthews was active in establishing Cincinnati's annual summer Festival of Negro Music, which continued until the mid-1950s and featured such artists as PAUL ROBESON, Clarence Cameron White, R. NATHANIEL DETT, and ROBERT TODD DUNCAN. Matthews served as organizer and music director for these events.

In the 1940s Matthews served as musical director for local African American World War II patriotic events, arranged music for the Cincinnati Symphony Orchestra and the Cincinnati Summer Opera, and continued his music education through summer studies at Northwestern University. In December 1951 Matthews married for a third time, to Hazel Anderson. They had one child, a son. During the 1950s Matthews continued to direct and lead the Cosmopolitan School of Music and to serve the black church as organist, choral director, and minister of music until his death in Cincinnati.

Artie Matthews's legacy reflects his multidimensional capacities. He was a pioneering and innovative composer and pianist who created some of the most significant ragtime music of the twentieth century. For more than three and a half decades Matthews's Cosmopolitan School of Music provided musical training and education for hundreds of African Americans, thus providing them career opportunities as performers, arrangers, composers, and educators.

FURTHER READING

Blesh, Rudi, and Harriet Janis. *They All Played Ragtime* (1950).

Dabney, W. P. *Cincinnati's Colored Citizens* (1926).

Gammond, Peter. *Scott Joplin and the Ragtime Era* (1975)

Hasse, John Edward. *Ragtime: Its History, Composers, and Music* (1985).

Jasen, David A., and Trebor Jay Tichenor. *Rags and Ragtime* (1978).

Obituary: *Cincinnati Enquirer*, 28 Oct. 1958.

This entry is taken from the *American National Biography* and is published here with the permission of the American Council of Learned Societies.

LEONARD L. BROWN

Matthews, Miriam (6 Aug. 1905–23 June 2003), public librarian and activist, was the second of three children born to the painter Reuben Hearde Matthews and the homemaker Fannie Elijah Matthews in Pensacola, Florida. Matthews's paternal grandparents were schoolteachers, and her maternal grandfather, Zebulon Elijah, was Pensacola's first postmaster. Despite a relatively comfortable life the Matthews chose to move Miriam and her siblings, Ella Shaw and Charles Hearde, to Los Angeles in 1907 in order to shield them from the inevitable limitations of racism and segregation in the South. The entire family flourished socially and professionally in their new city. Miriam Matthews distinguished herself as a trailblazer by becoming in 1927 the first known credentialed African American librarian in the Los Angeles Public Library system, where she enjoyed a thirty-three-year career first as a branch librarian, then as a regional librarian after 1949. During her tenure she became recognized for her expertise in documenting the early history of blacks in Los Angeles.

Of course, even in Los Angeles, the Matthews family could not entirely escape the slights and insults of racism and discrimination, even if it was often subtle and personal rather than overt and institutional. After completing her bachelor's degree in Spanish at the University of California, Berkeley, in 1926, Matthews remained for an additional year in order to earn her Certificate in Librarianship. A former supervisor had promised to notify her when the Civil Service exam for a permanent position in the library was to be given; however, it was a chance meeting with a family friend who told her that the exam was to be given the next day. Throughout her career Matthews consistently met and overcame obstacles to promotions and career advancement by gaining broader knowledge of library science, such as participating as an exchange librarian at the New York Public Library, 135th Street Branch (now known as the Schomburg Center for Research in Black Culture) for six months in 1940 and earning a Master of Library Science from the University of Chicago in 1945.

Matthews was involved in numerous youth, history, civic, and progressive organizations and always sought out a leadership role in each. After completing her master's degree, she was appointed chair of the California Library Association Intellectual Freedom committee in 1946 and served as the chair of the American Library Association Committee on Intellectual Freedom, where she served from 1947 to 1951 and contributed to the 1948 revision of the Library Bill of Rights, a declaration on the commitment of libraries to noncensorship and intellectual freedom.

Matthews was proud of the sophisticated public programming she organized for the libraries. She established an exhibition program for African American art in the libraries when there were few venues for black artists and intellectuals. In 1938 she invited the writers ARNA BONTEMPS and LANGSTON HUGHES to speak at the Vernon Branch on "Haiti, the Beautiful" and "Spain, Today and Yesterday," under the League of Allied Arts. She was an early promoter of Negro History Week (now Black History Month). She also wrote important biographical sketches, such as "William Grant Still—Composer," published in a 1940 edition of *Phylon*, an Atlanta University literary magazine, and compiled extensive bibliographies of primary source material, such as "The Negro in California from 1781–1910" (1944). Her growing expertise led her to serve as a primary consultant on numerous public projects documenting the central role blacks and other people of color had in founding the city.

In spite of her heavy workload and seemingly endless schedule of meetings and lectures, she enjoyed social events and traveled extensively around Mexico, Europe, and Scandinavia shortly before her retirement. After leaving the library system, she toured South America and the Caribbean, finally visiting Asia in 1971. In 1977 Governor Jerry Brown appointed her to the California Heritage Preservation Commission and the California State Historical Advisory Board in order to establish a set of best practices for the organization and preservation of institutional archives.

Matthews moved to the Seattle area in 1996 to be close to her nephew, Charles H. Matthews Jr., and his family. She died at age ninety-seven on Mercer Island, Washington. Matthews received numerous citations and awards for her service to the profession and to the people of the city of Los Angeles, and continued to be honored after her death. In 2003 the Los Angeles Historical Society established the annual Miriam Matthews Award and the Hyde Park Branch of the Los Angeles Public Library was renamed the Hyde Park Miriam Matthews Branch in 2004.

FURTHER READING

Parts of Miriam Matthews's extensive collection of papers, photographs, and ephemera are held by the Central Branch of the Los Angeles Public Library, the African American Museum and Library in Oakland, California, with the bulk of her papers at the UCLA Department of Special Collections, Charles E. Young Research Library.

Edmonds, Ruth, ed. *The Black Women's Oral History Project: From the Arthur and Elizabeth Schlesinger Library on the History of Women in America*, vol. 7 (1991).

Flamming, Douglas. *Bound for Freedom: Black Los Angeles in Jim Crow America* (2004).

Josey, E. J., and Marva L. DeLoach. *Handbook of Black Librarianship* (2000).

Wilkin, Binnie Tate. *African American Librarians in the Far West* (2006).

Obituary: *Los Angeles Times*, 6 July 2003.

KAREN MASON

Matthews, Victoria Earle (27 May 1861–10 Mar. 1907), writer, educator, and activist, was the youngest of nine children born to Caroline Smith, a former slave, in Fort Valley, Georgia. Oral family history has it that Victoria's father was her mother's owner. Her mother migrated to New York with her daughters Victoria and Anna around 1873. Victoria attended Grammar School 48 in New York City until she was compelled to leave because of poverty; she

took work as a domestic servant, the only employment available to many African American women at that time. HALLIE QUINN BROWN's *Homespun Heroines and Other Women of Distinction* (1926) notes of Matthews, however, that she "never lost an opportunity to improve her mind" (209). Matthews developed her own literacy program, acquiring knowledge from independent study, lectures, and contact with educated people. Marriage at the age of eighteen to William Matthews, a carriage driver, enabled her to escape her home life, but it led to an unhappy and perhaps lonely domestic situation.

During the early years of her marriage, Matthews contributed articles about her childhood to *Waverly Magazine*, the *New York Weekly*, and *Family Story Paper*. She was also a news correspondent for the *New York Times*, the *New York Age*, the *Brooklyn Eagle*, the *Boston Advocate*, the *Washington Bee*, and the *Richmond Planet*. In 1893, under the pen name Victoria Earle, she published her most ambitious work, the short story "Aunt Lindy." Five years later, with encouragement from the *New York Age* editor T. THOMAS FORTUNE, she edited *Black Diamonds: The Wisdom of* BOOKER T. WASHINGTON, a selection of his speeches and talks to students.

Matthews's writing brought her into contact with prominent white and black women and led to membership in the Women's National Press Association. Linking the written word and action, she organized a dinner to honor the achievements of the antilynching crusader and *New York Age* journalist IDA B. WELLS-BARNETT. This event inspired Matthews and Maritcha Remond Lyons, a Brooklyn schoolteacher, to organize the Woman's Loyal Union, which became involved in racial protest and women's issues. As a delegate of the union, Matthews attended the 1895 Congress of Colored Women in Atlanta and presented a stunning address, "The Value of Race Literature," emphasizing the importance of preserving the cultural contributions of African Americans. An outgrowth of the Congress was the founding of the National Federation of Afro-American Women (NFAAW). Matthews was appointed to the editorial board of the *Woman's Era*, the NFAAW's official journal, and chair of its executive committee. Her resourcefulness was invaluable in planning the 1896 convention in Washington, D.C., which merged the NFAAW and the National Colored Women's League of Washington into the National Association of Colored Women.

Matthews felt compelled to raise her voice and pen in defense of black womanhood. Addressing the San Francisco Society of Christian Endeavor in

1897, she expressed her indignation over the attacks on black females as immoral women. In her lecture "The Awakening of the Afro-American Woman," she also challenged black and white women to assume some responsibility for the less fortunate. Matthews believed that all women's educational, religious, and temperance organizations should cooperate to combat both negative public attitudes and discriminatory laws that degraded black womanhood.

After the death of her only child, Matthews dedicated her life to social welfare work among the black poor. On 11 February 1897 she established the White Rose Mission "as a Christian nonsectarian Home for Colored Girls and Women and to train them in the principles of practical self-help and right living" (August Meier, *Negro Thought in America, 1880–1915* [1978], 134). Incorporated in 1898 with a biracial board of directors, the White Rose Home and Industrial Association for Working Girls provided a space where black women newly arrived from the South were befriended, counseled, and prepared for jobs through courses in cooking, sewing, and housekeeping. The women were then found jobs, usually in domestic service. Seeking to protect rural women from the dangers of urban life, the White Rose Home rigorously enforced its rules and curfews.

To further race consciousness, Matthews established a library of African American history books and taught a course in black history. Ruth Alice Moore (later ALICE DUNBAR-NELSON) ran a kindergarten at the home, while other volunteers provided a range of programs, lectures, and clubs. Matthews's leadership of the White Rose Home allowed her to exchange ideas with like-minded white reformers and social workers, among them Mary Stone, Mary White Ovington, Grace Hoadley Dodge, and Frances Kellor.

Prior to Matthews, only a few reformers had addressed the influence of the urban environment on the behavioral patterns of black women in both the North and the South. She toured the South in 1895 and, appalled by the red-light districts in New Orleans and other southern cities, warned the Hampton Negro Conference of the dangers faced by young black female migrants to the cities. Matthews's Hampton address inspired the organization of volunteers at the nearby Norfolk, Virginia, docks to counsel arriving migrants. White Rose agents in New York likewise watched the docks to prevent the women from becoming victims of a "white slave" traffic that existed from New Orleans to New York. These developments led Matthews

to establish the White Rose Travelers' Aid Society in 1905.

When Matthews discovered that several New York employment agencies sent black women seeking work as domestic servants to houses of ill repute, she decided to "check the evil" of these "unprincipled men who haunted the wharves" (Gilbert Osofsky, *Harlem: The Making of a Ghetto: Negro New York, 1890–1930* [1971], 56). Afraid that this practice would prevent these migrants from acquiring respectable employment, Matthews expertly gathered evidence and reported similar conditions for black women in New York, Chicago, Boston, and San Francisco.

Matthews's death from tuberculosis at the age of forty-five left the White Rose Home without a public figure immersed in social work. She is recognized in connection with the organization not only of women's clubs but also of a movement in New York City to aid African American women. Her name is inextricably linked to the White Rose Home and its mission of providing social services for thousands of African American women.

FURTHER READING
The Empire State Federation of Women's Clubs Papers, SUNY, Albany, New York, contains information relating to the White Rose Mission and Industrial Association founded by Victoria Earle Matthews in 1897 and supported by the clubs of the Empire State Federation. Records of the National Association of Colored Women's Clubs, 1895–1992, contain the minutes of its national conventions, which Victoria Earle Matthews attended in both 1895 and 1896, and its publication, the *National Association Notes*.
Brown, Hallie Q. *Homespun Heroines and Other Women of Distinction* (1926, 1988).
Davis, Elizabeth. *Lifting as They Climb* (1933).
Wesley, Charles. *The History of the National Association of Colored Women's Clubs: A Legacy of Service* (1984).
Obituary: *New York Age*, 14 Mar. 1907.
FLORIS BARNETT CASH

Matthews, Vince (16 Dec. 1947–), track athlete, was born Vincent Edward Matthews in Queens Village, New York. His parents' names are not known, but his father was a fabric cutter in the clothing trade. Matthews spent much of his early childhood in some of New York's rougher neighborhoods. In 1949 his family moved from a cramped flat in Brooklyn to the Marcy Housing Projects, a collection of ramshackle apartment blocks near the Bedford-Stuyvesant section. After Matthews's mother had the astounding luck of winning a substantial sum of money playing the Irish Sweepstakes, his parents purchased a house in the more stable neighborhood of South Ozone Park, Queens. Matthews attended Andrew Jackson High School in a nearby neighborhood of Queens.

A bright, inquisitive youngster, Matthews began running competitive track at Andrew Jackson. But he devoted so much time to the sport that his schoolwork suffered, and he was dismissed twice from Jackson's track team. Finally, with a little extra effort in the classroom, he was able to maintain his eligibility as a senior and became one of New York's top prep quarter-milers. In 1965 he outran a talented field to take the citywide public school 440-yard dash championship. Recruited by several colleges, Matthews opted for the historically black Johnson C. Smith University in North Carolina. Like many other historically black universities, Johnson C. Smith was a member of the National Association of Intercollegiate Athletics (NAIA). At Johnson C. Smith Matthews met Dianne Freeman. The couple married in 1970, and would have one child, a daughter.

It did not take Matthews long to demonstrate his athletic prowess in college. As a freshman he won several meet titles, and came in a respectable fourth competing for the New York Pioneer Club—he had run for the track club since high school—at the 1966 Amateur Athletic Union (AAU) national championships at Randall's Island in New York. In 1967, his sophomore year, he garnered the national NAIA 440-yard dash title in 45.4 seconds. He also fared well against international competition. At the 1967 Pan-Am Games in Canada, Matthews earned a gold medal in the 1,600-meter relay, and a silver medal in the 400 meters. *Track and Field News* rated him as the world's number two quarter-miler for 1967. The following year, at a meet in California, he scorched through the 400 meters in a blazing 44.4 seconds—at the time a new world record. However, the International Association of Athletics Federation (IAAF), the organization overseeing international track and field, refused to acknowledge the time, citing the illegality of the brush spikes—dozens of little pin-like projections, which allegedly provided better traction than regular spikes—that Matthews wore on the bottom of his track shoes. That same year, however, he was vindicated. At the 1968 Olympic Games in Mexico City, the American 1,600-meter relay team of Matthews, Ron Freeman, Larry James, and Lee Evans not only won the gold medal but their time of 2:56.1 seconds also shattered

the existing world record by three and a half seconds. Not until 1992 was their record eclipsed.

Matthews stopped running competitive track in 1969 after his last season at Johnson C. Smith. Having not yet completed his degree—he would eventually graduate in May 1972—Matthews bounced from job to job, working briefly in a department store, practicing football and playing sparingly in one game with the National Football League's Washington Redskins during the preseason, and then taking a job with his local Neighborhood Youth Corps after he was released by the Redskins. But running was his life. In 1971, after reclaiming his amateur ranking, a classification he had lost because of his short stint with the Redskins, Matthews ended his hiatus from track and field. Racing in June 1972 for the Brooklyn Over the Hill Athletic Association, a track club he had helped establish, Matthews finished second at the AAU championships in Seattle. One month later, at the United States Olympic Trials in Eugene, Oregon, he surprised more than a few by coming in third. The position qualified him for the 1972 Olympic Games in Munich, where he continued to astound observers by taking the gold medal in the 400 meters in 44.66 seconds.

The luster of Matthews's Olympic triumph, however, soon became tarnished. During the medal ceremony, Matthews and his fellow African-American quarter-miler, Wayne Collett, winner of the silver medal, slouched, conversed with each other, and seemed indifferent to the victory. Making matters worse, Matthews spun his medal in circles and Collett raised his fist in what appeared to be a black power salute as the two made their way from the podium. The behavior provoked an avalanche of jeers and howls from the Olympic stadium crowd. The medal-stand controversy came less than forty-eight hours after Palestinian terrorists had murdered eleven Israeli officials and athletes, and several weeks after Olympic authorities were forced to exclude racially-segregated Rhodesia because of threats of an Olympic boycott from more than two dozen African countries. An angry International Olympic Committee (IOC), already upset over the intrusion of nationalist politics, imposed a ban on the two quarter-milers that prohibited them from ever again taking part in the Olympic Games. Because the number of eligible runners for the American 4 × 400-meter relay team had been reduced to five following teammate John Smith's injury in the 400-meter finals, the disqualification of Matthews and Collett forced the United States to withdraw its team. The Americans had been favored to win the event.

For many, Matthews and Collett's conduct brought to mind the controversial black power salutes of the American sprinters TOMMIE SMITH and John Carlos four years earlier at the Olympic Games in Mexico City, even though Matthews initially insisted that his and Collett's behavior on the victory platform had been misconstrued as a demonstration. The denial, however, did little to quell the outrage of those who believed that the two runners had dishonored the flag and the country, and Matthews later admitted his actions were a protest. As he explained in early 1973, "In my frame of reference, that flag and anthem didn't represent equality for everyone, so I couldn't stand at attention" (*Track and Field News*, 1 Mar. 1973).

Matthews was a product of an increasingly assertive racial consciousness among African Americans during the late 1960s and early 1970s. The Black Power movement and the efforts of the outspoken sports activist HARRY EDWARDS—most notably the Olympic Project for Human Rights (OPHR) and the suggested boycott of the 1968 Mexico City Olympic Games—greatly influenced him. At those Olympic Games in Mexico City, Matthews and the three other African American members of the victorious 1,600-meter relay team staged a mild demonstration atop the medal platform, though it was less politically explicit than Smith and Carlos's. In much the same way, Matthews and Collett's Munich demonstration lacked a clear political message, and it never became a symbol of racial pride among African Americans like Smith and Carlos's.

Following the Olympic Games in Munich, Matthews faded into relative obscurity, even as he remained connected to track and field. He ran in the International Track Association, a professional track and field competition that lasted only a few years, moved to Africa to help coach the Nigerian national team, and became the coach of the well-respected track team at Essex County College in Newark, New Jersey. Eventually his interests shifted away from coaching track, and he pursued a career working with inner-city youths in New York. His autobiography, *My Race Be Won* (1974), recounts the difficulties he encountered as both an athlete and as an African American. He is a member of New York City's distinguished Public Schools Athletic League Hall of Fame. Like several other African American athletes during the post–World War II era, Matthews tried to use his athletic prominence to expose the injustices of a racially biased society.

FURTHER READING
Matthews, Vincent, with Neil Amdur. *My Race Be Won* (1974).
Matthews, Vincent, with Neil Amdur. "Matthews: 'I'm an Athlete, Not a Politician,'" *New York Times*, 9 Sept. 1972.
Amdur, Neil. "Matthews Wins in 400; Munich Fans Boo Him," *New York Times*, 8 Sept. 1972.
Dunaway, Jim. "US Smashes Record: 2:56.1," *Track and Field News* (Oct./Nov. 1968).
Hanley, Reid M. *Who's Who in Track and Field* (1973)
Hendershott, Jon. "Life Not Changed Much by a Gold Medal," *Track and Field News* (1 Mar. 1973).
Hill, Garry. "The Victory Stand Incident," *Track and Field News* (Sept. 1972).
Hornbuckle, Adam R. "Matthews, Vincent Edward 'Vince,'" in *Biographical Dictionary of American Sports: 1992–1995 Supplement for Baseball, Football, Basketball, and Other Sports*, ed. David L. Porter, (1995).
"View from Mount Olympus," *Black Sports* (Aug. 1976).
CHRIS ELZEY

Matthews, William Clarence (7 Jan. 1877–9 Apr. 1928), athlete and attorney, was born in Selma, Alabama, to William Henry Matthews, a tailor, and Elizabeth Abigail Matthews. Little is known about his early childhood, but he attended Tuskegee Institute from 1893 to 1896 and came to the attention of BOOKER T. WASHINGTON, who arranged for him to attend Phillips Andover Academy in Massachusetts in 1896. At Andover Matthews excelled at football, baseball, and track as well as academics. He was also popular with his classmates who gave him a silver loving cup, a large cup that has multiple handles on it so it can be passed around to various people at a banquet, at graduation.

As successful as he was at Andover, Matthews truly came into his own as an athlete during his college career. Enrolling at Harvard in 1901, Matthews earned places on the varsity football and baseball teams in his freshman year at a time when baseball was America's premier sport and college teams were the training ground for the major leagues. Although he excelled at both sports, he quickly became a star on Harvard's baseball team, then considered one of the best college squads in the country. Relatively small (he stood five-feet eight-inches tall) and quick, Matthews was the complete baseball player. He could hit, field (he played shortstop), and run with equal ease, and he led his team in hitting every year he played. In his final Harvard season, he hit .400 and stole twenty-two bases in twenty-five games. Thanks in part to his efforts, Harvard compiled an impressive record of seventy-five wins and eighteen losses between 1901 and 1905.

Matthews was equally renowned for his character. In an era when college athletes often used aliases and took money under the table to play semi-professional ball during the summer, Matthews refused to compromise his amateur standing, even though he needed the money. Instead he worked summers in hotels and Pullman cars and taught at a Boston night school to pay his college tuition and expenses.

Despite the acclaim baseball brought him, Matthews's college career was far from idyllic. In 1902, his first full season (an injured knee caused him to miss more than half of the 1901 season), Matthews sat out a dozen games because players on opposing teams would not play against him or because a coach or manager threatened to cancel the game if he played. The next year Harvard cancelled its annual southern tour because of opponents' hostility to Matthews's presence.

Still Matthews persevered and after leaving Harvard in 1905 went to Vermont to play for Burlington in the all-white "outlaw" (so-called because it wasn't affiliated with the other major or minor leagues of the time) Northern League, then one of the many professional leagues just below the majors. Again he garnered attention for his play (his batting average ranged from a high of .314 to a low of .248) and his character. His fans called him "Matty," the same nickname given to Christy Matthewson, the most popular white player of the era.

Matthews also encountered prejudice from opposing players. Some purposely tried to injure him by running into him with their spikes while he was playing shortstop, and one former college foe, Sam Apperious, also a native of Selma, stirred up controversy when he refused to play against him professionally. Although Apperious's opposition was widely and, for the most part, unfavorably reported in the New England press, little changed for Matthews.

The hostility Matthews faced intensified when rumors began to circulate that the Boston National League Team wanted to hire him if it could obtain the permission from the other major league team owners. Press reaction around the country ranged from vehement opposition in the South to more temperate condescension in the North. Matthews himself described the situation as an "outrage. What a shame it is that black men are barred forever from participating in the national game," he said. "I should think that Americans should

rise up in revolt against such a condition. Many Negroes are brilliant players and should not be shut out because their skin is black" (Lindholm, *Cooperstown Symposium*, 38). Shut out he was, though. The league refused to authorize the hire, and Matthews never played professionally again.

Undaunted by the demise of his baseball career, Matthews returned to Boston where he enrolled in the law school at Boston University, paying his expenses by working as an athletics instructor at three local high schools. After marrying Penelope Belle Lloyd in 1907 and passing the bar in 1908, he continued to teach and practiced law in Boston.

In 1913 with help from his former mentor Booker T. Washington, Matthews was named special assistant to the U.S. District Attorney in Boston. From 1915 to 1919 he served as special counsel to the New York, New Haven and Hartford Railroad, and from 1920 to 1923 he was legal counsel to the black nationalist MARCUS GARVEY.

Matthews was active politically as well. In the 1924 presidential campaign he was the organizer of the "Colored Section" of the Republican National Committee, and he helped generate a million African American votes for Calvin Coolidge who subsequently named him an assistant attorney general. In that position, Matthews worked in Lincoln, Nebraska, and in San Francisco, California.

When Matthews died suddenly of a perforated gastric ulcer in Washington, D.C., his death was widely reported in both the white and African American press. One newspaper, the *Boston Post*, then a major daily, eulogized him as "no doubt the greatest colored athlete of all time ... the best infielder Harvard ever had, [and Harvard's] greatest big league prospect" (Lindholm, *A Review of Baseball History*, 72).

Despite the barrier of legalized segregation, William Clarence Matthews proved that an African American could successfully compete on an integrated baseball team. As such he was an early—and important—figure in the integration of the sport. Sixty years after he played his first and only professional season, the *Boston Globe* columnist Harold Kaese acknowledged Matthews's contribution when he called him the "JACKIE ROBINSON of his age" (*Boston Globe*, 17 Jan. 1965).

FURTHER READING

Chalk, Ocania. *Black College Sport* (1976)

Lindhom, Karl. "William Clarence Matthews," *The National Pastime: A Review of Baseball History* 17 (1997).

Lindholm, Karl. "William Clarence Matthews: 'The Jackie Robinson of His Day,'" in *The Cooperstown Symposium on Baseball and American Culture 1977*, ed. Peter M. Rutkoff (1999).

Lindholm, Karl. "William Clarence Matthews: Brief Life of a Baseball Pioneer 1877–1928," *Harvard Magazine* (Sept.-Oct.).

Peterson, Robert W. *Only the Ball Was White* (1970)

Reiss, Steven A., ed. *Sports in North America: A Documentary History Vol. 6* (1998).

Wiggins, David K. *African Americans in Sports* 2 (2004).

Obituary: *New York Times*, 11 Apr. 1928.

TODD M. BRENNEMAN

Matzeliger, Jan Ernst (15 Sept. 1852–24 Aug. 1889), inventor, was born in Paramaribo, Surinam (Dutch Guiana), the son of Carl Matzeliger, a Dutch engineer in charge of government machine works for the colony, and a native Surinamese mother. At the age of ten, Matzeliger began serving an apprenticeship in the machine works. In 1871 he signed on to the crew of an East Indian merchant ship and set out to seek his fortune overseas. After a two-year voyage, he landed at Philadelphia, where he probably worked as a cobbler. In 1877 he settled in the town of Lynn, Massachusetts, the largest shoe-manufacturing center in the United States. His first job there was with the M. H. Harney Company, where he operated a McKay sole-stitching machine. He also gained experience in heel-burnishing, buttonholing, machine repair, and other aspects of shoe manufacture. Later, he was employed in the shoe factory of Beal Brothers. In his spare time Matzeliger drove a coach, studied to increase his proficiency in the English language, and painted oils and watercolors (mostly landscape scenes). After covering rent and other essentials, his small earnings went into the purchase of books, including such useful reference tools as *Popular Educator* and *Science for All*.

At the time, a major challenge facing the shoe industry was how to improve the technique of "lasting"—or connecting the upper flaps to the soles of the shoe. Lasting was still done entirely by hand, an arduous process that slowed production. Several lasting machines had been tried without success. With characteristic zeal, Matzeliger took up this challenge, which had eluded the best mechanical minds. He spent long evening hours in his garret room experimenting and building models. In March 1883 he finally received Patent No. 274,207 for his "Lasting Machine." With sole and upper positioned on a lathe, the machine alternately drove tacks, rotated the shoe, and pleated the leather—an automated replication of the manual technique. Two years later he ran a successful factory test in which, over the course of a day, his machine lasted a record seventy-five pairs of shoes (a hand laster could produce no more than fifty in a ten-hour period). With further improvements, it lasted up to seven hundred pairs a day. This invention, dubbed the "niggerhead," came into universal use in the shoe industry. (It is unclear how the machine acquired its name. The term "niggerhead," applied in several contexts at the time, was used in the apparel industry to designate a type of fabric.)

Matzeliger's "dark complexion" made him stand out among his mostly white fellow workers, and his reception by the community varied. A religious man, he tried without success to join the local Unitarian, Episcopal, and Catholic churches. In 1884 he was accepted into the Christian Endeavor Society, the youth wing of the North Congregational Church. He was active in the society's Sunday school and fund-raising work. His diligence, polite bearing, and easygoing personality endeared him to those whose minds had not been completely closed by racial prejudice. Among his circle of friends were the younger group of factory workers and members of the Christian Endeavor Society. He never married.

Although he remained active in the developing shoe-machinery technology, and was awarded four related patents between 1888 and 1891, Matzeliger's financial benefit from the work was relatively modest. He sold the patents to his backers for fifteen thousand dollars' worth of stock in their company. By the end of the century, this company had become part of the United Shoe Machinery Corporation. Matzeliger's patents provided a nucleus of economic strength for the corporation in its early years. Matzeliger was long since gone, however, having died of tuberculosis. At the time of his death he was being cared for by friends at his home in Lynn. Three of his five patents were granted posthumously.

FURTHER READING

A small collection of correspondence, photographs, and other materials is preserved in the Manuscript Division of the Moorland-Spingarn Research Center, Howard University.

Haber, Louis. "Jan Earnst Matzeliger," in *Black Pioneers of Science and Invention* (1970), 25–33.

Kaplan, Sidney. "Jan Earnst Matzeliger and the Making of the Shoe," *Journal of Negro History* 40 (Jan. 1955): 8–33.

Mitchell, Barbara. *Shoes for Everyone: A Story about Jan Matzeliger* (1986).

This entry is taken from the *American National Biography* and is published here with the permission of the American Council of Learned Societies.

KENNETH R. MANNING

Maxwell, Campbell L. (1 Jan. 1846?–10 May 1920), was born in Fayette County, Ohio, one of ten children of Campbell and Henrietta (Hill) Maxwell. He is first mentioned in the 1850 census as being four years of age, although most official records list his birth year as 1851 or 1852. His father was a farmer and Methodist minister. Maxwell received his early education at home and in the Fayette County public schools before attending Wilberforce University, an African Methodist Episcopal (AME) school in Xenia, Ohio, where he attended preparatory classes and studied law.

By 1870 Maxwell worked as a schoolteacher in Xenia, while attending Wilberforce, and lived with his older brother Joshua, a local grocer. It was here that he met his future wife, Mary E. Cousins, a local schoolteacher, and they were married in June 1873. Two of their four children lived to adulthood: son Earl Frederick Maxwell, born in 1879, and daughter Minnie Pearl, born in 1884.

After graduating from Wilberforce, Maxwell was admitted to the Ohio state bar in the early 1870s. For four years, he served as principal of the African American public schools in nearby Springfield. He also became active in civic affairs and Republican Party politics after returning to Xenia, where he served as assistant commonwealth attorney and then town clerk from 1879 to 1885. In 1888, after being named alternate delegate at large from Ohio to the Republican national convention, Maxwell first came to the attention of national party leaders.

In January 1892 President Benjamin Harrison selected Maxwell to succeed JOHN S. DURHAM as U.S. consul to Santo Domingo—capital of the Caribbean nation now known as the Dominican Republic—a post frequently held by African American appointees. Durham himself had become consul only in 1890, but had been selected to replace FREDERICK DOUGLASS as U.S. minister to neighboring Haiti after Douglas resigned in June 1891. With Durham's elevation, Maxwell was quickly confirmed by the U.S. Senate, proceeding to Santo Domingo to handle consular and commercial affairs—ironically, as an aide to Durham, also the chargé d'affaires in Santo Domingo.

Maxwell held the consular position until his replacement in November 1893 by John R. Meade, a white appointee named by President Grover Cleveland. Maxwell's family returned to the United States in mid-1893. Within months of arriving, Meade died, and was replaced as consul in early 1894 by ARCHIBALD GRIMKÉ of Boston, one of Cleveland's few African American appointees, who held the post until 1898.

In March 1898, Maxwell was given two signal honors. First, the widow of former U.S. SENATOR BLANCHE K. BRUCE, then register of the U. S. Treasury, selected Maxwell among a select list of honorary pallbearers at Bruce's funeral in Washington, D.C., alongside such national race leaders as JOHN ROY LYNCH, GEORGE HENRY WHITE, and HENRY P. CHEATHAM (Washington, DC, *Evening Star*, 21 Mar. 1898).

A week later, President McKinley formally nominated Maxwell as the first U.S. consul general in Santo Domingo, signifying both Maxwell's stature and the increasing importance of the small Caribbean mission. Three days later, on 1 April 1898, Maxwell was confirmed by the Senate as consul general, becoming the third-ranking black diplomat in the U.S. State Department. He served under U.S. Minister William F. Powell in Port-au-Prince for the next six years.

Again, Maxwell's family accompanied him to Santo Domingo, where his daughter became fluent in French and Spanish and studied at the city's Instituto de Senoritas, later graduating from Wilberforce University to become a schoolteacher in Xenia. His son Earl, a student at Ohio State University during this period, visited regularly. Political turmoil marked Maxwell's second tour in Santo Domingo, including the assassination of Dominican strongman Ulysses Heureaux in July 1899. As senior resident U.S. diplomat, Maxwell represented the United States at President Heureaux's funeral, and the State Department depended on him for dispatches from the scene (*New York Times*, 28 July 1899).

In April 1904 President Theodore Roosevelt nominated Thomas C. Dawson of Iowa as the first U.S. minister resident and consul general in Santo Domingo, subsuming the responsibilities of Maxwell's position. Maxwell, his wife, and daughter soon returned to Xenia, while his son Earl remained behind for another two years as legation secretary to Minister Dawson.

Upon Earl's return from Santo Domingo in 1906, the Maxwells established a joint law practice in Xenia. Campbell Maxwell then joined the faculty of Wilberforce University as dean of the law school and became a life trustee of the school. He remained active in St. John's AME Church and the Masons until his death in 1920.

FURTHER READING
Talbert, Horace. *The Sons of Allen; Together with a Sketch of the Rise and Progress of Wilberforce University, Wilberforce, Ohio* (1906).

BENJAMIN R. JUSTESEN

May, Derrick (6 Apr. 1963–), DJ, recording artist, and producer, was born in Detroit to Eleanor May-Tankersley, a clerical worker, and Lawrence Todd, an entrepreneur and leathermaker. He was raised by his mother, and studied at Belleville High School. When his mother moved to Chicago during May's senior year, he remained in Belleville, living with his school friend Kevin Saunderson. Despite winning an athletic and football scholarship, May chose not to attend university. Another school friend, Juan Atkins—whom May later cited as the second most important influence on his life, behind his mother—convinced May to learn how to DJ and to produce electronic music. The futurologist Alvin Toffler, who argued that those who mastered technology would soon come to dominate society, had inspired Atkins. By 1981 he and May had formed a DJ collective called Deep Space Soundworks and were playing a combination of funk, electro, and European disco records to high school audiences in inner city Detroit, often augmenting the mix with live synths and drum machines.

Between 1981 and 1985, while Atkins recorded electronic music under the pseudonym Cybotron, May sampled the nascent house scene in Chicago and came under the influence of FRANKIE KNUCKLES and Ron Hardy. He also listened to and was influenced by the radio programs of Detroit's Electrifying Mojo (DJ Charles Johnson), which combined an eclectic selection of black and white music with Johnson's outlandish monologues about UFOs, aliens, and mystical philosophy. Following the demise of Deep Space in 1986, May established his own record label, naming it Transmat after a Cybotron track. Transmat's first release, the May-Atkins collaboration "Let's Go," met a muted reaction but the second Transmat record, "Nude Photo" (released under May's alias Rhythim is Rhythim) defined what became known as the Detroit techno sound. Further Rhythim is Rhythim releases between 1987 and 1989, notably "Kaos," "It Is What

It Is," "The Dance," and "Strings of Life," broadened the palette of Detroit techno. These compositions were characterized by heavily syncopated rhythm patterns over a 4/4 beat, synth riffs that revealed a debt to electronic music pioneers such as Georgio Moroder and Kraftwerk, P-Funk–influenced basslines, and a structure in which contrapuntal melodies wove around each other in a manner that hinted at postbop jazz. May layered these elements upon each other, building the tracks to irresistible crescendos. Many critics believed May's sparse production of these tracks to be an aural representation of post-industrial Detroit (May lived in the center of the city during this period); few noted that it remained resolutely optimistic. This optimism was driven by May's Toffler-influenced belief that technology and futurism offered a vision of salvation for the African American community.

In 1988 a compilation of Detroit music entered commercial space, which finally gave the music a name. *Techno!: The New Dance Sound of Detroit* (1988) featured tracks by the Belleville Three: May, Atkins, and Saunderson (whose Inner City track "Big Fun" became a worldwide chart hit). Asked to define techno, May flippantly but accurately replied, "The music is just like Detroit, a complete mistake. It's like GEORGE CLINTON and Kraftwerk stuck in an elevator" (Stuart Cosgrove, "Seventh City Techno," in *The Faber Book of Pop* [1995]: 678). That same year, May started DJing at the Music Institute in downtown Detroit, and soon attracted a large African American following. Although it lasted only until November 1989, the Music Institute became central to the development of Detroit techno, offering the music a true home and inspiring many in its crowd to start producing music themselves. By the early 1990s techno had developed an international following. Yet May was rapidly becoming alienated from the music that he had created. As the entertainment industry co-opted it and attempted to make the music more accessible to a wider popular audience, techno lost its Detroit elements and was transformed into something that many of its original adherents did not immediately recognize. Dispirited, he stopped recording altogether and allowed a second wave of Detroit producers to carry the baton, most notably his protégée, Carl Craig, whose work pushed the boundaries of techno almost to the breaking point and reemphasized techno's debt to postbop jazz. May instead cemented his reputation through DJing around the world and cultivating a mystical aura around his personality and work. In 1997 a Rhythim is Rhythim compilation was released to rapturous acclaim and hopes that May would start producing again, hopes that were boosted by the appearance of a Rhythim is Rhythim track on a video game and the resurrection of Transmat after years of inactivity. The 1999 Transmat *Time: Space* compilation included another new composition, although the track's ambiance suggested that May continued to work at a languid pace. In 2003 May started curating Detroit's annual electronic music festival, which he renamed Movement. The first Movement attracted an estimated 630,000 people but the 2004 event incurred large financial losses. Tensions between Movement organizers led to May's resignation in February 2005. He continued to DJ into the new century.

May's records were considered so distinctive that critics created a completely new genre of music in order to describe them. May was correctly identified as techno's innovator and has having established techno's aesthetic and aural parameters. He defined the image of the techno producer as an auteur, and contributed vastly to the reconstruction of the cultural and economic life of Detroit. While his body of recorded work was relatively thin, it buried the myth that electronic music was soulless and lacking in emotion, and ranks alongside the greatest musical accomplishments of the 1980s and 1990s. Indeed, the May template continued to influence electronic music over fifteen years after it was defined.

FURTHER READING

Bidder, Sean. *Pump Up the Volume: A History of House* (2001).

Reynolds, Simon Reynolds. *Energy Flash: A Journey through Rave Music and Dance Culture* (1998).

Sicko, Dan. *Techno Rebels: The Renegades of Electronic Funk* (1999).

JOE STREET

May, Lee (23 Mar. 1943–), baseball player, was born Lee Andrew May in Birmingham, Alabama. His father, Tommy, worked in a mattress and springs factory and his mother, Mildred, worked for a seasoning company. May had one younger brother, Carlos, who also would go on to play major league ball. May's parents divorced when he was young, and he saw his father only occasionally after that.

May played high school baseball, football, and basketball; starting at age 16, he also played on a semiprofessional industrial baseball league. He graduated from Birmingham's Parker High School in 1961, while living with his mother, brother, and grandmother Ernestine. The University of Nebraska offered him a football scholarship, and the Cincinnati Reds organization offered him $12,000 to play-for their minor league system. He signed with the Reds, and he joined the Tampa club of the Florida State League, batting .260 and racking up nine runs-batted-in (RBIs) in 26 games. In January 1962 he married his high school girlfriend, Terrye Perdue; they would have three children, two daughters and a son. That winter May attended classes at Miles College.

Over the next five years, May also played professional baseball in the off-season, spending three winters in Venezuela and two in Puerto Rico. After spending two seasons with the Tampa team, this six-foot-tall, 203-pound right-handed first baseman played for the Rocky Mount team in the Carolina league in 1963; he then played for the Macon, Georgia, team in the Southern Atlantic League in 1964, where he led the league in RBIs (110) and where he faced increasingly fierce racial prejudices. He joined the San Diego team in the Pacific Coast league in 1965; there he batted .321 with 34 homers, and earned 103 RBIs. That year, he also won the Most Valuable Player (MVP) Award.

On 1 September 1965 May debuted with the major league Cincinnati Reds. He played for this National League team—the "Big Red Machine"—through the 1971 season, except for a foray to the Buffalo Club of the International League in 1966. In 1967 May won the Rookie of the Year Award. In 1968 he hit 22 home runs, and over a period of 11 years May always had a minimum of 20 homers and 80 RBIs per season. He batted .290 in 1968, and he played his best season in 1969, with 38 home runs and a career-high 110 RBIs. In 1969, his first year to play in the All-Star game, he slammed six home runs during three consecutive games in May, tying a major league record. On 15 July 1969 May hit four home runs during a doubleheader.

In 1969 Carlos May, who was playing for the Chicago White Sox, played against his brother on the American League All-Star team. Carlos hit 18 home runs that year, and the two Mays still hold the second-highest home run output record for two brothers in a single season; the DiMaggios hold the record.

May hit 34 home runs in 1970, the year that the Cincinnati Reds won the National League pennant. Although the Reds lost the World Series to the Baltimore Orioles, Lee batted .389 during the Series and led the Reds with eight RBIs. He hit two home runs, as well, and his second one was a three-run homer that gave the Reds their only win in this five-game Series, a victory that broke the Orioles 17-game winning streak. May also fielded all 51 balls thrown to first base. In October 1970 May and his family moved to Cincinnati.

In 1971 Lee hit a career-high 39 home runs, and he played in another All-Star game. He was also the Reds MVP. Traded to the Houston Astros on 29 November 1971, May hit 29 home runs and 98 RBIs in 1972, and he participated on the All-Star team, again playing against his brother. In June 1973, he hit three home runs in one game and he ended the season with 28 home runs and 105 RBIs.

On 3 December 1974 he was traded to the Baltimore Orioles, where he played through 1980. In 1976, he led the American League in RBIs with 109, and he served as the Orioles MVP that year. In 1979, when the Orioles faced the Pittsburgh Pirates in the World Series, May pinch-hit. He has since been elected to the Oriole Hall of Fame.

Granted free agency on 23 October 1980, May signed with the Kansas City Royals on 9 December 1980; he played two seasons with this ball club, finishing off his major league career on 24 September 1982. May had played 2,071 major league games in his career, with a lifetime batting average of .267. He hit 354 home runs and posted 1,244 RBIs during an 18-year span. In 11 of those years, he hit 20 or more home runs and knocked in 80 or more runs. He also rated highly in strikeouts, fanning out 1,570 times; 10 times, he struck out at least 100 times during a season. After retiring in 1983 he returned to the Kansas City Royals in 1984 to serve as an assistant coach.

Throughout his baseball career, May was noted for his brawn and power, and he was praised for his perseverance and readiness to play. Born in a time and place in which racial prejudices could still serve as significant impediments, May faced down those who taunted him, and he won an impressive number of awards, ranging from the Rookie of the Year to the Most Valuable Player. His performance in the 1970 World Series was especially noteworthy.

FURTHER READING

Some of the information for this entry was gathered through personal interviews with Terrye Perdue May, wife of Lee May, and Lee May Jr., son of Lee May.

Devaney, John. "The Hard Scuffle to Be a Big-Leaguer," *Sport* 44.1 (July 1967): 50–55.

Hano, Arnold. "Lee May: The Man behind the Astros' Surge," *Sport* 54.2 (Aug. 1972): 68–76.

KELLY BOYER SAGERT

Mayes, Vivienne Lucille Malone (10 Feb. 1932– 9 June 1995), mathematician, educator, and activist, was born Vivienne Lucille Malone in Waco, Texas. Her parents, Pizarro Ray Malone and Vera Estelle (Allen) Malone, both worked as public school teachers and stressed the importance of education as a pathway to advancement and opportunity.

After graduating from the racially segregated A.J. Moore High School in 1948 at the age of sixteen, young Vivienne attended Fisk University, a historically black institution in Nashville, Tennessee. She wanted to become a doctor and might have achieved that goal had she not met and married James Jeffries Mayes, a dental student. Her husband-to-be convinced her that the professional demands of two doctors in the family would be a strain on them personally. So she switched her major from pre-med to mathematics. The decision proved fortuitous. During her junior year in 1950, the university hired two mathematicians who would serve as mentors: Lee Lorch, an outspoken white advocate for civil rights who headed the department until 1955, and EVELYN BOYD GRANVILLE, believed to be only the second African American woman to earn a Ph.D. in Mathematics. Even though Granville was only at Fisk for two years, the image of possibility she symbolized influenced her student. She later wrote, "I believe it was her presence and influence which account for my pursuit of advanced degrees in mathematics" (Kenschaft, 297).

In 1952, Vivienne Malone graduated from Fisk with a B.A. in Mathematics. She married James Jeffries Mayes on September 1 of that year. The newlyweds remained at Fisk for another two years to complete the master's degree, during which time Lee Lorch hired Mayes as his grader. After graduation, Mayes and her husband moved back to Waco, Texas, where he opened a dental practice, and she taught and chaired the mathematics department at the historically black Paul Quinn College for seven years, and later commuted to Dallas for a year to teach at the now defunct Bishop College, also a black institution.

Mayes wanted to continue studying mathematics. In 1961, she applied for admission to Baylor University, a private research university just a short distance from downtown Waco. Her application was denied; Baylor did not admit African Americans. Undeterred, Mayes was able to gain entry to the University of Texas (UT) at Austin, a public institution that had been required to desegregate under the 1954 *Brown v. Board of Education* Supreme Court decision. Federal law, however, did little to change the climate of hostility and alienation that Mayes experienced in a graduate program in mathematics where she clearly was not wanted. She had few friends, was ignored by her classmates, and was denied a teaching assistantship, despite having more than thirteen years of college-level teaching experience as a tenured faculty member at Paul Quinn and Bishop colleges. Mayes recalled a conversation she had with longtime UT-Austin faculty member Robert E. Lee Moore. As former head of the American Mathematical Society (1937–1938), Moore could not understand why blacks insisted on publicly demonstrating for civil rights instead of following Mayes's example of hard work and disciplined study. Mayes replied, "If it hadn't been for those hell-raisers out there, you wouldn't even know me" (Williams, 2007). White faculty presumptions aside about how she and other blacks should—or should not act—Mayes joined the protestors in the picket lines.

With so few African Americans, particularly women, earning advanced degrees in science in majority white universities, Mayes felt the weight of the race on her soldiers, as though eleven million marginalized African American citizens were being judged by her performance. She had no choice but to excel and that she did. Studying under Don Edmondson, Mayes was awarded a doctoral degree in Mathematics in 1966 with a dissertation on "A Structure Problem in Asymptotic Analysis." She was the first black woman to earn a doctorate in mathematics from UT-Austin and only the second black person since the university formally opened its doors on 15 September 1883 to earn such a degree. In a surprising move, Baylor University reversed its anti-black policy and recruited and hired Mayes in 1966 as the university's first African-American faculty member. Federal investigators monitored the institution for five years to ensure that Mayes was not subjected to discrimination in salary or promotion. The investigators' annual reports revealed no discriminatory practices.

Mayes taught at Baylor for nearly thirty years, rising to the rank of full professor. She published several articles based on her research in the areas of steady state properties of mathematical functions and summability theory. The first of these articles appeared in the *Proceedings* of the American Mathematical Society in 1969 (Vivienne Mayes, "Some steady state properties of [Int(f(t),t,o to x)]/f(x)," *Proc Amer Math Soc*, v. 22 (1969)). Two years later, in 1971, the Baylor student congress

voted her Outstanding Faculty of the Year. She served on the resolution and program committees of the Mathematical Association of America (1972–1973); was the first African American elected to the executive committee of the Association for Women in Mathematics; served on the board of the National Association of Mathematicians; and in 1988 participated on a panel of prominent mathematicians as part of the American Mathematical Society's Centennial Celebration. Mayes was also active in several nonprofit organizations and in her local Baptist church. She served on the boards of Goodwill Industries and Cerebral Palsy and was a member of the Texas State Advisory Council for Construction of Community Mental Health Centers.

In 1985 Mayes and her husband divorced. They had one daughter, Patsyanne, but Mayes was also legal custodial guardian for two Hispanic children. Mayes remained on the faculty at Baylor until 1994 when she was forced to retire due to complications from lupus, a chronic inflammatory disease. A year after retirement, she died of a heart attack in Temple, Texas. Writing in the *Association for Women in Mathematics Newsletter*, fellow mathematician ETTA ZUBER FALCONER and former Fisk faculty Lee Lorch eloquently summed up Mayes's legacy: "With skill, integrity, steadfastness and love she fought racism and sexism her entire life, never yielding to the pressures or problems which beset her path. She leaves a lasting influence" (Falconer and Lorch, 1995).

FURTHER READING

Malone-Mayes, Vivienne. "Black and Female," in *Association for Women in Mathematics Newsletter*, 5 (1975).

Cantwell, Catherine. "Biographies of Women Mathematicians, BU Math Professor's Life Filled with Firsts," *Waco Tribune-Herald*, 26 Feb. 1986.

Kenschaft, Patricia C. "Black Women in Mathematics in the United States," in Ivan Van Sertima, ed., *Blacks in Science: Ancient and Modern* (2001).

Sammons, Vivian Ovelton. *Blacks in Science and Medicine* (1990).

Simpson, Elizabeth, "'You Had to Make It All Alone.' Black Baylor Teacher Recalls Road to Success," *Waco Tribune-Herald*, 22 Aug. 1988.

Warren, Wini. *Black Women Scientists in the United States* (1999).

Obituary: *Association for Women in Mathematics Newsletter* (Nov.–Dec. 1995).

OLIVIA A. SCRIVEN

Mayfield, Curtis (3 June 1942–26 Dec. 1999), singer, musician, and composer, was born Curtis Lee Mayfield Jr. in Chicago, Illinois, the first child of Curtis Lee Mayfield (born Curtis Lee Cooper) and Marion Washington. He was raised in impoverished circumstances by his mother and his grandmother, Sadie Riley, and rarely saw his father, who deserted the family after the fifth child was born. By the time Mayfield attended Wells High School, the family had settled on Chicago's North Side in the Cabrini-Green housing project. His paternal grandmother, Anna Belle Mayfield, was a minister, and Mayfield sang in her church's gospel group, the Northern Jubilee Singers, which included his three cousins and the future rhythm and blues star JERRY BUTLER.

Mayfield in his sophomore year dropped out of school to become the guitarist and tenor vocalist in a vocal harmony group, the Impressions, which included Butler, Sam Gooden, and the brothers Arthur and Richard Brooks. In 1958 the group, with Butler's baritone lead, achieved a national hit with the moving ballad "For Your Precious Love." The song was considered one of the first examples of soul music. When Butler quit the group, the Impressions regrouped by featuring Mayfield, with his soft high tenor lead, and adding Fred Cash; in 1959, however, the Impressions temporarily disbanded. In 1960 Mayfield started touring, writing, and recording with Butler, creating songs that made the singer a major recording artist of hit records, notably "He Will Break Your Heart" (1960) and "Need to Belong" (1963). In 1960 Mayfield established his own publishing company, Curtom, for his songs, at the time a virtually unprecedented move for an African American songwriter.

In 1961 Mayfield married Helen Williams, but the union lasted no more than two years. They separated when Mayfield was around twenty-one (though the divorce did not come until years later). The couple had one son. About a year after his split with Williams, Mayfield began a relationship with Altheida Sims; they had six children and eventually

Curtis Mayfield, composer and songwriter, in an undated photograph. (AP Images.)

married. Mayfield also had two other children with another woman, Diane Fitzgerald.

Mayfield reunited the Impressions in 1961, and immediately they got a major hit record with the much-copied Mayfield composition "Gypsy Woman," a strongly melodious song with a cha-cha–inflected beat that typified his early output. Mayfield sustained the Impressions' popularity with similarly styled songs for the next two years. With "It's All Right," a hit record in 1963, however, he developed a more intense gospelized approach, with dramatic switching off of leads from the remaining three members—Mayfield, Fred Cash, and Sam Gooden (the Brooks brothers having dropped out). The energy level was likewise raised in the musical arrangements, with blaring horns and a stronger backbeat.

In 1962 Mayfield was hired as a composer by Carl Davis, head of A&R for Columbia's rhythm and blues subsidiary Okeh. For the label Mayfield provided a remarkable number of memorable hit songs, particularly "Monkey Time" (1963) for Major Lance, "It's All Over" (1964) for Walter Jackson, and "I Can't Work No Longer" (1965) for Billy Butler. Mayfield also provided songs to Chicago artists on other labels, particularly to Gene Chandler, who built a successful recording career with the songwriter's ballads, notably "Rainbow" (1963) and "Just Be True" (1964), and to Jan Bradley, who got a hit record with Mayfield's "Mama Didn't Lie" (1963). During the same period, Mayfield kept the Impressions high on the record charts with such hits as the stirring ballad "I'm So Proud" (1964), the rousing anthemlike number "Keep On Pushing," and the sublime secular gospel classic "People Get Ready" (1965). The latter was the centerpiece of the Impressions' most outstanding LP, *People Get Ready*.

In 1965, to better concentrate on the Impressions and his own entrepreneurial endeavors, Mayfield left the employ of Okeh and substantially reduced the number of songs he gave to other artists to record. The large catalog of hit songs he had composed during the previous five years was unrivaled by any single rhythm and blues composer of the time. He entered the record label business in 1966, forming Mayfield Records (on which he produced the girl group the Fascinations) and the Windy C label (on which he produced the vocal group the Five Stairsteps). Failing to sustain these small operations, in 1968 he founded Curtom Records, which became a $10 million-a-year business by the mid-1970s, primarily with Mayfield-composed and -produced film soundtrack albums featuring such artists as ARETHA FRANKLIN, GLADYS KNIGHT and the Pips, and the Staple Singers.

During the late 1960s, Mayfield helped pioneer the use of social commentary and political messages in black music, reflecting the greater militancy of the civil rights movement and the general social unrest in the country. His first message song with the Impressions, "We're a Winner" (1967), was banned by many stations as too militant; and after the summer of 1968, when the Impressions moved to Curtom, Mayfield made the social messages ever more overt with such hits as "This Is My Country" (1968) and "Choice of Colors" (1969). These were the first of his many humanistic songs in which he preached love, peace, understanding, and harmony among all racial and religious groups.

Mayfield left the Impressions in 1970 to begin a solo career. His *Superfly* album (1972) was a multimillion-selling soundtrack LP for a movie about a Harlem drug dealer; it yielded two million-selling singles, "Freddie's Dead" and "Superfly." Featuring conga-led and bass-heavy songs, *Superfly* put Mayfield in the forefront of the new funk music, which was pushing traditional soul music off the charts in the early 1970s. For the first time in his career, Mayfield reached a substantial white audience. Curtom, like many independent labels, succumbed to the competition from the major labels in the late 1970s, and Mayfield was forced to close his operation in 1980. He moved to Atlanta, Georgia, and continued his career there. In 1990 he was permanently paralyzed from the neck down when stage scaffolding fell on him. This accident essentially ended Mayfield's career as a musician and composer. He died in Roswell, Georgia.

Mayfield was inducted into the Rock and Roll Hall of Fame twice, as a member of the Impressions in 1991 and as a solo artist in 1999. He received the Grammy Legends Award in 1994. He is recognized as one of the principal architects of the Chicago soul music industry from the many hats he wore working as a recording artist, songwriter, producer, and record company entrepreneur. As a member of the Impressions and later as a solo artist, he forged distinctive musical styles out of his gospel roots that contributed significantly to the shaping of black popular music. As a composer, first with his traditional rhythm and blues love songs and later with his inspirational songs, he created an enduring legacy of African American songs.

FURTHER READING

Hewitt, Paolo. "So Proud: The Moral Standard of Soul," *New Musical Express* (9 July 1983).

Pruter, Robert. *Chicago Soul* (1991).

Obituary: *Chicago Sun-Times*, 27 Dec. 1999.

This entry is taken from the *American National Biography* and is published here with the permission of the American Council of Learned Societies.

ROBERT PRUTER

Mayfield, Percy (12 Aug. 1920–11 Aug. 1984), blues musician and songwriter, was born in Minden, Louisiana, a town not far from Shreveport. His parents' names are unknown, but his mother was reportedly a singer and his father was a dancer. Despite this musical background, Percy's early interest was in poetry, which he wrote in high school and which he then sometimes reworked as songs. A restless young man, Percy hit the rails when he was just fifteen, traveling first to Houston, Texas, where he struggled to find work as a singer, then in 1942 to Los Angeles, California, to live with a sister. Success was not immediate, so the young Mayfield made ends meet by working odd jobs: taxi driver, short-order cook, and laundry presser, among others. Still, Mayfield found work singing with a number of local orchestras, including George Como's, and he continued to write songs.

One of his songs, "Two Years of Torture," proved a breakthrough. Mayfield pitched the song as a possible number for the jazz singer Jimmy Witherspoon, but Supreme Records was so impressed by Mayfield's performance of the song that the company asked him to record it. The song proved to be a local hit, and Mayfield soon had an offer from Art Rupe of Specialty Records, for whom he turned out many of his best and most memorable songs. In 1950 Mayfield wrote and recorded "Please Send Me Someone to Love," a song that proved to be one of his enduring singles, as it rose to number one on the R&B charts, and sold approximately a quarter of a million copies. This was followed by respectable efforts like "Lost Love," "What a Fool Was I," and "Cry Baby." In the course of only three years Mayfield had soared from relative obscurity to national recognition as a premier blues and R&B performer.

In September 1952, however, while returning to Los Angeles from a performance in Las Vegas, Mayfield was involved in a serious automobile accident. The crash ravaged his face and changed his voice, altering it from the smooth and soft instrument of a melancholic balladeer to a huskier,

deeper timbre. Afterward Mayfield sharply reduced his touring and live performances, though he did continue to write and record, if less frequently than before. Disheartened, he returned to Minden, where, as he had in the beginning, he focused on his songwriting. He left Specialty Records in 1954 to sign with Chess Records in 1955 and later with Imperial and RAY CHARLES's Tangerine label. His stay in Minden was unhappy, as was the music he produced there, and he eventually returned to Los Angeles. In the early 1960s Mayfield became one of Ray Charles's favorite songwriters, penning such classic R&B hits as "At the Club," "But on the Other Hand Baby," and the inimitable "Hit the Road Jack." He also continued to record, but trips to the charts were rare. Throughout it all he struggled with depression and alcoholism, both of which he faced with surprising honesty and sensitivity in his music.

Mayfield recorded into the 1970s, with RCA and Atlantic, but he eventually was forced to fund his own studio sessions after record companies lost interest in his sound and style. Mayfield died of a heart attack on the day before his sixty-fourth birthday. He left behind a wife, Tina, and a legacy of blues and R&B music that, though not always fully appreciated or understood during his lifetime, influenced generations of young performers. Mayfield's strength lay in the sensitivity of his approach to material that in lesser hands would appear maudlin or self-pitying. The physical aftereffects of his accident, and their effect in turn on his performing and recording career, served only to deepen and darken this approach with such numbers as the suicide's siren song "River's Invitation" or the painful "Life Is Suicide." CD reissues of Mayfield's work, especially the popular *Poet of the Blues* compilation, made his work accessible to a new generation of listeners and devotees of the best of modern blues and R&B.

FURTHER READING

Shaw, Arnold. *Honkers and Shouters: The Golden Years of Rhythm and Blues* (1978).

DISCOGRAPHY

His Tangerine and Atlantic Sides (B0001MMG36).

Memory Pain, vol. 2. (B000000QN0).

Poet of the Blues (B000000QLY).

JASON PHILIP MILLER

Mayhew, Richard (3 Apr. 1924–), landscape painter, was born in Massapequa, New York (though some biographies list his birth place as Amityville, the town in which the attending doctor lived), the son of Alvin Mayhew, a contract painter and carpenter, and Lillian Goldman Mayhew, who worked at various times as a librarian and at the local phone company. His father was of African American and Long Island Shinecock Indian ancestry, and his mother was Cherokee and African American. Mayhew's interest in art developed in a twofold manner. He was inspired by the artists who visited Amityville during the summer, and he experimented with his own art, making off with his father's house painting brushes and paint. As a teenager he traveled to New York City and frequented art galleries and museums.

Mayhew moved to New York City in 1945, working as an illustrator for children's books and magazines but also indulging his passion for music, especially jazz. He attended nightclubs, sang, and acted. He began classes at the Brooklyn Museum School in 1951, studying with the painters Edwin Dickinson and Reuben Tam, who were noted for their light-filled, subjectively interpreted landscapes. The German-born painters Max Beckmann and Hans Hofmann also numbered among Mayhew's influential teachers. He continued his education at Columbia University from 1953 to 1957, graduating with a degree in Art History.

In 1955 Mayhew's first solo exhibition was held at the Brooklyn Museum. His second solo exhibition was held at the Morris Gallery in Greenwich Village in 1957. Following the success of this exhibit, he received a John Hay Whitney Fellowship and traveled to Italy to study at the Academia in Florence. After a year in Florence, he received a Ford Foundation grant that enabled him to travel in Europe for two more years. He studied the Dutch masters in the Netherlands, at the Louvre in France, and at the Prado in Spain.

Mayhew returned to the United States in 1962 and along with ROMARE BEARDEN, HALE A. WOODRUFF, CHARLES ALSTON, and other New York–based African American artists formed the collective known as the Spiral in 1964. According to Mayhew, this group came together as a result of the 1963 March on Washington, D.C., organized by BAYARD RUSTIN, the civil rights activist, and A. PHILIP RANDOLPH of the Brotherhood of Sleeping Car Porters, among others. Mayhew recalled: "We artists met, as a sort of think tank, to analyze the sensibility and creativity in the development of arts in African American Culture. We had questions about identity, of ourselves as people, as artists, as creators who might influence society" (Mayhew). Recalling the origins of the group, he said, "As a

symbol for the group, we chose the spiral ... the Archimedean one ... from the starting point it moves outward embracing all directions, yet constantly upward" (Mayhew). Spiral members, including Felrath Hines, James Yeargons, Norman Lewis, EMMA AMOS, Earl Miller, REGINALD GAMMON, and Perry Ferguson, discussed ways artists could support and advance the struggle for civil rights. The group met for two years, eventually drifting apart as they began to pursue the ideas and challenges they had discussed. Mayhew continued to explore abstract expressionism, but other artists, such as Bearden, focused on a motif of black culture and life.

Beginning in 1975 Mayhew began to travel yearly across the United States. He inserted these road trips between teaching and painting in order explore the country he would then paint, depending upon his memory and imagination to convey the sense of what he saw. With the intention of fully understanding his preferred subjects—light, color, and artistic textures—he studied optics, form, and chromatic theory to express his lyrical and often musically inspired reaction to the American landscape. Mayhew noted that the qualities evoked by blues and jazz music are reflected in his work. He often played the music of MILES DAVIS and CECIL TAYLOR in his studio while he painted.

Influenced by his rich multicultural heritage, Mayhew's landscapes and later figure drawings were luminous expressions of color and form and were his means of conveying emotions rather than illustrating a specific landscape. Bearden said, "Mayhew represents a bridge between the older black artists who developed through the WPA in the 1930s and those who, after World War II, attended art schools and matured during the turbulent civil rights movements of the 1960s and the rise of Abstract Expressionism."

Reminiscent of the Hudson River school of painters, Mayhew's work has also been compared to that of the early black landscape painter HENRY OSSAWA TANNER. Mayhew noted in his artist statement: "My paintings are based on an improvisational internalized creative experience of my native heritage. I paint the essence of nature, always seeking the unique spiritual mood of the land." He customarily created oil paintings on canvas and watercolor drawings on paper. His method was to saturate the canvas or paper with color and manipulate the flow of paint with brush, spritz bottle, and watercolors with salt mixed into the medium.

Mayhew had more than thirty solo exhibitions. New York institutions such as the Metropolitan

Museum of Art, the Whitney Museum of American Art, and the Brooklyn Museum acquired his work along with the Art Institute of Chicago, the Smithsonian Institution, and the Smithsonian Museum of American Art. He was a member of the National Academy of Design and taught at the Brooklyn Museum Art School and Hunter College of the City University New York. He retired from Pennsylvania State University in 1991, moving to Santa Cruz, California, to create in "self-indulged joy" (Mayhew) beside the light and sound of the ocean.

FURTHER READING

Mayhew, Richard. Interview with author (25 Aug. 2007).

Bearden, Romare, and Harry Henderson. *A History of African American Artists: From 1792 to the Present* (1993).

LeFalle-Collins, Lizzeta. "The Spiritual Realm of Richard Mayhew: The Life and Works of Painter Richard Mayhew," *American Visions* (Apr. 2000).

Lewis, Samella. *African American Art and Artists* (1990)

Patton, Sharon F. *African American Art* (1998)

ROBIN JONES

Maynard, Aubre de Lambert (17 Nov. 1901–20 Mar. 1999), surgeon, was born to Percival Conrad Maynard and Gertrude (Johnson) Maynard in Georgetown, British Guyana (later Guiana) and at age five moved with his family to New York City. Because his parents regarded him as sickly, each winter they sent him to stay with relatives in Barbados, where he attended private school. He returned to New York permanently when he was fourteen, hoping to enroll immediately in the elite Townsend Harris High School. However, because his prior education did not include enough American history he spent an additional year in eighth grade. From Townsend Harris, he entered the City College of New York (CCNY), at the time a highly competitive undergraduate school that male New York City residents could attend at no cost. Maynard thought of becoming an engineer but was discouraged by his father, who believed there was more opportunity for a bright young black man as a doctor. After graduating from CCNY in 1922, Maynard applied to several "white" medical schools but to neither of the two largely black schools then in existence (Howard and Meharry). Admitted to every school to which he applied, he decided to enroll at the College of Physicians and Surgeons of Columbia University. He angrily changed his mind, however, after being told that he would have to transfer to Howard or Meharry for his clinical years because white patients would not want to be seen by a black doctor-in-training. He then made arrangements to attend New York University—where he followed the full medical course of four years with the support of the faculty and administration, and no complaints from patients. Nonetheless, when his father died during his senior year in medical school, Maynard resolved to follow his advice and develop his career in an environment largely populated by African Americans.

From the time Maynard completed his medical degree his career was intimately connected to Harlem Hospital. Several years earlier, the Harvard-educated African American surgeon LOUIS T. WRIGHT demanded that blacks be represented on the hospital staff, and, in 1920, four African American doctors were appointed. The hospital committed itself to bringing more blacks onto the staff in 1926, and when Maynard scored higher than any other candidate of any race on the examination for interns he was welcomed to the uptown facility. The hospital's transformation into a racially integrated institution was completed in 1930, when Dr. Wright—a national leader of the NAACP—succeeded in lobbying the New York Democratic Party machine into supporting an increased black presence on the medical staff. Doctors who resisted—including a few blacks allied with the old guard—lost their privileges, and nearly all services were integrated, some with African Americans as department chiefs. Maynard was among the deserved beneficiaries of this change. With attending privileges at Harlem Hospital, he was poised to develop a lucrative surgical practice.

During World War II, Maynard emerged as the leader of Democracy in Action, a group organized to encourage support for the war among African Americans. A fellow of both the New York Academy of Medicine and the American College of Surgeons, Maynard presided in 1951 when the president of the college spoke at the academy and was honored for his support of African Americans in the profession. The following year, upon the death of Louis Wright, Maynard became chief of surgery at Harlem Hospital.

As chief, Maynard quickly established a division of thoracic surgery and within a few years he announced a gift of $100,000 from Dr. Godfrey Nurse, a successful black surgeon not affiliated with the hospital, for a surgical research laboratory.

When the College of Surgeons again met in New York in 1958, Maynard gave a talk on twenty years' experience with stab wounds, making the point that Harlem was, unfortunately, a good place to develop experience in this regard. Later that year, Maynard's skill with knife wounds came to national prominence when Dr. MARTIN LUTHER KING JR.—in Harlem signing copies of his book, *Stride toward Freedom*—was assaulted by a mentally disturbed woman. Maynard had taken the afternoon off to see a Brigitte Bardot film before visiting patients at a hospital downtown. As soon as he could be reached he was told to return to Harlem to attend to an emergency with an important but unnamed patient. Arriving at the hospital after his staff had stabilized King, Maynard found that the knife the woman had attacked King with had been left in place, because King's aorta was in danger of being punctured if the knife were not extracted very carefully. Maynard later claimed that one of King's aides expressed surprise that the surgeon for whom everyone was waiting turned out to be black.

Maynard married Janine Delcroix on 7 July 1960. That same year Harlem Hospital suddenly lost twenty-five resident physicians, the result of new rules governing foreign medical graduates in American hospitals, and the situation was described as "chaotic" in a *New York Times* article reporting the death of two patients due to lack of care. To resolve the crisis, an administrator asked doctors from nearby Mount Sinai Hospital to remove some patients to their own wards. This incensed Maynard, who acknowledged the problems at Harlem Hospital but insisted that adequate care could be given if the hospital were provided needed resources. The city government ultimately came up with an agreement with Columbia-Presbyterian Medical Center, whereby Harlem Hospital became an affiliated teaching facility. Maynard was then nominated to join the faculty at Columbia, and on 15 November 1961 he was made the first full-time salaried department head at the hospital. This was a model for other departments, whose chiefs became part of Columbia's clinical faculty and also received city salaries for their work at the hospital. In 1972 the hospital's cardiac operating suite was named for Maynard.

In retirement he remained an active participant in the medical and cultural life of Harlem and New York City.

FURTHER READING

Maynard's papers are at the Schomburg Center for Research in Black Culture of the New York Public Library, the Amistad Research Center of Tulane University, and the New York Academy of Medicine.

Maynard, Aubre. *Surgeons to the Poor: The Harlem Hospital Story* (1978)

Gamble, Vanessa. *Making a Place for Ourselves: The Black Hospital Movement, 1920–1945* (1995)

Pearson, Hugh. *When Harlem Nearly Killed King: The 1958 Stabbing of Dr. Martin Luther King, Jr.* (2002)

EDWARD T. MORMAN

Maynard, Robert Clyve (17 June 1937–17 Aug. 1993), journalist and champion of press diversity, was born in Brooklyn, New York, to Barbadian immigrants Robertine, a homemaker, and Samuel, a lay Pentecostal minister and furniture mover.

Maynard's ambition to excel in journalism and make the press reflect the diversity of American society sprang from his strict upbringing by striving, intensely religious parents who regarded education almost as highly as godliness, and denied their children most music, dancing, movies, and anything else they deemed frivolous. As the youngest of six, inhibited by a severe stutter and forced to compete with high-achieving siblings, Maynard began writing essays to read at family dinners, his first about the post–World War II "white flight" that cost him playmates and transformed his ethnically diverse Bedford-Stuyvesant neighborhood into a mostly black ghetto.

"We were mostly immigrants when the war began. We were all Americans when it was over. Or so I thought in my sheltered innocence," Maynard wrote in a *Washington Post* essay on the U.S. bicentennial. "I wanted to know how my world could have been so snug and secure in wartime and so cold and strange in peacetime" ("The Outsiders: Fear and Anger and Dreams Deferred," *July 4, 1976*, 70).

Maynard's budding intellect impressed his first grade teacher at P.S. 44, but he had a severe stutter, a communication barrier that was compounded by his deep West Indian accent. His teacher had him listen to and repeat recordings of Edward R. Murrow's radio war reports. Maynard spoke in oratorical tones thereafter. His mother kept a fierce watch on her children's learning, but Bob, enchanted with newspapers, defied her, quitting Brooklyn's Boys High at age 16 and setting out to launch his writing career in Greenwich Village, among the likes of JAMES BALDWIN, subsisting on freelance fees.

He never resumed formal education, but by his compulsive learning and boundless curiosity Maynard became a stunningly erudite adult, proud of the label "autodidact" bestowed by an editor. By his early twenties Maynard had worked for numerous black papers, applied in vain to three hundred white dailies, and gained a wife and daughter.

Fidel Castro's triumphant 1960 visit to the United Nations brought Maynard's first big break in journalism, when Castro abandoned his downtown hotel for Harlem's landmark Hotel Theresa. Maynard snared an assignment to cover the event for the *York* (Pennsylvania) *Gazette and Daily*. His graceful, mature account won him a job on the eccentric daily in a virtually all-white farming town. Maynard found it a splendid learning and reporting environment. Five years in York led to a coveted 1965 Nieman Fellowship to study at Harvard for a year. Friends teased that he compressed an entire Harvard education into nine months, immersing himself in libraries and impressing celebrated guest speakers, including the top editor of the *Washington Post*, who hired him in 1967.

Maynard's early career bridged two distinct journalism eras, the dimming lights of a once-mighty black press, undercut by the racial integration it had championed, and the rise of integration in mainstream newspapers, accelerated by 1960s racial violence. Segregation in daily papers cracked when the Watts, Los Angeles, riot of August 1965 awakened big city newspapers to the need for black reporters. Most hired at least one.

Maynard was among the first wave of "riot reporters" on metropolitan papers, arriving at the *Post* in 1967 to cover some of the decade's most devastating urban eruptions. From post-riot Detroit he wrote of black anger and disillusionment. "Time and space become irrelevant in ghettos. It is this sameness that bodes America ill, this mass of trapped humanity, fixed and frozen in yesterday's dream within a nation already in tomorrow" (Robert C. Maynard, "New Wall Rising between the Races," *Washington Post*, July 30, 1967).

Maynard became a barrier breaker, the *Washington Post*'s first black White House correspondent, first black national correspondent, and first black ombudsman. He began twenty years of creating opportunities for minority journalists in 1972 as co-director of Columbia University's Summer Program for Minority Journalists with Earl Caldwell of the *New York Times*. Created to rapidly integrate newsrooms in response to the Kerner Commission Report (President Johnson's 1968 riot study), the Summer Program evolved into the Institute for Journalism Education, renamed in Maynard's honor after his 1993 death and steered

into the twenty-first century by his journalist daughter Dori J. Maynard.

Maynard helped direct the Summer Program, commuting to New York, until Columbia suspended it in 1974. He led a group of journalists, including his future wife, the *New York Times* correspondent Nancy Hicks, to rebuild it at the University of California, Berkeley. Maynard's 1975 marriage to Hicks, a bright light at the *Times* and a widow with a young son, blended a personal and professional partnership. Maynard left the *Washington Post* and Hicks quit the *Times* in 1977 to work on press diversity full-time. He became affirmative action director for the Gannett newspapers. Moving to Oakland, they organized the 1978 National Conference on Minorities and the News, at the annual ASNE meeting in Washington, D.C. It concluded with ASNE's adoption of Maynard's vision, the "Year 2000 Plan" for racial parity in newsrooms.

In 1979 Maynard was named editor of Gannett's *Oakland Tribune*, becoming a sensation as the black editor of a major daily newspaper. Two years later he became publisher, and in 1982, purchased the paper. His was the first African American family to own a metropolitan daily in the U.S., albeit a struggling one.

In June 1987, at 50, Maynard was diagnosed with prostate cancer, then the second-deadliest cancer among men, and disproportionately deadly for African American men. By 1989 Maynard had rebounded. His national stature was growing and he had survived the cancer and the *Tribune*'s many trials. His column was being syndicated and he was a frequent commentator and essayist for two television programs, *This Week with David Brinkley* on ABC-TV and the *MacNeil/Lehrer NewsHour* on PBS. He was on the boards of the Pulitzer Prizes, the Associated Press, and the Rockefeller Foundation. His journalism awards continued to mount: the 1989 John Peter Zenger Award for Freedom of the Press, the 1990 Elijah Lovejoy Award for journalistic courage, and a George Chaplin Scholar recognition in Hawaii. Still, his newspaper remained highly vulnerable to a recession and competition from suburban and San Francisco papers.

When a 7.1 magnitude earthquake struck at the beginning of a World Series game in San Francisco on 17 October 1989, it brought the *Tribune* a 1990 Pulitzer Prize for photography, but losses included major advertisers, business tenants in its historic building, a staff reduction of 25 percent, and near-bankruptcy.

In 1992, with his cancer recurring and the *Tribune* unable to recover from multiple setbacks, Maynard sold it to William Dean Singleton's Alameda Newspaper Group, a competitor that had swallowed much of his suburban circulation and advertising. Within a year, Maynard died at his home in the Oakland hills, survived by his wife, Nancy, and their three children, Dori, David, and Alex.

In 1993, Maynard's final year, minority journalists in daily newsrooms topped 10 percent for the first time, up from less than 1 percent when he became a leader in press diversity twenty years earlier. It was a milestone reached slowly and arduously over the two decades of Maynard's activism.

Maynard served press diversity as a leading activist, philosopher, and spokesman. He was a symbol of that movement's best aspirations. Maynard's epitaph for Supreme Court Justice Thurgood Marshall proved an apt description of his own place in history. He said Marshall, by reshaping the legal landscape of American racial relations, "made America a different place." As did Bob Maynard.

FURTHER READING

Robert C. Maynard's papers are archived at the Robert C. Maynard Institute for Journalism Education, in Oakland, California.

Maynard, Robert C., with Dori J. Maynard, *Letters to My Children* (1996).

Bonner, Alice Carol. "Changing the Color of the News: Robert Maynard and the Desegregation of Daily Newspapers," Ph.D. diss., University of North Carolina, Chapel Hill, 1999.

Fong, Nancy Anne. "The 'Oakland Tribune' under Robert C. Maynard and the Alameda Newspaper Group: A Case Study," Master's Thesis, San Jose State University, 1995.

Grabowicz, Paul. "Maynard's Success Was Also Oakland's," *Oakland Tribune*, 19 Aug. 1993.

Lewis, Gregory, "Maynard Legacy: Diversity, Sensitivity," *San Francisco Examiner*, 19 Aug. 1993.

Obituary: *Washington Post*, 19 Aug. 1993.

ALICE BONNER

Mays, Benjamin E. (1 Aug. 1894–28 Mar. 1984), educator and clergyman, was born Benjamin Elijah Mays in Greenwood County, South Carolina, the youngest of eight children of Hezekiah Mays and Louvenia Carter, both tenant farmers who had been born in slavery. Mays's earliest memory was of the 1898 Phoenix riot in Greenwood County, which was sparked by internecine battles for control of the Democratic Party and white efforts to disfranchise African Americans. Mays, who was only four at the time, recalled a mob riding with guns and making his father kowtow to save his life. He also remembered the problems his parents had faced living as tenant farmers in the cotton economy of South Carolina.

Three things about his formative years were significant to Mays. The first was his father's abuse of alcohol. He recalled that his father drank even near the church, and he remembered the fights between his parents when his father was drunk. As a result of his father's behavior, Mays abstained from alcohol. The second formative influence on Mays was the religious life of his mother. She would lead the family in nightly ritual prayer, and her abiding faith instilled a disciplined spirituality into Mays's life. Her piety strongly influenced his religious sensibilities, and her belief in the power of education helped to shape his emerging worldview. Third, Mays benefited from support at church and school, and from his oldest sister, Susie, who taught him rudimentary reading and math. Throughout his adolescent years, such encouragement at home, church, and school persuaded Mays to seek an education as a means of overcoming rural poverty. Later in life, he would remember his prayers in the cotton fields to God to grant him the opportunity to get an education.

Mays left home after his father objected to his being a full-time student. He completed high school at South Carolina State College in Orangeburg, graduating as the valedictorian of his class in 1914. From there he would follow the abolitionist nexus, attending Virginia Union University in Richmond, a Baptist-affiliated historically black college founded by the American Home Mission Society in 1865. While a student at Virginia Union, Mays met two alumni of Bates College, who had joined Union's faculty; they encouraged him to transfer to Bates College, a predominantly white, Baptist-affiliated institution, in Lewiston, Maine. Bates was liberating for Mays. He attended the college so that he could compete academically with northern whites. The experience satisfied his need to gain respect and overcome the culture of inferiority with which segregated society had marked all African Americans. Mays became a member of Phi Beta Kappa Society and, at the age of twenty-six, graduated from Bates with honors.

After completing his degree at Bates, Mays decided upon a career in the ministry. Although numerous black Baptist congregations would have accepted him as pastor with only a bachelor's degree, he declined to take any such post and instead chose to enroll in the University of Chicago Divinity School in 1920. He initially wanted to attend Andover-Newton Seminary in Massachusetts, but he was not accepted because of his race. Chicago proved to be stimulating and on the cutting edge of theology and sociology. Unfortunately, the university offered him very little money to complete his master's work without interruption.

After having finished the first year of his program, Mays delayed his education for three years to teach at Morehouse College, in Atlanta, Georgia. Morehouse's president, JOHN HOPE, recruited Mays to teach math and psychology. Though the original contract was for one year, Mays remained at Morehouse for three years, during which he taught and influenced many students and colleagues who would go on to notable achievements, among them the sociologist E. FRANKLIN FRAZIER, the theologian HOWARD THURMAN, and the civil rights lawyer JAMES NABRIT. The high standards set at Morehouse under Hope's leadership was an inspiration to Mays. It was a model of how dedicated leadership could bring about racial uplift and inspire African Americans to even greater accomplishments.

Although Mays loved Morehouse, he still wanted to be an active church pastor. While at Morehouse, he served as pastor of a small congregation—Shiloh Baptist Church. Tragically for Mays, his first wife, Ellen Harvin, who had encouraged him in his pursuit of the ministry, died in Atlanta in childbirth in 1923. Although the tragic loss of his wife grieved him, Mays pursued his calling and returned to the University of Chicago in the academic year 1924–1925 to complete his master's thesis, titled "Pagan Survivals in Christianity," under the New Testament historian Shirley Jackson Case.

In the spring of 1925, Robert Shaw Wilkinson, the president of South Carolina State College, recruited Mays to teach at his alma mater. During his brief tenure in Orangeburg, Mays met Sadie Gray, a teacher and social worker, and married her in 1926. Their marriage broke the college's rule that married women could not be members of the faculty, which sent Mays and his wife in search of employment. The National Urban League soon employed them both as social workers in Tampa, Florida, where they stayed for two years, with Mays serving as director of the league. Although Mays did not find the job fulfilling, with characteristic dutifulness he completed a study of Tampa in 1928 with the white liberal sociologist Arthur Raper. In 1928 Mays and his wife returned to Atlanta, where he worked for

the national YMCA while continuing to seek the pastorship of a church. At the end of his term with the YMCA in 1930, Mays received a stipend from a Rockefeller Foundation–funded organization, the Institute for Social Religious Research, to study African American churches.

After the publication in 1933 of *The Negro's Church*, co-authored with Joseph Nicholson, Mays was able to return to the University of Chicago to complete a Ph.D. in Theology. His dissertation, *The Negro's God as Reflected in His Literature*, was published as a book in 1938. Upon completion of his degree, Mays once more sought a pulpit. Once again, however, the academy, not the church, called him. In 1934 MORDECAI JOHNSON, the president of Howard University, recruited Mays to be the dean of the university's School of Religion. Mays thought that if he could not actively lead a church, the next-best calling was to the train the clergy. During his six-year tenure at Howard, he recruited faculty and students, built the library, and secured accreditation for the School of Religion. As a result of his work at Howard and the internal struggle that took place after the death of John Hope, Mays was voted by the trustees to the post of president of Morehouse College in 1940.

From 1940 to 1967 Mays served as president of Morehouse College. While working in this capacity, he continued to build on the legacy of John Hope. Like Hope, he was active in the Federal Council of Churches, serving as the first African American vice president and on the central committee of the World Council of Churches as well as pursuing civil rights causes. In addition, he was widely sought after as a public speaker and weekly columnist for the *Pittsburgh Courier*. As president of the college, he mentored a generation of students engaged in the struggle for human rights. Mays's most famous student, MARTIN LUTHER KING JR., called him "his spiritual and intellectual mentor" (*New York Times*, 29 Mar. 1984, D23). For Mays, it was tragic that he was called upon to give the eulogies for King and, later, for WHITNEY YOUNG JR., the executive director of the National Urban League.

Upon his retirement, Mays nursed Sadie Gray Mays through her last illness; she died in 1969. He also wrote his autobiography, *Born to Rebel*, took speaking engagements, and served as the president of the Atlanta Board of Education. In 1982 the NAACP awarded him its highest honor, the Spingarn Medal. In 1984, just short of his ninetieth birthday, Mays died in Atlanta. He is buried on the campus of Morehouse College.

FURTHER READING

The Benjamin E. Mays Papers are held at Howard University's Moorland-Spingarn Research Center in Washington, D.C.

Mays, Benjamin. *Born to Rebel: An Autobiography* (1987)

Mays, Benjamin. *The People Have Driven Me On* (1981)

Burton, Vernon. "Foreword," in *Born to Rebel* (1987).

Jelks, Randal M. "The Academic Formation of Benjamin E. Mays, 1917–1936," in *Walking Integrity: Benjamin Elijah Mays, Mentor to Generations*, ed. Lawrence Edward Carter (1996).

Wills, David W. "An Enduring Distance: Black Americans and the Establishment," in *Between the Times: The Travail of the Protestant Establishment in America, 1900–1960*, ed. William R. Hutchinson (1989).

Obituary: *New York Times*, 29 Mar. 1984.

RANDAL MAURICE JELKS

Mays, Isaiah (16 Feb. 1858–2 May 1925), soldier and Medal of Honor recipient, was born into slavery at Carters Bridge, Virginia. His parents were likely Jacob and Sarah Mays, who had been enslaved before their move to Ohio by 1863 during the early years of the Civil War. By 1880 Jacob and Sarah Mays were living on a farm in Benton Township, in Pike County, Ohio, some fifty miles south of Columbus. Nothing is known of Isaiah Mays's life until he enlisted in the U.S. Army at Columbus in September 1881, listing his occupation as that of a laborer.

As an African American, Isaiah Mays was assigned to the 24th Infantry Regiment, one of the four all-black units in the army, along with the 25th Infantry and 9th and 10th Cavalry regiments, which Congress authorized as part of the regular peacetime army in 1869. These segregated regiments, which soon gained the collective nickname "Buffalo Soldiers" from their Native American opponents during their service on the western frontier, were commanded by white officers and were the only units open to African Americans who sought the career of a soldier. The Buffalo Soldiers served under extreme conditions of weather and performed a variety of duties. While the military campaigns to subdue Native Americans fighting to keep their tribal lands were their most publicized feats, black soldiers, men like Mays, WILLIAM MCBRYAR, THOMAS BOYNE, and many others who would gain recognition for their valiant service, were also employed in protecting frontier settlers from outlaws, building roads, and scouting duties. All these duties were critical elements facilitating America's great expansion westward in the decades following the Civil War.

Upon joining the 24th Infantry, Isaiah Mays was assigned to B Company and sent to serve at Fort Elliot, Texas. There he served for five years and saw little but garrison duty; at the end of his first term of service on 7 September 1886, he was noted as an excellent soldier and soon reenlisted for service at Fort Leavenworth, Kansas, on 19 September 1886. He continued to serve in Texas until June 1888, when the 24th Infantry was transferred to the Arizona Territory. In May 1889 Mays, now promoted to corporal, was serving at Fort Grant when he was assigned to a detachment of eleven men tasked with providing protection for the payroll wagon of Major Joseph Wham, carrying nearly $29,000 in gold coins destined for the garrison at nearby Fort Thomas. Corporal Isaiah Mays was second in command of the payroll escort, the senior man being his fellow Buffalo Soldier, Sergeant BENJAMIN BROWN. Despite the heavy escort, the payroll wagon was ambushed near Cedar Springs on 11 May 1889 by as

Isaiah Mays, U.S. Corporal and Medal of Honor Recipient (c. 1900). (Library of Congress/Daniel Murray Collection.)

many as twenty outlaws. Pinned down under heavy fire, the Buffalo Soldiers fought back fiercely, but caught in the open and outgunned, the odds were against them. Though wounded in both legs, Isaiah Mays ran and crawled for two miles to seek help for the embattled soldiers, while Sergeant Brown kept up a steady return fire. In the end, despite the efforts of Mays and Brown, the outlaws prevailed and made off with the entire payroll. Still, Major Wham, a veteran of sixteen battles in the Civil War, recognized a good soldier when he saw one and recommended both Mays and Brown for the Medal of Honor, stating that he had "never witnessed better courage or better fighting than shown by these colored soldiers" (Hanna, p. 61). Though the recommendation for the Medal of Honor for Mays and Brown was disputed by some officials because of the fact that the payroll was not saved, the heroism of these Buffalo Soldiers was undisputed, and the award was subsequently made on 19 February 1890.

Following this, Isaiah Mays continued his army service, reenlisting at Fort Grant on 15 September 1891. In February 1892, citing his parents and their failing health, Mays sought to be discharged and was supported by his commanding officer. However, when the army refused his request, Mays got into a heated argument with his company commander. He was subsequently court-martialed for his actions and reduced in rank to private and fined $60, and in June 1892 he was transferred to Company D at Fort Bayard, New Mexico. The following year, Private Isaiah Mays again sought a discharge based on his parents' failing health, which was this time approved. He was discharged on 4 September 1893 at Fort Bayard, New Mexico. However, Mays never returned eastward; he worked as a laborer in Arizona for years and was a resident of Guthrie, Arizona, in 1910. In 1922, with the help of Congressman Carl Hayden, Mays sought an invalid pension from the army, but was denied. By 1925 Isaiah Mays was a resident of the Territorial Insane Asylum (now the Arizona State Hospital) in Phoenix, an institution that cared for the ill and the indigent. Here it was that Isaiah Mays died and was buried in All Souls Cemetery in a grave marked only by a headstone with a number.

Isaiah Mays remained largely forgotten until efforts by hospital personnel and local veteran groups resulted in a Medal of Honor headstone being erected in 2001. In 2008 a veterans group, the Old Guard Riders, began an effort to have Mays's remains disinterred and transferred to Arlington National Cemetery in Virginia. In March 2009 Mays's remains were disinterred and cremated. Mays's ashes were subsequently placed in a specially designed urn and transported across the country, accompanied by an honor guard the entire journey. Isaiah Mays finally returned to his native state when he was interred at Arlington National Cemetery on 29 May 2009.

FURTHER READING

Hanna, Charles W. *African American Recipients of the Medal of Honor* (2002).
Schubert, Frank N. *Black Valor: Buffalo Soldiers and the Medal of Honor, 1870–1898* (1997).

GLENN ALLEN KNOBLOCK

Mays, Willie (6 May 1931–), baseball player, was born Willie Howard Mays Jr. in Westfield, Alabama. His paternal grandfather, Walter Mays, and his father, William Howard Mays Sr., were semiprofessional baseball players, and his mother was a high school track star. After his parents divorced when he was three years old, Mays was raised by his father and two adopted sisters in Fairfield, Alabama.

Mays starred in football and basketball at Fairfield Industrial High School. As the school had no baseball team, Mays began playing semiprofessional baseball as a young teenager. By age fourteen he was playing right field with his father's semiprofessional steel mill team. In 1947 his father introduced him to Piper Davis, the manager of the Birmingham Black Barons, a professional baseball team in the Negro American League. He got two hits in his first game for the Black Barons and was signed for $250 per month, even though he could play only home games because he was still in high school. In a sign of things to come, Mays hit a double in his first at bat against the great pitcher SATCHEL PAIGE of the Kansas City Monarchs. He played for the Black Barons from 1947 through 1949.

The Boston Braves scouted Mays in 1949 and 1950 but did not sign him. However, Eddie Montague, a scout for the New York Giants, reported that Mays was the greatest ballplayer he had ever seen, and the Giants signed him at a salary of five thousand dollars on the day Willie graduated from high school. They paid the Black Barons ten thousand dollars for Mays's contract. In 1950 Mays was assigned to a minor-league team in Sioux City, Iowa, but because the team would not accept black players, he was subsequently sent to the Trenton, New Jersey, minor-league team. In 1951 he was promoted to the New York Giants' top farm team, the Minneapolis Millers. He batted .477

during the first two months of the season and was promoted to the New York Giants on 25 May 1951. Despite his short stay in Minneapolis, he became such a fan favorite that the Giants placed an advertisement in the local newspaper to apologize to the community for promoting him. Mays's impact on the Giants was immediate and profound. Although he did not hit well in his first games, his fielding prowess was so extraordinary that the Giants' manager, Leo Durocher, affirmed that Mays was to be his regular center fielder no matter how poorly he batted. His hitting improved as he helped the Giants win the National League pennant in his first season. Mays's performance earned him the Rookie of the Year award. His enthusiastic "Say Hey" greeting and impassioned play led to his nickname, the "Say Hey Kid."

In 1952 Mays was drafted into the U.S. Army and assigned to Fort Eustis, Virginia. During this time he played baseball and created his distinctive technique of catching fly balls at the level of his belt buckle, his famous "basket catch." He finally returned to a languishing New York Giants team in 1954. When a fan noticed Durocher greeting

Mays, he remarked, "Leo is shaking hands with the pennant." Mays won the batting title, hit forty-one home runs, and was awarded the National League Most Valuable Player award. That year he led the Giants to the pennant and the World Series championship against the favored Cleveland Indians.

The 1954 World Series was marked by one of the most remarkable fielding plays in baseball history, known as "the Catch." In the eighth inning of the first game, with the score tied and two runners on base, Vic Wertz of the Indians hit a fly ball over Mays's head in center field. Mays turned around, ran straight back, and caught the ball over his shoulder 450 feet from home plate. He twirled around in one motion and threw to the infield, which kept any runners from scoring. "The Catch" epitomizes Mays's place as the greatest fielding center fielder in baseball history.

Mays married Margueritte Wendell in 1956, and they adopted a son, Michael, in 1959. Their marriage ended in divorce in 1961. The breakdown in his marriage coincided with the Giants' move to San Francisco in 1958. Although he was the star of the team, Mays was not immediately accepted

Willie Mays is doused with champagne in the dressing room at Chicago's Wrigley Field after his New York Mets defeated the Chicago Cubs to win the National League East division championship, 1 October 1973. (AP Images.)

into the community and was kept from buying a house in a white neighborhood when homeowners protested. On the diamond he was often unfavorably compared to San Francisco's local hero, Joe DiMaggio, who, ironically, had been Mays's boyhood idol. Mays let his play overcome the critics. He led the Giants to a pennant in 1962, and in 1964 he became the first African American ever to captain a Major League Baseball team. Two years later, Mays signed a contract with the Giants that made him the highest-paid player in baseball history. *Sporting News* voted him the Player of the Decade for the 1960s. Mays married Mae Louise Allen in 1971, a year before the Giants traded him to the New York Mets, and two years before he completed his career as the Mets' player-coach. In 1979 he became the ninth player to be elected to the Baseball Hall of Fame in his first year of eligibility.

Mays's greatness lies in his superiority in all areas of the game: running, fielding, throwing, power hitting, and hitting for average. The adulation of his fans for one of baseball's greatest all-around players rests on Mays's twenty-two-year career of consistently phenomenal statistics and defensive plays. From 1954 through 1962 he led the National League in at least one offensive category every year. He holds the records of 7,290 outfield chances and 7,095 putouts and led the league in outfield double plays from 1954 to 1956 and, remarkably, ten years later, in 1965. He also holds seven club records for the New York Giants (for which he played only five full seasons) and fifteen club records for the San Francisco Giants.

Mays's career totals put him in the top ten in nine offensive categories, including 2,992 games played, 660 home runs, 63 multiple-home-run games, 1,903 runs batted in, and 2,062 runs scored. He won the Most Valuable Player award in 1954 and 1965 and led the league in batting in 1954. He also led the National League four seasons in home runs and four consecutive seasons in stolen bases. He had ten seasons batting over .300, ten seasons batting in at least 100 runs, and twelve consecutive seasons scoring at least 100 runs. He hit at least 30 home runs in eleven seasons, 20 doubles in sixteen seasons, and 5 triples in twelve seasons. In 1971 he hit 5 triples at the age of forty.

Mays is one of only three players to have 500 home runs and 3,000 hits and one of only six players to hit 4 home runs in a single game. He was the first player to have 20 doubles, triples, home runs, and stolen bases in a season (1957), 30 home runs and 30 stolen bases in a season (1956 and 1957), and 50 home runs and 20 stolen bases in a season (1955). He also was the first player to reach 300 home runs and 300 stolen bases. In recognition of all these accomplishments, Mays was selected for the National League All-Star team twenty-four consecutive times.

Despite all Mays gave to the game, the baseball commissioner Bowie Kuhn banished him from baseball in 1979 because he was hired to work in public relations by Bally's Casino; Major League Baseball had long prohibited players and coaches from having any association with gambling entities. He was finally welcomed back into baseball in 1985 by Commissioner Peter Ueberroth. The San Francisco Giants then hired him in 1986 as a special assistant to the president and made this a lifetime appointment in 1993.

Mays's impact on baseball, sports, and society goes well beyond his statistics and awards. Remembering his humble beginnings, he has continuously promoted activities to help underprivileged children. During his adolescence he watched Saturday football games at Miles College, a black school in Birmingham. In 1968 he returned to Miles College as national chair of their fundraising campaign to build the Willie Mays Health and Physical Education Center. During his years as a New York Giant, he was famous for playing stickball with neighborhood children in Harlem; in San Francisco in the 1960s he became a mentor to O. J. SIMPSON, who was at that time a wayward teenager from the city's Potrero Hill housing projects. When Mays returned to New York with the Mets, he supported New York's Fresh Air Fund to allow inner-city children to spend time in summer camps outside the city. Mays's Say Hey Foundation, formed in 1980, is dedicated to providing higher education for underprivileged children.

Mays has actively promoted the inclusion of Negro League players into the Hall of Fame. When the Hall of Fame proposed setting up a separate exhibit for Negro League players and their accomplishments, he forcefully argued that Negro League baseball should be recognized as part of the highest level of baseball and that its players should be integrated into exhibits of baseball's greatest athletes. Although blacks and whites played separately, he believed they should be remembered together. In 2000 the San Francisco Giants honored Mays by addressing their new ballpark 24 Willie Mays Plaza and adorning it with a nine-foot-tall statue of the "Say Hey Kid."

FURTHER READING

Mays, Willie, with Lou Sahadi. *Say Hey: The Autobiography of Willie Mays* (1988).

Einstein, Charles. *Willie Mays: My Life and Times in and out of Baseball* (1972).

Einstein, Charles. *Willie's Time: A Memoir of Another America* (1979).

STANTON W. GREEN

Mazloomi, Carolyn (22 Aug. 1948–), one of America's most prominent quilters and African American quilt history advocates, was born Carolyn Stewart in Baton Rouge, Louisiana, to Edward Stewart, a chemical engineer, and Thelma Stewart, a librarian. The eldest of four children, she earned her undergraduate degree in 1977 at Northrop University in Inglewood, California. In 1984 she received her Ph.D. in Aerospace Engineering from the University of Southern California in Los Angeles. As a child, her favorite aunt encouraged Mazloomi's fascination with airplanes and flying. She became a licensed pilot in 1974 and retired from a career as an aerospace engineer and Federal Aviation Administration crash site investigator. Mazloomi and her husband, Rezvan, married in 1975 and resided in West Chester, Ohio. They had three children, Damian Patrick, Farzad, and Farhad.

Mazloomi taught herself to quilt after seeing a traditional patchwork quilt with American eagles in each corner at the Dallas Trade Market in 1980. She was mesmerized by the hand quilting and soon purchased quilting how-to books to teach herself. She started copying traditional patchwork and Baltimore Album appliquéd quilt patterns, but found the exact measurements too limiting for her creative energies. The Baltimore Album quilt pattern is composed of blocks of colorful appliquéd flowers and leaves on a white background. The pattern was popular in the mid-nineteenth century. In a Smithsonian Institution interview in 2002 she shared: "One night I became so angry at the indecision within myself to just choose colors for [a quilt] block, I took all of my quilt books … and I burned them. And that was a spiritual release for me" (www.aaa.si.edu/oralhist/mazloo02.htm). Over the years, Mazloomi remained true to her inner creative spirits. She created large-size pictorial or narrative quilts with bold colors. Her fabrics included cottons, silks, hand-dyed indigo fabrics, shibori cloths, and antique kentes. She often sewed beads onto her quilt tops.

In the early 1980s Mazloomi attended many quilting events but never saw other African American quilters there. The isolation she felt led her to place an advertisement in the February 1986 issue of *Quilter's Newsletter Magazine* requesting to correspond with other African American quilters. She heard from a number of black quilters who had felt similarly isolated, and they joined Mazloomi in founding the Women of Color Quilters Network (WOCQN) in 1986. They included Claire E. Carter, aRma Carter (*sic*), CUESTA BENBERRY, Melodye Boyd, MICHAEL CUMMINGS, Peggie Hartwell, and Marie Wilson. The goals of the organization were to foster and preserve the art of quilt making among men and women of color, to encourage research in African American quilt history, to offer authentic African American-made quilts to museums and galleries for exhibition, and to offer expertise in quilt making techniques. WOCQN membership swelled to 1,200 worldwide. WOCQN newsletters, often the only source of real news for and about quilters of color, were published between 1987 and 1993, and a complete set of newsletters is in the permanent collection of the American Folk Art Museum Library in New York City. Mazloomi also founded the African American Quilters of Los Angeles in 1986 with Ouida Braithwaite.

Mazloomi, a self-confident woman, decided to make a profession of selling her own quilts so she could stay home with her three children. Over her career, she made more than one hundred quilts. Her pictorial and improvisational works often depict personal and universal African American themes: family life, women's rights, political freedom, and musical legacy. She has remarked that "[n]one of [my] quilts are planned, they just give birth to themselves. Quilts are my equivalent to making music; I never know the final result. Much like the jazz instrumentalist who improvises his music with such radically eloquent rhythms, quilts have vibes all their own. Quilts are visual soul food and I hope the viewer can feel the spirit of the cloth" (www.quiltsforchange.net/judges.htm). She often worked in series creating three or more quilts of a similar theme. Her quilt series include the *Black Family* (1990s), *Big City Women* (1999–2002), and *Wise Women* (2002–2003).

A generation of contemporary African American quilters would not have their works exhibited but for the efforts of Mazloomi. She ensured that American and global audiences experience contemporary African American quilt designs by curating exhibitions seen by thousands of museum and gallery visitors. In 1995, she curated an international quilt exhibit at the Fourth Annual United Nations World Conference on Women in Beijing, China. She coedited the exhibit's 192-page catalog, *Star Quilts*, and showcased the works of 150 quilts by 63 nationally known artists in her book *Spirits of the Cloth: Contemporary African American Quilts* (1998). This catalog won the 1999 Best Non-Fiction Book of the Year award from the American Library Association. In 2004, Mazloomi partnered with Patricia C. Pongracz of the American Bible Society Gallery in New York to exhibit *Threads of Faith: Recent Works from the Women of Color Quilters Network*. This quilt exhibit, which featured more than 50 quilts by 33 quilters, broke opening day and total attendance records for the gallery.

Mazloomi's work was featured in close to fifty solo exhibitions and more than 145 group shows in museums and galleries in the United States and internationally. American venues have included the Autry Museum of Western Culture, the National Civil Rights Museum, the New England Quilt Museum, the New Orleans Museum of Art, the Ronald Regan Presidential Library, the Smithsonian Institution Renwick Gallery, and the Wadsworth Atheneum Museum of Art in Hartford, Connecticut. International venues have included the National Art Gallery of Namibia; the Museum for Textiles in Toronto, Canada; the Center for Intercultural Research of Women's Daily Lives, in Nuremberg, Germany; and the Cultural Palace in Beijing, China.

Important exhibitions included *Always There: The African-American Presence in American Quilts* (1993), *Uncommon Beauty in Common Objects* (1993), *Stop Asking/We Exist* (1999), *Women Designers in the USA: Diversity and Difference 1900–2000* (2000), *A Communion of the Spirits: African American Quilters, Preservers, and Their Stories* (2001), *Threads of Freedom: The Underground Railroad Story in Quilts* (2001), *Six Continents of Quilts* (2002, international touring display), *Common Threads: African American Quilts Past and Present* (2003), and *Gumbo Ya Ya: Contemporary African American Quilts* (2005).

Mazloomi's quilts are in the permanent collections of several museums and corporations such as the Mint Museum of Craft and Design in Charlotte, North Carolina; the National Civil Rights Museum in Memphis, Tennessee; the Quilters' Hall of Fame Museum in Madison, Indiana; the Rocky Mountain Quilt Museum in Denver, Colorado; and the Smithsonian Institution Renwick Gallery.

In 2003, Mazloomi was awarded the first Ohio Heritage Fellowship Award, honoring her for the high artistic achievement her body of work represents as well as for her dedicated service to quilting traditions. Mazloomi became one of America's most prominent quilters and an indispensable advocate of African American quilt history. In 2007, Mazloomi published *Textural Rhythms: Quilting the Jazz Tradition*.

FURTHER READING

Freeman, Roland. *A Communion of the Spirits: African-American Quilters, Preservers, and Their Stories* (1996).

National Afro-American Museum and Cultural Center. *Uncommon Beauty in Common Objects: The Legacy of African American Craft Art* (1993).

KYRA E. HICKS

McAdoo, Robert Allen, Jr. (Robert Bob Allen McAdoo) (25 Sept. 1951–), professional basketball player, was born in Greensboro, North Carolina. His mother was an elementary school teacher who had attained a master's degree, and his father was a custodian at North Carolina Agricultural and Technical College. McAdoo attended Ben L. mith High School in Greensboro. Though he lived closer to a black high school, he was bused to the integrated Ben L. Smith High School because he thought it would be easier to make the basketball team there. McAdoo was a basketball and track star in high school, leading his basketball team to the state semifinals. He was also a talented alto saxophone player. He did not have the requisite test scores to attend the four-year University of North Carolina at Chapel Hill (UNC-CH), which was well known for its basketball program. At first McAdoo attended Vincennes Junior College in Indiana, where he did well academically and excelled on the basketball court, leading the team to a national junior college championship in 1970. He was soon able to transfer to UNC-CH. He played one stellar season for the UNC-CH Tar Heels, leading them to the NCAA Final Four in 1972. McAdoo was named most valuable player (MVP) of the Atlantic Coast Conference Tournament. With an average of 19.5 points and 10.1 rebounds per game, he was named First Team All-American. In 1972 McAdoo left North Carolina for the National Basketball Association (NBA). It was not common at that time for players to leave college early to turn professional. McAdoo received permission to leave a year early owing to his family's economic troubles. Years later he revealed that the story was more complicated than that. His mother, who prized education, strongly discouraged his choice to leave school. It was through consultation with his father that he made up his mind to turn professional. His decision to leave the Tar Heels made him unpopular in North Carolina, and for a time he was harassed by people who defaced his car.

McAdoo joined the Buffalo Braves of the NBA in 1972 and stayed until 1977. With the Braves, he led the league in scoring for three seasons. He was named NBA Rookie of the Year in his first season and NBA Most Valuable Player in 1975. His offensive skills overshadowed his defensive skills, which were often the subject of critique. At the same time his tremendous offensive skills were highly praised by sports writers and even the great player and coach BILL RUSSELL. McAdoo was the first player of his (for that time) large size to be an offensive threat, not only from close to the basket but also from long distance. His long-distance shooting skills effected an important change in the dynamics of the professional game.

Bob McAdoo of the LA Lakers tries to retrieve the ball during a game against the Denver Nuggets in Los Angeles, 27 December 1983. (AP Images.)

In his first few seasons, McAdoo was not known as a particularly easygoing fellow and was highly sensitive to criticism. He often came across as aloof if not arrogant. This led to conflicts with both teammates and team management and resulted in his trade from the Buffalo Braves to the New York Knickerbockers in 1976. Between 1976 and 1981 he played for the New York Knicks, the Boston Celtics, the Detroit Pistons, and the New Jersey Nets. In 1978 he played in his fifth and final NBA All-Star Game. During this time his career was plagued with interpersonal conflicts. Though he continued to post impressive statistics, his status as a star began to diminish.

McAdoo's career turned around in late 1981, when he joined the powerhouse Los Angeles Lakers, which at that time included KAREEM ABDUL JABBAR and EARVIN "MAGIC" JOHNSON JR. Though he was not a starter for the Lakers, McAdoo was a crucial substitute, coming in from the bench at critical moments. He won his first NBA championship with the Lakers in 1982. He was also a member of the 1985 championship Lakers team. McAdoo's contract with the Lakers was not renewed after that year, and he played one disappointing season with the Philadelphia Seventy-Sixers before leaving the NBA. He retired with a scoring average of 22.1 points per game and 18,787 points in all. At the time that he achieved his ten thousandth point he was the youngest player to have done so.

In 1986 McAdoo joined the Tracer Milan team of the Italian League. In his first year he led Tracer Milan to both the Italian and the European championships. In Italy, McAdoo was a star and once again a dominant player, averaging 26.5 points per game over his 6 seasons. Although he retired from the European game in 1993, McAdoo came to greatly appreciate Italian culture. He married an Italian native, Patrizia, in 1995. He had six children, Robert, Rita, Ross, Russell, Rasheeda, and Ryan, the last four with Patrizia.

In 1994 McAdoo returned to the NBA as an assistant coach for the Miami Heat. In 1996 he was controversially left off a list of the fifty greatest players of all time. He was the only one-time MVP to have been left off the list. At a height of six feet nine inches, McAdoo played fourteen seasons in the NBA at center and power forward, amassing a set of statistics, particularly in shooting, that were unusual for a man of his size. He was inducted into the Naismith Memorial Basketball Hall of Fame in 2000.

FURTHER READING

McAdoo, Bob. "The Game I'll Never Forget," *Basketball Digest* (Nov. 2000).

May, Peter. "Finally Having It All, McAdoo Inducted into Hall of Fame," *Boston Globe* (Oct. 2000).

Vecsey, George. "McAdoo: More to Prove," *New York Times* (June 1985).

PAUL DEVLIN

McAfee, Walter Samuel (2 Sept. 1914–18 Feb. 1995), astrophysicist, was born in Ore City, Texas. His father, Luther McAfee, was a Colored Methodist Episcopal (CME) minister and graduate of Texas College. His mother, Susie (Johnson) McAfee, taught at the Wiley College Normal School, which Walter would attend years later. The family of nine children stayed in the rural community of Upshure County for about three months after Walter's birth before moving to Marshall, Texas.

Walter McAfee graduated with honors from high school and counted his chemistry and physics teacher Freeman Prince Hodge among his earliest influences. In 1930 he received a scholarship to Wiley College, where Charles Anthony McCain (who later taught at Howard University) would be his professor for general physics and sophomore mechanics. It was McCain whom McAfee credited with advising him to choose physics rather than engineering. In 1934, the nineteen-year-old Walter McAfee graduated magna cum laude from Wiley College.

Unable to find a job during the Great Depression, the young graduate worked as a farm laborer, carpenter's assistant, and door-to-door salesman before applying for a scholarship to attend graduate school at Ohio State University. In August 1934 he arrived in Columbus without a place to live. At the bus depot, a black baggage handler connected him with a local black family who would provide him with a place to stay in exchange for rent and work.

McAfee studied theoretical mathematical physics in courses with Alfred Lande, who was known for the Lande G-factor, the third of three "magnetic moments" in the position of an electron in an atom. Professor Llewellyn H. Thomas would advise his graduate work. In June 1937 he received his master's degree in Theoretical Physics and found his first job teaching general science, mathematics, and biology at a local junior high school. While at Ohio State, he met Viola Winston, who was working on her B.A. in Elementary Education. They married in 1941; they would have two daughters, Diana Mercedes and Marsha Ann-Bera.

Prior to the attack on Pearl Harbor that propelled the United States into World War II, civil service jobs were hard to come by. Young people took several exams in order to increase the likelihood of getting a position. When manpower needs became acute, hiring was changed to "War Services Indefinite Basis," which meant that workers could be let go after the war. It was common practice for employers to require an applicant to attach a photograph to his or her application forms. Groups like the NAACP actively fought against this requirement as African Americans stood a higher chance of being rejected than did whites.

The first job offer McAfee received was for a position at Langley Air Force Base in Virginia. After he returned his paperwork, McAfee was informed the position had been filled. Other offers came from a Texas site and the Great Lakes Naval Training Station in Michigan. He was rejected for both. As the McAfees were expecting their first child, he secured a position with the U.S. Army Signal Corps at Fort Monmouth, New Jersey. The Signal Corps had traditionally hired more African Americans than had other military units.

McAfee was assigned to the Theoretical Studies Unit, where he immediately focused on two problems: how to distinguish friendly aircraft from non-friendly ones using radar, and how to detect mortar-firing positions in the field. McAfee coauthored several papers on the scattering of electromagnetic waves, radar echoing areas, and radar coverage patterns, as well as other technical memoranda that solved these problems.

Fort Monmouth was a large campus with laboratories scattered over much of the state. The military head of Evans Laboratory, Lt. Col. John H. DeWitt Jr., had previously tried bouncing and retrieving radar signals off the moon. Having performed radar echoing and refraction studies McAfee was brought in to help solve the problem. He computed cross-sections of the lunar surface along with a distance and pattern analysis to determine the strength of the returning signal; the hope was that by bouncing and successfully receiving signals off the moon's surface (an object whose orbit is highly predictable) it would then be possible to move to the next step of experimentation: sending and receiving radio communications with man-made objects orbiting in space.

The first radar signal to be bounced and retrieved from the moon's surface was announced on January of 1946 as part of "Project Diana." The news was widely publicized and the team's accomplishments highlighted as paving the way for space exploration. Papers appeared in peer-reviewed journals and employment opportunities grew for those associated with its success. But McAfee's groundbreaking contributions were not mentioned.

Shortly thereafter McAfee received a Rosenwald Fellowship to Cornell University, where he completed his dissertation in 1949 with the future Nobel laureate Hans Bethe. McAfee was promoted to assistant section chief and his unit began the first of its postwar experiments in radiation physics. From 1949 until 1953 McAfee conducted a number of research projects in atomic and nuclear energy. In the fall of 1953 he took over as section chief of the Electromagnetic Wave Propagation Section, where experiments to place aboard orbiting satellites were planned.

By the time of the Korean conflict opportunities for promotion were still limited for African Americans, as racism continued to be a factor in hiring and promotion. McAfee and others offered training programs for technical and support staff with a curriculum that ranged from elementary mathematics to advanced engineering. Eventually this program was taken over by Fort Monmouth's Personnel Office.

Twenty-five years later McAfee's contributions to the Moon Radar Project were officially recognized. Nevertheless, he had many achievements in radiation detection and sensing. He received the first Secretary of the Army's Research Fellowship Award, was inducted into the Wiley College Science Hall of Fame, and scholarships in his name were established by the Armed Forces Electronics Command and the National Society of Black Physicists. He served as director of scientific studies for NATO and was promoted to scientific adviser at Fort Monmouth before retiring in 1985. McAfee died in 1995; two years later the U.S. Army Communications-Electronics Command posthumously dedicated the McAfee Center in his honor.

FURTHER READING

Cooper, Louise T. "Scholarships Established—Dr. McAfee Honored as a Black Leader and Outstanding Scientist," *Monmouth Message*, 24 Feb. 1989.

Johnson, Robert O. *An Oral History of African-Americans and the Development of Radar Defense Technology at Fort Monmouth, New Jersey—Dr. Walter S. McAfee.* Information Age Science Center (1994).

"Original Participants Mark Diana's 25th Anniversary." *Army Research and Development Newsmagazine* (1971).

Samuels, Vivian O. *Blacks in Science and Medicine* (1990).

Obituary: *Asbury Park (N.J.) Press*, 21 Feb. 1995.

ROBERT JOHNSON JR.

McBay, Henry Cecil Ransom (29 May 1914–23 June 1995), chemistry professor and research chemist, was born in Mexia, Texas, to William Cecil McBay, a drugstore and barbershop owner, and Roberta (Ransom) McBay, a seamstress. McBay's father also taught himself anatomy, became an embalmer's apprentice, and later established a mortuary business with his older brother. The parents' example of hard work as a prerequisite for success set a high standard for McBay, his brother and two sisters, all four of whom attended college and earned postgraduate degrees. Just prior to the 1920s, as the nation recovered from the social and economic trauma of World War I, Mexia, Texas, experienced a temporary economic boom that had a significant impact on McBay's early academic opportunities. Oil was discovered in that middle-Texas community, primarily on farmland owned by African Americans. Although McBay's immediate family did not own oil-laden property, McBay and his siblings benefited indirectly from the oil boom: because of the oil revenue in Mexia, the local racially-segregated school for African Americans, Paul Laurence Dunbar High School, was able to attract excellent teachers who established high academic standards for their students. The principal of the school had a master's degree in Mathematics from Northwestern University and established an outstanding curriculum in mathematics. This provided McBay with the foundation that was essential for his future studies in chemistry. Later in his career McBay often pointed out to his students that mathematics is the basic tool required for the study of the sciences, particularly chemistry and physics.

In 1930 at age sixteen McBay entered Wiley College in Marshall, Texas, with the initial career goal of becoming a physician. However, as the Great Depression engulfed the nation, McBay reconsidered his decision to pursue a career in medicine, partly because of the potential financial hardship of going to medical school. Instead, during his sophomore year he chose to major in chemistry and set a new career goal of becoming a research chemist. With his excellent academic preparation at Dunbar and Wiley, McBay was prepared to meet the challenges of a research career in chemistry; he graduated second in his class at Wiley in 1934.

McBay then received a scholarship to pursue a master's degree in chemistry at Atlanta University in Atlanta, Georgia. To assist with room and board McBay was hired as a research assistant in the laboratory of Kimuel A. Huggins, his faculty adviser and mentor. This began a long-standing academic and personal relationship between McBay and Huggins that extended over more than three decades. Huggins had received his master's degree in Chemistry from the University of Chicago in 1929 and was pursuing a doctorate in chemistry when McBay arrived at Atlanta University. Huggins later received his doctorate from the University of Chicago, as McBay himself did.

After earning his master's degree from Atlanta in 1936, McBay accepted a teaching position at Wiley, where he taught chemistry for two years. He later worked at a junior college in Kansas City, Kansas, and taught high school chemistry in Huntsville, Texas. While in Huntsville, McBay was invited to join the Tuskegee Institute's George Washington Carver Foundation as its first research fellow. At Tuskegee, McBay worked with Dr. Carver on a project to convert fiber from the okra plant into usable commercial products. Although the research project did not yield the expected results, McBay gained valuable experience as a research scientist. During this time McBay took summer courses in chemistry at the University of Chicago as preparation for entering the doctoral program.

In 1942, a few months after the United States had formally joined the Allies in World War II, McBay entered the University of Chicago's doctoral program in chemistry as a full-time student. As a graduate student McBay was assigned the position of departmental assistant, which at first provided him the opportunity to work with the chemistry professor H.I. Schlesinger, a renowned inorganic chemist. The position also provided valuable laboratory experience, as well as the same draft deferment available to teaching assistants. Later, McBay's mentor and thesis advisor for his Ph.D. was Morris Kharasch, an internationally known chemist who brought the esoteric free radicals into mainstream organic chemistry. Thus McBay became a part of what he described as "a whole new thrust in organic chemistry" (Manning, 24) through the research that he conducted on acetyl peroxide. This chemical was later used in the production of plastics and polymers, as well as in a synthetic hormone. During this time McBay was awarded the university's Elizabeth Norton Prize for Excellence at Research in Chemistry in 1944 and again in 1945.

During McBay's tenure as a graduate student at the University of Chicago, he was asked, and then pressured, to take a job with the famed Manhattan atom-bomb development project. Several outstanding African American scientists were recruited to work on the Manhattan Project including chemists Moddie Taylor, WILLIAM KNOX, and Lawrence Knox, and physicists George Reed and Edwin Russell. McBay's outstanding record in an analytical chemistry course made him a desirable recruit for the bomb project. He resisted the pressure to join the project, however, even though it would have provided him with a substantial increase in income. McBay, who was slightly older than the other graduate students, was committed to completing requirements for the doctorate as quickly as possible. As a result he continued his graduate research project and received his Ph.D. in Organic Chemistry in 1945.

In September 1945 McBay accepted a teaching position in the department of chemistry at Morehouse College in Atlanta, where BENJAMIN E. MAYS was president. Mays, who held a master's degree in Mathematics, was committed to academic excellence and to improving the college's science curriculum. He encouraged McBay to strengthen the chemistry program and raised $600,000 for the construction of a new chemistry building that included a research laboratory for McBay. Thus Mays and McBay began an academic partnership to provide Morehouse chemistry students with the training required to pursue doctoral studies in chemistry at graduate institutions throughout the nation. As a result of the rigorous teaching and training provided by McBay, more than fifty of his former students earned doctorates or medical degrees. At one time more African Americans with PhDs in Chemistry had been trained by McBay at the undergraduate level than by any other educator in the United States. He also served as chair of the Morehouse chemistry department from 1960 to 1981.

In addition to his teaching responsibilities, the position at Morehouse provided McBay with the opportunity to continue his research on acetyl peroxide and free-radical chemistry. A review of papers in the Atlanta University Center's Robert Woodruff Library Archives, Special Collections, indicates that soon after his arrival at the college McBay was awarded grants to conduct research on free-radical mechanisms and on new methods for generating free radicals in solutions. As part of a unique relationship between the Morehouse and Atlanta University chemistry departments, the two institutions shared facilities and resources; McBay taught graduate courses and directed the research of graduate students at Atlanta. Over the years McBay published his research in scientific journals co-authored with his graduate students, as well as with other research associates. In 1954 SHIRLEY MATHIS (McBAY) entered Atlanta University to pursue a master's degree in chemistry. As a graduate student she began working with McBay, and they were married soon after. They had two sons before the marriage ended in divorce.

While professor and chair of chemistry at Morehouse, McBay also served as a consultant for government organizations and private industry, and he accepted temporary academic and research appointments at other institutions. In 1951 McBay was appointed technical expert for the United Nations Educational, Scientific, and Cultural Organization (UNESCO) to assist in the development of a comprehensive program in chemistry for Liberia. He was a special research fellow at the Union Carbide Corporation and the DuPont Experimental Station, and he was visiting research officer at the National Research Council in Ottawa, Canada. In 1976 McBay accepted an appointment as visiting professor at the University of Minnesota; while there he pursued research in free-radical chemistry through electron-spin resonance technology.

McBay became the Fuller E. Callaway Professor of Chemistry at Atlanta University (later Clark Atlanta University) in 1981 and Distinguished Professor of Chemistry at Morehouse in 1988. In 1991 McBay became the first Martin Luther King Jr. Scholar at the Massachusetts Institute of Technology, and he was awarded an honorary doctor of science degree in 1992 by Emory University. Other awards and honors received by McBay included the Charles H. Henry Award for Outstanding Contributions to Chemistry (Georgia Section of the American Chemical Society), the Outstanding Teacher Award of the National Organization for the Advancement of Black Chemists and Engineers, the Kimuel A. Huggins Award in Science for Outstanding Contributions to Chemistry and Human Endeavors (Bishop College), the James Flack Norris Award for Outstanding Achievement in the Teaching of Chemistry (Northeastern Section of the American Chemical Society), and the Jones-McBay-Williams Award for Excellence in Teaching (Morehouse).

McBay died in Atlanta, Georgia, and was buried in his hometown of Mexia, Texas. Although McBay truly became a legend in his own time as a gifted and inspirational teacher, mentor, and role model, his true legacy remains in the careers of the many students whose lives he touched.

FURTHER READING

Blake, John. "A Classroom of Chemistry: 40-plus Years Prove Morehouse Prof Has a Formula for Success," *Atlanta Journal-Constitution*, 11 Mar. 1991.

Manning, Kenneth R. "Henry C. McBay: Reflections of a Chemist," in *Henry C. McBay, A Chemical Festschrift: Proceedings of a Symposium in Honor of the First Martin Luther King, Jr., Scholar at the Massachusetts Institute of Technology*, ed. William M. Jackson and Billy Joe Evans (1994).

"Morehouse College and Henry McBay: A Case of Good Chemistry," *The Morehouse College Alumni Magazine* 45 (1989).

"Seven Receive Honorary Degrees," *Emory Magazine* (Autumn 1992).

ROSALYN MITCHELL PATTERSON

McBay, Shirley Mathis (4 May 1935–), mathematician, chemist, and education advocate, was born Shirley Mathis in the small and racially segregated town of Bainbridge, Georgia, during the Great Depression. Her parents' names and occupations are unknown. By all accounts, McBay was a child prodigy who was often teased because she liked to study, especially mathematics. But McBay's mother supported her daughter's interest in mathematics and encouraged her to continue to work hard if she wanted to be successful. McBay would follow that principle throughout her professional career.

McBay found her mother's own hard work a source of inspiration and looked up to her as a role model. McBay's other role models were her teachers. One teacher in particular, Hattie Mae Mann, recognized early that McBay had potential and challenged her to excel. Yet, despite the support and involvement of her community, McBay learned early about the separation between black and white, which characterized relations in the Jim Crow South. Her most vivid childhood memory was of the body of a black man tied to the back of a Ford model-T car, dragged through the streets, and dumped on the lawn of the court house. Whites claimed the black man had raped a white woman. Blacks claimed three white men committed the act; the rape victim blamed the black man.

After graduating high school in 1950 at the age of fifteen, McBay attended Paine College, a private, historically black college, in Augusta, Georgia. She majored in chemistry because there weren't enough students interested in mathematics to offer advanced courses in the subject. She graduated summa cum laude from Paine College in 1954 with a bachelor's degree in chemistry. The Board of Trustees at Paine awarded McBay a small scholarship to attend graduate school. So, at age nineteen, she left the small-town environment to attend Atlanta University, also a historically black institution. At Atlanta University, McBay was able to pursue mathematics as she had always wanted to do, earning a master's degree in chemistry in 1957 and a second master's in mathematics the following year. It was also in graduate school that McBay met her future husband, HENRY CECIL MCBAY, an organic chemist who, as a graduate student in Chicago during World War II, turned down the chance to join the research team that developed the atomic bomb. Cecil McBay was twenty-one years older than his new wife and brought three children to the marriage. Having married, Shirley McBay was no longer eligible to receive her graduate scholarly funding. To earn money, she taught chemistry and physics at Spelman College, a historically black institution for women that was adjacent to the Atlanta University campus.

In 1961, after a brief period in Chicago, McBay returned to Atlanta and was appointed acting chair of the mathematics department at Spelman College. She would spend the next fifteen years at Spelman, in between earning a doctoral degree in mathematics from the University of Georgia while taking care of her family, which by this time included two sons, Michael and Ronald. For three years she made a nearly seventy-five-mile commute between Spelman in Atlanta on weekends and the University of Georgia in Athens during the week.

McBay was the first black graduate student admitted to the University of Georgia after it had been integrated by HAMILTON HOLMES and CHARLAYNE HUNTER-GAULT following the *Brown v. Board of Education* Supreme Court ruling in 1954. In 1966, McBay became the first African American to earn a doctoral degree, in any field, from the university. She also became the ninth known black woman in the United States with a Ph.D. in Mathematics. Her dissertation was entitled "The Homology Theory of Metabelian Life Algebras."

When McBay returned to Spelman as a full-time faculty in 1966, she resumed her role as chair of mathematics. Along with newly hired fellow mathematician ETTA ZUBER FALCONER and several other faculty members, McBay was concerned about the low number of students pursuing science majors. She reorganized the sciences into a divisional structure, hoping that the restructuring would place Spelman in a better position to compete for the millions of federal grant dollars available to support science education. The strategy was successful, and the college was awarded funding to support a number of student development and capacity-building initiatives. In 1973 McBay was appointed associate academic dean. She held her chair and her deanship until 1975, when she left Spelman to work at the National Science Foundation. At NSF she held several program management positions until the Massachusetts Institute of Technology (MIT) recruited her in 1980 to become dean of student affairs.

When McBay arrived at MIT in April 1980, the institution was taking steps to increase the number of minority and women students, which stood at 10.9 percent and 19.5 percent respectively. McBay was the first black dean for student affairs and the first black on the Academic Council, which was the highest level of MIT's organizational structure.

McBay could not understand why many of the black students who came to MIT with high SAT scores and excellent grade point averages weren't performing well. A small group McBay convened to examine the problem released its finding in the 1986 Racial Climate Report. The two-year study found that minority students felt overwhelmingly isolated, financially stressed, and under verbal attack by nonminority students and faculty who implied, both directly and indirectly, that African Americans, Latinos and other historically underrepresented minority students were not qualified to be there. Several subsequent reports were issued, followed by efforts to improve the campus' racial climate and minority student experiences. Several advances were made, including expansion of the student services infrastructure, an increase in financial aid packages, and intensified recruitment. Some of the interventions seemed to work. The number of under-represented minorities in MIT's entering class rose from 104 in 1986 to 169 in 1988. (Desai, "Minority Group Finishes Second Study," *The Tech*, 25 Apr. 1989).

In 1990 McBay took a two-year paid leave of absence from MIT to become president of the Quality Education for Minorities (QEM) Network, a national nonprofit organization dedicated to improving the education of African Americans,

Alaska Natives, American Indians, Mexican Americans, and Puerto Ricans. She would not return to MIT but remain at QEM. John Deutch, provost at MIT when McBay resigned, attributed her efforts as instrumental in changing institutional culture and climate to support the right of higher education access for under-represented minorities.

FURTHER READING

Kenschaft, Patricia C. "Black Women in Mathematics in the United States," *Journal of African Civilizations* (Apr. 1982).

Sammons, Vivian Ovelton. *Blacks in Science and Medicine* (1990).

Scriven, Olivia A. "The Politics of Particularism: HBCUs, Spelman College and the Struggle to Educate Black Women in Science, 1950–1997," Ph.D. diss., Georgia Institute of Technology, 2006.

Williams, Clarence G. *Technology and the Dream: Reflections on the Black Experience at MIT, 1941–1999* (2001).

OLIVIA A. SCRIVEN

McBride, James (1957–), writer and musician, was born in Brooklyn, New York, the youngest of eight children of Andrew Dennis McBride, a Baptist minister, and Rachel (Shilsky) McBride, an occasional typist. The exact date of his birth is not known. Part of a tide of African Americans who left the South in search of greater freedom and job opportunities in the North, McBride's father Andrew had moved in the 1940s from North Carolina to New York, where he found work in a small Manhattan leather factory. Similarly his mother, Rachel, had emigrated from Poland as a child in 1921 and settled with her family in Suffolk, Virginia, where her father, an Orthodox rabbi, ran a synagogue and managed a store that exploited the local black population. One of Rachel's jobs in that store was to watch the "shvartses" (a derogatory Yiddish term for blacks), who were always suspected of stealing. After one, in fact, stole her heart and virginity, she fled to New York to obtain an abortion and to escape her father's sexual abuse. Rachel found work and met Andrew in the leather factory, which was owned by her aunt.

Rachel converted to Christianity as a result of the support that she found at the Metropolitan Baptist Church in Harlem, where Andrew was a deacon and choir member and where she became a secretary. The two were married in the privacy of the church office in 1942 and lived openly and proudly together. Andrew was her guide as Ruth—as Rachel now called herself—immersed herself in the cultural ethos of Harlem. Disowned by her Jewish family, who formally mourned her as though she were dead, Ruth claimed the black community as her own.

In 1950 the McBride family moved into a two-bedroom apartment in the Red Hook Housing Projects in Brooklyn. Rather than seeing it as a ghetto, they felt fortunate to reside in a development that was then clean, new, and integrated. Andrew began studying for the ministry at Shelton Bible College and started a black congregation called New Brown Memorial, over which Ruth became the shouting-singing-testifying matriarch. James never knew his father, for in 1957 Andrew died after a short illness, leaving Ruth with eight small children. Shortly thereafter she married Hunter Jordan, a black man who worked as a furnace fireman. Together they had four children, which brought the clan to twelve. Ruth never spoke to her children about her ancestry. In fact, when James started school and began to learn to distinguish white people from black, he asked his mother if she were white, and she replied, "No, I'm light-skinned" (McBride, 21).

In 1963 the family moved to St. Albans, Queens, a neighborhood that was about to become part of a new black suburbia. As James was trying to find his place in the integrated public schools, he asked his mother, "Am I black or white?" She characteristically quipped back, "You're a human being.... Educate yourself or you'll be a nobody" (McBride, 92). At the height of the civil rights movement young James was internally torn: he identified strongly with the Black Power movement, but he feared for what might happen to his beloved mother should antiwhite rhetoric become a reality.

When James was fifteen his stepfather died, and despite his mother's insistence on academic excellence from all of her children, his grades at Benjamin Cardozo High School began to plummet. Lacking discipline and a goal, he sank into behavior that involved drinking, drugs, and a variety of street crimes for which, luckily, he was never arrested. In 1974 his mother abruptly moved the family to Wilmington, Delaware, where James attended the all-black Pierre S. Du Pont High School. There, with the help of a teacher, C. Lawler Rogers, he developed a serious interest in music as a saxophonist. He worked as a house servant and yardman for Ann Fox Dawson, who donated the funds for him to travel to Europe with the American Youth Jazz Band. His work experience with the Dawsons was demeaning, and it convinced him that he did not want the life of drudgery that a black man without education could expect; but the conversations and literature that he was exposed to helped instill a love of words that came to rival his love of music.

McBride attended Oberlin College in Ohio on a music scholarship. There, in order to complete the necessary paperwork, he pressed his mother for her maiden name. Rather than satisfying his curiosity, the name "Shilsky" lit a flame of interest that burned for years until he had fully discovered the details of his mother's identity, thus resolving questions about his own. His college sweetheart, like himself, was of mixed race and half-Jewish. By then he had come to realize that in America being of mixed race meant being all black in the eyes of most people. After graduating with a bachelor's degree in Musical Composition in 1979, McBride entered the Columbia University School of Journalism, receiving a master's degree in 1980. Uncertain whether to pursue a career in music or in journalism, he set out to succeed at both.

After a short stint with the *News Journal of Wilmington*, McBride's exceptional talent carried him to a coveted position with the *Boston Globe*. Quite fortuitously the *Globe Sunday Magazine* editor, Al Larkin, asked McBride to write a piece for Mother's Day in 1982. To pay homage to his mother McBride told a little of his family's remarkable story. From this article came the idea for the book that secured his place in the pantheon of great autobiographies about race: *The Color of Water: A Black Man's Tribute to His White Mother* (1996). Eventually the book sold millions of copies, was translated into a dozen languages, spent two years on the *New York Times* best-seller list, and had Hollywood producers clamoring for its movie rights. But all that came only after years of additional genealogical detective work and after overcoming his doubts (and his mother's fears) about quitting a lucrative and respectable position in journalism to become a freelance writer and struggling musician. Nevertheless McBride left the *Globe* and then turned down positions at *People*, *Us*, and the *Washington Post*, opting instead in 1987 to support himself as a substitute teacher in New York City so that he could devote himself to his twin dreams.

Although McBride's subsequent achievements as a musician, songwriter, and arranger have not equaled the fame or fortune that came with *The Color of Water*, they have been substantial and have won him critical acclaim. McBride worked with rhythm and blues vocalist Anita Baker on her Grammy-winning recording *Giving You the*

Best That I Got (1988). He also wrote songs for the saxophonist GROVER WASHINGTON JR. and for the popular children's television program *Barney*. In 1993 McBride won the American Music Theater Festival's Stephen Sondheim Award. As the leader of his own jazz group, he released a richly textured CD, *The Process*, in 2002.

On the literary side, McBride remained active. He was the ghostwriter behind *Q: The Autobiography of* QUINCY JONES (2001), and he occasionally published essays on a variety of topics. His first novel, *Miracle at St. Anna* (2002), was both artistically ambitious and challenging, telling the story of four fictional members of the army's Ninety-second Negro Division who witness the massacre of 560 Italian civilians by Nazis in the Church of St. Anna di Stazzema. The only survivor, a young boy, falls into the care of these black soldiers.

McBride said in interviews that his work attempted to transcend the simple statement of racial problems in an effort to discover something more meaningful and beautiful. To write, he rose at four in the morning, leaving his wife, Stephanie Payne, and their three children in Bucks County, Pennsylvania, and drove to his office in Manhattan, where he waited, as he put it, for "God to enter the room" with inspiration.

FURTHER READING

McBride, James. *The Color of Water: A Black Man's Tribute to His White Mother* (1996).

Budhos, Marina. "Black Man, Jewish Soul," *Nation* 262, no. 13 (22 April 1996).

Kovach, Ronald. "James McBride," *Writer* 116, no. 6 (June 2003).

SHOLOMO B. LEVY

McBryar, William (14 Feb. 1861–8 Mar. 1941), Indian Wars and Spanish-American War soldier and Medal of Honor recipient, was born in Elizabeth City, North Carolina. Nothing is known of his early life. By 1887 he was in New York City, where he enlisted in the U.S. Army, joining Company K of the 10th Cavalry Regiment.

The regiment in which William McBryar served was one of four units in the U.S. Army, the others being the 9th Cavalry and 24th and 25th Infantry regiments, in which African American soldiers were allowed to serve. Commanded by white commissioned officers, but often led in the field by black noncommissioned officers holding the rank of sergeant or corporal, these regiments performed skillfully during the time of America's great westward migration. Serving in harsh weather extremes and difficult terrain, these African American soldiers, men such as McBryar, ISAIAH MAYS, THOMAS BOYNE, and BENJAMIN BROWN, provided valuable, and in many cases heroic, service in building roads, protecting new settlements from attacks by outlaws, providing scouting services, and even preventing white settlers from encroaching on Indian Territory. However, these soldiers, nicknamed "Buffalo Soldiers" by their Native American adversaries, are best known for their battles with Native American warriors who were fighting to retain what remained of their native lands. These series of intermittent skirmishes with such renowned Native American leaders as Geronimo, Victorio, Crazy Horse, Big Foot, and Sitting Bull lasted from 1866 to 1890 and are collectively referred to as the Indian Wars by modern-day historians. Of the eighteen African American soldiers who were recipients of the Medal of Honor during the Indian Wars, William McBryar was one of last to be so honored and was the only man to later rise to the status of commissioned officer.

McBryar was stationed with the 10th Cavalry Regiment in the Arizona Territory in March 1890 when his unit, Company K, along with Company I of the white 4th Cavalry Regiment, was detached to pursue a group of five Apache warriors who had murdered a Mormon trader near Fort Thomas. The pursuit lasted for days and covered over 250 miles over rugged terrain; on the afternoon of 7 March 1890 the Apache warriors were taken by surprise at the Salt River near Globe, Arizona. Holed up in the rocks, the warriors put up a stiff resistance, but "coolness and bravery while under fire" (Hanna, p. 75) and fine marksmanship by McBryar and his fellow soldiers carried the day. By evening, two of the Apaches were killed, one wounded, and the remaining two had surrendered, while the soldiers suffered no casualties. William McBryar was one of three men of the detachment awarded the Medal of Honor for their actions at Salt River. Medal of Honor recipients during this time usually had to wait at least a year for their award paperwork to be processed and often much longer, but such was not the case with William McBryar. The first man of the 10th Cavalry to be so honored, McBryar received the Medal of Honor on 15 May 1890, just ten weeks later, a sure indicator of the "exceptional nature" (Schubert, p. 106) of his deeds.

Following this action, William McBryar continued with the 10th Cavalry until 1893, when he transferred to the 25th Infantry Regiment while serving in Montana. He rose to the rank of quartermaster sergeant of his company and was still with the 25th when the Spanish American War broke out in 1898. Sent to Cuba with the 25th Infantry in June 1898, McBryar soon distinguished himself in battle at El Caney and was thereafter recommended for an officer's commission by his commanding officer. In November 1899 McBryar finally received an officer's wartime commission as a second lieutenant and was assigned once again to the 25th Infantry while serving during the Philippine Insurrection. During his service in the Philippines, McBryar was promoted to first lieutenant and was widely regarded for his leadership skills, but after the war ended he was discharged from service, and though he reenlisted in the army he failed to gain a permanent officer's commission. Among those who worked on his behalf to obtain a commission was his mother, Rose Black, who wrote a letter to President William McKinley pleading his case. Of William McBryar, one of his superior officers would state that "few in the Army can equal his record" (Schubert, p. 112). However, while McBryar continued his army service, he never did gain a permanent commission and finally retired from the army in 1906. After leaving the army, William McBryar was married to Sallie Waugh, also a native of North Carolina, and worked for a time as a night watchman at Arlington National Cemetery and as a military instructor at the Saint Paul's Normal and Industrial School in Lawrenceville, Virginia, a small black school. When World War I broke out in 1914, McBryar tried to enlist in the army again, but was turned down due to his age. He died in Philadelphia, Pennsylvania, and was buried at Arlington National Cemetery, where a Medal of Honor headstone marks his final resting place.

FURTHER READING

Hanna, Charles W. *African American Recipients of the Medal of Honor* (2002).
Schubert, Frank N. *Black Valor: Buffalo Soldiers and the Medal of Honor, 1870–1898* (1997).

GLENN ALLEN KNOBLOCK

McCabe, Edwin Prescott (10 Oct. 1850–23 Feb. 1920), politician and land agent, was born in Troy, New York. Not long after his birth his family moved to Fall River, Massachusetts, then Newport, Rhode Island, and Bangor, Maine. When his father died McCabe quit school to support the family. As a young man McCabe worked on Wall Street in New York City before going to Chicago, where he clerked for the hotel owner Potter Palmer until 1872, when he received a clerkship at the Cook County federal Treasury office. In 1878, with his friend Abraham T. Hall Jr., editor of the African American newspaper the *Chicago Conservator*, McCabe journeyed to Kansas to join the African American Nicodemus colony, for which he served as secretary. In 1880 he married Sarah Bryant. They had two daughters who lived to adulthood and a son who died in infancy.

McCabe entered Republican politics in Kansas, and in 1880 he was elected clerk for Graham County and served as delegate-at-large to the Republican National Convention. In 1882 Republicans nominated him for state auditor. He won the election, becoming the first African American to hold state office in Kansas. McCabe moved to Topeka and enjoyed reelection in 1884, but he failed to be nominated in 1886. Although he reasoned that party leaders wished to limit officeholders to two terms, in fact anti-black sentiment had grown in the state while the number of African Americans in Kansas dwindled, thus reducing his political importance. In 1888 he failed to be chosen a delegate-at-large to the Republican National Convention. He attempted to be selected clerk of the Kansas State Republican Party Central Committee, but failed. In 1889 he sought to become registrar of the Kansas treasury, only to be defeated.

In 1889 McCabe turned his attention to the Indian Territory, where the Unassigned Lands (Oklahoma) were to be opened to settlers and where he envisioned all-black towns and a future state dominated by African Americans. Becoming the Washington, D.C., agent for the Topeka-based Oklahoma Immigration Association, he met with President Benjamin Harrison, broached his idea of Oklahoma as an African American enclave, and presented petitions for his appointment as territorial governor. The administration did not embrace McCabe's proposals but did offer him the post of immigration inspector in Key West, Florida, a position he declined. He then unsuccessfully sought to be named secretary of Oklahoma Territory.

Despite these political disappointments, McCabe continued to see Oklahoma Territory as a place where African Americans could prosper. In 1890 he moved to Guthrie, the territorial capital, to speculate in land. Joining the Republican Party there, he gained appointment as secretary to the territorial legislature and then as treasurer of Logan County.

In October 1890 McCabe founded the town of Langston with Charles H. Robbins, a white land speculator. The town was named for JOHN MERCER LANGSTON, a respected African American educator and politician from Virginia. Although he lived in Guthrie, McCabe functioned as Langston's main booster, especially through the *Langston City Herald*, the newspaper he established in 1891. Proclaiming Langston "the Only Distinctively Negro City in America," McCabe and the editor W. L. EAGLESON, a friend in the Oklahoma Immigration Association, encouraged economically independent African Americans to come to Langston. McCabe did not envisage Langston as a refuge for the destitute. Indeed, he imagined all-black communities in Oklahoma in which enterprising, financially stable African Americans could better themselves economically, socially, and politically. He promoted hard work, respectable behavior, and cleanliness—views associated with BOOKER T. WASHINGTON. Copies of the newspaper, which claimed to have the largest circulation of any weekly in Oklahoma, were widely distributed throughout the South. McCabe sold the *Langston City Herald* in 1892.

Also in 1892 McCabe found himself at odds with his fellow Republicans, and at the territorial convention he temporarily broke with the party. Many white Republicans considered him too aggressive in his desire for office, a viewpoint no doubt having much to do with his race and his continuing efforts to bring African Americans into the territory, as well as Eagleson's editorials advocating McCabe for territorial governor.

Despite the political rancor, the creation of all-black towns held McCabe's attention, and in 1893 he founded Liberty, but white hostility led to its demise. He helped to establish Vernon in 1895. McCabe also traveled to tribal lands being opened for settlement, inducing African Americans to stake claims, efforts that spurred hostility from both whites and Indians.

By 1894 McCabe had reconciled with the Republican Party and headed to Washington, D.C., for a job with the register of deeds there. However, he had returned to Oklahoma Territory by 1895, at which time he was selected assistant chief clerk to the Oklahoma territorial legislature. He also served on a committee that failed to convince the St. Louis and San Francisco Railroad to lay tracks to Langston. In 1897 he was appointed deputy auditor for Oklahoma Territory, and that year, too, Langston got a boost. Since 1892, residents of Langston had asked for a college, and in 1897 the governor proposed building a land-grant college for African

Americans at Langston. McCabe donated forty acres for the campus, and the Colored Agricultural and Normal University—later Langston University—was established, an occurrence that many attributed to McCabe's influence.

McCabe's status in Oklahoma diminished after Democrats assumed control of the government after statehood in 1907. Nevertheless, McCabe attempted to thwart passage of Jim Crow legislation by filing an ultimately fruitless lawsuit against the measure. In 1908, saddened by the death of a daughter, his loss of political influence, and legalized discrimination in Oklahoma, McCabe returned to Chicago, where he died poor and generally forgotten. His wife buried him in Topeka, where he had risen to prominence as a noted African American in the West.

FURTHER READING

Dann, Martin. "From Sodom to the Promised Land: E. P. McCabe and the Movement for Oklahoma Colonization," *Kansas Historical Quarterly* (1974).

Hamilton, Kenneth Marian. *Black Towns and Profit: Promotion and Development in the Trans-Appalachian West, 1877–1915* (1991).

Leiker, James M. "African Americans and Boosterism," *Journal of the West* (2003).

Littlefield, Daniel F., and Lonnie F. Underhill. "Black Dreams and 'Free' Homes: The Oklahoma Territory, 1891–1894," *Phylon* (1973).

Woods, Randall Bennett. *A Black Odyssey: John Lewis Waller and the Promise of American Life, 1878–1900* (1981).

THOMAS BURNELL COLBERT

McCain, Franklin (3 Jan. 1941–), one of the four North Carolina Agricultural and Technical State University freshmen who initiated the sit-in movement in Greensboro, North Carolina, was born Franklin Eugene McCain

in Union County, North Carolina, the son of Warner and Mattie McCain. McCain grew up in Washington, D.C., and graduated from Eastern High School in 1959. After graduating, he returned to his native North Carolina to attend college at North Carolina Agricultural and Technical State University (A&T). During his time as an undergraduate student at A&T, McCain roomed with DAVID RICHMOND and lived around the corner from Ezell Blair Jr. and Joseph McNeil on the second floor of Scott Hall. These four men challenged public accommodation customs and laws in North Carolina on 1 February 1960, launching a sit-in movement that became an important catalyst for much of the modern civil rights movement. They decided to sit at an all-white section in F.W. Woolworth in downtown Greensboro, believing that the concept that blacks could only be served in particular areas of the store and not with whites was unjust. The following day, two dozen students from North Carolina A&T and Bennett College joined the protest. By the end of the week 3,000 students were picketing in downtown Greensboro. The movement rapidly spread to nine other southern states and fifty-four cities. McCain and his friends watched the protest turn into a community-wide effort. Support for the demonstrations came from Dudley High School and the local NAACP. A&T president Warmoth T. Gibbs refused to discipline the protesters. Dr. MARTIN LUTHER KING JR. attributed the increased momentum of the civil rights struggle to these committed youths, signaled by actions of McCain and his friends. The "Greensboro Four" soon lent their support to the formation of the Student Nonviolent Coordinating Committee (SNCC) under the leadership of ELLA BAKER at Shaw University in Raleigh. They inevitably became national symbols of the struggle for racial justice. After graduating from A&T with a B.S. degree in Biology and Chemistry in 1964,

Franklin McCain (left) with David Richmond in Greensboro, North Carolina, 1 April 1960. McCain and Richmond are two of the four college students who started demonstrations against segregated lunch counters in February of 1959. (AP Images.)

McCain did graduate work at North Carolina A&T and North Carolina State University. He joined the Hoechst Celanese Corporation in Charlotte as a chemist in 1964 and rose through the corporate executive ranks to head the company's Shelby office before his retirement. As a longtime resident of Charlotte, North Carolina, McCain brought about social, civic, and political change by serving on many boards in the Charlotte-Mecklenburg area. His continued commitment to higher education was evidenced by his affiliations with the Board of Visitors for Bennett College and the Board of Trustees of North Carolina Central University. He was also an active force in national organizations, serving as chairman of the North Carolina Committee of the NAACP Legal Defense and Educational Fund, Inc., and as chairman of Sigma Pi Phi Social Action Committee.

McCain was honored for his continued dedication to service and leadership abilities by numerous organizations. Among the highlights was an honorary doctorate and a Distinguished Alumni Award from his alma mater North Carolina A&T University, a Black History Award from Barber Scotia College, a Distinguished Leadership Award from the National Conference for Community and Justice, and recognition by the North Carolina Humanities Council. A residential street in Greensboro was named for him in recognition of his important place in history.

McCain married Betty Davis, who was an active member of the Student Executive Committee for Justice, the planning committee for the sit-ins and marches that were held. The couple had three sons.

FURTHER READING

Chafe, William H. *Civilities and Civil Rights: Greensboro, North Carolina, and the Black Struggle for Freedom* (1980).

Gaillard, Frye. *The Greensboro Four: Civil Rights Pioneers* (2001).

Harrington, Walt. *Crossings* (1992).

Pfaff, Eugene F., Jr. Interview with Joseph McNeil, 14 Oct. 1979. North Carolina Agricultural and Technical State University Archives.

ROBERT "BOB" DAVIS

McCall, Herman Carl, Jr. (17 Oct. 1935–), minister, civil rights activist, New York state legislator and official, and ambassador, was born in Boston, Massachusetts, the oldest of six children of Herman Carl McCall Sr., a waiter on a train, and Carolesa McCall, a homemaker. During his early years, McCall's father lost his job and abandoned the family, leaving Herman's mother struggling to raise him and his five sisters. McCall grew up poor in the Roxbury section of Boston, shifting through low-income housing. His mother collected welfare as a means to support the family; they also received support from caring members of their United Church of Christ parish. Despite the difficulties of being a single parent, she was active in his life and stressed the importance of a good education and a close relationship with God. McCall was a talented student and knew he wanted to attend college. He was encouraged by parish members of his church to apply to Dartmouth College in Hanover, New Hampshire. Dartmouth had few blacks on campus, but was interested in increasing diversity. With the help of his Sunday school teacher, McCall was accepted as part of the first expanded class of blacks, doubling previous classes, with eight enrollees. Dartmouth also provided a scholarship that made it possible for McCall to attend.

While at Dartmouth, McCall began his involvement in politics. He was a registered Republican, encouraged by a family friend, EDWARD BROOKE, a black Republican who would serve as a senator from Massachusetts from 1967 to 1979. McCall graduated with a B.A. in 1958. Afterward, he traveled to Scotland to study at the University of Edinburgh before returning to Boston and joining the army in 1961. McCall then became a teacher at Jamaica Plain High School, but was disenchanted by the attitude and problems he saw in the educational system. He felt the school was more interested in managing the kids rather than teaching them. The experience inspired McCall to look for ways to make a change in the system. After six months he left teaching and returned to school, pursuing a master of divinity degree from Andover Newton Theological School in Newton, Massachusetts. After graduating in 1963, McCall was ordained by the United Church of Christ and moved to Brooklyn, New York, to become a social worker with the New York City Missionary Society's Church Community Service Program and a pastor of the Metropolitan United Methodist Church in Harlem. During this time, McCall decided to switch political loyalties and became a Democrat. He joined a number of political groups and became active in voter registration drives and assisting Harlem political leaders such as DAVID DINKINS, PERCY SUTTON, and CHARLES RANGEL. These were trying times. Racial tensions were high across the country, discrimination was

H. Carl McCall, holding a press conference on the steps of the New York Public Library during his gubernatorial campaign, 3 October 2002. (AP Images.)

rampant, and countless blacks and Puerto Ricans could not find work. McCall joined other local leaders in becoming an active voice in the civil rights movement. With a group of other ministers, he formed the Committee for Job Opportunities in Brooklyn, which designed strategy and organized protests around the city.

The same year, McCall participated in the largest civil rights demonstration New York had seen since the 1943 Harlem riots. The Rutgers Houses project protest was an effort to obtain more public construction jobs for blacks and Puerto Ricans and force trade unions to enlist minorities. Demonstrators picketed the site and blocked entry of construction vehicles. Over 200 people were arrested. McCall's activism proved successful in getting the attention of the political establishment. Both Governor John Rockefeller and Mayor Robert Wagner joined initiatives to increase the number of blacks and Puerto Ricans in employment and trade unions.

In 1966 McCall joined the administration of newly elected mayor John Lindsay as head of the New York City Council Against Poverty, which was considered a training ground for promising black leaders. In 1967 he became deputy administrator

for operations of the city's Human Resources Administration, dealing primarily with antipoverty programs. He resigned a year later to pursue a fellowship studying conflict between blacks and Jews in urban areas. During the 1970s McCall launched a remarkable political career. Across the city, he cultivated numerous relationships in government and community, as well as joining a powerful black group to purchase the *New York Amsterdam News*, one of the oldest black weeklies in the United States. Using his connections, McCall launched a successful campaign for New York State Senate. Beginning in 1974 he represented the West side of Manhattan and Harlem. In 1979 he was appointed third U.S. ambassador for the American mission to the United Nations under President Jimmy Carter. After leaving the administration in 1981, McCall entered the private sector as a television executive for WNET public television in New York and launched an unsuccessful bid for lieutenant governor in 1982.

During the 1980s, New York politics were still quite polarized and many Democratic administrations and campaigns lacked minorities in high-level positions. McCall returned to public service as the state commissioner for Human Rights in Governor

Mario Cuomo's administration. In 1983 McCall married Dr. Joyce Brown, an administrator in the SUNY Higher Education system and an associate of Dinkins. In 1984 he became a vice president for Citibank, dealing with governmental relations. During the 1986 election cycle, McCall served as cochairman for the unsuccessful state comptroller bid of Herman Badillo, a Hispanic candidate.

In the 1990s, with the support of then-mayor Dinkins, McCall was elected president of the New York City Board of Education and his wife served as deputy mayor for Public and Community Affairs. In 1993 McCall left the Dinkins administration to rejoin Governor Cuomo's administration with an appointment to finish the term of State Comptroller Edward Regan, who had resigned. As a result, McCall became the first black in New York to hold a statewide elected office. In 1994 McCall campaigned to keep his job as state comptroller and easily won, garnering more than 2 million votes, more than any candidate for any office. In 1998 he solidly won reelection and cemented his position as one of the most influential blacks in New York politics. In 1999 he became a member of the board for the New York Stock Exchange. Because of his popularity, he was encouraged to run for U.S. Senate in 2000, but opted to forgo a campaign and instead supported Hillary Clinton.

In 2002 McCall decided to run for governor in a competitive field. His most formidable opponent in the Democratic Primary was Andrew Cuomo, the son of his former employer. The campaign proved bruising for both candidates and the Democratic Party. Racial divisions were exposed, and substantial funds earmarked for the general campaign were depleted. Although McCall would win the primary, he lost support among Italians and was offered limited support from the Democratic National Committee, primarily because he was polling poorly against the incumbent Republican governor George Pataki. Shortly before the election, a scandal emerged involving his use of state letterhead to help friends and family, including his daughter Marci from a previous marriage, seek employment with companies that did business with the state. McCall suffered a substantial defeat from Pataki, getting little more than 30 percent of the vote, a low figure for a state controlled by Democrats.

McCall returned to the private sector and joined numerous boards. He resigned from the Stock Exchange board in 2003, but remained a member of influential groups like the Council on Foreign Relations, while serving as vice chairman of the private equity firm HealthPoint. He remained active in New York politics and in 2007 was invited to sit on a committee tasked with choosing a successor for State Comptroller Alan Hevesi, who resigned owing to a scandal.

MICHAELJULIUS IDANI

McCall, Nathan (25 Nov. 1954–), journalist and writer, was born in Norfolk, Virginia, and spent his earliest years in Key West, Florida, and Morocco, where his stepfather was stationed with the navy. McCall's biological father, who left the family when McCall was two, was named JL; after his departure McCall did not see him again until he was twenty-seven years old. His mother's name is unknown. From the age of nine McCall grew up in the Cavalier Manor area of Portsmouth, Virginia, with his mother, stepfather Bonnie Alvin, grandmother Sadie Benton, two older brothers, Dwight and Billy, a younger half-brother, Bryan, and a step-brother, Junnie.

In 1966 McCall began sixth grade as one of first black students at the recently desegregated Alfred J. Mapp Junior High School. After facing intense discrimination there he transferred to Cavalier Manor's W. E. Waters Middle School, of which McCall writes, "Before going to that school, I'd never considered the beauty and solace of being around my own people. Nor had I realized the danger in being away from them" (21). McCall attended Woodrow Wilson High School. In his early teens he worked a summer with his stepfather, who had retired from the navy and worked as a gardener. McCall would later write of his dismay at his stepfather's apparent subservience and reflect on the perspective working as a gardener in nearby wealthy neighborhoods allowed him on glaring disparities of experience across racial and economic groups.

Portsmouth was marked by fights between rival gangs and neighborhoods, and McCall supported himself through mugging, car theft, and robbery. McCall was caught shoplifting and later managed to escape arrest for stealing an ice cream truck. On 20 July 1973, during the summer after their high school graduation, McCall's high school girlfriend Elisabeth Miller gave birth to a son, Monroe, whom she would raise. McCall enrolled at Norfolk State University in 1973 with a major in psychology, but lacking preparation, focus, and funds, lost motivation and dropped out. In May 1974 McCall shot and wounded a local teenager who had insulted Elisabeth; he turned himself in and received a three-hundred-dollar fine and a thirty-day sentence, of which he served four weekends. In December 1974 McCall was caught, with two accomplices, robbing a McDonald's restaurant in Norfolk, Virginia. McCall was convicted of armed robbery and sentenced to twelve years in prison, of which he served three before being released on parole.

During his years in prison McCall worked in the library, joined a Christian fellowship group, and studied printing. He kept a regular journal and read widely, influenced by books including RICHARD WRIGHT's *Native Son*, Kahlil Gibran's *The Prophet*, Chaim Potok's *My Name Is Asher Lev*, and *The Autobiography of* MALCOLM X. While awaiting parole McCall wrote to the head of journalism at Norfolk State about reenrolling and won an essay competition for a scholarship. McCall was released on parole on 3 February 1978 and returned to Portsmouth to live with his family. At Norfolk State McCall worked on the school newspaper and studied with the psychologist Na'im Akbar. Under Akbar's mentorship, McCall decided to join the American Muslim Mission in 1979 and later that year married a fellow convert, Yvette X. After growing disenchanted with the group's social conventions and ideological boundaries, McCall left the group and separated from Yvette, divorcing her in 1981.

In 1981 McCall graduated with honors from Norfolk State with a B.A. in Journalism and began as a reporter at the *Virginian Pilot-Ledger Star*, where he had once worked as an intern. McCall flourished at the *Pilot-Ledger* but also endured harassment from neighborhood acquaintances suspicious of his professional success. This prompted him to move in 1983 to Atlanta and a job at the *Atlanta Journal-Constitution*, where he worked the city hall beat and later served as an editor. His wife, Debbie, who had moved to Atlanta with McCall, gave birth to a son, Ian Bakari, on 6 May 1983 and a daughter, Maya Nailah, on 19 August 1985. McCall and Debbie married in June 1986. Though he was a productive reporter and ascended the corporate hierarchy, McCall also writes of his persistent discomfort in working in the predominantly white environment at the *Journal-Constitution*.

In 1989 McCall moved to the *Washington Post*, where he wrote on subjects that included politics and the prison system. In 1991 McCall published in the *Post* a personal reminiscence, "Dispatches from a Dying Generation," in which he revisits his childhood neighborhood and mulls over the fates of his childhood peers. The enthusiastic popular response to the story led McCall to take a leave of absence from the paper to write about his life. His autobiography, *Makes Me Wanna Holler: A Young Black Man in America* was published in 1994 to significant acclaim. Following McCall's personal promise to "pull no punches" in his recollections and opinions, it featured frank and detailed accounts of his experiences with crime, prison life, the violent exploitation of black women by black men, and corporate racism. It became a *New York Times* best-seller and was selected as Blackboard Book of the Year, making McCall a prominent public commentator. His second book, *What's Going On*, a collection of essays on topics including sexism, the black middle class, white church racism, and gangster rap was published in 1997. Since 1998 Nathan McCall has been a professor at Emory University, where he has taught classes in journalism, creative writing, and African American studies. McCall's candid story of determined self-uplift has inspired and informed many, and his insights into American culture have made him an influential voice on topics including race, masculinity, and politics in America.

FURTHER READING

McCall, Nathan. *Makes Me Wanna Holler: A Young Black Man in America* (1994).

ALEX FEERST

McCarty, Oseola (7 Mar. 1908–26 Sept. 1999), washerwoman and philanthropist, was born in Shubuta, Mississippi, the only child of Lucy McCarty, a homemaker. Little is known about Oseola's father, as her mother was a victim of sexual assault. When McCarty was a baby, her mother married Willy Zinnerman, a laborer in the turpentine industry. Julia Smith McCarty, Oseola's maternal grandmother, decided to raise her because Oseola's mother would be migrating with her husband to one turpentine camp after the other. These camps were temporary quarters where workers extracted pine tree oils for solvents and were known for crime and gambling. Back in Shubuta, Oseola McCarty lived on her grandmother's farm and learned the virtues of industry and frugality. By 1918 McCarty's grandmother had grown weary of cultivating crops and livestock and moved the family to Hattiesburg, Mississippi. Once in town, her family started a laundry business. McCarty attended Eureka Elementary School and enjoyed spending time with her schoolmates. She also helped wash, dry, iron, and fold clothes when at home. With earnings from her after-school work, McCarty opened her first savings account at a local bank. Three months before McCarty finished the sixth grade, her aunt Evelyn fell ill. Since McCarty was the only unemployed family member living close to her aunt, she became her full-time caregiver and could not attend school. Her aunt recovered soon after, but by then McCarty's classmates had completed their course of study. McCarty looked upon these classmates with great affection and disliked the idea of repeating the sixth grade without them, so she left school permanently in her early teens.

McCarty began her career as a washerwoman immediately after leaving school and worked fifteen-hour days over boiling wash pots and a blistering iron. She entertained thoughts of becoming a nurse, but she soon learned that she lacked the educational credentials to pursue that occupation. McCarty laundered clothes and linens six days a week from the early 1920s until the early 1990s. She started each day by scouring clothes with a washboard and boiling them in a wash pot. Then she rinsed each load at least three times and dried them on a clothesline. The next day, she ironed the clothes. After McCarty's stepfather died in the Great Mississippi Flood of 1927, the most disastrous river flood in U.S. history, her mother returned to live in the family home. McCarty became a caregiver once again, as her grandmother began to experience frequent bouts of illness; her grandmother died in 1944. During World War II, McCarty laundered the uniforms of locally stationed servicemen. She lived alone after her aunt and mother died in the mid-1960s. Because of the obligation of caring for her grandmother, she had never married or had children. In her spare time McCarty enjoyed reading her Bible and attending a local Baptist church. She retired from her laundry business in December 1994, after symptoms of arthritis rendered her hands less useful.

After she retired, employees at McCarty's local bank urged her to make financial plans for health services and living expenses during her final years and to decide where to distribute her savings after her death. The bank calculated that McCarty would not outlive the sizable reserve in her bank accounts. During her career, she had minimized her monthly expenses and deposited surplus wages into the bank each month. She never owned a car, preferring instead to walk about Hattiesburg for weekly grocery trips and church gatherings. She had inherited a small amount of property upon the deaths of her mother and aunt, and an uncle had given her the frame house she occupied. Given that her basic needs were met, McCarty reflected on how her accumulated funds could be used to benefit the people or institutions of her choice. After she chose three recipients for these holdings upon her death, she notified the bank of her decision.

On 26 July 1995 the University of Southern Mississippi announced that McCarty had made a $150,000 gift to the institution. The rest of her estate was to be directed to her local church and relatives. The University of Southern Mississippi gift established the Oseola McCarty Endowed Scholarship Fund, created to help students pay tuition costs and living expenses while pursing a course of study. No other African American had given the formerly all-white institution a gift of this size, and McCarty requested that the university dispense the scholarships with a preference for African American students. She regretted not finishing school herself, but felt strongly about supporting the educational pursuits of generations after her. Financially needy students could realize the goal of a college education because of her economical lifestyle, steadfast commitment to regular savings, and selfless investment in their futures.

McCarty's gift touched the public, and her noble act attracted enthusiastic attention from the international community, government leaders, educational institutions, and a host of national organizations and media outlets. In 1995 she received the United Nations' Avicenna Medal from its educational, scientific, and cultural organization, and President Bill Clinton awarded her with the Presidential Citizens Medal, the second-highest civilian award granted to those acting in outstanding service to the country. In 1996 she carried the Olympic torch through a portion of her home state and accepted an honorary doctorate of humane letters from Harvard University. McCarty also accepted honors from the American Association of Retired Persons and the National Council of Negro Women, and she participated in interviews for major publications and television shows, including *Newsweek* magazine in 1995 and *The Oprah Winfrey Show* in 1997. Her $150,000 gift to the University of Southern Mississippi inspired a matching fund-raising drive soon after it was publicized, wherein outside donors raised more than three hundred thousand dollars for her scholarship fund. McCarty's gift served as a model of charitable giving in support of higher education. She died at her home from complications of liver cancer.

FURTHER READING

Oseola McCarty's oral history interviews and awards are housed in the McCain Library and Archives,

University of Southern Mississippi in Hattiesburg, Mississippi.

McCarty, Oseola. *Simple Wisdom for Rich Living* (1996)
Obituary: *New York Times*, 28 Sept. 1999.

DELAINA A. PRICE

McClain, Leanita (1951–28 May 1984), journalist, was born in Chicago, the daughter of Lloyd McClain, a clothing factory employee, and Elizabeth (maiden name unknown). McClain grew up in Chicago's South Side in the Ida B. Wells public housing project. Her parents stressed obedience and achievement and taught her that she was not to consider the "projects" a place where they would spend their lives. "We were brought up knowing we would not have to raise our children there," she later recalled. McClain attended local schools, including an all-girls public high school.

As a young girl McClain was beset by identity problems, most stemming from her physical appearance. She claimed an African American, Native American, and Caucasian heritage. Her mother was an albino, and McClain was by all accounts a lovely young woman with freckles and a light complexion, green eyes, and hair naturally streaked blonde. However, writings from her mid-teens indicate a girl not sure of her worth and acutely aware of "so much hate and contempt among people." Her mother taught her to type, and her father taught her to sew. Following completion of high school, McClain attended Chicago Teachers College (later Chicago State University) and graduated with a B.A. in Education in 1972. She then obtained her master's degree from Northwestern University's Medill School of Journalism in 1973.

During her time at Medill, McClain took a job in 1970 as a classified-ad taker at the *Chicago Tribune*. Upon graduation she was made a cub reporter. She later was made a copy editor as well as photo editor and editor of an opinion section of the *Tribune*. In 1974 McClain married fellow journalist CLARENCE PAGE; they had no children.

In 1980 McClain garnered national attention by submitting a column to *Newsweek* magazine's 30 October issue. Printed in the "My Turn" feature section and titled "The Middle-Class Black's Burden," she showed clearly how she was caught between the white-dominated world of professional journalism and her need to be cared about for who she was, not who the world thought that she should be: "I am burdened daily with showing whites that blacks are people. I am, in the old vernacular, a credit to my race ... though many have abandoned me

because they think that I have abandoned them.... I assuage white guilt. I disprove black inadequacy." Thereafter she received several promotions, going from an occasional columnist to a weekly columnist. In 1981 McClain and her husband separated, and she attempted suicide. She began a relationship that culminated in her having an abortion, a grave contradiction from a woman who openly wanted children. Moreover, she felt guilty that she lived in the mostly white North Side of Chicago. Yet through it all, she continued to write her columns.

In 1982 McClain was made a member of the editorial board of the *Tribune* as their specialist in minority and urban affairs. She was the first black and the first woman to achieve that status. The same year she became one of nine editorial writers, and in 1983 she was made a twice-weekly columnist. In "How Chicago Taught Me to Hate Whites," McClain, writing about the victory of HAROLD WASHINGTON, Chicago's first black mayor, called the campaign a "race war." She was bitterly disappointed by her white colleagues' reaction to the victory of a black man and was tired of what she called "the voice of this evil ... the voice going on about 'the blacks' this, 'the blacks' that.... It would make me feel like machine-gunning every white face on the bus" (*Washington Post*, 24 July 1983).

The furor over McClain's column went on for weeks. The white-controlled city council called for her resignation from the *Tribune*. She also received hate mail and threatening phone calls. Her elderly father was quoted at the time as saying, "She told the truth."

McClain moved to a new home in the integrated South Side. She appeared as a guest on television broadcasts, and in spring 1984 she taught a journalism seminar at Howard University. Yet in private she was moody and subject to crying jags and making late-night phone calls to friends. She became withdrawn when in her office, not really sure who her supporters were. On Memorial Day weekend in Chicago, she committed suicide, taking an overdose of antidepressants. Some colleagues blamed McClain's death on the stresses of racism; others blamed it on personal problems. In her newspaper columns she left behind no simple answers.

Despite McClain's short life and even shorter career as a journalist, she was responsible for creating a state- and citywide dialogue on ethnic relations in Chicago. Her teaching at the Medill School of Journalism spurred many black students to choose journalism as a career, and she broke barriers based on gender and ethnicity at the *Chicago*

Tribune. Her insistence on focusing on Chicago's race-related problems guaranteed that media organizations in Chicago continued to bring the ethnic dialogue to the public arena.

FURTHER READING

McClain, Leanita. *A Foot in Each World: Essays and Articles*, ed. Clarence Page (1986).

Obituaries: *Washington Post* and *Boston Globe*, 31 May 1984.

This entry is taken from the *American National Biography* and is published here with the permission of the American Council of Learned Societies.

MARIA ELENA RAYMOND

McClendon, Dorothy V. (12 Jan 1924–), microbiologist, was born Dorothy Varie McClendon in Minden, Louisiana, one of two daughters of Glennie J. Henry, a teacher.

McClendon got her early education in the segregated schools of the small predominantly white town of Minden, Louisiana, located twenty-eight miles east of Shreveport. When McClendon was a young teen she moved with her mother and older sister Melba to Detroit, Michigan. The value of education was instilled in McClendon throughout her life. Her mother, a veteran teacher for forty-two years, encouraged her early interest in the sciences, and McClendon applied to Detroit's Cass Technical High School, one of two public "magnet" type schools open to top-notch students from all over the city. McClendon explored her interest in the sciences at Cass, and excelled in her classes in chemistry, bacteriology, and biology.

After graduation from Cass Tech, McClendon attended the Tennessee Agricultural & Industrial State College in Nashville, which began as the Agricultural and Industrial State Normal School for Negroes and later became Tennessee State University. McClendon wanted a career in medicine. At Tennessee A&I she enrolled in the college's Division of Biological Sciences and pursued a pre-medical course of study. She had hoped to go on to the historically black Meharry Medical College in Nashville.

She delved into microbiology and the study of microorganisms, too small to be seen by the naked eye, such as protozoa, bacteria, and fungi. McClendon also found time to serve as president of the Pyramid Club for the Alpha Chi Chapter of Delta Sigma Theta Sorority, and the Sunday School Cabinet. She graduated Tennessee A&I in 1948 with a bachelor of science degree in Biology, one of only two women that year to graduate in the field.

Most black women graduating from college became teachers, but McClendon had the passion to pursue a career as a biological scientist. Unable at first to find a position in research, she took teaching positions, first in the public schools of Phoenix, Arizona, and later in Eldorado, Arkansas. When she left Arkansas, she returned to Detroit to look for a job in state government where she might utilize her academic training in the biological sciences, preferably with vertebrate research. It proved impossible for her; the state offered little or no job opportunities for a black woman in the sciences. She was heartbroken. Then the U.S. Army offered hope. The Army Tank Automotive Command (TACOM) in Warren, Michigan, was looking to increase minority representation in its civilian workforce and McClendon was a beneficiary of this affirmative action initiative. Hired in 1952, she began her affiliation at TACOM first as an aide in chemical analysis, then as a physical aide. Finally she moved to a position as an industrial microbiologist, providing her the opportunity to work in the field of biotechnology and study microorganisms that might produce useful products for the military.

McClendon joined TACOM's mission to find and implement technology and logistics solutions for their soldiers; to harness new technologies for emerging systems, and assure military personnel safer, better performing, more reliable ground vehicles. Her contribution to these efforts came with her coordination of microbial research and development programs. She worked to develop methods to prevent microorganisms from contaminating fuel and deteriorating military storage material. The only black woman in her department, McClendon conducted scientific studies to develop a fungicide, a chemical to protect storage materials without harm to the people who used them. This contribution to microbiological science bought McClendon wide recognition in the scientific community globally. While she continued to make scientific impact in her industry, McClendon broadened her scientific expertise with advanced courses at Wayne State University, the University of Detroit, and Purdue University. During her years at TACOM she made many important advances in her department and was very active in the American Institute of Biological Sciences, a nonprofit scientific association dedicated to advancing biological research and education. The Michigan Society of Professional Engineers, the Detroit Central Business Association, the Tennessee

State University, and many other professional associations also recognized her for her scientific accomplishments. McClendon held her civilian position with the army for thirty-two years, leaving in 1984.

In retirement, McClendon, who never married, maintained her home in Highland Park, Michigan. In her leisure she enjoyed playing bridge and fishing. She credited her Christian faith with sustaining her throughout her career and found a church home at Greater New Mount Moriah Baptist in Detroit. Though she had no children of her own, McClendon focused special attention on programs for children at Mount Moriah, where she volunteered for many years in youth ministries, the Sunday school, and scholarship programs.

While she received much public attention for her scientific contributions, McClendon kept a more modest profile with regard to her accomplishments, guarding her privacy, and even declining attempts to make a documentary film on her work in industrial microbiology.

By virtue of her service in the field of microbiology and within government and industry, Dorothy McClendon was unusual for her time. Women scientists had sought to improve their status within the scientific professions since the early twentieth century. Throughout her career there was a persistent underrepresentation of women, and an even greater underrepresentation of African American women, in the sciences. She lamented the rejection of affirmative action programs in the country, remembering the opportunity the initiative had provided her. She experienced firsthand the plight of women and blacks who consistently failed to get the positions, advancements, and pay that came to their male counterparts. Speaking of the difficulties McClendon had to overcome, SHIRLEY ANN JACKSON, chairman of the U.S. Nuclear Regulatory Commission, noted the uniqueness of McClendon's position in industrial microbiology with the army. Asking "Is There a Crack in the Darkened Glass Ceiling?" Jackson told the sixty-ninth National Technical Association Conference that McClendon, "like nearly every scientific practitioner before her, had the will to pursue her chosen career in the biological sciences despite obstacles" (1997). Not only did McClendon rise above the obstacles so many of her fellow black women scientists had to overcome, she also made a pioneering contribution with the invention of a fungicide.

FURTHER READING

Carwell, Hattie. *Blacks in Science: Astrophysicist to Zoologist* (1977).

"Speaking of People: Military Microbiologist," *Ebony* (November 1974).

Jackson, Shirley Ann. "Is There a Crack in the Darkened Glass Ceiling?" Keynote Address to the National Technical Association, Sixty Ninth Annual Conference, 7 Nov. 1997.

J. DEBORAH JOHNSON STERRETT

McClendon, James Julius (16 Mar. 1898–20 Apr. 1982), physician and civil rights activist, was born in Rome, Georgia, the son of Benjamin McClendon, who died when James was very young, and Louisa Buckner. With the assistance of siblings, James graduated from Atlanta University in 1921, and by his own efforts he earned an MD at Meharry Medical College in 1926. He then moved to Detroit, interned at the black-owned Dunbar Hospital, and served as a staff member of Hutzel Hospital for nearly fifty years. Assisting patients of all classes, "Doc Mac" never refused treatment to the poor. He cofounded the Fairview Sanatorium and served on several black and white staffs, including those of Parkside and Woman's Hospital. In 1932 he married college graduate Irene Hunter Scruggs; the couple had two daughters. McClendon actively participated at the Second Street Baptist Church and at St. Antoine Street Young Men's Christian Association.

McClendon also became a recruiter for the local National Association for the Advancement of Colored People (NAACP) chapter, and beginning in 1937 he served as its president. He led the organization for eight successive years, establishing its first office, hiring its first executive secretary, GLOSTER B. CURRENT, and expanding its membership from three thousand to nearly twenty-five thousand. Combining his own organizational skills, Current's relentless energy, and the city's importance as a center of defense production during World War II, McClendon forged one of the most effective chapters in NAACP history.

McClendon's presidency covered three interrelated yet distinct periods. From 1937 to 1942 he addressed issues associated with the Depression and, increasingly, with preparedness at home. His call for an end to police brutality resulted in the resignation of one police commissioner, and his request that blacks be represented in the selective service process caused the statewide appointment of fourteen black board members. He pressed less successfully for greater inclusion of blacks in the civil service, while protesting the treatment of black soldiers at nearby Fort Custer. Perhaps most significant, he both broadened the base of the NAACP to reach across ideological lines within the black community and embraced trade unionism for black workers; he also reinforced the NAACP national office's 1941 support of the United Automobile Workers' effort to organize the Ford Motor Company.

In 1942 McClendon helped form the Citizen's Committee on SOJOURNER TRUTH, headed by the Reverend CHARLES A. HILL, and provided it with seed money, financial oversight, and office facilities, as well as with legal advice from the national office. This collective, biracial effort overcame white opposition, which included a localized riot that forced all levels of government into action. The riot came on 29 April 1942, when military and police forces moved black defense workers into the two hundred federally funded units named after the famed abolitionist Sojourner Truth. The conflict also revealed escalating white resistance to black demands for a wartime "Double V"—a victory abroad against fascism and a victory at home against racism.

The housing controversy ushered in the second phase of McClendon's presidency, during which the focus on wartime issues of housing and employment deepened. The NAACP continued to provide space and funding for Hill's committee, which transformed itself in name and emphasis from housing to defense jobs. Increasingly, however, McClendon and his board expressed concern over Hill's ties to Communist-connected members of the National Negro Congress and leftist unionists seeking more militant action on behalf of the black masses and on the labor front. In a December 1942 showdown for control of the NAACP, McClendon handily defeated the write-in candidate Hill, opened the board to union representation, and severed all ties with the jobs committee. He also permitted board members more influence and gave executive secretary Current greater responsibility.

McClendon's second period ended with the worst race riot of the war, which began on 20 June 1943 and killed thirty-four people and injured 765, destroying $2 billion in property. He began his third presidential phase in the wake of this devastation and of charges by white officials that actions by the NAACP and black journalists had instigated the bloodshed. McClendon jousted with Wayne County prosecutor William E. Dowling of the governor's riot committee, as well as with Mayor Edward J. Jeffries Jr., whose reelection McClendon publicly opposed that fall. But he failed on all fronts, including in his call for a grand jury to investigate the upheaval and promote a more positive atmosphere for race relations.

Thereafter McClendon pressed for action, although less militantly than before. Like most leaders of both races, he feared another outburst. He criticized the newly formed Mayor's Interracial Committee only when necessary and cooperated with local groups to redress wrongs, most notably in black housing. In this atmosphere of status quo politics and racial tension, his NAACP chapter doubled its membership, but like other private and public organizations, it could not resolve the socioeconomic issues exacerbated by war.

When McClendon stepped down from his eight years as president in December 1945, he left a legacy that reached back to FREDERICK DOUGLASS. He grew up believing that reform required cooperation among blacks and conflict with whites. Active on the campus of NAACP cofounder W. E. B. DU BOIS and his own classmate, future NAACP executive secretary WALTER F. WHITE, McClendon became a full-blown neoabolitionist in Detroit. There he advocated democratic ideals such as biracial housing, believing that the end of segregation and discrimination was necessary for true racial progress. Throughout the war he spoke and acted boldly, though hardly recklessly, urging blacks to fight for their rights and fulfill their responsibilities as citizens. He pressured officials, joined coalitions, financed committees, sponsored conferences, and—despite NAACP policy—endorsed political candidates. An aristocratic member of the Talented Tenth, he adjusted to wartime circumstances by continuing to adopt various tactics and strategies as the situation required.

McClendon retired as chapter president, but he never left the NAACP, serving on its national board of directors until his death. A member of several medical associations, he also continued his practice, and between 1965 and 1971 he became a member and president of the Detroit Board of Health. He also remained active as an investor in ventures like Wayne County Better Homes. When he died in Detroit, the local Young Men's Christian Association, the state medical society, and his alma maters had already recognized and honored him. As "Mr. NAACP," McClendon had linked the struggle for racial equality of one generation with that of another.

FURTHER READING

Capeci, Dominic J., Jr. *Race Relations in Wartime Detroit: The Sojourner Truth Housing Controversy of 1942* (1984).

Meier, August, and Elliott Rudwick. *Black Detroit and the Rise of the UAW* (1979).

This entry is taken from the *American National Biography* and is published here with the permission of the American Council of Learned Societies.

DOMINIC J. CAPECI

McClendon, Rose (27 Aug. 1884–12 July 1936), actress, was born Rosalie Virginia Scott in Greenville, South Carolina, the daughter of Sandy Scott and Tena Jenkins. Around 1890 the family moved to New York City, where her parents worked for a wealthy family as a coachman and a housekeeper, respectively. An avid reader, McClendon and her brother and sister were educated at Public School No. 40 in Manhattan. Although she admitted to having no inclinations for the stage at this time, as a child she participated in plays at Sunday school and later performed in and directed plays at St. Mark's African Methodist Episcopal (AME) Church. In 1904 she married Henry Pruden McClendon, a licensed chiropractor and Pullman porter for the Pennsylvania Railroad. The couple had no children, and McClendon was content as a housewife for a number of years while also active in the community and at St. Mark's. In 1916 McClendon received

Rose McClendon, distinguished actress, director, organizer of the Negro People's Theater, and head of the sixteen "Negro Units" of the Federal Theater Project during the Depression, photographed as Medea in 1935. (Library of Congress/Carl Van Vechten.)

a scholarship to attend the American Academy of Dramatic Art at Carnegie Hall, studying acting under Frank Sargent and others. Three years later McClendon made her professional theatrical debut at the Davenport Theatre in New York during the 1919–1920 season, appearing in John Galsworthy's *Justice* with the Bramhall Players. For the next fifteen years McClendon appeared in almost every important drama about black life that was produced in New York, which earned her the title of the "Negro race's first lady."

McClendon gained some critical attention in a touring production of *Roseanne* (1924), which starred CHARLES GILPIN, but it was the small role of Octavie in Laurence Stallings's and Frank Harling's *Deep River* that first brought McClendon critical success and the acknowledgment of her peers. The play opened on 21 September 1926 in Philadelphia, Pennsylvania, and on 4 October moved to New York City. As Octavie, McClendon entered and walked slowly down a grand staircase and exited through a garden—all without saying a word. Of her performance, critic John Anderson of the *New York Evening Post* said McClendon created "out of a few wisps of material an unforgettable picture" (5 Oct. 1926). In Philadelphia, the director Arthur Hopkins convinced Ethel Barrymore to "watch Rose McClendon come down those stairs," and Barrymore later referred to McClendon's performance as "one of the memorable, immortal moments in the theatre" (*Journal of Negro History*, Jan. 1937).

On 30 December 1926 McClendon appeared as Goldie McAllister in Paul Green's Pulitzer Prize–winning play *In Abraham's Bosom* for the Provincetown Players at the Provincetown Theater, which also starred ABBIE MITCHELL and JULES BLEDSOE. The play was a success and ran for 277 performances. A revival was staged after the Pulitzer was awarded. In 1928 McClendon played Serena in Dorothy and DuBose Heyward's *Porgy*. The play had an extended run of 217 performances in New York, after which McClendon toured with the show across the country and abroad. McClendon was called "the perfect Aristocrat of Catfish Row" and won critical acclaim for her role. In 1931 she played Big Sue in Paul Green's *House of Connelly*, the first production of the Group Theatre. The production, which opened 23 February 1931, starred Franchot Tone and Morris Carnovsky and was sponsored in part by the Theatre Guild. *House of Connelly* was an immediate success and became an important part of the Group Theatre's contribution to American theater. In 1932 McClendon took the role of Mammy in *Never No More*, and for the 1933 season she played various roles in the radio series JOHN HENRY, *Black River Giant*.

In 1935 McClendon played Cora in LANGSTON HUGHES's *Mulatto*, which premiered at the Vanderbilt Theatre in New York on 24 October. *The Oxford Companion to American Theatre* asserts that the play itself was inferior but succeeded on the strength of McClendon's performance. Doris Abramson expressed a similar sentiment and praised McClendon, saying, "This great Negro actress brought power and dignity to the role" (Abramson, 79). The New York critics agreed. Brooks Atkinson called her "an artist with a sensitive personality and a bell-like voice. It is always a privilege to see her adding fineness of perception to the parts she takes" (*New York Times*, 25 Oct. 1935). The show ran 373 performances, a record for a play by a black author. However, ill health forced McClendon to leave the cast a few months after the opening. She died of pneumonia a year later in New York City.

Beyond her own acting, McClendon was deeply concerned with the state of the black theater art, and she used her influence to promote it during what became known as the Harlem Renaissance. She directed productions for the Harlem Experimental Theatre, founded in 1928, and helped found in 1935 the Negro People's Theatre, which through McClendon's guidance became incorporated into the Federal Theatre Project's Black Unit in Harlem. McClendon also served on the advisory board of the Theatre Union, a nonprofit producing company founded in 1932 to produce socially significant plays at popular prices. She saw the theater as an important medium for depicting a true picture of African American life. She hoped the Federal Theatre Project support would produce quality black actors and writers.

As one of the great actresses of her time, McClendon became a strong symbol for black theater at a time when African Americans were just gaining their theatrical voice; indeed, when McClendon first appeared on the stage, blacks were not yet allowed into theater audiences. In the year after her death, the Rose McClendon Players were organized by Dick Campbell in memory of her vision for the black theater. While the company faltered after the Second World War, it launched the careers of numerous artists who would make their mark in the postwar American theater—her vision fulfilled.

FURTHER READING

McClendon's scrapbook and clippings are in the Schomburg Center for Research in Black Culture of the New York Public Library.

Abramson, Doris. *Negro Playwrights* (1969).

Bond, Frederick. *The Negro and the Drama* (1940).

Isaacs, Edith J. R. *The Negro in the American Theatre* (1947).

Obituaries: *New York Times*, 14 July 1936; *Afro-American* and *New York Amsterdam News*, 18 July 1936; *Journal of Negro History* (Jan. 1937).

This entry is taken from the *American National Biography* and is published here with the permission of the American Council of Learned Societies.

MELISSA VICKERY-BAREFORD

McClennan, Alonzo Clifton (1 May 1855–4 Oct. 1912), physician and professional leader, was born in Columbia, South Carolina, the orphaned son of unknown parents. As with many African Americans of the post–Civil War era, it was Reconstruction that gave McClennan a chance at a larger life. In 1872, at the height of Reconstruction in South Carolina (and thanks to the influence of a guardian uncle), he became a page in the black-dominated state senate. There he won the notice and friendship of the influential legislator RICHARD H. "DADDY" CAIN. That fall Cain ran successfully for Congress, and in 1873, after McClennan passed a competitive examination, Cain appointed his young protégé to the U.S. Naval Academy at Annapolis, Maryland.

Only the second African American student to enter Annapolis, McClennan, who was light-skinned enough to pass for white but never denied his race, found that the navy had made no accommodation to the new racial ethic of Reconstruction. From midshipmen and officers alike the young South Carolinian met savage hatred and the most blatant injustice. Goaded into minor infractions (or falsely accused of them), McClennan was dealt the severest punishments, including several months' confinement on a training ship and a court-martial (whose judgment was stayed by his patron Cain). Soon McClennan's life at Annapolis was so desperately lonely that his one joy was the nightly visit of the black servant who cleaned his boots and tidied his room. After three terms, only his worry about letting down his people kept him from quitting. Finally, in January 1874, two sympathetic faculty members not only urged him to resign but also promised to help him enroll elsewhere. McClennan then decided that he could withdraw with honor.

But the hound of racism was still in pursuit. Following a brief stint at Wesleyan Academy in Massachusetts, McClennan returned home to Columbia in 1875 to take advantage of the recent integration of South Carolina College. His timing could not have been worse: a year later General Wade Hampton's "Red Shirts" ousted the Republican regime. One consequence was a resegregation of the college and the resignation of all its blacks. Once again McClennan was on the hunt for a place to complete his degree, which he was now determined to take in medicine.

Fortunately, Howard University Medical School, just ending its first decade, wanted the determined young South Carolinian badly enough to offer him a scholarship. The blond-haired, blue-eyed McClennan could finally pursue his training without harassment or unusual notice. His record, however, did get attention: in 1880 he completed the surgery program with distinction, as well as acquiring a degree in pharmacy, and he then was ready to let down his bucket among his people. He set up practice in Columbia but soon shifted to Augusta, Georgia, where he not only began to earn his way out of poverty but also found a wife. In 1883 he married Veronica Ridley, who, like her husband, could also have passed for white. They had two daughters.

In 1884 McClennan made his final move—to Charleston—and was soon enjoying a substantial income. Two things probably accounted for his remarkable rise (and a lifestyle that included a large home and a black domestic). The first was the existence in Charleston of a large black middle class; the second was his physiognomy and coloring. As under slavery, lightness of skin still translated into social standing and popularity in African American communities. McClennan's daughters, who took pride in their father's Caucasian features, probably reflected the community view. Yet there was nothing elitist about him. Unlike the storied black plutocrat who turned his back on his race to curry favor with whites, McClennan sought only to serve his people. Colleagues may have found him dictatorial in pushing his professional agenda, but there was no denying its usefulness or his sincerity.

A major component of McClennan's professional agenda was South Carolina's first black nurse training school, begun by McClennan in 1896. One of many responses to nursing reforms begun at the Johns Hopkins Hospital only a few years before, McClennan's school was more than just a reaction to professional need. With only a few black doctors in Charleston and no access for black people to existing hospitals (except the city hospital, where African Americans faced overcrowding and indifferent attention), McClennan's efforts to supply trained black nurses for home care met a critical community need. Plus, Charleston had a ready supply of underemployed young women to furnish a corps of students. What the school did not have was a clinical setting where students could practice and apply their book skills. Neither the private white hospitals (including that of the state medical college) nor the city hospital nor the poorhouse would accept black students. When, finally, local government rebuffed McClennan's appeal for aid—at the very moment when it was funding a white school—McClennan went to the black community for help. From meager resources, money began to trickle in—from individual gifts, community dances, food sales—until by 1897 there were sufficient funds to buy and improve a frame house on Cannon Street to accommodate ten students.

But the community-owned Cannon Street Hospital served more than novice nurses. Its twenty-four patient beds offered care not only to local blacks but also to those from throughout the Lowcountry as well as from states as far north as Virginia. Open to all city physicians—who donated their services—the hospital also provided rare clinical experience to doctors. But McClennan, the hospital director and surgery chief, saw the facility reaching far beyond its patients and staff; he wanted to extend health and medical education to the whole state. To that end, in 1899 he founded (and edited) the *Hospital Herald*, a monthly newsletter filled with information and advice for mothers, doctors, nurses, the sick, and the well. It also carried constant appeals for money; once the hospital's founding moment passed, contributions from hard-pressed blacks tailed off. To meet operating and debt-retirement expenses, its medical staff and trustees had little choice but to dig deeper into their own pockets.

McClennan never slackened in his commitment. By 1906 he had even won some funding from city government. Though there never was enough funding to equip the hospital adequately—McClennan had to outfit the operating room himself—or to give patients the kind of modern care that whites enjoyed, the most important thing was to keep Cannon Street Hospital in business. If blacks got less than they should have, they got far more than they would have without McClennan's efforts. Moreover, no matter how sharp the money pinch, McClennan never turned away a patient for lack of funds.

Yet, while staggering under the burden of a continually failing institution, McClennan found energy to tackle other professional problems. In 1897 he joined a handful of colleagues in creating the Palmetto Medical, Dental, and Pharmaceutical Association, South Carolina's first organization for black health professionals, and by 1900 he had served as its president for one year. But a lifetime spent battling high odds had taken its toll, and at the age of fifty-seven McClennan died in Charleston, still working for his hospital and his people.

FURTHER READING

Beardsley, Edward H. *A History of Neglect: Health Care for Blacks and Mill Workers in the Twentieth-Century South* (1987).

Gatewood, Willard B., Jr. "Alonzo Clifton McClennan: Black Mid-shipman from South Carolina, 1873–1874," *South Carolina Historical Magazine* 89 (Jan. 1988): 24–29.

This entry is taken from the *American National Biography* and is published here with the permission of the American Council of Learned Societies.

E. H. BEARDSLEY

McCline, John (1852–1948), autobiographer and former slave, was born at Clover Bottoms, the plantation of Dr. James Hoggatt in Davidson County, Tennessee. His father, John "Jack" McCline Sr., lived on a plantation in a neighboring county; he hired his time from his master and supported himself as a traveling huckster. Though John's mother died when he was two and his sister passed away before he was old enough to remember her, he felt continued family influence through the presence of his grandmother, Hanna, and three older brothers, Richard, Jefferson, and Armstead. McCline's narrative, *Slavery in the Clover Bottoms*, re-creates this early plantation life, though the majority of the text is concerned with his attachment to Company C of the Thirteenth Infantry of Michigan during the Civil War. Published in 1998, McCline first showed the manuscript to his employer, Herbert Hagerman, in 1930, and it is presumed, but not known, that he composed it some time during the previous decade. His book shares with other slave narratives both a disgust for slavery as an institution and the familiar personal trajectory from bondage to freedom. However, his postwar vantage point shaped his narrative and its aims. Unlike other slave narratives that have the explicit goal of convincing an audience of the evils of a present system, McCline's narrative, because he was re-creating a way of life that no longer existed when he wrote it, reinforces an understanding of slavery's destructive power.

Clover Bottoms, as one of Dr. Hoggatt's three plantations, was large, prosperous, and mostly self-contained, and McCline's descriptions of the plantation foreground the violence that produced such plenty. Mrs. Hoggatt's liberality with the rawhide whip was complemented by the brutality of the ignorant overseer, a Mr. Phillips, who maintained authority through his reliance on fierce hounds and instruments of restraint and torture, as well as a willingness to shoot a slave dead for disobedience. Despite his fear of both mistress and overseer, McCline recalled boyhood moments of peace and happiness: the excitement of corn husking, the pride he took in his job as cowboy, his interest in the outside world represented by the travelers he met on the road, and his enjoyment of brotherly fishing trips. McCline also recalled moments of unrest. The whispered news of John Brown's Kansas and Virginia activities, which began in 1856 and culminated in his failed attack on the Harpers Ferry armory in 1859, and later Abraham Lincoln's nomination by the Republican Party, brought fear to the white community and resulted in talk of civil war and greater restrictions and increased patrols to monitor slaves' movement. Once Lincoln was elected president, widespread change engulfed the plantation. The patrollers disappeared, Mrs. Hoggatt put away her rawhide, and the slaves were suddenly treated with kind solicitation as the Hoggatts struggled to keep slaves from leaving the plantation.

McCline was awed by the youthful, enthusiastic spectacle of Wilson County's three thousand soldiers marching off to war. In February 1862, General Grant's attack on Fort Donelson and the 1864 battle of Nashville brought the war to his doorstep. Later that year, five thousand Union soldiers encamped in the Hoggatt's pasture and headquartered in the main house presenting a far more appealing vision for McCline. The soldiers delivered the unexpected news that the slaves were now free, and encouraged them, if not prevented by family obligations, to follow the army in its march. In August more Union troops, as well as General Forrest's ragged and starving Confederate cavalry, stopped at the plantation. Upon a chance encounter with Yankee forces who kindly invited him to travel with them, promising him freedom "up North," McCline attached himself to the Union army.

Despite strong initial homesickness, McCline enjoyed the order of camp life and his responsibilities as an unofficial assistant to "Dick," the company's English teamster. He assisted Dick in feeding, grooming, and driving one of the regiment's thirteen six-mule teams. After a year and three months of service, McCline, much to his surprise, was granted a monthly salary of eight dollars. He found the company warm and hospitable and became close companions with another boy, Aron, also a former slave, who had joined the company as it passed through Kentucky. Staying with the company, Company C of the Thirteenth Infantry of Michigan, until June 1865, McCline witnessed firsthand the gore of the battlefield and the horror of dead and mutilated bodies. He performed feats of bravery and loyalty, driving his team to the battlefront with supplies when no adult teamster could be located for the dangerous duty and capturing a horse for his captain's use. He followed General Sherman's famed "march to the sea" in 1864 and even exchanged brief conversation with the general, when Sherman, remarking that he had seen McCline many times, told McCline that he was nearly big enough to carry a gun and that he should help all he could. McCline responded with a salute. His narrative occasionally engages with matters of strategy. Overall, however, McCline's experience of war is that of a boy, and is personal, concerned with the immediate need for friends and food. He feared for his comrades when they were on the field and was overjoyed at a chance meeting with his brother Jeff, fighting in the Sixth Ohio Battery. In a response that marks a shift from his days as a slave, he reacted with anger, not fear, when he was tied to a tree by a cruel lieutenant after he had stayed too long at headquarters. Apart from that one officer, McCline's relationship with his company was overwhelmingly positive, a far cry from the general African American experience with the Union army.

When his company dispersed after the war, McCline, still a teenager, left for Paw Paw, Michigan, with Colonel Culver, to whose regiment he had been attached, and boarded with Dr. Bathrick, a physician and Baptist minister. He lived with several other families in Michigan before moving to Chicago in 1871. The city was still in wartime ruins, but McCline found work as a waiter at the Sherman Hotel. He found similar work in Indianapolis, then traveled south with his brother Jeff to find their other siblings. They were able to locate McCline's two older brothers, Dick and Armstead, as well as other relatives. He attended the Nashville Institute, a school for blacks, for two terms, from 1875–1877; after his first term he was considered advanced enough to teach in a common school outside of Nashville.

In 1878 he moved to St. Louis, where he again worked as a waiter before being promoted to the charge of the hat rack, a job that required perfect memory and that McCline performed without error. He further increased his knowledge and capital by both reading and selling newspapers. After nine years, he moved to Colorado Springs for health reasons, malaria and a bad cough having made a change in climate advisable.

Beginning in 1892, he worked for Herbert Hagerman, who in 1906 became the territorial governor of New Mexico. McCline first served as Hagerman's stable manager in Colorado then followed him to Santa Fe in 1906 to oversee the governor's mansion. McCline remained in Santa Fe when Hagerman's tenure as governor ended, and rejoined him in 1923 when Hagerman returned to the city with a government job in the Indian Service. After McCline showed Hagerman his three hundred-page memoir manuscript in 1930, Hagerman agreed to serve as both editor and typist of *Slavery in the Clover Bottoms*, but the narrative was not published during either man's lifetime. It was at Hagerman's insistence that McCline expanded his discussion of boyhood and adolescence during the war years by adding a postscript on his later experiences, though he still left out the last two decades of his life. Hagerman finished his work on the manuscript in 1934, one year before he died. Since McCline's handwritten copy of the narrative is not extant, it is impossible to gauge the possible changes the draft underwent.

McCline married his wife, Bertha Slaughter, in 1937. Bertha, along with her daughter Ben Ethel, apparently boarded in McCline's house after her second husband, Ernest Slaughter, passed away in 1936. McCline died in Santa Fe, where he had been an active leader in the black community. He left Hagerman's copy of his book in Bertha's care; it was passed down through her family and finally published in 1998.

FURTHER READING

McCline, John. *Slavery in the Clover Bottoms* (1998).
Noe, Kenneth W., and Shannon H. Wilson, eds. *The Civil War in Appalachia: Collected Essays.* (1997).

SARA KAKAZU

McClinton, O. B. (25 Apr. 1940–23 Sept. 1987), country music singer, was born Obie Burnett McClinton in the Gravel Springs community of Senatobia,

Mississippi. Growing up on the 700-acre farm of his Baptist minister father G.A. McClinton, McClinton picked cotton alongside members of his family (which included his grandfather, his father, his mother, three brothers, and three sisters). By the time he was a teenager, McClinton would listen at night to radio programs broadcast from such stations as WLAC Nashville and WHBQ Memphis; since his family did not own a record player or any recordings, the radio was his only exposure to music that originated from outside his home community. While he enjoyed several genres of music, including blues, rhythm and blues, soul, and rockabilly, McClinton was particularly fond of country music, and he regularly listened to the Grand Ole Opry concerts on WSB Nashville. Not wanting to make his living through agricultural work, he moved in 1954 to nearby Memphis, Tennessee, where he lived with his older sister and attended high school. Occasionally performing music locally, McClinton at one point entered an on-air talent contest for teenaged musicians broadcast over WDIA Memphis, and he won the contest after singing "Sixteen Tons," the hit song associated with country music singer Tennessee Ernie Ford. After a year in Memphis, McClinton returned to his parents' home when his sister became concerned about the proximity of local gangs.

In 1958, after completing high school in Senatobia, McClinton returned to Memphis, where he worked at a Mexican restaurant and often attended concerts by performers of various music genres. Later, he worked as a disc jockey at radio station WDIA. In the fall of 1962 McClinton began attending Rust College in Holly Springs, Mississippi, having received a scholarship to sing in that school's choir. While a student at Rust, he began to write songs. The first McClinton song to be included on an album was "Keep Your Arms around Me," which the soul singer OTIS REDDING recorded in January 1965 for *Otis Redding Sings Soul Ballads*. Other soul performers who recorded songs by McClinton during the 1960s included Clarence Carter, James Carr, and Arthur Conley.

After graduating from Rust in 1966, McClinton was drafted into the U.S. army. Rather than enter that branch of the military, he enlisted in the U.S. Air Force. Based in Okinawa, McClinton performed soul and country songs at military talent shows (since he could not play an instrument, he relied on back-up bands in his performances). The servicemen particularly responded to his singing of country music, and McClinton started to write

country songs. In 1968 McClinton began writing songs for the Florence, Alabama-based Fame Publishing Company.

In January 1971, while working as a staff songwriter for the Memphis-based soul label Stax Records, McClinton was signed to a recording contract with Stax's subsidiary label, Enterprise Records. Despite his songwriting success in the soul genre, McClinton felt that he had no future in soul because, as he himself admitted, "I never had the voice for blues…. My voice was always more a narrative type—I always had a good speaking voice. Usually if you have a good speaking voice and can carry a tune you could sing a good country song because it is a lyric-oriented style" (Bowman, 24). Enterprise decided to market McClinton as a country singer and to make his recordings in Nashville rather than in the studios in Memphis. A fan of two major country singer-songwriters—Hank Williams Sr. and Merle Haggard—McClinton also emulated the breakthrough success in country music of his fellow black Mississippian CHARLEY PRIDE. Acknowledging the fact that he would be compared to the more famous African American country singer, McClinton wrote and recorded the self-deprecating song "The Other One." As it turned out, McClinton and the Oklahoman STONEY EDWARDS would become virtually the only African American musicians after Charley Pride to experience sustained commercial success within the country music industry, even if that success was modest when compared to Pride's. For Enterprise, McClinton notched two Top Forty country hits: the singles "Don't Let the Green Grass Fool You" (originally recorded by the soul star WILSON PICKETT; McClinton's cover version peaked at number thirty-seven on the country chart and became his signature song) and "My Whole World Is Falling Down" (which rose to number thirty-six). He also had several minor hits, such as "Six Pack of Trouble" (which peaked at number seventy). McClinton recorded several albums with that label, beginning with *O. B. McClinton Country* (1971) and *Obie From Senatobia* (1972).

Frustrated at his lack of creative control over his first two Enterprise albums, McClinton requested and was granted permission to serve as his own producer for his third Enterprise album, *Live at Randy's Rodeo* (1973). His final album for Enterprise, *If You Loved Her That Way* (1974), was recorded with an outside producer, and his singles from that album—"If You Loved Her That Way" and "Something Better"—briefly entered the country hits chart. McClinton began recording a fifth album for Enterprise, but the project was terminated as Stax struggled to survive as a business.

When Enterprise went out of business in the mid-1970s, McClinton recorded and released six country singles for such recording companies as Mercury, ABC, Sunbird, and Moonshine Records; none of those singles became country hits. He also produced records for several other musicians during this period. By the early 1980s, McClinton was writing songs, touring frequently, and performing on television (including a widely viewed appearance on the program *Nashville Now*). In the fall of 1986 his double album entitled *O. B. McClinton* was released by Suffolk Marketing, and McClinton promoted the album via commercials broadcast on the cable channel the Nashville Network. Shortly afterward, he was diagnosed with cancer.

In November 1986, suggesting the high degree of respect for McClinton within the country music industry, numerous country singers presented a benefit concert to raise funds to help defray McClinton's medical bills. He died of abdominal cancer in Nashville. That same fall, Epic Records released an album entitled *The Only One*, which featured McClinton's performances of ten of his own original songs.

FURTHER READING

Bowman, Rob. "O. B. McClinton, 'Country Music, That's My Thing,'" *Journal of Country Music* 14.2 (1992): 23–29.

From Where I Stand: The Black Experience In Country Music. Liner notes (1998).

TED OLSON

McCluskey, John A., Jr. (25 Oct. 1944–), author and educator, was born John Asberry McCluskey Jr. in Middletown, Ohio, the first of four children of John A. McCluskey Sr., a truck driver, and Helen McCluskey (née Harris), a domestic worker. McCluskey attended primary school at Middletown's all-black Booker T. Washington Elementary, where he demonstrated an early aptitude for literature by winning a school writing contest. Despite encouragement from his teachers, however, he didn't give creative writing much thought, though he was a voracious reader.

An honors student and star athlete, McCluskey entered Harvard in 1962, thinking he would study medicine or engineering before returning to Ohio. Although the concentration of his studies was on social relations, McCluskey also pursued his growing literary interests by writing his undergraduate honors thesis, "The Sociology of Literature," on works by RALPH ELLISON, JAMES BALDWIN, CHESTER HIMES, and RICHARD WRIGHT. Having been active in sports growing up, McCluskey easily made the transition to college athletics. At Harvard he made history in 1964 as the first African American starting varsity quarterback in Ivy League history. McCluskey credited his experience as an athlete for teaching him the discipline, preparation, and focus that would prove crucial to him as a writer and educator. Having completed his degree in 1966, McCluskey entered graduate school at Stanford University to study English and creative writing.

McCluskey interrupted his graduate education to teach freshman English and creative writing at Miles College in Birmingham, Alabama, from 1967 to 1968. A lifelong northerner, McCluskey had never experienced the South firsthand, and he was struck by southern African Americans' generosity as well as their moral courage in the face of racial violence. He told the story of eating dinner at his students' homes on "Dynamite Hill," so named because white supremacists bombed the houses there, and he credited his time in the South with teaching him a new way of viewing the world. "[Going South] forced me to the realization that you can develop sensible, meaningful stories out of ... seemingly meaningless acts" (Rowell, 915). McCluskey moved on to Valparaiso University in Valparaiso, Indiana, where he served as a lecturer and writer-in-residence from 1968 to 1969.

In 1969 McCluskey married Audrey Louise Thomas, and the two lived in Cleveland, Ohio, where he had accepted a post at Case Western Reserve University, which lasted until 1977. Their first son, Malik Douglass, was born in 1970, Jerome Patrice in 1975, and John Touré in 1978. While at Case Western Reserve, McCluskey rose from lecturer to assistant professor, teaching courses in Afro-American studies, American studies, and English. He also served as coordinator of Afro American studies and was a vocal advocate for the institutionalization of black studies and black literature. An active member of the Cleveland community, McCluskey was a consultant for a black studies pilot project in the East Cleveland elementary school district, a member of the Independent School of East Cleveland's board of directors, and director of a black drama troupe in the city. During his tenure at Case Western Reserve, McCluskey completed his master's degree at Stanford in 1972.

McCluskey's first published short story, "Nairobi Nights," appeared in the January 1973 issue of *Black*

World. Although he had published a poem in the periodical in 1969, this short story publication served to validate his desire to write fiction and reach a wider audience. His first novel, *Look What They Done to My Song,* appeared in 1974 and tells the story of a young musician who, according to the critic Frank Moorer, "wants to preach a message of love with his music, … an evangelist with a horn spreading a message of love and understanding" (Thadious M. Davis, ed., *Dictionary of Literary Biography,* vol. 33: *African American Fiction Writers after 1955* [1984]: 179–181). In his second novel, *Mr. America's Last Season Blues,* McCluskey explored "how performers—people who use their bodies like athletes and dancers—fare when the body grows old" (Rowell, 924). Roscoe Americus, a professional football player permanently sidelined by injuries early in his career, spends the novel trying to escape from his own glorious history and discover a new form of heroism. In his novels and short stories McCluskey demonstrated his keen ear for language, his knowledge of black cultural traditions, and his awareness of history. His work tied together multiple strands within twentieth-century literature: the bildungsroman quality of J. D. Salinger's *Catcher in the Rye* and Ralph Ellison's *Invisible Man,* the desperation of Richard Wright's *Native Son,* and the lyrical athleticism of Gabriel Garcia Marquez, TONI MORRISON, and JOHN EDGAR WIDEMAN. McCluskey identified some of these authors as influences, but he also noted that he drew inspiration from the visual artists ROMARE BEARDEN and JACOB LAWRENCE as well as musicians such as MILES DAVIS.

In 1977 McCluskey joined the faculty of Indiana University in Bloomington, where he chaired the African American studies program and directed the CIC Minority Fellowship Program, which included the Big Ten conference and the University of Chicago. McCluskey also served as associate dean of the graduate school and taught courses in African American literature and fiction writing. At times his work as a university administrator challenged his ability to concentrate on his writing, but he tried to maintain a disciplined routine, working for a couple of hours early each morning and returning to write late in the evening. His most recent fictional works include the novels-in-progress *The River People* and *Chicago Jubilee Rag.* The first focuses on a small group of people who have banded together to seek a place to establish and nurture their fellowship, and the second is a fictionalized account of FREDERICK DOUGLASS and his contemporaries

at the 1893 Chicago World's Fair. McCluskey's short stories appeared in *Full Court: A Literary Anthology of Basketball* (1999), *Ancestral House: The Black Short Story in the Americas and Europe* (1995), and *Breaking Ice: New African-American Fiction* (1990). Besides fiction, McCluskey pursued his interest in African American literature and culture through a number of edited works, including *Black Men Speaking* (coedited with Charles Johnson, 1997) and *The City of Refuge: The Collected Stories of* RUDOLPH FISHER (1987). He also coedited and contributed to *The Chicago Renaissance: Literature and Politics 1935–1960,* a cultural history whose publication is forthcoming. McCluskey crafted a dual legacy as an author and educator whose voice reaches far beyond the pages of a book and the walls of a classroom.

FURTHER READING

"John A. McCluskey." *Contemporary Authors Series* (2001).

Karrer, Wolfgang, and Barbara Puschmann-Nalenz, eds. *The African American Short Story 1970–1990* (1993).

Moorer, Frank. "John A. McCluskey, Jr." *Dictionary of Literary Biography* (1984).

Rowell, Charles. "An Interview with John McCluskey, Jr.," *Callaloo* 19.4 (1996).

Whirty, Ryan. "Goal-Oriented," *Harvard Magazine* (Nov.–Dec. 2004).

REBECCA S. WOOD

McCovey, Willie (10 Jan. 1938–), major league baseball player, was born Willie Lee McCovey in Mobile, Alabama, the seventh of ten children of Frank McCovey, a railroad worker, and Ester. Ester supervised the children, who were expected to work outside the home to help the family financially. Willie was hired as a newsboy at twelve and then worked for a bakery making cracker dough.

McCovey played baseball, football, softball, and basketball as a youth, and his advanced skills allowed him to play in three different men's leagues while he was still in high school. In basketball McCovey played center and led his team in scoring. He also played tight end in high school football and was a quarterback in a men's league after school. Softball games found the left-hander at first base.

At sixteen McCovey wanted to work full time. He dropped out of high school and went to California to live with an older brother. But before McCovey left for California, Alejandro "Alex" Pompez, a former executive and team owner in the Negro Leagues, scouted him for the New York Giants baseball team. Pompez recommended him as a prime prospect for the Giants. Soon after McCovey's arrival in Los Angeles in January 1955, he received a telephone call from the scout requesting that he fly to the Giants' camp in Florida. His play at the tryouts was weaker than Pompez had hoped; nonetheless, McCovey was signed to play with the Sandersville Giants class D farm team at a salary of $150 per month (along with a $500 signing bonus that he sent to his mother in Alabama). While playing for Sandersville, McCovey was mentored by Bill White, first baseman with the Giants' AA club in Dallas, Texas. McCovey played well in Sandersville, and in 1956 he was moved to Danville, Virginia, in the Carolina League. He was injured that season and performed poorly. In 1958 he was moved to a team in Phoenix, Arizona, one step below the majors in the Pacific Coast League, and his play improved after an injury he had sustained earlier in the year healed. During the latter part of the 1959 season, the Giants brought him up to the major league club. He was successful in his first game with the Giants on 30 July 1959, getting a hit in each of his four times at bat, including an impressive two triples off the future Hall of Fame pitcher Robin Roberts. That year, with a batting average of .354 that put him just a notch behind the National League (NL) leader HANK AARON, McCovey won the NL Rookie of the Year Award. His initial success did not last, and after a batting slump in 1960, he was sent to play for Tacoma in the Pacific Coast League before returning to the Giants at the end of the season. He had always played first base, but he spent some time that season playing in the outfield until an injury to the first baseman ORLANDO CEPEDA allowed McCovey to return to his favorite position. McCovey was also used as a pinch hitter. He hit a game-winning home run in the 1962 World Series against the Yankees.

McCovey tied Aaron for the home run title in 1963, but the next year was a different story. Plagued with injuries, including knee and foot problems, McCovey was also devastated in 1964 by the death of his father, who had always been his biggest supporter. From 1965 onward McCovey was a permanent fixture for the Giants at first base. He ranked first in both home runs and RBIs in both 1968 and 1969, tying the record of Bill Nicholson, who had been the first player to earn this honor two years in a row. McCovey's batting skill was feared by many pitchers, who often intentionally walked him. In 1969 he set a record by drawing forty-five intentional walks in a single season; the record stood until 2002. Also in 1969 he was voted the most valuable player by the Baseball Writers Association of America and hit two home runs in the All-Star Game. The following season McCovey was again injured (including blurred vision in one eye), but he still managed to hit home runs in all twelve NL ballparks.

McCovey was a soft-spoken player at the beginning of his career, but by 1970 he had become more outgoing and developed his own personal style. An automobile sponsorship from Chrysler provided him with free cars, and he enjoyed wearing expensive suits and wristwatches. At the height of the Black Power movement, some militant blacks were disappointed that the highly visible McCovey did not use his position to promote the struggle for black equality in other fields.

McCovey's move to the San Diego Padres expansion team in 1974 disappointed San Francisco fans. "Big Mac" McCovey (so nicknamed in reference to Ray Kroc, owner of both the Padres and the McDonald's franchises) played in San Diego until 1976, when his contract was sold to the Oakland Athletics. The A's released him after eleven games, and he returned to the San Francisco Giants, where he played from 1977 to 1980. He was voted comeback player of the year in 1977. The left-handed McCovey, who wore jersey number 44 (also Aaron's number), retired from baseball on 6 July 1980. That year he hit one home run, giving him a career total of 521. The score tied Ted Williams's record and was good for the tenth rank at the time that McCovey retired. McCovey's eighteen career grand slams put him second only to Lou Gehrig, who had hit twenty-three. McCovey won the NL home-run title three times and the RBI crown twice, and he played in six All-Star Games. The back-to-back hitting prowess of the Giants' right-handed WILLIE MAYS and the lefty "Stretch" McCovey was a challenge for opposing pitchers.

The popular McCovey was elected to the Baseball Hall of Fame in 1986. In his honor the Giants' new stadium features McCovey Cove, a flower garden and park on the stadium grounds that features a nine-foot statue of McCovey. Giants players voted the "Willie Mac" Award each year to the team's most inspirational player. Giant fans were allowed to vote on the award in 2006 for the player demonstrating the highest qualities of "competitive spirit, ability, and leadership." After his retirement McCovey worked on the Giants' management staff, and he opened a California restaurant in Walnut Creek with his business partner Jeff Dudum in 2003.

FURTHER READING

Allen, Bob. *The Five Hundred Home Run Club: Baseball's Fifteen Greatest Home Run Hitters from Aaron to Williams* (1999).

Peters, Nick. *Willie McCovey: Stretch* (1988).

PAMELA LEE GRAY

McCoy, Bill. *See* Railroad Bill.

McCoy, Elijah (27 Mar. 1843–1929), inventor, was born in Colchester, Canada West (now Ontario), the son of George McCoy and Mildred Goins, former slaves who had escaped from Kentucky. In 1849 his parents moved the family to Ypsilanti, Michigan, where Elijah began attending school. In 1859 he went to Edinburgh, Scotland, to undertake an apprenticeship as a mechanical engineer; he stayed there five years.

Unable to obtain a position as an engineer after he returned to the United States, McCoy began working as a railroad fireman for the Michigan Central Railroad. This position exposed him to the problems of steam engine lubrication and overheating. Locomotive engines had to be periodically oiled by hand, a time-consuming task that caused significant delays in railroad transport of commercial goods and passengers. Poorly lubricated locomotives also used more fuel than those that were efficiently lubricated.

McCoy began his career as an inventor by first examining and improving the lubrication of stationary machines. On 23 June 1872 he patented "an improvement in lubricators for steam engines," the first of his automatic lubrication devices for use on stationary engines. The rights for this patent were assigned to S. C. Hamlin of Ypsilanti. McCoy received several additional patents for improvements in lubricators that were all for use on stationary engines and on steam engines for ships.

In 1882 McCoy began receiving patents for lubricators specifically designed for railroad locomotive engines. His hydrostatic lubricator for locomotives made quite an impact. Largely constructed of brass, the lubricators, approximately twelve inches in height, had valves that fed the oil to the engine and that regulated the steam pressure. These lubricators were assigned to Charles and Henry Hodges and were manufactured by the Detroit Railway Supply Company. The money McCoy received from these patent assignments he used for further studies of the problems of lubrication.

McCoy continued to receive patents for improvements to his hydrostatic lubricator, and railroad officials soon took note. Even though other locomotive lubricators were on the market, McCoy's lubricators sold well. He became an instructor in the correct installation and maintenance of his lubricators and also served as a consultant for several lubricator manufacturing companies, such as the Detroit Lubricator Company.

In 1915 McCoy patented a graphite lubricator, specifically designed for use on the newly introduced "superheater" locomotive engines. Because of the extreme temperatures of the steam, it was difficult to control and regulate the supply of oil with which the superheater engines were lubricated. McCoy's new lubricator relied on the use of a solid lubricant, graphite, combined with oil that solved this problem. The basic design was economical and simple with few moving parts. The amount of lubricant was controlled by an

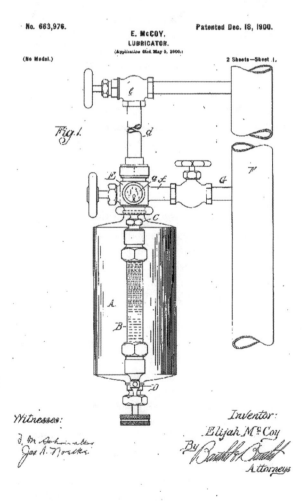

Patent illustration for Elijah McCoy's displacement lubricator, 1900. (US Patent and Trademark Office.)

equalizing valve that regulated the flow of oil and graphite over the engine cylinder. One enthusiastic customer reported that his locomotive made thirteen round trips between Chicago and the Mississippi River, and when the engine was examined it was in "perfect condition." On these trips the amount of oil used for lubrication was reduced by one-third to one-half, and the amount of coal was reduced by four to six tons. McCoy considered the graphite lubricator to be his greatest invention. The Elijah McCoy Manufacturing Company, located in Detroit, was established in 1916 to sell the graphite lubricator. But apparently McCoy was only a minor stockholder; the company went out of business a few years after it began. Many questions remain about the extent to which McCoy himself profited from his own inventions. McCoy could have become a very wealthy man given the commercial success of his lubricator design. But many of his patents were quickly assigned to others, and he merely served as a figurehead for the company bearing his name.

McCoy married Mary E. Delaney (MARY ELEANORA MCCOY), his second wife, in 1873. They later moved to Detroit, where she became a well-known civil rights and women's rights activist and clubwoman. The McCoys were very close, and after her death in 1923 Elijah McCoy's health began to deteriorate. Never a very sociable man, he began to withdraw from the world around him. In 1928 he was committed to Eloise Infirmary, suffering from senile dementia, and he died there. By the time of his death he had received at least fifty patents, many held in foreign countries and virtually all of them in the area of engine lubrication.

The theory is often propounded that one of McCoy's enduring legacies is the phrase "the real McCoy." The proposed explanation is that the quality of his lubricators was so outstanding in comparison to others on the market that railroad inspectors and engineers are said to have challenged their crews as to whether they had installed "the real McCoy." Actual evidence of such use has yet to be discovered. However, the phrase, in the form "the real Mackay" (pronounced *muh-KYE* in Scotland), may have been used as an advertising slogan by the G. Mackay and Co. distillery in Edinburgh, Scotland, as early as 1870, and it appears in a letter by the Scottish author Robert Louis Stevenson in 1883, only a year after McCoy patented his locomotive lubricator. In 1899 a San Francisco newspaper applied the idiom to a flamboyant white boxer known as "Kid McCoy." This

and other evidence suggests that "the real McCoy" could easily be applied to anyone of note named McCoy. Its application to Elijah McCoy has certainly helped in recent years to keep his memory alive.

FURTHER READING

Hayden, Robert C. *Eight Black American Inventors* (1972).
Klein, Aaron. *Hidden Contributors: Black Scientists and Inventors in America* (1971).
Marshall, Albert P. *The "Real McCoy" of Ypsilanti* (1989).
This entry is taken from the *American National Biography* and is published here with the permission of the American Council of Learned Societies.

PORTIA P. JAMES

McCoy, Mary Eleanora (7 Jan. 1846–1923), club organizer, community leader, and philanthropist, was born Mary Eleanora Delaney in Lawrenceburg, Indiana, to Jacob C. and Eliza Ann Montgomery Delaney. Her parents may have been runaway slaves since Mary was born in an Underground Railroad station. Little else is known about the Delaney family or Mary's early life. Her early education was sporadic, but she learned to read and write in mission schools that met in homes in Indiana. After the Civil War she also attended the Freeman's School in St. Louis, Missouri, for a brief time. In 1869, at age twenty-three, Delaney married Henry Brownlow of St. Louis. The Brownlows' union, however, was short-lived. On 25 February 1873 Mary married ELIJAH MCCOY in Ypsilanti, Michigan, where she had moved in 1870. Elijah McCoy, the famous inventor of the lubricator for steam engines, was a widower. Mary and Elijah were blessed the second time around with a marriage that lasted forty-six years.

Elijah had received six patents for his self-lubricating devices by 1879 and one patent for an ironing table. By 1882 Mary and Elijah McCoy had moved from Ypsilanti to Detroit, where Elijah worked as a mechanical consultant to several companies. Mary McCoy not only enjoyed the status of being the wife of a successful and highly visible inventor but she also blossomed as a conscientious socialite, community organizer, and church worker. In 1894 some of Detroit's prominent white women invited her to become a charter member of the exclusive Twentieth Century Club, organized in key cities across the country to fight against social evils.

McCoy accepted this offer, becoming the club's sole black member. The next year she cofounded the In As Much Circle of King's Daughters and Sons Club to promote philanthropy and charity among black women.

The success of this club prompted McCoy to help found the Michigan State Association of Colored Women in 1898. Lucinda Thomas of Jackson, Michigan, served as president, and McCoy was vice president. At the first meeting of the new association McCoy persuaded the ladies to establish the Phillis Wheatley Home for Aged and Infirm Colored Women. The Michigan Association's national counterpart, the National Association of Colored Women's Clubs, had been established in July 1896 in Washington, D.C., to help improve the quality of life for African American families in general, and women and children in particular. McCoy envisioned the Phillis Wheatley Home as a safe haven in which the residents' basic needs for shelter, food, and clothing could be met. Although she had no children of her own, McCoy established and financially supported the McCoy Home for Colored Children to protect the rights of children, expand the children's access to opportunities, and work for their moral, economic, social, and religious welfare.

McCoy became known as the "Mother of Clubs" because she founded or belonged to so many organizations. She was president of the Sojourner Truth Memorial Association and vice president of the Lydian Association of Detroit. The Lydian Association was organized in December 1899 by Elizabeth Johnson for the purpose of helping its members during sickness and death. McCoy persuaded the Lydian members to broaden their view and work to uplift people in the community. The Truth Memorial Association worked to establish scholarships in Truth's name at the University of Michigan, and to erect a monument to SOJOURNER TRUTH, who lived in Battle Creek from the 1850s to 1884. McCoy was also active in the Guiding Star Chapter of Freemasonry's Order of the Eastern Star and in several organizations at the Bethel African Methodist Episcopal Church, including the Willing Workers Club, organized in November 1887 to contribute to the Community Fund and the Scholarship Fund, to make and sell quilts, and to give baby garments to the needy.

When the Detroit chapter of the NAACP was established in the 1910s McCoy became a charter member. She also worked with the Democratic Party, campaigned against lynching and Jim Crow laws, and participated in the women's suffrage movement. She represented Michigan as a flag bearer in the women's suffrage parade that preceded Woodrow Wilson's inauguration in 1913. The following year, Governor Woodbridge Nathan Ferris appointed McCoy to the Commission for the Half-Century Exposition of Freedmen's Progress that would be held in Chicago in 1915. She collected material from Eastern Michigan to exhibit during the Exposition and for inclusion in the accompanying book, *Michigan Manual of Freedmen's Progress.*

In 1920 McCoy and her husband were involved in an automobile accident, and she sustained serious internal injuries from which she never fully recovered. After years of declining health, she died in Detroit. Organized groups of black women existed in Detroit before McCoy moved to the city. Indeed, the oldest society in the state, the Ladies Benevolent Society, had been organized in 1867 as a Baptist society devoted to giving sick and death benefits to its members. The society's work grew rapidly and became non-denominational. Nonetheless, it is appropriate to call Mary McCoy the mother of clubs because she helped found so many organizations. McCoy's altruism and determination are noteworthy, and she embodied the National Association of Negro Women's motto of lifting others as you climb.

FURTHER READING

"Black Clubwomen's Movement." *Reader's Companion to U.S. Women's History* (2005).

Davis, Elizabeth Lindsay. *Lifting as They Climb* (1933).

Dykes, De Witt S., Jr. "McCoy, Mary E." in *Black Women in America: The Early Years, 1616–1899,* ed. Darlene Clark Hine (1997).

"National Association of Colored Women." *Reader's Companion to U.S. Women's History* (2005).

ARTHUREE MCLAUGHLIN WRIGHT

McCray, Carrie Anderson Allen (4 Oct. 1913–25 July 2008), writer and activist, was born in Lynchburg, Virginia, the ninth of ten children of William Patterson Allen, a lawyer, and Mary Magdalene Rice Hayes Allen, a college professor. Across the street from the home where Carrie McCray was born is the campus of Virginia Seminary. McCray's mother served as interim president of this black Baptist seminary from 1906 to 1908. When she was almost seven years old McCray's family moved from Lynchburg to Montclair, New Jersey. Except for the first two years in New Jersey her family spent every summer back in Lynchburg. Throughout her childhood McCray's parents instilled in her a love of poetry, an appreciation for her ancestors, and an understanding of how education provided a path to freedom. In childhood McCray also learned how to remain optimistic even in dark times and how to treat all people with respect, kindness, and compassion. McCray attended Spaulding Elementary School in Montclair, New Jersey; Hillside Junior High; and Montclair High School. She received her bachelor of arts degree in 1935 from Talladega College in Alabama. When at home in Montclair during her college years, she taught at the Holcombe/Kenney School. McCray received her master of arts degree in 1955 from New York University's School of Social Work and Sociology.

In 1940 McCray married Winfield Scott Young, but the couple divorced five years later. With her second husband, JOHN H. MCCRAY, she had one son. For several years McCray served as a certified social worker in New York City, before returning to Talladega College to teach. In 1976 the United Negro College awarded its Teacher of the Year Award to McCray.

McCray organized several groups and grass-roots movements, including local chapters of the NAACP and Alpha Kappa Alpha Sorority. She has served on the Alabama Youth Commission and the Board of Governors of the South Carolina Academy of Authors. She helped found the South Carolina Writers Workshop, which named its literary award in her honor.

McCray published a book of poems, *Piece of Time*, in 1993, and her work was also anthologized in numerous magazines and literary quarterlies, including the *Crimson Edge, Older Women, Squaw Review, South Carolina Collection, Ms. Magazine, Cave Canem I, Point, River Styx, Reading Literature*, and *Moving Beyond Words*. Several radio stations, National Public Radio (NPR) among them, broadcast recordings of her poetry.

McCray's narrative poem, "A Song for Ota," paid tribute to OTABENGA, a Pygmy who lived with McCray's family for several years. Otabenga had been first "displayed" at the 1904 World's Fair in St. Louis and then at the Bronx Zoo. After furious protests from African Americans in the area, he was eventually removed from display and relocated

Carrie Allen McCray, talking with Wim Roefs of the University of South Carolina before the start of a panel titled "Spearhead for Reform: The Leadership of the NAACP," at The Citadel Conference on Civil Rights in Charleston, South Carolina, 6 March 2003. (AP Images.)

to Lynchburg, where he was reportedly tutored by poet ANNE SPENCER and others.

Although McCray wrote poems, short stories, and scholarly articles for many years, she only began to consider herself a writer at age seventy-three. She considered herself living proof that anyone can start to write at any age.

In the afterword of *Piece of Time*, McCray discussed her family background and her desire to know more about her grandfather, a white man who served as a general in the Confederate army during the Civil War. McCray continued this search in her most famous book, *Freedom's Child: The Life of a Confederate General's Black Daughter* (1998), part memoir, part history, but mostly a loving biography of her mother, Mary Magdalene Allen, a civil rights activist. Her book followed an old Yoruba proverb, "If you want to know the end, you have to start at the beginning." McCray wrote about her own family's history, but readers of *Freedom's Child* also learned about American history, especially the years between Reconstruction and the Depression.

Although McCray felt embarrassed that her grandfather was a white man who fought for slavery, she wanted to know more about him and her mother. To write *Freedom's Child*, she researched extensively, seeking truth wherever she could find it. She learned that her grandfather, General John Robert Jones, acted differently from most generals in the war: he openly acknowledged having black children and made sure they received a good education. Doing this prevented him from becoming a famed military hero. In her book McCray went from feeling intense anger toward her grandfather to embracing and loving him.

McCray devoted her life and writings to activist issues: she fought against racism, prejudice, and segregation, and for full freedom for all people, justice, equality, the importance of education, and kindness and compassion. The following verse from a poem McCray wrote after returning home from the Shenandoah Valley where she "spoke" with her deceased grandfather illustrates the love and optimism found in almost all of McCray's writings:

Perhaps there is a love that transcends,
that's unafraid, uncompromised
Perhaps there is a love that laughs in
the face of the shallow *Oh, mys*
of white gloved ladies
Perhaps there is a love that says
"To hell" (pardon me, Grandfather)
"with false barriers,"

and stands there unadorned,
in pure naked beauty,
like a field of wildflowers
unashamed of their unlike likenesses.

Carrie Allen McCray will be remembered especially for her influence on southern, African American, and women's literature. McCray died at the age of 94 in Columbia, South Carolina.

FURTHER READING
McCray, Carrie Allen. *Freedom's Child: The Life of a Confederate General's Black Daughter* (1998).
McCray, Carrie Allen. *Piece of Time* (1993).

LOIS J. EINHORN

McCray, John Henry (25 Aug. 1910–15 Sept. 1987), editor and political activist, was born near Youngstown, Florida, the eldest of eight children of Donnie McCray, a minister, and Rachel McCray, whose maiden name is unknown. When John was six his father moved the family to Lincolnville, South Carolina, an all-black town twenty miles north of Rachel McCray's hometown of Charles. In addition to his duties as assistant pastor of the Ebenezer African Methodist Episcopal (AME) Church, Donnie McCray served as Lincolnville's town marshal, while Rachel McCray, an early NAACP activist, had a seat on the local council. John McCray thus grew up believing that African American self-governance was the norm. That belief, he later admitted, may have emboldened him in his political career.

McCray shone at Lincolnville Grade School, where he graduated first in his class, and excelled at Charleston's Avery Normal Institute, where he graduated as class valedictorian in 1931, with the highest four-year grade average of any student since the 1870s. McCray was also president of the institute's debating society and editor of the *Avery Tiger*, the school newspaper. Charleston, unlike Lincolnville, had a clear and hardening color line, and McCray increasingly came to resent it. He later recalled his anger when city officials erected "For Whites Only" signs in the prestigious Colonial Lake section of the city, where he and his friends had once sat on benches, shooting the breeze while admiring the passing girls.

In 1931 McCray continued his interest in journalism and oratory at Talladega College in Alabama. He wrote several columns in the *Mule's Ear*, a campus monthly, which lambasted the conservatism of both the Talladega faculty and his fellow students. He also challenged their apathy about the fate of the Scottsboro Boys, at that time languishing in an Alabama prison. "We may not possess the financial or political influence necessary to save the lives of the boys," McCray wrote in 1935, "but we can offer our resentment to the manner in which many of the local and neighboring whites regard them" (quoted in Roefs, 466). McCray graduated in 1935 with a B.S. in Chemistry, but at that time in the South there were pitifully few jobs in the sciences for African Americans. He returned instead to Charleston, South Carolina, taking a position as a debit manager for a branch of the North Carolina Mutual Life Insurance Company, while also serving as city editor of the *Charleston Messenger* and as president of Charleston's moribund branch of the NAACP. In 1936 McCray married Satis Victoria Ballou. Following a second marriage, he later married CARRIE ALLEN [MCCRAY].

In Charleston as at Talladega, McCray challenged what he saw as black timidity in the face of white racism. He was determined to use his paper to counteract the negative images of blacks in the white media, particularly in the reporting of crime, but he also used his paper as a bully pulpit, urging black Charlestonians to conform to an ideal of race-conscious respectability. The paper's message to African Americans, he recalled later in an interview, was, "Don't go around making a lot of bad noise, using a lot of bad language.... Stop grinning every time you see a white face. Stand up and be a man." McCray's brash manner sat uneasily with many of Charleston's African American leaders, however, who feared that his establishment in 1936 of a defense fund for two black men accused of killing a policeman would unnecessarily provoke a violent white backlash.

In 1939, having tired of endless squabbles with the *Messenger*'s publisher about controversial news items, McCray founded his own newspaper, the *Charleston Lighthouse*. The following year he merged the *Lighthouse* with the Sumter, South Carolina, *People's Informer* and in 1941, at the urging of the NAACP activist MODJESKA SIMKINS, moved the *Lighthouse and Informer* to Columbia, the state capital. The move signaled the belief of Simkins, McCray, and his assistant editor, OSCEOLA McKAINE, that South Carolina blacks were now ready to mount a full-fledged statewide campaign to restore the right to vote that had been taken away by a white-supremacist-led constitutional convention in 1895.

The campaign began in earnest in May 1944 when the thirty-four-year-old McCray was elected

chairman of the South Carolina Progressive Democratic Party (PDP), established to campaign for the reelection of the Democratic president Franklin Roosevelt. (The organization had initially been known as the Colored Democratic Party, but its inclusion of a small cadre of white liberals prompted a name change.) By July 1944 the PDP enjoyed a presence in thirty-eight of the state's forty-six counties and claimed forty-five thousand members. When white officials in the state Democratic Party refused the PDP's request that it be given eight of South Carolina's eighteen delegates (a figure proportionate to the black percentage of the state population), McCray led an alternate delegation to the Democratic National Convention in Chicago. The PDP failed in its campaign to be seated at the convention—as BOB MOSES and FANNIE LOU HAMER of the Mississippi Freedom Democratic Party would fail twenty years later—but McCray's challenge highlighted the newfound confidence of South Carolina blacks.

McCray's confidence was often frustrated over the next four years, as South Carolina's white Democratic leadership established various roadblocks to keep blacks out of the primary process, even though the U.S. Supreme Court had ruled in *Smith v. Allwright* (1944) that such discrimination was unconstitutional. After a series of legal challenges, the federal courts ruled in the PDP's favor in 1948. Two years later black voters, encouraged by McCray in the *Lighthouse and Informer*, proved decisive in the defeat of Strom Thurmond for U.S. Senate. Thurmond's opponent, Senator Olin Johnston, was hardly a racial liberal, but he at least had accepted the new political reality in South Carolina by courting the PDP. Thurmond, whose "states' rights" views were attacked by McCray as "the same old kicking Negroes around," had not, and he paid the price (quoted in Roefs, 481).

McCray's abrasive personality resulted in frequent disputes with his colleagues, notably with OSCEOLA McKAINE, whose communist sympathies he viewed with suspicion. McCray's anticommunism could not protect him, however, from hate mail, death threats, and harassment by the Charleston police and other white city officials who resented his outspoken advocacy of black voting rights.

In 1950 McCray was charged with criminal libel for an October 1949 article in the *Lighthouse and Informer* in which he discussed the case of an African American man sentenced to death (and later executed) for raping a white woman. Though

McCray did not name the woman, he was convicted of criminal libel for publishing the condemned man's allegation that he had engaged in consensual sex. Believing that an all-white jury would almost certainly find against him, McCray pled guilty and was sentenced to three months' probation. A white reporter who had also discussed the case in print avoided prosecution. Although the court initially allowed McCray to leave the state for business purposes, his probation was revoked in August 1951 after he made two brief trips outside the state.

McCray thought that it was no coincidence that his new sentence—he served two months in leg irons on a chain gang—came shortly after his active support of black parents in Clarendon County who had initiated a school desegregation lawsuit, *Briggs v. Elliot*, that in 1954 became part of the U.S. Supreme Court's landmark *Brown v. Board of Education* ruling. McCray was certain that South Carolina governor Jimmy Byrnes, a former U.S. Supreme Court justice, secretary of state under Franklin Roosevelt, and a committed segregationist, had ordered his arrest, and also that Byrnes had persuaded the state supreme court to uphold the sentence when the NAACP Legal Defense Fund appealed his conviction. McCray had no regrets about the case, however, remarking stoically that "somewhere along the way I was bound to catch it" (quoted in Egerton, 550).

The court case—and McCray's continuing disputes with allies who did not always meet his expectations—exacted a major toll, however, and in 1954, with the circulation of the *Lighthouse and Informer* in decline, he left the paper. In the decade that followed, McCray continued to work as a journalist, covering the emerging civil rights movement in South Carolina for northern black newspapers like the *Pittsburgh Courier, Baltimore Afro-American*, and *Chicago Defender*. Unlike in the 1930s and 1940s, however, he was no longer part of the civil rights story himself. In 1964, after an unsuccessful attempt to establish a new black newspaper in Charleston, he returned to Talladega College in Alabama, where he served as director of public relations and as director of admissions until 1981.

In retirement, however, McCray returned to his first love, journalism, penning an occasional column, "The Way It Was," for the *Charleston Chronicle* from 1980 to 1987. His columns recalled for a younger audience the struggles of South Carolina blacks for voting rights and better education in the 1930s and 1940s, struggles in which McCray played a central but by then largely forgotten role.

Typically, he recalled in one column that the life of a crusading black journalist was not as glamorous as it sounded: "Invariably, you are committed to fighting for an ethnic group that doesn't patronize you enough to pay even the rent. You have to find some way of trading enough with whites ... that will work with you, while you consistently blast away at other whites. Sort of crazy business" (*Charleston Chronicle*, 21 Feb. 1982).

Yet despite those problems, McCray, who died in Talladega, possessed the necessary skills, political commitment, and self-confidence to make the crazy business work. In the words of his fellow campaigning editor, Durham's LOUIS AUSTIN, McCray's *Lighthouse and Informer* was in the 1930s and 1940s "truly the one burning torch in the benighted state of South Carolina" (*Carolina Times*, 18 Aug. 1951).

FURTHER READING

John McCray's papers are housed at the University of South Carolina's South Caroliniana Library, Columbia, South Carolina.

Interview with John McCray, *Southern Changes* (Spring 1997).

Egerton, John. *Speak Now against the Day: The Generation before the Civil Rights Movement in the South* (1994).

Roefs, Wim. "Leading the Civil Rights Vanguard in South Carolina: John McCray and the *Lighthouse and Informer*, 1939–1954," in *Time Longer than the Rope: A Century of African-American Activism (1850–1950)*, eds. Charles M. Payne and Adam Green (2003).

Sullivan, Patricia. *Days of Hope: Race and Democracy in the New Deal Era* (1996).

STEVEN J. NIVEN

McCray, Mary F. (26 May 1837–Nov. 1894), slave, minister, and religious activist, was born into slavery in Kentucky as Mary Frances Taylor. Known as "Fannie," she was the fifth of sixteen children and the reported favorite of her parents, Mary and Jonathan Taylor. Jonathan Taylor was the freeborn son of a slave mother and her white master, while Fannie's mother Mary was a slave. Although Mary and Jonathan were allowed by her owner to marry, he spent only part of each week on the plantation where Mary and their children worked as slaves. Fannie's family was not a religious family and although she had an understanding and acknowledgement of God she was anything but pious in her youth, and took pleasure in dancing. When Fannie was fourteen years old, her aunt, a religious woman, challenged her behavior explaining the evils of dancing and its sinful implications. This conversation ultimately led to Fannie's religious conversion.

Fannie and her family were owned by a spinster, Miss Polly Adams, who died in 1859, when Fannie was twenty-one years old. In her will Adams granted her slaves freedom and enough money for Fannie's family and Aunt Margaret's family to buy eighty acres of land each in Ohio. When Polly Adams's relations learned of her gratitude toward her slaves, they tried to break her will. That protest kept Fannie and her family in slavery for another three years until the validity and permanent nature of her will was established.

With the help of the white abolitionist Levi Coffin, known for his work on the Underground Railroad, Fannie and Margaret purchased two farms in Mercer County, Ohio. After the death of her mother, Fannie had been left to care for her father, an alcoholic incapable of providing physical or financial support to his family. Fannie cared for her father, mothered her siblings, worked the fields, and chopped wood to earn money. Occasionally she was able to hire on help to work the farms. It was Fannie who held her family together through the strength she attributed to her Christian faith.

Fannie was the only Christian in her family and sought to be an example and inspiration to them. This is not to say that her faith came easily. She lost three of her sisters within eighteen months of each other and was surrounded by people of disreputable character. Yet she was renewed with the spirit and more determined to live a life of righteousness when one of her sisters found Christ before she died. Burdened by the laborious nature of her life, as well as financial difficulties of sustaining the farms, Fannie remained steadfast in her faith and commitments.

In 1868 Fannie married S. J. "Mack" McCray, an acquaintance of her sisters, who had served in the Union army. Although he had never seen Fannie face-to-face he had struck up a correspondence with Fannie while he was living in Michigan and Chicago after the war. Like her he had become a committed Christian, and together they began a life of ministry and evangelism that would last until Fannie's death. The McCrays moved to Lima, Ohio, soon after their marriage and became the leaders (what is today known as Pastor and First Lady) of Lima's African Methodist Episcopal (AME) Church.

Mack and Fannie were innovative, committed, and stalwart individuals who provided the framework for modern-day missionary and evangelism ministries. In 1880 the McCrays, now with two sons, moved to Desmet in the Dakota Territory and purchased 160 acres of the government land Congress made available to veterans. Within weeks they held a church meeting in their home, the site of the first Sunday school in their area. In 1886 the church members decided to have a revival service. When discussions turned to procuring a preacher, Mack nominated his wife, who became one of the first black female preachers of the Methodist church in the Dakota Territory. That same year Fannie McCray, who could neither read nor write, organized a Free Methodist Church and was licensed to preach on 15 April 1886. This was significant because most northern Methodists believed that Methodists from the south saw religion as an immediate emotion or experience, as opposed to an intellectual and learned understanding through the written word. Southern Methodists were often not treated as true Christians because of their inability to read and write; they were assumed therefore to lack true understanding of the Bible. Fannie McCray, however, embraced a more sedate practice of religion and commanded a full understanding of the Bible that made her respectable and successful.

In addition to their work in the ministry, the McCrays built schools in their community. They founded the first public school house in the Dakota Territory on 1 March 1884, which unfortunately closed down within the same year. Not to be deterred however, they convinced the township to build seven schoolhouses, which would also be used for church meetings and Sunday school.

After a two-year drought destroyed their crops the McCrays were forced to leave Dakota and return to Lima in 1891. The couple visited several churches in Lima and were displeased, believing the spirit of the Lord was not present in these congregations, so they helped found the First Holiness Church of Lima, later named The Mission Church of Christ. In late November 1894, on a day when she was singing hymns and praising God with some church ladies, Mary Frances "Fannie" McCray died peacefully. After a life of devotion to evangelism, preaching, building schools, and organizing churches, she finally "went home."

FURTHER READING

Maffly-Kipp, L. F. *The Church in the Southern Black Community* (2001), available online at http://docsouth.unc.edu/church/intro.html.

McCray, S. J. *Life of Mary F. McCray: Born and Raised a Slave in the State of Kentucky* (1898), available online at http://docsouth.unc.edu/mccray/mary.html.

CAROL PARKER TERHUNE

McCree, Wade Hampton, Jr. (3 July 1920–30 Aug. 1987), lawyer, judge, Solicitor General of the United States, and law professor, was born in Des Moines, Iowa, the second of four children of Lucretia Harper McCree, a former schoolteacher, and Wade Hampton McCree Sr., a pharmacist, drugstore proprietor, and, later, federal narcotics inspector. Both parents were college graduates who highly valued education. Their example and expectations profoundly affected McCree who, throughout his career in public service and law, was deeply interested in education and involved in expanding educational opportunities for African Americans.

The senior McCree's pharmacy, established in 1914, was the first African American–owned drug store in Iowa. By 1924, however, following the postwar downturn of Iowa's agricultural economy, McCree's father had given up the business. He applied for and was the first African American to be appointed to a position as a U.S. Narcotics Inspector. That career took the McCree family, now including three children, to Hilo, Hawaii, Chicago, and finally Boston, where young Wade was educated at the prestigious Boston Latin School. There he developed a love for ancient history, mythology, poetry, and language.

Upon graduation from Boston Latin, McCree expected to enter the University of Iowa where, as a native Iowan, he would not have to pay tuition. His older sister was already enrolled at Fisk University, their parents' alma mater, and he wanted to avoid a further strain on the family's finances. But when he was informed by Iowa that, because of his race, he would not be allowed to live in a university dormitory, he accepted a tuition-only scholarship to Fisk, which he supplemented for four years by working as a waiter in the college dining hall and in various off-campus jobs.

McCree excelled at Fisk, serving as an associate editor of the Fisk *Herald*, a member of the student/faculty council, president of the student council, a teaching assistant in the History Department, and a member of Kappa Alpha Psi Fraternity. In 1941 he graduated *summa cum laude* with an AB in history and departmental honors. He was elected to Phi Beta Kappa in 1959, when the Fisk chapter of the honor society was established.

McCree entered Harvard Law School in the fall of 1941 and completed his first year before entering military service in World War II. Following Officer Candidate School at Fort Benning, Georgia, McCree served with the Ninety-second Infantry Division, the segregated Buffalo Soldiers Division, fighting in three Italian campaigns in the European Theater of Operations. At the time of his discharge in 1946, he had attained the rank of captain, become fluent in Italian, and received the bronze star for valor. Within weeks of leaving the Army, McCree married Dores McCrary, a Simmons College library science student, and resumed his studies at Harvard Law.

Completing the second and third years of law school in eighteen months, McCree graduated Harvard Law in the winter of 1947 as a member, *nunc pro tunc*, of the class of 1944, with which he had started, ranked twelfth in his class. Moving to Detroit, his wife's hometown, McCree was rebuffed by the city's elite law firms, then all-white, notwithstanding his class rank and letter of recommendation from the dean of his law school to the firms' hiring partners. Impressed by two pioneering African American lawyers, Harold Bledsoe and Hobart Taylor, McCree joined the firm of Bledsoe and Taylor in 1948. There, with Harold Bledsoe as his mentor, he became immersed in Detroit's African American community and Democratic Party politics.

In 1952 Michigan's Democratic governor, G. Mennen Williams, appointed McCree to the state's Workman's Compensation Commission, the first African American to hold such a post. While a workers' compensation referee, McCree also performed local legal research as part of the national effort behind the NAACP's *Brown v. Board of Education* project. In 1954, when a vacancy occurred on the Circuit Court for Wayne County, then the largest and busiest trial court in Michigan, Williams appointed McCree to the judgeship. He was not the first African American to be appointed to a Michigan court of record. Four years earlier, an African American appointed to the criminal court serving Detroit had failed to survive a retention election. Skeptics who viewed Williams's appointment of McCree, five months after the U.S. Supreme Court's *Brown v. Board of Education* decision, as a gesture to the state's African American voters, predicted a similar fate for McCree. Instead, in 1955 he made political history and became Michigan's first elected African American judge. In 1959 he won reelection handily.

In 1961, during his second term on the Wayne County Circuit bench, President John F. Kennedy appointed McCree to the United States District Court for the Eastern District of Michigan. He was the first African American to serve on that court; and the third

African American federal district judge in the nation. In 1966 President Lyndon B. Johnson elevated McCree to a seat on the United States Court of Appeals for the Sixth Circuit, where, again, he was the first judge of his race on the court. McCree served on the Sixth Circuit until 1977, when he accepted President Jimmy Carter's appointment to serve as Solicitor General of the United States, the second African American, after Thurgood Marshall, to hold that office.

As a judge, McCree was known for his superb intellect, impartiality, scholarship, incisive analysis, and the command of language reflected in his finely crafted judicial opinions. He also was known for composing impromptu limericks, including one that famously immortalized the snail darter, a two-inch-long inedible fish at the center of a case involving the Endangered Species Act decided by the Sixth Circuit in 1977. Although Judge McCree resisted labels and wanted to be known as a fair and impartial jurist who was right on the law, his opinions upholding civil liberties and civil rights nonetheless demonstrated his liberal leanings.

McCree delighted in the role of solicitor general, the lawyer who advocates for the United States Government in cases that come before the U.S. Supreme Court. Unlike arguments to a jury, a trial judge, or an appellate court, which are tied to the law as it exists, arguments to the highest court often invite theoretical discussions of what the law should be. McCree made such an argument, on behalf of the United States as a friend of the court, in the highly controversial reverse discrimination case of *The Regents of the University of California v. Bakke*. Arguing that the use of race as a factor in college and graduate school admissions was constitutionally permissible, although the use of quotas was not, the United States urged that the case be remanded for a lower court determination of whether Bakke's rights were violated by his denial of admission to medical school. Although the court ordered Bakke to be admitted, it agreed with the United States—and McCree—that affirmative action was constitutional.

In 1981 McCree resigned as solicitor general to accept appointment to the faculty of the University of Michigan Law School. McCree loved teaching; while a state and federal trial judge in Detroit, he had taught at local law schools as an adjunct professor. As a Court of Appeals judge and solicitor general, he had frequently lectured at law schools throughout the United States and in 1969 had been a member of the law faculty for the Salzburg Seminar in American Studies in Austria. He enjoyed the rigor of academic life at Michigan and found gratification in his mentoring of law students. Besides teaching, among other courses, Constitutional Law and Constitutional Litigation, he also accepted appointments from the U.S. Supreme Court to serve as a special master in three cases, the most notorious of which involved the multibillion-dollar estate of Howard Hughes. McCree was a member of the Michigan Law faculty until his premature death in 1987, from multiple myeloma, a form of bone cancer.

McCree's most significant contribution to education may not have been to legal scholarship, but to extending the opportunity to receive a college education to youngsters to whom it otherwise would have been denied. In Detroit in 1963, alarmed by the low rate of college matriculation by graduates of some of Detroit's inner city high schools, most of whom were African American, McCree co-founded, with Dean Arthur Neef, of the Wayne State University Law School, the Higher Education Opportunities Committee to mobilize community resources to enable qualified but economically disadvantaged high school graduates to attend and graduate from college. Beginning with privately raised funds, H.E.O.C. identified college-caliber high school students and provided special counseling and tutoring where needed. The students were accepted to colleges throughout the United States, some with significant scholarships, and, continuing to receive mentoring and support from the H.E.O.C. during their college careers, graduated at a higher than average rate. The success of the H.E.O.C. program attracted financial support of foundations and eventually the federal government. It became the model for similar programs in other states and across Michigan where, in 1988, it was renamed the Wade H. McCree, Jr. Incentive Scholarship Program.

FURTHER READING

Wade H. McCree, Jr.'s papers are housed in the Walter P. Ruther Library, Wayne State University, Detroit, Michigan.

Kalt, Brian C. "Wade H, McCree Jr., and the Office of the Solicitor General, 1977–1981." *Detroit College of Law Review* 794 (1998).

"Portrait Dedication Ceremony: Honorable Wade H. McCree, Jr., and Honorable Philip Pratt." *Federal Reporter* (1992).

"Presentation of the Portrait of the Honorable Wade H. McCree, Jr. United States Court of Appeals for the Sixth Circuit." *Federal Reporter* (1984).

Williams, Marcus D. "Lawyer, Judge, Solicitor General, Educator: A Tribute to Wade H. McCree, Jr." 12 *National Black Law Journal* 1 (1990–1993).

KATHLEEN MCCREE LEWIS